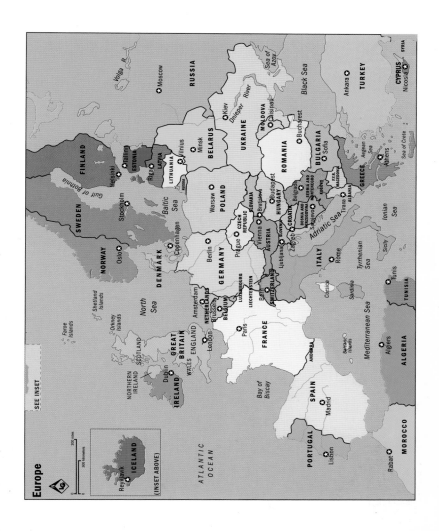

Europe

ICELAND

(INSET ABOVE)

SEE INSET

ATLANTIC
OCEAN

Reykjavik

300 miles
300 kilometers

Faroe
Islands

Shetland
Islands

Orkney
Islands

SCOTLAND

NORTHERN
IRELAND

IRELAND

Dublin

WALES ENGLAND

London

GREAT
BRITAIN

North
Sea

Amsterdam

NETHERLANDS

Brussels

BELGIUM

LUXEMBOURG

LIECHTENSTEIN

Paris

FRANCE

Bay of
Biscay

PORTUGAL

SPAIN

Madrid

Lisbon

ANDORRA

Balearic
Islands

MOROCCO

Rabat

ALGERIA

Algiers

Mediterranean Sea

TUNISIA

Tunis

NORWAY

Oslo

SWEDEN

Stockholm

Gulf of Bothnia

FINLAND

Helsinki

DENMARK

Copenhagen

Baltic
Sea

Tallinn

ESTONIA

Riga

LATVIA

LITHUANIA

Vilnius

RUSSIA

GERMANY

Berlin

Prague

CZECH
REPUBLIC

Vienna

AUSTRIA

SWITZERLAND

Bern

Warsaw

POLAND

SLOVAKIA

Bratislava

Budapest

HUNGARY

Ljubljana

SLOVENIA

Zagreb

CROATIA

BOSNIA AND
HERZEGOVINA

Sarajevo

ITALY

Rome

Corsica

Sardinia

Tyrrhenian
Sea

Sicily

Adriatic Sea

Minsk

BELARUS

UKRAINE

Kiev

Dnieper River

MOLDOVA

Chisinau

ROMANIA

Bucharest

Belgrade

SERBIA AND
MONTENEGRO

Tirana

ALBANIA

Podgorica

F.Y.R.
MACEDONIA

Skopje

BULGARIA

Sofia

GREECE

Athens

Ionian
Sea

Aegean
Sea

Sea of Crete

Black Sea

Sea of
Azov

Moscow

RUSSIA

Volga R.

TURKEY

Ankara

CYPRUS

Nicosia

SYRIA

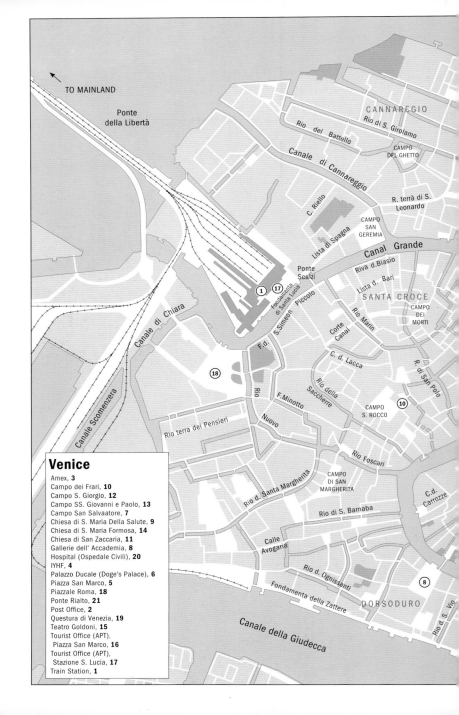

Venice

Amex, **3**
Campo dei Frari, **10**
Campo S. Giorgio, **12**
Campo SS. Giovanni e Paolo, **13**
Campo San Salvatore, **7**
Chiesa di S. Maria Della Salute, **9**
Chiesa di S. Maria Formosa, **14**
Chiesa di San Zaccaria, **11**
Gallerie dell' Accademia, **8**
Hospital (Ospedale Civili), **20**
IYHF, **4**
Palazzo Ducale (Doge's Palace), **6**
Piazza San Marco, **5**
Piazzale Roma, **18**
Ponte Rialto, **21**
Post Office, **2**
Questura di Venezia, **19**
Teatro Goldoni, **15**
Tourist Office (APT),
  Piazza San Marco, **16**
Tourist Office (APT),
  Stazione S. Lucia, **17**
Train Station, **1**

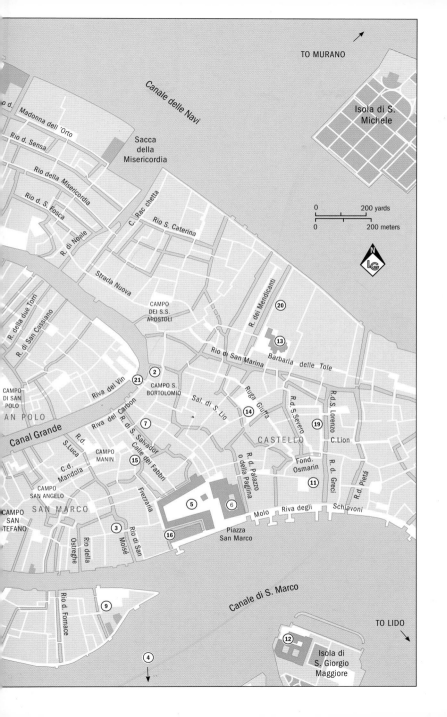

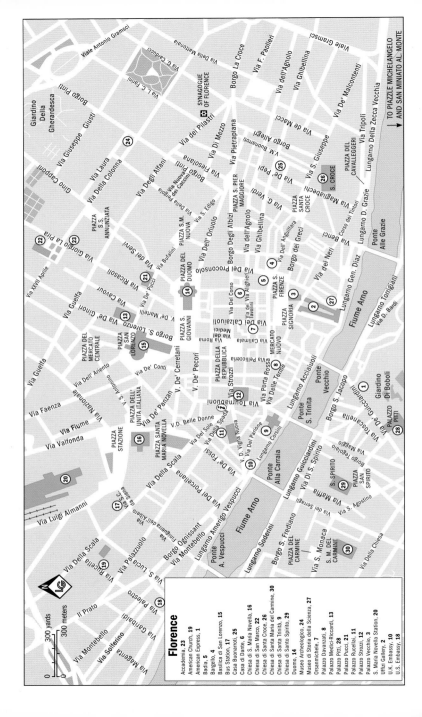

Florence

Accademia, **23**
American Church, **19**
American Express, **1**
Badia, **5**
Bargello, **4**
Basilica di San Lorenzo, **15**
Bus Station, **17**
Casa Buonarroti, **25**
Casa di Dante, **6**
Chiesa di S. Maria Novella, **16**
Chiesa di San Marco, **22**
Chiesa di Santa Croce, **26**
Chiesa di Santa Maria del Carmine, **30**
Chiesa di Santa Trinità, **9**
Chiesa di Santo Spirito, **29**
Duomo, **14**
Museo Archeologico, **24**
Museo di Storia della Scienza, **27**
Orsanmichele, **7**
Palazzo Davanzati, **8**
Palazzo Medici-Riccardi, **13**
Palazzo Pitti, **28**
Palazzo Pucci, **21**
Palazzo Rucellai, **11**
Palazzo Strozzi, **12**
Palazzo Vecchio, **3**
S. Maria Novella Station, **20**
Uffizi Gallery, **2**
U.K. Embassy, **2**
U.S. Embassy, **18**

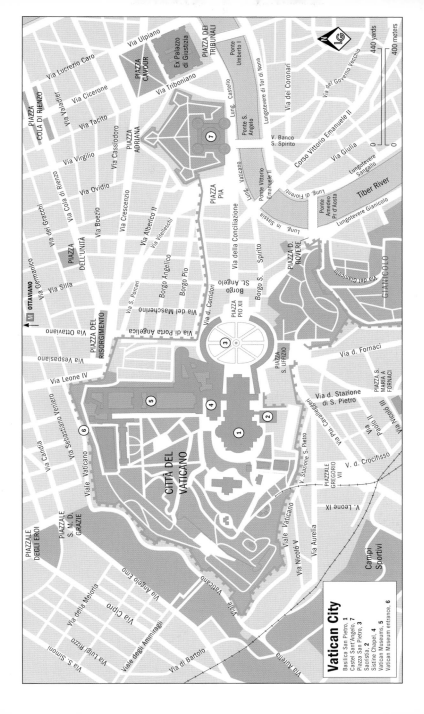

Vatican City

Basilica San Pietro, **1**
Castel Sant'Angelo, **7**
Piazza San Pietro, **3**
Sacristia, **2**
Sistine Chapel, **4**
Vatican Museums, **5**
Vatican Museum entrance, **6**

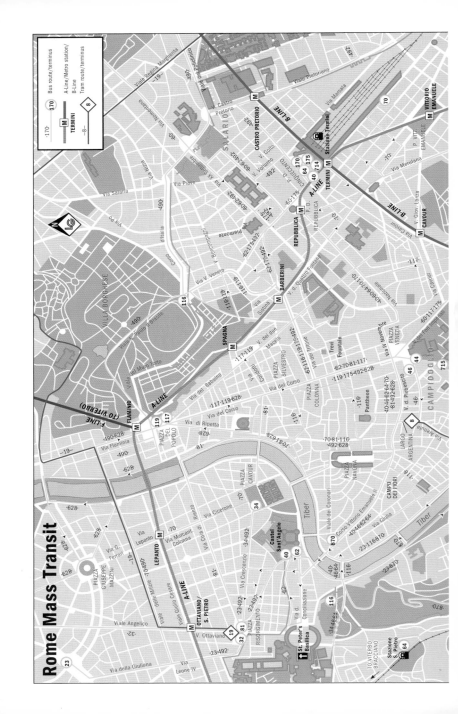

Rome Mass Transit

Legend:
- -170- Bus route/terminus
- A-Line/Metro station /
- TERMINI — A-Line
- -8- Tram route/terminus

VILLA BORGHESE

A-LINE
FLAMINIO (TO VITERBO)

LEPANTO

OTTAVIANO / S. PIETRO

St. Peter's Basilica

Stazione S. Pietro

PIAZZA DEL POPOLO

SPAGNA

BARBERINI

REPUBBLICA

CINQUECENTO

TERMINI
A-LINE
Stazione Termini

CASTRO PRETORIO

B-LINE

Castel Sant'Angelo

Tiber

PIAZZA NAVONA

CAMPO DE' FIORI

PIAZZA VENEZIA

CAMPIDOGLIO

LARGO ARGENTINA

Pantheon

Trevi Fountain

PIAZZA COLONNA

PIAZZA SILVESTRO

CAVOUR

VITTORIO EMANUELE

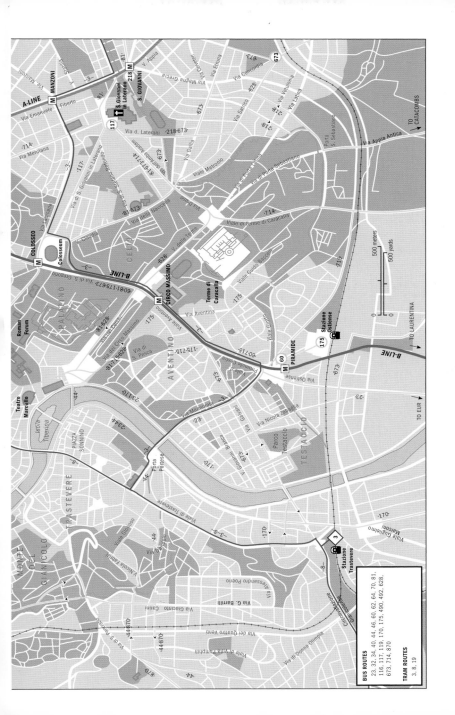

BUS ROUTES
23, 32, 34, 40, 44, 46, 60, 62, 64, 70, 81,
116, 117, 119, 170, 175, 490, 492, 628,
673, 714, 870

TRAM ROUTES
3, 8, 19

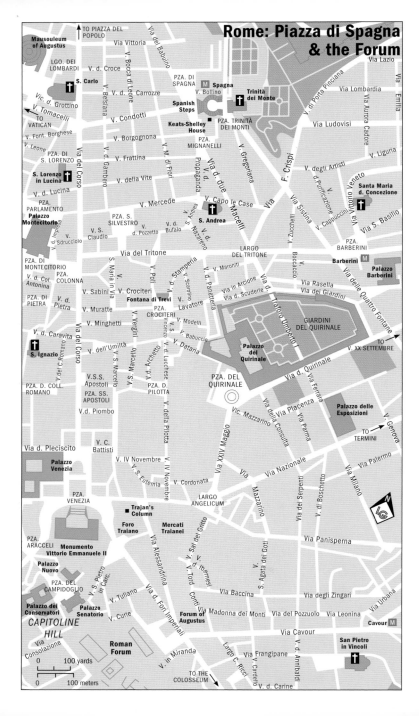

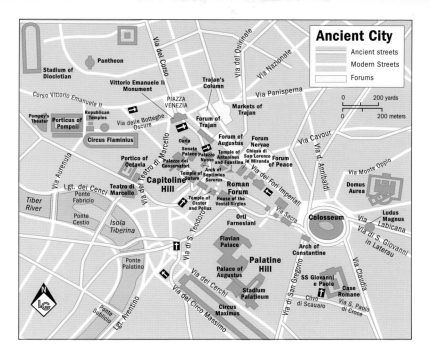

Ancient City

Ancient streets
Modern Streets
Forums

0   200 yards
0   200 meters

Stadium of Diocletian
Pantheon
Vittorio Emanuele II Monument
Trajan's Column
Via del Corso
Via del Quirinale
Via Nazionale
Via Panisperna
Corso Vittorio Emanuele II
PIAZZA VENEZIA
Markets of Trajan
Pompey's Theater
Porticus of Pompeii
Republican Temples
Via delle Botteghe Oscure
Forum of Trajan
Forum of Augustus
Forum Nervae
Chiesa di San Lorenzo in Miranda
Via Cavour
Circus Flaminius
Curia
Senate Palace
Palazzo del Conservatori
Temple of Antoninus and Faustina
Forum of Peace
Via Monte Oppio
Portico of Octavia
Palazzo Nuovo
Via dei Fori Imperiali
Domus Aurea
Via Aurenula
Lgt. dei Cenci
Ponte Fabricio
Teatro di Marcello
Via del Teatro di Marcello
Capitoline Hill
Temple of Saturn
Arch of Septimius Severus
Roman Forum
Via Sacra
Colosseum
Via Labicana
Ludus Magnus
Via di S. Giovanni in Laterau
Tiber River
Ponte Cestio
Isola Tiberina
Via di S. Teodoro
Temple of Castor and Pollux
House of the Vestal Virgins
Orti Farnesiani
Ponte Palatino
Flavian Palace
Palace of Augustus
Palatine Hill
Arch of Constantine
SS Giovanni e Paolo
Case Romane
Via Claudia
Via S. Paolo di Croce
Via dei Cerchi
Via di San Gregorio
Ponte Sublicio
Lgt. Aventino
Via del Circo Massimo
Stadium Palatinum
Circus Maximus
Clivo di Scauaro
N LG

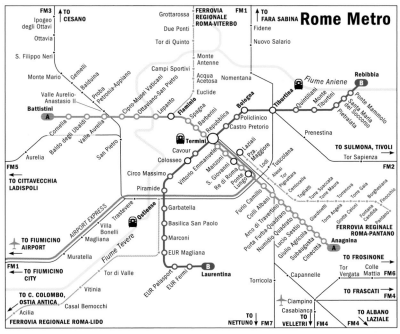

Rome Metro

FM3
TO CESANO
Ipogeo degli Ottavi
Ottavia
S. Filippo Neri
Monte Mario
Valle Aurelio-Anastasio II
Battistini A
Cornelia
Aurelia
FM5
TO CITTAVECCHIA LADISPOLI
Gemelli
Balduina
Proba Petronia-Appiano
Baldo degli Ubaldi
Valle Aurelia
San Pietro
Grottarossa
Due Ponti
Tor di Quinto
Campi Sportivi
Monte Antenne
Acqua Acetosa
Euclide
Cipro-Musei Vaticani
Ottaviano-San Pietro
Lepanto
Flaminio
Spagna
Barberini
Repubblica
Nomentana
FERROVIA REGIONALE ROMA-VITERBO
FM1
TO FARA SABINA
Fidene
Nuovo Salario
Bologna
Policlinico
Castro Pretorio
Termini
Cavour
Colosseo
Circo Massimo
Piramide
AIRPORT EXPRESS
Trastevere
Ostiense
Villa Bonelli
Magliana
Muratella
TO FIUMICINO AIRPORT
FM1
TO FIUMICINO CITY
TO C. COLOMBO, OSTIA ANTICA
Acilia
Casal Bernocchi
Vitinia
Tor di Valle
FERROVIA REGIONALE ROMA-LIDO
Garbatella
Basilica San Paolo
Marconi
EUR Magliana
EUR Palasport
EUR Fermi
Laurentina B
Fiume Tevere
Vittorio Emmanuele
Manzoni
S. Giovanni
Re di Roma
Ponte Lungo
Furio Camillo
Colli Albani
Arco di Travertino
Porta Furba-Quadrato
Numidio Quadrato
Lucio Sestio
Giulio Agricola
Subaugusta
Cinecittà
Anagnina A
Capannelle
Torricola
Ciampino
Casabianca
Flume Aniene
Tiburtina
Quintiliani
Monte Tiburtino
Pietralata
Santa Maria del Soccorso
Ponte Mammolo
Rebibbia B
Prenestina
TO SULMONA, TIVOLI
Tor Sapienza
FM2
Pza. Maggiore
Lodi
La Giustiniana
Tuscolana
Alessi
Tor Pignattara
Centocelle
Tagliati
Torre Spaccata
Torre Maura
Giardinetti
Grotte Celoni
Torrenova
Torre Gaia
Torre Nova
Fontana Candida
Finocchio
Pantano
Borghesiana
Grotte Celoni
Torre Angela
FERROVIA REGIONALE ROMA-PANTANO
TO FROSINONE
Tor Vergata
Colle Mattia
FM6
TO FRASCATI
FM4
TO ALBANO LAZIALE
TO NETTUNO
FM7
TO VELLETRI
FM4
FM4

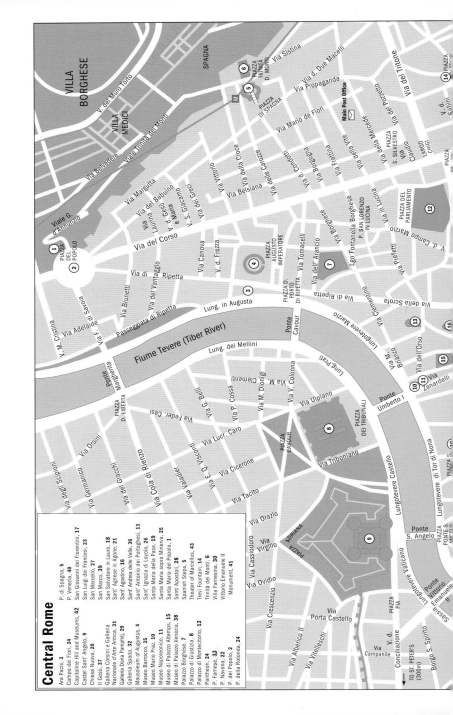

Central Rome

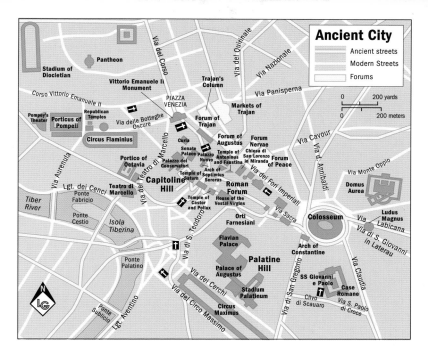

Ancient City

Ancient streets
Modern Streets
Forums

0   200 yards
0   200 meters

Stadium of Diocletian
Pantheon
Via del Corso
Via del Quirinale
Via Nazionale
Via Panisperna
Vittorio Emanuele II Monument
Trajan's Column
Corso Vittorio Emanuele II
PIAZZA VENEZIA
Markets of Trajan
Pompey's Theater
Republican Temples
Porticus of Pompeii
Via delle Botteghe Oscure
Forum of Trajan
Via Cavour
Circus Flaminius
Forum of Augustus
Forum Nervae
Via di Monte Oppio
Via d. Annibaldi
Curia
Senate
Palace
Palazzo
Temple of Antoninus and Faustina
Chiesa di San Lorenzo in Miranda
Forum of Peace
Portico of Octavia
Palazzo dei Conservatori
Temple of Nuovo
Temple of Saturn
Arch of Septimius Sererus
Domus Aurea
Teatro di Marcello
Via del Teatro di Marcello
Capitoline Hill
Roman Forum
Via dei Fori Imperiali
Colosseum
Via Labicana
Ludus Magnus
Tiber River
Lgt. dei Cenci
Ponte Fabricio
Temple of Castor and Pollux
House of the Vestal Virgins
Via Sacra
Via di S. Giovanni in Laterau
Ponte Cestio
Isola Tiberina
Orti Farnesiani
Via di S. Teodoro
Via Aurenula
Via Aventino
Ponte Palatino
Flavian Palace
Palatine Hill
Arch of Constantine
Via Claudia
Palace of Augustus
Via dei Cerchi
Stadium Palatinum
SS Giovanni e Paolo
Case Romane
Via S. Paolo di Croce
Ponte Sublicio
Via del Circo Massimo
Circus Maximus
Via di San Gregorio
Clivo di Scauro

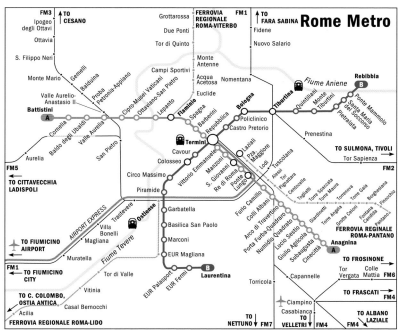

Rome Metro

FM3 TO CESANO
Ipogeo degli Ottavi
Grottarossa
FERROVIA REGIONALE ROMA-VITERBO
FM1
TO FARA SABINA
Ottavia
Due Ponti
Fidene
S. Filippo Neri
Tor di Quinto
Nuovo Salario
Monte Antenne
Monte Mario
Campi Sportivi
Acqua Acetosa
Nomentana
Fiume Aniene
Rebibbia
B
Gemelli
Balduina
Proba Petronia-Appiano
Euclide
Valle Aurelio-Anastasio II
Cipro-Musei Vaticani
Ottaviano-San Pietro
Leganto
Flaminio
Spagna
Bologna
Tiburtina
Quintiliani
Monte Tiburtino
Ponte Mammolo
Santa Maria del Soccorso
Pietralata
Battistini
A
Cornelia
Baldo degli Ubaldi
Valle Aurelia
San Pietro
Barberini
Repubblica
Policlinico
Castro Pretorio
Prenestina
Aurelia
Termini
TO SULMONA, TIVOLI
Tor Sapienza
FM5
TO CITTAVECCHIA LADISPOLI
Cavour
Colosseo
Vittorio Emanuele
Manzoni
S. Giovanni
Re di Roma
Laziali
Pza. Maggiore
Lodi
Tuscolana
FM2
Circo Massimo
Ponte Lungo
Alessi
Tor Pignattara
Centocelle
Piramide
AIRPORT EXPRESS
Trastevere
Ostiense
Garbatella
Furio Camillo
Colli Albani
Arco di Travertino
Porta Furba-Quadraro
Numidio Quadrato
Lucio Sestio
Giulio Agricola
Subaugusta
Cinecittà
Anagnina
A
Villa Bonelli
Magliana
TO FIUMICINO AIRPORT
Fiume Tevere
Muratella
Basilica San Paolo
Marconi
EUR Magliana
Togliatti
Torre Spaccata
Torre Maura
Torre Gaia
Giardinetti
Grotte Celoni
Borghesiana
Bolla
Finocchio
Pantano
FERROVIA REGIONALE ROMA-PANTANO
TO FROSINONE
FM1
TO FIUMICINO CITY
Tor di Valle
Vitinia
EUR Palasport
EUR Fermi
Laurentina
B
TO FRASCATI
FM4
TO C. COLOMBO, OSTIA ANTICA
Casal Bernocchi
Torricola
Capannelle
Tor Vergata
Colle Mattia
FM6
Acilia
FERROVIA REGIONALE ROMA-LIDO
Ciampino
Casabianca
TO NETTUNO
FM7
TO VELLETRI
FM4
FM4
TO ALBANO LAZIALE

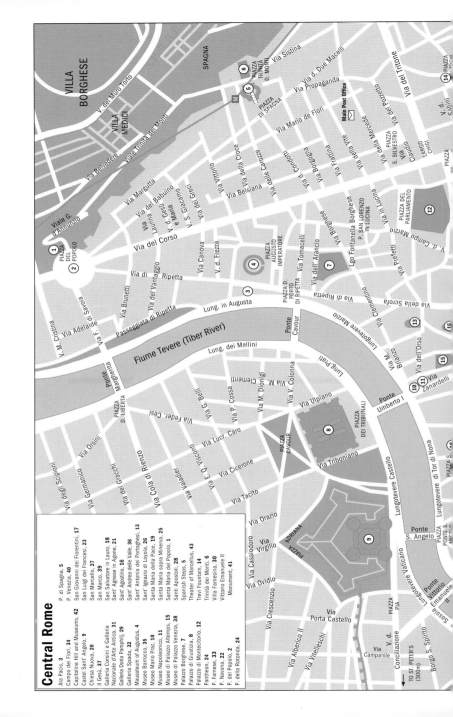

Central Rome

Ara Pacis, **3**
Campo dei Fiori, **34**
Capitoline Hill and Museums, **42**
Castel Sant' Angelo, **9**
Chiesa Nuova, **20**
Il Gesù, **37**
Galleria Corsini e Galleria
Nazionale d'Arte Antica, **31**
Galleria Doria Pamphilj, **29**
Galleria Spada, **32**
Mausoleum of Augustus, **4**
Museo Barrocco, **35**
Museo Mario Praz, **10**
Museo Napoleonico, **11**
Museo di Palazzo Altemps, **15**
Museo di Palazzo Venezia, **38**
Palazzo Borghese, **7**
Palazzo di Giustizia, **8**
Palazzo di Montecitorio, **12**
Pantheon, **24**
P. Farnese, **33**
P. Navona, **22**
P. del Popolo, **2**
P. della Rotonda, **24**

P. di Spagna, **5**
P. Venezia, **40**
San Giovanni dei Fiorentini, **17**
San Luigi dei Francesi, **23**
San Marcello, **27**
San Marco, **39**
San Salvatore in Lauro, **18**
Sant' Agnese in Agone, **21**
Sant' Agostino, **16**
Sant' Andrea delle Valle, **36**
Sant' Antonio dei Portoghesi, **13**
Sant' Ignazio di Loyola, **26**
Santa Maria della Pace, **19**
Santa Maria sopra Minerva, **25**
Santa Maria del Popolo, **1**
Santi Apostoli, **28**
Spanish Steps, **5**
Theater of Marcellus, **43**
Trevi Fountain, **14**
Trinità dei Monti, **6**
Villa Farnesina, **30**
Vittorio Emanuele II
Monument, **41**

VILLA
BORGHESE

VILLA
MEDICI

SPAGNA

PIAZZA
TRINITÀ
D. MONTI

PIAZZA
DI SPAGNA

Main Post Office

Viale G.
d'Annunzio

PIAZZA
DEL
POPOLO

Via del Corso

Via Margutta

Via del Babuino

Laurina

V. d. Maria

V.S. Giacomo

Via dei Greci

Via Vittorio

Via della Croce

Via delle Carozze

Via Mario de' Fiori

Via Propaganda

Via d. Due Macelli

Via Sistina

Via del Tritone

PIAZZA

Via Belsiana

Via Bocca

Via Frattina

Via delle Vite

Via della Mercede

Via del Pozzetto

PIAZZA
S. SILVESTRO

Via
Claudio

LARGO
CHIGI

PIAZZA

Via Canova

V. d. Frezza

PIAZZA
AUGUSTO
IMPERATORE

Via dell' Arancio

Lgo Fontanella Borghese

P. SAN LORENZO
IN LUCINA

PIAZZA DEL
PARLAMENTO

Via in Lucina

V. d. Campo Marzio

PIAZZA DI
PORTO
DI RIPETTA

Via di Ripetta

Via Borghese

Via Tomacelli

Via dei Prefetti

Via della Scrofa

Via Clementina

Lungotevere Marzio

Lung. in Augusta

Passeggiata di Ripetta

Lung. dei Mellini

Via Brunetti

Via di Vantaggio

Ponte
Cavour

Fiume Tevere (Tiber River)

Lung. Prati

Via M. Colonna

Via V. Colonna

Via M. Dionigi

Via P. Cossa

Via Ulpiano

PIAZZA
DEI TRIBUNALI

Ponte
Umberto I

Via M.
Brianzo

Via dell'Orso

Via
Lanardelli

Via Federi. Cesi

Via G. Belli

Via M.
Clementi

PIAZZA
D. LIBERTA

Ponte
Margherita

V. M. Cristina

Via Adelaide

Via F.

Via Orsini

Via degli Scipioni

Via Germanico

Via dei Gracchi

Via Cola di Rienzo

Via Valadier

Via E.Q. Visconti

Via Lucr. Caro

Via Cicerone

Via Triboniano

PIAZZA
CAVOUR

Via Tacito

Via Orazio

Via Crescenzio

Via
Virgilio

Via
Cassiodoro

Via
Ovidio

PIAZZA
ADRIANA

Lungotevere Castello

Lungotevere di Tor di Nona

Ponte
S. Angelo

Ponte
Vittorio
Emanuele II

PIAZZA
PIA

PIAZZA
PONTE S.

Lungotevere Vaticano

Via
Porta Castello

Via
Conciliazione

Via Alberico II

Via Vitelleschi

Via
Campanile

V. d.
Sabin

Borgo S. Spirito

TO ST. PETER'S
(300m)

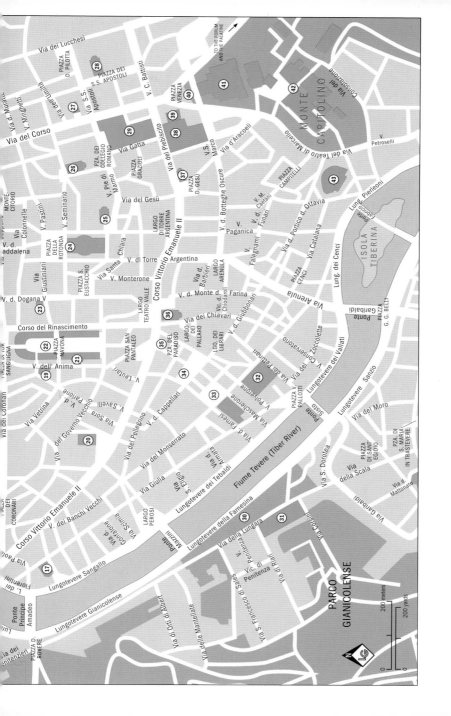

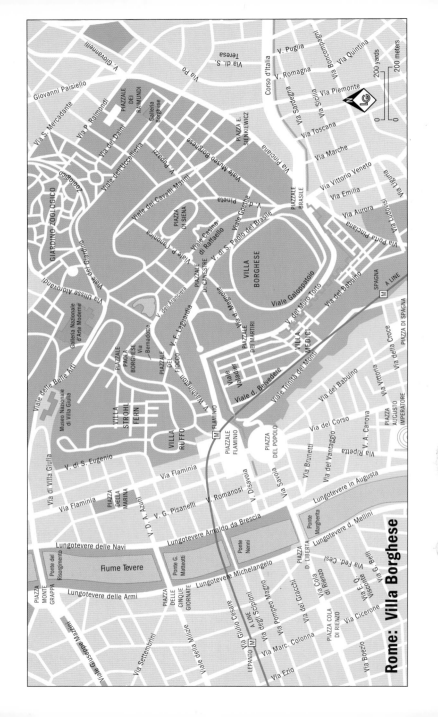

Rome: Villa Borghese

LET'S GO

PAGES PACKED WITH ESSENTIAL INFORMATION

"Value-packed, unbeatable, accurate, and comprehensive."

—The Los Angeles Times

"The guides are aimed not only at young budget travelers but at the independent traveler; a sort of streetwise cookbook for traveling alone."

—The New York Times

"Unbeatable; good sight-seeing advice; up-to-date info on restaurants, hotels, and inns; a commitment to money-saving travel; and a wry style that brightens nearly every page."

—The Washington Post

THE BEST TRAVEL BARGAINS IN YOUR BUDGET

"All the dirt, dirt cheap."

—People

"Let's Go follows the creed that you don't have to toss your life's savings to the wind to travel—unless you want to."

—The Salt Lake Tribune

REAL ADVICE FOR REAL EXPERIENCES

"The writers seem to have experienced every rooster-packed bus and lunar-surfaced mattress about which they write."

—The New York Times

"[Let's Go's] devoted updaters really walk the walk (and thumb the ride, and trek the trail). Learn how to fish, haggle, find work—anywhere."

—Food & Wine

"A world-wise traveling companion—always ready with friendly advice and helpful hints, all sprinkled with a bit of wit."

—The Philadelphia Inquirer

A GUIDE WITH A SPIRIT AND A SOCIAL CONSCIENCE

"Lighthearted and sophisticated, informative and fun to read. [Let's Go] helps the novice traveler navigate like a knowledgeable old hand."

—Atlanta Journal-Constitution

"The serious mission at the book's core reveals itself in exhortations to respect the culture and the environment—and, if possible, to visit as a volunteer, a student, or a teacher rather than a tourist."

—San Francisco Chronicle

LET'S GO PUBLICATIONS

TRAVEL GUIDES

Australia
Austria & Switzerland
Brazil
Britain
California
Central America
Chile
China
Costa Rica
Eastern Europe
Ecuador
Egypt
Europe
France
Germany
Greece
Hawaii
India & Nepal
Ireland
Israel
Italy
Japan
Mexico
New Zealand
Peru
Puerto Rico
Southeast Asia
Spain & Portugal with Morocco
Thailand
USA
Vietnam
Western Europe

ROADTRIP GUIDE

Roadtripping USA

ADVENTURE GUIDES

Alaska
Pacific Northwest
Southwest USA

CITY GUIDES

Amsterdam
Barcelona
Boston
Buenos Aires
London
New York City
Paris
Rome
San Francisco
Washington, DC

POCKET CITY GUIDES

Amsterdam
Berlin
Boston
Chicago
London
New York City
Paris
San Francisco
Venice
Washington, DC

LET'S GO

ITALY
2009

RAÚL CARRILLO EDITOR
SARA O'ROURKE ASSOCIATE EDITOR
MARY POTTER ASSOCIATE EDITOR
MATT ROLLER ASSOCIATE EDITOR

RESEARCHER-WRITERS
MATEO CORBY   **FABIAN POLIAK**
ASHLEY GRAND   **JULIA ROONEY**
PAIGE PAVONE   **KENNETH G. SAATHOFF**

GRETCHEN KRUEGER MAP EDITOR
LAUREN CARUSO MANAGING EDITOR

ST. MARTIN'S PRESS ⚑ NEW YORK

HELPING LET'S GO. If you want to share your discoveries, suggestions, or corrections, please drop us a line. We appreciate every piece of correspondence, whether a postcard, a 10-page email, or a coconut. Visit Let's Go at **http://www.letsgo.com,** or send email to:

> **feedback@letsgo.com**
> **Subject: "Let's Go: Italy 2009"**

Address mail to:

> **Let's Go: italy 2009**
> **67 Mount Auburn St.**
> **Cambridge, MA 02138**
> **USA**

In addition to the invaluable travel advice our readers share with us, many are kind enough to offer their services as researchers or editors. Unfortunately, our charter enables us to employ only currently enrolled Harvard students.

HOW TO USE THIS BOOK

COVERAGE LAYOUT. Welcome to *Let's Go: Italy 2009*. Our book begins in Rome, still the center of Italian pride, hope, and *la dolce vita*. From there, we travel to the rugged, alpine north; the flashy (and occasionally trashy) Mediterranean coast; and the top of the boot, containing beautiful lakes and cutting edge fashion. We visit the northeastern shores of Venice, Verona, and spots immortalized in literature; central Italy for culinary and artistic delights; and Campania, for lovers, ruins, and the occasional mobster. Finally, we move to the sunbaked southern heel, explosive Sicily, and mythic Sardinia. Black tabs on the side of each page and our extensive **Index** (p. 775) will help you navigate Italy's regions.

TRANSPORTATION INFO. Sections on intercity transportation generally list all major destinations, followed by trip duration, frequency, time range of departures, and price. A typical listing: Trains to Rome (1hr., 13 per day 4:30am-7pm, €10). For more general info on travel, consult the **Essentials** (p. 9) section.

COVERING THE BASICS. Discover Italy (p. 1), contains **Let's Go Picks** (our favorite places in Italy) and **Suggested Itineraries** to help you plan your trip. Essentials (p. 9) provides logistical information and useful tips for travelers in Italy. **Life and Times** (p. 56) explains Italy's 3000 years of history, culture, and customs. Along your Italian trek, reference the useful **Italian phrasebook** and **menu reader** in the **Appendix** (p. 765). For information on study abroad, volunteer, and work opportunities in Italy, consult Beyond Tourism (p. 91).

SCHOLARLY ARTICLES. To help travelers understand their destinations in a more in-depth fashion, Let's Go solicits experts for in-depth treatments of country-specific topics. Our extended articles discuss the cultural institution of *calcio* (soccer; p. 85), the emotional entanglement behind the influential *Laocoön* sculpture (p. 143), the role of ecotourism in southern Italy (p. 103), and a program in Rome that intends to resurrect Latin, Italian's ancestor (p. 151).

PRICE DIVERSITY. Our researchers list establishments in order of value from best to worst, with absolute favorites denoted by the Let's Go thumbs-up (🖐). Since the cheapest price does not always mean the best value, we have incorporated a system of price ranges for food and accommodations (p. XIII).

LANGUAGE AND OTHER QUIRKS. The English translations for cities are listed when applicable, followed by their Italian name. For pronunciation help, consult the phonetic spelling in each city introduction, or the Appendix (p. 765). In text and on maps, the names of streets and **piazze** have been shortened to the standardized abbreviations chart on the inside back cover.

PHONE CODES AND TELEPHONE NUMBERS. Phone codes for each city appear opposite the name of the city and are denoted by the ☎ icon. Phone numbers in text are also preceded by the ☎ icon. Emergency phone numbers have not been listed in every city, but are conveniently on the inside back cover.

A NOTE TO OUR READERS. The information for this book was gathered by Let's Go researchers from May through August of 2008. Each listing is based on one researcher's opinion, formed during his or her visit at a particular time. Those traveling at other times may have different experiences since prices, dates, hours, and conditions are always subject to change. You are urged to check the facts presented in this book beforehand to avoid inconvenience and surprises.

RESEARCHER-WRITERS

Mateo Corby *Sicily, Calabria*

The memories of most RWs fade into the dusty recesses of archived travel notes long after they have stepped off their route—not so with Mateo. The man is a legend in his own skin. Blazing through Sicily and Calabria in record time, this supersonic bomber also provided precise copy. He experienced *la dolce vita* in a way most never will—so quickly he was able to meet every backpacker on the lava-seared island at least twice. "Isa nice!"

Ashley Grand *Rome, Sardinia*

Ashley braved the summer heat—and the tourist hordes—in Rome to bring readers the inside pulse of the heart of *la città eterna*. The Poli-Sci major also got to see the flipside of Italy while rubbing shoulders with the *sardo* in rural Sardinia. Ashley finished her route just in time to study abroad in yet another cultural capital—Buenos Aires.

Paige Pavone *Liguria, Tuscany, Umbria*

Those pretty boys under the Tuscan sun never knew what hit 'em. Paige intrepidly toured the soul of Italy and sent back excellent, clever copy detailing the best of the Riviera, Florence, and Siena. Mastering Tuscan slang and rooting through the touristy Riviera to find the hottest of seaside spots, Paige used her researcher's instinct to get the inside scoop on the most path-not-taken of places. *Grazie mille* Paige! Your coverage=*ganza!*

Fabian Poliak *Campania, Puglia, Basilicata, Abruzzo, Molise*

Fabian had a special touch for the Wild South. Not even twin Swedish blondes or equally lascivious nuns could deter this well-traveled *gaucho* from his goal: creating nightlife and outdoors coverage where there once was none. Always down for another adventure, Fabian learned Italian on the fly, enjoyed special connections and protection from a certain family in Naples, and developed a motto that researchers will use for years to come: "There is no such thing as the wrong street."

RESEARCHER-WRITERS

Julia Rooney   *Emilia-Romagna, Friuli, Le Marche, Trentino, Veneto*

This former track star's painterly eye led her on a veggie-pizza-fueled whirlwind from rainy beaches up north to Giotto's Scrovegni Chapel in Padua to Italy's party capital, Rimini. Julia truly hit her stride in Venice, returning home to New York City energized, practically fluent in Italian, and with plenty of artistic inspiration. Her plaque now resides in the LG Hall of Fame.

Kenneth G. Saathoff   *Piedmont, Valle D'Aosta, The Lake Country, Lombardy*

This crafty outdoorsman with dashing good looks took his mountaineering skills and prolific prose to the rugged Italian Alps and beautiful isolated abbeys alike. There, touching the heavens, this soon-to-be senior composed copy to rival the *canti* of Dante, the novels of Stendhal, and the magna opera of all others who had drawn inspiration from the beautiful scene before him. Braving euro-less days and a veritable language barrier (at first), Kenny G prevailed. *Alooorrraaa, dimmi,* what more could an editor *vuole?*

CONTRIBUTING WRITERS

Alexander Bevilacqua was born in Milan and has lived in Germany, Australia, and the United States, but his heart remains in the wheat fields of southern Italy. He is a 2006 graduate in History of Harvard University and was a Researcher-Writer for *Let's Go: Germany 2005* in Bavaria.

Dr. Laura Flusche teaches art history at the University of Dallas's Rome campus. She is the founder of Friends of Rome (www.friendsofrome.org), a nonprofit dedicated to the preservation of Roman monuments. She's also president of The Institute of Design & Culture in Rome (www.idcrome.org).

Edoardo Gallo, from Cuneo, Italy, is currently working as a consultant in New York after researching for *Let's Go: Central America* in El Salvador, Nicaragua, and Honduras. He is a 2004 graduate in Physics and Mathematics of Harvard University and is also a passionate, lifelong fan of Juventus.

Clem Wood has spent summers in both Florence and Rome. He graduated from Harvard in the spring of 2008 with an A.B. in Classics and plans to return to Italy for further adventures and studies in the near future.

CONTENTS

ACKNOWLEDGMENTS

TEAM ITALY THANKS: Our super RWs!!!!!!! ◪Lauren for devotion, patience, and TLC. Prod! Gretchen for map perfection. ◩Jonathan for salvation. Team France for playing second fiddle. Kansas...for nothing. NOS. Sara for being clutch. Middle school R&B ballads. Gelfand for the help at the end. Ditto Gordon. We done!!!

RAÚL THANKS: Mama. Mary Potter for being a saint. The Jungle. Mateo and Fabian for hilarious and sometimes very touching marginalia. Weezy F Baby for that last push. Sammy G for always caring. LG of LG—the tension was awkward. Brain Break. ◪EM. RIP Rolldiggity, you understood me best.

MARY THANKS: *Grazie mille* Mommer 'n em & ◪Thomas Aquinas, Rennie & Sharon, Lauren, Ra-Raúl, mat-roller & sara-o. Char, Dee Dee & marycat, Julia, FRITA, the studs at LGHQ, the blocktopus+◪popkins, the Bro-tel, and all members of the little bookgroup that couldn't.

SARA THANKS: Lauren for schmeeks, Hwack, and being (my) superior. MPMP for my fresh pond map, ETC. Raúl. City Pod+Dube for lunch and other failed plans. LGHQ. Lyle&Brit for girls' nights. Family and friends for readership. ◪Nelly for TACK, surrealism, and other Awkward Moments. Siblings for fun, friendship, and bonding over chaos. Dad and Mom, as always.

GRETCHEN THANKS: Team Italia, for hard work, creativity, and patience. My RWs, for editing maps with care. Meg, shoop! Becca and Elissa, for laughing and appreciating little things. Illiana, for advice about life after graduating. Derek, for the music and for teaching me about maps. MNDC, for all the good times. Trish, Justine, and Eliz, for the love. My family.

Editor
Raúl Carrillo
Associate Editors
Sara O'Rourke
Mary Potter
Matt Roller
Managing Editor
Lauren Caruso
Map Editor
Gretchen Krueger
Typesetter
Jonathan B. Reed

LET'S GO

Publishing Director
Inés C. Pacheco
Editor-in-Chief
Samantha Gelfand
Production Manager
Jansen A. S. Thurmer
Cartography Manager
R. Derek Wetzel
Editorial Managers
Dwight Livingstone Curtis,
Vanessa J. Dube, Nathaniel Rakich
Financial Manager
Lauren Caruso
Publicity and Marketing Manager
Patrick McKiernan
Personnel Manager
Laura M. Gordon
Production Associate
C. Alexander Tremblay
Director of IT & E-Commerce
Lukáš Tóth
Website Manager
Ian Malott
Office Coordinators
Vinnie Chiappini, Jenny Wong
Director of Advertising Sales
Eric Alberto Claros
Business Manager of Advertising
Nicole J. Bass
Senior Advertising Associates
Kipyegon Kitur, Jeremy Siegfried,
John B. Ulrich
Junior Advertising Associate
Edward C. Robinson Jr.

President
Timothy J. J. Creamer
General Manager
Jim McKellar

Italy: Chapters

Zurich
Bern
SWITZERLAND
AUSTRIA
HUNGARY
SLOVENIA
Ljubljana
Zagreb
CROATIA

Trentino-Alto Adige
p. 356
Friuli-Venezia Giulia
p. 370

The Lake Country
p. 270
Lombardy
p. 235
The Veneto
p. 305
Trieste
BOSNIA AND HERZEGOVINIA
Sarajevo

Piedmont and Valle d'Aosta
p. 162
Milan
Venice

Turin
Emilia-Romagna
p. 385
Bologna
SAN MARINO

Genoa
FRANCE
Nice
Cannes
Liguria
p. 197
MONACO
Florence
Le Marche
p. 530

Corsica
FRANCE
Tuscany
p. 426
Umbria
p. 502
Abruzzo and Molise
p. 547

Rome
Bari
Brindisi

Rome
p. 104
Naples
Campania
p. 563
Puglia and Calabria
p. 620

Sassari
Sardinia
p. 725

Cagliari

N

0   200 kilometers
0   200 miles

Palermo
Sicily
p. 653
Catania

ALGERIA
TUNISIA
Tunis

2 PRICE RANGES ❸ ❹
❶ ITALY ❺

Our researchers list establishments in order of value from best to worst, honoring our favorites with a *Let's Go* thumbs-up (🔳). Because the best *value* is not always the cheapest *price*, we have incorporated a system of price ranges based on a rough expectation of what you will spend. For **accommodations,** we base our range on the cheapest price for which one traveler can stay for one night. For **restaurants** and other dining establishments, we estimate the average amount one traveler will spend in one sitting. The table below tells you what you'll typically find in Italy at the corresponding price range, but keep in mind that no system can allow for the quirks of individual establishments.

ACCOMMODATIONS	RANGE	WHAT YOU'RE *LIKELY* TO FIND
❶	under €20	Campgrounds, dorm rooms, *suores* (rooms in religious institutions), or dorm-style rooms. Expect bunk beds and a communal bath. You may have to provide or rent towels and sheets.
❷	€20-30	Upper-end hostels or lower-end *pensioni*. You may have a private bathroom, or there may be a sink in your room and a communal shower in the hall.
❸	€31-45	A small room with a private bath, probably in a budget hotel or *pensione*. Should have decent amenities, such as phone and TV. Breakfast may be included in the price of the room.
❹	€46-65	Similar to ❸, but may have more amenities or be in a convenient location.
❺	above €65	Large hotels or upscale chains. If it's a ❺ and it doesn't have the perks you want, you've paid too much.

FOOD	RANGE	WHAT YOU'RE *LIKELY* TO FIND
❶	under €7	Probably a fast-food stand, *gelateria*, bar, cafe, or pizzeria. Rarely ever a sit-down meal.
❷	€7-15	Sit-down pizzerias and most affordable *trattorie*. Should include *primi* and *secondi*.
❸	€16-25	Similar to ❷, but nicer setting and a more elaborate menu. May offer a cheaper lunch *menù*, and a pizza could be a less expansive alternative to a *primo* or *secondo* combination.
❹	€26-33	As in ❸, higher prices are likely related to better service, but in these restaurants, the food will tend to be fancier or more elaborate, or the location will be especially convenient or historic. While few restaurants in this price range will have a dress code, T-shirts, jeans, or shorts may be frowned upon.
❺	above €33	Venerable reputation, a 90-page wine list, or the freshest seafood and a harbor view. Elegant attire may be expected.

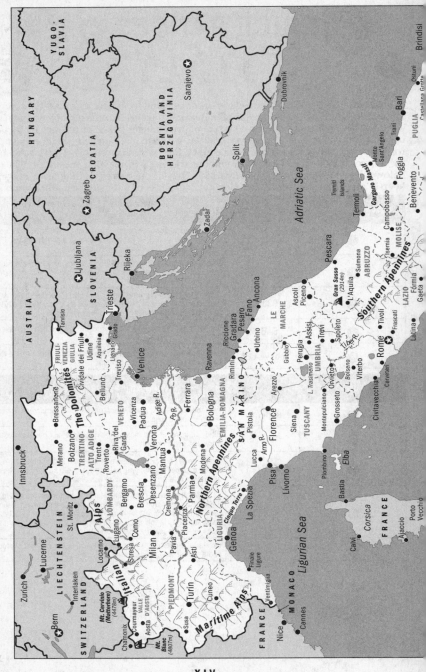

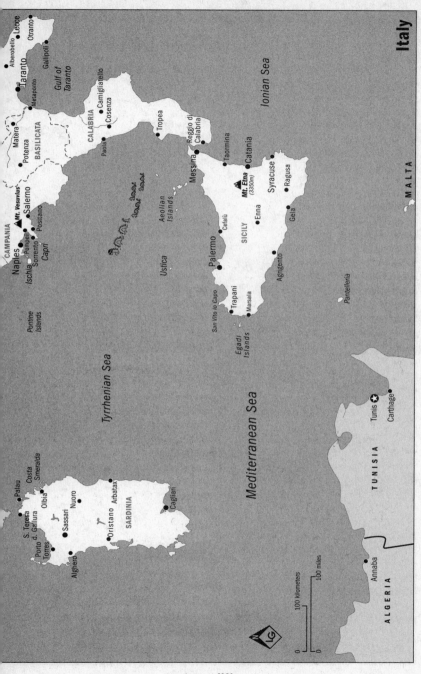

Italy

Alberobello
Leece
Otranto
Taranto
Galipoli
Gulf of
Taranto
Metaponto
Matera
BASILICATA
Potenza
Camigliatello
Cosenza
CALABRIA
Paola
Tropea
Reggio di
Calabria
Taormina
Messina
Catania
Mt. Etna
(3350m)
Syracuse
Ragusa
SICILY
Enna
Cefalù
Gela
Palermo
Agrigento
Aeolian
Islands
Ustica
San Vito lo Capo
Trapani
Marsala
Egadi
Islands
Ionian Sea
MALTA

CAMPANIA
Naples
Mt. Vesuvius
Salerno
Pompeii
Positano
Ischia
Sorrento
Capri
Pontine
Islands

Pantelleria

Tyrrhenian Sea

Mediterranean Sea

Carthage
Tunis
TUNISIA

Palau
Costa
S. Teresa
Smeralda
Porto d. Gallura
Olbia
Torres
Nuoro
Sassari
Arbatax
Alghero
Oristano
SARDINIA
Cagliari

Annaba
ALGERIA

0   100 kilometers
0   100 miles

XV

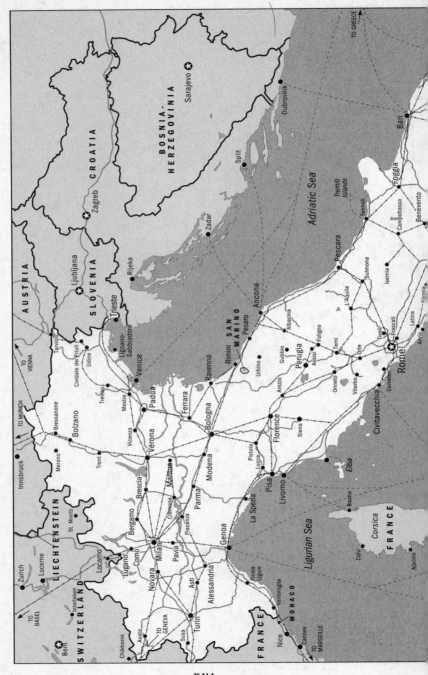

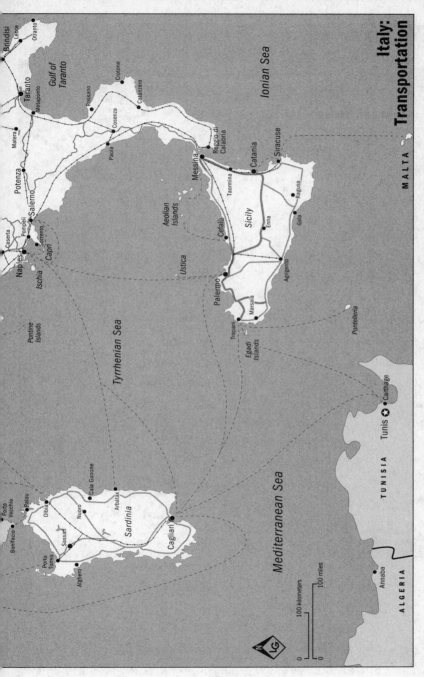

Italy:
Transportation

hostels of naples - italy

from 16 euros hostelofthesun

Located in the city center in front of the ferry port to Capri, Sorrento and Sicily, and two minutes by walk to "Sita" bus terminal to Pompei and Amalfi Coast.
Private rooms and dorms available.

We offer full kitchen, free breakfast, 24hrs reception, free lockers, hot showers, english speaking staff, free luggage storage, tourist information, internet access, lounge room, free maps, satellite tv, dvd room, laundry service.

Hostel of the Sun - via Melisurgo, 15 - 80133 Naples - Italy
phone and fax: 0039 081 420 63 93 (from anywhere outside Italy)
phone and fax: 081 420 63 93 (from anywhere inside Italy)
www.hostelnapoli.com - info@hostelnapoli.com - skype: hostelofthesun

from 16 euros bella capri hostel & hotel **bella capri**

Located in the centre of Naples right across the port for ferries to Capri, Ischia, Sorrento, Sicily and Aeolie Islands, and only three minutes on foot to "Sita" bus terminal to Pompei, Positano and Amalfi.

Beds from 16 €. Rooms from 50 €.

We offer mixed and female dorms and private rooms, some of which with a view on the bay of Naples.
Super friendly multilingual staff. Free breakfast. Free luggage storage. Common room with satellite TV and English DVD movies. Free internet. WiFi connection. Free maps. Fully equipped kitchen. Laundry facility. Air conditioning. Groups discounts.

Hostel and Hotel Bella Capri - via Melisurgo, 4 - 80133 Naples - Italy
phone: 0039 081 552 94 94 - fax: 0039 081 552 92 65 (from anywhere outside Italy)
phone: 081 552 94 94 - fax: 081 552 92 65 (from anywhere inside Italy)
www.bellacapri.it - info@bellacapri.it

from 13 euros hostel pensione *Mancini*

Small cozy hostel located right in front of Naples' central railway station and Circumvesuviana local trains to Herculaneum, Mt. Vesuvius, Pompei and Sorrento.

Beds from 13 €. Rooms from 40 €.

We offer mixed and female dorms and private rooms.
Very helpful English, Spanish and Polish speaking staff. Free breakfast. Free luggage storage. Common room with satellite TV and English DVD movies. Free internet. WiFi connection. Free maps. Fully equipped kitchen. Air conditioning. Groups discounts.

Hostel Pensione Mancini - via P.S. Mancini 33, 80139 Naples - Italy
phone: 0039 081 553 67 31 - fax: 0039 081 554 66 75 (from anywhere outside Italy)
phone: 081 553 67 31 - fax: 081 554 66 75 (from anywhere inside Italy)
www.hostelpensionemancini.com - info@hostelpensionemancini.com

Directions

Hostel of the Sun and Hostel Hotel Bella Capri
Exit the station cross the square and you will find the bus stop R2. The bus will drive through C.so Umberto and than turn to via Depretis. You get off at second stop of via Depretis. In front of the bus stop is via Melisurgo. At n° 4 is Hotel Bella Capri and at n° 15 is Hostel of the Sun.

Hostel Pensione Mancini
Exit the station square "piazza Garibaldi", till you enter via Mancini. We are at n° 33.

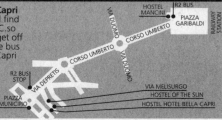

DISCOVER ITALY

The classic images of Italy—the vespas, the Vatican, the *vino*—are all enjoyable, but don't let them define your experience. Instead, stomp through volcanic ruins, masquerade with budget-friendly Bacchus, and saunter down cobblestone streets—in stilettos, of course. Slap on your Frauda sunglasses, slip into D&G, douse yourself in Gucci perfume, and indulge in some good ol' Italian elegance. Meet those eccentric restaurant owners, learn Italy's local secrets, and explore her untainted nature. In between action-packed adventures, don't forget to step back, as Italians often do, and experience *la dolce far niente* (literally, the sweetness of doing nothing). Don't just come to Italy to confirm the spaghetti-and-meatballs image; come to discover something you can't send home on a postcard. Discover the chaos, energy, and allure. Discover Italy.

FACTS AND FIGURES

ITALY 2009 POPULATION: 58 million

NUMBER OF CELL PHONES: 63 million

MONEY THROWN INTO ROME'S TREVI FOUNTAIN EACH DAY: about €3000

ANNUAL WINE CONSUMPTION PER PERSON: 26 gallons

REGULAR CHURCHGOERS: 18½ million

REGULAR SOCCER FANS: 30 million

VATICAN CITY: World's richest institution; world's smallest country

ANNUAL BREAD CONSUMPTION PER PERSON: 26 kg

READY, SET...DON'T GO YET!

Tourism enters overdrive in June, July, and August. Hotels are booked solid, rates skyrocket, and rows of lounge chairs take over pristine beaches. Around *Ferragosto*, a national holiday on August 15, Italians head to the coast, leaving a flood of closed businesses in their wake. Some larger cities avoid this summer hibernation and remain enjoyable in August, but late May through July make for a livelier trip. Traveling to Italy in early May or early September assures a calmer, cooler, cheaper vacation, with temperatures averaging a comfortable 25°C (77°F). Depending on the destination, a trip in April offers the advantages of lower prices and smaller crowds. The best weather for hiking in the Alps is from June to September; ski season generally lasts from December through late March, although some locations stay open year-round.

MOSAICS TO MODERNISM

Unsurprisingly, Italy, the birthplace of the Renaissance, is home to impressive art collections. The most important are found in the country's largest cities; however, virtually every small town has its own *museo archeologico* or *pinacoteca* (art gallery) that showcases collections that range from Greek pottery shards and Roman mosaics to Futurist paintings. Don't head to these if you're looking for a high concentration of famous works, but avoiding the crowds and finding that lone Caravaggio or da Messina in a regional museum can be a more rewarding experience than a barrage of masterworks. Also, note that some of Italy's greatest artwork is held within the sacred walls of her many churches.

DISCOVER

CITY	PRINCIPAL ART COLLECTIONS
Florence	Uffizi Gallery (p. 443) Galleria dell'Accademia (p. 449) Museo dell'Opera del Duomo (p. 443)
Milan	Pinacoteca di Brera (p. 247) Galleria d'Arte Moderna (p. 249)
Naples	Museo Archeologico Nazionale (p. 576) Museo di Capodimonte (p. 578)
Rome	Sistine Chapel (p. 146) Vatican Museums (p. 146) Galleria Borghese (p. 148) Museo Nazionale d'Arte Antica (p. 150)
Reggio di Calabria	Museo Nazionale (p. 643)
Rovereto	Museo d'Arte Moderna e Contemporanea—"Il Mart" (p. 360)
Siena	Pinacoteca Nazionale (p. 464) Museo dell'Opera Metropolitana (p. 463)
Trieste	Museo Revoltella (p. 374)
Turin	Museo Egizio (p. 170) Galleria Sabauda (p. 170)
Venice	Collezione Peggy Guggenheim (p. 325) Gallerie dell'Accademia (p. 325)

SO MUCH MORE THAN PIZZA

Pizza, beloved internationally as a quick takeout meal, is much more than fast food on its home turf. Originating in **Naples** (p. 563) in the 1800s after introduction of tomatoes, pizza has evolved beyond the basic *Margherita*. Italy's pizzerias may be good, but don't be afraid to branch out. Even pasta, an integral part of the Italian diet for thousands of years, faces competition for its claim as the Italian carb of choice. Italy's famous creamy rice dish, *risotto*, incorporates local specialties: wine and truffles in Piedmont, seafood in the Veneto, and saffron in Milan. In northern regions such as **Trentino-Alto Adige** (p. 356), polenta and gnocchi (potato and flour dumplings) enjoy popularity. To go beyond the nationwide staples, begin your regional tour of Italian cuisine with **Piedmont's** (p. 162) white truffles. Watch your wallet, though, because these 'white diamonds' go for US$850-1500 per lb. This region also saw the invention of Nutella, which is now consumed internationally in greater amounts than all peanut butter brands combined. **Genoa** (p. 197) flaunts colorful pesto, which gets its name from *pestatura* (a method of grinding using a mortar and pestle); imitations are marketed worldwide, but the best basil leaves—and therefore the best pesto—hail from Liguria. The **Friuli-Venezia Giulia region** (p. 370) has a subtle Slavic flair, apparent in ingredients like yogurt, fennel, cumin, and paprika. **Treviso** (p. 350), in the Veneto region, is famous for its tiramisu, a heavenly espresso-and-rum-soaked cake layered with mild *mascarpone* cheese. Its name, which literally means "pick me up," is rumored to have originated from its use by tired prostitutes. Check out **Tuscany's** (p. 426) saltless bread, whose popularity comes as a surprise to many; several theories explain the lack of salt, including one that claims a 12th-century salt price-hike protest that changed from boycott to tradition after prices came back down. Centuries ago, **Florence** (p. 426) birthed gelato, a milk-based frozen treat now available throughout the country. In the heart of Emilia-Romagna, **Bologna** (p. 385), birthplace of *tortellini bolognese* sauce, reigns as Italy's culinary capital, while **Modena** (p. 399) is renowned for its balsamic vinegar, and **Parma** (p. 403) boasts tender prosciutto. The region is perhaps most famous for its *parmigiano-reggiano* cheese. Besides Naples' pizza, southern Italy offers seafood, olive oil, and *granita*, **Sicily's** (p. 653) slushy version of gelato, and *cipolle rosse* (red onions) from **Tropea** (p. 161). To find the perfect wine to compliment your meal, see **In Vino Veritas** (p. 82).

BICEP CURLS GET THE GIRLS

Sandwiched between the Mediterranean and Adriatic Seas, the Italian coastline stretches over 2000 mi. In the northwest, the famous beaches of **Liguria** (p. 197) form the Italian Riviera, home to the picturesque fishing villages of **Cinque Terre** (p. 210) and the glitterati-packed resorts of **San Remo** (p. 226). Farther down, the hidden gem, **Ponza** (p. 160), provides a relaxing daytrip from sweaty Rome. Swing south along the Amalfi Coast to beach towns like **Positano** (p. 604) and **Capri** (p. 599) that offer sparkling waters, lapping against cliffs and lemon groves. After getting your dose of high culture in Venice's art museums, don't miss the nearby beach towns like **Caorle** (p. 347), **Lignano** (p. 379), and **Grado** (p. 376). On the Salento Peninsula, **Otranto** (p. 638) and **Gallipoli's** (p. 637)emerald waters entice visitors. In Abruzzo and Molise, the **Tremiti Islands (p. 561)** are home to rocky coves and secluded beaches, excellent for swimming and snorkeling. Also on the east coast, **Rimini (p. 415)** attracts a large student population with its beaches during the day as well as a smoking night club scene. Calabria and Sicily offer visitors variety, from the dark stone coasts of African-influenced **Pantelleria** (p. 721) to the resort towns of **Cefalù** (p. 664).

TAKE A HIKE!

Italy presents plenty of opportunities for the outdoor adventurer, whether you get your kicks staring into the fiery mouth of a volcano or strolling through the Tuscan countryside. The **Aeolian Islands (p. 667)** are home to both active and inactive volcanoes, while nearby **Mt. Etna** (p. 694) offers far-reaching views. Hike, bike, or ski through **Abruzzo National Park** (p. 554), the southern Apennines, the northeastern **Dolomites** (p. 356), or Calabria's **Sila Massif** (p. 648). Enjoy the hiking and beaches of Liguria's **Cinque Terre** (p. 210), a young backpacker's paradise. Slow things down by taking Grandma on a walk through the **Chianti region (p. 457)** of Tuscany, which offers travelers a less strenuous experience; walk along country roads past vineyards, olive groves, and ancient castles, all while enjoying views of the surrounding hills and valleys.

TAKE A BREAK ON A LAKE

Northern Italy is home to the gorgeous Lake Country. Take in its beauty on a stroll through citrus groves in **Limone** (p. 276) or catch some waves on a windsurfing board in **Domaso** (p. 286). A trek along **Stresa's** (p. 297) scenic trails will alleviate any stress, leaving you ready to hit the clubs in **Desenzano** (p. 280), reportedly home of the best *discoteche* on Lake Garda. *Mangia* in **Menaggio** (p. 290) to get a taste of some authentic regional cuisine. Be prepared to shell out a few extra euro for this paradise; however, the lakeside view from your balcony will remind you that it's worth it.

HOW TO RUIN A PERFECTLY GOOD TRIP

The Roman Empire may have fallen 1500 years ago, but it continues to bring global commerce into Rome. Some crumbling and wonderfully preserved arches, aqueducts, and amphitheaters give a sense of majesty, mystery, and poetry. Although many Italian cities, including **Spoleto** (p. 520), **Rimini (p. 415)**, **Aquileia** (p. 376), **Aosta** (p. 189), and **Acqui Terme** (p. 183) boast some sort of Roman relic, the most impressive ruins are scattered through the streets of **Rome** itself (p. 104), where travelers can admire the famous Colosseum, Pantheon, and Roman Forum. Daytrips from Rome lead to the extravagant Villa Adriana in **Tivoli** (p. 157). Farther south, **Naples** (p. 563) boasts a world-renowned archaeological museum and miles of subterranean Roman aqueducts open for exploration. Near Naples, **Pompeii** (p. 582) is a city eternally petrified in AD 79, when an eruption of Mt. Vesuvius covered it in lava. A neighboring excavation site, **Herculaneum** (p. 582), features another surprisingly intact 2000-year-old town. Across the peninsula, **Brindisi** (p. 628) is home to the column marking the end of the Appian Way, an ancient road that led to Rome. Italy also has numerous relics of pre-Roman inhabitants. Etruscan artifacts can be found in many Tuscan towns like **Fiesole** (p. 456). Sicily's proximity to Greece led to the establishment of many Greek colonies, which were the first great civilizations in Italy, including **Segesta** (p. 716), **Agrigento** (p. 705), and **Syracuse** (p. 699). On the mainland, **Paestum** (p. 618) is home to both Doric temples and Roman forums. Evidence of more ancient civilizations can be found in **Alberobello's** *trulli* (p. 626), and **Sardinia's** *nuraghi* (p. 761).

☒LET'S GO PICKS

BEST PLACE TO SHOW UP BACCHUS HIMSELF: In the vineyards of the **Chianti** region (p. 457).

BEST PLACE TO SAY A HAIL MARY TO ATONE FOR BACCHANALIAN EXCESS: The **Vatican** (p. 136) offers confession in numerous languages.

BEST PLACE TO SLEEP LIKE A ROCK: The white-washed, conical *trulli* of **Alberobello** (p. 626) are mortarless abodes used as residences, churches, and restaurants. **Pantelleria's** domed *dammusi* (p. 721) are constructed from petrified lava.

BEST PLACE TO REVEL IN INSOMNIA: Wild bars and themed clubs dominate the beachside party town of **Rimini** (p. 415) and nearby **Riccione** (p. 421).

BEST PLACE TO GET BLOWN AWAY: Scale **Mt. Vesuvius (p. 586)**, Europe's only active volcano; investigate—but not too closely—**Mt. Etna's** (p. 694) lava-seared wilderness.

BEST PLACE TO CORPSE-WATCH: Pace through the huge **Cappuchin Catacombs** (p. 661) in Palermo, where 8000 bodies rest in their moth-eaten Sunday best. Or check out the partially decayed body of **Ötzi** (p. 365), a 5000-year-old Iceman in Bolzano.

EATALY (4 WEEKS)

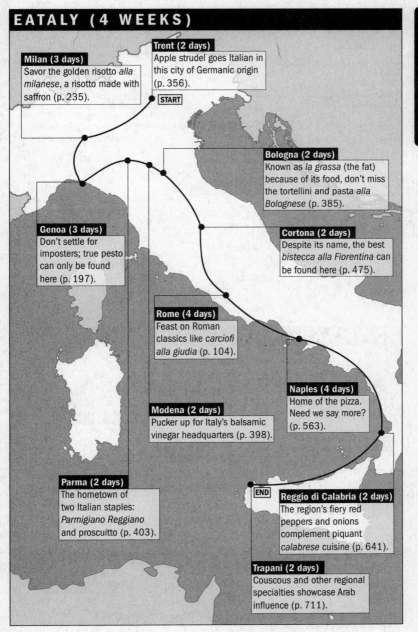

Milan (3 days)
Savor the golden risotto *alla milanese*, a risotto made with saffron (p. 235).

Trent (2 days)
Apple strudel goes Italian in this city of Germanic origin (p. 356).
START

Bologna (2 days)
Known as *la grassa* (the fat) because of its food, don't miss the tortellini and pasta *alla Bolognese* (p. 385).

Genoa (3 days)
Don't settle for imposters; true pesto can only be found here (p. 197).

Cortona (2 days)
Despite its name, the best *bistecca alla Fiorentina* can be found here (p. 475).

Rome (4 days)
Feast on Roman classics like *carciofi alla giudia* (p. 104).

Naples (4 days)
Home of the pizza. Need we say more? (p. 563).

Modena (2 days)
Pucker up for Italy's balsamic vinegar headquarters (p. 398).

Parma (2 days)
The hometown of two Italian staples: *Parmigiano Reggiano* and proscuitto (p. 403).

END
Reggio di Calabria (2 days)
The region's fiery red peppers and onions complement piquant *calabrese* cuisine (p. 641).

Trapani (2 days)
Couscous and other regional specialties showcase Arab influence (p. 711).

DEBEACHERY (3 WEEKS)

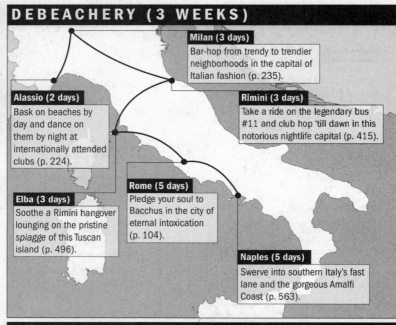

Milan (3 days)
Bar-hop from trendy to trendier neighborhoods in the capital of Italian fashion (p. 235).

Alassio (2 days)
Bask on beaches by day and dance on them by night at internationally attended clubs (p. 224).

Rimini (3 days)
Take a ride on the legendary bus #11 and club hop 'till dawn in this notorious nightlife capital (p. 415).

Elba (3 days)
Soothe a Rimini hangover lounging on the pristine *spiagge* of this Tuscan island (p. 496).

Rome (5 days)
Pledge your soul to Bacchus in the city of eternal intoxication (p. 104).

Naples (5 days)
Swerve into southern Italy's fast lane and the gorgeous Amalfi Coast (p. 563).

ROMP AROUND THE RUINS (2 WEEKS)

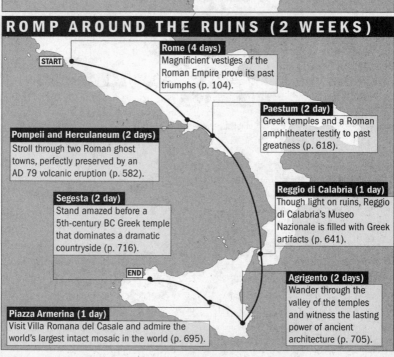

START

Rome (4 days)
Magnificient vestiges of the Roman Empire prove its past triumphs (p. 104).

Paestum (2 day)
Greek temples and a Roman amphitheater testify to past greatness (p. 618).

Pompeii and Herculaneum (2 days)
Stroll through two Roman ghost towns, perfectly preserved by an AD 79 volcanic eruption (p. 582).

Reggio di Calabria (1 day)
Though light on ruins, Reggio di Calabria's Museo Nazionale is filled with Greek artifacts (p. 641).

Segesta (2 day)
Stand amazed before a 5th-century BC Greek temple that dominates a dramatic countryside (p. 716).

END

Agrigento (2 days)
Wander through the valley of the temples and witness the lasting power of ancient architecture (p. 705).

Piazza Armerina (1 day)
Visit Villa Romana del Casale and admire the world's largest intact mosaic in the world (p. 695).

NORTHERN NATURAL WONDERS (2 WEEKS)

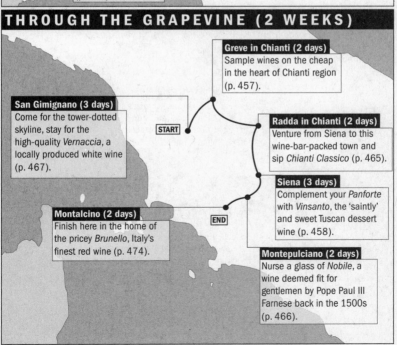

Aosta (3 days)
A heaven for every outdoorsman, with rock-climbing, hang-gliding, mountain biking, kayaking, and rafting in the surrounding valleys (p. 189).

Domaso (2 days)
Cool breezes in this lakeside town create the perfect conditions for windsurfing (p. 286).

Bressanone (3 days)
Throw your pack down in this sleepy town, then trek the extensive trails (p. 366).

START

Laghi di Fusine (2 days)
Lakes and mountains so beautiful you might not believe your eyes (p. 384).

Cuneo (2 days)
Renting a car will be worth the expense to experience some of Italy's least-trafficked Alpine hiking trails (p. 176).

END

Riva del Garda (2 days)
Feast on stunning views while hiking or mountain-biking by Lake Garda (p. 273).

THROUGH THE GRAPEVINE (2 WEEKS)

Greve in Chianti (2 days)
Sample wines on the cheap in the heart of Chianti region (p. 457).

San Gimignano (3 days)
Come for the tower-dotted skyline, stay for the high-quality *Vernaccia*, a locally produced white wine (p. 467).

START

Radda in Chianti (2 days)
Venture from Siena to this wine-bar-packed town and sip *Chianti Classico* (p. 465).

Siena (3 days)
Complement your *Panforte* with *Vinsanto*, the 'saintly' and sweet Tuscan dessert wine (p. 458).

Montalcino (2 days)
Finish here in the home of the pricey *Brunello*, Italy's finest red wine (p. 474).

END

Montepulciano (2 days)
Nurse a glass of *Nobile*, a wine deemed fit for gentlemen by Pope Paul III Farnese back in the 1500s (p. 466).

BEST OF ITALY (4 WEEKS)

Turin (3 days)
Enjoy the cultural offerings, hot nightlife, and nearby outdoor adventures in this rising star of the North (p. 162).

Milan (3 days)
Party it up in this fast-paced financial and fashion center that hasn't forgotten its past (p. 235).

Trieste (2 days)
Sample sapphire seas and sauerkraut in this multicultural hidden gem (p. 370).

START

Venice (5 days)
Dreams come true drifting down Venice's romantic canals (p. 305).

Florence (5 days)
This Renaissance city is brimming with world-class art, awe-inspiring churches, and high-class shopping (p. 426).

Cinque Terre (2 days)
Hike among five colorful towns and lounge on the beach in this backpacker's mainstay (p. 210).

Rome (5 days)
After more than 2700 years, powerful history and lively nightlife still echo in *la città eterna* (p. 104).

Naples (3 days)
Grab a slice in pizza's hometown and don't miss nearby Herculaeum and Pompeii (p. 563).

END

Catania (2 days)
Climb Mt. Etna and discover this Sicilian treasure's mixed architecture and lively student population (p. 688).

ESSENTIALS

PLANNING YOUR TRIP

ENTRANCE REQUIREMENTS
Passport (p. 10). Required for citizens of Australia, Canada, Ireland, New Zealand, the UK, and the US.
Visa (p. 11). Required only for citizens of Australia, Canada, Ireland, New Zealand, the UK, and the US for stays over 90 days.
Work Permit (p. 12). Required for all foreigners planning to work in Italy.

EMBASSIES AND CONSULATES

ITALIAN CONSULAR SERVICES ABROAD

Australia: 12 Grey St., Deakin, Canberra ACT 2600 (☎+61 262 733 333; www.ambcanberra.esteri.it/Ambasciata_Canberra). **Consulates:** 509 St. Kilda Rd., Melbourne VIC 3004 (☎+61 039 867 5744; www.consmelbourne.esteri.it); The Gateway, Level 45, 1 Macquarie Pl., Sydney NSW 2000 (☎+61 029 392 7900; www.conssydney.esteri.it).

Canada: 275 Slater St., 21st fl., Ottawa, ON K1P 5H9 (☎+1-613-232-2401; www.ambottawa.esteri.it). **Consulate:** 3489 Drummond St., Montreal, QC H3G 1X6 (☎+1-514-849-8351; www.consmontreal.esteri.it).

Ireland: 63/65 Northumberland Rd., Dublin (☎+353 16 60 17 44; www.ambdublino.esteri.it).

New Zealand: 34-38 Grant Rd., P.O. Box 463, Thorndon, Wellington (☎+64 44 735 339; www.italy-embassy.org.nz). **Consulate:** 102 Kitchener Rd., PO Box 31 121 Auckland (☎+649 489 9632).

UK: 14 Three Kings Yard, London W1K 4EH (☎+44 207 312 2200; www.embitaly.org.uk). **Consulates:** 32 Melville Street, Edinburgh EH3 7HA (☎+44 131 226 3631; www.consedimburgo.esteri.it); Rodwell Tower, 111 Piccadilly, Manchester M1 2HY (☎+44 161 236 9024; www.consmanchester.esteri.it).

US: 3000 Whitehaven St., N.W., Washington, DC 20008 (☎+1-202-612-4400; www.ambwashingtondc.esteri.it). **Consulates:** 600 Atlantic Ave., Boston, MA 02110 (☎+1-617-722-9201; www.consboston.esteri.it); 500 N. Michigan Ave., Ste. #1850, Chicago, IL 60611 (☎+1-312-467-1550; www.conschicago.esteri.it); 690 Park Ave., New York, NY 10021 (☎+1-212-737-9100; www.consnewyork.esteri.it).

CONSULAR SERVICES IN ITALY

Australia: V. Antonio Bosio 5, Rome 00161 (☎06 85 27 21, emergency ☎800 87 77 90; www.italy.embassy.gov.au). Open M-F 9am-5pm.

Canada: V. Zara 30, Rome 00198 (☎06 85 44 41; www.dfait-maeci.gc.ca/canada-europa/italy/menu-en.asp). Open M-Th 8:30-11:30am.

Ireland: P. di Campitelli 3, Rome 00186 (☎06 69 79 121; www.ambasciata-irlanda.it). Open M-F 10am-12:30pm and 3-4:30pm.

New Zealand: V. Zara 28, Rome 00198 (☎06 44 17 171; www.nzembassy.com). Open M-F 8:30am-12:45pm and 1:45-5pm. **Consulate:** V. Guido d'Arezzo 6, Milan 20145 (☎02 48 01 25 44). Open M-F 8:30am-5pm.

UK: V. XX Settembre 80a, Rome 00187 (☎06 42 20 00 01; www.britain.it). Open M-F Sept.-May 9am-5pm; June-Aug. 8am-2pm. Closed UK and Italian holidays.

US: V. Vittorio Veneto 121, Rome 00187 (☎06 46 741; www.usembassy.it). Consular services open M-F 8:30am-12:30pm. Closed US and Italian holidays. **Consulate:** V. Principe Amedeo 2/10, Milan 20121 (☎02 29 03 51). Open M-F 8:30am-noon.

TOURIST OFFICES

Italian Government Tourist Board (ENIT) provides information on Italy's culture, natural resources, history, and leisure activities. Visit their website, www.italiantourism.com, for info. Call ☎+1-212-245-4822 for a free copy of *General Information for Travelers to Italy*. The main office in Rome (☎06 49 71 11; sedecentrale@cert.enit.it) can help locate any local office not listed online.

Australia: 44 Market St., Sydney NSW 2000 (☎+29 26 21 666; enitour@ihug.com.au).

Canada: 175 E. Bloor St., Ste. 907 South Tower, Toronto, ON M4W 3R8 (☎+1-416-925-4882; enit.canada@on.aibn.com).

UK: 1 Princes St., London W1B 2AY (☎+20 7408 1254; www.italiantouristboard.co.uk).

US: 630 5th Ave., Ste. 1565, New York, NY 10111 (☎+1-212-245-5618; www.italiantourism.com).

DOCUMENTS AND FORMALITIES

PASSPORTS

REQUIREMENTS

Citizens of Australia, Canada, Ireland, New Zealand, the UK, and the US need valid passports to enter Italy and to re-enter their home countries. Returning home with an expired passport is illegal and may result in a fine.

NEW PASSPORTS

Citizens of Australia, Canada, Ireland, New Zealand, the UK, and the US can apply for a passport at any passport office or at selected post offices and courts of law. Citizens of these countries may also download passport applications from the official website of their country's government or passport office. Any new passport or renewal applications must be filed well in advance of the departure date; rush services may be available for a very steep fee. Note, however, that even "rushed" passports still take up to two weeks to arrive.

PASSPORT MAINTENANCE

Photocopy the page of your passport with your photo as well as your visas, traveler's check serial numbers, and any other important documents. Carry one set of copies in a safe place, apart from the originals, and leave another set at home. Consulates recommend also carrying an expired passport or an official copy of your birth certificate separate from other documents.

If you lose your passport, immediately notify the local police and your home country's nearest embassy or consulate. To expedite its replacement, you must show ID and proof of citizenship; it also helps to know all information previously recorded in the passport. In some cases, a replacement may take weeks to process, and it may be valid only for a limited time. Any visas stamped in your old passport will be lost forever. In an emergency, ask for immediate temporary traveling papers that will permit you to re-enter your home country.

ONE EUROPE. European unity has come a long way since 1958, when the European Economic Community (EEC) was created to promote European solidarity and cooperation. Since then, the EEC has become the European Union (EU), a mighty political, legal, and economic institution. On May 1, 2004, 10 South, Central, and Eastern European countries—Cyprus, the Czech Republic, Estonia, Hungary, Latvia, Lithuania, Malta, Poland, Slovakia, and Slovenia—were admitted into the EU, joining the original 15: Austria, Belgium, Denmark, Finland, France, Germany, Greece, Ireland, Italy, Luxembourg, the Netherlands, Portugal, Spain, Sweden, and the UK. On January 1, 2007, two others, Bulgaria and Romania, came into the fold, bringing the tally of member states to 27.

What does this have to do with the average non-EU tourist? The EU's policy of **freedom of movement** means that most border controls have been abolished and visa policies harmonized. Under this treaty, formally known as the **Schengen Agreement,** you're still required to carry a passport (or government-issued ID card for EU citizens) when crossing an internal border, but, once you've been admitted into one country, you're free to travel to other participating states. Most EU states are already members of Schengen (minus Bulgaria, Cyprus, Ireland, Romania, and the UK), as are Iceland and Norway. In 2009, Cyprus, Liechtenstein, and Switzerland will bring the number of Schengen countries to 27. Britain and Ireland have also formed a **common travel area,** abolishing passport controls between the UK and the Republic of Ireland.

For more important consequences of the EU for travelers, see **The Euro** (p. 14) and **Customs in the EU** (p. 13).

VISAS, INVITATIONS, AND WORK PERMITS

VISAS

EU citizens do not need a visa. Citizens of Australia, Canada, New Zealand, and the US do not need a visa for stays of up to 90 days, but this three-month period begins upon entry into any of the countries that belong to the EU's **freedom of movement** zone. For more information, see **One Europe** (p. 11). Those staying longer than 90 days may purchase a visa at the Italian consulate or embassy. A visa costs about €60 and allows the holder to spend between 90 and 365 additional days in Italy, depending on the type of visa. Double-check entrance requirements at the nearest Italian embassy or consulate (p. 9) for up-to-date info before departure. US citizens can also consult http://travel.state.gov.

Foreign nationals planning to spend over 90 days in Italy should apply within eight working days of arrival for a *permesso di soggiorno* (permit of stay). Generally, non-EU tourists are required to get a permit at a police station or foreign office *(questura)* if staying longer than 20 days or taking up residence in a location other than a hotel, official campsite, or boarding house. If staying in a hotel or hostel, the staff will fulfill registration requirements for you and the fee will be waived. There are steep fines for any failure to comply.

Entering Italy to study requires a special visa. For more information, see the **Beyond Tourism** chapter (p. 91) or visit www.ambwashingtondc.esteri.it.

WORK PERMITS

Admittance to a country as a traveler does not include the right to work, which is authorized only by a work permit. For more information on the regulations related to obtaining a work permit, see the **Beyond Tourism** chapter (p. 91).

IDENTIFICATION

When you travel, always carry at least two forms of identification on your person, including a photo ID. A passport and a driver's license or birth certificate will usually suffice. Never carry all of your IDs together; split them up in case of theft or loss and keep photocopies in your luggage and at home.

STUDENT, TEACHER, AND YOUTH IDENTIFICATION

The **International Student Identity Card** (ISIC), the most widely accepted form of student ID, provides discounts on some sights, accommodations, food, and transportation; access to a 24hr. emergency help line; and insurance benefits for US cardholders (see **Insurance,** (p. 21). Applicants must be full-time secondary or post-secondary school students at least 12 years old. Because of the proliferation of fake ISICs, some services (particularly airlines) require additional proof of student identity.

The **International Teacher Identity Card** (ITIC) offers teachers the same insurance coverage as the ISIC and similar but limited discounts. To qualify for the card, teachers must be currently employed and have worked a minimum of 18hr. per week for at least one school year. For travelers who are under 26 years old but are not students, the **International Youth Travel Card** (IYTC) also offers many of the same benefits as the ISIC.

Each of these identity cards costs US$22. ISICs, ITICs, and IYTCs are valid for one year from the date of issue. To learn more about ISICs, ITICs, and IYTCs, visit www.myisic.com. Many student travel agencies (p. 25) issue the cards; for a list of issuing agencies or more information, see the **International Student Travel Confederation** (ISTC) website (www.istc.org).

The **International Student Exchange Card** (ISE Card) is a similar identification card available to students, faculty, and children aged 12 to 26. The card provides discounts, medical benefits, access to a 24hr. emergency help line, and the ability to purchase student airfares. An ISE Card costs US$25; call ☎+1-800-255-8000 (in North America) or ☎+1-480-951-1177 (from all other continents). For more info visit www.isecard.com.

CUSTOMS

Upon entering Italy, you must declare certain items from abroad and pay a duty on the value of those articles if they exceed the allowance established by Italy's customs service. Goods and gifts purchased at duty-free shops abroad are not exempt from duty or sales tax; "duty-free" means that you won't pay tax in the country of purchase. Duty-free allowances were abolished for travel between EU member states on June 30, 1999, but still exist for those arriving from outside the EU. Upon returning home, you must likewise declare all articles acquired abroad and pay a duty on the value of articles in excess of your home country's allowance. In order to expedite your return, make a list of any valuables brought from home and register them with customs before traveling abroad. It's a good idea to keep receipts for all goods acquired abroad.

CUSTOMS IN THE EU. As well as freedom of movement of people (p. 11), travelers in the European Union can also take advantage of the freedom of movement of goods. This means that there are no customs controls at internal EU borders (i.e., you can take the blue customs channel at the airport), and travelers are free to transport whatever legal substances they like as long as it is for their own personal (non-commercial) use—up to 800 cigarettes, 10L of spirits, 90L of wine (including up to 60L of sparkling wine), and 110L of beer. Duty-free allowances were abolished on June 30, 1999, for travel between the original 15 EU member states; this now also applies to Cyprus and Malta. However, travelers between the EU and the rest of the world still get a duty-free allowance when passing through customs.

MONEY

CURRENCY AND EXCHANGE

The currency chart below is based on August 2008 exchange rates between local currency and Australian dollars (AUS$), Canadian dollars (CDN$), European Union euro (EUR€), New Zealand dollars (NZ$), British pounds (UK£), and US dollars (US$). Check the currency converter on websites like www.xe.com or www.bloomberg.com for the latest exchange rates.

EURO (€)		
AUS$1 = €0.62		€1 = AUS$1.63
CDN$1 = €0.63		€1 = CDN$1.59
NZ$1 = €0.48		€1 = NZ$2.08
UK£1 = €1.26		€1 = UK£0.79
US$1 = €0.63		€1 = US$1.58

As a general rule, it's cheaper to convert money in Italy than at home. While currency exchange will probably be available in your arrival airport, it's wise to bring enough foreign currency to last for at least 24-72 hours.

When changing money abroad, try to go only to banks or money chargers *(cambio)* that have at most a 5% margin between their buy and sell prices. Since you lose money with every transaction, it makes sense to convert large sums at one time (unless the currency is depreciating rapidly).

If you use traveler's checks or bills, carry some in small denominations (the equivalent of US$50 or fewer) for times when you are forced to exchange money at poor rates, but bring a range of denominations since charges may be applied per check cashed. Store your money in a variety of forms; ideally, at any given time you will be carrying some cash, some traveler's checks, and an ATM and/or credit card. All travelers should also consider carrying some US dollars (about US$50 worth), which are often preferred by local tellers.

TRAVELER'S CHECKS

Traveler's checks are one of the safest and most convenient means of carrying funds. However, they can also be one of the most frustrating means of spending money since fewer and fewer shops outside of tourist areas accept traveler's checks. American Express and Visa are the most-recognized brands. Many banks and agencies sell them for a small commission. Check issuers

ESSENTIALS

provide refunds if the checks are lost or stolen, and many provide additional services, such as toll-free refund hotlines abroad, emergency message services and assistance with lost and stolen credit cards or passports. Ask about toll-free refund hotlines and the location of refund centers when purchasing checks, and always carry emergency cash.

American Express: Checks available with commission at select banks, at all AmEx offices, and online (www.americanexpress.com; US residents only). AmEx cardholders can also purchase checks by phone (☎+1-800-528-4800). Checks available in Australian, British, Canadian, European, Japanese, and US currencies, among others. AmEx also offers the Travelers Cheque Card, a prepaid reloadable card. Cheques for Two can be signed by either of 2 people traveling together. For purchase locations or more information, contact AmEx's service centers: in Australia ☎+61 2 9271 8666, in New Zealand +64 9 367 4567, in the UK +44 1273 696 933, in the US and Canada +1-800-221-7282; elsewhere, call the US collect at +1-336-393-1111.

Travelex: Visa TravelMoney prepaid cash card and Visa traveler's checks. For info about Thomas Cook MasterCard in Canada and the US, call ☎+1-800-223-7373, in the UK +44 0800 622 101; elsewhere, call the UK collect at +44 1733 318 950. For info about Interpayment Visa in the US and Canada, call ☎+1-800-732-1322, in the UK +44 0800 515 884; elsewhere, call the UK collect at +44 1733 318 949. For more info, visit www.travelex.com.

Visa: Checks available (generally with commission) at banks worldwide. For the location of the nearest office, call the Visa Travelers Cheque Global Refund and Assistance Center: in the UK ☎+44 0800 895 078, in the US +1-800-227-6811; elsewhere, call the UK collect at +44 2079 378 091. Checks available in British, Canadian, European, Japanese, and US currencies, among others. Visa also offers TravelMoney, a prepaid debit card that can be reloaded online or by phone. For more info on Visa travel services, see http://usa.visa.com/personal/using_visa/travel_with_visa.html.

THE EURO. As of January 1, 2009, the official currency of 16 members of the European Union—Austria, Belgium, Cyprus, Finland, France, Germany, Greece, Ireland, Italy, Luxembourg, Malta, the Netherlands, Portugal, Slovenia, and Spain—will be the euro.

The currency has some important—and positive—consequences for travelers hitting more than one euro-zone country. For one thing, money-changers across the euro-zone are obliged to exchange money at the official, fixed rate (below) and at no commission (though they may still charge a small service fee). Second, euro-denominated traveler's checks allow you to pay for goods and services across the euro-zone, again at the official rate and commission-free. At the time of printing, €1 = US\$1.58 = CDN\$1.59 = NZ\$2.08. For more info, check a currency converter, visit www.xe.com or www.europa.eu.int.

CREDIT, DEBIT, AND ATM CARDS

Where they are accepted, credit cards often offer superior exchange rates—up to 5% better than the retail rate used by banks and other currency exchange establishments. Credit cards may also offer services such as insurance or emergency help and are sometimes required to reserve hotel rooms or rental cars. **EuroCard** and **Carte Bleue** are the most frequently accepted; **American Express** cards work at some ATMs and at AmEx offices and major airports.

The use of ATM cards is widespread in Italy. Depending on the system that your home bank uses, you can most likely access your personal bank account from abroad. Cirrus and BankMate are two of the most common financial networks. ATMs get the same wholesale exchange rate as credit cards, but there is often a limit on the amount of money you can withdraw per day (around US$500). There is also typically a surcharge of US$1-5 per withdrawal.

Debit cards are as convenient as credit cards but withdraw money directly from the holder's checking account. A debit card can be used wherever its associated credit-card company (usually MasterCard or Visa) is accepted. Debit cards often also function as ATM cards and can be used to withdraw cash from associated banks and ATMs throughout Italy.

The two major international money networks are **MasterCard/Maestro/Cirrus** (for ATM locations ☎+1-800-424-7787 or www.mastercard.com) and **Visa/PLUS** (for ATM locations ☎+1-800-847-2911 or www.visa.com). Most ATMs charge a transaction fee that is paid to the bank that owns the ATM.

PINS AND ATMS. To use a cash or credit card to withdraw money from a cash machine (ATM) in Europe, you must have a four-digit Personal Identification Number (PIN). If your PIN is longer than four digits, ask your bank whether you can just use the first four or whether you'll need a new one. Credit cards don't usually come with PINs, so, if you intend to hit up ATMs in Europe with a credit card to get cash advances, call your credit-card company before leaving to request one.

Travelers with alphabetic, rather than numerical, PINs may also be thrown off by the lack of letters on European cash machines. The following are the corresponding numbers to use: 1 = QZ; 2 = ABC; 3 = DEF; 4 = GHI; 5 = JKL; 6 = MNO; 7 = PRS; 8 = TUV; and 9 = WXY. Note that if you mistakenly punch the wrong code into the machine three times, it will swallow your card for good.

GETTING MONEY FROM HOME

If you run out of money while traveling, the easiest and cheapest solution is to have someone back home make a deposit to your bank account. Otherwise, consider one of the following options.

WIRING MONEY

It is possible to arrange a **bank money transfer,** which means asking a bank back home to wire money to a bank in Italy. This is the cheapest way to transfer cash, but it's also the slowest, usually taking several days or more. Note that some banks may only release your funds in local currency, potentially sticking you with a poor exchange rate; inquire about this in advance. Money transfer services like Western Union are faster and more convenient than bank transfers—but convenience comes at a price. **Western Union** has many locations worldwide. To find one, visit www.westernunion.com, or call in Australia ☎+1 800 173 833, in Canada and the US +1-800-325-6000, in the UK +44 0800 833 833, or in Italy at 800 788 935. To wire money using a credit card (Discover, MasterCard, Visa), call in Canada and the US ☎+1-800-CALL-CASH, in the UK +44 0800 833 833. Money transfer services are also available to **American Express** cardholders and at selected **Thomas Cook** offices.

US STATE DEPARTMENT (US CITIZENS ONLY)

In serious emergencies only, the US State Department will forward money within hours to the nearest consulate, which will then disburse it according to instructions for a US$30 fee. If you wish to use this service, you must contact the Overseas Citizens Services division of the US State Department (☎+1-202-501-4444, from US 888-407-4747).

TOP TEN WAYS TO SAVE IN ITALY

Homeland of Gucci, Prada, and Armani, Italy doesn't always cater to the frugal-minded, starving-artist types. But that doesn't mean that you can't spend your dough wisely. Keeping in mind that safety should always be a top priority when traveling, consider the following tips for saving money while living well in Italia:

1. For the best exchange rates, try using your trusty dusty **ATM card** instead of exchanging money.

2. Fly through London on **Ryanair** for the cheapest rates, if you're traveling from the US or Canada.

3. Register with **Hostelling International,** and save on hostels in Italy and around the world.

4. Take advantage of special days when you can get into monuments and museums for free.

5. Buy food at **open-air markets** and **grocery stores** instead of eating in restaurants.

6. To avoid an extra service charge in a *bar,* drink and eat at the counter instead of sitting at a table.

7. Find **free Internet access** in most libraries and tourist offices.

8. Swim and lounge at **public beaches** to avoid the cover charge at many private beaches.

9. Look for cafes and restaurants on **side streets** rather than on main squares or thoroughfares.

10. Bring a **sleepsack** to avoid paying extra for linen in hostels.

COSTS

The cost of your trip will vary considerably, depending on where you go, how you travel, and where you stay. The most significant expenses will probably be your round-trip (return) airfare to Italy (see **Getting to Italy: By Plane,** (p. 24) and a railpass or bus pass. Before you go, spend some time calculating a reasonable daily budget.

STAYING ON A BUDGET

To give you a general idea, a bare-bones day in Italy (camping or sleeping in hostels/guesthouses, buying food at supermarkets) would cost about US$50 (€32); a slightly more comfortable day (sleeping in hostels and the occasional budget hotel, eating one meal per day at a restaurant, going out at night) would cost US$90 (€57); and, for a luxurious day, the sky's the limit. Don't forget to factor in emergency reserve funds (at least US$200) when planning how much money you'll need.

TIPS FOR SAVING MONEY

Some simpler ways include searching out opportunities for free entertainment, splitting accommodation and food costs with trustworthy fellow travelers, and buying food in supermarkets rather than eating out. Bring a **sleepsack** (p. 17) to save on sheet charges in hostels and do your **laundry** in the sink (unless you're explicitly prohibited from doing so). Museums often have certain days once a month or once a week when admission is free; plan accordingly. If you are eligible, consider getting an ISIC or an IYTC (p. 12); many sights and museums offer reduced admission to students and youths. For getting around quickly, bikes are the most economical option. Don't forget about walking, though; you can learn a lot about a city by seeing it on foot. Drinking at bars and clubs quickly becomes expensive. It's cheaper to buy alcohol at a supermarket and imbibe before going out. That said, don't go overboard. Though staying within your budget is important, don't do so at the expense of your health or a great travel experience.

TIPPING AND BARGAINING

At many Italian restaurants, a service charge (*servizio*) or cover (*coperto*) is included in the bill. Locals sometimes do not give tips, but it is appropriate for foreign visitors to leave an additional 5-10% at restaurants for the waiter. Taxi drivers expect about a 5-10% tip, though Italians rarely tip them. Bargaining is common in Italy, but use discretion. Haggling is appropriate at markets, with vendors, and unmetered taxi fares (settle the price before getting in), but elsewhere, it is usually inappropriate. Hotel negotiation is more successful in uncrowded *pensioni*. To get lower prices, show little interest. Don't offer what you can't pay; you're expected to buy once the merchant accepts your price.

TAXES

The **Value Added Tax** (**VAT**; *imposto sul valore aggiunta*, or IVA) is a sales tax levied in the EU. Foreigners making any purchase over €155 are entitled to an additional 20% VAT refund. Some stores take off 20% on-site. Others require that you fill out forms at the customs desk when leaving the EU and send receipts from home within six months. Not all storefront "Tax-Free" stickers imply an immediate, on-site refund, so ask before making a purchase.

PACKING

Pack lightly: lay out only what you absolutely need, then take half the clothes and twice the money. The **Travelite FAQ** (www.travelite.org) is a good resource for tips on traveling light. The online **Universal Packing List** (http://upl.codeq.info) will generate a customized list of suggested items based on your trip length, the expected climate, your planned activities, and other factors. If you plan to do a lot of hiking, also consult **The Great Outdoors,** (p. 45). Some frequent travelers keep a bag packed with all the essentials: passport, money belt, hat, socks, etc. Then, when they decide to leave, they know they haven't forgotten anything.

Luggage: If you plan to cover most of your trip on foot, a sturdy **internal-frame backpack** is unbeatable. (For the basics on buying a pack, see (p. 17).) Unless you are staying in 1 place for a large chunk of time, a suitcase or trunk will be unwieldy. In addition to your main piece of luggage, a **daypack** (a small backpack or courier bag) is useful.

Clothing: No matter when you're traveling, it's a good idea to bring a warm jacket or wool sweater, a rain jacket (Gore-Tex® is both waterproof and breathable), sturdy shoes or hiking boots, and thick socks. Flip-flops or waterproof sandals are must-haves for grubby hostel showers, and extra socks are always a good idea. You may also want 1 outfit for going out and maybe a nicer pair of shoes. If you plan to visit religious or cultural sites, remember that you will need modest and respectful dress. Women traveling alone, especially in Southern Italy and Sicily, should dress modestly to avoid unwanted attention. Consult the table of Italy's average temperatures (p. 765) to determine what other clothes would best be suited for your trip.

Sleepsack: Some hostels require that you either provide your own linen or rent sheets from them. Save cash by making your own sleepsack: fold a full-size sheet in half the long way, then sew it closed along the long side and one of the short sides.

Converters and Adapters: In Italy, electricity is 230 volts AC, enough to fry any 120V North American appliance. 220/240V electrical appliances won't work with a 120V current, either. Americans and Canadians should buy an adapter (which changes the shape of the plug; US$10-20) and a converter (which changes the voltage; US$10-20). Don't make the mistake of using only an adapter (unless appliance instructions explicitly state otherwise). Australians and New Zealanders (who use 230V at home) won't need a converter but will need a set of adapters to use anything electrical. For more on all things adaptable, check out http://kropla.com/electric.htm.

Toiletries: Condoms, deodorant, razors, tampons, and toothbrushes are often available, but it may be tough to find your preferred brand; bring extras. Contact lenses are especially rare, so bring enough extra pairs and solution for your entire trip. Also bring your glasses and a copy of your prescription in case you need emergency replacements.

First-Aid Kit: For a basic first-aid kit, pack a variety of bandages, a pain reliever, antibiotic cream, a thermometer, a multifunction pocketknife, tweezers, moleskin, decongestant, motion-sickness remedy, diarrhea or upset-stomach medication, an antihistamine, sunscreen, insect repellent, and burn ointment.

Film: Film and developing in Italy are expensive, so consider bringing along enough film for your entire trip and developing it at home. If you don't want to bother with film, consider using a **digital camera.** Although it requires a steep initial investment, a digital camera means you never have to buy film again. Be sure to bring along a large enough memory card and extra batteries. Less serious photographers may want to bring a few disposable cameras. Despite disclaimers, airport security X-rays can fog film, so buy a lead-lined pouch at a camera store or ask security to hand-inspect it. Always pack film in your carry-on luggage, since higher-intensity X-rays are used on checked luggage.

Other Useful Items: For safety purposes, you should bring a **money belt** and a small **padlock.** Basic **outdoors equipment** (plastic water bottle, compass, waterproof matches, pocketknife, sunglasses, sunscreen, hat) may also be handy. Quick repairs of torn garments can be done on the road with a needle and thread; also consider bringing electrical tape for patching tears. Other things you're liable to forget include: an umbrella, sealable **plastic bags** (for damp clothes, soap, food, shampoo, and other spillables), an **alarm clock,** safety pins, rubber bands, a flashlight, earplugs, garbage bags, and a small calculator. A **cell phone** can be a lifesaver (literally) on the road; (p. 40) for information on acquiring one that will work in Italy.

Important Documents: Don't forget your passport, traveler's checks, ATM and/or credit cards, adequate ID, and photocopies of all of the aforementioned in case these documents are lost or stolen (p. 10). Also check that you have any of the following that might apply to you: a hosteling membership card (p. 42), driver's license (p. 12), travel insurance forms (p. 21), ISIC (p. 12), and railpass or bus pass (p. 29).

SAFETY AND HEALTH

GENERAL ADVICE

In any type of crisis, the most important thing to do is **stay calm.** Your country's embassy abroad (p. 9) is usually your best resource in an emergency; registering with that embassy upon arrival in the country is a good idea. The government offices listed in the **Travel Advisories** box (p. 20) can provide information on the services they offer their citizens in case of emergencies abroad.

LOCAL LAWS AND POLICE

In Italy you will mainly encounter two types of police: the *polizia* (☎113) and the *carabinieri* (☎112). The *polizia* are a civil force under the command of the Ministry of the Interior, whereas the *carabinieri* fall under the auspices of the Ministry of Defense and are considered a military force. Both, however, generally serve the same purpose—to maintain security and order in the country. In the case of attack or robbery both will respond to inquiries for help.

DRUGS AND ALCOHOL

Needless to say, **illegal drugs** are best avoided altogether. In Italy, drugs including marijuana, cocaine, and heroin are illegal. An increase in cocaine and heroin addiction and trafficking have led Italian authorities to respond harshly to drug-related offenses. If you carry **prescription drugs,** bring copies of the prescriptions and a note from a doctor, and have them accessible at international borders. The drinking age in Italy is 16. Drinking and driving is prohibited and can result in a prison sentence. The legal blood alcohol content (BAC) for driving is under 0.05%, significantly lower than US standards, which limit BAC to 0.08%.

SPECIFIC CONCERNS

NATURAL DISASTERS

Italy is crossed by several fault lines, the chief one running from Sicily to Friuli-Venezia Giulia in the northeast. The country's principal cities do not lie near these faults, though smaller tourist towns like Assisi do and thus may experience **earthquakes** (most recently in 1997).

DEMONSTRATIONS AND POLITICAL GATHERINGS

Americans should be mindful while traveling in Italy, as there is some anti-American sentiment. No matter where you travel in Italy, you will likely encounter some sort of anti-American or, more likely, anti-Bush statements. It is best to err on the side of caution and sidestep these discussions. In general, use discretion and avoid being too vocal about your citizenship.

TERRORISM

Terrorism has not been as serious a problem in Italy as in other European countries, though the general threat of terrorism still exists. Exercise common sense and caution when in crowded, public areas like train or bus stations and open spaces like *piazze* in larger cities. The box on **travel advisories** below lists offices to contact and webpages to visit to get the most updated list of your home country's government's advisories about travel.

PERSONAL SAFETY

EXPLORING AND TRAVELING

To avoid unwanted attention, try to blend in as much as possible. Respecting local customs (in many cases, dressing more conservatively than you would at home) may ward off would-be hecklers. Familiarize yourself with your surroundings before you set out and walk with purpose. Check maps indoors rather than on the street. If you're traveling alone, be sure someone at home knows your itinerary and never tell anyone you meet that you're by yourself. When walking at night, stick to busy, well-lit streets. If you ever feel uncomfortable, leave the area as quickly and directly as you can.

There is no surefire way to avoid all the threatening situations that you might encounter while traveling, but a good **self-defense course** will give you concrete ways to react to unwanted advances. **Impact, Prepare,** and **Model Mugging** can refer you to local self-defense courses in Australia, Canada, Switzerland, and the US. Visit the website at www.modelmugging.org for a list of chapters.

If you are using a **car,** learn local driving signals and always wear a seatbelt. Study route maps before you hit the road and, if you plan on spending a significant amount of time driving, consider bringing spare parts. For long drives in desolate areas, invest in a cellular phone (p. 40) and a roadside assistance program (p. 37). Park your vehicle in a garage or well-traveled area and use a steering-wheel locking device in larger cities. Sleeping in your car is the most dangerous way to get your rest. See p. 38.

TRAVEL ADVISORIES. The following government offices provide travel information and advisories by telephone, by fax, or via the web:

Australian Department of Foreign Affairs and Trade: ☎+61 2 6261 1111; www.dfat.gov.au.

Canadian Department of Foreign Affairs and International Trade (DFAIT): ☎+1-800-267-8376; www.dfait-maeci.gc.ca. Call for their free booklet, *Bon Voyage...But.*

New Zealand Ministry of Foreign Affairs: ☎+64 44 39 80 00; www.mfat.govt.nz.

United Kingdom Foreign and Commonwealth Office: ☎+44 20 7008 1500; www.fco.gov.uk.

US Department of State: ☎+1-888-407-4747; http://travel.state.gov. Visit the website for the booklet, *A Safe Trip Abroad.*

POSSESSIONS AND VALUABLES

Never leave your belongings unattended; crime occurs in even the most safe-looking hostel or hotel. Bring your own padlock for hostel lockers and don't ever store valuables in a locker. Be particularly careful on **buses** and **trains;** horror stories abound about determined thieves who wait for travelers to fall asleep. Carry your bag or purse in front of you where you can see it. When traveling with others, sleep in alternate shifts. When alone, use good judgment in selecting a train compartment: never stay in an empty one and use a lock to secure your pack to the luggage rack. Use extra caution for overnight trains. Try to sleep on top bunks with your luggage stored above you (if not in bed with you) and keep important documents and valuables on you at all times.

There are a few steps you can take to minimize the financial risk associated with travel. First, **bring as little with you as possible.** Second, buy a few combination **padlocks** to secure your belongings either in your pack or in a hostel or train-station locker. Third, **carry as little cash as possible.** Carry traveler's checks and ATM/credit cards in a **money belt**—not a "fanny pack"—along with your passport and ID cards. Fourth, **keep a small cash reserve separate from your primary stash.** This should be about US$50 (US dollars or euros are best) sewn into or stored deep in your pack, along with your traveler's check numbers, photocopies of your passport, your birth certificate, and other important documents.

In large cities, **con artists** often work in groups and may involve children. Beware of certain classics: sob stories that require money, rolls of bills "found" on the street, mustard spilled (or saliva spit) onto your shoulder to distract you while they snatch your bag. **Never let your passport and your bags out of your sight.** Hostel workers will sometimes stand at bus and train-station arrival points to recruit tired and disoriented travelers to their hostel; never believe strangers who tell you that theirs is the only hostel open. Beware of **pickpockets** in city crowds, especially on public transportation. Also, be alert in public telephone booths: if you must say your calling card number, do so very quietly; if you punch it in, make sure no one can look over your shoulder.

If you're will be traveling with a laptop computer, check whether your homeowner's insurance covers loss, theft, or damage when you travel. If not, you might consider purchasing a low-cost separate insurance policy. **Safeware** (☎+1-800-800-1492; www.safeware.com) specializes in covering computers and charges $90 for 90-day international travel coverage up to $4000.

PRE-DEPARTURE HEALTH

In your passport, write the names of any people you wish to be contacted in case of a **medical emergency** and list any allergies or medical conditions. Matching a prescription to a foreign equivalent is not always easy, safe, or possible, so, if you take **prescription drugs,** consider carrying up-to-date prescriptions or a statement from your doctor stating the medication's trade name, manufacturer, chemical name, and dosage. While traveling, be sure to keep all medication with you in your carry-on luggage. For tips on packing a **first-aid kit** and other health essentials, (p. 18). While it may be difficult to find brand name medications like Tylenol or Advil, these products can easily be identified by their drug names (such as acetaminophen or paracetamol and ibuprofen).

IMMUNIZATIONS AND PRECAUTIONS

Travelers over two years old should make sure that the following vaccines are up to date: MMR (for measles, mumps, and rubella); DTaP or Td (for diphtheria, tetanus, and pertussis); IPV (for polio); Hib (for *haemophilus influenzae* B); and HepB (for Hepatitis B). Adults traveling to the developing world on trips longer than four weeks should consider the following additional immunizations: Hepatitis A vaccine and/or immune globulin (IG), typhoid and cholera vaccines, particularly if traveling off the beaten path, as well as a rabies vaccine and yearly influenza vaccines. For recommendations on immunizations, consult the Centers for Disease Control and Prevention (CDC; below) in the US or the equivalent in your home country and check with a doctor for guidance.

INSURANCE

Travel insurance covers four basic areas: medical/health problems, property loss, trip cancellation/interruption, and emergency evacuation. Though regular insurance policies may well extend to travel-related accidents, you may consider purchasing separate travel insurance if the cost of potential trip cancellation, interruption, or emergency medical evacuation is greater than you can absorb. Prices for travel insurance purchased separately generally run about US$50 per week for full coverage, while trip cancellation/interruption may be purchased separately at a rate of US$3-5 per day, depending on length of stay.

Medical insurance (especially university policies) often covers costs incurred abroad; check with your provider. **Homeowners' insurance** (or your family's coverage) often covers theft during travel and loss of travel documents (passport, plane ticket, railpass, etc.) up to US$500.

ISIC and **ITIC** (p. 12) provide basic insurance benefits to US cardholders, including coverage of US$100 per day of in-hospital sickness for up to 100 days and US$10,000 of accident-related medical reimbursement (see www.isicus.com for details). Cardholders have access to a toll-free 24hr. helpline for medical, legal, and financial emergencies overseas. **American Express** (☎+1-800-338-1670) grants most cardholders automatic collision and theft car rental insurance on rentals made with the card.

USEFUL ORGANIZATIONS AND PUBLICATIONS

The American **Centers for Disease Control and Prevention** (**CDC;** ☎+1-877-FYI-TRIP; www.cdc.gov/travel) maintains an international travelers' hotline. Consult the appropriate government agency of your home country for consular information sheets on health, entry requirements, and other issues for various countries (see the listings in the box on **Travel Advisories**). For quick information on health and other travel warnings, call the **Overseas Citizens Services** (from overseas

☎+1-202-501-4444, from US 888-407-4747; line open M-F 8am-8pm EST) or contact a passport agency, embassy, or consulate abroad. For info on medical evacuation services and travel insurance firms, see the US government's website at http://travel.state.gov/travel/abroad_health.html or the **British Foreign and Commonwealth Office** (www.fco.gov.uk). For general health info, contact the **American Red Cross** (☎+1-202-303-4498; www.redcross.org).

STAYING HEALTHY

Common sense is the simplest prescription for good health while you travel. Drink lots of fluids to prevent dehydration, and wear sturdy, broken-in shoes.

ONCE IN ITALY

ENVIRONMENTAL HAZARDS

Arid summer weather in the south creates prime conditions for heat exhaustion and dehydration. Be especially careful at Pompeii; there may no longer be a threat of volcanic eruption, but a lack of water fountains and shade create new dangers. Trekking at high altitudes in the Dolomites, the Alps, and on Mt. Vesuvius and Mt. Etna should not be done too hastily; be especially careful in winter to protect yourself against hypothermia and frostbite.

Heat exhaustion and dehydration: Heat exhaustion leads to nausea, excessive thirst, headaches, and dizziness. Avoid it by drinking plenty of fluids, eating salty foods (e.g., crackers), abstaining from dehydrating beverages (e.g., alcohol and caffeinated beverages), and wearing sunscreen. Continuous heat stress can eventually lead to heatstroke, characterized by a rising temperature, severe headache, delirium, and cessation of sweating. Victims should be cooled off with wet towels and taken to a doctor.

Sunburn: Always wear sunscreen (SPF 30 or higher) when spending time outdoors. If you get sunburned, drink more fluids than usual and apply an aloe-based lotion. Severe sunburns can lead to sun poisoning, a condition that can cause fever, chills, nausea, and vomiting. Sun poisoning should always be treated by a doctor.

Hypothermia and frostbite: A rapid drop in body temperature is the clearest sign of overexposure to cold. Victims may also shiver, feel exhausted, have poor coordination or slurred speech, hallucinate, or suffer amnesia. Do not let hypothermia victims fall asleep. To avoid hypothermia, keep dry, wear layers, and stay out of the wind. When the temperature is below freezing, watch out for frostbite. If skin turns white or blue, waxy, and cold, do not rub the area. Drink warm beverages, stay dry, and slowly warm the area with dry fabric or steady body contact until a doctor can be found.

High Altitude: Allow your body a couple of days to adjust to less oxygen before exerting yourself. Note that alcohol is more potent and UV rays are stronger at high elevations.

INSECT-BORNE DISEASES

Many diseases are transmitted by insects—mainly mosquitoes, fleas, ticks, and lice. Be aware of insects in wet or forested areas, especially while hiking and camping. Wear long pants and long sleeves, tuck your pants into your socks, and use a mosquito net. Use insect repellents such as DEET and soak or spray your gear with permethrin (licensed in the US only for use on clothing). **Mosquitoes**—responsible for malaria, dengue fever, and yellow fever—can be particularly abundant in wet, swampy, or wooded areas like those found in Liguria and Trentino-Alto Adige. **Ticks**—which can carry Lyme and other diseases—can be particularly dangerous in rural and forested regions, especially in Friuli-Venezia Giulia, the Veneto, and Trentino-Alto Adige.

ESSENTIALS

Lyme disease: A bacterial infection carried by ticks and marked by a circular bull's-eye rash of 2 in. or more. Later symptoms include fever, headache, fatigue, and aches and pains. Antibiotics are effective if administered early. Left untreated, Lyme can cause problems in joints, the heart, and the nervous system. If you find a tick attached to your skin, grasp the head with tweezers as close to your skin as possible and apply slow, steady traction. Removing a tick within 24hr. greatly reduces the risk of infection. Do not try to remove ticks with petroleum jelly, nail polish remover, or a hot match. Ticks usually inhabit moist, shaded environments and heavily wooded areas. If you are going to be hiking in these areas, wear long clothes and insect repellent.

FOOD- AND WATER-BORNE DISEASES

Prevention is the best cure: be sure that your food is properly cooked and the water you drink is clean. Watch out for food from markets or street vendors that may have been cooked in unhygienic conditions. Other culprits are raw shellfish, unpasteurized milk, and sauces containing raw eggs. Buy bottled water or purify your own water by bringing it to a rolling boil or treating it with **iodine tablets;** note, however, that boiling is more reliable. While Italy's water is relatively clean (the ancient Roman aqueduct water still provides Rome with a reliable water source), it is important to be wary in places like some campgrounds and trains where water is not clean. The sign *"acqua non potabile"* means the water is not drinkable; the sign *"acqua potabile"* means the water is sanitary. Even as a developed nation, Italy experienced an outbreak of stomach flu due to contaminated drinking water in Taranto in 2006.

Traveler's diarrhea: Results from drinking fecally contaminated water or eating uncooked and contaminated foods. Symptoms include nausea, bloating, and urgency. Try quick-energy, non-sugary foods with protein and carbohydrates to keep your strength up. Over-the-counter anti-diarrheals (e.g., Imodium®) may counteract the problem. The most dangerous side effect is dehydration; drink 8 oz. of water with ½ tsp. of sugar or honey and a pinch of salt, try uncaffeinated soft drinks, or eat salted crackers. If you develop a fever or your symptoms don't go away after 4-5 days, consult a doctor. Consult a doctor immediately for treatment of diarrhea in children.

Giardiasis: Transmitted through parasites and acquired by drinking untreated water from streams or lakes. Symptoms include diarrhea, cramps, bloating, fatigue, weight loss, and nausea. If untreated, it can lead to severe dehydration.

OTHER INFECTIOUS DISEASES

The following diseases exist all over the world. Travelers should know how to recognize them and what to do if they suspect they have been infected.

AIDS and HIV: For detailed info on Acquired Immune Deficiency Syndrome (AIDS) in Italy, call the 24hr. National AIDS Hotline at ☎+1-800-342-2437. Note that Italy screens incoming travelers for AIDS, primarily those planning extended visits for work or study, and denies entrance to those who test HIV-positive. Contact the consulate of Italy for info.

Hepatitis B: A viral infection of the liver transmitted via blood or other bodily fluids. Symptoms include jaundice, appetite loss, fever, and joint pain. It is transmitted through unprotected sex and unclean needles. A 3-shot vaccination sequence is recommended for sexually active travelers and anyone planning to seek medical treatment abroad; it must begin 6 months before your trip to Italy.

Hepatitis C: Like Hepatitis B, but the mode of transmission differs. IV drug users, those with occupational exposure to blood, and recipients of blood transfusions are at the highest risk, but the disease can also be spread through sexual contact or sharing items like razors and toothbrushes that may have traces of blood on them. No symptoms are usually exhibited. If untreated, Hepatitis C can lead to liver failure.

Sexually transmitted infections (STIs): Gonorrhea, chlamydia, genital warts, syphilis, herpes, HPV, and other STIs are easier to catch than HIV and can be just as serious. Though condoms may protect you from some STIs, oral or even tactile contact can lead to transmission. If you think you may have contracted an STI, see a doctor immediately.

OTHER HEALTH CONCERNS

MEDICAL CARE ON THE ROAD

Although quality of care varies by region, Italy overall conforms to standards of modern health care. Medical facilities tend to be better in the north and in private hospitals and clinics. Doctors speak English in most large cities; if they don't, they may be able to arrange for a translator. *Let's Go* lists info on how to access medical help in the **Practical Information** sections of most cities.

Those concerned about obtaining medical assistance abroad may wish to employ special support services. The **MedPass** from **GlobalCare, Inc.,** 6875 Shiloh Rd. East, Alpharetta, GA 30005, USA (☎+1-800-860-1111; www.globalcare. net), provides 24hr. international medical assistance, support, and evacuation resources. The **International Association for Medical Assistance to Travelers** (**IAMAT;** US ☎+1-716-754-4883, Canada +1-519-836-0102; www.iamat.org) lists English-speaking doctors worldwide, and offers detailed info on immunization requirements and sanitation. If your regular insurance policy does not cover travel abroad, you may wish to purchase additional coverage (p. 21).

Those with medical conditions (such as diabetes, allergies to antibiotics, epilepsy, or heart conditions) may want to obtain a **MedicAlert** membership (US$40 per year), which includes among other things a stainless-steel ID tag and a 24hr. collect-call number. Contact the MedicAlert Foundation International, 2323 Colorado Ave., Turlock, CA 95382, USA (☎+1-888-633-4298, outside US 209-668-3333; www.medicalert.org).

WOMEN'S HEALTH

Women traveling in unsanitary conditions are vulnerable to **urinary tract** (including bladder and kidney) infections. Bring supplies from home if you are prone to infection, as they may be difficult to find on the road. **Tampons, pads,** and **contraceptive devices** are widely available, though your preferred brand may not be stocked—bring extras of anything you can't live without. Abortion (*aborto* or *interruzione volontaria di gravidanza*) is legal and may be performed in the first 90 days of pregnancy for free in a public hospital or for a fee in an authorized private facility. Except in urgent cases, a week-long reflection period is required. Women under 18 must obtain parental permission or a judge's decision. Availability may be limited in some areas, especially in the south, due to a "conscience clause" that allows physicians who oppose abortion to opt out of performing the procedure. The election of Pope Benedict XVI has sparked controversy over abortion, but no immediate policy changes are expected.

GETTING TO ITALY

BY PLANE

When it comes to airfare, a little effort can save you a bundle. Courier fares are the cheapest options for travelers whose plans are flexible enough to deal with the restrictions. Tickets sold by consolidators and standby seating are also good deals, but last-minute specials, airfare wars, and charter flights often beat these fares. The key is to hunt around, be flexible, and ask about discounts. Students, seniors, and those under 26 should never pay full price for a ticket.

AIRFARES

Airfares to Italy peak between April and early September; holidays are also expensive. The cheapest times to travel are from late September to mid-December and January to March. Midweek (M-Th morning) round-trip flights tend to be cheaper than weekend flights, but they are generally more crowded and less likely to permit frequent-flier upgrades. Not fixing a return date ("open return") or arriving in and departing from different cities ("open-jaw") can be pricier than round-trip flights. Flights into Rome and Milan tend to be cheaper.

If Italy is only one stop on a more extensive globe-hop, consider a round-the-world (RTW) ticket. Tickets usually include at least five stops and are valid for about a year; prices range US$1200-5000. Try **Northwest Airlines/KLM** (☎+1-800-225-2525; www.nwa.com) or **Star Alliance,** a consortium of 16 airlines including United Airlines (www.staralliance.com).

Fares for round-trip flights to Rome and Milan from the US or Canadian east coast cost US$700-1200, US$500-700 in the low season (mid-Sept. to mid-Dec. and Jan.-Mar.); from the US or Canadian west coast US$800-1600/600-1000; from the UK, UK£175-300/125-200; from Australia AUS$1700-2600/1320-2000; from New Zealand NZ$2000-3000/1800-2400.

 FLIGHT PLANNING ON THE INTERNET. The Internet may be the budget traveler's dream when it comes to finding and booking bargain fares, but the array of options is overwhelming. Many airline sites offer special last-minute deals. Look for sale fares on www.alitalia.com and www.flyairone.it.

STA (www.statravel.com) and **StudentUniverse** (www.studentuniverse.com) provide quotes on student tickets, while **Orbitz** (www.orbitz.com), **Expedia** (www.expedia.com), and **Travelocity** (www.travelocity.com) offer full travel services. **Priceline** (www.priceline.com) lets you specify a price and obligates you to buy any ticket that meets or beats it; **Hotwire** (www.hotwire.com) offers bargain fares but won't reveal the airline or flight times until you buy. Other sites that compile budget deals include www.bestfares.com, www.lowestfare.com, www.onetravel.com, and www.travelzoo.com.

SideStep (www.sidestep.com) and **Booking Buddy** (www.bookingbuddy.com) are online tools that can help sift through multiple offers; these two let you enter your trip information once and search multiple sites.

Air Traveler's Handbook (www.faqs.org/faqs/travel/air/handbook) is an indispensable resource on the Internet; it has a comprehensive list of links to everything you need to know before you board a plane.

BUDGET AND STUDENT TRAVEL AGENCIES

While knowledgeable agents specializing in flights to Italy can make your life easy and help you save, they may not spend the time to find you the lowest possible fare—they get paid on commission. Travelers holding ISICs and IYTCs (p. 12) qualify for big discounts from student travel agencies. Most flights from budget agencies are on major airlines, but in peak season some may sell seats on less reliable chartered aircraft.

STA Travel, 5900 Wilshire Blvd., Ste. 900, Los Angeles, CA 90036, USA (24hr. reservations and info ☎+1-800-781-4040; www.statravel.com). A student and youth travel organization with over 150 offices worldwide (check their website for a listing of all their offices), including US offices in Boston, Chicago, Los Angeles, New York, Seattle, San Francisco, and Washington, D.C. Ticket booking, travel insurance, railpasses, and more. Walk-in offices are located throughout Australia (☎+61 392 075 900), New Zealand (☎+64 93 09 97 23), and the UK (☎+44 8701 630 026).

The Adventure Travel Company, 124 MacDougal St., New York, NY, 10021, USA (☎+1-800-467-4595; www.theadventuretravelcompany.com). Offices across Canada and the US including Champaign, New York, San Diego, Seattle, and San Francisco.

USIT, 19-21 Aston Quay, Dublin 2, Ireland (☎+353 1602 1904; www.usit.ie). Ireland's leading student/budget travel agency has 20 offices throughout Northern Ireland and the Republic of Ireland. Offers programs to work, study, and volunteer worldwide.

Wasteels, Skoubogade 6, 1158 Copenhagen K., Denmark (☎+453 3314 4633; www.wasteels.com). A huge chain with 180 locations across Europe. Sells Wasteels BIJ tickets discounted 30-45% off regular fare, 2nd-class international point-to-point train tickets with unlimited stopovers for those under 26 (sold only in Europe).

COMMERCIAL AIRLINES

The commercial airlines' lowest regular offer is the **APEX (Advance Purchase Excursion)** fare, which provides confirmed reservations and allows "open-jaw" tickets. Generally, reservations must be made seven to 21 days ahead of departure, with seven- to 14-day minimum-stay and up to 90-day maximum-stay restrictions. These fares carry hefty cancellation and change penalties. Book peak-season APEX fares early. Use **Expedia** (www.expedia.com) or **Travelocity** (www.travelocity.com) to get an idea of low published fares, then use the resources outlined here to try to beat those fares. Low-season fares should be appreciably cheaper than the high-season (mid-June to Aug.) ones listed here.

Let's Go treats 🛫budget airlines (see opposite page) separately from commercial airlines. For travelers who don't place a premium on convenience, we recommend these no-frills airlines as the best way to jet around Europe. Even if you live outside the continent, you can save money by finding the absolute cheapest flight to Europe and then using budget airlines to reach your final destination.

TRAVELING FROM NORTH AMERICA

The most common ways to cross the pond are those you've probably heard of. Standard commercial carriers will probably offer the most convenient flights, but they may not be the cheapest.

American: ☎+1-800-433-7300; www.aa.com.

United: ☎+1-800-538-2929; www.ual.com.

Northwest: ☎+1-800-447-4747; www.nwa.com.

Lufthansa: ☎+1-800-399-5838; www.lufthansa.com.

British Airways: ☎+1-800-247-9297; www.britishairways.com.

Air France: ☎+1-800-237-2747; www.airfrance.us.

Alitalia: ☎+1-800-223-5730; www.alitaliausa.com.

TRAVELING FROM IRELAND AND THE UK

Cheapflights (www.cheapflights.co.uk) publishes bargains on airfare from the British Isles, but British and Irish globetrotters really looking to save should always fly on budget airlines. The following commercial carriers occasionally offer discounted fares or specials.

Aer Lingus: Ireland ☎+353 818 365 000; www.aerlingus.ie. Flights from Dublin, Cork, Kerry, and Shannon to Bologna, Milan, Naples, Rome, and Venice (EUR€30-200).

KLM: UK ☎+44 8705 074 074; www.klmuk.com. Cheap tickets between UK airports and over 23 Italian destinations (UK£60-200).

TRAVELING FROM AUSTRALIA AND NEW ZEALAND

Qantas Air: Australia ☎+61 13 13 13, New Zealand +64 800 808 767; www.qantas.com.au. Flights from Australia and New Zealand to Rome.

Singapore Air: Australia ☎+61 13 10 11, New Zealand +64 800 808 909; www.singaporeair.com. Flies from Auckland, Christchurch, Melbourne, and Sydney to Rome.

Thai Airways: Australia ☎+61 86 62 22 66, New Zealand +64 93 77 38 86; www.thaiair.com. Flies from Auckland, Melbourne, Perth, and Sidney to Rome.

BUDGET AIRLINES

Low-cost carriers are the latest big thing in Europe. With their help, travelers can often snag tickets for illogically low prices (i.e., less than the price of a meal in the airport food court), but you get what you pay for: namely, minimalist service and no frills. In addition, many budget airlines fly out of smaller regional airports several kilometers out of town. You'll have to buy shuttle tickets to reach the airports of many of these airlines, so plan on adding an hour or so to your travel time. After round-trip shuttle tickets and fees for services that might come standard on other airlines, that €1 sale fare can suddenly jump to €20-100. Prices vary dramatically; shop around, book months ahead, pack light, and stay flexible to nab the best fares. For a more detailed list of these airlines by country, check out www.whichbudget.com.

bmibaby: UK ☎0871 224 0224, elsewhere +44 870 126 6726; www.bmibaby.com. Round-trip London to Naples (UK£35-140) and Venice (UK£40-100).

easyJet: ☎+44 871 244 2366, UK£0.10 per min.; www.easyjet.com. London to Bologna, Milan, Naples, Pisa, Rome, Turin, and Venice (UK£25-200).

Ryanair: Ireland ☎0818 30 30 30, UK 0871 246 0000, elsewhere +353 1249 7791; www.ryanair.com. The cheapest flights (from £10 with taxes) from Dublin, Glasgow, Liverpool, London, and Shannon to over a dozen destinations throughout Italy.

AIR COURIER FLIGHTS

Those who travel light should consider courier flights. Couriers help transport cargo on international flights by using their checked luggage space for freight. Generally, couriers are limited to carry-ons and must deal with complex flight restrictions. Most flights are round-trip only, with short fixed-length stays (usually one week) and a limit of a one ticket per issue. Most of these flights also operate only out of major gateway cities, mostly in North America. Round-trip courier fares from the US to Italy run about US$150-600. Most flights leave from Los Angeles, Miami, New York, or San Francisco in the US; and from Montreal, Toronto, or Vancouver in Canada. Generally, you must be over 18 (in some cases 21). In summer, the most popular destinations usually require an advance reservation of about two weeks (you can usually book up to two months ahead). Super-discounted fares are common for "last-minute" flights (three to 14 days ahead). Round-trip courier fares from the US to Italy run about US$200-600. The **International Association of Air Travel Couriers** (**IAATC;** www.courier.org) offers services from 7 North American cities and London to Rome. Courier flights are also available from Auckland to Frankfurt and London. (1-year membership US$45.) A second service, **Courier Travel** (www.

couriertravel.org), utilizes a searchable online database, but with many available flights to Rome originating in London, New York, and Sydney. Note that the minimum age for couriers from the UK is usually 18.

STANDBY FLIGHTS

Traveling standby requires considerable flexibility in arrival and departure dates. Companies dealing in standby flights sell vouchers rather than tickets, along with the promise to get you to your destination (or near your destination) within a certain window of time (typically 1-5 days). You call in before your specific window of time to hear your flight options and the probability that you will be able to board each flight. You can then decide which flights you want to try to catch, show up at the appropriate airport at the appropriate time, present your voucher, and board if space is available. Vouchers can usually be bought for both one-way and round-trip travel. You may receive a monetary refund only if every available flight within your date range is full; if you opt not to take an available (but perhaps less convenient) flight, you can only get credit toward future travel. To check on a company's service record in the US, contact the **Better Business Bureau** (☎+1-703-276-0100; www.bbb. org). It is difficult to receive refunds, and clients' vouchers will not be honored when an airline fails to receive payment in time.

TICKET CONSOLIDATORS

Ticket consolidators, or **"bucket shops,"** buy unsold tickets in bulk from commercial airlines and sell them at discounted rates. The best place to look is in the Sunday travel section of any major newspaper (such as *The New York Times*), where many bucket shops place tiny ads. Call quickly, as availability is extremely limited. Not all bucket shops are reliable, so insist on a receipt that gives full details of restrictions, refunds, and tickets, and pay by credit card (in spite of the 2-5% fee) so you can stop payment if you never receive your tickets. For more info, see www.travel-library.com/air-travel/consolidators.html. When traveling from Canada and the US, some consolidators worth trying are **Rebel** (☎+1-800-732-3588; www.rebeltours.com), **Cheap Tickets** (www.cheaptickets.com), **Flights.com** (www.flights.com), and **TravelHUB** (www.travelhub.com). *Let's Go* does not endorse any of these agencies. As always, be cautious, and research companies before you hand over your credit-card number.

CHARTER FLIGHTS

Tour operators contract charter flights with airlines in order to fly extra loads of passengers during peak season. These flights are far from hassle free. They occur less frequently than major airlines, make refunds particularly difficult, and are almost always fully booked. Their scheduled times may change and they may be canceled at the last moment (as late as 48hr. before the trip, and without a full refund). In addition, check-in, boarding, and baggage claim for them are often much slower. They can, however, be much cheaper.

Discount clubs and fare brokers offer members savings on last-minute charter and tour deals. Study contracts closely; you don't want to end up with an unwanted overnight layover. **Travelers Advantage** (☎+1-800-835-8747; www. travelersadvantage.com; US$90 annual fee includes discounts and cheap flight directories) specializes in European travel and tour packages.

BY TRAIN

Traveling to Italy by train from within Europe can be as expensive as a flight, but allows travelers to watch the country unfold before them, and allows the possibility of spontaneous stopovers before reaching their ultimate destination. For info on traveling within Italy by rail, see **By Train**, p. 32.

MULTINATIONAL RAILPASSES

EURAIL PASSES. Eurail is **valid** in most of Western Europe but **not** the UK. Standard **Eurail Passes,** valid for a consecutive number of days, are best for those planning to spend an extended period of time on trains. **Eurail Global Pass,** valid for any 10 or 15 (not necessarily consecutive) days in a two-month period, is more cost-effective for those traveling long distances less frequently. **Eurail Pass Saver** provides first-class travel for travelers in groups of two or more people **Eurail Pass Youth** provides parallel second-class perks for 12- to 25-year-olds.

EURAIL PASSES	15 DAYS	21 DAYS	1 MONTH	2 MONTHS	3 MONTHS
1st class Eurail Pass	US$795	US$1029	US$1279	US$1809	US$2235
Eurail Pass Saver	US$675	US$875	US$1089	US$1539	US$1615
Eurail Pass Youth	US$519	US$669	US$835	US$1179	US$1455

EURAIL SELECTPASS	10 DAYS IN 2 MONTHS	15 DAYS IN TWO MONTHS
1st class Eurail Pass Flexi	US$879	US$1115
Eurail Pass Saver Flexi	US$745	US$949
Eurail Pass Youth Flexi	US$569	US$725

Passholders receive a timetable for routes and a map with details on possible bike rental, car rental, hotel, and museum discounts, as well as reduced fares or free passage on many boat, bus, and private railroad lines.

The **Eurail Selectpass** is a slimmed-down version of the Eurail Pass: it allows five to 15 days of unlimited travel in any two-month period within three to five bordering countries. Eurail Selectpasses (for individuals) and **Eurail Selectpass Savers** range from US$365-449 per person (5 days) to US$805 (15 days). The **Eurail Selectpass Youth** (2nd class), for those under 26, costs US$279-619. You are entitled to the same freebies as the Eurail Pass, but only when they are within or between countries that you selected with your purchase.

Eurail Regional Passes are valid in specific countries (Youth and Saver options also available). The France-Italy pass is available for four to 10 days in a two-month period, and costs €305-€589, €269-509 for the Saver pass, and €229-385 for the Youth pass. The Greece-Italy pass is also valid for four to 10 days in a 2-month period. The cost is €275-549/235-459/235-359. Though sold at some Italian and Greek train stations, it's cheaper to purchase in advance.

SHOPPING FOR A EURAIL. Passes are designed by the EU itself and must be sold at uniform prices determined by the EU. Some agents tack on a US$10 handling fee, and others offer certain bonuses, so shop around. Prices usually go up each year, so if you're planning to travel early in the year, save cash by purchasing before January 1 (you'll have 3 months to validate your pass).

Eurail passes should be bought before leaving; only a few places in major European cities sell them, usually at marked-up prices. You can get a replacement for a lost pass if you have purchased insurance under the **Pass Security Plan** (US$12). Eurail Passes are available through travel agents, student travel agencies like STA (p. 25), **Rail Europe** (US ☎+1-888-382-7245, Canada +1-800-361-7245; www.raileurope.com), or **Flight Centre** (US ☎+1-866-967-5351, Canada +1-877-967-5302; www.flightcentre.com). You can also buy directly from Eurail's website, www.eurail.com.

INTERRAIL PASS. If you have lived for at least six months in one of the European countries where **InterRail Global Pass** is valid, it provides an economical option. The InterRail Global Pass allows for travel within 30 European countries (excluding the country of residence). The five-day pass (€249, under 26 €159) must be used within 10 days, the 10-day pass (€359, under 26 €239) must be used within 22 days, the 22-day pass (€469, under 26 €309) is valid only for a 22-day period, and the one-month pass (€599, under 26 €399) is similarly valid only for a one-month period. Passholders receive discounts on many **ferries** in Europe. Passes can be purchased online at www.interrailnet.com.

FURTHER READING AND RESOURCES ON TRAIN TRAVEL
Info on rail travel and railpasses: www.raileurope.com.
Point-to-point fares and schedules: www.raileurope.com/us/rail/fares_schedules/index.htm. Allows you to calculate railpass savings.
European Railway Server: www.railfaneurope.net. Links to rail servers located throughout Europe.

BY BUS AND BOAT

Though European trains are popular, in some cases buses prove a better option. Often cheaper than railpasses, international bus passes allow unlimited travel on a hop-on, hop-off basis between major European cities. Amsterdam, Athens,

Istanbul, London, Munich, and Oslo are centers for lines that offer long-distance rides across Europe. Bus travel within Italy has its own benefits and disadvantages; in remote parts of the country private companies offer cheap fares and are often the only option, though schedules may be unreliable.

Eurolines, 4 Vicarage Rd., Edgbaston, Birmingham B15 3ES, UK (☎+44 0870 514 3219; www.eurolines.com). The largest operator of Europe-wide coach services. Unlimited 15-day (high season UK£195, under 26 and over 60 UK£165; low season UK£149/129); 30-day (high season UK£290/235; low season UK£209/169); or 60-day (high season UK£333/259; low season UK£265/211) travel passes that offer unlimited transit between 35 major European cities.

Busabout, 258 Vauxhall Bridge Rd., London SW1V 1BS, UK (☎+44 0207 950 1661; www.busabout.com). Offers 5 interconnecting bus circuits covering 60 cities and towns in Europe. Unlimited (consecutive-day) Passes, Flexipasses, and Add On Passes are available. Unlimited standard/student passes are valid for 2 weeks (US$469/419), 4 weeks (US$739/659), 6 weeks (US$919/819), 8 weeks (US$1049/939), 12 weeks (US$1319/1179), or for the season (US$1649/1469).

Most European ferries are quite comfortable; the cheapest ticket typically still includes a reclining chair or couchette. Fares jump sharply in July and August. Ask for discounts; ISIC holders can often get student fares, and Eurail Pass holders get many reductions and free trips. You'll occasionally have to pay a port tax (under US$10). Schedules are erratic, and different companies offer similar routes at varying prices. Shop around, and be wary of dinky, unreliable companies that don't take reservations. Mediterranean ferries may be the most glamorous, but they can also be the most rocky. Ferries run from Sicily to Tunisia and Malta, and from Sardinia to Tunisia and Corsica. Ferries float across the Adriatic from Ancona and Bari, Italy, to Split and Dubrovnik, Croatia, respectively. Ferries also run across the Aegean, from Ancona, Italy, to Patras, Greece, and from Bari, Italy, to Igoumenitsa and Patras, both in Greece. Eurail is valid on certain ferries between Brindisi, Italy, and a few Greek cities. Countless ferry companies operate these routes simultaneously; see the transportation sections of individual cities and towns for more specific info. **Ferriesonline.com** lists info on companies and schedules, and allows you to book online, but it's best to check with ferry lines directly to confirm information.

BORDER CROSSINGS

The surrounding countries of France, Switzerland, and Austria can make great daytrips from Italy's border cities. Multiple-country rail passes are available through RailEurope (www.raileurope.com). For more info on cross-border transportation in Europe, see p. 29.

As a part of the EU, Italy only requires that travelers present a valid passport and ID to travel between EU nations. When traveling to France and Austria, no currency exchange is necessary; yet, Switzerland uses the Swiss franc (CHF).

GETTING AROUND ITALY

Fares are either **one-way** or **round-trip.** "Period returns" require you to return within a specific number of days; "day return" means you must return on the same day. Unless stated otherwise, *Let's Go* always lists single fares. Round-trip fares on trains and buses in Italy are typically double the one-way fare.

ESSENTIALS

BY PLANE

With 25 major airports throughout Italy, there is no excuse for not making that hop, skip, and jump up to Venice to rendezvous with your newfound Italian lover. The main Italian hubs are Rome, Milan, Bergamo, Verona, Bologna, Genoa, Pisa, Florence, Turin, Venice, Naples, Bari, and Palermo, but suitable airports exist in nearly every corner of the country. The recent emergence of no-frills airlines has made hopscotching around Europe by air more affordable and convenient. Though these flights often feature inconvenient hours or serve less-popular regional airports, with one-way flights running as low as US$30, it's never been faster or easier to jet set across the Continent. **Ryanair** and **easyJet** (p. 27) are just two among many cheap airlines that fly throughout Italy and beyond. The **Star Alliance European Airpass** offers economy class fares as low as US$65 for travel within Europe to more than 965 airports in 42 countries. The pass is available to non-European passengers on Star Alliance carriers, including Air Canada, Austrian Airlines, BMI British Midland, Lufthansa, Scandinavian Airlines System, Thai International, and United Airlines, as well as on certain partner airlines. See www.staralliance.com for more info. In addition, a number of European airlines offer discount coupon packets. Most are available as tack-ons for transatlantic passengers, but some are stand-alone offers. Most must be purchased before departure, so research in advance.

BY BUS OR TRAIN

Trenitalia (☎89 20 21; www.trenitalia.com) is the main provider of railway transportation throughout Italy. Trenitalia is owned by Ferrovie dello Stato (FS), which is owned by the Italian government. Other (somewhat less reliable) companies include **Ferrovia Nord,** which runs several lines originating in Milan and expanding into the north, and **Ferrovie Sud-Est (FSE),** which runs mainly in Puglia. Local rail in some parts of Italy shuts down on Sunday, leaving buses as the principle weekend transportation option.

Several types of trains ride the Italian rails. The **locale** (sometimes called a **regionale**) stops at every station along a particular line, often taking twice as long. The **diretto** makes fewer stops than the *locale*, while the **espresso** only stops at major stations. The air-conditioned, more expensive, **InterCity (IC),** or **rapido,** train travels only to the largest cities; a few routes may require reservations. Tickets for the fast, comfortable, and pricey **Eurostar** trains (1st- and 2nd-class trains) require reservations. Eurail passes are valid without a supplement on all trains except the Eurostar. All InterRail holders must also purchase supplements (€2-20) for trains like Eurostar and InterCity. Train tickets may be purchased from *bigletterie* and automated ticket machines, which have instructions in English. There are often discounts for those under 26 or those traveling in a group of six or more.

 EASY COME, EASILY MISSED. Trenitalia stations are poorly labeled. Ask the conductor which is your stop to avoid missing it entirely.

Trains are not always safe. For long trips make sure you are on the correct car, as trains sometimes split at crossroads. For more specific travel safety concerns see **Personal Safety** (p. 19). Towns listed in parentheses on European schedules require a train switch at the town listed immediately before the parentheses. Note that unless stated otherwise, *Let's Go* lists one-way fares.

TRAIN TRAVEL DISTANCES AND TIMES

	Bari	Bologna	Bolzano	Florence	Genoa	Milan	Naples	Rome	Trieste	Turin	Venice
Bari	km\hr.	6	11	7	10	8	4	5	10	10	8
Bologna	681		3	1	3	2	5	3	4	3	2
Bolzano	950	291		5	5	3	10	7	5	5	3
Florence	784	106	397		4	3	4	2	5	5	3
Genoa	966	285	399	268		2	7	5	7	1	5
Milan	899	218	276	324	156		6	5	5	1	3
Naples	322	640	931	534	758	858		2	9	9	7
Rome	482	408	90	302	526	626	232		6	7	5
Trieste	955	308	338	414	535	420	948	715		7	2
Turin	1019	338	408	442	174	139	932	699	551		5
Venice	806	269	225	265	387	284	899	567	165	414	

NATIONAL PASSES. In general, trains in Italy are cheap enough not to warrant buying a national pass. **Eurail** sells a **National Pass** for Italy (Youth and Saver options also available). The **Italy pass** is available for three to 10 days in a two-month period, and costs US$225-424, US$191-361 for the Saver pass, and US$186-346 for the Youth pass. The Euro Domino pass became the InterRail **One Country Pass** in 2007 and is available to anyone who has lived in Europe for at least six months; it is only valid in one country (designated when bought). Passes can be bought for three to eight days within one month. A three-day pass is €109, under 26 €71; an eight-day pass costs €229/149. Reservations must be paid for separately. Supplements are included for many high-speed trains. The pass can be purchased online at www.interrailnet.com. In addition to simple railpasses, many countries (as well as Eurail) offer **rail-and-drive passes,** which combine car rental with rail travel—a good option for travelers who wish to visit cities accessible by rail and to make trips into the surrounding areas. Prices range US$308-728 per person, depending on the type of pass, car, and the number of people included. Additional days cost $46-104 per day. For price estimates, contact **Rail Europe** (p. 29).

NEED VALIDATION? Before boarding, always validate your ticket in the validation machines, colored yellow or orange. Failure to validate may result in steep fines, and train operators do not accept ignorance as an excuse.

RESERVATIONS. Seat reservations are rarely required, but you are not guaranteed a seat without one (€2.50 and up, depending on the ticket). Reservations are available up to two months in advance on major trains (IC and Eurostar). Italians often reserve far ahead, so strongly consider reserving during peak holiday and tourist seasons (at the very least, book a few hours ahead). If someone occupies your seat, be prepared to say politely, *"Mi scusi, ma ho prenotato questo posto"* (Excuse me, but I have reserved this seat). Purchase a **supplement** (€3.50-30) or special fare for faster or higher-quality trains. Eurail passes do not include reservations.

OVERNIGHT TRAINS. Night trains have their advantages: you don't waste daylight hours traveling, and you can forego the hassle and expense of securing a night's accommodation. However, they have their drawbacks, namely discomfort and sleeplessness. Consider paying extra for a **cuccetta** (couchette), one of six fold-down bunks in a compartment; private **sleeping cars** offer more comfort, but are considerably more expensive and not always available. Even if you're not willing to spend the money, some trains have more comfortable seating compartments with fold-out seats. If you are using a restricted-day railpass, inspect train schedules to maximize your pass use: a direct overnight train or boat journey uses up only one of your travel days if it departs after 7pm.

SHOULD YOU BUY A RAILPASS? Railpasses exist to allow you to jump on any train in Europe, go wherever you want whenever you want, and change your plans at will. In practice, it's not so simple. You still must stand in line to validate your pass, pay for supplements, and fork over cash for seat and couchette reservations. More importantly, railpasses don't always pay off. If you are planning to spend extensive time on trains, hopping between big cities, a railpass will probably be worth it. But in many cases, especially if you are under 26 or traveling in a large group, point-to-point tickets may prove a cheaper option.

You may find it tough to make your railpass pay for itself in Italy, where train fares are reasonable, distances short, and buses are often preferable. If, however, the total cost of your trips nears the price of the pass, the convenience of avoiding some ticket lines may be worth the difference.

BY FERRY

The islands of Sicily and Sardinia, as well as the smaller islands along the coasts, are connected to the mainland and to each other by **ferries** *(traghetti)* and the more expensive **hydrofoils** *(aliscafi)*; international trips are generally made by ferry. Italy's largest private ferry service, **Tirrenia** (www.gruppotirrenia. it), runs ferries to Sardinia, Sicily, Tunisia, and Albania. Other major ferry companies (**Siremar, Toremar, Saremar, Caremar, Moby Lines,** and **Corsica Ferries**) and the **SNAV** (www.snav.it) hydrofoil services travel between major ports like Ancona, Bari, Brindisi, Civitavecchia, Genoa, La Spezia, Naples, and Trapani. Ferry services also depart for the Tremiti, Pontine, and Aeolian Islands.

Ferry service is also prevalent in the Lake Country. These ferries can be expensive and time-consuming, but sometimes they are the best way to go from city to city, and many carry cars as well. Pick up a schedule brochure at the tourist office upon arrival at each lake. Some cities act as major hubs (e.g., Desenzano on Lake Garda) and require you to stop there between cities in order to catch a ferry to your next destination. Ferry times and fares vary, so check for information at major hub cities in your area.

For major trips reserve tickets at least one week in advance and even earlier if the ferry company permits it. Service is often infrequent on longer routes, with only one or two departures per week, and during peak travel seasons, these routes are booked quickly. Schedules change unpredictably—confirm your departure one day in advance. Some ports require check-in two hours before departure, or your reservation will be cancelled. **Posta ponte** (deck class; preferable in warm weather) is cheapest but is often only available when the **poltrona** (reclining cabin seats) are full. Port taxes often apply.

BY BUS AND METRO

 DON'T TRASH IT! Hold on to your (validated!) bus, metro, and train tickets throughout your entire journey. *Controllori* will spontaneously board at any given time to check for freeloaders and dole out hefty fines.

Though notoriously unreliable and uncomfortable, **buses** *(autobus)* are often cheaper than trains. Two bus systems exist within Italy: *pullman* or intercity, which run between towns and regions, and intra-city, which provide local transportation. Tickets can generally be purchased at private bus company offices near the bus station or departure point, or onboard. In many rural areas, where stops are unmarked, it is crucial to find out exactly where to stand to flag down the bus. On rare occasions, the tickets are actually sold by the side of the road out of a salesperson's car near where the bus will stop. Intra-city bus tickets are usually sold at *tabaccherie*, and must be validated using the orange machines immediately upon entering the bus. Failure to do so will result in fines around €30, but occasionally as high as €500 upon inspection. The websites www.bus.it and www.italybus.it are both helpful resources for finding bus companies in specific regions and routes to small towns.

Most large cities, including Rome, Naples, and Milan, have fast and cheap **metro systems** that connect major tourist destinations. Along with buses, the metro is the best form of local transport. The metro usually operates from 6am until midnight, and tickets usually cost approximately €1. Cabins and stations get packed during rush hour, so guard personal belongings carefully, as theft is rampant. Tickets are sold in stations at counters or from automated machines. Remember to validate them, or risk a heavy fine.

 FERMATA FRENZY. Taking the bus in Italy is easy, affordable, and a great way to get around, but most bus stops that aren't in major *piazze* are only *"fermata prenotata"* stops, meaning the bus driver won't stop there unless he/she sees somebody waiting or someone onboard requests a stop. Drivers often miss travelers waiting quietly on the side of the road, so make your presence known. Wave your hands, step out on the curb, and make eye contact; you might feel silly but you'll feel worse if the bus drives right by.

BY CAR

With a vast network of narrow, winding roads, loosely enforced speed limits, and aggressive native drivers, touring Italy by **car** is a memorable experience. Despite the initial intimidation that may come from cruising bumper to bumper on a cliffside road along the Amalfi coast, with a little bit of courage and a decent helping of driving competence, car travel opens up corners of Italy that are not easily reached by—or inaccessible altogether to—the average explorer.

RENTING

While the Italian bus and train systems are quite effective in negotiating travel between the major cities, travelers looking to explore smaller cities and rural villages might find renting a car to be a more viable option. A single traveler won't save by renting a car (especially considering the high gas prices), but four usually will. If you can't decide between train and car travel, you may benefit from a combination of the two; RailEurope and other railpass vendors offer **rail-and-drive** packages. **Fly-and-drive** packages are often available from travel agents or airline-rental agency partnerships.

RENTAL AGENCIES

You can generally make reservations before you leave by calling major international offices in your home country. It's a good idea to cross-check this information with local agencies as well. The local desk numbers are included in town listings; for home-country numbers, call your toll-free directory.

To rent a car from most establishments in Italy, you need to be at least 18 years old. Some agencies require renters to be 25, and most charge those 18-24 an additional insurance fee of €12 per day. Small local operations occasionally rent to people under 21, but be sure to ask about the insurance coverage and deductible, and always check the fine print. Rental agencies in Italy include:

Auto Europe (Italy, Canada, and the US ☎+1-888-223-5555; www.autoeurope.com).

Avis (Australia ☎13 63 33, Canada and the US +1-800-352-7900, Italy 19 91 00 133, New Zealand 0800 655 111, UK 0870 010 0287; www.avis.com).

Budget (Canada ☎+1-800-268-8900, UK 8701 565 656, US +1-800-472-3325, www.budget.com).

Europe by Car (US ☎+1-800-223-1516; www.europebycar.com).

Hertz (Canada ☎+1-800-654-3001; +1-US 800-654-3001; www.hertz.com).

COSTS AND INSURANCE

Rental car prices start at around US$39 a day from national companies. Expect to pay more for larger cars and for four-wheel-drive. Cars with **automatic transmission** can cost up to US$100 per day more than cars with manual transmission (stick shift), and, in some places, automatic transmission is hard to find in the first place. It is often difficult to find an automatic four-wheel-drive.

Remember that if you are driving a conventional rental vehicle on an unpaved road, you are almost never covered by insurance; ask about this before leaving the rental agency. Be aware that cars rented on an **American Express** or **Visa/ MasterCard Gold** or **Platinum** credit card in Italy might not carry the automatic insurance that they would in some other countries; check with your credit-card company. Insurance plans from rental companies almost always come with an **excess** of around US$5000 for conventional vehicles; excess ranges are even higher for younger drivers and for four-wheel-drive. This means that the rental company's insurance only applies to damages over the excess; damages up to that amount must be covered by your existing insurance plan. Many rental companies in Italy require you to buy a **Collision Damage Waiver (CDW)**, which will waive the excess in the case of a collision. **Loss Damage Waivers (LDWs)** do the same in the case of theft or vandalism.

National chains often allow one-way rentals (picking up in one city and dropping off in another). There is usually a minimum hire period and sometimes an extra dropoff charge of several hundred dollars.

DRIVING PERMITS AND CAR INSURANCE

INTERNATIONAL DRIVING PERMIT (IDP)

If you plan to drive a car while in Italy, you must be over 18 and have an **International Driving Permit (IDP)**, though certain regions will allow travelers to drive with a valid American or Canadian license for a limited number of months. It may be a good idea to get one anyway, in case you're in a situation (e.g., an accident or stranded in a small town) where the police do not know English; information on the IDP is printed in 11 languages, including Italian.

Your IDP, valid for one year, must be issued in your own country before you depart. An application for an IDP usually requires one or two photos, a current local license, an additional form of identification, and a fee. To apply, contact your home country's automobile association. Be vigilant when purchasing an IDP online or anywhere other than your home automobile association. Many vendors sell permits of questionable legitimacy for higher prices.

CAR INSURANCE

Most credit cards cover standard insurance. If you rent, lease, or borrow a car, you will need a **green card,** or **International Insurance Certificate,** to certify that you have liability insurance and that it applies abroad. Green cards can be obtained at car rental agencies, car dealers (for those leasing cars), some travel agents, and some border crossings. Rental agencies may require you to purchase theft insurance in countries that they consider to have a high risk of auto theft.

ON THE ROAD

Driving in Italy is similar to driving in the rest of Europe: vehicles drive on the right, pass on the left, and follow international rules and road signs established by the Geneva Convention. Roads range from the *autostrade*—superhighways with 130kph (80 mph) speed limit, increased to 150kph (93 mph) in some areas—to the narrow and sometimes unpaved *strade comunali* (local roads). Mountain roads can have steep cliffs and narrow curves; exercise caution if you must drive in the Dolomites or the Apennines. Highways usually charge expensive tolls, often best paid with a credit card. In cities the speed limit is usually 50kph (31 mph). Headlights must be on when driving on the *autostrada*. For more driving rules and regulations, check *Moto Europa* (www.ideamerge.com/motoeuropa) or *In Italy Online* (www.initaly.com/travel/info/driving.htm).

DRIVING PRECAUTIONS

When traveling in the summer or in the desert, bring substantial amounts of water (a suggested 5L of water per person per day) for drinking and for the radiator. You should always carry a spare tire and jack, jumper cables, extra oil, flares, a flashlight, and heavy blankets (in case your car breaks down at night or in the winter). If you don't know how to change a tire, learn before heading out, especially if you are planning on traveling in deserted areas. If your car breaks down, stay in your vehicle.

DANGERS

While road conditions are perfectly safe in most areas of Italy, the further you get from civilization, the narrower and more poorly paved roads are likely to be. Use caution on minor roads in the countryside, as many are not well maintained and best taken at a slow and steady pace.

CAR ASSISTANCE

The **Automobile Club d'Italia** (ACI) is at the service of all drivers in Italy, with offices located throughout the country (www.aci.it). In case of breakdown, call ☎116 for assistance from the nearest ACI. On superhighways use the emergency telephones placed every 2km. For long drives in desolate areas, invest in a roadside assistance program and a cell phone, but be aware that use of phones en route is only permitted with a hands-free device.

ESSENTIALS

BY BOAT, BICYCLE, MOPED, ETC.

Renting a **bike** is easy in Italy; look for *noleggio* signs. If you want to bring your own, some airlines will count a bike as your second piece of luggage; many now charge extra (one-way US$80-160). Bikes must be packed in a cardboard box with the pedals and front wheel detached; many airlines sell bike boxes at the airport (US$15). Most ferries let you take your bike for free or for a nominal fee, and you can always ship your bike on trains. Renting a bike beats bringing your own if you plan to stay in one or two regions, and some hostels rent bicycles for low prices. *Let's Go* lists bike rental stores in the **Transportation** section of towns and cities whenever possible. **Ciclismo Classico,** 30 Marathon St., Arlington, MA 02474, USA (☎+1-800-866-7314; www.ciclismoclassico. com), offers beginner to advanced level trips across Italy, including Sardinia, the Amalfi Coast, Southern Italy, Sicily, Piedmont, and the Veneto.

    Scooters or **mopeds** are available for rent in major cities, as well as in smaller or rural locations. Often a *motorino* (scooter) is the most convenient method of transportation to reach sights in places with unreliable bus or train connections. Rental companies are required by law to provide a helmet, which the driver must wear. Gas and insurance may or may not be included in the rental price. Even if riding a scooter is exhilarating, always exercise caution; practice in empty streets before you hit the open road and keep with the flow of traffic instead of just following street signs. Drivers in Italy—especially those enthusiastic southerners—are notorious for ignoring traffic laws.

    Some of Italy's grandest scenery can be seen only by **foot.** *Let's Go* features many daytrips, but native inhabitants and fellow travelers are the best source for tips. Professionally run hiking and walking tours are often your best bet for navigating *la bell'Italia*. Hiking tours generally range from six to nine days long and cost from US$2800-4000. Check out Ciclismo Classico (see above) for hiking options along the Amalfi Coast, and through Tuscany or Cinque Terre. The **Backpack Europe** website (www.backpackeurope.com) provides links to great hiking, walking, and kayaking options throughout Italy.

BY THUMB

LET'S NOT GO. Let's Go never recommends hitchhiking as a safe means of transportation. None of this information is intended to do so.

Let's Go strongly urges you to consider the risks before you choose to hitchhike. Hitching means entrusting your life to a stranger and risking assault, sexual harassment, theft, and unsafe driving. For women traveling alone (or even in pairs), hitching is just too dangerous. A man and a woman are a less dangerous combination; two men will have a harder time getting a lift, while three men will go nowhere. Because hitchhiking can be difficult in Italy, travelers usually pick a well-lit spot outside of urban areas, where drivers can stop, return to the road without causing an accident, and have time to look over potential passengers as they approach. Note that it is illegal to walk along the highway. Some travelers head to service areas *(le aree di servizio)* to get rides. Italian speakers will have an easier time getting where they want to go; knowing the Italian name of the destination is essential. Keep luggage on the seat next to you, instead of in the trunk, to facilitate a quick exit. Most Western European countries, including Italy, offer a ride service which pairs drivers with riders; the fee varies by destination. **Eurostop International** (www.eurostop.

be) is one of the largest. Or try **Viavai** (www.viavai.com/autostop). Not all organizations screen drivers; ask in advance. Request the ID number from the ride service of the driver you are paired with and give it to someone you trust; when you get picked up, make sure your driver confirms the ID number.

KEEPING IN TOUCH

BY EMAIL AND INTERNET

While Internet is a relatively common amenity throughout Italy, Wi-Fi is not, and as a general rule, the prevalence of both decreases the further you travel from urban areas. In large towns, it may be possible to find Internet but not Wi-Fi. In smaller towns, even a basic Internet connection may be hard to come by. Rates range from €2-6 per hour. While it's possible in some places to forge a remote link with your home server, in most cases this is a much slower (and more expensive) option than using free **web-based email accounts** (e.g., www.gmail.com and www.hotmail.com). **Internet cafes** and the occasional free Internet terminal at a public library or university are listed in the **Practical Information** sections of major cities. For additional cybercafes in Italy, check out http://cafe.ecs.net.

WARY WI-FI. Wireless hot spots make Internet access possible in public and remote places. Unfortunately, they also pose **security risks.** Hot spots are public, open networks that use unencrypted, unsecured connections. They are susceptible to hacks and "packet sniffing"—ways of stealing passwords and other private information. To prevent problems, disable ad hoc mode, turn off file sharing and network discovery, encrypt your email, turn on your firewall, beware of phony networks, and watch for over-the-shoulder creeps.

BY TELEPHONE

CALLING HOME FROM ITALY

Prepaid phone cards are a common and relatively inexpensive means of calling abroad. Each comes with a Personal Identification Number (PIN) and a toll-free access number. You call the access number and then follow the directions to enter your PIN. To buy prepaid phone cards, check online for the best rates; www.callingcards.com is a good place to start. Online providers generally send your access number and PIN via email, with no actual "card" involved. You can also call home with prepaid phone cards purchased in Italy (see **Calling Within Italy,** next page).

PLACING INTERNATIONAL CALLS. To call Italy from home or to call home from Italy, dial:
1. The **international dialing prefix.** To call from **Australia,** dial 0011; **Canada** or the **US,** 011; **Ireland, New Zealand,** or the **UK,** 00; **Italy,** 00.
2. The **country code** of the country you want to call. To call **Australia,** dial 61; **Canada** or the **US,** 1; **Ireland,** 353; **New Zealand,** 64; the **UK,** 44; **Italy,** 39.
3. The **city/area code.** *Let's Go* lists the city/area codes for cities and towns in Italy opposite the city or town name, next to a ☎, as well as in every phone number. If the first digit is a zero (e.g., 020 for London), omit the zero when calling from abroad (e.g., dial 20 from **Canada** to reach **London**).
4. The **local number.**

Another option is to purchase a **calling card,** linked to a major national telecommunications service in your home country. Calls are billed collect or to your account. To call home with a calling card, contact the operator for your service provider in Italy by dialing the appropriate toll-free access number (listed below in the third column).

COMPANY	TO OBTAIN A CARD:	TO CALL ABROAD:
AT&T (US)	☎800-364-9292 or www.att.com	☎800 17 24 44
Canada Direct	☎800-561-8868 or www.infocanadadirect.com	☎800 17 22 13
MCI (US)	☎800-777-5000 or www.minutepass.com	☎800 90 58 25
Telecom New Zealand Direct	www.telecom.co.nz	☎800 17 26 41
Telstra Australia	☎800 676 638 or www.telstra.com	☎800 17 26 10

Placing a collect call through an international operator can be expensive, but may be necessary in case of an emergency. You can frequently call collect without even possessing a company's calling card just by calling its access number and following the instructions.

CALLING WITHIN ITALY

The simplest way to call within the country is to use a coin-operated phone. Prepaid phone cards (available at newspaper kiosks and tobacco stores, or *tabaccherie*), usually save time and money in the long run.

CELLULAR PHONES

Cellular phones *(telefonini)* are a convenient and inexpensive option for those planning longer visits to Italy. Given the prevalence of cell phones in Italy, pay phones are increasingly hard to come by, making cell phones a good alternative for tourists. You won't necessarily have to deal with cell phone plans and bills; prepaid minutes are widely available and phones can be purchased cheaply or even rented, avoiding the hassle of pay phones and phone cards.

The international standard for cell phones is **Global System for Mobile Communication** (GSM). To make and receive calls in Italy you will need a GSM-compatible phone and a **SIM (Subscriber Identity Module) card,** a country-specific, thumbnail-sized chip that gives you a local phone number and plugs you into the local network. Many SIM cards are prepaid, and incoming calls are often free. You can buy additional cards or vouchers (usually available at convenience stores) to "top up" your phone. For more info on GSM phones, check out www.telestial.com, www.orange.co.uk, www.roadpost.com, or www.planetomni.com. Companies like **Cellular Abroad** (www.cellularabroad.com) rent cell phones that work in a variety of destinations around the world.

 GSM PHONES. Just having a GSM phone doesn't mean you're necessarily good to go when you travel abroad. The majority of GSM phones sold in the United States operate on a different frequency (1900) than international phones (900/1800) and will not work abroad. Tri-band phones work on all three frequencies (900/1800/1900) and will operate through most of the world. Additionally, some GSM phones are SIM-locked and will only accept SIM cards from a single carrier. You'll need a SIM-unlocked phone to use a SIM card from a local carrier when you travel.

TIME DIFFERENCES

Italy is one hour ahead of Greenwich Mean Time (GMT). The country observes Daylight Saving Time, which starts on the last Sunday in March, when clocks are moved ahead one hour, making Italy two hours ahead of GMT. Clocks are put back one hour on the last Sunday of October.

The following table applies from late October to early April.

4AM	5AM	6AM	7AM	8AM	1PM	10PM*
Vancouver Seattle Los Angeles	Denver	Chicago	Boston New York Toronto	New Brunswick	**Rome**	Sydney Canberra Melbourne

*Australia observes Daylight Saving Time from October to March, the opposite of the Northern Hemisphere. Therefore, it is 8hr. ahead of Rome from March to October and 10hr. ahead from October to March, for an average of 9hr.

BY MAIL

SENDING MAIL HOME FROM ITALY

Airmail is the best way to send mail home from Italy. **Aerogrammes,** printed sheets that fold into envelopes and travel via airmail, are available at post offices. Write "airmail" or *"per posta aerea"* on the front. Most post offices charge exorbitant fees or simply refuse to send aerogrammes with enclosures. Surface mail is by far the cheapest and slowest way to send mail. It takes one to two months to cross the Atlantic and one to three to cross the Pacific—good for heavy items you won't need for a while, such as souvenirs. Delivery times and package shipping costs vary; inquire at the post office *(ufficio postale).*

SENDING MAIL TO ITALY

To ensure timely delivery, mark envelopes "airmail," *"par avion,"* or *"per posta aerea."* In addition to the standard postage system whose rates are listed below, **Federal Express** (Australia ☎+61 13 26 10, Canada and the US +1-800-463-3339, Ireland +353 800 535 800, New Zealand +64 800 733 339, the UK +44 8456 0708 09; www.fedex.com) handles express mail services to Italy.

There are several ways to arrange pick up of letters sent to you while you are abroad. Mail can be sent via **Fermo Posta** (General Delivery) to almost any city or town in Italy with a post office, and it is generally reliable, if occasionally untimely. Address **Poste Restante** letters like so:

Dante ALIGHIERI

c/o Ufficio Postale Centrale

FERMO POSTA

48100 Ravenna

Italy

The mail will go to a special desk in the central post office, unless you specify a post office by street address or postal code. Note that the postal service may ignore this specification. It is usually safer and quicker, though more expensive, to send mail express or registered. Bring your passport (or other photo ID) for pickup; there may be a small fee. If the clerks insist that there is nothing for you, ask them to check under your first name as well. *Let's Go* lists post offices in the **Practical Information** section for each city and most towns.

American Express's travel offices throughout the world offer a free **Client Letter Service** (mail held up to 30 days and forwarded upon request) for cardholders

ESSENTIALS

who contact them in advance. Some offices provide these services to non-card-holders (especially AmEx Travelers Cheque holders), but call ahead to make sure. *Let's Go* lists AmEx locations for most large cities in **Practical Information** sections; for a complete list, visit www.americanexpress.com/travel.

ACCOMMODATIONS

HOSTELS

Many hostels are laid out dorm-style, often with large single-sex rooms and bunk beds, though private rooms that sleep two to four are becoming more common. They sometimes provide bike or moped rentals, lockers, transportation to airports, breakfast and other meals, laundry facilities, and Internet. However, there can be drawbacks: some hostels close during certain daytime "lockout" hours, have a curfew, don't accept reservations, impose a maximum stay, or, less frequently, require that you do chores. In Italy, a dorm bed in a hostel will average around €15-25 and a private room around €25-30.

A HOSTELER'S BILL OF RIGHTS. There are certain standard features that we do not include in our hostel listings. Unless we state otherwise, you can expect that every hostel has no lockout, no curfew, free sheets, free hot showers, some system of secure luggage storage, and no key deposit.

HOSTELLING INTERNATIONAL

Joining the youth hostel association in your own country (listed below) automatically grants you membership privileges in **Hostelling International (HI),** a federation of national hosteling associations. Non-HI members may be allowed to stay in some hostels, but will have to pay extra to do so. HI hostels are scattered throughout Italy, and are typically less expensive than private hostels. HI's umbrella organization's website (www.hihostels.com), which lists the web addresses and phone numbers of all national associations, can be a great place to begin researching hosteling in a specific region. Other comprehensive hosteling websites include www.hostels.com and www.hostelplanet.com.

Most HI hostels also honor **guest memberships**—you'll get a blank card with space for six validation stamps. Each night you'll pay a nonmember supplement (one-sixth the membership fee) and earn one guest stamp; six stamps make you a member. A new membership benefit is the **FreeNites program,** which allows hostelers to gain points toward free rooms. Most student travel agencies (p. 25) sell HI cards, as do all of the national hosteling organizations listed below. All prices listed below are valid for a one-year membership.

Australian Youth Hostels Association (AYHA), 422 Kent St., Sydney, NSW 2000 (☎+61 2 9261 1111; www.yha.com.au). AUS$52, under 18 AUS$19.

Hostelling International-Canada (HI-C), 205 Catherine St., Ste. 400, Ottawa, ON K2P 1C3 (☎+1-613-237-7884; www.hihostels.ca). CDN$35, under 18 free.

Hostelling International Northern Ireland (HINI), 22-32 Donegall Rd., Belfast BT12 5JN (☎+44 28 9032 4733; www.hini.org.uk). UK£15, under 25 UK£10.

Youth Hostels Association of New Zealand Inc. (YHANZ), Level 1, 166 Moorhouse Ave., P.O. Box 436, Christchurch (☎+64 3379 9970, in NZ 0800 278 299; www.yha.org. nz). NZ$40, under 18 free.

Youth Hostels Association (England and Wales), Trevelyan House, Dimple Rd., Matlock, Derbyshire DE4 3YH (☎+44 8707 7088 68; www.yha.org.uk). UK£16, under 26 UK£10.

Hostelling International-USA, 8401 Colesville Rd., Ste. 600, Silver Spring, MD 20910 (☎+1-301-495-1240; www.hiayh.org). US$28, under 18 free.

HOTELS, GUESTHOUSES, AND PENSIONS

Hotel singles in Italy cost about US$40-80 (€25-50) per night, doubles US$ 60-140 (€40-90). In many lower budget establishments, you'll typically share a hall bathroom; a private bathroom will cost extra. Some hotels offer "full pension" (all meals) and "half pension" (no lunch). Smaller guesthouses and pensions are often cheaper than hotels. If you make **reservations** in writing, indicate your night of arrival and the number of nights you plan to stay. The hotel will send you a confirmation and may request payment for the first night.

OTHER TYPES OF ACCOMMODATIONS

BED AND BREAKFASTS (B&BS)

For a cozy alternative to impersonal hotel rooms, B&Bs (private homes with rooms available to travelers) range from acceptable to sublime. In Italy, B&Bs, singles generally cost €20-50 and doubles generally cost €70-90. Any number of websites provide listings for B&Bs; check out **Bed & Breakfast Inns Online** (www. bbonline.com), **InnFinder** (www.inncrawler.com), **InnSite** (www.innsite.com), or **BedandBreakfast.com** (www.bedandbreakfast.com).

AGRITURISMO

Frequently omitted by mainstream travel guides and ignored by local tourist offices, *agriturismo* is a pleasurable, leisurely, and inexpensive way to visit the Italian countryside. Local families open their homes to guests and provide reasonably-priced meals. The host family and guests gather around the table each night, sharing bottles of homemade wine, fresh vegetables from the garden, and stories that last far into the night. These houses, however, are usually only accessible by car—a tranquil remoteness that simply adds to their charm, provided that you can reach them. If you're looking to truly experience the laid-back Italian lifestyle, hearty cuisine, local wines, and sweeping countryside vistas, *agriturismo* is the best way to spend your time and money. To find *agriturismo* options in your region, consult local tourist offices or check out the **Associazione Nazionale per l'Agriturismo, l'Ambiente e il Territorio** (www.agriturist.it).

UNIVERSITY DORMS

Many **colleges** and **universities** open their residence halls to travelers when school is not in session; some do so even during term time. Getting a room may take a couple of phone calls and require advanced planning, but rates tend to be low and many offer free local calls and Internet access. For a list of student housing opportunities in Italian cities, write to The Italian Ministry of Education, Vle. Trastevere 76/A, 00153 Rome (☎06 58 491; www.pubblica. istruzione.it), and ask for a "Guide for Foreign Students."

HOME EXCHANGES AND HOSPITALITY CLUBS

Home exchange offers the traveler various types of homes (houses, apartments, condominiums, villas, even castles in some cases), plus the opportunity to live like a native and to cut down on accommodation fees. For more information, contact **HomeExchange.com Inc.,** P.O. Box 787, Hermosa Beach, CA 90254, USA (☎+1-310-798-3864 or toll-free +1-800-877-8723; www.homeexchange.com) or **Intervac International Home Exchange** (☎05 19 17 841; www.intervac.com).

Hospitality clubs link their members with individuals or families abroad who are willing to host travelers for free or for a small fee to promote cultural exchange and general good karma. In exchange, members usually must be willing to host travelers in their own homes; a small fee may also be required. **The Hospitality Club** (www.hospitalityclub.org) is a good place to start. **Servas** (www.servas.org) is an established, more formal, peace-based organization, and requires a fee and an interview to join. An Internet search will find many similar organizations, some of which cater to special interests (e.g., women, GLBT travelers, or members of certain professions). As always, use common sense when planning to stay with or host someone you do not know.

LONG-TERM ACCOMMODATIONS

Travelers planning to stay in Italy for extended time periods may find it most cost-effective to locate an **apartment** for rent *(affittasi)*. A basic one-bedroom or studio apartment in Rome will range €500-2000 per month. Besides the rent itself, prospective tenants are frequently required to front a security deposit (usually one month's rent) and the last month's rent.

A good place to check for apartments is **craigslist** (www.craigslist.org), a forum for renters and rentees where you can see others' listings or post your own housing needs. For regional listings, try http://affittistudenti.studenti.it and www.secondamano.it. If it's Rome you're after, look at http://liveinrome. com. For listings in Rome, Florence, and Venice, check www.romepower.com. For traveler-written reviews of establishments throughout Italy, http://www. slowtrav.com/italy/index.asp is a useful resource.

CAMPING

Over 1700 campgrounds in Italy are designated between one and four stars; a four-star campground includes amenities such as a market, swimming pool, and a bar. Costs vary, but are generally under €10 per person. Some campgrounds offer bungalows as a cheap alternative for travelers without tents; others even have tents to rent. Camping is legal only at designated sites. A regional guide can be found through **Easy Camping** (☎33 96 09 41 04; easycamping.it). Reservations are recommended at some sites. Campgrounds are listed in the **Accommodations** section when available.

Renting an RV costs more than tenting or hosteling but less than staying in hotels while renting a car (see **By Car,** p. 35). The convenience of bringing along your own bedroom, bathroom, and kitchen makes RVing an attractive option, especially for older travelers and families with children. Rates vary widely by region, season (July and August are the most expensive months), and type of RV. Rental prices for a standard RV are around €600-800 per week.

Hikers might also be interested in the mountain refuges of the **Club Alpino Italiano,** P. Savonarola 3, I-48022 Lugo di Romagna, Ravenna (☎/fax 05 45 30 541; www.racine.ravenna.it/cailugo). These shelters range from €17 (€8.50 for members) to €26 (€13) per night, depending on accessibility and services.

THE GREAT OUTDOORS

The **Great Outdoor Recreation Page** (www.gorp.com) provides excellent general information for travelers planning on camping or enjoying the outdoors.

 LEAVE NO TRACE. *Let's Go* encourages travelers to embrace the "Leave No Trace" ethic, minimizing their impact on natural environments and protecting them for future generations. Trekkers and wilderness enthusiasts should set up camp on durable surfaces, use cookstoves instead of campfires, bury human waste away from water supplies, bag trash and carry it out with them, and respect wildlife and natural objects. For more detailed information, contact the **Leave No Trace Center for Outdoor Ethics,** P.O. Box 997, Boulder, CO 80306, USA (☎+1-800-332-4100 or 303-442-8222; www.lnt.org).

USEFUL RESOURCES

A variety of publishing companies offer guidebooks to meet the educational needs of novice or expert hikers. For info about camping, hiking, and biking, write or call the publishers listed below to receive a free catalog. Campers heading to Europe should consider buying an **International Camping Carnet.** Similar to a hostel membership card, it's required at a few campgrounds and sometimes provides discounts. It is available in North America from the **Family Campers and RVers Association** and in the UK from **The Caravan Club** (both below).

For Italian information, consult the **Touring Club Italiano (TCI)**, C. Italia 10, Milan (☎02 85 261; www.touringclub.com).

Automobile Association, Contact Centre, Lambert House, Stockport Rd., Cheadle SK8 2DY, UK (☎+44 8706 000 371; www.theAA.com). Publishes road atlases for Europe, Britain, France, Germany, Ireland, Italy, Spain, and the US.

The Caravan Club, East Grinstead House, East Grinstead, West Sussex, RH19 1UA, UK (☎+44 1342 326 944; www.caravanclub.co.uk). For UK£34, members receive access to sites, insurance services, equipment discounts, maps, and a monthly magazine.

Cicerone Press, 2 Police Sq., Milnthorpe, Cumbria UK LA7 7PY, (☎+44 1539 562 069; www.ciceroneguides.com). Walking, trekking, and climbing guides, including *Walking in Tuscany* (2006; UK£14) and *Walking in Sicily* (2006; UK£12).

European Rambler's Association (ERA), c/o Klub èeských turistù, Archeologická 2256, 155 00 Prague 5 - Lužiny, Czech Republic (☎+420 251 627 356; www.era-ewv-ferp. org). Umbrella organization for Rambler's Associations in countries throughout Europe. Maintains 11 long-distance, walk-able, inter-European trails with the aim of promoting sustainable travel and supporting European culture and heritage.

Family Campers and RVers Association, 4804 Transit Rd., Bldg. 2, Depew, NY 14043 (www.fcrv.org). For US$25, members receive access to special events, equipment discounts, maps, and a monthly magazine.

The Mountaineers Books, 1001 SW Klickitat Way, Ste. 201, Seattle, WA 98134, USA (☎+1-206-223-6303; www.mountaineersbooks.org). Over 600 titles on hiking, biking, mountaineering, natural history, and conservation.

The following bookstores in Italy carry maps as well as titles on outdoor adventure, travel, and mountaineering.

Monti in Città, Vle. Monte Nero 15, Milan (☎02 55 18 17 90; www.montiincitta.it).

Nuova Libreria Accursio, V. G. Oberdan 29/b, 40126 Bologna (☎051 22 09 83; accursio-wolit@tiscali.it)

Peakbook, V. Arco dei Banchi 3a, 00186 Rome (☎06 64 76 00 87; www.peakbook.it).

NATIONAL PARKS

Trekking through a national park can be a welcome escape from the touristed mayhem of Italy's big cities. With 22 national parks and more than five times as many regional parks and nature reserves, Italy protects nearly 10% of its land. Whether you seek mountains, lakes, forests, or oceans, Italy's parks have something to offer. Bears and lynxes inhabit the **Parco Nazionale d'Abruzzo** (www.parcoabruzzo.it; see p. 554), accessible by both car and train from Rome. The beautiful coast of the **Parco Nazionale delle Cinque Terre** (www.parconazionale-5terre.it; see p. 210) can be reached by bus, train, and boat. **Federparchi,** V. Cristoforo Colombo 163, 00147 Rome (☎06 51 60 49 40; www.parks.it.) publishes *Parchi,* a magazine devoted to the parks, their preservation, and other environmental concerns in Italy and throughout Europe. Its thorough website lists news, events, and other info for the parks.

WILDERNESS SAFETY

Staying **warm, dry,** and **well hydrated** is key to a happy and safe wilderness experience. For any hike, pack a first-aid kit, a reflector, a whistle, high-energy food, extra water, raingear, a hat, mittens, and extra socks. For warmth, wear wool or insulating synthetic materials designed for the outdoors.

Check weather forecasts often and pay attention to the skies when hiking, as weather patterns can change suddenly. Always let someone—a friend, your hostel, or a park ranger—know when and where you are going. See **Safety and Health,** p. 18, for information on outdoor medical concerns.

CAMPING AND HIKING EQUIPMENT

WHAT TO BUY

Good camping equipment is both sturdy and light. North American suppliers tend to offer the most competitive prices.

Sleeping Bags: Most sleeping bags are rated by season; "summer" means 30-40°F (around 0°C) at night; "4-season" or "winter" often means below 0°F (-17°C). Bags are made of **down** (warm and light, but expensive, and miserable when wet) or of **synthetic** material (heavy, durable, and warm when wet). Prices range US$50-250 for a summer synthetic to US$200-300 for a good down winter bag. **Sleeping bag pads** include foam pads (US$10-30), air mattresses (US$15-50), and self-inflating mats (US$30-120). Bring a **stuff sack** to store your bag and keep it dry.

Tents: The best tents are freestanding (with their own frames and suspension systems), set up quickly, and only require staking in high winds. Low-profile dome tents are the best all around. Worthy 2-person tents start at US$100, 4-person tents at US$160. Make sure your tent has a rain fly. Other useful accessories include a **battery-operated lantern,** a plastic **ground cloth,** and a nylon **tarp.**

Backpacks: Internal-frame packs mold well to your back, keep a lower center of gravity, and flex adequately to allow you to hike difficult trails, while **external-frame** packs are more comfortable for long hikes over even terrain, as they carry weight higher and distribute it more evenly. Make sure your pack has a strong, padded hip belt to transfer weight to your legs. There are models designed specifically for women. Any serious backpacking requires a pack of at least 4000 cu. in. (16,000cc), plus 500 cu. in. for sleeping bags in internal-frame packs. Sturdy backpacks cost anywhere from US$125 to US$420—your pack is an area where it doesn't pay to economize. On your hunt for the perfect pack, fill up prospective models with something heavy, strap it on correctly, and walk around the store to get a sense of how the model distributes weight. Either buy a rain cover (US$10-20) or store all of your belongings in plastic bags inside your pack.

Boots: Be sure to wear hiking boots with good **ankle support.** They should fit snugly and comfortably over 1-2 pairs of **wool socks** and a pair of thin **liner socks.** Break in boots over several weeks before you go in order to spare yourself blisters.

Other Necessities: Synthetic layers, like those made of polypropylene or polyester, and a pile jacket will keep you warm even when wet. A **space blanket** (US$5-15) will help you to retain body heat and doubles as a **ground cloth.** Plastic **water bottles** are vital; look for shatter- and leak-resistant models. Carry **water-purification tablets** for when you can't boil water. Although most campgrounds provide campfire sites, you may want to bring a small **metal grate** or grill. For those places (including virtually every organized campground in Europe) that forbid fires or the gathering of firewood, you'll need a **camp stove** (starts at US$50) and a propane-filled fuel bottle to operate it. Also bring a **first-aid kit, pocketknife, insect repellent,** and **waterproof matches** or a **lighter.**

WHERE TO BUY IT

The online and mail-order companies listed below offer lower prices than many retail stores. A visit to a local camping or outdoors store will give you a good sense of the look and weight of certain items before you buy.

Campmor, 400 Corporate Dr., P.O. Box 680, Mahwah, NJ 07430, USA (☎+1-800-525-4784; www.campmor.com).

Cotswold Outdoor, Unit 11 Kemble Business Park, Crudwell, Malmesbury Wiltshire SN16 9SH, UK (☎+44 8704 427 755; www.cotswoldoutdoor.com).

Eastern Mountain Sports (EMS), 1 Vose Farm Rd., Peterborough, NH 03458, USA (☎+1-888-463-6367; www.ems.com).

L.L.Bean, Freeport, ME 04033, USA (US and Canada ☎+800-441-5713, UK 0800 8912 97; www.llbean.com).

Mountain Designs, 443a Nudgee Rd., Hendra, Queensland 4011, Australia (☎+61 7 3114 4300; www.mountaindesigns.com).

Recreational Equipment, Inc. (REI), Sumner, WA 98352, USA (US and Canada ☎+800-426-4840, elsewhere +1-253-891-2500; www.rei.com).

The following retail stores offer camping and outdoor supplies in Italy.

Campo Base, V. Bartolo da Sassoferrato 11/11a, 00165 Rome (☎06 66 20 966).

Climb, V. Maragliano 149-151, Florence (☎05 53 24 50 74; www.climbfirenze.com).

Fini Sport, V. Indipendenza 52, 40100 Bologna (☎051 24 63 17; www.finisport.it).

La Montagna Sport, V. Mauro Macchi 13, 20100 Milan (☎02 29 53 20 27; www.lamontagnasport.it).

TuttoSport Montagna, V. G.B. Morgagni 24-26-28, Rome (☎06 44 25 46 17; www.tuttosport.it).

ORGANIZED ADVENTURE TRIPS

Organized adventure tours offer another way of exploring the wild. Activities include hiking, biking, skiing, canoeing, kayaking, rafting, climbing, photo safaris, and archaeological digs. Tourism bureaus can often suggest parks, trails, and outfitters. Organizations that specialize in camping and outdoor equipment like REI and EMS (above) also are good sources for info.

La Boscaglia (☎05 16 26 41 69; www.boscaglia.it). Offers walking tours and treks throughout Italy. Must pay a membership fee to participate (about €20

Specialty Travel Index, P.O. Box 458, San Anselmo, CA 94979, USA (US ☎1-888-624-4030, elsewhere 415-455-1643; www.specialtytravel.com).

SPECIFIC CONCERNS

SUSTAINABLE TRAVEL

ECOTOURISM RESOURCES. For more info on environmentally responsible tourism, contact one of the organizations below:

Conservation International, 2011 Crystal Dr., Ste. 500, Arlington, VA 22202, USA (☎+1-800-406-2306 or 703-341-2400; www.conservation.org).

Green Globe 21, Green Globe vof, Verbenalaan 1, 2111 ZL Aerdenhout, the Netherlands (☎+31 23 544 0306; www.greenglobe.com).

International Ecotourism Society, 1333 H St. NW, Ste. 300E, Washington, DC 20005, USA (☎+1-202-347-9203; www.ecotourism.org).

Sustainable Travel International, P.O. Box 1313, Boulder, CO 80306 USA (☎+1-800-276-7764; www.sustainabletravelinternational.org).

United Nations Environment Program (UNEP), 39-43 Quai André Citroën, 75739 Paris Cedex 15, France (☎+33 1 44 37 14 50; www.uneptie.org).

In Italy, attention is often focused on cultural restoration while natural resources are overlooked and under appreciated. As the number of travelers on the road rises, the detrimental effect they can have on natural environments is an increasing concern. *Let's Go* promotes the philosophy of sustainable travel. Through a sensitivity to issues of ecology and sustainability, today's travelers can be a powerful force in preserving and restoring the places they visit.

Ecotourism, a rising trend in sustainable travel, focuses on the conservation of natural habitats—mainly, on how to use them to build up the economy without exploitation or overdevelopment. Travelers can make a difference by doing advance research, by supporting organizations and establishments that pay attention to their carbon "footprint," and by patronizing establishments that strive to be environmentally friendly. Recently, ecotourism has been getting more creative, interesting and diverse. Opportunities in Italy can be found at **www.ecoturismo-italia.it,** an Italian nonprofit that works in conjunction with other international organizations. For information on environmental conservation, see the resources below or the **Beyond Tourism** (p. 91) section of this book.

RESPONSIBLE TRAVEL

Your tourist dollars can make a big impact on the destinations you visit. The choices you make during your trip can have powerful effects on local

ESSENTIALS

communities—for better or for worse. Travelers who care about the destinations and environments they explore should make themselves aware of the social and cultural implications of their choices. Simple decisions such as buying local products, paying fair prices for products or services, and attempting to speak the local language can have a strong, positive effect on the community.

Community-based tourism aims to channel tourist dollars into the local economy by emphasizing tours and cultural programs that are run by members of the host community. This type of tourism also benefits the tourists themselves, as it often takes them beyond the traditional tours of the region. *The Ethical Travel Guide* (UK£13), a project of Tourism Concern (☎+44 20 7133 3330; www.tourismconcern.org.uk), is an excellent resource for community-based travel, with a directory of 300 establishments in 60 countries. For more on the role of tourism in Southern Italy, see *"Saving Alta Irpinia"* (p. 103).

TRAVELING ALONE

Traveling alone can provide a sense of independence and a greater opportunity to connect with locals. On the other hand, solo travelers are more vulnerable targets of harassment and street theft. If you are traveling alone, look confident, try not to stand out as a tourist, and be especially careful in deserted or very crowded areas. Stay away from areas that are not well lit. If questioned, never admit that you are traveling alone. Maintain regular contact with someone at home who knows your itinerary, and always research your destination before traveling. For more tips, pick up *Traveling Solo* by Eleanor Berman (Globe Pequot Press; US$18), visit www.travelaloneandloveit.com, or subscribe to **Connecting: Solo Travel Network,** 689 Park Rd., Unit 6, Gibsons, BC V0N 1V7, Canada (☎+1-604-886-9099; www.cstn.org; membership US$30-48).

WOMEN TRAVELERS

Women exploring on their own inevitably face additional safety concerns. Single women can consider staying in singles that lock from the inside in hostels or in religious organizations with single-sex dorms. It's a good idea to stick to centrally located accommodations and to avoid traveling alone at night.

Always carry extra cash for a phone call, bus, or taxi. **Hitchhiking** is never safe for lone women, or even for two women traveling together. Look as if you know where you're going and approach older women or couples for directions if you're lost or feeling uncomfortable. Generally, the less you look like a tourist, the better off you'll be. Dress conservatively, especially in rural areas. Wearing a conspicuous **wedding band** may help to prevent unwanted advances.

Your best answer to verbal harassment is no answer at all; feigning deafness, sitting motionless, and staring straight ahead at nothing in particular will usually do the trick. The extremely persistent can sometimes be dissuaded by a firm, loud, and very public *"Vai via"* or *"Vattene"* ("Go Away!"). Don't hesitate to seek out a *poliziotto* (police officer) or a passerby if you are being harassed. Memorize the emergency numbers in places you visit, and consider carrying a whistle on your keychain. A self-defense course will both prepare you for a potential attack and raise your level of awareness of your surroundings (see **Personal Safety,** p. 19). Also, it might be a good idea to talk with your doctor about the health concerns that women face when traveling (p. 24).

GLBT TRAVELERS

It is difficult to characterize the Italian attitude toward gay, lesbian, bisexual, and transgendered (GLBT) travelers. Homophobia is still in issue in some regions. Rome, Florence, Milan, and Bologna all have easily accessible gay scenes. Away from the larger cities, however, gay social life may be difficult to find. **Out and About** (www.planetout.com) offers a comprehensive site addressing gay travel concerns. The online newspaper **365gay.com** also has a travel section (www.365gay.com/travel/travelchannel.htm). **Babilonia** and **Guida Gay Italia** (www.guidagay.com) can be found at newsstands, and **Pride** and **GayClubbing** (both free) can be found at most gay venues. Travelers can also expect the larger cities to have gay *discoteche* and bars. Listed below are contact organizations and publishers that offer materials addressing some specific concerns.

Arcigay, V. Don Minzoni 18, 40121 Bologna (☎051 64 93 055; www.arcigay.it). National organization provides resources for homosexuals and helps combat homophobia throughout the peninsula. Holds dances and other special events. Website contains addresses and phone numbers of city centers.

Gay.It, S.p.A., V. Ravizza 22/E, 56121 Pisa (www.gay.it). Provides info on gay life in Italy. Associated website in English (www.gayfriendlyitaly.com) gives regional info on nightlife, homophobia, gay events, and more.

Gay's the Word, 66 Marchmont St., London WC1N 1AB, UK (☎+44 20 7278 7654; http://freespace.virgin.net/gays.theword). The largest gay and lesbian bookshop in the UK, with both fiction and non-fiction titles. Mail-order service available.

Giovanni's Room, 345 S. 12th St., Philadelphia, PA 19107, USA (☎+1-215-923-2960; www.queerbooks.com). An international lesbian and gay bookstore with mail-order service (carries many of the publications listed below).

International Lesbian and Gay Association (ILGA), Avenue des Villas 34, 1060 Brussels, Belgium (☎+32 2 502 2471; www.ilga.org). Provides political info, such as homosexuality laws of individual countries.

ADDITIONAL RESOURCES: GLBT

Spartacus International Gay Guide 2008, by Bruno Gmunder Verlag (US$22).

Damron Men's Travel Guide, Damron Road Atlas, Damron Accommodations Guide, Damron City Guide, and *Damron Women's Traveller* (US$18-24). For info, call ☎+1-800-462-6654 or visit www.damron.com.

The Gay Vacation Guide: The Best Trips and How to Plan Them, by Mark Chesnut. Kensington Books (US$15).

Gayellow Pages USA/Canada, by Frances Green. Gayellow Pages (US$20). They also publish regional editions. Visit Gayellow pages online at http://gayellowpages.com.

TRAVELERS WITH DISABILITIES

Those with disabilities should inform airlines and hotels of their disabilities when making reservations; some time may be needed to prepare special accommodations. Call ahead to restaurants, museums, and other facilities to find out if they are wheelchair-accessible. Guide-dog owners should inquire as to the quarantine policies of each destination country.

Rail is probably the most convenient form of transport for disabled travelers in Europe: many stations have ramps, and some trains have wheelchair lifts, special seating areas, and specially equipped toilets. All Eurostar, some InterCity (IC), and some EuroCity (EC) trains are **wheelchair-accessible,** and CityNightLine trains and Conrail trains feature special compartments. For those who wish to rent cars, some major **car-rental** agencies (e.g., Hertz) offer hand-controlled vehicles. Look for pamphlets on accessibility from local tourist offices; a list of publications and where to find them can be found at **www. coinsociale.it/tourism/services/guide.php.** A good wheelchair accessible tour of Rome is available at **www.slowtrav.com/italy/accessible/rome/index.htm.**

USEFUL ORGANIZATIONS

Accessible Italy, V. C. Manetti 34, 47891 Dogana, Repubblica di San Marino (☎378 05 49 94 11 11; www.accessibleitaly.com). Provides tours to Italy for travelers with disabilities. Proceeds go toward improving handicap-access to attractions in Italy. Also organizes handicap-accessible weddings in Italy.

Accessible Journeys, 35 W. Sellers Ave., Ridley Park, PA 19078, USA (☎+1-800-846-4537; www.disabilitytravel.com). Designs tours for wheelchair users and slow walkers. The site has tips and forums for all travelers.

Flying Wheels Travel, 143 W. Bridge St., Owatonna, MN 55060, USA (☎+1-507-451-5005; www.flyingwheelstravel.com). Specializes in escorted trips to Europe for people with physical disabilities; plans custom trips worldwide.

The Guided Tour, Inc., 7900 Old York Rd., Ste. 114B, Elkins Park, PA 19027, USA (☎+1-800-783-5841; www.guidedtour.com). Organizes travel programs in Italy for persons with developmental and physical challenges.

Mobility International USA (MIUSA), P.O. Box 10767, Eugene, OR 97440, USA (☎+1-541-343-1284; www.miusa.org). Provides a variety of books and other publications containing information for travelers with disabilities.

Society for Accessible Travel and Hospitality (SATH), 347 5th Ave., Ste. 610, New York, NY 10016, USA (☎+1-212-447-7284; www.sath.org). Advocacy group publishes free online travel information. Annual membership US$49, students and seniors US$29.

MINORITY TRAVELERS

Like much of Western Europe, Italy has experienced a wave of immigration from Africa, Eastern Europe, and South America in recent years that has spurred some racial tension, especially over competition in the local economy. Particularly in southern Italy, travelers belonging to racial minorities or members of non-Christian religions may feel unwelcome or experience some hostility. Tension has always existed in Italy regarding gypsies from Romania and other parts of Eastern Europe. In terms of safety, there is no easy answer. Men and women should always travel in groups and avoid unsafe parts of town. The best answer to verbal harassment is often not to acknowledge it. A number of advocacy groups for immigrant rights have sprouted up throughout Italy, including **Associazione Almaterra** (☎01 12 46 70 02; www.arpnet.it/alma/) and **NOSOTRAS** (☎05 52 77 63 26; www.nosotras.it). The following organizations work to combat discrimination in Italy and can give advice and help in the event of an encounter with racism.

Associazione Arci, V. dei Monti di Pietralata 16, 00157 Rome (☎06 41 50 95 00; www.attivarci.it). Extensive organization that promotes citizen rights, democracy, and inclusivity. Fights to end discrimination and racism on the peninsula.

Casa dei Diritti Sociali FOCUS, V. dei Mille 6, 00185 Rome (☎06 44 64 61 13; www.
dirittisociali.org). Volunteer organization promoting solidarity with and among immigrant
populations and multiculturalism through youth outreach and political advocacy.

European Network Against Racism (ENAR), 43 rue de la Charité, B-1210 Brussels,
Belgium (☎+32 02 229 35 70; www.enar-eu.org). Umbrella organization of European
associations combatting racism. Website has extensive list of groups by country.

Società Cooperativa Sociale Camelot, V. Contrada della Rosa 14, 44100 Ferrara (☎05
32 20 29 45 24 14 19; www.coopcamelot.org). Youth organization to advocate social
justice for young people, the elderly, and immigrant populations in Italy.

Ucodep, V. Madonna del Prato 42, 52100 Arezzo (☎05 75 40 17 80; www.ucodep.org)
Works to advance human rights, social justice, nonviolence, and intercultural exchange.

DIETARY CONCERNS

With all of Italy's delicious carnivorous offerings, vegetarians may feel left out.
While there are not many strictly vegetarian restaurants in Italy, it is not difficult to find vegetarian meals. To avoid confusion in restaurants, make sure
you tell your waiter *"Non mangio carne"* (I don't eat meat) or say that you
would like your pizza or pasta sauce *"senza carne, per favore"* (without meat,
please). Before you head to Italy, check out the **Italian Vegetarian Association (AVI),**
V. XXV Aprile 41, 20026 Novate Milanese, Milano (www.vegetariani.it), which
also offers *Good Vegetarian Food* (Italian Vegetarian Association, 2004; €12), a
guide to vegetarian tourism up and down the peninsula.

The travel section of **The Vegetarian Resource Group's** website, at www.vrg.org/
travel, has a comprehensive list of organizations and websites that are geared
toward helping vegetarians and vegans traveling abroad. For more info, visit
your local bookstore or health food store and consult *The Vegetarian Traveler: Where to Stay if You're Vegetarian, Vegan, Environmentally Sensitive,*
by Jed and Susan Civic (Larson Publications; US$16). Vegetarians will also
find numerous resources on the web; try www.vegdining.com, www.happy-
cow.net, and www.vegetariansabroad.com.

Lactose intolerance also does not have to be an obstacle to eating well in Italy.
Though it may seem like everybody but you is devouring pizza and gelato, there
are ways for even the lactose intolerant to indulge in local cuisine. In restaurants ask for items without *latte* (milk), *formaggio* (cheese), *burro* (butter), or
crema (cream); or order the cheeseless delicacy, *pizza marinara.*

Travelers who keep **kosher** should contact synagogues in larger cities for
info on kosher restaurants. Your own synagogue or college Hillel should
have access to lists of Jewish institutions across the nation. Check out **www.
shamash.org/kosher/** for an extensive database of kosher establishments in
Italy. If you are strict in your observance, you may have to prepare your own
food on the road. A good resource is the *Jewish Travel Guide,* edited by
Michael Zaidner (Vallentine Mitchell; US$18). Travelers looking for halal res-
taurants may find www.zabihah.com a useful resource.

OTHER RESOURCES

Let's Go tries to cover all aspects of budget travel, but we can't put everything
in our guides. Listed below are books and websites that can serve as jumping-
off points for your own research.

USEFUL PUBLICATIONS

Culture Shock!: Italy, Alessandro Falassi and Raymond Flower. Helpful tips for travelers about Italian life and culture. Marshall Cavendish, July 2008 (US$16).

Italy: The Best Travel Writing from the New York Times, Umberto Eco and New York Times writers. With stunning photographs, this anthology shows and tells the wonders of each town and city of Italy. Harry N. Abrams, Inc., 2005 (US$50).

Living, Studying, and Working in Italy: Everything You Need to Know to Live la Dolce Vita, Monica Larner and Travis Neighbor Ward. A comprehensive guide for an extended stay or permanent Italian move. Holt Paperbacks, 2003 (US$17).

Touring Club Italiano (TCI), C. Italia 10, Milan (☎02 85 261; www.touringclub.com). Detailed maps, as well as guides on the food, heritage, and nature of Italy's regions.

I(TALIAN)TUNES. Got an iPod? Bored on the plane ride over? Here are a couple Italian favorites to get you tapping your feet on your way to the boot:

1. **L'Italiano** (The Italian; Toto Cutugno): Sing it and you'll basically become one of them.
2. **Il Canto degli Italiani** (The Song of Italians; the national anthem): If you don't become an *Italiano,* you can at least show your love and dedication.
3. **O Sole Mio** (Oh, My Sun; Giovanni Capurro): Usually sung by Pavorotti, Italy's other famous son.
4. **Bella** (Beautiful; Giovanotti): A bad boy sings about a beauty. A basic descriptor of the Italian populace.
5. **Caruso** (Lucio Dalla): Pretend this is your last name to fit in?
6. **Tu Sei l'Unica Donna Per Me** (You're the Only Woman for Me; Alan Sorrenti): Use it to pick up an Italian lover.
7. **Bella Ciao** (Unknown): An old anti-Fascist song. Not to be confused with "Ciao, bella!"
8. **The Godfather Theme—Speak Softly, Love** (Andy Williams): Prep for the mobsters.
9. **Gli Ostacoli del Cuore** (Obstacles of the Heart; Elisa): Those Italians are just so good at love songs.
10. **Arrivederci Roma** (Renato Rascel): Well, maybe for the return flight...

WORLD WIDE WEB

Almost every aspect of budget travel is accessible via the web. In 10min. at the keyboard, you can make a hostel reservation, get advice from other travelers, or find out how much a train from Ravenna to Naples costs.

Listed here are some regional and travel sites to start your surfing; other relevant websites are listed throughout the book. Because website turnover is high, use search engines (e.g., www.google.com) to head out on your own.

THE ART OF TRAVEL

Backpacker's Ultimate Guide: www.bugeurope.com. Tips on packing, transportation, and where to go. Also tons of country-specific travel information.

BootsnAll.com: www.bootsnall.com. Numerous resources for independent travelers, from planning your trip to reporting on it when you get back.

Expats in Italy: www.expatsinitaly.com. Offers advice from non-Italians living in Italy.

How to See the World: www.artoftravel.com. A compendium of great travel tips, from cheap flights to self defense to tips on local culture.

Slow Travel Italy: www.slowtrav.com/italy. Advocates longer stays at major destinations, emphasizing quality over quantity. Provides comprehensive instructions on navigating Italian roads, railways, customs, and much more. Includes numerous links to helpful websites. Also posts personal blogs and travel stories.

Travel Intelligence: www.travelintelligence.net. A large collection of travel writing by distinguished travel writers.

Travel Library: www.travel-library.com. A fantastic set of links for general information and personal travelogues.

World Hum: www.worldhum.com. An independently produced collection of "travel dispatches from a shrinking planet."

INFORMATION ON ITALY

CIA World Factbook: www.odci.gov/cia/publications/factbook/index.html. Tons of vital statistics on Italy's geography, government, economy, and people.

Geographia: www.geographia.com. Highlights, culture, and people of Italy.

TravelPage: www.travelpage.com. Links to official tourist office sites in Italy.

PlanetRider: www.planetrider.com. A subjective list of links to the "best" websites covering the culture and tourist attractions of Italy.

World Travel Guide: www.travel-guides.com. Helpful practical info.

LET'S GO ONLINE. Plan your next trip on our newly redesigned website, **www.letsgo.com.** It features the latest travel info on your favorite destinations, as well as tons of interactive features: make your own itinerary, read blogs from our trusty researcher-writers, browse our photo library, watch exclusive videos, check out our newsletter, find travel deals, and buy new guides. We're always updating and adding new features, so check back often!

LIFE AND TIMES

From Michelangelo to Armani, Italy has carved a distinct path through the centuries, consistently setting a world standard for innovation and elegance. Defined by the legacy of the Roman Empire and the prominence of the Catholic Church, its artistic, intellectual, and cultural developments have carried forward from ancient times to form the foundations of a modern civilization. As a result, modern Italy boasts more UNESCO World Heritage Sites than any other country in the world. Despite this distinction, the country's history has been marked as much by its unresolved conflict as by its accomplishments. Haunted by centuries of foreign rule, fragmented governments, and regional disputes, Italy's allegiances are often torn between past and present, local and national. Even in the last century Italy has continued to rely on its past tradition, struggling to overcome the vestiges of fascism, delaying the passage of women's suffrage until 1945, and strictly observing the Catholic custom. Though both Roman rule and the Risorgimento came close to uniting the country's varied regions, distinct regional identities and social tensions between North and South persist. Italy is today in constant negotiation between tradition and progress, unity and independence, as it endeavors to transform its triumphant past into an equally glorious future the Italian way—slowly but surely.

HISTORY AND POLITICS

ITALY BEFORE ROME (UNTIL 753 BC)

3000 BC
Ötzi, the prehistoric hunter, goes on his last hunt.

1600 BC
Paintings of bikini-like garments are drawn on cave walls. Who knew cave-women could be so scandalous?!

753 BC
Romulus and Remus found Rome, but brotherly love soon deteriorates to fratricide.

Italy before Rome? Impossible! That's what most might think at least. In fact, a somewhat lengthy and quasi-exciting and rich history proceeded the grand Empire.

Archaeological excavations at Isernia date Italy's earliest inhabitants to the Paleolithic Era (100,000-70,000 BC). Perhaps the most important discovery has been **Ötzi**, a 5000-year-old iceman (p. 365) found in 1991 encased deep inside the icy Dolomites, just chillin'. The Bronze Age brought the development of more sophisticated settlements, and by the seventh century BC, the **Etruscans** had established their stronghold in present-day Tuscany, conquering much of Italy in the process. Though initially powerful, their growth was gradually checked by an increasing Greek presence along the Mediterranean coast. And so the Greco-Roman rivalry commenced. Forming what the Romans would later call **Magna Graecia**, the Greeks established colonies along the coast of Puglia, at Cumae in Campania, and throughout Calabria and Sicily. By the third century BC, however, the power of both Greeks and Etruscans declined as a third force swelled on the mainland—the Romans. By conquering *Magna Graecia*, the Romans inherited their predecessors' cultural history. It was only a matter of time before they set up their legacy.

ANCIENT ROME (753 BC-AD 476)

THE MONARCHY (753-509 BC)

Though numerous stories recount the founding of Rome, the tale of the brothers **Romulus** and **Remus** is by far the most famous. According to legend, one of the seven Vestal Virgins, priestesses who protect Rome's Eternal Flame, conceived the twins Romulus and Remus when she lost her virginity to Mars, the god of war. In a fury over the shame his niece brought to the family name, the priestesses's royal uncle ordered the infants killed. The servant commissioned for the task found himself unable to do so, and instead laid the children in a basket by the Tiber River. Various accounts describe their rescue, though one of the most common depictions is of Romulus and Remus suckling at the teats of a she-wolf who adopted them (an excellent example can be found in a sculpture dating to 500 BC, in the Musei Capitolini; p. 148). In 753 BC, the brothers founded Rome together on the Palatine Hill. While Romulus was building the wall around the Palatine, however, Remus challenged the height of the wall by showing he could jump over it. Angered by this insult, Romulus killed his brother and became the first king of Rome, which was named in his honor. Despite the early successes of Romulus and his successors, Etruscan kings eventually forced themselves back into power. By 616 BC, their **Tarquin** dynasty, short-lived though it may have been, was infamous for its tyranny. This era of kings ended in 509 BC, when Prince Sextus Tarquinius raped the noblewoman Lucretia, compelling her relative Lucius Brutus to expel the Tarquins and establish the **Roman Republic.**

734 BC
The Corinthians send a boatload of ancient adventurers to found Syracuse on the island of Sicily.

616 BC
The Etruscan kings come to power in Rome and become known for tyranny.

THE REPUBLIC (509-27 BC)

The end of the monarchy and the foundation of the Republic raised new debates over equality. The Republic faced social struggles between upper-class patricians, who enjoyed full participation in the Senate, and middle- and lower-class plebeians, who were denied political involvement. In 450 BC, the **Laws of the Twelve Tables,** the first codified Roman laws, made a slight concession to the lower classes, requiring that the law be made public and allowing them some political liberties.

As the Republic made efforts to placate those within its territory, it continued in its efforts to dominate those outside it. The defeat of Tarentum (modern day Taranto) in 272 BC completed the Roman conquest of mainland Italy. Never satisfied, the Romans went on to conquer **Sicily** in 241 BC and to wrest **Sardinia** in 238 BC from the **Carthaginians,** an extremely successful Phoenician colony. With this conquest, the Romans gained control of all of modern-day Italy.

The spoils of war that supposedly enriched Rome actually undermined its stability by creating further class inequality. In 133 BC Tiberius Gracchus, the first of the two **Gracchi brothers,** attempted to push through land reforms, but

509 BC
The Roman Republic is established. Also becomes known for tyranny.

450 BC
Roman Law is codified in the Twelve Tables.

390 BC
In one of France's most recent military triumphs, the Gauls sack Rome.

91 BC
Riots against the patrician class lead to the Social War.

73 BC
Spartacus leads a revolt of 70,000 slaves.

47 BC
Antony and Cleopatra get it on.

45 BC
Julius Caesar names himself Dictator for Life.

44 BC
Caesar is assassinated on the Ides of March.

27 BC
Augustus becomes the first Roman Emperor.

19 BC
Virgil finishes his *Aeneid.*

AD 37
Emperor Caligula tries to make his horse a senator.

AD 64
Nero plays his fiddle while Rome burns.

was assassinated. Ten years later his brother Gaius again attempted reforms with the same results. Demands for land redistribution led to riots against the patrician class and then to the **Social War** in 91 BC. The patrician general **Sulla** saw his chance for glory in the unrest, defeated his rivals in 82 BC, and quickly named himself dictator.

In 73 BC, **Spartacus,** an escaped gladiatorial slave, led an army of 70,000 slaves and impoverished farmers on a two-year rampage around the Italian peninsula. Sulla's close associates, **Marcus Crassus** and **Pompey the Great,** quelled the uprising and took control of Rome for themselves. They joined forces with ambitious **Julius Caesar,** the conqueror of Gaul, but their alliance rapidly fell apart as their absolute power corrupted them absolutely. By 45 BC, Caesar had defeated his "allies" and emerged as the Republic's leader, naming himself Dictator for Life. Angered by Caesar's pandering to the poor, an aristocratic coalition, led by **Brutus,** assassinated the reform-oriented leader on the Ides (15th) of March, 44 BC. Caesar's death created yet another power vacuum as would-be successors struggled for the helm. In 31 BC, Octavian, Caesar's adopted heir, emerged victorious over Marc Antony and his exotic mistress Cleopatra; he was granted the title **Augustus** (meaning "majestic") in 27 BC.

THE EMPIRE (27 BC-AD 476)

As the center of the world's largest and most powerful empire, Rome eventually reached as far as modern Britain in the north and Iran in the east. Political power and economic prosperity brought about great cultural achievement, and Roman civilization and language made a lasting impact on every corner of the Empire, and often beyond.

Augustus was the first of the Empire's **Julio-Claudian** rulers (27 BC–AD 68). Superficially following Republican traditions, he did not call himself *rex* (king), but *princeps* (first citizen). His principate (27 BC–AD 14) is considered the Golden Age of Rome, and this period of relative stability and prosperity, the *Pax Romana* (Roman Peace), continued until AD 180. During this time, Augustus extended Roman law and civic culture, beautified Rome, and reorganized its administration. For all of his excellent reforms, Augustus ran a tight ship. He even exiled his daughter, **Julia,** for reasons of promiscuity.

The Empire continued to expand despite the fact that two of its emperors during this time, **Caligula** (AD 37-41) and **Nero** (AD 54-68), were violent, economically irresponsible, and likely mad: a veritable trifecta of political incompetence. Following a series of civil wars after Nero's death in AD 68, the **Flavian** dynasty (AD 69-96) ushered in a period of prosperity, extended to new heights by **Trajan** (AD 98-117), who conquered the regions at the borders of the Black Sea. By this point, the Empire had reached astounding geographical limits, encompassing Western Europe, the Mediterranean islands, England, North Africa, and part of Asia. Following Trajan, **Hadrian** (AD 117-130) established the **Antonine** dynasty, which lasted until AD 193. The Antonines, especially philosopher-emperor **Marcus Aurelius**, were known for their enlightened leadership. When **Septimius Severus** (AD 146-211) won the principate after yet another civil war, he founded the robust **Severan** dynasty (AD 193-235).

Weak governments and rapid inflation led to near anarchy in the AD third century, until a formerly obscure general, **Diocletian** (AD 284-305), divided the empire into two eastern and two western regions, each with its own ruler. As a result of his persecution of Christians, Diocletian's reign became known as the "Age of Martyrs." While Diocletian's economically successful four-part empire eventually crumbled under his successor, **Constantine** (AD 272-337), Christian fortune took a turn for the better. Before the Battle of the Milvian Bridge in AD 312, he claimed he saw a cross of light in the sky, emblazoned with the words "by this sign you shall conquer." When victory followed, he converted to Christianity and issued the **Edict of Milan** in AD 313 abolishing religious discrimination. In AD 330 he began the process of moving the capital to Byzantium, renaming the city **Constantinople** (present-day Istanbul) in his honor. These changes split the Empire permanently into the stronger, wealthier Byzantine Empire and the down-sized Roman Empire, which struggled to integrate a large barbarian immigrant population. **Alaric,** king of the Visigoths, sacked Rome in AD 410, dealing a crushing blow to Roman morale. Roman leadership proved little help in this situation: Emperor **Honorius** so uninformed of the state of his Empire that he believed news of the imminent fall of Rome referred to the death of his pet rooster, Roma. The final symbolic blow came in AD 476 when the German chief **Odoacer** crowned himself king and put the last western emperor, Romulus Augustulus, under house arrest.

MIDDLE AGES (476-1375 AD)

Though sometimes called the "Dark Ages," the near millennium between the fall of Rome and the emergence of the Renaissance was not, in fact, a cultural wasteland. Instead, this complex period of secular and religious power struggles resulted in the establishment of institutions like the royal court and feudal society. External influences from barbarian tribes, Arabic kingdoms, and the Germanic empire brought a blast of fresh air to counteract the former empire's decay.

While the East continued to thrive as the **Byzantine Empire,** the fall of the Roman Empire in the West left room for the growing strength of the papacy. **Pope Gregory I** (the Great; also known for the Gregorian chant; see p. 75) began to negotiate treaties independent of the Emperor instead of relying on him for protection. With Arabs and Byzantines advancing on Italian territory, the Pope called upon the barbarian chieftain **Charlemagne** to uphold **Roman Catholicism.** Adding Italy to the Holy Roman Empire (not to be confused with the fallen Roman Empire), Charlemagne was crowned emperor of

AD 79
Mount Vesuvius erupts and destroys Pompeii and Herculaneum.

AD 80
The Colosseum hosts its inaugural games.

AD 313
The Edict of Milan grants all, though particularly Christians, freedom to worship.

AD 380
Christianity becomes the official religion of the Roman Empire.

AD 476
The last western Roman Emperor abdicates.

LIFE AND TIMES

Christian Europe by Pope Leo III on Christmas Day, AD 800. Pope Urban II increased the Church's strength by launching the **First Crusade** to liberate the Holy Land in 1095.

Charlemagne's successors were unable to maintain the new Empire, and in the following centuries, Italy became a playing field for petty wars. The instability of the 12th, 13th, and 14th centuries resulted in a division of power between city-states and rival families, leading to intense regional divisions that still exist today. Both European ruling houses and the Vatican enjoyed setting Italians, most notably the **Guelphs** and **Ghibellines** in the 12th and 13th centuries, against each other. The pro-papal Guelphs managed to expel the imperial-minded Ghibellines from major northern cities by the mid-13th century. The victorious Guelphs then split into two rival factions, the **Blacks** and the **Whites,** and battled for dominion. After the Whites exiled the Blacks from Florence in 1300, the Blacks came back with a vengeance in 1302 and expelled the Whites. Politically minded Florentine poet **Dante Alighieri** was permanently exiled to Ravenna for his loyalty to the Whites, and wrote *La Divina Commedia* (p. 74) as an attempt to vindicate himself in the eyes of his fellow Florentines.

Church separated from state when Holy Roman Emperor **Henry IV** (1084-1105) denounced **Pope Gregory VII** (1073-85) as a "false monk." Gregory in turn threatened the Emperor's nobles with excommunication. The terrified Emperor gave in to the Pope, but then came back with an army that defeated the Church's forces. The destabilization of Church power reached its zenith during the **Babylonian Captivity** (1309-77), when the papacy was moved from Rome to Avignon and was supposedly held "captive" by the French kings. The disorder and confusion sparked the **Great Schism** (1378-1417), when three popes simultaneously claimed the holy title. The conflict was overshadowed by an outbreak of the **Black Death** (also called the bubonic plague) in 1347, which killed one-third of Europe's population, and recurred in Italy each July over the next two centuries.

RENAISSANCE (1375-1540)

After the Middle Ages came the great rebirth, or **Rinascimento** (Renaissance), growing out of a rediscovery of Greek and Latin texts and a new emphasis on high culture. Pinpointing its origins has always been problematic, though historian Hans Baron has argued that the Italian tendency toward friendly competition spurred the rise of **civic humanism** by compelling city officials to bid for the best minds of the era, creating a market for intelligence.

Rising out of medieval obscurity were the exalted **Medici** clan in Florence, the **Visconti** in Milan, and the **House of Este** in Ferrara. When not stabbing each other in cathedrals, these ruling families instituted a series of humanist-minded economic and social reforms. **Cosimo** and **Lorenzo (Il Magnifico)** consolidated power and broadened the scope of

1088
The Bologna School of Law becomes Europe's first university.

1266-1273
Thomas Aquinas writes the *Summa Theologica.*

1314
Dante's *Inferno* is published.

1347-1351
"Bring out your dead! Bring out your dead!" The Black Death sweeps Europe.

14th century
Eyeglasses are invented in Italy.

the Medici family's activities from banking and warring to patronizing the arts. They engaged in a high-stakes political battle with sword-wielding **Pope Julius II** to bring Michelangelo to Florence and would have prevailed were it not for his Sistine Chapel commission (p. 70).

Just as things were getting interesting, an ascetic Dominican friar set out to spoil the fun. Infamous **Girolamo Savonarola** was ferociously opposed to what he perceived as the excesses of the Church. In 1497, Savonarola's followers did the priest's bidding by collecting and burning thousands of "immoral" books and other objects of vanity, including cosmetics, fine dresses, and musical instruments. The event became known as **The Bonfire of the Vanities,** and participants ranged from enraged Florentine clergy to a reformed Botticelli, who even threw several of his own paintings of mythological figures onto the pyre. Savonarola's power over the Florentine public pushed him into such great criticism of the clergy that **Pope Alexander VI** tried to silence the friar by excommunicating him. Savonarola persevered until the fickle Florentines—tired of his nagging—tortured and hanged him from the top of the **Palazzo Vecchio,** and burned him at the stake.

Power-hungry princes continued the Italian tradition of petty warfare, leaving the door open for foreign invasion. The weakened cities yielded in the 16th century to the invading Spanish armies of **Charles V.** The fighting continued until 1559 when Spain finally gained control over all Italian cities except Venice. Despite the political unrest plaguing Italy at the time, several prominent Italians embarked to make a splash on the world scene. **Christopher Columbus,** a native of Genoa funded by Queen Isabella of Spain, set sail in 1492 to discover a faster route to Asia, inadvertently opening the door to a whole New World of exploration with his discovery of the Caribbean. The Florentine **Amerigo Vespucci** made his own expeditions across the Atlantic, leaving his name on both Americas, and **Galileo Galilei,** despite the Church's opposition, suggested that the Earth spins around the sun. During Galileo's trial for heresy, he recanted, but mumbled *"eppur si muove"* ("but it does move") after the Inquisition ruled him guilty. He died under house arrest in 1642.

FOREIGN RULE (1540-1815)

Once the seat of the mightiest empire of the Western world, by the 18th century the Italian peninsula could no longer support the economic demands of the Holy Roman Empire. **Charles II,** the last Spanish Habsburg ruler, died in 1700, sparking the War of the Spanish Succession. Italy, weak and decentralized, became the booty in battles between the Austrian Habsburgs and the French and Spanish Bourbons.

A century later, **Napoleon** decided to solve the disputes the easy way: he began taking all the spoils for himself. During his march through Europe, the little emperor united much of Italy into the Italian Republic and incidentally fostered

1420
Brunelleschi begins a lifetime of work on the *duomo* in Florence.

1492
Columbus sails the ocean blue.

1504
Michelangelo sculpts David.

1503-1506
Lisa Gherrardini sits for Leonardo da Vinci's *Mona Lisa.*

1512
Michelangelo finishes the Sistine Chapel, earning international fame and a very sore neck.

1513
Machiavelli writes *The Prince.*

1564
Gabriele Falloppio invents the condom.

1633
Galileo is condemned for heresy by papal authorities.

LIFE AND TIMES

1725
Vivaldi writes *The Four Seasons.*

1748
The first excavations begin at Pompeii.

1797
Napoleon invades. "Who's short now?" he allegedly demanded.

1804
Napoleon declares himself the monarch of the Kingdom of Italy.

1815
The Congress of Vienna breaks up the Kingdom of Italy.

1848-1860
Camillo Cavour struggles to unite the peninsula.

1861
Italy's first parliament meets in Turin.

1883
Carlo Collodi writes *Pinocchio.*

1895
Italo Marcioni invents the ice cream cone.

1915
Italy enters WWI.

1919
Mussolini heads the world's first fascist regime.

national sovereignty. Napoleon declared himself the monarch of the newly united **Kingdom of Italy** in 1804. After Napoleon's fall in 1815 at the **Battle of Waterloo,** the **Congress of Vienna** carved up Italy, unsurprisingly granting considerable control to Austria. Exiled, Napoleon spent his last days amidst the charms of Elba (p. 496), an island off the Tuscan coast. Despite his exile, the consequences of his unification efforts would have a permanent impact on the Italian landscape.

THE ITALIAN NATION (1815-PRESENT)

UNIFICATION

Following the Congress of Vienna, a long-standing grudge against foreign rule sparked the **Risorgimento,** a nationalist movement that culminated in political unification in 1860. **Giuseppe Mazzini, Giuseppe Garibaldi,** and **Camillo Cavour,** the movement's leaders, are honored on countless street signs throughout the country. **Vittorio Emanuele II,** whose name also crowds Italian maps, was crowned as the first ruler of the independent Kingdom of Italy in 1860. He expanded the nation by annexing the north and central regions, with Rome and the Veneto joining in 1870.

Though Italy was united under a single name, tensions arose between the different regions. The north sought to protect its money from the needs of the agrarian south, and cities were wary of surrendering power to a central administration. The defiant **Pope Pius IX** (1846-78), who had lost power to the kingdom, refused to acknowledge Italian acquisition of Rome and began calling himself a prisoner in the Vatican. Despite these tensions, nationalism increased during **World War I,** as Italy fought against Austria, having been promised territory for its alliance with Russia, Britain, and France.

THE FASCIST REGIME

The chaotic aftermath of WWI paved the way for fascism under **Benito Mussolini,** *Il Duce* ("the leader"), who promised strict order and stability. He established the world's first fascist regime in 1919 and expelled all opposing parties. As Mussolini initiated domestic development programs and aggressive foreign policies, sentiments toward the fascist leader ran the gamut from intense loyalty to belligerent discontent. In 1940, Italy entered **World War II** on the side of its **Axis** ally, Nazi Germany. Success for the Axis powers came quickly but was short-lived: the Allies landed in Sicily in 1943, pushing Mussolini from power. Later that year, Mussolini established the **Republic of Salò,** a Nazi puppet state based in Salò (p. 279). As a final indignity, he and his mistress, **Claretta Petacci,** were captured in Milan and executed, their naked bodies hung upside-down in public. In 1945, after nearly three years of occupation, Italy was finally freed from Nazi control, but tension persisted between supporters of a more liberal government and those who favored a return to fascism.

POST-WAR POLITICS

The end of WWII did little but highlight the Italian peninsula's intense factions. In the 63 years since the end of the war, Italy has changed governments more than 60 times, with no evidence to suggest the trend is slowing. The **Constitution,** adopted in 1948, established a democratic Republic, with a president, a prime minister, a bicameral parliament, and an independent judiciary. The **Christian Democratic Party (DC)** soon triumphed over the **Socialists (PSI)** as the primary player in the government. Over 300 parties fought for supremacy in parliament; unsurprisingly, none could claim a majority. Ultimately, tenuous party compromises were formed, and the coalition system that exists to this day was arranged.

Italian economic recovery began with industrialization in the 1950s—Lamborghini billboards and factory smokestacks quickly appeared alongside old cathedral spires and large glowing crucifixes on northern cities' skylines. Despite the **Southern Development Fund,** which was established to build roads, construct schools, and finance industry, the traditionally agrarian south lagged behind the more industrial north during this period of growth; the resulting economic inequality contributed to much of the regional strife that persists today. Economic success gave way to violence in the late 1960s, especially the *autunno caldo* (hot autumn) of 1969, a season of strikes, demonstrations, and riots by university students and factory workers, which foreshadowed greater violence in the 70s. During the period of *Strategia della Tensione* (Strategy of Tension) in the early 70s, rightwing terrorists detonated bombs as public manifestations of political discontent, typically trying to blame them on political opponents. The most shocking episode was the 1978 kidnapping and murder of ex-Prime Minister **Aldo Moro** by a group of left-wing terrorists, the *Brigate Rosse* (Red Brigades). The demonstrations and violence of the 70s challenged the conservative Social Democrats. In 1983, **Bettino Craxi** became Italy's first Socialist prime minister, but fell from grace in a corruption scandal, avoiding jail time by fleeing to Tunisia, where he died in 2000.

RECENT DEVELOPMENTS

Italians have always been enamored with powerful, charismatic leaders. Living up to expectations, Italian government officials have rarely shied away from questionable maneuvers intended to bring them more power. Recognizing corruption in his own government, **Luigi Scalfaro,** elected in 1992, launched the *Mani Pulite* (Clean Hand) campaign. With the help of anti-corruption judge **Antonio di Pietro,** he uncovered the *Tangentopoli* (Bribesville) scandal, an unprecedented political crisis that found over 1200 public officials guilty of bribery. Fallout from the investigation included the 1993

1938
Enrico Fermi wins the Nobel Prize for Physics for directing the first controlled nuclear chain reaction.

April 28, 1945
Mussolini and mistress Clera Petacci are hanged.

1946
Corradino d'Ascanio invents the Vespa Scooter, so named for its resemblance to a wasp (*vespa*).

1948
Italy adopts a constitution, establishing a democratic Republic.

1957
Europeon Economic Community (EEC) founded.

1972
Francis Ford Coppola directs *The Godfather.*

1975
The Giorgio Armani Company is founded.

1978
Aldo Moro, a five-time Italian Prime Minister, is kidnapped and murdered by left-wing terrorists.

1982
Italian soccer team wins the World Cup in Spain.

LIFE AND TIMES

1994
Berlusconi becomes prime minister, but is forced to resign eight months later.

1999
Roberto Benigni wins three Oscar for *La Vita è Bella*.

1999
Italy enters the European Monetary Union and adopts the euro.

2001
Berlusconi becomes Prime Minister (again).

April 2005
Pope John Paul II dies after a 26-year reign, and Pope Benedict XVI is elected.

April 20, 2005
Berlusconi resigns as Prime Minister.

April 23, 2005
Not so fast— Berlusconi's back! The embattled ruler becomes Prime Minister once again.

2006
Turin hosts Winter Olympics.

May 2, 2006
Berlusconi begrudgingly resigns as Prime Minister, leaving Romano Prodi in his place for the second time.

July 9, 2006
Italian football team withstands headbutt and defeats France in penalty kicks to win the World Cup.

bombing of the Uffizi Gallery in Florence, suicides of 10 indicted officials, and the murders of anti-Mafia investigators. Out of the ruins of the old system came the origins of the modern, (generally) less corrupt political system.

ENTER BERLUSCONI. The election of media tycoon **Silvio Berlusconi** as prime minister in 1994 raised eyebrows. The self-made billionaire's empire included three private TV channels, political influence over three state-run channels, a major newspaper, and the AC Milan soccer team. The fragile web of coalitions that enabled Berlusconi's election collapsed after just eight months, forcing him to resign.

Shortly after the collapse of Berlusconi's government, the platform of the reactionary Northern League became separatist under the extremist (and some say racist) **Umberto Bossi.** Aiming to push the economy to meet the European Union's economic standards, the Northern League called for a split from the south in order to create the **Republic of Padania**, a nation for northerners only. The 1996 elections brought the center-left coalition, **l'Ulivo** (Olive Tree), to power, with **Romano Prodi,** a Bolognese professor, economist, and non-politician, serving as prime minister. Ultimately, Prodi helped stabilize Italian politics. For the first time in modern history, Italy was run by two equal coalitions: the center-left l'Ulivo and the center-right **Il Polo** (Berlusconi's Freedom Alliance, without the Northern League). Despite Prodi's optimism, his coalition lost a vote of confidence in 1998.

Prodi was succeeded by former communist **Massimo D'Alema.** D'Alema and **Carlo Ciampi** introduced fiscal reforms and pushed a "blood and tears" budget that qualified Italy for entrance into the European Monetary Union in January 1999. Despite D'Alema's successes, he stepped down in May 2000 and was replaced by former Treasury Minister **Giuliano Amato.** Nicknamed "Dr. Subtle," Amato is one of the people credited with the institution of the 1999 budget reforms. Perhaps the nickname also derives from Amato's ability to avoid scandal; he was one of few to emerge unscathed from corruption crack-downs in the early 90s.

BERLUSCONI: TAKE TWO. Somehow or another Italy's richest man, Berlusconi, secured his re-election as prime minister again in May 2001. Downplaying corruption charges, he won 30% of the popular vote to head Italy's 59th government since WWII with his **Forza Italia** party. Berlusconi reaffirmed his commitment to the US, courting President George W. Bush in several meetings and sending 2700 troops to Iraq, in spite of left-wing opposition. In European foreign policy, the Prime Minister focused more on domestic than on European issues, creating some tension between Italy and its neighbors. Most notable was Berlusconi's 2004 comparison of one German European Parliament member to a guard in a Nazi concentration camp, a comment which caused considerable discord between the governments of Italy and Germany, and caused a miffed Chancellor Gerhard Schroeder to cancel his summer holiday in Italy.

BERLUSCONI: TAKE THREE? Berlusconi's unpopularity mounted as a result of troop deployment in Iraq, and an economic recession caused some to call for the reinstitution of lira. Berlusconi resigned again as Prime Minister in April 2005, only to form a new coalition several days later. History repeated itself as Romano Prodi won over Berlusconi in the national elections of April 2006, much like he did 10 years earlier. Prodi did not find ruling the Italians to be any easier. A controversy over funding the Italian troops in Afghanistan in early 2007 followed by a dispute over expanding the US Army Base in Vicenza (p. 338), pushed Prodi to the limit. He offered his resignation to President Giorgio Napolitano in February 2007. Napolitano did not accept the resignation enthusiastically and called for a vote of confidence in the legislature. After a narrow survival of the vote of no confidence, Prodi decided to remain in office. However, a short time later in January 2008, a new crisis caused Prodi to lose a vote of confidence. In an early election that was scheduled for April 2008, Berlusconi regained his post as Prime Minister.

February 21, 2007
Frustrated by his opposition, Romano Prodi attempts to resign.

January 24, 2008
Resignation attempt part two a success: following a vote of no confidence, Romano Prodi resigns.

April 14, 2008
Third time's the charm: Billionaire media mogul Silvio Berlusconi elected Prime Minister.

PEOPLE

DEMOGRAPHICS

Despite the stereotype of large families, Italian women today have an average of only 1.3 babies each, contributing to a lag in population growth that has persisted for several decades. In fact, with a death rate that narrowly outstrips its birth rate and increasing immigration, Italy's population is barely growing at all, holding approximately steady at its current 58 million. Immigration from China, Africa, Eastern Europe, and Middle Eastern countries functions to counteract the dwindling number of Italians in the workforce. Although some consider immigration to be necessary for the economy, many Italians associate undocumented migrant labor with sex work or drug trafficking, despite efforts by the government to eliminate illegal immigration. The situation is only made worse by Italy's aging population distribution. Altogether, these problematic statistics present a perfect storm of population crisis, which represents a legitimate threat to the traditional Italian way of life.

LANGUAGE

A descendant of Latin, Italian is part of the family of Romance languages, which includes French, Spanish, Portuguese, and Romanian. Due to the number and variety of dialects that exist in various regions of the country (a vestige of Italy's past division into city-states), many Italians, especially those in the South, will ironically claim that the first foreign language they learn is Italian. The claim is not unfounded: the throaty **Neapolitan** of southern Italy may indeed sound foreign to a northerner, and even be difficult to understand. Ligurians use a mix of Italian, Catalan, and French. Many Tuscan dialects substitute an "h" for every "c;" an American might be called an "Amerihano." **Sardo,** spoken in Sardinia, bears little resemblance to standard Italian, constituting a separate language in itself. In the northern region of Friuli-Venezia Giulia, you may encounter as many as four languages spoken in one small city—Slovene,

FROM THE ROAD

FALSE FRIENDS

Italian, like any romance language, is chalk-full of false cognates, often called "false friends." These words seem like a word in another language, but mean something entirely different. This list might spare you some embarrassment on the road, and if not, hopefully tickle your tummy.

Educato does not always mean educated, it means well mannered. You could be a genius and still not be *educato*, like Robert DeNiro.

A **fattoria** is not something you find in a midwestern town. It's a farm. A **fabbrica**, meanwhile, is a factory. There's no such thing as a "fat factory" in either language.

Fame is most often not associated with stars and entertainers, unless they're the starving artist type. It means hunger.

An **orso** is not an animal you ride, but something you run from. It means bear.

The **genitore** is usually not paid for cleaning up the house. The word means parent, not janitor, though the two can surely overlap.

In the same vein, **parente** means relative, not parent. Often still annoying, but more distant.

A **preservativo** is not something found in strawberry jam. It means condom. **Conservativi** go in the jam, or elsewhere if you so choose.

Italian, German, and Friulian coexist in Canale. Conversely, citizens in some northern regions do not speak any Italian at all: the population of Valle d'Aosta speaks mainly French, and Trentino-Alto Adige has a German-speaking minority. Standard Italian, developed in the 13th and 14th centuries as a literary dialect, today serves as the language used by schools, media, and literature. North of Rome, dialects are dying out in favor of this standard language, but accents persist. Locals do their best to employ standard Italian with foreigners, although some may be hesitant to do so. Many Italians, especially older people or those living in rural areas, do not speak English, but most young people, big-city dwellers, and those in the tourist industry do.

TALK TO THE HAND. Italians don't just talk with their mouths, they also use hand gestures. When dialects (or basic language skills) fall short, these are universal and instantly understood. To express frustration, as in, "*Mamma mia*, are you seriously going to fine me even though the signs says I can park here on Sundays?" put your hands together in a prayer-like position and shake them down and up, imploringly. Indignant? Hold all your fingers together, point them upward, and shake your wrist lightly back and forth. Don't care? Point your palm downwards and drag your fingers outwards from where your chin and neck meet. Ask around for more gems. Don't get confused; the best of friendships could go south if an inexperienced gesturer were to offer up the wrong finger .

LISTEN WITH YOUR EYES. First published in 1958 and re-released in 2005 by Chronicle Books, Bruno Munari's *Speak Italian: The Fine Art of the Gesture* waves its hands in every conceivable Italian way and provides a 'supplement to the Italian dictionary' by demystifying Italian hand gestures. A fun collection of photos accompanied by explanations in Italian and English, this book will give you 'words' when you find yourself speechless in the stickiest of situations.

RELIGION

As the home of the pope, Italy has been the center of the Roman Catholic faith for almost 2000 years. The **Lateran Pacts,** a treaty in 1929 between Pope Pius XI and Benito Mussolini, made the Vatican City a sovereign state within the city of Rome. It is the traditional and administrative capital of the

Catholic Church. The treaty also made Catholicism the official religion of Italy, which it remained until 1984. Unsurprisingly, roughly 90% of Italians identify themselves as Catholic, although only 40% consider themselves active members of the church. Additionally, the country is home to a substantial number of Protestants and nearly a million Muslims.

The death of **Pope John Paul II** in April 2005 stirred Catholics around the globe. Tens of thousands flooded the square in front of St. Peter's Basilica (p. 140) as the College of Cardinals gathered in the Sistine Chapel (p. 70) to elect a new Pope. Sworn to secrecy (a full transcript of the voting will not be made public for 100 years), the Cardinals locked inside the chapel cast four votes per day until a two-thirds majority was reached. After each round of voting, smoke from the chimneys of the Sistine Chapel signaled the results—gray smoke for failure to reach a consensus, and white smoke for a successful election. The process could have taken up to three and a half months (as it did in AD 180), but **Cardinal Ratzinger** of Munich (now **Pope Benedict XVI**) was elected on the second day of voting. At 78, Cardinal Ratzinger became the oldest elected pope since Clement XII in 1730. Though his past career indicated he might be overly dogmatic, Benedict has in fact displayed a softer touch. His first encyclical, *Deus Caritas Est* (God is Love), stressed the love of God and neighbor as the core of Christian life. Yet, he has also placed great emphasis on opposing what he calls "the dictatorship of relativism" in the West and advocating the Church's conservative position on social issues like abortion, birth control, and same-sex marriage, putting the Church at odds with many progressive activists.

The Church continues to play a substantial role in the lives of ordinary Italians. Most Italians continue to celebrate the feast day of their town's patron saint in annual celebrations, but church attendance is declining. Currently about one-third of the nation attends weekly services. Nevertheless, Italians are very conscientious about respecting churches, cathedrals, and other religious domains. In general, tourists are not allowed in religious spaces unless dressed modestly: covered shoulders for women and long pants for men. Furthermore, some churches do not allow visitors to take pictures because camera flashes damage fragile paintings and mosaics. When visiting churches, remember that the buildings are places of worship first, and tourist attractions second.

ART AND ARCHITECTURE

In Italy, great works of art and architecture seem to spring from every street corner. In Rome, the Colosseum (p. 128) hovers above a city bus stop; in Florence, couples flirt in front of the *duomo* (p. 441); in Sicily, diners sit beneath Greek columns. Modern Italians may seem immune to this stunning visual history, but to anyone who hasn't grown up amid ancient ruins and medieval fortresses, it's a feast for the senses.

ANCIENT ITALIAN ART

GREEKS. In the eighth century BC, the Greeks established colonies in southern Italy, covering the region with magnificent **temples** and **theaters.** The best-preserved examples of Greek ruins are in Sicily—not Greece!—in the Valle dei Templi at Agrigento (p. 708) and Taormina (p. 684). Italy is also home to Roman copies of Greek **statues** and original Greek **bronzes;** the prized *Bronzi di Riace*, recovered from the Ionian Sea in 1972 after 2500 years underwater, are now in Reggio di Calabria's Museo Nazionale della Magna Grecia (p. 643).

AND ETRUSCANS. The history of native Italian art begins with the Etruscans, a people who lived on the Italian peninsula before the Romans. Loosely influenced by Greek art and inspired by both the everyday and the afterlife, Etruscan artwork is best known for its narrative quality; beneficial, as the Etruscan language is largely undeciphered. The Etruscan works that remain today include decorated **funeral statues, tomb paintings,** and **ceramic ash burial urns,** all of which depict Etruscan scenes and legends. However, because the Romans either destroyed or melted down a large portion of Etruscan sculptures and bronzes, our modern perception of Etruscan art as solely funerary is skewed. Just like their art, the Etruscans mysteriously disappeared in the third century BC. The Museum at the Villa Giulia (p. 149) in Rome houses many Etruscan gems.

AND ROMANS (OH MY!). Roman art (200 BC-AD 500) is known for its vivid portrayal of the political aims and cultural values of Imperial Rome. Sculptures, architecture, and other masterpieces fall into two principle categories: private household art and art in service of the state. Although art historians have traditionally used Greek statues as benchmarks for beauty and artistic skill, the sculpted portraiture developed by the Romans deserves separate recognition. Portraits of the **Republican period** (510-27 BC) were brutally honest, immortalizing wrinkles, scars, and even warts. The later **Imperial sculpture** (27 BC-AD 476) tended to blur the distinction between mortal and god in powerful, idealized images like *Augustus of Prima Porta* (Vatican Museums; p. 146). Later in the period, Roman art developed a flattened style of **portraiture,** with huge eyes looking out in an "eternal stare." The government sponsored **statues, monuments,** and **literary narratives** to commemorate leaders, heroes, and victories. Augustus was perhaps the best master of this form of self-promotion, as evidenced by his impressive **mausoleum** and **Ara Pacis** (Altar of Peace), both gracing the Piazza Augusto Imperatore in Rome (p. 152). Roman monuments evolved into decorated concrete forms with numerous arches and columns, like the **Colosseum** (p. 128) and the **Pantheon** (p. 125).

Upper-class Romans had an appetite for sumptuous interior decoration. Scenes depicting gods and goddesses, exotic beasts, and street entertainers decorated villas, courtyards, and shops. Some wealthy patrons had their walls adorned with **frescoes,** which used the Greek technique of painting onto wet plaster walls to create a time-resistant effect. It was also popular to hire craftsmen to fashion wall and floor **mosaics,** works of art created using thousands of finely shaded *tesserae* (geometrically-shaped fragments of colored pottery, tile or glass) cemented with mortar. The luxurious **Villa Romana del Casale** (p. 696), just outside Piazza Armerina, holds 40 rooms of stone mosaics, making it the world's largest work of intact artistic mosaics of the Late Roman period.

EARLY CHRISTIAN AND BYZANTINE ART

Fearing persecution, early Christians in Rome, Naples, and Syracuse hid inside haunting **catacombs** to worship their Christian God. But following Emperor Constantine's **Edict of Milan** (AD 313), the religion quickly became Rome's faith *du jour*. Even the Roman magistrate's basilica was altered to accommodate Christian services. **Transepts** were added to many Roman churches, creating crucifix-shaped architecture. Except for a few **sarcophagi** and **ivory reliefs,** Christian art slowly transitioned from sculpture to pictorial forms in order to depict religious narratives for the illiterate. Ravenna (p. 410) is a veritable treasure trove of the first Byzantine Golden Age, which ran from AD 526 to 726. Examples of these "instructional" mosaics can be seen in Ravenna's octagonal **Basilica of San Vitale** (p. 413), a UNESCO World Heritage Site that is one of the first churches to boast a free-standing *campanile* (bell tower).

MIDDLE AGES

ROMANESQUE. Although true classical Roman style was not revived until the Renaissance, rounded Roman arches, heavy columns, and windowless churches came back in style in the period from AD 800 to 1200. The earliest Italian example of Romanesque architecture is Milan's **Basilica di Sant'Ambrogio** (p. 248), notable for its squat nave and groin vaults. In Tuscany, competition among Italian cities (particularly Florence and Pisa) resulted in great architectural feats, most notably **San Miniato al Monte** (p. 453) and the **Duomo** in Pisa with its famously leaning *campanile* (p. 490). In the south, most notably in **Cattedrale di Monreale** (p. 660), sculptural detailings and intricate mosaics reflect Arab, Byzantine, and Norman influences on the Romanesque style.

GOTHIC. Beginning in the late 13th century, the Gothic movement filtered into Italy from France. Artists and architects rejoiced at the fantastic spaces and light created by the new vaulted technology and giant, multi-colored rose windows. The most impressive Gothic cathedrals include the **Basilica di San Francesco** (p. 518) in Assisi, the **Basilica di Santa Maria Gloriosa dei Frari** (p. 324) in Venice, and the **Santa Maria Novella** (p. 448) in Florence. Secular structures like Florence's **Ponte Vecchio** (p. 446) followed this stylistic trend too. The **Palazzo Ducale** (p. 321) in Venice, spanning several canals with ornate bridges, represents the brilliant marriage of airy, lace-like Islamic stonework and Gothic style. In sculpture, **Nicola Pisano** (c. 1220-78) created pulpits at both Pisa and Siena that combined Roman reliefs, Gothic form, and early Byzantine mosaics. By the end of the 13th century, Italians were bored by the emaciated torsos of suffering martyrs. **Cimabue** (c. 1240-1302) and **Duccio** (c. 1255-1318) introduced new dimensions and brighter colors to their works, though bleeding Christians remained their subject of choice. Straddling the late Gothic and early Renaissance, **Giotto** (c. 1267-1337) is credited with noting that humans—not giants—look at pictures. He placed his work at eye level, putting the viewer on equal footing with his realistically rendered holy subjects. His masterpieces are on display at the Basilica di San Francesco and the **Scrovegni Chapel** (p. 335).

RENAISSANCE

EARLY RENAISSANCE. Donatello's (1386-1466) *David* (c. 1430; at the **Bargello** in Florence; p. 446), a now-world-famous free-standing nude, marked the "rebirth" of sculpture without boundaries. His wooden *Mary Magdalene* (p. 443) in Florence similarly represents a departure from earlier, restrained traditions, emphasizing the woman's fallen and repentant side, depicting her in rags and with a sorrowful facial expression. Just as Donatello's expressive portraiture became a model for artists to come, **Brunelleschi's** (1377-1446) mathematical studies of ancient Roman architecture became the cornerstone of Renaissance building. His engineering talent allowed him to raise the dome over **Santa Maria del Fiore** (p. 441) and showcase his mastery of proportions in the **Pazzi Chapel** (p. 451). **Lorenzo Ghiberti** (c. 1381-1455) designed two sets of bronze doors for the baptistry in Florence (p. 442), defeating Brunelleschi's doors in the contest of 1401. **Leon Battista Alberti** (1404-72), a champion of visual perspective, designed Florence's **Santa Maria Novella (p. 448)** and Rimini's **Tempio Malatestiano** (p. 418), prototypes for future Renaissance palaces and churches. In painting, **Sandro Botticelli** (1444-1510) and his *The Birth of Venus* (p. 444), depicting the goddess floating on her tidal foam, epitomize the Italian Renaissance. **Masaccio** (1401-28) filled chapels with angels and gold-leaf and is credited with the first use of the mathematical laws of perspective. His figures in the **Brancacci Chapel** (p. 452) of Florence served as models for Michelangelo and Leonardo. An unlikely artist, **Fra Angelico** (c. 1400-55) personified the tension between medieval and Renaissance Italy. Though a member of a militant branch of Dominican friars which opposed humanism on principle, Fra Angelico's works, seen at the **Museo della Chiesa di San Marco** (p. 450) in Florence, exhibit the techniques of space and perspective endorsed by humanistic artists.

HIGH RENAISSANCE. From 1450 to 1520, the torch of distinction passed between two of art's greatest figures: Leonardo and Michelangelo. Branching out from the disciplines of sculpture and painting, **Leonardo da Vinci** (1452-1519) excelled in subjects ranging from geology, engineering, and musical composition to human dissection and armaments design. *The Last Supper*, or *Il Cenacolo* (p. 247), in Milan, pays a level of attention to the individuality of its figures previously unrivalled for that particular biblical subject. His experimentations with *chiaroscuro*, or contrasts between light and shadow that highlight contours, and *sfumato*, which is a smoky or hazy effect of brushwork, secured his place as the century's great artistic innovator.

Michelangelo Buonarroti (1475-1564) was an artistic jack of all trades, despite what he told Julius II after painting the Sistine Chapel ceiling: "I am not a painter!" Julius was so fond of the artist's work on the ceiling (p. 146) that he commissioned *The Last Judgment* for the wall above the chapel's altar. Michelangelo painted like a sculptor, boldly emphasizing musculature and depth, and sculpted like a painter, with lean, smooth strokes. The artist also completed architectural designs for the **Laurentian Library** (p. 450) in Florence and the dome on **St. Peter's Basilica** (p. 137) in Rome. Classic examples of his sculptures include the *Pietà* in St. Peter's and the *David* and unfinished *Slaves* in Florence's Accademia (p. 449).

Other prominent Renaissance artists include **Raffaello** (1483-1520), a draftsman who created technically perfect figures. His frescoes in the papal apartments of the Vatican, including the *School of Athens* (p. 147), show his debt to classical standards. In addition to Michelangelo, the Venetian Renaissance school of artistic thought produced **Giorgione**, known as "The Great" (1478-1510); **Giovanni Bellini** (c. 1430-1516), the pre-eminent teacher within the school; and Bellini's protégé, the prolific **Titian** (1488-1576). Titian's works are notable for their realistic facial expressions and rich colors. In the **High Renaissance,** the greatest architect after Michelangelo was **Donato Bramante** (1444-1514), famed for his work on the *Tempietto of St. Peter* in Rome.

MANNERISM

A heightened sense of aestheticism led to Mannerism, the style that dominated the High Renaissance from the 1520s until the birth of the Baroque style around 1590. Starting in Rome and Florence, Mannerist artists experimented with juxtapositions of color and scale. For example, **Parmigianino** (1503-40) created the *Madonna of the Long Neck*, a piece emblematic of the movement's self-conscious distortions. Another painter, **Jacopo Tintoretto** (1518-94), a Venetian Mannerist, was the first to paint multiple light sources within a single composition. The Mannerist period is also known for its architecture, designed by artisans such as **Giulio Romano** (c. 1499-1546) who rejected the Renaissance (p. 448) deal of harmony. The villas and churches of architect **Andrea Palladio** (1508-80) were also remarkably innovative, particularly the **Villa Rotonda** (p. 340) outside Vicenza. His other lasting contribution, the *Four Books of Architecture*, promoted his work and influenced countless architects.

BAROQUE AND ROCOCO

A 17th-century stylistic hybrid born of the Counter-Reformation and monarchy, Baroque composition combined Mannerism's intense emotion with the Renaissance's grandeur to achieve a new expressive theatricality. Heavy on drama, emotion, and richness, Baroque art attempted to inspire faith in the Catholic Church and respect for earthly power. Painters of this era favored naturalism, a commitment to portraying nature in its raw state. **Caravaggio** (1573-1610), the epitome of Baroque painters, relied heavily on *chiaroscuro* and naturalism to create dramatically unsettling images. It is even rumored that he used the corpse of a prostitute recovered from Rome's Tiber River as a model for the Virgin Mary's body in *Death of the Virgin* (1606). **Gianlorenzo Bernini** (1598-1680), a prolific **High Baroque** sculptor and architect, designed the overwhelming colonnade of St. Peter's Piazza and the awesome *baldacchino* inside. Drawing inspiration from Hellenistic works, Bernini's sculptures were orgies of movement, portraying violent interactions of light and space. **Francesco Borromini** (1599-1667), Bernini's rival, was even more adept than his rival at shaping the walls of his buildings into lively, serpentine architectural masterpieces, as in his **San Carlo alle Quattro Fontane** (p. 136). Toward the end of the Baroque period, however, this grand style began to give way to the delicacy and elaborate ornamentation of **Rococo,** a light and graceful method originating in 18th-century France. Rococo motifs include seashells, clouds, flowers, and vines carved into woodwork and stone edifices. **Giovanni Battista Tiepolo** (1696-1770), with his brilliant palette and vibrant frescoes, was a prolific Venetian painter of allegories and the premier exemplar of the Italian Rococo style.

NINETEENTH-CENTURY ART

With the decline of Rococo came French-influenced **Neoclassicism,** which abandoned the overly detailed Rococo and dramatic Baroque methods in favor of a purer, more ancient construction. At first, the shift was almost too subtle to notice, primarily because the Neoclassical artists had no new materials on which they could base their Neotraditional works. With the early 17th-century discovery and excavation of Herculaneum and Pompeii, however, Neoclassical artists quickly found their ancient muses in the forms of recovered artifacts. One such Neoclassical artist was the sculptor **Antonio Canova** (1757-1822) who explored the formal Neoclassical style in his giant statues and bas-reliefs. His most famous work is the statue of *Pauline Borghese*, which displays Neoclassical grace and purity of contour. Rebelling against the strict Neoclassical style, **Telemaco Signorini** (1835-1901), **Giovanni Fattori** (1825-1908), and **Silvestro Lega** (1826-1895) spearheaded the **Macchiaioli** group in Florence (c. 1855-65)—a group anticipating French Impressionism that believed a painting's meaning lay in its *macchie* (spots) of color rather than in its narrative. A technique called "blotting," which abruptly juxtaposed patches of color through manipulations with a dry paint brush, was used to depict politicized scenes of battle and outspoken responses to everyday life.

TWENTIETH-CENTURY ART

The Italian **Futurist** painters, sculptors, and architects of the early 20th century brought Italy to the cutting edge of art. Inspired by **Filippo Tommaso Marinetti's** (1876-1944) *Futurist Manifesto* of 1909, these Italian artists loved to glorify danger, war, and the 20th-century machine age. With pieces displayed in the 1912 Futurist exhibition in Paris, painters **Gino Severini** (1883-1966) and **Carlo Carrà** (1881-1966) and sculptor **Umberto Boccioni** (1882-1916) went beyond

MOST COMMON STREET NAMES

After only a day or two in Italy, it's apparent that just a few big names run Italy's streets.

1. In 1849 **Vittorio Emanuele II** became unified Italy's 1st king.

2. Giuseppe Garibaldi, a 19th-century military hero, was crucial to Italy's unification.

3. Count Camillo Benso di Cavour designed the constitutional structure of the "Kingdom of Italy" in the 19th century.

4. Guglielmo Marconi sent three beeps to Canada in 1901—the first transatlantic telegraph signals.

5. XX Settembre (1870) is the date of Italy's final unification.

6. Giacomo Matteoti, a socialist born in 1885, wrote a book critical of fascism in 1924, but was murdered in response.

7. Cesare Battisti, a native of Trent, was a WWI martyr.

8. Giuseppe Mazzini tried to instigate popular uprisings to unify Italy, but failed time and again.

9. Solferino was a battle fought on June 24, 1859 for the the unification of Italy in the region between Milan and Verona. Italy, along with French ally Napolean III, defeated Austria.

10. Umberto I reigned as King of Italy from 1878 until 1900 when he became and remains the only modern Italian head of state to be assassinated.

Cubism to celebrate the dynamism and energy of modern life by depicting several aspects of moving forms. The work of **Giorgio de Chirico** (1888-1978), some of which is currently on display at the Collezione Peggy Guggenheim in Venice (p. 325), depicts eerie scenes dominated by mannequin figures, empty space, and steep perspective. Although his mysterious and disturbing style, called *Pittura Metafisica*, was never successfully imitated, de Chirico inspired early Surrealist painters. Other 20th-century Italian artists include **Amadeo Modigliani** (1884-1920), a sculptor and painter who was highly influenced by African art and Cubism, and **Marcello Piacentini** (1881-1960) who created fascist architecture that imposed sterility upon classical motifs. In 1938, Piacentini designed the looming **EUR** in Rome (Esposizione Universale Roma) as an impressive reminder of the link between Mussolinian fascism and Roman imperialism.

In the Postwar Era, Italian art lacked unity but still produced noteworthy artists. **Lucio Fontana** (1899-1968) started **Spatialism,** a movement to bring art beyond the canvas towards a synthesis of color, sound, movement, time, and space. His *taglio* (slash) canvases of the mid-1950s created a new dimension for the 2D surface with a simple linear cut. Conceptual artist **Piero Manzoni** (1933-63) created a scandal in 1961 when he put his feces in 90 small cans labeled *Artist's Shit*, setting the price of the excrements at their weight in gold. In May 2007 Sotheby's sold a can for €124,000. In the late 1960s **Arte Povera** bridged the gap between art and life by integrating cheap everyday materials into pieces of art. **Michelangelo Pistoletto** (1933-) caused a clamor with his *Venus in Rags* (1967), a plaster cast of a classical Venus facing a pile of old rags, on display at the **Castello di Rivoli Museo d'Arte Contemporanea** (p. 170) in Turin. While eclipsed by its Renaissance past, contemporary art in Italy thrives in select museums and at the bi-annual **Venice Biennale** (p. 330), showcasing the recent work of artists from Italy and around the world.

LITERATURE

SEX, DRUGS, AND ROMAN MYTHOLOGY

The Romans stole their religion and mythology from anyone and everyone. Though much Roman folklore comes from their own early traditions and Etruscan beliefs, much more of their mythology is a filtered form of Greek mythology. It is important to remember that Greek civilization across the Mediterranean flourished centuries before Rome. When Greek poets were reciting the Odyssey and Iliad, Rome was still an obscure farming village. During the last two centuries of the Roman Republic, roughly the last two centuries BC, interaction between the Greeks and Romans increased because the Romans were conquering the Greeks. When they were not forcing the city-states into submission, they took the time to embrace the Greek mythological system in the form of beautiful poems typically depicting lustful and petty gods. Until this time, the Romans had relied only on boring and ambiguous agricultural gods, as well as the famous story of Romulus and Remus (p. 57).

LATIN LOVERS

ET IN ARCADIA EGO. As they gained dominance over the Hellenized Mediterranean, the Romans discovered the refined joys of literature. **Plautus** (c. 259-184 BC) and **Terrence** (d. 159 BC), for example, adapted Greek comedies into Latin while giving them their own Roman flair. The lyric, though occasionally obscene, poetry of **Catullus** (84-54 BC) demonstrates the complex relationship between Greece and Rome. **Cicero** (106-43 BC), a fiery and complicated Roman politician, orator, and author, whose prose has been central to Latin education since ancient times, is the definitive example of classical Latin. History buffs should check out the writing of **Julius Caesar** (100-44 BC), who gave a first-hand account of the expansion of Rome's empire in his Gallic Wars.

WHEN IN ROME. As a result of Augustus's patronage and the relative peace and prosperity of the time, Augustan Rome produced an array of literary talents. **Livy** (c. 59 BC-AD 17) wrote a mammoth history of Rome from the city's founding to his own time in *Ab Urbe Condita* (From the Founding of the City). Coining the phrase *carpe diem*, **Horace** (65-8 BC) wrote on love, wine, service to the state, hostile critics, and the pleasure of pastoral life in his Odes. **Ovid** (43 BC-AD 17) gave the world the *Metamorphoses*, a beautiful and sometimes racy collection of poetry. For unknown reasons, he angered Augustus so much that he was eventually exiled to modern-day Romania where he eventually died a broken man. **Suetonius's** (c. AD 69-130) *De Vita Caesarum* presents tabloid biographies of the first twelve Emperors, and **Tacitus's** (c. AD 55-116) *Histories* offers a biting synopsis of Roman war, diplomacy, scandal, and rumor during AD 69, the year of notorious Emperor Nero's death. It is widely considered stylistically the greatest work of history in Latin.

DARK AGES TO CULTURAL REBIRTH

DARK TIMES. Between classical antiquity and the Renaissance, authors usually remained anonymous, with the exception of notable religious figures like **St. Thomas Aquinas** (1225-74). By the 13th century, Christianity had become the uniting factor of much of chaotic Europe. While this religious zeal was sometimes oppressive, it also ensured the survival of ancient texts and ideas, since monks of this period typically spent their days and nights copying ancient texts. Despite this tendency to preserve ancient thoughts, writers of the Dark Ages also began using a degraded form of Latin. Adding to this evolution of literature were troubadour songs (usually detailing romance at court) and Carolingian and Arthurian adventure stories which developed at the intersection of northern Italy, southern France, and northern Spain. These served as models for the medieval verses delivered by singers and poets who traveled throughout Europe. The invasion of Norman and Arab rulers into Sicily and southern Italy (1091-1224) also introduced diverse literary traditions.

ABANDON ALL HOPE, YE WHO ENTER HERE! Although the tumult of medieval life discouraged most literary musing in the late 13th century, three Tuscan writers, known as the *Tre Corone* (Three Crowns), resuscitated the written art: **Dante, Petrarch,** and **Boccaccio.** Although scholars do not agree on the precise dates of the literary Renaissance, many argue that the work of Dante Alighieri (1265-1321) marked its inception. Considered the father of modern Italian literature, Dante was one of the first poets in all of Europe to write using the *volgare* (common vernacular; Florentine, in Dante's case) instead of Latin. In his epic poem *La Divina Commedia*, he roams the three realms of the afterlife *(Inferno, Purgatorio, Paradiso)* with Virgil as his guide, meeting famous historical and mythological figures and his true love, Beatrice. In the work, Dante calls for social reform and indicts all those who contributed to Florence's moral downfall, including Popes and political figures—especially those who ordered his own political exile. **Petrarch** (1304-74), the second titan of the 13th century, more clearly belongs to the literary Renaissance. A scholar of classical Latin and a key proponent of humanist thought, he wrote sonnets to a married woman named Laura, collected in *Il Canzoniere*. The third member of this literary triumvirate, **Giovanni Boccaccio** (1313-75), wrote the *Decameron*, a collection of 100 stories that range in tone from suggestive to vulgar. In one, a gardener has his way with an entire convent.

RENAISSANCE MEN. The 14th century saw the rise of **la Commedia dell'Arte,** a form of improvised theater with a standard plot structure and characters. Each character had its own mask and costume and a few fixed personality traits. The most famous character, *Arlecchino* (Harlequin), was easily identified by his diamond-patterned costume. By the 15th and 16th centuries, Italian authors were reviving classical sources in new ways. **Alberti** (1404-72) and **Palladio** (1508-80) wrote treatises on architecture and art theory. In 1528 **Baldassare Castiglione** (1478-1529) wrote *Il Cortegiano,* which instructed the Renaissance man on etiquette and other fine points of behavior. At the pinnacle of the Renaissance, **Ludovico Ariosto's** (1474-1533) *Orlando Furioso* (1516) described a whirlwind of military victories and unrequited love, and **Niccolò Machiavelli** (1469-1527) wrote *Il Principe* (The Prince), a grim assessment of what it takes to gain political power. In the spirit of the Renaissance, specialists in other fields tried writing: **Giorgio Vasari** (1511-74) stopped redecorating Florence's churches to produce the ultimate primer on art history and criticism, *The Lives of the Artists;* **Benvenuto Cellini** (1500-71) wrote about his art in *The Autobiography;* and **Michelangelo** (1475-1564) proved to be a prolific composer of sonnets.

MODERN TIMES

The 19th century brought Italian unification and the need for one language. Nationalistic "Italian" literature, an entirely new concept, grew slowly. *Racconti* (short stories) and poetry became popular in the 1800s. **Giovanni Verga's** (1840-1922) brutally honest depiction of destitute Italians ushered in a new tradition of portraying the common man in art and literature, a movement known as *verismo* (contemporary, all-too-tragic realism). In 1825, **Alessandro Manzoni's** (1785-1873) historical novel, *I Promessi sposi,* established the Modernist novel as a major avenue of Italian literary expression. **Carlo Collodi's** (1826-1890) *Storia di un burattino* (Adventures of a Marionette), also called *Le avventure di Pinocchio,* continues to enchant children, now in its innocuous Disney classic format, with the precocious and sometimes diabolic antics of a puppet.

ITALY SEEN THROUGH FOREIGN EYES

SHAKESPEARE, WILLIAM. *Romeo and Juliet; Othello; Julius Caesar; Merchant of Venice.* Fun and games and death all over.

ELIOT, GEORGE. *Romola.* Deceit, politics, and martyrdom in Savonarola's Florence.

JAMES, HENRY. *The Wings of the Dove.* Unscrupulous seduction in Venice's canals.

FORSTER, E.M. *A Room with a View.* Victorian love and coming-of-age in Florence.

MANN, THOMAS. *Death in Venice.* A writer's obsession with a beautiful boy.

LAWRENCE, D.H. *Twilight in Italy.* An intimate connection with sun-soaked Italy.

HEMINGWAY, ERNEST. *A Farewell to Arms.* Soldier learns to love in WWI Italy.

STONE, IRVING. *The Agony and the Ecstasy.* More of the latter than the former in this biography of Michelangelo.

MAYES, FRANCIS. *Under the Tuscan Sun.* A woman's soul-searching in the heart of Italy, which inspired the 2003 movie by the same name.

POSTMODERNISM. Twentieth-century Italian writers sought to undermine the concept of objective truth that was so dear to the *verismo* movement. Nobel Prize winner **Luigi Pirandello** (1867-1936) deconstructed theatrical convention and explored meta-theater in works like *Sei personaggi in cerca d'autore* (*Six Characters in Search of an Author*; 1921). During the terror of Mussolini, anti-fascist fiction exploded as writers related their horrific personal and political experiences under the dictator. The most prolific of these writers, **Alberto Moravia** (1907-90), wrote the ground-breaking *Gli indifferenti* (*The Time of Indifference*), which was promptly censored for its subtle attacks on the fascist regime. **Primo Levi** (1919-87) wrote *Se questo è un uomo* (1947) about his experience as a prisoner in Auschwitz. Several female writers also gained popularity, including **Grazia Deledda** (1875-1936), **Elsa Morante** (1912-85), and **Natalia Ginzburg** (1916-91). Writers such as **Cesare Pavese** (1908-50) and **Beppe Fenoglio** (1922-63) brought the cinematic trend of *neorealismo* to the novel. **Italo Calvino** (1923-85) exemplified the postmodern era with the magic realism of *Il barone rampante* (*The Baron in the Trees*, 1957) and by questioning the act of reading and writing in *Se una notte d'inverno un viaggiatore* (*If On A Winter's Night A Traveler*; 1979). In 1997, playwright **Dario Fo's** (b. 1926) satires brought him both a denunciation by the Catholic Church and the Nobel Prize for literature.

MUSIC

GREGORY'S FAMOUS CHANTING MONKS

Biblical psalms are some of the earliest known songs of both Italian and Western culture. Roman and Ambrosian rites (Italy's medieval liturgies), which originated in Jewish liturgy, were characterized by monophonic vocal **plainchant,** also known as plainsong. Although the Ambrosian chant can still be heard in Milan, it is the Roman Gregorian chant that prevails. The **Gregorian Chant,** named for **Pope Gregory I** (c. 540-609) is characterized by a repeated reciting note, interrupted only by periodic deviations. Further advancements were made by Italian monk **Guido d'Arezzo** (c. 995-1050), who came up with the modern system of staff-notation and explored the emerging concept of polyphony. Blind organist and composer **Francesco Landini** (c. 1335-97) made significant contributions to the development of the song during the 14th century **Ars Nova** period. This era also brought *madrigales*, musical poems, and *caccia*, musical and poetic narratives describing hunting scenes.

OPERA LIRICA: THE FAT LADY SINGS

Italy's most cherished musical art form was born in Florence in the mid-1590s, nurtured in Venice and Naples, and popularized in Milan's famed Teatro alla Scala (p. 246). Conceived by the **Camerata,** a circle of Florentine writers, noblemen, and musicians including Vincenzo Galilei (famed music theorist and father of Galileo, c. 1525-91), **opera lirica** originated as an attempt to recreate the dramas of ancient Greece by setting lengthy poems to music. The earliest surviving opera is *Euridice* (1600), a collage of compositions by **Jacobo Peri** (1561-1633), **Ottavio Rinuccini** (1562-1621), and **Giulio Caccini** (c. 1550-1618). Opera found a perfect equilibrium between music and poetry for the first time in *L'Orfeo* (1607), a breakthrough piece by **Claudio Monteverdi** (1567-1643), who drew freely from history and juxtaposed high drama, love scenes, and uncouth humor (see **Cremona,** p. 266). Still-popular **Alessandro Scarlatti** (1660-1725) was arguably the most talented composer of Italian operas, pioneering advances in the overture during the 17th century. Meanwhile, the simple and toneful aria became the dominant form of opera, and castrated men the singers of choice. These *castrati*, thanks to their masculine strength of voice and feminine tone, became the most celebrated and envied group of singers in all of Europe.

BAROQUE: THE BIRTH OF VIVALDI AND THE VIOLIN

The Baroque period, known for its heavy ornamentation and emphasis on musical contrasts, saw the birth of the string orchestra. The violin's modern form was perfected by **Antonio Stradivari** (1644-1737) and became popular in pieces by fellow Cremonese Monteverdi and his contemporaries (visit the Museo Stradivariano, p. 268). In 1698, Florentine **Bartolomeo Cristofori** (1655-1731) invented the pianoforte. The work of violinist **Antonio Vivaldi** (1675-1741), who composed over 600 concertos, continues to awe contemporary audiences, with innovative works like *The Four Seasons* (1725). Vivaldi established the concerto's present form, in which an orchestra accompanies a soloist through three movements.

VIVA VERDI!

LAYING THE GROUNDWORK. Despite its convoluted plots and powerful, dramatic music, 19th-century Italian opera had not yet adopted the French tradition of visual spectacle. A famous composer of tragedies and comedies and a master of the light, flexible *bel canto* (beautiful song), **Gioacchino Rossini** (1792-1868) composed *Cinderella* in 1817. Rossini's rough contemporary, **Giacomo Puccini** (1858-1924), helped further the reputation of Italian opera with his brilliant orchestral works and world-famous operas, including *La Bohème* (1896), *Tosca* (1900), and *Madama Butterfly* (1904).

AND, OF COURSE, THE MAN HIMSELF. Giuseppe Verdi (1813-1901), whose lyrical half-century domination of Italian opera emphasized human themes and the human voice, remains the crowning musical figure of 19th-century Italy and, along with his German contemporary Wagner, of all of opera. *Nabucco* (1842), a pointed and powerful *bel canto*, typifies Verdi's early works. The opera's chorus, *Va pensiero*, became the hymn of Italian freedom and unity during the Risorgimento. Verdi also produced the touching, personal dramas and memorable melodies of *Rigoletto* (1851), *La Traviata* (1853), and *Il Trovatore* (1853) in mid-career. His later work brought the grand and heroic conflicts of *Aïda* (1871), the dramatic thrust of *Otello* (1887), and the mercurial comedy *Falstaff*

(1893). Verdi's support of the Risorgimento in the 1850s encouraged patriots to invoke his name—a convenient acronym for "Vittorio Emanuele, *Re d'Italia*" (King of Italy)—as their popular battle cry: "*Viva Verdi!*"

TWENTIETH-CENTURY OPERA. In the 20th century, **Ottorino Respighi** (1879-1936) explored his fascination with orchestral color in the popular *Roman Trilogy* (1924-29). The Italian-American composer, **Gian Carlo Menotti** (1911-2007) wrote Pulitzer Prize-winning operas *The Consul* (1950) and *The Saint of Bleecker Street* (1954). **Luigi Dallapiccola** (1904-75) achieved success with surrealist choral works, including *Canti di prigionia* (*Songs of Prison*, 1941), which protested fascism. His student, avant-garde composer **Luciano Berio** (1925-2003), pioneered the composition of electronic music. Grammy-winning tenor **Luciano Pavarotti** (1935-2007) made his world debut in the 60s and helped bring opera into mainstream popular culture with his televised operas in the 1990s. **Andrea Bocelli** (b. 1958) has continued to bridge the expanse between opera and pop with chart-topping songs such as "*Con Te Partirò*" in 19995. Visitors looking to experience Italian opera firsthand can visit Milan's Teatro alla Scala (p. 246), Rome's Teatro dell'Opera (p. 152), and Palermo's Teatro Massimo (p. 659), or one of Italy's countless other opulent opera houses.

ARRIVEDERCI, VERDI

More recent Italian music has reversed its centuries-long role as a groundbreaker, drawing inspiration instead from American pop culture. Melodic rockers of the 60s included **Enzo Iannacci**, a dentist-turned-musician; the crooning, politically-minded, Genoese **Fabrizio De Andre**, and **Adriano Celentano,** whose career spanned 40 years. Emerging in the 60s and 70s, **Lucio Battisti** now enjoys a popularity rivalling that of the Beatles in his own country. In the 70s and 80s, **Eduardo Bennato** used rock to spread a progressive political message; his successor **Vasco Rossi,** drew an unprecedented 300,000-member crowd to a free concert he gave in 2004. **Eros Ramazzotti** gained universal appeal by recording every album in Spanish as well as Italian, often teaming up with Cher and Tina Turner. Italians **Laura Pausini, Elisa,** and **L'Aura** followed suit by recording English albums. More recently, **Jovanotti's** rap has entered the global scene, along with socially conscious **Frankie-Hi-NRG** and **99 Posse**. For a more relaxed beat, try **Lucio Dalla**'s internationally popular *Caruso*.

FILM

OLDIES AND GOLDIES

Italy's golden position within the film industry began in 1905, when **Filoteo Alberini** released *La Presa di Roma (The Taking of Rome)*. This film ushered in the Italian "super-spectacle," an extravagant recreation of historical events through film. Throughout the early 20th century, most Italian film followed this melodramatic pattern, and many Italian film stars were consequently thought of as superhuman. Before WWI, celebrated actors like **Francesca Bertini** (1888-1985), **Pina Menichelli** (1890-1984), and **Lyda Borelli** (1884-1959) epitomized the Italian diva.

SEEING IS BELIEVING

No one ever accused Benito Mussolini of missing out on an opportunity. Recognizing film's potential as propaganda in the late 30s, Mussolini revived an industry that had been in decline since the golden age of the silent era by creating

BEEN THERE, SCENE IT

Picturesque Italy has provided a backdrop for artistic genius, breathtaking romance, and feature films. Relive the cinematic moments of the following movies by visiting their original settings.

1. La Dolce Vita (1960): Since dancing like Sylvia in Rome's Trevi Fountain (p. 135) is now illegal, you'll just have to imagine yourself in this famous scene from Fellini's Oscar-winning feature.

2. The Italian Job (2003): Innocently stand by and see the peaceful Venetian canals where the opening scene's high-speed boat chase took place (p. 323).

3. The Godfather III (1990): Escape Michael Corleone's fate by visiting Palermo's Teatro Massimo (p. 659) and going home unscathed.

4. The Bourne Supremacy (2004): Feel like an amnesiac former CIA assasin on the run in Naples (p. 563)—just don't flee to Berlin the way Jason did.

5. Star Wars Episode II: Attack of the Clones (2002): Re-enact Anakin and Princess Padmé's wedding, which took place at the Villa del Balbianello in Lenno, on Lake Como (p. 282).

the gargantuan **Cinecittà Studios,** Rome's answer to Hollywood. Yet the boost to the industry came at a price: Mussolini also enforced a few "imperial edicts" that dictated the production of films, one of which even forbade laughing at the Marx Brothers's 1933 film, *Duck Soup.* Films created under fascist rule between the years 1936 and 1943 glorified Italian military conquests (linking them to Classical Roman success) and portrayed comfortable middle-class life. This era of Italian film is often referred to as the era of *telefoni bianchi* (white telephones) in reference to the common prop. Rare compared to their black cousins, these phones were a symbol of prosperity, and during the short-lived glory days of Italian Fascism, these films kept the chaos in other parts of Europe out of sight, out of mind. A few renegade leaders in the film industry, however, opposed fascist rule. **Luigi Chiarini,** for instance, was instrumental in the founding of Italy's *Centro Sperimentale della Cinematografia*, the film school that despite funding by Mussolini's government, slowly shifted away from propaganda and became the alma mater of many neorealist directors.

NEOREALISM

The fall of fascism brought the explosion of **neorealismo** in cinema in the 1940s, which rejected contrived sets and professional actors, emphasizing instead on-location shooting and "authentic" drama based in reality. These low-budget productions created a film revolution and brought Italian cinema international prestige. Neorealists first gained attention in Italy with **Luchino Visconti's** (1906-76) French-influenced *Ossessione* (1942). Because fascist censors suppressed this so-called "resistance" film, it wasn't until **Roberto Rossellini's** (1906-77) film *Roma, città aperta* (1945) that neorealist films gained international exposure. The film began his Neorealistic WWII Trilogy, which also included *Paisà* (1946) and *Germania anno zero* (1948). **Vittorio De Sica's** 1948 *Ladri di biciclette* (The Bicycle Thief) was perhaps the most successful neorealist film. The film's simple plot explored the human struggle against fate. A demand for Italian comedy gave birth to **neorealismo rosa**, a more comic version of the intense and often dismally authentic glimpse into daily Italian life. Actor **Totò** (1898-1967), the illegitimate son of a Neapolitan duke, was Italy's Charlie Chaplin. With his dignified antics and clever lines, Totò charmed audiences and provided subtle commentary on Italian society.

THE GOLDEN AGE

The golden age of Italian cinema, which took place in the 60s, began *la commedia all'italiana*, during which the prestige and economic success of Italian movies was at its height. **Mario Monicelli** (*I Soliti Ignoti*, 1958; *La Grande guerra*, 1959) brought a more cynical tone to the portrayal of daily Italian life, which was in a stage of rapid transformation and social unease. Italian comedy struggled to portray cultural stereotypes with as much wit as its public demanded. Actors **Marcello Mastroianni, Vittorio Gassman,** and **Alberto Sordi** gained fame portraying self-centered characters lovable for their frailties.

By the 1960s, post-neorealist directors like **Federico Fellini** (1920-93) and **Michelangelo Antonioni** (1912-2007) valued careful cinematic construction over mere real-world experience. With the Oscar-winning *La Strada* (1954), Fellini went beyond neorealism, scripting the vagabond life of two street performers, Gelsomina and Zampanò, in the most poetic of terms. Fellini's *8½* (1963) interwove dreams with reality in a semi-autobiographical exploration of the demands of the artist that has earned a place in the international cinematic canon. His *La Dolce Vita* (1959) was condemned by both religious and political authorities for its portrayal of decadently stylish celebrities in 50s Rome on the Via Veneto. The film coined the term *paparazzi* and glamorized dancing in the Trevi Fountain (p. 135), an act that is now legally off-limits. Antonioni's haunting trilogy, *L'Avventura* (1959), *La Notte* (1960), and *L'Eclisse* (1962) presents a stark world of estranged couples and isolated aristocrats. His *Blow-Up* was a 1966 English-language hit about miming, murder, and mod London. Controversial writer-director **Pier Paolo Pasolini** (1922-75) may have spent as much time on trial for his politics as he did making films. An ardent Marxist, he set his films in the underworld of shanty neighborhoods, poverty, and prostitution. His later films include scandalous adaptations of famous literary works including famous works, *Il Decameron* (1971) and *The Arabian Nights* (1974).

INTROSPECTION

Aging directors and a lack of funds led Italian film into an era characterized by nostalgia and self-examination. **Bernardo Bertolucci's** (b. 1940) *Il conformista* (1970) investigates fascist Italy by focusing on one "comrade" struggling to be normal. Other major Italian films of this era include **Vittorio de Sica's** (1901-74) *Il Giardino dei Finzi-Contini* (1971) and **Francesco Rosi's** *Cristo si è fermato a*

6. Under the Tuscan Sun (2003): Soak up Tuscany's luscious landscape and stunning sunsets in Cortona (p. 475) and wonder if you too can purchase a villa like divorcee Frances Mayes.

7. The Talented Mr. Ripley (1999): Dive into the to-die-for crystal waters that surround beautiful Ischia on the Amalfi Coast (p. 604) where Jude Law's Dickie Greenleaf was murdered by Matt Damon's Mr. Ripley.

8. Life is Beautiful (1997): Visit the picturesque Arezzo (p. 478), hometown to actor/director Roberto Benigni, who chose the town as the backdrop for many key scenes of his touching Oscar-winning WWII drama.

9. Ocean's Twelve (2004): Find Villa Erba, the Night Fox's mansion, on the shores of Lake Como in Bellagio (p. 287) and start scheming to compete with mastermind and thief Danny Ocean. This villa was also the vacation home for Italian director Luchino Visconti's family.

10. Romeo and Juliet (1968): Although the Shakespearean original was set in fair Verona, director Franco Zeffirelli filmed in locales across Italy. Challenge your enemy to a duel in the streets of Gubbio (p. 511) where Franco set the fatal fight between Romeo and Tybalt.

Eboli (1979), both of which are adaptations of classic post-war, anti-fascist novels. In the 80s, the **Taviani brothers,** Paolo and Vittorio, catapulted to fame with *La notte di San Lorenzo* (1982), which depicted an Italian village during the last days of WWII, and *Kaos* (1984), a film based on stories by **Pirandello.** Inheriting the *commedia all'italiana* tradition of the golden age, actor-directors like **Nanni Moretti** (b. 1953) and **Maurizio Nichetti** (b. 1948) delighted audiences with macabre humor in the 80s and early 90s. Both men usually choose projects that required them to play neurotic, introspective, or ridiculous characters. In his psychological comedy-thriller *Bianca* (1984), Moretti stars as a slightly deranged high school math teacher, and in *Volere Volare* (1991), Nichetti plays a confused cartoon sound designer who turns into an animated figure.

BUONGIORNO, PRINCIPESSA!

Oscar-winners **Gabriele Salvatores** (for *Mediterraneo*, 1991) and **Giuseppe Tornatore** (for *Nuova Cinema Paradiso*, 1988) have earned the attention and affection of audiences worldwide. Oscars have been bestowed upon a handful of other contemporary Italian filmmakers, as well. In 1996 **Massimo Troisi's** (b. 1953) *Il Postino* won Best Original Score and was nominated in four additional categories, including Best Picture, Screenplay, Director, and Actor. Three years later **Roberto Benigni** (b. 1952) won several Oscars for *La vita è bella (Life is Beautiful)*, which juxtaposed the tragedy of the Holocaust with a father's devoted love for his son. Most recently, **Nanni Moretti** snagged the Palm D'Or at Cannes in 2001 for the film, *La Stanza del Figlio (The Son's Room)*, and **Leonardo Pieraccioni** (b. 1965) released *Il Paradiso all'improvviso (Suddenly Paradise)* to international acclaim in 2003.

MEDIA

PRINT

The media in Italy is anything but impartial, and has been known to lambaste everyone from public officials to popular actresses. The most prevalent national daily papers are *Il Corriere della Sera*, a center-right publication based in Milan, and *La Repubblica*, a somewhat liberal paper based in Rome. Other popular papers include *La Stampa* (center-right, based in Turin), *Il Messaggero* (center-left, based in Rome), and *Il Giornale* (based in Milan and owned by ex-Prime Minister Silvio Berlusconi's brother). Dailies like the pink *La Gazzetta dello Sport* and *Il Corriere dello Sport* are the true mainstays, covering soccer victories and losses, which cause more uproar than elections. For weekly entertainment listings, large cities have their own magazines, including *Roma C'è; Firenze Spettacolo;* and *Qui Napoli*. English-language Italian papers include *Italy Daily*, an insert in the *International Herald Tribune*, the monthly *talk aBOut*, and the weekly newsletter *Wanted in Rome*.

TELEVISION

Italian television offers three state-owned channels, **RAI1, RAI2,** and **RAI3,** and a handful of cable options from Italy and abroad. It is important to note, however, that everyone's favorite ex-Prime Minister, **Silvio Berlusconi,** owns all three of the RAI channels and is in control of three others. Television in Italy is a flashy affair. Whether they are game shows or the nightly news, Italian shows overwhelm viewers with disco balls, scantily-clad women, hit Europop songs, and general frivolity. In addition to its domestic sensational spectacles, Italian TV also incorporates international flair in its programming. The evening news reports on domestic and international issues, dubbed re-runs of American shows figure prominently, and bad 80s movies play late into the night.

DESIGN

From the Roman aqueducts to Leonardo's flying machine to Dolce & Gabbana's spacesuit-inspired winter 2008 line, Italians have always had a penchant for design. Compare **Enzo Ferrari's** original 1929 cars to Ford's Model T's, **Bialetti's** 1930 art deco Moka Express coffeemaker to one by Mr. Coffee, or a Gucci leather shoe to the American sneaker, and it's obvious that Italians designers deserve the prestige they enjoy. Aside from cars and appliances that achieve statuesque beauty, Italian design produced the **Vespa**—still adored by Italians and hated by fearful tourists—in 1946, and the 1957 **Fiat,** a tiny 2-door car. Before the days of sleek laptops, **Olivetti's** 1969 Valentine typewriter by designer **Ettore Sottass** combined style and practicality. This combination of streamlined beauty and simple functionality frequently characterizes Italian design.

FASHION FOR POCKET CHANGE. Save 25-75% at end-of-season sales. These happen in January and July and last until the collection sells out. Many stores also offer previews of the next collection at this time.

Equally stunning and more widely recognized is Italian fashion design. Italian domination began in 1881 when **Cerruti** opened his doors and began his lasting impact on Italian fashion, serving as a mentor and teacher for later designers such as **Giorgio Armani.** Still-famous **Salvatore Ferragamo,** whose love affair with shoes would later produce Dorothy's ruby slippers in *The Wizard of Oz* (1939), opened his first shoe shop in his parents' home in 1912. The illustrious **Fendi** line began as a tiny fur and leather business in Rome at the end of WWI, but was revolutionized by the five Fendi sisters who took control after WWII. Two years later, **Guccio Gucci** opened a leather store in Florence originally intended as a saddle shop that later moved to Rome and became an international fashion powerhouse. In the early 50s, **Gian Battista Giorgini** organized a series of runway shows that re-introduced the phrase "Made in Italy" as a universally accepted indication of quality and established Milan as a fashion capital on par with Paris. Italy soon became host to now-famous designers such as **Max Mara** (1951), **Valentino** (1962), the **Giorgio Armani Company** (1975), **Versace** (1978), and **Dolce & Gabbana** (1985), all of whose designs litter the red carpet, often overshadowing the stars they adorn. To become a star for the day, go shopping in **Milan** (see **Milan: Shopping,** p. 250), and find out what makes this the fashion capital of the world. Take notes on the classic cuts, quality fabrics, and liberal use of black that make Italians so effortlessly stylish. If you have assimilated to Italian culture and decided that football (p. 86) is your passion, take a look at Dolce & Gabbana's AC Milan uniforms (see **Milan: Sports,** p. 250) or their 2006 men's underwear campaign featuring well-cut *calcio* stars.

FOOD AND WINE: LA DOLCE VITA

MANGIAMO!

In Italy, food preparation is an art form, and culinary traditions constitute a crucial part of the culture. Each region of Italy has a distinct culinary identity to complement its personality that often includes its own unique shape of pasta. The words *"Buon appetito!"* and *"Cin cin!"* chime around the table as friends and families sit down to dine. As much an institution as the meal itself, the after-dinner *passeggiata* (promenade) attracts Italians into the main square late into the evening. Small portions and leisurely paced meals help keep locals looking svelte despite their rich cuisine.

Breakfast is the least elaborate meal in Italy. Often taken at a neighborhood bar, *la colazione* consists—at most—of a quick coffee and a *cornetto* (croissant). For *il pranzo* (lunch), Italians usually grab a *panino* (sandwich) or salad. Lunch is generally the most important meal of the day in rural regions, where daily work comes in two shifts and is separated by a lengthy lunch and *pisolino* (nap). Most common in northern cities, Italians will end a none-too-stressful day at work with an *aperitivo* (aperitif) around 5 or 6pm. Try a *spritz*, a northern specialty made with *prosecco*, *campari*, or *aperol* and a splash of mineral water. *La cena* (dinner) usually begins at 8pm, although in Naples it's not unheard of to go for a midnight pizza. Traditionally, dinner is the lengthiest meal of the day, usually lasting through much of the evening and consisting of an *antipasto* (appetizer), a *primo piatto* (starch-based first course like pasta or *risotto*), a *secondo piatto* (meat or fish), and a *contorno* (vegetable side dish). Finally, *la cena* is capped off with the *dolce* (dessert), then *caffè* (espresso), and often an after-dinner liqueur. Many restaurants offer a fixed-price *menù turistico* including *primo*, *secondo*, bread, water, and wine. While the cuisine may vary regionally, the importance of relaxing over a meal does not. For example, many restaurants in Bologna do not seat more than one party per table per night, and dinners throughout Italy can last for hours. It's easy to see why Italians champion the Slow Food movement to combat Americanized fast food.

FOOD ON THE RUN

In Italian, *un bar* refers to a spot to grab a quick, inexpensive meal. Calm dining can be found at a *tavola calda* (cafeteria-style snack bar), *rosticceria* (grill), or *gastronomia* (food shop that prepares hot dishes for takeout). Although some fast-food chains have infiltrated Italy, the ample seafood, salad, beer, and espresso offerings at most McDonald's demonstrate that Italians do fast food their way. The typical bar sells hot and cold *panini*, gelato, and coffee. The *bars* on major tourist thoroughfares have prices that reflect location—not necessarily service or quality. In small towns, the *bar* is a social center; children come to meet playmates and eat gelato, young adults to flirt and sip beer, and older men to drink wine and reminisce. In crowded *bars*, clients often purchase food at the cashier's desk and take the *scontrino* (receipt) to a bartender for service. Standing at the counter may be cheaper than sitting at a table. A *salumeria* or *alimentari* (meat and grocery shop) or the popular **STANDA** or **Coop** supermarkets sell food basics, while open-air markets have fresher produce and negotiable prices. Customers must carry receipts for 100m after making a purchase to avoid accusations of theft.

IN VINO VERITAS

Despite its reputation for living in the shadow of wine-loving French neighbors, Italy is the world's leading exporter of vintage spirits. Today, over 2000 varieties of grapes are grown in Italy's warm climes and rocky hills before *la vendemmia* (the grape harvest) in September or October. To make red wine, *rosso*, vintners pump the juice and skins into glass, oak, or steel fermentation vats; white wines, *biancos*, are made from skinless grapes. Whether a wine is *dolce* (sweet) or *secco* (dry) is largely determined by the ripeness and sugar content of its grape. After fermentation, the wine is racked and clarified to remove sediment. The wine is then stored in barrels or vats until bottling.

IT'S ALL IN THE NAME. Look for one of four classifications on your bottle to determine the wine's quality. Independently tested wine will bear the label DOCG *(Denominazione di Origine Controllata e Garantita);* wines that follow regional regulations are labeled DOC *(Denominazione di Origine Controllata);* the label IGT *(Indicazione Geografica)* means that a wine has been produced in a specific area; and *Vino da Tavola* is a catch-all term for otherwise unclassifiable table wines.

Wine tasting is made easy by *enoteche* (wine bars), especially government-run bars, which serve as regional exhibition and tasting centers in order to promote local vineyards and sponsor educational events. *Cantine* (wine cellars) do not typically offer tastings unless accompanied by a wine bar. If touring by car, ask the local tourist office about *Strade del Vino* (wine roads). **Tuscany** (see p. 426, birthplace of the *Movimento del Turismo del Vino* (wine tourism), is especially accessible for wine tasting. Reservations are recommended at some vineyards, so be sure to call ahead.

REGIONAL WINES

WINE FROM WINE LAND. Piedmont (p. 162), Italy's most distinguished wine region (followed closely by Tuscany), produces the touted (and expensive) *barolo*, a full-bodied red made from the region's *nebbiolo* grapes. *Barolo* is aged for up to twenty years, much longer than its lighter cousin, *Barbaresco*. Celebrate Piedmont's lighter side with the sparkling and sweet *asti spumante* after biking through the vineyards. The **Veneto** (p. 305) region yields everyday wines such as *bianco di custoza*, a dry *Soave* white, and *Valpolicella*, a sweet dessert wine. Go to **Friuli** (p. 370) for smooth merlots and soothing whites like *Tocai Friulano*. Prepare for the *parmigiano-reggiano* and parma ham of **Emilia-Romagna (p. 385)** with a red *Sauvignon*, or *Frizzantino Malvasia*, both typical aperitifs or dessert wines. *Lambrusco*, known elsewhere as a cheap export, is enjoyed in Emilia-Romagna as a refreshing red. Tuscany's *Sangiovese* grapes are crushed to make the region's popular *Chianti Classici*, 'noble' red *vino Nobile di Montepulciano*, and white *Trebbiano*.

IN RECENT NEWS

SLOW FOOD SPREADS FAST

The Slow Food movement sprung in 1986 when Carlo Petrini of Bra, Italy decided enough was enough with grab-n-go fast-food chains. In a mere 22 years, his movement has grown to 80,000 members from all points of the globe who are attempting to counteract consumers' dwindling interest in the food they eat. Where is it from? What does it taste like? Sometimes we eat so quickly that we can't even remember.

Slow Food's requirements are three-fold; the food must be good, clean, and fair. In other words, it must taste good, not harm the environment, and food producers must receive fair compensation for their work. Ultimately, their view is that when you lift your fork to swirl that first bite of linguine, you are not a consumer, but an informed co-producer.

Keep an eye out for Slow Food's snail symbol on the doors of many restaurants in Italy for assured quality. They even opened a University of Gastronomical Sciences in 2004, offering Bachelor's and Master's degrees, along with many cultural seminars.

So before you grab that *panini* "da portare via" ("to go"), take a moment to step back and remember where your food is coming from. Even a little acknowledgement is a start.

CORK YOUR WALLET! Wine snobs may spend €50 on a bottle of aged *riserva*, but wines in the €6-12 range can often be sublime. The most respected wine stewards in the nation regularly rank inexpensive wines above their costly cousins. Expense can equal quality, but it's wiser to go for the high end of a lower-grade wine than the low end of a higher-grade wine.

DOWN SOUTH. When in **Rome** (p. 104), drink cold *Frascati*, a clean white wine invented over 2000 years ago. In **Umbria** (p. 502), where wine production dates back to the ancient Etruscans, the world-famous *Orvieto* is a golden white whose versatility is still being explored, as French chardonnay grapes have recently been incorporated to produce the world-class *Cervaro della Sala*. **Naples** (p. 563) boasts *Lacryma Cristi* ("Christ's Tear"), while the red *Aglianico* hails from the coutryside of Campania (p. 563). The hotter climate and longer growing season of Southern Italy and the islands produces fruitier, more sugary wines. Try the **Sicilian** (p. 653) *Marsala*, excellent when served as an apertif between *primi* and *secondi*, with Parmesan cheese, or as a dessert wine.

REGIONAL LIQUEURS

DOPO LA CENA. Liqueurs are often enjoyed at the end of the meal as palate-cleansing *digestivi*. Don't pass up the ubiquitous *limoncello*, a heavy lemon liqueur especially famous in **Sorrento** (p. 588), which also features the walnut-flavored *nocino*. *Amari* cordials, served after festival meals, are often infused with so much sugar that they contradict their name—"bitter" in Italian. Unusual wild fruit and nut essences found in Italian liqueurs include blueberry (in *mirto*), artichoke (in *cynar*), and melon (in *melone*). Other Italian specialties include almond-flavored *amaretto* (originally made from apricot pits), hazelnut-flavored *frangelico*, and licorice *sambuca*, often served with three coffee beans to represent health, happiness, and prosperity. Once known as "firewater" (or, to some Italians, a morning boost), *grappa* is usually uncontaminated by sugars and leaves the palate disinfected. After grapes are pressed, the remaining *pomace* (seeds, stalks, and stems) is used for this national favorite.

 SO A GUY WALKS INTO A BAR... In Italy a *"bar"* doesn't refer to a beer-serving nightspot but to an establishment where you can get a coffee and a bite to eat. For alcohol, head to *un bar americano* or a *discoteca*.

WAKE UP AND SMELL THE CAFFÈ!

THE ART OF ESPRESSO. Italians drink coffee at breakfast, lunch, dinner, and any time in between—and still manage to close shop in the afternoon for a snooze. But espresso in Italy isn't just a beverage; it's an experience, from the harvesting of the beans to the savoring of the beverage. High altitude *Arabica* beans compose 60-90% of most Italian blends, while the remaining 10-40% are made of woody-flavored *robusta* beans. Italians are partial to a high concentration of *robusta* beans because they emit oils that produce a thick, foamy *crema* under the heat and pressure of the espresso machine. Espresso beans are roasted longer than other coffee beans, and give the drink fuller volume. After roasting, the beans are then ground, tapped into a basket, and mixed with hot, pressurized water. In a good cup of espresso, the foamy *crema* should be caramel-colored and thick enough to support a spoonful of sugar for a good

Calcio

Calcio, known to Anglophones as football or soccer, isn't just a sport in Italy; it's a religion. If culture is what people identify with most strongly, then calcio is arguably the most important aspect of Italian culture. La Gazzetta dello Sport is by far the most popular Italian daily. The ten most-watched TV broadcasts include ten *calcio* matches, most of them featuring a match of the Italian national team.

The *azzurri* (or Blues, the traditional name of the Italian national team derived from their jersey color) are famous worldwide, and one of the few elements uniting Italians under the same flag. Watching locals cheer the *azzurri* to victory in a local bar is an indescribable show. After every victory, street parades go on for hours with cars full of Italian flags honking throughout the *piazze* and impromptu pool parties in public fountains.

However, the *azzurri* are an exception to the daily *calcio* environment, typically characterized by undestroyable affiliations with one team and profound rivalries with all the others. The main competition is the Serie A, the Italian championship that assigns the *scudetto*, the title of Italian Champion, every year. The matches take place every Sunday at 3pm, and to many Italians this time is as sacred as Holy Mass. Recently the Champions' League, with matches on Tuesday and Wednesday nights, has become more prestigious as the best teams in Europe compete for the title of European champion.

Like every estimable religion, *calcio* has its temples with their traditions. Here is a brief guide to the most famous stadiums in Italy:

—Home of the Best: Delle Alpi, Turin (71,000). Juventus, the most successful team in Italian history, with 27 Italian Championship wins, plays here. They have the highest number of supporters of any team in Europe, and their black-and-white jerseys are a universally respected symbol of nobility.

—La Scala of *calcio*: San Siro, Milan (84,000). One of Italy's most beautiful stadiums, with a perfect view from any seat. Home to AC Milan, the team owned by Berlusconi that has won many titles in the last two decades, and Inter, the only team that has never been in the second division.

—Best Choreography: Olimpico, Rome (83,000). The *tifosi* (fans) in Rome are the loudest and most creative. The main team is Roma, but Lazio is almost at the same level and their rivalry permeates every Roman conversation.

—Southern Passion: fans in the south are the most passionate. Every game is a matter of life or death, and regional matches often lead to street fights. San Paolo (Naples; 80,000) is as respectable a stadium as San Siro and for several years has been the home of Maradona, the greatest *calcio* player of all time. The arenas La Favorita (Palermo; 50,000) and San Nicola (Bari; 58,000) are always feared by the home team's opponents.

> ## "Calcio ... isn't just a sport in Italy; it's a religion."

A tip for first-time match-goers: don't sit in the curve, the curved sides of the stadium where the very hot *tifosi* are. Overly zealous fans are often nerve-wrackingly active, waving giant flags, brandishing flares, and chanting insults at the opposing team. By no means wear any other jersey except the home team's while watching a match from this section.

Now that you know about the *calcio* world, buy La Gazzetta, a ticket, and a *sciarpa* (scarf), and be ready for the time of your life.

Edoardo Gallo, from Cuneo, Italy, is currently working as a consultant in New York after researching for Let's Go: Central America in El Salvador, Nicaragua, and Honduras. He is a 2004 graduate in Physics and Mathematics of Harvard University and is also a passionate, lifelong fan of Juventus.

couple of seconds. Heavy *crema* prevents the drink's rich aroma from diffusing into the air and is the sign of a quality brew.

 COFFEE STAINED. While Italians drink coffee with every meal, they do not drink cappuccino after 10am. If you order a cappuccino after lunch or dinner, you might as well open your map on the table and wave your country's flag; every Italian in the surrounding area will know you're a tourist.

HOW TO ORDER. For a standard cup of espresso, request a *caffè*. Stir in sugar and down it in one gulp like the locals. If you take a little milk with it, ask for *caffè macchiato* (*macchia* means "stain" or "spot"). Cappuccino, which Italians drink only before lunch, is espresso and steamed milk "capped" by frothed milk; *caffè latte* or *latte macchiato* is heavier on the milk, lighter on the coffee. Note that good espresso is supposed to have a layer of foam on the top due to the compression process. For coffee with a kick, try a *caffè corretto* (corrected): espresso with a drop of strong liqueur (usually *grappa* or brandy). *Caffè americano*, scorned by Italians, is watery espresso served in a large cup. *Caffè freddo* is a refreshing, chilled coffee. For dessert, the *caffè affogato* (drowned coffee) is espresso with a scoop of vanilla gelato.

SPORTS AND RECREATION

ANCIENT TIMES. The Romans liked their athletic spectacles fast and violent. Gladiatorial combat originated as part of a funeral custom: gifts to the dead were offered in amphitheaters across the Empire. Examples include a site at **Pompeii (p. 582)** and, of course, the Roman **Colosseum** (p. 128). Romans also hosted *venationes* (wild beast hunts), and even giant mock naval battles. Greek athletics, like wrestling, running, and javelin throwing, were slower to catch on in the Capital of the Ancient World—perhaps there just wasn't enough killing.

SOCCER. Slightly less violent—and only slightly—today's *calcio* ("soccer" to Americans, "football" to everyone else) surpasses all other sports in popularity and competes with politics, fashion, and religion as national pastime (see "*Calcio:* An Italian Religion," previous page). **La Squadra Azzurra** (The Blue Team) is a source of pride: there are claims that Italy's 1982 World Cup victory inspired more national unity than any of the country's political movements. However, Italian *calcio* fans, or *tifosi*, are also divided by their undying devotion to local teams. Enthusiasm peaks in June for the **Coppa Italia** championship. During games between big-city rivals like Naples, Milan, and Rome, don't be surprised to find hauntingly empty streets and bars stifled with fans either commiserating or celebrating in communal agony or ecstasy. To become one with the mob, catch a game at Rome's **Stadio Olimpico (p. 153)** or Milan's **San Siro** (p. 250).

WORLD CUP 2006. Veni, Vidi, Vici: Italy came. Italy saw. Italy conquered. Despite French player Zinedine Zidane's "head-butt felt 'round the world" in the final match, the Italian national team officially became **the world's best soccer team in 2006.** The victory served as Italian football's saving grace: around the same time as the Cup, *Calciopoli*, or the **Serie A scandal,** incriminated Juventus and other teams in Italy's professional soccer league for fixing match results.

CYCLING. Home to both cyclists and cycling aficionados, Italy hosts the annual **Giro d'Italia**, a 21-stage cross-country race, in May. Second only to the Tour de France, the race was inaugurated in 1909 and has since been interrupted only twice—by the First and Second World Wars. The Giro's victor receives the **maglia rosa,** whose pink hue represents the color of paper used by *La Gazzetta dello Sport*, Italy's top sports newspaper.

SKIING. From December to April, skiers flock to the Italian Alps and Apennines. Head to resorts near **Turin** (p. 162), host of the 2006 Winter Olympics, or to the **Aosta Valley** (p. 186) for summer skiing, helicopter skiing, and a large assortment of other exciting possibilities. Annual World Cup competitions at Italian ski slopes appeal to less adventurous ski fans.

FESTIVALS AND HOLIDAYS

Though most Italians work 35hr. per week, take 2hr. lunch breaks, close some businesses on Mondays, and take elaborate month-long coastal vacations each August, they still enjoy a seemingly constant stream of festivity. Despite often religious origins, celebrations aren't necessarily pious. Revelry during **Carnevale,** which is particularly enthusiastic in Venice, prepares Italian towns for Lent with 10 days of celebration. At **Scoppio del Carro,** held in **Florence** on Easter Sunday, Florentines set off a cart of explosives in keeping with medieval tradition (except for the addition of the mechanical dove used to light the cart). Countless other quirky local festivals pay homage to medieval customs, often in the form of jousts and period costumes. For a complete list of festivals, write to the **Italian Government Tourist Board** (p. 10).

DATE	FESTIVAL	LOCATION
Jan. 1	Capodanno (New Year's Day)	National Holiday
Jan. 6	Epifania (Epiphany)	National Holiday
Jan. 30-31	Fiera di Sant'Orso	Aosta (p. 193)
Feb.-March	Carnevale; see www.carnivalofvenice.it or www.viareggio.ilcarnevale.it	Venice (p. 331); Viareggio (p. 495)
Apr.-June	Verdi Opera Festival	Parma (p. 407)
Palm Su to Easter Su (Apr. 5-12, 2009)	Settimana Santa (Holy Week)	National Holiday
Apr. 10, 2009	Venerdi Santo (Good Friday)	National Holiday
Apr. 12, 2009	Pasqua (Easter Sunday)	National Holiday
Apr. 13, 2009	Pasquetta (Easter Monday)	National Holiday
Apr. 25	Festa della Liberazione (Liberation Day)	National Holiday
Late Apr.-June	Maggio Musicale (May of Music)	Florence (p. 454)
May	Land of Motors Festival	Modena (p. 402)
May-June	Monteverdi Opera Festival	Cremona (p. 269)
May 1	Festa del Lavoro (Labor Day)	National Holiday
May 1	Primo Maggio Concert	Rome (p. 156)
May 1	Sagra di Sant'Efisio	Cagliari (p. 733)
1st Sa in May (May 2, 2009) and Sept. 19	Festa di San Gennaro	Naples (p. 594)
Su after Ascension Day (May 21, 2009)	Festa del Grillo (Festival of the Cricket)	Florence (p. 454)

DATE	FESTIVAL	LOCATION
May 7-9	Festa di San Nicola	Bari (p. 626)
May 15	Corsa dei Ceri (Race of the Candles)	Gubbio (p. 514)
3rd week in May	Calvacata Sarda (Sardinian Cavalcade)	Sassari (p. 735)
Last Su in May (May 31, 2008)	Palio di San Giorgio	Ferrara (p. 398)
Last Su in May (May 31, 2008)	Palio dei Balestrieri (Crossbow Competition between Gubbio and Sansepolcro)	Gubbio (p. 514) Sansepolcro (p. 481)
50 days after Easter	Festa della Palombella (Pentecostal Festival of the Dove, or Holy Spirit)	Orvieto (p. 529)
June	Calcio Storico (old-fashioned soccer)	Florence (p. 464)
Early June	Giostra dell'Archidado (Crossbow Contest)	Cortona (p. 478)
June-July	Festival di Ravenna (classical music)	Ravenna (p. 414)
June-July	Festival dei Due Mondi (2 week Spoleto arts festival)	Spoleto (p. 525)
June-July	Mostra Internazionale del Nuovo Cinema (International New Cinema)	Pesaro (p. 532)
June-Sept.	Verona Opera Festival	Verona (p. 346)
June 2	Festa della Repubblica (Republic Day)	National Holiday
June 3	Festa della Madonna della Lettera	Messina (p. 684)
3rd Su in June (June 21, 2009) and 1st Su in Sept.	Giostra del Saracino (Joust of the Saracen)	Arezzo (p. 481)
June 24	Festa di San Giovanni Battista (Feast of St. John)	Florence (p. 454)
Last Su in June (June 28, 2009)	Gioco del Ponte (Battle of the Bridge)	Pisa (p. 495)
July	Festival di Musica Antica	Urbino (p. 532)
July	Umbria Jazz Festival	Perugia (p. 508)
July	Luglio Musicale Trapanese (July of Music in Trapani)	Trapani (p. 713)
July 2 and Aug. 16	Corsa del Palio	Siena (p. 464)
July 2	Festa della Madonna (Feast of the Virgin Mary)	Enna (p. 698)
2nd weekend in July	Pistoia Blues Festival	Pistoia (p. 484)
July 12 and Sept. 14	Palio della Balestra (Crossbow Contest)	Lucca (p. 490)
Mid-July	ArezzoWave Love Festival	Arezzo (p. 481)
Mid-July	International Jazz Festival	Pescara (p. 532)
3rd Su in July (July 19, 2009)	Festa del Redentore (Feast of the Redeemer)	Venice (p. 331)
July 25	Giostra del Orso (Joust of the Bear)	Pistoia (p. 484)
Last week of July	Giostra Cavalleresca di Sulmona (Horse Joust)	Sulmona (p. 553)
Last Su of July (July 26, 2009)	Festa di Sant'Anna	Enna (p. 698)
Early Aug. to Sept.	Rossini Opera Festival	Pesaro (p. 532)

DATE	FESTIVAL	LOCATION
1st Su in Aug. (Aug. 2, 2009)	Torneo della Quintana (Joust of the Quintana)	Ascoli Piceno (p. 544)
Aug. 13-15	Ferragosto Messinese, Processione dei Giganti	Messina (p. 684)
Aug. 13-15	Festa dei Martiri d'Otranto	Otranto (p. 640)
Aug. 14	Processione dei Candelieri (Procession of Candle Holders)	Sassari (p. 736)
Aug. 14-15	Sagra della Bistecca (Steak Feast)	Cortona (p. 478)
Aug. 15	Ferragosto (Feast of the Assumption)	National Holiday
Aug. 16 and July 2	Corsa del Palio	Siena (p. 464)
3rd Su of Aug. (Aug. 16, 2009)	Ceremonia della Rievocazione (Ceremony of the Revocation)	Urbino (p. 538)
Aug. 18-19	Festa dei Porcini (Porcini Mushroom Festival)	Cortona (p. 478)
Aug. 24	Festa di San Bartolomeo	Lipari (p. 672)
Last Su of Aug. (Aug. 30, 2009)	Festa della Madonna di Valverde	Enna (p. 698)
Late Aug.-Early Sept.	Venice International Film Festival	Venice (p. 331)
Sept.	Sagra Musicale Umbria (Umbrian Classical Music Festival)	Perugia (p. 509)
Early Sept.	Palio delle Balestre	San Marino (p. 425)
Sept. 3	San Marino Independence Day	San Marino (p. 425)
1st 2 weekends in Sept.	Festival del Prosciutto	Parma (p. 407)
1st Su in Sept. (Sept. 6, 2009)	Festa della Madonna dell'Altomare (Festival of the Virgin of the High Seas)	Otranto (p. 640)
1st Su in Sept. (Sept. 6, 2009)	Festa dell'Aquilone (Kite-flying Competition)	Urbino (p. 538)
1st Su in Sept. (Sept. 6, 2009)	Regata storica (Historical Regatta)	Venice (p. 331)
1st Su in Sept.; also 3rd Su in June	Giostra del Saracino (Joust of the Saracen)	Arezzo (p. 481)
2nd week of Sept.	Annuale della morte di Dante Alighieri (Dante Festival)	Ravenna (p. 414)
2nd and 3rd week of Sept.	D'ouja d'Or (Wine Festival)	Asti (p. 182)
Mid-Sept. (4 days)	Festa della Madonna della Consolazione	Reggio di Calabria (p. 643)
Sept. 13-22	Settembre Lucchese (Procession of the Holy Cross)	Lucca (p. 490)
Sept. 14; also July 12	Palio della Balestra (Crossbow Contest)	Lucca (p. 490)
Sept. 19	Festa di San Gennaro	Naples (p. 580)
3rd Su in Sept. (Sept. 20, 2009)	Palio di Asti	Asti (p. 182)
Early Oct.	Sagra dell'Anguilla (Festival of the Eel)	Ferrara (p. 398)

LIFE AND TIMES

DATE	FESTIVAL	LOCATION
Oct. 4	Festa di San Francesco	Assisi (p. 519)
Late Oct.	EuroChocolate Festival	Perugia (p. 509)
Nov. 1	Ognissanti (All Saints' Day)	National Holiday
Nov. 2	Giorno dei Morti (All Souls' Day)	National Holiday
Nov. 21	Festa della Salute	Venice (p. 331)
Dec. 8	Immacolata (Day of Immaculate Conception)	National Holiday
Dec. 13	Festa di Santa Lucia	Syracuse (p. 704)
Dec. 24	Le Farchie di Natale (Christmas Eve)	National Holiday
Dec. 25	Natale (Christmas Day)	National Holiday
Dec. 26	Festa di Santo Stefano (Saint Stephen's Day)	National Holdiay
Dec. 29-Jan. 1	Umbria Jazz Winter	Orvieto (p. 529)
Dec. 31	Festa di San Silvestro (New Year's Eve)	National Holiday

LIFE AND TIMES

BEYOND TOURISM

A PHILOSOPHY FOR TRAVELERS

> **HIGHLIGHTS OF BEYOND TOURISM IN ITALY**
>
> **TRACK** endangered dolphins near the volcanic island of Ischia (p. 94).
>
> **PLANT** grapevines on a vineyard in Naples recently reclaimed from the mob (p. 94).
>
> **LEARN LATIN** for free from Father Reginald Foster *et carpe diem* (p. 98).
>
> **COOK** traditional Tuscan cuisine with locals at culinary classes in Florence (p. 98).

As a tourist, you are always a foreigner. Sure, hostel-hopping and sightseeing can be great fun, but connecting with a foreign country through studying, volunteering, or working can extend your travels beyond tourist traps. We don't like to brag, but this is what's different about a *Let's Go* traveler. Instead of feeling like a stranger in a strange land, you can understand Italy like a local. Instead of being that tourist asking for directions, you can be the one who gives them (and correctly!). All the while, you get the satisfaction of leaving Italy in better shape than you found it (after all, it's being nice enough to let you stay here). It's not wishful thinking—it's Beyond Tourism.

As a **volunteer** in Italy, you can take part in everything from preserving rare Neolithic rock art in an alpine valley to teaching English to school children in Sardinia. This chapter is full of ideas on how to get involved, whether you're looking to pitch in for a day or run away from home for a whole new life in Italian activism. For even more regional Beyond Tourism opportunities, flip to our "Giving Back" sidebar features (p. 216, p. 651, and p. 716, p. 390).

The powers of **studying** abroad are beyond comprehension: it actually makes you feel sorry for those poor tourists who don't get to do any homework while they're here. Aside from being home to some of the oldest universities in Europe, Italy hosts a slew of unique educational institutions, from art schools in Florence to archaeological camps in Rome. A little research in advance is all you need to discover your ideal study abroad program.

Working abroad immerses you in a new culture and can bring some of the most meaningful relationships and experiences of your life. Yes, we know you're on vacation, but these aren't your normal desk jobs. (Plus, it doesn't hurt that it helps pay for more globetrotting.) Opportunities in Italy include interning at a museum in Venice or teaching English in schools around the country.

 SHARE YOUR EXPERIENCE. Have you had a particularly enjoyable volunteer, study, or work experience that you'd like to share with other travelers? Post it to our website, www.letsgo.com!

VOLUNTEERING

Feel like saving the world this week? Volunteering can be a powerful and fulfilling experience, especially when combined with the thrill of traveling in a new place. Whatever shape your philanthropic cravings may take, opportunities to satisfy them exist throughout Italy. As the former home to the ancient Etruscans, Greeks, and numerous iterations of the Roman Empire, Italy has more than its share of relics and tourists who want to explore them. As the country strives both to share its ancient treasures and protect them, demand is high for volunteers willing to assist in the preservation effort. Even with minimal prior experience, hundreds of opportunities exist for English speakers interested in the art, architecture, and culture of the many groups that have occupied the Italian peninsula throughout history.

Most people who volunteer in Italy do so on a short-term basis at organizations that make use of drop-in or once-a-week volunteers. The best way to find opportunities that match your interests and schedule may be to check with local or national volunteer centers similar to those listed below, which organize work camps devoted to a number of cultural and environmental causes. Opportunities range from programs for community development to camps dedicated to ecological and historical preservation. Demand for volunteers among these programs varies depending on the time of year and the duration of a volunteer's stay, so it's always best to check with an organization before making any definitive plans. As always, read up before heading out.

Those looking for longer, more intensive volunteer opportunities usually choose to go through a parent organization that takes care of logistical details and often provides a group environment and support system—for a fee. There are two main types of organizations—religious and secular—although there are rarely restrictions on participation for either. Websites like **www.volunteerabroad.com, www.servenet.org,** and **www.idealist.org** allow you to search for volunteer openings both in your country and abroad.

ECOTOURISM

Italy's expansive coastline and mild mainland environment play host to thousands of visitors annually. Tourists and locals alike are able to play a role in preserving the environment that has made Italy such a popular travel destination. Taking advantage of opportunities to work with wildlife and restore local habitats can be a great way to experience Italian culture at its best.

Via dei Sediari,
8 00186 Roma
Tel. +39 06 6864203
www.hotelnavona.com

Hotel Navona is situated in the historical center of
Rome, only a few steps away from the splendid Piazza
Navona, an ancient palace of the 1400s where you can
see Roman ruins.

Our convenient location also allows you to reach the
beautiful squares and famous monuments of Rome in just
a few minutes. The Pantheon, the Trevi Fountain, Piazza
di Spagna, St. Peter's and the Colosseum are all easily
accessible and just a stone's throw from Hotel Navona.

Elegantly restructured with care given to every detail,
Hotel Navona offers spacious rooms designed with
ancient caisson ceilings and delicate frescoes and
equipped with every modern amenity—satellite TV, air
conditioning, safes, hair dryers and telephones.

Singles: 90-120 €
Doubles: 120-150 €
Triples: 170-190 €

Benvenuto!

Residenza Zanardelli is an intimate, family-run, 4 star hotel located in the
historical center of Rome. Many well-known sites and monuments,
including St. Peter's Basilica, the Pantheon, the Trevi Fountain, and the
Spanish Steps, are within walking distance.

The hotel is a palazzo constructed in the "Barocchetto Romano" style, one
of the architectural designs most characteristic of the late 19th century in
Rome.

Newly renovated and beautifully furnished rooms await our guests. Each
room has its own private bathroom, satellite plasma TV, telephone and air
conditioning.

Several of the rooms have a direct view of the Palazzo Altemps, which has a
wonderful collection of ancient sculpture.

Residenza Zanardelli

Canadian Alliance for Development Initiatives and Projects (CADIP), 129-1271 Howe St., Vancouver, British Columbia, V6Z 1R3, Canada (☎+1-604-628-7400; www.cadip.org). Offers over 100 2- to 3-week projects in Italy with an emphasis on environmental and historical preservation. Room and board provided by the program. Most projects 18+. US$285; some projects have extra fees.

Ecovolunteer: Common Dolphin Research, CTS-Centro Turistico Studentesco e Giovanile, Dept. Ambiente, V. Albalonga 3, 00183 Rome (☎06 64 96 03 27; www.ecovolunteer.org). Volunteers in the Gulf of Naples live on a research boat while tracking dolphins and other marine mammals. 1-week programs June-Oct. 18+. Program fee €750-850 per week. Student discounts available.

Greenwood Cooperation Society (Società Cooperativa Greenwood), V. Pozzillo 21, 87045 Dipignano (☎0984 44 55 26; www.scgreenwood.it). Conducts research in National Park of Calabria and encourages ecotourism. Volunteers help with ecological studies, like studying and tracking wolves with GPS devices and topographic maps. Check website for current studies. €350 covers food, camping, and research supplies.

Lega Italiana Protezione Uccelli (LIPU), LIPU Sede Nazionale, V. Trento 49, 43100 Parma (☎05 21 27 30 43; www.lipu.it/tu_voluntario.htm). Volunteers at this bird sanctuary nurse injured animals back to health and help with grounds maintenance.

Parco Nazionale d'Abruzzo, Lazio e Molise, V. Roma s.n.c., 67030 Villetta Barrea, AQ (☎08 64 89 102; www.parcoabruzzo.it). Hosts over 100 summer volunteers for 1-3 weeks. Responsibilities range from park maintenance to visitor assistance. 18+. Program fee 1 week €110, 2 weeks €170, 3 weeks €230.

World-Wide Opportunities on Organic Farms (WWOOF Italia), V. Casavecchia 109, 57022 Castagneto Carducci, Livorno (www.wwoof.it). Provides a list of organic farms that introduce volunteers to tasks like harvesting olives, grapes, and even bamboo. Knowledge of farming not necessary, although volunteers should be physically capable and willing to work hard. Required €25 membership fee.

ART, CULTURE, AND RESTORATION

Italy's rich cultural heritage, which dates back to Ancient Rome, is increasingly in danger of crumbling or being overrun by modern life. Volunteers looking for a labor-intensive way to engage with Italy's historical past should research groups that specialize in landmark preservation.

Archeo Venezia, Cannaregio 1376/a, 30121 Venezia (☎41 71 05 15; www.archeove.com). Offers 1-week programs in archeological field work, including ceramics, metalwork, and painting. €150-330. Fee includes room and board.

Footsteps of Man, Ple. Donatori di Sangue 1, 25040 Cerveno, Brescia, Italy (☎03 64 43 39 83; www.rupestre.net/field/index.html). Accepts volunteers for a minimum stay of 7 days to analyze rock art in the Italian Alps, with over 300,000 samples dating from the Neolithic era to the Middle Ages. Training provided. 16+. €370 per week.

ResponsibleTravel.com, 3rd Floor, Pavilion House, 6 Old Steine, Brighton BN1 1EJ, UK (☎+44-127-360-0030; www.responsibletravel.com). Various volunteer opportunities including cultural and environmental preservation projects of variable length. Program fee €460-975, depending on project.

YOUTH AND THE COMMUNITY

Community-based projects are among the most rewarding volunteer experiences. Programs listed below promote interactive humanitarian work through

English language programs and projects aimed at assisting the disadvantaged. Due to their one-on-one nature, knowledge of Italian is often necessary.

Agape Centro Ecumenico, Segreteria di Agape, Borgata Agape 1, 10060 Prali, Torino (☎01 21 80 75 14; www.agapecentroecumenico.org). Help maintain this international Protestant conference center in the Italian Alps. Clean and cook for the center for as little as 2 days to as long as 5 weeks in return for free room and board during spring and summer. Knowledge of Italian useful. 18+.

Global Volunteers, 375 East Little Canada Rd., St. Paul, MN 55117, USA (☎+1-800-487-1074; www.globalvolunteers.org). Teach English to students in southern Italy. 2-week sessions available throughout the year. Program fee US$2695-2995.

Pueblo Inglés, Rafael Calvo 18, 4A, Madrid 28010, Spain (☎+34 913 913 400; www.puebloingles.com). Week-long program in Umbria hires native English-speaking volunteers to provide English-language immersion for Italians. Room and board provided. Ages 22-80; alternative opportunities for ages 13-18. Free.

Service Civil International, 5505 Walnut Level Rd., Crozet, VA 22932, USA (☎+1-434-823-9003; www.sci-ivs.org). Places volunteers in small, 2- to 4-week work camps that range from festival assistance to social work to environmental or historical restoration. Long-term opportunities are also available. 18+. Program fee €50-150.

United Planet, 11 Arlington St., Boston, MA 02116, USA (☎+1-617-267-7763; www.unitedplanet.org). Places volunteers in 6-month to 1-year programs, including many aimed at helping children and the disabled in Italy. 18+. Maximum age varies by program. Fee of US$5000 for 6 months and $8000 for 1 year includes local transportation costs, training, a monthly stipend, and room and board with a host family.

Volunteers for Peace, 1034 Tiffany R., Belmont, VT 05730, USA (☎+1-802-259-2759; www.vfp.org). Provides info on volunteer programs. Most programs 18+. Program fee US$300.

STUDYING

It's hard to dread the first day of school when Rome is your campus and heaping bowls of *pasta al dente* and creamy *gelato alla fragola* make up your meal plan. A growing number of students report that studying abroad is the highlight of their university, or post-educational experience. If you've never studied abroad, you don't know what you're missing—and if you have studied abroad, your former destination certainly could not hold a candle to Italy's many sunny cities. Either way, opportunities to immerse yourself in *la dolce vita italiana*—while hitting the books every once and awhile—can be found in every corner of the beautiful, bold, and boisterous boot.

Study-abroad programs range from basic language and culture courses to university-level classes, often for college credit. In order to choose a program that best fits your needs, research as much as you can before making your decision—determine costs and duration, as well as what kind of students participate in the program and what sorts of accommodations are provided.

In programs that have large groups of students who speak the same language, there is a trade-off. You may feel more comfortable in the community, but you will not have the same opportunity to practice a foreign language or to befriend other international students. For accommodations, dorm life provides a better opportunity to mingle with fellow students, but there is less of a chance to experience the local scene. If you live with a family, you could potentially build lifelong friendships with natives and experience day-to-day life in more depth, but you might also get stuck sharing a room with their pet iguana. Conditions can vary greatly from family to family.

VISA INFORMATION. Italian bureaucracy often gives international visitors the run-around, but there are ways to minimize paperwork confusion. Just remember that all **non-EU citizens** are required to obtain a visa for any stay longer than three months. For info and applications, contact the Italian embassy or consulate in your country. Before applying for a student visa, however, be sure to obtain the following documentation: valid passport, visa application form (available from most embassy websites), four passport-size photographs, proof of residency, and complete documentation on the course or program in which you are participating. If you are under the age of 18, you will also need an affidavit of financial support from parents, and your parents' most recent bank statement. All **non-EU citizens** are also required to register with the *Ufficio degli Stranieri* (Foreigners' Bureau) at the *questura* (local police headquarters) to receive a *permesso di soggiorno* (permit to stay) within eight days of arrival. The kit required to complete the *permesso di soggiorno* can be obtained and submitted at most major *ufficio postali* (post offices). The same documentation is necessary for the *permesso di soggiorno* as for the visa; additionally, applicants must have the required *permesso di soggiorno* form and a *Marco da Bollo*, which costs €15 and is available at most Italian *tabaccherie*. **EU citizens** must apply for a *permesso di soggiorno* within three months, but they do not need a visa to study in Italy. Once you find a place to live, bring your *permesso di soggiorno* (it must have at least one year's validity) to a records office. This certificate will both confirm your registered address and expedite travel into and out of Italy.

UNIVERSITIES

Most university-level study-abroad programs are conducted in Italian, but many programs offer classes in English as well as lower-level language courses. Savvy linguists may find it cheaper to enroll directly in a university abroad, although getting college credit may be more difficult. You can search **www.studyabroad.com** for various semester-abroad programs that meet your criteria, including your desired location and focus of study. If you're a college student, your friendly neighborhood study-abroad office is often the best place to start.

AMERICAN PROGRAMS

American Institute for Foreign Study (AIFS), College Division, River Plaza, 9 W. Broad St., Stamford, CT 06902, USA (☎+1-800-727-2437; www.aifsabroad.com). Organizes programs for high-school and college study in universities in Italy.

CET Academic Programs: Italian Studies Program in Siena, Florence, and Sicily, 1920 N St. NW, Ste. 200, Washington, D.C. 20036, USA (☎+1-800-225-4262; www.cetacademicprograms.com). Only open to the public for the summer term, this Vanderbilt University program offers art history courses and traveling seminars. Summer program US$7790-8490. Includes medical insurance and housing.

Council on International Educational Exchange (CIEE), 300 Fore St., Portland, ME 04101, USA (☎+1-207-553-4000 or +1-800-40-STUDY/407-8839; www.ciee.org). A comprehensive resource for work, academic, and internship programs in Italy.

International Association for the Exchange of Students for Technical Experience (IAESTE), Politecnico di Milano, Centro per le Relazioni Internazionali, Piazza Leonardo da Vinci 32, 20133 Milan (☎2 23 99 97 64; www.iaeste.org). Offers hands-on technical internships in Italy. You must be a college student studying science, technology, or engineering. Most programs last 8-12 weeks.

School for International Training (SIT) Study Abroad, 1 Kipling Rd., P.O. Box 676, Brattleboro, VT 05302, USA (☎+1-888-272-7881 or +1-802-258-3212; www.sit.edu/studyabroad). Semester-long programs cost about US$6800. Also runs **The Experiment in International Living** (☎+1-800-345-2929; www.usexperiment.org), which offers 3- to 5-week summer programs for high-school students that involve cross-cultural home-stays, community service, ecological adventure, and language training. US$6800.

LANGUAGE SCHOOLS

Enrolling at a language school has two major perks: a slightly less rigorous courseload and the ability to teach you exactly what those kids in Milan are calling you under their breath. There can be great variety in language schools—independently run, affiliated with a larger university, local, international—but one thing is constant: they rarely offer college credit. Their programs are also good for younger high-school students who might not feel comfortable with older students in a university program.

Centro Culturale Giaccomo Puccini, V. Amerigo Vespucci 173, 55049 Viareggio (☎05 84 43 02 53; www.centropuccini.it). 2- to 24- week language courses at all levels. Professional Italian and cultural courses available. 16+. Additional accommodations fee for apartment or homestay. Program costs €260-2520. €70 registration fee.

Centro Fiorenza, V.S. Spirito 14, 50125 Florence (☎05 52 39 82 74; www.centrofiorenza.com). Students live in Florence and are immersed in Italian. Program also offers courses on the island of Elba, although hotel accommodations there are expensive. 1- to 5-week course (20 lessons per week) from €185. Enrollment fee €55.

Eurocentres, 56 Eccleston Sq., London SW1V 1PH, UK (☎+44 20 7963 8450; www.eurocentres.com). Language programs with homestays in Florence.

Istituto Venezia, Campo S. Margherita 3116/a, Dorsoduro, 30123 Venice (☎04 15 22 43 31; www.istitutovenezia.com). Language and art history classes at all levels, taught in small groups. Courses 1-24 weeks. Language classes also taught in Trieste. Accommodation arrangements upon request; costs and housing types vary, but start at €220.

Italiaidea, V. dei Due Macelli 47, 1st fl., 00187 Rome (☎06 60 94 13 14; www.italiaidea.com). 1-week to 6-month Italian language and culture courses near the Spanish Steps for individuals and groups of 10 or fewer. Courses qualify for credit at many American universities. Students live in private homes, homestay, or apartments; reserve ahead. Program costs €300-1200. €50 registration fee.

Koinè, V. de' Pandolfini 27, I-50122 Florence (☎05 52 13 881; wwww.koinecenter.com). Language lessons (group and individual), cultural lessons, wine tastings, and cooking lessons. Courses offered in Florence, Lucca, Bologna, Cortona, and Elba. 1-4 week courses €190-4780. Accommodations not included. Deposit €150.

Language Immersion Institute, State University of New York at New Paltz, 1 Hawk Dr., New Paltz, NY 12561, USA (☎+1-845-257-3500; www.newpaltz.edu/lii). Short, intensive summer language courses and some overseas courses in Italian. Program fees are around US$1000 for a 2-week course, not including accommodations.

ITALIAN SCHOOLS: SPECIAL INTEREST

FINE ARTS

Aegean Center for the Fine Arts, Paros 84400, Cyclades, Greece (☎+30 22 84 02 32 87; www.aegeancenter.org). Italian branch located in Pistoia. Instruction in arts, literature, creative writing, voice, and art history. Classes taught in English. Fees cover housing in 16th-century villa, meals, and excursions to Rome, Venice, and Greece. University credit on individual arrangement. 14-week program in the fall €8500.

Art School in Florence, Studio Art Centers International, Palazzo dei Cartelloni, Via Sant'Antonio 11, 50123 Florence (☎+1-212-248-7225; www.saci-florence.org). Affiliated with Bowling Green State University. Studio arts, art history, Italian studies. Apartment housing. 6 credits summer US$5550; 15 credits semester US$14,900.

Scuola Arte del Mosaico, V. Francesco Negri 14, 48110 Ravenna (☎34 96 01 45 66; www.sira.it/mosaic/studio.htm). Participants learn the history and techniques behind both ancient and modern mosaics, and get to create their own. 5-day course (40hr.) for beginner and intermediate levels conducted in English. Program fee €660.

COOKING IN LA CUCINA

Apicius, The Culinary Institute of Florence, V. Guelfa 85, Florence 50129 (☎05 52 65 81 35; www.apicius.it). Professional and non-professional food and wine studies in historic Florence. Cooking courses in English; Italian language classes available. Prices for weekly, non-professional programs €1265-5750. Include room and board. Masters in Italian cuisine €10,550. Enrollment fee €115.

Cook Italy, (☎34 90 07 82 98; www.cookitaly.com). Region- or dish-specific cooking classes. Venues include Bologna, Cortona, Florence, Lucca, Rome, and Sicily. Courses 3- to 6- nights from €950. Housing, meals, and recipes included.

The International Kitchen, 330. N. Wabash #2613, Chicago, IL 60611, USA (☎+1-800-945-8606; www.theinternationalkitchen.com). A leading provider of cooking school vacations to Italy. Traditional cooking instruction in beautiful settings for individuals and groups. Program locations include the Amalfi Coast, Liguria, Tuscany, and Venice. Courses 2-10 nights. Programs start at US$400.

ROCKIN' RELICS

Aestiva Romae Latinitatis, Summer Latin in Rome, P. Reginald Foster OCD, Tersianum, P. S. Pancrazio 5A, I-00152 Rome. Free 6-week summer Latin program in Rome with legendary Father Reginald Foster, an American priest who works in the "Latin Letters" section of the Vatican's Secretariat of State. Foster has taught this program for nearly 25 years. Lessons in written and conversational Latin for intermediate and advanced students. Optional lesson "sub arboribus" (under the trees in the monastery garden) given in the evenings. Write for info and application materials.

ArchaeoSpain, PO Box 1331, Farmington, CT 06034 USA (☎+1-866-932-003; www.archaeospain.com). Archeology buffs help out in Rome at Monte Testaccio. Once an ancient pottery dump, the site is now the best record of ancient Roman commerce. English speakers and all ages welcome. University credit on individual arrangement. 2-week program US$2745. Housing and meals included.

WORKING

Nowhere does money grow on trees (though *Let's Go*'s researchers aren't done looking), but there are still some pretty good opportunities to earn a living and

BEYOND TOURISM

travel at the same time. As with volunteering, work opportunities tend to fall into two categories. Some travelers want long-term jobs that allow them to integrate into a community, while others seek out short-term jobs to finance the next leg of their travels. In Italy, short-term work in agriculture, the service sector, and tourism is the easiest to come by. Though job hunters must navigate the inevitable challenge of Italy's soaring unemployment rates and the premium that Italian employers place on both practical experience and advanced degrees, take heart: with a little research in advance, long-term opportunities are not out of the realm of possibility. **Transitions Abroad** (www.transitionsabroad.com) offers updated online listings for work over any time span.

Check out weekly job listings in *Corriere della Sera*'s "Corriere Lavoro" (online at trovolavoro.it) or *Il Sole 24 Ore*'s "Cercolavoro Giovani," which specializes in listings for recent university graduates. **GoAbroad.com** (www.internabroad.com/Italy.cfm) has a user-friendly online database of internship listings in Italy. **Youth Info Centers Informagiovani** (www.informagiovani-italia.com) in each region target both Italians and visitors and offer free information on work regulations, employment trends, volunteer programs, and study opportunities. Note that working abroad often requires a special work visa.

MORE VISA INFORMATION. Working legally in Italy as a foreigner is a bureaucratic challenge regardless of your nationality. **EU passport holders** do not require a special visa to live or work in Italy. They do require a permit to stay *(permesso di soggiorno per lavoro)*, which grants permission to remain in Italy for the duration of employment. To obtain a *permesso di soggiorno*, EU citizens must register at the local police headquarters *(questura)* within eight days of arrival for a permit to search for work *(ricevuta di segnalazione di siggiorno)*. **Non-EU citizens** seeking work in Italy must possess an Italian work permit *(autorizzazione al lavoro in Italia)* before entering the country. Only a prospective employer can begin the process, guaranteeing that the individual has been offered a position. Permits are authorized by the Provincial Employment Office and approved by the police headquarters before being forwarded to the employer and prospective employee. The prospective employee must then present the document, along with a valid passport, in order to obtain a work visa. **Non-EU citizens** must also obtain both the *permesso di soggiorno* and a workers' registration card—*libretto di lavoro*—which will function as an employment record for up to ten years. Visit the **Italian Ministry of Foreign Afffairs** website (www.esteri.it) or the **US Embassy** site (http://italy.usembassy.gov) for more information.

BEYOND TOURISM

LONG-TERM WORK

If you're planning on spending a substantial amount of time (more than 3 months) working in Italy, search for a job well in advance. International placement agencies are often the easiest way to find employment abroad, especially for those interested in teaching. Although they are often only available to college students, **internships** are a good way to ease into working abroad. Many say the interning experience is well worth it, despite low pay (if you're lucky enough to be paid at all). Because Italian students typically spend more years in university than their American, British, and Australian counterparts, *stage* (internships) are not as prevalent. Strong language skills will certainly make you a more desirable candidate. Be wary of advertisements for companies claiming to be able get you a job abroad for a fee—often the same listings are available online or in newspapers. Some reputable organizations and resources for student internships and job opportunities in Italy include:

Center for Cultural Interchange, 746 N. LaSalle Dr., Chicago, IL 60610, USA (☎312-944-2544; www.cci-exchange.com/abroad/intern.shtml). 1-3 month volunteer internships in Florence. Opportunities in business, accounting and finance, tourism, and social service. At least 2 years of college-level Italian required. US$7090-10,590. Tuition includes Italian language course, health insurance, and homestay with half-board.

English Yellow Pages, V. Belisario 4/B, 00187 Rome (☎06 474 0861 and 06 97 61 75 28; www.englishyellowpages.it). Resources for English-speaking expats in Italy run by an American who relocated to Italy in 1982 to teach English. Includes job listings, classifieds, photos, blogs, and more.

Global Experiences, 168 West St., Annapolis, MD 21401, USA (☎877-432-27623; www.globalexperiences.com). Arranges internships with companies in Florence, Rome, Verona, and Milan. Fields include law, international business, tourism, graphic design, and fashion. 8-week programs start at €4000 and include intensive language training, accommodation, emergency medical travel insurance, and full-time on-site support.

Institute for the International Education of Students, 33 N. LaSalle St., 15th fl., Chicago, IL 60602, USA (☎800-995-2300; www.iesabroad.org). Internships for academic credit in Rome, Milan, and Siena based on availability, background, skills, and language ability. Past assignments in fashion, photography, journalism, business consulting, and psychological research. Semester-long programs from around US$17,000. Includes tuition for up to 19 credits, orientation, housing, and medical insurance.

Peggy Guggenheim Collection, Palazzo Venier dei Leoni, Dorsoduro 701, 30123 Venice (☎041 2405 401; www.guggenheim-venice.it). Interns assist museum operations such as gallery preparation, tour guidance, workshops with children, and administrative matters for 1-3 months. Offers a stipend. Italian skills a plus.

World Endeavors, 3015 E. Franklin Ave., Minneapolis, MN 55406, USA (☎+1-866-802-9678; www.worldendeavors.com/Italy). 3- to 6-month internships in Florence in a wide variety of fields from craft apprenticeships to sports management with professional football teams. 4-month internships start at US$4700 and include intensive Italian training and various English-speaking support services.

TEACHING ENGLISH

While some elite private American schools offer competitive salaries, let's just say that teaching jobs abroad pay more in personal satisfaction and emotional fulfillment than in actual cash. Perhaps this is why volunteering as a teacher instead of getting paid is a popular option. Even then, teachers often receive some sort of a daily stipend to help with living expenses. In almost all cases, you must have at least a bachelor's degree to be a full-fledged teacher, although college undergraduates can often get summer positions teaching or tutoring. Though the demand for English teachers in Italy is high, the competition is stiff. Finding a teaching job as a non-EU citizen can be especially tough. Beyond the usual difficulty of obtaining permits, many language schools require EU citizenship and most prefer British citizens to other English speakers.

Many schools require teachers to have a **Teaching English as a Foreign Language (TEFL)** certificate. You may still be able to find a teaching job without one, but certified teachers often find higher-paying jobs. Some schools within Italy that grant TEFLs will even offer both classroom instruction and practical experience or a leg up in job placement when you earn your certificate. The Italian-impaired don't have to give up their dream of teaching, either. Private schools usually hire native English speakers for English-immersion classrooms where no Italian is spoken. (Teachers in public schools will more likely work in both English and Italian.) Placement agencies or university fellowship programs are the best resources for finding teaching jobs. The alternative is to contact schools directly or to try your luck once you arrive in Italy. In the latter case, the best time to look is several weeks before the start of the school year, or as early as February or March for summer positions. The following organizations are extremely helpful in placing teachers in Italy.

Associazione Culturale Linguista Educational (ACLE), V. Roma 54, 18038 San Remo, Imperio (☎01 84 50 60 70; www.acle.org). Non-profit association working to bring theater, arts, and English language instruction to Italian schools. Employees create theater programs in schools, teach English at summer camps, and help convert a medieval home into a student art center. Knowledge of Italian useful. On-site accommodations and cooking facilities included. Ages 20-30. Camp counselor salary of €220-260.

International Schools Services (ISS), 15 Roszel Rd., P.O. Box 5910, Princeton, NJ 08543, USA (☎+1-609-452-0990; www.iss.edu). Hires teachers for more than 200 overseas schools, including in Italy. Candidates should have teaching experience and a bachelor's degree. 2-year commitment is the norm.

Office of Overseas Schools, US Department of State, 2201 C St. NW, Washington, D.C. 20520, USA (☎+1-202-647-4000; www.state.gov/m/a/os). Provides an extensive list of general info about teaching overseas. See also the **Office of English Language Programs** (http://exchanges.state.gov/education/engteaching).

AU PAIR WORK

Au pairs are typically women (although sometimes men) aged 18-27 who work as live-in nannies, caring for children and doing light housework in foreign countries in exchange for room, board, and a small spending allowance or stipend. One perk of the job is that it allows you to get to know Italy without the high expenses of traveling. Drawbacks, however, can include mediocre pay and long hours. Unfortunately, with the recent adoption of laws that severely limit the availability of work visas for non-EU citizens in Italy, au pairing has become less common, especially for stays longer than 3 months (the maximum visa-free visiting period). The Italian government will not grant au pair-specific visas so it is imperative that au pairs take necessary steps with prospective employers to obtain work permits and visas (see **More Visa Information,** p. 99). In Italy, average weekly pay for au pair work is about €65. Much of the au pair experience depends on the family with which you are placed. The agencies below are a good starting point for looking for employment.

Childcare International, Trafalgar House, Grenville Pl., London NW7 3SA, UK (☎+44 20 8906 3116; www.childint.co.uk).

InterExchange, 161 6th Ave., New York City, NY 10013, USA (☎+1-212-924-0446 or 800-AU-PAIRS/287-2477; www.interexchange.org).

Roma Au Pair, V. Pietro Mascagni 138, 00199 Rome (☎33 97 79 41 26; www.romaaupair.it). Provides information on au pair placement throughout Italy.

SHORT-TERM WORK

Believe it or not, traveling for long periods of time can be hard on the wallet. Many travelers try their hand at odd jobs for a few weeks at a time to help pay for another month or two of touring around. Romantic images of cultivating the land in a sun-soaked vineyard may dance in your head, but in reality, casual agricultural jobs are hard to find in Italy due to the prevalence of foreign migrant workers who are often willing to work for minimal pay. Those looking for agricultural jobs will have the best luck looking in the northwest during the annual fall harvest or volunteer with **WWOOF** (p. 94). Another popular option is to work several hours a day at a hostel in exchange for free or discounted room and/or board. Most often, these short-term jobs are found by word of mouth or by expressing interest to the owner of a hostel or restaurant. Due to high turnover in the tourism industry, many places are eager for help, even if it is only temporary. *Let's Go* lists temporary jobs of this nature whenever possible; look in the Practical Information sections of larger cities.

FURTHER READING ON BEYOND TOURISM

Alternatives to the Peace Corps: A Guide of Global Volunteer Opportunities, edited by Paul Backhurst. Food First, 2005 (US$12).

The Back Door Guide to Short-Term Job Adventures: Internships, Summer Jobs, Seasonal Work, Volunteer Vacations, and Transitions Abroad, by Michael Landes. Ten Speed Press, 2005 (US$22).

Green Volunteers: The World Guide to Voluntary Work in Nature Conservation, by Fabio Ausenda. Universe, 2007 (US$15).

How to Get a Job in Europe, by Cheryl Matherly and Robert Sanborn. Planning Communications, 2003 (US$23).

How to Live Your Dream of Volunteering Overseas, by Joseph Collins, Stefano DeZerega, and Zahara Heckscher. Penguin Books, 2001 (US$20).

International Job Finder: Where the Jobs Are Worldwide, by Daniel Lauber and Kraig Rice. Planning Communications, 2002 (US$20).

Live and Work Abroad: A Guide for Modern Nomads, by Huw Francis and Michelyne Callan. Vacation Work Publications, 2001 (US$20).

Volunteer Vacations: Short-Term Adventures That Will Benefit You and Others, by Doug Cutchins, Anne Geissinger, and Bill McMillon. Chicago Review Press, 2006 (US$18).

Work Abroad: The Complete Guide to Finding a Job Overseas, edited by Clayton A. Hubbs. Transitions Abroad, 2002 (US$16).

Work Your Way Around the World, by Susan Griffith. Vacation Work Publications, 2007 (US$22).

Saving Alta Irpinia
How Ecotourism Might Save One of Italy's Poorest Regions

Anywhere but these rolling hills of wheat. Such a thought is not uncommon in Alta Irpinia, a region in Campania. Here, the problems that mark the entire South are exacerbated by the mountainous terrain that makes agriculture unprofitable, unlike in the fertile Puglian plains. Modern industry and economy have failed here, and the few factories that once provided jobs are moving overseas. Unemployment is around 20%. In addition, Irpinia is at high seismic risk. The effects of the terrible earthquake of November 1980, which claimed 5000 lives and completely destroyed 30 towns, are still visible. While government subsidies flowed in to revitalize the region, there was little long-term success. In recent years, Irpinia's best and brightest have migrated to Naples or north to Turin or Milan. Those who remain are faced with an obsolete traditional lifestyle and continued, ineffective attempts to adopt more modern ways.

Some Irpinians believe that their traditional culture is worth fighting for. A new buzzword, agriturismo, or ecotourism, denotes this push to save Irpinia by moving closer to nature and to rural ways of life. The region's riches include beautiful mountains, famous wines, archaeological sites, and ancient castles and churches. Not all was destroyed by earthquakes or by building speculation, although often the potential of a site is wasted because of a lack of resources to develop it. A number of castles dot a region once ruled by the medieval court of Frederick II. The medieval period also left behind many churches and monasteries, but archaeological sites are Irpinia's real hidden treasure. Prior to the Roman invasion, a local population of Sannites flourished here. Little is known about them, as there have never been funds to excavate the region

properly. The situation is a vicious circle: without fully developed cultural sites, there will be no tourism; yet without a tourist industry, there will never be money to excavate ruins or restore churches.

The Zampaglione family is a good example of a business that has completely embraced the agriturismo ethos. Their farm near Calitri has produced organic wheat since 1990, which is then made into organic pasta. In 1998 they transformed their old barns into a guesthouse. A visit to the Zampaglione farm presents northern Italians with the chance to connect to the rural culture of their grandparents. The Zampagliones also hope to attract international travelers who already know Italy and wish to see the country from a different angle. However, often weeks pass when no one ventures to the farm, and the post-9/11 tourism slump has not helped.

Ethnographic museums have been more successful in taking root and matching the ideals of agriturismo. Museums attempt to preserve and

> ## "A new buzzword, *agriturismo,* or ecotourism, denotes [a] push to save Irpinia."

present what is known of traditional village culture. Visitors are fascinated by the handicrafts, such as ceramics, still practiced in Irpinia. Yet, industrial procedures threaten to replace these ancient crafts. The last original practitioners of Irpinian pottery fire their pots only once a year in a large, purpose-built oven, which is then destroyed. Local cuisine, fortunately, does not face the same risk, as the healthy, rural diet strong in fresh pastas and cheeses continues to thrive.

Agriturismo is still the work of individuals, and does not reflect a greater policy on the part of the Avellino province. Nonetheless, agriturismo is an important validation for those who refuse to modernize or leave.

Alexander Bevilacqua was born in Milan and has lived in Germany, Australia, and the United States, but his heart remains in the wheat fields of southern Italy. He is a 2006 graduate in history from Harvard University, and was a Researcher-Writer for Let's Go: Germany 2005 in Bavaria.

ROME

ROME (ROMA)   ☎ 06

The sight of the Eternal City is daunting, whether you're an old hand or are taking it in for the first time. Rome (RO-ma; pop. 2.8 million) is a city of constant renewal. Crumbling pagan ruins are the backdrop, and often the main stage, for the buildings of the Papacy, while hip, modern clubs and bars buzz alongside grand cathedrals. Though inextricably linked to its past, Rome lives in the present and often surges toward the future. The aroma of homemade pasta, the friendly tinkling of wine glasses, and the hum of vespa engines will greet you at every turn on Rome's maze of cobblestone. Augustus once boasted that he found Rome a city of brick and left it one of marble. No matter how you find it, you'll undoubtedly leave it with a new appreciation for *"la dolce vita."*

HIGHLIGHTS OF ROME

CHANNEL Rome's Golden Age with a trip to the Ancient City (p. 127).

SURVEY Rome's art scene, and let collections from the Vatican Museums (p. 146) to the Galleria Borghese (p. 148) prove the city deserving of its reputation.

TOSS a coin into the Trevi Fountain for a speedy return to the Eternal City (p. 135).

EVADE the temptations of Circe on the Pontine Islands (p. 160), where the likes of Mussolini, Nero, and even Odysseus were reputedly held captive.

✈ INTERCITY TRANSPORTATION

FLIGHTS

Most international flights arrive at **Da Vinci International Airport,** known as **Fiumicino** (☎ 06 65 21 01). After exiting customs, follow the signs for **Stazione Trenitalia/Railway Station.** The **Termini line** (the colorful Leonardo Express) runs nonstop to Rome's main train station, **Termini** (30min., 2 per hr., 6:35am-11:35pm, €11). Buy a ticket at the Trenitalia ticket counter, the *tabaccheria* on the right, or from one of the machines in the station. Beware of scam artists attempting to sell fake tickets. A train leaves Termini for Fiumicino from track #24 (30min., 2 per hr., 5:52am-10:52pm; €12). Buy tickets at the Railway Information Center (open 7am-9:45pm), by track #4, at the Leonardo Express kiosk on track #24, or from other designated areas in the station. Failure to validate your ticket in one of the yellow machines before boarding could lead to a €50 fine.

EARLY AND LATE FLIGHTS. For flights that arrive after 10:30pm or leave before 8am, the most reliable option to go between Rome and the airport is a **taxi.** (Request one at the kiosk in the airport or call ☎ 06 49 94 or 66 45.) **Decide upon a price with the driver before getting into the cab**—it should be around €40. Factors such as the amount of luggage and the time of day will affect the price. The cheapest option is to take the blue **COTRAL bus** (☎ 06 80 01 50 008) outside the main exit doors after customs to Tiburtina (1:15, 2:15, 3:30, 5am; €5 onboard). From Tiburtina, take buses #492 or 175 or Metro B to Termini. To get

to Fiumicino from Rome late at night or early in the morning, take bus #492 or 40N (which takes over for Metro B at night) from Termini to Tiburtina (every 20-30min.), then catch the blue COTRAL bus to Fiumicino from the *piazza* (12:30, 1:15, 2:30, 3:45am; €5). The **24hr. airport shuttle** service (☎06 47 40 451 or 42 01 34 69; www.airportshuttle.it) is a good deal for two or more. Call or visit the website to reserve a spot. (€28 from Fiumicino to the city center, each additional passenger €6; early mornings, nights, and holidays prices rise 30%.)

CIAMPINO AIRPORT. Most charter flights and a few domestic ones, including **Ryanair,** arrive at **Ciampino Airport** (☎06 79 49 41). To get to Rome from Ciampino, take the **COTRAL bus** (every 30min. 6:10am-11:40pm, €1) to Anagnina station on Metro A. The public shuttle buses (☎06 59 16 826; www.sitbusshuttle. com) or the **Terravision Shuttle** (☎06 79 34 17 22; www.terravision.it) are slightly more convenient options, especially for late or early flights. They both go to V. Marsala, outside Termini, at the Hotel Royal Santina (40min.; 25 per day per carrier, first shuttles to Ciampino 4:30am, last shuttles to Rome around midnight; public shuttle €5, Terravision €5). Schedules are online and at the hotel. After 11pm and before 7am, take a **taxi** (€35-40).

TRAINS

Stazione Termini is the train and subway hub, though it's closed between midnight and 5:30am. During this time trains usually arrive at Stazione Tiburtina or Stazione Ostiense; both connect to Termini at night by bus #175. Station services include: shopping; **ATMs;** hotel reservations, across from track #13; **luggage storage,** underneath track #24; **police,** track #13, make a report at track #1. Termini's **bathrooms** (€0.70) beneath track #1 are a surreal black-lit wonderland. Trains (Direct, or D, is the slowest; IC is the intercity train; ES, or Eurostar, is the fastest and most expensive) leave Termini for: **Bologna** (IC 3hr., €33; ES 2hr., €42); **Florence** (D 3hr., €14; IC 2hr., €24; ES 1hr., €33); **Milan** (D 8hr., €30; IC 6hr., €41; ES 4hr., €50); **Naples** (D 2hr., €10; IC 2hr., €19; ES 1hr., €25); **Venice** (D overnight, €33; IC 5hr., €39; ES 4hr., €50). Hours and prices are updated every six months; check **www.trenitalia.it** for the most up-to-date schedules and prices.

ROME

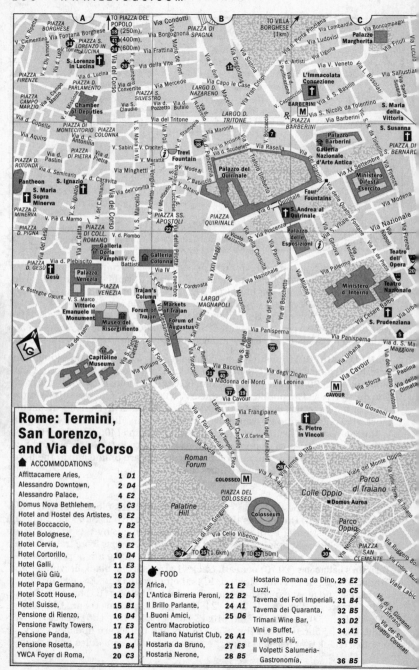

Rome: Termini, San Lorenzo, and Via del Corso

🏠 ACCOMMODATIONS

Affittacamere Aries,	**1 D1**
Alessandro Downtown,	**2 D4**
Alessandro Palace,	**4 E2**
Domus Nova Bethlehem,	**5 C3**
Hotel and Hostel des Artistes,	**6 E2**
Hotel Boccaccio,	**7 B2**
Hotel Bolognese,	**8 E1**
Hotel Cervia,	**9 E2**
Hotel Cortorillo,	**10 D4**
Hotel Galli,	**11 E3**
Hotel Giù Giù,	**12 D3**
Hotel Papa Germano,	**13 D2**
Hotel Scott House,	**14 D4**
Hotel Suisse,	**15 B1**
Pensione di Rienzo,	**16 D4**
Pensione Fawlty Towers,	**17 E3**
Pensione Panda,	**18 A1**
Pensione Rosetta,	**19 B4**
YWCA Foyer di Roma,	**20 C3**

🍎 FOOD

Africa,	**21 E2**
L'Antica Birreria Peroni,	**22 B2**
Il Brillo Parlante,	**24 A1**
I Buoni Amici,	**25 D6**
Centro Macrobiotico Italiano Naturist Club,	**26 A1**
Hostaria da Bruno,	**27 E3**
Hostaria Nerone,	**28 B5**
Hostaria Romana da Dino,	**29 E2**
Luzzi,	**30 C5**
Taverna dei Fori Imperiali,	**31 B4**
Taverna dei Quaranta,	**32 B5**
Trimani Wine Bar,	**33 D2**
Vini e Buffet,	**34 A1**
Il Volpetti Piú,	**35 B5**
Il Volpetti Salumeria-Gastronomía,	**36 B5**

TO 42 (500m)

Via Nomentana

D | E | F

1

PIAZZALE D.
PORTA PIA

Via Belissiario

Via Piave

Via S. Tullio

Via Collina

CAFES
Enoteca Cavour 313,   37 B4
Il Gelato di San Crispino,   38 B2
Il Gelatone,   39 B4
L'Impiccione Viaggiatore,   40 B4
Lion Bookshop & Café,   41 A1

NIGHTLIFE
Alien,   42 E1

PIAZZA
D. CROCE
ROSSA

Via di Villa

Viale del
Policlinico

Castro
Praetorio

Via G. M. Lancisi

POLICLINICO

M

PIAZZA
SASSARI

Via Quintino Sella

A. Salandra

Via Carducci

Via Flavia

Via XX Settembre

Ministeri del
Bilancio e del Tesoro

PIAZZA DELLE
FINANZE

Via Pastrengo

Via Parigi

Musei Nazionali Romani

S. Maria
d. Angeli

Terme di
Diocleziano

Via L. Einaudi

M
PUBBLICA
AZZA D.
UBBLICA

Via Cernaia

Via Montebello

Via Calatafimi

Via Gaeta

Via Volturno

Via Gaeta

Via Goito

Via Castelfidardo

Via Castro Pretorio

Via Sapri

Via Gaeta

CASTRO
PRETORIO

M

Biblioteca
Nazionale

CITTÀ
UNIVERSITARIA

Viale delle Scienze

Via di Terme
Diocleziano

21

PIAZZA
INDIPENDENZA

Via S. Martino d. Battaglia

Via Solferino

6

9

Via Mentana

Via Palestro

29

Enjoy
Rome
i

Via Marghera

Viale dell'Università

Min. Di festa
Aeronautica

Viale Piero Gobetti

Viale della Scienze

Warner
illage
Moderno

Via Viminale

Via P. Mondio

Via Principe Amedeo

12

PIAZZA DEI
CINQUECENTO

Via Vicenza

Via dei Mille

Via Magenta

Via Marsala

Via Milazzo

Via Castro Pretorio

11

11

TERMINI

M

Termini
Station

M

TERMINI

27

Splashnet
Internet,
Laundry,
and Luggage
Storage

PIAZZA
DELL'ESQUILINO

Via Daniele Manin

Via Gioberti

i

14

S. Maria
Maggiore

10

16

Via Carlo Cattaneo

PIAZZA
M. FANTI

2

Via Filippo Turati

Via Giovanni Giolitti

Via Principe Amedeo

Via Ratazzi

Via Carlo Alberto

Prassede

Via di S.
Prassede

Via di S. Vito

ESQUILINO

Via Statuto

Via Merulana

Museo
zionale
d'Arte
ientale

Auditorium of
Maecenas

Via Mecenate

Via A.
Poliziano

Via Leopardi

PIAZZA
VITTORIO
EMANUELE II

VITTORIO
EMANUELE

M

Via B. Ricasoli

Via Buonarroti

Via Michelangelo Buonarroti

Via Ferruccio

Via Giusti

S. Bibiana

Via Bibiana

PIAZZALE
TIBURTINO

V. Tiburtina
Antica

Via T. Mamiani

Via La Marmora

Via Macchiavelli

PIAZZA
DANTE

Via Guicciardini

Via Alfieri

Via Conte Verde

Via Nino Bixio

Via Principe Umberto

Via Cairoli

Via Pianciani

Via Foscolo

Via Tasso

Via Ariosto

Via Galilei

Via Villari

VITTORIO

Viale Alessandro Manzoni

M

MANZONI

TO S. GIOVANNI
IN LATERANO
(300m)

25

Via Aleardi

Via Emanuele Filiberto

Via di Porta Maggiore

Via Alessandro Manzoni

Viale Alessandro Manzoni

Via S. Croce In Gerusalemme

Via S. Vittorio

Via Carlo Emanuele I

Via S. Quintino

Via Grattoni

Via Statilia

PIAZZA DI
PORTA
MAGGIORE

Tomb of
the Baker

Via Giovanni Giolitti

Viale dello Scalo
di S. Lorenzo

Via Prenestina

LARGO
E. TALAMO

SAN
LORENZO

Via dei Sabelli

Via dei Marsi

Via degli Apuli

Via di Campani

Via dei Lucani

Via dei Liguri

Via degli Aurunci

Via dei Volsci

Via dei Sarti

Disfunzioni
Musicali

Via Tiburtina

Via dei Etruschi

Via dei Latini

Via dei Equi

Via degli Ausoni

LARGO
D. OSCHI

LARGO
D. FALISCI

Via dei Falisci

V. Ernici

Via dei Ramni

Via Cesare de Lollis

Via dei Dalmati

Via dei Marucchi

Via dei Corsi

Via dei Luceri

Via di Tizi

V. Tiburtina

Via dei Taurini

Via Pelasgi

Via Caudini

Via d. Frentani

Viale Pretoriano

Via Dauni

PIAZZALE
ALDO MORO

Via Porta Tiburtina

Via Porta Labicana

0   200 meters
0   200 yards

2

3

4

5

6

ROME

**Rome:
Centro Storico
and Trastevere**

▲ ACCOMMODATIONS

Albergo del Sole,	1 E3
Colors,	2 C1
Hotel Fontanella Borghese,	3 F1
Hotel Lady,	4 C1
Hotel Navona,	5 E3
Ostello Per La Gioventù	
Foro Italico,	6 B1
Hotel San Pietrino,	7 B1

● FOOD

Bar da Benito,	10 E4
Il Cantinone,	11 D6
Cacio e Pepe,	12 D1
Cul de Sac,	13 D2
Enoteca Trastevere,	14 D4
Franchi,	15 C1
Il Gelato di San Crispino,	16 F2
L'Insalata Ricca,	17 E3
Miscellanea,	18 F2
The Old Bridge,	19 B1
Pellachia,	20 D1
Pizza Art,	22 E4

Il Pollarola,	25	E3
Il Portico,	26	E4
Ristorante Grappolo d'Oro	27	D3
Zampàno,	29	E4
La Taverna del Ghetto,	30	E4
Trattoria da Giggetto,	32	F2
Trattoria dal Cav. Gino,		
Trattoria da Settimio		
all'Arancio,	33	F2
CAFES		
Bar Giulia,	35	C2
Biscotti cio Artigiano		
Innocenti,	36	D5
Caffè della Pace,	37	D2
Da Quinto Gelateria,	38	D2
Della Palma,	39	F2
Giolitti,	40	F2
Pasticceria Ebraico		
Boccione,	41	E4
Sant'Eustachio Il Caffè,	42	E3
Tazza d'Oro,	43	F2
NIGHTLIFE		
Artu Café,	44	C4
Caffè della Scala,	45	C4
Charro Café,	46	D6
Coyote,	47	D6
Express,	48	C4
Jonathan's Angels,	49	C4
Proud Lion Pub,	50	B1
Freni e Frizioni,	51	D4
Big Hilda Caffè,	52	C4
Alien,	53	F1
THEATERS		
Cinema Reale,	54	D5
Metropolitan,	55	F1
Nuovo Olimpia,	56	F2
Nuovo Sacher,	57	D6

⊞ ORIENTATION

Rome's size and myriad of narrow, winding streets can make it difficult to navigate, so it's helpful to orient yourself by using major landmarks and main streets. The **Tiber River,** which snakes north-south through the city, is also a useful reference point. Most trains arrive at **Stazione Termini** east of Rome's historical center. The neighborhood surrounding **Termini** and **San Lorenzo** to the east is home to the city's largest university and most budget accommodations. **Via Nazionale** originates two blocks northwest of Termini Station in **Piazza della Repubblica** and leads to **Piazza Venezia,** the city's focal point, recognizable by the immense white **Vittorio Emanuele II monument.** From P. Venezia, **Via dei Fori Imperiali** runs southeast to the Ancient City, where you can find the **Colosseum** and the **Roman Forum. Via del Corso** stretches north from P. Venezia to **Piazza del Popolo,** which has an obelisk in its center that is visible all the way from P. Venezia. The **Trevi Fountain, Piazza Barberini,** and the fashionable streets around **Piazza di Spagna** and the **Spanish Steps** lie to the east of V. del Corso. **Villa Borghese,** home to impressive gardens and museums, is northeast of the Spanish Steps. West of V. del Corso is the **centro storico** (historical town center), the tangle of streets around the **Pantheon, Piazza Navona, Campo dei Fiori,** and the old **Jewish Ghetto. Largo Argentina,** west of P. Venezia, marks the start of **Corso Vittorio Emanuele II,** which runs through the *centro storico* to the Tiber River. Across the river to the northwest is **Vatican City** and the **Borgo-Prati** neighborhood. South of the Vatican are **Trastevere** and residential **Testaccio.** Be sure to pick up a free color map in English at the tourist office (**Practical Information,** see opposite page).

⊏ LOCAL TRANSPORTATION

SUBWAY (METROPOLITANA) AND BUSES

MI SCUSI! MI SCUSI! Romans often prepare for their descent from the bus or subway well in advance. If you are not getting off at the next stop, step away from the doors and allow people to move to the front as early as the preceding stop. They may ask you, *"Scende la prossima fermata?"* (Are you getting off at the next stop?) to which you should respond *"si"* or *"no."*

Rome's subway, the **Metropolitana** (www.metroroma.it), has two lines, A and B, which intersect at Termini. Station entrances are marked by poles with a white "M" on a red square. The subway usually runs daily 5:30am to 11:30pm, but due to construction of the forthcoming C line, the subway occasionally closes at 10pm. At night, bus #55N replaces Metro A and 40N or 80N replaces Metro B.

The network of routes may seem daunting, but Rome's buses are an efficient means of getting around the city, especially since the Metro doesn't serve the *centro storico.* The **ATAC** transportation company has booths throughout the city, including one in Termini. (☎06 800 431 784; www.atac.roma.it. Open daily 7:30am-8pm.) Grab a map (€1) at **biglietteria ATAC,** V. Gaeta 78 (open daily 7am-7pm). ATAC tickets (€1) are valid for the Metro and buses, and are sold at *tabaccherie,* newsstands, vending machines, and some bars. Vending machines are in metro stations, on street corners, and at major bus stops; look for ATAC labels. Tickets are valid for one Metro ride or 1 hr. of unlimited bus travel. A **BIG daily ticket** (€4) covers unlimited bus or train travel in the metropolitan area (including Ostia but not Fiumicino) until midnight the day of purchase; a **CIS ticket** (€16) is good for a week; a three-day tourist ticket is €11.

Each bus stop *(fermata)* is marked by yellow signs, which list all routes that stop there and the key stops along those routes. Some buses run only on weekdays *(feriali)* or weekends *(festive)* while others have different routes on different days. Most buses run from 5am to midnight, after which the less reliable night buses *(notturni)* take over and run at 30-60min. intervals.

Enter buses through the front and back doors; exit through the middle door. A few useful bus routes are: **#40/64,** Vatican area, C. V. Emanuele, Largo Argentina, P. Venezia, Termini; **#81,** P. Malatesta, San Giovanni, Colosseo, Bocca della Verità, P. Venezia, Largo Argentina, V. del Corso, P. Cavour, V. Cola di Rienzo, Vatican; **#170,** Termini, V. Nazionale, P. Venezia, Bocca della Verità, Testaccio, Stazione Trastevere, V. Marconi, P. Agricoltura; **#492,** Tiburtina, Termini, P. Barberini, P. Venezia, C. Rinascimento, P. Cavour, P. Risorgimento; **#175,** Termini, P. Barberini, V. del Corso, P. Venezia; **tram 8,** Largo di Torre d'Argentina to Trastevere; **Linea H,** Termini to Trastevere; **#910,** Termini to Villa Borghese.

TAXIS, BIKES, AND MOPEDS

Taxis in Rome are expensive. Try to flag down a stray cab, head to stands near Termini, or find one in the major *piazze*. Ride only in yellow or white taxis, and make sure the taxi has a meter. If it doesn't, settle on a price before getting in the car. Expect to pay around €10-12 for a ride from Termini to the Vatican during the day; prices rise significantly at night. The meter starts at €2.33 (M-Sa 7am-10pm), €3.36 (Su and holidays 7am-10pm), or €4.91 (daily 10pm-7am). Surcharges are levied when heading to or from Fiumicino (€7.23) and Ciampino (€5.50), with a €1 charge per suitcase larger than 35cm by 25cm by 50cm. Standard tip is 10%. **RadioTaxi** (☎06 35 70) responds to calls, but be aware that the meter starts the moment the taxi is dispatched.

Rome's cobblestone streets, dense traffic, and reckless drivers make the city a challenge for bikes and mopeds. **Bikes** cost around €5 per hr. or €10 per day. There are several self-service rental stands around the *centro storico*. The price of **scooters** changes based on their size, but is around €35-55 per day. Be aware that the length of a "day" sometimes depends on the shop's closing time. In summer, try the stands (open daily 10am-7pm) on V. del Corso, at P. di S. Lorenzo and V. Pontifici, or **Treno e Scooter,** Termini. (☎06 48 90 58 23; www.trenoescooter.191.it. Open daily 9am-2pm and 4-7pm. AmEx/MC/V). **Bici & Baci,** V. del Viminale 5, is in front of Termini. (☎06 48 28 443 or 48 98 61 62; www.bicibaci.com. Open daily 8am-7pm. AmEx/MC/V.) The minimum rental age is 16. Helmets, included with rental, are strictly required by law. Prices often include a 20% sales tax. For those just interested in an afternoon on a bike, **Enjoy Rome** offers an informative, if harrowing, tour of the city. Villa Borghese is another popular destination for biking. Recently, **Segways,** P. Popolo, have made an appearance on Rome's labyrinthine streets. (☎06 38 03 01 29 13 www.segwayroma.ne. €8 per 30min., €15 per hr.)

🔢 PRACTICAL INFORMATION

TOURIST AND FINANCIAL SERVICES

Tourist Offices:

Enjoy Rome, V. Marghera 8/A (☎06 44 51 843; www.enjoyrome.com). From the middle concourse of Termini (between the trains and the ticket booths), exit right. Cross V. Marsala. The office is 3 blocks down V. Marghera on the left. Helpful, English-speaking staff makes reservations at museums and shows, books accommodations, orients travelers in the city, and leads walking tours of all the major areas of the city (€27, under 26 €22). Along with info on excursions and bus lines, the office also provides 2 useful publications: a detailed and accurate map and a *When in Rome* booklet, with practical info and insider tips for making the most of a trip to Rome. Open Apr.-Oct. M-F 8:30am-7pm, Sa 8:30am-2pm; Nov.-Mar. M-F 9am-6pm, Sa 9am-2pm.

PIT Info Points (☎06 48 90 63 00). Run by the city, these round green kiosks provide limited info on events, hotels, restaurants, and transportation, as well as brochures and a basic map of sights. Open daily 8am-9pm. **Branches:** Castel Sant'Angelo, Trevi Fountain, Fori Imperiali, P. di Spagna, P. Navona, Trastevere, Santa Maria Maggiore, P. S. Giovanni in Laterano, V. del Corso, V. Nazionale, and Termini. The same info is available by phone from the **Call Center Comune di Roma** (☎06 36 00 43 99), which operates daily 9am-7pm.

Embassies and Consulates: See **Essentials,** p. 9.

Currency Exchange: Banca di Roma and **Banca Nazionale del Lavoro** have good rates, and **ATMs** are readily available all over town. Open M-F 8:30am-1:30pm.

American Express: P. di Spagna 38 (☎06 67 641; for lost or stolen cards and checks, 80 08 72 000). Open M-F 9am-5:30pm, Sa 9am-12:30pm.

LOCAL SERVICES

Luggage Storage: Splashnet, V. Varese 33. €2 per day. In Termini, below Track #24. Open daily 6am-midnight. €3.80 1st 5hr., €0.60 per hr. up to 12hr., €0.20 per hr. thereafter.

Lost Property: Oggetti Smarriti, V. Nicolo Bettoni 1 (☎06 58 16 040), at Termini, at the glass booth in main passage. Open M and W 8:30am-1pm and 2:30-6pm, Tu and F 8:30am-1pm, Th 8:30am-6pm. **Lost property on bus:** ☎06 58 16 040; **Metro A:** ☎06 48 74 309; M, W, and F 9am-12:30pm **Metro B:** F 8am-6:30pm ☎06 57 53 22 65.

Bookstores:

▪**The Lion Bookshop and Café,** V. dei Greci 33-36 (☎06 32 65 40 07 or 32 65 04 37), off V. del Corso. Open M 3:30-7:30pm and Tu-Sa 10am-7:30pm.

Libreria Feltrinelli International, V. V. Emanuele Orlando 84/86 (☎06 48 27 878), near P. della Repubblica. Open M-Sa 9am-8pm, Su 10am-1:30pm and 4-8pm.

Anglo-American Bookshop, V. della Vite 102 (☎06 67 95 222; www.aab.it), off V. del Corso near the Spanish Steps. Open M-F 10am-7:30pm, Sa 10am-2pm; closed mid-Aug. AmEx/MC/V.

Mel Bookstore, V. Nazionale 252-255 (☎06 48 85 405). Open in summer M-Sa 9am-8pm, Su 10am-1:30pm and 4:30-8:30pm; in winter M-Sa 9am-8pm, Su 10am-1:30pm and 4-8pm.

GLBT Resources:

ARCI-GAY, V. Goito 35/B (☎06 64 50 11 02 or 349 197 6191; www.arcigayroma.it), holds discussions, dances, and special events. Welcome group every Th 7-9pm. Open M-F 4-8pm. Helpline (☎06 800 713 713) open M, W, Th and Sa 4-8pm.

Circolo Mario Mieli di Cultura Omosessuale, V. Efeso 2/A (☎06 54 13 985; www.mariomieli. org). Ⓜ️B-San Paolo. From the metro stop, walk to Largo Beato Placido Riccardi, turn right on V. Corinto. Promotes GLBT rights and holds cultural activities. AIDS activists offer psychological and legal assistance. Welcome group Su at 3:30pm. Open daily 10am-7pm.

Libreria Babele, V. dei Banchi Vecchi (☎06 68 76 628; www.libreriababeleroma.it), across from Castel Sant'Angelo. Library focusing on gay literature. Open M-Sa 11am-7pm.

Laundromats:

▪**Splashnet,** V. Varese 33 (☎06 49 38 04 50; www.splashnetrome.com), 3 blocks from Termini. Wash €3 per 6kg., dry €3 per 7kg. Internet €1.50 per hr. Free maps. Helpful, English-speaking staff. Ask for the *Let's Go* discount. Open daily in summer 8:30am-1am; in winter 8:30am-11pm.

BollaBlu, V. Milazzo 20/B (☎06 44 70 30 96), near Termini. Wash and dry approx. €10, includes 15min. of free Internet; €2 per additional hr. Luggage storage €2. Open daily 8am-midnight.

OndaBlu, V. Pricipe Armideo 70B (info ☎06 80 08 61 346; www.ondablu.com). 17 locations in the city. Wash €3.50 per 6.5kg, dry €3.50 per 6.5kg. Detergent €1. Open daily 8am-10pm.

Supermarkets: Standa, DìperDì, and **Despar,** have stores scattered throughout Rome.

Standa: V. Cola di Rienzo 71/73, in Borgo Prati, open daily 8am-9pm; V. Trastevere 62, in Trastevere, open M-Sa 8:30am-8pm, Su 9:30am-1:30pm and 4-8pm. AmEx/MC/V.

DìperDì: V. del Gesu 58, in *centro storico*, open M-Sa 8am-9pm, Su 9am-8pm; V. Carlo Tavolacci 1-7, in Trastevere, open M-Sa 8am-8pm, Su 8:30am-1:30pm; V. S. S. Quattro 53/54, near the Colosseum, open M-Sa 8am-9pm, Su 9am-7:30pm. AmEx/MC/V.

Despar: V. del Pozzetto 119, in P. di Spagna and environs, open M-Sa 9am-9pm, Su 10am-9pm; V. Nazionale 211/213, open daily 8:30am-9pm. AmEx/MC/V.

Supermercato SMA Rocca, P. S. Maria Maggiore 1-5, open daily 8am-9pm.

Conad, P. dei Cinquecento, lower level of Termini, open daily 6am-midnight.

EMERGENCY AND COMMUNICATIONS

Rape Crisis Line: Centro Anti-Violenza, V. di Torrespaccata 157 (☎06 23 26 90 49 or 23 26 90 53). Branches throughout city. Open 24hr. **Samaritans,** V. S. Giovanni 250 (☎06 70 45 44 44), in Laterano. English speakers. Counseling available; call ahead. Open daily 1-10pm. For additional resources consult www.controviolenzadonne.org.

Counseling Hotlines: Alcoholics Anonymous (☎06 47 42 913); **Narcotics Anonymous** (www.na.org); **Refugee Center** (☎06 47 45 603).

Pharmacies: Farmacia Internazionale, P. Barberini 49 (☎06 48 25 456). Ⓜ A-Barberini. Open daily 9am-12:30pm and 3-9pm. MC/V. **Farmacia Piram,** V. Nazionale 228 (☎06 48 80 754). Open 24hr. MC/V.

Hospitals:

International Medical Center, V. Firenze 47 (24hr. ☎06 48 82 371; www.imc84.com). Prescriptions filled. Paramedic crew on call. Referral service to English-speaking doctors. General visit €100, house visits at night €150. Call ahead. Open M-F 9am-8pm; house calls after hours.

Rome-American Hospital, V. Emilio Longoni 69 (24hr. ☎06 22 551, appointments 22 55 290; www.rah.it). Private emergency and laboratory services, HIV tests, and pregnancy tests. Visits average €100-200. Doctors on call 24hr.

Policlinico Umberto I, Vle. del Policlinico 155 (emergency ☎06 49 911, automated phone line for first aid and appointments 49 971). Ⓜ B-Policlinico or bus #649. Open 24hr.

THE BLOOD OF THE ROMANS. When it is hot and humid outside, mosquitoes swarm Rome. While the nasty little buggers love feasting upon foreign blood, Romans seem to avoid the pestilent attacks. Consequently, insect repellents are extremely overpriced in the city. If you are prone to allergic reactions, bring antihistamine cream and bug spray.

Internet Access: Splashnet (see **Laundromats,** opposite page). **Padma Internet Point,** V. Cavour 131 (☎06 48 93 03 80). €2 per hr. Printing €0.20 per page, graphics €0.75 per page. Open daily 8am-midnight. **Yex Internet Points** are located throughout the city. 2 located between P. Navona and Campo dei Fiori at C. V. Emmanuele 106 (☎06 45 42 98 18) and P. Sant'Andrea della Valle 1 (☎06 97 84 42 46). €2.90 per 30min., €4.80 per hr. Also offer wire transfer and currency exchange. Open daily 8am-9pm.

Post Office: V. Giolitti 14, in Termini, and P. S. Silvestro 19 (☎06 69 73 72 13). Both open M-F 8am-7pm, Sa 8am-1:15pm. Dozens of locations throughout the city; see www.poste.it/online/cercaup for a full listing. **Postal Codes:** 00100 to 00200; V. Giolotti 00185; P. S. Silvestro 00187.

▌ ACCOMMODATIONS

Rome swells with tourists around Easter, from May to July, and in September; be sure to book well in advance for those times. Most establishments also raise their prices during long weekends and holidays, and also throughout the high season. In general, prices vary widely with the time of year, and a proprietor's willingness to negotiate increases with length of stay, number of vacancies, and group size. Termini is swarming with hotel scouts. Many are legitimate and have IDs issued by tourist offices; however, some impostors have fake badges and direct travelers to run-down locations with exorbitant rates, especially at night. In some neighborhoods, like Trastevere, hotels are pricey, but good deals on apartments can still sometimes be found. The neighborhood surrounding Termini is notorious for budget accommodations, including cheap hotels and youth hostels, but be discerning and find out as much as you can about your prospective accommodation before making a commitment.

ACCOMMODATIONS BY PRICE

€20-29 (❷)	
▨ Ostello Per La Giovent (HI) (115)	VC
▨ Alessandro Palace (116)	TE
Alessandro Downtown (116)	TE
Legends Hostel (116)	TE
Hostel Des Artistes (117)	SL
▨ Hotel Papa Germano (117)	VIA

€30-40 (❸)	
▨ Colors (115)	VC
▨ Hotel San Pietrino (p. 115)	VC
Hotel Cervia (116)	SL
Hotel Bolognese (117)	VIA
▨ Hotel Scott House (117)	ES
Hotel Giù Giù (118)	ES
YWCA Foyer di Roma (116)	AA

€41-60 (❹)	
Pensione Panda (115)	PS
Hotel Boccaccio (115)	PS
Pensione Fawlty Towers (117)	SL
Affittacamere Aries (117)	VIA
Pensione di Rienzo (118)	ES

Over €60 (❺)	
Pensione Rosetta (114)	CS
Albergo del Sole (115)	CS
Hotel Navona (114)	CS
Hotel Fontanella Borghese (114)	CS
Hotel Suisse (115)	PS
Hotel Elite (115)	PS
Hotel Lady (116)	VC
Hotel Des Artistes (117)	SL
Hotel Galli (116)	SL
Hotel Cortorillo (118)	ES

CS Centro Storico and Ancient City **ES** Esquilino and West of Termini **PS** Piazza di Spagna and Environs **RH** Religious Housing **SL** San Lorenzo and East of Termini **TE** Termini and Environs **VIA** Via XX Settembre and North of Termini **VC** Vatican City

CENTRO STORICO AND ANCIENT CITY

Due to their proximity to the major sights, these small hotels come at a price.

Hotel Navona, V. dei Sediari 8, 1st fl. (☎06 68 64 203; www.hotelnavona.com). Bus #64 to C. V. Emanuele II or #70 to C. del Rinascimento. Take V. de Canestrari from P. Navona and cross C. del Rinascimento. The choice of both Keats and Shelley. English spoken. A/C, TV, luggage storage, and breakfast included. Reservations with 1st night deposit. Singles €100-125; doubles €135-155; triples €180-210. Occasional online discounts; *Let's Go* discount 5%; cash discount for stays longer than 5 days. MC/V. ❺

Hotel Fontanella Borghese, Largo Fontanella Borghese 84, 2nd fl. (☎06 68 80 95 04; www.fontanellaborghese.com). Heading north from P. Venezia, take a left on Largo Fontanella Borghese. Once owned by the Borghese princes, this centrally located hotel oozes character. Comfy rooms with A/C, minibar, phone, and satellite TV. Singles €128-180; doubles €195-260; triples €230-340. Frequent online discounts. AmEx/MC/V. ❺

Pensione Rosetta, V. Cavour 295 (☎06 47 82 30 69; www.rosettahotel.com), past the Fori Imperiali. Buzz at large front doors and walk through courtyard. Affordable for the location. Spacious rooms have bath, TV, phone, and fan. A/C €10. Reservations recommended in high season. Singles €60; doubles €85; triples €95. AmEx/MC/V. ❺

Albergo del Sole, V. del Biscione 76 (☎06 68 80 68 73; www.solealbiscione.it), off Campo dei Fiori. 1 of the best deals in the *centro storico.* Comfy, modern rooms with antique furniture. Elevator from 2nd to 5th fl. Parking €18-21. Reserve ahead in high season. Singles €75, with bath €90-125; doubles €100-105/120-140; triples €200; quads €240. Discount for groups of 10+. Cash only. ❺

PIAZZA DI SPAGNA AND ENVIRONS

Though prices at hotels near P. di Spagna can be very steep, the accommodations offer the convenience of being closer to the Metro and are often newer than those found in the *centro storico.* In this luxurious part of town, higher prices translate into lusher fabrics and more amenities.

Hotel Suisse, V. Gregoriana 54, 3rd fl. (☎06 67 83 649 or 67 86 172; www.hotelsuisserome.com). Ⓜ A-Spagna. From the Spanish Steps, veer right facing away from P. di Spagna. Antique furniture, huge rooms, and an opulent lounge in a former *palazzo.* Private baths. Elevator. English spoken. Breakfast included. A/C €10. Free Wi-Fi. Singles €90-110; doubles €150-170; triples €190. Low-season deals online. MC/V. ❺

Hotel Elite, V. Francesco Crispi 49. (☎06 67 83 083, www.elitehotel.eu). Ⓜ A-Barberini. Beautiful hotel with restaurant and wine bar. Plush rooms have bath, phone, A/C, and TV. Free Wi-Fi and computer in lounge area. 24hr. reception. Singles €70-110; doubles €90-150; triples €120-185; quads €160-210. AmEx/MC/V. ❺

Pensione Panda, V. della Croce 35, 2nd fl. (☎06 67 80 179; www.hotelpanda.it). Ⓜ A-Spagna. Between P. di Spagna and V. del Corso. Spotless rooms with faux marble statues and frescoed ceilings on a quiet street. English spoken. A/C €6. Free Wi-Fi. Reservations recommended. Singles €65-75, with bath €68-80; doubles €75-98/78-108; triples €130/140; quads €180. 5% discount when paying with cash. AmEx/MC/V. ❹

Hotel Boccaccio, V. del Boccaccio 25, 1st fl. (☎06 48 85 962; www.hotelboccaccio.com). Ⓜ A-Barberini. Off V. del Tritone near P. Barberini. Simple rooms with high ceilings and a cozy terrace in a quiet hotel. No A/C or TV. Elevator. Singles €45; doubles €80, with bath €100; triples €108/135. Ask about low-season discounts. AmEx/MC/V. ❹

VATICAN CITY

Pensions near the Vatican offer some of the best deals in Rome as well as extensive amenities. Though definitely not devoid of good times, the area is somewhat more sober than other parts of the city.

▨ **Colors,** V. Boezio 31 (☎06 68 74 030; www.colorshotel.com). Ⓜ A-Ottaviano. Take a right on V. Terenzio, off V. Cola di Rienzo, then left on V. Boezio to reach this truly special hotel. As the name suggests, a variety of colorful rooms are available. 2 hostel floors and a newly renovated 3rd floor with private rooms. A/C and English-speaking staff. Kitchens and tranquil terraces on all floors. Breakfast included. Internet access €2 per hr. Reserve dorms by 9pm night before. Dorms €27; singles €90, with bath €105; doubles €100/130; triples €120. Low season discount up to 30%. Cash only. ❸

▨ **Hotel San Pietrino,** V. Giovanni Bettolo 43, 3rd fl. (☎06 37 00 132; www.sanpietrino.it). Ⓜ A-Ottaviano. Exit on V. Barletta and turn left on V. Bettolo. A distinct amphibian motif manifests itself in small frog statues, stuffed frogs, and other frog trinkets in the hallways. Spacious rooms are simple and clean with A/C, TV, and DVD players. Internet access available. Laundry €8. In high season, reserve 2-3 months ahead. Singles €32-90; doubles €48-118; triples €72-148; family quad €92-168. Negotiable discount for stays over 1 week. Check website for low-season specials. AmEx/MC/V. ❸

Ostello Per La Gioventù Foro Italico (HI), V. delle Olimpiadi 61 (☎06 32 36 267; www.hihostels.com or www.ostellionline.org). Ⓜ A-Ottaviano, then bus #32 from P. del Risorgimento to the 2nd "LGT Cadorna Ostello Gioventù" stop (10-15min.); hostel is the

ROME

barracks-like building behind the bushes across the street. Common area and cafeteria. Single-sex floors with giant communal baths feel like a college dorm. English-speaking staff. No A/C. Breakfast included. Laundry available. Internet €5 per hr. Reception 7am-11pm. Curfew 1-1:30am. Dorms €18. Non-HI member fee €3. AmEx/MC/V. ❷

Hotel Lady, V. Germanico 198, 4th fl. (☎06 32 42 112; www.hotelladyroma.it), between V. Fabbio Massimo and V. Paolo Emilio. Cozy and old-fashioned. Dimly lit halls with rich wood beams. Rooms have antique furniture, desk, phone, and fan. Internet access. Singles €50-90; doubles €70-111, with bath €90-150; triples €90-145. AmEx/MC/V. ❺

TIP **MO' MONEY, NO PROBLEMS.** Most independently run hostels and hotels will offer discounts if you pay in cash in order to avoid a 10% tax from credit companies. So put your credit card away and hit up the ATMs.

TERMINI AND ENVIRONS

Welcome to budget traveler central. Any of the hostels that make up Alessandro's empire are your best bet—if you can get a reservation. Use caution in the area, especially at night; keep an eye on your purse and pockets.

 Alessandro Palace, V. Vicenza 42 (☎06 44 61 958; www.hostelalessandropalace.com). From Termini's track #1, turn left on V. Marsala and right on V. Vicenza. Renovated dorms with bath and A/C. Fun bar with flatscreen TV. English spoken. Breakfast included; free pizza nightly in summer with drink purchase (€3). Lockers available. Towels €2; included with doubles, triples, and quads. Internet €2 per hr. Check-in 3pm. Check-out 10am. Dorms €25-30; doubles €90-100; triples and quads €118-€140. AmEx/MC/V. ❷

Alessandro Downtown, V. Carlo Cattaneo 23 (☎06 44 34 01 47; www.hostelalessandrodowntown.com). From Termini's track #22, take a left on V. Giolitti and a right on V. C. Cattaneo. Worthwhile alternative to the Palace, with the same social environment. Dining room, sitting room with TV, and new kitchen. Breakfast included; free pasta party weeknights. Lockers available. Towels €2. Internet €2 per hr. Check-in 3pm. Check-out 10am. Dorms €23-33; doubles €70, with bath €90; quads €120/140. AmEx/MC/V. ❷

Legends Hostel, V. Curtatone 12 (☎06 44 70 32 17; www.legendshostel.com). Pop in a DVD from the hostel's collection and enjoy a complimentary cup of hot chocolate. Kitchen. Breakfast included; free pasta party weeknights. Free lockers. Towels €2. Internet access available. Family friendly. 10-bed dorms with bath €32; 8-bed single-sex dorms €34; 6-bed co-ed and single-sex dorms with bath €36. AmEx/MC/V. ❷

YWCA Foyer di Roma, V. Cesare Balbo 4 (☎06 48 80 460 or 48 83 917; foyer.roma@ywca-ucdg.it). From Termini, take V. Cavour. Turn right on V. Torino and left on V. C. Balbo. The YWCA (pronounced EEV-kah, known as the *Casa per Studentesse*) has a pretty courtyard and spotless rooms. Rooms come with fan and towels. Breakfast included; lunch €12. Reception 7am-midnight. Check-out 10am. Curfew midnight. Private rooms co-ed; dorms women only. Dorms €26; singles €40, with bath €50; doubles €66/80. Stays longer than 1 week. require €10 membership fee. AmEx/MC/V. ❸

SAN LORENZO AND EAST OF TERMINI

Hotel Galli, V. Milazzo 20 (☎06 44 56 859; www.albergogalli.com). From Termini's middle concourse, exit right. Turn right on V. Marsala and left on V. Milazzo. Reception on 2nd fl. English spoken. Clean rooms with bath, minifridge, phone, TV, and safe. A/C €5. Check-in noon. Check-out 10am. Singles €25-75; doubles €40-110; triples €65-120; quads €80-160. Check discounts online. 3-day cancellation policy. AmEx/MC/V. ❺

Hotel Cervia, V. Palestro 55, 2nd fl. (☎06 49 10 57; www.hotelcerviaroma.it). From Termini, exit on V. Marsala, head down V. Marghera, and take the 4th left. Clean rooms with fans. Multilingual staff. Identical sister hotel, **Restino,** on the 5th fl. Breakfast €3. Check-out 11am. Reserve online. Singles €35-55, with bath €50-80; doubles €55-80/70-120; triples €75-110/90-150; quads €80-130/100-160. 5% *Let's Go* discount when paying in cash; discounts negotiable for longer stays. AmEx/MC/V. ❸

Hotel and Hostel Des Artistes, V. Villafranca 20, 5th fl. (☎06 44 54 365; www.hoteldesartistes.com). From Termini's middle concourse, exit right, turn left on V. Marsala, right on V. Vicenza, and take 5th left. Rooftop terrace and small bar. English spoken. Hotel: private bath, A/C, TV, safe, fan, and hair dryer. Breakfast included. Doubles €100, with bath €146. Rates vary seasonally. Discount when paying cash. AmEx/MC/V. Hostel: pastel-colored common room with TV. Private rooms have TV, safe and fan. Luggage storage. €10 key deposit. Dorms €12-23 per person. Cash only. Hotel ❺/hostel ❷

Pensione Fawlty Towers, V. Magenta 39, 5th fl. (☎06 44 50 374; www.fawltytowers.org). From Termini, cross V. Marsala onto V. Marghera, and turn right on V. Magenta. Distinct Bohemian feel. Brightly colored rooms. English spoken. Kitchen available. Comfortable common room with TV, A/C, DVD player, library, microwave, and free Internet access. Check-out 9:30am. No reservations for dorms—arrive as early as possible. Singles €25, with shower €30; doubles €45, with full bath €53; triples with shower €65, with full bath €75. Must pay cash in advance. Check website for seasonal specials. ❹

I SAY TOMATO, YOU SAY TOMAHTO. In Italy, the 1st floor is actually floor 0 (known as *pianterreno*). Consequently, every floor thereafter is numbered 1 less than you might expect.

VIA XX SETTEMBRE AND NORTH OF TERMINI

Dominated by government ministries and private apartments, this area is less noisy and touristy than nearby Termini.

Hotel Papa Germano, V. Calatafimi 14/A (☎06 48 69 19; www.hotelpapagermano. com). From Termini, exit right; turn left on V. Marsala, which becomes V. Volturno, and take the 4th right on V. Calatafimi. Clean, simple rooms with TV. English spoken. Breakfast included. A/C €5. Internet access €2 per hr. Dorms €25-30; singles €40-55; doubles €65-85, with bath €85-110; triples €75-95/95-125; quads €100-125/110-145. Check online for discounts. Discount cash payment. AmEx/MC/V. ❷

Hotel Bolognese, V. Palestro 15, 2nd fl. (☎/fax 06 49 00 45; www.hotelbologneseinrome.com). From Termini, exit right; walk down V. Marghera and take the 4th left onto V. Palestro. The proud artist/owner's impressive paintings and the cleanliness and comfort of the newly renovated rooms, set this hotel apart. Private baths. Breakfast included. Singles €30-60; doubles €50-90; triples €90-120. AmEx/MC/V. ❸

Affittacamere Aries, V. XX Settembre 58/A (☎06 42 02 71 61; www.affittacamerearies. com). From Termini, turn left onto V. Marsala, which becomes V. Volturno, and right onto V. Cernia. Make a left on V. Goito and follow it to V. XX Settembre. Comfy rooms with fridge, TV, towels, and A/C. English spoken. Breakfast €5-7. Singles €35-80; doubles €45-100, with bath €50-120; triples €70-150. Ask about *Let's Go* discount. MC/V. ❹

ESQUILINO AND WEST OF TERMINI

Esquilino, south of Termini, has tons of cheap hotels closer to the major sights. The area west of Termini is also inviting, with busy streets and shopping.

Hotel Scott House, V. Gioberti 30 (☎06 44 65 379; www.scotthouse.com). Exit Termini on V. Giolitti and turn left. Cross the street and take a right on V. Gioberti. Colorful, modern rooms have private bath, A/C, phone, safes, and TV. English spoken. Breakfast included. Internet available. Singles €35-68; doubles €63-93; triples €75-114; quads €88-129. Discount for cash payments. AmEx/MC/V. ❸

Hotel Giù Giù, V. del Viminale 8, 2nd fl. (☎06 48 27 734; www.hotelgiugiu.com). Exit Termini on V. Giolitti, turn right and walk past P. dei Cinquecento to V. Viminale. Turn left. Elegant but fading *palazzo* filled with porcelain knick-knacks and Victorian furniture feels like Grandma's house. Rooms have A/C, TV, and safe. English spoken. Breakfast €8. Check-out 10am. Singles €40-60; doubles with bath €70-95; triples €105-140; quads €140-190. Check website for low-season specials. Cash only. ❸

Pensione di Rienzo, V. Principe Amedeo 79/A, 2nd fl. (☎06 44 67 131; www.hoteldirienzo.it). Tranquil, family-run retreat just 2 blocks from Termini. Well-furnished rooms are fresh and airy. English spoken. Breakfast €10. Check-out 10am. Singles €25-65, with bath €50-60; doubles €30-70/35-80; triples with bath €90. MC/V. ❹

Hotel Cortorillo, V. Principe Amedeo 79/A, 5th fl. (☎06 44 66 934; www.hotelcortorillo.it). Renovated, modern hotel. Spacious rooms with bath, TV, minifridge, and A/C. Breakfast included. Check-in 11am. Check-out 10am. Singles €50-100; doubles €60-130. Extra bed €15-30. Online discounts. Credit card required for deposit. AmEx/MC/V. ❺

ALTERNATIVE ACCOMMODATIONS

BED AND BREAKFASTS

B&Bs in Rome differ from their American counterparts. Some are private homes with guest rooms; generous owners typically provide breakfast. Others are apartments with kitchens that clients can use. The rooms and apartments vary in quality, location, and size. There is generally a 2 night minimum. The multilingual staff at **Bed and Breakfast Association of Rome,** V. Antonio Pacinotti 73, coordinate B&B bookings and apartment rentals. (☎06 55 30 22 48; www.b-b.rm.it. Call M-F 10am-2pm or 3-7pm for an appointment.) **Your Flat in Rome,** Borgo Pio 160, also rents spacious, short-term apartments near St. Peter's Square to individuals or groups for as little as €24 per person per night. (☎338 95 60 061; www.yourflatinrome.com.) **Hotel Trastevere,** V. Luciano Manara 24a/25 (☎06 58 14 713; www.hoteltrastevere.com), in Sq. San Cosimato, also has short-term apartments available. **Short Let's Assistance,** V. Zucchelli 26 (☎48 90 58 97; www.shortletsassistance.com), by P. Barberini, oversees 120 apartments.

RELIGIOUS HOUSING

Don't automatically assume that religious housing is cheap; a single can cost up to €155. While a few establishments require letters of introduction from local Catholic dioceses, most are open to guests of all denominations. The rooms in religious housing are similar to hotel rooms in terms of amenities; the only difference is that the profits go toward church missions. Do think sober: early curfews or chores are standard. Check www.santasusanna.org/comingtorome/convents.html for a comprehensive listing of religious housing.

Domus Nova Bethlehem, V. Cavour 85/A (☎06 47 82 44 14; www.suorebambinogesu.it). From Termini, pass P. dell'Esquilino, Domus is on the right. Modern, centrally located, hotel decorated with religious art. Rooms have A/C, bath, and TV. Breakfast room, courtyard, and rooftop terrace. Breakfast included. Safes and Internet access available. Dinner in restaurant available for €13. Parking €15.50 per day. Curfew in summer 2am; in winter 1am. Singles €75; doubles €110; triples €140; quads €150. AmEx/MC/V. ❺

FOOD

Romans love to eat, and eat often. Whether it's a multi-course meal or an afternoon gelato, Romans settle for nothing but the best—so should you. Don't fall into the tourist traps around major sights; you'll miss out on authentic Roman cuisine and find yourself paying high prices for mediocre food. Popular Roman dishes include *spaghetti alla carbonara* (egg and cream sauce sprinkled with bacon), *spaghetti all'amatriciana* (spicy thin tomato sauce with chili peppers and bacon), *carciofi alla giudeia* (deep-fried artichokes common in the Jewish quarter), and *fiori di zucca* (stuffed, fried zucchini flowers). Pizza—eaten with fork and knife, of course—is unsurprisingly popular in Rome. Rome's proximity to the sea makes *pesce* (fish) popular as well. Expect to pay an extra €1-1.50 for *coperto* (service) and bread—whether or not you eat it.

FOOD BY PRICE

Under €7 (❶)		Ristorante Grappolo d' Oro Zampanò (123)	CF
▩ Miscellanea (121)	CS	L'Insalata Ricca (123)	CF
Pizza Art (122)	CS	Il Pollarola (123)	CF
Trattoria dal Cav. Gino (122)	CS	Vini e Buffet (123)	PS
Luzzi (122)	AC	Il Brillo Parlante (123)	PS
L'Antica Birreria Peroni (122)	AC	Cacio e Pepe (124)	VC
Franchi (124)	VC	Paninoteca da Guido e Patrizia (124)	VC
Hosteria Romana da Dino (124)	TER	Africa (124)	TER
Hostaria da Bruno (124)	TER	Arancia Blu (124)	TER
▩ Pizzeria San Callisto (125)	TRA	Pizzeria San Marco (125)	TRA
Augusto (125)	TRA	La Piazzetta (125)	PS
▩ Bar Da Benito (125)	JG	Trattoria da Giggetto (125)	JG
Il Portico (125)	JG	La Taverna del Ghetto (125)	JG
▩ Il Volpetti Pù (126)	TES	Il Cantinone (126)	TES
		Volpetti Salumeria-Gastronomia (126)	TES
€7-15 (❷)			
▩ Buoni Amici (122)	AC	**€16-22 (❸)**	
Taverna dei Fori Imperiali (122)	AC	Trattoria da Settimio all'Arancio (123)	PS
Hostaria Nerone (122)	AC	Centro Macrobiotico Italiano Naturist	
Taverna dei Quaranta (123)	AC	Club (123)	PS

AC Ancient City **CF** Campo dei Fiori **CS** Centro Storico **JG** Jewish Ghetto **PS** Piazza di Spagna and Environs **TRA** Trastevere **TER** Termini and Environs **TES** Testaccio **VC** Vatican City

CENTRO STORICO

▩ **Miscellanea,** V. delle Paste 110a (☎06 67 80 983), around the corner from the Pantheon. A proven student and local favorite. Dedicated owner, Mickey, will make your meal memorable. With fresh food, gigantic portions, low prices, and above all else, *"simpatia and respetto"* for the customers, Miscellanea exemplifies what a true *ristorante* should be. Sweet *fragoli*, a free "sexy wine" (as the owner calls it), included with every meal. Salads €6. Antipasto. *Panini* €3. Desserts €2-3. Open daily 11am-2am. AmEx. ❶

Pizza Art, V. Arenula 76 (☎06 687 316 0378). From C. V. Emanuele II, cut through Largo di Torre Argentina and walk toward the river. Delicious, thick focaccia pizza, topped with delicious ingredients like arugula and goat cheese. Try the candy-like *pizza con nutella* (from €2.50 per slice). Open daily 8am-10:30pm. Cash only. ❶

ROME

Trattoria dal Cav. Gino, Vicolo. Rosini 4 (☎06 68 73 434), small red-and-white sign, off V. di Campo Marzio, across from P. del Parlamente. Affable owner Gino greets guests himself. Dine under the blue sky, grapevines, and birds painted on the ceiling. Primi €6-8. Secondi €7-12. Open Sept.-July M-Sa 1-2:30pm and 8-10:30pm. Cash only. ❶

ANCIENT CITY

The area around the Fora and the Colosseum is home to some of Italy's finest tourist traps. Head to side streets where cheap and delicious culinary outposts are oases in a desert of color-photograph menus.

▨ **I Buoni Amici,** V. Aleardo Aleardi 4 (☎06 70 49 19 93). ⓂB-Colosseo. From the Colosseum, take V. Labicana, then take a right on V. Merulana and a left on V. A. Aleardi. Look for a blue *osteria* sign. Exceptional service. Try the popular *linguine alle vongole* (pasta with clams; €8). Self-serve antipasto bar. Primi and secondi €7-12. Wine €8-15. Dessert €4. Cover €1. Open M-Sa 12:30-3pm and 7-11pm. AmEx/MC/V. ❷

▨ **L'Antica Birreria Peroni,** V. San Marcello 19 (☎06 67 95 310; www.anticabirreriaperoni.it). From the Vittorio Emmanuele monument, turn right on V. Cesare Battisti and left into P. dei S. S. Apostoli. 1 block down on the left. Energetic *enoteca* with a German twist. Wash down a *wurstel* (€7) with 1 of 4 delicious beers on tap (€2-5). Fantastic *fiori di zucca* (€1). Primi €5-7. Cover €1. Open M-Sa noon-midnight. AmEx/MC/V. ❶

Luzzi, V. San Giovanni in Laterano 88 (☎06 70 96 332), just down V. dei Fori Imperiali from the Colosseum. No-fuss *osteria* packed with locals. Specials like *penne con salmone* (€7) will leave you wanting more. Wine €4 per L. Primi €5-7. Secondi €7-11. Dessert €4. Open M-Tu and Th-Su noon-3pm and 7pm-midnight. AmEx/MC/V. ❶

Taverna dei Fori Imperiali, V. della Madonna dei Monti 16 (☎06 67 98 643). ⓂB-Colosseo. Walk up V. dei Fori Imperiali, and turn right through the park at the beginning of V. Cavour. V. della Madonna dei Monti runs parallel to V. Cavour on the left. Steps away from Trajan's Forum. Creative twists on traditional Roman favorites like *tagliolini cacio e pepe e zafferano* (wide, flat noodles in a cheese and pepper saffron sauce; €7.50). Primi €7-8. Secondi €11-14. Cover €1.50. Open M and W-Su 12:30-3:30pm and 7-10:30pm. Reservations recommended for dinner. AmEx/MC/V. ❷

Hostaria Nerone, V. delle Terme di Tito 96 (☎06 48 17 952), between the Colosseum and the Domus Aurea. ⓂB-Colosseo. Take V. Nicola Salvi, turn right, and then left on V. delle Terme di Tito. Traditional dishes include *spaghetti all'amatriciana* (€8). House wine €2 per L. Self-serve antipasto €8. Primi €8-9. Secondi €9-13. Cover €1.50. Open Sept.-July M-Sa noon-3pm and 7-11pm. AmEx/MC/V. ❷

Taverna dei Quaranta, V. Claudia 24 (☎06 70 00 550). ⓂB-Colosseo. Up the hill past P. del Colosseo. Delicious dishes in the quiet shade ascending the Caelian Hill. Try the *oliva ascolane* (fried olives stuffed with meat; €4). 20 types of pizza available only at dinner. House wine €11 per L. Primi €8-10. Secondi €7-12.50. No pizza on M. Cover €1. Open daily 12:15-3:30pm and 7:30pm-11:30pm. AmEx/D/MC/V. ❷

CAMPO DEI FIORI

Il Pollarola, P. Pollarola 25/27 (☎06 68 80 16 54), just behind the Campo dei Fiori. Exquisite renditions of traditional dishes. Try the *cannelloni specialista* (pasta filled with meat, tomato, and mozzarella; €8). Daily specials €8-12. Primi €7-9. Secondi €9-13. Dessert €5. Cover €1. Open M-Sa 12:30-3pm and 5:30-11pm. AmEx/D/MC/V. ❷

Ristorante Grappolo d'Oro Zampanò, P. della Cancelleria 80/84 (☎06 68 97 080), between C. V. Emanuele II and the Campo. Enjoy delicious homemade pasta or the mouth-watering Argentine angus steak in balsamic vinegar (€15) to the soothing sound of the *piazza*'s fountain. Primi €7.50-10. Secondi €12-15. Cover €1.50. Open M and W-Sa noon-4:30pm and 7:30-11pm, Su noon-3pm and 7:30-11pm. MC/V. ❷

L'Insalata Ricca, Largo dei Chiavari 85-6 (☎06 68 80 36 56; www.linsalataricca.it), off C. V. Emanuele II near P. S. Andrea della Valle. 10 locations throughout Rome. Casual takeout joint meets full service restaurant. Friendly servers bring Parma ham, *pantesca* (tomatoes, capers, and potatoes), mammoth salads (€7-8). Pastas €7-8. Desserts €4. Cover €1.10. Open daily noon-4pm and 7pm-midnight. AmEx/D/MC/V. ❷

PIAZZA DI SPAGNA AND ENVIRONS

▧ **Il Brillo Parlante,** V. della Fontanella 12 (☎06 32 43 334; www.ilbrilloparlante.com). Ⓜ A-Flaminio. Take V. del Corso away from P. del Popolo and turn left on V. Fontanella. While the wood-burning oven cooks perfect pizza (€4.50-10), it's the handmade pasta, delectable sauces, and smaller dishes like *pecorino* cheese with honey and walnuts (€8.50) that set this place apart. Primi €8-9.50. Secondi €9.50-18. Open M 5pm-1am, Tu-Su 12:30pm-1am. Bar open 5-7:30pm. Reservations recommended. MC/V. ❷

Vini e Buffet, V. della Torretta 60 (☎06 68 71 445), near P. di Spagna. From V. del Corso, turn on P. di San Lorenzo in Lucina. Turn left on V. Campo Marzio and right on V. della Torretta. A favorite among local wine enthusiasts. Antipasti €4-9. Crepes €7.50-8. Salads €7.50-11. Regional wines €10-24 per bottle. Open M-Sa 12:30-3pm and 7:30-11pm. Reservations recommended. Cash only. ❷

Trattoria da Settimio all'Arancio, V. dell'Arancio 50-52 (☎06 68 76 119). Take V. dei Condotti from P. di Spagna; after V. del Corso bear right on V. Tomacelli and take 1st left. Generous portions of decadent dishes. Try handmade *ravioli all'arancio* (cheese ravioli in cream sauce with a hint of orange). Primi €8-15. Secondi €8-20. Open M-Sa 12:30-3pm and 7pm-midnight. Reservations recommended. AmEx/MC/V. ❸

Centro Macrobiotico Italiano Naturist Club, V. della Vite 14, 4th fl. (☎06 67 92 509). Heading toward P. del Popolo on V. del Corso, take a right on V. della Vite. Wonderful for health-conscious travelers. All organic vegan menu with Italian specialties. "Natural snacks" €8-10. Lunch *menù* €14. Dinner *menù* €20-25. Open M-F 12:30-3pm and 7:30-11pm, Sa 7:30-11pm. Reservations required for dinner. AmEx/MC/V. ❸

VATICAN CITY

Venture down V. Cola di Rienzo towards P. Cavour and explore the residential side streets to escape touristy bars and *pizzerie*. The area west of P. Risorgimento and north of Vatican City is also full of packed, family-run eateries.

Cacio e Pepe, V. Giuseppe Avezzana 11 (☎06 32 17 268). From P. Mazzini, turn right on V. Settembrini, right at P. dei Martiri di Belfiore, and left on V. Giuseppe Avezzana (about a 20min. walk from P. del Risorgimento). Worth the walk from the Vatican. In summer, rub elbows with locals at the close-packed tables outside. Namesake specialty is perfectly *al dente*, topped with olive oil, grated cheese, and fresh-ground pepper (€6). Open M-F 12:30-3pm and 7:30-11pm, Sa 12:30-3pm. Cash only. ❷

Paninoteca da Guido e Patrizia, Borgo Pio 13 (☎06 68 75 491), near Castel Sant'Angelo. Casual atmosphere and homey decor—perfect for a quick afternoon bite. Popular with locals. Owner Guido holds court behind a well-stocked *tavola calda* (snackbar). Full meal (primo, secondo, and drink) around €11. Open M-Sa 8am-6pm. Cash only. ❷

Franchi, V. Cola di Rienzo 200-204 (☎06 68 74 651; www.franchi.it). Luxurious picnic supplier for nearly 50 years. Cheaper and of better quality than most Vatican-area snack bars. Try the delicious *fritti misti* (deep-fried zucchini flowers, artichoke hearts, and zucchini) or the house ravioli. A snack-size pizza (€2.60) is great for those lines at the Vatican Museums. Stuff yourself for around €8. Open M-Sa 9am-8:30pm. AmEx/MC/V. ❶

Peccato Divino, V. Properzio 30 (☎06 45 423 168). Ⓜ A-Ottaviano. Steps from P. Risorgimento. Sinfully delectable cuisine to match this romantic *enoteca*'s name—"divine sin."

Pair top-notch wine with gourmet cheeses (€12) and indulge in a chocolatey dessert. Secondi €20-25. Open M-Sa noon-3pm and 6:30pm-2am. AmEx/MC/V. ❹

TERMINI AND ENVIRONS

San Lorenzo offers inexpensive food with local character to the budget-conscious student with a discriminating palate. There's a **Conad** supermarket on the lower floor of Termini Station. (Open daily 8am-midnight.)

 NOT SO SICURO. Termini and the surrounding areas are unsafe at night. Stay alert and avoid walking alone in the neighborhood at night.

Hostaria da Bruno, V. Varese 29 (☎06 49 04 03). Take V. Milazzo from V. Marsala. Turn right on V. Varese. A bastion of authenticity in a sea of tourist traps. Try *tortellini al sugo* (meat tortellini; €7). Open M-F noon-3pm and 7-10pm, Sa 7-10pm. AmEx/MC/V. ❶

Hostaria Romana da Dino, V. dei Mille 10 (☎06 49 14 25). From Termini's track 1, turn left on V. Marsala, right on V. Vicenza, and left on V. dei Mille. Delicious dishes for dirt-cheap prices. Loyal local following. Delectable pizza (€5-7) and pasta (€4.50-5). House wine €1.10 per L. Open M-Tu and Th-Su noon-3pm and 6:30-11pm. ❶

Africa, V. Gaeta 26-28 (☎06 49 41 077), near P. Indipendenza. 32-year tradition of affordable Eritrean and Ethiopian cuisine. Vegetarian menu available. Secondi €8-11. Cover €1. Open Tu-Su 8am-2am. AmEx/MC/V. ❷

Arancia Blu, V. Prenestina 396 (☎34 54 73 18 18), in San Lorenzo southeast of Termini. Elegant and popular vegetarian restaurant greets you with 3 glasses of wine (white, red, and sparkling). Adventurous yet affordable. Enjoy the warm pesto salad (€7.50) under soft lighting. Wine from €12 per bottle. Open daily 8:30pm-midnight. Cash only. ❷

JEWISH GHETTO

The Jewish Ghetto, about 10min. south of the Campo dei Fiori and near the Tiber, serves tempting kosher and traditional Jewish specialties with an Italian twist—a welcome break from pasta and pizza. Keep in mind that much of the Ghetto is closed on Saturdays for the Sabbath.

▨ **Portico,** V. del Portico D'Ottavia 1/D (☎06 68 64 642). Pleasant patio perfect for people-watching and filling pizza (from €6.50) with plentiful toppings. Salads €5-8. Primi €5.50-8. Secondi €7-14. Open daily noon-3:30pm and 7pm-midnight. MC/V. ❶

La Taverna del Ghetto, V. del Portico d'Ottavia 8 (☎06 68 80 97 71; www.latavernadelghetto.com). Popular kosher *taverna* prides itself on homemade pasta and delicacies like *lingua all'ebraica* (veal tongue). The *stracotto di manzo* (braised beef; €14) goes nicely with red wine. Primi €11. Secondi €14-17. Open M-Th and Sa-Su noon-3pm and 6:30-11pm, F noon-3pm. Reservations recommended. Cover €1.50. AmEx/MC/V. ❷

Trattoria da Giggetto, V. del Portico d'Ottavia 21-22 (☎06 68 61 105; www.giggettoalportico.com), next to the Portico d'Ottavia ruins. Traditional Roman fare like *fritto misto* (mixed fried vegetables; €12) and Jewish delicacies. Primi €11-16. Secondi €9-20. Dessert €5-6. Cover €1.50. Open Tu-Su 12:30-3:30pm and 7:30-11pm. Closed last 2 weeks of July. Dinner reservations required. AmEx/MC/V. ❷

Bar Da Benito, V. dei Falegnami 14 (☎06 68 61 508), easiest to approach from V. del Portico d'Ottavia or V. Arenula. Lightning-quick bus boys clear tables faster than a NASCAR pit crew. Fresh, delicious food. Primi €4.50. Secondi €4.50-7.50. Dessert €2-3.50. Open M-Sa 6:30am-7pm. Closed Aug. Cash only. ❶

ROME

TESTACCIO

▩ **Il Volpetti Più,** V. Alessandro Volta 8 (☎06 57 44 306; www.volpetti.com). Turn left on V. A. Volta, off V. Marmorata. Relive high school as you slide down the lunch line at this *tavola calda*—but replace day-old sloppy joes with authentic Italian fare. Pasta and pizza from €4. Open M-Sa 10:30am-3:30pm and 5:30-9:30pm. AmEx/MC/V. ❶

Il Cantinone, P. Testaccio 31/32 (☎06 57 46 253). Ⓜ B-Piramide. Turn left on V. Giovanni Batista Bodoni off V. Marmorata; P. Testaccio is just past V. Luca della Robbia. Patrons slurp down *pappardelle* with boar sauce (€8) and hearty meat-and-gravy dishes (€10-20). Enormous brick oven pumps out delicious pizza (€5-7). Terrific house white wine €6 per L. Open M and W-Su noon-3pm and 7pm-midnight. AmEx/MC/V. ❷

Volpetti Salumeria-Gastronomia, V. Marmorata 47 (☎06 57 42 352), around the corner from its sister restaurant, Il Volpetti Più. Duck to avoid hanging meat shanks at this spiffy shop and wander among shelves lined with fresh gourmet cheeses, homemade pasta, and baked goods (priced per kg). Open M-Sa 8am-2pm and 5-10:15pm. AmEx. ❷

GELATERIE AND PASTICCERIE

While gelato is everywhere in Rome, good gelato is less common. And lest you think that gelato is the only sweet Rome has to offer, numerous bakeries sell cookies and small cakes all priced by the *etto* (100g).

▩ **Pellachia,** Vatican, V. C. di Rienzo 103 (☎06 32 10 807; www.pellachia.com). After an afternoon of budget-friendly boutique shopping on V. Cola di Rienzo, drop by this beloved *gelateria,* which serves simple, fresh flavors with finesse. Ask for the "kiss" (chocolate with hazelnuts) on a date, or *fragole con panna e gelato* (strawberries with gelato and fresh cream; €4.50). Cones €1.50-3. Open Tu-Su 6am-1:30am. AmEx/MC/V. ❶

▩ **The Old Bridge,** Vatican, V. dei Bastioni di Michelangelo 5 (☎06 39 72 30 26), off P. del Risorgimento, across from the bend in the Vatican Museum's outer wall. Your wait in the Vatican museums lines will seem much shorter (and sweeter) with a heaping, melty cone—that is if you make it past the gelato lines at this local favorite. 20 homemade flavors. Cup or cone €1.30-3. Cash only. Open M-Sa 10am-2am, Su 3pm-2am. ❶

▩ **Pasticceria Ebraico Boccione,** Jewish Ghetto, V. del Portico d'Ottavia 1 (☎06 68 78 637), on the corner of P. Costaguti. Tiny, family-run bakery serves only about 8 specialties, including delicious custard-filled challah (€0.60) and sugar-dusted *ciambelle* (doughnuts; €0.80). Open in winter M-Th and Su 8am-7:30pm, F 8am-3:30pm; in summer M-Th 8am-7:30pm, F 8am-3:30 pm, and Su 8am-2pm and 4-7:30pm. ❶

Biscottificio Artigiano Innocenti, Trastevere, V. della Luce 21 (☎06 57 03 926). From P. Sonnino, take V. Giulio Cesare Santina and turn left on V. della Luce. This haven of baked goodness sells a dizzying variety of cookies and biscuits, and has been featured in countless international culinary magazines. Stock up on hazelnut, almond, chocolate, and jam cookies (about €2.50 for 10). Open Tu-Sa 8am-8pm, Su 9:30am-2pm. ❶

Della Palma, *centro storico,* V. della Maddalena 20/23 (☎06 68 80 67 52), steps from the Pantheon, with another location near the Trevi Fountain. Over 100 flavors of gelato, including meringue and spicy dark chocolate. Famous for its mousse. Small (2 flavors, €2). Medium (4 flavors, €3). *Granita* €2. Open daily 8am-1:30am. Cash only. ❷

Giolitti, *centro storico,* V. degli Uffici del Vicario 40 (☎06 69 91 243; www.giolitti.it). From the Pantheon, follow V. del Pantheon, take V. della Maddalena to its end, and turn right on V. degli Uffici del Vicario. Always crowded. More than 50 unique flavors of gelato, such as *limoncello,* champagne, and *crema* (€2-4). Top off your cone with homemade *panna* (whipped cream). Open daily 7am-1am. AmEx/MC/V. ❶

Il Gelatone, Ancient City, V. dei Serpente 28 (☎06 48 20 187). From V. dei Fori Imperiali, take a left on V. Cavour, then left on V. dei Serpente. Neon-colored *gelateria* with creamy, smooth gelato. Try the specialty *gelatone,* a blend of chocolate and vanilla with chocolate chips. The cool and refreshing *pompelmo rosa* (pink grapefruit) complements *limoncello* nicely. Over 65 flavors, including soy-based gelato. Cones €1.50-3, 4-flavor cone-bowls €4. Open daily 9:30am-midnight. Cash only. ❶

Da Quinto Gelateria, Ancient City, V. di Tor Millina 15 (☎06 68 65 657), off P. Navona on a side street next to the church. Walls plastered with pictures of the hot-pink-aproned owner posing with famous clientele, including Ben Stiller and various cardinals. Fresh fruit *frullati* (smoothies) made to order. Gelato €1.50-3. Gelato *affogato* (drenched in whiskey, brandy, or rum) €3.50. Open in summer daily 11am-3am. Cash only. ❶

CAFFÈ

Caffè della Pace, *centro storico,* V. della Pace 3-7 (☎06 68 61 216; www.caffedella-pace.it), off P. Navona. More of a laid-back, swanky *enoteca* than a cafe; take your time and don't rush through with counter service. Espresso €3. Prosecco €8. Mixed drinks €10. Open M 4pm-2am, Tu-Su 9am-2am. ❷

Caffè Tazza d'Oro, *centro storico,* V. degli Orfani 84 (☎06 67 92 768 or 67 89 792; www.tazzadorocoffeeshop.com). Boasts *"il migliore caffè nel mondo"* (the best coffee in the world) as well as an extensive tea selection. Try the *granita di caffè con panna* (with fresh whipped cream; €2). Coffee from €0.80. Open M-Sa 7am-8pm. ❶

Sant'Eustachio Il Caffè, *centro storico,* P. di Sant'Eustachio 82 (☎06 68 80 20 48). Turn right on V. Palombella behind the Pantheon. Since 1938, this cafe has built a reputation as one of Rome's finest. Muscle your way to the front of the line for signature *gran caffè speciale* (€2.20 standing; €4.20 table service). Ground coffee €22 per kg. Open M-Th 8:30am-1:30am, F and Su 8:30am-1am, Sa 8:30am-2am. Cash only. ❶

ENOTECHE (WINE BARS)

The tinkling of crystal, low lighting, and an intimate atmosphere distinguish true *enoteche* from more rough-and-tumble pubs. Serving a variety of small dishes and plates, like cheese, smoked meats, antipasto, and salads, *enoteche* are usually frequented by Romans looking for a small bite before a late dinner or those who plan to simply stay and sip the night away.

Enoteca Cavour 313, V. Cavour 313 (☎06 67 85 496). A short walk from ⓂB-Cavour; near the Colosseum. Sip wine from crystal glasses in this French bar's intimate booths, where the sweaty tourist crowds feel oceans away. Try a *misto di formaggi* (mixed cheese plate; €8-10). Meats (mixed plate €7-14) listed by region or type. Wine €3-8 per glass; from €13 per bottle. Rich desserts €4-6. Open M-Sa 12:30-2:30pm and 7:30pm-12:30am, Su 7:30pm-12:30am. Closed Aug. AmEx/MC/V. ❷

Cul de Sac, P. Pasquino 73 (☎06 68 80 10 94), off P. Navona. One of Rome's 1st wine bars. Specialty homemade *pâtés* (including boar and chocolate or pheasant with truffle) are exquisite, as is the *escargot alla bourguignonne* (€6.40). Wine from €2 per glass. Primi €7-8. Secondi €7-9. Open daily noon-4pm and 6pm-12:30am. MC/V. ❷

Enoteca Trastevere, V. della Lungaretta 86 (☎06 58 85 659). A block off P. Santa Maria. Small but high-caliber wine list. Wine €3.50-5 per glass. Meat and cheese plates €10-12. Desserts €3-5. Open M-Sa 6pm-2:30am, Su 6pm-1am. ❷

Trimani Wine Bar, V. Cernaia 37/B (☎06 44 69 630), near Termini, perpendicular to V. Volturno, with a shop around the corner at V. Goito 20. Escape the summertime heat in this chilled fine wine haven that exudes easy, unpretentious class. Suggested wines complement meat plates (€9-13.50). Famous chocolate mousse €6.50. Wines from €2 per glass. Happy hour 11:30am-12:30pm and 6-7pm. Open M-Sa 11:30am-3pm and 6pm-12:30am. Open daily in Dec. AmEx/MC/V. ❷

◉ SIGHTS

CENTRO STORICO

VIA DEL CORSO AND PIAZZA VENEZIA. Following the ancient V. Lata, V. del Corso began as Rome's premier race course and now plays host to many parades, including **Carnevale.** Running between P. del Popolo and P. Venezia, it is full of restaurants, hotels, *gelaterie*, and affordable boutiques (see **Shopping,** p. 154). From P. del Popolo, take V. del Corso to **Piazza di Colonna Romana** where **Palazzo Wedekind,** home to the newspaper *Il Tempo*, was built in 1838 with columns from the Etruscan city of Veio. Running south from P. del Popolo, V. del Corso ends at P. Venezia, home to the massive white marble **Vittorio Emanuele II monument.** Lovingly referred to as "the wedding cake" or "Mussolini's typewriter," the monolithic monument makes a good reference point. At the top of the exterior staircase is the **Altare della Patria,** which has two eternal flames guarded night and day by the Italian Navy in remembrance of the Unknown Soldier. Walk upstairs to the **Museo Centrale del Risorgimento** for a comprehensive exhibit on Italian unification. *(Open daily 9:30am-6:30pm. Free.)* The **Palazzo Venezia,** right off P. Venezia, once used by Mussolini as both an office and a soapbox, is one of Rome's earliest Renaissance structures.

PANTHEON AND PIAZZA DELLA ROTONDA. The granite columns, bronze doors, and soaring dome of the Pantheon's still, cool interior have changed little over the building's 2000 years. Architects still puzzle over the engineering; its dome, a perfect half-sphere constructed from poured concrete without the support of vaults, arches, or ribs, is the largest of its kind. It was built under Hadrian from AD 118 to 125 over the site of an earlier Pantheon destroyed in AD 80. In AD 608 the Pantheon was consecrated as the **Chiesa di Santa Maria ad Martyres.** Several noteworthy figures are buried within: Renaissance painter Raphael; King Vittorio Emanuele II, the first king of united Italy; his son, Umberto I, second king of Italy; and finally, Umberto's wife, Queen Margherita, after whom the *pizza margherita* was named in the 19th century. *(Open M-Sa 8:30am-7:30pm, Su 9am-6pm, holidays 9am-1pm. Closed Jan. 1, May 1, Dec. 25. Free. 20min. audio tour €3.)*

In front of the Pantheon, an **Egyptian obelisk** dominates the ever-crowded P. della Rotonda. Around the Pantheon's left side and down the street, another obelisk, supported by Bernini's curious **elephant statue,** marks the center of tiny P. Minerva. Behind the obelisk is Rome's only Gothic church: **Chiesa di Santa Maria Sopra Minerva.** Built on the site of an ancient Roman temple, the unassuming exterior of this hidden gem hides some Renaissance masterpieces, including Michelangelo's *Christ Bearing the Cross*, Antoniazzo Romano's *Annunciation*, and a statue of St. Sebastian recently attributed to Michelangelo. The **Cappella Carafa** in the southern transept boasts a brilliant series of Fra Filippo Lippi frescoes. A decapitated St. Catherine of Siena is reportedly buried under the altar; her head rests in Siena's *duomo. (Open daily 7am-1pm and 3-7pm.)* From the upper left corner of P. della Rotonda, V. Giustiniani heads north to V. della Scrofa and V. della Dogana Vecchia, where you'll find **Chiesa di San Luigi dei Francesi,** France's national church in Rome, and home to three of Caravaggio's most famous paintings: *The Calling of St. Matthew, St. Matthew and the Angel,* and *The Crucifixion. (P. San Luigi dei Francesi 5. 1 block down V. di Salvatore from C. del Rinascimento, opposite P. Navona. Open daily 7:30am-12:30pm and 3:30-7pm.)*

ROME

IMBIBE THIS! Remember that Rome's water is *potabile* (drinkable), and many fountains or spigots run throughout the city. Take a drink, or fill up your water bottle from these free sources of cold, refreshing *acqua naturale.*

PIAZZA NAVONA. Originally a stadium built by Domitian in AD 86, P. Navona is now filled with artists, puppeteers, and mimes. Bernini's **Fontana dei Quattro Fiumi** (Fountain of the Four Rivers) commands the *piazza.* Each river god represents a continent: the Ganges for Asia, the Danube for Europe, the Nile for Africa (veiled because the river's source was at the time of construction), and Rio de la Plata for the Americas. Giacomo della Porta's 16th-century **Fontana del Moro** and the **Fontana di Nettuno** stand at opposite ends of the *piazza.* The **Chiesa di Sant'Agnese** in Agone holds the tiny skull of its namesake saint. Legend has it that Agnes was condemned to death for refusing to marry the son of a Roman prefect. To circumvent the law against executing virgins, she was dragged naked to a brothel, but her hair miraculously grew to cover her body. Then, when they tried to burn her alive, she would not light, so one indefatigable Roman soldier swiftly chopped off her head. *(West side of P. Navona, opposite Fontana dei Quattro Fiumi. Open daily 9am-noon and 4-7pm.)* West of P. Navona, at the intersection of V. di Tor Millina and V. della Pace, the **Chiesa di Santa Maria della Pace** houses Raphael's *Sibyls* in its Chigi Chapel. *(Open M-F 10am-noon and 3-6pm, Sa 10am-10pm, Su 10am-1pm.)* On nearby C. del Rinascimento, the **Chiesa di Sant'Ivo's corkscrew cupola** hovers over the Palazzo della Sapienza, originally home to the University of Rome before it was enlarged under Mussolini. *(Open M-Sa 9am-6pm; Chiesa di S. Ivo alla Sapienza services Su 9am-noon.)* Down C. V. Emanuele II, Jesuit church **Il Gesu** houses Andrea Pozzo's masterful *Chapel of S. Ignazio* and Bernini's *Monument to S. Bellarmino. (Open daily 6:45am-12:45pm and 4-7:45pm.)*

CAMPO DEI FIORI. Campo dei Fiori is across C. V. Emanuele I from P. Navona. By day, the *piazza*'s fountain and colorful, peeling facades play host to a bustling **market.** *(Open daily 9am-1:30pm.)* By night, the Campo transforms into a hip young person's magnet. Under papal rule, the area was a popular execution site; an eerie statue pays tribute to Giordano Bruno, one of the deceased. The English and Irish pubs that dominate today's Campo create an odd juxtaposition between traditional, laid-back Italy and the inescapable Anglo influence that dominates much of the peninsula. South of the Campo, the **Palazzo Farnese** dominates P. Farnese. **Palazzo Spada** and its **art gallery** are to the east.

LARGO DI TORRE ARGENTINA. This busy square is named for the **Torre Argentina** that dominates its southeast corner. The sunken area in the center of the Largo is a complex of four Republican temples unearthed in 1926 during Mussolini's project for demolishing the medieval city. The site is now a cat shelter, and dozens of felines patrol its grounds, providing photo opportunities for cat calendar photographers everywhere. The shelter welcomes donations and volunteers to help take care of the cats. The *piazza* also serves as a handy point of orientation, as it lies along C. V. Emanuele between the P. Navona area and the area surrounding C. dei Fiori and the Jewish Ghetto. *(At the intersection of C. V. Emanuele II and V. di Torre Argentina. Shelter ☎ 06 45 42 52 40; www.romancats.com.)*

MUSEI NAZIONALI ROMANI. The **Museo Nazionale Romano Palazzo Massimo alle Terme** is devoted to art from the Roman Empire, including the Lancellotti *Discus Thrower*, a rare mosaic of Nero's time, as well as ancient coins and jewelry. *(Largo di Villa Peretti 1. In the left corner of P. dei Cinquecento. www.roma2000.it/zmunaro.html. Open Tu-Sa 9am-2pm, Su 9am-1pm. €15, includes admission to Baths of Diocletian. Cash only.)*

ROME

Nearby, **the Museo Nazionale Romano Terme di Diocleziano,** a beautifully renovated complex partly housed in the huge **Baths of Diocletian,** has exhibits devoted to ancient writing and Latin history as well as a cloister by Michelangelo. *(Vle. Enrico de Nicola 78. Open Tu-Sa 9am-2pm, Su 9am-1pm. €15. Cash only.)* The **Aula Ottogonale,** in another wing, holds Classical sculptures in a gorgeous octagonal space. *(V. Romita. Open daily 9am-1pm and 3-6pm. Included with Baths of Diocletian admission.)*

ANCIENT CITY

PALATINE HILL
South of the Roman Forum, this hill was home to the Roman emperors. Purchase tickets or Archeologica Card at the biglietteria 100m down V. di San Gregorio from the Colosseum. Open daily Mar.-Aug. 8:30am-7:15pm; Sept. 9am-7pm; Oct. 9am-6:30pm; Nov. to mid-Feb. 9am-4:30pm; mid-Feb. to Mar. 9am-5pm. Last entry 1hr. before closing. Combined ticket with the Colosseum €11, EU citizens 18-24 €6.50, EU citizens under 18 or over 65 free. Combined ticket requires you to see both sites in 1 day, unless tickets are purchased after 1:30pm, in which case they are valid until 1:30pm the next day. Cash only.

Legend has it that the Palatine Hill, a plateau between the Tiber River and the Roman Forum, was home to *la lupa,* the she-wolf that suckled Romulus and Remus. During the Republic, the Palatine was the most fashionable residential quarter, where aristocrats and statesmen, including Cicero and Marc Antony, built their homes. Augustus lived here in a modest house, but later emperors capitalized on the hill's prestige and built gargantuan quarters. By the end of the AD first century, the imperial residence covered the entire hill, whose Latin name, *Palatium,* became synonymous with the palace.

The best way to approach the Palatine is from the northeast by the stairs near the **Arch of Titus.** The path ascends to the 17th-century **Farnese Gardens (Orti Farnesiani),** the world's oldest botanical gardens. Views of the Roman Forum make the gardens perfect for a picnic; *"Affacciata sul Foro"* (Facing the Forum) signs point to a lookout over reflecting pools at the **House of Vestal Virgins.**

On the southwest side of the hill directly below the Farnese Gardens, the remains of an ancient village feature the **Casa di Romulo,** alleged home of Romulus, as well as the **Temple of Cybele.** These remains can be dated to roughly the same period as the Forum's Archaic necropolis, which supports the theory that Rome was founded in the eighth century BC. To the left of Casa di Romulo is the **Casa di Livia,** where Augustus's wife Livia resided. The house used to connect to the **Casa di Augusto** (not to be confused with Domus Augustana) next door. Around the corner to the left, stretching along the Farnese Gardens, is the mosaic-tiled **Cryptoporticus,** a tunnel which connected Tiberius's palace with nearby buildings and was used by slaves and couriers as a secret passage.

To the left of the Casa di Livia at the center of the hill is the sprawling **Domus Flavia,** the site of an octagonal fountain that occupied almost the entire courtyard. Romans have traditionally associated octagons with power; you will see

ROME

many octagonal rooms in places of important significance, such as the Vatican and at the bases of important statues. To the left of the Domus Flavia stands the solemn **Domus Augustana,** the emperor's private space. Visitors are only allowed on the upper level, from which they can make out the shape of two courtyards down below. The palace's east wing contains the curious **Stadium Palatinum,** a sunken oval space used as a riding school.

 PALATINE PROBLEMS. There is no English audio tour available for the Palatine Hill. Be sure to catch the ⚔ **guided English tour** (daily 4:15pm; €3.50, with Archeologica Card €2.50).

Visitors can also see the **Circus Maximus,** which lies right behind the hippodrome. The fire of AD 64 started from there and spread to the Palatine, causing everything in the residences, except for the marble and stone constructions, to burn. The **Museo Palatino,** between the Domus Flavia and the Domus Augustana, displays archaeological artifacts from the early Archaic period on the lower level. The upper floor of the museum displays sculptures of well-to-do Romans and their deities. (Open daily 9:10am-6:20pm. Visiting slots every 20min.; only 30 people per fl. per slot. Free with admission to the Palatine.)

COLOSSEUM

☎06 70 05 469. Ⓜ B-Colosseo. Open daily 8:30am-7:15pm. Last entry 6:15pm. ⚔ **Tours with archaeologist** in Italian Sa-Su, English and Spanish daily every 30-45min. from 9:45am-1:45pm and 3-5:15pm. The same sticker you get for the Palatine/Roman Forum will get you an English tour at the Colosseum as well. Tours €3.50. Audio tour €4.50 in Dutch, English, French, Italian, Japanese, and Spanish. Video tour €5.50. Cash only.

 CUT THE LINE. To avoid waiting up to 20min. for tickets to the Colosseum, purchase from the less-crowded biglietteria on V. di San Gregorio.

The Colosseum—a hollowed-out ghost of Travertine marble that once held more than 50,000 bloodthirsty spectators and now dwarfs every other ruin in Rome—stands as an enduring symbol of the Eternal City. The arena's name comes from the legendary 35m statue of Nero that used to stand beside it. The gilded bronze statue was referred to as "The Colossus," and hence the building became known as the Colosseum. The gaping holes in the bricks are the only signs left of where the brilliant marble ornamentation used to lie. Romans repeatedly stripped monuments of their marble to re-use in new monuments, a process called spoilage. You can see signs of spoilage throughout the ancient city's ruins—look for the holes where iron hooks were ripped out of the wall.

Within 100 days of the Colosseum's AD 80 opening, some 5000 wild beasts perished in its bloody arena, and the slaughter continued for three more centuries. The labyrinth of cells, ramps, and elevators used to transport exotic animals from cages to arena level was once covered by a wooden floor and layers of sand. Upon release, the beasts would suddenly emerge into the arena, surprising spectators and hunters alike. Animals weren't the only beings killed for sport; men were also pitted against men. Though these gladiators were often slaves and prisoners, if they won their fights, they were idolized like modern athletes—at least until the next fight. Contrary to popular belief, not all gladiator matches ended in death. Some fights stopped after the first knockdown, or the loser could ask the emperor—who would defer to the crowd—for mercy.

A section of seating has been reconstructed using original Roman marble to represent what the stands used to look like. Spectators sat according to a hierarchy of class and gender, with senators, knights, and vestal virgins closest to the arena and women of lower classes on the highest tier.

Next to the Colosseum, on the corner of V. di San Gregorio, stands the **Arco di Costantino,** one of the area's best preserved Imperial monuments. The arch commemorates Constantine's bold victory at the Battle of the Milvian Bridge in AD 312, using fragments from monuments to Trajan, Hadrian, and Marcus Aurelius.

ROMAN FORUM

Main entrance: V. dei Fori Imperiali, at Largo Corrado Ricci, halfway between P. Venezia and the Colosseum. Other entrances are opposite the Colosseum, at the start of V. Sacra, and at the Clivus Capitolinus, near P. del Campidoglio. ⓂB-Colosseo, or bus to P. Venezia. Access to the Forum is unpredictable, as areas are sometimes fenced off for excavation or restoration. Open daily in summer 8:30am-7:15pm; in winter 9am-4:15pm. Last entry 1hr. before closing. Free. Guided tour in English with archaeologist daily 12:30pm. €3.50. Inquire at Biglietteria Palatino, at the end of V. Nova past the Arch of Titus, for the audio tour in Dutch, English, French, German, Italian, and Japanese. €4. Cash only.

Because this valley between two of Rome's most famous hills—the Palatine and Capitoline—was originally a marshland prone to flooding, Rome's Iron Age inhabitants (1000-900 BC) avoided it in favor of the Palatine Hill, descending only to bury their dead. In the eighth and seventh centuries BC, Etruscans and Greeks used the Forum as a marketplace. The Romans founded a thatched-hut shantytown here in 753 BC, when Romulus and Sabine leader Titus Tatius joined forces to end the war triggered by the infamous rape of the Sabine women. Today, the Forum bears witness to centuries of civic building.

From the Arch of Constantine by the Colosseum, take V. Sacra, the oldest street in Rome, to the **Arch of Titus.** On the left as you approach the arch lie the **Thermae** (Baths) and the **Temple of Jupiter Stator.** On the right is a series of 10 columns, all that remain of Hadrian's **Temple of Venus and Rome.** Built in AD 81 by Domitian, the Arch of Titus stands in the area of the Forum called the **Velia** and celebrates Jerusalem's sack by Domitian's brother Titus. The right panel shows a triumphal Titus on a quadriga chariot, while his soldiers carry back the spoils of war on the left panel. It is missing the two-sided arches typical of a triumphal arch (2 lower arches flanking a taller middle arch) because they were damaged when it was removed from its original location.

The Chronicle

IN RECENT NEWS

NO MORE ROMA IN ROMA?

For years, tourists visiting Italian cities have been warned to clutch their cameras and wallets around major monuments to guard against gypsies who frequently ensnare visitors by begging for spare change or claiming to sell souvenirs. Problems have grown so serious in recent years that it's more than just tourists who worry about the ethnic minority that has served as a public scapegoat for the past generation.

The LA Times reports that due to certain crimes attributed to the Roma, the Italian government decided to address the huge nomadic settlements surrounding Italian cities with gypsy round ups, and by raiding and destroying their dwellings. The Italian government is even fomenting plans to have all gypsies—children included—fingerprinted, with the ultimate aim of deporting most Roma adults. The authorities claim that the suddenly parentless children will be resettled in safer, cleaner environments.

This presents an obvious concern for many European Parliament members, who have decried the move as racist and deeply unsettling. With no nation to turn to for support or protection, the Roma may have hope only in allies in neighboring European countries.

ROME

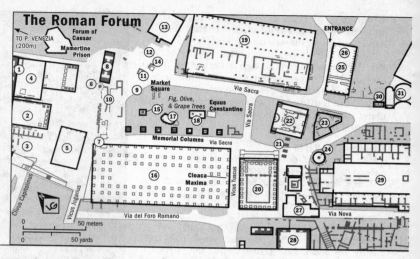

The Roman Forum

Turn right to face the Baroque facade of the **Chiesa della Santa Francesca Romana** (or **Santa Maria Nova**), which was built over Hadrian's Temple of Venus and Rome. It hides the entrance to the **Antiquarium Forense,** a museum displaying necropolis urns and skeletons (open daily 9:30am-noon and 4:30-7pm). Turn left, and as you pass the Upper Forum, check out the colossal ruins of the **Basilica of Maxentius and Constantine** on the right. Emperor Maxentius began construction in AD 308, but Constantine deposed him and completed the project himself. Farther down you pass the **Temple of Romulus,** named for the son of Maxentius (not the legendary founder of Rome), on the right. The original bronze doors have a AD fourth-century working lock.

Just after the Temple of Romulus is the **Archaic Necropolis,** a flat platform where Iron Age graves lend credibility to Rome's legendary eighth-century BC founding. Farther down on the right, the columns and rigid lattice ceiling help preserve the **Temple of Antoninus and Faustina.** In the AD seventh and eighth centuries, after numerous unsuccessful attempts to demolish it, confirmed by gashes near the at the top, the **Chiesa di San Lorenzo in Miranda** was built in the temple's interior. The church is an example of the medieval approach to the pagan ruins—either tear down the temples or convert them to churches.

Continuing down V. Sacra's right fork, on the left lie the remains of the **Regia,** which once served as the office of the Pontifex Maximus, Rome's high priest and the titular ancestor of the pope. Next on the left is the **Temple of the Deified Julius,** a shrine built by Augustus in 29 BC to honor the great leader and proclaim himself the inheritor of Julius Caesar's divine spirit. This is believed to be the site of Caesar's cremation, where he was burned in a funeral pyre with a piece of wood, flowers, and a cage with an eagle over his body. As the fire was started, the eagle was released from the cage, a symbol of the soul of the dead emperor flying away towards the heavens. Every year on July 12, Caesar's alleged birthday, people bring flowers to the shrine.

Back on V. Sacra, the **Basilica Aemilia** is on the right as you enter the **Civic Forum.** Built in 179 BC, the Basilica housed the guild of the *argentari* (money changers). It was rebuilt several times after fires until one started by Alaric and his merry band of Goths in AD 410 left it in its current state. Melted coins are now

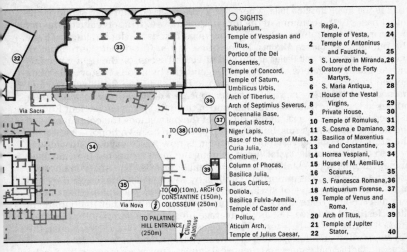

○ SIGHTS

Tabularium,	1	Regia,	23
Temple of Vespasian and		Temple of Vesta,	24
Titus,	2	Temple of Antoninus	
Portico of the Dei		and Faustina,	25
Consentes,	3	S. Lorenzo in Miranda,	26
Temple of Concord,	4	Oratory of the Forty	
Temple of Saturn,	5	Martyrs,	27
Umbilicus Urbis,	6	S. Maria Antiqua,	28
Arch of Tiberius,	7	House of the Vestal	
Arch of Septimius Severus,	8	Virgins,	29
Decennalia Base,	9	Private House,	30
Imperial Rostra,	10	Temple of Romulus,	31
Niger Lapis,	11	S. Cosma e Damiano,	32
Base of the Statue of Mars,	12	Basilica of Maxentius	
Curia Julia,	13	and Constantine,	33
Comitium,	14	Horrea Vespiani,	34
Column of Phocas,	15	House of M. Aemilius	
Basilica Julia,	16	Scaurus,	35
Lacus Curtius,	17	S. Francesca Romana,	36
Doliola,	18	Antiquarium Forense,	37
Basilica Fulvia-Aemilia,	19	Temple of Venus and	
Temple of Castor and		Roma,	38
Pollux,	20	Arch of Titus,	39
Aticum Arch,	21	Temple of Jupiter	
Temple of Julius Caesar,	22	Stator,	40

shiny studs in the pavement. On the left you'll see the Forum's central section, **Market Square.** The **Column of Phocas** in the square was erected in AD 608 for the visiting Byzantine emperor, Phocas, and was the last monument erected in the Forum. The **Lacus Curtius** to its left is marked by concentric marble semicircles in the ground and a small frieze of a man on horseback; it commemorates the heroism of the legendary Roman warrior Marcus Curtius, who threw himself into a deep chasm in 362 BC to save the city from collapse. In the center of the square, **Three Sacred Trees of Rome**—olive, fig, and grape—were planted by the Italian state in honor of Curtius remarkable heroism. Off V. Sacra to the right is one of the Forum's oldest buildings, the **Curia** (Senate House). Contrary to popular belief, it was not in the square outside the Curia where the group of (literally) back-stabbing senators murdered Julius Caesar in 44 BC. Caesar was actually murdered in the Theater of Pompey in the Campus Martius.

The area in front of the Curia holds several noteworthy ruins. The **Imperial Rostra,** now a single, right angle of stone, was once a speaker's platform erected by Julius Caesar just before his death. The **Comitium,** now a marble semicircle in the ground, was the assembly place where citizens voted, where representatives gathered for public discussion, and where Rome's first laws, the Twelve Tables, were first inscribed on bronze tablets. The **Lapis Niger** (Black Stone) is the volcanic rock that marks the location of the underground sixth-century BC altar to the god Vulcan, where archaeologists discovered the oldest-known Latin inscription, which warns against defiling the shrine.

Back on V. Sacra, the **Arch of Septimius Severus** is straight ahead, built in AD 203 to celebrate Septimius's victories in the Middle East. Next to it stands the **Umbilicus Romae,** a circular solid brick structure marking the mythological center of Rome. Turn left to reach the **Temple of Saturn** in the **Lower Forum.** Though built in the early fifth century BC, the Temple of Saturn achieved larger-than-life status during the Golden Age of Rome (AD 1st-3rd centuries). The temple became the site of **Saturnalia,** a raucous Roman winter party where class and social distinctions were forgotten and anything was permitted. The **Tabularium** is the structure built into the rock face which forms the base of the **Campidoglio.** Turn left in front of the Temple of Saturn on the other branch of V. Sacra. To the

ROME

right is the large **Basilica Julia,** where the well-preserved floor plan supports the intact bases of the columns of the former courthouse. To appreciate the luxury that is modern plumbing, take a right on Vicus Tuscus and look right; you'll see the remnants of **Cloaca Maxima,** Rome's first sewer. Check out the remains of the **Temple of Castor and Pollux** at the end of Vicus Tuscus, on the right when facing the Basilica Aemelia. According to legend, the twin gods Castor and Pollux helped Romans defeat the Etruscans at the Battle of Lake Regillus in 499 BC. Immediately after the battle, the twins appeared in the Forum to water their horses at the nearby **Basin of Juturna,** one of the only springs in ancient Rome.

Once again on V. Sacra, in the middle of the path stands the column base of the former **Arch of Augustus,** built by the emperor in his own honor. Uphill from the arch, the **Temple of Vesta,** once circular, is now just a vaguely curved wall next to the **House of the Vestal Virgins.** Among the most respected individuals in ancient Rome, the Vestal Virgins were female priests. The six women were chosen from the most important families by the Pontifex Maximus; they had to be between the ages of six and ten and without physical imperfections. A virgin served 30 years, after which she could choose whether to continue in the priesthood or leave, but as the average lifespan was around 35 years, few made it to the end of their term. The Virgins could walk unaccompanied in the Forum, pardon prisoners, travel in private chariots, and sit in special reserved seats at gladiatorial games and theatrical shows. They were responsible for the city's sacred eternal flame, keeping it lit for over 1000 years. A small statue of Minerva, which Aeneas took from Troy, occupies the **Palladium,** a secret room accessible only to the Virgins. This esteem had its price: a virgin who strayed from celibacy was buried alive (so that no sacred blood would be spilled).

FORI IMPERIALI. The sprawling Imperial Forums lie along V. dei Fori Imperiali, a boulevard Mussolini paved to connect the old empire to his own in P. Venezia, destroying a third of the ruins in the process. The temples, basilicas, and public squares that make up the Imperial Forums were constructed between the first century BC and AD second century in response to increasing congestion in the old Forum. Much of the area is currently being excavated and is closed to the public, but visitors can peer over the railing along the sidewalk on the east side of V. dei Fori Imperiali and side street V. Alessandrina, or take a ◼**guided archaeological tour** to get closer to the ruins. (*Reservations ☎ 06 67 97 702. English tour given Su at 4:30pm. €7. Inquire within the visitor's information center on V. dei Fori Imperiali.*)

Built between AD 107-113, the **Forum of Trajan** celebrated Trajan's victorious campaign in Dacia (mostly present-day Romania). Its creation rendered the older Roman Forum a tourist attraction of sorts. The complex served practical functions, housing two important libraries of Latin and Greek documents, as well as a colossal equestrian statue of Trajan and a triumphal arch. At one end stands **Trajan's Column,** an extraordinary specimen of Roman relief-sculpture depicting 2500 legionnaires. In 1588, Pope Sextus V replaced Trajan's statue with one of St. Peter. Nearby, the three-floor, semicircular **Market of Trajan** is essentially Rome's first shopping mall, featuring an impressive—albeit crumbling—display of sculpture. A bit farther down V. Alessandrina, the **Forum of Augustus** commemorates Augustus's victory over Caesar's murderers at the Battle of Philippi in 42 BC. The nearby **Forum Transitorium** (also called the **Forum of Nerva**) was a narrow, rectangular space connecting the Forum of Augustus with the Republican Forum. Emperor Nerva dedicated the temple in 97 BC to the goddess Minerva. In the shade of the Vittorio Emanuele II monument, the paltry remains of the **Forum of Caesar** hold the ruins of Julius Caesar's **Temple to Venus Genetrix** (Mother Venus, to whom he claimed ancestry). In **Vespatian's Forum,** the mosaic-filled **Chiesa della Santi Cosma e Damiano** is across V. Cavour, near the Roman Forum. *(Closed for excavations. Tourist office on V. dei Fori Imperiali has maps, guidebooks, and an exhibition about the Imperial Forum. Free.)*

OTHER SIGHTS

DOMUS AUREA. Take a break from the relentless sun and enjoy the cacophony of chirping birds in the shade. Joggers, wildflowers, and ruins now occupy the Oppian Hill. The park houses part of Nero's "Golden House," a 35 hectare palace, which covered much of Ancient Rome. An enclosed lake used to be at the base of the hill, and the hill itself was a private garden. The Forum was reduced to a vestibule of the palace; Nero crowned it with a colossal statue of himself as the sun. He also pillaged all of Greece to find works of art worthy of his abode, including the famous *Laocoön* now held in the Vatican's collections. Apparently, decadence didn't buy happiness: the megalomaniacal Nero committed suicide five years after building his hedonistic pad. *(From P. Venezia, follow V. dei Fori Imperiale past the Colosseum; the park is on the left. Open daily 6:30am-9pm. Free.)*

CHIESA DI SAN PIETRO IN VINCOLI. This fourth-century church is named for the sacred *vincoli* (chains) that bound St. Peter in prison. The two chains were separated for more than a century in Rome and Constantinople, brought back together in the fifth century, and now lie beneath the altar. Michelangelo's ▓**statue of Moses** is tucked in the back right corner. The two horns on his head are actually supposed to be beams of light, indications of wisdom. *(ⓂB-Cavour. Walk along V. Cavour toward the Forum and take the seemingly endless stairs on the left to P. San Pietro in Vincoli. Open daily 8am-12:30pm and 3-6pm. Modest dress required.)*

CIRCUS MAXIMUS AND BATHS OF CARA-CALLA. Today's Circus Maximus is only a grassy shadow of its former glory as Rome's largest stadium. After its construction in 600 BC, the circus held more than 300,000 Romans who came to watch chariots careen around the track. Today the ruins are all but gone, and the Circus is mainly a concert venue. The mosaic-coated Baths of Caracalla, about a 10min. walk down V. dei Terme di Caracalla, are the largest and best-preserved in Rome. *(ⓂB-Circo Massimo, bus #118, or walk down V. di San Gregorio from the Colosseum. Circus open ☎06 39 96 77 00. 24hr. Baths open Apr.-Oct. M 9am-2pm, Tu-Su 9am-7:15pm; Nov.-Mar. M 9am-2pm, Tu-Su 9am-3:30pm. Last entry 1hr. before closing. €6, EU residents ages 18-24 €3, EU residents under 18 and over 65 free. Audio tour €4.)*

THE LIES OF MARCH

"Beware the Ides of March"—more like, "beware the lies of March." After all, our dear friend Shakespeare fictionalized the setting of the toga gang stabbing in his famous play, Julius Caesar. As a result, centuries of Roman travelers have mistakenly made pilgrimages to the Roman Forum's curia (senate house) instead of the Theater of Pompey. Shocker, huh?

On the Ides of March in 44 BC, Caesar was slated to address the senate near the Theater of Pompey. Despite bloody omens from a soothsayer and his wife, he was coerced into attending the meeting. Senator Casca made the first move and stabbed Caesar in the neck. The senatorial snake pit grew chaotic, and following a mass stabbing, Caesar looked into the eyes of his close aide, Brutus, and gasped "Et tu Brute?"

1600 years later, Shakespeare rewrote the event. History buffs who would like to see the actual site of Caesar's assassination should look no farther than the basements around Rome's Palazzo Pio, off Campo dei Fiori. While the theater is now ruined, remnants of the assassination site still exist underground. When visiting the Palazzo Pio area, be sure to check the cellars of nearby buildings. But beware the Ides of March—the 2000-year-old ghost of Julius Caesar might be lurking there.

CAPITOLINE HILL. Home to the original "capital," the Monte Capitolino still houses the city's government, topped by Michelangelo's spacious **Piazza di Campidoglio.** *(To get to the Campidoglio, take bus to P. Venezia, face the Vittorio Emanuele II monument, and walk around to the right to P. d'Aracoeli. Take the stairs up the hill.)* At the far end of the *piazza,* the turreted **Palazzo dei Senatori** houses the Roman mayor's offices. Pope Paul III moved the famous **statue of Marcus Aurelius** here from the Palazzo dei Conservatori and then asked Michelangelo to fashion the imposing statues of Castor and Pollux. Framing the *piazza* are the twin Palazzo dei Conservatori to the right and Palazzo Nuovo on the left, home of the **Capitoline Museums** (p. 148). From the Palazzo Nuovo, stairs lead up to the rear entrance of the seventh-century **Chiesa di Santa Maria in Aracoeli.** Its stunning **Cappella del San Bambino** to the left of the altar is home to the *Santo Bambino,* a cherubic statue that receives letters from sick children. *(Santa Maria open daily 9am-12:30pm and 3-6:30pm. Donation requested.)* The gloomy **Mamertine Prison,** consecrated as the **Chiesa di San Pietro in Carcere,** lies downhill from the back of the Aracoeli. St. Peter baptized his captors here with water that flooded his cell. *(Entrance underneath the church of S. Giuseppe dei Falegnamis. ☎ 06 67 92 902. Open daily in summer 9am-7pm; in winter 9am-12:30pm and 2-5pm. Donation requested.)*

CAELIAN HILL. The Caelian and the Esquiline are the biggest of Rome's seven original hills. In ancient times Nero built his decadent Domus Aurea (see previous page) between them. **San Clemente** consists of a 12th-century addition on top of an AD fourth-century church, with an ancient **mithraeum** and sewers at the bottom. The upper church holds mosaics of the Crucifixion, saints, and apostles, and a 13th-century Masolino fresco cycle graces the **Chapel of Santa Caterina.** The fourth-century level contains the tomb of St. Cyril, a pagan sarcophagus, and a series of frescoes depicting Roman generals. Farther underground is a dank second-century *mithraeum,* below which is the **insulae,** a series of brick and stone rooms where Nero is said to have played his lyre while Rome burned in AD 64. In summer, the **New Opera Festival of Rome** performs abridged productions in the church's outdoor courtyard. *(ⓂB-Colosseo. Bus #85, 87, 810. Tram #3. Turn left down V. Labicana, away from the Forum, then turn right into P. San Clemente. From ⓂA-Manzoni, walk west on V. A. Manzoni; turn left into P. San Clemente. ☎ 06 77 40 021. Open M-Sa 9am-12:30pm and 3-6pm, Su and holidays 10am-12:30pm and 3-6pm. Last entry 20min. before closing. Lower basilica and mithraeum €5, students €3.50. Cash only. For New Opera Festival of Rome, tickets ☎ 77 07 27 68; visit www.newoperafestivaldiroma.com.)*

THE VELABRUM. The Velabrum lies in a flat, flood plain of the Tiber, south of the Jewish Ghetto. At the bend of V. del Portico d'Ottavia, a shattered pediment and a few columns are all that remain of the once magnificent **Portico d'Ottavia.** The 11 BC **Teatro di Marcello** next door bears the name of Augustus's nephew; the Colosseum was modeled after its facade. One block south along V. Luigi Petroselli is the P. della Bocca della Verità, the site of the ancient Foro Boario (Cattle Market). Across the street, the **Chiesa di Santa Maria in Cosmedin** harbors lovely medieval decor. The portico's **Bocca della Verità,** a drain cover with a river god's face, was made famous by Audrey Hepburn in 1953's *Roman Holiday.* But beware, medieval legend has it that the "mouth of truth" bites any liar's hand. Inside, perhaps St. Valentine's skull and bones will ignite your romantic side. Nothing says *amore* like centuries-old relics. *(Chiesa ☎ 06 67 81 419. Currently undergoing restorations, but still open to public daily 9:30am-5:50pm.)*

 WHEN NATURE CALLS. It's hard to find public restrooms without buying anything. Duck into a department store, such as La Rinascente or COIN, or a large bookstore, such as Feltrinelli, to use a free restroom.

PIAZZA DI SPAGNA AND ENVIRONS

▓FONTANA DI TREVI. Nicolo Salvi's bombastic Fontana di Trevi has enough presence and grace to turn even the most jaded jerk into a sighing, romantic mush. The fountain's name refers to its location at the intersection of three streets *(tre vie)*, perpetually crowded with people wanting to catch a glimpse of the fountain and tenacious vendors taking advantage of the masses of potential customers. Neptune, in the center, stands in front of the goddesses of abundance and good health; the two horsemen in the water represent the mercurial sea, either covered by rough waves or in placid ripples. Although you should hold back to avoid a steep fine, actress Anita Ekberg couldn't resist taking a dip in the fountain's cool waters in Fellini's famous scene in *La Dolce Vita*. Legend has it that a traveler who throws a coin into the fountain is ensured a speedy return to Rome, and one who tosses two will fall in love there. Three coins ensure that wedding bells soon will ring. For a less crowded view, head to the fountain in the late evening. The water flows all night, even after most tourists have gone to bed. On a less poetic note, the crypt of the **Chiesa dei Santi Vincenzo e Anastasio,** opposite the fountain, preserves the hearts and lungs of popes from 1590 to 1903. Fortunately or unfortunately, depending on your preference, the crypt is not open for public viewing. *(Church open daily 7am-noon and 4-7pm.)*

SPANISH STEPS. Designed by an Italian, paid for by the French, named for the Spaniards, occupied by the British, and currently featuring American greats like Ronald McDonald, the **Scalinata di Spagna** is, to say the least, multicultural. Piazza di Spagna is also home to designer boutiques like Gucci, Prada, and Valentino, and thousands of tourists and Romans alike flock here daily to shop, people-watch, and socialize. John Keats died in 1821 in the pink-orange house by the Steps; it's now the small **Keats-Shelley Memorial Museum,** displaying several documents of the Romantic poet and his contemporaries, including Lord Byron, Percy Bysshe Shelley, and his wife Mary Shelley. *(☎06 67 84 235; www. keats-shelley-house.org. Open M-F 9am-1pm and 3-6pm, Sa 11am-2pm and 3-6pm. €3.50.)*

PIAZZA DEL POPOLO. Once a favorite venue for the execution of heretics, this is now the "people's square." In the center is the 3200-year-old Obelisk of Pharaoh Ramses II, which Augustus brought from Egypt in AD 10. Climb the hill on the east side of the *piazza* for a spectacular view. **Santa Maria del Popolo** holds Renaissance and Baroque masterpieces. Two exquisite Caravaggios, *The Conversion of St. Paul* and *Crucifixion of St. Peter*, are in the **Cappella Cerasi,** next to the altar. Raphael's **Cappella Chigi** was designed for the Sienese banker Agostino Chigi, reputedly once the world's richest man. Niches on either side of the altar house sculptures by Bernini and Lorenzetto. With so much artwork, an exquisite portrait of the late Pope John Paul II seems orphaned, leaning against a chapel wall. *(☎06 36 10 836. Open M-Sa 7am-noon and 4-7pm, Su and holidays 8am-1:30pm and 4:30-7:30pm.)* At the southern end of the *piazza* are Carlo Rinaldi's 17th-century twin churches, **Santa Maria di Montesano** and **Santa Maria dei Miracoli.** *(☎06 36 10 250. Open M-Sa 6:30am-1:30pm and 4-7:30pm, Su 8am-1:30pm and 5-7pm.)*

VILLA BORGHESE

VILLA BORGHESE. Imagine NYC's Central Park, but a little less central, a little more Mediterranean, and of course, with a little more marble sculpture and Roman grace. To celebrate becoming a cardinal, Scipione Borghese financed construction of the **Villa Borghese,** a stunning park northeast of the *centro storico*, replete with hidden fountains and meandering paths, and home to three art museums—the **Galleria Borghese** (p. 148), **Museo Nazionale**

ROME

PLACES TO SMOOCH IN ROMA

While you may be close enough to pucker up with strangers on the subway, save your saliva for these dreamy destinations.

1. Stroll through **Villa Borghese (see previous page)** find a secluded, shaded spot, and go in for the kill.
2. Bottle of red. Bottle of white. **Trevi Fountain** (p. 135) at night.
3. With the sun setting behind St. Peter's and the swirling Tiber beneath you, **Ponte Sisto** is the perfect place to lay it on. Hard.
4. St. Peter's Square (p. 137). Just try and keep it PG—his Holiness may be watching.
5. Look out over **Circus Maximus** (p. 133) from Palatine Hill and imagine thousands of fans cheering on you and your sweetie.
6. The terrace of the **Vittorio Emanuele II** monument (p. 125). There's a reason people call this spot the "wedding cake."
7. Top of the **Spanish Steps** (p. 135). If it fails, you can always push the person down them.
8. Waiting for the **Metro.** You'd be surprised—it can get pretty steamy. Plus you'll make a stranger's day.
9. Chiesa di Santa Maria in Cosmedin (p. 134). Forget chocolates and roses; the skull and relics of St. Valentine are the key ingredient in any love potion.
10. Over a shared bowl of spaghetti, *Lady and the Tramp* style.

Etrusco di Villa Giulia (p. 149), and the **Galleria Nazionale d'Arte Moderna,** which is actually a Vatican Museum located in the park. (ⓂA-Spagna and follow the signs. Or, from the A: Flaminio stop, take V. Washington under the archway. From P. del Popolo, climb the stairs to the right of Santa Maria del Popolo, cross the street, and climb the small path. ☎06 32 16 564. Free.)

THE GLOBE THEATER. This circular, wooden structure is an exact replica of the 16th-century Elizabethan theater. Shakespearean plays are performed in Italian on the outdoor stage. (Reservations ☎06 82 05 91 27; www.globetheatreroma.com. M-F 2-7pm, Sa-Su noon-7pm. July-Sept. tickets €5.50-17.50.)

QUIRINAL HILL. At the southeast end of V. del Quirinale, the ◼**Piazza del Quirinale** occupies the summit of the tallest of Rome's seven hills. In the center, the statues of Castor and Pollux (Roman copies of the Greek originals) stand on either side of an obelisk from the Mausoleum of Augustus. The president of the Republic resides in the Palazzo del Quirinale, a Baroque architectural collaboration by Bernini, Maderno, and Fontana. Farther along the street lies the facade of Borromini's **Chiesa di San Carlo alle Quattro Fontane.** Bernini's ◼**Four Fountains** are built into the corners of the intersection of V. delle Quattro Fontane and V. del Quirinale. Be careful when viewing the fountain; sidewalks are nonexistent. (Palazzo closed to the public. Chiesa open daily 8:30am-12:30pm and 3:30-6pm.)

PIAZZA BARBERINI. Though the busy traffic circle at V. del Tritone feels more like a modern thoroughfare than a Baroque square, P. Barberini features two Bernini fountains, **Fontana Tritone** and **Fontana delle Api.** Maderno, Bernini, and rival Borromini are responsible for the **Palazzo Barberini,** home to the Galleria Nazionale d'Arte Antica. The severe **Chiesa della Immacolata Consezione** houses the morbidly fascinating ◼**Capuchin Crypt,** decorated with hundreds of human skulls and bones, in themed rooms. (V. V. Veneto 27. www.cappucciniviaveneto.it. Open M-W and F-Su 9am-noon and 3-6pm. Cash donation requested.)

VATICAN CITY

☎06 69 81 662. ⓂA-Ottaviano; bus #40, 64, 271, or 492 from Termini or Largo Argentina; or tram #19 from P. Risorgimento, 62 from P. Barberini, or 23 from Testaccio. The official Comune di Roma tourism kiosk has helpful English-speaking staff who will provide free maps, brochures, hours, location, and ticket info for any of the sites related to the Vatican or Rome. Located at Castel Sant'Angelo, P. Pia (☎06 58 33 34 57). Open daily 8:30am-7pm. 10 other locations in the city around the major tourist sites.

The administrative and spiritual center of the Roman Catholic Church, once the mightiest power in Europe, occupies 108 independent acres within Rome. The Lateran Treaty of 1929 allows the Pope to maintain legislative, judicial, and executive powers over this tiny theocracy, but also requires the Church to remain neutral in national politics and municipal affairs. The Vatican has historically and symbolically preserved its independence by minting coins (Italian *lire* and euros with the Pope's face), running a separate press and postal system, maintaining an army of Swiss Guards, and hoarding some of the world's finest art in the **Musei Vaticani.** Devout pilgrims and atheists alike are awed by the stunning grace and beauty of its two famous churches, the Sistine Chapel and St. Peter's Basilica, and the Vatican Museums are some of Italy's best.

BASILICA DI SAN PIETRO (SAINT PETER'S BASILICA)

The multilingual staff of the Pilgrim Tourist Information Center, located on the left between the rounded colonnade and the basilica, provides Vatican postage, brochures, and currency exchange. A first-aid station and free bathrooms are next to the tourist office. Open daily Apr.-Sept. 7am-7pm; Oct.-Mar. 7am-6pm. Mass M-Sa 8:30, 9, 10, 11am, noon, 5pm; Su and holidays 9, 10:30, 11:30am, 12:15, 1, 4, 5, 5:30pm. Vespers 5pm. Free guided tours Tu and Th 9:45am and W 3pm; meet at Info Center. Modest attire strictly enforced: no shorts, short skirts, or exposed shoulders allowed.

PIAZZA AND FACADE. The famous artist Bernini's colonnade around **Piazza San Pietro,** lined with the statues of 140 saints perched around the perimeter, was designed to provide a long, impressive vista to pilgrims after their tiring journey through the tiny, winding streets of Borgo and the *centro storico.* The open circle created by the two sides of the colonnade leading away from San Pietro are said to represent the welcoming arms of the Church, embracing its followers as they enter the *piazza.* Mussolini's broad V. della Conciliazione, built in the 30s to connect the Vatican to the rest of the city, opened a broader view of the church than Bernini ever intended. Round disks mark where to stand so that the quadruple rows of colonnades seem to merge into one perfectly aligned row. Statues of Christ, John the Baptist, and all the apostles except Peter are on top of the basilica. In warm months, the Pope holds papal audiences on a platform in the *piazza* on Wednesday mornings. *(To attend an audience, contact the Prefettura della Casa Pontificia ☎ 06 69 88 46 31 or stop by the Bronze Door, located on the right after you pass through security. Ascend the steps and ask the Swiss Guard for a ticket.)*

 COLOR-CODED. The Virgin Mary can usually be recognized in art by her red dress and bright blue mantle. Blue became her trademark color because the pigment was made from *lapis lazuli,* the most expensive of all paint.

INTERIOR. The iconic basilica rests on the reputed site of St. Peter's tomb. In Holy Years the Pope opens the **Porta Sancta** (Holy Door)—the last door on the right side of the entrance porch—by knocking in the bricks with a silver hammer. The interior of St. Peter's Cathedral measures 187m by 137m along the transepts. Metal lines on the marble floor mark the lengths of other major world churches. To the right of the entrance, Michelangelo's glowing *Pietà* has been encased in bullet-proof glass since 1972, when an axe-wielding fanatic attacked it, smashing Christ's nose and breaking Mary's hand

Bernini's **baldacchino** (canopy) rises on spiraling columns over the marble altar, reserved for the Pope's use. The Baroque structure, cast in bronze pillaged from the Pantheon, was unveiled on June 28, 1633, by Pope Urban VIII, a member of the wealthy Barberini family. Bees, the family symbol, buzz whimsically around the canopy, and vines climb toward Michelangelo's cavernous

cupola. Seventy oil lamps glow in front of the *baldacchino* and illuminate Maderno's sunken *Confessio,* a 17th-century chapel. Two staircases directly beneath the papal altar descend to St. Peter's tomb. The staircases are closed to the public, but the underground grottoes offer a better view of the tomb, as well as the tombs of countless other popes, including John Paul II. *(Open daily Apr.-Sept. 7am-6pm; Oct.-Mar. 7am-5pm. Free. The entrance is to the right of the basilica.)*

High above the *baldacchino* and the altar rises **Michelangelo's dome,** designed as a circular dome like that of the Pantheon (p. 125). Out of reverence for that ancient architectural wonder, Michelangelo is said to have made this *cupola* a meter shorter in diameter than the Pantheon's; the difference is not noticeable, however, as the dome towers 120m high and 42.3m across. When Michelangelo died in 1564, only the drum of the dome had been completed. Work remained at a standstill until 1588, when 800 laborers were hired to complete it. Toiling round the clock, they finished the dome on May 21, 1590.

BASILICA ENVIRONS

To the left of the basilica is a courtyard protected by Swiss Guards. The **Ufficio Scavi,** administrative center for the Pre-Constantinian Necropolis, is here. Ask Swiss Guards for permission to enter. To the right of the basilica, at the end of the colonnade, the **Prefettura della Casa Pontifica** gives free tickets to papal audiences in the morning on Wednesdays when the Pope is speaking.

CUPOLA. The cupola entrance is near the Porta Sancta. Ascend 551 stairs to the top or take an elevator to the walkway around the dome's interior. Beware: even using the elevator, you'll still have to climb 320 steps to see the top ledge's panorama. *(Open daily Apr.-Sept. 8am-5pm; Oct.-Mar. 8am-4pm. Stairs €4, elevator €7.)*

TREASURY OF SAINT PETER. The Treasury contains gifts bestowed upon St. Peter's tomb. At the entrance, look for a list of all the popes. Highlights include the dalmatic of Charlemagne (the Holy Roman Emperor's intricately designed robe), a Bernini angel, and the magnificent bronze tomb of Sixtus IV. *(Inside the basilica on the left. Open daily Apr.-Sept. 9am-6:15pm; Oct.-Mar. 9am-5:15pm. Last entry 30min. before closing. Closed when the Pope is celebrating mass in the basilica and on Christmas and Easter. Wheelchair-accessible. Photographs forbidden. €6, under 13 €4.)*

TOMB OF SAINT PETER AND PRE-CONSTANTINIAN NECROPOLIS. After converting to Christianity, Constantine built his first basilica directly over St. Peter's tomb. In order to build on that exact spot, the emperor had to level a hill and destroy a necropolis that once stood on the site. The basilica's history was mere legend until 1939, when workers came across ancient ruins underneath. Unsure of finding anything, the Church secretly set about looking for St. Peter's tomb. More than 20 years later, the tomb was identified under a small temple beneath the altars of Constantine's basilica. The saint's bones, however, were not found. A hollow wall nearby held what the church later claimed to be the holy remains. Some believe that the bones were displaced from the tomb during the Saracens' sack of Rome in AD 849. Multilingual tour guides will take you around the streets of the necropolis, which hold several well-preserved pagan and Christian mausolea, funerary inscriptions, mosaics, and sarcophagi. *(Entrance to the necropolis is on the left side of P. S. Pietro, beyond the info office. ☎ 06 69 88 53 18; scavi@fsp.va. Office open M-Sa 9am-5pm. To request a tour, arrange in person or write to: The Delegate of the Fabbrica di San Pietro, Excavations Office, 00120 Vatican City. Give a preferred range of times and languages. Phone calls only accepted for reconfirmations. Reserve as far ahead as possible. Instructions available on website. €10.)*

CASTEL SANT'ANGELO

☎ *06 68 19 111, reservations 39 96 76 00. Along the Tiber River on the Vatican side when going from St. Peter's toward the Tiber River. From centro storico, cross Ponte Sant'Angelo. Bus #40, 62, 64, 271, 280 to Ponte V. Emanuele or P. Pia. Dungeon. Open in summer Tu-Su 9am-7pm; in winter daily 9am-7pm. Last entry 1hr. before closing. Tours Su 12:30pm in Italian, 2:30pm in English. €5, EU students 18-25 €2.50, EU citizens under 18 or over 65 free. Additional €2 fee for traveling exhibits. Audio tour €4.*

Built by Hadrian (AD 76-138) as a mausoleum for himself and his family, this gigantic brick-and-stone mass overlooking the Tiber has served as a fortress, prison, and palace. When a plague struck in AD 590, Pope Gregory the Great saw an angel sheathing his sword at the top of the complex; the plague abated soon thereafter, and the building was rededicated to the angel. Military aficionados will relish the armory, located on one of the top floors and offering an incomparable view of Rome and the Vatican. Outside, the marble **Ponte Sant'Angelo,** lined with statues by Bernini, is the beginning of the traditional pilgrimage route from St. Peter's to **San Giovanni in Laterano** (p. 144).

TERMINI AND ENVIRONS

◪**BASILICA DI SANTA MARIA MAGGIORE.** One of the four "Patriarchal" churches in Rome granted extraterritoriality, this basilica crowns the **Esquiline Hill** and is officially part of Vatican City. In AD 352, Pope Sixtus III commissioned it when he noticed that Roman women were still visiting a temple dedicated to the pagan mother-goddess, Juno Lucina. He tore down the pagan temple and built a basilica in celebration of the Council of Ephesus's recent ruling that Mary was the mother of God. This gigantic basilica is home to a wealth of holy and artistic wonders. Upon entering, marvel at the beautiful coffered ceiling in the nave and the statues, mosaics, and frescoes that decorate the adjourning chapels. Set in the floor to the right of the altar, a marble slab marks **Bernini's tomb.** Don't miss the **baptistery,** featuring a magnificent statue of St. John the Baptist covered with animal skins and holding a clam shell. The glorious 14th-century mosaics in the church's **loggia** recount the story of the August snowfall that showed the Pope, who had dreamed of snow brought by the Virgin Mary, where to build the church; every mid-August, this miracle is re-enacted as priests sprinkle white petals from the top of the church. Below the altar are what some believe to be relics from Jesus's manger. Since 2001, Santa Maria Maggiore has hosted a museum containing art and papal artifacts significant to the history of the basilica. *(From Termini, exit right on V. Giolitti, and walk down V. Cavour. Tickets in souvenir shop. ☎ 06 48 31 95. Open daily 7am-7pm. Suggested donation €4. Museum open 9:30am-6:30pm. Loggia only accessible with guided tour daily 1pm. Multilingual confession available. Modest dress required. Loggia tour €3; audio tour €4. Cash only.)*

BATHS OF DIOCLETIAN. From AD 298 to 306, 40,000 Christian slaves built these 3000-person-capacity public baths, the largest and most lavishly appointed in Rome. They contained a marble public toilet with seats for 30 people, several pools, gymnasiums, art galleries, gardens, brothels, sports facilities, libraries, and concert halls. The AD fourth-century rotunda displays statues from the baths, and the entrance holds gorgeous, stained-glass windows. In 1561, in keeping with the grand tradition of converting pagan structures into centers of Christianity, Michelangelo undertook his last architectural work and converted the ruins into a church, **Chiesa di Santa Maria degli Angeli.** On the bronze door to the left, a startling cross cuts deeply into Christ's body, symbolizing his resurrection. *(Baths on V. Enrico De Nicola 79, in P. dei Cinquecento, across the street from Termini. ☎ 06 39 96 77 00. Closed for restoration. Church is in P. della Repubblica. ☎ 06 48 80 812; www. santamariadegliangeliroma.it. Open M-Sa 7am-6:30pm, Su and holidays 7am-7:30pm.)*

VIA XX SETTEMBRE. V. del Quirinale becomes V. XX ("VEN-tee") Settembre at its intersection with V. delle Quattro Fontane, where a spectacular Bernini fountain sits on each of the four corners. A few blocks down, the colossal **Fontana dell'Acqua Felice** graces P. S. Bernardo. Opposite, **Chiesa di Santa Maria della Vittoria** houses an icon of Mary that accompanied the Catholics to victory in a 1620 battle near Prague. Bernini's fantastically controversial ⧄**Ecstasy of Saint Theresa of Ávila** continues to amaze and bemuse visitors in the Cornaro Chapel. At the time of its creation, people were outraged by the depiction of the saint in a pose resembling sexual climax; today, many viewers don't notice the innuendo until told of the controversy. The statue illustrates St. Theresa's heart being pierced by an arrow wielded by an angel, filling her with ardent love for God. *(Open daily 6:30am-noon and 4:30-6pm. Modest dress required.)*

VIA NOMENTANA. This road runs northeast from Michelangelo's **Porta Pia** out of the city. Hop on bus #36 in front of Termini or head back to V. XX Settembre and catch bus #60. A 2km walk or bus ride from Pta. Pia past villas, embassies, and parks leads to **Chiesa di Sant'Agnese Fuori le Mura** on the left. Its apse displays a Byzantine-style mosaic of St. Agnes. Underneath the church wind some of Rome's most impressive **catacombs**. While St. Agnes's body is buried here, her head resides in the church bearing her name in P. Navona, the location of her beheading. *(V. Nomentana 349. ☎06 86 10 840 to reach the tour guide service. Open M-Sa 9am-noon and 4-6pm, Su 4-6pm. Modest dress required. Catacombs €5, under 16 €3.)*

TRASTEVERE

Take bus #75 or 170 or tram #8 to V. Trastevere to reach these sights.

ISOLA TIBERINA. According to Roman legend, Isola Tiberina emerged with the Roman Republic. After the Etruscan tyrant Tarquin raped the virtuous Lucretia, her outraged family killed him and then tossed his body into the Tiber; so much muck and silt collected around his corpse that an island eventually formed. For centuries the river's fast-flowing water was harnessed by mills, which were destroyed by the great flood of 1870. Home to the Fatebene-fratelli Hospital since AD 154, the island has long been associated with health and cures. The Greek god of healing, Aesclepius, notoriously appeared to the Romans as a snake and slithered from the river. The eclectic 10th-century **Basilica di San Bartolomeo** has a Baroque facade, a Romanesque tower, and 14 antique columns. *(☎06 68 77 973. Open M-Sa 9am-12:30pm and 3:30-6:30pm. Free.)* The **Ponte Fabricio,** known as the **Ponte dei Quattro Capi** (Bridge of Four Heads), was built in 62 BC, making it the oldest in the city.

CENTRAL TRASTEVERE. Off Ponte Garibaldi stands the statue of poet G. G. Belli in his own *piazza*, which borders P. Sonnino and marks the beginning of Vle. di Trastevere. Follow V. Giulio Cesane Santina, which turns into V. dei Genovesi, and take a right on V. di S. Cecilia. Beyond the courtyard is the **Basilica di Santa Cecilia** in Trastevere and its fantastic mosaic above the altar. *(Open daily 9:30am-12:30pm and 4-6:30pm. Donation requested. Crypt €2.50. See Cavallini's frescoes M-F 10:15am-12:15pm, Sa-Su 11:15am-12:15pm. €2.50.)* From P. Sonnino, V. della Lungaretta leads west to P. di S.Maria in Trastevere, home to the Chiesa di Santa Maria in Trastevere, built in the AD fourth century by Pope Julius II. The mosaics and the chancel arch are quite impressive. What appears to be a trash heap around the statue of the friar and the infant at the entrance is actually a pile of prayers written on anything from Metro tickets to napkins. *(Open M-Sa 9am-5:30pm, Su 8:30-10:30am and noon-5:30pm.)*

GIANICOLO HILL. At the top of the hill, the **Chiesa di San Pietro** in Montorio stands on what is believed to be the site of St. Peter's upside-down crucifixion. The church contains del Piombo's *Flagellation*, from designs by Michelangelo. *(Open daily May-Oct. Tu-Su 9:30am-12:30pm and 4-6pm; Nov.-Apr. 9:30am-12:30pm and 2-4pm. Free.)* Next door in a small courtyard behind locked gates is Bramante's tiny ▪**Tempietto.** A combination of ancient and Renaissance architecture, the Tempietto was constructed to commemorate the site of St. Peter's martyrdom, and it provided the inspiration for the dome of St. Peter's in Vatican City. *(Courtyard open Tu-Sa in summer 9:30am-12:30pm and 4-6pm; in winter 9:30am-12:30pm and 2-4pm. Free.)* Check out an aerial view of Rome from a viewing spot in front of **Acqua Paolo.** The sprawling public **gardens** behind Acqua Paolo continue up V. Garibaldi. Rome's botanical gardens lie at the bottom of Gianicolo and contain a garden for the blind as well as a rose garden that holds the bush from which all the world's roses are supposedly descended. *(Reach the summit on bus #41 from the Vatican, 115 from Trastevere, 870 from P. Fiorentini, where C. V. Emanuele meets the Tiber, or walk up the medieval V. Garibaldi, from V. della Scala in Trastevere for 10min. Botanical Gardens, Largo Cristina di Svezia 24, at the end of V. Corsini, off V. della Lungara. ☎ 49 91 71 06. Open M-Sa Apr.-Oct. 9:30am-6:30pm; Nov.-Mar. 9:30am-5:30pm. Closed holidays. Guided tours Sa 10:30am-noon. Comes with leaflet and audio tour in Italian, English, or French. Call for reservations and more info. €5, ages 6-11 and over 60 €3, under 6 free.)*

THE JEWISH GHETTO

Rome's Jewish community is the oldest in Western Europe—Israelites came in 161 BC as ambassadors of Judas Maccabee, asking for Imperial help against invaders. The Ghetto, the tiny area to which Pope Paul IV confined the Jews in 1555, was dissolved in 1870, but it is still the center of Rome's Jewish population of 15,000. Take bus #64; the Ghetto is across V. Arenula from Campo dei Fiori. Alternatively, walk down V. Arenula from C. V. Emanuele and make a left at the river. The Ghetto will be on your left. The neighborhood's main attractions and eateries are located on and around V. del Portico d'Ottavia.

PIAZZA MATTEI. This square, site of Taddeo Landini's 16th-century **Fontana delle Tartarughe,** marks the Ghetto's center. Nearby in the Portico d'Ottavia, the AD eighth-century **Chiesa di Sant'Angelo in Pescheria** was named for the fish market that once flourished there. Jews were once forced to attend mass here, an act of evangelism that they quietly resisted by stuffing their ears with wax. *(V. dei Funari. Heading toward the Theater of Marcellus on V. del Teatro Marcello, go right on V. Montavara, which becomes V. dei Funari after P. Campitelli. The church is under restoration indefinitely.)*

SINAGOGA ASHKENAZITA. Built between 1901 and 1904 at the corner of Lungotevere dei Cenci and V. Catalana, this temple incorporates Persian and Babylonian architectural techniques and features a rainbow-colored dome intended to symbolize peace. Take note of the stained glass high up on the right hand side of the synagogue, commemorative of a tragic terrorist bombing in 1982, which killed a small child. The broken glass was replaced by clear glass, in honor of the victim. In response to the attacks, guards now search all visitors, and *carabinieri* patrol the vicinity. In 1986 Pope John Paul II made the first-ever papal visit to a Jewish synagogue here, declaring that Jews are the oldest brothers of Christians. The synagogue houses the **Jewish Museum,** a collection of ancient Torahs and Holocaust artifacts that document the community's history. *(☎ 06 68 40 06 61. Open for services only. Museum open June-Sept. M-Th and Su 10am-7pm, F 9am-4pm; Oct.-May M-Th and Su 10am-10pm, F 10am-4pm. Last entry 45min. before closing. Closed Sa, Jewish holidays from 1pm the day before, and after 1pm on Catholic holidays. €7.50, students €3, under 10 free. Groups €6.50. Reservations required. Cash only.)*

ROME

TESTACCIO AND OSTIENSE

Take Metro B to Piramide, Garbatella, or San Paolo.

South of the Aventine Hill, the working-class neighborhood of Testaccio is known for its cheap trattorie and raucous nightclubs. The area centers around the castle-like **Porta San Paolo,** a remnant of the Aurelian walls built in the AD third century to protect Rome from barbarians. Another attraction is the colossal **Piramide di Gaius Cestius,** built in 330 days by Gaius Cestius's slaves under Augustus at the height of Roman Egyptophilia, and the namesake of the metro stop/train station. Piramide also shuttles droves of sun-loving Romans to the beach on the weekends, so don't be surprised if you're sitting next to bathing-suit-clad *signore* on the metro. Ostiense is the district south of Testaccio, and is made up of mostly apartment buildings and industrial complexes.

BASILICA DI SAN PAOLO FUORI LE MURA. The massive Basilica di San Paolo Fuori le Mura is the Rome's second-largest church after St. Peter's Basilica. St. Paul's body, after his beheading at the Tre Fontane, is said to have been buried beneath the altar, while his head remained with St. Peter's at the **Arcibasilica of San Giovanni.** The exact point above the body's resting place is marked by a tiny red light on the front of the altar. San Paolo is also home to many less-significant relics; they are held in the **Capella delle Reliquie,** which you can access through the cloister. In addition to an impressive cadelabrum, the basilica also displays the likenesses of every pope since the beginning of the church, with a light shining on face of the current pope, Benedict XVI. Before leaving, pick up a bottle of monk-made Benedictine liqueur (€5-15) in the gift shop. If you have the time, stick around for the daily Gregorian chants sung by the monks at vespers at 5pm. (Ⓜ B-Basilica S. Paolo, or take bus #23 or 769 from Testaccio, at the corner of V. Ostiense and P. Ostiense. ☎ 06 45 43 41 85. Basilica open daily in summer 7am-7pm; in winter 7am-6pm. Cloister open daily in summer 9am-1pm and 3-6:30pm; in winter 9am-1pm and 3-6pm. Mass daily at 7, 8, 9, 10:30am, and 6pm. Modest dress required. Donation requested. Audio booths for short history of basilica €1. Audio tour €5. Gift shop cash only.)

CIMITERO ACATTOLICO PER GLI STRANIERI. This peaceful Protestant cemetery, the Non-Catholic Cemetery for Foreigners, is one of the only burial grounds in Rome for those who don't belong to the Roman Catholic Church. Notable non-Catholics, including Keats, Shelley, von Goethe, and Antonio Gramsci, rest here. Keats's grave, in his typically self-effacing style, is dedicated to "A Young Poet." (From Piramide, walk in between the pyramid and the castle. Once on V. Marmorata, turn left on V. Caio Cestio. Ring the bell. www.protestantcemetary.it. Cemetery open M-Sa 9am-5pm. Last entry 4:30pm. €2 donation requested. Cat sanctuary open daily 2:30-4:30pm.)

ABBAZIA DELLE TRE FONTANE (ABBEY OF THE THREE FOUNTAINS). Legend has it that when St. Paul was beheaded here in AD 67, his head bounced on the ground three times and created a fountain at each bounce. The supposed column upon which Paul was decapitated lies in the back-right corner of the chapel. Far from the busiest streets of the city, and heavy with spiritual significance, the chapels have a serenity entirely distinct from the dramatic exuberance of Rome's Baroque churches; visit the Abbey for an hour of quiet contemplation. (Ⓜ B-Laurentina. Walk straight and take a right on V. Laurentina; proceed about 1km north, and turn right on V. delle Acque Salve. About a 15min. walk, or take bus #761 from Laurentina, get off after 2 stops, and walk the rest of the way. The abbey is at the bottom of the hill. ☎ 06 54 60 23 47. Open daily 8am-1pm and 3-6pm. Free.)

The Agony and The Ecstasy

Everyday, visitors rush through the Vatican Museum's Belvedere courtyard, eager to bask in the glory of the nearby Sistine Chapel. One by one, however, each courtyard on-looker becomes paralyzed at the sight of the Laocoön and his sons. As his marble muscles ripple, Laocoön's grimace seems ever more deeply etched on his face. His anguished expression

year, Julius triumphantly transported the sculpture through Roman streets. Throngs of citizens lined the streets and showered the Laocoön with flower petals while the Sistine Chapel Choir heralded the sculpture's journey to the Belvedere Courtyard of the Vatican Palace. Without a doubt, the Laocoön was the find of the century. The Laocoön was revered by Renaissance artists who admired the skill required to sculpt a work of such intense pathos and anatomical precision. Michelan-

"The *Laocoön* became the artistic standard of beauty."

is almost the opposite of beauty, and those who stop to witness his struggle react with awe and terror. The struggle and writhing of this dying man gave rise to much beauty—and not just that of Michelangelo's Sistine Chapel—for arguably, the Laocoön was the most influential work of art in the Western world for some 300 years after its discovery.

On January 14, 1506, a momentous discovery was made in the city of Rome. While digging in his vineyard on the Esquiline Hill, a farmer uncovered nine fragments of an ancient marble statuary. Pope Julius II promptly dispatched the architect Giuliano da Sangallo to inspect the new discovery. Though ancient sculptures were regularly pulled from the ground in Renaissance Rome, this find proved to be of extraordinary interest. Almost immediately, the fragments were identified as being from the Laocoön, a sculpture that had belonged to the Roman Emperor Titus, and that was known to Renaissance humanists because it had received the highest of praise from the first-century writer Pliny the Younger.

Finding the Laocoön was a dream come true for well-educated Renaissance artists and patrons intent on restoring Rome to its ancient glory. At the very moment in which the idea of "Rome Reborn" was being made manifest in art and architecture projects, the Laocoön emerged from the earth, further fueling the Renaissance dream. In July of the same

gelo, the greatest of them all, found himself humbled by the ancient sculpture. Asked to replace the sculpture's missing arms, he declined, claiming his talents to be less than those of the Greek sculptors who had created the work 1500 years earlier.

The Laocoön became the artistic standard, thereby establishing a canon of beauty that influenced art for the next 400 years. Almost without a doubt, the artist most influenced by the sculpture was Michelangelo himself, whose representation of the human figure in motion was fundamentally changed by his study of the Laocoön. Michelangelo's work clearly demonstrates that he was intrigued by the sculpture's muscular tension and by the central figure's spiraling motion as he struggles to free himself from the strangling snakes. On the Sistine Chapel ceiling, Michelangelo created numerous figures in serpentinata positions reminiscent of the central figure in the Laocoön.

It's not just artists who found themselves stimulated by the Laocoön, however. The intense pain suffered by Laocoön and his sons, and the contrast of this pain with the beauty of the sculpture, was a topic of discussion for the 18th-century father of art history, J. J. Winckelmann. How, Winckelmann asked, can a viewer cope with the inevitable mental conflict that arises when one admires the beauty of the Laocoön, but is at the same time painfully aware that the sculpture portrays the final, painful moments of a man who has failed to save his own life and those of his own children? Unanswered for centuries, this question continues to enthrall mankind to this very day.

Dr. Laura Flusche teaches art history at the University of Dallas's Rome campus. She is the founder of Friends of Rome (www.friendsofrome.org), a nonprofit dedicated to the preservation of Roman monuments. She's also president of The Institute of Design & Culture in Rome (www.idcrome.org)

SOUTHERN ROME

█SAN GIOVANNI IN LATERANO. The immense **Arcibasilica of San Giovanni in Laterano,** the cathedral of the diocese of Rome, was home to the Papacy until the 14th century. Founded by Constantine in AD 314, it is the city's oldest Christian basilica. The golden *baldacchino* (canopy) rests over two golden reliquaries with the skulls of St. Peter and St. Paul. Note the immense statue of Constantine, the fresco by **Giotto,** the octagonal Battistero, and the intimate **cloister.** A museum of Vatican history is on the right when facing the church. *(Enter the church at the left. Cathedral open daily 7am-6:30pm. Free. Cloister open 9am-6pm. Cloister €2, students €1. Audio tour €5, students €4. Let's Go discount €1. Battistero open 7am-12:30pm and 4-7pm. Free. Museum open M-Sa; entrances at 9, 10, 11am, noon. €4, students €2. Cash only.)*

The **Scala Santa,** outside the church and to the left facing out of the front doors, are revered as the marble steps used by Jesus outside Pontius Pilate's home in Jerusalem. Indulgences are still granted to pilgrims if they ascend the steps on their knees, reciting prayers on each step. Martin Luther took a break from Catholicism here when he was unable to experience true piety in the act and left without finishing. The steps lead to the chapel of the **Sancta Sanctorium,** which houses the Acheiropoieton, or "picture painted without hands," said to be the work of St. Luke assisted by an angel. *(Ⓜ A-S. Giovanni or bus #16 from Termini. Walk through the archway of the city walls to the P. S. Giovanni. Church ☎06 69 88 63 92. Open daily in summer 6:15am-noon and 3:30-6:45pm; in winter 6:15am-noon and 3-6:15pm. Modest dress required. Free. Scala Santa and Sancta Sanctorium ☎06 77 26 641. Open daily in summer 6:30am-noon and 3-6:30pm; in winter 6:30am-noon and 3-6pm. Donation requested.)*

PORTA SAN GIOVANNI. The **Chiesa della Santa Croce in Gerusalemme** holds the Fascist-era **Chapel of the Relics,** with fragments of the "true cross" as well as other relics purportedly from the Crucifixion. Perhaps the most intriguing of the relics is St. Thomas's dismembered finger, which, when still attached, was used to probe Christ's wounds. On a lighter note, the building's bright, sweeping frescoes seem to leap off the ceiling. *(P. S. Paolo della Croce in Gerusalemme Ⓜ A-S. Giovanni. From Pta. S. Giovanni north of the stop, go east on Vle. Carlo Felice; church is on the right. Or, from P.V. Emanuele II, take V. Conte Verde. ☎06 70 14 769; www.basilicasantacroce.com. Open daily 7am-12:45pm and 2:30-6pm. Modest dress required. Donation requested.)*

AVENTINE HILL. Enjoy awe-inspiring and sparsely traversed vistas from this exclusive area of town. V. di Valle Murcia climbs past some of Rome's swankiest homes and the **Roseto Comunale,** a beautiful public rose garden. Formerly a Jewish cemetery, the gardens are now marked by commemorative pillars at each entrance that contain the Tablets of Moses. Up the hill, along the left side of the gardens, the street turns into V. di S. Sabina. On the right side of V. di S. Sabina, just before the hill's crest, a park with orange trees and offers sweeping views of southern Rome. Nearby the **Chiesa di Santa Sabina** has a wooden portal that dates to AD 450. The top, left-hand panel contains one of the earliest-known Crucifixion images. V. di Sabina continues along the crest of the hill to **Piazza dei Cavalieri di Malta,** home of the once-crusading order of the Knights of Malta. On the right as you approach the *piazza* is a large, cream-colored, arched gate; peer through its tiny, circular █**keyhole** for a hedge-framed view of the dome of St. Peter's Cathedral. *(Take V. di S. Gregorio from the Colosseum. Turn right at the intersection with V. del Cerchi, and take the stairs across the Circus Maximus to P. Ugo la Malfa and V. di Valle Murcia. Rose garden open May-June 8am-7:30pm. Free.)*

█THE APPIAN WAY

Ⓜ A-San Giovanni. Exit onto P. Appio and follow the signs back through the brick archways to P. S. Giovanni, where you will see the giant basilica. Then take bus #218 to V. Appia

Antica; get off at the info office, just before Domine Quo Vadis; hit the button to stop after you turn left onto V. Appia Antica. Or, Ⓜ B-Circo Massimo or Piramide, then take bus #118 to the catacombs; Ⓜ A-Colli Albani, then bus #660 to Cecilia Metella. Info office of the Parco dell'Appia Antica, V. Appia Antica 60/62. ☎ 06 51 35 316; www.parcoappiaantica. org. Provides maps and pamphlets about the ancient road and its history, excavations, and recreational opportunities. Also rents bikes €3 per hr., €10 per day. Open in summer daily 9:30am-5:30pm; in winter M-Sa 9:30am-4:30pm. Free.

About 30min. outside the city center, V. Appia Antica, also known as the Appian Way, was the most important thoroughfare of Ancient Rome. In its heyday it stretched from Campania to the Adriatic Coast and rightfully gained the nickname "The Queen of Roads." Marcus Linius Crassus, a first-century BC tycoon and sometime general, crucified 6000 slaves along this road as punishment for joining the rebellion of the legendary gladiator Spartacus. Today, all remnants of such macabre displays are ancient history, leaving a perfect oasis away from the grind of Rome's streets, vendors, and Vespas. Third-century catacombs, medieval and Baroque churches, and a wealth of ancient Roman ruins remain on the Appian Way. On Sundays, when the street is closed to vehicles, take the opportunity to bike through the countryside.

▓BASILICA OF SAN SEBASTIANO. Perhaps second only to St. Peter's in overall quality, this basilica should not be missed. Originally dedicated to St. Peter and St. Paul, it now honors St. Sebastian. When Sebastian, a captain in the Roman army, was discovered to be a Christian, he was shot with arrows and left for dead. Miraculously, he was nursed back to health and continued to practice his faith, but was eventually executed. He is the patron saint of athletes because of this remarkable endurance, of soldiers due to his profession and perseverance, and of archers—despite his vested interest in their doing poorly. His likeness is reproduced on the gorgeous ceiling, the work of a Flemish artist. In 2000, the magnificent statue of Jesus Christ the Redeemer was attributed to Bernini as his final masterpiece, completed at age 81. However, the oldest but most recently discovered of the church's relics are the snail fossils. Allegedly 120 million years old, the fossils are visible in the marble floor, which sports the fitting nickname *lumacella*, or "little snails," though the snails seem gigantic by today's standards. *(V. Appia Antica 136. ☎ 06 78 08 847. Open daily 8:30am-6pm. Free.)*

CHIESA DELLA SANTA MARIA IN PALMIS. On the site of this church, also called **Domine Quo Vadis,** St. Peter had a vision of Christ. Allegedly, he asked Jesus, *"Domine, quo vadis?"* ("Lord, where are you going?"). When Christ replied that he was going to Rome to be crucified again because Peter had abandoned him, Peter returned to Rome to suffer his own martyrdom: he was crucified upside down. In the middle of the aisle, just inside the door, Christ's alleged footprints are set in stone. *(At the intersection of V. Appia Antica and V. Ardeatina. Open daily in summer 8am-12:30pm and 2:30-7:45pm; in winter 8am-12:30pm and 2:30-6:45pm. Free.)*

CATACOMBS. Since burial inside the city walls was forbidden during ancient times, fashionable Romans buried their beloved along Appian Way, while early Christians dug maze-like catacombs—an economic solution for pricey land. **San Callisto** is the largest catacomb in Rome, with nearly 22km of subterranean paths. Its four levels once held 16 popes, seven bishops, St. Cecilia, and 500,000 other Christians. *(V. Appia Antica 126, entrance on road parallel to V. Appia. ☎ 06 51 30 15 80; www.catacombe.roma.it. M-Tu and Th-Su 9am-noon and 2-5pm. €5, ages 6-15 €3. Cash only.)* **Santa Domitilla** holds a third-century portrait of Christ and the Apostles, along with other colorful frescoes. *(V. delle Sette Chiese 282. Facing V. Ardeatina from San Callisto exit, cross street, and walk right up V. Sette Chiese. ☎ 06 51 10 342; www.catacombe. domitilla.it. Open Feb.-Dec. M and W-Su 9am-noon and 2-5pm. €5, ages 6-15 €3. Cash only.)* **San**

ROME

Sebastiano houses the massive underground tomb of St. Sebastian himself, and was reputedly the home to the bodies of Peter and Paul before their relocation to their final resting places. San Sebastiano also contains three impressive stucco-ceiling tombs from the pre-Christian period. Visit the info office for maps, booklets, and advice. *(V. Appia Antica 136. ☎06 78 50 350. www.fratilazio.it. Open M-Sa 9am-noon and 2-5pm. €5, ages 6-15 €3. MC/V. All catacombs accessible only with guided tours in English, Italian, and Spanish, which run every 20min.)*

VILLA AND CIRCUS OF MAXENTIUS. Emperor Maxentius built this complex, which contains a villa and a 10,000-spectator chariot racetrack. *(V. Appia Antica 153. ☎06 78 01 324. Open 9am-1:30pm. €3, students €1.50. Cash only.)*

🏛 MUSEUMS

Rome is home to some of the world's most renowned museums. Though contemporary exhibits do occasionally pass through the city, permanent masterpieces have been secured through the wealth and influence of prominent Roman families and the Vatican. Reserving or buying tickets in advance saves time. Keep your eyes on the ceilings—in many museums they are covered in frescoes. For more info on Rome's museums, visit www.beniculturali.it.

🖾VATICAN MUSEUMS (MUSEI VATICANI)

From P. S. Pietro, walk 10 blocks north along the Vatican City wall. From Ⓜ️Ottaviano, turn left on V. Ottaviano to reach the Vatican City wall; turn right and follow the wall to the museum's entrance. Several signs along the wall pointing to the entrance. ☎06 69 88 49 47; www.vatican.va. Major galleries open Mar.-Oct. M-Sa 8:30am-6pm, last entrance 4pm. Last entry 2hr. before closing. Closed on major religious holidays. Snack bar between the collection of modern religious art and the Sistine Chapel; full cafeteria near main entrance pavilion. Most of the museums are wheelchair-accessible, though less visited parts, such as the upper level of the Etruscan Museum, are not. Admission €13, ISIC members €8, with guided tour €21.50, children under 1m tall free. Free last Su of the month 8:30am-12:30pm. Info and gift shop sell a useful guidebook (€7.50) on ground level past the entrance. Audio tour €6.

The Vatican Museums hold one of the world's greatest collections of art, with ancient, Renaissance, and modern paintings, sculptures, and of course papal odds and ends. After a day of art overload, be sure to admire the famous **bronze double-helix ramp** as you ramble down it towards the exit.

 ARE WE THERE YET? Lines for the Vatican Museums, which begin forming around 6:30am, only become more unbearable. It's not a bad idea to drag yourself out of that rock-hard hostel bed at an ungodly hour.

🖾SISTINE CHAPEL. Since its completion in the 16th century, the Sistine Chapel, named for its founder, Pope Sixtus IV, has been the site of the College of Cardinals' election of new popes, most recently **Pope Benedict XVI** in April 2005. Michelangelo's **ceiling,** the pinnacle of artistic creation, gleams from its 20-year restoration, which ended in 1999. The simple compositions and vibrant colors hover above, each section depicting a story from Genesis. The scenes are framed by the famous *ignudi* (young nude males). Michelangelo painted the masterpiece by standing on a platform and craning backward—he never recovered from the strain to his neck and eyes. *The Last Judgement* fills the altar wall; the figure of Christ as judge lingers in the upper center, surrounded by his saintly entourage and the supplicant Mary. Michelangelo painted himself as a flayed human skin that hangs symbolically between the realms of heaven and hell. The frescoes on the side walls predate Michelangelo's ceiling; they were completed between 1481 and 1483 by a team of artists under Perugino including Botticelli, Ghirlandaio, Roselli, Signorelli, and della Gatta. On one side, scenes from the life of Moses complement parallel scenes of Christ's life on the other. Sitting is only allowed on the benches along the side. Guards will ask you to be silent, as the chapel is a holy place.

OTHER VATICAN GALLERIES. The **Museo Pio-Clementino** houses the world's greatest collection of antique sculpture. The world-famous statue of **Laocoön,** who was strangled by Neptune's sea serpents for being suspicious of the Greek's gift of the wooden horse, is located in the octagonal courtyard. Proceeding through the courtyard, two slobbering hounds guard the entrance to the **Stanza degli Animali,** a marble menagerie highlighting Roman brutality. The statues of **Apollo Belvedere** and **Hercules** are both masterful works. The last room of the gallery has the red sarcophagus of Sant'Elena, Constantine's mother. From here, the Simonetti Stairway climbs to the **Museo Etrusco,** filled with artifacts from Tuscany and northern Lazio. Back on the landing of the Simonetti Staircase is the **Stanza della Biga** (room of an ancient marble chariot) and the **Galleria della Candelabra,** which contains over 500 smaller statues. The route to the Sistine Chapel begins here, passing through the dimly lit **Galleria degli Arazzi** (tapestries), the **Galleria delle Mappe** (maps), the **Apartamento di Pio V** (where there is a shortcut to the Sistine Chapel), the **Stanza Sobieski,** and the **Stanza dell'Immacolata Concezione.** From the Stanza dell'Immacolata Concezione, a door leads into the first of the four **Stanze di Rafaele,** apartments built for Pope Julius II in the 1510s. A door at the back of the second room, originally called the **Room of the Parrot,** depicts St. John the Baptist with parrots on either side of him. The door below leads to the Room of the Swiss Guard and is closed to the public. Another room features Raphael's **School of Athens,** painted as a trial piece for Julius, who was so impressed that he fired his other painters, destroyed their frescoes, and commissioned Raphael to decorate the entire room. From here, there are two paths: one to the Sistine Chapel, and the other a staircase to the frescoed Borgia apartments and the **Museum of Modern Religious Art.**

PINACOTECA. This collection, one of Rome's best, includes Filippo Lippi's *Coronation of the Virgin,* Perugino's *Madonna and Child,* Titian's *Madonna*

IN RECENT NEWS

HOT TO TROT

What could possibly be more romantic than sharing a bottle of wine with your sweetheart as you clip-clop along the streets of Rome at sunset? Despite all of its old-world charm, this tradition has recently come under fire from animal activists, who claim that the horses are forced to work in inhumane conditions, one of which is the sweltering summer heat.

New city ordinances forbid horse-drawn carriage service between 1 and 5pm from July to September—hours now officially deemed "too hot to trot."

But the ENPA, the principal animal rights group concerned, remains unimpressed. The group has proposed another law that will essentially transform the four-legged taxis into four-wheeled ones, by giving the carriage drivers new permits to tout tourists around in taxis instead.

This proposition, as expected, was not well-received by the horse-drawn-carriage-driving community, whose skills with the animals are quite specialized and not so easily interchangeable with the skills required of a taxi driver. And so, the heated debate continues.

While it will probably be some time before another law passes, you shouldn't risk missing out on your chance to "horse around" Rome!

of San Nicoletta dei Frari, and Raphael's ▧**Transfiguration.** On the way out of the Sistine Chapel, take a look at the **Room of the Aldobrandini Marriage,** which contains a series of rare, ancient Roman frescoes.

PRINCIPAL COLLECTIONS

▧**GALLERIA BORGHESE.** The crown jewel of the beautiful Villa Borghese, the Galleria Borghese may be Rome's most enjoyable museum. The spellbinding collection, housed in the Villa Borghese, was begun by Cardinal Scipione Borghese in the 1600s. It includes some of the greatest masterpieces by Bernini, Titian, Raphael, Caravaggio, and Rubens—and can be appreciated in one unforgettable afternoon. Without a doubt, a visit to the Galleria Borghese should be a part of any Roman itinerary. Reservations are required, however, as tickets sometimes sell out one month in advance.

Upon entering, don't miss Mark Antonio's **ceiling,** depicting the Roman conquest of Gaul. After perusing the Roman mosaics on the floor, check out the dragon and eagle statues, symbols of the Borghese family, on opposite ends of the room. **Room I** houses Canova's steamy statue of Paolina Borghese portrayed as a reclining Venus triumphant, holding the golden apple given to her by Paris. The myth is also depicted in elaborate frescoes on the ceiling. The next rooms display two of Bernini's most momentous works: the breathtaking ▧**Apollo and Daphne,** in which Daphne's hands and feet appear to be sprouting leaves and roots as she begins her mythical transformation into a laurel tree, and a magnificent and thought-provoking *David* crouching with his slingshot.

Feel free to marvel at more of Bernini's splendor while taking in Pluto and Prosperina's seemingly weightless bodies in *The Rape of Proserpina.* A trip to the Galleria is not complete without a visit to the renowned ▧**Caravaggio Room,** featuring six staggeringly impressive works, including his self-portrait, **The Sick Bacchus,** which he painted during a stay in the hospital (supposedly recuperating from either depression or a horse kick to the head). *The Sick Bacchus* bears a striking resemblance to *Young Boy with Basket of Fruit,* as it is more commonly referred to, but the Galleria has it labeled as *Young Girl.* The questionable gender of the main subject and his/her pose of nonchalant suggestiveness (slightly parted lips, tenderly revealed shoulder) has led some art historians to psychoanalyze Caravaggio's sexuality. The stark ▧**David and Goliath** is another self-portrait, one that epitomizes the artist's tragic reputation.

The collection continues in the *pinacoteca* upstairs, accessible from the gardens around the back by a staircase. **Room IX** holds Raphael's *Deposition,* a masterpiece showing the midpoint between the traditional moments of the Pietà and the Entombment, while Sodoma's *Pietà* graces **Room XII.** Look for self portraits by Bernini, del Conte's *Cleopatra and Lucrezia,* Rubens's *Pianto sul Cristo Morto,* and Titian's famous *Amor Sacro e Amor Profano.* (Ple. Scipione Borghese 5. Ⓜ A-Spagna; take exit labeled "Villa Borghese," walk to the right past the Metro stop to V. Muro Torto and then to P. Pta. Pinciana; Vle. del Museo Borghese is ahead and leads to the museum. Or take bus #116 or 910 to V. Pinciana. ☎ 06 84 216 542; www.galleriaborghese.it/borghese/it/default.htm. Open Tu-Su 8:30am-7:30pm. Entry every 2hr.; last entry 5pm. Limited capacity; reservation required. Tickets for high season may become booked a month in advance. Reservations ☎ 06 32 810, group reservations 06 32 65 13 29 M-F 9am-6pm, Sa 9am-1pm; www.ticketeria.it. The ticket office and a bookshop share the villa's basement. Tickets including reservation and bag charge €13.50, EU citizens ages 18-25 €10.25, EU citizens under 18, over 65 and students €7. Audio tour €5. Guided tours in English at 9:10 and 11:10am. €5. MC/V.)

MUSEI CAPITOLINI. This collection of ancient sculptures is the world's oldest public museum of ancient art, and one of its largest. Pope Clement XII Corsini bought the *palazzo* to exhibit Cardinal Alessandro Albani's ancient sculptures in 1733. The *palazzo*'s courtyard contains fragments of the somewhat frightening **Colossus of Constantine,** whose muscular right arm measures almost two meters. The original statue of **Marcus Aurelius,** Bernini's **Head of Medusa,** and the famous **Capitoline Wolf,** which has symbolized the city of Rome since antiquity, occupy the first floor. At the top of the stairs, the **pinacoteca** houses the museum's non-sculpture masterpieces, including Bellini's *Portrait of a Young Man,* Titian's *Baptism of Christ,* Rubens's *Romulus and Remus Fed by the Wolf,* and Caravaggio's *St. John the Baptist* and *Gypsy Fortune-Teller.* The collection continues in the Palazzo Nuovo, which can be accessed through the **Tabularium,** a hall of ancient Rome built in 79 BC. The entryway patio holds **Maforio,** one of Rome's five original "talking statues," to which people would give messages for the public. This gallery also holds the **Galata,** one of the oldest specimens of Roman sculpture. (☎*06 82 05 91 27; info.museicapitolini@comune.roma.it. Open Tu-Su 9am-8pm. Musei Capitolini's wheelchair-accessible entrance at V. del Tempio di Giove; Tabularium's wheelchair entrance at Palazzo Nuovo. Reservations ☎06 82 05 91 27. Reservations necessary for groups Sa and Su. €6.50, reduced €4.50, EU residents under 18 and over 65 free; with temporary exhibition €8; combined Musei Capitolini and Centrale Montemartini valid for 7 days €8.50, ISIC & EU students €6.50. Musei Capitolini, Centrale Montemartini, and temporary exhibition €10, ISIC and students €8, EU citizens under 18 or over 65 free. Reservations for groups of 12 or more €25. Audio tour €5. Guidebook €7.75, exact change required.)*

MUSEO NAZIONALE ETRUSCO DI VILLA GIULIA. This 16th-century villa was built under Pope Julius III. Today, it houses one of the most extensive collections of Etruscan artifacts in the world. Highlights include the noted sarcophagus of a married couple in **Room 9.** Upstairs, archaeologists have put together fragments of a facade of an Etruscan temple, complete with terra-cotta gargoyles, chips of paint, and a relief of the warrior Tydaeus biting into the brain of a wounded adversary. The museum is also home to a chaotic collection of Greek artifacts found in the region, evidence of the extensive trade relationships that once existed between the Etruscans and the Greeks. More interesting than the jewelry, ceramics, and other artifacts is the villa itself. Make sure to stroll around the well-manicured grounds and check out the lily pads and goldfish in the discreetly hidden pond in the center courtyard. (*P. Villa Giulia 9, just south of Villa Borghese, near P. Thorvaldsen.* Ⓜ*A-Flaminio; then tram #30 or 225, or bus #19 from P. Risorgimento or 52 from P. S. Silvestro. From Galleria Borghese, follow V. dell'Uccelliera to the zoo, and then take V. del Giardino to V. delle Belle Arti. Museum is on the left after Galleria d'Arte Moderna.* ☎*06 32 01 951, reservations 82 45 29. Open daily 8:30am-7:30pm. €4, EU citizens ages 18-24 €2, EU citizens under 18 and over 65 free. Mandatory bag check. English audio tour €4.)*

VILLA FARNESINA. The villa belonged to Agostino "Il Magnifico" Chigi, once Europe's wealthiest man. For show, Chigi had his banquet guests toss gold and silver dishes into the Tiber River after every course; ever the miser, he secretly hid nets under water to recover his treasures. To the right of the entrance lies the breathtaking **Sala di Galatea,** mostly painted by the villa's architect, Baldassare Peruzzi, in 1511. The vault displays symbols of astrological signs that represent 9:30pm on November 29, 1466, the moment of Agostino's birth. The room's masterpiece is Raphael's **Triumph of Galatea.** The ceiling of the Loggia di Psiche depicts the marriage of Cupid and Psyche. Returning to the entrance, a stunningly detailed stairway ascends to the **Salone delle Prospettive.** This room, decorated by Peruzzi, incorporates five different colored marbles in the floor design and offers views of Rome between fictive columns. The adjacent bedroom, known as the **Stanza delle Nozze** (Marriage Room), is the real reason for coming here. Il Sodoma, who had previously been busy painting the pope's rooms in the Vatican, frescoed the chamber until Raphael showed up and took over. Il Sodoma bounced back, creating this masterful fresco of Alexander the

Great's marriage to the beautiful Roxanne. *(V. della Lungara 230. Across from Palazzo Corsini on V. della Lungara. Bus #23, 271, or 280; get off at Lungotevere della Farnesina or Ponte Sisto.* ☎ *06 68 02 72 67; www.lincei.it. Open M-Sa 9am-1pm; 1st Su of the month 9am-1pm. Last entry 20min. before closing. €5, under 18 €4, EU citizens over 65 free.)*

MUSEO NAZIONALE D'ARTE ANTICA. This collection of 12th- to 18th-century art is split between Palazzo Barberini and Palazzo Corsini. Barberini contains paintings from the medieval through Baroque periods. Don't miss Rafael's lover delicately cradling her exposed breast in *La Fornarina. (V. Barberini 18.* Ⓜ*A-Barberini. Bus #492 or 62.* ☎ *06 48 14 591. For tours call* ☎ *06 85 55 952. Open Tu-Su 8:30am-7:30pm. €5; EU citizens ages 18-24 €2; EU citizens under 18, over 65, and EU students free. Cash only.)* Galleria Corsini's 17th- to 18th-century collection includes works by Rubens, Caravaggio, Bernini, and Brueghel. *(V. della Lungara 10. Opposite Villa Farnesina in Trastevere. Take bus #23; get off between Ponte Mazzini and Ponte Sisto.* ☎ *06 22 58 24 93. Open Tu-Su 8:30am-7:30pm. Wheelchair-accessible. €4, EU students €2, Italian art students and EU citizens over 65 free. Guidebooks in Italian €10.50. Cash only.)*

GALLERIA SPADA. Cardinal Bernardino Spada bought a large assortment of paintings and sculptures, and commissioned an even more opulent set of great rooms to house them. Time and good luck have left the palatial seventh-century apartments nearly intact—a visit to the gallery offers a glimpse of the luxury of Baroque courtly life. Before heading into the gallery rooms upstairs, check out Borromini's fantastic example of ▨**3D perspective** in the courtyard. Watch in awe as the seemingly distant, life-size statue through the corridor is revealed to be only three feet tall and less than 35 ft. away. In **Room 1** of the gallery's four rooms, the modest cardinal hung portraits of himself by Guercino, Guido Reni, and Cerini. In **Room 2,** look for paintings by the Venetians Tintoretto and Titian and a frieze by Vaga, originally intended for the Sistine Chapel. In **Room 4** are three canvases by the father-daughter team of Orazio and Artemisia Gentileschi. *(P. Capo di Ferro 13, in the Palazzo Spada. From Campo dei Fiori, take any of the small streets leading to P. Farnese. Facing away from Campo dei Fiori, turn left on Capo di Ferro. Bus #64.* ☎ *06 68 32 409. Open Tu-Su 8:30am-7:30pm. Last entry 7pm. Guided tour Su 10:45am from museum book shop. Pamphlet guides in English available for each room of the exhibit. €5, EU students €2.50, EU citizens under 18 or over 65 free. Guidebooks €10.50. Cash only.)*

OTHER COLLECTIONS

GALLERIA DORIA PAMPHILI. The Doria Pamphili family, whose illustrious kin include Pope Innocent X, maintain this stunning private collection in their palatial home. The Classical art is organized by size and theme, and Renaissance and Baroque masterpieces include Caravaggio's *Rest During the Flight in Egypt*, Raphael's *Double Portrait*, and Velasquez's portrait of Pope Innocent X, generally considered to be one of the most outstanding papal portraits of all time. The pope was shocked by the depiction, exclaiming, "It's too real!" The back gallery's mirrors and windows evoke the feeling of a miniature Versailles. *(V. del Corso 305. Bus #40 Express or 64 to P. Venezia. From P. Venezia, walk up V. del Corso and take the 2nd left.* ☎ *06 67 97 323; www.doriapamphilj.it. Open M-W and F-Su 10am-5pm. Last entry 4:15pm. Closed Jan. 1, Easter, May 1, Aug. 15, and Dec. 25. €9, students and seniors €5.70. Informative audio tour in English, French, or Italian included. Cash only.)*

MUSEO CENTRALE MONTEMARTINI. The building, a former turn-of-the-century electrical plant, has a striking collection of Classical art. Highlights include *Hercules's Presentation at Mount Olympus*, a huge well-preserved floor mosaic of a hunt, and a statue of Dionysus, the god of wine and revelry, whose hair is interwoven with grapes. *(V. Ostiense 106.* Ⓜ*B-Piramide. From P. Ostiense take V. Ostiense, then walk or take bus #23 or 702 3 stops.* ☎ *06 82 05 91 27; www.centralemontemar-*

A Dead Language Lives
A Young Classicist Experiences Italy Yesterday and Today

Although I had heard of Father Reginald Foster as a child, it was only seven years later as a Classics major that I made the pilgrimage to Rome to study with Fr. Reggie, one of the Vatican's chief Latinists. I had traveled to Italy several times before and thought I would immerse myself exclusively in the old lingua franca. But I soon found that the more I read and spoke Latin, the more I came to understand and appreciate the modern Italian language and culture around me.

Since class did not begin until 2pm, I spent the mornings wandering. The irresistible scents wafting from the bakery on a side street off Vle. di Trastevere, the midday street festival in the Jewish Ghetto, or the cats prowling around the Mausoleum of Augustus are the city's best attractions—and are conveniently free.

In the afternoon, I journeyed back to the basement schoolroom at the top of the Gianicolo Hill. Fr. Reggie teaches Latin as if it were a living lanuage. He often began with musings—in Latin, naturally—on his arduous commute to work in the Vatican that morning in the face of the two-week-long taxi strike or on the intricacies of the national rail service. He devoted a portion of class every week to translating acta diurna (headlines) from English-language news magazines into Latin. We read everything from Thomas More to 1999 Papal marriage court decisions.

After three 1½hr. sessions, we would break for an evening of casual Latin conversation or reading sub arboribus (under the trees) in the garden of the Carmelite monastery.

Because of the length and pace of the course, I engaged Rome as a resident rather than as a tourist. Every day, during the break after the first class, I would wander down the street to the Star Café, where Remo, the jovial owner, would give me an espresso with an extra cookie. I spent the second recess selecting fruits from the neighborhood vendor. I got to know my neighborhood, Trastevere, through regular excursions to the nearby cheese shop and Standa supermarket and morning runs up the slopes of the Gianicolo hill and through the Doria Pamphilj Gardens. This routine helped ensure that I was not just studying a "dead language" and insulating myself from the very living city.

My Latin and Italian experiences came together while watching the final match of the World Cup with 200,000 fans in the Circus Maximus, the old Roman racetrack. The triumphant march of the azzurri through the tournament fostered a camaraderie that manifested itself in distinctly Italian ways. With gleeful grins, the owners of a local pizzeria not far from Fr. Reggie's class carved up watermelons and offered them gratis to us after the semifinal win over Germany. The victory over France

"I wasn't studying a 'dead language' and tuning out the living city around me"

even inspired T-shirts with a Latin slogan—a welcome sight despite a grammatical error.

A traveler to Rome armed with knowledge of Latin can unlock mysteries of the Eternal City that would remain otherwise indecipherable. Latin inscriptions everywhere tell stories of ceremony, betrayal, victory, and defeat. Engaging the language in Fr. Reggie's way—as a living embodiment of a humanistic tradition—gives the traveler a sense of how Italy has evolved into what it is today. It doesn't take long to realize that Rome is a city with an amazing past; Latin and its connection to Italian bridges that gap between the Rome of Caesar and chariots and the Rome of Prodi and Vespas.

Clem Wood has spent summers in both Florence and Rome. He will graduate from Harvard in the spring of 2008 with an A.B. in Classics and plans to return to Italy for further adventures and studies in the near future.

tini.org. Open Tu-Su 9:30am-7pm. €4.20, with entry to the Capitoline Museums €8.50; EU citizens ages 18-24 €2.60/7.80; EU citizens under 18 or over 65 free. Reservations €1.50. Cash only.)

MUSEO NAZIONALE D'ARTE MODERNA E CONTEMPORANEA. This museum holds a splendid collection of 19th- and 20th-century art, ranging from nationalistic Italian paintings and pastoral scenes to abstract works. In **la sala giardiniere** (the gardener's room), Van Gogh's *L'Arlesiana* and Edgar Degas's *Dopo il bagno* hang among works completed by Italians in Paris. The museum's soaring galleries also house an impressive array of sculptures and temporary traveling exhibitions. *(Vle. delle Belle Arti 131, in Villa Borghese, near Museo Nazionale Etrusco. ⓂA-Flaminio; then tram #30 or 225, or bus #19 from P. Risorgimento or #52 from P. S. Silvestro. From Galleria Borghese, follow V. dell'Uccelliera to the zoo and take V. del Giardino to V. delle Belle Arti. ☎06 32 29 82 21; www.gnam.arti.beniculturali.it. Open Tu-Su 8:30am-7:30pm. Last entry 6:45pm. €9, EU citizens ages 18-24 €7, EU citizens under 18 or over 65 free. Cash only.)*

MUSEO MARIO PRAZ. This small, eccentric museum was once the home of Mario Praz (1896-1982), an equally small and eccentric professor of English literature and an 18th- and 19th-century art collector. This evil-eye-wielding, club-footed man preferred books, fans, and serpent-like musical instruments to people. Superstitious neighbors spat when they saw him. *(V. Zanardelli 1, top fl. At the east end of Ponte Umberto, next to Museo Napoleonico. ☎06 68 61 089; www.gnam.arti.beni-cultural.it/prazco.htm. Mandatory 35-45min. tour in Italian, given every hr. Open M 2:30-6:30pm, Tu-Su 9am-1pm and 2:30-6:30pm. Max. 10 people on tour. Free.)*

MUSEO NAZIONALE D'ARTE ORIENTALE. This museum contains artifacts from prehistory to the 1800s along with exhibits on Near Eastern, Islamic, Nepalese, Tibetan, Indian, Southeast Asian, and Chinese art. *(V. Merulana 248. In Palazzo Brancaccio on Esquiline Hill. ☎06 48 74 415; museorientale.it. Open M, W, and F 9am-2pm; Tu, Th, and Su 9am-7:30pm. Closed 1st and 3rd M of each month. €4, reduced €2. Cash only.)*

MUSEO NAZIONALE ROMANO PALAZZO ALTEMPS. This sculpture museum displays the famous AD fifth-century Ludovisi Throne. *(P. Sant'Apollinare 44, just north of P. Navona. Bus #30 Express, 492, 70, 81, 87, or 628 to C. del Rinascimento/P. Cinque Lune. Museum ☎06 78 33 566, ticket office 68 33 759. Open Tu-Su 9am-7:45pm. Last entry 7pm. €9, EU citizens ages 18-24 €6.50, EU citizens under 18 or over 65 free. Audio tour €4. Cash only.)*

MUSEO DEL RISORGIMENTO. Underneath the left side of the Vittoriano monument in P. Venezia, this museum contains items relating to the Risorgimento, the 19th-century "resurgence," which ultimately led to the unification of Italy in 1861. *(Entrance on V. di S. Pietro in Carcere. ☎06 67 93 526. Open daily 9:30am-6pm. Free.)*

MUSEO DELL'ARA PACIS. Right beside Augustus's Mausoleum, this museum highlights the art of the restored first-century BC Ara Pacis (Altar of Peace), a temple built to celebrate Augustus's return from Spain and Gaul. Check out the impressive floral frieze on its lower half and noteworthy Romans on top. *(Lungotevere in Augusta. From P. Popolo, walk down V. di Ripetta. The museum is the white building on the right. ☎06 82 05 91 27; http://en.arapacis.it. Open Tu-Su 9am-7pm. €6.50, EU citizens ages 18-25 €4.50, under 18 and over 65 free. Audio tour €3.50. AmEx/MC/V.)*

🎵 ENTERTAINMENT

Weekly *Roma C'è* (with an English section) and *Time Out*, which are both available at newsstands, have up-to-date club, movie, and event listings.

LIVE MUSIC

Rome hosts a variety of performances in fantastic venues, especially in the summer. Local churches often host free choral concerts. Perhaps most interesting, the *carabinieri* band gives rousing (and free) concerts in P. di Sant'Ignazio and other outdoor venues on the occasional holiday or festival.

Alexanderplatz Jazz Club, V. Ostia 9 (☎06 39 74 21 71; www.alexanderplatz.it). ⓂA-Ottaviano. Head left on V. G. Cesare, take 2nd right on V. Leone IV and 1st left on V. Ostia. Night buses to P. Venezia and Termini leave from P. Clodio. Italy's oldest jazz club in Italy, considered Europe's best. Shows start at 10pm. Open daily Sept.-May 9pm-2am. Moves outside to Villa Celimontana in summer. €10.

Teatro Ghione, V. delle Fornaci 37 (☎06 63 72 294; www.ghione.it), near the Vatican. This red velvet theater hosts Euromusica's classical concerts. Box office open Oct.-Apr. daily 10am-1pm and 4-8pm. Tickets €12-22. Call for occasional discounts. MC/V.

Parco della Musica, Vle. Pietro de Coubertin 30 (info ☎06 80 24 12 81, tickets ☎19 91 09 783; www.auditorium.com), near P. del Popolo. Incredible venue with everything from Verdi and to orchestral arrangements of Jimi Hendrix. Box office open Sept.-June daily 11am-6pm and from 8pm until the start of the performance on concert nights.

OPERA AND DANCE

Arias of world-famous operas, especially those by national composer Giuseppe Verdi fill the air in Rome throughout the summer. Countless flyers and posters list performances at fantastic outdoor venues as well as in the famous **Teatro dell'Opera** near P. della Repubblica (P. Gigli 7; ☎06 48 16 01). *Roma C'è* also lists the week's upcoming performances, and tourist offices can often help you book tickets at a reduced rate.

THEATER

For info on English theater, visit www.musical.it or www.comune.roma.it.

Teatro Argentina, Largo di Torre Argentina 52 (☎06 68 40 00 111; www.teatrodiroma. net). Bus #64 from Termini or tram #8, right off V. Arenula. Home to the Teatro di Roma company. Hosts plays, concerts, ballets, and festivals. Box office open M-F 10am-2pm and 3-7pm, Sa 10am-2pm. Performances €12-27, students €12-22. AmEx/MC/V.

Teatro Colosseo, V. Capo d'Africa 5 (☎06 70 04 932). ⓂB-Colosseo. Walk down V. dei Fori Imperiali past the Colosseum, then go right through P. Colosseo; V. Capo d'Africa is 2 blocks down on the left. Occasional English productions. Box office open Sept.-Apr. Tu-Sa 6-9:30pm. €10-20, students €8.

CINEMA

Unfortunately, most theaters in Rome show dubbed movies. For foreign films with Italian subtitles, look for a "v.o." or "l.o." in listings (*versione originale* or *lingua originale*). In summer, huge screens spring up in *piazze* around the city for **outdoor filmfests.** Cinemas citywide offer discounts on Wednesdays and for 5pm showings. Visit **www.ilteatrodiroma.it** for more info.

Nuovo Olimpia, V. in Lucina 16G (☎06 68 61 068), off V. del Corso. Olympic film haven shows American films for 1 week before dubbing. €7, matinees and M and W €5.

Warner Village Moderno, P. della Repubblica 45/46 (☎06 47 77 92 01). Periodically shows films in English prior to dubbing. 5 screens.

Nuovo Sacher, Largo Ascianghi 1 (☎06 58 18 116). Take V. Induno from V. di Trastevere. Famed Italian director Nanni Moretti's theater shows a host of indie films. Films in original language M. Tickets €7, matinee and W €5.

SPECTATOR SPORTS

Rome is *calcio*-obsessed. The city has two *Serie A* teams: **S.S. Lazio** and **A.S. Roma.** The two annual Roma-Lazio games often prove decisive in the championship

ROME

race. Matches are held at the **Stadio Olimpico**, in Foro Italico, almost every Sunday from September to June. Buy tickets (from €16) at team stores like **A.S. Roma**, P. Colonna 360 (www.asroma.it.), and **Lazio Point**, V. Farini 34/36, near Termini. (☎06 48 26 688. Open daily 9am-7pm. AmEx/MC/V.) They are also available at **Orbis**, P. Esquilino 102 (☎06 48 27 403).

 CALCIO CRAZIES. Tickets to intense soccer matches can be obtained at the stadium before a game, but beware long lines and sold-out games; if you're buying last minute, watch out for price gouging and fake tickets.

🛍 SHOPPING

Rome is a shopper's paradise, versatile enough to accommodate a wide spectrum of tastes and budgets. First, there are the ubiquitous chain stores like **Motivi, Mango, Stefanel, Intimissimi, Zara,** and **United Colors of Benetton.** Then there are the heart attack-inducing prices of designer shrines like **Cavalli, Dolce & Gabbana,** and **Prada,** followed by the techno-blasting teen stores that dominate central thoroughfares. Finally, tiny boutiques in the *centro storico,* including **Ethic** and **Havana,** often have locations throughout the city. Below is a list of notable boutiques, budget stores, and fashionable streets, since no trip to Italy is complete without a bit of shopping. **Via del Corso,** the main street connecting P. del Popolo and P. Venezia, offers a mix of high- and low-end, disco-pumping stores with leather goods, men's suits, and silk ties as well as plenty of fashionable women's apparel. Beware of high-priced tourist traps, however, since V. del Corso is littered with them. **Etam** (no. 170) and **Motivi** (no. 318) are two lower-priced Italian chains. **Calzedonia** (no. 140 and 190) and **Yammamay** (no. 309 and 139) are fabulous for cheap, colorful, and fun tights, socks, and bikinis. **La Rinascente** (no. 191) is a magnificent major department store. Try your luck with higher-end labels like **Diesel** (no. 186/655), **Ferrari** (no. 402), **Lacoste** (no. 221), and **Puma** (no. 403). Across the river from V. del Corso, **Via Cola di Rienzo** offers a more leisurely shopping experience sans throngs of tourists. Meander down this thoroughfare of shops and stop by stylish chain stores. **COIN** department store, V. Cola di Rienzo 171/173, won't leave you penniless.

BOUTIQUES

Unique boutiques and hot haute couture designer stores cluster around the Spanish Steps and V. dei Condotti. Purchases of over €155 at a single store are eligible for a tax refund for non-EU residents. Most of the fancy-schmancy stores—**Bruno Magli, Dolce & Gabbana, Armani, Gianni Versace, Gucci, Prada, Salvatore Ferragamo**—can be found on **Via dei Condotti** (near the Spanish Steps). Fendi, an Italian favorite, is an exception, holding its purse strings nearby in Largo Goldini, off V. del Corso. If you feel dissatisfied after your trip to this chic street, there's always **Via dei Governo Vecchio,** near P. Navona. Lined with vintage clothing, furniture, and art stores, this avenue offers ageless goodies at a price.

CHEAP YET CLASSY

Tezenis, V. del Corso 148 (☎06 67 93 569; open M-Sa 10am-8pm, Su 10:30am-8pm), offers women's, men's, and children's intimate apparel (underwear €3, shirts €5-6). The **General Store**, V. della Scala 62a (☎06 58 17 675; open daily 10am-1pm and 4-8pm), sells discounted overstock Diesel, Adidas, and Nike goods. Off Campo dei Fiori, **Via dei Giubbonari** is dotted with authentic European clothing stores, and will have you dressed to the nines before eight.

OUTDOOR MARKETS

Street vendors will often try to sell fake Prada bags for exorbitant prices, insisting they're from the hands of Miuccia herself. Seemingly miraculous bargains can end up costing you dearly in the end: a 2005 Italian law stipulates that buyers of fake designer items can be fined €10,000.

Mercato Andrea Doria, on V. Andrea Doria, northwest of the Vatican Museums. Ⓜ Cipro; bus #23 or 70. Caters to the local population, so don't expect to find many English-speaking folks here. Fruits, vegetables, fish, groceries, and clothes sold in a huge open square and in permanent vendor stalls all along the street. Open M-Sa 7am-1:30pm.

Campo dei Fiori, *centro storico.* Tram #8 or bus #64. Transformed daily by stalls of fruits and vegetables, meat, poultry, and fish. Open M-Sa 7am until the individual vendors decide their food has run out—usually around 1:30pm.

Porta Portese, in Trastevere. Tram #8 from Largo di Torre Argentina. This gigantic flea market is a surreal experience, with booths selling clothing, shoes, jewelry, bags, toilets, and millions of other items you never knew you needed. Keep your friends close and your money closer, as the place swarms with pickpockets. Open Su 5am-1:30pm.

Mercato delle Stampe, Largo della Fontanella di Borghese. Bus #81, 116, 117, or 492. A bookworms' haven specializing in old books, both used and genuine antiquarian magazines, and other pieces of art. Open M-Sa 9:30am-6pm.

 HAGGLING RULES. Name your bottom price; if the vendor refuses, walk away. If he wants to make the sale, he will call you back.

🔊 NIGHTLIFE

Romans find nighttime diversion at the pubs of San Lorenzo, the clubs of Testaccio, and everywhere in between. Pick up *Roma C'è* for updates on clubs' hours. *Time Out* covers Rome's sparse but solid collection of gay nightlife listings, many of which require an **ARCI-GAY pass** (1 year. €10; p. 112). Also check with **Circolo di Cultura Omosessuale Mario Mieli** (☎ 06 54 13 985).

PUBS AND BARS

Though *enoteche* tend to be the primary destination for locals, bars and pubs are still a fun way to knock back a few without covers or sweaty polyester. There are many Irish pubs in Rome; the best are around **Campo dei Fiori.** Crowds of people flood P. Navona after the bars close at 2am to continue the revelry.

Caffè della Scala, V. della Scala 4 (☎ 06 58 03 610), on V. della Scala before it intersects with P. S. Egidio. Friendly proprietress/bartender extraordinaire Frances offers creative drinks with unusual ingredients. Try the potent Christian Alexander (Canadian whiskey, creme de cacao, and cardamom pods; €7.50) and the Black Velvet (Guiness and prosecco; €7.50) in the dim, sexy interior. Open daily 5pm-2am. Cash only.

Big Hilda Caffe, Vicolo del Cinque 33/34 (☎ 06 580 3303). Enjoy Sunday brunch or head there after midnight when a festive crowd squeezes into the cozy interior. Pints €3.50. Open M-Sa 5:30pm-2am, Su 11am-2pm and 5:30pm-2am. Cash only.

Frenzi e Frizioni, Travestere, V. del Politeama 4/6. (☎ 58 33 42 10). From Ponte Sisto, turn left on Lungotevere Raffaello Sanzio; the bar is in the *piazza* on the right. Hip, energetic music spills out the doors. Young locals gather for mojitos (€7), delicious wine (€4), wine spritzers (white wine with either peach, kiwi, or strawberry cream; €6), mixed drinks (€6), and frozen mixed drinks (€7). Open daily 10am-2am.

Express, Trastevere, V. del Moro 10. (☎33 82 07 44 63). From Ponte Sisto, cross the street to P. Trilussa and go left. College crowd. Bartenders juggle bottles in the pint-sized interior while classic rock blasts in the background. Beer and mixed drinks from €4. Shots €3. Happy hour 6-11pm. Open daily 6pm-2am.

CLUBS

Italian discos are flashy and fun, but many clubs close for the summer; Testaccio is dependable through early August.

Charro Cafe, V. di Monte Testaccio 73 (☎06 57 83 064). Music booms from this Latin-themed open-air club. Plenty of tropical drinks, Mexican appetizers, and women dancing on top of the benches. Cover €5. Open daily midnight-3:30am.

Coyote, V. di Monte Testaccio 50, (☎06 339 463 9667). The line outside is as long as the one at the Vatican, but it leads to blaring music and an energetic young crowd instead of a silent Sistine Chapel. No cover. Open daily 9:30pm-5am.

Alien, V. Velletri 13-19 (☎06 84 12 212; www.aliendisco.it). One of Rome's biggest discos. Attracts a well-dressed, slightly more mature crowd. Mostly house music. Cover about €15, includes 1 drink; Sa €20. Open Tu-Su midnight-4:30am.

❊ FESTIVALS

From June to August, thousands (often over 30,000) celebrate all things Latin American at **Fiesta,** in the Ippodrome delle Capannelle. Famous artists like Ricky Martin help Romans enjoy *la vida loca*. (Reach the venue using Ⓜ A-Colli Albani or bus #664. For advance tickets, call ☎06 71 82 139, or visit www.fiesta.it.) Music lovers enjoy an auditory feast at the **Cornetto Free Music Festival Roma Live,** which showcases popular international acts. Past performers have ranged from Pink Floyd and the Cure to the Backstreet Boys. (Enter to win free tickets at www.cornettoalgida.it.) On May 1 of every year, Romans are joined by hundreds of thousands of Italians for the **Festa della Primo Maggio** (Festival of the First of May). With roots dating back to the late 1800s, this festival has transformed over the past century from an often violent celebration of labor rights to a crazy, Woodstock-like music mania. Featuring big-name Italian artists like Elisa, Carmen Consoli, Tiromancino, and Articolo 31, this festival continues late into the night, with close to one million students packed into P. di S. Giovanni in Laterno. Don't be surprised to see a pot-smoking, communist-flag-waving Italian youth rocking out next to you. September brings an end to Rome's summer festivals with the traditional **La Notte Bianca** (The White Night), typically held during the first week of the month. Rome's "White Night" refers to an evening when the Metro, shops, museums, and restaurants remain open all night for one last hurrah, thereby leaving the city's streets illuminated all night. Most museums offer free admission.

⬛ DAYTRIPS FROM ROME

▧SPERLONGA

Trains run daily from Rome to the Fondi-Sperlonga station (70min., every hr. 4:57am-11:32pm, €6.20). Take either the COTRAL bus or the Autoservizi Piazzoli urban bus from the Fondi-Sperlonga station to Sperlonga. Purchase tickets on the bus (15-20min, every 2hr., €1). Get off at P. Europa at the top of hill, or, for those wishing to hit the beach, at any of the stops along Vle. Cristoforo Colombo. With a decrepit church to the left and a restaurant to the right, walk 30m to the Tourist Info Center, C. S. Leone 23. (☎0771 55

70 00; www.communedisperlonga.it. Open daily 8am-8pm.) In P. Repubblica, there is a tabaccheria that sells maps (€5) and tickets for COTRAL buses. Facing the tabaccheria, the street to the right of the piazza, V. Ottaviano, winds its way down to the sea and to Vle. Cristoforo Colombo. From here, there are also several paths and stairways that lead down the hill to the shore. Note that because Sperlonga's main road is so long, addresses are identified using kilometers rather than plain numbers. However, since the main attractions are fairly close together, you won't really be walking that far.

Sperlonga (spehr-LON-ga; pop. 3102) served as Emperor Tiberius's imperial getaway until he moved to Capri in AD 26. Well worth the trip from Rome, Sperlonga's curving, whitewashed streets lead through cobblestoned *piazze* to sparkling white sands and sapphire waters. Lounging inside his seaside *speluncae* (grottoes), which gave the town its name, Tiberius would invite his wealthy Roman friends to enjoy this Tyrrhenian heaven with him. A few feet away from the grottoes is the modern and well-exhibited **Museo Archelogico,** where you can see the statuary ruins of Tiberus's villa. This impressive collection represents scenes from Homer's *Odyssey*, including the blinding of Polyphemus the cyclops and the attack of Ulysses's boat by the monstrous Scylla. (V. Flacca 16,600km. 10-15min. walk from P. Europa. ☎0771 54 80 28. Open daily 8:30am-7:30pm. €2, under 18 and over 65 free.) Sperlonga also served as a refuge for those fleeing barbarian attacks on Rome in the AD sixth century—watchtowers along the coast remain from this period of unrest. In 1534, the town was destroyed by Barbarossa, and it wasn't until the 18th and 19th centuries that Sperlonga regained its popularity as a vacation spot. Today, Emperor Tiberus's villa and fish-filled grottoes remain popular sights for all who visit this dreamworld beach getaway.

TIVOLI

From Metro B: Rebibbia, exit the station, turn right, and follow signs for Tivoli through an underpass to reach the other side of V. Tiburtina. Take the blue COTRAL bus to Tivoli. Tickets (€1.60) are sold in the subway station and the bar next door. Once the bus reaches Tivoli (35-45min.), disembark at Ple. delle Nazioni Unite. The return bus to Rome stops across the street from the tourist office, which offers maps, bus schedules, and info on the villas. (☎0774 31 12 49 or 0774 31 35 36. Open Tu-Su 10am-6pm.) An info kiosk in Ple. delle Nazioni Unite distributes free maps. Trains run from Roma Tiburtina to Tivoli (1 hr., €2.30). Exit the train station and make a right, heading down the hill. Cross the roundabout at the bottom of the hill to reach the entrance of Villa Gregoriana.

Tivoli (TEE-vo-lee; pop. 49,342) is an awe-inspiring hilltop town poised 120m above the Aniene River where poets Horace, Catullus, and Propertius all once had homes along the rocky cliffs. Today, Tivoli is a beautifully preserved medieval city, with narrow, winding streets and panoramic views of surrounding valleys. Though the three main villas listed below are Tivoli's chief attractions, the tourist office provides a fantastic ▓map detailing lesser known sites, including a 15th-century castle, an ancient Roman amphitheater, several churches, and Gothic-style houses, all within walking distance of the bus stop.

Villa d'Este, a castle and garden, was laid out by Cardinal Ercole d'Este (the son of Lucrezia Borgia) and his architect Piero Ligorio in 1550 to recreate an ancient Roman pleasure palace. The villa is known for the ingenious and abundant **fountains,** particularly the hydraulic organ. Beneath these famed bubblers lie dank grottoes and three reflecting pools filled with fish. The **Fontana di Diana Efesia,** a statue of a decaying multi-breasted goddess, lies behind the sprinkler-infested gardens. Additionally, the villa itself has a fantastic collection of frescoes and some modern art. One room tells the tale of Hercules, legendary founder of the house of Este. In the summer, concerts are held on the villa's grounds. (Walk through the P. Trento's souvenir stands to reach Villa d'Este. ☎07 74

HOSTEL WATERS

As any budget traveler knows, not all hostels are created equal. There's an especially pronounced difference between hostels on land and hostels...on water? Univelica, L'Università della Vela (University of Sailing), the newest member of Hostelling International, is a training ground for the aspiring young sailors from around the world. The program, called Navigando Peter Pan, accommodates eight adventurous youth who want an Italian experience at sea. A professional instructor from the Italian Sailing Federation transform novices into a legitimate sailing crew.

Based in Porto di Ostia, 30km from Roma Termini, and 9km from the Rome Leonardo Da Vinci airport, Peter Pan travels up and down the coast, hitting Agropoli, Amalfi, Capri, Formia, Giannutri Island, Giglio Island, Ischia Island, Nettuno, Palmarola Island, Ponza Island, Procida Island, Riva of Traiano, and Ventotene Island along the way. You can climb on at any port and stay as long as you want (within reason).

After exploring Italy's churches, museums, and trattorie, Univelica is a veritable nautical escape.

To book, email the hostel the dates you wish to stay and learn. Open year-round. August €80 per night; September and June-July €70; Oct.-May €55. Reservations required. For more info, call ☎ 579 55 84 55, fax 0691 90 00 51, or email info@univelica.it.

31 20 70; www.villadestetivoli.info. Open Tu-Su May-Aug. 8:30am-6:45pm; Sept. 8:30am-6:15pm; Oct. 8:30am-5:30pm; Nov.-Jan. 8:30am-4pm; Feb. 8:30am-4:30pm; Mar. 8:30am-5:15pm; Apr. 8:30am-6:30pm. €9, EU citizens 18-24 €6, EU citizens under 18 or over 65 free. Audio tour €4.)

🖾**Villa Gregoriana,** at the other end of town, is a park with hiking trails that wind over majestic waterfalls and the alleged caves of Neptune and the Sirens. Tivoli's **Temple of Vesta,** a better-preserved version of the one in the Roman Forum, can be admired from lookouts. The trail winds down the cliffs to the base of the waterfalls and up across the Valley of Hell, ending at the Temple of Vesta. A nice respite from crowded Rome, the villa has many benches and grottoes for reading and relaxing. Give yourself at least an hour to explore, and wear comfortable shoes. (From P. Garibaldi, walk down V. Pacifici, which becomes V. del Trevio; turn left on V. Palatina and left again on V. di Ponte Gregoriano. Cross the bridge; the entrance to Villa Gregoriana is on the left. ☎ 39 96 77 61. Open daily Apr.-Oct. 15 10am-6:30pm; Oct. 16-Nov. and Mar. 10am-2:30pm; Dec.-Feb. by reservation only. €4, ISIC holders €3.20, ages 4-12 €2, EU citizens under 18 or over 65 free. Audio tour €4.)

Return to the square and catch bus #4 (€1) by the playground in P. Garibaldi to reach the remains of **Villa Adriana,** the largest and most expensive villa built under the Roman Empire. Ask the bus driver to let you off close to the entrance. Emperor Hadrian, inspired by his travels, designed its AD second-century buildings with an international flair. He often retired here to escape bad moods and pursue artistic endeavors. Look for the *pecile*, built to recall the famous *Stoa Poikile* (Painted Porch) of Athens, and the *canopus*, a statue-lined expanse of water built to replicate a canal in Alexandria, Egypt. (6km from Tivoli proper; take the orange bus #4 from P. Garibaldi's *tabaccheria*, which sells bus tickets. From the parking lot, head uphill away from the villa until you reach a small COTRAL bus sign. ☎ 07 74 38 27 33. Open daily 9am-7:30pm. Last entry 1hr. before close. Parking €2. €6.50, EU citizens 18-24 €3.25, EU citizens under 18 or over 65 free. Archaeological tour €3.50. Audio tour €4.)

OSTIA ANTICA

From Rome, take Metro B to Piramide (€1). At the top of the stairs, turn left and follow signs to Ferrovia Roma-Lido. Your Metro ticket includes the train ride to Ostia Antica (30min., every 15min. daily 5:40am-11:30pm). After disembarking at Ostia Antica, exit the station and cross the road using the blue pedestrian footbridge. Walk down V. della Stazione di Ostia Antica, cross Viale dei Romagoli; entrance is on the left at the end of V. degli Scavi di Ostia Antica. Ticket booth is on the right, after the parking lot.

An immense archaeological park, Ostia Antica is an ideal environment to experience ancient Roman life away from the hoi polloi in the Roman Forum. According to legend, Ostia was founded in the seventh century BC by King Ancus Martius to protect the *ostium* (mouth) of the Tiber River from would-be invaders. As the years progressed, Ostia blossomed into Rome's busiest commercial port. The Tiber's sedimentary deposits have pushed this former seaside spot 4km from the coast. Nevertheless, Ostia continues to awe travelers with its extensive and intimate **ruins**—in unparalleled glimpse into Roman life.

The **necropolis**, located on V. Ostiense outside of the city walls, greets visitors upon entering the ruins. Tombs vary in size and simplicity, depending on the economic standing of the deceased. V. Ostiense ends at the **Porta Romana**, the entrance to the ancient city, which was once guarded by two towers. From here, **Decumanus Maximus**, the city's main road, leads to the **forum**. As you walk down Decumanus Maximus, an amazing AD first-century statue of Minerva graces the left side, followed by the *horrea* (warehouses), where everything from grain to perfume was stored. Further down on the right lie the **Terme di Nettuno** (Baths of Neptune). Walk up the steep stairs to see the magnificent black and white ▓**mosaic** of Neptune riding a quadriga of *hippocampi*, mythical creatures with the heads of horses and bodies of fish. Continuing down the main road, an ancient *enoteca*, as well as the **teatro**, built by Agrippa and enlarged by Commodus and Septimus Severus. Inside, 4000 Romans would enjoy lewd plays filled with obscene puns, performed strictly by men wearing brown masks for male roles and white masks for female roles. Two millennia later, the theater continues to entertain Romans during the summer.

The forum lies at the center of the city, with the imposing **Capitolium** dominating the *piazza*. Merchants, politicians, and travelers used to flood this formidable center of global commerce in its glory days. In addition to baths, a 20-person **foriza** (latrine) remains well preserved. Make a right on V. dei Mollini to reach a small **museum** contains sarcophagi, busts, and Roman copies of Greek statues found among the ruins. Besides being a great place for a game of hide and seek, Ostia Antica offers a personal, engaging look into Rome's history, away from the mobs of tourists and honking horns of the Fori Imperiale. Wear sturdy, comfortable shoes, as the ancient streets are often uneven and rocky. (Museum ☎06 56 35 02 15. Ruins open daily Apr.-Oct. 8:30am-7pm; Nov.-Feb. 8:30am-5pm; Mar. 8:30am-6pm. Parking €2.50, maps €2.50 at ticket booth. Museum open M-F 9am-1:30pm and 4:15-6:30pm, Sa-Su 9am-1:30pm. Last entry 1hr. before closing. Ruins and museum €6.50, EU citizens ages 18-25 €3.25, under 18 and over 65 free. Audio tour €2.50.)

CASTEL GANDOLFO

Take Metro A: Anagnina. From Anagnina, take blue COTRAL buses to Albano (30-40min., every 20min. daily 6am-11pm, €1); tickets sold at counter or from machines. Disembark at P. Mazzini, then take another COTRAL bus, which you can catch on the opposite side of the piazza in front of the Derby Bar, toward Frascati. (Daily every 35min.) Your COTRAL ticket from Rome to Albano should still be valid if used within 75min. If it's no longer valid, replace it at the Derby Bar. Get off at either of the two Castel Gandolfo stops (5min. from Albano). Take a COTRAL bus back to Albano. (M-F every 15-30min., Sa-Su and holidays every 40min.) Alternatively, take the train from Termini to Castel Gandolfo. From the train station, walk up the stairs and cross the street. Head right until you see a sign that says "centro," to the left of which is a pedestrian staircase/walkway that leads up the hill to Piazza della Libertà.

Named after the Gandolfini family who ruled the area from the 11th to the 13th centuries, Castel Gandolfo (pop. 6927) was chosen by the popes as the official papal summer residence in the 17th century. Designed by Carlo Maderno, the palace was constructed beginning in 1624. The seemingly peculiar 6hr. clock recalls the Italian system of timekeeping in place before Napoleon instituted the European system in the early 19th century. The *palazzo* also contains a *specola*, a Vatican astronomical observatory. During the Pope's stay Swiss Guards man the portal and an increased *carabinieri* presence is noticeable. Although the palace is closed to tourists, the Pope holds summer papal audiences Sunday mornings in July and August. Visitors who attend a papal audience typically stand inside the **Piazza della Liberta,** which abuts the residence. Designed by Bernini in the latter half of the 18th century, this *piazza* also showcases **Bernini's Fountain.** The church to the right of the papal residence, **Chiesa di San Tommaso da Villanova,** was also designed by Bernini and contains works by Pietro da Cartona, Gemignani, and Cortese as well as a crypt with statues of the three wise men bearing gifts. (Open daily 8am-1pm and 4:30-8pm. Mass 8:30am, 6:30pm; Sun 10 and 11:30pm. Modest dress required. Donation requested.)

Nature lovers will find plenty to pique their arborial and aquatic interests at pristine **Lake Albano.** Believed to have been formed when the two prehistoric craters of the Lazio Volcanio merged into one, Lake Albano continued its fiery path to glory when it housed the 1960 Olympic canoe races. The crystal clear water still tempts travelers with opportunities for swimming, kayaking, canoeing, and sun bathing. (About a 20min. walk from Piazza della Liberta. Take the zig-zagging V. del Stazione down the hill to V. Antonio Gramsci. Take a right, cross the train tracks, and take another right on V. del Emissario. Take a right on V. dei Pescatori and a *balneare* (bath) is on the left, across the street from V. dei Pescatori 10. ☎3476 66 63 34. Open May-Sept. 9am-7pm. Lounge chair €5, chair €3. Canoe €5 per hr., paddleboat €8 per hr.)

On the last Sunday of July, take a bite of a juicy peach with the Pope at the **Peach Festival.** After mass, children offer gifts to the Pope, and a peach-dominated, folksy revelry overtakes the town. Castel Gandolfo also comes together to celebrate its patron saint at the **Feast of Saint Sebastian** in September. Enjoy music, merriment, and beautiful fireworks over Lake Albano. **September for Youths** is dedicated to young men and women, with concerts, parades, and exhibitions. Don't miss the **antique market** on the last Sunday of each month.

Along with the many shops selling artisanal crafts and local foods, restaurants, trattorie, cafes, and *gelaterie* line the town's main street, C. della Repubblica. **Bucci ❸,** V. dei Zecchini 31, while pricey, is worth it for the view from the flower-bedecked terrace overlooking the lake below. (☎06 93 23 334. Open M-Tu and Th-Su 12:30-2:30pm and 7:30-10pm. AmEx/MC/V.) A cheaper sit-down option is **Hosteria La Fraschetta ❶,** C. della Repubblica 58. (☎06 93 61 312. Primi €5.50-9.50. Secondi €6.50-9. Open Tu-Su 12:30-3pm and 7pm-midnight. MC/V.)

To get from the bus stop to the town **info kiosk,** which offers free maps and brochures, walk up the winding V. Palazzo Pontificio to the right. At the top of the summit sits P. Liberta. The info kiosk is located through P. Liberta on V. Massimo D'Azeglio. (☎06 93 59 18 235. Open Tu-Su 10am-6pm.)

PONTINE ISLANDS

The Pontine Islands are accessible by aliscafi (hydrofoils) or slower, cheaper traghetti (ferries). The closest port to Rome with service to the islands is Anzio. Take the Termini-Nettuno train to Anzio (1hr., every hr. 6am-11pm, €3.20). From the station head downhill on V. Paolini, then go through P. Battisti onto V. dei Fabbri, and through the next piazza to C. del Popolo. Or take a taxi from the station to the quay (€10). From the port, take the CAREMAR ferry to Ponza (2hr.; June 16-Sept. 15 M-F 9:25am, Sa 8:30am, Su and holidays 8:30am and 3pm; return M-F 5pm, Sa 5:15pm, Su and holidays 11am and 5:15pm; €23.40; cash only). The CAREMAR ticket office is in the white booth labeled "traghetto" on the quay (☎06 98 60 00 83; www.

caremar.it) and in Ponza (☎07 71 80 565). The Linee Vetor hydrofoils are smaller and faster. (70min.; 3-5 per day 8:15am-7pm; M-Th and Su €27, F-Sa and Aug. €32. Suitcases €2.50-25 depending on weight. Bikes €7.50. Windsurfing equipment €25. Cash only, unless reserved ahead online.) Linee Vetor ticket office also on the quay in Anzio. Open 1hr. before departure. (☎06 98 45 083; www.vetor.it.) 2nd office on dock in Ponza (☎07 71 80 549).

The Pontine Islands (pop. 4000), a stunning archipelago 40km off the coast of Anzio, offer both striking beauty and intriguing history and lore. These small islands were once believed to be home of the sorceress Circe, who captured and seduced the Greek hero Odysseus and transformed his crew into pigs. Nero was exiled here and Mussolini cast enemies of the state into the 30 million-year-old volcanic residuum, only to be imprisoned here himself. The cliff-sheltered beaches, turquoise waters, coves, tunnels, and grottoes have also provided pirates a place to unwind after pillaging and plundering. You'll be hard-pressed to find an English speaker in this isolated area. Ferries run from Anzio to **Ponza,** an island with superb beaches and picturesque cliffside residences. A 10min. walk from the port leads to **Chiaia,** a beach set at the foot of a spectacular 200m cliff. A beautiful, though slightly pulse-quickening ▓**bus ride** (€1; buy onboard) around hairpin turns and blind drives leads to the even lovelier ▓**Piscine Naturali.** Take the bus to Le Foma, and ask to be let off at the *piscine*, or just follow the throngs of people who get off there. Facing the water, the bus stop is to your left, along V. Carlo Pisacane, just past the San Antonio Tunnel, about 3-5min. from the quay. Look for the hordes of people around the blue buses. Once you exit the bus at the Piscine stop go down the long, steep path marked by a sign. It takes approximately 5min. to get to the bottom of the hill. Cliffs crumbling into the ocean create a series of deep, crystal-clear natural pools separated by smooth rock outcroppings perfect for sunbathing. Snorkeling, exploring the rocks, and jumping off the cliffs will make you feel like a modern-day Jacques Cousteau. The western-most island is **Palmarola,** with irregular volcanic rock formations and steep, white cliffs. To get to Palmarola, rent a boat (from €45 per day), or take a boat tour advertised at the port. The tiny island of **Zannone** is home to a wildlife preserve. Try **Cooperativa Barcaioli Ponzesi,** V. Carlo Piscacane, at the S. Antonio tunnel, for boat tours. (☎07 71 80 99 29. Open 9am-12:30pm and 5-11pm. Tours 9am; return 7pm. Must reserve day before. €20.) Tours of Zannone, which is part of the **Circeo National Park,** take visitors around the coast, with time for walks through the forests on the islands filled with wild sheep, and to the medieval, legend-filled **San Spirito monastery.**

R O M E

PIEDMONT (PIEMONTE) AND VALLE D'AOSTA

PIEDMONT (PIEMONTE)

More than just the source of the Po River, Piedmont (pee-yeh-MON-tay) is a fountainhead of nobility and fine cuisine. The area rose to prominence in 1861 when the Savoys selected Turin as capital of their reunified Italy in 1861. The capital relocated only four years later, and Piedmont fell back into obscurity. Today, European tourists escape whirlwind urban pace on the banks of Lake Maggiore, while outdoor enthusiasts and expert skiers conquer Alpine mountains to the northeast. Sometimes called the "Prussia of Italy," Piedmont is renowned for its high standard of living and modern, well-organized infrastructure. Since Turin hosted the Winter Olympics in 2006, the region's profile has only continued to rise.

HIGHLIGHTS OF PIEDMONT AND VALLE D'AOSTA

EAT at Turin's enormous Eataly, a combination between a restaurant, a cooking school, a museum, and a fresh food market (p. 168).

SIP *Barbera, Barbaresco,* and *Asti Spumante* in Piedmont's wine country (p. 179).

JUMP into the icy blue waters of the streams of the Gesso Valley (p. 176).

CONQUER the glacial slopes beneath the great Matterhorn (p. 193).

PIEDMONT AND VALLE D'AOSTA

TURIN (TORINO) ☎011

A century and a half before Turin (toh-REE-no; pop. 910,000) hosted the 2006 Winter Olympics, it served as the first capital of unified Italy. The city is characterized by contemporary art masterpieces, and some of Italy's best nightlife. Though Turin's cultural offerings rival Milan's, it manages to avoid pollution and crime problems that plague larger cities. One of the greenest Italian metropolises, Turin is a pedestrian dream: numerous parks and charming Po River treat visitors to everything from boating tours to outdoor nightlife.

▣ TRANSPORTATION

Flights: Caselle Airport (www.aeroportoditorino.it) services European destinations. From Pta. Nuova, take blue Sadem buses to "Caselle Airport," via Pta. Susa (☎011 30 00 611; 40min., €5.50). Buses run regularly to the airport (5:15am-11:15pm) and to the city (6:05am-12:05am). Buy tickets at Bar Cervino, C. V. Emanuele II 57; Bar Mille Luci, P. XVIII Dicembre 5, at newsstand on corner of Corso V. Emanuele II and P. Felice, on left when exiting station, or onboard (€0.50 surcharge). Airport train goes from Torino Dora to airport (20min., every 30min., €3.40). To get to Torino Dora station, take tram #10 from Torino Porta Susa, or buses #46 or 49.

Trains: Stazione Porta Nuova (☎011 66 53 098), on C. V. Emanuele II. The station has a **post office**, luggage storage. To: **Genoa** (2hr., every hr. 5:20am-11:50pm, €8.80); **Milan**

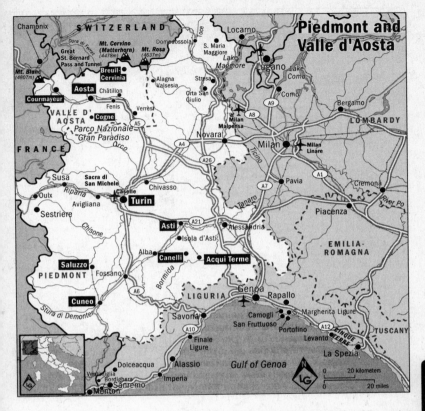

Centrale (2hr., every hr. 4:50am-10:50pm, €9); **Rome Termini** (6-7hr., 25 per day 4:50am-11:50pm, from €64); **Venice Santa Lucia** (5hr., 20 per day 4:50am-10:50pm, from €22). Turin's **Stazione Porta Susa** is one stop toward Milan and runs TGV trains to **Paris** via **Lyon, France** (5-6hr.; 8:11, 9:40am, 5:35, 7:05, 9:18pm; around €95).

Buses: Autostazione Terminal Bus, C. V. Emanuele II 131/H in front of the Court (☎011 43 38 100). From Pta. Nuova, take tram #9 or 15 (5 stops). Ticket office open daily 6:30am-1:15pm and 2-8:30pm. Serves ski resorts, the Riviera, and the valleys of Susa and Pinerolo. To **Aosta** (2hr., M-F 3 per day, €7.50), **Courmayeur** via Aosta (4hr., €8.40), and **Milan** (2hr., every hr., €8.70).

Public Transportation: Buy tickets at *tabaccherie*, newsstands, or bars. Buses run daily 5am-1am, some routes stop at midnight. 70min. ticket to **city buses** and **trams** €1; 1-day ticket €3. Metro tickets single-use only, but valid for 70min. for other modes of transport. Get public transport map with buses and trams from tourist office.

Taxis: ☎011 57 37, 57 30, or 33 99.

Car Rental: in Stazione Porta Nuova, on the right side by the platforms. **Avis**, C. Turati 37 (☎011 50 11 07). Open M-F 8:30am-noon and 2:30-6:30pm, Sa 8:30am-noon. **Europcar**, V. Nizza 346 (☎011 69 60 284). Open daily 7am-11pm. C. Grosetto 152 (☎011 22 29 802). Open daily 8:30am-1pm and 2:30-6:30pm.

Turin

ACCOMMODATIONS

Albergo Azalea,	1 C3
Campeggio Villa Rey,	2 F2
La Foresteria degli Artisti,	3 E2
Nicosia Schaya,	4 E2
Open 011,	5 A2
Ostello Torino (HI),	6 F5

FOOD

Caffè Cioccolateria al Bicerin,	
Caffè Gelateria Fiorio,	
Eataly,	
Hafa Café,	

Il Punto Verde,	11 E3
Le Vitel Etonné,	12 D3
Spaccanapoli,	14 D4
Stars & Roses,	15 C4
Angoletti & Friends,	28 C2

7 B2
8 D3
9 D6
10 B2

PIEDMONT AND VALLE D'AOSTA

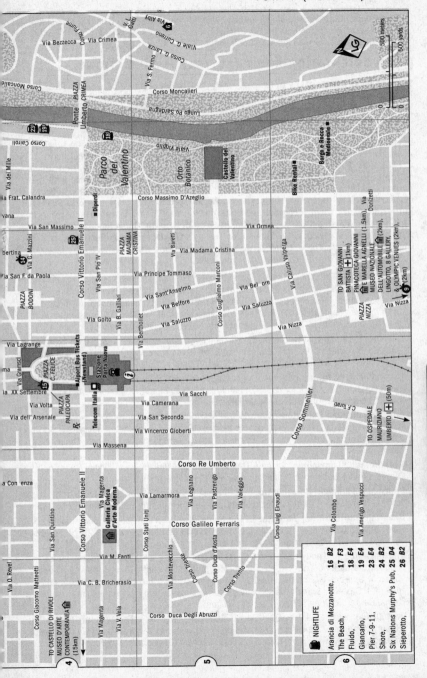

NIGHTLIFE	
Arancia di Mezzanotte,	16 B2
The Beach,	17 F3
Fluido,	18 E4
Giancarlo,	19 E4
Pier 7-9-11,	23 E4
Shore,	24 B2
Six Nations Murphy's Pub,	25 D4
Sieperotto,	26 B2

Bike Rental: Club Amici della Bicicletta, V. S. Domenico 28 (☎011 56 13 059; cluba-micidellabici@email.it) and **Bici & Dintorni,** Vle. Bistolfi 20/a (☎011 339 582 9332 and 44 23 014; www.biciedintorni.org). Both €4 per 6hr., €8 per day.

🗺️ 🛈 ORIENTATION AND PRACTICAL INFORMATION

Stazione Porta Nuova, in the heart of the city, is the usual place of arrival. The city itself is an Italian rarity: its pre-designed streets meet at right angles, making it easy to navigate by bus and foot. **Corso Vittorio Emanuele II** runs east past the station to the **Po River,** where it intersects **Parco del Valentino** on the south and the **Murazzi** district on the north. **Via Roma,** the major north-south thoroughfare, houses many banks and the principal sights and shops. North of the station, it heads through **Piazza Carlo Felice, Piazza San Carlo,** and **Piazza Castello.** From P. Castello, **Via Pietro Micca** extends southwest to **Piazza Solferino** where the tourist office is located, while **Via Po** veers southeast to **Piazza Vittorio Veneto** and the University district, intersecting the river above the Murazzi. **Via Giuseppe Garibaldi** stretches west from P. Castello to **Piazza Statuto** and **Stazione Porta Susa,** a launching point for international trains and the metro to the suburbs. Above P. Castello, the **Palazzo Reale** and **Giardini Reali** lie below the **Corso Regina Margherita,** which connects **Piazza della Repubblica** west to the **Docks Dora** district north of the Giardini Reali. **Via Nizza** heads south from Stazione Pta. Nuova to the **Lingotto** area which housed the former Olympic district.

Tourist Office: Turismo Torino, P. Castello 161 (☎011 53 51 81; www.turismotorino. org), at the intersection of P. Castello and V. Garibaldi. English, French, German, and Spanish spoken. Excellent map of Turin. Info on museums, cafes, hotel booking, and tour reservations. Open daily 9:30am-7pm. **Info booth** at Pta. Nuova, opposite platform 17. Open daily 10am-7pm. Volunteer-run info points near main attractions.

Currency Exchange: In Pta. Nuova. Open M and W-Sa 8am-8pm, Tu and Su 10am-5:30pm. MC/V. Otherwise try the **banks,** most with **24hr. ATMs** along V. Roma and V. Alfieri. Generally open M-F 8:20am-1:20pm and 2:20-4:20pm.

Beyond Tourism: Informagiovani, V. delle Orfane 20 (☎011 800 998 500 or 44 24 977; www.comune.torino.it/infogio). Provides info on jobs, volunteering, and enterprises for young people. Internet access. Open Tu-Sa 9:30am-6:30pm.

English-Language Bookstore: Libreria Internazionale Luxembourg, V. Accademia delle Scienze 3 (☎011 56 13 896), across from P. Carignano. Staff helps navigate 3 floors of English, French, German, and Spanish books, papers, and magazines. Open M-Sa 8am-7:30pm, Su 10am-1pm and 3-7pm.

Laundromat: "Lavasciuga" Laundrettes and Internet Points (www.lavasciuga.torino.it) are located throughout the city. Check website for complete list.

Pharmacy: Farmacia Boniscontro, C. V. Emanuele 66 (☎011 54 12 71). 3 blocks east of Pta. Nuova. Open 9am-12:30pm and 3pm-9am. Posts after-hours rotations. MC/V.

Hospital: San Giovanni Battista, C. Bramante 88-90 (☎011 63 31 633; molinette. piemonte.it), commonly known as Molinette. **Maria Adelaide,** V. Zuretti 29 (☎011 69 33 111; www.cto.to.it). **Mauriziano Umberto I,** Largo Turati 62 (☎011 50 81 111).

Internet Access: 1pc4you, V. Verdi 20/G (☎011 81 22 179; www.1pc4you.com), in front of the Mole. €4 per hr.; €2 per hr. with purchased card (€5, includes €3 of use). Open M-Sa 9am-10pm, Su noon-10pm. **Telecom Italia Internet Corners,** V. Roma 18, just off P. Castello. **Branch** inside the Pta. Nuova station. Both have phone card web stations. €3 per hr. Open M and W-Su 8am-10pm.

Post Office: V. Alfieri 10 (☎011 50 60 260), off P. S. Carlo. Facing north (toward P. Reale), head left 2 blocks down on the right. Fax and telegram service. Grab ticket slip by door. Open M-F 8:30am-7pm, Sa 8:30am-1pm. **Postal Code:** 10100.

ACCOMMODATIONS AND CAMPING

Turin's budget accommodations are not clustered together, but several are located near Stazione Pta. Nuova. Many new hotels and residences were built to accommodate Olympic crowds. Family-run B&Bs are in some of the city's best areas, though they're required by law to close for two months each year. Many take this time in July and August, but call ahead to verify exact dates.

> **TIP**
> **WEEKEND OF TOURIN'.** The embodiment of Turin's warm welcome to visitors, the **Turin Week-End offer** includes a 2-night stay (F-Sa or Sa-Su nights) with a hotel breakfast as well as a **Torino Card** with wide access and discounts. Prices start at €59 per person; 4- to 5-star hotels cost about €89-150. Considering the hotels involved and the long list of benefits, this is a steal. All hotels bestow guests with special offers and welcome gifts. Check *www.turismotorino.org* for a list of hotels and offers. Reserve directly through the hotel; be sure to specify that you want the Turin Week-End offer.

Open 011, C. Venezia 11 (☎011 25 05 35; www.openzero11.it). To reach this brand-new hostel, take bus #52 (#64 on Su) from Pta. Nuova to V. Chiesa della Salute. 5min. walk from Stazione Dora. 34 gleaming rooms (2-4 beds with bathroom). Services include restaurant, bar, TV, terrace, Wi-Fi, and library. Check-in until 10pm. Reception 24hr. Dorms €16.50; singles €30; doubles €42. Reserve ahead. Cash only. ❶

Ostello Torino (HI), V. Alby 1 (☎011 66 02 939; www.ostellotorino.it). Bus #52 (#64 on Su) from Pta. Nuova to the Lanza stop at V. Crimea and follow the "Ostello" signs to C. Giovanni Lanza. Turn left at V. Luigi Gatti. Breakfast included; dinner €10. Laundry €4. Reception M-Sa 7am-12:30pm and 3-11pm, Su 7-10am. Lockout 10am-3pm. Curfew 11pm; ask for key if staying out later. Closed Dec. 21-Jan. 14. Single-sex and co-ed 3- to 8-bed dorms €15; doubles €35, with bath €40; triples €51; quads €68. MC/V. ❶

La Foresteria degli Artisti, V. degli Artisti 15 (☎011 83 77 85; www.foresteriadegliartisti.it). Ring bell for Coss F&G, then walk to 2nd door on left and ring again. La Foresteria is a furnished apartment with wood floors, antique furniture, DVD player, library, laundry, and kitchen. Breakfast included. Reservations required. Closed Aug. Singles €50; doubles €80. Extra bed €20. Cash only. ❹

Albergo Azalea, V. Mercanti 16, 3rd fl. (☎011 53 81 15 or 333 24 67 449; albergo.azalea@virgilio.it). Exit Pta. Nuova. Take bus #58, 72 to V. Garibaldi. Turn left on V. Garibaldi, away from P. Castello, and left on V. Mercanti. If you take bus #52, turn right from the stop. 10 spic-and-span rooms with floral wallpaper and white furniture in central location. No reception; call ahead. Singles €40, with bath €50; doubles €55/65. MC/V. ❸

Nicosia Schaya, Largo Montebello 33, top fl. (☎011 19 71 28 73 or 347 00 21 184; www.bedandbnicosia.it). Take bus #3, 68, 13, 16 or 18; get off near Largo Montebello. Sliding-glass door leads to the privacy of comfortable rooms with framed family pictures, phone, fridge, balcony, and bath. Breakfast included. No reception; call ahead. Singles €50; doubles €70. Cash only. ❹

Campeggio Villa Rey, Strada Superiore Val San Martino 27 (☎/fax 011 81 90 117). From Pta. Nuova take the #72 or 63 bus to Pta. Palazzo, change to tram #3 on C. Regina, and ride to the end of the line (stop: Hermada). From there, walk 500m uphill or take bus #54. Quiet hillside location with views of the Basilica Superga has caravans and tent campers. Bar, small market, and restaurant. 2-course meal €15. Laundry €3. Office open daily 8am-10pm. €6 per person, €4 per child; €4-7 per tent; €10-11 per car; €11 per site. Electricity €1. Shower €0.80. MC/V. ❶

FOOD

Ever since the Savoys started drinking an evening cup of *cioccolato* in 1678, Turin has grown into one of the great international centers of chocolate production. Ferrero Rocher and Nutella are its most famous products. Napoleonic restrictions on buying chocolate brought the hazelnut substitute *gianduiotto*, now the key ingredient in a distinctly *torinese* ice-cream flavor known as *gianduia*, available at cafes around P. Castello. On the savory side, *Piemontese* cuisine is a blend of northern Italian peasant staples and elegant French garnishes. Butter replaces olive oil, while cheese and mushrooms, occasionally served with white truffles, are used more than vegetables or spices. *Agnolotti*, ravioli stuffed with lamb and cabbage, is the local pasta specialty, but polenta, warm cornmeal often topped with fontina cheese, is the more common starch. The three most outstanding red wines in Italy—*Barolo, Barbaresco, and Barbera*, in descending price order—are available in markets and restaurants. To sample the true flavors of *Piemontese* cuisine, be ready to pay—restaurants that specialize in regional dishes are expensive. Self-caterers can head to **DiperDì** supermarket, all over the *centro*. (V. S. Massimo 43. Open M-Tu and Th-Sa 8:30am-1:30pm and 3:30-7:30pm, W 8:30am-1pm. MC/V.) Find food at **Porta Palazzo** in P. della Repubblica, in what claims to be Europe's largest **open-air market** (M-F 7:30am-2pm, Sa until sunset). Many restaurants participate in **Torino Gourmet,** offering fixed-price *menù* for cheap (€22-30).

> **TIP**
> **CHOCOHOLICS UNITE.** Sample Turin's best with a **ChocoPass** (www.turismotorino.org), offering tastings of chocolate products, including *gianduiotti,* pralines, and ice cream. Buy a coupon book for €15 (3 days; 23 tastings) at any tourist office. This is the pass for the truly dedicated chocoholic.

Eataly, V. Nizza 224 (☎011 19 50 68 11; www.eataly.it). Take bus #1, 18 or 35 to the "Biglieri" stop, near Lingotto Expo Center. Turin's new culinary amusement park is a 10,000 sq. ft. facility that could realistically take at least a half day of sightseeing on its own. Tastings of wine and beer are just the beginning: classrooms feature scheduled cooking classes by famous guest chefs (in English by group reservation), meat and cheese lockers, and museum-quality exhibits demonstrate various foods and preparation techniques. Browse the restaurants, each with its own daily specialty. Open daily 10am-10:30pm; meat and fish restaurants daily 10am-3:30pm and 5:30-10pm. ❷

Agnoletti and Friends, P. Corpus Domini 18/b (☎011 43 38 792; www.agnolettiandfriends.it). Blends time-honored traditions with cutting edge decor. Perfect location in a quiet square lets patrons relax and focus on the food, from the *agnolotti* (€10-12) to the adventurous meat offerings. Open M-F 6-8pm, Sa-Su noon-3pm and 6-8pm. ❷

Hafa Café, V. Sant'Agostino 23/C (☎011 43 67 091; www.hafa.it). Sit among Moroccan decor and sip creamy *Hafa Café* (tea with spices, milk, and *amaretto;* €5) or Moroccan mint tea (€3). Mixed drinks €7. Open Tu-Sa 1pm-2:30am, Su 5pm-1am. MC/V. ❷

Stars & Roses, P. Paleocapa 2 (☎011 51 62 052), near P. Carlo Felicehead. Head upstairs and pick a room to match your mood: the color scheme, lighting, and furniture change through each doorway. Celebrity photos decorate the walls. Takeout available. Calzones €7-10. Pizza €6.50-15.50. Primi €5-7. Secondi €8-15. Cover €2. Open M and Su 7:30pm-12:30am, Tu-Sa noon-3pm and 7:30pm-12:30am. AmEx/MC/V. ❷

Il Punto Verde, V. S. Massimo 17 (☎011 88 55 43), off V. Po, near P. Carlo Emanuele II. California juice bar meets traditional Italian trattoria. Vegan options. Student lunch *menù* €5, 3-course *menù* €9; dinner *menù monopiatti* (3 courses plus wine, dessert, and coffee) €12, lunch €6. Primi €6.50-11. Secondi €5-11. Dinner cover €1.80. Open M-F 12:30-2:30pm and 7:30-10:30pm, Sa 7-10:30pm. Closed Aug. MC/V. ❷

Caffè Gelateria Fiorio, V. Po 8 (☎011 81 73 225 or 81 70 612; www.fioriocaffegelateria.com), just off P. Castello. Famous for lunch buffet (€14-15). Hangout for the student movement. Fiorio is frequented by artists and noblemen alike. Cones from €1.50. Sundaes €4.50-9. Open M-Th and Su 7am-1am, F-Sa 7am-2am. AmEx/MC/V. ❸

Le Vitel Etonné, V. S. Francesco da Paola 4 (☎011 81 24 621; www.leviteletonne.com). A popular spot for Turin's casual professionals, Le Vitel Etonné has a wine cellar in the basement (€3-5 per glass) and an artisan cafe upstairs, with a menu that changes depending on what's fresh. Primi €9-11. Secondi €13-15. Open Tu-Sa 10:30am-1am, Su 10:30am-3:30pm. Closed 1 week in Aug. MC/V. ❹

Spaccanapoli, V. Mazzini 19 (☎011 81 26 694). Pizza by the meter (€20-36); try gorgonzola or the special *"spaccanapoli"* pizza, large enough to feed an army. Worth the trip for groups of 4 or more people. Delicious desserts. Primi €6-10. Secondi €10-15. Cover €2. Open daily noon-2:30pm and 7pm-midnight. AmEx/MC/V. ❸

Caffè Cioccolateria al Bicerin, P. della Consolata 5 (☎011 43 69 325; www.bicerin.it). The cafe has sold its namesake drink (€4), a hot mixture of coffee, chocolate, and cream since 1763 to such notables as Nietzche, Dumas, and Puccini. Open M-Tu and Th-F 8:30am-7:30pm, Sa-Su 8:30am-1pm and 3:30-7:30pm. ❶

🎯 SIGHTS

█MOLE ANTONELLIANA. Once the largest structure in the world built using traditional masonry (a title sadly lost in the 1900s with the addition of some concrete), and still the world's tallest museum, the Mole dominates Turin's skyline. The towering spire is gloriously reproduced today on the euro two-cent coin. Begun as a synagogue in 1863, it ended as an architectural eccentricity. The glass elevator that leads through the middle of the building goes to the observation deck. Today, the Mole houses the **Museo Nazionale del Cinema.** The ground floor has a mod bar with color-changing tables and movie screens. Interactive exhibits chronicle the history of cinema. At the center of the museum on the second floor, **Temple Hall** holds a field of red velvet chairs for visitors to watch Italian films projected on screens high above. A variety of movies screen in wild settings, like a 60s living room, a Neolithic cave, and a giant fridge with toilets for seats. A suspended staircase nearby winds to hundreds of movie posters. Every hour, images on the dome disappear and music plays, while the Mole's walls are drawn up to reveal the building's skeleton beneath. (*V. Montebello 20, east of P. Castello. ☎011 81 25 658; www.museonazionaledelcinema.org. Open Tu-F and Su 9am-8pm, Sa 9am-11pm. Last entry 1hr. before closing. Museum €5.20, students €4.20. Elevator €3.62/2.58; combined ticket €6.80/5.20.*)

CATTEDRALE DI SAN GIOVANNI (DUOMO) AND CHIESA DI SAN LORENZO. The **█Holy Shroud of Turin,** one of the most enigmatic relics in Christendom, has been housed in the Cappella della Santa Sindone of the **Cattedrale di San Giovanni Battista** since 1694. Said to be Jesus's burial cloth, the 3 ft. by 14 ft. cloth first entered official accounts when the Crusaders brought it back from Jerusalem in the 13th century. Transferred to Turin from Chambéry, France, by the Savoys in 1578, today the shroud rests in a climate-controlled case. With rare exceptions, a photograph of the unfolded shroud to the left of the cathedral's entrance is as close as visitors will get to the real thing. A negative below the photograph of the shroud reveals more detail, including the countenance of a man with a fractured nose and bruised cheek. It was initially carbon-dated to 1350, but recent studies have suggested that a newer, repaired piece of the shroud from the Middle Ages may in fact be 2500 years old. *(Behind Palazzo Reale where V. XX Settembre crosses P. S. Giovanni.* ☎ *011 43 61 540. Open daily 7am-noon and 3-7pm. Modest dress required. Free.)* Nearby, to the left of the Palazzo Reale, the 16th-century **Chiesa di San Lorenzo** served as temporary home to the shroud before completion of San Giovanni in the 15th century. Its soaring dome was designed by Guarino Guarini, and its ribs form an overlapping, eight-pointed star reminiscent of the Islamic architecture that influenced Guarini on his travels. In the sacristy to the right hangs an exact-size replica of the shroud. *(V. Palazzo di Città 4, at the corner with P. Castello.* ☎ *011 43 61 527; www.sanlorenzo.torino.it. Open daily 8am-noon and 3-6pm. Free.)*

TOURIN' CARD. The best deal in the city the **Torino Card** (48hr. €18, 72hr. €21), provides free entrance to all museums and monuments in Turin and throughout Piedmont; access to the **TurismoBus Torino,** the panoramic lift in the Mole, the Sassi-Superga cable car, and the boats for river navigation on the Po; and discounts on guided tours, transportation, and shows. The card is available at any Turismo Torino info point and at most hotels.

■CASTELLO DI RIVOLI MUSEO D'ARTE CONTEMPORANEA. This museum houses one of Europe's most impressive contemporary art collections in a 14th-century Savoy residence. The sleek venue holds works from the 50s onward, and many exhibits, including Sol Lewitt's 1992 *Panels and Towers*, were designed specifically for the *castello's* cavernous spaces. Other featured artists include Bruce Nauman, Claes Oldenburg, and Michelangelo Pistoletto. *(P. Mafalda di Savoia in Rivoli, 22km outside Turin. Take bus #36 or 66 from Turin, or subway from Pta. Susa to Fermi Station and then bus #36 to Rivoli. Inquire at the bus station about the direct shuttle bus.* ☎ *011 95 65 222; www.castellodirivoli.org. Open Tu-Th 10am-5pm, F-Su 10am-9pm. €6.50, students €3.50. Under 11 free.)*

PALAZZO DELL'ACCADEMIA DELLE SCIENZE. The *palazzo* houses two of Turin's best museums—the **Museo Egizio** and the **Galleria Sabauda.** From 1903-37, the Italian Archaeological Mission brought thousands of artifacts home to Turin, making Museo Egizio the second largest Egyptian collection outside Cairo. Museum highlights include both wrapped and unwrapped mummies, life-size wooden Nubian statues, the massive Ellesiya temple, and the well-furnished tomb of Kha, a 14th-century BC architect; Kha's tomb was one of the few Egyptian tombs spared by grave robbers. The ground floor also holds a cast of the Rosetta Stone. *(V. Accademia delle Scienze 6. 2 blocks from P. Castello.* ☎ *011 56 17 776; www.museoegizio.it. Open Tu-Su 8:30am-7:30pm. €6.50, ages 18-25 €3, under 18 or over 65 free.)* On the third floor, the **Galleria Sabauda** houses art collections from Palazzo Reale and Palazzo Carignano, and is renowned for its 14th- to 18th-century Flemish and Dutch paintings, including Van Eyck's *St. Francis Receiving the Stigmata* (1427), Memling's *Passion* (1470), and Rembrandt's *Old Man Sleeping* (1629), among others. *(V. Accademia delle Scienze 6.* ☎ *011 54 74 40; www.museitorino.it/galleriasabauda. Open Nov.-May Tu and F-Su 8:30am-2pm, W 2-7:30pm, Th 10am-7:30pm; June-Oct. Tu and F-Su 8:30am-2pm, W 2-7:30pm, Th 2-7:30pm. €4, 18-25 €2, under 18 or over 65 free. Combined ticket for both museums €8.)*

PINACOTECA GIOVANNI E MARELLA AGNELLI. This tiny museum atop a former Fiat factory holds 26 pieces from the last 300 years. The collection features Venetian landscape works by Il Canaletto, Impressionist works by Matisse and Renoir, and pieces by Tiepolo, Picasso, and Modigliani. *(V. Nizza 230.* ☎ *011 00 62 713. Open Tu-Su 9am-7pm. €4, students €2.50. Special exhibits €6.)*

PIEDMONT AND VALLE D'AOSTA

GALLERIA CIVICA D'ARTE MODERNA E CONTEMPO-RANEA (GAM). The city's premiere modern and contemporary art museum devotes four floors to 19th- and 20th-century works made mostly by Italians, including some Modiglianis and de Chiricos. Though its collection is not the most representative of the diverse styles of these periods, it does contain Andy Warhol's gruesome *Orange Car Crash* and a few works by Picasso, Chagall, Klee, and Renoir. *(V. Magenta 31. On the corner of C. Galileo Ferraris, off Largo V. Emanuele. Take tram #1, 9, or 15.* ☎ *011 44 29 610; www.gamtorino.it. Open Tu-Su 9am-7pm. €7.50, under 26 or over 65 €6, Tu free.)*

BASILICA DI SUPERGA. When the French siege on Turin culminated in the attack on September 6, 1706, King Vittorio Amedeo II made a promise to the Virgin Mary to build a basilica in her honor should the city withstand the invasion. Turin stood unconquered, and famous architect Juvarra helped fulfill the vow, erecting a Neoclassical portico and high drum to support the basilica's spectacular dome. The church houses the tombs of the Savoys. In 1949, a plane carrying the entire Turin soccer team crashed into the basilica; a memorial stands at the accident site today, listing the names of the victims. The basilica is built on a 640m summit outside Turin, once described by Le Corbusier as "the most enchanting position in the world." It offers panoramic views of the city, the Po Valley below, and the Alps beyond. *(Tram #15 from V. XX Settembre to Stazione Sassi, then bus #79 or a small cable railway for an 18min. ride uphill. Cable Car* ☎ *011 57 64 733; www.gtt.to.it. Every hr. M and W-F 9am-noon and 2-8pm, Sa-Su 9am-8pm. Round-trip €3, Su and holidays €4. Basilica* ☎ *011 89 97 456; www.basilicadisuperga.com. Open daily Apr.-Oct. M-F 9am-noon and 3-6pm, Sa-Su 9am-noon and 3-6:45pm; Nov.-Mar. M-F 9am-noon and 3-5pm, Sa-Su 9am-noon and 3-5:45pm. Dome of basilica and Savoy tombs each €3, students €2.)*

PALAZZO REALE. The Palazzo Reale forms part of the *"Corona di Delitie,"* a ring of Savoy royal residences that came under the UNESCO's protection as a World Heritage site in 1997. Home to the Princes of Savoy from 1645 to 1865, the ornate *palazzo* contains over 300 rooms. Thirty of the rooms, mostly unfurnished, are covered on the long Italian-language tour. Those with short attention spans beware, as there is no leaving or separating from the group once this one-hour tour has begun. André le Nôtre, famous for his work on the gardens of Versailles, designed the grounds in 1697, but the gardens have since been deeply reduced. *(In Piazzetta Reale, at the end of P. Castello.* ☎ *011 43 61 455; www.ambienteto.arti.beniculturali.it. Palazzo Reale open Tu-Su*

LOCAL LEGEND

THE AXIS OF... MAGIC?

Those who refer to Turin as a "magical" destination aren't always talking about its enchanting green riverbank or renowned museums. According to legend, the city is actually a hub of supernatural activity: a rare locus of both white and black magic.

Staunch believers insist that Turin forms one point of a white magic triangle with Lyon and Prague. The black magic triangle is more obtuse, extending to London and San Francisco. These conflicting forces create an exponentially higher mystical charge than cities containing white or black magic alone.

To explore the darker side, begin at **Piazza Statuto,** a former Roman burial ground and site of public hangings and medieval massacres. Today's dark power is limited to a monument honoring the death of railway workers and a statue held to be Lucifer himself. Below, a manhole cover is said to lead to the gates of hell.

Cheer up with a trek to Turin's center of white magic, **Piazza Castello,** which lies directly between two of the most powerful forces of good in the city: the Holy Shroud and the **Chiesa della Gran Madre di Dio,** allegedly built above the Holy Grail. Turin, a city divided against itself.

*For more on Turin's magical side(s), take the **Magic Turin Tour**, a 2½hr. odyssey. (€20. Begins at Piazza Statuto Th and Sa 9pm.)*

EAT. SHOP. LEARN.

In January 2007, a new restaurant opened in Turin. Actually, 10 of them did, all under one roof. More than just a food court, **Eataly** (p. 168) is a culinary theme park.

Each of Eataly's restaurants specializes in a different food group and prepares your meal in front of you. Including the €1 cover, dishes generally cost €8-15 at each station, a bargain for their high quality. Splitting meals is highly recommended in order to taste from more stations. The daily menus of meat, seafood, vegetables, deli meat, cheese, pizza, and pasta are only the beginning. A coffee shop and gelato stand are also on the ground floor, while the basement has meat and cheese selections. The basement also has two more restaurants, one dedicated to wine and the other to beer. The bottled wine selection is overwhelming but, if you are the mood for something simple, you can fill up your own liter of wine from the tap for €1.30-4 per L.

You can take the cooking into your own hands at the expansive organic food store or at the learning center, which offer varied and valuable cooking lessons from world-famous guest chefs (€20-100). While the calendar of classes is in Italian, many of the cooking lessons are also available in English for groups. (V. Nizza 224. Take bus #1, 18, or 35 to the Biglieri stop. Reservations ☎011 19 50 68; www.eataly.com.)

8:30am-7:30pm. Visit only with mandatory guided tour. €6.50, students €3.25. Gardens open 9am-1hr. before sunset. Free.) In the right wing of the Royal Palace lies the **Armeria Reale** (Royal Armory), with medieval and Renaissance war tools. (P. Castello 191. ☎011 54 38 89. Open Tu-F 9am-2pm, Sa-Su 1-7pm. €4, under 18 or over 65 free.)

PARCO DEL VALENTINO. One of Italy's largest parks and the country's first public park, the designer Valentino's lush grounds on the banks of the Po provide a safe haven for whispering lovers and children. Upon entering the park from C. V. Emanuele, **Castello del Valentino** is on the left. Its distinctly French air honors the royal lady Christina of France, who made the castle her favorite residence. It now houses the University's Facoltà di Architettura and is open to the public only by appointment (☎011 66 94 592). Nearby, a fake *rocca* (castle) is open to the public. Located in the nearby **Borgo e Rocca Medievale**, it was built for the Italian Industry and Crafts Exhibition of 1884, and today has a shop-filled village attached. (Park and castle at Vle. Virgilio 107, along the Po. ☎011 44 31 701; www.borgomedievaletorino.it. Castle open Tu-Su 9am-7pm. €5, students €4. Village open daily 9am-7pm. Free.)

SANTUARIO DELLA CONSOLATA. This ornate Baroque church belongs to Turin's cult of the Virgin, with gold and jeweled offerings of gratitude from the wealthy in glass boxes by the entrance. The room to the right is a collection of ex-voto paintings. Reminiscent of children's drawings, they depict catastrophes averted across the decades, as well as scenes from WWI and WWII. (P. della Consolata. ☎011 43 63 235; www.laconsolata.org. Open daily 6:30am-12:30pm and 3-7:30pm. Free.)

PALAZZO AND TEATRO CARIGNANO. This *palazzo* designed by the Guarini family in 1679 to house the Princes of Savoy was also the seat of the first Italian parliament. The building contains the **Museo Nazionale del Risorgimento Italiano,** which commemorates Italy's unification between 1706 and 1946. (V. Accademia delle Scienze 5. ☎011 56 21 147.) Across from the *palazzo* is the Baroque **Teatro Carignano,** where Italian poet Vittorio Alfieri premiered his tragedies. (☎011 54 70 54. Call for info on tours. Free.)

PALAZZO MADAMA. On the site of the ancient Roman military camp, this palace was converted to a castle in the Middle Ages. It lost its defensive function in the 17th century, became a museum in 1934, and today houses an enormous Baroque collection of paintings and artifacts from churches. Highlights include the view from the castle's tower and a small circular room on the ground floor with four medieval marble carvings. *(P. Castello. ☎ 011 44 33 501; www.palazzomadamatorino. it. Open Tu-F and Su 10am-6pm, Sa 10am-8pm. €7.50, over 65 and students under 25 €6.)*

MUSEO DELL'AUTOMOBILE. With an emphasis on Italian cars and racing, this museum documents the automobile's evolution through prints, drawings, more than 150 original cars, and first models by Ford, Benz, Peugeot, Oldsmobile, and Fiat. *(C. Unità d'Italia 40. Head south 20min. along V. Nizza from Stazione Porta Nuova. ☎ 011 67 76 66; www.museoauto.it. Open Tu-Su 10am-6:30pm. €7.)*

♫ ENTERTAINMENT

For the most updated calendar of Turin's yearly events, visit www.torinocul-tura.it (mostly in Italian) or www.turismotorino.org (in English). If you want the news in print, Turin's daily newspaper, *La Stampa*, publishes *Torino Sette*, a thorough Friday section on cultural events. Turin's **Teatro Regio**, in P. Castello, is home to the city's beloved **opera, ballet**, and **orchestra**, which showcase a combined 130 events a year. (☎ 011 88 15 557; www.teatroregio.torino.it. Ticket office open Tu-F 10:30am-6pm, Sa 10:30am-4pm, and 1hr. before shows.) Eclectic music, theater, and cinema events enliven Turin between June and August, when **Torino d'Estate** draws many local and international acts to the city. Included in the summer festivities are **Torino Puntiverdi**, 19 July nights of dance and music from tango to orchestra in the Giardini Reali and other venues. (☎ 011 50 69 967 or 80 00 15 457. Tickets €10-15, available from ticket office at V. S. Francesco da Paola 6. Open M-Sa 10:30am-6:30pm.) Head to the turn-of-the-century glamour of **Cinema Romano**, Galleria Subalpina, P. Castello 9, near the beginning of V. Po. (☎ 011 56 20 145. Movies daily, usually 4-10:30pm. Tickets €6-10.)

❅ FESTIVALS

During the 20s, Turin was home to over 100 movie production companies, and its love affair with cinema still lives on today. During the academic year, Turin's university organizes screenings of **foreign films** in their original languages. Two prestigious film festivals take place annually. The **Turin Film Festival** in November (www.torinofilmfest.org) is one of the liveliest festivals of contemporary cinema in Italy, paying particular attention to up-and-coming cinema auteurs. The various categories explore the many diverse aspects of contemporary cinema: feature films by famous directors, experimental cinema, and documentaries and retrospectives. In addition, **Da Sodoma ad Hollywood** is Turin's GLBT Film Festival held in April (www.tglff.com), one of the most important queer festivals in the world. In the fall, the tourist office organizes guided city tours with a cinematic bent. The ■**TRAFFIC Turin Free Festival**, during early July, attracts international acts to the free celebration of contemporary youth culture (www.trafficfestival.com). Previous performers include Franz Ferdinand and The Strokes. Last but not least, chocoholics venture to Turin every year at the end of February for the **Chocolate Fair** (www.cioccola-to.it).

⌐ SHOPPING

One of Turin's unique events is the **Gran Balon flea market,** held every second Sunday of the month behind Porta Palazzo. A smaller-scale **Mercato del Balon** (www.balon.it) occurs every Saturday. The biggest **open-air market** in Europe takes place under Porta Palazzo in P. della Repubblica. (M-F 8:30am-1:30pm, Sa 8:30am-6:30pm.) Over 600 vendors sell food, clothing, and odds and ends. Though clothing stores line Turin's streets, the big-name designer shops on **Via**

Roma are more conducive to window-shopping. Turin's student population has attracted trendy and affordable clothing shops to **Via Garibaldi** and **Via Po;** the latter is also home to antique bookshops and record stores. In the **Quadrilatero Romano,** up-and-coming designers have set up shop on the renovated streets within the rectangle outlined by V. Bligny, V. G. Garibaldi, V. XX Settembre, and P. della Repubblica. **8 Gallery,** V. Nizza 262 (www.8gallery.it), is housed inside Lingotto's former Fiat factory in Turin's future cultural center, and features over 100 shops, restaurants, bars, and movie theaters.

NIGHTLIFE

Turin's raging options are impressive in scope and variety, with something to offer all ages, ranging from good wine and grooving background music to vodka and tonics in a packed club. Clubs are less pretentious, covers are cheap, and choices are conveniently concentrated—mostly along the Po River. Especially in summer, Turin's social scene centers on **I Murazzi,** two stretches of boardwalk, one between Ponte V. Emanuele I and Ponte Umberto and another smaller stretch downstream from the Ponte V. Emanuele I. Some establishments charge covers late at night, but free bars or clubs can be easily found (many distribute consumption cards at the door that must be stamped, paid for, and returned upon departure; lost card fee €30). **Quadrilatero Romano,** the recently renovated collection of buildings between P. della Repubblica and V. Garibaldi, attracts partygoers who would rather sit and chat than dance to techno music. English and Irish pubs line C. V. Emanuele II from Stazione Porta Nuova to the Po, attracting an English-speaking student crowd. Head south on the I Murazzi side of the river for a few blocks to reach the growing Valentino Park riverfront nightlife, near the Valentino castle.

The Beach, V. Murazzi del Po 18-22 (☎011 88 87 77). With strobe lights and an energetic crowd, this club easily has the best dance floor in Turin. By 1am, this large, modern club fills with the young trendsetters, electronica music, and Redbull and vodkas. During the week, it hosts occasional performance-art pieces, film openings, and book signings. Mixed drinks €6-7. Open W and Su 5-11pm, Th-Sa 11pm-5am. MC/V.

Giancarlo, V. Murazzi del Po 47 (www.arcitorino.it), closest to Ponte V. Emanuele. 1st bar to invade I Murazzi. Rock and punk music draws an alternative crowd to its cavernous dance floor, and after 4am almost everyone who is not sitting by the river will be here. Beer €3-4. Mixed drinks €5-7. Student night Tu. Open M-Sa 10pm-6am. Cash only.

Pier 7-9-11, V. Murazzi del Po 7-11 (☎011 83 53 56). Flashy dance club. The most outdoor seating in I Murazzi. Shots €3. Beer €4. Mixed drinks €8. Cover with 1 drink included €8. F-Sa every drink €8. Open M-Sa midnight-6am.

Fluido, Vle. Umberto Cagni 7 (☎011 66 94 557; www.fluido.to). Riverside wine bar and restaurant, with a dance club downstairs. On warm evenings, the young clientele spread out in the grassy expanse surrounding the club. Shots €3. Mixed drinks €6. Open Tu-W 10am-2am, Th 10am-3am, F-Sa 10am-4:30am, Su 10am-1am.

Six Nations Murphy's Pub, C. V. Emanuele 28 (☎011 88 72 55). Exit Pta. Nuova, and turn right; the pub is a few blocks down on the left. Beer taps glow in the dim interior, filled with British expats, TVs, darts, and billiards. Sept.-May weekly Erasmus party for international students on W nights. Beer €3-4.50. Open daily 6pm-3am. MC/V.

Seiperotto, V. delle Orfane 17 (☎011 43 38 738; www.seiperotto.com). Specializing, as it claims, in "art, food, and drink," any trip to Seiperotto will inspire through tasty wines and rotating art exhibits. In addition to the photographs and paintings on display, don't neglect the giant bottom half of a stuffed ballerina hanging from the ceiling, tutu and all. Wine €3-4 per glass. Dinner €25. Open Tu-Su 7pm-2am. MC/V.

Shore, P. Emanuele Filiberto 10/G (☎011 43 63 495; www.shorecocktailclub.it). Serves large mixed drinks until the wee hours. Chill-out fusion music completes the mood. Mixed drinks €7. Open daily 6:30pm-2:30am. Cash only.

Arancia di Mezzanotte, P. E. Filiberto 11/I (☎011 52 11 338; www.aranciadimezzan-otte.it). Set in a quaint interior, this is a popular place for an aperitif away from the noisy and hectic river area. Beer €4-5. Mixed drinks €8. Open daily 6pm-4am. MC/V.

◤ DAYTRIPS FROM TURIN

◼ SACRA DI SAN MICHELE

From Turin, take a train to Sant'Ambrogio (30min.; 8 per day, last return 7:10pm; €2.50) to tackle the scenic 1½hr. climb from the village of Sant'Ambrogio to the monastery. Exiting the station, walk straight up V. Caduti per la Patria, and turn right on V. Umberto. Continue straight until Chiesa Parrocchiale. Behind the church on the right is a "Sacra di San Michele Mulattiera" sign. The rest of the hike is clearly marked. Do not hike alone, as the unpaved path can be difficult and slippery. Wear sturdy shoes and bring water. Alternatively, take the train to Avigliana (30min., 15 per day, €2.20). From there, either take a taxi (☎011 93 02 18; around €30) or tackle the 14km, 3hr. hike.

On a bluff above the town of Avigliana, the Sacra di San Michele (sa-cra dee san mee-KEH-leh) grows from the very rock on which it was built. *The Name of the Rose,* a movie based on a novel by Umberto Eco, was not filmed at this megalithic stone monastery, but it probably should have been. Eco based his book's plot on the Sacra's history, and even in full summer sunshine, there is an ominous air about the place. Ugo di Montboissier, an Alevernian pilgrim, founded it in 1000, and the **Scalone dei Morti** (Stairway of the Dead), a set of steps chiseled from the mountainside, helps to buttress the structure. Monks' corpses were once draped across the staircase for the faithful to pay their last respects; today, their skeletons are tactfully concealed in the cavities on the side. The stairs ascend to the **Porta dello Zodiaco** (Door of the Zodiac), a door sculpted by 11th-century artist Nicolao with zodiac signs and symbols. Steps in the middle of the nave descend into the shrine of St. Michael and three tiny **chapels.** The oldest dates to the time of St. Michael's earliest known veneration. In 966, St. John Vincent built the largest chapel; today, it holds the medieval members of the Savoy family. (☎011 93 91 30; www.sacradisanmichele.com. Open Mar. 16-Oct. 15 Tu-Sa 9:30am-12:30pm and 2:30-6pm, Su 9:30am-noon and 2:40-6:30pm; Oct. 16-Mar. 15 Tu-Sa 9:30am-12:30pm and 2:30-5pm, Su 9:30am-12:30pm and 2:40-6pm. Last entry 30min. before closing. €4, children and over 65 €3.) For a map of the arduous trek, head to Avigliana's **Informazione Turistica,** C. Torino 6/d, a 5-10min. walk straight ahead from the train station. (☎011 93 66 037. Open M-F 9am-noon and 3-6pm.)

PARCO DELLA MANDRIA AND VENARIA CASTLE

By car: from the by-pass in Turin, take the Venaria Reale exit. By train: take the Torino-Ceres (Airport) line from Stazione Dora to Venaria. By bus: take the blue GTT line #11, 72, or 72b from the centro to Venaria. Ask at tourist office or nearby tabaccherie for the most convenient bus stop. Alternatively, a shuttle bus conveniently runs between C. Stati Uniti, Porta Nuova, Porta Susa, and the palace. (45min.; 14 departures per day 8:05am-6:55pm, 16 returns per day 9am-7:50pm; round-trip €5. Info: ☎011 800 329 329; www.parks.it/ parco.mandria or www.lavenariareale.it.)

An immense project mostly constructed by a single architect during the 17th and 18th centuries, this newly restored royal palace has an immaculate contemporary garden and over 5000 sq. m of frescoes and decorations. Parco Della Mandria is a rural, historical park characterized by alluvial terraces where woods alternate with pastures, lakes, and fields. The variable countryside landscape invites you to relax and enjoy the ancient churches and royal residences, which date back to the times of King Vittorio Emanuele II. The area's vegetation includes an ancient forest rich in oaks and ash trees that shelters many animal species. Many activities, such as horseback riding, trekking, and cycling are available. The plan for the building of the castle was begun in 1659 at the request of Duke Carlo Emanuele II. The layout by Amedeo di Castellamonte was finished in 1675, and consists of a village, a palace, and gardens. (La Venaria Reale, P. della Republica 4. ☎011 45 93 675; www.reggiavenariareale. it. Open Tu, Th, and Sa-Su 9:30-11:30am and 2:30-5:30pm.)

CUNEO   ☎0171

Cuneo's (COO-neh-oh; pop. 55,000) name means "wedge," and for good reason: it's wedged between the Stura di Demonte River and the Torrente Gesso. Over the years, no fewer than nine different armies have besieged strategically located Cuneo, but the town has lived up to its motto, *"ferendo"* (to bear), surviving each onslaught. These days, invasion comes in the form of bargain hunters, who overwhelm serene Cuneo during its open-air market every weekend. While other Italian cities of its size and historical presence retain a village-like atmosphere, Cuneo is built on a grand scale, with imposing *piazze* and *vie*. Its 14km of *portici* (arcades) provide ample space for an afternoon of window-shopping and people-watching, and on warm nights, residents of all ages flock to the broad avenues and grand squares, enjoying gelato or a glass of wine. However, most travelers visit Cuneo as a launching point for excursions into the nearby valleys and Maritime Alps National Park.

TRANSPORTATION AND PRACTICAL INFORMATION. The **train station** (ticket office open 6am-midnight) in P. Libertà provides service to Mondovì (40min., 13 per day 6:20am-7:09pm, €2.70), Saluzzo (30min., 14 per day 5:35am-7:38pm, €2.70-4), and Turin (1½hr., 30 per day 4:35am-10pm, €5.30). Local **buses** also depart from the station, serving Mondovì (12 per day 7am-7:35pm, €2.70), Saluzzo (1hr., 21 per day 6:45am-7:35pm, €2.45), and Turin via Saluzzo (4:55am-8:25pm, €5.30). Schedules vary daily and seasonally; the tourist office provides up-to-date timetables. To explore the Cuneo Valleys, rent a **car** from Europcar, V. Torino 178 (☎017141 23 63), inside the Hyundai dealership. To get there from Cuneo, take a cab or bus 4, 8, or 15 from the center (bus stops directly in front of dealership). For those over the age of 25, try Avis, C. Francia 251 (☎0171 49 34 86; open M-F 8:30am-12:30pm and 2:30-6:30pm, Sa 8:30am-12:30pm; AmEx/MC/V). Borrow a free **bike** from the town hall next to the tourist office and grab a copy of the brochure, *Cuneo's Bicycle Touring District*. Also at the tourist office, *Cuneo In Your Pocket*, outlines an artistic and historical walking tour.

Cuneo lies 80km south of Turin. **Piazza Galimberti,** in the eastern extreme of the town, is the heart of Cuneo's shopping, accommodation, and nightlife district, with main thoroughfares **Via Roma** and **Corso Nizza** extending out of it. The rest of the streets form a navigable grid. To reach C. Nizza from the train station, follow **Corso Giolitti** from **Piazza Libertà**. The **tourist office**, V. Roma 28, provides info and helps find lodgings. (☎0171 69 32 58; www.comune.cuneo.it. Open M-Sa 10am-12:30pm and 3-6:30pm.) For info on the Cuneo province, contact **ATL**, V. Amedeo 82. From C. Nizza, turn onto V. Amedeo one block before the *piazza*. (☎0171 69 02 16. Open daily 8:30am-noon and 2:30-6pm.) **Banks** with **ATMs** line V. Roma and C. Nizza. In case of emergency, call the **police** (☎0171 67 777) or **paramedics** (☎0171 44 13 37). Several **pharmacies** on C. Nizza post after-hours rotations, including one at P. Galimberti 5. (Open M, W-Th, Sa-Su 9am-12:30pm and 3:30-7:30pm, Tu and F 8:30am-12:30pm.) The Santa Croce **hospital** is at V. Coppino 26 (☎0171 45 01 11). **Internet access** is available at the **Call Center,** V. Fossano 19. (☎0171 60 54 75. €4 per hr. Open M-Sa 9am-9pm, Su 2:30-9pm.) The **post office** is at V. Francesco Andrea Bonelli 6. (☎0171 69 33 06. Open M-F 8:30am-7pm, Sa 8:30am-1pm.) **Postal Code:** 12100.

▮▮ ACCOMMODATIONS AND FOOD. Find comfortable, newly renovated hotel rooms, all with A/C, Wi-Fi (€5 per day), TV, phone, and bath or shower at **Hotel Ligure ❹,** V. Savigliano 11. Exit P. Galimberti on V. Roma and turn right; V. Savigliano runs parallel to V. Roma. A kitchen is available for stays over a week. (☎0171 63 45 45; www.ligurehotel.com. Breakfast included. Parking €7. Singles €50-65; doubles €70-80; triples €90-98. MC/V.) At **Bisalta ❶,** V. S. Maurizio 33, on the outskirts of the city, 200 campsites offer plenty of recreational activities. (☎0171 49 13 34; campingbisalta@libero.it. €5-6.50 per person, €5-6.50 per site. Bungalows €20-40 per person. Electricity €2. Cash only.)

Cafes line the arcades of V. Roma and C. Nizza, providing cheap spots to stop for a sandwich or gelato. At ▨**Ristorante Les Gourmands ❸,** V. Statuto 3/e, bright colors and a classily off-beat, ever-changing decorating scheme will delight even the most jaded restaurant-goer, while the cuisine innovatively fuses cuisines from around the world. Try the strawberry risotto with shrimp and rosemary for €8. (☎0171 60 56 64; www.lesgourmands.it. Primi €7-10. Secondi €5-17. 3-course lunch *menù* €10. Cover €2. Open Tu-F and Su noon-3pm and 7pm-midnight, Sa 7pm-midnight. AmEx/MC/V.) For a traditional dinner, head to **Ristorante Zuavo ❷,** on V. Savigliano, directly across from Hotel Ligure, where a simple menu, wood tables, and walls adorned with family mementos guarantee an authentic meal. (☎0171 60 20 20. Primi €6. Secondi €8-9. Open M-Tu and F-Su 12:30-2pm and 7pm-1am, Th 7:30-1am. AmEx/MC/V.) Nearby, **Cristal ❸,** V. Savigliano 17, presents an intimate place to sip wine just outside the bustle of V. Roma. (☎0141 69 47 64. Mixed drinks €5-8. Wine €3.50-5 per glass. Open daily 6pm-1am. AmEx/V.) There's a **Maxisconto** supermarket at the corner of V. Cesare Battisti and V. Ponza di S. Martino, off P. Galimberti. (Open M-W 8:30am-1pm and 3-7:30pm, Th 8:30am-1pm, F-Sa 8:30am-7:30pm.)

▯▧ SHOPPING AND SIGHTS. Cuneo's famous **open-air market** sprawls over 1km, filling P. Galimberti, most of V. Roma, and much of C. Nizza—not to mention all the side streets. Stalls full of clothes, antiques, postcards, cookware, and all else imaginable delight shoppers, but make parking a nightmare. (Every Tu during daylight hours. In summer approximately 7am-6pm; in winter 8am-4pm.) There is also an **antiques market** on the last Saturday of every month in P. Europa. The facade of the **duomo,** at the corner of C. Nizza and V. Bologna, may blend in with the municipal government buildings around it, but inside there is a Baroque wonderland, accented with attractive modern stained glass. (Open daily 8am-noon and 3-7pm.) The **Museo Civico di Cuneo,** V. S. Maria 10, occupies the retired convent of S. Francesco, and displays archaeological artifacts that showcase Cuneo's history as well as its Bronze Age cave drawings. (☎0171 63 41 75. Open Tu and Sa 8:30am-1pm and 2:30-5:30pm, W-F 8:30am-1pm and 2:30-5pm, Su 3-7pm. Closed June 15-30. €2.60, students €1.55.)

SALUZZO   ☎0175

For over four centuries, the hilltop town of Saluzzo (sa-LOOT-so; pop. 16,400) reigned as the capital of a fiercely independent marquisate before falling under the influence of the House of Savoy in 1601. The arcade-lined *centro storico* and churches of the "Siena of the North" remain well preserved and tourist-

PIEDMONT AND VALLE D'AOSTA

free—unless you count the crowds of farmers who visit on weekend nights for a glass of wine in the trattorie. Saluzzo is the perfect place to relax before hiking in the nearby mountains, or to use as a base for exploring the Po Valley.

TRANSPORTATION AND PRACTICAL INFORMATION. Saluzzo lies 33km north of Cuneo. **Trains** depart from the P. Vittorio Veneto station off C. Roma for Cuneo (1hr., M-Sa every 45min. 6:55am-8:20pm, €5) and Turin (1hr., M-Sa 7:10am-9:05pm, €4.70) via Savigliano. Local ATI **buses** (www.atibus.com) leave from V. Circonvallazione 19, connecting Saluzzo to villages in the surrounding valleys, including Turin (1hr., 1-2 per hr. 4:25am-8:25pm, €3) and Cuneo (1hr., 1-2 per hr. 6:10am-7:25pm, €2.45). On the weekend, the train station closes, but buses still run. Purchase tickets at the machine behind the station; buses pick up passengers in front of the station. For a **taxi**, call ☎0175 45 098.

Saluzzo's main street, **Via Spielberg** becomes **Corso Italia**, and then **Corso Piemonte** as it moves east to west. From the train station, head straight up **Via Piave** and turn right to walk toward the *centro storico;* from the bus station, turn left on **Via Circonvallazione,** then immediately right on **Via Torino.** The *centro storico* and most of the sights lie uphill on the north side of town. To reach the **tourist office,** Piazzetta dei Mondagli 5, enter the old town through the arched passageway at V. Volta, near the junction of V. Spielberg and C. Italia. It provides detailed info on bike routes and sights in nearby villages and valleys. (☎0175 46 710; www.comune.saluzzo.cn.it. Open Apr.-Sept. Tu-Sa 9am-1pm and 2:30-5:30pm, Su 9am-1pm and 2:30-6pm; Oct.-Mar. Tu-Sa 9am-12:30pm and 2-5:30pm, Su 9am-12:30pm and 2-6pm.) **Unicredit Banca,** C. Italia 28, has an **ATM.** (Open M-F 8:20am-1:20pm and 2:30-4pm.) The public library, **Biblioteca Civica,** V. Volta 39, offers free **Internet** access. (Open Tu-Th 9:30am-12:30pm and 3-7pm, F 3-7pm, Sa 9:30am-1pm and 2:30-5:30pm. Internet available Tu-F 3-7pm, Sa 9:30am-1pm and 2:30-6:30pm.) **Farmacia Chiaffredo,** C. Italia 56, posts a list of after-hours rotations. (Open daily except for rotating rest day 8:30am-12:30pm and 3:30-6pm.) The **Ospedale Civile** lies on V. Spielberg 58 (☎0175 21 51 11), two blocks outside the *centro storico.* The **post office,** V. Peano 1, is on the other side of the river, near the train station. (Open Jan.-July and Sept.-Dec. 8:30am-7pm, Sa 8:30am-1pm; Aug. M-F 8:30am-2pm, Sa 8:30am-1pm.) **Postal Code:** 12037.

ACCOMMODATIONS AND FOOD. As with many small towns in the area, true budget digs of the hostel variety are tough to find in the town proper; visitors with cars should inquire at the tourist office about B&Bs in the countryside. Meanwhile, Turin's hostels are a short train ride away. For a good value located in the center of town, try the **Hotel Përpoin ❹,** V. Spielberg 19, through a covered passage. The hotel offers spacious modern rooms with TV, phone, and bath and has an English-speaking staff. The restaurant serves rich *piemontese* cuisine. (☎0175 42 552; www.hotelsaluzzo.com. Breakfast included; full pension €15 per extra meal. Wheelchair-accessible. Singles €40; doubles €70. Extra bed €15. AmEx/MC/V.) **Albergo Persico ❹,** Vco. Mercati 10, is near P. Cavour. (☎/fax 0175 41 213; www.albergopersico.net. Singles with breakfast €40-42; doubles €60, with breakfast €68; triples €75/85. AmEx/MC/V.)

The menu changes seasonally at **Le Quattro Stagioni D'Italia ❸,** V. Volta 21. Traditional dishes like *tajarin* (homemade pasta made with egg yolks; €9.50) and pizza (€6.50-8.50) are served in a dimly lit interior or a bamboo-accented garden outside. The lunch buffet (€9.50), offers a veritable rainbow of tempting fresh dishes. Peaches stuffed with chocolate and hazelnut sauce (€5) are a knockout. (☎0175 47 470; www.ristorantele4stagioni.it. Primi €7.50-10. Secondi €10-20. 3-course *menù* €17. Open M-Tu and Th-Su noon-2:30pm and 7-11pm. AmEx/MC/V.) **Hotel Përpoin's restaurant ❷,** on the ground floor, lists its affordable local fare on a chalk board transported between tables. You can't go wrong with the €12-25 *menù*. (Primi €4-6. Secondi €6-8. Cover €1.50. Open M-Th and Sa-Su noon-2:30pm and 7:30-9:30pm. AmEx/MC/V.) **Albergo Persico's restaurant** ❸ specializes in *piemontese* cuisine, including the farmer's *fritto misto* (€12), a plate of all the food groups—meat, vegetables, fruit, and bread—deep fried. (☎0175 41 213. Primi €7-9. Secondi €9-12. Open M-Th and Sa-Su noon-2pm and 7:30-10pm. AmEx/MC/V.) **Supermercati Maxisconto** offers cheap groceries at C. Piemonte 21. (Open Jan.-June and Aug.-Dec. M-Sa 9am-7:30pm. MC/V.)

▣ SIGHTS. The **Cattedrale di Maria Assunta** lies on C. Italia. The recently restored Lombard Gothic cathedral is decorated with bright Baroque frescoes that contrast sharply with the somber exterior. (Open daily 7-11:30am and 3:30-7pm. Free.) To reach the *centro storico*, where many of the city's noteworthy sights are located, head uphill from the tourist office along Salità Castello. At the summit in P. Castello, visit **La Castiglia**, which was the town fortress and prison until the 80s. When current renovations are completed, it will be reborn as a cultural center. As you turn right on V. S. Giovanni, the 48m tall **Torre Civica**, built in 1556, commands a sweeping view of the Po Valley. (☎0175 41 455. Open daily 9:30am-12:30pm and 2:30-6:30pm. €1.30; combined ticket with Casa Cavassa €5.) The **Museo Civico** (also called the **Casa Cavassa**), V. S. Giovanni 5, one of Saluzzo's most important Renaissance buildings, was once home to the politically important Cavassa family and features pieces like Hans Clemer's *Madonna della Misericordia*. (☎0175 41 455; cavassa@comune.saluzzo.cn.it. Open Th-Su Apr.-Sept. 10am-1pm and 2-6pm; Oct.-Mar. 10am-1pm and 2-5pm. €4.) The most important building after the *duomo* is the **Chiesa di San Giovanni**, V. S. Giovanni 15, that holds a rare wood choir in the Gothic-flamboyant style sitting behind the altar. The ceiling of the adjoining chapel, accessible through the cloisters to the church's left, is decorated with frescoes representing the night sky. (Open daily 8am-noon and 3-7pm. Free.) In Piasco, 15km from Saluzzo toward Cuneo lies the **Museo dell'Arpa Victor Salvi**, V. Rossana 7, the world's first museum dedicated solely to the harp. Inaugurated in 2005, the *museo* has 100 antique harps. (☎27 05 10; www.museodellarpavictorsalvi.it. Open M-F and Su 10am-1pm and 2-5pm. €5, under 10 and over 65 €2.50.) To reach the extensive **Giardino Botanico Villa Bricherasio**, V. Giambattista Bodoni 88, follow V. Bodoni west out of the centro, 800m past V. Matteo Olivero. (☎075 41 061 or 340 80 54 313. Open Apr.-Oct. during daylight hours. €5.)

ASTI ☎0141

Set in the hillsides of Piedmont's wine country, the provincial seat of Asti (AHS-tee; pop. 73,000) has bustled with activity since it was founded by the Romans in the AD first century. A trading power during the Middle Ages, Asti had become one of Italy's richest cities by 1200. Today, it is best known for its wines—limestone-rich soils on gentle south-facing slopes produce grapes destined for bottles of *Moscato*, dark red *Barbera*, and sparkling *Asti Spumante*. Though Asti is filled with iconic medieval brick towers, much of the city is today dominated by automobiles (read: ample parking for visitors with cars and a headache for pedestrians).

▮ TRANSPORTATION

Trains: Station in P. Marconi, where V. Cavour meets C. Luigi Einaudi. Ticket office open daily 6am-9:30pm, or use ticket machine. Connections to most destinations via Alessandria. To: **Acqui Terme** (1hr., 19 per day 6:22am-8:35pm, €3.50); **Alba** (40min., 20

PIEDMONT AND VALLE D'AOSTA

per day 5:49am-8:34pm, €2.70); **Alessandria** (30min., 55 per day 12:27am-11:40pm, €2.70); **Cuneo** (2hr., 23 per day 4:32am-10:54pm, €7); **Milan Centrale** (2hr., 23 per day 5:25am-11:32pm, €8.75); **Turin Porta Nuova** (1hr., 53 per day, 4:32am-11:51pm, €3.90).

Buses: in P. Medaglie d'Oro, to the right when exiting the train station (☎0141 43 329 or 43 34 53). To: **Canelli** (every 2hr. 7:20am-7:10pm); **Castagnole** (every 2hr. 7:20am-6:40pm); **Costigliole** (9 per day 7:15am-6:50pm); **Isola d'Asti** (6 per day 10am-6:50pm). Buy tickets (€1.60-2.20) onboard or at *tabaccherie*.

Taxis: in P. Alfieri (☎0141 53 26 05) or at the train station (☎0141 59 27 22).

➕ 🛈 ORIENTATION AND PRACTICAL INFORMATION

The *centro* lies in the triangular **Piazza Alfieri**. From the station, go up **Via Cavour** through **Piazzetta San Paolo, Piazza Statuto,** and **Piazza San Secondo,** then right on **Via Garibaldi.** Most sights are along **Corso Vittorio Alfieri**, the major east-west road, connecting with the top of P. Alfieri. Between P. Alfieri and the train station sits **Piazza Campo del Palio,** now used for parking and weekly markets.

Tourist Office: ATL, P. Alfieri 29 (☎0141 53 03 57; www.astiturismo.it). Open M-Sa 9am-1pm and 2:30-6:30pm, Su 9am-1pm.

Banks: Currency exchange available along C. Vittorio Alfieri and V. Dante. There are **ATMs** in the train station and on V. Dante, or at **Banca Popolare di Lodi,** P. Alfieri 15. Open M-F 8:20am-1:20pm and 2:30-4pm.

English-Language bookstore: Libreria Mondadori, C. Alfieri 324. Open in summer M 3-7:30pm, Tu-Sa 9:30am-noon and 3-7:30pm; in winter hours vary.

Police: C. XXV Aprile 19 (☎0141 41 81 11).

Pharmacy: Farmacia Alfieri, P. Alfieri 3 (☎0141 59 46 05 or 35 43 05). Open daily 8:30am-12:30pm and 3:30-7:30pm. Closes 1 month in summer.

Internet Access: Mari Mina Phone Center, C. L. Einaudi 144 (☎0141 32 65 82). €1.50 per hour. Open daily 8am-midnight.

Post office: C. Dante 55 (☎0141 35 72 51. Open M-F 8:30am-7pm, Sa 8:30am-1pm.), at the intersection of P. Alfieri and V. Verdi. **Postal Code:** 14100.

🛏 ACCOMMODATIONS

For a better value, those with cars should consider a B&B in the scenic wine country just outside of Asti. Ask at the tourist office for more info.

Hotel Cavour, P. Marconi 18 (☎/fax 0141 53 02 22; www.hotelcavour-asti.com), across from the train station. Clean, modern rooms with shower or large bath, TV, and phone. Most have A/C. Handicapped-accessible. Free parking. Reception 6am-1am. Singles €45-50; doubles €65-73; triples €85. AmEx/MC/V. ❹

Hotel Genova, C. Alessandria 26 (☎0141 59 31 97). Cross P. Marconi, in front of the train station, and continue down V. Cavour. Cross through P. Alfieri. Turn right onto C. Vittorio Alfieri, which becomes C. Alessandria after P. Maggio. Simple, homey establishment offers rooms with TV and sink. Reception 6:30am-11pm. Singles €32-42; doubles €52, with bath €65. Call ahead if arriving on Su. AmEx/D/MC/V. ❸

Campeggio Umberto Cagni, Località Valmanera 152 (☎0141 27 12 38). 4km from P. Alfieri, turn on V. Arò, which becomes C. Volta, then left onto V. Valmanera. Open Apr.-Sept. Bungalows €40. Electricity €3. Showers free. Cash only. ❶

🍴 FOOD

Astigiana cuisine is known for its reliance on a few crucial ingredients, especially gorgonzola and other pungent cheeses. *Coniglio* (rabbit), *cinghiale* (wild boar), truffles, and mountain herbs make up classic *piemontese* dishes. Restaurant cellars are stocked with Asti's local wines, including the sparkling white *Moscato*. Local vineyards also produce *grappa*, a strong grape liqueur. An extensive fruit and vegetable **market** is at P. Campo del Palio and P. Alfieri. (Open W and Sa 7:30am-1pm. Clothing booths open until sunset.) The **DìperDì** supermarket, P. Alfieri 26, has low prices and a wide selection. A **second location** is on V. Bruno, off P. S. Secondo. (☎0141 34 759. Open M-Tu, Th-F, and Su 8:30am-1pm and 3:30-7:45pm, W and Sa 8:30am-7:45pm. MC/V.)

▨ **Ristorante Tacabanda/L'Osteria della Barbera,** V. al Teatro 5 (☎0141 53 09 99), off P. S. Secondo. Waiters double as wine experts in the candlelit dining room. Heaping portions of dishes like surprisingly tasty *agnolotti di asino* (ravioli stuffed with donkey meat; €8). Lunch *menù* (€11) includes a primo, secondo, and wine. Primi €8-8.50. Secondi €8.50-14. Open Tu-Su noon-2:30pm and 8-10pm. AmEx/MC/V. ❸

Ristorante La Vecchia Carrozza, V. Carducci 41 (☎/fax 0141 53 86 57). Homestyle food beneath arched brick ceilings in a quiet back room. Family-owned. Primi €7-8. Secondi €8-14. Open Tu-Su noon-2pm and 7:30-10pm. AmEx/MC/V. ❸

L'Angolo del Beato, V. Guttuari 12 (☎/fax 0141 53 16 68), off V. Cavour. Quiet, intimate dining room with unadvertised entrance. Antipasto €7.50. Primi €9-11. Secondi €13-15. Cover €1.50. Open M-Sa noon-2pm and 7:30-10:30pm. AmEx/MC/V. ❹

Pizzeria Francese, V. dei Cappellai 15 (☎0141 59 23 21; www.pizzerie-italia.it), off P. S. Secondo. Chef Francese knows his pizza—he's written a 668-page guide to Italy's best pizzerias. Try the *pizza di tartufo* (€20-25). Pizza from €5.50. Primi and secondi €7-9. Cover €1.50. Open in summer daily 10:30am-3pm and 6:30pm-1am; in winter M-Tu and Th-Su 10:30am-3pm and 6:30pm-1am. Closed mid-Aug. AmEx/MC/V. ❷

Al Volo Food in motion, C. Vittorio Alfieri 335 (☎0141 30 271). Pizza, primi, and secondi all under €4, even during the mid-afternoon siesta. Open M-Th 10:30am-10:30pm, F-Sa 10:30am-midnight, and Su 3-10:30pm. ❶

◙ SIGHTS

CATTEDRALE. The 14th-century cathedral is a noteworthy example of the *piemontese* Gothic style. Its *piazza* entrance is decorated by statues of monks and priests. In the 11th century, artists blanketed the floor around the altar with mosaics, while in the 16th and 17th centuries, local artists covered every inch of the walls with frescoes. (*Walk down C. V. Alfieri and turn right at P. Cairoli.* ☎0141 59 29 24. *Open daily 8:30am-noon and 3-5:30pm. Free.*)

CHIESA DI SAN PIETRO IN CONSAVIA. This 15th-century church served as a WWII army hospital. Beside it sits the 12th-century octagonal baptistry. On the first floor of the *chiesa*, the **Museo Paleontologico** has a small collection of fossils and bones from the astiano area. On the second floor, the **Museo Archeologico** showcases fourth-century BC Greek vases. (*On C. V. Alfieri.* ☎0141 43 74 54. *Museums open Apr.-Oct. Tu-Su 10am-1pm and 4-7pm; Nov.-Mar. Tu-Su 10am-1pm and 3-6pm.*)

PIAZZA SAN SECONDO. This piazze is home to the 18th-century **Palazzo di Città** and the Romanesque-Gothic **Chiesa Collegiata di San Secondo,** the latter built in the 14th century for Asti's patron saint. The first chapel holds colorful banners from past *Palio* festivals. Statues of San Secondo represent the saint holding a sword in one hand and the city of Asti in the other. (*From P. Alfieri, walk west on V. Garibaldi.* ☎0141 53 00 66. *Open M-Sa 8:30am-noon and 3:30-5:30pm, Su 3:30-5:30pm.*)

CRIPTA E MUSEO DI SANT'ANASTASIO. Here visitors will find wall fragments and ornate columns of ruins of the former church of Sant'Anastasio juxtaposed against exhibits of political posters of the past century and record album covers of the 1960s and 70s. Don't miss the almost completely intact chapel, complete with tiny brick stairwells that lead nowhere. (*C. Alfieri 365/A.* ☎ *0141 43 74 54. Open in summer 10pm-1am and 4-7pm; in winter Tu-Su 10am-1pm and 3-6pm. Free.*)

TOWERS. During the city's medieval prominence, feuding nobles constructed brick towers to flaunt their wealth. In the 13th century, the city was famed for having more than 100 examples, but now only 30 or so remain, many of them in ruin. The city's symbol, **Torre Troyana**, in P. Medici, was built in the 13th and 14th centuries. (☎ *0141 39 94 60 or 43 74 54. Open Sa-Su Apr.-Oct. 10am-1pm and 4-7pm; Nov. 10am-1pm and 3-6pm. €1.50.*) The 16-sided **Torre Rossa** in P. S. Caterina, at the western end of C. V. Alfieri, is much older, with foundations dating to the late first century BC. Connected to the tower is the elliptical Baroque **Chiesa di Santa Caterina.** (*Open daily 7:30am-noon and 3-7pm. Free.*)

OTHER SIGHTS. The **Giardini Pubblici**, between P. Alfieri and P. Campo del Palio, are great for a picnic or stroll. On the edge of the city, the **Tapestry Museum Scassa** is located in the **Antica Certosa di Valmanera** (Ancient Monastery of Valmanera) and features impressive modern tapestries and designs made using ancient looms. (*V. dell'Arazzeria 60.* ☎ *0141 27 13 52; ugscasa@tin.it. Guided tours with reservation.*)

❋ ♫ FESTIVALS AND ENTERTAINMENT

Other than at annual festivals, the only place to hear live music in Asti is at **Diavolo Rosso**, P. S. Martino 4. The name, which translates to "red devil," is a bit ironic considering that it is housed in a desecrated church. The building serves as a community center and political forum during the day. (☎ 0141 35 56 99; www.diavolorosso.it. Mixed drinks €4. Wine €2. Open Th-Su 7:30pm-2am. Closed during most of July and Aug.) For more festival info and exact dates, contact the tourist office (see **Practical Information,** p. 180.)

Douja d'Or (www.doujador.it), 2nd and 3rd week of Sept. Agricultural Asti revels in a 10-day local wine fair, with tastings and competitions.

Palio di Asti, 3rd Su in Sept. The culmination of the Douja d'Or. Commemorates the town's liberation in 1200, followed by Italy's oldest bareback horse race, which dates to 1275. Each jockey represents a quarter of the city, and the winner takes a banner with the city's coat of arms and patron saint.

Paisan, P. Campo del Palio, 2nd weekend in Sept. A.k.a. the **Festivale delle Sagre.** 45 regional towns serve specialty dishes amid 19th-century costumes and parades.

Asti Teatro, a series of theatrical performances, is held in **Teatro Alfieri,** V. al Teatro 2, from June through July. (☎ 0141 39 90 32; www.astiteatro.it. Reserve tickets in advance. Some events are free, others cost €15.)

Asti Musica in P. Cattedrale (☎ 0141 39 93 99), throughout July. Showcases bands for dancing crowds nightly starting at 10pm. Tickets range from free to €25.

⬛ DAYTRIP FROM ASTI

CANELLI

Trains run to Asti (1hr., 6:45am-7:57pm, €3) via Castagnole. Buses run from Canelli (30min., every 1hr. 6:05am-6:15pm, €2.50).

The sparkling *Asti Spumante* and super-sweet *Moscato* bubble forth from the famous countryside vineyards surrounding Canelli (ca-NEH-lee; pop. 11,000). Though wine has flowed from the verdant, vineyard-striped hills since Roman times, the first Italian sparkling wine matured in the Gancia family winery just 150 years ago. The region's long-standing wine-making tradition has created kilometers of vaulted underground tunnels used as wine cellars. The "underground cathedral," as the interconnected brick cellars are known, may soon earn designation as a UNESCO World Heritage site: the distinction would provide enough money to finish the tunnels, which will enable visitors and residents to walk underground from one end of the city to the other.

At **Cantine Gancia,** C. Libertà 66, tour the wine-bottling facilities, the cellar, and the museum of the Gancia family's winery. The factory has come a long way since Carlo Gancia invented the classic method of creating sparkling wine from Moscato grapes through in-bottle refermentation; while it was originally all done by hand, today, a machine slowly turns the bottles for 70 days to sift the sediments against the cork. Gancia's annual production is now 30 million bottles a year, making the modern facility Italy's biggest producer of sparkling wine. *(☎0141 83 02 53; www.gancia.it. Open daily 9am-6pm, but hours vary. Free 30min. guided tour in English; reservations required. Wine tasting. Wine from €4 per bottle.)* Afterward, head to the neighboring AD ninth-century cellar of **Enoteca Regionale di Canelli e dell'Astesana,** C. Libertà 65/A, located under a palace, for a taste of Canelli's finest wines, most notably the *Moscato d'Asti, Barbera d'Asti,* and *Dolcetto d'Asti.* *(☎0141 83 21 82; enotecacanelli@inwind.it. Open Th-F 5pm-midnight, Sa-Su 11am-1pm and 5pm-midnight. Tastings after 8pm.)* On the third Saturday of June, over 2000 townspeople in medieval garb reenact the **Siege of Canelli,** a 1613 battle. Entrance is free, but obtain a pass from military authorities at the gate, or risk being thrown in the stocks. Inn-keepers and restaurants participate by serving 17th-century feasts (€8-21). A **market** held every Tuesday has over 100 stalls, with goods in P. Gancia, produce in P. Gioberti, and other foods in P. Zoppa. A small market is held on Fridays. Canelli's annual **Fiera Regionale di Tartufo** (2nd Su in Nov.), is a truffle fair that dates back to the 14th century.

Banca Popolare di Novara, V. Roma 1, has an **ATM.** *(Open M-F 8:20am-1:20pm and 2:35-3:35pm, Sa 8:20-11:50am.)* A **pharmacy, Bielli Dott. Renata Farmacia,** V. XX Settembre 1 (☎0141 82 34 46), is in the *centro.* The **tourist office** is at V. Roma 37. *(☎0141 82 01 11; www.comune.canelli.at.it. Open M, W, F 8:30am-12:30pm, Tu and Th 8:30am-12:30pm and 3-5pm. Hours subject to change; call ahead.)*

ACQUI TERME   ☎0144

Steaming-hot fountains, brick archways, and aqueduct ruins have drawn vacationers seeking luxury to Acqui Terme's (AH-kwee TEHR-meh) healing waters and mud baths since Roman times when the town was known as "Aquae Statiellae." Subterranean sulfuric springs at temperatures of 75°C (167°F) gurgle in P. della Bollente and across the Bormida River in the private Lago delle Sorgenti. Today, Acqui Terme might just be the perfect Italian town: its *vie* and *piazze* overflow with warmth, relaxation, and unique personality.

▣ ◨ TRANSPORTATION AND PRACTICAL INFORMATION. The **train station** (☎0144 89 20 21) is in P. Vittorio Veneto. (Ticket booth open M-F 6am-7:30pm, Sa-Su 6am-12:35pm and 1-7:30pm.) **Trains** run to: Alessandria (43min., 23 trains per day 5:35am-8pm, €2.70); Asti (1hr., 17 trains per day 5:15am-7:50pm, €3.50); Genoa (1hr., 51 per day 5:18am-8:55pm, €3-3.50); Savona (1hr., 13 trains per day 6am-8:08pm, €4.80), and Turin (1½hr., 6:58am, €6.80). **Taxis** wait at the station (☎0144 32 32 80 or 32 20 40). To reach town from the station, turn left on **Via Alessandria,** which becomes C. Vigano and ends in **Piazza Italia.** From here, most sights are found by taking **Corso Italia,** along an ancient riverbed.

To reach the **IAT tourist office,** P. Levi 12, follow Corso Italia and make a left onto V. Garibaldi followed by a right into P. Levi. The office rents **bikes** and provides info on itineraries for the city and surrounding region. (☎0144 32 21 42; www.comuneacqui.com. Bikes €3 per ½-day, €5 per day. Open M-Sa

STAYING SANE THE SAINTLY WAY

Whether you're in Italy to celebrate your graduation from your all-girls Catholic high school or you don't know the Pope from Melissa Etheridge, you've probably noticed that in Italy it's difficult to take more than a couple steps without running into a saint. Churches and monasteries abound and generally have saints to thank for their names and for the lovely statuaries all over their naves and courtyards, but saints also crop up to give their patronage to streets, hotels, banks, and pastries.

Many saints have quite colorful life stories, and learning about them can enrich your experience of the hotels you sleep in and the cookies you eat. Devout Catholics often ask saints to intercede on their behalf with Christ, and in that vein, have determined specific fields for each saint, so that prayers can be appropriately directed. Here are some that may come in handy during your trip:

1. St. Raphael: patron saint of travelers and of lovers.
2. St Christopher: patron saint of safe travel.
3. St. Anthony: patron saint of lost things
4. St Eustace: patron saint of difficult situations.
(And, in case the situation is truly at its most dire:)
5. St. Jude: patron saint of hopeless causes.

9:30am-12:30pm and 3:30-6:30pm, Su 10am-1pm. Closed Su Jan.-Feb.) **Banks** line C. Dante, including **Unicredit Banca,** C. Dante 26, with a branch in P. Italia, both with **ATMs** and currency exchange. (Open M-F 8:20am-1:20pm and 2:30-4pm, Sa 8:20am-12:45pm.) The **public library,** located on V. Maggiorino Ferraris, off V. Crenna, offers **Internet access.** (☎0144 77 02 67. Open in summer M and Th 8:30am-1:30pm and 4-6pm, Tu-W and F 8:30am-1pm, Sa 9am-noon; in winter M and Th 2:30-6pm, Tu-W and F 8:30am-12:30pm, Sa 9am-noon.) In an emergency, call ☎112. For health-specific emergencies, call ☎118. There's a **pharmacy** at P. Italia 2. (Open M-F and Su 8:45am-12:30pm and 3-6:45pm. MC/V.) The **hospital, Ospedale Civile,** is located at V. Fatebenefratelli 1 (☎0144 77 71). **Internet** is available at **Internet Cafe Balalah,** on V. Giacomo Bove off V. Garibaldi. (☎0144 32 54 19. Open Tu-Sa 7:30am-9pm, Su 3-9pm.) Take V. XX Settembre from P. Italia through P. Matteotti to the **post office,** V. Trucco 27. (☎0144 38 21 11. Open M-F 8am-7pm, Sa 9am-12:30pm.) **Postal Code:** 15011.

▐ ACCOMMODATIONS. Reserve in advance during the thermal bath rush of the second half of August and much of September. Many hotels, budget and otherwise, line Vle. Einaudi behind the station and across the Ponte Carlo Alberto. For an affordable, centrally located hotel, head to ▨**Albergo San Marco** ❸, V. Ghione 5. From P. Italia, take C. Bagni and make the first right on V. Ghione. Comfortable and spacious rooms with TV are well kept by a welcoming staff. A restaurant is downstairs. (☎0144 32 24 56; fax 35 64 65. Half pension and full pension available. Free parking. Closed Dec. 24-Feb. 1 and mid-July. Singles €30-35; doubles €55. Cash only.) **Villa Glicinia** ❸, Vle. Einaudi 11, is a quiet and enormous pink accommodation outside of town, near the Centro Fitness Regina. The non-English-speaking management offers a homey living room and well-maintained guest rooms with large, pink bathrooms and antique furniture. (☎0144 32 28 74. Breakfast €3-5. Half and full pension available. Open May-Oct. Singles €36-38; doubles €50. Extra bed €13. Cash only.)

▐ FOOD. Acqui Terme offers a wide selection of excellent, well-priced restaurants, serving traditional Roman fare and lining the consequently fragrant V. Mazzini. ▨**Albergo San Marco's restaurant** ❷ serves some of the best home-cooked meals and stocks some of the best wine in town. There is no written menu, as the delightfully fresh offerings vary based on the chef's inclination. Don't skip the pasta—it may be the most exquisite you'll ever eat. (Primi €5-6.50. Secondi €6.50-9. Open Tu-Su noon-2pm and 7:30-10pm.) At the ◪**Enoteca Regionale Acqui "Terme e Vino" ❷**, P. Levi 7, off V. Garibaldi, choose from over 230 types of wine, including the local specialties *Dolcetto* and *Bracchetto*, from the shelves along the cavernous brick walls. (☎0144 77 02 73. Tastings €1. Open Tu and Th-Sa 9:30am-1pm and 3:30-7pm, Su 10am-1pm and 4-7pm. MC/V.) For fine dining, take C. Dante from P. Italia across V. Mariscotti to reach the white awnings of **Il Nuovo Ciarlocco ❸**, V. Don Bosco 1. Courteous service accompanies a high-quality fish and meat menu. (☎0144 57 720. Primi €7-8.50. Secondi €10-17. Cover €2.50. Open Tu-Sa noon-2pm and 7:30-10pm, Su noon-2pm. AmEx/MC/V.) At **Antica Osteria da Bigat ❶**, V. Mazzini 30/32, a town fixture since 1885, the crisp and exquisitely seasoned *farinata* (chickpea-flour pancake; €3) tempts hungry patrons. (☎0144 32 42 83. Pizza €3-4. Primi. Secondi €6.50-8. Open M and Th-Su noon-2pm and 5:30-9pm, Tu noon-2pm. Closed last 2 weeks of Feb. and July. MC/V.) **Il Sarto ❷**, C. Italia 97, serves food all day long and also provides practically the town's only nightlife option. The trendy leather couches and modern glass tables provide seating for drinking either beer (€3) or tea. (☎0144 32 27 65; www.ilsarto.eu. Open M-Tu and Th 8am-2am, F-Su 8am-3am. AmEx/MC/V.) The **DìperDì** supermarket, V. Garibaldi 50, sells groceries. (Open M-Tu and Th-Sa 8:30am-12:30pm and 3:45-7:45pm, W 8:30am-12:30pm, Su 9am-12:30pm. AmEx/MC/V.) Every Tuesday and Friday morning from 8:30am to 1pm, a **market** fills the *centro storico* around P. Addolorata, C. Italia, and P. Ferraris. During the same time, vendors hawk fruit, vegetables, cheese, and fish products in P. Orfo S. Pietro and P. S. Franceso. A bustling **antique market** is held on the fourth Sunday of every month along C. Bagni (9am-7pm).

◪ **SIGHTS.** Down V. Garibaldi, P. Addolorata is home to the 11th-century restored Romanesque **Basilica di San Pietro e Addolorata;** its floor is located at the same land elevation as the pre-Christian temple that previously occupied the site. (☎0144 32 27 91. Open daily 7am-noon and 3-6pm.) From P. Bollente, take V. Bollente across town and up a hill to P. Duomo, where the **Cattedrale di Santa Maria Assunta** (1067) holds Bartolomeo Bermejo's famous 15th-century triptych of *Madonna our Lady of Montserrat* in its **sacristy.** In the late 18th century, the masterpiece was spared by Napoleon's troops because they found the triptych closed. Look closely—the Madonna is seated on the blade of a sword. (Cathedral open M-Sa 7-11:30am and 3-6pm, Su 3-6pm. Sacristy open daily 4-6pm. Ask church caretaker at the sacristy to view the triptych. Free.) Up V. Barone from the *duomo*, the 11th-century **Castello dei Paleologi**, V. Morelli 2, houses the **Museo Civico Archeologico.** The museum displays a small but allusive collection of Roman tombs and mosaics. More evocative is the view of the town and surrounding hillsides from the park. (☎0144 57 555; www.acquimusei.it/archeo. Open W-Sa 9:30am-12:30pm and 3:30-6:30pm, Su 3:30-6:30pm. €5, ages 18-25 €3, under 18 or over 65 free. Park open from dawn until dusk. Free.)

No trip to Acqui is complete without dipping at least a toe in the steamy sulfuric water. Beneath the marble chapel in **Piazza Bollente** (from C. Italia, enter through the Torre Civica), hot water streams out from a fountain, sending up visible steam even in summer. P. Bollente is the former site of the Jewish ghetto, pulled down between 1870 and 1880 and transformed into the city's civic center. The beautiful law courts are located in Acqui's former synagogue. To see where four arches of the ◪**Roman Aqueduct** overlook the banks of the Bormida River, exit P. Italia, part of Pisterna's medieval *centro*, by taking C. Bagni through Borgonuova. The view is otherworldly at night, when the arches are illuminated with strategically placed spotlights. Though the Roman public baths are gone, you can still see the ruins along C. Bagni. (Open Sa-Su

PIEDMONT AND VALLE D'AOSTA

3:30-5:30pm) The **Grand Hotel Nuove Terme,** P. Italia 1, has a spa right near the town center which offers thermal baths (sulfur content is weak, but detectable) and a Turkish bath, among other services. (€13; hair net, robe, and locker €10.) The **Terme Regina,** V. Donati 2, in the *zona bagni*, offers many options for pampering, as well as serious alternative medicine. A dip in the **sulfuric pool** with hydro massage runs as little as €18 per day. (☎0144 32 90 74; www.reginaterme. com. Open M-F 10am-9pm, Sa-Su 10am-6pm. Reservations recommended.) To bathe in non-sulfuric water, head down the street to the enormous **Piscine di Acqui Terme,** a public pool equipped with trampolines, a bar, and a beach volleyball court. (☎0144 32 20 65. Open June-Sept. daily 9am-6:30pm. €6.50-8.50.) Next door to the **Museo Civico Archeologico,** off P. della Conciliazione, the outdoor **Teatro Estivo Giuseppe Verdi** hosts performances in summer, including the **Acqui in Palcoscenico** international dance festival in July and early August. (Contact tourist office for info and schedules. €15, students €10; some events free.)

VALLE D'AOSTA

Stunning peaks, pine forests, waterfalls, and tiny villages color Italy's least-populated and most-elevated region, Valle d'Aosta (VA-leh da-OS-ta). The valley is a key transportation hub; Hannibal and his elephants once traversed Aosta's St. Bernard Pass, and today an even greater stampede of heavy-goods vehicles barrel through the Monte Bianco tunnel. Some locals fear that Aosta's status as a trade gateway damages the natural splendor and destabilizes the tourist economy. Before the tractor trailers and even before the skiers, Aosta welcomed elites seeking hot springs and alpine freshness. Living so close to their Swiss and French neighbors, *valdostani* take on much of their continental cousins' cultural character, evident at intersections of a *via* with a *rue* or *Strasse*. Though not the Italy of the popular imagination, Valle d'Aosta's unique setting and culture, its relative seclusion from the masses, and the stunning Alps make it the perfect destination to taste Alpine glory.

⚑ HIKING

The scenic trails of Valle d'Aosta are a hiker's paradise: whether day hiking or taking a longer trip, they offer a unique opportunity to see Northern Italy's pristine peaks up close and personal. Hiking is the least expensive of Aosta's outdoor pursuits, as most other activities require expensive package deals or group outings organized by professionals. The best time to hike is between July and the first week of September, when much of the snow has melted and public buses run frequently. In April and May, thawing snow can cause avalanches. Monte Bianco and surrounding peaks are classic climbs, but only pros should attempt them. Because of the snow, spring hiking should only occur below 1000m. Each area's tourist office or Alpine guide office assists hikers of all levels with suggested itineraries and info on weather and trail conditions. Offices in Aosta and in the smaller valleys also provide details on campgrounds, *pranzo al sacco* (bagged lunches), *rifugi alpini* (mountain refuges or chalets overseen by a proprietor, which offer filling meals and dorm rooms; €15-20 per night, half pension €35-40), and *bivacchi* (empty public huts)—ask for *Mountain Huts and Bivouacs in Aosta Valley*, which offers a list of accommodations and prices. For information, call the guide societies in the appropriate valleys or the tourist office. They offer insurance and *rifugi* discounts. For explorations on foot, most regional tourist offices also carry the booklet *Alta Vie* (High Roads), with maps, photographs, hiking recommendations, and helpful advice

Valle d'Aosta

SWITZERLAND

PIEDMONT

FRANCE

LAUSANNE (112km)

Biella

Ivrea

TURIN (55km)

Alagna Valsèsia

Monte Rosa 4637m

Mt. Cervino (Matterhorn) 4478m

Gressoney-la-Trinité

Val di Gressoney

Gaby

Pont-Saint-Martin

Dora Baltea

Breuil-Cervinia

St. Jacques

Gressoney St. Jean

Masognaz

Valle d'Ayas

Champoluc

Antagnod

Brusson

Verrès

Valtournenche

Saint Vincent

Châtillon

Parco Naturale del Monte Avic

Alte Valle

Fenis

Grand Eyvia

Lake Place Moulin

Nus

Quart

Dora Baltea

Valpelline

Saint Christophe

Cogne

Val di Cogne

Oyace Ollomont

Valpelline

Aosta

Sarre

Grand Eyvia

Valnontey

Saint-Oyen Etroubles

Valle del Gran San Bernardo

Gran Paradiso 4061m

Parco Nazionale del Gran Paradiso

Val Savarenche

Pont

Saint-Rhémy

Morgex

Rhêmes St. Georges

Punta Helbronner (3462m) Rifugio Torino (3375m)

Pavillon du (2173m) Mont Fréty

Dora di Rhêmes

Val di Rhêmes

Courmayeur

La Palud

Pré-Saint-Didier

Rhêmes Notre-Dame

Valgrisenche

Valsrisenche

Chamonix

Plan de l'Aiguille (2137m)

Aiguille du Midi (3842m)

Dora di Ferret

Val Ferret

La Thuile

Lake Beauregard

Mt. Blanc (Monte Bianco) 4807m

Val Veny

Mt. Fortin 2753m

Mt. Percé 2844m

Dora di Verney

A5

A5

26

26

26

26

27

21

11

pertaining to the two serpentine mountain trails that wind around the valley and link the region's most dramatic peaks. These trails require no expertise, but still offer adventure and beautiful panoramas. Beginning in Cogne, **Parco Nazionale del Gran Paradiso** is also nearby. This park, replete with *rifugi*, is paradise for any outdoor enthusiast. Its endless hiking, skiing, and climbing possibilities could even serve as an entire vacation on their own.

⛷ SKIING

Skiing Valle d'Aosta's mountains and glaciers is a fantastic experience; unfortunately, doing so isn't cheap. One-week **Settimane Bianche** (White Weeks) packages for skiers are one source of discounts. For info and prices, call the **Aosta Ufficio Informazioni Turistiche** (☎0165 23 66 27; www.regione.vda.it/turismo) or go to the AIAT Aosta office, P. Chanoux 45 (☎0165 33 352; www.aiataosta. com), and request the pamphlet *White Weeks: Aosta Valley*, detailing skiing packages (from €168-210), hotels, prices, and tourist office info. Or contact the tourist offices of the ski resorts directly: **Courmayeur** (☎0165 84 20 60; www.aiat-monte-bianco.com) and **Breuil-Cervinia** (☎0166 94 91 36; www.montecervino. it) are the best-known ski resorts in the 11 valleys, though **Val d'Ayas** (☎0125 30 71 13; www.aiatmonterosa.com) and **Val di Gressoney** (☎0125 35 51 85) offer equally challenging terrain for lower rates with a joint pass. **Cogne** (☎0165 74 040; www.cogne.org) and **Brusson** (☎0125 30 02 40), halfway down Val d'Ayas, have cross-country skiing and less demanding trails. Pick up descriptions and maps of all resorts at most tourist offices in the region.

⚠ OUTDOOR SPORTS

A host of activities—rock climbing, biking, hang-gliding, hydrospeeding, and rafting—will keep your adrenaline rushing in the valleys. Rafting and other water expeditions are available from many companies. For a full list, contact the tourist office. One unique program put on by **Rafting: Morgex & Valsesia** (☎0165 80 00 88) offers 8km of rafting from (3 to 6pm), then gives access to the thermal baths until the 10pm closing. (☎1065 86 72 72. June-Sept M-F €49-72.) Run by a band of Argentine brothers, **Rafting Adventure**, Località Perole, to the right off the A5 "Chatillon" exit, offers rafting, hydrospeeding, canyoning, and kayaking. (☎346 30 90 856; www.raftingadventure.com. Guides available in English, French, and Spanish upon request. Reservations recommended. Open May-Sept. M-Su 9am-7pm. Rafting packages from €40 for 2hr.; kayaking and hydrospeeding from €50; canyoning from €60. Cash only.) On the road to Cogne, **Grand Paradis Emotions**, in Aymavilles, also offers rafting, kayaking, and canyoning. (☎0165 90 06 05; www.gpemotion.com. Call ahead to reserve. Open June-Sept. daily 9am-6:30pm. Packages for rafting or hydrospeeding €40, canyoning €60. Cash only.) The **Società delle Guide** in most cities around the valley arranges ice- and rock-climbing lessons and excursions, as well as mountain biking trips. Ask a local tourist office for a complete list of recreational activities. Near the Aosta airport, **Club Aerostatique Mont Blanc** flies hot air balloons up to over the Alps. (☎339 85 26 950. 1hr. flight €180 per person; to France or Switzerland €500. Call ahead to reserve.) Take the ▣funicular (20-30min.) at the **Pila Ski Resort** for amazing mountain biking. One trail even runs from the top of Pila's lift all the way to Aosta, a descent of over 1000m. (☎0165 52 10 45 or 0165 52 10 55; www.pila.it. Chairlift pass €11 per ½-day, €16 per day.)

AOSTA   ☎ 0165

Aosta (ah-OS-ta; pop. 37,000) straddles the line between Italian and French *valdostana* cultures. For many years, Aosta was ancient Rome's launching point for military expeditions. Boutiques and food shops now pack the *centro storico*, but even here you can admire the jagged peaks and their frosty caps. Within the walls that once defended the imperial Alpine outpost.

◩ TRANSPORTATION

Trains: In P. Manzetti. Ticket window open M-Th 7:20am-2pm and 2:15-5:25pm, F-Sa 6:15am-7:40pm, Su 11:30am-6:10pm. MC/V.) Trains run to: **Turin** (2hr., 14 per day 5:10am-9:41pm, €7.35) via **Châtillon** (20min., €2.10); **Chivasso** (2hr., 5 trains per day, €5.10); **Ivrea** (1hr., 5 per day 6:12am-5:12pm, €4.10); **Milan Centrale** via **Chivasso** (4hr., 12 per day 5:10am-8:40pm, €11.20); **Pré-Saint-Didier** (1hr., 14 per day 6:41am-7:46pm, €2.70); **Verrès** (30min., €3).

Buses: (☎0165 26 20 27; www.savda.it), on V. Carrel off P. Manzetti, to the right exiting the train station. Office open daily 6:40am-7:20pm. Tickets also available on bus. To: **Chamonix** (1hr., 6 per day 8:15am-4:45pm, €14.40); **Châtillon** (30min.; 5:30am, 1:35, 3:15, 5:40, and 8pm; €2.60); **Courmayeur** (1hr., every hr. 6:45am-9:45pm, €3); **Great St. Bernard Pass** (1hr., in summer 2 per day, €3); **Turin** (2-3 per day, €80). Regional buses serve **Cogne** (1hr., 7 per day 8:05am-7:45pm, €3) and **Fenis** (1hr.; 12 per day 6:20am-8pm, reduced service Su; €2.70). Buses also leave from the Châtillon train station for **Breuil-Cervinia** and **Valtournenche**. Local buses are orange and are operated by **SVAP** (www.svap.it). Tickets can be purchased onboard.

Taxis: P. Manzetti (☎0165 36 36 23 or 31 831).

Car Rental: Europcar, P. Manzetti 3 (☎0165 41 432), to the left of the train station. 18+. Open M-F 8:30am-12:30pm and 3-7pm, Sa 8:30am-12:30am. AmEx/MC/V.

Bike and Ski Rental: Gal Sport Shop, V. Paravera 6/B, 3rd fl. (☎0165 23 61 34; shop@galsport.com), past the funicular base. Open M-Sa 9am-12:30pm and 3-7pm. MC/V.

CONNECTION PERFECTION. Aosta makes a good base for exploring the Italian Alps, but be aware that daytrips to surrounding valleys often require tricky train and bus connections, so plan carefully.

Taxis: P. Manzetti (☎0165 36 36 23 or 31 831).

Car Rental: Europcar, P. Manzetti 3 (☎0165 41 432), to the left of the train station. 18+. Open M-F 8:30am-12:30pm and 3-7pm, Sa 8:30am-12:30am. AmEx/MC/V.

Bike and Ski Rental: Gal Sport Shop, V. Paravera 6/B, 3rd fl. (☎0165 23 61 34; shop@galsport.com), past the funicular base station. Offers bike rentals and sells equipment. Open M-Sa 9am-12:30pm and 3-7pm. MC/V.

◩◪ ORIENTATION AND PRACTICAL INFORMATION

Trains stop at **Piazza Manzetti.** From there, take **Avenue du Conseil des Commis** past the ruins of the Roman wall until it ends in the enormous **Piazza Chanoux,** Aosta's *centro.* The main street runs east-west through P. Chanoux. Running east it changes its name from **Via de Tillier** to **Via Aubert;** running west, **Via Porta Praetoria** leads to the historical gate, **Porta Praetoria** (and becomes **Via Sant'Anselmo**).

Tourist Office: P. Chanoux 2 (☎0165 23 66 27; www.aiataosta.com), down Ave. du Conseil des Commis from train station. Provides town maps, maps of the valley, accommodations booking, and art guides. English spoken. Open July-Sept. daily 9am-1pm and

PIEDMONT AND VALLE D'AOSTA

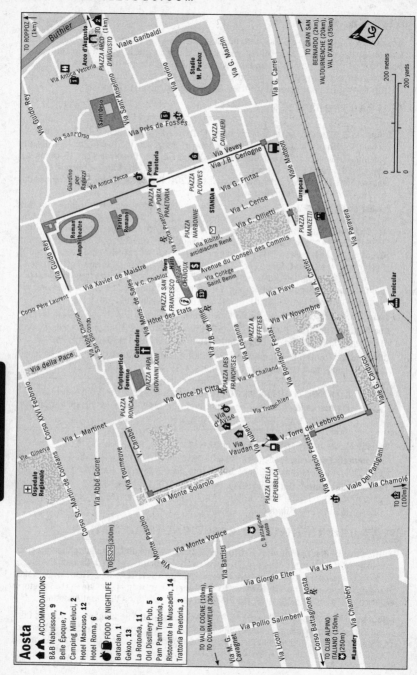

Aosta

ACCOMMODATIONS
B&B Nabuisson, 9
Belle Époque, 7
Camping Milleluci, 2
Hotel Mancuso, 12
Hotel Roma, 6

FOOD & NIGHTLIFE
Bataclan, 1
Gekoo, 13
La Rotonda, 11
Old Distillery Pub, 5
Pam Pam Trattoria, 8
Ristorante la Muscadin, 14
Trattoria Praetoria, 3

2:30-8pm; Oct.-June M-Sa 9:30am-1pm and 3-6:30pm, Su 9am-1pm. **Branch:** P. Arco d'Augusto, across from the Roman arch, offering info only on the city of Aosta itself. In winter, a tourist office opens in **Pila**, at 11020 Gressan, near the top of the funicular.

Alpine Information: Club Alpino Italiano, C. Battaglione Aosta 81, 3rd fl. (☎/fax 0165 40 194; www.caivda.it), off P. della Repubblica. Open Tu 7-8:30pm, F 8-10pm. **Interguide,** V. Monte Emilius 13 (☎0165 40 939; www.interguide.it).

Tours: Associazione Guide Turistiche (☎0165 338 695 1558; www.guideturisticheval-dostane.it). Guided group tours.

Currency Exchange: Monte dei Paschi di Siena, P. Chanoux 51 (☎0165 27 68 88). **ATM** outside. Open M-F 8:30am-1:30pm and 2:40-4:10pm. Another ATM at post office.

Laundromat: Onda Blu, V. Chambéry 60. Wash and dry €8. Detergent €1, softener €0.50. Snack machines on premises. Open daily 8am-10pm.

Police: at C. Battaglione Aosta (☎0165 27 91 11).

Pharmacy: Farmacia Chenal, V. Croix-de-Ville 1 (☎0165 26 21 33), near V. Aubert. Posts after-hours rotations. MC/V.

Hospital: Vle. Ginevra 3 (☎0165 54 31).

Internet: Public Library, V. Torre del Lebroso 2 (☎0165 27 48 43). Reserve ahead. Open M 2-7pm, Tu-Sa 9am-7pm. **Aosta Web Service Internet Point** (☎0165 06 00 15), at C. Padre Lorenzo and C. XXVI Febbraio. Open M-Sa 9am-10pm and Su 2-10pm.

Post Office: P. Narbonne 1a (☎0165 27 62 11), in the huge semi-circular building. Open M-F 8am-6:30pm, Sa 8am-1pm. **Postal Code:** 11100.

🏠 🏠 ACCOMMODATIONS AND CAMPING

Prices vary seasonally in Aosta. Rates are lowest from January to April and from October to mid-December, and highest in early August and around Christmas. The **Valle d'Aosta Pass,** managed by the Association of Hoteliers of Aosta Valley, allows you to book hotels online or by phone for free with at least two days advance notice. (☎0165 23 00 15; www.valledaostapass.com.)

Bed & Breakfast Nabuisson, V. Aubert 50 (☎0165 36 30 06 or 339 609 0332; www. bedbreakfastaosta.it). In a building through the iron gate under the arch between the *tabaccheria* and *libreria*. Near the *centro*. 2 large, rustic-themed rooms have wooden floors, antique furniture, TV, and bath. 1 has kitchen. Breakfast €4. Reservations recommended. Doubles €50-65. Extra bed €10-15. Cash only. ❹

Belle Époque, V. d'Avise 18 (☎0165 26 22 76; fax 26 11 56). Central location and affordable price partially compensate for small rooms. Breakfast €6.50. Singles €22-26; doubles €50-60; triples €65-85. MC/V. ❸

Hotel Mancuso, V. Voison 32 (☎0165 34 526; www.albergomancuso.com). 15min. walk from P. Chanoux. Affordable, clean rooms have great views, bathroom, TV, and hair dryer; some with balcony. Free parking. Singles €30-40; doubles €38-48; triples €55-60; quads €65-70. Let's Go discount 10%. ❷

Hotel Roma, V. Torino 7 (☎0165 41 000; hroma@libero.it), close to the train station and *centro*, around the corner from Hotel Turin (enter off Rue Vevey). Large, recently renovated rooms; all have bath, phone, and TV. Breakfast €6. Parking €6. Singles €40-54; doubles €68-76. Extra bed 30% surcharge. AmEx/MC/V. ❹

Camping Milleluci, Località Roppoz 15 (☎0165 23 52 78; www.campingmilleluci.com), a 1km hike from station. Reception in Hotel Milleluci. Each site has a cabin connected to a trailer. Quiet location with great views. Most crowded June-Sept. Laundry €5. €8-10 per person, €5-7 per child under 10; €15 per tent; €15 per RV. Showers free. Free access to swimming pool. Free electricity. AmEx/MC/V. ❶

FOOD

Aosta's cold climate and predominantly agricultural lifestyle have created unique cuisine. *Fonduta*, a cheese sauce made from the local *fontina*, usually served with toast, is a local specialty. Regional wines include *blanc de morgex* and *pinot gris*. Pick up local varieties of *fontina* and groceries at **STANDA**, on V. Festaz 10. (☎0165 35 757. Open M-Sa 8am-8pm, Su 9am-1pm and 3:30-7:30pm. AmEx/D/MC/V.) A Tuesday **market** is in P. Cavalieri di V. Veneto.

Pam Pam Trattoria, V. Maillet 5/7 (☎0165 40 960). Romantic trattoria tucked in a centrally located ivy-festooned lane. Rustic fare presented with elegance. Try the *polenta grassa* (polenta with butter and *fontina;* €7.50). Primi €7.50-9. Secondi €8-18. Open Tu-Sa 12:30-2pm and 7:30-10pm. AmEx/MC/V. ❸

Trattoria Praetoria, V. Sant'Anselmo 9 (☎0165 44 356), past Pta. Praetoria. A calm trattoria with a rotating menu that frequently includes the delicious *fonduta valdostana* (cheese fondue with toast; €10) or the *crespelle alla valdostana* (French crepe layered with cured ham and baked cheese; €7.50). Primi €7-10. Secondi €6.50-15. Cover €1.50. Open in summer daily 12:15-2:30pm and 7:15-9:30pm; in winter M-Tu and Sa-Su 12:15-2:30pm and 7:15-9:30pm, W and F 12:15-2:30pm. AmEx/MC/V. ❷

Ristorante la Muscadin, V. Torino 23 (☎0165 363 119). For one of the best values in town, opt for their special *menù,* which includes 2 courses, wine, coffee, and dessert (€10). Open M-F noon-2:30pm, Sa noon-2:30pm and 8-10pm. ❷

La Rotonda, Vle. dei Partigiani 30 (☎0165 43 927). Overwhelmingly large portions at low prices keep the large restaurant full and lively. Beer and wine from €2. Pizza €4.50-6. Primi €5-6.50. Secondi €5.50-11. Cover €1.10. Open M-Tu and Th-Su noon-2:30pm and 6:30pm-midnight. AmEx/MC/V. ❷

⊙ SIGHTS

Vestiges of the Roman Empire are thoroughly integrated with modern Aosta; a partially intact, 2000-year-old wall surrounds the *centro,* and modern streets run neatly through its gaps. The **Porta Praetoria,** on the street bearing its name, once served as a guard house. To its left lie the remains of the massive **Teatro Romano.** (Open daily Apr.-Aug. 9am-8pm; Sept. and Mar. 9am-7pm; Oct. and Feb. 9am-6:30pm; Nov.-Jan. 9am-5pm. Free.) Through Pta. Praetoria, V. Sant'Anselmo leads to the **Arco d'Augusto,** built in 25 BC. The monument has sported a hanging Christian cross inside the arch since the Middle Ages. Between Pta. Praetoria and Arco d'Augusto, the renowned **Complex of Sant'Orso** includes the Collegiate Church of Saints Pietro and Orso, the *campanile,* and the cloister. (Open daily July-Aug. 9am-8pm; Oct.-Feb. 10am-12:30pm and 1:30-5pm; Mar.-June 9am-7pm. Free.) **Museo Archeologico,** P. Roncas, has a model of the old town and info on its history. (☎0165 27 59 02. Open daily 9am-7pm. Free.) The ruins of the ancient forum, **Criptoportico Forense,** are off P. Papa Giovanni XXIII. Because the forum has not been excavated, there is not actually much to tour here. (☎0165 27 59 11. Open Apr.-Sept. 2-6pm; Nov.-Feb. 2-5pm upon request. Free.)

▓ NIGHTLIFE

▓ **Gekoo,** P. Chanoux 28 (☎0165 36 14 45; www.myspace.com/gekooaosta). Picnic tables, ski lift benches, and an old Volkswagen van compete for prominence in the quirky but somehow gimmick-free interior. Frequent parties and concerts in the *piazza.* Try their signature drink, a *Caipiroska* with violet syrup (€4). Open Tu-Su 4pm-1am.

▓ **Bataclan,** P. Arco d'Augusto 40 (☎0165 36 39 21; www.bataclan.it). One of the town's newest and most popular nightlife establishments. Lounge upstairs beneath the stars, or order a bottle of wine from a candlelit table while listening to live jazz in a grass court-yard. Staff all play instruments and keep them around, so live music may break out at any time. Primi €7-9. Secondi €12-16. Open Tu-Su 12:30-3pm and 7:15pm-12:30am. Kitchen open 12:30-3pm and 7:15-11pm; pizza available until closing. MC/V.

Old Distillery Pub, V. des Prés Fossés 7 (☎0165 23 95 11; www.olddistillerypub.com). From Pta. Praetoria, walk down V. S. Anselmo and turn right on V. des Prés Fossés. A Scottish-themed local favorite. Beamish €5 per pint. Open daily 6pm-2am.

FESTIVALS

The **Fiera di Sant'Orso,** the region's 2000-year-old craft fair, takes place January 30-31 and the second weekend of August in the *centro storico* between P. Arco d'Augusto and P. della Repubblica (open 8am-6pm). The heart of the fair is **L'Atelier,** P. Chanoux, where local craftsmen typically offer demonstrations. The schedule changes annually, so ask at the tourist office.

▶ DAYTRIPS FROM AOSTA

VALTOURNENCHE: THE MATTERHORN AND BREUIL-CERVINIA

SAVDA buses (☎0166 94 90 54, www.savda.it) run to Breuil-Cervinia (1hr., 9 per day 6:10am-7:25pm, €2.60) from Châtillon, on the Aosta-Turin line. Once in Chatillon, exit the train station and walk up the road for 15min. until you come to the circular building that marks the bus stop. Buses run daily from Milan's P. Castello (5hr.) and from Breuil-Cervina to Turin (4hr.; M-Sa 3 per day, Su 1 per day; €7.80).

The most famous mountain in Switzerland, the **Matterhorn (Il Cervino)** looms majestically over the Italian town of **Breuil-Cervinia** in Valtournenche. Despite high costs in this heavily touristed area, fresh-air fiends consider it a small price for the chance to climb up the glaciers of one of the world's most spectac-ular mountains. A funicular services **Plateau Rosà,** where die-hard skiers tackle the slopes in bathing suits for ✪**summer skiing.** (July-Sept. 7-11am. €24 per day, students and children €18; 2-day pass €40/25. Combo pass with slopes in Zer-matt, Switzerland €38/19 per day, 2-day €71/36.) Most hiking trails start near the funicular. Follow **Trail 15** for a day hike with breathtaking views between two waterfalls beneath the Matterhorn (1-2hr.; follow Trail 13 when the trails part). Hikers can also attempt the 3hr. ascent to **Colle Superiore delle Cime Bianche** on Trail 16 (2982m), with views of Val d'Ayas to the east and the Cervino glacier to the west. A shorter trek (1hr.) on the same trail leads to **Lake Goillet.** In Breuil-Cervinia, the Monte Cervino **tourist office,** V. Carrel 29, is off highway A5 next to a Total gas station by the Châtillon Exit; follow signs for the Info Exit. The English-speaking staff has detailed maps and itineraries, as well as info on the winter *Settimana Bianca* (White Week) packages and *Settimane Estive,* the summer equivalent. (☎0166 94 91 36 or 94 44 11; www.cervinia.it. Open high season daily 9am-6pm; low season 9am-12:30pm and 2-5:30pm.) The **Società Guide** (☎0166 94 81 69), across from the tourist office, arranges outings.

 HIKE SMART. Don't forget your passport on hiking excursions; many trails enter Switzerland.

VAL D'AYAS

Trains run from Aosta to Verrès (30min.; 6:20am, 2:20, 10:15pm; €2.45). SAVDA buses run from the train station at Verrès to Champoluc (1hr.; 6 per day 8:55am-12:25am, 6 returns per day 6:50am-5:30pm; €2.10), as do VITA buses (☎0125 96 65 46; 1hr., 9 per day 7:12am-9:22pm). VITA also runs between Val d'Ayas towns (6:27am-11:04pm). When entering Champoluc, look for the tourist office, V. Varase 16, on the right side of the main road. It may be difficult to identify with signs; look for 5 flags flying above the wooden lodge. It has accommodations info and trail maps. (☎0125 30 71 13; infoayas@ aiatmonterosa.com. Open daily 9am-12:30pm and 3-6pm.)

Budget-minded sports enthusiasts should visit the gently sloping Val d'Ayas, which offers the cheapest **skiing** in the region at **Monterosa Ski Resort.** (☎0125 30 31 68; www.monterosa-ski.com. Open M-F 8:30am-noon and 1-5:30pm. Dec. 19-Apr. 2 €33 per day, children €24; start of season to Dec. 18 and Apr. 3-19 €27/20.) The small town of **Saint Jacques** is the last along the valley road and offers the most **hiking** trails. This should be your departure point if you plan to stay in one of the many *refugi*. The town of **Champoluc** offers the most tourist amenities; the tourist office here should be your stop to plan out any excursions from the valley. An easy hike is the 45min. **Trail #14** from Champoluc to the hamlet of **Mascognaz,** home to a farming population of 10, the charming **Capella di San Grato,** and an excellent restaurant. **Trail #105** wanders over rocks and through pastures to the impressive ▧**Mount Zerbion** (2700m). A 360° panorama displays the soaring Five Giants: the **Matterhorn, Mont Blanc, Monte Rosa, Grand Combin,** and **Gran Paradiso.** Expert hikers may try the **Walser Trail,** staying overnight in tents and following the path of the Germanic migration through Champoluc, Gressoney, St. Jacques, and Valtournenche. For the best views of the valley, turn left after Champoluc and follow the road up the hill to **Antagnod,** which has numerous B&Bs along the steep slope and its own ski lift. **Rafting** is a great way to enjoy the scenery. **Totem Adventure,** Route Mont Blanc 4, has €40-60 packages. (☎0165 87 677; www.totemadventure.com. Reservations recommended. Open July-Aug. daily 8:30am-7:30pm. Cash only.)

COURMAYEUR   ☎0165

Italy's oldest Alpine resort lures tourists to the spectacular shadows of Europe's highest peak. French Mt. Blanc (known in Italy as Monte Bianco), with its jagged ridges and snowy fields, is perfect for hiking and skiing. Unfortunately, attractions often cater to the elegant vacationing styles of Europe's rich. However, in May and June, when the snow has melted, quiet descends upon Courmayeur (coor-ma-YUHR; pop. 2800), leaving a sleepy little town surrounded by the beautiful peaks that provide its raison d'être.

🚍🚶 **TRANSPORTATION AND PRACTICAL INFORMATION.** A single large complex, the **Centro Congressi Courmayeur,** in **Piazzale Monte Bianco,** houses most travel services, including the **bus station. Buses** run to Aosta (1hr.; every hr. 6:45-9:55pm; €3.10, round-trip €5.30), Milan (4hr.; 3-4 per day; €16, round-trip €29), and Turin (3hr.; M-F 6:45 and 9:45am, Sa-Su 6:45am; €9.30, round-trip €15.80). SAVDA and SADAEM buses, Ple. Monte Bianco 3, buses have frequent service to larger towns. (☎0165 84 20 31 or 84 13 97. Office open daily July-Aug. 8am-7:30pm; Sept.-June 8:45am-12:30pm and 2-7pm. Tickets also sold onboard.) **Taxis** (☎0165 84 29 60) are available 24hr. at Ple. M. Bianco. Pick up a map from the multilingual staff at the **AIAT tourist office,** Ple. M. Bianco 13 (☎0165 84 20 60; www.aiat-monte-bianco.com. Open M-Sa 9am-12:30pm and 3-6:30pm, Su 9am-noon and 3-6pm.) An accommodations board, next to the office, can also help you find a room. (Open Tu-Sa 9am-12:30pm and 3-6:30pm, Su 9am-noon and 3-6pm.). Free **Wi-Fi** is available at the **Cafe des Guides,** though in order to use it, you must be able to register a mobile number; you will receive your access code via text message. The bus station ticket office has currency exchange, as does the **San Paolo Istituto Bancario di Torino,** P. Brocherel 1, which also has an **ATM.** (☎0165 84 20 23. Open M-F 8:25am-1:25pm and 2:40-4:10pm.) In case of **emergency,** go to the **police,**

Strada della Margherita 8. A **pharmacy,** V. Circonvallazione 69, posts after-hours rotations. (Open M-F 9am-12:30pm and 3-7:30pm, Sa 9am-12:30pm and 3:30-7:30pm. MC/V.) The **post office** is at Ple. M. Bianco 5, behind the main complex. It also offers currency exchange. (☎0165 84 08 11. Open M-F 8am-1:30pm, Sa 8am-12:30pm.**Postal Code:** 11013.

🛏🍴 **ACCOMMODATIONS AND FOOD.** You can't book accommodations far enough ahead, especially if you are hoping to be in Courmayeur for snow season. While hotels abound in Courmayeur, most are expensive without being luxurious. **Pensione Venezia ❸**, Strada delle Villete 2, is by far the best deal in town. From Ple. M. Bianco, head uphill, then left on V. Circonvallazione. This centrally located chalet with rustic rooms, shared bathroom, and TV lounge. (☎/fax 0165 84 24 61. Breakfast included. Singles €35; doubles €46; triples €69. Cash only.) For slightly pricier digs, try the **Hotel Croux ❺**, V. Croux 8, with a convenient location and flowered window-boxes that make it a stand-out. (☎0165 846 735; www.hotelcroux.it. Singles €68-88; doubles €108-135. AmEx/MC/V.)

🍝**Pastificio Gabriella ❶**, Passaggio dell'Angelo 2, at the end of V. Roma, has freshly made sides, breads, pastries, pasta, and sauces. It's the perfect place to pack for a picnic in the shadow of Mt. Bianco. (☎0165 84 33 59. Open July-Aug. daily 8am-12:45pm and 4-7:30pm; Sept.-June M-Tu and Th-Su 8am-12:45pm and 4-7:30pm. MC/V.) Off-piste skiers recharge in the center of town at **Cafe des Guides ❶**, Vle. Monte Bianco 2, below the Società delle Guide. (☎0165 84 24 35. Panini €4-5. Beer €5-6. Mixed drinks €6-8. Cover €1. Free Wi-Fi for those with text messaging services. Open daily 7:30am-2:30am. Cash only.) **Petit Bistrot ❶**, V. Marconi 6, whips up cheap crepes in a city with few budget eateries. (☎0165 347 508 4158. Crepes €4 for takeout, €6.50 inside. Open 11:30am-midnight. Cash only.) Many restaurants close in summer, but **La Terraza ❺**, V. Circonvallazione 73, stays open year-round. Uphill from Ple. Monte Bianco, it specializes in *valdostano* cuisine, like fondue with chestnuts and honey. (☎0165 84 33 30; www.ristorantelaterrazza.com. Pizza €7-12. Primi €12-14. Secondi €17-30. Cover €3. Open daily noon–2:15pm and 7pm-late. MC/V.)

🏔⛷ **OUTDOOR ACTIVITIES AND SKIING. Courmayeur Ski Resort** is famous for its scenic downhill runs, off-piste itineraries, and cross-country offerings (info ☎0165 84 20 60, downhill tickets ☎0165 84 66 58, cross country tickets ☎0165 86 98 12.

High season is Dec. 19-Apr. 2. In high season ski passes €41 per day, €224 per week; inquire at the tourist office for the most up-to-date prices.) The brochure Settimane Bianche lists rental prices and often offers discounts. **Buses** also run to **Pré-Saint-Didier** (15min., 8 per day 7:55am-7:15pm, €1.20), which has thermal baths. Pré-Saint-Didier then connects to **La Thuile** (20min., 11 per day 7:55am-8:40pm, €1.20), another ski resort with 150km of intermediate and expert downhill trails and five cross-country skiing tracks.

Buses run from Courmayeur to the trailheads in **Val Veny** and **Val Ferret,** which branch in opposite directions along the base of Monte Bianco. Inquire at the tourist office for a *Valdigne Mont-Blanc: Les Sentiers* map and the brochure *Seven Itineraries around Mont Blanc, Val Veny, and Val Ferret.* The most popular hike in Val Veny is the 1hr. path past the Lac du Miage to **Refuge Elisabetta** (2197m). In Val Ferret, the two short hikes to the **Refuge Bonatti** (2150m) from Lavachey (45min.) and to the **Refuge Elena** (2055m) from Arp Nouva (40min.) make for a relaxing trip. Several trailheads can be accessed directly from Courmayeur. An excellent place to ask questions is **Società delle Guide di Courmayeur,** Strada Villair 2, to the left behind the church. Since 1850, the office has been providing free advice to hikers and finding guides for all major treks and climbs. This headquarters also houses a small museum with photos and exhibits of the original society of mountain guides, established in 1850. (☎0165 84 20 64; guidecourmayeur@tiscali.it. Open in summer M-Tu and Th-Su 9am-noon and 4-7pm, W 4-7pm; in winter Tu-Su 9am-7pm. Museum €3, children €1.50.) A number of excellent **biking** trails traverse Monte Bianco. **Scott Center,** Ple. M. Bianco 15 (☎0165 84 82 54), runs a ski-school and ski-rentals during the winter. During the summer, it becomes **Sirdar** (☎0165 346 578 9776; www.sirdar-montagne.com), and organizes hiking and biking trips.

To explore Monte Bianco, use the ⬛**Funivie Monte Bianco** (☎0165 89 925; www.montebianco.com). *Funivie* depart from **La Palud,** which is accessible by bus from Courmayeur's Ple. Monte Bianco (10min., 8:30am-4:20pm, €1). Head first to the glacier terrace at **Punta Helbronner** (3462m), then across the border to **Aiguille du Midi** (3842m), then to **Chamonix** (1030m). You can take the funicular to La Palud and then to Punta Helbronner, Italy's highest point (round-trip €36; €17 surcharge to continue to Chamonix in summer). In winter, Chamonix is reachable by skiing with a guide. Punta Helbronner affords views of Monte Bianco and the **Matterhorn, Monte Rosa,** and **Gran Paradiso National Park.**

LIGURIA

Liguria (lih-GOO-ree-ah), which stretches along 350km of the Italian riviera, is home to terraced hillsides, the Apennine Mountains, vineyards, and lush olive groves. Every restaurant boasts the best *frutti di mare* (seafood) and *pesto alla Genovese* (sauce made of basil, pine nuts, and garlic), and rarely do they exaggerate. With trains chugging along the coast, Liguria is easy to explore. Stroll through winding streets lined with colorful houses and elaborately painted architectural in Portofino, trek the coastal cliffs of Cinque Terre, and gaze at Caravaggio masterpieces in Genoa's *Palazzo Bianco*. No matter your destination in Liguria, trade that pair of Italian leather shoes for flip flops and follow the locals' lead through this laid-back vacation oasis.

HIGHLIGHTS OF LIGURIA

TRAIPSE among the villas of Genoa's Via Garibaldi, the "Golden Street" (p. 202).

TREK the trails that connect the colorful towns of the Cinque Terre (p. 210).

BEACH BUM with classy Italians on the sandy shores of the Alassio coast (p. 224).

DOUBLE your money in San Remo's casino, a turn-of-the-century gem (p. 228).

GENOA (GENOVA)   ☎010

As any Genovese will proclaim, *"Si deve conoscerla per amarla"*—you have to know Genoa to love her. A city of grit and grandeur, Genoa (JEH-no-va; pop. 600,000) has little in common with neighboring beach towns, except of course impeccable focaccia and pesto. The ugly port and large monuments are the most apparent features of the city, but much of central Genoa is a hidden maze—the narrow, tangled *vicoli* by the port are full of stores, churches,

197

and charm. The world-famous aquarium and the nearby miniscule fishing village of Boccadasse (where people still speak *zenese*, an Italian dialect) attract travelers in the know, but truth be told, most Italians will look at you funny if you say you spent time in Genoa on purpose. Like, for fun. So most travelers just pass through, using the city as a base for exploring the spectacular Ligurian coast. Those who do stick around come to appreciate Genoa as the historic port whose rich intellectual history, financial success, and distinctive culture may just have the rest of Italy a little bit jealous. And we're not just saying that. This place has class.

TRANSPORTATION

Flights: Cristoforo Colombo Internazionale (☎010 60 151), in Sesti Ponente, sends flights to European destinations. **Volabus #100** runs to the airport from Stazione Principe (every hr. 5:40am-10:40pm, €4.50).

Trains: Stazione Principe, in P. Acquaverde, and **Stazione Brignole,** in P. Verdi. Trains (5min., every 15min., €1.40) and buses #18, 19, 20, 33, and 37 (25min., €1.20) connect the 2 stations. Both offer **luggage storage** (☎010 27 43 4 63). €3.80 for 1st hr., €0.60 per additional hr. for 12hr., €0.20 per hr. thereafter. Open 7am-11pm. Cash only. Ticket validation good for 1hr. Open daily 7am-11pm. Trains run from stations to points along the Riviera and major Italian cities including **Rome** (5-6hr., 10 per day, €27.50) and **Turin** (2hr., every 20-30min., €8-12).

Ferries: At Ponte Assereto arm of the port. Take bus #20 from Stazione Principe or bus #1 from the aquarium. Purchase tickets at travel agency or Stazione Marittima. Arrive at Terminal Traghetti Ponte Assereto at least 1hr. before departure. Tirrenia (☎010 08 13 17 29 99; www.tirrenia.it) runs ferries to **Sardinia.** Grandi Navi Veloci (☎010 20 94 591; www.gnv.it) heads to **Sardinia, Sicily, Spain,** and **Tunisia.** EnerRmaR (☎010 11 97 60 003) goes to **Olbia** and **Palau.** Moby lines (☎010 19 93 03 040; www.moby.it) runs to **Olbia, Bastia,** and **Porto Torres**.

Public Transport: AMT (☎010 80 00 85 311) buses leave from V. Gramsci, in front of the aquarium, or Stazione Brignole. 1-way tickets within the city €1.60. Day passes €4. Passport required for foreigners. Tickets also valid for funicular and elevator rides.

Taxis: (☎010 59 66). From P. de Ferrari.

 BUS IT. Though the *centro* is compact, many of Genoa's sights are just beyond a comfortable walking distance. City buses are a frequent and convenient alternative. A 24hr. pass with unlimited rides is just €3.50; if you're traveling with friends, pick up a 24hr. pass for 3 for just €7. Longer stays merit the €12 week long pass with unlimited rides.

ORIENTATION AND PRACTICAL INFORMATION

Genoa has two train stations: **Stazione Principe,** in P. Acquaverde, and **Stazione Brignole,** in P. Verdi. From Stazione Principe take bus #18, 19, or 30, and from Stazione Brignole take bus #19 or 40 to **Piazza de Ferrari** in the center of town. To walk to P. de Ferrari from Stazione Principe, take **Via Balbi** to **Via Cairoli,** which becomes **Via Garibaldi,** and at **Piazza delle Fontane Marose** turn right on **Via XXV Aprile.** From Stazione Brignole, turn right out of the station, left on **Via Fiume,** and right onto **Via XX Settembre,** ending in P. de Ferrari. To get to the **Porto Antico** from P. de Ferrari, take V. Boetto to **Piazza Giacomo Matteoti,** and follow **Via di San Lorenzo** to the water. Genoa's streets stump even natives, so pick up a map.

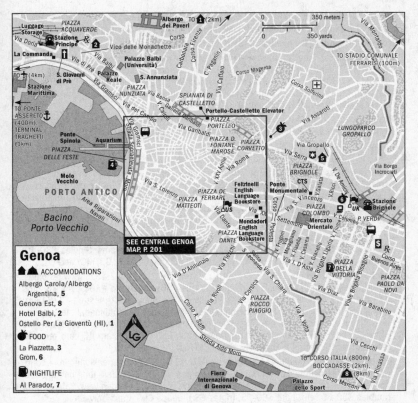

Genoa

🔺🔺 ACCOMMODATIONS

Albergo Carola/Albergo
    Argentina, **5**
Genova Est, **8**
Hotel Balbi, **2**
Ostello Per La Gioventù (HI), **1**

🍴 FOOD
La Piazzetta, **3**
Grom, **6**

🎵 NIGHTLIFE
Al Parador, **7**

Tourist Offices: GenovaInforma, Palazzo Ducale, P. G. Matteoti (☎010 86 87 452).
Open daily 9am-1pm and 2-6pm. **Kiosks** in Stazione Principe (☎010 24 62 633), and
airport (☎010 60 15 247). Both open M-Sa 9:30am-1pm and 2:30-6pm.

Budget Travel: CTS, V. S. Vincenzo 117r (☎010 56 43 66 or 53 27 48), off V. XX Settembre, near Ponte Monumentale. Walk up 1 flight of stairs at the shopping complex to
the left. Student fares available. Open M-F 9:30am-6:15pm. MC/V.

Consulates: UK, P. Guiseppe Verdi 6/A (☎010 57 40 071; fax 53 04 096). Take bus #30
(dir.: Sampierdarena) from Stazione Principe to last stop. Open M-Th 9:30am-12:30pm.
US, V. Dante 2, 3rd fl., 43 (☎010 58 44 92). Open M-Th 11am-3pm.

Beyond Tourism: Informagiovani, Palazzo Ducale, P. G. Matteotti 24r (☎010 55 73 952
or 55 73 965; www.informagiovani.comune.genova.it). Youth center offers info on apartment rentals, jobs, volunteer opportunities, and concerts. Free **Internet** access (1hr.
limit). Open M-F 9am-1pm and Tu-Th 2-5:30pm.

English-Language Bookstore: Mondadori, V. XX Settembre 210r (☎010 58 41 40).
Huge, with a full wall of classics and some bestsellers. Open M-Sa 9am-8pm, Su
10:30am-1pm and 4:30-8pm. AmEx/MC/V. For a larger selection, check out **Feltrinelli,**
V. XX Settembre 231. (Open M-Sa 9:30am-8pm, Su 10am-1pm and 4-8pm. MC/V.)

Pharmacy: Pescetto, V. Balbi 185r (☎010 26 16 09), near Stazione Principe. After-
hours rotation posted outside. Open M-F 7:30am-12:30pm and 3:30pm-midnight,

Sa-Su 8pm-midnight. AmEx/MC/V. **Farmacia Ghersi,** C. Buenos Aires 18r, across town. Open M-F midnight-12:30pm and 3:30pm-midnight, Sa-Su 7:30pm-midnight. MC/V.

Hospital: Ospedale Evangelico, C. Solferino 1a (☎010 55 221).

Internet Access: Free at **Informagiovani** (see **Beyond Tourism** above). **Number One Bar/Cafe,** P. Verdi 21r (☎010 54 18 85), near Stazione Brignole. €4 per hr. Open M-Sa 7:30am-11:30pm. MC/V. **In-Centro.it Agenzia Viaggi,** V. Roccatagliata Ceccardi 14r, between V. Dante and V. XX Settembre. €3 per hr., students €2.50. Also a bookstore and travel agency. Open M 3-7:30pm, Tu-Sa 9:15am-7:30pm. MC/V.

Post Office: P. Dante 4/6r (☎010 25 94 687). 2 blocks from P. de Ferrari. *Fermoposta* available. Open M-F 8am-6:30pm, Sa 8am-1:30pm. **Postal Code:** 16121.

🏠 🏕 ACCOMMODATIONS AND CAMPING

Rooms are scarce in October, when the city hosts a wave of nautical conventions. Some budget lodgings in the *centro storico* and near the port rent rooms by the hour for reasons best left uninvestigated. Establishments are more refined around Stazione Brignole and P. Corvetto. The area around Genoa offers plenty of campgrounds, but they fill up in summer, so book ahead.

Albergo Argentina, V. Gropallo 4 (☎/fax 010 83 93 722), near Stazione Brignole, 2 flights down from Albergo Carola. 9 large, clean, comfortable rooms. Singles €30-40; doubles €50-65, with bath €60-75; triples €75-90; quads €85-100. MC/V. ❷

Ostello Per La Gioventù (HI), V. Costanzi 120 (☎/fax 010 24 22 457; www.geocities. com/hostelge). From Stazione Principe, take bus #35; transfer to #40 at the 1st stop on V. Napoli. From Stazione Brignole, take bus #40 (evening #640; last bus 12:50am) 30min. all the way up the hill. Cafeteria, free lockers, and TV. Multilingual staff. Breakfast included. Laundry €7 per 5kg. Wheelchair-accessible. Reception 7-11:30am and 3pm-12:30am. Check-out 10am. Lock-out 10am-3pm. Curfew 2am. HI card required (sold at hostel). Dorms €16; family rooms €16-20 per person. ❶

Albergo Carola, V. Gropallo 4/12, 3rd fl. (☎010 83 91 340; www.pensionecarola.com), near Stazione Brignole. Look for big doors with lion heads on the left. Ring bell to enter. English-speaking staff and 9 rooms with soft beds, some with garden view. Singles €30; doubles €50-65, with bath €60-75; triples €80; quads €90. Cash only. ❸

Hotel Balbi, V. Balbi 21/3 (☎/fax 010 27 59 288), close to Stazione Principe. Beyond the unpromising exterior stairwell lie spacious, comfortable rooms and a well-stocked bar and TV area. All rooms with bath. Breakfast included. Internet access €4 per hr. Singles €65; doubles €80; triples €110; quads €125. AmEx/MC/V. ❺

Genova Est (☎010 34 72 053; www.camping-genova-est.it), on V. Marconi, Località Cassa. Take the train from Stazione Brignole to the suburb of Bogliasco (10min., 6 per day, €1.70); from here, take the free van (5min., every 2hr. 8am-7:50pm) to the campground. While getting there may seem daunting, the campground's website provides train and bus schedules. Shaded sites overlook the sea, with clean bathroom facilities. Laundry €3.50 per load. €6 per person; €5.60-8.60 per tent. Electricity €2.20. ❶

 JESUS! THOSE PRICES ARE HIGH. For travelers visiting Genoa during Easter, be aware: prices jump for most accommodations.

🍴 FOOD

A dish prepared *alla Genovese* is served with Genoa's pride and joy—pesto. The *genovesi* put it on just about everything and claim that Ligurian water is why true pesto can only be made from basil in this region of Italy. Other

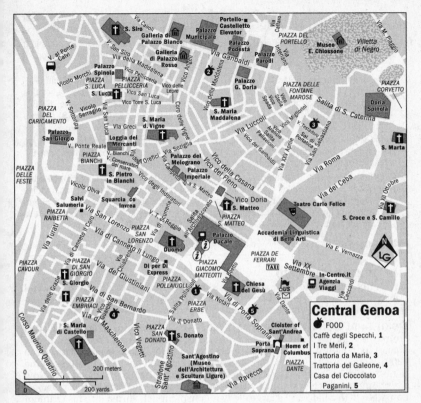

Central Genoa

🍎 FOOD

Caffè degli Specchi, 1
I Tre Merli, 2
Trattoria da Maria, 3
Trattoria del Galeone, 4
Casa del Cioccolato
Paganini, 5

delectables include *farinata* (a fried, chickpea flour pancake), focaccia filled with cheese, and *pansotti* (ravioli stuffed with spinach and ricotta in a creamy walnut sauce). To sample a slice of Genoa's famous salami or pick up a jar of pesto, stop by **Salvi Salumeria,** V. di S. Lorenzo 2, near Porto Antico. Also, don't forget to sample the fresh seafood sold along the port-side arcade. For groceries, head to **DiperDì Express,** V. di Canneto Il Lungo 108-112. From P. Matteotti go down Salita Pollaioli, take a right onto V. di Canneto Il Lungo; the supermarket is on the right. (Open M-Sa 8am-7:45pm, Su 9am-1pm and 4-7pm. MC/V.)

▧ **Trattoria da Maria,** V. Testadoro 14r (☎010 58 10 80), near P. delle Fontane Marose, off V. XXV Aprile. Typical Italian restaurant with checkered tablecloths and a faithful lunch crowd. Outgoing staff serves fresh, delicious dishes of the day. *Menù* includes primo, and secondo, and drink (€9). Open M-Sa 11:45am-3pm. MC/V. ➋

▧ **I Tre Merli,** V. della Maddalena 26r (☎010 24 74 095), on a narrow street off V. Garibaldi. A hidden gem with soft music and a mellow atmosphere. Impeccable service and delicious food make the price well worth it. Wine connoisseurs take note—the list is 16 pages long and very well compiled. Primi €10-12. Secondi €14-16. Open M-F 12:30-3pm and 7:30-11pm, Sa 7:30-11pm. AmEx/MC/V. ➍

Trattoria del Galeone, V. di S. Bernardo 55r (☎010 24 68 422). From P. G. Matteoti, take Salita Pollaiuoli, and turn right on V. di S. Bernardo. Galeone is 100m up on the left.

Nautically themed dining rooms are crowded with lively yet somewhat older locals. Primi €5-6. Secondi €7-11. Open M-Sa 12:30-2:30pm and 7:30-10pm. Cash only. ❷

La Piazzetta, V. Calatafimi 9 (☎010 87 70 28), off P. Marsala. Convenient location in a quiet *piazza* offers Ligurian specials on an outdoor wooden deck. Primi €8-15. Secondi €11-15. Open M-F 12:30-3pm and 7:30-11pm, Sa 7:30pm-midnight. MC/V. ❸

Caffè degli Specchi, Salita Pollaiuoli 43r (☎24 68 193), on the left, down Salita Pollaiuoli from P. G. Matteotti. *Specchio* means mirror, and narcissists will surely enjoy this sophisticated, mirror-lined cafe. The crowds enjoy *bicchierini* (glasses of wine; €3.60) or mixed drinks (€5-5.50) at pleasant outdoor seating. Mini *panini* (€1.50-3) make a tasty snack. Open M-F 7am-9pm, Sa 8am-9pm. AmEx/MC/V. ❶

Grom, V. S. Vincenzo 53r (☎010 56 54 20; www.grom.it), near Stazione Brignole. All you ever wanted gelato to be, made daily with fresh ingredients. Cups and cones from €2. Open M-Th and Su 10am-10pm, F-Sa 10am-midnight. Cash only. ❶

Casa del Cioccolato Paganini, V. di Porta Soprana 45r (☎010 25 13 662). Like the composer of its namesake, the chocolate here just might draw tears of passion. Indulge in unique homemade sweets, from Niccolo Paganini chocolate (boxes from €6.50) to signature *sciroppo di rosa,* a sublime liquid made from sugar, water, and rose petals (€7.30 per bottle). Open M-Sa 12:30-7:30pm. AmEx/V/MC. ❶

🜨 SIGHTS

THE CENTRO STORICO

The eerily beautiful *centro storico* is a mass of narrow, winding streets and cobblestone alleyways bordered by **Porto Antico, Via Garibaldi,** and **Piazza de Ferrari.** Remember that walking alone after hours in the *centro storico* is unsafe.

🜨CHIESA DI SANTA MARIA DI CASTELLO. With foundations from 500 BC, this church is a labyrinth of chapels, courtyards, cloisters, and crucifixes. In the chapel to the left of the high altar looms the spooky **Crocifisso Miracoloso** (circa 1200). According to legend, the wooden Jesus moved his head to attest to the honesty of a damsel betrayed by her lover, and his beard is still said to grow every time a crisis hits the city. To see the painting of **San Pietro Martire di Verona,** complete with a halo and a large cleaver conspicuously thrust into his cranium (the handiwork of incensed adversaries), go up the stairs to the right of the high altar, turn right, and right again. Go through the doorway and turn around. The painting is above the door. After walking through the door, check out the famous **L'Annunciazione** by Jost di Favensburg (circa 1400) on the right. The real beauty of this sight, though, comes with wandering up stairwells, down porticoes, and through courtyard gardens; there is far more to this church than initially meets the eye. *(From P. G. Matteotti, head up V. di S. Lorenzo toward the water and turn left on V. Chiabrera. A left on serpentine V. di Mascherona leads to the church in P. Caricamento. Open daily 9am-noon and 3:30-6:30pm. Closed Su during masses. Free.)*

🜨PALAZZO SPINOLA DI PELLICCERIA. Built at the end of the 16th century, this *palazzo* once hosted Peter Paul Rubens, who described it warmly in a 1622 book on pleasing palaces. Today it houses the **Galleria Nazionale,** a collection of art and furnishings, most donated by the family of Maddalena Doria Spinola. The building tells its own compelling history, as different sections represent architectural styles from throughout the ages. The 18th-century kitchen simulation is particularly intriguing, with a lit stove and flour on the countertop. The museum also contains enormous maps of the world drawn during different eras of exploration, highlighting Genoa's importance in seafaring and cartography of the past. The fourth floor displays Antonello da Messina's 1460 masterpiece *Ecce Homo,* and Van Dyck's portraits of the evangelists reside on the second floor. *(P. di Pellicceria 1, between V. Maddalena and P. S. Luca. ☎010 27 05 300. Open Tu-Sa 8:30am-7:30pm, Su 1:30-7:30pm. €4, ages 18-25 €2.)*

> **TROUBLE IN PARADISE.** Though most of Genoa's crime problems are a thing of the past, travelers should avoid **Via di Prè** entirely and be especially cautious in the area around **Via della Maddalena**. At night, or on weekends when stores are closed, the **centro storico** is also dangerous.

▓**PORTA SOPRANA.** The city's gate was built in 1115 to intimidate Genoa's enemies. The Porta is both the historical centerpiece of P. Dante and the passageway from the modern *piazza* into the *centro storico*. Would-be assailant Emperor Federico Barbarossa took one look at the arch, whose Latin inscription welcomes all coming in peace but proclaims doom to enemy armies, and abandoned his attack. Christopher Columbus's boyhood **home** lies nearby, alongside the remains of the Cloister of St. Andrew's Church. *(From P. G. Matteotti, head down V. di Porta Soprana. ☎010 25 16 714. Porta and Columbus's home open daily 10am-6pm. Porta €4, home €4; both €7. Cash only.)*

DUOMO (SAN LORENZO). The *duomo* was reconstructed between the 12th and 16th centuries after religious authorities deemed it "imperfect and deformed." The result may have been an improvement, but it sure wasn't symmetrical; because only one of the two planned bell towers was completed, the church has a lopsided appearance. Climb the completed *campanile* (bell tower) for dizzying city views. On the left in the church, the golden **Cappella di San Giovanni** houses a relic from St. John the Baptist. *(In P. S. Lorenzo, off V. di S. Lorenzo. Open daily 9am-noon and 3-6pm. Guided tour every 30min. Modest dress required. Tickets for campanile sold M-Sa in Museo del Tesoro on left side of church. Campanile €5.50, duomo free. Cash only.)*

CHIESA DEL GESÙ. Also known as **Sant'Andrea e Ambrogio,** this former Jesuit church, completed in 1606, houses two Rubens canvases: *The Circumcision* over the altar and *The Miracle of St. Ignatius* in the third alcove on the left. *(From P. de Ferrari, take V. Boetto to P. G. Matteotti. Open M-Sa 7am-12:45pm and 4-7:30pm, Su 8am-12:45pm and 5-9:45pm. Closed Su during masses 7:15, 10, 11am, noon, 6:30pm. Free.)*

PALAZZO DUCALE. The majestic centerpiece of the *centro storico*, this *palazzo* was constructed in 1290 as the seat of Genoa's government. The neoclassical facade was completed a few years before the end of the Republic of Genoa in 1797 by architect Simone Cantoni, while the interior is done up in Rococo decor. Visit the **museum** on the second floor for rotating exhibits of international artwork. *(P. G. Matteotti 9. ☎010 55 74 000; www.palazzoducale.genova.it. Museum open Tu-Su 9am-7pm. Ticket office closes at 6:30pm. €7, students €6. AmEx/MC/V.)*

FROM STAZIONE PRINCIPE TO THE CENTRO STORICO

Outside the winding alleys of the *centro storico*, Genoa boasts a multitude of *palazzi*, many of which have been converted to museums that showcase 16th- and 17th-century Flemish and Italian art. **Via Garibaldi,** which skirts the edge of the *centro storico*, and **Via Balbi,** which runs through the university quarter from Stazione Principe to P. Nunziata, offer the best city views.

PALAZZO REALE. Built in the 15th century, this *palazzo* was originally home to the Balbi family. It became the Royal Palace in 1823. The *piemontese* Rococo throne room, covered in red velvet, remains untouched, along with the royal waiting room and sleeping quarters. The resplendent **Galleria degli Specchi** is modeled after the Hall of Mirrors at Versailles. In the queen's bedroom, the **queen's clock** is really a *notturlabio*, a clock with stenciled numbers lit from behind by a candle. Don't miss the spectacular view from the *palazzo*'s terrace, off Room 22. To see paintings by Tintoretto, Van Dyck, and Bassano, ascend the red-carpeted stairs on the left after purchasing a ticket. *(V. Balbi 10. 5min. walk west of V. Garibaldi. ☎ 010 27 10 236; www.palazzorealegenova.it. Open Tu-W 9am-1:30pm, Th-Su 9am-7pm. Entrances on the ½hr. €4, ages 18-25 €2, under 18 or over 65 free. Cash only.)*

AQUARIUM. Genoa's most elaborate tourist attraction has the most water of any European aquarium. Wander the exhibits, then board **Grande Nave Blu,** a huge barge filled with habitat recreations, from the forests of Madagascar to the Caribbean reefs. There's also a touch tank with sea rays. Guides offer multilingual "Behind the Scenes" tours. *(On Porto Antico, across from tourist kiosk. ☎ 010 23 45 666; www.acquariodigenova.it. Open July-Aug. daily 9am-11pm; Mar.-June and Sept.-Oct. M-F 9:30am-7:30pm, Sa-Su 9am-8:30pm; Nov.-Feb. daily 9:30am-7:30pm. Last entry 1hr. before closing. Various entrance packages, starting at €20. Discounts for groups and children. AmEx/MC/V.)*

VIA GARIBALDI. The most impressive street in Genoa, V. Garibaldi deserves its nickname, *Via Aurea* (Golden Street). In the 17th century, wealthy families lined the way with elegant palaces. Today, the **Palazzi** have been converted into a series of museums that give the paintings center stage. **Galleria di Palazzo Rosso,** built in the 16th century, earned its name when it was painted red a century later. Red carpets cover the floors of exhibit halls that feature several hundred years' worth of *genovese* ceramics. The second floor now holds several Van Dyck portraits of nobility. Across the street, the **Galleria di Palazzo Bianco** exhibits a large collection of Ligurian art. The third floor contains Van Dyck's *Red-Eyed Christ*, as well as works by Caravaggio, Rubens, and Vasari. Several doors down lies **Palazzo Tursi** (also known as the **Palazzo Municipale**). The former home of the Savoy monarchy built between 1565 and 1579, now serves as the city hall and showcases a courtyard and Niccolo Paganini's violin, *Il Cannone*, made by the legendary Giuseppe Guarneri. This instrument is still played by the winner of Premio Paganini, an international violin competition held annually on October 12. *(Galleria di Palazzo Rosso: V. Garibaldi 18. Galleria di Palazzo Bianco: V. Garibaldi 11. Palazzo Tursi: V. Garibaldi 9. All 3 sights ☎ 010 27 59 185. Open Tu-F 9am-7pm, Sa-Su 10am-7pm. Ticket office, V. Garibaldi 9, open daily 9am-8pm. Admission to all 3 museums covered by single ticket. €8, €6 students and seniors, under 18 free. AmEx/MC/V.)*

PORTELLO-CASTELLETTO ELEVATOR. Walk down the tunnel in P. Portello to ride this elevator with locals, who take it as regularly as the bus. A plaque in the entrance tunnel quotes Giorgio Caproni: *"Quando mi sarò deciso d'andarci, in paradiso ci andrò con l'ascensore di Castelletto."* ("When I have decided to go there, in paradise I will go with the elevator of Castelletto.") The 30-second ride, which connects the *centro storico* with neighborhoods in surrounding hills, leads commuters to perfect panoramas one step closer to paradise. *(Through the tunnel entrance in P. Portello. Open daily 6:40am-midnight. Single-use tickets can be purchased for €0.50 from machines at the entrance to the elevator or from newsstands nearby.)*

PORTO ANTICO. Genoa's enormous port yields a mixture of fascinating history and commercial bustle. The port is sectioned into several wharves. The oldest, 15th-century **Molo Vecchio**, on the far left facing the water, is home to Genoa's former cotton warehouses as well as a movie theater and restaurants. The central *Quartieri Antichi* (historical districts) still hold some 16th-century bond houses. Nearby Ponte Spinola is the site of Genoa's famed **aquarium,** and the adjacent **Piazza del Caricamento** is lined with fruit and produce vendors.

VILLETTA DI NEGRO. This relaxing park offers waterfalls, grottoes, and terraced gardens. *(From P. delle Fontane Marose, take Salita di S. Caterina to P. Corvetto. Entrance along V. Piaggio. Open daily 8am-dusk.)*

LIGURIA

ART-STARVED? If you plan on visiting many museums, invest in a museum pass. The 24hr. pass (€9), covers Palazzo Reale and Palazzo Spinola, while the 2-day pass (€16, €20 including bus fare) covers every museum in Genoa. Purchase passes at the tourist office or participating museums.

🎵 🎭 ENTERTAINMENT AND NIGHTLIFE

Genoa's new **Cineplex**, V. Magazzini de' Cotone, at Molo Vecchio, shows American movies dubbed in Italian. (☎010 89 90 30 820; www.cineplex.it. Box office open M-F 4-10:30pm, Sa 2:15pm-1am, Su 2-11:30pm. Tickets €7.30, matinees €5.) A walk farther down the port, to the end of the pier, reveals myriad wine bars which offer views of the highly commercial port and surprisingly cheap glasses of wine. As with most bars, to get the cheapest price, order at the bar rather than sitting at a table. **Corso Italia** is a trendy promenade, home to much of Genoa's nightlife. A 20min. ride down the long boulevard on bus #31 leads to **Boccadasse**, a fishing village and seaside playground for wealthy *genovesi*. Unfortunately for tourists, many clubs are difficult to reach on foot, so travelers in Genoa often drive to reach their nightlife destinations. Local university students flock to bars in **Piazza delle Erbe** and along **Via San Bernardo**. Closer to Stazione Bringole, **Al Parador**, P. della Vittoria 49r, is located in the northeast corner of P. Vittoria, near the intersection of V. Cadorna and V. B. Liguria. Upscale bar by day, by night this watering hole is frequented by both real celebrities like Uma Thurman and Claudia Schiffer and the wannabes who idolize them. (☎010 58 17 71. Mixed drinks €4.50. Open M-Sa 24hr. Cash only.)

RIVIERA DI LEVANTE

CAMOGLI ☎0185

Lounge, eat, and hike your way to happiness in the postcard-perfect town of Camogli (ca-MOL-yee; pop. 5516). A warm breeze rises off the sea, diffusing the tempting smells of fried fresh seafood from the restaurants that line the promenade. Waitresses at beachside cafes wear bikinis and aprons. Less ritzy and more youth-friendly than nearby Portofino and Santa Margherita, Camogli is a gem in Liguria's aptly named Golfo Paradiso (Gulf of Paradise).

🚆 **TRANSPORTATION.** Camogli is on the Genoa-La Spezia train line. (Ticket office open M-Sa 6:15am-3pm, Su 10am-7pm.) **Trains** run to Genoa (40min., 2 per hr., €1.90); La Spezia (1hr., 1-2 per hr., €4.20) via Santa Margherita; (5min., every 30min., €1.40); and Sestri Levante (30min., every 30min., €3). Tigullio **buses** leave from P. Schiaffino for nearby towns. Buy tickets at the tourist office or at *tabaccherie*. Buses go to Santa Margherita (20min., 20 per day, €1.10), Rapallo, Ruta, and San Lorenzo. For Golfo Paradiso **ferries**, V. Scalo 2 (☎0185 77 20 91; www.golfoparadiso.it), look for the *"Servizio Batelli"* sign near P. Colombo by the water. Buy tickets at dock or on the ferry (cash only). Round-trip ferries go to Monterosso (July and Aug. Su, check at office for more info and summer specials; €20), Portofino (June 10-Sept. 5 Tu-Su depart morning, return late afternoon; €13), and San Fruttuoso (June-Sept. every hr. 8am-7pm, €9).

LIGURIA

⚞ ⚟ ORIENTATION AND PRACTICAL INFORMATION. Camogli extends uphill from the sea to pine and olive groves and downhill from the train station to the beach. To get to the **centro,** turn right out of the **train station** on **Via XX Settembre,** walk 100m, and turn left down the stairs to **Via Garibaldi.** Walk down a second flight, marked by the sign: "Scalinata Martiri delle Forbe" to reach the beach. Services include: the **tourist office,** V. XX Settembre 33 (☎0185 77 10 66; Internet access €1.50 per 30min; open in summer M-Sa 9am-12:30pm and 3-6:30pm, Su 9am-12:30pm); **Banco di Chiavari della Riviera Ligure,** V. XX Settembre 19 (☎0185 77 51 13; open M-Sa 8:20am-1:20pm and 2:30-4pm); **police,** G. B. Ferrari (☎0185 77 07 25); **carabinieri,** V. Cuneo 30/F (☎0185 77 00 00); a **pharmacy,** V. Repubblica 4-6 (☎0185 77 10 81; open daily July-Aug. 8:30am-12:30pm and 4-8pm; Sept.-June 3:30-7:30pm; MC/V); and the **post office,** V. Cuneo 4. (☎0185 77 68 31. Open M-F 8am-6:30, Sa 8am-12:30pm. Cash only.) **Postal Code:** 16032.

⚑ ACCOMMODATIONS. Prices and availability vary greatly according to season and day of the week. Though the tourist office can help with last-minute rooms, reserve ahead and be prepared to pay a higher price in summer. Renovated **⚞Hotel Augusta ❸,** V. Piero Schiaffino 100, has 14 blue and yellow rooms; all have bath, TV, A/C, and phone. Some overlook the harbor from private balconies. From the train station, turn right and keep walking until V. Repubblica turns into V. P. Schiaffino. (☎0185 77 05 92; www.htlaugusta.com. Breakfast included. Internet access free; limit 15min. Singles €40-78; doubles €55-115. AmEx/MC/V.) The **⚞Albergo La Camogliese ❹,** V. Garibaldi 55, is just steps from the beach. Exit train station, walk down the long stairway to the right, and look for the blue sign. Large rooms are as comfortable as the English-speaking staff is helpful. All have bath, TV, safe, and phone. (☎0185 77 14 02; www.lacamogliese.it. Breakfast included. Internet access available. Singles €50-90; doubles €70-110; triples €95-120. Extra bed €10. 10% discount with cash payment. AmEx/MC/V.) The **Pensione Faro ❹,** V. Schiaffino 116-118, above a restaurant of the same name, offers quiet rooms with bath, TV, and some sea views. (☎/fax 0185 77 14 00. Breakfast €4. Singles €40-50; doubles €60-80. AmEx/MC/V.)

⚞ FOOD. Focaccia is the specialty in Camogli, as is fresh seafood caught by local fishermen. **⚞Focacceria Pasticceria Revello ❶,** V. Garibaldi 183, is famous in the region for fresh, crispy flatbreads and delectable pastries. This shop invented the town's beloved *camogliesi* (dense and crumbly cookies; €21 per kg). Make like the locals and lunch on focaccia with onions or *formaggio.* (☎0185 77 07 77; www.revellocamogli.com. Focaccia €8.50 per kg. Open daily 8am-2pm and 4-8pm. MC/V.) **Il Portico Spaghetteria ❷,** V. Garibaldi 197A, offers creative pastas (€6.50-9.50) at excellent values that will satisfy every craving; try the *spaghetti alla carbonara.* (☎0185 77 02 54; www.ilporticodicamogli.it. Cover €1.50. Open daily 12:30-3pm; 8-11pm. Cash only.) The creamy gelato at **Gelato e Dintorni ❶,** V. Garibaldi 104/105, puts national rivals to shame. They specialize in parfaits made with creamy homemade yogurt and fresh fruit. (☎0185 77 43 53. 2 scoops €1.70. Sicilian *granita* €2. Open daily 11:30am-11pm. Cash only.) Find groceries and picnic supplies at shops on V. Repubblica (one block from the harbor) or at the **Picasso** supermarket, V. XX Settembre 35. Walk down the stairs immediately past the tourist office. (Open M-Sa 8:15am-12:30pm and 4:30-7:30pm, Su 8:30am-12:30pm. MC/V.) On Wednesdays, an **open-air market** fills P. del Teatro with local produce and cheap clothing. (Open 8am-noon.)

⚞ ⚟ OUTDOOR ACTIVITIES AND NIGHTLIFE. The Camogli tourist office has a useful **trail map.** Painted red shapes mark the paths, which start at the end of V. Cuneo near the *carabinieri* station. Bike paths line the city and rentals are

LIGURIA

available through the tourist office. Ferry or snorkeling trips also make inter-esting—if more costly—diversions. **B&B Diving Center,** V. S. Fortunato 11/13, off V. Schiaffino, offers scuba diving. (☎/fax 0185 77 27 51; www.bbdiving.it. Open daily June 15-Sept. 15 9am-1pm and 2:30-7:30pm; Sept. 16-June 14 9am-1pm and 3:30-7pm. 1-person canoe €17 per ½-day, 2-person €30 per ½-day. Scuba tours with guide and equipment Sa-Su 4 per day, €39; equipment only €18-23. 10-person boat capacity. Cash only.) The **Sagra del Pesce,** an enormous fish fry, is held annually on the second Sunday in May. The night before the big fry, the town gathers for a procession honoring the patron saint of fishermen, followed by a fireworks display and a bonfire-building contest on the beach. The next day the fryers cook in a gargantuan frying pan, which measures 4m in diameter and holds 2000 fish to feed the jolly crowd. After the sardine rush, the colossal pan hangs on a city wall along the stairs to the beach.

Spend nights in peaceful Camogli with a cool drink and a sea view. Order a mojito (€5.50) or sangria loaded with pineapple chunks (€4.50) to cap off the day at upscale **Il Barcollo,** V. Garibaldi 92. (☎0185 77 33 22. Open M-F 4pm-3am, Sa-Su 11am-3am. Cash only.) Down the boulevard is the pirate-themed **Hook,** V. al Porto 4, decorated like a ship's cabin and offering over 60 types of rum (€3.50-20) to wash down the good food. (☎0185 77 07 11. Panini €3-4. Happy hour 6-9pm; drinks €6. Open M, W, Su 8am-3am, Tu 6pm-3am. AmEx/MC/V.)

▌⚡ DAYTRIP FROM CAMOGLI: SAN FRUTTUOSO. The hikes from Camogli to tiny San Fruttuoso (san FROO-too-OH-so; pop. 8, 10 including dogs) fol-low two labeled trails that wind through Portofino's nature reserve. The easier 2hr. hike along **Trail #1,** marked by a red circle, climbs up and around Mt. Por-tofino through ancient forests and olive groves, with a descent to the harbor on a stone path that can be very slippery when wet. Only experts should ven-ture out on the 2hr. **Trail #2.** Marked by two red dots, Trail #2 winds along the coast past Nazi anti-aircraft bunkers and through forests to sea vistas before it descends into town. Proper footwear is essential.

San Fruttuoso is named for its abbey, the Benedictine **Abbazia di San Frut-tuoso di Capodimonte,** constructed during the 10th through 13th centuries. The monastery and tower rotate archaeological exhibits. *(☎0185 77 27 03. Abbazia open daily 10am-6:30pm. Tower open daily 10am-1pm and 2-5:30pm. Last entry 30min. before closing. €7, children €4.)* Fifteen meters offshore and 17m underwater, the bronze *Christ of the Depths* stands with arms upraised in memory of the sea's casual-ties. The statue now protects scuba divers, and a replica stands in **Chiesa di San Fruttuoso,** enticing visitors to make an offering to the *Sacrario dei Morti in Mare* (Sanctuary for the Dead at Sea). Friendly locals with small boats offer rides to the underwater statue from the docks for €2.50. *(San Fruttuoso is accessible by trails from Portofino Mare 1hr., Portofino Vetta 1hr., or Camogli 2hr. Golfo Paradiso (☎0185 77 20 91; www.golfoparadiso.it) runs boats from Camogli to San Fruttuoso in summer; Tu and Th-Sa every hr. 8am-5pm, last return 6-7pm; round-trip €9.)*

SANTA MARGHERITA LIGURE ☎0185

For the most part, Santa Margherita Ligure (SAN-ta Mar-ge-REE-ta LEE-goo-reh; pop. 10,210) leads a calm existence as a fishing village far from the Levante limelight. The little popularity it has stems from a *National Geographic* feature in the 50s, while the beachfront and palm-tree-lined harbor provides plenty of photo ops. As a resort town, every inch of the manicured coast boasts scenes of natural beauty situated between big-name fashion outlets.

LIGURIA

◪ TRANSPORTATION

Trains: on the Genoa-La Spezia line. To: **Genoa** (50min., €2.30) and **Monterosso** (1hr., €3.90). Ticket office is inside the station. Open daily 6am-7pm. MC/V.

Buses: Tigullio (☎0185 28 88 34) departs from the small green kiosk in P. Vittorio Veneto. To: **Camogli** (30min., every 45min., €1.30) and **Portofino** (20min., 3 per hr., €1). Ticket office open daily 7am-7pm. Tickets available after hours at the *tabaccheria*.

Ferries: Servizio Marittimo del Tigullio, V. Palestro 8/1B (☎0185 28 46 70; www. traghettiportofino.it). Docks at P. Martiri della Libertà. To: **Cinque Terre** (1st Su of May through last Su of Sept. 9am, round-trip €23) and **Portofino** (M-F every hour 10:15am-4:15pm, Sa-Su every hour 9:15am-5:15pm; €5, round-trip €8.50).

Taxis: in P. Stazione (☎0185 28 65 08) and on V. Pescino (☎0185 28 79 98).

◪ 🛈 ORIENTATION AND PRACTICAL INFORMATION

From the **train station,** turn right on **Via Roma,** and follow it along the water. At the end of the road turn left on **Corso E. Rainuso** to reach **Piazza Vittorio Veneto.** Turn right on V. Pescino, which winds around **Piazza Martiri della Libertà. Piazza Caprera** is between them set back from the water. From P. V. Veneto, V. Guglielmo Marconi winds around the port and V. XXV Aprile leads to the tourist office, becoming **Corso Matteotti** near the town's main square, **Piazza Mazzini.**

Tourist Office: Pro Loco tourist office, V. XXV Aprile 2/B (☎0185 28 78 17; www.santamargheritaturismo.it). Open M-Sa 9:30am-12:30pm and 3-7:30pm, Su 9:30am-12:30pm and 4:30-7:30pm. **info point,** P. Veneto. Open 10am-12:30pm and 3-5pm.

Police: P. Mazzini 46. ☎0185 20 54 50.

Pharmacy: Farmacia Dr Machi, V. Palestro 44 (☎0185 28 70 02), off P. Caprera. Posts after-hours rotation. Open M-W and F-Su 8:30am-12:30pm and 4-8pm. MC/V.

Hospital: V. Fratelli Arpe. ☎0185 68 31.

Internet Access: The Internet Point, V. Giuncheto 39 (☎0185 29 30 92; liguriacom@ tigullio.it). Follow V. Dogali from P. Mazzini; it's on the left. €2.50 per 20min. Open M-Sa 10am-1pm and 3-7:30pm. Cash only.

Post Office: V. Roma 36 (☎0185 29 47 51). Offers currency exchange, *fermoposta,* and an **ATM.** Open M-F 8am-6:30pm, Sa 8am-12:30pm. Cash only. **Postal Code:** 16038.

◪ ACCOMMODATIONS

Ritzy waterfront accommodations are by no means the only options, but be prepared to shell out a few more euro than usual in Santa Margherita. Luckily nothing is far from the beach.

▨ Hotel Conte Verde, V. Zara 1 (☎0185 28 71 39; www.hotelconteverde.it), off V. Roma. From train station turn left down V. Trieste, which becomes V. Roma. Cozy beds and private showers make for a truly heavenly stay. Gold tasseled pillows and other indulgent luxuries. Breakfast included. Singles €50-60, with bath €65-120; doubles €65-90/70-150; triples €90-120; quads €100-230. AmEx/MC/V. ❹

Hotel Nuova Riviera, V. Belvedere 10 (☎0185 28 74 03; www.nuovariviera.com). Run by an English-speaking family. Large, bright rooms decorated in the Victorian style all have private bath. Breakfast included for hotel rooms, €5 for annex rooms. Internet access €5 per 30min. Hotel singles €65-105; doubles €85-110, annex doubles €60-90; triples €75-110. Cash only for annex rooms; MC/V for hotel rooms. ❺

Albergo Annabella, V. Costasecca 10/1 (☎0185 28 65 31), behind P. Mazzini. Kind owner makes guests feel at home in comfortable rooms, some with bath. Breakfast €4. Singles €40-45; doubles €60; triples €80-90; quads €100-120. Cash only. ❹

Hotel Metropole, V. Pagana 2. Recently renovated, this 57-room hotel is located in a beautiful private garden. Rooms with A/C, TV, bath, safe, and minibar. Some rooms have balconies overlooking the water. Doubles €90-160. AmEx/MC/V. ❹

FOOD

Markets and bakeries line **Corso Matteotti;** pick up some focaccia for a cheap picnic lunch. Buy essentials at the **Coop,** C. Matteotti 8, off P. Mazzini. (☎0185 28 43 15. Open M-Sa 8:30am-1pm and 3:30-8pm, Su 8:30am-1pm. AmEx/MC/V.)

Trattoria Da Pezzi, V. Cavour 21 (☎0185 28 53 03). Locals descend on the famous trattoria for its home-style cuisine and jovial atmosphere. *Farinata* (€4.50) and *torta pasqualina* (pork quiche; €5.20-6) are great choices. Takeout available. Primi €4-7.50. Secondi €6-15. Cover €1. Open M-F and Su 10am-2:15pm and 5-9:15pm. MC/V. ❶

Trattoria Baicin, V. Algeria 5 (☎0185 28 67 63), is off P. Martiri della Libertà. Mama Carmela serves glorious plates of *spaghetti carbonara* (pasta in a cream sauce with chopped eggplant, peppers, capers, and garlic; €6.50). Primi €5.50-7.50. Secondi €9.50-16.50. Cover €1.50. Open Tu-Su noon-3pm and 7-11:30pm. AmEx/MC/V. ❸

La Locanda Azzura, V. S. Bernardo 3 (☎0185 28 53 94). From the shore, turn right off C. Matteotti. The *pansotti alla salsa di noci* (vegetable-filled pasta in walnut cream sauce; €7) is tough to beat. Primi €6-10. Secondi €8.50-18.50. Cover €2. Open M-Tu and Th-Su 12:10-2pm and 7:10-10:30pm. MC/V. ❸

L'Approdo, V. Cairoli 26 (☎0185 28 17 89). This place is worth the extra expense for its exquisite presentation and succulent dishes like shrimp scampi with peas (€28). Primi €12-17. Secondi €18-42. Cover €3. Open Tu 7:30pm-midnight, W-Su 12:30-2pm and 7:30pm-midnight. AmEx/MC/V. ❺

Gelateria Centrale, Largo Giusti 14 (☎0185 28 74 80). Crowds gather nightly for *pinguini* (€2.50), chocolate-dipped gelato cones. Open daily 9am-midnight. Cash only. ❶

SIGHTS AND NIGHTLIFE

If lapping waves at the pebbly public **beach** across from the main promenade, C. Doria, aren't sufficiently invigorating, visit the Rococo **Basilica di Santa Margherita,** in P. Caprera, dripping with gold and crystal chandeliers. The church also contains fine Flemish and Italian artwork commissioned by the Catholic Church. (☎0185 28 65 55. Open daily 7:30am-noon and 3-6:30pm.) Off V. della Vittoria, paths wind uphill to the pink-and-white **Villa Durazzo,** which is surrounded by gardens and holds 16th-century paintings. (Basilica open daily July-Aug. 9am-8pm; Sept. and May-June 9am-7pm; Oct. and Apr. 9am-6pm; Nov.-Dec. 9am-5pm. Villa open daily 9am-1pm and 2:30-6pm. Both free.) **Chiesa di San Francesco,** at the end of Salata al Castello off P. Martiri della Liberta, holds the monuùt of St. Francis. (Open daily 8:30am-noon and 3:30-5:30pm. Free.)

Come nightfall, youthful crowds claim the multi-colored tables at **Sabot American Bar,** P. Martiri della Libertà 32, which offers appetizers, drinks, sushi platters, and a nightly DJ. (☎0185 28 07 47. Beer €4.50-7. Mixed drinks €8-9. Open daily 5pm-4am. MC/V.) Mingle with the *fashionistas* a few doors down at **Miami,** P. Martiri della Libertà 29, amid with neon lights and vinyl booths. (☎0185 28 34 24. Primi €7-12. Secondi €10-20. Open daily 5pm-3am. AmEx/MC/V.) Next door, **Soleado Cafe** is another stop on the P. Martiri della Liberta bar hop. Cheap drinks draw in a large crowd throughout the week. (Open M-F 5pm-2am and Sa-Su midnight-2am. AmEx/MC/V.)

LIGURIA

DAYTRIP FROM SANTA MARGHERITA

PORTOFINO

Take bus #82 to Portofino Mare from green kiosk in P. Martiri della Libertà in Santa Margherita, where tickets are sold behind the train station. From Portofino's P. Martiri della Libertà, Tigullio buses run to Santa Margherita (3 per hr., €1.10). Portofino is also accessible by ferry from Santa Margherita (every hr. 10:30am-4pm, €4.70), and Camogli (2 per day, €11.70).

Portofino (POR-toh-FEE-no; pop. 529) is a perfect half-day outing from Santa Margherita. Yachts fill the harbor, chic designer boutiques and art galleries line cobblestone streets, and luxury cars crowd parking lots. Nevertheless, the tiny bay of this fine port can be enjoyed by the glamorous and the budget-minded alike. The nature reserve that surrounds Portofino and nearby resort village Paraggi boasts a small but beautiful public beach. Treks through the hilly terrain past ruined churches and stately villas lead to Rapallo (2hr.), Santa Margherita (1hr.), and San Fruttuoso (2hr.). Information regarding hikes and necessary trail maps are available at the tourist office. Facing the water, head right, around the port, and climb hundreds of steep stone stairs for 10min. to reach the cool, stark interior of the **Chiesa di San Giorgio.** Don't forget your camera for the views of the port from the nearby lookout. Another 10min. up the hill you'll find the 16th-century **Castello Brown,** V. alla Penisola 13/A. The castle was once a fortress, but the wealthy Brown family converted it into a summer home after Consul Montague Yeats Brown bought it in 1867 from the Kingdom of Sardinia for 7000 lire. (☎0185 26 71 01 or 26 90 46. Open daily 10am-6pm. €4.50.)

Back in town, **Alimentari Repetto ❷,** P. Martiri dell'Olivetta 30, in the main square in front of the harbor, sells sandwiches (from €3) like the special prosciutto *panini,* as well as regional goods like *limoncello* for around €10. (Open daily in summer 8am-10pm; in winter 9am-6pm. Cash only.) **Trattoria Concordia ❸,** V. del Fondaco 5, behind P. della Libertà, serves authentic Ligurian cuisine in a small, nautical-themed dining room. Local favorites are cheaper here than at many other harbor haunts. (☎0185 26 92 07. Primi €10-26. Secondi €14-32. Service 10%. Open M and W-Su noon-3pm and 7:30-10pm. AmEx/MC/V.) The English-speaking staff at the **APT tourist office,** at V. Roma 35, distributes trail maps. (☎0185 26 90 24. Open daily 10:30am-1:30pm and 2:30-6:30pm.)

> **TIP**
>
> **A FERRY TALE.** Though the hikes and train rides through Portofino's nature reserve are gorgeous, the real charm of the small coastal towns is best experienced from the sea. Hop on one of the many ferries between Camogli, San Fruttuoso, Portofino, and Santa Margherita for incomparable panoramas of colorful buildings nestled in the mountains.

CINQUE TERRE ☎0187

Cinque Terre (CHEEN-kweh TEHR-reh; pop. 6000) is the outdoor enthusiast's Spring Break region. An exorbitant number of American cliques crowd the area for beach-bumming and hiking. The tourist office claims strong hikers can cover all five villages in about 5hr., but the word on the cliff says 3½hr. will do. Both the speedy and slothful can find numerous opportunities for kayaking, cliff jumping, scuba diving, and horseback riding. Rather than rushing through, take time to wander through villages with tiny clusters of rainbow-colored houses amid hilly stretches of olive groves and vineyards. Each town has its own identity: Bustling Monterosso is the ideal destination for *gelaterie*, upscale Vernazza the best swim-spot, Corniglia is a perfect rocky shore getaway, tiny Manarola maintains a steady stream of backpackers, and Riomaggiore offers stunning cliff views and wild nightlife. So reserve ahead, put on your hiking boots, and step away from the modern world for a few days.

 TERRE TRIPPING. The train stations and Cinque Terre National Park offices in each of the 5 towns sell 1-day (€8.50), 2-day (€14.70), 3-day (€19.50), and 7-day (€36.50) Cinque Terre Cards with unlimited train, bus, and path access among the 5 villages, La Spezia, and Levanto.

⌕ TRANSPORTATION

Trains: The towns lie on the Genoa-La Spezia line. Find schedules at tourist offices. Most trains stop at **Monterosso** and **Riomaggiore**, making them the most accessible of the 5 towns. From the station on V. Fegina, trains run to: **Florence** (3hr., every hr., €9) via **Pisa** (2hr., €5.50); **Genoa** (90min., every 2hr. 4:55am-11:35pm, €5); **La Spezia** (20min., every 30min., €1.40); **Rome** (7hr., every 2hr., €24) via **Livorno**. Local trains connect the 5 towns (2-19min.; every 50min.; M-F €1.40, Sa-Su €1.50.).

Ferries: Monterosso can be reached by ferry from **La Spezia** (2hr., 4 per day, €12). Ferries from Monterosso also connect the towns. Navigazione Golfo dei Poeti (☎0187 81 84 40 or 73 29 87), in front of the IAT office at the port (in the old town; see **Practical Information**, below). To: **Manarola** (7 per day, €7); **Portovenere** (7 per day, €12); **Riomaggiore** (8 per day, €8.50); **Vernazza** (7 per day, €3).

Taxis: ☎0187 335 616 5842.

Boat Rental: Samba (☎0187 339 681 2265), across from the train station and along the beaches in Monterosso, rents 2-person canoes for €25 per 3hr. Open daily 9am-6pm. Cash only. **Il Corsaro Rosso** (☎0187 328 693 5355), on the harbor in Riomaggiore, rents kayaks and 3-person canoes for €18 per hr. Snorkeling €10 per day. Snorkeling plus boat tour €12. Cash only.

⎘ PRACTICAL INFORMATION

The five villages string the coast between Levanto in the northwest and La Spezia in the southeast, and are connected by trains, roads (although cars are not allowed inside the towns), and inland and coastal footpaths that traverse the rocky shoreline. **Monterosso** is the largest and western-most town, followed from west to east by **Vernazza, Corniglia, Manarola**, and **Riomaggiore**.

Tourist Offices:

Cinque Terre National Park Office, P. Garibaldi 20, Monterosso (☎0187 81 70 59 or 80 20 53; www.parconazionale5terre.it). Info on trails. **Cinque Terre Cards** available. Open daily 8am-8pm.

Pro Loco, V. Fegina 38 (☎/fax 0187 81 75 06), below the Monterosso train station. Provides info on boats, hikes, and accommodations. Open daily 9am-7pm.

Tourist Office, in the train stations of all 5 towns. Open daily June-Sept. 6:30am-9pm. Tourist offices in Manarola, Riomaggiore, and Monterosso have **Internet** access.

Tours: Navigazione 5 Terre Golfo dei Poeti (☎0187 81 84 40; fax 73 03 36) offers boat tours to **Vernazza** (€3, round-trip €5.50), **Manarola** (€7, round-trip €12), and **Riomaggiore** (€8.50, round-trip €13) from **Monterosso** (7 per day noon-6:30pm) and **Vernazza** (7 per day 10:40am-6pm). Round-trip boats also go to **Portovenere** (€20) and **Lerici** (€20). Dates and times vary seasonally.

First Aid: (☎0187 338 853 0949) for doctor on call M-W and F-Su. **Carabinieri:** in Monterosso (☎0187 81 75 24); in Riomaggiore (☎0187 92 01 12).

Post Office: Main branch in Monterosso, V. Roma 73 (☎0187 81 83 94). Open M-F 8am-1:15pm, Sa 8am-12:30pm. **Postal Codes:** 19016 (Monterosso); 19017 (Manarola and Riomaggiore); 19018 (Corniglia and Vernazza).

TREK THE TERRE. If pressed for time, take the train (€1.40) to Monterosso or Corniglia and hike the 2 paths connecting those 2 towns. The better of the 4 trails along the Cinque Terre, the footpaths that connect Monterosso, Vernazza, and Corniglia, while strenuous, provide great vistas of the precariously positioned Cinque Terre towns.

MONTEROSSO

The largest and most developed of the five villages, Monterosso (Mohn-teh-ROS-so; pop.1600) lacks some of the natural wonders of the other towns, but compensates with conveniences like multiple grocery stores, Internet points, and endless strips of *gelaterie*. By day, visitors flood into town to take advantage of the free beach and shopping opportunities. By night, most retreat to other towns, leaving bustling Monterosso tranquil just in time for sunset.

ORIENTATION AND PRACTICAL INFORMATION. Descend the steps from the **train station** (where there is a **tourist office**) and turn left on **Lungomare di Fegina** through a tunnel into **Piazza Garibaldi,** the heart of town. From here, **Via Vittorio Emanuele** veers left; **Via Roma** veers right. Exchange currency at **Cassa di Risparmio della Spezia,** V. Roma 47 (open M-F 8:10am-1:10pm and 2:30-3:30pm, Su 8:10-11:30am) and **Banca Carige,** V. Roma 69 (open daily 8:05am-1:15pm and 2:30-3:45pm; **ATM** outside). Do **laundry** at **Laundry Matic,** one on V. Molinelli 12, and one on the corner of V. Roma and V. Mazzini. (Wash, detergent, and dry €12 per 5kg. Open daily 9am-1pm and 2-7pm. Cash only.) The **pharmacy,** V. Fegina 44, posts after-hours rotations outside. (☎0187 18 18 394. Open M-Sa 8:30am-12:30pm and 4-7:30pm, Su 9am-12:30pm and 4-7:30pm. Cash only.) The **Net,** V. V. Emanuele 55, offers **Internet** access. (☎0187 81 72 88. €1 per 10min., €0.10 per min. thereafter, or €10 per 2hr. Open daily 9:30am-12:30pm and 3:30-7:30pm. Cash only.) **InNet,** Vcl. Martini 39, off V. V. Emanuele, also offers Internet. (€2.50 per 20min., €5 per hr. Wi-Fi available. Open daily 9am-10pm.)

ACCOMMODATIONS AND FOOD. While most of Cinque Terre's hotels are in Monterosso, they generally fill up in early June. Inquire at the tourist office for help finding the more plentiful *affittacamere* (room rentals). The lively ⑤**Hotel Souvenir** ❷, V. Gioberti 24, popular with students, has bunk beds in comfortable rooms. The common areas and private garden are perfect for socializing. (☎/fax 0187 81 75 95; hotel_souvenir@yahoo.com. Breakfast €5. Rooms with shared bath for students €26; private rooms €44. Cash only.) The friendly owners of nearby Cantina di Sciacchetrà also rent rooms at **Alle 5 Terre** ❷, V. Molinelli 87. The five rooms have bath, TV, and fridge; some have a balcony. (☎0187 81 78 28 or 328 55 05 623. €25 per person. MC/V.) To get to **Albergo La Pineta** ❹, V. Padre Semeria 3, turn right from the train station, then right on V. Padre Semeria. The amiable owners keep a private beach and no-frills rooms with bath and TV, some with sea views. It's close enough to the *centro,* but out of earshot of nightlife noise. (☎0187 82 90 29; hotel_lapineta@virgilio. it. Breakfast included. Singles from €42-52; doubles from €62. Cash only.)

To avoid high prices, consider a picnic of items from the grocery store: pesto-spread focaccia and juicy local fruit; wash it all down with a glass of light, dry *Cinque Terre bianco* or some *Sciacchetrà* dessert wine made from raisins. **█Il Ciliegio ❸**, Località Beo 2, cooks fantastic meals with ingredients fresh from the owner's gardens. Savor the exceptional *trofie al pesto* (pasta with pesto; €7.50) and *cozze ripiene* (stuffed mussels; €9) featured in reviews worldwide, in the flowered garden overlooking the coastline. The restaurant is a 10min. drive from town; friendly management offers free shuttle service from V. Roma on request. (☎0187 81 78 29. Primi €7-10.50. Secondi €8-15. Cover €2. Open Tu-Su 12:30-2:30pm and 7-11pm. AmEx/MC/V.) In a narrow alley off V. Roma, **Ristorante Al Carugio ❸**, V. S. Pietro 9, serves traditional Ligurian dishes. Share the excellent *risotto con frutti di mare* (seafood risotto; €9.50) with at least two people. (☎/fax 0187 81 73 67. Primi €7-11. Secondi €8-16. Open M-W

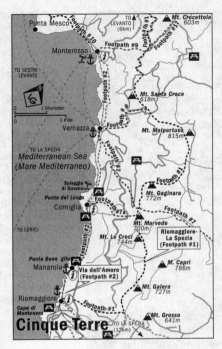

and F-Su noon-2:30pm and 6-10:30pm. AmEx/MC/V.) **Focacceria Il Frantoio ❶**, V. Gioberti 1, bakes tasty *farinata* and hot focaccia stuffed with olives, onions, peppers, cheese, or herbs. (☎0187 81 83 33. Slices €1-3. Open M-W and F-Su 9am-2pm and 3:30-8pm. Cash only.) Those interested in fine wine should visit **█Cantina di Sciacchetrà**, V. Roma 7, which has free tastings, delicious *antipasti*, deals on gourmet treats, and a patient English-speaking staff. (☎0187 81 78 28. Bottles of *Cinque Terre bianco* €5-20, *Sciacchetrà* €29. Open Feb.-Dec. daily 9am-11pm. AmEx/MC/V.) **SuperConad Margherita**, P. Matteotti 9, stocks basic groceries. (Open June-Sept. M-Sa 8am-1pm and 5-8pm, Su 8am-1pm. MC/V.)

█▓ SIGHTS AND NIGHTLIFE. Monterosso has Cinque Terre's largest **free beach**, surrounded by a cliff-cove in front of the *centro storico* to the left and down the stairs from the train station. Umbrella and chair rentals available. About 200m to the right of the train station, **Il Gigante**, a craggy giant carved into the rocky cliff, watches over the sunbathers below. The 15th-century **Chiesa dei Cappuccini**, in the center of town, yields broad vistas of the five towns. In the chapel to the left is the 17th-century *Crucifixion* by Flemish master Anthony Van Dyck, who stayed here during his most productive years. (Open daily 9am-noon and 4-7pm. Free.)

For a midnight snack, chow down on hot sandwiches named after American bands (from €4.50) and sip mixed drinks (€5.50) beneath hanging electric guitars and televisions broadcasting MTV at **FAST**, V. Roma 13. (☎0187 81 71 64. Beer €3-4, tap €2.80-8. Open in summer daily 8am-2am; in winter M-W and F-Su 8am-noon. MC/V.) Enjoy seaside views from the patio over beer, liquor, and snacks at **Il Casello**, V. Lungo Ferravia 70. (☎0187 81 83 30 or 333 49 27 629. Mixed drinks

TOP TEN LIST

PICNIC ON THE TERRE

These pretty (tough) paths will leave any trekker with a hearty appetite. Rather than ducking into an overpriced 4-walled eatery, stop at a market, find a coveted outdoor cove, and bask in the natural wonders of the Riviera.

1. Campiglia: The perfect spot to settle those pre-trek munchies, surrounded by trees and weeds.

2. Valico di Sant'Antonio: Fellow hikers are a rare sight at this secluded forest patch.

3. Il Telegrafo: The cantine is a lifesaver when you forget that carefully packed meal at the hostel.

4. Montenero: Horse and man unite in fatigue at this spot, with the horse refresher station and picnic tables.

5. Via dell'Amore: Lunch with your sweetie under garden canopies.

6. Punta Bonfiglio (Point of the Good Son): After lunch, enhance your Cinque Terre trivia at the Museum of the Territory.

7. Volastra: Grab a light lunch at the snack bar at this serene stop on the coastal path next to the sanctuary.

8. Corniglia: Dip into the cool, tourist-free waters after you eat.

9. San Bernardino: Gulp down water and chow down on *panini* with every level of trekker.

10. Soviore: Take a spiritual lunch break at this inland spot next to a church shaded by palm trees.

€7-9. Open daily 11am-midnight. Cash only.) **Nuovo Eden Bar,** V. Fegina 7, above the beach, offers salad and pasta (€5-7). At night, grab a gelato (from €1.60) for a beachside stroll. (Open daily 8am-midnight.)

HIKING: MONTEROSSO-VERNAZZA. The hardest of the four town-linking treks, this 1hr. hike climbs steeply up a cliff-side staircase, winding past terraced vineyards and hillside cottages before the steep descent into Vernazza.

DAYTRIP FROM MONTEROSSO: LEVANTO. Sandy beaches and seaside promenades are the main attractions at this beach town, a busier and bigger alternative to the laid-back Cinque Terre towns, but with fewer tourists. The trek to Levanto (LE-van-toh) is more uncultivated and rugged than most of the hikes in Cinque Terre. The trail leaves Monterosso for a harsh 45min. climb to **Punta del Mesco,** a 19th-century lighthouse converted from the ruins of an Augustinian monastery. Before descending to Levanto, it wraps around cliffs and passes vineyards, orchards, and the remains of a 13th-century castle. Private and public beaches line the promenade.

Ostello Ospitalia del Mare ❷, V. S. Nicolo 1, is the perfect option for an overnight stay and only a 5min. walk from the beach. The rooms are spacious, sunny, and have baths. (☎0187 80 25 62; www.ospitaliadelmare.it. Last train from Cinque Terre arrives at 12:35am. Breakfast included. Internet access €5 per hr. Reception 8am-1pm, 4-8pm, and 9:30-11pm. Dorms €28; doubles with bath €30-32. MC/V.) At **Hotel Dora ❺,** V. Martiri Liberta 27 (☎0187 80 81 68; fax 80 80 07), sun streams through the yellow curtains and spills onto wood headboards and flower pots. Not more than 250m from the ocean, the beach is as much a hotel amenity as the A/C, bar, and common area. (Minimum 3 night stay. Singles €67; doubles €90; triples €120; quads €150.) Load up for a beach picnic at **La Focacceria Dome ❶,** V. Dante Alghieri 18, serving fresh focaccia, *farinata*, and pizza (€1-2) in heaping portions. (Open Sept.-Apr. daily 9am-9pm. Closed Oct.-Mar. Tu. Cash only.) Those staying for dinner shouldn't miss **Da Rino ❸,** V. Garibaldi 10, for a family-style Ligurian feast where the fish is always fresh. (☎0187 328 389 0350. Primi €6-10. Secondi €11-18. Cover €1.50. Open daily 7-10pm. Cash only.)

A 2hr. hike connects Levanto to Monterosso. Trains run to Levanto from Monterosso (5min., every 30min. 4:46am-11:42pm, €1.40). To reach the tourist office, P. Mazzini, cross the *piazza*, go down the stairs, cross a bridge, and take C. Roma. ☎0187 80 81 25. Open M-Sa 9am-1pm and 3-6pm, Su 9am-1pm.

VERNAZZA

Graced by a turquoise lagoon of multicolored motorboats surrounded by restaurant-filled *piazze* and a small but beautiful stretch of sandy beach, Vernazza (Vehr-NAT-sa; pop. 1000) is historically the wealthiest of the five Cinque Terre towns. Climb to the remains of the 11th-century Castello Doria, up a staircase on the left of P. Marconi, for great views of the other four towns.

 TUNNEL VISION. Depending which train car you're in, stops in Cinque Terre stations, particularly Vernazza and Riomaggiore, are in tunnels! This may not appear to be the station stop, but often it is; ride in the center of the train and watch for your stop to be sure.

ORIENTATION AND PRACTICAL INFORMATION. Lined with shops and restaurants, **Via E. Q. Visconti** runs from the station toward the sea and turns into **Via Roma** about halfway to the beach. **Piazza Marconi** overlooks the harbor at the end of V. Roma. There is a **tourist office** in the train station. Check email at **Internet Point,** V. Roma 32. (€0.15 per min. for the first 30min; €0.10 per min. thereafter. Wi-Fi available. Open daily 9am-1:30pm and 3-8pm.)

ACCOMMODATIONS AND FOOD. Vernazza has some great hotels and private rooms. **Hotel Gianni Franzi** ❸, P. Marconi 1, has 23 rooms, all with antique decor, in several small rustic buildings at the top of the town. Some sport balconies with postcard views of the coast and Corniglia. Quiet private courtyard with manicured bright green grass makes an ideal relaxation spot. (☎0187 82 10 03; www.giannifranzi.it. Singles €45, with bath €70; doubles €65/80, with balcony €100; triples with bath €120. AmEx/MC/V.) The friendly owners of **Albergo Barbara** ❸, P. Marconi 30, on the top floor, make their guests feel at home. The nine rooms are bright and some have views of the port. Attic rooms have wood-beamed ceiling and are located up multiple flights of stairs. (☎0167 81 23 98; www.albergobarbara.it. Ring bell to enter. Doubles €50, with bath €60-65, with bath and view €100. Extra bed €10. Closed Dec.-Feb. Cash only.)

Reputedly home to the best restaurants in Cinque Terre, P. Marconi fills with hungry tourists each evening. The oldest trattoria in Vernazza, **Trattoria Gianni Franzi** ❷, P. Marconi 1, is famed for its pesto and friendly local charm. Dine casually in the roomy stone-walled interior or outside on the *piazza*. (☎0187 82 10 03; fax 81 22 28. Primi €5-12. Secondi €7-22. Open M-Tu and Th-Su noon-3pm and 7:30-9:30pm. AmEx/MC/V.) For a delicious splurge, visit **Gambero Rosso** ❺, P. Marconi 7. Touted by *vernazzesi*, the service is excellent and the food superb. (☎0187 81 22 65; fax 82 12 60. Primi €12-18. Secondi €16-26. Cover €3. Open Tu-Su noon-3:15pm and 7-10pm. AmEx/MC/V.) For a slice of pizza (€3), pop in to **Pizzeria Baja Saracena** ❶, P. Marconi 16, to enjoy a quick snack between rounds of hiking and sunbathing. Try the warm and tasty pesto lasagna (€9), available to go or to enjoy on terrace seating overlooking the ocean. (Open daily 10am-10:30pm. Cash only.) Fresh produce, and gourmet foods are available at **Salumi e Formaggi,** V. Visconti 19. (☎0187 82 12 40. Open M-Sa 8am-2pm and 5:20-7:30pm, Su 8am-1:30pm. Cash only.) For groceries, visit **Coop,** V. Roma 25. (Open daily 8:15am-1pm and 5-8pm; closed Tu afternoons. AmEx/MC/V.)

HIKING: VERNAZZA-CORNIGLIA. Geographic diversity and **unparalleled views** are the rewards along this 1hr. hike. The trail climbs harshly from Vernazza, passing through vineyards and olive groves before curving through uncultivated landscape. Scents of rosemary, thyme, lemon, and lavender fill

GIVING BACK

THE BEATEN PATH

Cinque Terre is doubtless a paradise for hikers, with trails connecting cliff-hugging towns along the mountainous shore of the Ligurian coast. Its beauty has even earned it inclusion on the UNESCO World Heritage List. Yet the uniqueness of this land is far from undiscovered, and the tourist stands that line the main streets of the towns offer proof of just that.

Even the picturesque trails, far into the brush, have been unable to escape tourism's impact. The shoes that have packed down the dirt trails have caused deterioration to the landscape, causing it to go (literally) downhill. In response, Cinque Terre was placed on the "World Monument Fund's List of 100 Sites at Risk," and dedicated workers at the Parco Nazionale delle Cinque Terre are committed to its restoration.

The Park's Landscape University organizes work camps to rebuild stone walls and stabilize trails. In exchange for your able hands, you will gain knowledge of the region's geography, customs, and specialized work techniques, while contributing to an effort that will ultimately enhance and preserve this vibrant patch of earth.

For further information, contact the Parco Nazionale delle Cinque Terre (☎0187 76 00 00; info@ parconazionale5terre.it).

the summer air. At one point, the trail bends to reveal the secluded, clothing-optional **Guvano beach** hundreds of feet below, occupied largely by students and adventurous types willing to make the trek down the cliff, then get intimate. Corniglia, perched spectacularly in the distance, is in view for the duration of the hike.

CORNIGLIA

Three hundred sixty-five steps and a 15min. climb from the station bring travelers to this colorful village on a seaside cliff. Without the beachside glitter of the other towns, Corniglia (cor-NEEL-ya; pop. 500) has a more peaceful ambience with considerably fewer tourists. A rocky strip of public beach beneath the tracks is a popular morning stop for local sunbathers, while more secluded beaches beckon hikers off the trail on the way to Vernazza.

◼ **ORIENTATION.** **Via Alla Stazione** begins at the top of the station steps and turns into **Via Fieschi** in the *centro.* To the right of the *centro,* down **Via Serra,** is the entrance to the trail from Vernazza. To reach the free beach beneath the station, walk down the stairs and turn left after the tunnel. Do not follow misleading signs that read "Spiaggia," as these refer to the distant **Guvana Beach.**

◤◪ **ACCOMMODATIONS AND FOOD.** Due to its small size and cliffside location, Corniglia is best as a daytrip. If you do plan to stay, private rooms are the way to go, as there are few hotels. See a list of available *affitacamere* in front of the stairs leading to the *centro storico* from the train station. **Ristorante Cecio ❹,** V. Serra 58, on the road from Corniglia to Vernazza, rents eight rooms above the restaurant with views of the sea and mountains, and eight rooms in the village with terraces. Seaside rooms all have bath. Request the corner room for more space and more windows. (☎0187 81 20 43 or 334 350 6637; www.cecio5terre.com. Singles €55; doubles €60; triples €80. Cash only.)

Pizzerias serve hungry hikers all over town. Follow your nose to **La Gata Flora ❶,** V. Fieschi 109, for delicious slices. Crispy *farinata* (€1.10) is also available. (☎0187 82 12 18. Focaccia €1.20-2.10. Whole pizza €4.50-8, slice €2.60 . Open M and W-Su 9:30am-4pm and 6-8:30pm; also open Tu in Aug. Cash only.) To get to **La Posada ❸,** V. Alla Stazione 11, climb the staircase from the train station. Turn right on the road at the top; follow for about 50m. (Primi €6-8. Secondi €8-11. Cover €2. Open daily noon-3pm and 7-10:30pm. MC/V.) The cavernous **Cantina de**

Mananan ❸, V. Fieschi 117, offers a cool setting in which to enjoy hearty home-made dishes like stuffed pasta, potato pasta, and spaghetti. (☎0187 82 11 66. Primi €9-11. Secondi €12-16. Cover €1.80. Open M and W-Su 12:45-2:15pm and 7:45-9:15pm. Cash only.) Sip wine and twirl spaghetti on the terrace of **Ristorante Cecio ❸**, V. Serra 11. (☎0187 81 20 43. Primi and secondi €8-22. Cover €2.50. Open M-Tu and Th-Su noon-3pm and 7:30-10pm. Closed Nov. MC/V.)

◢ **HIKING: CORNIGLIA-MANAROLA.** Take the stairs down to the station from V. Alla Stazione and turn left, following the path along the railroad tracks. The 1hr. trail begins just after the public beach. Though less pictur-esque than the hikes between the previous towns, the gentle trail to Manarola boasts an easier, flatter trek and has some sweeping, open-sea vistas. Experi-enced hikers can finish this portion of the trek in 30min.

MANAROLA

Two large swimming coves, sheltered by rocky inlets, attract swimmers and sunbathers to Manarola (ma-na-RO-la; pop. 900). Its laid-back pace and newly renovated hostel make this the ideal hangout for the backpacking crowd.

◤◥ **ORIENTATION AND PRACTICAL INFORMATION.** From the train station, walk through the tunnel and emerge onto **Via Antonio Discovolo.** Turn left and cross **Piazza Dario Capellino,** after which **Via Birolli** runs to the sea, or turn right and head uphill for the hostel and stunning views.

◤◥ **ACCOMMODATIONS AND FOOD.** To reach the ◪**Ostello Cinque Terre ❶**, V. B. Riccobaldi 21, turn right from the train station, continue uphill 300m and turn left at the sign. Forty-eight beds, a bright dining room, a rooftop terrace with 360° of perfection, and a shelf full of board games contribute to the sum-mer-camp atmosphere. Ask about kayaking, biking, and snorkeling equipment rental. (☎0187 92 02 15; www.hostel5terre.com. Breakfast €4. 5min. shower and linens included. Laundry wash €4, dry €2 per 30min. Internet access €1.50 per 15min. Wheelchair-accessible. Lockout 10am-5pm. Curfew in summer 1am; in winter midnight. Reserve at least 1 week ahead. Dorms €20-23; double with bath €55-65; quad with bath €88-100. Closed Nov. 9-Feb. 28. Advanced payment of 1st night required. AmEx/MC/V.) The cheery **Bed and Breakfast La Torretta ❺**, Vico Volto 20, is filled with flowers. Canopied beds are spacious and rooms have balcony, TV, and A/C in this fully staffed villa available for rent for a paltry €2000 per night. The terrace yields some of the town's best sea views. (☎0187 92 03 27; www.torrettas.com. Breakfast included. Singles €100; doubles €120; quads €190. AmEx/MC/V.) The restaurant **Il Porticciolo ❸**, V. Renato Birolli 92, rents rooms with bath, TV, and balcony. (☎/fax 0187 92 00 83; www.ilporticciolo5terre.com. Breakfast €5. Singles €30; doubles €50-60. AmEx/MC/V.) **Da Paulin ❸**, V. Disco-volo 126, offers rooms with quilted comforters, bath, hair dryer, balcony, Wi-Fi, and TV. (☎39 018 792 0706; www.dapaulin.it. Doubles €60-75.)

At **Trattoria da Billy ❸**, V. Rollandi 122, get away from the town center and eat lunch with the locals. (☎0187 92 068. Primi €6-8. Secondi €7-14. Open M-W and F-Su 12:30-2:30pm and 7-10:30pm. MC/V.) **Marina Piccola ❸**, V. lo Scalo 16, just off V. Renato Birolli, is a little place with big meals. Savor *risotto di frutta di mare* (with large pieces of shrimp on a plate lined with mussels) on the edge of a rocky cove. (☎0187 92 09 23. Primi €8-16. Secondi €9-17. Open Jan.-July and Sept.-Dec. M and W-Su noon-2:30pm and 7pm-midnight. AmEx/MC/V.) **Trattoria Il Porticciolo ❷**, V. Renato Birolli 92, serves hearty meals in a casual ambience at a good value. **Il Porticcioto** boasts excellent *gnocchi al pesto* (€6) and superb

LIGURIA

torta di frutta e noci (fruit and nut cake) for €4.50. (☎0187 92 00 83. Primi €5-9. Secondi €7-16. Open M-Tu and Th-Su 7am-3:30pm and 5-11pm. AmEx/MC/V.)

🔊 **NIGHTLIFE.** One of the quieter towns of the five, a night in Manarola is more likely to be a low-key evening than a bass-pumping rager, though a few times each summer, Manarola hosts disco parties in a *piazza*, advertised on posters around town with themes like "Havana Nights." **Bar Enrica**, on V. Renato Birolli in Punta Bonfiglio, serves gelato by day and mixed drinks by night. (☎0187 92 02 77. *Bruschette* €3-5. Hot panini €4-4.50. Beer €2.50-5. Mixed drinks €5. Open daily 8:30-11am and 8-11pm. Cash only.)

🥾 **HIKING: MANAROLA-RIOMAGGIORE.** Via dell'Amore, the most famous stretch of Cinque Terre hikes (20min.), passes through a stone tunnel of love decorated by romantic graffiti scenes and colorful mosaics. With elevators at its beginning and end, the slate-paved walk is almost wheelchair-accessible except for some steps in the middle, and is a good way to ease into the hikes and views the park provides for all its visitors.

RIOMAGGIORE

A castle crowns a cliff above the bright houses that cascade down the valley of Riomaggiore (REE-yo-ma-JO-reh; pop. 1736). Here, fishermen varnishing boat hulls are as common as sunbathers rubbing in lotion. There are rooms for rent around the harbor; Riomaggiore is the best bet to find last-minute lodging, and as a result, houses a busy population of young travelers and lively nightlife.

🗺️ **ORIENTATION AND PRACTICAL INFORMATION.** Turn right from the back of the **train station** and walk through a tunnel to the *centro*. Do not follow the train tracks, as that tunnel is not for pedestrians. The main street, **Via Cristoforo Colombo,** runs up the hill to the left. A **Pro Loco tourist office** in the train station provides info on trails, hotels, and excursions. (☎0187 92 06 33. Open M-F 6:30am-8pm, Sa-Su 7am-9pm.) The **National Park Office** next to the station offers **Internet** access for €0.08 per min. and currency exchange. (☎0187 76 05 15. Open daily 8am-9:30pm.) You can also find currency exchange at **Banca Carige,** V. C. Colombo 215. (Open M-F 8:20am-1:20pm and 2:30-4pm. AmEx/MC/V.) A 24hr. **ATM** can be found at the foot of V. C. Colombo. **Farmacia del Mare,** V. C. Colombo 182, posts a list of late-night pharmacies. (☎0187 92 01 60. Open M-Sa 9am-noon and 4-8pm, Su 9am-noon. AmEx/MC/V.) **Wash and Dry Lavarapido** is at V. C. Colombo 109. (Wash €3.50 per 30min. Detergent €1. Open daily 8am-8pm. Cash only.) A **post office** is at V. Pecunia 7, up the stairs from V. C. Colombo and to the left. (☎0187 80 31 60. Open M-F 8am-1pm and Sa 8am-noon.)

🏠 **ACCOMMODATIONS AND FOOD.** The clean and welcoming ▪**Mar-Mar ❷**, V. Malborghetto 4, rents dorms and rooms with bath. Some have TV and balcony. Apartments for two to six people are also available, and the community terrace lined with plastic furniture overlooks the harbor. (☎/fax 0187 92 09 32; www.5terre-marmar.com. Dorms Nov. to Easter €15-€20; doubles €60-80; apartments €65-120. Cash only.) **Hotel Ca Dei Duxi ❹**, V. C. Colombo 36, is pleasant and well situated, offering wood furnishings, white tiled floors and 60s-style floral bedspreads. Six rooms all have bath, TV, A/C, and fridge; some have a terrace. (☎0187 92 00 36; www.duxi.it. Breakfast included. Doubles €60-90; triples €90-130. *Let's Go* discount. AmEx/MC/V.) At **5Terre Affitti ❷**, V. C. Colombo 97, Papa Bernardo rents rooms located mostly on the harbor with bath and satellite TV; some have a balcony. (☎0187 92 03 31; www.immobiliare5terre.com.

Doubles €50-60; studios with kitchen and views for 2 or 3 people €65-75; quad with kitchen and terrace €90-120. Cash only.) **La Dolce Vita ❷**, V. C. Colombo 120, has a young, friendly staff that attract similar clientele. Rents doubles with bath and minibar, and four-person apartments. (☎0187 76 00 44. Reception open 9:30am-7:30pm. Doubles €55-70; triples €80; quads €95-125. Cash only.) **Edi ❸**, V. C. Colombo 111, rents rooms with bath and fridge as well as apartments for up to four people. Reserve ahead via fax. (☎/fax 0187 92 03 25. Doubles €60, with view €75; apartment doubles €80/135; quads €120/155. AmEx/MC/V; cash only for some privately owned properties, ask ahead.)

At popular **Trattoria La Lanterna ❸**, V. S. Giacomo 46, off V. C. Colombo, enjoy delicious fresh fish or pasta and watch the fishing boats roll by. (☎0187 92 01 20. Primi €7-9. Secondi €7-22. MC/V.) On a cliff above town, eat fried fish off chinaware at the glass-enclosed **Ripa del Sole ❹**, V. de Gasperi 282. The *gnocchi* with scampi and white truffles (€11.50) is excellent. (☎0187 92 01 43. Primi €10-13. Secondi €12-24. Open Tu-Su noon-2pm and 6:30-9:30pm. AmEx/MC/V.) For groceries, stop by one of the many *alimentari* lining V. C. Colombo, enticing backpackers with fresh fruit displays. Try **Alimentari della Franca**, V. C. Colombo 253. (☎0187 92 09 29. Open daily 7:45am-1pm and 3-8pm. MC/V.)

🔫🏄 **OUTDOOR ACTIVITIES AND NIGHTLIFE.** **Coopsub Cinqueterre Diving Center,** on V. S. Giacomo, conducts supervised dives off the coast, where dolphins frolic in June and September. Boat trips include stops to the natural waterfalls of nearby Caneto Beach. (☎0187 92 00 11; www.5terrediving.com. Single kayak €7 per hr.; double kayak €12 per hr. Open daily Easter-Sept. 8:30am-6pm. Cash only.) At night, groups of young tourists hang at the harbor. During the warmer months, restaurants with outdoor seating fill until late, and live performers, serenade guests. The bar and outdoor patio at **Bar Centrale**, V. C. Colombo 144, fill up with young international backpackers. Ivo, the energetic bartender, serves a cold brew and turns up swingin' Motown. (☎0187 92 02 08. Beer €3-5.50. Mixed drinks €5.50-7. Open daily 7:30am-1am. Cash only.) **A Pie de Ma, Bar and Vini,** with sweeping views of turquoise waters below on V. dell'Amore, is a hot spot to grab pre-dinner drinks. (☎0187 92 10 37. Focaccia €3.50. Mixed drinks €5. Live music some F and Sa nights. Open daily 10am-midnight. Cash only.)

LA SPEZIA ☎0187

Though the upscale beach ambience of Cinque Terre is only a short ride away, La Spezia's poor, urban atmosphere seems like another world. Heavily bombarded in during WWII because of its naval base and artillery, La Spezia (la SPET-see-ya; pop. 91,391) has since evolved into a proud commercial port. Though La Spezia boasts none of the majestic architecture or cobblestone passageways that grace some neighboring villages, it does make a great starting point for daytrips to the small fishing village of Porto Venere, the beach resorts of San Terenzo and Lerici, and the beautiful coves of Fiascherino; it's also an unavoidable stopover on the way to and from Cinque Terre.

ROCK THE BEACH. Free beaches are easy to find in Cinque Terre if you don't mind rocks. Grab a towel and picnic lunch and avoid the private beaches near the city centers. A great stretch of surf and sand lies beyond the ferry dock in Riomaggiore. Or, pay for a 1-day trail pass and seek out a cliffside sun-bathing spots on the coast between Riomaggiore and Corniglia.

LIGURIA

⎀ TRANSPORTATION. La Spezia lies on the Genoa-La Spezia-Pisa **train** line. The station is included in the **Cinque Terre Card,** which allows unlimited train use between destinations. One-way tickets are €1.40. Navigazione Golfo dei Poeti, V. Don Minzoni 13 (☎0187 73 29 87; www.navigazionegolfodeipoeti.it), runs **ferries** to each of the Cinque Terre towns (€12; round-trip M-Sa €21, Su €23); Capraia (3hr., round-trip July-Aug. €40); Portovenere (€3.50, round-trip €6.50). Call ahead for schedule. For a **taxi,** call ☎0187 52 35 23 or hail one at the train station. A 12km **footpath** also links La Spezia to Riomaggiore.

▰ ▰ ORIENTATION AND PRACTICAL INFORMATION. From the **train station,** turn left, and walk down the stairs. Turn left on **Via Fiume,** which goes through P. S. Bon and P. Garibaldi before turning into **Via del Prione,** the city's main drag. Continue 15min. on V. del Prione until it hits **Via Chiodo. Via Mazzini** runs parallel to V. Chiodo, closer to the water. The main **tourist office** is at the train station. (☎0187 25 43 11. Open daily 9am-1pm and 2-7pm.) Another branch is at V. Mazzini 45. (Open M-Sa 9am-1pm and 2-7pm, Su 2-7pm.) **CTS,** V. Sapri 86, helps with ferry tickets to Greece and Sardinia as well as car rentals. (☎0187 75 10 74. Open M-F 9:30am-12:30pm and 3:30-7:30pm, Sa 9:30am-12:30pm. MC/V.) **Farmacia dell'Aquila,** V. Chiodo 97, posts a list of late-night pharmacies. (☎0187 23 162. Open daily 8:30am-12:30pm and 4-8pm. Closed in July but posts a list of other open locations. MC/V.) **Phone Center,** P. Saint Bon 1, has **Internet access** and **Western Union.** (☎0187 76 77 24; fax 71 21 11. €4 per hr. Open M-Sa 9:15am-1pm and 3-9pm, Su 3-9pm. Cash only.) For currency exchange and an **ATM** try **Banca Carige,** C. Cavour 154. (☎0187 73 43 69. Open M-F 8:20am-1:20pm and 2:30-4pm.) Have a cappuccino while your surf the Internet at centrally located **Map Caffe',** V. Sapri 78. (☎0187 77 84 88. €5 per hr. Open M-Sa 8am-1am.) The **post office,** P. Verdi 1, a few blocks from the port, offers currency exchange. (☎0187 25 84 31. Open M-Sa 8:15am-6:30pm. Cash only.) **Postal Code:** 19100.

▰ ▱ ACCOMMODATIONS AND FOOD. *Affitacamere* are available for nightly rental throughout La Spezia, and are a convenient option for those planning a long-term stay. Not all rentals are budget-friendly, so compare prices and obtain *affitacamere* listings through the tourist office near the train station. Try the family-run **Albergo Il Sole ❷,** V. Cavalotti 31, close to the port. English-speaking staff keeps basic, spacious rooms decorated in yellow and rose with large windows. (☎0187 73 51 64; www.albergoilsole.com. Breakfast €4. Singles €28-40; doubles €50, with bath €60; triples €55-65; quads €80-92. MC/V.) The next street over, **Albergo Teatro ❷,** V. Carpenino 31, near the Teatro Civico, offers six comfortable rooms with TV; some have bath. (☎/fax 0187 73 13 74. Singles €25-30; doubles €40-50, with bath €50-65. Extra bed 15% of room price.) If you're willing to splurge, try **Hotel Firenze & Continentale ❺,** V. Paleocapa 7, across from the train station. The hotel retains a *fin de siècle* look, with marble floors and plush sitting areas. The rooms are decorated with oriental rugs and wood furniture, and all have bath, A/C, TV, and phone; some have balcony. (☎0187 71 32 00. Breakfast included. Wi-Fi €10 per day. Wheelchair-accessible. Singles €70-92; doubles €93-155; triples €125-185. AmEx/MC/V.)

Inexpensive trattorie line V. del Prione. Join the young crowd at **▰Osteria Duccio ❷,** V. Roselli 17, off V. del Prione, for typical Tuscan dishes prepared with the freshest organic ingredients from local farms. (☎0187 25 86 02. Primi €6.50-7.50. Secondi €7-10. 3-course lunch *menù* with wine €11; dinner €15. Cover at dinner €1. Open Tu-Su noon-2:30pm and 7:30-11pm.) **La Pia ❶,** V. Magenta 12, also off V. del Prione, is a small place with big portions, and an even grander reputation. (☎0187 73 99 99. Most items €2.80-4.50. Takeout available. Open M-Sa 10am-3pm and 5-11pm. MC/V.) **Osteria con Cucina all'Inferno ❷,** V. Lorenzetti Costa 3, off P.

Cavour, has been serving Ligurian specialities since 1905. Try fish fresh from the gulf in a *zuppa di pesce* (fish soup; €5.50) and hearty *mesc-ciua* (a thick soup of white cannellini beans and chickpeas, cornmeal, olive oil, and pepper; €4.50) served with extra dry bread. (☎0187 29 458. Primi €5.50-6.50. Secondi €5-9. Open M-Sa 12:15-2:30pm and 7:30-10:30pm. Cash only.) For lighter snacks refreshing *granite* (€1.50-2) or *prosciutto e melone* (€4) head to **Cellini Roma ❷**, P. Cavour 48. (Open Tu-Su 8am-3:30pm and 8pm-12:30am.) You'll also find a **market** on P. Cavour (Open M-Sa 7am-1pm). For groceries and fresh produce, try **Supermercato Spesafacile**, V. Colombo 101, down V. Roselli off V. del Prione. (Open M-Sa 8:30am-1pm and 4:15-8pm. MC/V.)

◪ SIGHTS. Seaside La Spezia offers more than just palm trees, boutiques, and people-watching when it comes to sights. Three-day **museum passes** (€12) are sold at any city museum. The unique collection of the **Museo Navale**, in P. Chiodo next to the entrance of the Maritime Military Arsenal, features diving suits dating from WWII and carved prows of 19th-century ships (including a huge green salamander). Check out the gargantuan iron anchors and tiny replicas of Egyptian, Roman, and European vessels. (☎0187 78 30 16. Open M-Sa 8am-6:45pm, Su 8am-1pm. €2. Cash only.) **Museo Amadeo Lia**, V. del Prione 234, houses a collection of paintings from the 13th-17th centuries, including Raphael's *San Martino and the Beggar* in Room 6. Find Titian's *Portrait of a Gentleman* and Bellini's *Portrait of an Attorney* in Room 7. The 17th-century building, is a former Franciscan convent. Remnants of religious artifacts remain. (☎0187 73 11 00; www.castagna.it/mal. Open Tu-Su 10am-6pm. Last entry 30min. before closing. €6, students €4.) Next door, the **Museo del Sigillo**, V. del Prione 236, in the Palazzina delle Arti, displays a large collection of civic wax seals from around the globe. (☎0187 77 85 44; www.castagna.it/musei/museodelsigillo. Open Tu 4-7pm, W-Su 10am-noon and 4-7pm. €3.) The **Museo Entografico**, V. del Prione 156, has an important collection of traditional costumes, furniture, jewelry, and pottery from the surrounding region. Marvel at the colors and intricate details on the central urn. (☎/fax 0187 25 85 70; www.comune.sp.it/citta/guida/podenzana.htm. Open F-Su 10am-12:30pm and 4-7pm. €4.)

RIVIERA DI PONENTE

FINALE LIGURE ☎019

A plaque at the base of a statue along the promenade claims that Finale Ligure (fee-NA-leh LEE-goo-reh; pop. 11,845) is the place for *"il riposo del popolo,"* or "the people's rest." Whether *riposo* involves bodysurfing in the choppy waves, browsing chic boutiques, or sipping coffee in Finalborgo's medieval *piazze*, there are countless ways to pass the time in this sleepy town.

▣ TRANSPORTATION

The **train station** (☎019 27 58 777 or 89 20 21) is in P. Vittorio Veneto. The ticket office is open daily 6am-7pm. Trains run to Genoa (1hr., every 30min 7:53am-10:55pm, €14.50.) via Savona, and Ventimiglia (30min., every 30min. 7:12am-11:46pm, €5.50) via San Remo. ACTS **buses** depart from a side street left of the train station to Finalborgo (5min., every 30min., €1.40) and Savona (45min., every 30min., €2.20). Buy tickets at the bar in the train station. For **taxis**, call Radio Taxi ☎019 69 23 33, or 69 23 34.

✈ 🔀 ORIENTATION AND PRACTICAL INFORMATION

The city is divided into three sections: **Finalpia** to the east, **Finalmarina** in the center, and **Finalborgo,** the *centro storico,* to the northwest. The train station and most services are in Finalmarina. The area's main street winds through the town between the station and **Piazza Vittorio Emanuele II,** whose name changes from **Via di Raimondi** to **Via Pertica** to **Via Garibaldi.** From P. V. Emanuele II, **Via della Concezione** runs parallel to the shore. To reach Finalborgo, turn left from the station, go under the tracks, and keep left on **Via Domenico Bruneghi** for 10min.

The **IAT tourist office** is at V. della Concezione 27. From the station, walk to the water, and then take the only left; signs lead the way. (☎019 68 10 19; www. inforiviera.it. Open M-Tu and Th-Su 7am-7pm. Closed Su in winter.) Currency exchange and an **ATM** are available at **Banca Carige,** V. Garibaldi 4. (Open M-F 8:20am-1:20pm and 2:30-4pm.) In an emergency, call the **police,** V. Brunenghi 67 (☎019 69 26 66). **Farmacia della Marina,** V. Ghiglieri 2, at the intersection where V. Raimondi becomes V. Pertica, lists after-hours rotations. (☎019 69 26 70. Open M-Sa 8:30am-12:30pm and 4-8pm. Ring bell for emergencies.) **Internet** access is available at **Net Village Internet Cafe,** V. di Raimondi 21, across from the train station. (☎019 68 16 283. €5 per hr. Open daily 8am-10pm.) For rock climbing in the area, the **Mountain Shop,** V. Nicotera 4, in Finalborgo, provides maps and the necessary gear. (☎019 68 16 230. Open M and W-Su 9:30am-1pm, 5-8pm, and 9pm-midnight. MC/V.) The **post office** is at V. della Concezione 29. (☎019 69 04 79. Open M-F 8:15am-6:30pm, Sa 8:15am-12:30pm.) **Postal Code:** 17024.

🏠 🏕 ACCOMMODATIONS AND CAMPING

The youth hostel has the best prices—not to mention the best view. While it may also have the only available rooms, especially in July and August, it's still best to call ahead. The tourist office can help find *affitacamere.*

Castello Wuillerman (HI), V. Generale Caviglia 46 (☎/fax 019 69 05 15). From the station, turn left on V. Raimondo Pertica (just after the intersection), and continue straight. Turn left at the corner of V. Pertica and V. Alonzo, and climb the thigh-burning stairs to the top. The cliffside castle-turned-hostel has locking cabinets in rooms, a beautiful courtyard, and a good restaurant. Breakfast included. Laundry €4 per load. Reception 7-10am and 5-10pm. Curfew midnight. Dorms €14. HI members only. Cash only. ❶

Albergo Carla, V. Colombo 44 (☎019 69 22 85; fax 68 19 65). Across from the seaside walkway. All rooms with bath and phone; some with sea view. Restaurant downstairs. Breakfast €4. Reservations recommended. Singles €28-40; doubles €48-60. MC/V. ❸

Alba Chiara, Vico Tubino 5 (☎019 69 34 18; fax 019 69 07 02). 1-star hotel with long rooms that have blue comforters and white-lace curtains. All rooms have TV and phone. English spoken. Doubles €55-90. AmEx/MC/V. ❸

Petit Hotel, Corso Europa 83 (☎019 60 17 50; fax 019 60 31 30). Modern, colorful rooms have phone, TV, and safe. English spoken. Doubles €60-88. AmEx/MC/V. ❹

Del Mulino (☎019 60 16 69; www.campingmulino.it), on V. Castelli, 15min. from the center of town. From the station, take the Calvisio bus to Boncardo Hotel, then turn left at P. Oberdan and right on V. Porro. Follow signs uphill. Tents pitched on cement on a hill overlooking water and vegetation. Bar, pizzeria, and mini-market. Hot showers. Laundry €5. Reception 8am-8pm. Open Apr.-Sept. €6-7 per person; €5-7 per tent. MC/V. ❶

🍴 FOOD

Reservations are helpful for dinner; restaurants fill up quickly. Get basics at **DìperDì Express,** V. Alonzo 10. (Open M-Sa 8:15am-1pm and 4:30-7:30pm. MC/V.)

NO FOOD FOR YOU. During the high season in towns along the Riviera, dinner reservations are harder to come by than a hostel bed. Make reservations a few nights in advance if you're set on a restaurant, otherwise you might find yourself staring at a *completo* sign on the door instead of a menu.

Spaghetteria Il Post, V. Porro 21 (☎019 60 00 95). Follow V. Colombo from the beachfront past P. Cavour. Turn left onto V. Genova, which becomes V. Porro. Try *formaggi*, including Ligurian specialty *pecorino*, made from sheep's milk (€6.50). Lots of vegetarian options. Bring a few friends, as each dish is made for 2. Cover €1. Open Tu-Su 7:30-11pm. Closed 1st 2 weeks of Mar. Cash only. ❶

Farinata Vini, V. Roma 25 (☎019 69 25 62). Small, popular trattoria serves fresh seafood and pasta. Enjoy yellow *farinata* (pie made from chickpeas, sometimes filled with meat and vegetables) on the table at every meal. Menu changes daily. Primi €8-11. Secondi €10-16. Open M and W-Su 12:30-2pm and 7:30-9pm. MC/V. ❸

Sole Luna, V. Barrili 31 (☎019 68 16 160). A distance from the beach for those who need relief from the sun. *Farinata* €1.50. Pizza €2-2.50 per slice. Grilled focaccia *panini* €2-3.50. Savory crepes €3-4. Open daily 10am-8pm. Cash only. ❶

La Taverna dei Brontoloni, V. della Concezione 7. Considering the beachfront seating overlooking water and palm trees, these prices can't be beat. Try the *trofie alla gevonese* (€9). *Menù turistico* (primo, secondo, and contorno) €15. Pizza €4-8. Primi €7-10. Secondi €8-18. Open M-Tu and Th-Su noon-2:30pm and 6-10:30pm. AmEx/MC/V. ❷

⊙ ♪ SIGHTS AND ENTERTAINMENT

Finalmarina is best known for its sandy **beaches.** The free beach is perfect: small and well-populated, but not crowded, the strip of yellow sand is caressed by sparkling waters. For more seclusion but less ready access to snack bars, walk 15min. east along V. Aurelia and through the first short tunnel to another beach, cradled by overhanging cliffs. **Finalborgo,** Finale Ligure's historical district, is a 1km walk or 2min. bus ride up V. Bruneghi from the station. Past the **Porta Reale** (its main entrance), the Chiostro di Santa Caterina houses the **Museo Archeologico del Finale,** dedicated to Ligurian history with displays ranging from Paleolithic artifacts to Roman and Byzantine finds. (☎019 69 00 20. Open Tu-Su Sept.-June 9am-noon and 2:30-5pm; July-Aug. 10am-noon and 4-7pm. Free.) Enjoy the town's medieval architecture and quiet ambience while sipping a *caffè* in one of many small *piazze*. If you crave the small-town charm of narrow streets and ancient churches, consider making a short bus trip to nearby villages of **Borgio** and **Verezzi** (every 15min. 6:15am-10:30pm, round-trip €2.20). Consider visiting during July and August, when the annual **Festival Teatrale** holds live theater performances by national touring companies. (V. IV Novembre. ☎019 61 29 73; www.festivalverezzi.it. Tickets €23, reduced €20.)

In Finalmarina, late summer nights are the norm, and bars, *gelaterie*, and even restaurants are packed until the wee hours. A few blocks from the shore is **Pilade,** V. Garibaldi 67, with live music ranging from blues to soul on some Friday nights and rock and techno during the week. Posters of jazz legends fill the walls and an older crowd fills the tables, ordering mixed drinks (€5) or beer (from €3). Pizza (€2 per slice) and delicious *panini* (€2.60-3) are available for a sit-down meal or takeout. (☎019 69 22 20. Open daily 10am-2am. Closed Th in winter.) Each Saturday night, locals pile into **El Trucadero Cocktail Bar,** V. della Concezione 13, for DJ-hosted "Palm Beach Parties," beginning at 10pm. (Mixed drinks €5-8. Open W-Sa 10pm-3am.) As the sun sets, it's easy to find more nightlife—just follow the crowds to the waterfront, where bathhouses host dance parties and bars fill up with sunbathers along **Via della Concezione.**

ALASSIO   ☎0182

Sun-splashed Alassio (ah-LA-see-yo) has attracted high-class Italians and dedicated beachgoers to its sparkling seas for over a century. Though its residential population is only about 13,000, this number seems to triple in summer thanks to sun-worshipping resort-frequenters. Vacationers come for the white-sand beaches, excellent cuisine and nightlife, or a case of the town's signature Baci chocolate pastries (see opposite page). Even with these luxuries, Alassio maintains a cheery, unpretentious character that makes it perfect for young travelers.

▐ TRANSPORTATION

Trains: between V. Michelangelo and V. Giuseppe Mazzini (☎0182 89 20 21). Ticket office open daily 6am-7pm. 24hr. self-service ticket machines available. To: **Finale Ligure** (20min., every 30min., €3.30); **Genoa** (2hr., every 2hr., €6.40); **Milan** (3hr., every 3hr., €14); **Ventimiglia** (1hr., every 30min., €4.90).

Buses: SAR buses run along V. Aurelia, connecting Alassio to nearby towns.

Bike Rental: Ricciardi, C. Dante Alighieri 144 (☎0182 64 05 55). €5 per hr., €15 per day. Open M-Sa 9am-7pm, Su 10am-12:30pm and 4:30-7pm. AmEx/MC/V.

▐▐ ORIENTATION AND PRACTICAL INFORMATION

Alassio is a small, navigable town with activity centering around the boardwalk. Head straight out of the **train station** and turn right on **Via Giuseppe Mazzini** in front of the park. V. G. Mazzini forms one part of the city's main street, **Via Aurelia.** Three streets, V. Aurelia, **Corso Dante Alighieri,** and **Via Vittorio Veneto,** run parallel to the sea. Head straight from the train station to hit the shore.

Tourist Office: APT tourist office, V. G. Mazzini 68 (☎0182 64 70 27; alassio@inforiviera.it). Open M-Sa 9am-12:30pm and 3-6:30pm, Su 9am-noon.

Banks: Unicredit Banca, V. Gibb 14, 2 blocks from the train station on V. Aurelia. Open M-F 8:20am-1:20pm and 2:20-4:20pm, Sa-Su 10am-12:30pm and 4:30-7pm.

Luggage storage is available to the left of the train station's main exit. Open daily 7am-noon and 2:15-6:30pm. €3.50 per day.

Farmacia Nazionale is at V. V. Veneto 3. (☎0182 64 06 06). Open daily 8:30am-12:30pm and 3:30-7:30pm. MC/V.

Internet Access: Punto.it, V. Torino 30 (☎0182 47 01 24). Open M 4-7:30pm, Tu-Sa 9:30am-12:30pm and 4-7:30pm. MC/V.

Post Office: P. Airaldi Durante (☎0182 66 091). Open M-F 8am-6pm, Su 8am-1:15pm. Cash only. **Postal Code:** 17021.

▐▐ ACCOMMODATIONS AND CAMPING

Hotel Fiorenza & Banksia, V. Privata Marconi 11-13 (☎0182 64 05 04; www.alassio.it/banksia). From the station, walk along V. Hanbury and turn right on V. P. Marconi. Welcoming staff provide rooms with TV, phone, and private bath. Breakfast included. Parking €5 per day. Doubles €60-90. Extra bed 25% of room price. Cash only. ❸

Hotel Panama, V. Brennero 27 (☎0182 64 59 16; www.panamavacanze.com). From the station, turn right on V. G. Mazzini and left on V. Torino. Follow to the sea, and then turn right on V. V. Veneto, which becomes V. Brennero. Private beach and cheery dining room with beachwood cabinets. Rooms have flatscreen TV, A/C, and phone. Breakfast included. Lockers and Internet access available. Doubles €80-180. Weekly rates available. Extra bed €20. Full-pension €50-115. AmEx/MC/V. ❸

Hotel Rosa, V. Maddalena Conti 10. Family-run. Rooms with have embroidered duvets. Private garden, 2 terraces, 3 common rooms, and bar. Doubles €75-110. ❸

Camping La Vedetta Est, V. Giancardi 11 (☎0182 64 24 07; fax 64 24 27), 1.5km from Alassio. From V. G. Mazzini, take bus toward Albenga. Bus stops in front on the highway, so be careful. Bungalows and tent sites overlook the sea. Open daily 8:30am-12:30pm and 3-10pm. Campsites €7-8 per person; 2-person bungalows with car and tent €24-35; bungalows €30-145. Cash only. ❶

🛒 FOOD

Alassio is overrun with pizzerias and *gelaterie*. Don't leave without sampling the famed *Baci di Alassio* (fudge pastry) at **Balzola**, P. Matteotti 26. (☎0182 64 02 09. Open daily in summer 9am-4am; in winter 9am-2am.) Buy basics from the **STANDA** supermarket at V. S. Giovanni Bosco 36/66, part of V. Aurelia. (Open daily 8am-8:30pm. AmEx/MC/V.)

🍴 **Osteria Mezzaluna,** V. Vico Berno 6 (☎0182 64 03 87; www.mezzaluna.it), on the waterfront. Intimate, Spanish-influenced atmosphere and delectable Mediterranean cuisine. Large platters of meats and cheeses served family-style. Salads €6.50-8.50. Secondi €7.50-10. Live music nightly. Open daily 7:30pm-2am. AmEx/MC/V. ❸

Pizzeria Italia, Passeggiata Toti 19 (☎0182 64 40 95). Ultra-thin-crust pizza just steps from the beach. The *boscaiola* (grilled eggplant, prosciutto, and fresh mozzarella; €7.50) packs a flavorful punch. Primi €8-10. Secondi €10-16. Cover €1. Open daily May-Aug. noon-3:30pm and 7pm-4am. Cash only. ❷

Ristorante Sail Inn, V. Brennero 34-38 (☎0182 64 02 32). Attentive waiters and a waterfront patio make this *ristorante* a classy choice for a fishy feast. Primi €12-24. Secondi €15-40. Open Tu-Su for lunch and dinner. AmEx/MC/V. ❹

Gelateria Acuvea, P. Matteotti 3 (☎0182 66 00 60). After 25 years in business, the Sicilian wizards at Gelateria Acuvea have the whole town in their power, scooping out fresh, whipped gelato. Watch flavors being hand-churned while you wait. 2 scoops €1.70 Open daily in summer 10am-2am; in winter 10am-midnight. Cash only. ❶

👁 📷 SIGHTS AND NIGHTLIFE

Kilometers of pristine, sandy **beaches** stretch in both directions along the coast, leaving little reason to venture inland. There are a few **free** public beaches about a 15min. walk down the shore, but if central location and lively activity are a priority, then a private beach may be worth the price of admission. Most entries requires a €12-20 fee for two to four chairs and umbrella. Take a short stroll down the beach to the east to join the throng of older fishermen at the **pier,** a favorite spot for loafing, line-casting, and relaxed sea-gazing. If you need a beach break, the fishing village of **Laigueglia** offers colorful houses, tiny *piazze*, and twisting stone streets. (30min. coastal walk or 5min. bus ride toward Andorra. SAR buses leave from points on V. Aurelia every 20 min., buy tickets for €1.40 at nearby *tabaccherie*.)

Stoked by tourists and youth from nearby towns, Alassio comes to life at night. Decorated with red lanterns, **Tokai Bar,** V. V. Veneto 151, draws an international crowd for beachfront refreshments and animated conversation. (Mixed drinks and sangria from €5.50. Open M-W and F-Su 10:30am-3am. Cash only.) Local favorite **Bar Cabaret,** V. Hanbury 58, has live music on weekends and a raucous crowd that sings along. Grab a pint (€3-7) and one of many *panini* named after classic rock legends. (☎0182 347 961 5372. Open daily 9:30pm-3am. Cash only.) Trendy **Caffe Roma**, V. Dante 308-310, is the new place to see and be seen among the Euro-chic. All-white decor adorns the two-story lounge, and a young and hip crowd flirts on red-and-black polka-dotted plush couches. (☎0182 64 03 78. Panini €3-5. Mixed drinks €5-9. Open Tu-Su noon-4am.)

SAN REMO   ☎0184

With all the cheapness and tacky glamor of a casino town, and yet the tranquility of a resort refuge, this former Russian-elite retreat now hosts a medley of international tourists seeking unadulterated freedom. Despite the crowds that converge to play slots in the largest casino resort town on the Italian Riviera, San Remo (san RAY-mo; pop. 50,608) offers a plethora of urban comforts and entertainment opportunities. The city's many boutiques and upscale shops help winners and indulgent losers alike live like big spenders. Upholding the reputation of the *Riviera dei Fiori* (Riviera of Flowers), San Remo blooms with colorful carnations year-round. Adding to the musical click of poker chips, the town resounds with an international jazz competition each summer.

TRANSPORTATION

Trains: Stazione F.S., V. Carlo Pisacane, facing C. Felice Cavalotti. Ticket office open daily 6:30am-8pm. To: **Genoa** (2-3hr., every hr. 5:24am-10:24pm, €7.90), **Milan** (4hr., 7 per day 5:22am-5:15pm, €15), and **Ventimiglia** (20min., 1-2 per hr. 7:25am-12:55am, €1.90). 5min. walk from ticket booth to train. Prices listed vary seasonally.

Buses: Stazione Autolinee, P. Colombo (☎0184 59 27 06). To: **Ventimiglia** (30min., every 15-30min. 5am-12:55am, €2) via **Bordighera** (20min., €1.40).

Taxis: Radio Taxi, ☎0184 54 14 54.

ORIENTATION AND PRACTICAL INFORMATION

The city is comprised of three main streets that run east-west, parallel to the beach. The train station faces the northern-most of the three, **Corso Felice Cavalotti**, which becomes **Corso Giuseppe Garibaldi** and then **Corso Giacomo Matteotti** on its way west through the *centro*. To the south is **Via Roma**, followed by **Via Nino Bixio** closest to the water. To get to the *centro* from the station, turn right on C. F. Cavalotti, cross the roundabout **Rondo Giuseppe Garibaldi**, and veer left down C. G. Garibaldi. At **Piazza Colombo**, continue straight, bearing left while crossing the *piazza* to reach swanky C. G. Matteotti, which leads to the *lungomare* and the sea. The tourist-free old town, **La Pigna**, is uphill from P. Colombo.

Tourist Office: APT, V. Nuvoloni 1 (☎0184 59 059; www.rivieradeifiori.travel). From P. Colombo, go left onto C. G. Matteotti and follow it to the end. The office is slightly up the hill on the corner on the right. Open M-Sa 8am-7pm, Su 9am-1pm.

Bank: There are plenty of banks for the high rollers in San Remo. **Banca Intesa**, V. Roma 62 (☎0184 59 23 11), offers currency exchange and **ATM**. Open M-F 8:30am-1:30pm and 2:45-5pm, Sa 8:30am-noon.

Bookstore: Libreria Mondadori, V. Roma 91 (☎0184 50 57 12). Large English selection. English-speaking staff. Open 9am-8pm daily.

Laundromat: Blu Acquazzura, V. Alessandro Volta 131 (☎0184 340 417 8480), off Rondo Garibaldi. Wash and dry €3.50 each. Open daily 8:30am-7:30pm.

Pharmacy: Farmacia Centrale, C. G. Matteotti 190 (☎0184 50 90 65). After-hours rotation posted outside. Open M-Sa 8:30am-8:30pm.

LIGURIA

Hospital: Ospedale Civile, V. Giovanni Borea 56 (☎0184 53 61).

Internet: Mailboxes, Etc., C. Cavallotti 86 (☎0184 59 16 73). €2.50 per 30min., €4 per hr. Photocopies and fax available. Open M-F 9am-6:30pm. AmEx/MC/V.

Post Office: V. Roma 156. Open M-F 8:15am-6:30pm, Sa 8:15am-1pm. **Postal Code:** 18038.

ACCOMMODATIONS

San Remo enjoys a high standard of accommodations. Though this means high prices, it also means that even one-star hotels are clean and comfortable.

Albergo Al Dom, C. Mombello 13, 2nd fl. (☎0184 50 14 60). From the train station, turn right onto C. F. Cavallotti and pass through Rondo G. Garibaldi. Follow C. G. Garibaldi and turn left on C. G. Matteotti to reach C. Mombello. Buzz to enter. Welcoming owners tend rooms with full bath, fans, and TV. Breakfast €5. Singles €30; doubles €60. ❷

Hotel Graziella, Rondo Garibaldi 2 (☎0184 57 10 31; fax 57 00 43), 2min. from the train station. Turn right on C. F. Cavalotti, then right around Rondo G. Garibaldi. Hotel is in a villa set back from the road. Elegant rooms with high ceilings, stone balconies, TV, fridge, and phone; most with A/C. Breakfast €5. Singles €65; doubles €85. Prices jump €10-15 per person in August. MC/V. ❹

Hotel Sorriso, C. Raimondo 73 (☎0184 50 03 56; www.soloalberghi.com/hotelsorriso). From the train station, turn right on C. F. Cavalotti, left on V. Fiume, and right on C. Orazio Raimondo. Plush crimson carpeting, in-room TVs, A/C, and showers. English-speaking staff happily points the way to nearby dining and entertainment. Breakfast included. Singles €40-60; doubles €60-120. Prices soar in summer. AmEx/MC/V. ❸

Camping Villaggio dei Fiori, V. Tiro a Volo 3. (☎0184 66 06 35; info@villaggiodeifiori. it). A 10min. bus ride west of town. Take bus from station in P. Colombo to Villa Elios (every 20min., €1) or any bus to Ventimiglia and stop at Villa Elios. The shaded sites and relaxed atmosphere, combined with on-site pool and restaurant, make this a solid option. 2-person tent pitch €20-32; 4-person €29-53. High season 3- to 5-person bungalows €99-128, low season €64-120. Electricity €2. Cash only. ❶

Trattoria A Cuvea, C. G. Garibaldi 110 (☎0184 50 34 98). Follow C. F. Cavalotti away from the train station. Tasty cuisine served in this hole-in-the-wall favored by locals. Primi €5.70-7.60. Secondi €7.30-8.75. Open M-Sa noon-3pm and 7:30-10pm, Su 7:30-10:30pm. Cash only. ❷

FOOD

Some unique and affordable dining options exist among the pizzerias and pricey restaurants. Try *sardinara*, a local focaccia-like specialty topped with tomato sauce, herbs, and olives. Buy basics at **Casitalia** supermarket in P. Eroi 44. (Open M-F 8:15am-12:45pm and 2-7:30pm, Sa 8:15am-1pm and 4-7:45pm. Closed W afternoon. MC/V.) **Mercato Ortofruitticolo,** in neighboring P. Mercato, sells fresh produce, meat, and bread. (Open M-Sa 6am-1:30pm, Sa 4-7:30pm.)

Vin D'Italia, C. Mombello 5 (☎0184 59 17 47). Upscale restaurant accented with modern vases. Down-to-earth staff. Local food is their middle name; be sure to try *sardinara* (€0.80), hot from a wood-burning oven. Primi and secondi €9-16. Open M-Sa 11am-3pm and 7-10pm. AmEx/MC/V. ❸

Urbicla Vivas, P. dei Dolori 5/6 (☎0184 75 55 66; www.urbiciavivas.com), in a charming *piazza* in the old city. From V. Palazzo, turn left on V. Cavour, and walk through the archway, turn left onto V. S. Sebastiano and continue straight until you reach the 1st *piazza*. Join locals for generous helpings of *ravioli di erbette* (with herbs). Primi €10-14. Secondi €10-17. Open daily 8am-3pm and 7pm-midnight. AmEx/MC/V. ❸

RistoPizza Grill da Giovanni, V. Cesare Pesante 7 (☎0184 50 49 54), off V. XX Settembre. Innovative pizza in 32 varieties. Traditional *pizza margherita* (€5.50) can't be beat. On a quiet side street away from the crowds by the water. Pizza €5.50-8. Primi €6-12. Secondi €9-25. Open M-W and F-Su noon-3pm and 7-11:30pm. AmEx/MC/V. ❷

Liberty, V. Imperatrice 70 (☎0184 53 14 96; fax 0184 50 15 74). Traditional Ligurian fare and 90 wines. Elegant dining room overlooks the water. Primi and secondi €22-42. Cover €2.70. Open Dec. 22-Nov. 2, Tu-Su 12-2:30pm and 7-10:30pm. AmEx/MC/V. ❺

👁 🏖 SIGHTS AND BEACHES

San Remo has many historical treasures. Across from the tourist office stands the Byzantine-style, onion-domed Russian Orthodox **Chiesa di Cristo Salvatore,** V. Nuvoloni 2. The intricate exterior is the highlight; the simple interior has a few gleaming icons and plain walls. (Open daily 9:30am-12:30pm and 3-6:30pm. Suggested donation €1.) Leaving the church, follow C. G. Matteotti away from the sea. Turn left onto V. Pietro Calvi, which leads to P. S. Siro, where you'll find the city's most sacred monument, the 13th-century **Basilica di San Siro.** (Open M-Sa 8:30am-noon and 3-6pm, Su 8:30am-noon and 3-8pm. Free.) From the basilica, steer through the vendors along the *gelateria*-lined V. Palazzo and turn left on V. Cavour to **La Pigna,** San Remo's *centro storico,* which most tourists miss. Narrow streets are crowded with tiny medieval churches connected by private secret underground passageways. The streets can be confusing; be sure to ask for a map that includes La Pigna when you stop by the Tourist Office. From La Pigna, follow the tree-lined road upward to P. Assunta, to the elaborate **Il Santuario della Madonna della Costa.** This 17th-century monument features a high dome covered in frescoes and twisting rose marble columns. The *Madonna and Child* painting above the altar, attributed to Fra Nicoló of Voltri, dates to the late 14th century. (☎0184 50 30 00. Open daily 9am-noon and 3-6pm. Modest dress required. Free; donations welcome.)

In the daytime, Speedo- and bikini-clad crowds pack the beach and numerous *bagni* that line the water, so get there early to snag a patch of sand. Most commercial beaches are open from 8:30am to 7:30pm, while the public beach closes at 7pm. Lounge chair and umbrella rental run around €12 per day. Most public beaches require rentals for entrance. Penny-pinchers can head to the end of V. Roma for a well-kept public beach.

🎵 🎭 ENTERTAINMENT AND NIGHTLIFE

When darkness hits in San Remo, so do the gamblers who frequent the enormous **Casino Municipale,** C. Inglesi 18, at the end of C. G. Matteoti. Built in 1905, the casino is a dazzling example of *Belle Époque* architecture. No sandals or shorts are allowed upstairs, and a coat and tie for men and formal wear for women are required in winter. Five hundred slot machines clang away on the lower floors, while the swanky rooms upstairs host the Riviera's most dapper, sipping mixed drinks and hoping to win the famed "Mystery Jackpot." (☎0184 59 51; www.casinosanremo.it. 18+. Passport required. Cover F-Su €7.50. Open M-F 2:30pm-2am, Sa-Su 2:30pm-4am.) After dark, couples meander along the swanky **Corso Matteotti** for gelato and liqueurs. **Mellow Sax Pub,** V. Roma 160, has a sports- and jazz-inspired decor and outdoor seating to attract an all-ages crowd. Drinks run €3-7 and come with *torta di verde* and focaccia. (☎0184 50 37 43; www.saxpub.it. Open M and W-Su 8pm-4am. AmEx/MC/V.) Ten minutes from the casino is **Pico de Gallo,** Lungomare V. Emanuele 11/13, where the liquor starts flowing long before sundown. Sip a Caribbean-inspired drink (€5) as you sit on the beach. The *bagni* (beach area) is open daily 9:30am-7:30pm. (☎0184 57 43 45; www.picosanremo.com. Cash only. Bar open 24hr. Restaurant open

12:30-3pm. MC/V.) On a side street off C. G. Matteotti, **Zoo Bizarre,** V. Gaudio 10, is a small, trendy spot with electric-green tables and a ceiling plastered with movie posters. The hip, though unpretentious, crowd kicks off its weekend evenings here around 9pm with drinks (€4.50-7) and free munchies. (☎0184 50 57 74. Open M-F 5:30pm-2am, Sa-Su 5:30pm-3am. Cash only.)

Alternatives to dice and drinking are harder to find. At the end of January, a float parade livens up the city streets for the annual festival **San Remo in Fiore.** The **Jazz and Blues Festival,** held in late July and early August, draws international artists to soothe the sunburned crowds.

BORDIGHERA ☎0184

A seaside residential locale dominated by middle-class Italian vacationers, Bordighera (bor-dee-GEH-ra; pop. 10,292) first hit the tourist spotlight in the early 20th century, with high profile guests like Claude Monet and Louis Pasteur. Its outer edges are busy with traffic and cheap shops, though the humble *centro storico* offers quiet, palm-tree lined routes for a *passeggiata* (stroll). For those seeking sun, Bordighera also offers small gray stretches of beach, though they pale in comparison to the French Riviera just minutes away.

▐ TRANSPORTATION. The **train station** is in P. Eroi Libertà. **Trains** run to: Genoa (3hr., 6 per day 4:53am-10:23pm, €7.35); Milan (4hr., 4 per day 6:25am-7:05pm, €24.70); San Remo (15min., every hr. 4:53am-10:23pm, €1.70); Ventimiglia (5min., every hr. 7:35am-12:57am, €1). The ticket office is open daily 6:15am-7:35pm. Riviera Transporti **buses** stop every 300m on V. V. Emanuele and run to San Remo (25min., every 15min. 5:42am-1:22am, €1.20) and Ventimiglia (15min., every 15min. 5:42am-1:22am, €1.20). Buy tickets at *tabaccherie* on V. V. Emanuele or at the post office. Tourist office provides more detailed bus schedules. **Taxis** available outside train station.

▟▐ ORIENTATION AND PRACTICAL INFORMATION. The bus from Ventimiglia stops on the main street in the busy, modern city, **Via Vittorio Emanuele,** which runs parallel to the sea and the scenic **Lungomare Argentina.** To get to the *lungomare,* walk down V. Agostino Noaro or V. Generale Luigi Cadorna, and go through the tunnels under the train tracks. The **train station** is located between V. V. Emanuele and the sea, at **Piazza Eroi della Libertà.** To reach the **centro storico,** follow V. V. Emanuele to P. Ruffini. Bear left across the *piazza* and continue straight. This road changes names to V. Libertà, V. Matteotti, and V. Arziglia. Turn left and walk uphill on V. Botafogu Rossi and follow it to the top. **Via Roma,** which becomes **Corso Italia,** runs straight from the station.

For extensive info on all Riviera towns, head to the **tourist office,** V. V. Emanuele 172. From the train station, walk left and turn right onto **Via Sant'Antonio.** (☎0184 26 23 22; fax 26 44 55. Open in summer M-Sa 9am-12:30pm and 3:30-7pm, Su 9am-12:30pm.) **Currency exchange** and **ATM** are available at **Banca Intesa,** V. Roma 4. (☎0184 26 67 77. Open M-F 8:30am-1:30pm and 2:45-4:15pm, Sa 8:30am-noon.) In case of emergency, call the **police,** V. Primo Maggio 49 (☎0184 26 26 26). **Farmacia Centrale,** V. V. Emanuele 145, posts a list of after-hours service. (☎0184 26 12 46. Open M-F and Su 8:30am-12:30pm and 3:30-7:30pm.) The **post office,** P. Eroi della Libertà 5/6, has an ATM outside. (☎0184 26 91 51 or 26 91 31. Open M-F 8:15am-6:30pm, Sa 8:15am-12:30pm.) **Postal Code:** 18012.

▐▗ ACCOMMODATIONS AND FOOD. In the high season, many hotels in Bordighera require that clients accept full or half-pension. It is also standard practice to raise prices for guests staying under three days, usually by €5-10.

The city's few hotels tend to charge upwards of €125 a night for a double with simple furnishings. Across from the train station, on the left, **Albergo Nagos ❷**, P. Eroi della Libertà 7, third fl., has nine small rooms with long beds; three have private showers. The shared bath is clean and well-stocked. (☎0184 26 04 57. Singles €32; doubles €45. Half-pension €36; full-pension €45. MC/V.)

To escape the beach crowds, head to ⬛**Ristorante la Piazzetta ❷**, P. del Popolo 13, in the *centro*. Savor the specialty wood-fired pizza (€5-8.50) and other Ligurian fare in bountiful portions. (Primi €7-9.50. Secondi €10-16. Cover €1.20. Open M-Tu and Th-Su noon-2:30pm and 6:30-11pm. AmEx/MC/V.) Locals crowd the marble tables of **Creperie-Caffè Giglio ❷**, V. V. Emanuele 158. A dizzying selection of creative dinner crepes with many vegetarian options complement the seven-page drink menu. Dessert crepes (€3.50-6) are sweet and satisfying. (☎0184 26 15 30. Open Tu-Su 5:30pm-3am. Cash only.) The lively, beach-themed **La Reserve ❹**, V. Arziglia 20, at the eastern end of the *lungomare*, is a great place to grab a seaside drink—follow the blaring island music. (☎0184 26 13 22. Primi €10-16. Secondi €15-30. Bar open 24hr. Kitchen open 8-10am, 12:30-2:30pm, and 8-10pm.) **Osteria La Sfusa**, 144 V. Emanuele (☎0184 345 348 0650), bottles award-winning olive oil (½ liter €7.50; 1 liter €12.50) and uses it in its daily specials. *Giovedi gnocchi* and *sabato trippa* are excellent local draws. (Daily specials and primi €8. Secondi €12. Open Tu-Su noon-2:30pm and 7-10pm.) An outdoor **market** on the *lungomare* sells produce. (Th from early morning to 1pm. There is also a **STANDA** at V. della Libertà 32. (Open M-Sa 8am-8pm, Su 9am-8:30 pm. AmEx/MC/V.)

◨◪ SIGHTS AND BEACHES. Bordighera's **beach** is crammed with locals and tourists who arrive early to rent lounge chairs, umbrellas, and cabanas from one of the many *bagni* (each around €5 per day). A popular free beach is accessed through the subway beneath the train station. To rent jet skis, wind-surf boards, or motorboats, call ☎0184 348 518 3835. For sailing, windsurfing, kayaking, or canoeing, contact the **Nautical Club of Bordighera** (☎0184 26 00 94; www.clubnauticobordighera.it). The tourist office also has windsurfing info. Follow V. Arziglia for 20min. to reach the **Giardino Esotico Pallanca.** It's on the left past the tunnel. Buses from V. V. Emanuele heading in the direction of San Remo also stop at the *Giardino* upon request. The exotic garden, once open only to scientists, contains over 3000 species of cacti and flora. The walking tour (1hr.) leads along meandering terraces. (☎0184 26 63 47; www.pallanca. it. Open Tu-Su 9am-12:30pm and 2:30-7pm. €6, under 13 free, groups more than 8 €5.) Returning to town, the **Giardini del Capo** offer spectacular sea views and a glimpse of the statue of Queen Margherita Di Saviolo, one of Italy's first queens. The park leads to the town's **centro storico**, established in 1471, which is too narrow for cars. Walk through the parking lot at the top of the park and through the archway at the end of V. del Campo to explore the narrow stone streets.

◧❀ NIGHTLIFE AND FESTIVALS. Il Barretto is Bordighera's most renowned spot for beachside nightlife—you'll know it when you see it. A town staple since 1960, it has a spring break vibe and no-frills attitude. Come for cheap eats, packed dance floors, and ample amounts of liquor. (☎0184 26 25 66. Pizza €1.50. Shots €3.50. Open daily 9am-4am. Cash only.) A raucous, mostly male crowd fills the dim interior and outdoor tables under an arched arcade at **Graffiti Pub/Risto House**, V. V. Emanuele 122. Along with a wide choice of liquor (€3.50-5), beer on tap (€2.50-4), and wine (€11-15), they also serve cheap meals, including *panini* for €3.50-4. (☎0184 26 15 90. Open M-Sa 5:30pm-3am. Cash only.) A classier, more upscale *discoteca*, the **Kursaal Club**, Lungomare Argentina 7, has both live and recorded underground, house, and industrial music. A younger crowd floods the dance floor on Saturday, and locals from neighboring

LIGURIA

towns say it's the area's best club. (☎0184 26 46 85. 25+ on F and Su. Open Sept.-July F-Su 7pm-midnight; Aug. daily 11pm-5am. AmEx/MC/V.)

Despite its small size, Bordighera loves revelry. In April each year, the city becomes **La Città dell'Umorismo** (The City of Humor), when comedians, cartoonists, and cabaret performers descend upon the town for a celebration of laughter. For 10 days surrounding May 14, the church hosts the **Festa di Sant'Ampelio**, when the whole town gathers in celebration with fireworks, a feast of savory specialties, dancing, and music. Summer brings a host of outdoor festivities, including an international ethnic music festival at the end of July and a series of concerts and plays at the seaside gazebo **Chiosca della Musica.**

VENTIMIGLIA ☎0184

"Bonjour" is as common as *"buongiorno"* in this quiet, commercial town. Ventimiglia (VEN-tee-MEEL-ya; pop. 25,000) is only a 10min. train ride from the French border; the coastline between the town and Monaco were part of the same state until Napoleon's 1860 invasion drew clearer boundaries. Ventimiglia lacks the spunk of its more touristy neighbors, though the 11th-century *città alta* and the pebbly beaches are worth a visit. Ventimiglia's proud bilingual citizens and restaurant signs reading *"jambon di Parma"* and *"piatti du jour"* attest to the truly unique blend of French and Italian cultures.

◧ TRANSPORTATION

Trains: P. Cesare Battisti (☎0184 89 20 21). Ticket office open daily 5:15am-8:40pm. To **Genoa** (3hr., 1-2 per hr. 5am-7:51pm, €9), **Milan** (4hr., 7 per day 4:45am-6:58pm), and **Nice, FRA** (40min., 2 per day, €9). Trains to **Monaco, Cannes,** and Nice are frequently through the French lines.

Buses: Riviera Transporti (☎0183 70 01; www.rivieratrasporti.it). Runs to regional and local destinations, including **San Remo** (35min., 4 per hr. 5:30am-1:10am, €1.50) via **Bordighera** (15min., €1.20) and **Dolceacqua** (20min., 2 per hr., €1.25). Bus stops every 100m along V. Cavour. Tickets available in *tabaccherie* in V. Cavour and at **Turismo Monte Carlo** (see below), which also provides schedules.

✦ ⁊ ORIENTATION AND PRACTICAL INFORMATION

From the **train station,** walk down **Via della Stazione** to the *centro*. The second crossroad is **Via Cavour,** where V. della Stazione becomes **Corso Repubblica** as it continues toward the waterfront. A footbridge at the end of C. Repubblica leads to *Ventimiglia Alta* (or *città alta*), the medieval section of town. Turn left directly before the footbridge onto **Lungo Roia Giolamo Rossi** to stroll along a restaurant-lined promenade in the newer, commercial part of town.

Tourist Office: V. Cavour 61 (☎0184 35 11 83; infoventimiglia@rivieradefiori.org), 5min. from the train station. English spoken. Open M-Sa 9am-12:30pm and 3:30-7pm. **Turismo Monte Carlo,** V. Cavour 57 (☎0184 35 75 77; fax 35 26 21), 2 doors down, has currency exchange and bus and hotel info. Open M-Sa 9am-12:30pm and 2:30-7pm.

Bank: Cariparma, V. Roma 18/D. Open M-F 8:30am-1:30pm and 2:45-4:15pm.

Bookstore: Libreria Casella, V. della Stazione 1/D (☎0184 35 79 00). Small English selection. Open M-Sa 9am-1pm and 3:30-7:30pm. AmEx/MC/V.

Emergency: ☎800 55 44 00.

Police: V. Aprosio 12 (☎23 821).

Red Cross: V. Dante Alighieri 16 (☎23 20 00).

LIGURIA

Pharmacy: Farmacia Internazionale, V. Cavour 28/A (☎0184 35 13 00). Open M-F 8:30am-12:30pm and 3:30-7:30pm, Sa 9am-12:30pm. AmEx/MC/V.

Hospital: Ospedale Bordighera, V. Aurelia 122 (☎0184 53 61), in Bordighera.

Internet Access: Mail Boxes, Etc., V. Vittorio Veneto 4/B (☎0184 23 84 23), just past the Giardini Pubblici from C. Repubblica. €3 per 30min. **Western Union** available. Open M-Sa 8:30am-12:30pm and 3-8:30pm. Closed W morning.

Post Office: V. della Repubblica 8/C (☎0184 23 63 31). **24hr. ATM** outside. Open July and Aug. M-F 8:15am-1:15pm, Sa 8:15am-12:30pm; Sept.-June M-F 8:15am-6:30pm, Sa 8:15am-12:30pm. **Postal Code:** 18039.

▐▛ ▞▌ ACCOMMODATIONS AND CAMPING

Though less crowded than neighboring cities, Ventimiglia fills up quickly in July and August; reserve ahead to benefit from the town's budget options. Large rooms with simple, modern decor and spotless baths await at █Calypso Hotel ❸, V. Matteotti 8/G. This charming hotel in a calm, central location has a friendly, English-speaking staff. Vibrant seascape frescoes adorn the walls. (☎0184 35 15 88; www.calypsohotel.it. Breakfast included. Parking €10 per day. Reception 7am-midnight. Open Feb. 11-Jan. 14. Doubles for single use €50-64; doubles €65-82, with A/C €86; triples €90-112. AmEx/MC/V.) To reach **Camping Roma ❶,** V. Freccero 9, from the station, follow V. della Repubblica, turn right on V. Roma, cross the Ponte Doria, and make an immediate right onto C. Francia; after 50m it becomes V. Freccero. Family-friendly spot with large common areas and a playground has well-maintained, brightly painted bungalows and immaculate facilities. (☎0184 23 90 07; informazioni@campingroma.it. Camper service 8-10am and 3-6pm. Open Jan.-Oct. and Dec. 24-Dec. 31. €7 per person; €8-10 per tent; €5 per car. 4-person bungalows with kitchen €45-65, with private bath €60-100, with both €90. Showers free. MC/V over €50.)

▐ FOOD

The **covered market** (M-Sa 6am-1pm) displays a staggering array of fruit, vegetable, and fish stands along V. della Repubblica, V. Libertà, V. Aprosio, and V. Roma. There's a **STANDA** supermarket at the corner of V. Roma and V. Ruffini. (Open M-Sa 8am-8pm. AmEx/MC/V.) Pizzerias along the water all offer similar fare for €8-12. Head away from the beach and into the city for more variety.

Ristorante Cuneo, V. Aprosio 16/D, off V. della Repubblica. Tables decorated with fresh flowers and orange-and-yellow silk cloths create a welcoming atmosphere. Delicious Ligurian cuisine, including homemade gnocchi (€9.50). Primi €8.50-13. Secondi €13-25. *Menù* €20 includes service, primi, secondi, salad, and dessert. Open M-Sa 11:45am-3pm and 7-10:30pm, Su 11:45am-3pm. MC/V. ❸

Pasta & Basta, Passeggiata Giacomo Marconi 20/A (☎0184 23 08 78). Take the Passerella Squarciafichi bridge to the *città alta,* turn left onto V. Trossarelli and follow it until it becomes Passeggiata G. Marconi. Pick one of 22 sauces (€7-11) to pair with any of 8 pastas (€1-3.50) or try one of the house seafood specials (€13-16). A/C and ocean views. Open Tu-Th noon-midnight. MC/V. ❷

Ristorante Marco Polo, Passeggiata Felice Cavalotti 2 (☎0184 35 26 78). Candlelit waterfront terrace is the perfect place to splurge or to bring a date. Don't miss the *tagliatelle* with lobster (€25) or any special from the dessert cart. Service is poised and professional. Primi €15-27. Secondi €18-33. Open daily noon-2:30pm and 7-10:30pm; closed M Sept.-June. AmEx/MC/V. ❺

Gelateria Haiti, V. Roma 28C (☎0184 35 16 18). Serves odd but delicious flavors like violet, "liquorice," and blue bubblegum. Opt for a medium with 3 huge scoops and a

LIGURIA

bunny tipped spoon (€2.70). 12 flavors of *granita*. Scoopers pile on up to 7 flavors. Open daily 10am-12:30pm and 2:45-11pm. ❷

🏛 SIGHTS

Though Ventimiglia isn't known for its pebbly beaches, insistent beachgoers will find the quietest ones are on the *alta* side, along **Passeggiata Marconi.**

■BOTANICAL HANBURY GARDENS. Begun in 1867 by British aristocrat Sir Thomas Hanbury, the gardens hold exotic flora from three continents and cascade down the summit of Cape Mortola. Hike down to the seaside cafe for *panini* (€3.50) or gelato (€1.50). The steep, challenging course mapped out in the brochure takes about two hours. *(C. Montecarlo 43. Follow V. Guiseppe Verdi around the città alta until it becomes V. Biancheri. At P. della Costituente, bear left and walk 15min. down V. Francia. Riviera Transporti buses also stop at La Mortola. ☎0184 22 95 07. Open daily June 16-Sept. 15 9:30am-6pm; Sept. 16-Oct. 16 9:30am-5pm; Oct. 16-Feb. 28 9:30am-4pm; Mar.-June 15 9:30am-5pm. Last entry 1hr. before closing. €7.50. MC/V.)*

SPIAGGIA LE CALANDRE. For those set on sunbathing, a 15min. walk down a footpath from the end of Passeggiata Marconi leads to Spiaggia Le Calandre, the town's only sandy beach. A snack bar serves drinks and *panini* and rents essential beach equipment. It's best to head home before sundown (in summer around 8pm) to avoid navigating the cliff-side path in the dark. *(☎03 474 315 393. Open daily 8am-8:30pm. 2 lounge chairs and umbrella €18 per day. Cash only.)*

CITTÀ ALTA. Follow Passeggiata Giacomo Marconi for a pleasant walk along the water until it becomes V. Trossarelli, which leads up to the historic *città alta*, Ventimiglia's cliff-side medieval area. To reach the *città alta* from the main town, cross the footbridge and turn right on V. Trossarelli. Fifty meters ahead is Discesa Porta Marina; climb to V. Galerina and then V. Falerina. From there, streets lead to P. Cattedrale, where the ancient **Cattedrale dell'Assunta** stands guard over the town below. The 11th-century church of **San Michele** is on the other side of the old town, off V. Garibaldi, at P. Colleta. Its crypt was constructed using pilfered Roman columns. *(Open daily 9am-noon and 3-7pm. Free.)*

MUSEO ARCHEOLOGICO. Accessible by the Blue Riviera Transporti, the museum displays Roman artifacts found in the area, including 12 marble heads. It also holds rotating exhibits by town artists. *(V. Giuseppe Verdi 41. Buses leave from V. Cavour and V. Martiri della Libertà. Dir.: Ponte San Luigi (15min., 10 per day from 9:05am, €1.25). ☎0184 35 11 81; http://fortedellannunziata.it. Open Tu-W, F, and Sa 9am-12:30pm and 3-5pm; Th 9am-12:30pm and 8:30-10:30pm; Su 8:30-10:30pm. €3; under 18 €2. Cash only.)*

BALZI ROSSI (RED CLIFFS). From the neighboring town of Latte, take the Riviera Transporti Bus along C. Europa or walk 40min. through two large tunnels 700m to these cliffs. Prehistoric men once lived in the enormous grottoes. Enter to see a cave drawing of a horse painted thousands of years ago. The small buildings of the **Museo Preistorico** contain skeletons and fossils over a million years old. *(☎0184 38 113. Open Tu-Su 8:30am-7:30pm. €2.20. Cash only.)*

🔜 DAYTRIP FROM VENTIMIGLIA

■DOLCEACQUA
Riviera Transporti runs buses from Ventimiglia's V. Cavour, near C. Repubblica. (20min.; 18 per day 6am-7:05pm, last return 7:32pm; round-trip €2.60.) In Dolceacqua, the bus stops at P. Garibaldi, the new town's central square. The medieval town is across the river.

Dolceacqua (DOL-chay-AH-kwa; pop. less than 2000) is a hidden treasure not to be missed on any Ligurian vacation. Narrow cobblestone streets, low-ceilinged shops, and a towering castle give travelers a sense of the local character. Though the city's origins are ancient—dating as far back as the fifth century BC—its landmark year came in 1270, when a Genoan captain constructed the famous **Doria Castle.** During the Middle Ages, Dolceaqua became the largest and strongest of a string of villages that rose up along the Roya River to accommodate traders between Ventimiglia and the rest of northern Italy.

Cross the **Roman footbridge,** which Monet called a "jewel of lightness" for its high arch and ingenious construction. Turn right after the bridge and follow the walkway to a *piazza*, where the 15th-century parish church of **San Antonio Abate** overlooks the river. Decorated with paintings and a frescoed ceiling, the church is as traditional as the sea-pebble mosaics in the *piazza* outside. (Open M-Sa 11:30am-5pm. Mass Su 8am and Sa noon. Free.) From the *piazza*, follow the multilingual signs, which detail the town's history, through the narrow cobblestone streets of the old city. Many of the ancient stone houses have been converted into artist's studios, containing everything from Monet knockoffs to sculptures made from bathroom tiles. Admission to most galleries is free, but the artist may hover over your shoulder, expecting a sale.

Those who stay the night shouldn't miss a meal at **Pizzeria La Rampa ❷**, V. Barberis Colomba 11, on the left side of P. Garibaldi. In 2002, the National Agency of Pizza Chefs named La Rampa's pesto pizza the "Best Typically Regional Pizza" in Italy, selecting it from a pool of 900 contenders. (☎0184 20 61 98. Open Aug. 24hr.; Sept.-July Tu-Su 7pm-midnight. Pizza €5-9; gluten-free pizza available. Primi €5-7.50. Secondi €5-9. AmEx/MC/V.) Ask at the **tourist office** in P. Garibaldi, for info on August's **Ferragosto,** which fills the *piazza* with swirling traditional *balletti* costumes. (Tourist office open Tu-Su 10am-12:30pm and 3:30-6pm.) The **Festa della Michetta,** which takes place on August 16, celebrates the town's local take on brioche, the mouthwatering *michetta*. Local *alimentari* dotting the medieval stone streets sell the pastry year-round.

LIGURIA

LOMBARDY
(LOMBARDIA)

Lombardy ("lom-bar-DEE-ah") specializes in the finer things in life. Though coveted by the Romans, Goths, French, Spaniards, Austrians, and Corsicans, the disputing European powers failed to rob Lombardy of its prosperity. The region is filled with ornate art and architecture; from Milan's fashion runways to Cremona's Stradivari violin shops, cultural sophistication permeates the region.

HIGHLIGHTS OF LOMBARDY

GET DIZZY looking over Cremona from the Torazzo, Italy's tallest *campanile* (p. 268).

DAYTRIP to Certosa di Pavia, where the monastery stands as a monument to the evolution of northern Italian art from early Gothic to Baroque (p. 254).

SPOT the *moda* of the moment in Milan, as stylish *Milanesi* show off Europe's latest cutting-edge fashion (p. 250).

WANDER the streets of Mantua, where Renaissance artists Verdi and Mantegna got their inspiration (p. 262).

MILAN (MILANO)   ☎02

Milan ("mee-LA-no"; pop. 1,200,000) is a proud modern metropolis. Tire giant Pirelli, fashion master Armani, and various executive banks make it Italy's economic powerhouse. Rushed, refined, and unapologetically cosmopolitan, Milan has its share of problems, including traffic congestion and a high cost of living. But its beautifully ornate *duomo* and stunning La Scala theater, thriving alongside big designer shopping and even bigger spenders, attract throngs of visitors. Generally overlooked as a center of commerce, this Italian urban center also hides artistic treasures: Leonardo's *Last Supper*, the Pinacoteca di Brera, and the Pinacoteca Ambrosiana. Today, the city flourishes as Italy's leading producer of cutting-edge style, hearty risotto, and die-hard soccer fans. The city's pace quickens twice a year when local soccer teams AC Milan and Inter Milan face off in matches with fanfare that rivals many religious festivals. Milan's bustling lifestyle has established it as a northern capital.

⚔ INTERCITY TRANSPORTATION

Flights: 24hr. flight info (☎02 74 85 22 00; www.sea-aeroportimilano.it).

Malpensa Airport (MXP), 48km from the city. Intercontinental flights. **Luggage storage** and lost-and-found available. Shuttles run to and from right side of Stazione Centrale (1hr.; every 20min. to airport 5am-9:30pm, to Stazione Centrale 6:20am-12:15am; €4.50). Malpensa Express **train** departs Cadorna Metro station and Stazione Nord (40min.; every 30min. to airport 5:50am-8:20pm, to Stazione Centrale 6:45am-9:45pm; onboard €11/13, round-trip €15/17).

Linate Airport (LIN), 7km from town. Domestic, European, and intercontinental flights with European transfers. Starfly **buses** (☎02 58 58 72 37) run to Stazione Centrale (20min.; every 30min. to airport 5:40am-9:35pm, to Stazione Centrale 6:05am-11:35pm; €2.50). City bus #73 runs to Milan's San Babila Metro station (€1), even though it's less convenient than Starfly.

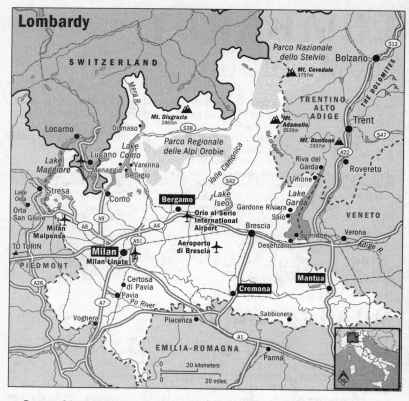

Lombardy

SWITZERLAND

Parco Nazionale
dello Stelvio

Bolzano

Mt. Cevedale
3757m

Locarno

Domaso

Mt. Disgrazia
2865m

Lake
Lugano

Lake
Como

TRENTINO-
ALTO
ADIGE

Trent

Mt.
Adamello
3539m

Mt. Bondone
1537m

Rovereto

Lake
Maggiore

Menaggio

Varenna

Bellagio

Parco Regionale
delle Alpi Orobie

Valle Camonica

Val d'Agogne

Riva del
Garda

Limone

Lake
Orta

Stresa

Como

Lake
Iseo

Lake
Garda

VENETO

Orta
San Giulio

Bergamo

Gardone Riviera

Salò

Verona

Milan
Malpensa

Orio al Serio
International
Airport

Brescia

Sirmione

TO TURIN

Aeroporto
di Brescia

Desenzano

Adige R.

PIEDMONT

Milan

Milan Linate

Mantua

Certosa
di Pavia

Pavia

Cremona

Voghera

Po River

Piacenza

Sabbioneta

EMILIA-ROMAGNA

Parma

0   20 kilometers

0   20 miles

Bergamo Orio al Serio Airport (☎035 32 63 23; www.orioaeroporto.it), 58km from town, serves some budget airlines including **RyanAir**. Shuttle runs to Stazione Centrale (1hr.; to airport 4:15am-10pm, to Milan 8am-1am; €6.70).

Trains:

Stazione Centrale (☎02 89 20 21), in P. Duca d'Aosta. Ticket office open daily 6am-8:40pm. To: **Bergamo** (1hr., every hr. 7:20am-11:37pm, €4.10); **Florence** (3hr., every 1-2hr. 5:30am-8pm, €37); **Rome** (Eurostar 5hr., €56; TBIZ 5hr., €62; sleeper car 8hr., €73); **Turin** (2hr., every hr. 5:18am-12:30am, €8.75); **Venice** (2hr., every hr. 6:05am-9:05pm, €30).

Stazione Cadorna (☎199 15 11 52). Part of Ferrovia Nord, the local rail system that connects to **Como** (1hr., every 30min. 6:12am-9:12pm, €3.70) and **Varese** (1hr., every 30min. 7:06am-1:03am, €4). Malpensa Express runs from the station to the airport (40min., every 30min. 4:20am-11:27pm, €11). **Lockers** available at the station to the left of the Express Cafe (small bag €3.50 per 2hr., medium €4.50, large €6.50).

Stazione Porta Genova, in P. Stazione di Pta. Genova, is on the western line to **Alessandria** (1hr., every hr. 5:10am-8:09pm) and **Mortara** (1hr., every hr. 5:57am-10:42pm).

Stazione Porta Garibaldi (☎02 65 52 078; ticket office open daily 6:30am-9:30pm). Runs to: **Bergamo** (1hr., every hr. 4:50am-6:45pm); **Domodossola** (2hr., every 1hr. 5:05am-8:47pm); **Lecco** (1hr., every hr. 5:35am-9:41pm); **Piacenza** (1hr., every hr. 8:26am-11:04pm).

Buses: At Stazione Centrale. Signs for destinations, times, and prices posted outside. Ticket office open 6:30am-8:10pm. Shuttle bus tickets also available from the *tabaccherie* outside the station on V. Vitruvio. **Intercity** buses depart from locations on the periphery of town. **Autostradale** departs from P. Garibaldi; **SAL, SIA,** and many others depart from P. Castello (M1: Cairoli) around V. Jacini near Stazione Nord, and Porta Garibaldi for **Bergamo, Certosa di Pavia,** the **Lake Country, Rimini, Trieste,** and **Turin.**

ORIENTATION

Milan's layout is a series of concentric squares. There are four central squares: **Piazza del Duomo,** where **Via Orefici, Via Mazzini,** and **Corso Vittorio Emanuele II** meet; **Piazza Castello** and the attached **Largo Cairoli,** near Castello Sforzesco; **Piazza Cordusio,** connected to Largo Cairoli by V. Dante and P. del Duomo by V. Orefici; and **Piazza San Babila,** the entrance to the business and fashion district. The **duomo** and **Galleria Vittorio Emanuele II** are at the center of town. Two parks, the **Giardini Pubblici,** with several museums, and **Parco Sempione,** home to the Castello Sforzesco and its **Musei Civici,** sit to the northeast and northwest respectively. **Stazione Centrale,** Milan's transportation hub, lies northeast of the *centro* in a commercial district above the Giardini Pubblici. To reach P. del Duomo, take M3 to the Duomo stop. From there, head through the station's main entrance into **Piazza Duca d'Aosta.** Follow **Via Pisani** as it becomes **Via Turati** and veers into **Via Manzoni,** which leads to **Piazza della Scala,** home to Milan's opera house, and through the Galleria Vittorio Emanuele II to P. del Duomo. From V. Manzoni, turn on **Via della Spiga** to the **fashion district.** From P. S. Babila take **Corso Venezia** north, which will become **Corso Buenos Aires,** and leads to the *pensioni* (budget hotels) district by **Piazzale Loreto. Via Torino,** going away from P. del Duomo, runs to **Corso Porta Ticinese** and the **Navigli Canal District.**

> **ATTENTION!** Avoid walking alone after dark in the areas east of Stazione Centrale, north of Porta Garibaldi, and below the Navigli.

LOCAL TRANSPORTATION

The layout of Milan's streets makes it difficult to navigate by car. Pick up a map with a street index at the tourist office or any bookstore, or a public transit map at the **ATM Point** (☎800 80 81 81; www.atm-mi.it; open M-Sa 7:45am-8:15pm) in the Metro station under Stazione Centrale or P. del Duomo.

Public Transportation: The **Metropolitana Milanese,** the city subway, operates 6am-midnight and is by far the most useful branch of Milan's transportation network. **Line #1** (red; M1) stretches east to west from the *pensioni* district east of Stazione Centrale (M1: Sesto FS) through the *centro* and west to the youth hostel (**Molino Dorino** northwestern end; **Bisceglie** at the southwestern end). **Line #2** (green; M2) links Milan's 3 train stations from **Cologno Nord** and **Gessate** in the east to **Abbiategrasso (Famagosta)** in the west, and crosses M1 at **Cadorna** and **Loreto. Line #3** (yellow; M3) runs south from the area north of Stazione Centrale at **Comasina** to **San Donato,** crossing M2 at **Stazione Centrale** and M1 at the **duomo.** Use the **bus system** for trips outside the city. **Trams #29** and **30** travel the city's outer road; **buses #94** and **61** traverse the inner road. **Azienda Trasporti Milanese (ATM)** tickets (€1) are good for buses, trams, and Metro for 1hr. Tickets €1.30 per night; 10 tickets €9.50; 24hr. pass €3. Metro tickets can be purchased at station machines.

Taxis: White taxis are omnipresent in the city. Call **RadioTaxi** (☎85 85 or 02 40 40).

Car Rental: Both have offices in **Stazione Centrale** facing P. Duca d'Aosta.

Avis (☎02 66 90 280 or 67 01 654). Open M-F 8am-8pm, Sa 8am-2pm.

Europcar(☎02 66 98 78 26). Open daily 7am-midnight. AmEx/MC/V.

LOMBARDY

Central Milan

▲ ACCOMMODATIONS

Albergo Villa Mira,	1 F2
Campeggio Città di Milano,	2 A4
La Cordata Ostello,	3 C6
Hotel Aurora,	4 F2
Hotel Eva and Hotel Arno,	5 F2
Hotel Cà Grande,	6 F2
Hotel San Tomaso,	7 F2
Hotel Kennedy,	8 F2
Ostello Piero Rotta (HI),	9 A3
Hotel Aliseo,	37 D5

● FOOD

Big Pizza: Da Noi 2,	10 B6
Caffè Vecchia Brera,	11 C3
Il Forno dei Navigli,	12 B6
L'Osteria del Treno,	13 F1
Il Panino Giusto,	14 F2
Obika Mozzarella Bar,	38 C3
Peck,	17 C4
Princi,	18 C4
Ristorante Asmara,	19 F2
Rugantino,	20 B5
Savini,	21 D4
Trattoria Milanese,	22 C4
Z2,	39 B5
Fratelli la Bufala,	40 B5

NIGHTLIFE	
Bar Magenta,	23 B4
Café Capoverde,	24 F2
Cave Montmarte,	25 C3
Club 2,	26 C3
L'elephant,	27 C4
Exploit,	28 B5
Flying Circus,	29 C5
Hollywood,	30 C1
Loolapaloosa,	31 C1
Old Fashion Café,	32 A3
Scimmie,	33 B6
Spazio Movida Cocktail Bar,	34 B6
Le Trottoir,	35 B6
Yguana Café Restaurant,	36 C5
La Hora Feliz,	41 C5

LOMBARDY

Milan Metro

M1	Rete Metropolitana Terminal Station	
	Transfer Station	
- - -	Airport Bus Connection	
i	Tourist Information	
✈	Airport	
P	Parking	
🚌	Bus Connection	
🚆	Rail Connection	

M1 Red
M2 Green
M3 Yellow

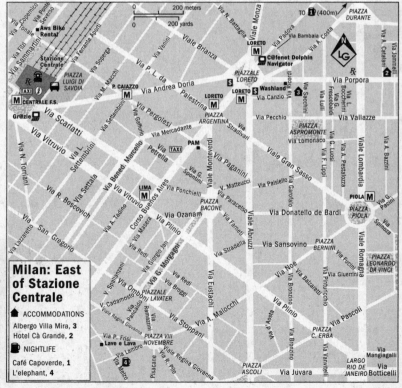

Milan: East of Stazione Centrale

🏠 ACCOMMODATIONS

Albergo Villa Mira, **3**
Hotel Cà Grande, **2**

🎵 NIGHTLIFE

Café Capoverde, **1**
L'elephant, **4**

LOMBARDY

Bike Rental: Companies require €100 security deposit and ID. **Rossignoli,** C. Garibaldi 65/71 (☎02 80 49 60). €6 per ½-day, €10 per day, €18 per weekend, €35 per week. Open M 2:30-7:30pm, Tu-Sa 9am-12:30pm and 2:30-7:30pm. **AWS,** V. Ponte Seveso 33 (☎02 67 07 21 45). €5.50 per ½-day. Open Th-Su 9am-1pm and 3-7pm.

⁊ PRACTICAL INFORMATION

TOURIST AND FINANCIAL SERVICES

Tourist Office: IAT (Informazioni Accoglienza Turistica), P. Duomo 19A (☎02 77 40 43 43; www.visitamilano.it). Next to the *farmacia* and down the stairs. *Hello Milano* has info in English on events and nightlife. Walking tours depart the tourist office every hr. M-Sa 10am-3pm; €10-20. Office open M-Sa 8:45am-1pm and 2-6pm, Su 9am-1pm and 2-5pm. **Branch:** Stazione Centrale (☎02 77 40 43 18/19), on ground fl. Smaller venue with shorter lines. Open M-Sa 9am-6pm, Su 9am-1pm and 2-5pm.

Tours: Autostradale (☎02 33 91 07 94; www.autostradale.it). Offers hop-on-hop-off sightseeing tours that circle the *centro*. Taped commentary in 8 languages. Buy tickets by phone, at the tourist office, online, or at M2: Garibaldi. Tours (from €40) depart P. del Duomo, usually at 9:30am. Some tours (€55) include admission to all the stops, including La Scala Theater and Leonardo's *Last Supper*.

Consulates: Australia, V. Borgogna 2 (☎02 77 70 41). M1: S. Babila. Open M-Th 8:30am-1pm and 1:30-5pm, F 8:30am-1pm. Appointments recommended. **Canada,** V. Vittor Pisani 19 (☎02 67 58 34 20; www.canada.it). M2/3: Centrale FS. Open M-F 9am-noon. **New Zealand,** V. Guido d'Arezzo 6 (☎02 49 90 201). M1: Pagano. Open M-Sa 8:30am-noon and 1:30-5:30pm. **UK,** V. S. Paolo 7 (☎02 72 30 00 08; emergency 03 35 81 06 857; www.britain.it). M1/3: Duomo. Open daily 9am-1pm and 2-5pm. **US,** V. Principe Amedeo 2/10 (☎02 29 03 51; www.milan.usconsulate.gov). M3: Turati. Open M-F 8:30am-noon.

Banks and Currency Exchange: Most banks open M-F 8:30am-1:30pm and 3-4pm. **ATMs** abound; some with automated currency exchange. **Western Union:** In Stazione Centrale. Open daily 9am-7:45pm. Also at **Money Transfer Point,** V. Porpora 12 (☎02 20 40 07 63). Open M-Sa 9:30am-9pm.

American Express: V. Larga 4 (☎02 72 10 41). Near the *duomo,* at the corner of V. Larga and V. S. Clemente. Holds cardholder mail for up to 1 month for free. Moneygram international money transfer. Also **exchanges currency.** Open M-F 9am-5:30pm, Sa 9am-12:30pm. Also at corner of V. dell'Orso and V. Brera. Open M-F 9am-5:30pm.

Beyond Tourism: InformaGiovani, Vco. Calusca 10 (☎02 88 46 57 60; www.comune.milano.it/giovani), enter at C. Porta Ticinese 106. Take trams #3, 15, 9, 29, 30 or bus #59 or 94. Info for young people looking to work, volunteer, study, or tutor. Also has resources on social events and professional associations, as well as apartment listings. Open M-W 10am-6pm, Th-F 2-6pm. Also at V. Laghetto 2. Open M-F 2-6pm. **Easy Milano** (www.easymilano.it), a biweekly publication for Milan's English-speaking community. Lists work opportunities including childcare and tutoring.

LOCAL SERVICES

Luggage Storage: Malpensa Airport (☎02 58 58 02 98), ground fl. €3.50-4 per bag per day. Open daily 6am-10pm. **Linate Airport** (☎02 71 66 59), ground fl. €3.50-4 per bag per day. Open daily 7am-9:30pm.

Lost Property: Ufficio Oggetti Smarriti Comune, V. Friuli 30 (☎02 88 45 39 00). Open M-F 8:30am-4pm. **Malpensa Airport** (☎02 74 86 83 31; lostpropertymalpensa@sea-aeroportimilano.it). Open M-F 10am-noon. **Linate Airport** (☎02 70 12 44 51). **Stazione Centrale** (☎02 63 71 22 12). Open daily 7am-1pm and 2-8pm.

English-Language Bookstore: The American Bookstore, V. Camperio 16 (☎02 87 89 20), at Largo Cairoli. Open M 1-7pm, Tu-Sa 10am-7pm. AmEx/MC/V. **English Bookshop,** V. Ariosto 12 (☎02 46 94 468). Open M-Sa 10am-7pm.

GLBT Resource: ARCI-GAY "Centro D'iniziativa Gay," V. Bezzeca 3 (☎02 54 12 22 25; www.arcigaymilano.org). Open M-F 3-8pm.

Handicapped/Disabled Services: AIAS Milano Onlus, V. Paolo Mantegazza 10 (☎02 33 02 021; www.milanopertutti.it).

Laundromat: Washland, V. Porpora 14 (☎02 34 00 81 44 77). Wash €3.50 per 7kg, dry €3.50 per 18min. Open daily 8am-10pm. **Lavanderia Self-Service ad Acqua,** V. Vigevano 20 (☎02 49 83 902). Wash €3.50 per 7kg, dry €3.50. Detergent €0.60. Open daily 8am-10pm. **Lava e Lava,** V. Melzo 17 (☎02 34 71 40 42 37). Wash €2, dry €3. Detergent €0.75. Open daily 8am-9:30pm.

EMERGENCY AND COMMUNICATIONS

Police: in P. Beccaria, ☎02 77 271.

Pharmacy: Farmacia Stazione Centrale (☎02 66 90 735). In Stazione Centrale's ground fl. galleria across from the tracks. Open 24hr. **Farmacia Carlo Erba,** P. del Duomo 21 (☎02 86 46 48 32), next to tourist office. Open M 2-7pm, Tu-F 9:30am-1:45pm and 3-7pm. **Farmacia Lombardia,** V. Porpora 65. Open M-F 8:30am-12:30pm and 3:30-7:30pm, Sa 8:30am-12:30pm. **Farmacia Stazione Porta Genova** (☎02 58 10 16 34), Ple. Stazione Porta Genova 5. Open M-F midnight-12:45pm and 3:30pm-midnight, Sa 3:30pm-8:30am, Su 8pm-midnight. AmEx/MC/V. All post after-hours rotations.

Hospital: Ospedale Maggiore di Milano, V. Francesco Sforza 35 (☎02 55 031), 5min. from *duomo* on inner ring road. **Ospedale Niguarda Ca'Granda,** in P. Ospedale Maggiore, is north of the city. **Ospedale Fatebenefratelli,** in C. Pta. Nuova.

Internet Access:

Gr@zia, P. Duca d'Aosta 14 (☎02 89 69 57 33; www.grazianet.com). M2/M3: Centrale FS. To the left and across the street from Stazione Centrale's main door. Wi-Fi and free webcam. €2.80 per 30min., €4 per 1hr., €8 per 3hr. Open daily 8am-midnight.

C@fenet Dolphin Navigator, V. Padova 2 (☎02 28 47 209). M1/M2: Loreto. Frappes, *panini,* and focaccia €3. Fast connection. €1.30 per 15min., €5 per hr. Open M-Sa 6:30am-7pm.

Post Office: P. Cordusio 4 (☎02 72 48 21 26), near P. del Duomo. Offers currency exchange and **ATM.** Open M-F 8am-7pm, Sa 8:30am-noon. **Postal Code:** 20100.

ACCOMMODATIONS AND CAMPING

Milan is a wealthy city with a high standard of living, and its accommodations tend to be priced accordingly. Booking two weeks to one month in advance is strongly advised for most hotels, especially during summer and theater seasons. Prices vary considerably from low season (Dec. and July-Aug.) to high season (Sept.-Nov. and Mar.-May), when room prices often triple. The tourist office assists travelers booking accommodations.

EAST OF STAZIONE CENTRALE

Unless stated otherwise, all hotels are easily accessible from M1 or M2: Loreto, or by tram #33 from Stazione Centrale. Women should exercise caution when traveling alone at night in this area.

Hotel Cà Grande, V. Porpora 87 (☎02 26 14 52 95; www.hotelcagrande.it), 7 blocks from Ple. Loreto. Tram #33 stops 50m from the hotel. Though a bit far, it is a pleasant option with English-speaking owners and a pleasant garden. All rooms have A/C, TV, sink, and phone. Breakfast included. Singles €40-65, with bath €45-80; doubles €55-85/60-110. AmEx/D/MC/V. ❹

Albergo Villa Mira, V. Sacchini 19 (☎02 29 52 56 18). Despite the barbed wire over the entrance, the small rooms in this family-run hostel are colorful. A few of the rooms overlook the garden patio. Singles €26-35; doubles €45-62; triples €70-85. Cash only. ❷

NEAR GIARDINI PUBBLICI

▓ **Hotel Eva and Hotel Arno,** V. Lazzaretto 17, 4th fl. (☎02 67 06 093; www.hotelevamilano.com or www.hotelarno.com). M1: Pta. Venezia. Follow V. Felice Casati, then take a right on V. Lazzaretto. Ring bell. Quirky, mirrored decor and spiral staircases make for an intriguing and inviting atmosphere. Note the life-size porcelain snow leopard. 18 large rooms with wood floors, TV, and phone. Shared bathroom. Free luggage storage. Free Internet. Singles €30-45; doubles €50-100; triples €65-90. AmEx/MC/V. ❸

Hotel San Tomaso, Vle. Tunisia 6, 3rd fl. (☎02 29 51 47 47; www.hotelsantomaso.com). M1: Porta Venezia. Exit at C. Buenos Aires; turn left on Vle. Tunisia. Rooms with TV and phone. Elevator. Singles €30-65; doubles €50-100; triples €70-150. AmEx/MC/V. ❸

Hotel Kennedy, Vle. Tunisia 6, 6th fl. (☎02 29 40 09 34; www.kennedyhotel.it). M1: Pta. Venezia. Exit at C. Buenos Aires, turn left on Vle. Tunisia. Simple rooms with clean bathrooms. Elevator. Singles €36-75; doubles €55-80, with bath €70-120; triples €90-120; quads €100-160. AmEx/D/MC/V. ❸

Hotel Aurora, C. Buenos Aires 18 (☎02 20 47 960; www.hotelaurorasrl.com). M1: Pta. Venezia. On the right side of hectic C. Buenos Aires after V. Felice Casati. Offers rooms with new furniture, large beds, A/C, TV, and thick blackout curtains. Reservations recommended. Singles €50-90; doubles €70-130; triples €90-160. AmEx/MC/V. ❹

Hotel Aliseo, C. Italia 6 (☎02 86 45 01 56). Located near the city center and convenient to the metro, this hotel is on the top floor of a building with a small, quiet courtyard. Red lobby is lushly decorated. Rooms available with shared or private bath. Singles €45-60; doubles €60-75. AmEx/MC/V. ❹

ON THE CITY PERIPHERY

▓ **La Cordata Ostello,** V. Burigozzo 11 (☎02 58 31 46 75; www.ostellimilano.it). M3: Missori. From P. Missori, take tram #15 2 stops to Italia San Luca; continue in the same direction for 1 block and turn right on V. Burigozzo. Entrance around the corner on V. Aurispa. Close to the Navigli area, a lively crash pad for a young, international crowd ready to party. Colorful, plant-filled common rooms with TV and large kitchens. Laundry €3. Free Internet and Wi-Fi. 7-night max. stay. Reception 24hr. except 1-2:30pm. Check-out 11am. Closed Aug. 10-20 and Dec. 23-Jan 2. Single-sex dorms €21-25; doubles €70-100; triples €90-110; quads €100-140. MC/V. ❷

Ostello per la Gioventù AIG Piero Rotta (HI), at the corner of V. Salmoraghi and V. Calliano (☎02 39 26 70 95; www.ostellomilano.it). M1: QT8. Facing Santa Maria Nascente, turn right on V. Salmoiraghi. Though slightly far from the Metro and most sites, this enormous hostel has 400 beds. Breakfast included. Laundry €5.50. 3-night max. stay. 24hr. reception. Check-out 10am. Lockout 10am-2pm. Reserve online one day in advance; book well ahead for Apr.-Oct. Closed Dec. 24-Jan. 12. 6-bed dorms €22; private rooms €25 per person. HI-member discount €3. MC/V. ❷

Campeggio Città di Milano, V. Gaetano Airaghi 61 (☎48 20 01 34). M1: De Angeli. From metro, take bus #72 to San Romanello Togni. Backtrack 10m and turn right on V. Togni. Campground is 20min. walk straight ahead. Enter at Aquatica water park.

Modern facilities, volleyball, and barbecue. Laundry €5. Reservations recommended. Closed Dec.-Jan. €7.50 per person; €11 per tent; €6.50 per car. 2- to 6-person cabins €37-88; bungalows with bath and A/C €80-120. Electricity free. MC/V. ❶

◧ FOOD

Choose between chowing down on focaccia with the lunch-break crowd, clinking crystal glasses, or taking your palate on a world tour through the city's ethnic neighborhoods. Old-style trattorie still follow Milanese culinary traditions with *risotto alla milanese* (rice with saffron), *cotoletta alla milanese* (breaded veal cutlet with lemon), and *osso buco* (lamb, beef, or veal shank). Many local bars offer happy-hour buffets of focaccia, pasta, and risotto that come free with drink purchase. In the *centro*, weary tourists near the *duomo* often succumb to P. del Duomo's pricey and mediocre offerings, but cheap and delicious rewards await those who look a little harder.

▨ Princi, V. Speronari 6 (☎02 87 47 97; www.princi.it), off P. del Duomo. Take V. Torino and make 1st left. Stone walls and glass countertops make this more zen than you imagined an Italian bakery could be. Local favorite for authentic food on-the-go. Pastries €1-4. Pizza €3.50-5. Primi and secondi €5. Open M-Sa 7am-8pm. Cash only. ❶

Z2, Corso di Porta Ticinese 32 (☎02 89 42 02 41). Savvy, minimalist decor contributes to a relaxing and elegant atmosphere. Watch chefs in glassed-in kitchen prepare dishes such as *gnocchi agli spinaci* (€10). Primi €9-10. Secondi €10-19. Dessert €7-8. ❸

Fratelli la Bufala, Corso di Porta Ticinese 16 (☎02 83 76 529; www.fratellilabufala. com). Relax in the lively atmosphere of this buffalo-meat inspired pizzeria. Don't miss out on the lunch *menù*, with 2 courses, 1 side, and water (€10). Pizza €5.50-9.50. ❷

Trattoria Milanese, V. S. Marta 11 (☎02 86 45 19 91). M1/3: Duomo. From P. del Duomo, take V. Torino; turn right on V. Maurilio and again on V. S. Marta. Serves *costolette alla milanese* (breaded veal; €18) and *mondeghili milanesi* (breaded meatballs; €14) under brick arches. Primi €6-11. Secondi €8-23. Cover €2. Open M-F noon-3pm and 7-11:30pm. Closed last 2 weeks of July. AmEx/MC/V. ❸

Peck, V. Spadari 9 (☎02 80 23 161; www.peck.it). Aromas from the ground floor spread from the wine cellar in the basement to the deli and cafe above. Open M 3:30-7:30pm, Tu-F 9:15am-7:30pm, Sa 8:45am-7:30pm. AmEx/MC/V. ❷

Savini, Galleria V. Emanuele II (☎02 72 00 34 33; www.savinimilano.it). This world-famous restaurant keeps its decor extravagant and attracts a clientele that matches. Exquisite food, like raw umbrine fish with sherbet of *vermentino di Gallura*. Primi €25-30. Secondi €35-45. Cover €7. Open M-Sa noon-3:30pm and 7:30-10:30pm. AmEx/MC/V. ❺

Caffè Vecchia Brera, V. dell'Orso 20 (☎02 86 46 16 95; www.vecchiabrera.it). M1: Cairoli. Take V. Cusani, which becomes V. dell'Orso, out of P. Cairoli for 2 blocks. Sweet, meaty, or liqueur-soaked crepes €4-8. Primi €7.50-9. Secondi €12-14. Cover €1. Service 10%. Happy hour 5-8:30pm; drinks €5. Open M-Sa 7am-2am. AmEx/MC/V. ❸

Obika Mozzarella Bar, intersection of V. Mercato and V. dei Fiori Chiari (☎02 86 45 05 68; www.obika.it). Sleek, cosmopolitan establishment has a relaxed atmosphere. Don't pass up a slice of one of the several offered mozzarella rolls (like a jelly roll, filled with various savory Italian fillings), €4-6. At night, morphs seamlessly into a classy bar. Open M-F noon-3:30pm and 6-11:30pm, Sa-Su noon-3pm and 6-11:30pm. AmEx/MC/V. ❶

NAVIGLI AND ENVIRONS

An area packed with students means cheap grub. Many bars serve dinner or offer happy-hour buffets with the purchase of mixed drinks, and some happy-hour benefits apply to wine or soda. The **Fiera di Sinigallia**, a bargaining extravaganza, occurs Saturdays on Darsena Banks, a canal around V. d'Annunzio. **PAM** supermarket, Vle. Olona 1/3, is by the Museo "da Vinci." (M2: Sant'Ambrogio. Open M-Sa 8am-9pm, Su 9am-7:30pm.) A **DìperDì Express** supermarket is located at Vigevano 22. (M2: Porta Genova F. S. ☎02 58 10 00 20. Open M-Sa 8:30am-1pm and 3:45-8:15pm. Closed M morning in late July and Aug. MC/V over €15.)

■ **Big Pizza: Da Noi 2,** V. Giosué Borsi 1 (☎02 83 96 77). Takes its name seriously. Beer and house wine flow liberally at this riverfront location, which has a restaurant feel but the prices of a small pizza joint. The *pizza della casa* is topped with pasta (€8). If not in the mood for pizza, try the crab pasta (€5). Calzoni €5-7. Pizza €4-8.50. Cover €1. Open M-Sa 10am-2:30pm and 7pm-midnight. MC/V. ❶

■ **Il Forno dei Navigli,** Alzaia Naviglio Pavese 2 (☎02 83 23 372). Some of the most delicious pastries in the city, fresh out of "the oven of Navigli." The *cestini* (pear tart with Nutella; €2.25) defines decadence. Pastries and breads €0.50-6. Open M-Sa 7am-2pm and 6pm-1am, Su 6pm-1am. Cash only. ❶

Rugantino, V. Fabbri 1 (☎02 89 42 14 04), between the Chiesa di San Lorenzo and the Roman pillars of C. Porta Ticinese. From M2: Sant'Ambrogio, walk down V. Edmondo De Amicis. Savor famous oven-baked dishes. Beer €4. Pizza €7-10. Primi and secondi €9-18. Open daily 12:30-3pm and 7:30pm-midnight. AmEx/MC/V. ❸

NEAR GIARDINI PUBBLICI AND STAZIONE CENTRALE

Avoid the *menù turistico* at a typical trattoria in favor of foods from the neighborhood's immigrant populations. **Unes** supermarket is on V. Melzo, just off C. Buenos Aires (open M-Sa 8am-8:30pm). A **PAM** supermarket, V. Piccinni 2, is just off C. Buenos Aires. (M1: Loreto. ☎02 29 51 27 15. Open M-Sa 8am-9pm.) **Punto SMA** is on V. Noe between P. Piola and P. Bernini. (Open M-F 8:30am-1:30pm and 3:30-7:45pm, Sa 8:30am-7:45pm.)

Ristorante Asmara, V. Lazzaro Palazzi 5 (☎02 89 07 37 98; www.ristoranteasmara.it). M1: Pta. Venezia. Eat spicy Eritrean food, including a *zighini* platter with flavorful meat and vegetables served on *injera* (thin flatbread; €10) with your hands. Vegetarian options available. Antipasti €4-5.50. Entrees €8-11.50. Cover €1.60 Open M-Tu and Th-Su 10am-4pm and 6pm-midnight. AmEx/MC/V. ❸

Il Panino Giusto, V. Malpighi 3 (☎02 29 40 92 97). M1: Pta. Venezia. From the *piazza*, head down Vle. Piave and turn left on V. Malpighi. If you believe sandwiches should contain goat cheese, truffled olive oil, or veal pâté for under €8, welcome home. Beer €4-5. Artisan panini €5-8. Open daily noon-1am. AmEx/MC/V. ❷

Shun Feelin' Sushi, Vle. Tunisia 6 (☎02 29 40 30 96). The fountains and bamboo at this modern sushi restaurant come as a welcome surprise amid the hubbub of nearby C. Buenos Aires. Try *gunkan* (1 piece) from €1.70-3.50 or 8 pieces from €7-10. ❸

L'Osteria del Treno, V. S. Gregorio 46/48 (☎02 67 00 479). M2/3: Centrale F. S. From P. Duca d'Aosta, take V. Pisani; turn left on V. S. Gregorio. Primi €8-9. Secondi €12-14. Cover €2.20. Open M-F 11am-7pm and 8:30pm-12:30am, Sa 7pm-1am, Su 10am-1pm and 3pm-12:30am. AmEx/MC/V. ❹

◉ SIGHTS

NEAR THE DUOMO

■**DUOMO.** As Milan's geographical and spiritual center, the *duomo* is a good starting point for any walking tour. Built over the remains of three other basilicas, it is Italy's second-largest church. The structure is home to more than

3400 statues, 135 spires, and 96 gargoyles. The newly renovated facade juxtaposes Italian Gothic with later Baroque elements that Archbishop Borromeo commissioned to show allegiance to Rome during the Protestant Revolution. The imposing 16th-century marble tomb of **Giacomo dei Medici** in the southern transept was inspired by the work of Michelangelo. Climb (or ride) to the top of the cathedral from outside the northern transept to the ◪**roof walkway** for prime views of the city. The rooftop statue of the *Madonnina* has become the symbol of Milan. *(M1/3: Duomo. ☎ 02 72 02 33 75; www.duomomilano.com. Cathedral open daily 7am-7pm. Modest dress strictly enforced. Roof open daily Feb. 16-Nov. 14 9:30am-9:30pm. Stairs €5, elevator €7.)* The **Museo del Duomo** is currently closed for restoration, but normally displays paintings, tapestries, jewels, and stained glass related to the *duomo*'s construction. *(P. del Duomo 14, next to the Palazzo Reale.)*

◪**PINACOTECA AMBROSIANA.** The 23 palatial rooms of the Ambrosiana display exquisite works from the 14th to 19th centuries, including Botticelli's *Madonna of the Canopy*, Leonardo's *Portrait of a Musician*, Caravaggio's *Basket of Fruit* (the first Italian still-life), Titian's *Adoration of the Magi*, and works by Flemish landscape painters Brueghel and Bril. Raphael's immense ◪**School of Athens** sketch is dramatically displayed in a darkened room where the life-like nuances of its professors and students as they engaged in lively discussion are plainly visible. The courtyard's statues, fountains, and staircase are also enchanting, as is Bertini's 1867 two-story *Vetrata Dantesca*, a stained-glass window with allusions to Dante's *Inferno*. *(M1/3: Duomo. P. Pio XI 2. Follow V. Spadari off V. Torino, and turn left on V. Cantù. ☎ 02 80 69 21; www.ambrosiana.it. Open Tu-Su 10am-5:30pm. Last entry 30min. before closing. €8, under 18 or over 65 €5.)*

TEATRO ALLA SCALA. Founded in 1778, La Scala has established Milan as the opera capital of the world. Its understated Neoclassical facade and lavish interior set the stage for works by Rossini, Puccini, Mascagni, and Verdi, performed by virtuosos like Maria Callas and Enrico Caruso. Visitors can peek into the theater's interior and soak up La Scala's history at the **Museo Teatrale alla Scala.** Replete with portraits, pianos, and porcelain figurines, the most compelling exhibit is the highly personal account of Maria Callas' contribution to modern opera. From poster art to a plaster cast of Toscanini's hand, the museum offers a glimpse into the operatic past. *(M1/3: Duomo. Largo Ghiringhelli 1 or P. della Scala. From P. del Duomo, walk through the Galleria Vittorio Emanuele II. Museum on left side of building. ☎ 02 88 79 24 73; www.teatroallascala.org. Open daily 9am-12:30pm and 1:30-5:30pm. Last entry 30min. before closing. See Entertainment, p. 249, for info about performances. €5, students €4.)*

MUSEO POLDI PEZZOLI. Poldi Pezzoli, an 18th-century nobleman and art collector, bequeathed his house and art to the city "for the enjoyment of the people." Wind past the 19th-century fountain with bronze cherubs to famous paintings that include Mantegna's *Virgin and Child*, Botticelli's *Madonna and Child of Mary Teaching Christ to Read*, and the signature piece, Pollaiuolo's *Portrait of a Young Woman*. The house itself is a treat, as are the smaller collections of china, marble busts, ancient Roman jewelry, Tiepolo oil sketches, and 18th-century clocks that fill Pezzoli's museum. *(M3: Montenapoleone. V. Manzoni 12, near La Scala. ☎ 02 79 48 89; www.museopoldipezzoli.it. Open Tu-Su 10am-6pm. €8, students and seniors €5.50, under 10 free. English-language audio tour free.)*

GALLERIA VITTORIO EMANUELE II. A 48m glass-and-iron cupola, groundbreaking at the time of construction both in its concept and in the combination of materials, towers over a five-story arcade of offices, overpriced shops, and cafes. Intricate mosaics representing the continents sieged by the Romans adorn the floors and walls. In the years before electricity, a miniature train circled the top of the arcade, keeping the candles lit along the glass. Once known as "Milan's Living Room," this 1870s gallery is now a tourist hub, connecting P. del Duomo to P. della Scala. Spin on the mosaic bull clockwise three times for good luck. *(To the right of the duomo. Free.)*

PALAZZO REALE. This *palazzo* served as the town hall before becoming the residence of Milanese royalty until the 19th century. Giuseppe Piermarini, architect of La Scala, designed its facade. *(To the left of the duomo. P. del Duomo 12. ☎ 02 88 451. Only open during exhibitions. Prices vary; usually €8, students €6.)*

NEAR CASTELLO SFORZESCO

⬛CASTELLO SFORZESCO. Restored after WWII damage in 1943, the Castello Sforzesco is one of Milan's best-known monuments. Its towers and courtyard were constructed in 1368 by the Visconti to defend against the Venetians, and Leonardo had his studio here before invaders used the grounds as army barracks and horse stalls. Inside are the ten **Musei Civici** (Civic Museums). Highlights include the **⬛Museum of Ancient Art,** which is housed in rooms and quiet courtyards just as awe-inspiring as the artifacts they contain, among them Michelangelo's unfinished **Pietà Rondanini** (1564), and Leonardo's frescoes on the ceiling of the **Sala delle Asse;** his design was once considered so insignificant it was whitewashed over, actually protecting the original colors. The **Museum of Decorative Art** showcases furnishings, Murano glass, and a giant porcelain crab. At the superb **Museum of Musical Instruments,** check out the amusing display on the history of the glass harmonica, and don't miss the African harps made from rattlesnake heads. *(M1: Cairoli or M2: Lanza. ☎ 02 88 46 37 03; www.milanocastello.it. Castello grounds open daily Apr.-Oct. 7am-7pm; Nov.-Mar. 7am-6pm. Free. Museums open Tu-Su 9am-5:30pm. Combined admission €3, students and over 65 €1.50. 3-day pass for Castello, Museo Archeologico, Museo di Storia Naturale e Museo del Risorgimento €7/3.50. F 2-5:30pm free.)*

CHIESA DI SANTA MARIA DELLE GRAZIE. The church's elaborately frescoed Gothic nave contrasts with the airy Renaissance tribune added by Bramante in 1497. Observe the intricate blue and red geometric drawings on the white walls and the gold sunbursts in the middle of each arch on the ceiling. *(P. S. Maria delle Grazie 2. M1: Conciliazione or M2: Cadorna. From P. Conciliazione, take V. Boccaccio and then right onto V. Ruffini for 2 blocks. Open M-Sa 7am-noon and 3-7pm, Su 7:30am-12:15pm and 3:30-9pm. Modest dress required. Free.)* To the left of the church entrance is the Cenacolo Vinciano (Vinciano Refectory, the convent dining hall), home to one of the best-known pieces of art in the world: Leonardo da Vinci's **⬛Last Supper.** Following a 20-year restoration effort, the painting was re-opened to the public in 1999; pieces have been flaking off almost since the day it was finished in 1498. As a result, only groups of 25 or fewer are allowed in the refractory for no more than 15min. Reservations are mandatory; book at least a month ahead in summer. At the tourist office, some tours with same-day booking include admission to the *Last Supper.* *(Reservations ☎ 02 89 42 11 46; www.cenacolovinciano.org. Refectory open Tu-Su 8:15am-6:45pm. Wheelchair-accessible. €6.50, EU residents 18-25 €3.25, EU residents under 18 or over 65 free. Reservation fee €1.50. Tours €3.25. Audio tour €2.50.)*

PINACOTECA DI BRERA. The Brera Art Gallery presents a superb collection of 14th- to 20th-century paintings, with an emphasis on the Lombard School. Works include Bellini's *Madonna col Bambino* and *Pietà*, Mantegna's innovative *Dead Christ*, Raphael's *Marriage of the Virgin*, Caravaggio's *Supper at Emmaus*, and Francesco Hayez's *The Kiss*. A small collection of modernist works includes pieces by Modigliani and Picasso. A glass-enclosed chamber in **Gallery 14** allows visitors to watch conservationists at work on the aged canvases. *(V. Brera 28. M2: Lanza or M3: Montenapoleone. Walk down V. Pontaccio, and turn right on V. Brera. Or from La Scala, walk up V. Verdi until it becomes V. Brera. ☎ 02 72 26 31; www.*

brera.beniculturali.it. Open Tu-Su 8:30am-7:15pm. Last entry 30min. before closing. Wheelchair-accessible. €5, EU citizens 18-25 €2.50, under 18 or over 65 free. Audio tour €3.50.)

MUSEO NAZIONALE DELLA SCIENZA E DELLA TECNOLOGIA "DA VINCI". This family-friendly museum traces the development of science and technology from Leonardo's age to the present. The hall of computer technology features a piano converted into a typewriter. Don't miss the **da Vinci room**, which contains wooden mock-ups of his flying machines, cranes, and bridges. *(V. S. Vittore 21, off V. Carducci. M2: Sant'Ambrogio. ☎ 02 48 55 51; www.museoscienza.org. Open Tu-F 9:30am-5pm, Sa-Su 9:30am-6:30pm. Last entry 30min. before closing. €8, students €6.)*

BASILICA DI SANT'AMBROGIO. A prototype for Lombard-Romanesque churches throughout Italy, Sant'Ambrogio is the most influential medieval building in Milan. The AD fourth-century **Cappella di San Vittore** in Ciel d'Oro is through the chapel on the right, and the asymmetrical **campanili** are the result of an intense eighth-century feud between Benedictine monks and priests, each of whom owned one tower. *(P. Sant'Ambrogio 15. M2: Sant'Ambrogio. Walk up V. Giosuè Carducci; the church bulwark rises up to the right. ☎ 02 86 45 08 95. Open M-Sa 7:15am-noon and 2:30-7pm, Su 7:15am-1pm and 3-8pm. Free. Mosaics ☎ 86 45 08 95. Open Tu-Su 9:30am-11:45am and 2:30-7pm. €2, students €1.)*

FROM NAVIGLI TO THE CORSO DI PORTA TICINESE

BASILICA DI SANT'EUSTORGIO. Founded in the fourth century to house the bones of the Magi, it lost its function when the dead sages were spirited off to Cologne in 1164. The 1278 building hosts a Lombard-Gothic interior of low vaults and thick columns. A great masterpiece of early Renaissance art is the 1468 Portinari Chapel to the left of the entrance. The frescoes in the chapel below the rainbow dome illustrate the life of St. Peter. The elevated sarcophagus in the center is supported by eight statues representing the five cardinal virtues and the three theological virtues; different images of Prudence take the faces of a young, middle-aged, and old woman. *(P. S. Eustorgio 1. M2: Sant'Ambrogio. From V. E. de Amicis, turn right on C. Porta Ticinese, and follow it toward the Navigli. Basilica: open daily 7:30am-noon and 3:30-6:30pm; closed 2 weeks in mid-Aug. Free. Cappella: ☎/fax 02 89 40 26 71. Open Tu-Su 10am-6pm. €6, students and seniors €3.)*

NAVIGLI DISTRICT. As the Venice of Lombardy, Milan's Navigli district boasts canals, elevated footbridges, open-air markets, and trolleys. The Navigli are sections of a larger medieval canal system that transported thousands of tons of marble to build the *duomo* and linked Milan to northern cities. Leonardo designed the original canal locks. *(From the M2: Pta. Genova station, take V. Vigevano.)*

CHIESA DI SAN LORENZO MAGGIORE. The oldest church in Milan, San Lorenzo Maggiore testifies to the city's medieval glory. Begun as a Christian church according to an octagonal plan, it was later rebuilt to include a 12th-century *campanile* and 16th-century dome. Next to the church sits the 14th-century **Cappella di Sant'Aquilino.** Inside, an AD fifth-century mosaic of a beardless Christ with his apostles looks over St. Aquilino's remains. *(M2: Sant'Ambrogio to V. E. de Amicis, which leads to P. Vetra and the church. V. Porta Ticinese 39. ☎ 02 89 40 41 29. Open M-Sa 7:30am-12:30pm and 2:30-6:45pm, Su 9am-6:45pm. Cappella €2, students and seniors €1.)*

PARCO DELL'ANFITEATRO ROMANO. This archaeological park is home to the remains of Milan's Roman **amphitheater**, which stretched from V. E. de Amicis to V. Arena and south to V. Conca del Naviglia. Known as *Mediolaum*, it served as the capital of the western Roman Empire and included a gladiatorial stadium, which was destroyed in the AD sixth century so the Lombards couldn't use it as a stronghold. Pieces of the stadium now make up the town walls and Chiesa

San Lorenzo. Another testament to Milan's ancient past can be found in the columns along C. Porta Ticinese. *(In the courtyard of V. E. de Amicis 17. M2: Sant'Ambrogio.* ☎ *02 89 40 05 55. Park open in summer M-F 9am-7pm, Sa 9am-2pm; in winter Tu-F 9am-4:30pm. Free. Museum open W and F-Sa in summer 9am-7pm; in winter 9am-2pm. Free.)*

IN THE GIARDINI PUBBLICI

GALLERIA D'ARTE MODERNA (MUSEO DELL'OTTOCENTO VILLA BELGIOJOSO BONAPARTE). Napoleon and Josephine lived here when Milan was the capital of Napoleonic Italy (1805-1814). The gallery displays modern Lombard art as well as works from the Impressionist period onward. Of special note are Modigliani's *Beatrice Hastings*, Picasso's *Testa*, Klee's *Wald Bau*, and Morandi's *Natura Morta con Bottiglia*, as well as pieces by Dufy, Matisse, and Mondrian. *(V. Palestro 16. M1/M2: Palestro.* ☎ *02 76 34 08 09; www.villabelgiojosobonaparte.it. Open Tu-Su 9am-1pm and 2-5:30pm. Free.)* The adjacent **Padiglione D'Arte Contemporanea (PAC)** contains contemporary photographs, paintings, and temporary exhibitions. *(V. Palestro 14.* ☎ *02 76 00 90 85; www.comune.milano.it/pac. Open M 2:30-7:30pm, Tu-W and F-Su 9:30am-7:30pm, Th 9:30am-10:30pm. €6, students €4.)*

🎵 ENTERTAINMENT

Milan sponsors many free events, all of which are detailed in the free, monthly **Milano Mese,** distributed at the tourist office. *Hello Milano* (www.hellomilano. it), an English monthly publication, can also be found at the tourist office.

OPERA AND BALLET

Milan's operatic tradition and unparalleled audience enthusiasm make 🔳**La Scala** one of the best places in the world to see opera. The theater's acoustics are phenomenal; even those in the cheap seats appreciate a glorious sensory experience. Opera season runs from December to July and September to November, overlapping the **ballet** season. In December and March, La Scala hosts **symphony concerts.** (Infotel Scala ☎ 02 72 00 37 44; www.teatroallascala.org. Open daily noon-6pm. Closed Aug. Ticket office at theater, V. Filodrammatici 2. Opens 3hr. before performances and closes 15min. after performance begins. Remaining tickets sold at a discount 2hr. before a show. Ticket prices vary widely, but many options are quite affordable; ask for student discounts.) **Teatro degli Arcimboldi,** Vle. dell'Innovazione 1, has modern concert performances. (☎ 02 80 01 21 121; www.teatroarcimboldi.org. Open M-Sa 8am-6:45pm, Su 1-6:30pm.)

THEATER, MUSIC, AND FILM

Founded after WWII as a socialist theater, the **Piccolo Teatro,** V. Rovello 2, near V. Dante, specializes in small-scale classics and off-beat productions. (☎ 02 72 33 32 22. Performances Tu-Sa 8:30pm, Su 4pm. €20-28 student rush tickets €13.) **Teatro delle Erbe,** V. Mercato 3, hosts lyrical opera from October to April. (M1: Cairoli or M2: Lanza. www.felixcompany.it.) Teatri d'Italia sponsors **Milano Oltre,** a drama, dance, and music festival (June-July). Call the **Ufficio Informazione del Comune** for the latest updates (☎ 02 86 46 40 94; www.comune.milano.it). In July the **Brianza Open Jazz Festival** (☎ 02 23 72 236; www.brianzaopen.com) draws jazz fans. Brianza is accessible by car from Milan. The **Milan Symphony Orchestra** season runs from September to May. Concerts are primarily at **Auditorium di Milano** at Largo Gustav Mahler. (☎ 02 83 38 92 01, reservations 89 40 89 16; www. orchestrasinfonica.milano.it. Ticket office open daily 10am-7pm. Tickets are also sold at the tourist office. Tickets €13-50, students €10-25.) Concerts also held at the **Conservatorio,** V. Conservatorio 12 (☎02 76 21 20), and **Dal Verme,** V. S. Giovanni sul Muro 2 (☎02 87 90 52 01). For concert listings look under *"Spetta-coli"* in the *'Tempo Libero"* section of the daily papers. Movie listings are also in every major paper (check Th editions). Many cinemas screen English-language films, listed on the back cover of *Hello Milano*.

SPORTS

In a country where *calcio* is taken as seriously as Catholicism, nothing compares to the rivalry between Milan's soccer clubs, **Inter Milan** and **AC Milan.** The sport's feverish competition has political overtones: Inter fans are said to be left-wing, while AC fans allegedly lean toward the right. The face-off takes place in their shared three-tiered stadium, packing in 87,000 fans. For Inter tickets, check out www.inter.it or head to the team's offices at V. Durini 24. (☎02 77 151; www.acmilan.com. M1: S. Babila.) AC tickets are available at the team offices at V. Turati 3. (☎02 62 281 or 622 85 660. M3: Turati.) **Milan Point** has tickets, C. S. Gottardo 2, or on V. Marino by P. della Scala (☎02 89 42 27 111; www.bestticket.it). **Ticket One,** located in FNAC department stores, one on V. Torino off P. del Duomo, sells tickets for games, concerts, and other events. (☎02 39 22 61; www.ticketone.it.) Tours (M-Sa on non-game days 10am-6pm) of the **San Siro stadium,** V. Piccolomini 5, with its unique spiraling ramps, include a visit to the *calcio* museum. (M1: Lotto. Take Vle. Federico Caprilli or tram #16. ☎02 40 42 432; fax 40 42 251. Enter Gate 21. €13, under 18 or over 65 €10.)

◻ SHOPPING

Milan is a city where clothes really do make the man (or woman): fashion pilgrims arrive in spring and summer to watch the newest styles take their first steps down the runway. Shows are generally by invitation only, but once designers take their bows, window displays and world-renowned biannual *saldi* (sales) in July and January usher new collections into the real world at more reasonable prices. With so many fashion disciples in the city, the fashion district known as the **Quadrilatero d'Oro** has become a sanctuary in its own right. This posh land—where denim jackets can sell for €2000 and Bentley limos transport poodles dressed-to-impress—is the block formed by V. Monte Napoleone, Borgospresso, V. della Spiga, and V. Gesu. Giorgio and Donatella live in the suites above the stores that sell their designs. Although most stores close at 7:30pm, have no fear. You can shop 24/7 at the touchscreens outside Ralph Lauren, so long as you don't mind waiting for delivery until the morning.

Designer creations are available to mere mortals at the trendy boutiques along **Corso di Porta Ticinese,** which extends from **Piazza XXIV Maggio** in the **Navigli district** toward the *duomo,* and its offshoot **Via Molino delle Armi.** Trendsetters and savvy shoppers flock to the affordable mix of shops along **Via Torino** near the *duomo* and the stores along **Corso Buenos Aires.** Another option is the department store **La Rinascente,** V. S. Radegonda 3, where Giorgio Armani began his illustrious fashion career. (☎02 88 52; www.rinascenteshopping. com. Open M-Sa 10am-10pm, Su 10am-8pm.)

Fashionistas who are fine with being a season behind can buy discounted top names from *blochisti* (wholesale clothing outlets). The well-known **Il Salvagente,** V. Fratelli Bronzetti 16, is off C. XXII Marzo. (☎02 76 11 03 28. M1: San Babila. Walk up C. Monforte across P. Tricolore to C. Concordia, which becomes C. Indipendenza. Turn right on V. F. Bronzetti. Open M-Tu 3-7pm, W-Sa 10am-7pm.) **Gruppo Italia Grandi Firme,** V. Montegani #7/A, stocks popular brand names at 70% off regular price. (☎02 89 51 39 51; www.gruppoitaliagrandifirme.

it. M2: Famagosta. Head along Vle. Famagosta, then Cavalcavia Schiavoni, under the overpasses and across the river to V. Montegani; turn right. Open M 3:30-7:30pm, Tu-F 10am-1pm and 3:30-7:30pm, Sa 10:30am-7:30pm.) For those who want to stay in the famous fashion center, **DMAGAZINE Outlet**, V. Monte Napoleone 26, sells big names for more reasonable prices. Just don't be surprised when you see that the 90% discounts still leave €300 price tags. (☎02 76 00 60 27. Open daily 9:30am-7:45pm.)

There are also markets and secondhand stores located around C. Porta Ticinese, the Navigli district, and C. Garibaldi. True bargain hunters attack the bazaars on Tuesday mornings and all day Saturday on **Via Fauché** (M2: Garibaldi). Also on Saturday, **Viale Papinian** (M2: Agostino) and the 400-year-old **Fiera di Sinigallia**, on V. Valencia (M2: Porto Genova), have a mix of junk and deals.

▐ NIGHTLIFE

Milan is known internationally for its too-cool nightlife. Each of the town's neighborhoods has its own personality. To make the most of a night out, choose a district and wander the streets. The **Brera district** calls to those with creative flair, inviting tourists and *milanesi* alike to test their vocal skills at one of its piano bars. In the nearby **Porta Ticinese**, the young and beautiful meet after a long workday to sip fancy concoctions in the shadow of ancient ruins. Students descend upon the ▣**Navigli canal district's** endless stream of cafes, pizzerias, pubs, bars, barges, and bars on barges. A single block of **Corso Como** near Stazione Garibaldi is home to Milan's most exclusive clubs, where bouncers reject the underdressed. Bars and clubs dot the rest of the city, especially around **Largo Cairoli,** home to Milan's hottest outdoor dance floor, as well the areas southeast of **Stazione Centrale** and east of **Corso Buenos Aires,** which features a mix of bars along with much of Milan's gay and lesbian scene. The best jazz clubs are on the town's periphery.

GET BUZZED IN BARS, NOT BY BUGS. Before heading out, don't underestimate Milan's sizable mosquito population, especially around the Navigli, where insect repellent is the cologne of choice.

Check any paper on Wednesday or Thursday for info on clubs and events. *Corriere Della Sera* publishes an insert called **Vivi Milano** on Wednesday, and La *Repubblica* produces **Tutto Milano** every Thursday. The best guide to nightlife is **Pass Milano,** published in Italian every two months and available in bookstores (€12.50). **Easy Milano** (www.easymilano.it), published biweekly by the city's English-speaking community, contains the latest on hot night spots and is free in many bars and restaurants. Free booklets listing bars and club venues, as well as calendars of performances, are available at almost any club or bar: look through **2night** (www.2night.it), a guide to the city's top bars, and **Zero2,** the Milanese edition of an Italian biweekly guide to music, disco, and bar acts.

BRERA DISTRICT

You won't find any clubbing here; instead, mostly older couples stroll the pedestrian thoroughfares between V. Brera and V. Mercado Vetero. Karaoke is one of the main highlights of an exciting evening in the Brera district. To reach the heart of the district from M2: Lanza, head to V. Pontaccio, turn right on V. Mercato and then left on V. Fiori Chiari.

Club 2, V. Formentini 2 (☎02 86 46 48 07), down V. Madonnina from V. Fiori Chiari. This bar sets the mood with red lights and a grand piano on the ground floor and a maze of cushions in its dark downstairs "discopub." Loud bass downstairs. F-Sa DJ and karaoke. Basement open daily in winter. Beer €6. Mixed drinks €10. Open daily 8:30pm-3am.

Cave Montmartre, V. Madonnina 27 (☎02 86 46 11 86). With dozens of outdoor tables at a perfect people-watching corner, Cave Montmartre serves gelato and mixed drinks to help the weary partygoer enjoy the catwalk of Milan locals. Gelato cones and cups €1.50-2.60, sundaes €3.70-7.80. Beer €3.50-5. Mixed drinks €6.50-7. Open Apr.-Sept. M-Sa 7am-2am, Su 5pm-2am. Oct.-Mar. M-Sa 7am-2am.

CORSO DI PORTA TICINESE AND PIAZZA VETRA

Welcome to the land of the nightly happy hour buffet—one mixed drink buys you dinner. Chilled-out, well-dressed crowds of locals come to socialize at bars that charge no cover. This area is accessible by M2 stop Sant'Ambrogio.

◪ Yguana Café Restaurant, V. Papa Gregorio XIV 16 (☎89 40 41 95), just off P. Vetra, a short walk down V. E. de Amicis and V. Molino delle Armi. Beautiful people sip fruity mixed drinks (€8-10). Lounge on a couch outside, or groove to hip hop downstairs. Su brunch noon-4pm. Happy-hour buffet (M-Sa 5:30-9:30pm, Su 5:30-10pm) with 50 rotating dishes makes other bars' offerings look downright pedestrian. Open M-Th and Su 5:30pm-2am, F-Sa 5:30pm-3am. Kitchen open M-F 12:30-3pm.

Flying Circus, P. Vetra 21 (☎02 58 31 35 77; www.flyingcircusmilano.com). Walk down V. E. de Amicis and V. M. delle Armi to P. Vetra. A relaxed lounge welcomes guests to this airplane-themed, red-walled, glass-encased wine bar. Mixed drinks and wine €7-8. W night €3 beers 9pm-2am. Happy-hour buffet daily 6-9:30pm. Open M-Sa 6pm-2am.

Exploit, V. Pioppette 3 (☎02 89 40 86 75; www.exploitmilano.com), on C. Porta Ticinese near Chiesa di San Lorenzo Maggiore down V. E. de Amicis. Where the old meets the new: a chic bar-restaurant next to Roman ruins. Free Wi-Fi. Mixed drinks €7-9. Wine €6 per glass, €18-20 per bottle. Primi €10. Secondi €18-25. Diverse happy-hour buffet daily 6-9:30pm. Open daily noon-3pm and 6pm-2am.

◪THE NAVIGLI

On summer nights Navigli's sidewalks fill with outdoor vendors, and students flock to its bars for their wallet-friendly prices. From M2: Pta. Genova, walk along V. Vigevano until it ends, and turn right on V. Naviglio Pavese. After you see the canals, look for ◪**Via Sforza,** which has countless bars and cafes, most with outdoor seating. Less refined and younger than the other neighborhoods, Navigli lets you have fun in Milan and still afford a plane ticket home.

◪ Le Trottoir, P. XXIV Maggio 1 (☎/fax 02 83 78 166; www.letrottoir.it). Located in the center of P. XXIV Maggio as its own island in a sea of roads. This self-proclaimed *"Ritrovo d'Arte, Cultura, e Divertimento"* (House of Art, Culture, and Diversions) may be the Navigli's loudest, most crowded bar and club. A young, alternative crowd comes nightly to get down to live underground music 10:30pm-3am on ground fl., while upstairs features a DJ or jazz (M and W). Check schedule for weekly roster and other music nights. Mixed drinks €6-9. Pizza and sandwiches €8. Cover depends on act; usually €8, includes 1 drink. Happy hour daily 6-8pm with beer €4. Open daily 11am-3am. AmEx/MC/V.

Scimmie, V. Sforza 49 (☎02 89 40 28 74; www.scimmie.it). Near the end of a street filled with nightlife choices is a nightclub in 3-part harmony: pub on a river barge, polished *ristorante,* and cool bar with nightly performances. Talented underground musicians play fusion, jazz, blues, Italian swing, and reggae. Concert schedule online. Mixed drinks €4-9. Primi €8-10. Secondi €18-20. Open daily 8pm-2am.

Spazio Movida Cocktail Bar, V. Sforza 41 (☎02 58 10 20 43; www.spaziomovida.it). Like its namesake Spanish cultural movement, Movida changes the tone of the social scene, spilling Latin music out onto the street from the sleek, colorful indoors. Free Wi-Fi. Mixed drinks €7. Happy hour 6-9pm; mixed drinks €6. Open daily 6pm-2am.

La Hora Feliz, V. S. Vito 5 (☎02 837 6587; www.lahorafeliz.com). For those looking for a Cuban feel, this "rumeria" is the place for you. With festive Latino flair and a wide selection of drinks, including their famous mango daiquiri (€6), it's a little different than your average Italian bar. Happy hour 6-9pm. Open daily 1pm-2am. MC/V.

AROUND CORSO COMO

While models mingle with movie stars over €15 mojitos inside the clubs, crowds of people are served curbside drinks and share a smoke along C. Como and C. Garibaldi. Many clubs close in August. Take the M2 metro line to Garibaldi FS, and go one block south on C. Como.

Loolapaloosa, C. Como 15 (☎02 65 55 693). Guests are invited to dance on the bar while the bartenders entertain by swinging lamps and ringing bells. Mixed drinks €6-8. Cover from €6. Buffet 6:30-10:30pm. Open M-Sa noon-4am, Su 2pm-4am.

Hollywood, C. Como 15 (☎02 65 98 996; www.discotecahollywood.com). Slip into something stunning and pout for the bouncer: this club selects revelers with discretion. Mixed drinks from €10. Tu hip hop. W house. Th-Sa mixed music by resident DJs. Su tends to be invite-only party for celebs. Cover €12-30. Open Tu-Su 11pm-5am.

AROUND LARGO CAIROLI

Take the Metro to M2: Cairoli. While the bars don't exactly cluster into one scene, it's one of the few places west of the Castello Sforzesco worth the trip.

🌑 **Old Fashion Café,** Vle. Emilio Alemagna 6 (☎02 80 56 231; www.oldfashion.it). M1/2: Cadorna F. N. Walk up V. Paleocapa next to the station, and turn right on Vle. Alemagna before the bridge. Club is to left of Palazzo dell'Arte along a dirt path. Summer brings stylish clubgoers to couches encircling an outdoor dance floor and stage, with live music and DJ. Tu is the most popular night, with mixed music. Su brunch noon-6pm; €20. Appetizer buffet 7:30-10pm; €13. Open M-Tu and Th-Sa 10:30am-4:30am, W 10:30pm-4am, Su 11am-4pm and 7:30pm-midnight.

Bar Magenta, V. Carducci 13 (☎02 80 53 808; www.barmagenta.it). M1/M2: Cardona. A short walk down V. G. Carducci to C. Magenta. More masculine than the name would imply. A popular music- and sports-filled institution that dates back to 1807. Free Wi-Fi. Pints €5.50. Happy-hour buffet 6-9pm €6 with 1 drink. Open daily 2pm-3am.

EAST OF CORSO BUENOS AIRES

The establishments southeast of Stazione Centrale are mostly frequented by locals. Most are accessible from M1/2: Loreto or M1: Pta. Venezia.

🌑 **L'elephant,** V. Melzo 22 (☎02 29 51 87 68; www.lelephant.it). M2: Pta. Venezia. From C. Buenos Aires turn right on V. Melzo and walk 5 blocks. An almost entirely male crowd socializes at tables under chandeliers, and on the street corner. Gay- and lesbian-friendly. Mixed drinks €7-8. Happy hour 6:30-9:30pm; €6. Open Tu-Su 6:30pm-2am.

Café Capoverde, V. Leoncavallo 16 (☎02 26 82 04 30; www.capoverde.com). M1/M2: Loreto. A long 30min. walk along V. Costa, which becomes V. Leoncavallo. Greenhouse/bar/restaurant. Pick a cactus for mom; grab a strawberry daiquiri for yourself. Mixed drinks €8. Organic happy-hour buffet 6:30-9:30pm with a drink. Large, tasty assortment of gluten-free dishes. Open M-Sa noon-3pm and 6pm-2am, Su 6pm-2am.

✿ FESTIVALS

Rival to Venice's famed festivities, Milan's increasingly popular **Carnevale** is Italy's oldest. The masked mystique and medieval revelry radiates from the *duomo* and spreads through the city annually during the days that precede Ash Wednesday. The **Mercatone dell'Antiquariato sul Naviglio Grande** (☎02 89 40 99 71; www.navigliogrande.mi.it), a giant antiques extravaganza, takes place the last Sunday of each month, except July. Experience true flower power during the **Fiori sul Naviglio,** the first Sunday of April, when flowers fill the district. **Festa di Naviglio** is usually the first Sunday of June, and is accompanied by another special market. The second week of May, don't miss **Arte sul Naviglio Grande,** when the Naviglio plays host to the creativity of over 300 young Italian artists whose work takes over a 10,000m long area. **La Notte Bianca** (White Night) occurs annually one night in June when the Metro, theater, shops, and restaurants stay open all night from 3pm-6am. The *Assessorato alla Cultura* publishes a special summer edition (in Italian) of **Milano Cultura,** found at the tourist office, highlighting all summer events. The **Feast of Sant'Ambrogio,** the patron saint of Milan, is December 7. During the first weeks of December, a special market named **Oh Bej** sets up around the basilica. The **Serate al Museo** celebration with free concerts (both classical and contemporary) spreads throughout Milan's museum courtyards and great halls; check the schedule at the tourist office.

▣ DAYTRIPS FROM MILAN

▨CERTOSA DI PAVIA

SILA buses F5 or F6 from M2: Milan-Famagosta serve Certosa (30min.; €2.40). In Certosa, return tickets to Milan are sold at Il Giornale newsstand in the bus lot. Bus to Milan stops next to the stand. Exiting the bus in Certosa, go to the traffic light, and turn right; continue straight for a few blocks on the road, which becomes the long, tree-lined V. Certosa. The monastery is at the end. Trains also run from the Milano Rogoredo station to Certosa (dir: Voghera, via Certosa; 20min., every hr. 5:44am-10:37pm, €2.65), and arrive quite a distance behind the walled city. From the train station, head through the parking lot and turn left in front of the wall, right at the cross street at the end, then right at the 1st street after the wall (500m). Continue 400m, and go through the portal on the right.

Seven kilometers north of Pavia stands the ▨**Monastero della Certosa di Pavia** (chehr-TOH-zah dee pa-VEE-ya). Gian Galeazzo Visconti founded it in 1396 as a mausoleum for the Visconti clan, who ruled the area from the 12th to 15th centuries. Consecrated as a monastery in 1497, the building testifies to the evolution of Italian art. Inlaid marble, bas-reliefs, and sculptures embellish every available surface. Completion of the work required over 250 craftsmen during the 15th-century Lombard Renaissance. Statues of biblical figures, carvings of narratives, and 61 medallions adorn the base, while the upper half relies more on geometric patterns formed by the contrasting colors of marble for embellishment. Today, the Cistercians oversee the monastery in place of the Carthusian monks. Past the gate in the left apse, note the figures of Ludovico il More and Beatrice d'Este. On Beatrice's feet, note the oldest artistic rendition of platform shoes, which she wore to match her husband's height. The old **sacristy** houses a Florentine triptych carved in ivory; 99 sculptures and 66 bas-reliefs depict the lives of St. Mary and Jesus. Encircling the **choir** are 42 intricate wood inlay representations of saints, prophets, and apostles. Beyond Gian Galeazzo's mausoleum, walk through an unoccupied monk's quarters and its peaceful courtyard. Worlds away from Milan's sleek, modern style, visiting the Monastero is a deeply moving experience not to be missed. (☎02 92 56 13; www.comune.pv.it/certosadipavia. Open Tu-Su Apr. 9-11:30am and 2:30-5:30pm; May-Aug. 9-11:30am and 2:30-6pm; Sept.-Oct. and Mar. 9-11:30am and 2:30-5pm; Nov.-Feb. 9-11:30am and 2:30-4:30pm. Modest dress required. Free.)

BRESCIA

Brescia is on the Turin-Trieste line. Trains run to: Bergamo (1hr., 10 per day 5am-10:16pm, €3.50); Cremona (45min., 15 per day 6:21am-9:25pm, €4.10); Milan (1hr., every hr. 4:15am-10:37pm, €5.40); Venice (2hr., every hr. 6:05am-9:57pm, €10); Verona (45min., 11 per day 5:45am-1:46am, €3.70). SIA buses, Vle. Stazione 14, run to many cities along the western shore of Lake Garda. (☎030 37 74 237. Ticket office open 7am-7pm; use machine in front of station for after hours purchases.) SAIA buses run every hour Monday-Saturday, from V. Solferino 6 to Cremona, Verona, and Sirmione. (☎840 62 00 01 or 44 915; www.saiatrasporti.it. Ticket office open M-F 7am-7pm, Sa 7am-3pm.)

In an attempt to shed its reputation for being dirty and dangerous, Brescia (BREH-shyah; pop. 200,000) has begun new tourism initiatives such as a self-guided audio tour through the tangled cobblestone streets of the *centro storico*. **Piazza del Foro**, the ancient commercial, religious, and political center, houses Emperor Vespasian's vast AD first-century ▓**Tempio Capitolino.** (V. dei Musei 55, off V. Gabriele Rosa. Open daily 10am-1pm and 2-5pm. Free.) Dating to the Middle Ages, the ▓**Museo della Città di Santa Giulia** was the final retreat of Charlemagne's ex-wife, Ermengarda, before it was converted to a convent in AD 753. Today, it displays over 10,000 archaeological finds amid stunningly preserved frescoes. (V. dei Musei 81/B. From P. della Loggia, turn left off V. Cesare on La Provincia and right on V. dei Musei. ☎800 76 28 11 or 030 29 77 834; www.museiarte.brescia.it. Open June-Sept. Tu-Su 10am-6pm; Oct.-May Tu-Su 9:30am-5:30pm. €8, groups €6, ages 14-18 or over 65 €4.) The somewhat overwhelming 22-room ▓**Pinacoteca Tosio-Martinengo** displays artwork by local masters Moretto, Ferramola, Romanino, Foppa, and Lotto. (P. Moretto 1. From V. V. Emanuele II, take V. Francesco Crispi and turn right on V. Martinengo da Barco. ☎030 37 74 999. Open June-Sept. Tu-Su 10am-1pm and 2:30-6pm; Oct.-Mar. 9:30am-1pm and 2:30-5pm. €5, students and over 65 €4.) Italy's third highest dome, **Duomo Nuovo** tops the courthouse-like structure of Brescia's newer cathedral. The smaller, older ▓**Rotonda,** or Duomo Vecchio, built in the 11th and 12th centuries, contains remnants of AD sixth-century mosaics from the basilica that originally stood in its place. (Take V. S. Martino della Battaglia, which becomes V. Mazzini and runs into P. Paolo VI. *Duomo* open M-F 7:30am-noon and 4-7pm, Sa-Su 8am-12:45pm and 4-7:15pm. Rotonda open Apr.-Oct. Tu-Su 9am-noon and 3-7pm; Nov.-Mar. Sa-Su 9am-noon and 3-6pm. Modest dress required. Free.) The medieval **castello,** which hosts an outdoor cinema from late June to September, is also home to the **Musei delle Armi** (Weapons v) and the **Museo Civico del Risorgimento.** (V. del Castello. 20min. climb up Cidneo Hill. Approaching the castle, keep to residential streets and the main road, then cross through the archway and climb the steps on the right. ☎030 29 77 833. Open daily in summer 10am-1pm and 2-6pm; in winter 9:30am-1pm and 2:30-5pm. Both museums €3, with guide €4.50; ages 14-18 or over 65 €1. Films €3-4.) In late May, **Mille Miglia** (Thousand Miles; ☎28 00 36; www.1000miglia.eu), a round-trip car race between Brescia and Rome, brings a fine showing of Ferraris, Maseratis, and Astin Martins.

If you plan to stay overnight, try **Hotel Solferino ❷**, V. Solferino 1/A, which offers large rooms with balconies that overlook the courtyard. From the train station, take the first right off Vle. Stazione. Buzz to enter; reception is on the second floor. (☎030 46 300. Singles €15-26; doubles €35-42. Cash only.) Brescia's culinary specialties are *manzo all'olio* (beef prepared in olive oil) and *tortelli di zucca* (pumpkin-stuffed pasta). For a pizza and *panini* fix, try the area around the train station. Upscale restaurants line **Via Beccaria**, between P. della Loggia and the *duomo*. ◼**Martha ❷**, P. Tito Speri 10, serves luscious *tortellini di zucca* on an outdoor patio in the heart of the green *piazza*. (Primi €7. Secondi €7. Open Tu-Sa 6pm-2am, Su 6pm-midnight.) Schmooze with locals after hours at **Da Franco Bar**, Contrada Pozzo dell'Olmo 14, where you'll likely be the only tourist. Poetry is scrawled across the walls of this lively bar, which stocks no commercial products. (☎335 707 5504; www.bardafranco.com. Mixed drinks €8-9. Open M-Sa 8pm-2am, Su 5:30pm-2am. MC/V.)

The area around the **train station** and west of **Piazza della Loggia** is dangerous at night; use caution and avoid walking alone. Take V. Foppa from the station. Turn right on **Via XX Settembre** and left onto **Via Gramsci** into **Piazza della Vittoria**. The **tourist office**, P. della Loggia 6, is behind the post office. (☎030 24 00 357; www.comune.brescia.it. Free bike rental with ID and €20 deposit. Must be returned before 5:30pm. Open in summer M-Sa 9am-6:30pm, Su 9am-1pm; in winter M-F 9:30am-12:30pm and 2-5:30pm, Sa 9:30am-1pm.) Other services include: **police**, V. Alessandro Volta 6 (☎030 45 001); **Internet** access at **Biblioteca di Largo Torrelunga**, in P. Arnaldo (free; open Tu-F 1:30-6:30pm, Sa 9:30am-noon and 1:30-6:30pm); and the **post office**, P. della Vittoria 1 (☎030 44 421; open M-F 8:30am-7pm, Sa 8:30am-12:30pm). **Postal Code:** 25100.

BERGAMO   ☎035

A trip to Bergamo (BEHR-ga-mo; pop. 115,000) is a visit to two different worlds. The *città bassa* (low city) is a modern commercial town. On the bluff above, however, lies the historical *città alta* (high city), with palaces, churches, and huge stone fortifications. Through its narrow cobblestone streets, the modern world disappears. On Viale Gombito, brochure-clutching tourists share *pasticcerie*, *piazze*, and museums with a smattering of locals. The city's history is dynamic: recent cathedral restorations unearthed very old ruins, and Bergamo is still trying to rediscover all of its hidden history.

▐⊏ TRANSPORTATION

Flights: Bergamo Orio al Serio Airport (☎035 32 63 23; www.orioaeroporto.it) Some budget airlines, including **RyanAir.**

Trains: Ple. Marconi. (☎035 24 79 50 or 035 98 20 21). Ticket office open 5:50am-8:45pm. AmEx/MC/V. To: **Brescia** (1hr., every hr. 5:20am-11:11pm, €3.50), **Cremona** (1hr., every 3hr. 6:16am-8:34pm, €5.40), and **Milan** (1hr., every hr. 5:01am-11:11pm, €4.10). Connections to all major cities from Milan.

Buses: SAB station serves suburbs and nearby towns. Buses to **Lake Como** more frequent in the summer beginning in mid-June. Check www.sptlinea.it for schedule.

Local Transportation: Airport bus runs between Colle Aperto, the train station, and Bergamo's airport (30min., 5:30am-10:05pm, €1.60). **ATB** runs buses in Bergamo as well as between *città alta* and *città bassa;* for a complete route map, inquire at the ATB Point, Largo Porta Nuova (☎035 23 60 26; www.atb.bergamo.it), or at the tourist office in *città bassa*. Tickets for both buses and funiculars €1 per 1hr., from €2.55 per day.

Taxis: ☎035 45 19 090, 035 24 45 05, or 035 24 20 00.

Car Rental: Avis, V. Pietro Paleocapa 3 (☎035 27 12 90 or 31 60 41), inside the central parking lot, or V. Aeroporto 13 (☎035 31 60 41 or 31 01 92).

Bergamo

NIGHTLIFE

Birreria Pozzo
Bianco, 10
Enoteca al
Donizetti, 8
La Birreria, 5
Papageno Pub, 2
Bierschenke
Marienplatz, 12

ACCOMMODATIONS

Hostel Novecento ("900"), 3
La Torretta Città Alta, 9
Locanda Caironi, 14
Ostello Città di Bergamo (HI), 11

FOOD

Trattoria Casa Mia, 13
Trattoria Tre Torri, 7
Trattoria Margi, 18
Trattoria da Ornella, 4

TO CASTELLO (400m)

Via Roccolino

Porta
Sant' Alessandro
(Funicular Station)

Colle
Aperto

Viale delle Mura

Cittadella

PIAZZA
MASCHERONI

Porta di
San Lorenzo

Via Maironi
da Ponte

Museo
Donizettiano

Via della Boccola

Via della Fara

V. della
S. Grata
V. San
Salvatore
V. Salvecchio
Via B. Colleoni
V. d'Agata
Via Vagine
Via Tassis
Via Tassis

PIAZZA
DUOMO

S. Maria
Maggiore

PIAZZA
VECCHIA

Biblioteca
Civica

Via S. Lorenzo

P. MERCATO
DEL FIENO

TO 3 (100m)
V. C.Ca

Via delle Mura

Via Tre Armi

PIAZZA
DUOMO

P. ROSATE

S. Alessandro

P. GIULIANI

Via San
Pancrazio

San
Gottardo

Via
Gombito

Parco delle
Rimembranze

Galleria S. Lucia Vecchia

V. F. Ardeatina

Palazzo della
Ragione

Via M. Lupo

Via G. Donizetti

La Rocca

La Solata

Via San Giacomo

P. MERCATO
DEL SCARPE

PIAZZATE
B. LEGNANO

S. Agostio

Prato della
Fara

V. S. Giacomo

Porta
San Giacomo

Funicular

CITTÀ ALTA

Via Fara

Via Porta Dipinta

Galleria Sant'Alessandro

Via San Carlo

Via Salita d. Scaletta

Sca. San
Bertello

Mura di S.
Giacomo

Sant'Andrea

Via Porta Dipinta

S. Michele
al Pozzo Bianco

Porta
Sant'Agostino

Il
Fortino

Via
Buttaro

Mura di S. Agostino

Viale Vittorio Emanuele II

Galleria
dell'Accademia
Carrara

Via della Noca

Pelicano
Supermarket

Via Zambelli

Via Antonio Locatelli

Via Cornasello

Via Pignolo

Via Pelabrocco

PIAZZA
GIACOMO
CARRARA

Via Don C. Botta

Via Brigata Lupi

Via Monte Ortigara

Via M. Domini

Via Zambianchi

Via Albini

Via San Tomaso

Galleria
d'Arte
Moderna

Vicolo d. Torni

Viale Vittorio Emanuele II

Via G.E.R. Zelasco

PIAZZALE
DELLA
REPUBLICA

Via Masone

Pradello

Via Elisabetta

Via Pignolo

TO 11
(2km)

TO (1km)

G. Garibaldi

V. F. Cucchi

V. S. Benedetto

PIAZZA
DELLA
LIBERTÀ

Via Petrarca

Via Giuseppe Verdi

S. Bernardino

Via San Giovani

Via C. Battisti

ROTUNDA
D. MILLE

Via Tasca

Via Roma

Via Adamello

Via Orobica

PIAZZA
DANTE

Via dei Partigiani

PIAZZETTA SAN
BARTOLOMEO

LARGO
BELOTTI

Giardini
Caprotti

Via Pignolo

Parco
Marenzi

Via San Giovanni

Via A. Pitentino

TO
(100m)

V. F. Crispi

PIAZZA
VITTORIO
VENETO

S. Bartolomeo

Via Torquato Tasso

CITTÀ BASSA

S. Spirito

LARGO DEL
GALGARIO V. Suardi

Via Borfuro

Via XX Settembre

PIAZZA
MATTEOTTI

Teatro
Donizetti

Via Gabriele Camozzi

PORTA SAN
ANTONIO

Via T. Frizzoni

Muraine

V. A. Mazzi

TO 13
(400m)

Via G. Tiraboschi

LARGO
PORTA
NUOVA

S. Maria
della Grazie

Via Gallicciolli

Via Taramelli

Via Clara Maffei

Via dei Casalino

Via Madonna della Neve

Via Borgo Palazzo

Morla R.

V. A. da Calepio

Via d'Alzano

Via Ghislanzoni

Via Papa Giovanni XXIII

V. S. Francesco
d'Assisi

Via Pascoli

Via Sottocorno

Via M. Cefalonia

SISA
Supermarket

Via Torretta

V. Caterina

Avis
Via Pietro
Paleocapa

Supermarket

PIAZZA
DEGLI ALPINI

Via Angelo Maj

Via Foro Boario

Via M. Manzoni

v. d. Cappuccini

PIAZZA
S. ANNA

Via A. da Calepio

Via Malfassi

Via G. Bonomelli

Stazione
Autolinee

Stazione
Autolinee
SAB

Via Bartolomeo Bono

Via Moretti

Via A. Fantoni

Via Div. Julia

Laundry

PIAZZALE G.
MARCONI

TO (5km)

0   200 meters
0   200 yards

N

ORIENTATION AND PRACTICAL INFORMATION

The train and bus stations, as well as a few budget hotels, are found in the **città bassa,** the industrial part of the city. To get to the *città alta* from the bus and train stations in Piazza Marconi, use line 1A (8 per hr., 7:08am-midnight). **Viale Papa Giovanni XXIII** becomes **Viale Vittorio Emanuele II** and ends as **Viale della Fara.** If you dare to walk to the *città alta*, climb the stairs on **Via Salita della Scaletta,** which starts to the left of the funicular on Vle. V. Emanuele II. Both sets of stairs go to **Porta San Giacomo** along **Via Tre Armi.** Continue through the stone Pta. S. Giacomo for another 15min. to reach the tourist office on V. Gombito.

> **TIP** **BERGAMO ON A BUDGET.** A great, cheap way to see the city is to purchase an all-day ATB ticket (€2.50) from a vending machine or *tabaccheria*. Tickets are good on both ATB city buses and the funiculars that climb to the *città alta* and the Castello San Vigilio.

The walled *città alta* is a well-preserved medieval town, home to most of Bergamo's major sights and churches. Enter through Pta. S. Giacomo, following V. S. Giacomo to the **Mercato delle Scarpe** and then up **Via Gombito,** which passes through **Piazza Vecchia,** where V. Gombito turns into **Via Bartolomeo Colleoni** before reaching the **Cittadella.** Just beyond the Cittadella, through **Colle Aperto** and **Porta Sant'Alessandro,** the **San Vigilio funicular** heads to Bergamo's highest point.

Tourist Offices: *Città alta:* V. Gombito 13, on the ground fl. of the tower (☎035 24 22 26; www.turismo.bergamo.it). *Città bassa:* building in center of P. Marconi (☎035 21 02 04 or 21 31 85). English spoken. Both open M-F 9am-12:30pm and 2-5:30pm.

Tours: Gruppo Guide Città di Bergamo (☎035 34 42 05; www.bergamoguide.it). 2hr. tours in English (Su), French (F), German (Sa), and Italian (F-Su). €10, children free. **Associazione Guide Interpreti e Accompagnatori Turistici** (☎035 42 844 68; www. agiatguidebergamo.it) also offers informative walking tours of the city. Seasonal schedule; check with the tourist office.

Currency Exchange: Banca Nazionale del Lavoro, V. Petrarca 12 (☎035 23 80 16), off Vle. Roma/Vle. V. Emanuele II, near P. della Libertà. Open M-F 8:20am-1:20pm and 2:35-4:05pm, Sa 8:20-11:50am. Also at the post office and other banks.

Western Union: Locations throughout the *città bassa,* especially on V. Giacomo Quarenghi, including **Multi Link Business Center,** V. G. Quarenghi 39/C, right off V. Pietro Paleocapa. Offers cheap long-distance calls. English spoken. Open M-Sa 9:30am-9pm.

Police: V. Noli in the *città bassa,* or P. della Citadella 2 (☎035 541 071).

Pharmacy: *Città alta:* **Farmacia Guidetti,** V. S. Giacomo 2 (☎035 23 72 20), in Mercato delle Scarpe. Open M-F 9am-12:30pm and 3-7:30pm. Posts after-hours rotations. *Città bassa:* Farmacia Internazionale, V. Maj 2/A. Head up V. Giovanni from the station and turn right. Open M-F 9am-12:30pm and 3-7:30pm. AmEx/MC/V.

Hospital: Ospedale Riuniti, Largo Barozzi 1 (☎035 26 91 11).

Internet Access: In many phone centers within *città bassa,* especially along V. G. Quarenghi. **Chiocciola,** V. D'Alzano 2d (☎035 24 52 36). €1 per 10min., €2.70 per 30min., €4.80 per hr. Open M-F 9:30am-7:30pm.

Post Office: *Città alta:* Mercato di Fieno 13 (☎035 23 95 23; fax 21 17 96). From V. Gombito, turn on V. S. Pancrazio. Open M-F 8:30am-2pm, Sa 8:30am-12:30pm. *Città bassa:* V. Locatelli 11 (☎035 53 22 11). Take V. Zelasco from Vle. V. Emanuele. Open M-F 8:30am-7pm, Sa 8:30am-12:30pm. **Postal Codes:** 24121, 24124, 24129.

ACCOMMODATIONS

Prices usually rise with altitude; the most affordable hotels are in the *città bassa*, but many have easy access to bus routes that go to the *città alta*.

Ostello Città di Bergamo (HI), V. G. Ferraris 1 (☎035 36 17 24; www.ostellodibergamo. it), located 2.5km from train station. Walk up Vle. Papa Giovanni to Largo Pta. Nuova and take bus #6 to Montesorro (every 15min.; M-Sa 5am-11pm, Su 5am-8:30pm). Walk to top of the hill. Also accessible by line #3 from *città alta*. This colorful, gleaming new hostel is a joy. Rooftop terrace, filled with flowering plants, has an amazing view of *città alta*. Blue and yellow rooms have bath or shower and balcony. Common room has TV, microwave, and fridge, as well as art lent by a local school. Breakfast included. Wi-Fi cards €2.50 for the first hour, €1.50 for each hr. thereafter. Internet access €3 per hr. Reserve at least a week in advance during summer. Dorms €17; singles €30; doubles €42; 4- to 8- bed family rooms €19 per person. HI-member discount €3. MC/V. ❶

Hostel Novecento ("900"), V. Statuto 23 (☎035 25 46 96 or 337 42 32 71). From train station, take bus #2 to Ospedale stop. Large, spotless rooms with phone and private bath. Affordable restaurant downstairs, filled with locals. No reception; call ahead and check in at pizzeria. Singles €30; doubles €40. Extra bed €10. AmEx/MC/V. ❸

La Torretta Città Alta, V. Rocca 2 (☎331 68 91 955; www.latorrettabergamoalta. com). Bed and breakfast within a historic tower. Unbelievable *piazza* view from balcony. Large common area. Breakfast included. Reservation required. Singles €60-70; doubles €80-95; triples €90-110. Cash only. ❹

Locanda Caironi, V. Torretta 6E (☎035 24 30 83; hotelcaironi@virgilio.it). From train station, take Vle. Papa Giovanni XXIII to V. Maj, turn right, and walk for 1.5km to P. Sant'Anna. Turn left on V. Borgo Palazzo, then right at 2nd block. Or take bus #5 or 7 from V. Maj. Clean rooms with shared bath. Reception inside Caironi Trattoria. Reservations recommended. Singles €25-40. MC/V. ❷

FOOD

Polenta, a yellow cornmeal paste, is a staple of the *bergamasco* plate, often found accompanying meals of *cavallo* (horse) or *asino* (donkey). Polenta is also used in pastries called *polentine*, which are filled with rum and chocolate and coated in sugar. Traditional meals in Bergamo conclude with a *formaggio*—try sharp *branzi* or *taleggio* cheese accompanied by local red and white Valcalepio wines. Many of Bergamo's best restaurants and cozy bakeries are on the main tourist drag, V. Bartolomeo, and its continuations, V. Colleoni and V. Gombito. Restaurants in the *città bassa* have fewer tourists than their *città alta* counterparts. Pick up staples at **Pellicano supermarket,** Vle. V. Emanuele II 17, past P. Repubblica from the train station. (Open M 8:30am-1:30pm, Tu-F 8:30am-1:30pm and 3:30-8pm, Sa 8:30am-8pm. MC/V.)

Trattoria Casa Mia, V. S. Bernardino 20 (☎035 22 06 76). From Pta. Nuova, go down V. Gerolamo Tiraboschi, which becomes V. Zambonate. Turn left at the last intersection to V. S. Bernardino. Intimate setting, genial staff, and a strong local flavor. Prices are low, but the delicious cuisine is on par with the nicest restaurants in town. Lunch *menù* (€10) includes primi, secondi, dessert, wine or water, and coffee. Dinner *menù* (€12) includes a primo and secondo. Open M-Sa noon-2pm and 7-10pm. Cash only. ❷

Trattoria Magri, V. Camozzi 73 (☎035 248 808; www.trattoriamagri.it). Walking past this funky and unexpected restaurant is like a quick glimpse into a friend's apartment—if the friend were a hip, quirky chef with a killer urban loft. 1 dish meal €10; 2 dishes €15; 3 dishes €18. Open M-Sa 12-2:30pm and 7-11pm. MC/V. ❷

Trattoria Tre Torri, P. Mercato del Fieno 7/A (☎035 24 44 74). Heading downhill from P. Vecchia, turn left off V. Gombito on to V. S. Pancrazio. Small homestyle menu. Larger covered patio and 5 tables in the stone interior. Antipasti €8. Primi €8. Secondi €10-14. Cover €1.50. Open M-Tu and Th-Su noon-1:30 pm and 7-10:30pm. MC/V. ❸

Trattoria da Ornella, V. Gombito 15 (☎035 23 27 36; www.paginegialle.it/trattoriadaornella). After exiting the funicular, walk up V. Gombito. This tourist hot spot with a *piazza* view specializes in rich *polenta taragna,* made with butter, local cheeses, and rabbit (€15). Primi €8-10. Secondi €12-15. Cover €2. Open M-W and F-Su 12:15-3:15pm and 7:15-11:15pm. Reservations recommended. AmEx/MC/V. ❸

👁 SIGHTS

CITTÀ ALTA

▨BASILICA DI SANTA MARIA MAGGIORE. This 12th-century basilica is Bergamo's most famous church. Tapestries and paintings depicting biblical scenes adorn the walls that surround the tomb of Bergamo's famous son, composer Gaetano Donizetti, who earned world renown through more than 70 compositions. Don't miss the particularly arresting—and startlingly emaciated—crucifix. *(Head through the archway flanking P. Vecchia to reach P. del Duomo. ☎035 22 33 27. Open Apr.-Oct. M-Sa 9am-12:30pm and 2:30-6pm, Su 9am-1pm and 3-6pm; Nov.-Mar. M-F 9am-12:30pm and 2:30-5pm, Sa 9am-12:30pm and 2:30-6pm, Su 9am-noon and 3-6pm. Free.)*

CAPPELLA COLLEONI. Marble braids weave through the colorful Renaissance facade and 18th-century ceiling frescoes illuminate the interior of the *cappella*, designed by G. A. Amadeo in 1476 as a funerary chapel for the celebrated *bergamasco* mercenary Bartolomeo Colleoni. Elaborate exterior carvings combine the biblical and the classical—saints wear togas and Julius Caesar and Augustus obtain divine status. *(To the right of the basilica. ☎035 21 00 61. Open Tu-Su Nov.-Feb. 9am-12:30pm and 2-4:30pm; Mar.-Oct. 9am-12:30pm and 2-6pm. Free. Audio tour €1.)*

PIAZZA VECCHIA. This *piazza* is filled with medieval and Renaissance buildings set among restaurants and cafes in the heart of the *città alta*. Locals lounge on the steps of the 400-year-old **Biblioteca Civica,** which houses Bergamo's 16th-century manuscripts. On summer weekends, artists sell paintings on the library steps. Across the *piazza* is the 12th-century Venetian Gothic **Palazzo della Ragione (Court of Justice),** which features St. Mark's lion symbol. Behind is the **Cattedrale di San Alessandro,** a cathedral for Bergamo's patron saint. To the right, connected to the *palazzo* by a walkway, stands the 12th-century **Torre Civica** (Civic Tower). The 230 steps to the top of the 54m tower lead to a 360-degree view of Bergamo. The 15th-century bell rings 180 times at 10pm each night to commemorate the town's medieval curfew. *(Check tower opening schedule at the tourist office. Wheelchair-accessible.)*

PARCO DELLE RIMEMBRANZE. Views from this former Roman military camp make the hike up to the *città alta* worthwhile. Inscriptions immortalize Italian battle casualties. Above the park, La Rocca houses the **Museo Storico,** which features weaponry, uniforms, and historical city plans. *(P. Brigata Legnano 12. At the end of V. Rocca. ☎035 22 10 40; www.bergamoestoria.org. Open June-Sept. Tu-F 9:30am-1pm and 2-5:30pm, Sa 9:30am-7pm; Oct.-May Tu-Su 9:30am-1pm and 2-5:30pm. La Rocca and tower €3, with admission to all Bergamo museums €5. Ask about group discounts. Cash only.)*

MUSEI DI CITTADELLA. Housed within the Citadella near the top of the *città alta*, the Civic Museums of Bergamo include the **Museo di Scienze Naturali,** which features a collection of fossils and taxidermy specimens native to Bergamo as well as an exhibit on Bergamo's silk industry that includes live silk worms. (*P. Cittadella 10. ☎ 28 60 11; www.museoscienzebergamo.it.*) The **Museo Archeologico** presents cultural memorabilia from Africa. (*P. Cittadella 9. ☎ 035 24 28 39; www.museoarcheologicobergamo.it. Both open Apr.-Sept. Tu-F 9am-12:30pm and 2:30-6pm, Sa-Su 9am-7pm; Oct.-Mar. Tu-Su 9am-12:30pm and 2:30-5:30pm. Free.*)

ABOVE THE CITTÀ ALTA. The San Vigilio funicular runs from a location just past Pta. Sant'Alessandro and Colle Aperto in the *città alta* to Castello San Vigilio, Bergamo's castle in the clouds. (*3min.; every 15min. M-Th 10:14am-11:51pm, F-Sa 10:15am-1:24am; €1 ticket good for 75min. on funicolare and city buses.*) While few halls and staircases are open for exploration, the fortification's isolation and the 360° views of Bergamo make it worth the ride. Hiking trails run down to the *centro storico*, including one just to the left of the funicular station, Salita dello Scorlassone. (*Head right up V. S. Vigilio after exiting the funicular; castle on left. Open daily Apr.-Sept. 9am-8pm; Mar. and Oct. 10am-6pm; Nov.-Feb. 10am-4pm. Free.*)

CITTÀ BASSA

GALLERIA DELL'ACCADEMIA CARRARA. In June 2010, the *galleria*, freshly renovated, will once again take its place on Bergamo's art scene. The cornerstone of the gallery's collection resides on the villa's top floor, where 13th- to 15th-century canvases showcase the work of Titian, Rubens, Brueghel, Bellini, Van Dyck, and El Greco. Works on display include Botticelli's *Ritratto di Giuliano dei Medici*, Lotto's *Ritratto di Giovinetto*, and Rizzi's *Maddalena in Meditazione*, in which Mary Magdalene looks down on a crucified Christ. (*P. Giacomo Carrara 82/A. From Largo Pta. Nuova, take V. Camozzi to V. Pignolo, then turn right onto V. S. Tomaso. ☎ 035 39 96 77; www.accademiacarrara.bergamo.it. Closed until June 2010. Open Tu-Su 10am-1pm and 2:30-5:30pm. €3.*)

GALLERIA D'ARTE MODERNA E CONTEMPORANEO. This art museum hosts a modest collection of works primarily from the 50s to the 70s, including many bronze sculptures completed by local artist Manzu, as well as a few notable works by painters such as Kandinsky. View Raphael's *San Sebastiano* and Antonio Pisano's *Ritratto di Lionello d'Este*. Don't miss Jean Fautrier's *Petite Construction en Bleu*. A separate building hosts temporary exhibitions. (*V. S. Tomaso 53. ☎ 035 39 96 77; www.gamec.it. Temporary exhibitions open Tu-W and F-Su 10am-9pm, Th 10am-10pm. Permanent collection open Apr.-Sept. daily 10am-1pm and 3-6:45pm; Oct.-Mar. Tu-Su 9:30am-1pm and 2:30-5:45pm. €4, reduced €2.50.*)

OTHER SIGHTS. In the heart of *città bassa* is P. Matteotti, where the first glimpse of the *città alta* stops you in your tracks. Continuing away form the *piazza*, V. Torquato Tasso leads to the **Chiesa del Santo Spirito,** marked by its stone and brick facade and Modernist iron sculpture over the door. The stark gray Renaissance interior contrasts strongly with decorative paintings by Lotto, Borgognone, and Previtali. (*V. Torquato Tasso. ☎ 035 22 05 18. Open July-Aug. M-Sa 7-11:3045am and 4-6:30pm, Su 5-7pm; Sept.-June M-Sa 7-11:30am and 4-6:30pm, Su 8am-noon and 4-7pm. Free.*) On the left, V. Pignolo connects the upper and lower cities, winding past 16th- to 18th-century villas whose large doors open into elaborate inner courtyards. At the intersection with V. S. Giovanni is tiny **Chiesa di San Bernardino,** whose bright interior features icons celebrating the town's agricultural and industrial heritage. (*V. Pignolo 59. ☎ 035 23 00 37. Open M-F 8-11am and 4-6pm, Sa and holidays 8-11:30am, Su 9am-noon. Free.*) If you are interested in finding out more about native composer Gaetano Donizetti, check out **Museo Donizetti** is housed in the palace of **Misericordia Maggiore** in the *città alta*. (*V. Arena 9.*

☎035 39 92 69. Open June-Sept. daily 9:30am-1pm and 2-5:30pm; Oct.-May M-F 9:30am-1pm, Sa-Su 9:30am-1pm and 2-5:30pm. Same prices and package tickets as Museo Storico).

🎵 🎭 ENTERTAINMENT AND NIGHTLIFE

Even outside its museums, the arts thrive in Bergamo. The **opera** season lasts from September to November and includes a celebration of native composer Gaetano Donizetti's works. The **drama** season follows, from November to April, at Teatro Donizetti, P. Cavour 15 (☎035 41 60 602 or 41 60 603), off P. Matteotti in the *città bassa*. (Box office open daily 1-9pm.) Between May and June, the spotlight falls on the highly acclaimed **Festival Pianistico Internazionale Arturo Benedetti Michelangeli** (☎035 24 01 40; www.festivalmichelangeli. it.), a celebration of classical works co-hosted by the city of Brescia. (Tickets €8-35.) Complementing these traditional offerings is **Andar per Musica** (☎035 41 75 453; www.bgavvenimenti.it), a contemporary folk extravaganza in June, July, and August, featuring cultural dance and music offerings in the city and surrounding area. During the summer, the tourist office provides a program of free monthly events, **Estate Viva la Tua Città.**

The *città alta* comes alive at night as people pack the restaurants, pubs, and *enoteche* along V. Colleoni and V. Gombito. The 200 different types of Belgian beers at **Papageno Pub,** V. Colleoni 1/B, make for a good time even on weekdays. (☎035 23 66 24. Open daily 11am-3pm and 7pm-2am. MC/V.) Continuing along the central street of *la città alta*, **La Birreria** at 1/B V. Gombita, has a young clientele and offers both free Wi-Fi and a special menu available only to university students. (Open daily 9am-2pm and 7pm-2am.) A bit off the beaten path, **Birreria Pozzo Bianco,** V. Porta Dipinta 30/B, offers a late-night kitchen. (☎035 24 76 94. Beer €2.50-8. Wine €12-19 per bottle. Primi and secondi €6.50-16.50. Open daily 11:30am-3pm and 7pm-2am. MC/V.) One sure bet in the *città bassa* is **Bierschenke Marienplatz,** V. Pignolo 37, which can be found about 30 yd. off the cobblestone street, through a courtyard. German beer and waitresses in traditional Bavarian dress set a kitschy, jovial tone. (☎035 23 89 64. Open daily noon-2:30pm and 7pm-midnight. MC/V.) **Enoteca al Donizetti,** V. Gombito 17/A, has platters of local *bergamaschi* cheeses and salami as well as wine tastings. There is limited indoor seating and a crowded patio. (☎035 24 26 61. Cover €2. Specialty plate €9-17. Open M and W-Su 10:30am-midnight. AmEx/MC/V.)

MANTUA (MANTOVA) ☎0376

Although Mantua (in Italian, "MAHN-toh-vah"; pop. 46,372) did not become a bustling cultural haven until the Renaissance, art and culture have shaped the city's history since the birth of the poet Virgil in 70 BC. Having provided inspiration for native and foreign artists alike including Verdi (1813-1901), the Renaissance writer Castiglioni (1478-1529), and artist Pisanello (1380-1456), the town is brimming with art. Mantova has a quiet energy, but an energy nonetheless —with great shopping along Corso Vittorio Emanuele II and small personable restaurants tucked in side streets around the sprawling *centro*, the town is constantly active. Surrounding towns like Castellaro, Cavriana, and Solferino house scenic vineyards with Lombardy's greatest gem, sparkling red wine.

📍 **TRANSPORTATION.** The **train station** is in P. Don Leoni, at the end of V. Solferino. (☎32 16 47. Ticket office open M-Sa 5:40am-7:45pm, Su 6am-7:45pm.) **Trains** run to Cremona (1hr., 8 per day 5:20am-8:50pm, €4.50); Milan (2hr., 9 per day 5:20am-7:43pm, €8.55); Modena (1hr., 5:57am-8:49pm, €3.70); Verona (40min., 20 per day 6am-10:41pm, €2.55). APAM **buses** (☎0376 23 01; www. apam.it) run locally and to nearby towns, including the village of Sabbioneta.

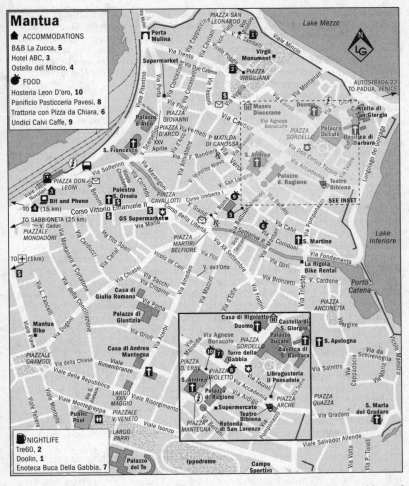

Mantua

🏠 ACCOMMODATIONS
B&B La Zucca, **5**
Hotel ABC, **3**
Ostello del Mincio, **4**

🍴 FOOD
Hosteria Leon D'oro, **10**
Panificio Pasticceria Pavesi, **8**
Trattoria con Pizza da Chiara, **6**
Undici Calvi Caffe, **9**

🎵 NIGHTLIFE
Tre60, **2**
Doolin, **1**
Enoteca Buca Della Gabbia, **7**

Check the *biglietteria* to the left of the train station for schedule booklets of urban and interurban buses. There are two stations: one directly in front of the train station and the other at Stazione Risorgimento, in front of Palazzo Te. **Taxis** (☎0372 32 53 51, 36 88 44, or 32 44 08) are available 5am-1am. For **bike rentals** try La Rigola, on V. Trieste, next to Antica Osteria ai Ranari. (☎0376 36 66 77 or 335 60 54 958. €2.50 per hr., €10 per day. Open daily 9:30am-8pm. Cash only.)

🚆🚇 **ORIENTATION AND PRACTICAL INFORMATION.** Getting to most of the city's sights and shops from the train station takes 10-15min. From **Piazza Don Leoni,** turn left on **Via Solferino,** then right on **Via Bonomi** to the main street, **Corso Vittorio Emanuele II.** Follow it to **Piazza Cavallotti,** crossing the **Sottoriva River,** to get to **Corso Umberto I.** This leads to **Piazza Marconi, Piazza Mantegna,** and the main **Piazze d'Erbe** and **Sordello.** Find a helpful, English-speaking staff at the

tourist office, P. Mantegna 6. (☎0376 43 24 32; www.aptmantova.it. Open daily 9:30am-6:30pm.) Check out the **museum tourist office,** P. Sordello 23, located in the Casa di Rigoletto. (☎0372 36 89 17. Open Tu-Su 9am-noon and 3-6pm.) C. V. Emanuele II is lined with **banks,** most with **ATMs,** including **UniCredit Banca,** C. V. Emanuele II 26. (Open M-F 8:20am-1:20pm and 2:35-4:05pm.) In an emergency, call the **carabinieri** (☎0376 32 88 88) or the **police,** P. Sordello 46 (☎0376 20 51). Call the **Ospedale Carlo** (☎0376 28 61 11 or 28 60 11), V. Albertoni, for medical assistance. **Farmacia Silvestri** (☎0376 32 13 56), V. Roma 24 (open Tu-Sa 8:30am-12:30pm and 4-8pm; MC/V), is one of many **pharmacies. Bit and Phone,** V. Bertinelli 21, across from the train station, offers **Internet** access and Western Union. (☎0376 22 05 94; www.bitandphone.it. Open M-Tu and Th-Sa 10am-10pm, Su noon-10pm. €2 per hr.) For English-language books, check out **Librogusteria il Pensatoio,** V. Accademia 56. (☎0376 618 107 88; www.pensatoio-inrete.it. Open Tu-Su 10am-9pm. MC/V.) The **post office,** P. Martiri Belfiore 15, up V. Roma from the tourist office, has currency exchange. (☎0376 31 77 11; fax 32 53 04. Open M-F 8:30am-7pm, Sa 8:30am-12:30pm.) **Postal Code:** 46100.

⌂ ACCOMMODATIONS. Accommodations in neighboring towns like Castellaro and Monzambano are less expensive than Mantua itself. In Mantua, accommodations near the train station and main *piazze* are pricey and hard to find. B&Bs as well as *affittacamere* are the least expensive options, though prices everywhere skyrocket in early September during Festivaletteratura. At **B&B La Zucca ❷,** V. Giovanni Battista Spagnoli 10, you won't have to sacrifice location for price. (☎339 61 89 870. Call ahead. Double €20-60, with bath €30-120.) **Hotel ABC ❹,** P. Don Eugenio Leoni 25, across from train station, is a modern hotel with comfortable rooms and an outdoor patio. All rooms have TV, A/C, and new bathrooms. Ring bell to enter after 11pm. (☎/fax 32 23 29; www.hotelabcmantova.it. Breakfast included. Luggage storage free for guests, €5 for others. Parking €12-20. Singles €44-165; doubles €66-165; triples €77-222; quads €88-250.) **Ostello del Mincio ❶,** V. Porto 23/25, is 15km away from Mantua. To the left of the train station, buy a ticket for bus #1; take it to Stazione Risorgimento. Find bus #13 (last departure at 7:40pm) to Rivalta. Though far, it is the only youth hostel in the area. Bear in mind that the bus does not run on Sundays. (☎0376 65 39 24; www.ostellodelmincio.org. Free Wi-Fi. Dorms €16-18.)

▯ FOOD. Mantuan cuisine is known for its *tortelli di zucca* (pumpkin-filled ravioli). Specialties include parmesan cheese, risotto, Mantuan salami (identifiable by its light color due to the proportion of quality meat) and *sbrisolona,* a crumbly almond cake. In July and August many small restaurants and bars close for anywhere from a week to two months, but you can generally rely on the series of nearly indistinguishable outdoor restaurants lining **Piazza delle Erbe** and **Piazza Sordello,** whose popularity with tourists ensures they seldom close. For tasty and reasonably priced local cuisine, head to **Hosteria Leon D'oro,** V. Leon D'oro 6, where the candlelit interior is dappled with partially revealed frescoes. (☎338 124 21 11; www.hosterialeondoro.net. Primi €8.50-13. Secondi €14-18.50. Open daily noon-3pm and 8pm-midnight.) To get to **Trattoria con Pizza da Chiara ❸,** V. Corridoni 44/A, from P. Cavallotti, follow C. Libertà and turn left on V. Roma, then right on V. Corridoni. Young professionals dine in this chic but unpretentious restaurant. Try the delicious *tortelli di zucca* for €8. (☎0376 22 35 68. Pizza and primi €4.50-9. Secondi €9-14.50. Cover €2. Open M and W-Su noon-2:30pm and 7-10:30pm. MC/V.) For a sleek and metropolitan cafe, check out **Undici Calvi Caffe ❷,** V. Calvi 11. Go for a cappuccino (€1.30) or a mixed drink (€3.50) while listening to the jazzy soundtrack. (☎0376 355 036. Open M-F 7:30am-8:30pm, Sa 8am-8:30pm, Su 9am-9pm. Cash only.) A **market** is held every Thursday morning in P. delle Erbe. **GS Supermarket** is on P. Cavallotti. (Open M-Sa 8am-8pm, Su 9am-7pm. AmEx/MC/V.)

🄪 SIGHTS

PALAZZO DUCALE. The behemoth Palazzo Ducale, home of the Gonzaga family since the start of the 14th century, dominates the Mantuan skyline. In medieval times, this was the largest palace in Europe, with 500 rooms and 15 courtyards constructed by the best architects and artists of the 14th to 17th centuries. Originally many separate buildings, the *palazzo* expanded as the Gonzagas annexed surrounding structures, the most prominent being the **Castello di San Giorgio.** This four-towered castle once served as a fortress and boasts an elaborate 17th century ceiling in its **Hall of Mirrors**, modified to suit Neoclassical tastes by Giocondo Albertoli a century later. In the Pisanello Room, the recent removal of a painted plaster frieze revealed a heroic cycle of frescoes depicting the knights of King Arthur. The **New Gallery** houses dozens of locally produced altarpieces from the 16th-18th centuries, removed from monasteries during the Hapsburg and Napoleonic eras. (*P. Sordello 40. ☎ 0372 22 48 32; www.mantovaducale.it. Open Tu-Su 8:45am-7:15pm. Last entry 45min. before closing. Ticket office under porticos facing the piazza. €6.50, EU students €3.25, EU citizens under 18 or over 65 free. Audio tour €4.*)

TEATRO BIBIENA. Commissioned by Maria Theresa of the Hapsburgs to serve as a venue for cultural events and scientific expositions, this theater resembles a miniature fairy-tale castle and is one of few in northern Italy not modeled after Milan's La Scala. Four tiers of stone balconies with intricately painted wood rise to the ceiling, illuminated by soft lantern light. Music lovers first filled the velvet couches when a 14-year-old Mozart inaugurated the building in 1769. Patrons continue to pour in today to attend musical and theatrical performances. (*V. Accademia 47, at the corner with V. Pomponazzo. ☎ 32 76 53. Open Tu-Su 9:30am-12:30pm and 3-6pm. Last entry 30min. before closing. €2.50, under 18 and over 60 €1.20.*)

PALAZZO TE. Built by Giulio Romano in 1534 for state guests of Federico II Gonzaga, who seldom stayed there himself, this opulent *palazzo* combines the layout of a Roman villa with the flamboyant ceiling frescoes that range in theme from the mythological to the Biblical. Pause in the **Sala dei Cavalli** (Room of Horses) to ponder the Gonzaga family's passion for animals, then continue past racy murals of **Cupid and Psyche.** The ▧**Room of Giants** is adorned with a fresco that depicts the demise of the Titans at the hands of Jupiter. In summer, concerts are often held in the courtyard. Meanwhile, the oft-overlooked **hidden garden** of the *palazzo* and **grotto** at the far end are not to be missed. (*At the southern end of the city through P. Veneto and down Largo Parri. ☎ 32 32 66. Open M 1-6pm, Tu-Su 9am-6pm. Last entry 30min. before closing. €8, over 60 €5.50, ages 12-18 and students €2.50.*)

PALAZZO D'ARCO. The former residence of the prominent D'Arco family, this *palazzo* is still furnished as it was during the 18th century. A separate wing houses a library and a kitchen, complete with pots, pans, and a dilapidated staircase. Navigate through the Neoclassical statues that dot the rose gardens to reach the *palazzo*'s highlight: the extraordinary Giovan Maria Falconetto-designed **zodiac chamber.** The room is divided into 12 sections, each decorated with frescoes dedicated to an astrological sign. The **murals** along the top of the walls are drawn from Ovid's *Metamorphoses*. (*P. d'Arco 4. ☎ 0376 32 22 42; www.museodarco.it. Open Mar.-Oct. Tu-Su 10am-12:30pm and 2:30-6pm; Nov.-Feb. Sa-Su 10am-12:30pm and 2-4:30pm. Visit only by guided tour in Italian with English brochure. €3.*)

CHIESA DI SANT'ANDREA. Passed on to the Pope by Matilde di Canossa, a powerful countess of Mantua, the oldest church in Mantua (built in the 11th century) is dwarfed by the surrounding buildings, including the **Palazzo della Ragione** (Palace of Justice) next door. (☎ 0376 22 38 10 or 22 00 97. *Open only during exhibitions Tu-Su 10am-1pm and 4-7pm. €3.)* Opposite the **Rotunda di San Lorenzo,** Mantua's most important Renaissance creation, Leon Battista Alberti's **Chiesa di Sant'Andrea** (1472-1594), was the first monumental space constructed in the Classical style since the days of imperial Rome. The church's plan served as a prototype for ecclesiastical architecture for the next 200 years. Giorgio Anselmi painted the dome's frescoes in muted colors. Mantegna's (1431-1506) tomb rests in the first chapel on the left after the entrance. The church's **sacri vasi del preziosissimo sangue** (sacred vases of the precious blood), a piece of earth believed to be in Christ's blood, parades through the streets in two intricate gold vessels during the annual Good Friday procession. The rest of the year, this relic is kept in a crypt under the nave. To view the relic, ask a *chiesa* volunteer, to the right of the entrance. *(Open daily 7:30am-noon and 3-7pm. Free.)*

📻 🎭 **ENTERTAINMENT AND FESTIVALS.** Located in the park near the monument to Virgil, the popular outdoor bar 🔲**Tre60,** P. Virgiliana 17, has raised outdoor patios scattered with lounge-style furniture. Bartenders experiment with a few new drinks (€5-6) every summer. (☎ 0376 22 36 05. Wine €5. Open Apr.-Oct. daily 5:30pm-1am. MC/V.) Irish pub **Doolin,** V. Zambelli 8, near P. Virgiliana, is a hidden bar popular with the locals. (☎ 36 25 63. Open Tu-Sa 6:30pm-2am, Su 6pm-1am. Cash only.) New pubs in P. Mantegna that have recently grown in popularity are **La Cantina** and **Cafe degli Artisti** (V. Galana 19). Both are small, and their central location make them easily accessible at night from all over the city. A more traditional night spot is **Enoteca Buca Della Gabbia,** V. Cavour 98, a semi-underground restaurant in a wine cellar with over 650 vintages. (☎ 36 69 01. Open M-F 10:30am-3pm and 6:30pm-1am, Sa 10:30am-3pm and 5:30pm-2am, Su 10:30am-1pm. Cash only.) The **Teatro Bibiena** (☎ 0376 32 76 53), V. Accademia 4, hosts countless events, including the **Concerti di Fine Settimana,** a series of operettas and recitals every Sunday, and the similar **Concerti della Domenica** series from November to February. Between October and April, enjoy the first classical concert season, while April to June hosts round two of classical concerts as well as the jazz season. In early September, Italian scholars pack Mantua for the five-day **Festivaletteratura,** which attracts hordes of literary buffs from around the world to attend discussions, lectures, book signings, and writers' workshops with Nobel Prize winners and international best-selling authors. (Office at V. Accademia 47. ☎ 0376 36 70 47; www.festivaletteratura.it.)

CREMONA   ☎ 0372

Viewed from the top of the Torazzo, the tallest bell tower in Italy, Cremona (cre-MO-na; pop. 71,313) is a sea of terra-cotta rooftops and warm red brickwork. Perhaps even more impressive, however, is the view of the *duomo* and accompanying *campanile* in Piazza del Comune, one of the most striking *piazze* in the country. Above all, Cremona is awash in music, proud to be the home of violin genius Antonio Stradivari and the birthplace of the father of modern opera, Claudio Monteverdi. The city thus draws tourists looking to admire its violin-makers, the University of Music Palaeography and Philology, and the International School of Violin Making. Whether you're looking for scenery or serenading, Cremona is worth at least a day of your travels.

🚆 **TRANSPORTATION.** The **train station** is at V. Dante 68 (☎ 0372 89 20 21). The ticket office is open daily 6am-7:30pm. **Trains** run to: Bergamo (1hr., 6 per day 7:11am-9:34pm, €5.40); Brescia (45min., 15 per day 5:24am-9:34pm, €4); Mantua

(1hr., 19 per day 5:12am-9:20pm, €4.50); Milan (1hr., 15 per day 5:02am-9:34pm, €5.85); Parma (1hr., 5:52am-9:37pm, €5.10); Pavia (2hr., 5:15am-9:05pm, €4.95); Piacenza (1hr., 11 per day 5:32am-9:37pm, €2.70). The **bus station,** V. Dante 90 (☎0372 29 212), is one block to the left of the train station. (Open M-F 7:40am-12:15pm and 2:30-6pm, Sa 7:40am-12:15pm.) **Buses** run to small surrounding towns and also to Brescia (2hr.; M-Sa every hr. 6:05am-8pm, Su 4 per day). The new service Prenotabus offers buses on demand. (☎800 19 05 20. Available M-F 7am-7pm, Sa 7am-noon. Tickets available at *tabaccherie*. Check with tourist office for more info.) Orange **local buses** run from the train station throughout the city. **Taxi** stands are in P. Roma (☎0372 21 300) and at the train station (☎0372 26 740). Mata Store, on V. Eridano (☎0372 45 74 83 or 333 62 26 061), rents city and mountain **bikes.** (Prices vary, call for rates.) Astrocar, V. Brescia 77 (☎0372 45 24 67), provides **car rental.**

🔳🔳 **ORIENTATION AND PRACTICAL INFORMATION** From the train station, walk straight ahead toward **Via Palestro,** which becomes **Corso Campi,** then **Via Verdi,** before ending in **Piazza Stradivari.** Cross P. Stradivari and follow **Via Baldesio** to reach the **tourist office,** P. del Comune 5, which sells a "City Card" for discounts around town. (☎0372 23 233; www.provincia.cremona.it. Open daily 9am-12:30pm and 3-6pm. July-Aug. closed Sunday afternoons.) Those seeking info on alternatives to tourism should visit **Informagiovani di Cremona,** V. Palestro 11/A, for job listings, course offerings, and other opportunities for long-term residents. **Internet** access is also available. (☎0372 40 79 50; informagiovani@comune.cremona.it. Open M-Tu and Th-F 10am-1:30pm, W 10am-6pm, or call for an appointment.) **Banco Nazionale del Lavoro,** C. Campi 4-10, has currency exchange and a **24hr. ATM.** (☎0372 39 117. Open M-F 8:20am-1:20pm and 2:30-4pm, Sa 8:20-11:50am.) A **laundromat, S. Agata a Gettone,** is located at C. Garibaldi 132 (☎0372 30 314). In case of **emergency,** call the **police,** Vle. Trento e Trieste 58 (☎112), or for health emergencies, dial ☎118. The **hospital** (☎0372 40 51 11) is in Largo Priori. **Farmacia (Centrale) Communale,** is at V. del Gesù 2. (☎0372 27 581. Open M 3:30-7:30pm, Tu-F 9am-1pm and 3:30-7:30pm, Sa 9am-1pm and 3-8pm. After-hours rotation posted outside. MC/V.) **Libreria Giramondo,** V. Palestro 44, near the train station, offers **Internet** access. (☎22 414. €1 per 15min., €1.50 per 30min., €3 per hr. Open M 3:30-7pm, Tu-Sa 9:30am-12:30pm and 3:30-7pm.) The **post office,** V. Palestro 53, exchanges currency. (☎0372 20 425. Open M-F 8:30am-2pm, Sa 8:30am-12:30pm.) **Postal Code:** 26100.

🔳🔳 **ACCOMMODATIONS AND CAMPING. Albergo Duomo** ❹, V. Gonfalonieri 13, is in the center of everything. Well-kept rooms have bath, TV, phone, and A/C. Hotel restaurant is always crowded. (☎0372 35 242 or 35 255. Breakfast €5. Parking free. Singles €45; doubles €65; triples €75-80. AmEx/MC/V.) Owned by an English-speaking violin-maker, **B&B La Mansarda** ❸, V. Larga 8, a 5min. walk from the *centro*, will charm you to pieces. The rooms are located in a bright and airy modern apartment with attractive architectural touches. An ideal place for musicians, the convenient location is quiet enough to play music without disturbing neighbors. (☎0372 30 374; www.heyligerscremona.com/beb.html. Singles and doubles €35 per person.) **Camping Parco al Po** ❶, Lungo Po Europa 12, on the banks of the Po River, is a 40min. walk outside the *centro* along V. del Sale. Camper hookups, tent spaces, and cabins are available. (☎0372 27 137; www.campingcremonapo.it. €10 key deposit. Open Apr.-Sept. €6 per person; €9 per tent; €10 per car. Cabins for 2-4 people €30-50 per person. Showers €0.50.)

🔳 **FOOD.** *Mostarda di Cremona,* first concocted in the 16th century, consists of cherries, figs, apricots, and melons. It has a honey-like consistency, is a bit

LOMBARDY

spicy, and is traditionally eaten with meat. Delicious *grana padano*, a sophisticated cousin of parmesan cheese, is available in any *salumeria* (deli). In addition, every sweet shop sells bars of *torrone* (egg, honey, and nut nougat). The oldest sweets store in town, **Sperlari ❶**, V. Solferino 25, has been selling treats since 1836. (☎0372 22 346; sperlari.negozio@tin.it. Candy €0.40-15. Open daily 8:30am-12:30pm and 3:30-7:30pm. AmEx/MC/V.) At **Pierrot ❷**, Largo Boccaccino 2, sit at one of the wicker tables, gaze out onto the lively P. del Comune, and agonize over picking one of the tantalizing gelato sundaes. (☎0372 29 318. Gelato and coffee €1.50-3. *Granita* €2-3. Panini €2.50-3.50. Fruit and sundaes €4-8. Open daily 7:30am-1am. AmEx/MC/V.) Packed with locals, an open-air market in P. Stradivari sells fresh produce, meats, and cheeses. Vendors also sell clothing. (☎0372 40 74 50. Open W and Sa 8am-1pm.) A **GS Supermarket,** V. S. Tomaso 13, is close to P. del Comune. (Open M 9am-8:15pm, Tu-Sa 8am-8:15pm, Su 9am-1pm.) **Supermarket Quice** is on C. V. Emanuele. (Open M-Sa 8am-1pm and 3:30-10pm.) On weekends, bars and cafes fill Piazza della Pace, off P. Stradivari and down V. Lombardini, with live music.

◪ SIGHTS. The **Piazza del Comune** has historically been the center of Cremonese life, housing the *duomo*, Torrazzo, the baptistry, Palazzo Comunale, and Loggia dei Militi. With an excellent collection of Amati, Ceruti, and Stradivari violins (like the evocatively named "Vesuvius" violin, crafted in 1727), the **Civica Collezione di Violini** at the **Palazzo Comunale** draws in musically minded tourists. Reserve ahead for brief performances on Stradivari and Amati instruments. Performances are unfortunately suspended June-Aug. *(Reservations ☎0372 20 502, questions 22 138; www.comune.cremona.it. Buy tickets at the bookshop to the right inside the courtyard. Open Tu-Sa 9am-6pm, Su 10am-6pm; also Apr.-Oct. M. Wheelchair-accessible. €6, students €3.50. Concerts €1.50.)* Directly across from the Palazzo Comunale, **Santa Maria Assunta,** a pink-marble, 12th-century *duomo*, towers above the Gothic lions that guard its entrance. The interior displays 16th-century frescoes and an ornate Grand Cross. *(Open daily 7:30am-noon and 3:30-7pm. Free.)* To the left of the *duomo* rises the late 13th-century **Torrazzo.** Standing at 111m, it is Italy's tallest *campanile.* Climb the 487 steps to the top where you and the pigeons can enjoy the view of the city and surrounding countryside. *(☎0372 49 50 29. Open Tu-Su 10am-12:30pm and 2:30-5:30pm; last entry 30min. before close. €4, students €3. Combined with battistero €5/4.)* The dome of the **battistero** (baptistry), built in 1167, ascends in an octagonal pattern. The unadorned brick of the inside stone dome is somehow far more stunning than many far more ornate buildings. The **Museo delle Pietre Romaniche** shelters treasures that include a wooden crucifixion piece and the disturbing 17th-century *Altare dell'Addolorata*, complete with a dagger piercing the heart of a golden Virgin. *(☎0372 49 50 29; beniculturali@diocesidicremona. it. Open Tu-Su 10am-1pm and 2:30-6pm. €2, students €1. Combined ticket for Torazzo and baptistry €5/4.)* At the Palazzo Affaitati, V. Ugolani Dati 4, off V. Palestro, a grand marble staircase leads to the **Museo Civico** and the **Museo Stradivariano** within. The Museo Civico exhibits a diverse collection of paintings from the 15th to 19th centuries, including works by Boccaccio, the Campi family, Caravaggio, and Il Genovesino. Soft violin music plays as visitors enter the Museo Stradivariano, which boasts a room of the artisan's tools, molds, models, and drawings donated after his death in 1737. There is also a collection of violins from other famous makers. An English video tour and interactive exhibit explain the violins' production. *(Both museums ☎0372 31 222. Open Tu-Sa 9am-6pm, Su 10am-6pm. €7, students and groups of more than 15 €4.)* The 250-year-old Baroque **Teatro Ponchielli,** C. V. Emanuele 52, once provided the testing ground for the Stradivari and Amati violins, but today plays home to Cremona's artistic and cultural events. One of the largest stages in Italy, it's also one of the world's most beautiful, lavishly

LOMBARDY

decorated opera houses. Unless you're there for a performance, visits are by reservation only. (☎02 20 01; www.teatroponchielli.it. Ticket office open M-Sa June-Sept. 4:30-7:30pm; Oct.-May 4-7pm. €1.)

FESTIVALS. In Cremona, music and festivity are in the air year-round; tickets and info can be found at the Teatro Ponchielli ticket booth. (☎02 20 01; www.teatroponchielli.it. Open June-Sept. M-Sa 4:30-7:30pm; Oct.-May daily 4-7pm.) October 2009 will bring the biggest music festival of all, the **Fondazione Antonio Stradivari Cremona La Triennale,** in which 550 contestants from 34 countries exhibit newly crafted instruments, followed by performances. The actual contest takes place every three years, but every October there are related performances. (☎/fax 21 454; www.cremonamondomusica.it or www.entetriennale. com.) The **Monteverdi Festival,** from May to June, honors the great Cremonese composer's. (Info and tickets ☎02 20 10/01; info www.teatroponchielli.it, tickets www.vivaticket.it. Tickets €10-22.) From June to August, Cremona sponsors theatrical performances, musicals, culinary *degustazioni*, and fireworks displays in the surrounding towns on the Po River as part of the annual **Il Grande Fiume** (☎0521 37 40 77; www.ilgrandefiume.it). Complementing these fine-art offerings is Arena Giardino's **Festival di Mezza Estate,** in Parco Tognazzi, along Vle. Po southeast of the city, a summer festival from June to September that mainly celebrates Italian cinema, but also features drama, concerts, and ballet. (☎333 39 55 235; www.cinemacremona.it. Tickets about €5.) Lastly, the **Strada del Gusto Cremonese** (www.stradadelgustocremonese.it) aims to boost ecological production and encourage culinary tourism by having local restaurants feature special menus; contact the tourist office for the schedule.

LOMBARDY

THE LAKE COUNTRY

Travelers who need some serious rejuvenation should follow the example of artistic visionaries like List, Longfellow, and Wordsworth: retreat to the serene shores of the northern lakes, Italy's pocket of paradise. Summer attracts droves of foreign and Italian visitors, and each gorgeous lake has its own vibe. A young, mostly-German crowd descends upon the more affordable Lake Garda, enjoying aquatic sports by day and bars by night. The mansion-spotted coast of Lake Como fills its abundant hotels year-round with visitors seeking Kodak moments and a resort getaway. A playground for the rich and famous, Lake Como's shoreline harbors a couple well-run and inexpensive hostels in addition to its famous villas, including George Clooney's. In the neighboring province of Piedmont, palatial hotels dot Lake Maggiore's sleepy shores.

HIGHLIGHTS OF THE LAKE COUNTRY

BASK in the sun along the grass "beaches" in Riva del Garda (p. 273).

CATCH A WAVE while windsurfing in breezy, relaxed Domaso (p. 286).

DE-STRESS in Stresa, a resort town that draws visitors from all over (p. 297).

PICK LEMONS in Limone, home to a heart-saving protein found only in its residents. (p. 276)

LAKE GARDA (LAGO DI GARDA)

Lake Garda, the largest lake in Northern Italy offers freshness and energy thanks to the youthful tourists and sports enthusiasts that flock to its striking blue-green waters and rocky shores. Stretching 52km into the regions of the Veneto, Lombardy, and Trent, Lake Garda's shores are popular with Europeans seeking aquatic sports on the breezy beaches or hiking in the gorgeous Dolomite mountains. In the south, the more crowded cities emphasize the good life that comes from quality food and wine.

SIRMIONE ☎ 030

Isolated on a peninsula from the surrounding lakeside towns, tiny Sirmione (seer-mee-OH-neh; pop. 7000) retains some of the old-world charm that once moved the poet Catullus to praise the beauty of his home here. Among the town's attractions are the healing powers of its spa waters, which have been renowned since ancient times. The *centro storico* is a pedestrian-only zone; nevertheless, the heavy tourist traffic gives Sirmione the feel of a bustling resort. Trendy boutiques, restaurants, and hotels line the sidewalks, sharing the space with traces of Sirmione's Roman history and medieval architecture. Despite all of the class, Sirmione remains the beachiest of the lake towns, with scads of people soaking up sun or splashing in its aquamarine waters.

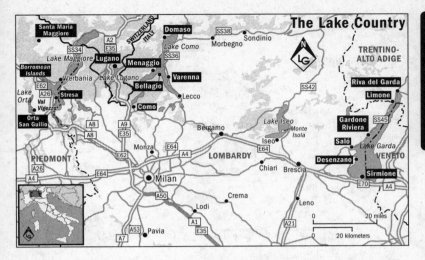

The Lake Country

▐▓ TRANSPORTATION AND PRACTICAL INFORMATION. SAIA **buses** run from the station, V. Marconi 26, to all stops along the Brescia-Verona line, including Desenzano, the nearest **train station.** (Ticket office open M-Tu 9am-1pm and 2-6pm, W-Su 7am-1pm and 2-8pm. After hours, purchase bus tickets from the *tabaccheria* on Vle. Marconi, about 200m from the ticket counter.) Navigazione Lago di Garda (☎030 91 49 511; www.navigazionelaghi.it), at the end of P. Carducci, runs **ferries** to Desenzano (15min.; 17 per day 10am-8pm; €3, express €5.10), Gardone via Salò (1-2hr.; 11 per day 8:27am-5:41pm; €6.90, express €9.80), and Riva del Garda via Limone (2-3hr.; 9:46, 10:20, 10:28am, 2:15, 3:00, 4:55pm; €9.70, express €13.10). Schedules are sold in the tourist office and at the ferry ticket offices. For a **taxi,** call ☎030 91 60 82. Rent **bikes, scooters,** and **motorbikes** at Adventure Sprint, P. Virgilio 31 (☎030 91 90 00). (Bikes €12 per day; scooters €50-75; motorbikes €110-140. Open daily 9am-6:30pm. MC/V.)

The **tourist office,** V. Guglielmo Marconi 8 (☎030 91 61 14; www.comune.sirmione.bs.it), is in the circular building in front of the SAIA station. (Open Apr.-Oct. daily 8am-8pm; Nov.-Mar. M-F 9am-1pm and 2-6pm, Sa 9am-12:30pm.) Other services include: **Banca Popolare di Verona,** P. Castello 3/4 (open M-F 9am-1:20pm and 2:35-3:35pm, Sa-Su 9-11:20am); the **police** (☎030 99 05 772); the **Tourist Medical Clinic,** P. Virgilio 35 (☎347 97 16 620); and **Farmacia di Turno,** V. S. Maria Maggiore (open M-W and F-Su 9:45am-12:15pm and 4:30-7pm, Th 9:45am-12:15pm), in the *centro storico.* The **post office,** V. G. Marconi 28, is behind the SAIA station (open M-F 8:30am-2pm, Sa 8:30am-12:30pm). **Postal Code:** 25019.

▐▐ ACCOMMODATIONS AND FOOD. A thorough exploration of Sirmione takes only an afternoon, but those looking for prolonged relaxation can choose from among a number of fairly pricey hotels or slightly cheaper accommodations in Colombare. Reserve early in summer, when rates are steeper. Closer to the end of the island by Grotte di Catullo, lovely host Sordelli's **⬛Villa Paradiso ❸**, V. Arici 7, offers accommodations inside a privately-owned, almost regal house. Rooms provide nearly 360-degree views of the lake from atop Sirmione. (☎030 91 61 49. Doubles €66. Cash only.) **Albergo Grifone ❸**, V. Bocchio 4, off V. Dante to the right of V. Vittorio Emanuele II past the castello, has country-style rooms

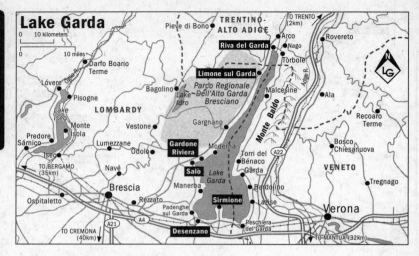

Lake Garda

all with small bathrooms and lake views. (☎030 91 60 14; fax 91 65 48. Doubles €67. Extra bed €23. Cash only.) Closer to the *centro storico*, **Hotel Speranza ④**, V. Castello 2, feels brand-new and has a breakfast room that would make Martha Stewart proud. Though still expensive, it is one of the more reasonable options in the older part of the town. (☎030 91 61 16; www.hotelsperanza.sitonline.it. Breakfast included. Open late Feb. to mid-Nov. Singles €50-60; doubles €85-100; triples €90; quads €105. AmEx/MC/V.) **Campeggio Sirmione ❶**, V. Sirmioncino 9, in Colombare, offers some of the least expensive accommodations on the peninsula for two or more people. It boasts a swimming pool and beach access as well as a small market and cafe. (☎030 99 05 089; www.camping-sirmione.it. Open late Mar.-Oct. €6-9 per person, €6-16 per tent. 2-person cabins €48-78; for a third person, add €7-11; 4-person cabins €63-113. MC/V.)

Sirmione's restaurants are numerous, but there are few that fit well in a budget. **Ristorante Pizzeria Valentino ❷**, P. Porto Valentino 10, off V. V. Emanuele II, is one of the more affordable establishments. It offers delicious fare, including homemade gnocchi and trout with Garda sauce and *polenta* (€14). (☎030 61 13 14. Pizza €4.50-9.50. Primi €8-19. Secondi €10-20. Cover €1.50. Open daily 11:15am-4pm and 6:30-10:30pm. AmEx/MC/V.) The gelato is piled high at **Master del Gelato Artigianale ❶**, near P. Castello. **Ristorante-Pizzeria Roberto ❷**, on V. Garibaldi 6, specializes in shrimp pizza (€8.70), *tagliolini* in cream sauce, and mushroom ravioli (both €7). After getting off the Colombare bus stop, walk 5min down V. Colombare. (☎030 919 359; www.ingarda.com/roberto. *Bruschetta* €2. Pizza €5-83.50-8.70. Antipasti €5-11.50. Primi €5-9.50. Secondi €8-22. Service 10%. Open Tu-Su 11:45am-2:30pm and 5:30-11pm.)

◙ **SIGHTS.** At the far end of the peninsula along V. Catullo is the **Grotte di Catullo,** perhaps the best-preserved and most impressive aristocratic Roman villa in northern Italy, spread over five acres of olive groves, it offers some of the most spectacular panoramas of Lake Garda. Although named for the poet Catullus, the ruins appear to date from the late first century BC, after the poet's death. Artifacts in the **archaeological museum** inside the grotto have English explanations. (☎030 91 61 57. Ruins and museum open Tu-Su Mar.-Oct. 8:30am-7pm;

THE LAKE COUNTRY

Nov.-Feb. 8:30am-5pm. €4, EU students 18-25 €2.) A small train runs between Sirmione and the grotto (€1, 8:30am-6:30pm). The 13th-century **Castello Scaligero** sits in the center of town as a testament to the power of the della Scala family who controlled the Veronese region from 1260 to 1387. Completely surrounded by water, the *castello's* commanding views are its main attraction. Except for some dirt and cannonballs, the interior is empty. (☎030 91 64 68. Open Tu-Su 8:30am-7pm. €4, EU students 18-25 €2.) Ruins of the city's **fortified walls** lie above Lido delle Bionde, near the ruins of a Lombardian church. **Chiesa di San Pietro in Mavino,** Sirmione's oldest church, dating to the AD 8th century, lies just off V. Catullo but is temporarily closed, due to newly discovered artifacts during excavation. Sixteenth-century frescoes decorate the church's interior.

◪◪ **ENTERTAINMENT AND NIGHTLIFE.** Sirmione's renowned thermal waters and mud baths at **Terme di Sirmione**, V. Punto Staffalo 1, are available only for those with prescriptions from a doctor. However, even the young and healthy can take advantage of the wellness packages (starting at €28) at the attached **Aquaria Spa,** which offers a range of services including thermal water soaks, massages, mud baths, and more. (☎030 91 60 44. Open Mar.-Oct. M 1-10pm, Tu-Su 10am-10pm; Nov.-Mar. M-F 4-10pm, Sa-Su 10am-10pm. AmEx/ MC/V.) Though slightly rocky, the free **public beach**, Lido delle Bionde, on Sirmione's east shore may be a better choice. **Canoes** and **paddleboats** are available for rent just below the **Lido delle Bionde** bar, off V. Catullo. (☎333 54 05 622. €6 per 30min., €8 per hr.; beach chair with umbrella €7 per day. Open daily Apr.- Sept. 8:30am-7pm. Cash only.) Walk around the tip of the peninsula to reach the **Punta Grotte,** a striking line of jagged cliffs slicing through the water. The town also has summer events, which generally include musical and dance performances, art exhibits, and fish tastings. Ask at the tourist office or look for Sirmione d'Estate flyers (www.commune.sirmione.bs.it).

A few bars and *enoteche* can be found on V. S. Maria Maggiore, off V. V. Emanuele II, the most scenic place to have a drink at night may be the beachside **Bar La Torre,** off V. Antiche Mura, behind the *castello.* (Drinks €3-8. Food €4-5. Open daily 10am-8pm, Sa until 2am. MC/V.) There is live jazz in P. Carducci on Friday evenings during the summer.

RIVA DEL GARDA ☎0464

With aquamarine lake waters lapping at the foot of the Brenta Dolomites, Riva del Garda (REE-va del GAR-da; pop. 14,500) is a spot for budget travelers looking to experience the Lake Country's beautiful views. Gentle mountain winds make Riva del Garda ideal for windsurfing, and its aquatic sports schools are world-renowned. The area is also a prime location for hiking, canoeing, whitewater rafting, kayaking, bicycling, swimming, and, above all else, relaxing on its extensive beaches—all made accessible and affordable by the attractive youth hostel. A walk or swim along the coast offers a view of the most stunning portion of the lake, where cliffs crash dramatically into the sea.

▆ **TRANSPORTATION**

Buses: Vle. Trento 5 (☎0464 55 23 23). Ticket office open M-Sa 6:30am-7:15pm, Su 9:05am-noon and 3:35-7:05pm. Local tickets available at dispenser in station. Buses run to: **Brescia** (2hr., 4 per day 7:45am-7:35pm, €5.30); **Desenzano** (6 per day 5:40am-5:10pm); **Limone** (20min., 6 per day 5:40am-5:10pm, €1.55); **Milan** (3hr.,

7:45am and 3:45pm, €8.60); **Rovereto** (1hr., 15 per day 5:50am-7:05pm, €2.45); **Salò** (6 per day 5:40am-5:10pm, €3.35); **Verona** (every hr. 5am-8pm).

Ferries: Navigazione Lago di Garda (☎0464 91 49 511; www.navigazionelaghi.it) in P. Catena, next to an information booth. Pick up a schedule in the tourist office or at the ferry ticket offices. To **Limone** (30min.; 17 per day 8am-6:05pm; €3.40, express €5.20); **Sirmione** (2-4hr.; 5 per day 8:35am-5pm; €9.70, express €14) via **Gardone Riviera** (1-3hr.; 5 per day 8:35am-5pm; €8.60, express €12); **Salò** (€8.60, express €12). Ticket office open 20min. before each departure.

Taxi: ☎848 80 07 79.

Bike Rental: Cicli Pederzolli, Vle. dei Tigli 24 (☎/fax 0464 55 18 30). Bikes €8-15 per day. **Bike Shop Girelli,** Vle. Damiano Chiesa 15/17 (☎0464 55 66 02). €15 per day. Both open M-Sa 9am-noon and 3-7pm. MC/V.

Scooter Rental: Sembenini Moto, Vle. Dante 3 (☎0464 55 45 48). €19 per 2hr., €49 per day. Open Tu-Su 9:30am-12:30pm and 4-7pm. MC/V.

⚒ 🔢 ORIENTATION AND PRACTICAL INFORMATION

To reach the **centro** from the bus station, head down **Viale Trento,** then cross the traffic circle. Go behind the church on **Via Roma** to reach **Piazza Cavour.**

Tourist Office "Ingarda Trentino": Largo Medaglie d'Oro 5 (☎0464 55 44 44; www.gardatrentino.it), at the old bus station at the end of V. della Liberazione. Lists hotel vacancies and offers a variety of cheap regional tours. Ask for a city map and hiking routes. City tour Sa 9:30am (3hr., €3); book 1 day in advance. English spoken. Wheelchair-accessible. Open M-Sa 9am-noon and 3-6:30pm, Su 9am-noon and 3:30-6:30pm.

Laundry: Vle. Rovereto 74. Take V. D. Alighieri, which becomes V. Giosuè Carducci and then Vle. Rovereto.

Internet Access: Internet Point, V. Dante Alighieri 70/B, has individual hookups for laptops. €3 per 30 min., Open M-Sa 10am-12:30pm and 3:30-10pm, Su 3:30-10pm.

English language books: Giunti, just outside the arched gate of P. Cavour. Open M-W 9am-8pm, Th 9am-10pm, F-Sa 9am-midnight, Su 10am-8pm.

Police: V. Brione 5 (☎0464 57 80 11).

Pharmacy: V. D. Alighieri 12/B (☎0464 55 25 08). Open M-F 8:45am-12:30pm and 3:30-7:30pm.

Post Office: V. S. Francesco 26 (☎0464 57 87 00). Open M-F 8am-6:30pm, Sa 8am-12:30pm. Also has ATM. **Postal Code:** 38066.

🏠 🔢 ACCOMMODATIONS AND CAMPING

▨ **Ostello Benacus (HI),** P. Cavour 10 (☎0464 55 49 11). From bus station, head right down V. Trento; cross through the traffic circle to V. Roma, turn left after the arch, and cross left through P. Cavour. Central location and clean facilities. Breakfast included; dinner €10. Laundry €4. Internet €2 per hr. Reception 7-9am and 3-11pm. Check-out 9am. Bathrooms closed 10am-3pm. Curfew 11pm; ask for key if returning after 11pm. Reservations recommended. Dorms €16. HI-member discount €3. MC/V. ❶

Albergo Garni Rita, V. Brione 19 (☎0464 55 17 98; www.garnirita.com). B&B located in a quiet area 25min. outside the *centro* within a cluster of similarly priced accommodations. Breakfast included. Reservations recommended. Located in a cluster of hotels and B&Bs with similar prices. Open Mar. 10-Nov. 3. €38 per person. Cash only. ❸

Bavaria, V. Rovereto 100 (☎0464 55 25 24), on the road toward Torbole. Pizzeria and *gelateria* in front of campground. Take lessons in windsurfing and sailing right behind the campground at Surfsegnana. Hot shower €1. Reception 9am-1pm and 3-6pm. Quiet hours 3-5pm and 11pm-8am. No entry by car 11pm-7am. Open Apr.-Oct. €8 per person, €6 per child. Site €10. AmEx/MC/V for €100 or more. ●

Camping Monte Brione, V. Brione 32 (☎0464 52 08 85; www.campingbrione.com). Offers a pool, bar, laundry services, and minimarket situated 800m from the lake, next to biking trails. Free hot showers. Internet €4 per hr. Reception 8am-1pm and 3-7pm. Reservations recommended. €6.50-8.50 per person. Small site without electricity €7-9; large site with electricity and parking €9.50-12. MC/V. ●

◨ FOOD

An **open-air market** sells produce in P. delle Erbe. (Open M-Sa mornings.) A **Despar** supermarket sells groceries just outside the *centro* at V. Roma 19. (Open M-Sa 8:30am-1pm and 3:30-7:30pm, Su 9am-12:30pm. Cash only.)

▧ **La Casa del Pane,** V. Disciplini, 3 (☎0464 5508 39). Outside of P. Cavour. Look no further for a delicious and cheap breakfast or lunch. Pizza cut by the slice will fill you up on the go (priced by weight, most slices €2-3.50). Absolutely don't miss one of their fantastic *brioche con cioccolato* (€1); baked fresh every morning, these warm and flaky beauties are the perfect way to start the day. Friendly owners will occasionally slip an additional cookie or slice of foccacia in with your order. ●

Leon d'Oro, V. Fiume 28 (☎0464 55 23 41). A general openness allows this energetic and traditional restaurant to spill pleasantly out onto the bustling street. Try the *risotto mantecato alle code di gambero* (with lemon-marinated prawns; €12) with local wine. Primi €7.50-13. Secondi €8.50-17. Cover €1.50. Open daily mid-March to mid-Nov. 11am-3:30pm and 5pm-11pm. AmEx/MC/V. ❸

Ristorante Ancora, V. Montanara 2 (☎0464 52 21 31). Maritime decor and sunkissed rooftop terrace. Pizza €3-8. Salads €4-6. Primi €8-13. Secondi €9-19. Open daily noon-midnight. AmEx/MC/V. ❸

◨ ◪ SIGHTS AND OUTDOOR ACTIVITIES

Take local bus #1, 2, or 6 from V. Martiri to reach **Cascata Varone,** which has a waterfall, stunning views, swimming, and sunbathing on amazing ▧**grass beaches.** Follow the lakeside path behind the tourist office and head away from the mountains to **Lungolago dei Sabbioni** and **Lungolago dei Pini**. Three kilometers outside town, the 20,000-year-old waterfall **Cascata Varone** has shaped a huge 110m gorge in the mountain. Foliage arches over surrounding mountain paths, making them ideal for easy strolls. (☎0464 52 14 21; www.cascata-varone.com. Open May-Aug. daily 9am-7pm; Sept. daily 9am-6pm; Oct. daily 9am-5pm; Nov.-Feb. Su 10am-5pm; Mar. daily 9am-5pm; Apr. daily 9am-6pm. €5. Cash only.) The **Ponale,** a road previously used by the military to connect Riva del Garda with Valle di Ledro during WWI, begins south of the city, a few hundred meters down the western shore, just before tunnel leading to Limone. The road boasts impressive views, tunnels, and mountain bike paths. For fun in the water, **Noleggio Rudderboat Rental,** in front of P. Battisti, by the castle, rents paddleboats. (☎0464 55 44 75. Rental for 2 people €7 per hr., €8 per 4hr., €9 per 5hr. Pay 2hr., get 1 free. Open daily 8:30am-7pm. Cash only.) **Surfsegnana,** behind campground Bavaria, offers windsurfing, sailing, and canoeing lessons. (☎0464 50 59 63; www.surfsegnana.it. Open daily 8am-6pm.) The cliffs above the lake draw hikers out of the city *centro*. Follow V. D. Alighieri to the mountains as it changes to V. Bastione; then, take a left up the ramp and follow the winding cobblestone path for 20min. to the 15th-century **Bastione** (the white building seen from below), a circular fortress that survived Napoleon's onslaught in 1796 but lost its upper half in the process. Today, hikers can explore the edges of the historical treasure or admire the aerial view of the vibrantly blue Lake Garda, speckled with tiny boats. Farther up, a steep 1hr. ▓hike leads to **Chiesetta Santa Barbara,** a tiny chapel poised over misty mountains and the valley below. Just look into the mountains for the white speck to locate it. There are numerous well-regarded **mountain biking** paths; for details, go to the tourist office.

█ NIGHTLIFE

The *centro* is peppered with English-style pubs that cater to a large German tourist contingent. The tourist office keeps a schedule of free beach parties during the summer that offer lakeside fireworks.

▓ **Pub All'Oca,** V. S. Maria 9 (☎0464 55 34 57; www.puballoca.com). Jazz and more upstairs, in an old leather booth or around the horseshoe bar. Downstairs is more fashionable, with black modern furniture. Young, international clientele and English-speaking staff. Mixed drinks €6. Open daily 6pm-2am. Cash only.

Nuovo 900, V. Gazzoletti 6 (☎0464 030 900; www.nuovo900.it). This jazzy, relaxing wine bar features surprisingly colorful futuristic decor and a candle-lit deck on the street. Wine starting at €3 per glass; ask about regional specialties. Open 6pm-2am. MC/V.

J24, P. Catena 7a (☎0464 55 31 73). J24 has plenty of seats that look out onto the lake and one of the more youthful clienteles along the *piazza*. Offers fresh fruity concoctions as well as a wide selection of rum and whiskey (€3.50-7 per glass). Open daily in summer 10am-1am; in winter 6pm-1am. MC/V.

LIMONE   ☎0365

On the northwestern coast of Lake Garda, jagged mountainsides dive deeply into the waters of Limone's (lee-MO-neh; pop. less than 1000) shores. Many adventurers come to windsurf or kayak, and Limone's small *centro* caters to tourism and provides a wonderful starting point for hikes to the surrounding mountaintops. Above all, Limone is best recognized as the lemon capital of Europe. Over the past thirty years, Limone has garnered the curiosity of scientific researchers who found a protein, Apolipoproteina A-1 Milano, unique to Limone locals. The wonder protein seems to naturally combat heart plaque in these lucky residents—or maybe it's just the beautiful views.

█ **PRACTICAL INFORMATION. Ferries** are run by Navigazione Lago di Garda (☎0365 91 49 511; www.navigazionelaghi.it) in P. Catena, next to an information booth. Pick up a schedule in the tourist office or at the ferry ticket offices. Ferries run to Desenzano (4 per day 10:25am-4:27pm; €9.60, express €13), Riva (17 per day 9:20am-7:36pm; €3.40, express €5.20), and Sirmione (8 per day 8:56am-5:21pm; €9.70, express €14). Located across from the bus stop, the **tourist office,** V. IV Novembre 29 (☎0365 95 47 20), offers maps and info on the town. To get there from the ferry stop, walk straight through the square, take your first left and follow V. Roma through Pta. Vecchio. After P. Garibaldi, the road becomes V. Camboni. Turns right on the steep Cottili. Follow the road uphill when it dead ends, then make a left on V. Capitelli. Take the next right; the tourist office is across the street. (Open daily 8:30am-9pm.) In case of **emergency,** contact the **police** (☎0365 95 47 44), Ufficio Piazzetta Erminia 3 or an **ambulance** (☎118). Call ☎95 40 27 for the **carabinieri,** V. Tamas 6. Other services include: **Banco di Brescia,** V. Comboni 24 (☎0365 95 40 24; open June-Sept. M-F 8:25am-1:25pm and 2:40-4:10pm, Sa 8:30am-12:30pm; Oct.-May M-F 8:25am-1:25pm and 2:40-4:10pm); **pharmacy,** V. IV Novembre 29 (☎0365 95 40 45; open June 15-Sept. 15 8:30am-12:30pm and 3:30-7:30pm; Sept. 16-June 14 M-W and F-Sa 8:30am-12:30pm and 4:30-7:30pm); **Internet at Caffè Milennio,** V. IV Settembre 29d, near the pharmacy and post office (☎0365 95 42 37, open

8am-9:30pm); and the **post office,** V. Caldogno 1, uphill from the tourist office, behind the parking garage (☎0365 95 47 46; open M-F 8:30am-2pm, Sa 8:30am-12:30pm). **Postal Code:** 25087.

▐▐ **ACCOMMODATIONS AND FOOD.** As with lower Lake Garda towns, affordable accommodations are scarce. Your best bet is the B&B ▓**Pensione Silvana ❷,** V. Nanzello 6. From the tourist office, walk south down V. IV Novembre for about 10min. After a bridge, make a right onto V. Luigi Einaudi, then a quick left by the "Silvana" sign. Though it is a rather hilly hike to and from the beach and the center of town, Silvana compensates with the lowest prices around. (☎0365 95 40 58. Breakfast included. €25-30 per person. No single rooms. Cash only.) More convenient rooms can be found directly by the bus stop at **Hotel Susy ❸,** V. IV Novembre 46. (☎0365 95 41 49. Breakfast included. Single €36; double €62. Reserve ahead. AmEx/MC/V.) **Hotel Alla Noce ❸,** V. Monsignor Daniele Comboni 33, three blocks from the bus stop, has stunning views of the town below. (☎0365 95 40 22; www.albergoallanoce.it. Breakfast included. Singles €35-42; doubles €60-74. AmEx/MC/V.). Overpriced restaurants filled with German tourists line the waterfront; venture inland to find more interesting (and wallet-friendly) fare. The various cakes at **Pasticceria Piva ❶,** V. Cortili 12, downhill from the bus stop. Stand alongside variety of sizable *panini* for less than €4-6. (☎0365 95 41 96. Open daily 9am-11pm. Cash only.)

▐▐ **SIGHTS AND ENTERTAINMENT.** Perched uphill from the quaint *centro* near the water, **La Limonaia del Castèl,** V. IV Novembre 25, transports tourists into the world of a functioning 18th-century citrus farm spread over 1633 sq. yd. of terraces. This impressive structure, with many of its original pillars and walls, grows a variety of citrus fruits. (☎0365 95 40 08; www.limone-sulgarda.it. €1.) Another source of pride for Limone is the **Tesöl,** the homestead of Monsignor Daniele Comboni, a Limone native and missionary whose dream to "save Africa through Africa" led him far from home in the late 1800s. The house, church, and surrounding park invite tourists to contemplate Saint Comboni's perseverance embodied in his motto *"O Nigrizia o Morte"* ("Africa or Death"). His relationship with Africa is captured in letters he wrote before eventually dying of Malaria in what is today the Sudan. Comboni was canonized by Pope John Paul II in 2003. The homestead is a long walk uphill from the beach—get a map from the tourist office

WHEN LIFE GIVES YOU LIMONE...

If you notice a surprisingly high number of elderly locals in Limone looking remarkably fit, you may be witnessing the effects of Limone's pride and joy, a medical anomaly that put the city on the world's health map in 1979. Perhaps the only thing more astonishing than the medical facts is the story of the people behind the numbers.

In 1979 a Limone-born railroad worker was hospitalized in Milan. In the course of his standard check-up, doctors discovered extremely high levels of cholesterol and triglycerides in his blood, though strangely, he showed no signs of the expected accompanying heart damage. The improbability of this phenomenon led to the discovery a previously unknown protein—Apoliproteina A-1 Milano—in the patient's blood, and further research revealed that there are no known carriers born outside of Limone. In other words, "Milano" is a misnomer.

To uncover the protein's source, genealogists traced carriers back to a pair of ancestors married in 1644. Limone's near complete isolation from the rest of the world until the construction of an access road in 1932 led to plenty of intermarriage, which kept the protein "in the family." Plaque-fighitng Milano burst onto the international scene in 2003. Heart disease may have finally met its match in this inbred underdog from Limone.

'ANNUNZIO, THE MAN, IE MYTH... WAIT, WHO?

A visit to D'Annunzio's villa will eave any visitor wanting to know more about the Oz-like enigma of a man. The reasons are two-fold: for one the villa is so quirky—nviting and forbidding, hilarious and tragic—it's hard not to crave a closer glimpse of the man behind he house. Secondly, the villa's mandatory tour offers little background on D'Annunzio, assuming his legacy to be common knowledge. Lest you find yourself leaving ascinated but confused, here are the basics of his biography.

Born in 1863 in Abruzzo, D'Annunzio rose to prominence as a journalist, novelist, and playwright, gaining acclaim after collaborating with artists like Claude Debussy and Sarah Bernhardt. Fuming after the territorial concessions made by Italy at the end of WWI, hawkish D'Annunzio seized the city of Fiume and tried to declare his own independent kingdom. His quest for glory insatiable, the "king" of Fiume then declared all-out war with Italy.

The campaign was short-lived and D'Annunzio soon retreated to his now-famous villa. His bold tactics and personality lived on as a model for Mussolini, as his writings foreshadowed Italian fascism, though D'Annunzio envisioned a more artistic form with music as he central focus. While he indeed lived a mythic reality, D'Annunzio need no longer remain a mystery.

and bring water. (Religious services Su 10am and 4pm; contact tourist office for seasonal opening hours and ask about free tours Th July 6-Aug. 31). **Chiesa San Benedeto** is one of the Lake Country's hidden treasures, overflowing with realistic and emotive artwork. Much of the moving artwork is by Andrea Celesti, a late 17th-century painter. The building itself was built in the 17th century. (Mass Su 8am and 10:30am.) Maps given at the tourist office note the locations of **public beaches.** Any significant visit to Limone wouldn't be complete without a lesson in **windsurfing,** and although generally quite expensive, Limone's one option, **Windsurfing Lino,** is fairly reasonable. This small company is run by a German expat who was once a windsurfing World Cup participant. (10min. walk down the beach to Foce San Giovanni. €40 per hr.; multiple day packages available: 3hr. lessons 10am and 1pm. Open daily 9:30am-5:30pm. Discount coupons available at the tourist office.)

The town's one nightclub is **Pub Alì,** V. Einaudi 4; walk down V. IV Novembre for about 10min. until V. Einaudi. Regular live music performances, posh white seats, a large dance floor, and a game room provide many entertainment options. Expect a crowd in July and August. (☎0365 91 41 42. Large beers €3. Mixed drinks €6. Open F-Su 10pm-3am.) Don't be dismayed by the name of **Bar Turista,** IV Novembre 48; in fact, it is frequented by a fairly equal mixture of tourists and locals, who are all drawn to its live music. (Large beers €4. Mixed drinks €5. Open daily 8am-1am. Cash only.)

GARDONE RIVIERA ☎0365

For tranquility far removed from its heavily touristed neighbors, Gardone will work wonders. A trip here was once commonly prescribed by doctors for European elites. The collection of villages that comprise the Gardone Riviera (gar-DOH-neh REE-vee-yeh-ra; pop. 2500) now serve as laid-back lake vacation destinations for many British visitors. Gracefully aging villas of colored stucco and lush gardens of Mediterranean citrus and olive trees surround the calm town. ▓**Il Vittoriale** is the sprawling estate of Gabriele D'Annunzio, a poet, novelist, WWI soldier, and latter-day Casanova. Inside, there are ornate rooms and artifacts, and the **Museo della Guerra** (Museum of the War). Absolutely do not miss touring the villa itself—a truly quirky playwright, D'Annunzio's house reflects his fascination with poetry, world religions, and leprosy, and is filled with various architectural features designed to teach his guests lessons on D'Annunzio's strange standards of behavior. (Museum and Villa open daily 9:30am-7pm. Mandatory guided tour available in many languages. Grounds and gardens open 8:30am-8pm.). The Fondazione al Vittoriale sponsors the **Festival d'Estate** in music: dance, theater, and lyrical opera in the 1500-seat open-air **Teatro del Vittoriale**, V. Vittoriale 12. (Festival d'Estate ☎0522 45 51 93; fax 0522 45 43 19. Ticket office ☎0365 29 65 06; www.teatrodelvittoriale.it. Performances July-Aug. Tickets €20-40.) Gardone's fairly new museum **Il Divino Infante**, V. dei Colli 34, features over 200 sculptures of the baby Jesus in every scene and costume imaginable. (☎0365 29 31 05; www.il-bambino-gesu.com. Open June-Aug. Tu-Su 3-7pm, Nov.-Jan. Tu-Su 3-7pm. €5, children and over 65 €4.) Climbing stairs from Zanardelli past the Bank from P. Marconi leads to the **Giardino Botanico** (Botanical Gardens), an oasis of criss-crossing brooks and bridges built from 1910 to 1970, at the corner of V. Roma and V. Disciplina. Thickets of bamboo and altars overgrown with palms transport visitors into a Southeast Asian jungle. Admire 2000 varieties of plants and modern sculptures by Haring and Lichtenstein, but beware getting into a spitting contest between two sculpted heads. (☎336 41 08 77. Open daily 9am-7pm. €9.)

Southbound **buses** stop in front of Grand Hotel (off P. Wimmer), northbound in front of the newsstand. Speedier, more frequent service to major cities is available on the Milan-Verona **train** line. Take the bus to Desenzano; the bus stop is next to the train station. Take V. Repubblica on the left from the ferry dock for about 250m to reach the English-speaking **tourist office**, V. Repubblica 8, which lists area establishments and events as well as maps. (☎/fax 0365 20 347; www.gardoneit.com. Open daily June-Sept. 9am-12:30pm and 3-6:30pm; Oct.-May 9am-12:30pm and 2:30-6pm.) For currency exchange and **ATM**, head to **Banco di Brescia**, V. Roma 6, across the street from the Grand Hotel on C. Zanardelli. (☎0365 20 081. Open M-F 8:25am-1:25pm and 2:40-3:40pm.) In case of **emergency**, dial the **police** (☎0365 20 179), located in Gardone Sopra (high village), where V. Carere leads away from V. Disciplina. A **pharmacy**, P. Wimmer 4, is located just past the travel agency. (☎0365 20 117. Open M-Sa 8:30am-12:30pm and 3:30-7:30pm.) The **post office**, V. Roma 8, is next door to the bank. (☎0365 20 862. Open M-F 8:30am-2pm, Sa 8:30am-12:30pm.) **Postal Code:** 25083.

SALÒ ☎0365

During the peak of WWII (Sept. 1943-Apr. 1945), Salò (sa-LO; pop. 10,000) was the "Capital of a Divided Italy" and was declared the Republic of Salò as a last attempt by Mussolini and Hitler to reorganize fascism in Italy. Hotel Laurin was once Mussolini's headquarters. The town, which is typically filled with yachters coming ashore, totally lacks affordable accommodations. If you seek stately allure and refined charm, try Salò as a daytrip from Sirmione or Desenzano. Head right toward the lake on Lungolago Zanardelli from the ferry stop to reach Salò's beautiful Gothic Venetian **duomo**, built by Filippo della Vacche. Stand underneath the intensely realistic wooden crucifix, which hangs in the center and look into Jesus's eyes. It almost seems as if you can see him exhale. (Open daily 8:30am-noon and 3:30-7pm. Free.) Two of the town's three museums, **Museo Archeologico** and **Museo Storico**, V. Fantoni 49, offer a comprehensive and overarching historical account of the region. (☎29 68 34. Museo Storico open Su 10am-noon and 3-5pm. €4. Museo Archeologico M-F 10am-noon. €2.)

Transporti Brescia Nord Buses (☎0365 840 62 00 01) stop at the bus stop on V. Calsone, where it meets Vco. Oratorio. Buses serve Desenzano (30min., 6 per day 6:57am-6:27pm, €2.50), and Gardone (5min., 6 per day 6:33am-7:03pm, €1), continuing on to Limone (1hr., €3) and Riva (1hr., €3.45). Tickets can be purchased at the *tabaccheria* in front of the stop; if it is closed, purchase tickets on the bus for €1 extra. **Navigazione Lago di Garda** (☎0365 91 49 511; www.navigazionelaghi.it) runs **ferries** to Desenzano (4 per day 10:25am-4:27pm; €9.70, express €13.10), Riva (17 per day 9:20am-7:36pm; €3.40, express €5.20), and Sirmione (8 per day 8:56am-5:21pm; €9.70, express €13.10). From the ferry station, head inland and left through P. della Vittoria to reach the **tourist office**, P. Sant'Antonio 4, which offers a great map of the town. (☎/fax 0365 21 423. Open daily 9:30am-1pm and 3-6:30pm.) **Postal Code:** 25087.

DESENZANO   ☎030

As the only town with train access and home to the largest port in the region, Desenzano (deh-sen-ZA-no; pop. 23,000) is the gateway to Lake Garda. It also holds extensive shopping and nightlife that is unavailable in most of its quieter neighboring towns. With lovely pedestrian streets, good restaurants, and a weekly lakeside open-air market, this town never lets a traveler down.

⚏ 🔢 TRANSPORTATION AND PRACTICAL INFORMATION. Trains, on the corner of V. da Vinci and Vle. Cavour, serve Milan (24 per day 6:33am-10:16pm; €6.80), Venice (22 per day 6:30am-10:13pm; €8.40), and Verona (14 per day 6:09am-11:39pm, €2.60). **Buses** leave across the street from the train station and stop by the port (tickets sold in a yellow newsstand there), serving Gardone (45min., 6 per day 6am-6pm, €2.80); Limone (1hr., 6 per day 6am-6:30pm, €4.90); Riva (2hr., 6 per day 6am-6:30pm, €5.60); Salò (30min., 6 per day 6am-6:30pm, €2.60); Sirmione (19 per day 5:40am-7:05pm, €1.60-4). The tourist office provides bus schedules. From the port in P. Matteotti on V. Anelli, Navigazione sul Lago di Garda runs **ferries** to Garda (8 per day 10:15am-5:40pm; €6.90, express €9.80) and Riva del Garda (4 per day 10am-4:55pm; €11, express €15). (☎030 91 49 511 or 800 55 18 01; www.navigazionelaghi.it. Ticket office open 20min. before departure time.) For **taxis**, call ☎030 91 41 527.

The **tourist office** is at V. Porto Vecchio 34. (☎030 91 41 510. Open M-Tu and Th 9am-12:30pm and 3-6pm.) Other services include: **Banco di Brescia,** V. Guglielmo Marconi 18, with **ATM** (open M-F 8:25am-1:25pm and 2:40-4:10pm); **police** (☎030 91 43 572); **medical emergency** (☎030 91 20 393); **pharmacy,** V. S. Maria 1, off P. Matteotti (open 9am-12:30pm and 3:30-7:30pm; MC/V); **Internet** and **Western Union,** V. Mazzini 3 (€1 per 15min., €3 per hr.; open daily 9am-10pm); **post office,** V. Crocefisso 27-29, near Villa Romana (open M-F 8:30am-7pm, Sa 8:30am-12:30pm). **Postal Code:** 25015.

🔢 🖪 ACCOMMODATIONS AND FOOD. Accommodations are plentiful in Desenzano, though they can be expensive, especially compared to those in nearby towns. **Hotel Flora ❸,** V. Guglielmo Marconi 22, on the main road entering the city, and walking distance from the water, has spacious rooms in addition to free parking, Wi-Fi, and fax. Rooms include TV, telephone, A/C, and a small safe. From the train station, take V. Cavour until V. G. Marconi, then make a right. (☎030 99 12 547; www.hotelflora.org. Breakfast included. Singles €40-60; doubles €60-80; triples €80-100. AmEx/MC/V.) **Hotel Trattoria Alessi ❸,** V. Castello 3, (not to be confused with the connecting V. Stretta Castello) boasts an ideal location, right beneath the *castello.* (☎030 91 41 980; www.hotelalessidesenzano.com. Breakfast included. Singles €40-50; doubles €60-70. AmEx/MC/V.) Another conveniently located hotel is **Albergo Moniga ❹,** V. Canonica 16, which overlooks a quiet street. (Singles €50; doubles €70. Breakfast included. MC/V.)

Restaurants line P. Giacomo Matteotti, as well as the pedestrian streets parallel to the waterfront, V. S. Maria, V. Papa, and V. Roma. Walk a while west on V. Roma until it becomes V. Cesare Battisti to get to Spiaggia Desenzanino, the home of **Ristorante-Pizzeria Desenzanino ❷,** C. Battisti. (☎030 91 28 096. Pizza €3-10. Open Tu-Su noon-2:15pm and 7-10:30pm. MC/V.) On the east end of town, **La Briciola ❶,** V. Tommaso dal Molin 5, offers inexpensive self-service food. Menu changes daily; most items under €7. (Open M-Sa noon-4:20pm. AmEx/MC/V.) To escape the heavy tourist feel of the center, make the short uphill trip to P. Garibaldi and try **La Frasca Osteria ❸,** which combines high-end cuisine with a homey yet sophisticated atmosphere. (030 991 27 98; www.osterialafrasca.com. Primi €8-9.50. Secondi €9-15. Open daily 12:15-2:30pm and 6:30-117-10:30pm. Cash only.) Discounts fall like manna from heaven upon the extremely cheap **Supermercato,** V. G. Marconi 17. (Open M-Sa 8:30am-12:30pm and 3:30-7:30pm, Su 9am-1pm.)

◙ SIGHTS. Beaches, Desenzano's chief appeal, are on the far west end of town (Desenzanino), as well as some short cultural attractions. ◙**Pedal-boats** run €6 per 30min. and €15 per 2hr., and kayaks cost €6-10 per hr. Views from the **Castello,** in the center of town, are striking. Inquire at the tourist office about free performances inside the castle. (Open Tu-Su 10:30am-12:30pm and 4-7pm. €1. Th free.) The **Villa Romana,** constructed before the AD first century, offers some of the most important remnants of Roman villas in northern Italy built during the demise of the Empire. Don't expect imposing columns or domed ceilings, however—the site brings to mind the word ruins, consisting mostly of low stone walls and mosaic-covered floors. For a more impressive set of debris, head to nearby Sirmione for the Grotte di Catullo. (☎030 91 43 547. Open daily Mar.-Oct. 8:30am-6:30pm; Nov.-Feb. 8:30am-5pm. €2.) The **Galleria Civica di Palazzo Todescini,** around the corner from the tourist office, has rotating art exhibits. (Open M-F 10:30am-12:30pm and 5pm-8pm, Sa-Su 10:30am-12:30pm, and 5-10pm. Hours depend on exhibition. Some exhibits free; for others prices vary.)

▒ ▐ FESTIVALS AND NIGHTLIFE. From the end of June to the first days of July, Desenzano celebrates its revered saint, **San Luigi.** Check www.commune.desenzano.brescia.it for more festivals. Many of the restaurants along P. Matteotti and P. Capelletti double as bars; check out the (relatively) hip offerings along P. Matteoti. For youthful glamour, check out **Circus,** P. Matteotti 23, where the sleek, vaguely circus-themed decor is more sexy than goofy. (☎030 25 015. Open daily in summer 7pm-3am, winter closes at 2am.) The area on V. Castello is less mainstream, but is home to unique establishments like the Irish pub **Fiddler of Dooney,** V. Castello 36. (☎030 91 42 262. Pints €3.50. Pizza €2.50. F and Sa live music. Open M-F 6pm-2am, Sa 5:30pm-2am, Su 4pm-2am.)

NO WORK, ALL PLAY

VON-TRAPPED IN DESANZANO

Every year in mid-July, residents of Desenzano and the tourists who flock to its shores welcome a group of very special guests–a troupe of all ages from Tyrol, a state in western Austria. While world-famous for its unsurpassed skiing, the remote Austrian region deflates in size when the snow melts and the crowds of visitors go with it. The tourism agency has thus elected to send emissaries of Tyrolean goodwill to its Italian sister city. For three nights, these men and women in traditional costume descend on Desenzano's castle, serving up fragrant, hearty messes of Wurst and Weizenbier, piping hot slices of strudel, and an extra helping of alpine spirit. Aside from sampling the delicious food–a welcome respite from the ubiquitous risotto–visitors and Desenzano residents can gawk at the hard-at-work Tyrolean blacksmiths forging their wares.

As a symbol of peace, the northern visitors bring with them the accordions of love and understanding. Not only do they come yodeling in five-part harmony bearing jovial oompa bands, but as the night wears on, dancers emerge–breeches, dirndls, and all–and make their way from the stage to the town's central square.

If you want to see just how alive these hills really are, look no further than to this soulful Italo-Austrian meeting of the minds!

LAKE COMO (LAGO DI COMO)

As indicated by the luxurious villas lining its shores, Lake Como has been a refuge for the well-to-do since before the Roman Empire. But the area is not all about glitz and glamor: the stately beauty surrounding one of Europe's deepest lakes (410m) has provided inspiration for revered artists like Rossini, Bellini, and Shelley alike. Bellagio, Menaggio, and Varenna, the three central lake towns, make for a more relaxing stay than Como, holding peaceful villages quietly tucked into the densely green slopes.

COMO   ☎031

Situated on the southwestern tip of Lake Como, closest to Milan, Como (CO-mo; pop. 86,000) is the lake region's comparative metropolis, where physicist Alessandro Volta (who brought us the battery) was born and where Giuseppe Terragni immortalized his fascist architectural designs. Como is a livelier, more youthful city than others on the lake, with visitors coming for the cutting edge shopping, eateries, and nightlife. For those interested in nature, Como's nearby hiking is more than enough to entertain those passing through.

◱ TRANSPORTATION

Trains: Stazione San Giovanni (☎031 89 20 21). Open daily 6:40am-8:25pm. Ticket office open daily 6:40am-8:25pm. To: **Chiasso** (10min., every hr. 6:29am-1:29am, €1); **Milan Centrale** (1hr., 15 per day 6:25am-11:08pm, €3.50); **Milan Porta Garibaldi** (1hr., 21 per day 5:08am-10:20pm, €3.50); **Basel, Switzerland** (5hr., 9 per day 6:29am-7:59pm, €58); **Zurich, Switzerland** (4hr., 10 per day 7:43am-8pm, €46). **Ferrovia Nord** runs trains from **Stazione Ferrovia Nord** (☎031 30 48 00), near P. Matteotti, to **Cadorna Stazione Nord** and **Milan** (1hr., 32 per day 5:46am-9:16pm, €3.45).

Buses: SPT (☎031 24 71 11; www.sptlinea.it) in P. Matteotti runs buses to nearby lake towns. Ticket office open M-Sa 6:15am-8:15pm, Su 8:10am-12:25pm and 1:25-7:40pm. Info booth open M-F 8am-noon and 2-6pm, Sa 8am-noon. **C30** to **Bel-**

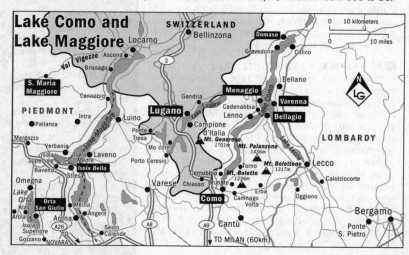

Iagio departs from Station San Giovanni. (1hr.; M-Sa 16 per day 6:25am-8:14pm, Su 8 per day 8:45am-8:14pm; €2.40). **C46** to **Bergamo** departs from P. Matteotti (2hr.; M-Sa 6:45, 9:30am, 12:10, 3:45, 6:30pm; Su 9:10am, 1:10, 4, 6:20pm; €4.60). **C10** to **Domaso** departs from P. Matteotti (dir.: Colico), but some end in **Menaggio** (2hr.; M-Sa 12 per day 7:10am-8:35pm, Su 9 per day 8:20am-8:15pm; €4).

Ferries: Navigazione Lago di Como (☎031 57 92 11; www.navigazionelaghi.it). Ticket office open 8:10am-6:50pm. Ferries depart daily to all lake towns from piers along Lungo Lario Trieste in front of P. Cavour. Ferries run to: **Bellagio** (1-2hr.; 21 per day 7:33am-7:10pm; €7.90, express €11); **Domaso** (1-4hr.; 11 per day 8:45am-7:10pm; €9, express €13); **Menaggio** (1-2hr.; 20 per day 7:33am-7:10pm; €7.90, express €11); **Varenna** (1-2hr.; 13 per day 8:45am-7:10pm; €7.90, express €11). Day-passes €20. Pick up the booklet *Orario* for a schedule, including summer night service.

Public Transportation: Buy bus tickets (€1) at *tabaccherie*, bus station, or hostels.

Taxis: RadioTaxi (☎031 26 15 15) in front of both train stations.

Car Rental: Europcar, Vle. Innocenzo XI 14. (☎031 24 16 43).

◀▶ ORIENTATION AND PRACTICAL INFORMATION

From Como's **Stazione San Giovanni,** head down the stairs, and then straight ahead through the park. At **Piazzale San Rocchetto,** take V. Fratelli Recchi on the left, and then turn right on Vle. Fratelli Rosselli, which becomes **Lungo Lario Trento** and leads to **Piazza Cavour. The bus station** and **Stazione Ferrovia Nord** are in **Piazza Matteotti,** 2min. farther down the lake along **Lungo Lario Trieste.**

Tourist Office: ATC, P. Cavour 17 (☎031 26 97 12; www.lakecomo.it), on the right when facing the *piazza*. Open M-Sa 9am-1pm and 2:30-6pm, Su 9:30am-12:30pm. **Como Viva,** a booth on V. Comacini next to the *duomo*, also offers info. Open Su 10am-6pm.

Currency Exchange: Banca Nazionale del Lavoro, P. Cavour 32 (☎031 31 31), near tourist office, has a **24hr. ATM.** Open M-F 8:30am-1pm and 2:30-4pm.

Carabinieri: V. Borgo Vico 171. (☎112).

Pharmacy: Farmacia Centrale, V. Caio Plinio Secondo 1, off P. Cavour. Posts after-hours rotations. Open M 3:30-7:30pm, Tu-Su 8:30am-12:30pm and 3:30-7:30pm.

Hospitals: Ospedale Valduce, V. Dante 11 (☎031 32 41 11). **Ospedale Sant'Anna,** V. Napoleana 60 (☎031 58 51 11).

Internet Access: Bar Black Panther, V. Garibaldi 59 (☎031 24 30 05). €3 per hr. Open Tu-Su 7am-midnight. **Como Bar,** V. Alessandro Volta 51 (☎031 26 20 52). Free drink with 2hr. Internet use. €1.40 per 30min., €3 per hr. Open M-Sa 8am-9pm. Cash only.

Post Office: V. V. Emanuele II 99 (☎031 27 63), in the *centro*. Open M-F 8:30am-7pm, Sa 8:10am-12:30pm. Branch on V. Gallio. **Postal Code:** 22100.

▮ ACCOMMODATIONS

▨ **In Riva al Lago,** P. Matteotti 4 (☎031 30 23 33; www.inriva.info), near the bus station. Soothingly airy new rooms with attractive architectural touches, bath, TV, and A/C. Some have minifridge. Internet €1.50 per 30min. Wi-Fi €3 per day, €5 per 2 days. Free luggage storage. Bustling restaurant-pub on ground fl. Reception 8am-11:30pm. Reservations recommended. Singles €35-45, with bath €40-53; doubles €40-63; triples €58-80; quads €68-98; 4- to 6-person apartments €95-115. AmEx/MC/V over €110. ❸

Ostello Villa Olmo (HI), V. Bellinzona 2 (☎031 57 38 00; ostellocomo@tin.it). From Stazione San Giovanni, turn left and walk 20min. down V. Borgo Vico to V. Bellinzona. Or take bus #1, 6, or 11 to Villa Olmo (€1). Summer-camp feel. Single-sex rooms. Ask about discounts for local attractions. Breakfast included; dinner €12. Laundry €4, dry

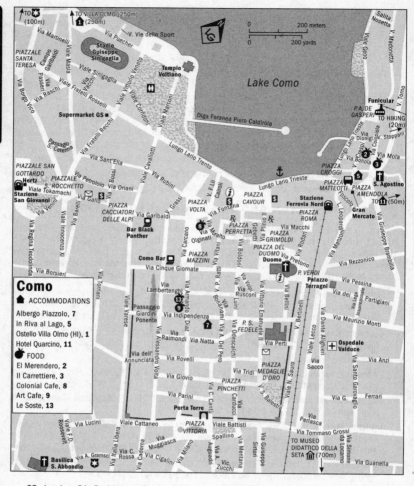

€3; ironing €1. Parking available. Bike rental €12.50 per day. Reception 7-10am and 4pm-midnight. Check-out 10am. Lockout 10am-4pm. Curfew midnight. Reservations recommended. Open Mar. 1-Nov.15. Dorms €18; family room €16.50 per person (only for families with children). HI-member discount €3. Cash only. ❶

Hotel Quarcino, Salita Quarcino 4 (☎031 30 39 34; www.hotelquarcino.it), offers spacious and calming rooms, some with terraces overlooking the nearby Chiesa di San Agostino. Pleasant garden. Free private parking. Singles €50, with breakfast €52; doubles €75/82; triples €100/110; quads €110/120. AmEx/MC/V. ❹

Albergo Piazzolo, V. Indipendenza 65 (☎/fax 031 27 21 86). From P. Cavour, take V. Bonta, which becomes V. Boldini, then V. Luni. V. Indipendenza is on the right. Tastefully decorated rooms above restaurant, all with bath, TV, and phone. Breakfast €6.50. Closed Nov. Doubles €60; triples €90; quad €110. AmEx/MC/V. ❹

🍴 FOOD

Piazza Mazzini and the streets branching out from it are a veritable Mecca of trendy, modern cafes and art galleries. *Resta* (sweet bread with dried fruit) is a Como specialty sold at **Beretta Il Fornaio,** Vle. Fratelli Rosselli 26/A. (Open Sept.-June M 7:30am-1:30pm, Tu-Sa 7:30am-1:30pm and 4-7pm; July-Aug. M-Sa 7:30am-1:30pm.) Local cheeses, like the pungent *semuda* and *robiola*, are available at supermarkets. Try **GS,** on the corner of V. Fratelli Recchi and V. Fratelli Roselli. (☎031 57 08 95. Open M 9am-8pm, Tu-Sa 8am-8pm, Su 9am-1pm. AmEx/MC/V.) **Gran Mercato** is by the bus station in P. Matteotti. (Open M and Su 8:30am-1pm, Tu-F 8:30am-1:30pm and 3:30-7:30pm, Sa 8am-7:30pm.) An **open-air market** is held in P. Vittoria (Tu and Th mornings, all day Sa.)

Le Soste, V. Diaz 52/A (☎031 266 024; www.lesoste.biz), is a small, youthful restaurant for those tired of the traditional *ristorante/pizzerie* combination. Try the Nettle dumplings with melted butter and poppy seeds (€10). Open M-Th noon-2:30pm and 6:30-10:30pm, F-Sa noon-2:30pm and 6:30pm-11:30pm. ❸

Art Cafe, V. Diaz 56 (☎031 268 013; www.i5sensi.it) operates not only as a cafe with a tasty array of wines and *aperitivi*, but also as an art gallery, with exhibits changing monthly and ranging from photos and paintings to multimedia sculptures and woven tapestries. Wine €4. Mixed drinks €5. Open daily noon-3pm and 6pm-2am. ❷

Colonial Cafe, V. Olginati 14 (☎031 449 1535; www.colonial-cafe.com), near P. Mazzini. A lush fusion of decor from various colonized nations around the world serving over-the-top tea and coffee creations. Specializes in countless varieties of profoundly sweetened espresso drinks, spiked with liqueurs and topped with a mountain of fresh whipped cream. Open daily 8am-midnight. ❷

Il Carrettiere, V. Coloniola 18 (☎031 30 34 78), off P. Alcide de Gasperi, near P. Matteotti. Draws crowds with Sicilian cuisine like *risotto con filote di pesce persico.* Pizza €5-8. Primi €8.50-10. Secondi €8.50-19.50. Cover €1.30. Open Tu-F 7pm-1am, Sa-Su noon-2:30pm and 7pm-2am. Reservations recommended. AmEx/MC/V. ❸

El Merendero, V. Crespi 4 (☎031 30 44 77). A lively hangout for nearly 30 years, offering 75 different types of beer to all types of locals. Try the potent Devil's Kiss (€2). Beer €3.50-6. Mixed drinks €4. Panini €4. Secondi €6-8. Open daily noon-3pm and 7:30pm-2am. Closed May-Sept. all day W and Su afternoon. Cash only. ❷

👁 SIGHTS

DUOMO. A gleaming white beacon in the center of the city, Como's recently restored octagonal *duomo* dates from 1396 and harmoniously combines Romanesque, Gothic, Renaissance, and Baroque elements. The Rodari brothers' life-like sculptures of the Exodus from Egypt animate the exterior, while a collection of 16th-century tapestries brighten the cavernous interior. Statues of Pliny the Elder and Pliny the Younger, long-past Como residents, flank the main door; inside, each massive column hosts its own illuminated statue. *(From P. Cavour, take V. Caio Plinio II to P. Duomo. Open daily 7am-noon and 3-7pm.)*

TEMPIO VOLTIANO. The Neoclassical structure was dedicated to Como's native son Alessandro Volta, inventor of the battery. The collection includes early attempts at wet-cell batteries the size of a kitchen table, and apparatuses used for experimenting on frog muscles. *(From P. Cavour, walk left along the waterfront, and turn onto Lungolago Mafalda di Savoia; look for the small building with a dome.* ☎031 57 47 05 and 27 13 43. Open Tu-Su Apr.-Sept. 10am-noon and 3-6pm; Oct.-Mar. 10am-noon and 2-4pm. €3.)*

VILLA OLMO. Around the western edge of the lake right next to the youth hostel,the light yellow ambassadorial Villa Olmo, built in Lombard style, sits in a spacious, statue-lined waterfront park of the same name. It hosts one art exhibit a year, from March to July. Last year's focus was Viennese painters Klimt, Schiele, and Kokoschka. *(On V. Cantoni. ☎ 031 25 24 43. Gardens open daily Apr.-Sept. 8am-11pm; Oct.-Mar. 9am-7pm. Exhibit prices vary.)*

MUSEO DIDATTICO DELLA SETA. The worms and silk looms that put Como on the textile map are now displayed in all their finery at this museum just outside of town. *(V. Vallegio 3. Entrance at V. Castelnuovo 1. ☎ 031 30 31 80; www.museosetacomo.com. Open Tu-F 9am-noon and 3-6pm. Wheelchair-accessible. €8.)*

HIKING

For some of the best hiking in the lake region, start by taking the **funicular** from P. dei Gasperi 4, at the far end of Lungo Lario Trieste, to **Brunate** (8min.) for an excellent hike back down to Como. (☎031 30 36 08; info@funicolarecomo.it. Daily every 15-30min. June-Sept. 6am-midnight; Oct.-May 6am-11:30pm. €2.45, under 12 €1.60; round-trip €4.25/2.70, 8:30pm-midnight €1.50. AmEx/MC/V.) The tourist office provides excellent trail descriptions of the lands above Brunate and the Lecco district east of Como. Adventures of all levels start in Brunate, where you can even launch a two-day hike all the way to Bellagio. For more effortless panoramas, take the red-brick *passeggiata pedonale* to the left of the pink church and hike toward **Faro Voltiano** (906m), a lighthouse dedicated to Volta (30min.). On a clear day, views from the Faro stretch from Milan to the Matterhorn. A bus runs from Brunate to near the Faro (every 30min. 8:15am-6:45pm, €1). From Faro Voltiano, another 15min. of hiking leads to **San Maurizio,** and another hour will take you to **Monte Boletto** (1236m). If the hike to Monte Boletto isn't too exhausting, keep strolling to reach **Monte Bolettone** (1317m).

Another option is to head northwest past San Maurizio after the restaurant Baita Carla before reaching Monte Boletto, on a path to lakeside **Torno,** 8km north of Como (1hr.); this is a good place to catch a ferry back to Como (every hr. 7am-7pm, €2). In Torno, check out the **Chiesa di San Giovanni** (open daily 8am-6pm) or the **Villa Pliniana,** 15min. north of the dock, closed to visitors but worth a look from afar. For extensive exploration of the mountains near Como, take bus C40 to **Erba** (30min.; every hr. 5:25am-10:20pm, last return 10:56pm; €1.90). From Erba, hike to **Caslino D'Erba,** which leads to **Monte Palanzone** (1436m). It is also possible to reach Erba by hiking south from Monte Bolettone (2hr.). Head to the cool recesses of **Buco del Piombo** for an encounter with prehistory— caves formed during the Jurassic Period over 150 million years ago.

DAYTRIP FROM COMO: DOMASO

Domaso lies 50km away from Como and can be reached by hydrofoil (1hr.; €11.50) or bus (2hr.; €4). Contact the tourist office in Como for more info.

The breezes in Domaso (doh-MA-zoh; pop. 1500), located at the top of the lake, create perfect **windsurfing** conditions. **Windsurfcenter Domaso,** V. Case Sparse 24, at Camping Paradiso, outfits sailors and windsurfers and offers classes from May 1 to October 14. (☎380 70 00 010; www.windsurfcenter-domaso.com. Board and sail rental €37 per half-day, €45 per day. Private lessons €55 per hr. not including equipment rental. Bikes €16 per half-day. Cash only.) If the wind isn't cooperating, travel 30min. farther along the main road to **Canottieri Domaso,** V. Antica Regina 36, where waves take out **wakeboarders.** (☎034 497 462; www.canottieridomaso.it. Wakeboarding €108 per hr., water skiing €120 per hr. Open daily 9am-noon and 1-6pm. AmEx/MC/V.) The **tourist office,** in Ple. Madonnina, has maps and info on aquatic sports. (☎96 322; www.comunedomaso.it. Open June-Sept. daily 10am-1pm and 3:30-6pm.)

BELLAGIO ☎031

Once favored by the upper-crust of *milanese* society, Bellagio (beh-LA-jee-yo; pop. 3000, in summer 6000) is one of the loveliest—and certainly the most heavily visited—of the central lake towns. While the tiny town center is generally crowded with tourists, a trip to the grounds of the Villa Melzi allows visitors to stretch their legs in the peaceful splendor of carefully manicured nature. Its name is a compound of *bello* (beautiful) and *agio* (comfort); fittingly, the town is filled with lakeside promenades, sidewalk cafes, and shaded streets.

TRANSPORTATION AND PRACTICAL INFORMATION. The best way to reach Bellagio is by **ferry.** The ferry next to the *biglietteria* in P. Mazzini serves people, while the one across the port also serves cars. Ferries depart to most lake towns, including Menaggio (10-15min., 8:36am-7:53pm, €3.50), Varenna (10-15min., 9:08am-10:20pm, €3.50), and Como (45min.-2hr., 6:47am-8:34pm, €7.90). SPT C30 **buses** run to Como (1hr., 19 per day 5:55am-6:55pm, €2.65). Lecco Trasporti runs buses to Lecco (1hr., 4-6 per day 6:30am-7:50pm, €2.10.). Ferries dock at **Piazza Mazzini,** which becomes **Via Roma** to the left and **Lungo Lario Manzoni** to the right. The English-speaking staff at the **tourist office,** in P. Mazzini, gives detailed daytrip info. (☎031 95 02 04; www.bellagiolakecomo.com. Open M-Sa 9am-12:30pm and 3-6:30pm, Su 9am-2:30pm.) In case of emergency, call the **carabinieri** (☎112) or the 24hr. **doctor** on-call (☎031 84 00 06 61). A **pharmacy** is at V. Roma 12. (☎031 95 06 23. Open June-Sept. M-Sa 8:30am-12:30pm and 3:30-7:30pm, Su 9am-12:30pm; Sept.-June M-Tu and Th-Sa 8:30am-12:30pm and 3:30-7:30pm.) **Banks** with **ATMs** are on Lungo Lario Manzoni, including **Banco San Paolo,** Lungo L. Manzoni 32. (Open M-F 8:20am-1:20pm and 2:35-4pm.) Use the **Internet** or taste wine at **bellagiopoint.com,** Salita Plinio 8/10/12, off V. Garibaldi. (☎031 95 04 37. €2 per 15min., €6 per hr. Open daily 10am-10pm. AmEx/MC/V.) The **post office,** Lungo L. Manzoni 10, also offers currency exchange. (☎031 95 19 42. Open M-F 8:30am-2pm, Sa 8:30am-12:30pm.) **Postal Code:** 22021.

ACCOMMODATIONS AND FOOD. Expect higher rates in Bellagio than in other lake towns. **Albergo Giardinetto ❹,** V. Roncati 12, off P. della Chiesa, is by far the best deal in town, with simple rooms overlooking beautiful gardens and grape arbors. (☎031 95 01 68; tczgne@tiscali.it. Breakfast €6. Open Easter-Nov., weather permitting. Singles €45; doubles with bath €60, with balcony €65; triples with bath €75. Cash or traveler's checks only.) **Hotel Suisse ❺,** P. Mazzini 8/10, is the only other choice for less expensive accommodations in the city, even though it is a bit pricey. (☎031 95 03 35; www.bellagio.co.nz/suisse. Breakfast €10. Doubles €85, with lake view €100; triples €125. AmEx/MC.) Another option is the **Albergo Europa ❸,** V. Roma 21, with a cheery restaurant and lobby. (☎031 950 471; www.hoteleuropabellagio.it. Doubles €78-90.)

Baba Yaga ❶, V. Eugenio Vitali 8, serves huge pizzas until late at night. For those not eagerly anticipating a walk to get their food, Baba Yaga also offers a free taxi service for customers. Call them and they will dispatch a cab to pick you up. (☎031 95 19 15. Takeout available. Primi and secondi until 10:30pm, pizza until 11pm.) Walk down a winding street away from the *centro,* starting from P. della Chiesa, to reach **Ristorante La Punta ❹,** V. Vitali 19. The cheese-and-walnut ravioli in cream sauce (€13) is a dream. (☎031 95 18 88. Primi €9-13. Secondi €12-14. Cover €2.50. Open daily noon-2:30pm and 7-10pm. AmEx/MC/V over €50.) **Ristorante Barchetta ❺**, Salita Mella 13, is on a shaded second-floor terrace in the heart of the old town and has featured Lombard cuisine since 1887. Try the gnocchi with shrimp and asparagus tips for €14.50. (☎031 95 13 89. Primi €14.50-17. Secondi €14-23. Cover €4. Open M and W-Su noon-2:30pm and 7-10:30pm. AmEx/MC/V.) The **Gelateria del Borgo**, V. Garibaldi 48, is said to have the creamiest and lightest gelato in Bellagio.

🎵 NIGHTLIFE. Far Out, Salita Mella 4, has live jazz every night at 9pm. Well-dressed couples come here for their mixed-drink fix. (☎031 95 17 43; www.farout.it. Primi €6-12. Secondi €10-17.50. Cover €2. Open noon-3pm and 7pm-midnight. Kitchen open noon-3pm and 7-10pm.) **La Divina Commedia "Spiritual Cafe" ❷**, near Far Out on Salita Mella, is one of the town's few nightlife options, with quirky decor and a devoted clientele. (Mixed drinks €7. Open 9pm-2am.)

◪ SIGHTS. The 17th-century **Villa Serbelloni** (not to be confused with the stately, five-star Grand Hotel Villa Serbelloni down the hill) offers spectacular views from the fortifications on the promontory and a lovely, cyprus-lined garden with artificial grottoes. Today, it is home to the Rockefeller Foundation and can be toured (except for the interior) twice daily in a guided group. (☎/fax 031 95 15 55. 1hr. tours Apr.-Oct. Tu-Su 11am and 3:30pm. Purchase tickets ¾-1hr. before at P. Chiesa 14. Small info office only open 1hr. before tours. €7, children €3.50.) From the ferry dock, 800m along Lungo Largo Europa, down Lungo Largo Manzoni to reach **Villa Melzi**. The lakeside gardens here, constructed by famous architect Albertolli at the beginning of the 19th century, are perhaps the most sublime place in the north country to take in the lake view while strolling or lounging. The villa is still a private residence, but the grounds are open to the public. (Open daily Mar.-Oct. 9am-6pm. €6.) The **Basilica di San Giacomo**, namesake of the P. della Chiesa, is an excellent example of 10th- to 12th-century Lombard Romanesque architecture—worth a stop for the glittering mosaic scenes in the cupolas of the chapels on either side of the main altar and the life-like wooden carving of Jesus, encased in glass along the left wall. (Open daily 8am-6pm.) While many simply stroll Bellagio's streets, most aquatic sports and organized recreation activities are based in the town. **Sports and Adventures-Cavalcalario Club**, Località Gallasco 1, offers sailing, motorboats, lake fishing, rock climbing, kayaking, canyoning, horseback riding, mountain biking, and paragliding. (☎031 33 95 308 138; www.bellagio-mountains.it.)

▰ DAYTRIP FROM BELLAGIO: VILLA DEL BALBIANELLO. Central Lake Como is known for its grandiose villas, a testament to the luxurious Como of days past. Reputed to be the lake's most gorgeous, **Villa del Balbianello** in Lenno, originally a Franciscan convent, was rebuilt in 1787 by Cardinal Durini as a "splendid palace of delights." The motto, "Do what you would like," welcomes visitors at the entrance. More recently, it was featured as the other-worldly site of the wedding in *Star Wars II: Attack of the Clones* (2002). The highlight of the villa's peninsula is a panoramic, terraced garden dominated by an elegant loggia. (*Lenno is accessible by ferry. 20-40min., 18 per day 6:37am-6:28pm, €3-4.60. From ferry, go left on the Lungolago Lomazzi all the way to the end. From there, villa is accessible by 1km walk, or by taxi boat Th-F only. ☎ 031 333 410 3854. 10min. ride every 30min.; round-trip €5. Villa ☎034 456 110. Open Mar. 17-Oct. 31 Tu and Th-Su 10am-6pm. Last entry 5:30pm. Garden €5, ages 4-12 €2.50. Guided tour of villa €11/6, with reservation €8/4.*)

VARENNA   ☎0341

A short ferry ride from Bellagio or Menaggio, Varenna (va-REHN-na; pop. 900) is a smaller, slower-paced version of its more famous neighbors. Varenna distinguishes itself from other lake towns with its relaxed, pedestrian feel and the easily accessible hamlets dotting its hillsides. The 14th-century **Chiesa di San Giorgio** looms above the main *piazza* overlooking the city. The ornate, Baroque-style confessional, built in 1690 by Giovanni Albiolo, offers a strong contrast to the exceedingly simple interior, which features frescoes painted by locals. (☎0341 83 02 28. Open daily 7am-noon and 2-7pm. Free.) Varenna's most famous sights are the two lakeside gardens of **Villa Monastero**, in a former Cistercian monastery. Facing the church, walk 150m to the right. The grounds contain 2km of paths past dark cyprus groves and giant aloe plants, and are also home to a museum. (☎031 29 54 50; www.villamonastero.it. Gardens open daily Mar. 28-Nov. 1 9am-7pm. Museum open Sa 1-5pm, Su 10am-1pm and 2-6pm. Museum €2; gardens €2. Combined ticket with Villa Cipressi €4.) Smaller, terraced gardens of 16th-century **Villa Cipressi**, once the strolling grounds of aristocrats, now serve patrons of the villa's luxury hotel. Enter through the Hotel Villa Cipressi, past Villa Monastero. (Gardens open daily Mar.-Oct. 9am-7pm. €2, with Villa Monastero €4.) From the tourist office, a 30min. hike up V. IV Novembre, then on V. Roma, leads to **La Sorgente del Fiumelatte,** so named for the *latte*-like foam on the river. Fiumelatte, the shortest river in Italy (250m), disappears in mid-October only to reappear in March. Walk straight out from the ferry and veer left to reach a cherry tree-lined cobblestone path leading 20min. uphill to the nearby village of Vezio. In the tiny central *piazza* lies the small ornate **Chiesa di San Antonio Abate di Vezio,** built in 1458 to honor the village's patron saint. A five minute walk uphill from the church leads to the ruins of Queen Teodolinda's castle, with excellent views of the lake and old Varenna.

One of Varenna's few affordable accommodations is **Albergo Beretta ❷**, V. per Esino 1, on the corner on the way to the train station. All 10 rooms have TV, telephone, and view. The ground-floor bar sells Italian translations of Agatha Christie books and offers a home-style €12 *menù*, available throughout the day upon request. (☎/fax 0341 83 01 32. Breakfast €6. Doubles €58, with bath €68, with balcony and sofa for 3rd person €80. Extra bed €12. MC/V.) **B&B Orange House di Mara Angeloni ❸,** V. Venini 156, is the only other affordable accommodation in town. Located on the fourth floor of the vaguely orange apartment building across the street from Albergo Beretta. (☎0341 347 918 7940; www.orangehouse.org. Reservations recommended. Singles €39; doubles €58. MC/V.) **Ristorante Montecodeno ❸,** V. Croce 2, uphill from the ferry station, is a local favorite for lake fish. (☎0341 83 01 23; www.hotelmontecodeno.com. Primi €9-10. Secondi €12-19. *Menù* €25-38. Open M and W-Su noon-2pm and 7-9pm. AmEx/MC/V.) Huge crepes (€5-8.50) at waterfront **Nilus Bar ❶**, Riva Garibaldi 4, burst with fillings. (☎0341 81 52 28. Panini €4-4.50. Pizza €4.50-7. Mixed drinks €4-6. Open Mar.-Dec. daily 10am-1am. Kitchen opens at noon.) The superb **Vecchia Varenna ❹**, V. Scoscesa 10, lets guests dine in a terrace over the water. Serves leg of lamb stuffed with prunes (€16), pumpkin ravioli (€11), and other fine cuisine. (☎0341 83 07 93. Primi €11-12. Secondi €15-16. Cover €3. Open Tu-Su 12:30-2pm and 7:30-9:30pm. Closed Nov.-Jan. MC/V.)

Varenna is one of few towns with a **train station,** directly uphill from the ferry dock, linking the eastern side of the lake to Milan. You cannot buy tickets at the train station, so get them en route at the travel agency next to Albergo Beretta. (Travel agency open M-F 8:30am-12:30pm and 3-7pm, Sa 8:30am-12:30pm.) **Trains** run to Lecco (30min., 23 per day 5:25am-10:29pm, €2.10) and Milan (15 per day 5:25am-9:23pm, €4.95). From other parts of the lake, the best way to access Varenna is by **ferry,** arriving at the northern point of town. Pick up a ferry schedule from the tourist office. Part of the central lake route, ferries serve Bellagio (15-20min., every 1-2hr. 6:33am-7:52pm, €3-4.60), Como (1-2hr., 6:33am-6:36pm, €7.20-10.50), and Menaggio (10-15min., every 30min.-

1hr. 6:33am-6:36pm, €3-4.60). For a **taxi**, call ☎0341 81 50 61. The **tourist office** is in the train station. (☎0341 830 651; www.varennaitaly.com. Open daily 10am-1:30pm and 3-7:30pm.) If arriving by ferry, see ticket office for the location of the closest tourist office. Off P. S. Giorgio, **Banca Popolare di Lecco**, V. IX Novembre 4, has an **ATM**. (☎0341 81 50 15. Open M-F 8:20am-1:20pm and 2:45-3:45pm.) **Pharmacy Pedrani** is at V. Venini 2. (☎0341 83 02 03. Open M-Tu and Th-Sa 9am-12:30pm and 3:30-7:30pm, W 9am-12:30pm. AmEx/MC/V.) **Internet** access is available at **al Barilott**, V. IX Novembre 6, which is also a wine bar. (€2.50 per 15min., €5 per hr. Open M-Sa 7am-8pm.) In case of emergency, dial ☎118 or call the **carabinieri** (☎0341 81 10 21) or an **ambulance** (☎0341 82 91 11), both based in nearby Bellano. The **post office** is at V. del Prato 13. (☎0341 83 02 31. Open M-F 8:30am-2pm, Sa 8:30am-12:30pm.) **Postal Code:** 23829.

MENAGGIO ☎0344

Menaggio (meh-NA-jee-yo; pop. 3200) is home to terra-cotta rooftops and stunning scenery. Travelers have recently caught on, though Menaggio is somehow less overwhelmed by tourists than other lakeside towns, while offering an equal number of sites and conveniences. Menaggio's beauty, central location, cheap accommodations, and excellent ferry connections make it the perfect base for exploring any part of Lake Como or the nearby mountains.

TRANSPORTATION AND PRACTICAL INFORMATION. SPT **buses** (☎0344 32 118) leave from the waterfront stop in front of P. Garibaldi. The C12 serves Lugano (1hr., 11 per day 6:02am-5:34pm, €4.30) and the C10 serves Como (1hr., 17 per day 5:20am-7:04pm). Navigazione Lago di Como (☎0344 32 255), in P. Traghetto, 6 blocks south of the *centro*, runs **ferries** to Bellagio (15min., 31 per day 6:37am-8:24pm, €3-4.60); Como (2hr., 22 per day 6:37am-8:24pm, €7.90); Domaso (1hr., 12 per day 9:39am-8pm, €4.10-6.10); Varenna (15min., 16 per day 8:13am-8:52pm, €3-4.60). There are three **taxi** drivers in Menaggio: Pozzi (☎0344 335 803 6670), Ezio (☎338 20 47 279) and Diego (☎333 86 01 035). There is a yellow callbox in front of P. Garibaldi if you can't get to a phone.

In the *centro*, the **tourist office**, P. Garibaldi 4, has info and maps to plan lake excursions. The multilingual staff has helpful pamphlets with details on hikes and other excursions. The office hosts myriad other services, including a multilingual free book exchange. (☎0344 32 924; www.menaggio.com. Open Apr.-Sept. daily 9am-12:30pm and 2:30-6pm; Oct.-Mar. M-Tu and Th-Sa 9am-12:30pm and 2:30-6pm, Su 9:30am-12:30pm.) In case of **emergency**, call the **carabinieri**, V. Regina, in the neighboring town of Nobiallo (☎0344 32 025). **Antica Farmacia Kluzer** is at V. IV Novembre 30. (Open M-W and F-Su 8:30am-12:30pm and 3-7:15pm.) The **hospital** (☎0344 33 111) is on V. Cazertelli, off V. Cadorna above the *centro*. **Internet** access is available at the **library**, V. Camozzi 21, two blocks north of the tourist office. (☎0344 32 379. Available Tu 9:30am-1pm, W-Th 9:30am-noon, and F 9am-12:30pm; €1.50 per 30min.) Internet access also available at **Video Mix**, V. IV Novembre 52, across from the Grand Hotel Menaggio. (☎0344 34 110. €1.50 per 15min. Open Tu-Sa 9:30am-12:30pm and 4-7pm. AmEx/MC/V.) The **post office**, V. Lusardi 50, has currency exchange and **ATM**. (☎0344 369 511. Open M-F 8:30am-2pm, Sa 8:30am-12:30pm.) **Postal Code:** 22017.

ACCOMMODATIONS AND FOOD. With the recent closing of Menaggio's one youth hostel, Menaggio's budget accommodations have taken a hit, though you'll still find cheaper digs here than in many of the other lakeside towns. **Vecchia Menaggio ❶**, V. al Lago 13, offers hotel rooms at extremely reasonable prices, in a fantastic location right next to the *centro*. Traditional, affordable Italian dining downstairs. (☎0344 32 082. Doubles €40, with bath €60.) **Albergo il Vapore ❸**, P. T. Grossi 3, off P. Garibaldi, has rooms with bath and phone; some have TV and balcony facing the lake. (☎0344 32 229; il.vapore@ email.it. Reception 8am-midnight. Breakfast €6.50. Singles €35; doubles €55; triples €75. Reservations only for stays over 3 days; fax confirmation required. Cash only.) For slightly pricier rooms but a great location, try the **Hotel Garni Corona ❹**, Largo Cavour 3. Some rooms have lovely river views. (☎0344 320 06; www.hotelgarnicorona.com. Breakfast included. Singles €55; doubles €85-€95.) **Lakeside Camping Europa ❶**, V. Cipressi 12, a pleasantly brief 15min. walk from the ferry docks down V. Lusardi, then V. Roma, comes complete with a rocky beach. (☎0344 31 187. Open daily 8am-11pm. €5.70 per person; €9.10 per tent. 1-person bungalow €30; 4- to 6-person €60. Cash only.)

Enjoy a waterfront dinner at the classy **Il Ristorante di Paolo ❹**, Largo Cavour 5, off P. Garibaldi, where you can listen to arias and watch as dusk falls across the lake. Try the homemade ravioli with beef, pear, veal sauce and parmesan for €10. (☎0344 32 133. Primi €8-10. Secondi €14-19. Cover €2.50. Open daily noon-3pm and 7-10pm. AmEx/MC/V.) Head uphill at the junction near Banca San Paolo for **Pizzeria Lugano ❶**, V. Como 26. Try peppers, eggplant, and a litany of other flavors on the *pizza della casa* for €6.50. (☎0344 31 664. Pasta €5.50-6. Open Tu-Su 11:30am-2:45pm and 6:30-11pm. No cover. MC/V.) Near the ferry dock, **Super Cappa Market,** V. IV Novembre 107, stocks groceries. Be warned, they have a strictly enforced policy on not bringing bags into the store. (☎0344 32 161. Open M 8am-12:30pm, Tu-Sa 8am-12:30pm and 3:30-7pm. MC/V.)

🄶🄽 **SIGHTS AND HIKING.** The only sandy **beach** in Menaggio is toward the campground, near the end of V. Benedetto Castelli and past the miniature golf course. This large beach club has a sand-side soccer field, a pool, a bar, and tons of chairs. However a recent change of ownership makes the fate of the club uncertain, and amenities may be scaled back in the meantime. (Open M-F €9, under 14 and over 65 €6; after 2:30pm €4. Sa-Su €12/8; after 2:30pm €9/7.) The tourist office and hostels stock informative printouts (available in Italian, English, French, and German): suggested scenic **boat trips,** recommended **driving excursions** by car or bus, and a collection of **hiking itineraries,** in the mountains flanking the lake. Explore the romantic park, breathtaking waterfall, local rural settlements, or archaeological sites. The tourist office's printouts on hikes include detailed directions, as well as history and anecdotes regarding sites near the trail. The Rifugio Menaggio mountain station is the starting point for a 2hr. round-trip hike to **Monte Grona** (1736m), which offers views of the pre-Alps and the three lakes or a 2hr. hike to **Chiesa di San Amate** (1623m) that takes you over a mountain ridge to sneak a peak at alpine pastures and Val Menaggio. To reach the Rifugio, take the C13 bus from Menaggio center to Breglia. The Rifugio is occasionally closed for repairs, so check with the tourist office before setting off. A number of shorter hikes start in Menaggio. A 2hr. hike (1-way) winds through outlying villages and farms to the picturesque **Sass Corbee Gorge,** overlooking a waterfall. Another option is the 2hr. hike toward **Lake Lugano** and **Lake Piano,** which intersects a small nature reserve in **Val Menaggio,** (bus C12 heads back). For a less strenuous adventure, take the 30min. walk through an old mule track up to **La Crocetta** (450m), a small cross located above Menaggio. On your way to the cross, you'll pass by *linea cadorna*—trenches built in 1915 and used during WWI as a defense against German invasion.

🄽 **NIGHTLIFE.** While Menaggio is in many ways an early to bed, early to rise town, a few nightlife options are available for those looking to burn the midnight oil. The provocatively named 🄿**Pub Chic and Freak,** V. IV Novembre 43, has

THE LAKE COUNTRY

a small but picturesque terrace overlooking the water where patrons enjoy a wide assortment of beers (€3.70-4.20) and snacks, ranging from deliciously savory crepes (€5-5.50) to a daily *menù* (€10). The kitchen is open all day, a rarity in these parts. (☎0344 32 463. Open M-Tu and Th-Su 10am-midnight.) Just around the corner is **Tanamana**, V. IV Novembre 79, which becomes the center of Menaggio's music scene every Friday night with live rock and pop. Enjoy a rum and coke (€5) or a beer (€3.50 per bottle) as you sway with the crowds. (☎0344 325 58; www.tanamana.it. Open Tu-Th and Su 7am-2am, F-Sa 7am-4am). Head for the *centro* to find the eclectic, multitasking **Il Ritrovo (White Bar)**, V. Calvi 10, which contains a bookstore, CD store, *gelateria*, and bar. The bookstore has a fair sized collection of English-language books, and past the espresso bar lurks an enormous selection of stuffed animals. The *gelateria* is also a standout, serving huge, softball-sized scoops of the creamiest, most flavorful gelato (€1.50-2.50) in all of town. (☎0344 31 400. Open M-Tu 8am-9pm, W-Sa 8am-12:30am, Su 9am-12:30am.)

ACROSS THE BORDER FROM LAKE COMO

LUGANO, SWITZERLAND ☎091

Lugano (loo-GAH-no; pop. 53,000), Switzerland's third largest banking center, rests on Lake Lugano in a valley between the San Salvatore and Monte Brè mountain peaks. Though it officially joined the Swiss Confederation in 1803, the town still feels like part of the Italian *famiglia* due to its shop-filled cobblestone streets and arcade-lined *piazze*. Influence by Italy since the Roman era, Lugano today is a popular spot for Swiss retirees and young travelers alike.

REMEMBER! Bring your **passport** for excursions into Switzerland. Also exchange your currency for **Swiss Francs (CHF)**, since euros are not accepted in many shops and bus ticket offices. As of Aug. 2008, **exchange rates** for the Swiss Franc are as follows: 1CHF=€0.62; €1=1.61CHF.

TRANSPORTATION AND PRACTICAL INFORMATION. To reach Lugano from Menaggio take bus #1 (€4) from V. Borgo Vico into Chiasso, on the border with Switzerland. Walk uphill to reach the **train station,** on V. Motta (☎091 058 122 792 33; www.fts.ch), to take the direct route to Lugano (1-3 per hr. 4:55am-1:41am, 9CHF). **Trains** in Lugano (☎091 92 35 120; station open M-Sa 6:30am-8pm, Su 7:30am-8pm) run from P. della Stazione to Chiasso (30min., every hr. 6:10am-1:14am, 9.60CHF), Bellinzona (30min., every 30min.-1hr. 5:26am-12:12am, 12CHF), and Milan (45min., every hr. 6:10am-9:48pm, 28CHF).

YOU GOT TOLLED. All cars entering Switzerland are charged 40CHF to use the A9. This charge is a yearly toll applying to any car that comes through. If you aren't in a hurry, get off the road in Chiasso and take side streets to Lugano. Or, coming from Malpensa, take the 233 to Lugano. The extra 20min. will buy your bed for the night.

SPT **buses** (www.sptlinea.it) run to and from neighboring towns, including Menaggio (C12; 1hr., every hr. 7:19am-6:46pm, €7.60). Buses are occasionally unreliable. Catch SPT buses in Lugano on V. Campo Marzio, next to the parking lot; the bus stop is between the two red benches on the north side of the lot. Tickets must be bought before boarding the buses; try the *tabaccheria* in the green building on the south side of the parking lot. The large bus station at C. Pestalozzi and V.le Carlo Cattaneo only provides service to destinations within Lugano. (Tickets 1.60-3.20CHF, Carta Giorno day-pass 5CHF.) For **taxis**, call ☎091 92 28 833, 97 12 121, or 92 20 222, or find one in front of the train station. The 15min. downhill walk from the train station to the classically Italian **Piazza della Riforma**, the *centro*, winds through Lugano's large pedestrian zone. For those who would rather avoid the walk, a **funicular** runs between the train station and the waterfront **Piazza Cioccaro**. (Open 5:20am-1150pm. 1.10CHF.)

DIALING ACROSS THE BORDER. To dial out of Italy, start with its **international dialing prefix**, 00. Switzerland's **country code** is 41, and Lugano's **city code** is 091. Drop the 0 if calling from within Switzerland.

The **tourist office** is found in the Palazzo Civico; its entrance faces the waterfront on Riva Albertolli. Ask about free, guided city walks in English: the **Classic Tour** (M) focuses on the architectural monuments from the past; the **Testimony of History Tour** (Th) which tours the whole city to find the evidence of past events still seen in its *piazze;* and the **Garden Tour** (Su) allows you to catch a glimpse of thriving oak and olive trees. (☎091 91 33 232; www.lugano-tourism.ch. Open Apr.-Oct. M-F 9am-7pm, Sa 9am-6pm, Su 10am-6pm; Nov.-Mar. M-F 9am-noon and 2-5:30pm, Sa 10am-noon and 1:30-5pm.) A tourist office representative also has a desk in the travel agency to the right when exiting the train station, and offers maps and hotel booking. Lockers for **luggage storage** (5-7CHF per locker) are at the train station. There are **pharmacies** in all major *piazze* and along the waterfront. In case of emergency, call the **police,** in P. Riforma, (☎091 80 08 111 or 117), **ambulance** (☎144) or **medical information** (☎18 11). The **hospital** is located on V. Tesserete 46 (☎091 81 16 111). **MondialPay**, V. Canova 9, has **Internet** access, **Western Union**, and international calling. (☎091 92 22 569. 3CHF per 15min., 8CHF per hr. Open M-F 9am-6pm, Sa 10am-5pm.) Cash travelers checks at the **post office,** on V. della Posta 7, two blocks up from the lake near V. al Forte. (Open M-F 7:30am-6:15pm, Sa 8am-4pm.) **Postal Code:** CH-6900.

⌂☐ ACCOMMODATIONS AND FOOD. Inexpensive accommodations are nearly impossible to find near the lake, where hotels with a view of the water tend to charge 250CHF and up for double rooms. View-touting budget accommodations should be reserved well in advance in summer. Converted from a 19th-century villa, the palm-tree-enveloped ▧**Hotel & Hostel Montarina ❶,** V. Montarina 1, has a large swimming pool amidst grape vines, TV room, kitchen, reception stocked with maps and travel guides, and a terrace overlooking the city. From the station, walk right 200m, cross the train tracks, then walk uphill and up the stairs to the left. (☎091 96 67 272; www.montarina.ch. Common area with fridge open 7:30am-9:30pm. Pool open 9am-7pm. Breakfast 12CHF. Linen 4CHF. Laundry 4CHF; detergent 2CHF. Internet access 10CHF per hr. Reception 7:30am-11pm; after 11pm, ring buzzer. Reservations recommended. Dorms 25CHF; singles 70CHF, with bath 80CHF; doubles 100/120CHF. AmEx/MC/V.) **Hotel Pestalozzi ❸,** P. Indipendenza 9, is just outside the city center, only two blocks from Casino Lugano along C. Elezia. Its location makes this hotel a steal for the price. Entrance on V. Bianchi. (☎091 92 14 646. Breakfast included. Internet access and Wi-Fi available. Singles 64CHF, with bath

WAYS TO CELEBRATE CROSSING THE SWISS BORDER

1. Take a gander at the colorful CHE currency! Unlike the rather staid Euros, Swiss Francs are psychedelically vivid.

2. When your diet says fondon't, the Swiss say fondue. This savory dish of melted cheese is a national indulgence. Watch it expand your waistline as it expands your soul.

3. Make time more whimsical. Switzerland, birthplace of the cuckoo clock, may be just the place to burst out in song and dance with each passing hour.

4. Open a Swiss bank account. Or don't. But you know you've thought about it.

5. The hills are alive! Try your hand—and lips—at yodeling.

6. Speak softly, but carry a big... knife? They may be notoriously neutral, but let's not forget the Swiss Army Knife. Revel in the paradox with one of your own.

7. Multilingualize yourself. The Swiss have four official languages (German, French, Italian, and Rheto-Romansch); most citizens are proficient in three or more.

8. Scale one of the small nation's beautiful alps and build some killer calves.

9. Feast on Toblerone and/or Lindor and wander about Bern in a chocolate-induced stupor.

10. Love humanity: home to the Red Cross and the UN, this peaceful nation can bring out the softer side of the sourest of scrooges.

84-106CHF; doubles 102/168-188CHF. Extra bed 40CHF.) Family-run **Ostello della Gioventù (HI) ❶**, V. Cantonale 13, is in Lugano-Savosa. Walk 350m left from the station, pass the parking lot, and cross the street to the bus stop; take bus #5 to "Crocifisso." Backtrack and turn left up V. Cantonale. Gardens and pool complement comfortable rooms that are popular with families. (☎091 96 62 728; www.luganoyouthhostel.ch. Kitchen access 1CHF after 7pm. Breakfast 9CHF. Towels 2CHF. Laundry 5CHF. Internet access available. Reception 6:30am-noon and 3-10pm. Curfew 10pm. Reservations recommended. Open mid-Mar. to Oct. Dorms 26CHF; doubles 68-88CHF; family rooms 35CHF per person. HI-members 6CHF discount. AmEx/MC/V.) There are several campgrounds near Lugano in Agno. To reach the lakeside **La Palma ❶**, V. Molinazzo 21 (☎091 60 52 561; fax 60 45 438), located at the mouth of the Vedeggio River, or the convenient **Eurocampo ❶** (☎091 60 52 114; www. eurocampo.ch), take the 20min. Ferrovia-Lugano-Ponte-Tresa (FLP; ☎091 60 51 305; www.flpsa.ch) tram from V. Stazione 8, to Agno (departs every 20min., 4.80CHF) via Ponte Tresa. From the station, turn left, then left again on V. Molinazzo. (La Palma: 9CHF per person; 10-12CHF per tent. Eurocampo: 9CHF per person; 10-12CHF per tent. Both include showers. Both cash only.)

Satisfying fare is easy to find at the outdoor restaurants and cafes that pay homage to Lugano's Italian heritage by serving delicious penne, gnocchi, and freshly spun pizzas. Avoid restaurants in the square; they tend to be overpriced and of low quality. To reclaim the feeling of being a kid in a toy store, head to **Ristorante Manora ❷**, in the Manor Department Store in P. Dante, 3rd fl. Scrumptious grab-as-you-please food will make your mouth water. Hungry budget travelers will love this gourmet spot's salad bar (5-11CHF), pizza (5-13CHF), pasta (8-11CHF), hot daily specials (10-15CHF), and beer (2.50-5CHF). (Wheelchair-accessible. Open M-Sa 7:30am-10pm, Su 10am-10pm. AmEx/MC/V.) Vegetables hang from the ceiling in the romantic **La Tinèra ❷**, V. dei Gorini 2, a dimly lit restaurant specializing in Lombard cuisine, and thus the most "Italian" restaurant you'll find near the water. Try the *risotto a la gorgonzola* for 15CHF. (☎091 92 35 219. Daily *menù* 12-26CHF. Open Tu-Sa 8:30am-3pm and 5:30-11pm. AmEx/MC/V.) The classy **Osteria Del Portico ❺**, C. Pestalozzi 21a, draws a lively crowd with its frequently changing specials. (☎091 921 02 95. Primi 16-22CHF. Secondi 19-35CHF. Open M-F 9am-11:30pm. AmEx/MC/V.) For quick eats, the **outdoor market** in P. della Riforma sells seafood,

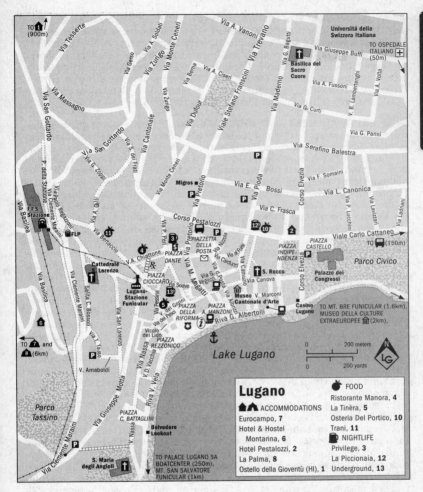

Lugano

FOOD
Ristorante Manora, **4**

ACCOMMODATIONS
La Tinèra, **5**

Eurocampo, **7**
Osteria Del Portico, **10**

Hotel & Hostel
Trani, **11**

Montarina, **6**
NIGHTLIFE

Hotel Pestalozzi, **2**
Privilege, **3**

La Palma, **8**
La Piccionaia, **12**

Ostello della Gioventù (HI), **1**
Underground, **13**

produce, flowers, and sandwiches for 4CHF. (Open Tu and F 8am-noon.) Also try the **outdoor stands** on V. Pessina, off P. della Riforma.

◨ SIGHTS. Housed in a lakeside villa, the **Museo delle Cultura,** V. Cortivo 24-28, showcases cultural artifacts, like carved masks and statues, from Africa, Oceania, and Indonesia. From the tourist office, take bus #1, (dir.: Castagnola), to San Domenica and walk to the street below; the villa is on the right. Or, take the ferry to Museo Helenum. (☎091 058 86 66 960; www.lugano.ch/cultura. Open daily 10am-6pm. 12CHF, students 8CHF.) The ornate frescoes filling the 16th-century **Cattedrale San Lorenzo,** located downhill from the train station and overlooking the whole city, still gleam with vivid colors. (☎091 92 28 842. Open daily 9:30am-6pm. Free.) The small 14th-century **Chiesa San Rocco,** in P. Maghetti, two blocks left of P. della Riforma, houses an ornate altarpiece and a series of frescoes depicting the life of its patron saint. (Open daily 10:30am-12:30pm and 3:30-6:30pm. Free.) Diagonal to Chiesa San Rocco, the **Museo Cantonale d'Arte,** V. Canova 10, exhibits a rotating collection of 5000 pieces of 19th- and 20th-century art from regional artists, as well as works by Degas, Renoir, and Pisarro. The collection is frequently complemented by contemporary art exhibits. (☎091 91 04 780; www.museo-cantonale-arte.ch. Wheelchair-accessible. Open Tu 2-5pm, W-Su 10am-5pm. Permanent collection 7CHF, students 5CHF. Special exhibits 12/8CHF. MC/V.)

■ ▨ ENTERTAINMENT AND NIGHTLIFE. Music fills Lugano's *piazze* year-round. Summer heat ushers in **Lungolago ai Pedoni** every Friday and Saturday evening, featuring classical and Latin music concerts as well as cabaret shows by the lake (July-Aug. 8:30pm-midnight). During the first two weekends of July, Lugano's **Estival Jazz** (www.estivaljazz.ch) fills P. della Riforma with free nightime jazz concerts by contemporary artists. Past performers include Miles Davis and Bobby McFerrin. In June and August, the young and old trek down to the beach for **Cinema Lago,** where movies are screened lakeside (15CHF). On August 1, Swiss-flag-studded parades, fireworks, and a choreographed air-show over Lake Lugano ring in the **Swiss National Day** celebration. During the beginning of September, the looser **Blues to Bop Festival** (www.bluestobop.ch) celebrates R&B and blues with free performances by well-recognized international singers alongside local amateurs throughout the city. At the beginning of October, Lugano reaffirms its Italian associations and celebrates the end of summer by honoring the country's *aqua vitae* at the **Festa D'Autunno,** where food- and wine-tastings are accompanied by traditional music.

Though Lugano has plenty of nightlife options, ranging from discos to night-clubs to piano bars, most of the action is located in Paradiso, an area southwest of central Lugano and accessible by bus. For those eschewing public transportation, there is a smattering of nightlife easily accessible by foot. If venturing to Paradiso, check the tourist office's brochure on Lugano resources, which includes an extensive nightlife section. At the basement club **Privilege,** P. Dante 8, sit and relax with a drink, or opt to join others at the crowded dance floor playing house, 70s, and 80s music (☎091 92 29 438 or 079 62 01 235; www.privi-legelugano.ch. Open W-Sa 10pm-2am.) For an all-inclusive nightlife experience, try **La Piccionaia,** C. Pestalozzi 21, which has a disco with a DJ and dancing, as well as a piano bar. Late-night hours and a central location make it a good bet for a great time. (☎091 923 45 46; www.classcafe.ch. Open nightly 10pm-5am. AmEx/MC/V). Not surprisingly, **Underground,** V. Soave 5a, is a slightly subterranean club with infectious beats and swarms of dancers. (Beer 8-10CHF. Mixed drinks 7-15CHF.) Another nighttime attraction is the **Casino Lugano,** V. Stauffacher 1, sitting by the water at Riva G. Albertolli and C. Elvezia. Equipped with roulette tables, a poker room, and slot machines, this maze will surely keep you occupied. (☎091 97 37 111; www.casinolugano.ch. Minimum gambling age 18. Open Mu-Th and Su noon-4am, F-Sa noon-5am.)

▨ OUTDOOR ACTIVITIES. The dock for the **Società Navigazione del Lago di Lugano,** V. Castagnola 12 (☎091 97 15 223; www.lakelugano.ch) is across the street from the tourist office. Tours of Lake Lugano pass tiny, lakeside towns, many with attractions like chocolate museums or miniature Swiss houses.

Reach the peaks of **Monte Brè** (933m) and **Monte San Salvatore** (912m) by funic-ular. The **◪Monte Brè funicolare** (☎091 97 13 171; www.montebre.ch) is a 20min. ride down the river along Riva Albertolli from the *centro.* (Every 20min. Open 9:10am-6:45pm.) An easier way is to take bus #1 (dir.: Castagnola) to the Cas-sarate-Monte Brè stop, or to catch the tourist train at the tourist office. (☎091

079 685 7070. Tourist train runs every 40min. daily 10am-8pm. 8CHF, children 5CHF.) The funicular takes travelers to a number of biking and hiking paths. Rent bikes at the top and return them at then bottom; tell employee that you would like to rent a bike when purchasing lift ticket (one-way ticket and half-day bike rental 23CHF; bring passport). A map of routes is available in the tourist and funicular offices; difficulty ranges from easy (30min.) to difficult (5hr.). The **San Salvatore funicolare** is 20min. from the tourist office at the intersection of V. delle Scuole and V. S. Salvatore in Paradiso; from the lakefront, follow V. E. Bosio inland and turn right on V. delle Scuole. (☎091 98 52 828; www.montesansalvatore.ch. Open June 17-Sept. 17. 10min., every 30min. 8:30am-11pm. 17CHF, round-trip 24CHF; ages 6-16 7-9/10-16CHF.)

Bike rental is available at the Stazione Trenitalia, next to ticket office #1. (☎091 051 221 5642; www.rentabike.ch. Open daily 8:30am-6pm. 23CHF per half-day, 31CHF per day; 38CHF to return the bike at a different location; lock and helmet included.) **Balmelli's Sport Shop,** V. Pioda 12 (☎091 92 35 867), also rents bikes. **Boatcenter Palace Lugano** (☎091 92 35 733; www.boatcenterpalace. ch) in P. Luini rents *motoscafi* (speedboats) for 30min. (from 25CHF) or an hour (from 40CHF), as well as windsurfing boards (10CHF per hr.), waterskis, and wakeboards. Boatcenter Palace rents boats with or without a license, but for those interested, sailing permits for foreigners are available from **Malcantone Turismo,** in the Piazza al Lago (☎091 606 28 86; www.malcantone.ch). For a more relaxing lake trip, rent paddleboats from the hut to the left of the Navigazione del Lago office. (☎091 079 621 3530. 3-person boat 8CHF per 30min.; 4-person boat 9CHF per 30min. Open daily 10am-7pm.)

LAKE MAGGIORE AND LAKE ORTA

"If it should befall that you possess a heart and shirt, then sell the shirt and visit the shores of Lago Maggiore."
—Stendhal

Steep green hills punctuate the dark blue shoreline, and to the west, the glaciated outline of Monte Rosa (4634m) peers across the temperate mountain waters of Lake Maggiore, also known as Lake Verbano. Though many writers and artists have been seduced by the lake's beauty—Byron, Stendhal, Flaubert, Dickens, Hemingway, and da Vinci have all spent time here—today, Lake Maggiore, provides an alternative to the getaway cities along Lake Como. Stresa and Verbania serve as convenient bases for exploring the Borromean Islands and nearby Lake Orta, while secluded Santa Maria Maggiore in Valle Vigezzo offers hiking trails and inexpensive skiing.

STRESA   ☎0323

Stresa (STREH-zah; pop. 5000) retains much of the manicured charm that lured visitors like Queen Victoria, in the 19th and early 20th centuries. Hydrangeas and Art Nouveau hotels line the waterfront, giving the small town a romantic, old-fashioned feel. Stresa is very much a resort town, albeit one that caters emphatically to those in their silver years. Those looking for bronzed and uninhibited coeds playing beach volleyball or doing tequila shots late into the night should look elsewhere. Families and the elderly come here for a trip to the Borromean Islands or for a ride up the funicular with options to bike or hike back down. The real draw, however, is in an evening walk along the lake.

☞🚊 TRANSPORTATION AND PRACTICAL INFORMATION. Stresa lies 1hr. from Milan on the Milan-Domodossola train line. (Ticket office in lobby open M-Sa 6:10-10:45am, 11am-4:15pm, and 4:30-7:20pm; Su 7-10:45am, 11am-4:15pm, and 4:30-8:10pm.) **Trains** run to Milan (1hr., every 30min. 5:23am-10:32pm, €4.60) and Domodossola (40min., 14 per day 6:37am-10:46pm, €3). **Buses** going to Orta (1hr.; 10am, 2, 5pm; €2.45) and Verbania-Pallanza depart from the lake-side church. The best way to see the region's scenery is to make the complete circuit through Lake Maggiore to Switzerland by **ferry** and return through Valle Vigezzo on rail, connecting from Locarno-Domodossola-Stresa. This loop can be easily done by Lago Maggiore Express. (☎0323 23 32 00 or 091 75 18 731. Ferries run Apr.-May Th-Su; June 1-Sept. 23 daily. Departures from Stresa 10:50am and 11:30am. Last connection between Locarno to Domodossola 7:25pm, connection from Domodossola to Stresa 9:55pm. 1-day round-trip €28, children €14; 2-day round-trip €34/17. Bring passport.) **Bikes** can be rented from Sapori d'Italia, V. de Martini 35. (☎0323 93 46 42. €10 per half-day, €18 per day, €45 per 3 days. Insurance €4.) For mountain biking, try Bici Co, at the base of the funicular. (☎0323 30 399; www.bicico.it. €21 per half day, €26 per day. Includes helmet and lock. Ask for detailed trail map. Open daily Apr.-Sept. 9:30am-5:30pm; funicular stops 12:30-1:30pm. Cash only.)

Most of Stresa's services line the water on **Corso Umberto, Piazza Marconi, Corso Italia** or the major north-south thoroughfares, **Via Principe Tomaso** and **Via Roma,** which run uphill from the water. To reach the *centro* and the **IAT tourist office,** P. Marconi 16, on the ferry dock, exit the train station, turn right on V. Principe di Piemonte, take a left on V. Duchessa di Genova, walk downhill toward the waterfront, and turn right. (☎0323 30 150. Open Mar.-Oct. daily 10am-12:30pm and 3-6:30pm; Nov.-Feb. M-F 10am-12:30pm and 3-6:30pm, Sa 10am-12:30pm.) For currency exchange and **ATM,** try **Banca Popolare di Intra,** C. Umberto 1, just off P. Marconi. (☎0323 30 330. Open M-F 8:20am-1:20pm and 2:35-4pm, Sa 8:20am-12:15pm.) In case of emergency, call the **carabinieri,** on Vle. D. di Genova, at ☎0323 30 118, or an **ambulance** (☎0323 33 360). **Farmacia Dott. Polisseni,** V. Cavour 16, posts after-hours rotations. (Open M-W and F-Sa 8:30am-1pm and 3:30-8pm, Th 8:30am-1pm.) **New Data,** V. De Vit 15/A, off P. Cadorna, provides **Internet** access, including connections for personal laptops. (☎0323 30 323. €3 per 30min. Open daily 9:30am-12:30pm and 3:30-10pm.) **Lidrovolante Internet Cafe,** Ple. Lido 6 (☎0323 31 384; www.lidrovolante.com), offers Internet access near the funicular. The **post office** is at V. Anna Maria Bolongaro 44. (☎0323 30 065. Open M-F 8:30am-7pm, Sa 8:30am-1pm.) **Postal Code:** 28838.

🖪🏠 ACCOMMODATIONS AND FOOD. The pristine 🏨**Albergo Luina ❸,** V. Garibaldi 21, centrally located and on the water, has vast, welcoming rooms with TV, bath, and phone. From the train station, walk to the waterfront and head right until you pass the ferry dock. Multilingual proprietress Renata makes guests feel at home and offers extensive advice on travel options. (☎0323 30 285; luinastresa@yahoo.it. Breakfast €3.50. Reservations recommended in summer. Singles €35-52; doubles €55-80; triples €56-80. *Let's Go* discount. MC/V.) With a prime location on the coveted waterfront, **Gigi Meuble ❹,** P. S. Michele 1, has seven rooms with bath and some with balconies. Don't miss the fantastic panoramic view of the lake from the breakfast room. (☎0323 30 225; gigihotel@email.it. Singles €50; doubles €60. AmEx/MC/V.) With numerous four-person rooms, **Hotel Meeting ❺,** V. Bonghi 9, is a popular choice for groups and families. Don't leave without experiencing the stellar panoramic view of the city, lake, and islands from the large rooftop sundeck. (☎0323 32 741; hotelmeeting@stresa.it. Singles €50-90; doubles €70-100; quads €90-120. AmEx/MC/V.)

Popular **Taverna del Pappagallo ❷**, V. Principessa Margherita 46, serves great brick-oven pizza (€4.50-10) and various pastas in a lively indoor seating or in the grapevine-covered courtyard. Greet the embalmed parrot on your way in. (☎0323 30 411. Primi €6.50-13. Secondi €7.50-14. Cover €1.30. Open M-Tu and Th-Su noon-2:30pm and 6:30-11pm. AmEx/MC/V.) Lounge bar **El Gato Negro Café ❷**, V. Principessa Margherita 52, is the most youthful hangout in this heavily silver-lined town. (☎0323 33 621. Mixed drinks €5. Panini €3.50. Salads €6. Primi €5.50. Secondi €6-9. Cover €0.50. Open daily 8:30am-midnight. AmEx/MC/V.) For refuge from the more expensive restaurants, **Il Capriccio ❶**, V. de Vit 15, offers creative pizza slices for only €2-2.20. (☎0323 31 687. Open Tu-Su 10:30am-2pm and 4:30-9pm. Cash only.) **Lago Maggiore ❷**, V. Cavour 34-36, is tucked behind the lakeside church. (☎0323 32 746. Primi €6-10. Secondi €7-15. Lake fish €9-21. Open daily 11:30am-3pm and 6:30pm-11:30pm. AmEx/MC/V.) Food in Stresa can be overpriced and often unsatisfying; a great option is to stock up on groceries at **GS**, V. Roma 11, and eat by the water or on the mountain. (Open M-Sa 8:30am-1pm and 3-8pm, Su 8:30am-12:30pm. AmEx/MC/V.)

◐ ♫ SIGHTS AND ENTERTAINMENT. Turn right out of the tourist office and follow the waterfront all the way to Vle. Lido to reach the **Stresa-Alpino-Mottarone Funivia**, P. Lido 8, which allows visitors to explore Mottarone's (1491m) extensive hiking and mountain biking trails. (☎0323 30 295; www.stresa-mottarone. it. Open daily 9:30am-12:30pm and 1:50-5:30pm; often closed Nov. for repairs. 20min.; every 20min., last return 5:40pm; €5-7.50.) Close to the water, **Villa Pallavicino**, down C. Italia, boasts 50 acres of gardens filled with over 40 species of exotic animals such as flamingoes and zebras. (☎0323 31 533; www.parcozoopallavicino.it. Open Mar.-Oct. daily 9am-6pm. €9, children €5.) From the last week in July to the second week in September, classical musicians and fans gather for the **Settimane Musicali di Stresa e del Lago Maggiore,** a celebration of the full canon of classical music. Performances crowd Stresa's Palazzo dei Congressi or Isola Bella. Contact the ticket office at V. Carducci 38. (☎0323 31 095 or 30 459; www.settimanemusicali.net. Open daily 9:30am-12:30pm and 3-6pm. Tickets €20-100, under 26 half-price, limited number of tickets €10. Package tickets available.) Stresa's new and only nightclub, **Loco Beach Club**, P. Lido, is next to the funicular. The rooftop bar, swanky beachside patio, and modern dining room draws a crowd of older tourists after 9pm. (☎0323 93 47 40. Mixed drinks €5-6. Primi €11. Secondi €15-18. Open daily 9pm-3am.) For a more low-key scene, try the wine bar, **Da Giannino**, V. Garibaldi 32, which serves reasonably priced wines indoors at a few wooden kegs-turned-tables, or outside where large groups socialize. While you sip, peruse their large selection of wines for purchase, organized by region with a heavy emphasis on Piedmont wines. Also check out the collection of liquors, distilled from everything from grapes to honey.(☎0323 30 781. Wine from €1.50. Open daily 9am-midnight. Kitchen open noon-2pm and 7pm-midnight. AmEx/MC/V.)

THE BORROMEAN ISLANDS (ISOLE BORROMEE) ☎0323

Beckoning visitors with dense greenery and stately villas, the lush beauty of the Borromean Islands (in Italian "EE-so-leh bo-ro-MEY") is one of the lake's major attractions. Situated between Stresa and Pallanza, the islands are easily accessible by ferry. The opulent **◪Palazzo e Giardini Borromeo** is set on the pearl of Maggiore, **Isola Bella.** This Baroque palace, built in 1670 by Count Vitaliano Borromeo, features meticulously designed rooms constructed over 300 years, with priceless tapestries and Van Dyck paintings. Napoleon and Josephine slept in the alcove of the grand **Napoleon Room** during his first Italian campaign in 1797. The **Sala della Musica** hosted Mussolini, Laval, and MacDonald at the 1935

Conference of Stresa, the last attempt to stave off WWII. Six underground man-made **grottoes** are covered in mosaics; for years, peasants collected black stones to complete the masterpieces. Ten terraced gardens rise up like a wedding cake, punctuated by statues of gods and topped with a unicorn, the symbol of the Borromeo family, whose motto, *Humilitas* (humility), is not so apparent here. (☎0323 30 556; www.grandigiardini.it. Open daily Mar. 21-Oct. 21 9am-6pm, garden until 6:15pm. Last entry 30min. before closing. Tours for 2-50 people can be arranged at least one day in advance by phone or at info@borromeoturismo. it. €11, ages 6-15 €5. Combined ticket for the *palazzo* and the Villa Taranto on Isola Madre €16, children €7. Audio tour €2.50. €35 per group.)

From Isola Bella, a short ferry ride leads to **Isola Superiore dei Pescatori,** a quaint fishing village full of souvenir vendors and cats, who come for the daily catch. There's a little-used rocky swimming beach on the west end of the island, but keep in mind this is an alpine lake; the water may be more chilling than refreshing. On top of the hill in the village, the only other attraction is the **Chiesa di San Vitore,** dedicated to a martyred second-century *borromese* native who later became a saint. While most of the church dates from 1638, portions of the altar date from the first century. (Open daily 9am-6pm. Free.) There is no such thing as a non-touristy restaurant on these popular islands, but head left when exiting ferry to reach **Ristorante Italia ❸**, V. Ugo Ara 58, which specializes in local fish and serves it in a charming blue-and-white house overlooking the lake. (☎0323 30 456; www.stresaonline.com/italia. Primi €7-10. Secondi €10-15. Cover €1.50. Open daily noon-3pm and 7-10pm. AmEx/MC/V.)

Isola Madre, almost entirely covered by its garden, is the largest and most tran-quil of the islands, and thus predictably the local favorite—perhaps because it also feels like a step back in time. Its elegant **Villa Taranto** was started in 1502 by Lancelotto Borromeo and finished by Count Renato 100 years later, after Lancelotto reputedly met his end in the mouth of a 🐉dragon. A far cry from many stuffy residences of European nobility, the villa has a number of room-sized puppet theaters, set with scenery and marionettes ranging from whimsi-cal to creepy. The villa's gardens have exotic flora and fauna—a flock of white peacocks and various other flamboyantly plumed birds guard the 200-year-old Cashmir Cyprus. Visit in July to see the rare lotus blossoms in bloom. (☎/fax 0323 31 261. Open daily Mar.-Sept. 9am-noon and 1:30-8:30pm; Oct.-Feb. 9:30am-12:30pm and 1:30-5pm. €10, ages 6-15 €5. Combined ticket with the Palazzo e Giardini Borromeo €16.50, children €7.50. Audio tour €2.50.)

If you've budgeted a day for island hopping, stop across the lake from Stresa at the small monastery ◼**Santa Caterina del Sasso.** Tucked along the coast, a few miles away from Baveno, the monastery is difficult to reach other than by boat; the complete isolation is worth exploring for the amount of late-Renaissance artwork inside, the highlight being a 17th-century fresco *God the Father*. Boats depart from Stresa (7-8 per day from 9:20am-4:35pm) for the monastery. (www. provincia.va.it/preziosita/ukvarese/itin/maggiore/gemonio.htm. Open daily Apr.-Oct. 8:30am-noon and 2:30-6pm; Nov.-Mar. 9am-noon and 2-5pm. Free.)

Ferries (☎0323 800 551 801; www.navigazionelaghi.it) run from Stresa to Car-ciano, Isola Bella, Isola Superiore, Baveno, Isola Madre, then Pallanza, and ending in Intra. Ferries leave Stresa every 15-30min. from 7:10am to 7:10pm and return from Intra until 6pm. A one-day ticket for unlimited travel between Stresa, Pallanza, and the three islands costs €11.50. Individual tickets from Stresa to Isola Bella or Superiore cost €6.60, and to Isola Madre €8.40. All tick-ets are valid until returning to departure point. A single day combined ride to Isola Bella, Isola Superiore, and Isola Madre with ferry ride costs €28.

SANTA MARIA MAGGIORE ☎ 0324

Carved out by the same glaciers that melted to Lake Maggiore and Lake Orta, Valle Vigezzo (VAL-lay vee-JET-soh) is a gorgeous valley with few tourists. The area has sparked artistic inspiration so often that it is now known as "Painter's Valley." Santa Maria Maggiore (SAN-ta ma-REE-ah ma-JO-reh; pop. 1280), the lake's largest town, is bordered by the smaller towns of Arvogno, Craveggia, Re, and Toceno. Perhaps the biggest highlight, however, is journeying through the valley to witness its stunning landscape, resplendent with enormous mountains, fields, villages, waterfalls, and streams.

⌂⓭ TRANSPORTATION AND PRACTICAL INFORMATION. From Stresa, take the **train** to Domodossola (☎0324 24 20 55; 40min., 20 per day 6:37am-10:34pm, €3), then transfer to the SSIF (or Centovalli) line by turning left out of the train, walking underground, taking the train toward Locarno, and getting off at Santa Maria Maggiore (40min.; 17 per day 5:30am-7:58pm, last return 8:15pm; €2.60.) The ticket office (☎0324 24 20 55) is open 20min. before departures. For a **taxi,** call ☎0324 92 405 or 98 045.

From the train station on **Piazzale Diaz,** cross **Via Luigi Cadorna** to **Via Dante,** which ends at **Via Antonio Rosmini.** Turn right to reach **Piazza Risorgimento,** the *centro.* The **Ufficio Turistico Pro Loco,** P. Risorgimento 4, offers free maps of the town and valley, and **Internet** access. (☎0324 94 565. Internet €3 per 30min. Open in summer M-Sa 10am-noon and 4-6pm, Su 10am-noon; in winter Sa 10am-noon and 4-6pm, Su 10am-noon.) Follow V. Cavalli from P. Risorgimento until it becomes V. Rossetti Valentini to reach **Banca Popolare di Novara.** (☎0324 95 002. Open M-F 8:20am-1:20pm and 2:35-3:35pm.) In case of emergency, call the **carabinieri** (☎0324 95 007) or the **guardia medica turistica,** V. Guglielmo Marconi 4. (☎0324 94 360. Open daily July-Aug. 2-6pm.) A **pharmacy** is on V. Matteotti 5. (☎0324 95 018. Open M-Sa 9am-12:30pm and 3:30-7:30pm, Su 9am-12:30pm.) The **post office** is at V. R. Valentini 26. (☎0324 90 53 87. Open M-F 8:30am-2pm, Sa 8:30am-1pm.) **Postal Code:** 28857.

⌂⌂ ACCOMMODATIONS AND FOOD. There are few budget accommodations in Santa Maria Maggiore. **Albergo Oscella ❸,** V. Matteotti 84, offers the best value in town, located just outside of the *centro.* (☎0324 951 70. Singles €35; doubles €65; triples €75.) For delicious and conscientiously prepared local food, head to **Osteria Bar Al Cortiletto ❸,** V. Cavalli 20. Save room for the homemade desserts. (☎0324 90 56 78. Pizza €4-7.50. Primi €6.50-8. Secondi €8.50-14. Cover €1.80. Open daily Dec.-Oct. 9am-10pm. AmEx/MC/V.)

◗◗ SIGHTS AND OUTDOOR ACTIVITIES. One of the main attractions in Santa Maria Maggiore is the **Museo dello Spazzacamino (Chimney Sweep Museum)** in the Parco Villa Antonia, which has a collection of equipment, and sends visitors through a tunnel of pictures, sounds, and smells. As the land was unsuitable for farming, young Vigezzo inhabitants, emigrated en masse to cities throughout Europe as chimney sweeps; the museum is a dedication to those who returned and used their earnings to boost the valley's economy. (☎0324 90 56 75; www.museospazzacamino.it. Open June-Sept. Tu-Su 10am-noon and 3-6pm; Oct.-May Sa-Su 10am-noon and 3-6pm. €2.) The ◪**Santuario della Madonna del Sangue** houses the painting *Madonna del Sangue* (Madonna of the Blood), which is said to have bled for 20 days in 1494 after being hit with a stone. To get to the sanctuary, take the Piana di Vigezzo Funivia (see below) to the stop in the town of Re. (☎0324 97 016. Open daily 8am-9pm. Free.) The best outdoor excursions in the area are in the ◪**Parco Nazionale Val Grande,** created in 1992. The 15,000 hectare park is less than 100km from Milan; it can be accessed only by car from the A8 motorway from Milan or the A26 from Genoa/Turin. Exit at "Gravellona Toce" and take Ossola highway toward the Simplon Pass. The park is not only known for its wilderness but also its relics of a once-major alpine civilization. Ask the tourist office for park info, and acquire hiking itineraries and maps at the office inside the park entrance. (☎0323 55 79 60; www.parcovalgrande.it.) **Arvogno** (1260m), starts hiking paths toward high peaks, and the **La Cima chair lift** takes visitors ever higher on summer weekends (8:30, 11:30am, 2:30, 5pm). In winter, it becomes part of the Valle Vigezzo ski ticket, which includes the **Piana di Vigezzo Funivia** (cable car) that mounts to **Colma Trubbio** (2064m) from **Prestinone.** (Ascents daily 8am-5:30pm. 1-way €7, children €4; round-trip €10/6. Full-day ski pass M-F €20, Sa-Su €24; ages 4-12 €15/18. Half-day pass €13/15, ages 4-12 €10/13. Equipment rental available at top of *funivia*. AmEx/MC/V.)

ORTA SAN GIULIO   ☎0322

Orta San Giulio (OR-ta san JOO-lee-oh; pop. 1120) is the gateway to Lake Orta—by far the smallest and least touristed of the lakes—though just as striking as any of them. The 19th-century villas that line the narrow, cobblestone streets evoke the very best of old Italy. Though difficult to reach without a car, the town has drawn many to its secluded location. In fact, the privacy is precisely what drew Friedrich Nietzsche here in 1882 with his young love, Lou Salome, in order to escape the watchful eye of her mother. Nietzsche claimed he couldn't remember whether or not the two had kissed because the views had sent him into a state of grace.

⬛ TRANSPORTATION. If coming by train from Stresa, switch lines at Premosello (1hr.; 4 per day 6:37am-6:47pm, return 6:28am-8:17pm; €3), getting off at Orta-Miasino. In Orta, buy train tickets at the nearby bar. (Open M-F 6:30am-midnight, Sa 7:30pm-midnight.) You can also access Orta-Miasino from Domodossola, north of Stresa on the Milan-Domodossola line. If coming or going to Milano Centrale, switch trains at Novara to the line ending in Domodossola (9 per day 6:39am-7:20pm, €4.70). Down the hill from the train station, a small red train-shaped vehicle, Il Trenino di Orta, shuttles passengers between the intersection of V. Panoramica and V. Giuseppe Fava (in front of the tourist office that is halfway on the walk) and the *centro;* the train also stops in front of Sacro Monte. (☎0322 347 488 3509. 5min.; Apr. 15-Oct. 15 M-Tu and Th-Su every 15-30min. 9am-8pm, Oct. 16-Apr. 14 Su; €4, children €2; round-trip €5/3.) **Bus 30** (or Nerini Mini-Bus; ☎0323 55 21 72; €3) runs to Orta from Stresa. In Stresa the bus departs from in front of the church near the ferry station (5 per day 7:40am-5pm, 1hr.). In Orta the bus departs from Ple. Prarondo (1hr., 3 per day 11am-6pm). Be early and stand in a visible location in the parking lot; as the bus doesn't stop if no one appears to be waiting for it. Small **motoscafi** (motorboats) in P. Motta weave back and forth from Isola di San Giulio to the mainland during the summer upon request. (☎0323 333 605 0288; www.motoscafipubblicorta.it. 10min.; daily Apr.-Oct. every 15min. 9am-6:30pm; Nov.-Mar. every 40min. 9am-5pm; €4). Navigazione Lago d'Orta runs larger boats between the island and the mainland. (☎0323 84 48 62. 5min.; Apr.-Sept. daily every 30min. 9:55am-7:10pm, Oct. Sa-Su, Nov. Su; €4.) On the mainland call a **taxi** (☎0323 328 391 1670 or 335 65 56 340).

⬛ PRACTICAL INFORMATION. The *centro* is **Piazza Motta.** Amble along **Via Olina,** which becomes **Via Bossi,** then **Via Gippini** to reach **Via Motta** and the footpath, Strada del Movero, and ultimately ⬛**Lungo Lario 11 Settembre,** a sublime path hugging the shore where you can sunbathe on the docks or jump off them into the clear blue water. There are two **tourist offices** in Orta. The primary one is on V. Panoramica, across the street and downhill from Villa Crespi. To reach the office from the train station, exit left from the station, make the first left downhill, and continue through the rotunda straight ahead. (☎0323 90 56 14 or 90 51 63; inforta@distrettolaghi.it. Open W-Su 9am-1pm and 2-6pm.) The second office is in the Palazzo Comunale, V. Bossi 11, straight past P. Motta. (☎0323 90 155; www.ortainfo.com. Open Apr.-Oct. M and W-F 11am-1pm and 2-6pm, Sa-Su 10am-1pm and 2-6pm.) **Banca Popolare di Novara** is at P. Ragazzoni 16. (☎0323 90 57 01. Open M-F 8:20am-1:30pm and 2:35-3:35pm, Sa 8:20-11:20am.) A **pharmacy**, V. Albertolletti 10, is off P. Motta. (☎0323 90 117. Open M-W and F-Sa 9am-12:30pm and 3:30-7:30pm. MC/V.) In case of emergency, call the **carabinieri**, V. Circonvallazione 4 (☎0323 90 114), in nearby Omegna or an **ambulance** (☎0323 81 500). The only **Internet** access inside the city is at the hotel booking center on V. Poli 13. (☎0323 90 55 32. €4 per 5min., €10 per 30min. Open daily 9am-7pm. Cash only.) They also rent bikes. **Il Cantuccio**, across from the train station, also has InternetThe **post office**, P. Ragazzoni 5, offers currency exchange. (☎0323 90 157. Open M-F 8:30am-2pm, Sa 8:30am-1pm.) **Postal Code:** 28016.

ACCOMMODATIONS AND FOOD. Orta's relative seclusion means high accommodation prices. Down the street from Villa Crespi, **B&B Villa Pinin** ❸, on V. Fava, is one of the best deals in town. Admire a gorgeous view of the lake from any spot in the spacious yard. (☎0323 90 55 05 or 340 00 69 323. Reservations required. High-season doubles €80, low-season €60. Cash only.) The enormous **Villa Francesco** ❸, V. Prisciola 6, has huge, bountiful rooms opening onto a spectacular terrace, as well as a breakfast room, restaurant, bar, garden, and chapel, all just a few short minutes from the station. Facing the train station, go left and continue 300m down the road. (☎0323 90 258; www.hotelsanfrancesco.it. Breakfast included. Singles €34; doubles €56. MC/V.) **Hotel Santa Caterina** ❺, V. Marconi 10, has what are undoubtedly the hippest Scandanavian-themed lodgings in Orta. The included buffet breakfast is an impressive value. Walk from the train station toward town, and the hotel is on the left several minutes before passing the tourist office. (☎0323 915 865 75; www.ortainfo.com. Singles €70-80; doubles €95-105. AmEx/MC/V.) The lakeside **Camping Orta** ❶, V. Domodossola 28, welcomes campers with a private

LOCAL LEGEND

IT'S A BLOODY MIRACLE!

The small town of Re, near Santa Maria Maggiore, has been a center for pilgrims since 1494. In that year a man named Zuccone and his friend were gambling over the Italian game *piodella*. Zuccone, unfortunately for him, was the loser. Furious and defeated, Zuccone trudged through the streets until he came upon a painting of the Virgin and Child beneath the arcade of the church. He became enraged at the expression of the Madonna, which seemed calm and unconcerned with his misfortune. In his rage, he hurled the rock from the game at the Virgin, striking her on the forehead. Immediately after realizing what he had done, he fell to his knees, but his remorse quickly turned into fear and he ran away.

Around dawn, an old man came by to open up the church only to discover that the Virgin was bleeding from her forehead! For the next day and night, people came from far and wide to see the miracle; the painting continued to pour out thick blood intermittently for 20 days.

Today, the sanctuary (p. 301) holds the tablecloth covered in blood and lights up a slightly blood-speckled wall behind the altar. Pilgrims still come to venerate the Madonna del Sangue, and it is said that the Virgin bestows health and safety upon them for their piety.

beach and Internet access. (☎0323 90 267; www.campingorta.it. Wash €3, dry €3. Internet €3 per 30min. Reception open 8:30am-12:30pm, and 2-7:30pm. €5-7 per person, €3.50-4.50 per child under 12; €8-15 per tent; €5-6 per car. Bungalows €65-90. Electricity €2. Showers €0.20 for 4 min. Cash only.)

Local cuisine is known for *tapulon* (spiced, minced donkey and horse meat cooked in red wine) eaten with cornmeal polenta, typically only served in winter. There isn't a better place to try the locally produced wine, *Ghemme*, or the native cheese, *Tomo di Motarone*, than at ◪**Al Boeuc ❷**, V. Bersani 28, a tiny, dimly lit wine bar one street inland from P. Motta. Large *bruschette* (€10) or mixed *salame* plates go well with wine. While *Ghemme* is only available by the bottle, other local wines come by the glass, such as *Traversa*, made from the same grapes. (☎0323 339 584 0039. Open M and W-Su 11am-3pm and 6:30pm-1am. Cash only.) Though most restaurants in the town center are quite touristy, **Ristorante Edera ❷**, V. Bersani 15, off the main square, is slightly less so. Primi €6-8. Secondi €8-13. (☎0322 9055 34. Open for dinner F-Sa.) At night, the mature crowd heads to classy **Caffè and Jazz ❷**, V. Olina 13, where Thursday (July-Sept.) means live jazz at 10pm. (☎0323 333 923 2522. Wine €4-5 per glass. Bruschette €7. Salads €8-9. Open Tu-Su 11am-3pm and 6pm-1am. Cash only.) Since 1228, P. Motta has had a weekly Wednesday **market.** The food market **La Dispensa,** V. Bersani 38, off P. Motta, and the fruit market next door offer *panini* (€2.30-4) and picnic basics. (Open M-Tu and Th-Sa 9am-6:30pm, W 9am-2pm, Su 10am-6:30pm.)

◪ **SIGHTS.** At the intersection of V. Panoramica and V. G. Fava, the ornate **Villa Crespi,** which now houses a hotel, was built in 1873 in an Arabian style to satisfy cotton pioneer Cristoforo Crespi's nostalgia for his trips to the Orient. The large stone columns of the ground floor portico of the beautiful city hall, also known as the **"Palazzoto,"** dominate P. Motta. Right up V. Albertoletti is the **Chiesa Santa Maria Assunta,** a church built to celebrate the end of the 1485 plague. (Open daily 9am-6pm.) On the lake across from Orta lies the **Isola di San Giulio.** According to legend, the island was inhabited by ◪**dragons** and serpents until they were destroyed by Julius, a traveler from Greece, in the AD fourth century. Today, it is inhabited by three families as well as a convent of 72 nuns who have taken a vow of seclusion. While the convent is not open to the public, the island can be visited by ferry or motorboat. Pedestrians cover the tiny island on a cobblestone path (10min.), known as **The Way of Meditation,** where periodic multilingual markers offer sage advice on the art of introspection. Walking the path in reverse will take you on **The Way of Silence,** where signs comment on the beauty of silence. The 12th-century Romanesque **Basilica di San Giulio,** built on fourth-century foundations, is filled with Baroque ornamentation and adorned with pink cloud frescoes. The true masterpiece is the **pulpit,** carved from black *oira* stone. Downstairs, the skeleton of San Giulio, dressed in brocade robes and mask, rests in a gold and glass sarcophagus. (Open daily 9:30am-12:15pm and 2-6:30pm. Modest dress required. Free.) A short 15min. hike off V. Panoramica onto V. della Cappelletta leads to the **Sacro Monte** monastic complex, a UNESCO World Heritage site. The complex holds 20 chapels filled with life-size, terra-cotta statues and frescoes that chart the life of St. Francis of Assisi. (☎0323 91 19 60; www.sacromonteorta.it. Open daily in summer 9am-5pm; in winter 9am-7pm. Free guided tours with reservations. Park open 24hr. Free.)

THE VENETO

From the rocky Dolomite foothills to the fertile Po valleys, the diversity of the Veneto (VEH-neh-toh) begins with its dramatic topography. Once loosely united under the Venetian Empire, the Veneto's towns and cities have retained their cultural independence; today, visitors are more likely to hear regional dialects than standard Italian. The region's marine supremacy, enviable location near the center of the peninsula, and heavy international and inter-provincial traffic have brought a variety of cuisines and cultural traditions. The influx of Austrian and Slovenian cultures in the mountain villages in the North creates a pleasant surprise for visitors expecting to find only gondolas and mandolins.

HIGHLIGHTS OF THE VENETO

BEHOLD St. Mark's remains at Venice's Basilica di San Marco (p. 320).

SERENADE your loved one during a gondola ride on Venice's Grand Canal (p. 323).

WANDER the hallowed halls of the Università di Padova, where luminaries such as Dante, Galileo, and Copernicus set the academic world on fire (p. 336).

VENICE (VENEZIA) ☎041

From its hedonistic, devil-may-care Carnevale, to the repentant God-may-care-too services of its soaring marble cathedrals, Venice (in Italian, "ve-NET-see-ah"; pop. 60,000) is a mystical, waterlogged city. Founded by Roman fishermen in the 11th century, the city soon became the major meeting point between East and West. Global commerce depended on Venetian merchants to supply silks, spices, and coffee for over a century before the city's trade dominance diminished. Since then, sea-bound ships have been replaced with gondolas as Venice trades naval prowess for a booming tourism industry. Though the busiest *piazze* and major sights may be overrun with visitors, Venice's beauty remains intact, and continues to defy guidebook descriptions. The awe of its seemingly untouched artistic masterpieces, the serene quiet of its hidden *piazze,* and the size and strength of its mighty canals will overtake you. Plus, the tourist hordes aren't all bad—some of the most memorable moments may be when you grab a fellow confused map-toting tourist and together muster up enough broken Italian to ask for directions, only to find a local who is as lost as you are. Venice is impossible to master, but the reward of discovering an authentic *enoteca* or a tiny residential neighborhood will lure you back again and again.

✈ INTERCITY TRANSPORTATION

Flights: Aeroporto Marco Polo (☎041 26 09 260; www.veniceairport.it), 10km north of the city. **ATVO shuttle** (☎042 13 83 671) links the airport to P. Roma on the main island (30min., every hr. 8am-midnight, €3). ATVO ticket office open daily 5am-8:40pm.

Trains: Stazione Santa Lucia (☎041 89 20 21), the main station, is in the northwestern corner of the city. Upon arrival, disembark at S. Lucia, not Mestre on the mainland. Info office open daily 7am-9pm. Ticket windows open M-F 8:30am-7:30pm,

THE VENETO

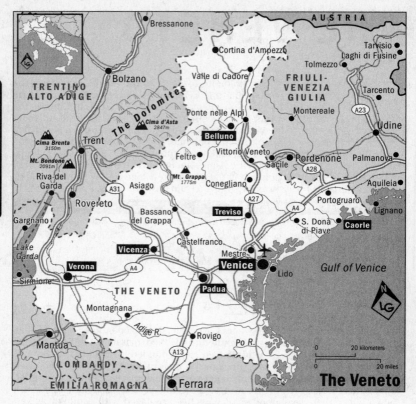

The Veneto

Sa-Su 9am-1:30pm and 2-5:30pm. AmEx/MC/V. To: **Bologna** (2hr., 32 per day 3:11am-11:30pm, €8.20); **Florence** (3hr., 19 per day 3:11am-7:57pm, €23.50); **Milan** (3hr.,26 per day 3:11am-8:03pm, €13.75); **Padua** (45min., 83 per day 12:17am-11:34pm, €2.90); **Rome** (4hr., 23 per day 12:17am-11:30pm, €41.50); **Trieste** (2hr., 32 per day 12:10am-10:47pm, €8.75). Reservations often required; check info booth. Prices, frequency, and travel time vary by company. **Lost and found** near track 5 (*oggetti rinvenuti;* ☎041 78 56 70; open daily for luggage retrieval 8am-noon; open for info 7am-9pm) and **luggage storage** by track #14 (see **Practical Information,** p. 312).

Buses: ACTV (☎041 24 24; www.hellovenezia.it), in Ple. Roma. Office open daily 7am-8pm. Ticket window open daily 6am-11:30pm. **ACTV long-distance carrier** runs buses to **Padua** (1hr., every 15-30min. 4:45am-12:45am, €4.50) and **Treviso** (1hr., every 15-30min. 4:55am-8:55pm, €3). Cash only.

⊞ ORIENTATION

Venice comprises 118 islands in a lagoon, connected to the mainland city of Mestre by a thin causeway. With the **Canale Grande** snaking throughout, the city is divided into seven *sestieri* (sections): **San Marco** in the center, encircled by

Cannaregio to the north, **San Polo** and **Santa Croce** to the west, **Dorsoduro** along the southwestern shore, **Castello** along the eastern shore, and **Giudecca** to the south, separated from Venice proper by the large Giudecca canal. *Sestieri* boundaries are vague but should be of some use in navigating the city's narrow alleys.

Venice's layout consists of a labyrinth of *calli* (narrow streets), *campi* (squares), *liste* (large streets), and *ponti* (bridges). It's practically impossible to avoid getting lost—maps are of little use, as many streets are either too narrow to be plotted, lack street signs, or have erratic street numbers. To get by, simply learn to navigate like a true Venetian. Locate the following sights on the map: **Ponte di Rialto** (in the center), **Piazza San Marco** (central south), **Ponte Accademia** (southwest), **Ferrovia** (or Stazione Santa Lucia, the train station; northwest), **Ponte Scalzi** (in front of the station), and **Piazzale Roma** (southwest of the station). These are Venice's main orientation points. A plethora of yellow signs posted throughout the city point the way to major landmarks and bridges.

When trying to find a place, locate the *sestiere*, then find a nearby landmark, and follow signs in that general direction. As you get closer, use the address numbers and busier streets to work your way toward the destination. As a general rule, follow the arrows on the yellow signs as precisely as possible. If a street suddenly leads into a *campo* and branches in five different directions, pick the street that follows the original direction of the arrow as closely as possible until reaching the next sign. Note that in Venice, addresses are not specific to a particular street, and every building in a *sestiere* is given a number ("San Marco 3434" is a typical address). Buildings are generally numbered consecutively, but there are also often large jumps, so the next number could be one block away or down an alleyway.

To get to **Piazza San Marco** or the **Rialto Bridge** from the train station, take V # 1 (15min. to Rialto, 35min. to San Marco, every 10min.) or V #2 (10min. to Rialto, 25min. to San Marco, every 10min.). On foot, follow signs to P. S. Marco, starting left of the station on Lista de Spagna.

V MARKS THE SPOT. Vaporetti stops appear in the text as V.

LOCAL TRANSPORTATION

The cheapest—and often the fastest—way to see the city is to walk through it. Pedestrians can cross the Grand Canal at the *ponti* Scalzi, Rialto, and Accademia. **Traghetti** (gondola ferry boats) traverse the canal at seven locations, including Ferrovia, San Marcuola, Cà d'Oro, and Rialto (€0.50). *Vaporetti* (water buses) provide 24hr. service around the city, with reduced service after midnight. Tickets vary in price based on the duration of their validity. 1hr. *traghetti* tickets cost €6.50. Longer-term **travel cards** allow unlimited access to both *traghetti* and buses running to Mestre and Lido. (12hr. €14, 24hr. €16, 36hr. €21, 2 day €26, 3 day €31.) Students aged 14-29 may purchase a 3-day pass (€22) that includes the perks of the Rolling Venice card and unlimited access to *traghetti* and buses. Travel cards can also be a time-saver; they come prevalidated whereas single fare tickets must be validated at the yellow boxes at each stop. Unvalidated tickets risk a fine; the "confused foreigner" act won't work in a town where tourists often outnumber residents two to one. Schedules, route maps, and tickets are available at tourist offices (**Practical Information**, p. 312). Tickets are also sold in front of stops.

THE VENETO

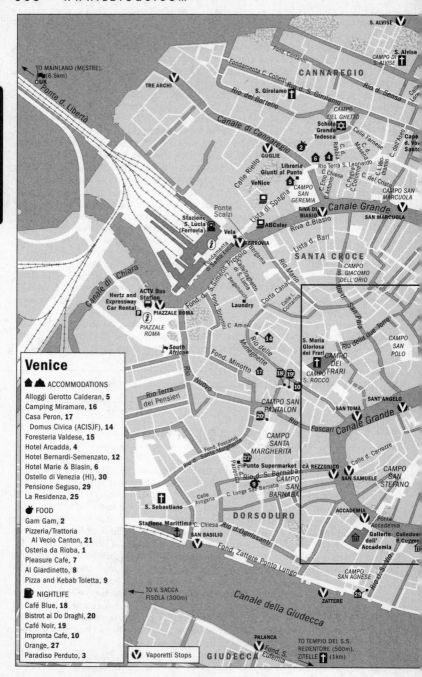

Venice

🏠🏠 ACCOMMODATIONS

Alloggi Gerotto Calderan, **5**
Camping Miramare, **16**
Casa Peron, **17**
Domus Civica (ACISJF), **14**
Foresteria Valdese, **15**
Hotel Arcadda, **4**
Hotel Bernardi-Semenzato, **12**
Hotel Marie & Blasin, **6**
Ostello di Venezia (HI), **30**
Pensione Seguso, **29**
La Residenza, **25**

🍴 FOOD

Gam Gam, **2**
Pizzeria/Trattoria
  Al Vecio Canton, **21**
Osteria da Rioba, **1**
Pleasure Cafe, **7**
Al Giardinetto, **8**
Pizza and Kebab Toletta, **9**

🍸 NIGHTLIFE

Café Blue, **18**
Bistrot ai Do Draghi, **20**
Café Noir, **19**
Impronta Cafe, **10**
Orange, **27**
Paradiso Perduto, **3**

V Vaporetti Stops

TO MURANO (1.5km),
TORCELLO (4km), BURANO (7km),
AEROPORTO MARCO POLO (10km).

CIMITERO

ORTO

Chiesa della
Madonna dell'Orto

Rio d.
Madonna dell'Orto

Sacca
della
Misericordia

Isola di San
Michele

Canale delle Fondamente Nuove

Campo dei Mori

Rio della Misericordia

S. Maria
Valverde

Rio di
Noale

Calle Lunga Santa Caterina

CAMPO
SANTA
FOSCA

S. Fosca

Chiesa
dei Gesuiti

FONDAMENTA NUOVE

Fondamenta Nuove

STAE

Billa
Supermarket

Calle i Rachetta

Calle delle Vele

Ruga Dui Pozzi

CAMPO
DEL GESUITI

Calle Larga
dei Botteri

Strada Nuova

Rio d. San Cassiano

Cà d'Oro

CÀ D'ORO

del Pistor

CAMPO S.S.
APOSTOLI

C. del Fumo

OSPEDALE

Internet
Station

Rio dello Squero

Calle dei Mendicanti

Ospedale
Civile

c. d. Cappuccine

CELESTIA

SAN POLO

Ponte
di Rialto

Riva del Vin

Campo S.
BARTOLOMEO

Rio d. San Marina

S.S. Giovanni
e Paolo

Barbaria delle Tole

S. Francesco
della Vigna

CAMPO D.
CELESTIA

TO 16
(10km)

SAN SILVESTRO

RIALTO

Riva del Carbon

Sal. di S. Lio

CAMPO
S. MARIA
FORMOSA

Ponte
Rosso
Farnes

Rio di S. Lorenzo

CAMPO SAN
LORENZO

Rio di S. Lucia

Rio di S. Salvador

Calle dei Fabbri

S. Maria
Formosa

Ruga Giuffa

Rio del Mezzo

B. Lorenzo

C. Castello

Calle Lion

Scuola Dalmata
San Giorgio
degli Schiavoni

C. d. Furlani

CAMPO
MANIN

Calle d. Mandola

Calle del Palazzo

CASTELLO

C. d.
Madonna

CAMPO
BANDIERA
E MORO

Rio dell'Arsenale

Rio di Gorne

CAMPO
SANT'ANGELO

Frezzaria

C. Corrona

C. d.
Osmarin

S. S. Provolo

S. Zaccaria

Calle della Pietà

C. Pietà

TO ARSENALE
(150m)

SAN MARCO

San
Marco

PIAZZA
SAN MARCO

Palazzo
Ducale

CAMPO
S. ZACCARIA

C. del Vin

C. del
Doxe

C. del
Forno

C. Crosera

Rio d. San
Mois

Rio della
Ostreghe

S. ZACCARIA

Riva degli Schiavoni

ARSENALE

TO GIARDINI
PUBLICI (250m)

GIGLIO

SALUTE

S. Maria
della Salute

Rio d. Fornace

Canale di San Marco

SEE CENTRAL VENICE MAP, P. 310

SAN GIORGIO

S. Giorgio
Maggiore

Isola di
S. Giorgio
Maggiore

Fond. Zattere ai Saloni

Fond. delle Zitelle

ZITELLE

TO 31 (100m)

TO LIDO (2km)

0   200 meters
0   200 yards

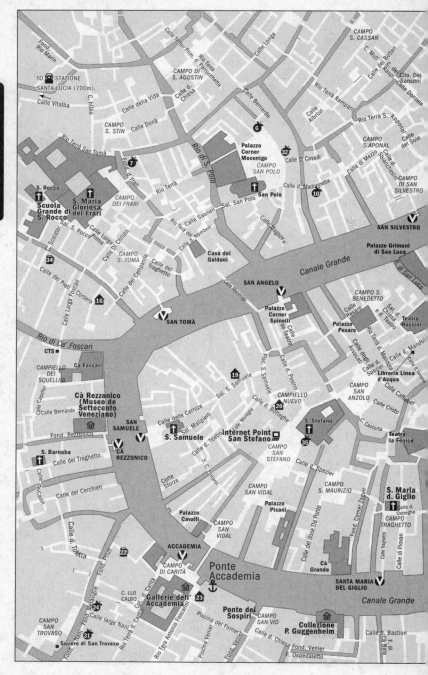

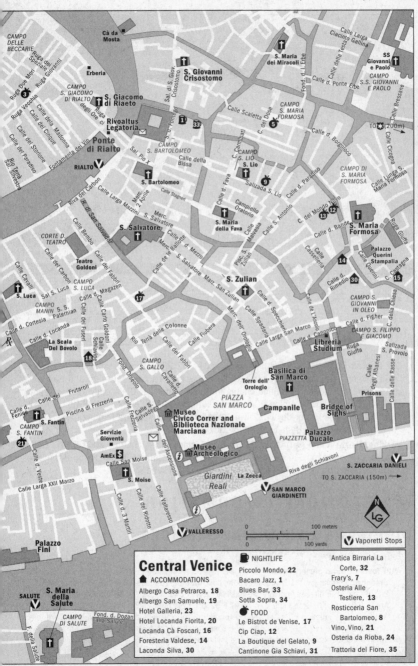

Central Venice

ACCOMMODATIONS
Albergo Casa Petrarca, **18**
Albergo San Samuele, **19**
Hotel Galleria, **23**
Hotel Locanda Fiorita, **20**
Locanda Cà Foscari, **16**
Foresteria Valdese, **14**
Laconda Silva, **30**

NIGHTLIFE
Piccolo Mondo, **22**
Bacaro Jazz, **1**
Blues Bar, **33**
Sotta Sopra, **34**

FOOD
Le Bistrot de Venise, **17**
Cip Ciap, **12**
La Boutique del Gelato, **9**
Cantinone Gia Schiavi, **31**

Antica Birraria La
    Corte, **32**
Frary's, **7**
Osteria Alle
    Testiere, **13**
Rosticceria San
    Bartolomeo, **8**
Vino, Vino, **21**
Osteria da Rioba, **24**
Trattoria del Fiore, **35**

Vaporetti Stops

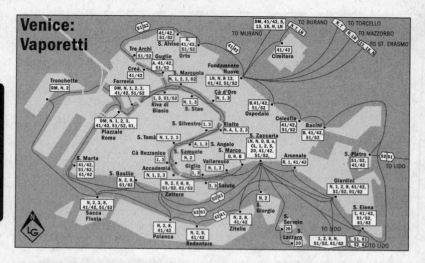

Venice: Vaporetti

MAIN VAPORETTO LINES
V #2, 4: Run from P. S. Marco, up the Giudecca Canal, to the station, down the Grand Canal, back to P. S. Marco, and then to Lido. Always crowded, with long lines.
V #1: Has a similar route to #2, but stays on the Grand Canal, skips Giudecca, and makes more local stops. Also 10min. slower than #2 but less crowded.
V #41, 42, 51, 52: Circumnavigate Venice. #41 and 51 run from the station to San Michele, Murano and Giudecca, ending up back at the station. #42 and 52 follow the same route in the opposite direction.
V #LN: Runs from F. Nove to Murano, Burano, and Lido with connections to Torcello.

Car Rental: Expressway, P. Roma 496/N (☎041 52 23 000; www.expressway.it). From €65 per day (€45 for smaller cars), €285 per week. Free car delivery to and from airport. 18+, with added insurance charge for those under 21. Open daily 7:30am-7pm. *Let's Go* discount 15%. AmEx/MC/V. **Hertz,** P. Roma 496/F (☎041 52 84 091; fax 52 00 614). From €93 per day (€72 without insurance). Credit card required. 25+. Open M-F 8am-6pm, Sa-Su 8am-1pm. AmEx/MC/V.

Parking: Piazza Roma (☎041 27 27 301) and island of Tronchetto (☎041 52 07 555; asm@asmvenezia.it). €24 per day. 24hr. Parking is considerably cheaper on the mainland. Consider parking in Mestre (1st train stop out of Venice).

🛈 PRACTICAL INFORMATION

TOURIST AND FINANCIAL SERVICES

Tourist Services:

APT Tourist Offices are located all over the city. Avoid the train station office, as it is always packed. **Branches:** P. Roma (☎041 24 11 499; open daily 9:30am-1pm and 1:30-4:30pm; AmEx/MC/V); P. S. Marco 71/F, directly opposite the Basilica (☎/fax 041 52 98 711 open daily 9am-3:30pm; AmEx/MC/V); Lido, Gran Viale 6/A (☎041 52 65 721; open daily June-Sept. 9am-noon and 3-6pm). Every location offers pricey city tours, *vaporetto* tickets, the **Rolling Venice Card**, city maps and guides (€2.50), and theater and concert tickets. Ask for the magazine *Leo* or visit www.turismovenezia.com for info on history, sights, and activities.

VeneziaSi (☎041 522 2264; www.veneziasi.it info@veneziasi.it), in train station, to right of tourist office. Finds available hotel rooms and makes same-day reservations in Venice and Rome (€2). Open daily 8am-9pm. **Branches** at P. Roma (☎041 52 28 640) and airport (☎041 54 15 133). Also book rooms (€2); call (instead of going in person), to avoid a charge for booking.

Rolling Venice Card: Provides discounts at over 200 restaurants, cafes, hotels, museums, and shops for those aged 14-29. Tourist offices has a list of participating vendors. (€4; valid for 1 year.) A 3-day *vaporetto* pass with card discount saves €9. Purchase it at the **ACTV VeLa** office (☎041 27 47 650), in P. Roma, at all APT tourist offices, and at ACTV VeLa kiosks next to the Ferrovia, Rialto, S. Marco, and Vallaresso *vaporetto* stops. Open daily 7am-8pm.

Budget Travel: CTS, Fondamenta Tagliapietra, Dorsoduro 3252 (☎041 52 05 660; www.cts.it). From Campo S. Barnaba, cross bridge closest to the church and follow the road through the small *piazza*, then turn left at the foot of the large bridge. Sells ISICs (€10) and discounted plane tickets. Open M-F 9:30am-1:30pm and 2:30-6pm. MC/V.

Consulates: UK consulate in Mestre, Ple. Donatori di Sangue 2 (☎041 50 55 990). Closest **US** (☎02 29 03 51) and **Australian** (☎02 77 70 41) consulates in Milan; **Canadian** consulate (☎049 87 64 33) in Padua.

Currency Exchange: Use banks whenever possible for best rates, and inquire about additional fees beforehand. The streets around San Marco, San Polo, and the train station are full of banks and **ATMs.** Note that banks close Sa-Su in Venice.

American Express: Calle San Moisè, San Marco 1471 (toll free ☎800 87 2000 for lost or stolen checks). Exit P. S. Marco facing away from the basilica and walk 2min. **Currency exchange** available. Open M-F 9am-1pm and 2-5:30pm.

LOCAL SERVICES

Luggage Storage: At the train station. €3.80 for 1st 5hr., €0.60 per hr. up to 12hr., €0.20 thereafter. Open daily 6am-midnight. Cash only. Maximum of 5 days and 20 kg weight limit. **Deposito Pullman Bar,** P. Roma 497/M (☎041 52 31 107). €3.50 per day. Open daily 6am-9pm. Cash only.

English-Language Bookstore: Libreria Studium, San Marco 337/C (☎/fax 041 52 22 382). From P. S. Marco, turn left on Calle delle Canonico between the basilica and the clock tower; it's the last shop on the right. Rolling Venice discount 10%. Open M-Sa 9am-7:30pm, Su 9:30am-1:30pm. AmEx/MC/V.

Laundromats: Speedy Wash, Calle dei Colori, Cannaregio 1520. Wash €6-8, dry €3 for 15min. Detergent €1. Purchase a key next door at Planet Internet for a 30% discount. Open daily 8am-10pm.

Public Toilets: AMAV W.C. Under white and blue signs. €1. Open daily 8:30am-8:45pm.

Disabled travelers: Informa Handicap (☎041 27 48 144) offers assistance to physically disabled and hearing-impaired travelers in Italy. Free Braille maps. Open Th 9am-1pm and 3-5pm. APT tourist office provides a list of wheelchair-accessible lodgings in Venice. Pick up a free map of the city outlining wheelchair-friendly routes in each *sestiere*, keys for wheelchair lifts at the bridges. V #1 is wheelchair-accessible.

EMERGENCY AND COMMUNICATIONS

Carabinieri: 112 Campo San Zaccaria, Castello 4693/A. Questura, Fondamenta S. Lorenzo, Castello 5056.

Pharmacy: Farmacia Italo-Inglese, Calle della Mandola, San Marco 3717 (☎041 52 24 837). Follow Calle Cortesia out of Campo Manin. There are no 24hr. pharmacies in Venice, but late-night and weekend pharmacies rotate hours. After-hours rotations posted outside. Open M-Sa 9am-1:30pm and 2:30-7:30pm. AmEx/MC/V.

Hospital: Ospedale Civile, Campo Giovanni e Paolo Santissimi, Castello (☎041 52 94 111).

Internet Access:

ABColor, Lista di Spagna, Cannaregio 220 (☎041 52 44 380; www.abcolor.it). Look for the "@" symbol on yellow sign, left off the main street heading from train station. Regular rate €6 per hr.; students €4 per hr. For longer than 5hr., purchase an Internet card at €3 per hr. Printing €0.20 per page. CD burning (€4) and international calls available. Open daily 10am-10pm. Cash only.

Internet Station, Cannaregio 5641. Just over the bridge from C. Apostoli. €4 per 30min., €7 per hr. 20% discount for students with ID. Open M-F and Su 10am-10pm, Sa 10am-8pm. Cash only.

VeNice, Lista di Spagna, Cannaregio 149 (☎041 27 58 217; www.ve-nice.com) has fax, webcams, and CD burning (€5). 20% discount for Venetian students. International calling cards are available. €4.50 per 30min., €8 per hr. Printing €0.35 per page. Open daily 9am-11pm. MC/V over €10.

Internet Point San Stefano, Campo San Stefano, San Marco 2967 and 2958 (☎041 52 20 402). €8 per hr., 33% discount with ISIC or Rolling Venice. Open daily 10am-midnight. MC/V.

Post Office: Poste Venezia Centrale, Salizada Fontego dei Tedeschi, San Marco 5554 (☎041 24 04 158), off Campo S. Bartolomeo. *Fermoposta* at window #16. Open M-F 8:30am-6:30pm, Sa 8:30am-1pm. **Postal Codes:** 30121 (Cannaregio), 30122 (Castello), 30123 (Dorsoduro), 30124 (San Marco), 30125 (San Polo), 30135 (Santa Croce).

ACCOMMODATIONS AND CAMPING

Unsurprisingly, Venetian hotels can break the bank, but savvy travelers can find cheap alternatives, especially during the low season. Agree on a price before booking and reserve at least one month ahead, especially in summer.

SAN MARCO

Surrounded by designer boutiques, souvenir stands, scores of restaurants, practically domesticated pigeons, and many of Venice's most popular sights, these lodgings are pricey options for those in search of Venice's showy side.

Albergo San Samuele, Salizada S. Samuele, San Marco 3358 (☎041 52 28 045; www. albergosansamuele.it). Follow C. delle Botteghe from Campo Santo Stefano and turn left on Salizada San Samuele. Spacious and simple rooms on a quiet street 10min. from P. S. Marco. Breakfast (€5) served 5min. away at Ribo Restaurant. Free Wi-Fi. 24hr. reception. Reserve 1-2 months ahead. Singles with shared bath €45-65; doubles €65-85, with bath €85-120. Check website for special deals. AmEx/MC/V. ❸

Albergo Casa Petrarca, C. Schiavine, San Marco 4386 (☎041 52 00 430; www.casape-trarca.com). From Campo San Luca, follow C. Fuseri; take 2nd left, and then turn right. Cheerful, English-speaking owner keeps 7 sunny rooms, most with bath and A/C. Breakfast included. Singles €95; doubles €125-135. Extra bed €35. Cash only. ❺

Hotel Locanda Fiorita, Campiello Nuovo, San Marco 3457/A (☎041 52 34 754; www. locandafiorita.com). From Campo S. Stefano, take C. del Pestrin and climb onto the raised *campiello*. Elegant rooms with flatscreen TV, phone, bath or shower, free Wi-Fi, and A/C in a quiet courtyard with small garden. Breakfast included. Reception 24hr. Singles €110-140; doubles €145-165. Extra bed €20. AmEx/MC/V. ❺

CANNAREGIO

The area around the Lista de Spagna has excellent budget options. Though it requires a 20min. *vaporetto* ride or a 15-25min. walk to most sights, the proximity to the train station and bustling nightlife make it a good home base.

Alloggi Gerotto Calderan, Campo San Geremia, Cannaregio 283 (☎041 71 55 62 or 041 71 53 61; www.283.it). From the train station, turn left on Lista di Spagna; continue for 5min. until you reach C.S. Geremia. Half hostel, half hotel with accommodating owner in a great location. All rooms have bath. Internet access €4 per hr. Wi-Fi available. Check-in 2pm. Check-out 10am. Lock-out for dorms 10:30am-2pm. Curfew 1am. 4- to

6-person dorms €23-25; singles €35-65; doubles €50-90; triples €75-105. Rolling Venice discount 10%; rates lowered with extended stay. Cash only. ❷

Hotel Marte & Biasin, Ponte delle Guglie, Cannaregio 338-1252 (☎041 71 63 51; www.hotelmarteebiasin.com). From train station, turn left and follow Lista di Spagna until you reach Campo S. Geremia. Cross the bridge; hotel is on the corner. Canal location just 5min. from the train station makes this hotel a steal. Large rooms with cheery decor, TV, A/C, minibar, safe and phone. Breakfast included. Singles €25-50, with bath €50-85; doubles €40-60/60-100; triples €60-80/75-120; quads €80-100/100-140; quints €90-110/110-150. 5% student discount. AmEx/MC/V. ❷

Hotel Arcadia, Cannaregio 1333/D (☎041 717 355 www.hotelarcadia.net). Housed in a 17th-century palace, this hotel offers luxurious rooms 5min. from the train station. Rooms are equipped with private baths, TV, and safe. Singles €25-80; doubles €40-120; triples €60-150; quads €80-160. Rates vary seasonally. MC/V. ❷

Hotel Bernardi-Semenzato, C. dell'Oca, Cannaregio 4366 (☎041 52 27 257; www.hotelbernardi.com). From V: Cà d'Oro, go right on Strada Nuova, left on C. del Duca, and right on C. dell'Oca. Sunny hallways and large, elegantly furnished rooms all with A/C and TV, some with private bath. Breakfast included. Free Internet access. Check-out 10:30am. Reception open 7am-midnight. Singles €35; doubles €80-95 (with bath); quads €120-130. Rolling Venice discount 10% on larger rooms. AmEx/MC/V. ❸

SAN POLO AND SANTA CROCE

In the heart of western Venice, these neighborhoods hug the city's winding river, providing easy *vaporetto* access to the city's sights.

Domus Civica (ACISJF), Campiello Chiovere Frari, San Polo 3082 (☎041 72 11 03; www.domuscivica.com). From train station, cross Ponte Scalzi, and turn right. Turn left on Fondamenta dei Tolentini and left through the courtyard on Corte Amai; hostel is to the right after the bridge. Amusing owner offers rooms with shared bath and common TV room. Free Internet access. Reception 7am-12:30am. Strict curfew 12:30am. Open June-Sept. 25. Singles €35, €31.50 with Rolling Venice, €27 ISIC and students under 26; doubles €30/27/24 per person. AmEx/MC/V. ❸

Casa Peron, Salizada S. Pantalon, Santa Croce 84 (☎041 71 00 21 or 041 71 10 38; www.casaperon.com). From train station, cross Ponte Scalzi, turn right, and then left before the bridge; continue down Fondamente Minotto. Casa Peron is on the left. Lace-accented lobby with English-speaking receptionist. Modest but cozy rooms. Some have bath and A/C. Breakfast included. Reception until 1am. Single with shared bath €50; doubles €85, with bath €100; triples €100/120. V. ❹

DORSODURO

Situated near the Grand Canal between Chiesa dei Frari and Ponte Accademia, this *sestiere* is home to many pricey hotels. Spartan facades line the canals that trace Dorsoduro's quiet streets. Art museums here draw visitors to canal-front real estate, while the interior remains a little-visited residential quarter surrounding Campo Santa Margherita, the city's most vibrant student social hub.

Pensione Seguso, Fondamente Zattere ai Saloni, Dorsoduro 779 (☎041 52 86 858; www.pensioneseguso.it). From V: Zattere, walk right. Right on the canal. Antique decor. Breakfast included; half- and full-pension available. Reception open 8am-9pm. Singles €40-122, with bath €50-160; doubles €65-180/70-190; triples €150-235/160-245; quads €190-255. Prices vary seasonally; closed Dec. and Feb. AmEx/MC/V. ❺

Locanda Cà Foscari, Calle della Frescada, Dorsoduro 3887/B (☎041 71 04 01; www.locandacafoscari.com), in a quiet neighborhood. From V: San Tomà, turn left at the dead end, cross the bridge, turn right, then turn left at the alley. Carnevale masks embellish this tidy hotel, which offers basic rooms, some with private bath. Breakfast included. Reception 24hr. Reserve 2-3 months ahead. Singles €60-70; doubles €80-100; triples €110-130; quads €130. Prices vary greatly with season, length of stay, and availability. Minimum 2 night stay on weekends. Check online for deals. AmEx/MC/V. ❺

Hotel Galleria, Rio Terrà Antonio Foscarini, Dorsoduro 878/A (☎041 52 32 489; www.hotelgalleria.it), on the left facing the Accademia museum. Hardwood floors and stunning Grand Canal views lend an aura of elegance. Breakfast included. Reception 24hr. Singles €85; doubles €115-130, with bath €140; large doubles €175-185. Extra bed 30% surcharge. Cash only; confirm reservation with credit card. ❺

CASTELLO

Castello, where most locals live, is arguably the prettiest part of Venice. A 2nd-or 3rd-floor room with a view of the sculpted skyline is worth the confusion of navigating some of the city's narrowest and most tightly clustered streets.

La Residenza, Campo Bandiera e Moro, Castello 3608 (☎041 52 85 315; www.venicelaresidenza.com). From V: Arsenal, turn left on Riva degli Schiavoni and right on C. del Dose into the campo. Great location 5min. from P. S. Marco. Lavish carpets and paintings and a sunny terrace overlooking the *campo* greet guests in this renovated 15th-century *palazzo*. Spacious and elegantly furnished rooms with TV, A/C, private bathroom, safe, and minibar make for a regal stay. Breakfast included. Free Wi-Fi. Reception 24hr. Singles €50-100; doubles €80-180. Extra bed €35. MC/V. ❹

Foresteria Valdese, Castello 5170 (☎041 52 86 797; www.diaconiavaldese.org/venezia). From Campo Santa Maria Formosa, take Calle Lunga Santa Maria Formosa; it's over the 1st bridge. An 18th-century house with 75 beds run by a Protestant church. Excellent location. Breakfast included. Internet access €5 per hr. Lockout 10am-1pm. Reception 9am-1pm and 6-8pm. Reservations required for bedrooms, though not possible for dorms. Dorms €24 for 1-night stays, €22 otherwise; doubles with bath €78-82, with kitchen €82-86; triples €90-96, with bath €96-102; quads with bath €114-122, quints with bath €132-142. Apartments €104. Rolling Venice discount €1. MC/V. ❷

Albergo Doni, C. del Vin, Castello 4656 (☎041 52 24 267; www.albergodoni.it). From P. San Marco, turn left immediately after the 2nd bridge on C. del Vin and stay left when the street splits. Cheery staff, headed by proprietress Annabella, and proximity to P. San Marco make this hotel an amazing deal. A rickety staircase leads to lovely rooms with antique decor and furnishing. Many come with private bathroom and fan or A/C. Breakfast included. Reception 24hr. Singles €45-65 (without bath); doubles €70-95, with bath €80-120. Discount with cash payment. MC/V. ❸

Locanda Silva, Fondamenta del Rimedio, Castello 4423 (☎041 52 27 643 or 52 37 892; www.locandasilva.it). From P. S. Marco, walk under clock tower, turn right on C. Larga S. Marco, and left on C. de l'Anzolo before the bridge. Head right on C. del Rimedio before next bridge; follow to the end. Rustic rooms with exposed beams and a sunny 18th-century breakfast room near P. San Marco overlooking the canal. Reception 24hr. Singles €35-60, with bath €50-80; doubles €60-85, with bath €70-100, with shower €80-126; triples €110-150; quads €130-160. MC/V. ❸

Hotel Casa Linger, Salizada Sant'Antonin, Castello 3541 (☎041 52 85 920; www.hotelcasalinger.com). From San Marco follow Riva degli Schiavoni until you reach C. del Dose; turn left and continue until you reach C. Bandiera e Moro. Walk until you hit S. Sant'Antonin; hotel is on the right. Large, simple rooms are sunny and clean, and come with great views. Some have TV and private bath. Reception 24hr. Singles €40-80, with bath €60-100; doubles €60-90/80-100; rooms with kitchen and bathroom (max. 7 people) €25-35 per person. AmEx/MC/V. ❸

Antica Locanda Casa Verardo, Castello 4765 (☎041 52 86 127; www.casaverardo.it). From the basilica, take C. Canonica, turn right before bridge and left over the bridge on Ruga Giuffa into Campo Santi Filippo e Giacomo. Follow C. della Chiesa left out of the *campo* until the bridge. Housed in a national monument, this 16th-century hotel's mosaic floors make travelers feel like Venetian royalty. Private courtyard, lounge, and terraces overlook the canal. Rooms with A/C, safe, minibar, and TV. Buffet breakfast and Internet access included. Singles €60-180; doubles €75-360; junior suites €110-650. Extra bed €15-60. Discount for web reservations or cash payment. AmEx/MC/V. ❹

GIUDECCA

Separated from Venice's center by the 400m-wide Giudecca canal, this neighborhood is often forgotten by tourists. It will take about 5-10min. by *vaporetto* to reach Venice proper from the island of Giudecca, where travelers looking for a peaceful respite from tourist hordes will be rewarded by quiet streets. Remember to factor in transportation costs to and from the city center.

Ostello di Venezia (HI), Fondamenta Zitelle, Giudecca 87 (☎041 52 38 211; www. ostellovenezia.it). Take V: #41, 42, 2, or N to Zitelle. Turn right along canal; the hostel is 3min. down on the left. This efficiently managed hostel has 270 beds in dorms for 4-6 guests with adjacent bathrooms, a restaurant, and sweeping city views. Breakfast included; other meals €10. Internet €3.50 per hr. Lockers €3.50. Reception 7-9:30am and 1:30pm-midnight. Lock-out 9:30am-1:30pm. Curfew 1:30am. Reserve through website. Dorms €21. HI members only. MC/V. ❷

CAMPING

While the low cost of camping is appealing, take into account that you'll be paying for pricey transportation to and from Venice (about €13-16 per day, €31 for 3 days), which may cost more than just staying in the city. Plan on at least a 40min. commute to Venice. In addition to this campground, the Litorale del Cavallino, on the Lido's Adriatic side, has multiple beach campsites.

Camping Miramare, Lungomare Dante Alighieri 29 (☎041 96 61 50; www.camping-miramare.it). A 40min. ride on V: #LN from P. S. Marco to Punta Sabbioni. 700m along the beach on the right. Handicapped facilities. Reception open 8am-9pm. Check-out 10am. During high season, min. 2-night stay in campground, 5 nights for bungalows. Open Mar.-Nov. €4.70-7.20 per person, €9.60-15 per tent. Bungalows €30-70 plus camping charge per person. Rolling Venice discount 15% with cash payment. MC/V. ❶

🖸 FOOD

In Venice, authentic dining may require a search, since many of the best restaurants lie in less-traveled areas. Avoid restaurants near major sights; they're typically overpriced and inauthentic. Naturally, Venetian cuisine is dominated by fish. *Sarde in saor* (sardines in vinegar and onions) is available only in Venice and can be sampled at most bars and *enoteche* with *cicchetti* (Venetian appetizers similar to *tapas*). The Veneto and Friuli regions produce many wines. Local whites include *prosecco della marca*, the dry *tocai*, and *bianco di custoza*. For reds, try *valpolicella*. The least expensive option is by no means inferior: a simple *vino della casa* (house wine) is usually a fine local merlot or chardonnay. For informal alternatives to traditional dining, visit an *osteria* or *bacaro* for pastries, seafood, or *tramezzini* (bread with any delicious filling).

Venice's Rialto **markets,** once the center of trade for the Venetian Republic, spread between the Grand Canal and the San Polo foot of the Rialto every morning from Monday to Saturday. Smaller produce markets are set up in Cannaregio, on Rio Terà San Leonardo by Ponte delle Guglie, and in many of the city's *campi*. The **BILLA** supermarket, Strada Nuova, Cannaregio 5660, has groceries and a small bakery and deli near Campo San Fosca. (Open M-Sa 8:30am-8:30pm, Su 9am-8:30pm. AmEx/MC/V.) A **Punto** supermarket is at Campo Santa Margherita 5017. (☎041 52 26 780. Open M-Sa 7:30am-8pm. MC/V.)

SAN MARCO

▨ **Trattoria da Fiore,** Santo Stefano 3461, San Marco (☎041 52 35 310; www.trattoriadafiore.com). Neighbors claim this is the only true *bacaro* left in San Marco. Serves a simple menu with wine (from €2 per glass) and tasty *cicchetti* (from €0.50). Try *spaghetti pinoli* with fresh tomatoes and basil (€10). Brush up on your Italian; this place is filled with locals. Plates €9-15. Open M and W-Su 8:30am-12:30am. Cash only. ❷

Vino, Vino, Ponte delle Veste, San Marco 2007/A (☎041 24 17 688). From C. Larga XXII Marzo, turn on C. delle Veste. Jazz plays quietly as guests sip wine (€4.50-11) and enjoy delicate Venetian dishes like salmon with peppers, capers, and ginger (€14.50). Wine list has over 350 vintages. Pasta €8-11.50. Fish and meat €13-16.50. Cover €2. Open M and W-Su 11:30am-11:30pm. Cash only. ❷

Rosticceria San Bartolomeo, C. della Bissa, San Marco 5424/A (☎/fax 041 52 23 569). From Campo S. Bartolomeo, follow the C. de la Bissa to the neon sign. A haven for weary tourists, the *rosticceria* serves food upstairs in its full-service restaurant and downstairs in the laid-back cafe. Try the famous fried mozzarella with prosciutto (€1.50). Wide selection of *tramezzini* (€1-1.50). Pizza €5.80-11. Primi €6-8. Secondi €8.50-15.50. Upstairs cover €2. Open daily 9am-9:30pm. AmEx/MC/V. ❸

Le Bistrot de Venise, C. dei Fabbri, San Marco 4685 (☎041 52 36 651; www.bistrotdevenise.com). From P. S. Marco, head through 2nd Sottoportego dei Dai under the awning. Follow road over bridge and turn right. Scrumptious Venetian dishes and over 50 wines, based on medieval and Renaissance recipes. Share the €45 tasting *menù* with the table or try dishes like marinated *umbrine* in black grape sauce with yellow garlic and almond pudding (€28). *Enoteca: cicchetti* €3-4, meat/cheese plates €12-24. Restaurant: Primi €18-22. Secondi €28-32. Wine from €5 per glass. Service 12%. Kitchen open daily noon-3pm and 7pm-midnight. Rolling Venice discount 10%. MC/V. ❺

CANNAREGIO

Gam Gam, Canale di Cannaregio, Cannaregio 1122 (☎041 71 52 84). From Campo S. Geremia, cross the bridge and turn left. Canal-side tables and a unique mix of Italian and Jewish cuisines. Try their *Pasticcio Gam Gam* (vegetable lasagna; €9) or their special Israeli appetizer plates (€9.80). Main courses €7.50-15. Kosher. Open M-Th and Su noon-10pm, F noon-4pm. Let's Go discount 10%. Cash only. ❷

Osteria ai Osti, Corte dei Pali Testori, Cannaregio 3849 (☎041 52 07 993). Coming from Campo S. Felice, cross 1st bridge onto Strada Nuova and take 1st left. Laid-back and filled with locals. Serves classic Italian seafood. White stucco walls and low ceilings create a cozy, informal atmosphere as customers enjoy simple dishes like pesto pasta (€7.50) or fresh *cicchetti* (€0.80-4). Primi €6.50-12. Secondi €13-14. Wine €0.70-9. Cover €1. Open M-Sa 9am-3:30pm and 4:15-8pm. ❸

Osteria da Rioba, Fondamenta della Misericordia, Cannaregio 2553 (☎041 52 44 379). Paintings of distant mountains on the walls give this canal-side eatery a far-away feel. Enjoy dishes like eggplant stuffed with ricotta and toasted pine nuts. Salads €8-9. Primi €8-13. Secondi €15-20. Cover €1.50. Open Tu-Su 12:30-2:30pm and 7:30-10:30pm. Call ahead on summer weekends to reserve outdoor seating. AmEx. ❹

Pleasure Cafe, Strada Nuova, Cannaregio 2208 (☎041 09 94 746). From Ca' d'Oro, continue west on Strada Nuova until you reach Campo S. Felice; cafe is practically on the bridge. Tiny *bacaro* and restaurant serves healthful cuisine. Jazz, handwritten menu,

THE VENETO

and artsy decor accompany fresh pasta dishes (€8). Excellent selection of vegetarian plates and salads €8-10. Meat and fish dishes €8-10. Wine €2.50-8.50. Open in summer daily 7am-11pm; winter daily 7am-8:15pm. V. Credit card min. €50. ❷

Trattoria da Bepi, Cannaregio 4550 (☎/fax 041 52 85 031). From Campo S. S. Apostoli, turn left on Salizada del Pistor. Staples like potato *tortelli* with ricotta and spinach (€9) served in a warm atmosphere. Primi €7-12. Secondi €12.50-17. Cover €1.50. Open M-W and F-Su noon-3pm and 7-11pm. Reservations recommended. MC/V. ❸

SAN POLO AND SANTA CROCE

Antica Birraria La Corte, Campo S. Polo, San Polo 2168 (☎041 27 50 570; www.birrarialacorte.it). The expansive interior of this former brewery houses a large restaurant and bar as well as outdoor tables on the peaceful *campo*. Filling salads (€11) hit the spot in the summer heat. Pizza €5.50-9. Primi €10-12. Secondi €13.50-19. Cover €2. Restaurant open daily noon-2:30pm and 7-10:30pm. Pizzeria open summer 10am-midnight; winter 10am-3pm and 9pm-midnight. AmEx/MC/V. ❸

Al Giardinetto, San Toma, 2910 Rio della Frescada (☎ 041 52 24 100; www.algiardinetto.it). From Campo S. Rocco, follow Salizada S. Rocco until Campo S. Toma then cross bridge. Smells of tasty grilled meat waft from the kitchen as the sound of birds from patio cages chirping overhead mingles with loud Italian music. Meat *menù* €6-18. Seafood €12-16. Open daily 11am-3pm and 7:30pm-12:30am. AmEx/MC/V. ❸

Frary's, Fondamenta dei Frari, San Polo 2559 (☎041 72 00 50). Across from entrance to S. Maria Gloriosa dei Frari. Right on the river. Serves Greek and Arab cuisine with many vegetarian options. Try the lunch *menù*, which includes 1 appetizer and 1 main course (€12). Appetizers €4-6. Main courses €8.50-14. Cover €1.50. Open M and W-Su noon-3:15pm and 6-10:30pm. AmEx/MC/V. ❸

Al Nono Risorto, Sotoportego de Siora Bettina, Santa Croce 2338 (☎041 52 41 169). From Ponte Rialto, follow yellow signs for Ple. Roma until you reach Campo S. Cassiano; restaurant is under the bridge. Serves hearty dishes in its casual interior and sunny garden. *Menù* changes weekly to reflect social issues; past themes have included "*menù* of women" and "*menù* of the refuges." Primi €8-9. Secondi €10-15. Pizza €5-9. Cover €1.70. Open M-Tu and Th-Su noon-2:30pm and 7pm-11pm. Cash only. ❸

Osteria Enoteca "Vivaldi," San Polo 1457 (☎041 52 38 185). From the Campo S. Polo, opposite the church, cross the bridge to Calle della Madonnetta. Violins cover the walls of this small neighborhood place. Multilingual menu with fish specials like *bigoli* noodles with anchovies (€10) and some vegetarian dishes. Primi €8-15, secondi €11-24. Cover €1.50. Service 10%. Open M-Tu and Th-Su 11am-2:30pm and 6pm-midnight. AmEx/MC/V. ❸

DORSODURO

▨ Cantinone Gia Schiavi, Fondamenta Meraviglie, Dorsoduro 992 (☎041 52 30 034). From the Frari, follow signs for the Accademia bridge. Just before Ponte Meraviglie, turn toward the Chiesa di San Trovaso. Cross the 1st bridge. Choose from hundreds of wines (€2-5) and dozens of fresh *cicchetti* (€1) with toppings like pumpkin cream in this old *enoteca*. Standing room only. Open M-Sa 8am-11pm, Su 8am-noon. Cash only. ❶

Pizza and Kebab Toletta, Dorsoduro 1215 (☎041 24 13 324). Walk to the south side of C. S. Margherita until you reach Rio Tera della Scoazzera. Turn right onto Rio Tera Canal and then left. Skip overpriced restaurants next to the museums and grab a huge slice (€1.80) or falafel sandwich (€3) at this simple pizzeria just a few blocks away. Pies €3.50-7. Open daily 11am-4pm and 5:30pm-midnight. Cash only. ❶

THE VENETO

CASTELLO

Cip Ciap, C. del Mondo Novo, Castello 5799/A (☎041 52 36 621). From Campo S. Maria Formosa, follow C. del Mondo Novo. Perhaps Venice's best pizzeria for the price. Uses fresh ingredients on Sicilian slices sold by weight (€1.20 per 100g). Their best deals are the huge prosciutto-filled calzones and *margherita* pies (€2.50). No seating; nab a bench in the nearby *campo*. Open M and W-Su 9am-9pm. Cash only. ❶

La Boutique del Gelato, Salizada S. Lio, Castello 5727 (☎041 52 23 283). From Campo Bartolomeo, walk under Sottoportego de la Bissa, then cross the bridge into Campo S. Lio. Follow Salizada S. Lio; *gelateria* is on the left. Tiny *gelateria* dishes up gigantic scoops acclaimed by locals and tourists as Venice's best. 1 scoop €1, 2 scoops €1.70. Open M 10:30am-8pm, T-Su 10:30am-11pm. Cash only. ❶

Osteria Alle Testiere, C. del Mondo Novo, Castello 5801 (☎/fax 041 52 27 220), off Campo S. Maria Formosa. Small restaurant with simple decor and authentic, rich Venetian cuisine. Dishes like ravioli with pistachio and ricotta (€17) are worth the splurge. Primi €17. Secondi €25-26. Open Tu-Sa noon-2pm and 7-9:30pm. Closed Aug. Reservations recommended. MC/V. ❺

Pizzeria/Trattoria Al Vecio Canton, Castello 4738/A (☎041 52 85 176). From Campo S. Maria Formosa, with church on right, cross the bridge and follow Ruga Giuffa. Turn right at the end. A 2-floor local favorite. Try any of the 50+ pizzas, or the *menù veneziano* (€14), which overflows with spaghetti and seafood. Pizza €5.50-10. Primi €8-22. Secondi €12-22. Cover €2. Open M and W-Su 12:30-4pm and 6:30-11pm. MC/V. ❸

SIGHTS

> **TIP**
>
> **ALL FOR ONE AND ONE FOR ALL.** Those planning to visit several museums in Venice should consider investing in a museum pass. Valid for 6 months, the pass grants one-time admission to 10 museums, including those on P. S. Marco, as well as those on the islands of Murano and Burano. It is available at all participating museums and costs €18 or €12 for students and Rolling Venice cardholders. The San Marco Plus pass, valid from April through October, grants access to the Museums of St. Mark's square and one of the museums run by the Musei Civici Veneziani. €13, reduced €7.50.

AROUND PIAZZA SAN MARCO

BASILICA DI SAN MARCO. The **basilica** is the city's most popular tourist attraction—and rightly so. Venice's crown jewel is a spectacular fusion of gold mosaics, marble walls, and rooftop balconies, graced with ultra-realistic mosaic portals and guarded by rooftop winged lions. The long lines move surprisingly quickly; unfortunately, this makes for crowded walkways inside. Visit in the early morning for the shortest wait or in late afternoon for the best natural illumination. Construction of the basilica began in the AD 9th century, when two Venetian merchants stole St. Mark's remains from Alexandria and packed them in pork meat to smuggle them past Arab officials. After the first church dedicated to St. Mark burned down in the 11th century, Venice designed a new basilica, choosing a Greek-cross plan with four arms and five domes instead of the Church's standard cross-shaped layout. A cavernous, eerily quiet interior sparkles with Byzantine and Renaissance mosaics and elaborate gold ornaments. The blue-robed **Christ Pantocrator** (Ruler of All) sits above the high altar. The floor, covered in colorful geometric 12th-century stone mosaics, is a sight unto itself. Behind the altar screen, the rectangular **Pala d'Oro** relief frames a parade of saints in gem-encrusted gold. Within the altar rests the tomb of St. Mark, adorned with a single gold-stemmed rose. Steep stairs lead to the **Galleria della Basilica,** which offers an eye-level view of the tiny golden tiles of the ceiling mosaics, a balcony overlooking the *piazza* below, and an intimate view of the bronze **Cavalli di San Marco** (Horses of St. Mark). Nearby, the **Cassine** displays mosaic heads (the most valuable and artistically challenging section of any masterpiece) removed during 1881 renovations. *(Basilica open M-Sa 9:45am-5pm, Su 2-4pm; illuminated 11:30am-12:30pm. Modest dress required. Baggage prohibited; follow signs to free storage at nearby Ateno San Basso on Calle San Basso; open daily 9:30am-5:30pm. Pala d'Oro and Treasury open in summer M-F 9:45am-5pm, Sa-Su 2-4:30pm, €3; in winter M-F 9:45am-4pm, Sa-Su 2-4pm, €2. Galleria open M-S 9:45am-4:45pm, €4.)*

IT'S A MIRACLE! The foundation for the Churches of Venice sells the **Chorus Pass** that covers admission to all of Venice's churches. A yearly pass (€9, students age 11-29 €6) includes S. Maria dei Miracoli, S. Maria Gloriosa dei Frari, S. Polo, Madonna dell'Orto, Il Redentore, and S. Sebastiano, and is available at participating churches. (For info, ☎041 27 50 462; www.chorusvenezia.org.)

PALAZZO DUCALE (DOGE'S PALACE). Home for eight centuries to the Doge, Venice's mayor, the Palazzo Ducale displays spectacular artwork, including Veronese's *Rape of Europa*. In the courtyard, Sansovino's enormous sculptures, *Mars* and *Neptune*, flank the **Scala dei Giganti** (Stairs of the Giants), upon which new Doges were crowned. On the balcony stands the **Bocca di Leone** (Lion's Mouth), into which the Council of Ten, the Doge's assistants, who also acted as judges and administrators, would drop the names of criminal suspects. Admire the sculptures of Hercules slaying the Hydra and Atlas bearing a brilliant blue, starry world on either side of the elaborate **Scala D'Oro.** From there, climb up to the **Sala delle Quattro Porte** (Room of the Four Doors), whose ceiling is covered in biblical judgments and representations of mythological tales related to events in Venetian history. More doors lead through the courtrooms of the much-feared Council of Ten, the even-more-feared Council of Three, and the **Sala del Maggior Consiglio** (Great Council Room), dominated by Tintoretto's harrowing *Paradise*, the largest oil painting in the world. Near the end, thick stone lattices line the covered **Ponte dei Sospiri** (Bridge of Sighs) and continue into the prisons. The bridge gets its name from 19th-century Romantic writers' references to the mournful groans of prisoners descending into the small, damp cells. The rest of the palace is best enjoyed by getting lost in the endless maze of tunnels. *(☎041 52 09 070; www.museivenezia.it. Open daily Nov.-Mar. 9am-5pm; Apr.-Oct. 9am-7pm. Last entry 1hr. before closing. Wheelchair accessible. €16, students and Rolling Venice cardholders €10, ages 6-14 €3. Includes entrance to P. San Marco museums. Audio tours in multiple languages €5, 2 for €8. Special English tours offered daily 9:55am-12:25pm, every 50min. Book 2 days in advance. MC/V.)*

CHIESA DI SAN ZACCARIA. Dedicated to the father of John the Baptist and designed in the late 1400s by Coducci, the Gothic-Renaissance church holds S. Zaccaria's corpse in an elevated, glass-windowed sarcophagus along the nave's right wall. Nearby, watch for Bellini's *Virgin and Child Enthroned with Four Saints,* one of the masterpieces of the Venetian Renaissance. Ask the custodian for entrance into the 10th-century crypt, which features paintings by Tintoretto and others. *(V: S. Zaccaria. From P. S. Marco, turn left along the water, cross two bridges, and turn left through the tunnel marked "San Zaccaria." ☎041 52 21 257. Open daily 10am-noon and 4-6pm. Church free. Crypt entrance €1.)*

The Chronicle

IN RECENT NEWS

VENICE: IN HOT WATER?

It's hard to picture Venice without water. Images of drifting gondolas, glistening canals, and apartments on stilts lend as much flavor to the city as do its history and cuisine. But ironically, Venice's most essential element has recently become the bane of its existence, causing flooding and pollution in the now "sinking city."

While *la acqua alta* has always been a subject of Venetian concern, debate over how best to handle the situation erupted after a storm left parts of the city under six feet of water, permanently damaging historic buildings and priceless works of art.

The most significant preventative effort currently underway is the MOSE project (Experimental Electromechanical Module), a $5 billion endeavor to protect the city from tides higher than 50 in. By 2012, MOSE hopes to resolve water-related concerns. Meanwhile, it has created a controversy among Venetians, many of whom claim that the issue of flooding is greatly exaggerated. MOSE poses its own consequences for the city as well. The cost of the project has forced many to move out and has halted business growth, and MOSE may cause pollution, damage to biodiversity, and dangerous changes in tidal patterns.

Should the topic arise, try to keep your head above water and remain respectful; you will likely face a cascade of debate.

PIAZZA SAN MARCO. Unlike the rest of Venice's labyrinthine streets, P. S. Marco, Venice's only official *piazza*, is a magnificent expanse of light, space, architectural harmony, and pigeons. Although hordes of photo-snapping tourists jostling each other may be annoying, the *piazza* is certainly worth it: it contains some of the city's best sights. Enclosing the *piazza* are rows of cafes and expensive glass and jewelry shops along the ground floors of the Renaissance **Procuratie Vecchie** (Old Treasury Offices), the Baroque **Procuratie Nuove** (New Treasury Offices), and the Neoclassical **Ala Napoleonica** (more Treasury Offices). At the end of the *piazza* near the shoreline of the lagoon sits the **Basilica di San Marco** (see p. 320), where mosaics and marble horses overlook the chaos below. Between the basilica and the Procuratie Vecchie perches the **Torre dell'Orologio** (Clock Tower), constructed between 1496 and 1499, according to Coducci's design. The 24hr. clock indicates the hour, lunar phase, and ascending constellation. A 96m brick **campanile** provides one of the best elevated views of the city. Though it originally served as a watchtower and lighthouse, cruel and unusual Venice took advantage of its location to create medieval entertainment by dangling state prisoners in cages from its top. The practice ceased in the 18th century, but public tower fascination did not. The *campanile* collapsed during a 1902 restoration project, but was reconstructed in 1912 with the enlightened addition of an elevator. (☎041 52 25 205. Campanile open daily May-Oct. 9am-9pm; Nov.-Apr. 9:30am-4:15pm. €8. Audio tour €3.)

MUSEUMS OF PIAZZA SAN MARCO. Beneath the arcade at the short end of P. S. Marco lies the entrance to a trio of museums. The **Museo Civico Correr,** a Venetian history museum, fills most of the two-story complex with curiosities from the city's imperial past, including naval maps and models, ornate Neoclassical artwork, and weapons, like a 16th-century key that fires poison darts. Highlights of the collection include Antonio Canova's sculptures *Winged Cupid* and *Daedalus and Icarus* in the first room. Near the end of the first floor, the **Museo Archeologico** houses a sizable collection of ancient pieces, from first-century Egyptian funeral parchment to Greek and Roman sculptures. A series of ceiling paintings by seven artists, including some from Verona, adorn the dark gilded reading room of the **Biblioteca Nazionale Marciana,** built between 1537 and 1560. (☎041 52 24 951. Museums open daily Apr.-Oct. 9am-7pm; Nov.-Mar. 9am-5pm. Last entry 1hr. before closing.)

Either purchase museum pass (€18, students €12) or a single ticket (€12). Ticket also includes entrance to the Doge's Palace and all 3 museums.)

LA SCALA DEL BOVOLO. This marble "staircase of the snails," as it translates into English, takes guests up five stories of tightly spiraling marble loggia to a circular portico at the top. Legend has it the staircase was designed by Leonardo da Vinci. Once leading to a now-destroyed palace, today the top affords views of the green courtyard below as well as an eye-level view of red rooftops and the distant domes of S. Marco. *(From the Campo Manin, facing the bridge, turn left down the alley, and look for the signs. ☎ 041 53 22 920. Closed for renovations until 2009.)*

AROUND THE RIALTO BRIDGE

◼**THE GRAND CANAL.** Over 3km long, the Grand Canal loops through the city and passes under three bridges: **Ponte Scalzi, Ponte Rialto,** and **Ponte Accademia.** (There are discussions of building a fourth bridge, but local politics have stalled the plan.) Coursing past the facades of cheek-to-cheek palaces that crown their banks, the blue-green waters are a constant reminder of Venice's history and immense wealth. Although each *palazzo* displays its own unique architectural blend of loggia, canal-side balconies, and marble sculptures, most share the same basic structural design. The most decorated floors, called *piani nobili* (noble floors, or 2nd and 3rd stories), housed luxurious salons and bedrooms. Rich merchant families stored their goods in the ground-floor rooms, and servants slept in tiny chambers below the roof. At night the facades are illuminated, producing a dazzling display of reflections. The candy-cane—called *bricole*—posts used for mooring boats on the *canalare* are painted with the family colors of the adjoining *palazzo*. *(For great facade views, ride V #2 or the slower #1 from the train station to P. S. Marco. For the best public canal views open to the public, visit Collezione Peggy Guggenheim or Ca Rezzonico.)*

RIALTO BRIDGE. Named after Rivo Alto, the first Venetian colony, the bridge's wood original collapsed in the 1500s. Antonio da Ponte designed the present-day stone structure, where strips of boutiques separate a wide central lane from two side passages. Don't expect to see much during the day, however, as camera-toting, souvenir-happy tourists will do everything in their power to stand between you and the picture-perfect views. Expensive stores also dominate the bridge, but unauthorized vendors selling overpriced, cheaply made goods manage to find their way onto the thoroughfare as well.

CANNAREGIO

JEWISH GHETTO. In 1516, the Doge forced Venice's Jewish population into the old cannon-foundry area, creating the first Jewish ghetto in Europe. (*Ghetto* is the Venetian word for foundry.) At its height, the ghetto housed 5000 people in buildings up to seven stories high, making them among the tallest European tenements at the time. Now, locals gather in this sequestered spot for the tranquility of the **Campo del Ghetto Nuovo,** where delicious smells from nearby local bakeries inevitably waft. In the *campo*, the **Schola Grande Tedesca** (German Synagogue), the oldest synagogue in the area, now houses the **Museo Ebraica di Venezia** (Hebrew Museum of Venice). In the adjacent Campiello delle Scuole stand the opulent **Schola Levantina** (Levantine Synagogue) and **Schola Spagnola** (Spanish Synagogue), both designed at least in part by Longhena. The Canton and Italian synagogues also occupy the area. *(Cannaregio 2899/B. V: S. Marcuola. Follow signs straight, then turn left into Campo del Ghetto Nuovo. ☎ 041 71 53 59. Hebrew Museum open M-F and Su June-Sept. 10am-7pm last entrance 5pm; Oct.-May 10am-4:30pm. 40min. Eng-*

lish and Italian tours leave from the museum every hr. June-Sept. 10:30am-5:30pm; Oct.-May 10:30am-4:30pm. €3, students €2. Museum and tour €8.50, students €7. MC/V.)

CHIESA DELLA MADONNA DELL'ORTO. Tintoretto's 14th-century church on the city's northern tip, the painter's final resting place, contains 10 of his largest paintings as well as some works by Titian. Look for Tintoretto's *Last Judgment*, a spatially intense mass of souls, and *The Sacrifice of the Golden Calf*, near the high altar. The right apse holds the brilliantly nuanced *Presentation of the Virgin at the Temple*. To illuminate the works, use light switches at each of the far corners. *(V: Madonna dell'Orto. ☎ 041 27 50 462; www.chorusvenezia.org. Open M-Sa 10am-5pm. Last entry 4:45pm. Included in the Chorus Pass. €3. Cash only.)*

CHIESA DEI GESUITI. Founded in the 12th century and reconstructed in the 18th, Dei Gesuiti features a gilt-rimmed stucco ceiling with painted portals to heaven. Exterior columns open onto a sea of marble that stretches from the floor to the realistic stone curtain in the pulpit. Titian's *Martyrdom of Saint Lawrence* hangs in the altar to the left of the entrance, while Tintoretto's lighter *Assumption of the Virgin* shows Mary, Heaven-bound. *(V: Fondamenta Nuove 4885; turn right, then left on Sala dei Specchieri. Open daily 10am-noon and 4-6pm. Free.)*

CÀ D'ORO. Built between 1421 and 1440, this "Golden House" houses the **Galleria Giorgio Franchetti.** Highlights include Andrea Mantegna's *Saint Sebastian* (temporarily out for restoration) in the small chapel on the first floor, Bonaccio's *Apollo Belvedere* (one of the 15th century's most important bronzes), several Bernini sculptures and Titian frescoes on the second floor, and two balconies above the Grand Canal. Don't miss the back courtyard, which contains a stunning mosaic floor designed by Baron Giorgio Franchetti. Take in the best view of the balconies and Cà d'Oro's tiered "wedding cake" facade from a *traghetto* crossing the canal toward the Rialto Markets. *(V: Cà d'Oro. ☎ 041 52 03 652; www.cadoro.org. Open M 8:15am-2pm, Tu-Su 8:15am-7:15pm. Last entry 30min. before closing. €5, EU students and EU citizens age 18-25 €2.50, EU citizens under 18 and over 65 and art students free. Audio tour €4, 2 for €6. Cash only.)*

SAN POLO

▨**BASILICA DI SANTA MARIA GLORIOSA DEI FRARI.** Even if churches aren't your thing, this Venetian marvel is worth it. The all-star collection of paintings, looming sculptures, and dangling chandeliers will awe any visitor. Franciscans began construction on the Gothic church, also known as *I Frari*, in 1340. Today, the cavernous gray interior boasts two Titian paintings as well as the corpse of the Renaissance master himself, who is entombed within the cathedral's cavernous terra-cotta walls. His ▨**Assumption** (1516-18), on the high altar, marks the height of the Venetian Renaissance. Titian's other work, *The Madonna and Child with Saints and Members of the Pesaro Family* (1547), is on the left from the entrance. Titian's elaborate tomb, a lion-topped triumphal arch with bas-relief scenes of Paradise, lies directly across from the enormous pyramid where the sculptor Canova (1757-1822) rests. Donatello's gaunt wooden sculpture, ▨**St. John the Baptist** (1438), stands framed in gold in the Florentine chapel to the right of the high altar. *(V: S. Tomà. Follow signs back to Campo dei Frari. ☎ 041 27 28 618; www.basilicadeifrari.it. Open M-Sa 9am-6pm, Su 1-6pm. Last entry 30min. before closing. Included in the Chorus Pass. €3. Audio guide €3. Cash only.)*

CHIESA DI SAN GIACOMO DI RIALTO (SAN POLO). Smack in the middle of the chaos between the Rialto and the surrounding markets, Venice's first church, diminutively called "San Giacometto," is remarkably peaceful. An ornate clock-face adorns its *campanile*. Across the *piazza*, a statue called *Il Gobbo* (The

Hunchback) supports the steps, once used for public announcements. It was at the foot of this sculpture that convicted thieves could finally collapse after being forced to run naked—chased by spectators along the way—from P. S. Marco. *(V: Rialto. Cross bridge and turn right. Church open M-Sa 10am-5pm. Free.)*

SCUOLA GRANDE DI SAN ROCCO. The most illustrious of Venice's *scuole*, or guild halls, is a monument to Jacopo Tintoretto, who left Venice only once in his 76 years, and who sought to combine the techniques of Titian and Michelangelo. Tintoretto's works are scattered all over the city, but most are concentrated here. The school commissioned Tintoretto to complete all the paintings in the building, a task that took 23 years. The large room on the second floor provides hand mirrors to admire the delicate paintings mounted on the ceiling, but the wall-to-wall *Crucifixion* in the last room upstairs is the collection's crowning glory. Lined with intricately carved columns and colored marble, the *scuola* is a masterpiece in itself; step outside to admire it amid the din of street musicians. *(Behind Basilica dei Frari in Campo S. Rocco. ☎ 041 52 34 864; www.scuolagrandesanrocco.it. Open daily Apr.-Oct. 9am-5:30pm; Nov.-Mar. 10am-4pm. Last entry 30min. before closing. €7; students, under 26, and Junior Rolling Venice cardholders €5; under 18 free with parents. Audio tour in Spanish, English, and German free. AmEx/MC/V.)*

CAMPO SAN POLO. The second largest *campo* in Venice, Campo San Polo is quiet and devoid of crowds. It was once host to bull-baiting matches during *Carnevale*, when a wild bull was released into the crowds, dogs at its tail. After the dogs began tearing at the bull's flesh, the animal would be decapitated before a cheering mob. A painting depicting the chaos hangs in the **Museo Correr** in P. S. Marco. Fortunately, modern visits generally involve less bloodshed; instead, visitors usually enjoy a drink or meal at a nearby cafe. *(V: S. Silvestro. Straight back from the vaporetto. Or from in front of the Frari, cross bridge, then turn right, left on Rio Terà, right on Seconda Calle dei Saoneri, and left at the end.)*

DORSODURO

▓COLLEZIONE PEGGY GUGGENHEIM. Guggenheim's elegant waterfront **Palazzo Venier dei Leoni,** once Guggenheim's home and a social haven for the world's artistic elite, now displays a private modern collection maintained by the Solomon Guggenheim Foundation. The museum holds works by Duchamp, Klee, Kandinsky, Picasso, Magritte, Pollock, Dalí, and Guggenheim's confidante, Max Ernst. Especially stunning are Constantine's blue glass figurines in the window, watching over the canal below, each modeled after Picasso sketches from 1964. Ms. Guggenheim and her beloved pet shih tzus are buried in the peaceful garden. The Marini sculpture *Angel in the City*, which sits (apparently aroused) on horseback on the terrace, was designed with a detachable penis so Peggy could make emergency alterations depending on the church groups that happened to be riding by on the Canal. The ivy-lined marble terrace offers a rare unobstructed view of the Grand Canal. See **Beyond Tourism** (p. 100) for internship opportunities. *(Fondamenta Venier dei Leoni, Dorsoduro 701. V: Accademia. Turn left, and follow the yellow signs. ☎ 041 24 05 411; www.guggenheim-venice.it. Open M and W-Su 10am-6pm. Last entry 15min. before closing. €10; seniors €8; students, ISIC, and Rolling Venice cardholders €5; under 12 free. Audio tour €5. AmEx/MC/V.)*

▓GALLERIE DELL'ACCADEMIA. This colossal gallery boasts the most extensive collection of Venetian art in the world. Start at the top of the stairs in **Room I,** then continue behind Veneziano's ornate *Lion Polyptych with the Annunciation.* Giovanni Bellini's *Madonna Enthroned with Child, Saints, and Angels* stands in **Room II. Rooms IV** and **V** display more works by Bellini, including the magnificent *Madonna and Child with Magdalene and Saint Catherine,* and two works by Giorgione, who defied contemporary convention by creating works with no apparent narrative. *The Tempest*, for instance, continues to foil even art historians today's art historians; an x-ray has revealed that Giorgione originally painted a bathing woman where the young man now stands. In **Room VI,** three paintings by Tintoretto—*The Creation of the Animals, The Temptation of Adam and Eve,* and *Cain and Abel*—become progressively darker. Venetian Renaissance works line the rooms leading to **Room X,** home to Veronese's colossal *Supper in the House of Levi.* Originally painted as a *Last Supper,* the infuriated Inquisition council tried to force Veronese to modify his unorthodox interpretation of the memorable event, which depicts a Protestant German, a midget, dogs, and fat men. Instead, Veronese cleverly changed the title, saving his artistic license and his life. On the opposite wall is Titian's last painting, a *Pietà* intended for his tomb, a request that was apparently ignored. Art historians speculate that this final painting was an autobiographical statement, and that the luminous figure is Titian suffering in the raging plague. In **Room XX,** works by Bellini and Carpaccio display Venetian cityscapes so accurately that scholars use them as "photos" of Venice's past. *(V: Accademia. ☎ 041 52 00 345. To pre-order tickets, call Teleart M-F ☎ 041 52 22 247. Open M 8:15am-2pm, Tu-Su 8:15am-7:15pm. Last entry 45min. before closing. Guided tours in English Tu-Su 11am-noon. €6.50, EU students age 18-25 €3.25, EU citizens under 18 or over 65 free. Tours €5. Audio tour €4. Combined ticket to with Ca' d'Oro and Museo Oriental €11. Cash only.)*

CHIESA DI SANTA MARIA DELLA SALUTE. The *salute* (Italian for "health") is a hallmark of the Venetian skyline; perched on Dorsoduro's peninsula just southwest of San Marco, the church and its domes are visible from anywhere in the city and afford a spectacular view. Inside, the central area is roped off, so stroll its circumference for a glimpse of its paintings, including one by Titian by the sacristy entrance. In 1631, the city commissioned Longhena to build the church for the Virgin, whom they believed would end the plague. These days, Venice celebrates the plague's end on the third Sunday of November by building a pontoon bridge across the Canal and lighting candles in the church (see **Festivals,** (p. 331). Next to the *salute* stands the *dogana,* the old customs house, where ships sailing into Venice were required to stop and pay appropriate duties. *(V: Salute. ☎ 041 52 25 558. Open daily 9am-noon and 3-5:30pm. The inside of the dogana is closed to the public. Church free. Entrance to sacristy €2, students €1.)*

CÀ REZZONICO. Longhena's great *palazzo* houses the newly restored **Museo del Settecento Veneziano** (Museum of 18th-Century Venice), which holds 18th-century art from all over the city. Known as the "Temple of Venetian Settecento," this grand palace features a regal ballroom, complete with flowing curtains and Crosato's frescoed ceiling. To reach the ballroom on the first floor, ascend the elaborate staircase near the courtyard entrance. Other rooms contain elaborate Venetian Rococo decor. Upstairs, two extensive portrait galleries display works by Tiepolo, Tintoretto, Guardi, and Longhi. *(V: Cà Rezzonico. ☎ 041 24 10 100. Open M and W-Su Apr.-Oct. 10am-6pm; Nov.-Mar. 10am-5pm. Last entry 1hr. before closing. €6.50, students and Rolling Venice cardholders €4.50. Multi-lingual audio tour. €4. AmEx/MC/V.)*

CHIESA DI SAN SEBASTIANO. This church is completely covered in paintings by Veronese, who took refuge in this white-marble and brown-stucco 16th-century church when he fled Verona in 1555 after allegedly killing a man. By 1565 he had filled the church with an amazing cycle of paintings and frescoes. His *Stories of Queen Esther* covers the ceiling, while the artist himself rests under the gravestone by the organ. Several works by Titian are also displayed in the church. *(V: S. Basilio. Continue straight ahead. Open M-Sa 10am-5pm, Su 1-5pm. Last entry 15min. before closing. Included in the Chorus Pass. €3. Cash only.)*

CASTELLO

CHIESA DI SANTISSIMI GIOVANNI E PAOLO. Also called San Zanipolo, this imposing structure is primarily built in the Gothic style, but has a Renaissance portal and an arch supported by Greek marble columns. Inside, monumental ceilings enclose tombs and monuments of the Doges. One fresco depicts the gory death of Marcantonio Bragadin, who valiantly defended Cyprus from the Turks in 1571, only to be skinned alive after his surrender. His remains rest in the urn above the monument. Next to Bragadin is an Bellini altarpiece depicting St. Christopher, St. Sebastian, and St. Vincent Ferrer. The bronze equestrian statue of local mercenary Bartolomeo Colleoni stands outside. Colleoni left his inheritance to the city on the condition that a monument in his honor be erected in front of San Marco; the city, unwilling to honor anyone in such a grand space, decided to place the statue in front of the Scuola di San Marco to loosely satisfy the conditions of the will and claim his fortune. The statue was designed in 1479 by Leonardo's teacher Verrochio. *(V: Fondamenta Nuove. Turn left, then right on Fondamenta dei Mendicanti. ☎ 041 52 35 913. Open M-Sa 9am-6:30pm, Su noon-6:30. €2.50, students €1.25. Cash only.)*

CHIESA DI SANTA MARIA DEI MIRACOLI. The Lombardi family designed this small Renaissance jewel in the late 1400s. Inside the tiny pink-, white-, and blue-marble exterior sits a fully functional church with a dark gold ceiling and pastel walls interrupted only by the vibrant blue-and-yellow window above the apse; the pastel marble wall panels make the church's interior glow blue. *(From SS. Giovanni e Paolo, cross the bridge directly in front of the church, and continue down Calle Larga Gallina over 2 bridges. Open July-Aug. M-Sa 10am-5pm; Sept.-June M-Sa 10am-5pm, Su 1-5pm. Last entry 15min. before closing. Included in the Chorus Pass. €3. Cash only.)*

GIARDINI PUBBLICI AND SANT'ELENA. For a short respite from urban crowds, walk through the shady lanes of Napoleon's public gardens, where children swarm over playgrounds and the local geriatric elite gossip on benches. Throughout the year, the Giardini plays host to the Biennale, Venice's international art festival. For a larger lounging area, continue past the gardens, and bring a picnic lunch to the lawns of Sant'Elena. *(V: Giardini or S. Elena. Free.)*

SCUOLA DALMATA SAN GIORGIO DEGLI SCHIAVONI. Carpaccio's finest paintings, which depict episodes from the lives of St. George, Jerome, and Tryfon, are on the ground floor of this early 16th-century building. *(Castello 3259/A. V: S. Zaccaria. From the Riva Schiavoni, take Calle Dose to Campo Bandiera e Moro. Follow S. Antonin to Fondamenta Furlani. ☎ 041 52 28 828. Open M 2:45-6pm, Tu-Sa 9:15am-1pm and 2:45-6pm, Su 9:15am-1pm. Modest dress required. €4.)*

GIUDECCA

BASILICA DI SAN GIORGIO MAGGIORE. Standing on its own monastic island, S. Giorgio Maggiore contrasts sharply with most other Venetian churches and is a gorgeous sight from the southern edge of San Marco. Palladio, the building's architect, ignored the Venetian fondness for color and opted for an austere design. Light fills the enormous interior, though unfortunately it does not hit Tintoretto's *Last Supper* by the altar. Don't miss the 16th-century carved wood chorus hiding behind the main altar. Take the elevator to the top of the *campanile* for an amazing city view. *(V: S. Giorgio. ☎ 041 52 27 827. Church open daily in summer 9am-12:30pm and 2:30-6pm. Free. Guided tours in French, English, and Italian every hr. Sa-Su 10am-5pm, M-F by reservation only for groups of 15+. €12, €10 reduced, €8 for students and age 6-12. For tour reservations call ☎ 041 52 40 119. Campanile open 9am-1pm and 2:30-6pm. €3. Purchase ticket in the elevator.)*

TEMPIO DEL SS. REDENTORE. Palladio's religious masterpiece is small, but striking from across the Giudecca Canal. Like the **Salute (p. 326)**, it commemorates a deal that Venice struck with God to end a plague. Every year the city celebrates with fireworks at the Festa del Redentore (see **Festivals,** p. 331). Paintings by Veronese and Bassano hang in the sacristy. *(V: Redentore. Open M-Sa 10am-5pm, last entry 15min. before closing. Included in the Chorus Pass. €3.)*

ISLANDS OF THE LAGOON

ISLAND HOPPING. *Vaporetto* ticket prices border on extortionate. The best way to visit all the islands is the 12 or 24hr. *vaporetto* pass for €14 and 16, respectively—hop between islands as often as you'd like for a full day!

LIDO. The breezy resort island of Lido provided the tragic setting for *Death in Venice*, Thomas Mann's haunting novella of love and lust. Visconti's film version was also shot here at the famous Hotel des Bains, Lungomare Marconi 17. Tree-lined streets, crashing blue waves, and the popular public beach seem miles away from Venice's mobbed urban seafront. An impressive shipwreck looms at one end. The island also offers a casino, horseback riding, and one of Italy's finest golf courses. *(V #1: Lido. From the vaporetto stop, cross the street, and continue until you reach Gran Viale, which traverses the island to the beach. Beach open daily 9am-8pm. Free. Lockable changing rooms €16 per day, €8 after 2:30pm. Beach umbrella and chair €21; long deck chair €9; small safe free. AmEx/MC/V.)*

MURANO. Famous since 1292 when glass artisans were forced off Venice proper because their kilns started fires, the six-island cluster of Murano affords visitors the opportunity to witness resident artisans blowing and spinning crystalline creations free of charge. Quiet streets are lined with tiny shops and glass boutiques with jewelry, vases, and delicate figurines for a range of prices; for demonstrations, check signs directing to the *fornace,* concentrated around the Colona, Faro, and Navagero *vaporetto* stops. The speed and grace of these artisans are stunning, and some studios let visitors blow their own glass creations. The **Museo Vetrario** (Glass Museum) houses a collection that begins with funeral urns from the AD 1st century and ends with pieces like an ornate model garden made entirely of glass and a cartoonish, sea-green octopus presumably designed by Carlo Scarpa in 1930. *(Fondamenta Giustianian 8. V #DM, LN, 5, 13, 41, 42: Faro from either S. Zaccaria or Fondamenta Nuove. ☎/fax 041 73 95 86. Open Apr.-Oct. M-Tu and Th-Su 10am-6pm; Nov.-Mar. M-Tu and Th-Su 10am-5pm. €5.50; EU students, EU residents age 6-14 and over 65, and Rolling Venice cardholders €3.)* Down the street, a marble loggia lines the second story of the 12th-century **Basilica di Santa Maria e San Donato,** which features hundreds of mosaics on the church floor, blue chandeliers in the side apses, and a holy waterfront with fused pieces of bright yellow, red, green, and blue glass. A huge crucifix, blown from a single piece of glass, hangs right of the altar. *(☎041 73 90 56. Open daily 8am-7pm. Modest dress required. Free.)*

BURANO. As you approach Burano, the lagoon's most postcard-worthy island, you'll immediately notice the brightly colored houses that distinguish this destination. Carefully handmade lace has become the art form of choice for this traditional fishing village. The small and somewhat dull **Scuola di Merletti di Burano** (Lace Museum), once the home of the island's professional lace-making school, features 16th-century lace strips and yellowing lace-maker diplomas. **Chiesa di San Martino** sits across from the museum, and its altar features gorgeous blue stained-glass windows as bright as Burano's pastel buildings. *(40min.*

by boat from Venice. V #LN: Burano from Fondamenta Nuove. Museum in P. Galuppi. ☎041 73 00 34. Closed through Nov. 2008. Church open daily 8am-noon and 3-7pm. Free.)

TORCELLO. Torcello, originally a safe haven for fishermen fleeing barbarians on the mainland, was the most powerful island in the lagoon before Venice usurped its 14th-century glory. The cathedral **Santa Maria Assunta** contains a resplendent wall, which has tiers of 11th- and 12th-century mosaics depicting the Last Judgment and the Virgin Mary. The soaring *campanile* affords splendid views of Torcello, distant Burano, and the outer lagoon, but the rambling walk along an undisturbed canal is a pleasure in itself. *(45min. by boat from Venice. V #T: Torcello from Burano. Cathedral ☎041 29 60 630. Open daily 10am-noon and 4-6pm. Last entry 30min. before closing. Modest dress required. €3. Combined church, campanile, museum admission, and audio tour €8; groups €5.50. Combined ticket sales end 4:30pm. Cash only.)*

ISOLA DI SAN MICHELE. You'll find much fewer crowds on Venice's cemetery island. The closest island to Venice proper, San Michele is home to Coducci's tiny **Chiesa di San Michele in Isola** (1469), the first Renaissance church in Venice. Enter the cyprus-lined grounds through the church's right-hand portal, which is ornamented by a relief of St. Michael slaying a ◼dragon. Quiet grounds offer the opportunity for peaceful reflection away from the bustle of Venice. Poet, fascist sympathizer, and enemy of the state Ezra Pound is buried in the Protestant cemetery, while Russian composer Igor Stravinsky and choreographer Sergei Diaghilev are entombed in the Orthodox graveyard. *(V: Cimitero, from Fondamenta Nuove. Church and cemetery open daily Apr.-Sept. 7:30am-6pm; Oct.-Mar. 7:30am-4pm. Free.)*

◻ SHOPPING

Venice offers the dedicated shopper everything from international designer chains to authentic, family-run holes in the wall. Be wary of shopping in the heavily touristed P. S. Marco or around the Rialto; shops in other areas often have better selection and quality for about half the price. Boutiques selling clothing, glass, and masks line the streets leading from the Rialto to Campo S. Polo and Strada Nuova and from the Rialto toward the station, but even these are mobbed with visitors in summer and on weekends. The map accompanying the Rolling Venice Card lists many shops that offer cardholder discounts. The most concentrated and varied selections of Venetian glass and lace require trips to the nearby islands of Murano and Burano, respectively.

◪ ENTERTAINMENT

The weekly guide *A Guest in Venice*, free in hotels, tourist offices, and at www. unospitedivenezia.it, lists current festivals, concerts, and gallery exhibits.

GONDOLAS

Gondolas were once displays of multicolored brilliance. Winding slowly through the city's tiny canals, gondolas have become the emblem of Venetian beauty and culture. Legend has it that their lavish reds and purples turned to black when the Plague struck: wooden boats were supposedly coated with tar and pitch to stop further contamination from spreading throughout the disease-infested canals. The morbid color was also a sign of respect for the dead and dying. A more likely story, however, is that a 17th-century city ordinance ordered all boats painted black to prevent noble families from launching gondola-decorating feuds. Certain dignitaries, of course, were exempt. These days the boats are mainly filled with tourists seeking up-close views of Venetian houses and palaces from the original canal pathways. Rides are

THE VENETO

most romantic about 50min. before sunset and most affordable if shared by six people. Gondolas are a private service; the rate that a gondolier quotes is negotiable, but expect to pay €80-100 for 40min. (and don't pay more). The most bargain-friendly gondoliers are those standing by themselves, rather than those in the groups at "taxi stands" throughout the city.

ORCHESTRAL MUSIC

Venice swoons for orchestral music, from the outdoor chamber orchestras in P. S. Marco to costumed concerts. **Vivaldi** (p. 76), the priest and choirmaster of the Chiesa di S. Maria della Pietà (a few blocks along the waterfront from P. S. Marco), was forgotten for centuries after his death. Today, his compositions, particularly *The Four Seasons*, can be heard regularly in the summer and during the winter. The **Chiesa di San Vidal**, next to Campo S. Samuele in San Marco, hosts performances using period instruments. (☎041 27 70 561. Open daily 9am-5pm. Concerts M-Sa 9pm. €23, students €18. Tourist office has information. Purchase tickets at the church or visit www.interpretiveneziani.com.)

THEATER, CINEMA, AND ART EXHIBITIONS

Teatro Goldoni, C. del Teatro, San Marco 4650/B, showcases varying types of live productions, often with a seasonal theme. Check with the theater for upcoming listings. (☎041 24 02 011; teatrogoldini@libero.it. Rolling Venice discount 10%. AmEx/MC/V.) The **Mostra Internazionale di Cinema** (Venice International Film Festival), held annually from late August to early September, is a worldwide affair, drawing both rising talents and more established names like Steven Spielberg. Movies are shown in their original languages. (☎041 52 18 878. Tickets €20, students €10, available for purchase throughout city. Some late-night outdoor showings free.) Venice's main cinemas include the **Giorgione,** Campo S. Apostoli, Cannaregio (☎041 52 26 298), and the **Rossini,** San Marco 3988 (☎041 52 30 322), off Campo Manin, which generally shows films in Italian. The famed **Biennale di Venezia,** an international contemporary art exhibition with musical and dance performances, takes over the Giardini Pubblici and the Arsenal with provocative art in odd-numbered years and contemporary architecture exhibits in even. Check the website for exact dates. (Info ☎041 52 18 898; for tickets, HelloVenezia ☎041 24 24; www.labiennale.org. Open daily 10am-6pm. Reservations required for dance performances; call ☎041 21 88 28 M-F 10am-5pm. Tickets €15, reduced €12, students and under 26 years €8. Consider buying a 6 performance pass for €75, students €48.)

⚑ NIGHTLIFE

While pubs and bars are not uncommon in Venice, most residents agree that a vibrant nightlife is virtually nonexistent. The majority of locals prefer an evening spent sipping wine in a *piazza* to bumping and grinding in a disco, but the island's fluctuating population means that new establishments spring up (and wither and die) regularly. Student nightlife is concentrated around **Campo Santa Margherita,** in Dorsoduro, and tourists swarm **Lista di Spagna,** in Cannaregio.

▨ **Café Blue,** Campo S. Pantalon, Dorsoduro 3778 (☎041 52 27 613). Popular, laid-back local hangout that is busy any time of day. Grab a glass of wine (€1.50-3.20) or a distinctly Venetian "sex on the bridge" (€6). Live jazz and blues F. Free Wi-Fi and one computer for Internet. Open M-F 10am-2am, Sa-Su 6pm-2am. Cash only.

Paradiso Perduto, Fondamenta della Misericordia, Cannaregio 2540 (☎041 72 05 81). From Strada Nuova, cross Campo S. Fosca, cross bridge, and continue in same direction, crossing 2 more bridges. Students flood this bar, where a young staff doles out filling plates like homemade pasta *al pesto* (€10), and generous *cicchetti* (€2-5). Outdoor canal-side seating and a spacious interior. Live jazz Su. Primi €10-16. Wine €4. *Grappa* €3.50-4.50. €2 cover for meals. Open daily 11am-3pm and 6pm-2am.

Impronta Cafe, Dorsoduro 3815/17 (☎041 27 50 386). Hip, modern decor distinguishes this cafe from its neighbors. A sleek restaurant by day (pasta from €10), the bar is just as lively at night. Frozen drinks €5. Beer €2.20-5. Wine €2.50-3.50. Primi €6.50-12. Secondi €9-15. Open M-Sa 7am-2am. AmEx/MC/V.

Sotto Sopra, Dorsoduro 3740/1 (☎041 52 42 177). From C. Santa Margherita, follow C.d. Chiesa, cross bridge and continue towards the right until you reach C. S. Pantalon. Funky bar features 2 floors of stain-glass windows, pop-art, and rock music near student nightlife. Flatscreen TV and bar downstairs. Cozy upstairs seating. Beers €2-5.50. Mixed drinks €5. Wine €1.20. Open M-Sa 10am-2am. MC/V.

Blues Bar, Campo S. Stin 2532 (☎041 347 575 5566). With the quiet *campo* all to themselves, customers sit leisurely under white umbrellas, enjoying cold drinks and *panini*. Inside, lively music, exposed brick walls, and hanging instruments add flavor to this hip bar. Live jazz and blues Th night. Wine €2.50-4. Beer €1.50-6. Mixed drinks €4.50-7. Open daily 7am-midnight. Cash only.

Bacaro Jazz, San Marco 5546 (☎041 52 85 249; www.bacarojazz.com), across from the post office. From the Rialto bridge, turn left and walk 100m. Bras dangle from the ceiling and an illuminated red Bellini sign greets customers in this eclectic bar. Dark interior and upbeat tunes. Mixed drinks €9. Beer from €3. Happy hour daily 2-7:30pm with 2-for-1 drinks. Open M-Tu and Th-Su 1pm-2am. AmEx/MC/V.

Orange, Campo S. Margherita, Dorsoduro 3054/A (☎041 52 34 740; www.orangebar. it). The painted bar seems to be on fire at this crowded spot, where an attentive staff serves everything from *panini* (€3.50) to mixed drinks (€3.50-7). For a break from the orange, retreat to the quiet garden out back or the white umbrella seats in front. Beer €2.50-6. Wine from €2. Open daily 9am-2am. AmEx/MC/V.

Café Noir, Dorsoduro 3805 (☎041 71 09 25). Low-ceilinged sparse interior, flatscreen TV, and a sophisticated vibe. The windows in front offer great people-watching, while the more private back room is perfect for an intimate drink. *Panini* loaded with fresh veggies €3-4.50. Mixed drinks €3.50-6. Open M-Sa 7am-2am, Su 9am-2am. Cash only.

Bistrot al Do Draghi, Campo S. Margherita 3665 (☎041 52 89 731). Maybe not as fierce as the name implies, but certainly more artsy than its C. S. Margherita neighbors. A cozy spot for a late night drink with old-fashioned, wood decor and dim lighting. Extensive wine list (€1.20-1.80). Famous spritz €1.20. Open daily 7am-2am. Cash only.

Piccolo Mondo, Accademia, Dorsoduro 1056/A (☎041 52 00 371). Facing away from the canal toward the Accademia, turn right and follow the street around. Heavy, locked doors open up late at this self-advertised "disco club." Disco, hip hop, and vodka Red Bulls (€10) keep a full house—even if it's because it's the only game in town. Heats up around 1am. Photos of famous clientele include notables from Boy George to Shaquille O'Neal to Mick Jagger. Ring bell to enter. Drinks from €7. Cover varies, usually €10 with free drink. Open nightly 11pm-4am. AmEx/MC/V.

❋ FESTIVALS

Banned by the church for several centuries, Venice's famous **Carnevale** was successfully reinstated in the early 70s. During the 10 days preceding Ash Wednesday, masked figures jam the *piazze* and street performances spring up throughout the city. On Mardi Gras, the city's population doubles. Contact the tourist office (see **Practical Information,** p. 312) in December or January for details and make lodging arrangements far in advance. Venice's 2nd most colorful festival is the **Festa del Redentore** (3rd Sa in July), originally held to celebrate the end of a 16th-century plague. It kicks off on Saturday night with a fireworks display at 11:30pm. On Sunday, craftsmen build a pontoon bridge across the Giudecca Canal, connecting Il Redentore to the Zattere. On the first Sunday in September, Venice stages its classic **regata storica,** a gondola race down the Grand Canal. During the religious **Festa della Salute** (Nov. 21), the city celebrates with another pontoon bridge, this time over the Grand Canal.

PADUA (PADOVA) ☎049

It is the oldest institutions of Padua (PA-do-va; pop. 215,000) that still draw visitors: pilgrims flock to San Antonio's tomb, athletes skate around peaceful picnickers along the looping Prato della Valle, and lecturers and academics frequent the hallowed university halls. Dante, Petrarch, Galileo, Copernicus, and Donatello built the city's long-standing reputation as an intellectual center. Home to Italy's second oldest university, Padua brings scores of 20-somethings into its busy *piazze,* where crowds linger late into the night.

⌐ TRANSPORTATION

Trains: In P. Stazione, at the northern end of C. del Popolo, the continuation of C. Garibaldi. Station open daily 5am-midnight. Ticket office open daily 6am-9pm. Info booth open daily 7am-9pm (☎049 89 20 21). To: **Bologna** (1hr., 32 per day 12:41am-8:33pm, €6.40); **Milan** (2hr., 25 per day 5:51am-8:24pm, €12.20); **Venice** (30min., 82 per day 12:41am-11:07pm, €2.90); **Verona** (1hr., 44 per day 5:51am-11:28pm, €5).

Buses: SITA (☎049 82 06 834), in P. Boschetti. From the train station, walk down C. del Popolo, turn left on V. Trieste, and bear right at V. Vecchio. Ticket office open M-Sa 5:30am-8:30pm, Su 6:20am-8:40pm. To: **Venice** (45min., 30 per day, every 15-30min 5:25am-10:25pm, €3.10) and **Vicenza** (1hr., 31 per day 5:50am-8:15pm, €3.20). Reduced service Sa-Su. Cash only.

Public Transportation: APS (☎049 82 41 111), at the train station, runs local buses. Ticket office open daily 6am-midnight. To get downtown, take buses #8, 12, or 18 M-F and #8 and 32 Sa-Su. 1hr. pass €1; purchase tickets at the *tabaccheria.*

Taxis: RadioTaxi (☎049 65 13 33).

Car Rental: Europcar, P. Stazione 6 (☎049 65 78 77), across parking lot from the station. 19+. Open M-F 8:30am-noon and 3-7pm, Sa 8:30am-12:30pm. AmEx/MC/V. **Maggiore National,** P. Stazione 15 (☎049 87 58 605; fax 87 56 223). Open M-F 8:30am-12:30pm and 2:30-7pm, Sa 9am-noon. AmEx/MC/V.

✈ ? ORIENTATION AND PRACTICAL INFORMATION

The train station is on the northern edge of town, outside the 16th-century walls. A 10min. walk down **Corso del Popolo,** which becomes **Corso Garibaldi,** leads to the heart of town and main area of the **Università degli Studi di Padova.**

Tourist Office: Vco. Cappellato Pedrocchi 7 (☎049 87 67 927; info@turismopadova.it), off P. Cavour. Free Internet with 15min. limit. Open M-Sa 9am-1:30pm and 3-6:50pm. Branches: P. del Santo (☎049 87 53 087), across from the basilica. Open Mar.-Oct. M-Sa 9am-1:30pm and 3-6pm, Su 10am-1pm and 3-6pm. In the train station (☎87 52 077). Open M-Sa 9:15am-7pm, Su 9am-noon.

Budget Travel: CTS, V. S. Sofia 96. (☎049 87 51 719). Sells ISICs and train tickets. Open M-F 9am-12:30pm and 3-6:30pm, Sa 9am-noon. Cash only.

English-Language Bookstore: Feltrinelli International, V. S. Francesco 14 (☎049 87 50 792). From the train station, turn left off V. Cavour. Wide selection of magazines, novels, and travel guides. Open M-Sa 9am-1pm and 3:30-7:30pm. AmEx/MC/V.

Hospital: Ospedale Civile, V. Giustiniani 1 (☎049 82 11 111), off V. Ospedale.

Internet Access: Free at the main tourist office (see above). **Internet Point Padova,** V. Altinate 145 (☎049 65 92 92). Printing, fax, and photocopy. €1 per 20min., €3 per hr. Open M-Sa 10am-midnight, Su 4pm-midnight. MC/V.

Post Office: C. Garibaldi 25 (☎049 87 72 111). Open M-Sa 8:30am-6:30pm. **Postal Code:** 35100.

ACCOMMODATIONS

Belludi 37, V. Luca Belludi 37 (☎049 66 56 33; www.belludi37.it). Too good to be true. Modern decor with simple stone steps, smooth hardwood floors, and glass tables in the heart of the city. Huge rooms have AC, cordless phones, orthopedic beds, LCD TVs, free DSL Internet, and private baths. Buffet breakfast or breakfast in bed at no extra cost. Parking €10. Singles €50-70; doubles €90-110. Extra bed €30. AmEx/MC/V. ❹

Ostello Città di Padova (HI), V. Aleardi 30 (☎049 87 52 219; www.ostellopadova. it). From station, take bus #12 or 18 to Prato della Valle, or walk 25min. Large, efficiently run hostel rents 6-bed dorms. TV room and good location 10min. from *centro*. Breakfast included. Laundry wash €3, dry €2.50. Internet €5 per hr. €3 key deposit for locker in room. Wheelchair-accessible. 5-night max. stay. Reception 7:15-9:30am and 4:30-11pm. Lockout 9:30am-4:30pm. Curfew 11:30pm. Call ahead. 6-bed dorms €18; 4-person family rooms €64, with private bath €84. MC/V. ❶

Al Giardinetto, Prato della Valle 54 (☎049 65 67 66; www.hotelalgiardinetto.it). Impeccable service, a lovely garden, and a great location overlooking the majestic *piazza*. Red-carpeted hallways and pink walls lead to large rooms adorned with coordinating flowers. All rooms have TV, phone, A/C, fridge, and private bath. Free Wi-Fi. Breakfast included. Singles €40, with bath €60; doubles €90. AmEx/MC/ V. ❸

Hotel Mignon, V. Luca Belludi 22 (☎049 66 17 22; www.hotelmignonpadova.it). Sunny rooms and a cheery staff, just 5min. from Basilica di San Antonio. Humbly furnished but comfortable and spacious rooms have private bath, TV, AC, and phone; some have balconies. Breakfast €2.50. Singles €52; doubles €67; triples €82; quads €97. MC/V. ❹

Hotel Al Santo, V. del Santo 147 (☎049 87 52 131; www.alsanto.it), near the basilica. Recently renovated, spacious rooms with modern decor, TV, A/C, Wi-Fi, phone, and bath. Breakfast included. Lunch or dinner *menù* €16. Restaurant downstairs. Singles €65; doubles €80-100; triples €120. Prices may drop with longer stays. AmEx/MC/V. ❺

Locanda la Perla, V. Cesarotti 67 (☎049 87 58 939), a 5min. walk from the Basilica di San Antonio. Friendly owner Paolo rents clean, fairly large rooms with comfortable beds, simple decor, phone, and shared bath on each floor. Fan and TV provided upon request. Closed last 2 weeks of Aug. Singles €35; doubles €45, triples €60. Cash only. ❸

FOOD

Morning **markets** are held in P. delle Erbe and P. della Frutta where sidewalk vendors also sell fresh produce, meats, and cheeses. (M-F 7am-1:30pm, Sa 7am-8pm). There's a **PAM** supermarket downtown in Piazzetta della Garzeria 3, past Palazzo Bo to the right of Caffè Pedrocchi. (Open M-Tu and Th-Sa 8am-8:30pm, W 8am-2pm. MC/V.) For an inexpensive taste of the gourmet, visit the specialty store, **Franchin,** V. del Santo 95. (☎049 87 50 532. Open M-Tu and Th-Su 8:30am-1:30pm and 4:30-8pm, W 8:30am-1:30pm. MC/V.) Wine lov-

Padua

🏠 **ACCOMMODATIONS**
Hotel Al Santo, **11**
Locanda la Perla, **10**
Ostello Città di
  Padova (HI), **13**
Hotel Mignon, **1**
Al Giardinetto, **2**
Belludi 37, **3**

🍎 **FOOD**
Antica Trattoria
  Paccagnella, **9**
Lunanuova, **7**
Il Grottino, **4**
Pizza Shop di Andrea
  Bettini, **5**
Osteria all'Antica
  Colonna, **6**

🍸 **NIGHTLIFE**
Fly, **8**
Da Tempo, **12**
Via Roma, **16**
Il Gottino, **14**
Osteria l'Anfora, **15**

ers should sample a glass from the nearby **Colli Euganei** district. Visitors to the **Basilica di Sant'Antonio** can nibble on *dolci del santo* (saint's sweets), a flaky, powdered cake with creamy nut and fig filling, in nearby *pasticcerie*.

🔹 **Il Grottino,** V. del Santo 21. (☎049 66 41 76). Locals crowd this casual spot where simple dishes like *tortellini in brodo* (€5) are served in an unimposing, warmly lit interior. Menu changes daily. Primi €5-7. Secondi €10-18. Open in winter M-Tu and Th-Sa 8:30am-3:30pm and 7pm-12:30am, Su 9am-3:30pm and 7pm-12:30am; in summer M-Tu and Th-Su 9am-3:30pm and 7pm-12:30am. MC/V. ❹

🔹 **Pizza Shop di Andrea Bettini,** V. G. Morgagni 48/B (☎049 87 51 648). Friendly owner Andrea has been making the best-priced and tastiest pizza in town for ages. Small interior, so take your slice to the nearby *piazza* or park. Marinara pies (€2.60) with toppings up to €6. Slices €1-1.30. Open Tu-Sa 11am-2:45pm and 6-10:45pm. Cash only. ❶

Osteria all'Antica Colonna, V. Altinate 127 (☎049 65 50 85). Colorful flags, clocks displaying world times, and overflowing wine bottles line the walls of this old trattoria, which specializes in Tuscan cuisine. Long wine list. Primi €6.50-9. Secondi €7-17. Wine from €2.50. Open M 6pm-midnight, Tu-Sa 10am-3pm and 6pm-midnight. MC/V. ❸

Lunanuova, V. S. Gregorio Barbarigo 12 (☎049 87 58 907), heading off P. Duomo. Buzz at stained-glass doors for entrance. Mix of healthy Middle Eastern and vegetarian cuisine. Handwritten daily menu with dishes like creamed fennel in sesame sauce (€4.50). Individual plates €4.50-5.30, 2 plates €8.80, 3 plates €9.80, 5 plates €11. Open Tu-Sa 12:30-2:30pm and 7:30pm-midnight. Cash only. ❷

Antica Trattoria Paccagnella, V. del Santo 113 (☎/fax 049 87 50 549). The place to go for authentic Paduan cuisine. Regional favorites like *cappellaci with rucola* and smoked *provola* (€9) in a relaxed atmosphere. Primi €7-11. Secondi €12-17. Cover €2.50. Open M-Sa 8am-4pm and 6:30pm-midnight. AmEx/MC/V. ❹

 GIMME TEN. Padua's sights are best visited with either the 48hr. or 72hr. **Padova Card** (€15/20), which covers all major sights in Padua, excluding the *duomo*. The card also provides free transport on local buses and discounts from participating merchants. Visit the tourist office for more info.

◎ SIGHTS

▩**CAPPELLA DEGLI SCROVEGNI (ARENA CHAPEL).** Enrico Scrovegni dedicated this tall brick chapel to the Virgin Mary in an attempt to save the soul of his father Reginald, a usurer famously lambasted in the 17th canto of Dante's *Inferno*. Pisano carved the chapel's statues and Giotto covered the walls with frescoed scenes from the lives of Jesus, Mary, and her parents, Saints Joachim and Anne. Completed between 1305 and 1306, this 38-panel cycle is one of the earliest examples of depth and realism in Italian Renaissance painting. A brilliant blue ceiling is adorned with bright gold stars and images of Jesus and Mary, each surrounded by prophets. Across the top panel, the marriage of Joachim and Anne is depicted with startlingly crisp perspectival lines and vibrant hues. The next two rows depict the life of Jesus, the players in the story portrayed with unprecedented emotion and realism. Note that the chapel has two entrances; one belonged to the citizens of the city, while the other, which is now the visitor entrance, was reserved for the Scrovegni family. Down a short gravel path from the museum, there is a multimedia room, featuring a short multilingual video on the chapel's history (narrated amusingly from Scrovegni's perspective) and an in-depth explanation of the fresco-painting technique. Additionally, the Musei Civici Eremitani has assembled an art collection including ancient Roman inscriptions and a beautiful crucifix by Giotto that once adorned the Scrovegni Chapel. *(P. Eremitani 8. ☎049 20 10 020; www.cappelladegliscrovegni.it. Reservations by phone or website required. Call M-F between 9am-7pm and Sa 9am-6pm. Museum and chapel open M-F 9am-7pm. Museum €10; combined ticket €12, students €8, disabled €1. Evening visits to chapel €8, reduced €6. AmEx/MC/V.)*

 GIOTTO'S JUDGMENT. In the **Last Judgment,** Giotto painted himself among the blessed as a signature and perhaps a self-assessment. Check him out: he's fourth from the left, with the pink robe and yellow hat.

▩**BASILICA DI SANT'ANTONIO (IL SANTO).** An array of rounded gray domes and conical spires caps Padua's enormous brick basilica. Bronze sculptures by Donatello grace the high altar, which is surrounded by the artist's *Crucifixion* and several Gothic frescoes. Upon entering, walk along the left side to reach the **Tomba di Sant'Antonio**, which sits on a platform underneath a huge marble arch. Each year, thousands of pilgrims crowd the marble bas-reliefs to cover the black stone of the sepulcher with framed photographs and prayers. Along the right side, the **Cappella di San Giacomo** is marked by a luminous blue ceiling with gold stars that recall Giotto's signature chapel. Along the pane of glass that now protects the frescoed wall, scratched-in and graffiti-written names can be detected by past couples and visitors. Behind the main altar in the apse sits the **Cappella delle Reliquie,** where ornately carved sculptures look down on shrines containing everything from St. Anthony's tunic to his jawbone and tongue; frightening cupids holding skulls line the way. A multimedia show in the courtyard (follow "Mostra" signs) details St. Anthony's life. To the right on the way out of the basilica, the tiny **Oratorio di San Giorgio,** which briefly served as a prison under Napoleon, displays Giotto-inspired frescoes. (*P. del Santo.* ☎ *049 82 42 811; www.basilicadelsanto.org. Basilica open daily Apr.-Sept. 6:15am-7:45pm; Nov.-Mar. 6:15am-6:45pm. Modest dress strictly enforced. Free. Capella delle Relinque open daily 8am-12:45pm and 2:30-7:30pm. Mostra open daily 9am-6pm. Free multilingual audio tour available at front desk. Oratorio and Scuola ☎/fax 049 82 42 831. Oratorio open daily Apr.-Oct. 9am-12:30pm and 2:30-7pm; Nov.-Mar. 9am-12:30pm and 2:30-5pm. Scuola open daily 10-11am and 3-4pm. Wheelchair-accessible. €2.50, Padova Card €2. Cash only.*)

ORTO BOTANICO (BOTANICAL GARDEN). Leafy trees and high stone walls surround a circular grid of iron fences, gravel walkways, and low fountains in Europe's oldest university botanical garden, recognized as a UNESCO World Heritage site. Take your time wandering through the oasis of water lilies, cacti, and medicinal herbs, or inhale the fresh scents from one of the many benches. **"Goethe's palm,"** planted in 1585, was given the name after the poet visited and developed his own pre-Darwinian theory of evolution based on the garden's leaves. (*V. Orto Botanico 15. Follow signs from basilica.* ☎ *049 82 72 119. Open Apr.-Oct. daily 9am-1pm and 3-7pm; Nov.-Mar. M-F 9am-1pm. €4, over 65 €3, students €1. Cash only.*)

PALAZZO BÒ AND ENVIRONS. The university campus is spread throughout the city but centers around two interior stone courtyards of **Palazzo Bò,** adorned with students' coats of arms and a war memorial. The **Teatro Anatomico** (1594), the first medical lecture hall of its kind. Nearly all Venetian noblemen received their mandatory law and public policy instruction in the **Great Hall,** which is decorated with the coat-of-arms of university directors and administrators. **Galileo's chair** is preserved in the **Sala dei Quaranta,** where the great physicist once lectured. (*V. VIII Febbraio.* ☎ *049 82 73 047. Entrance with 45min. guided tour only. Tours Mar.-Oct. M, W, and F 3:15, 4:15, 5:15pm; Tu, Th, and Sa 9:15, 10:15, 11:15am. Buy tickets 15min. before tour. €5, students €2.*) Across the street, **Caffè Pedrocchi,** founded in 1831, once served as headquarters for 19th-century supporters of the Risorgimento. The battle that exploded here between students and Austrian police in 1848 was a turning point in the movement—check out the spear hole in the left wall near the entrance that it left behind. Though considerably less revolutionary these days, it still serves coffee. (*V. VIII Febbraio 15.* ☎ *049 87 81 231; www.caffepedrocchi. it. Open M-W and Su 9am-9pm; Th-Sa 9am-1am. AmEx/MC/V.*) The **Museo Risorgimento e dell'Eta Contemporanea** carefully follows the city's development within the larger political cycles of Italy up through the middle of the 20th century. (☎ *049 87 81 231. Open Tu-Su 9:30am-12:30pm and 3:30-6pm. €4, students €2.50. Cash only.*)

PALAZZO DELLA RAGIONE (LAW COURTS). A long balcony that overlooks the busy P. delle Erbe marks the entrance to this giant *palazzo*. The building's vast interior awes visitors under a barrel vault roof. Admire the giant wooden horse at the western end of the hall, then trace the frescoes depicting the astrological cycle all the way around. To the right of the entrance is the **Stone of Shame.** Inspired by the exhortations of St. Anthony in 1231 to abolish debtors' prisons, Padua adopted the practice of forcing half-clothed debtors onto the stone, surrounded by hundreds of heartless hecklers. *(At P. delle Erbe. ☎049 82 05 006. Open Tu-Su Feb.-Oct. 9am-7pm; Nov.-Jan. 9am-6pm. €4.)*

PRATO DELLA VALLE. Originally a Roman theater, the Prato is one of Europe's largest *piazze.* Joggers and bikers on the outermost track orbit dog walkers, teenagers, and families who cross the moat to stroll the pebbly paths, sit by the fountain, or relax on the grass among statues of 78 famous *padovani.*

DUOMO. Michelangelo supposedly participated in the design of this hulking church, erected between the 16th and 18th centuries. The *duomo's* white-walled simplicity makes the steps of the apse especially unusual—chunky, half-carved, marble statues of Saints Prosdocimo, Gregorio, and Giustina accompany a golden, praying figure whose flowing hair melds with a marble tree to create the church's lectern. *(P. Duomo. ☎049 66 28 14. Open M-Sa 7:20am-noon and 4-7:30pm, Su 8am-1pm and 4-8:30pm. Free.)* Next door, the striking 12th-century ▧**battistero** (baptistry) is dedicated to St. John the Baptist. The interior walls are covered in colorful frescoes of New Testament scenes, while a massive, wide-eyed Christ and rings of painted saints look down from the hollow dome above. *(☎049 65 69 14. Open daily 10am-6pm. €2.80, students €1.80. Cash only.)*

▨ ▧ NIGHTLIFE AND FESTIVALS

Pilgrims pack the city on June 13, as Padua commemorates the death of its patron saint, Saint Anthony, with a procession bearing his statue and jawbone. An **antique market** is held in the Prato della Valle on the third Sunday of the month. The area holds a **clothing market** on Saturdays. As the sun sets on summer evenings, Padua's *piazzas* fill with crowds spilling out from nearby bars and cafes. Nightlife rages during the school year, but dies down in summer.

Il Gottino, V. S. Martino e Solferino 29 (☎049 87 74 647). Students liven up this nearly bare room. Funky floral wallpaper, rustic wood floors, dim lighting, and techno. Free *cicchetti.* Wine €2-4. Mixed drinks €5. Open M-Sa 10am-midnight. AmEx/MC/V.

Da Tempo, V. S. Sofia 70 (☎049 87 60 319; www.datempo.it). Bohemian bar with ample seating, a cool garden, and reasonable prices. An ideal student hangout. Flatscreen TV. Beer €2-4.50. Wine €1.50-3. Mixed drinks €3-5. Open M-T and Th 6:30am-8pm; W and F 6:30am-midnight; Su 4pm-midnight. Cash only.

Via Roma, V. Roma 96 (☎049 87 52 712). Upscale mix of modern and antique with funky mirrors and glittering chandeliers, complemented by fluorescent blue lighting, leopard print seating, and ▧**Klimt posters.** A lively crowd lounges outside under white umbrellas. Mixed drinks €6. Wine €3-7. Open daily 7am-2am. AmEx/MC/V.

Osteria l'Anfora, V. dei Soncin 13 (☎049 65 66 29). Great for both a hearty meal or an evening drink. Large wood tables among brick columns and bookshelves seat large groups, while the bar is ideal for traditional *sarde in saor* (€6) and wine (€1.50-5). Beer €3-4.50. Food €5.50-15. Open M-Sa 8am-midnight. AmEx/MC/V.

Fly, Galleria Tito Livio 4/6, (☎049 87 52 892) between V. Roma and Riviera Tito Livio. Fly is a pedestrian cafe by day and a swinging hot spot by night. This bar's great location near V. Roma and student nightlife make it a great choice for an evening out. Wine €2-3.50. Mixed drinks €3.50-4.50. Open daily 8am-1am.

VICENZA ☎ 0444

Vicenza (vee-CHEN-za; pop. 106,000) found its hero in Renaissance architect Andrea Palladio, who designed the *centro*'s magnificent Teatro Olimpico and whose work inspired villas far and wide, including Thomas Jefferson's Monticello. The iconic *manses* outside the city are present-day legacies of the 15th-century real estate boom that moved nobles from Venice to the mainland. Don't let the glamorous inhabitants and priceless art intimidate you; Vicenza's easily navigable streets and friendly locals welcome all visitors.

THE VENETO

⌐ TRANSPORTATION

Trains: P. Stazione, at the end of V. Roma, across from Campo Marzo. Currency Exchange available. Info office open daily 7am-9pm. Ticket office open daily 6am-8:30pm. AmEx/MC/V. To: **Milan** (2hr., 25 per day 6:10am-9:04pm, €10); **Padua** (30min., 51 per day 5:20am-10:50pm, €2.90); **Venice** (1hr., 44 per day 5:20am-10:48pm, €4.30); **Verona** (40min., 43 per day 5:42am-11:47pm, €3.90).

Buses: FTV, Vle. Milano 7 (☎0444 39 49 09) left after exiting the train station. Ticket office open M-F 6am-7:40pm, Sa-Su 6:15am-7:40pm. Cash only. Runs to Padua (30min.; 30 per day 5:50am-8:20pm, reduced service Sa-Su; €3.50).

Taxis: RadioTaxi (☎0444 92 06 00).

◼▮ ORIENTATION AND PRACTICAL INFORMATION

The train station and adjacent intercity bus station occupy the southern part of the city. **Viale Roma** leads from the station into town. At the **Giardino Salvi,** turn right under the Roman archway onto **Corso Palladio.** Walk several blocks to the old Roman wall that serves as a gate to the **Teatro Olimpico.** The tourist office is just to the right. **Piazza Matteotti** lies in front, at the end of C. Palladio.

Tourist Office: P. Matteotti 12 (☎0444 32 08 54; www.vicenzae.org). Free maps. Open daily 9am-1pm and 2-6pm. Branch at P. dei Signori 8 (☎0444 54 41 22; iatvicenza2@ provincia.vicenza.it). Open daily 10am-2pm and 2:30-6:30pm.

Budget Travel: AVIT, Vle. Roma 17 (☎0444 54 56 77; www.avit.it). Open M-F 9am-12:30pm and 3-7pm, Sa 9:30am-12:30pm. AmEx/MC/V for plane tickets only.

Pharmacy: Alla Pigna d'Oro, P. dei Signori 49 (☎0444 32 12 41). Open June-Aug. M-F 8:45am-12:30pm and 4-7:30pm, Sa 8:45am-12:30pm; Sept.-May M-F 8:45am-12:30pm and 3:30-7pm, Sa 8:45am-12:30pm. Closed 2 weeks in Aug. MC/V.

Internet Access: Bhai Bhai, Roma 19 (☎0444 52 73 77). €2 per hour. Open M-Tu and Th-F 9:30am-9:30pm, Sa-Su 9:30am-10pm.

Post Office: Contrà Garibaldi 1 (☎0444 33 20 77), between *duomo* and P. Signori. Open M-F 8:30am-6:30pm, Sa 8:30am-1:30pm. Cash only. **Postal Code:** 36100.

▮ ▮ ACCOMMODATIONS AND CAMPING

Due Mori, Contrà do Rode, 24/26 (☎0444 32 18 86; www.hotelduemori.com). Huge rooms with hardwood floors, plants, warm lighting, and private baths. Some have TV. Elegant lobby and a homey, relaxed feel. Breakfast €8. Wi-Fi €2 per hr. Wheelchair-accesible. Singles €45; doubles €80-90. MC/V. ❸

Hotel Castello, Contrà P. del Castello 24 (☎0444 32 35 85/83; www.hotelcastelloitaly. com), off P. del Castello. Centrally located hotel offers small but well-decorated rooms with A/C, satellite TV, Internet, phone, and minibar. Big windows. Modern lobby features piano bar, funky furniture, and colorful art. Breakfast and parking included. Singles €70-90; doubles €100-120; triples €120-150. AmEx/MC/V. ❺

Ostello Olimpico Vicenza (HI), V. Giuriolo 9 (☎0444 54 02 22). From the train station, walk up Vle. Roma until you reach Ple. de Gasperi. Turn right onto C. Palladio and continue 10min. until the tourist office at P. Matteotti. With the Museo Civico on the right, walk down Vle. Giuriolo; the *ostello* is the yellow building on the left. Buses #1, 2, 4, 5, and 7 also run from the station; ask bus driver for hostel stop. Small dorms within sight of the Teatro Olimpico. Breakfast included. Lockers free. Internet card (€1.80) includes 15min.; €3.50 per hr. thereafter. Wheelchair-accessible. Reception 7:30-9:30am and 3:30-11:30pm. Dorms €18; singles €21, with bath €23; doubles €56. MC/V. ❶

Campeggio Vicenza, Strada Pelosa 239 (☎0444 58 23 11; www.ascom.vi.it/camping). Take bus #1 (€1) from the train station and ask for camping; the *campeggio* is a 10min. walk from the bus stop. Small minigolf course on-site, showers, and electricity. Restaurant, TV, and free Internet access available at adjacent hotel. Laundry €6. Open Apr.-Sept. €5.90-7.60 per person; €12-16 per tent. Showers free. AmEx/MC/V. ❶

🍴 FOOD

Vicenza's specialties include dried cod with polenta, asparagus with eggs, and *torresani* (pigeon). An enormous **market** sprawls across P. delle Erbe, P. Signori, and Vle. Roma, and sells cheese, fish, produce, and clothing. (Open Tu-Th 7:30am-2pm.) **PAM** supermarket, Vle. Roma 1, has essentials and a huge wine selection. (Open M-Tu and Th-Sa 8am-8pm, W 8am-2pm. AmEx/MC/V.)

- 🍽 **Righetti,** P. del Duomo 3 (☎0444 54 31 35), with a second entrance at Contrà Fontana 6. Regulars fill this cozy self-service restaurant. Traditional dishes like *risotto al pesto* are made fresh and rotate daily. Primi €3.50-4.50. Secondi from €5-10. Cover €1. Open 10am-3pm and 6pm-midnight; closed 1st 3 weeks of Aug. Cash only. ❷

- 🍽 **Dai Nodari,** Contrà do Rode 20 (☎0444 54 40 85). Delicious menu with savory local cuisine like potato *gnochetti* with tomatoes and *mozzarella di bufala* (€5) or *morlacco* cheese with grape peels (€6). Eclectic, expansive interior. Lunch *menù* (€7-9) includes 2 courses. Salads €5. Cheeses €6. Primi €5-7. Secondi €8.50-13. Cover €1.50. Open Tu-Su noon-2:30pm and 7-10:30pm. AmEx/MC/V. ❸

- **Zi' Teresa,** Contrà S. Antonio 1 (☎0444 32 14 11), at the end of the street, to the left of the post office. Huge restaurant with multiple dining rooms decorated with frescoes of Naples. Try the *zi' teresa pizza* (with mushrooms and grilled peppers; €8) or the 3-course *menù* (€20 with meat, €26 with fish). Pizza €4-10. Primi €7-16. Secondi €10-17. Cover €2.50. Open M-Tu and Th-Su noon-2:30pm and 6:30pm-12:30am. AmEx/MC/V. ❹

- **Nirvana Caffè Degli Artisti,** P. Matteotti 8 (☎0444 54 31 11). From C. Palladio, enter the *piazza* and turn left. Buddha statues, incense, and books on healthy eating adorn this laid-back restaurant. Full menu of veggies, tofu, and tea. Try *panini* like "the tartaruga" (spiced tofu, tomato, arugula and parsley on whole-wheat; €4.10). Panini €3.60-4. Primi €5.50. Secondi €4.50-8. Open M-Sa 7am-8pm, Su 7am-3pm. Cash only. ❷

- **Ristorante Agli Schioppi,** Contrà P. del Castello 26 (☎0444 54 37 01), right off P. del Castello. Traditional dishes like black noodles with smoked trout and *zucchine* (€8) and beef with rosemary and roasted potatoes (€13), served in a warm, sunny interior or on the laid-back patio out front. Primi €7-9. Secondi €12-14. Cover €2.50. Open M-F noon-2pm and 7-10pm, Sa noon-2pm. AmEx/MC/V. ❸

👁 SIGHTS

For a view of Vicenza and Palladio's architecture, exit the train station and turn right on Vle. Venezia. Walk for about 10min., then turn left and go uphill at V. X Giugno. A long loggia to the left contains a staircase and ramp leading up Monte Berico to **Piazzale Vittoria,** where balconies jut out over the hillside.

■TEATRO OLIMPICO. Palladio did not live to see construction on his Teatro completed. The *Accademia Olimpica*, the city's organization for promotion of culture and the sciences, commissioned the construction project; the architect insisted that the Greek and Roman amphitheater style was the only one appropriate for the dramas the Accademia hoped to stage. Inside the *teatro*, carved statues—one for each of the Academy's members—fill the walls under a ceiling fresco of cloudy skies. Three main doors onstage and two side doors reveal the main streets of Thebes, crafted in perspective with excruciating detail for the theater's 1585 debut, *Oedipus Rex*. A beautiful sculpture garden and excellent English explanations lead to the ticket office and portrait gallery. (*In P. Matteotti. ☎0444 22 28 00; www.olimpico.vicenza.it. Open Tu-Su 9am-5pm. Last entry 4:30pm. €8, students €5, under 14 free; includes entrance to Museo Civico for 3 days after purchase. Audio tour available in many languages €3. Cash only.*) Summer brings local and imported talent to the Teatro. (*☎0444 22 28 01; www.comune.vicenza.it. MC/V.*)

PIAZZA DEI SIGNORI. The *piazza* was Vicenza's showpiece while the town was under Venetian control. Andrea Palladio's revamping of the **Basilica Palladiana** brought the architect his first taste of fame. (*Basilica closed indefinitely for renovations.*) The **Torre di Piazza,** a brick clock tower to the left of the basilica reveals a glimpse of the building's pre-Palladio architecture. The **Loggia del Capitano,** a municipal building across from the Torre, shows the results of the reconstruction, with two stories of marble pillars masking the crumbling brick beneath.

MUSEO CIVICO. Housed in Palladio's stately Palazzo Chiericati, this collection includes Renaissance art from Venetian powerhouses Tintoretto, Veronese, and Alessandro Vittoria. Giovanni Battista's first signed and dated work, *The Madonna of the Pergola* is in the last room, after Montagna's *Madonna Enthroned* and Tintoretto's *Miracle of St. Augustine*. (*☎0444 32 13 48. Open Tu-Su 9am-5pm. Last entry 4:30pm. Entrance included with Teatro Olimpico ticket.*)

◪ NIGHTLIFE

Somma Campagna Ugo, Corta Fontana 2 (*☎328 82 57 018*). Loud pop music and a nice selection of wine and beer to enjoy with *panini* and appetizers. Wine €2, beer €2.50. Open Tu-Su 8am-2pm and 5pm-midnight. Cash only.

◪ DAYTRIP FROM VICENZA: THE PALLADIAN VILLAS

Venetian expansion to the mainland began in the 15th century as Venice's maritime supremacy faded and nobles turned their attention to the acquisition of mainland real estate. The Venetian senate ordered nobles to build villas rather than castles to preclude the possibility of fiefdoms. The estate rush provided ample opportunity for renowned architect Andrea Palladio to showcase his talent. Some villas offer classical music concerts during summer; others can be rented for exorbitant rates—Neoclassical luxury doesn't come cheap. Check with tourist offices for details and contact info on regional villas. Though many of the Palladian villas scattered throughout the Veneto are difficult to reach, some of the most famous lie within a scenic 30min. walk of Vicenza. Stop for a moment at the **Villa Valmarana ai Nani,** 2km from the town center, to admire its perfectly manicured rose gardens and to see Tiepolo frescoes. (*Open Mar. 11-Nov. 5 Tu-Su 10am-noon and 3-6pm. €8, under 12 free.*) Begun in 1550, the ■**Villa Rotonda's** precision and alignment with the cardinal points produced one of the 16th century's most harmonious architectural achievements. The villa became a model for buildings in England, France, and the US, most notably Thomas Jefferson's Monticello. Don't feel badly if you miss a look at the villa's interior; the majesty of Villa Rotonda can just as easily be appreciated from outside. *(From Mt. Berico's P. Vittoria, head straight, keeping the mountains on the right. Bear left and continue down Stradella Valmarana. Or from Vle. Roma, just to the right of the train station, take bus #8 (€1) and ask for "La Rotonda."* ☎ *0444 32 17 93. Open from mid-Mar. to Nov. 5. Interior open W 10am-noon and 3-6pm. Tours Tu-Su 10am-noon and 3-6pm. Grounds €5, with interior €10.)* For those devoted to Palladio's architectural vision, **Palladio by the Hand Tour Company,** run through the tourist office, offers tours of Vicenza and some of the villas, with bus transportation to the villas provided. *(☎ 0444 32 08 54; www.vicenzae.org. Su 9am-3pm and 5:30pm, €12-15; Apr.-Nov. Sa 2:30-4:30pm, €10.)*

VERONA
☎ **045**

Verona (veh-RO-nah; pop. 4000) offers visitors much more than a Romeo and Juliet gimmick. From the winding river Adige to the city's dizzying towers, Verona offers the perks of a large city while maintaining a reputation for authentic local cuisine, rich wines, and an internationally renowned opera.

▎▋ TRANSPORTATION

Flights: Aeroporto Valerio Catullo (☎045 80 95 666; www.aeroportoverona.it), 16km from *centro*. For shuttles from train station (☎045 80 57 911; www.atv.verona.it; 5:40am, then every 20min. 6:10am-11:10pm; €4.50), buy tickets on the bus.

Trains: In Verona Porta Nuova P. XXV Aprile (☎045 89 20 21). Ticket office open daily 6am-9pm. To: **Bologna** (2hr., 22 per day 3:05am-10:38pm, €7.50); **Milan** (2hr., 34 per day 4:05am-10:42pm, €7); **Rome** (7hr., 4 per day 5:30am-11pm, €45); **Trent** (1hr., 25 per day 12:46am-10:48pm, €4.65); **Venice** (1hr., 41 per day 5:52am-10:43pm, €8); **Vicenza** (45min., 55 per day 5:52am-10:42pm, €3.40).

Buses: ATV, P. XXV Aprile (☎045 88 71 111; www.atv.verona.it), in the gray building in front of the train station. Station open M-Sa 6am-8pm, Su 6:30am-8pm. Buses run to **Brescia** (2hr., every hr. 6:40am-6:10pm, €5.30), **Riva del Garda** (2hr., 15 per day 6:40am-6:45pm, €5.20), and **Sirmione** (1hr., 17 per day 6:40am-10pm. Reduced service Sa-Su.)

Taxis: RadioTaxi (☎045 53 26 66; www.radiotaxiverona.it). 24hr.

Car Rental: Avis (☎045 80 06 636). Open M-F 8am-noon and 3-7pm, Sa 8am-noon. **Europcar** (☎045 92 73 161). Open M-F 8:30am-noon and 2:30-7pm, Sa 8:30am-noon. **Hertz** (☎045 80 00 832). 21+. Open M-F 8am-noon and 2:30-7pm, Sa 8am-noon. All 4 have offices at the train station. AmEx/MC/V.

◢▋ ORIENTATION AND PRACTICAL INFORMATION

From the **train station,** in P. XXV Aprile, walk 20min. up **Corso Porta Nuova,** or take bus #11, 12, 13, 51, 72, or 73 (weekends take #91, 92, or 93; tickets €1, full day €3.50) to Verona's *centro,* the **Arena di Verona,** in **Piazza Brà.** Most sights lie between P. Brà and the **Adige River. Via Mazzini** connects the Arena to the monuments of **Piazza delle Erbe** and **Piazza dei Signori.** The **Teatro Romano** and the **Giardino Giusti** lie across the bridges **Pietra, Navi,** and **Nuovo** on the Adige.

Tourist Office: At V. degli Alpini 9 (☎045 80 68 680; www.tourism.verona.it). From C. Pta. Nuova, enter P. Brà; office is on the right. Open M-Sa 9am-7pm, Su 9am-3pm.

Luggage Storage: At the train station (☎045 80 23 827; info@grandistazioni.it). €3.80 for 1st 5hr., €0.60 per hr. for 6-12hr., €0.20 per hr. thereafter; 5-day max. 20kg max. per bag. Open daily 6am-10pm. Cash only.

English-Language Bookstore: Ghelfi & Barbato, V. Mazzini 21 (☎045 80 02 306), at the intersection with V. Quattro Spade. Small, yet balanced English section with cafe upstairs. Open M-Sa 9am-12:30pm and 3:30-7pm. MC/V.

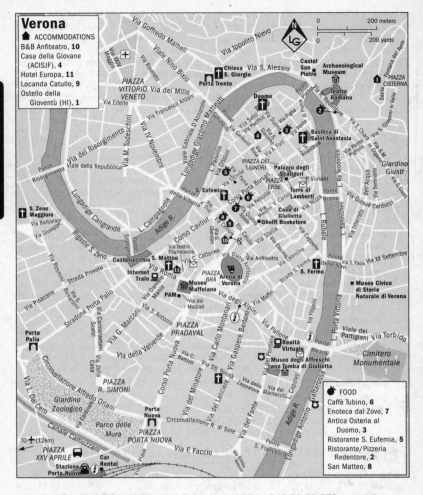

Verona

🏠 ACCOMMODATIONS

B&B Anfiteatro, **10**
Casa della Giovane
   (ACISJF), **4**
Hotel Europa, **11**
Locanda Catullo, **9**
Ostello della
   Gioventù (HI), **1**

🍴 FOOD

Caffè Tubino, **6**
Enoteca dal Zovo, **7**
Antica Osteria al
   Duomo, **3**
Ristorante S. Eufemia, **5**
Ristorante/Pizzeria
   Redentore, **2**
San Matteo, **8**

Beyond Tourism: Informagiovani, V. Ponte Aleardi 15 (☎045 80 78 770; www.informa-giovani.comune.verona.it), helps find work or study opportunities in Verona. Open M and F 9am-1pm, Tu and Th 3-6:30pm, W 9am-1pm and 3-6:30pm.

Police: V. del Pontiere 32/a (☎045 80 78 411).

Pharmacy: Farmacia Due Campane, V. Mazzini 52 (☎045 80 06 660). Open M-F 9:10am-12:30pm and 3:30-7:30pm, Sa 9:10am-12:30pm. MC/V.

Hospital: Ospedale Civile Maggiore (☎045 80 71 111), on Borgo Trento in P. Stefani in the north part of town.

Internet Access: Internet Train, V. Roma 17/A (☎045 80 13 394). From P. Brà, turn right on V. Roma; 2 blocks down on left. High-speed PCs, color printers, photocopiers, and scanners. €3.50 per hr. Open M-F 10am-11pm, Sa-Su 2-8pm. MC/V.

Post Office: V. Cattaneo 23 (☎045 80 03 998). Open M-F 8:30am-6:30pm, Sa 8:30am-1pm. **Postal Code:** 37100.

ACCOMMODATIONS

Budget hotels are sparse in Verona; those that do exist fill up quickly. Make reservations ahead, especially during opera season (June-Sept.). Prices rise when there are opera performances, and drop precipitously in the low season.

Bed and Breakfast Anfiteatro, V. Alberto Mario 5 (☎347 24 88 462; www.anfiteatro-bedandbreakfast.com). Walking toward P. Brà, V. Alberto Mario branches off from V. Mazzini to the right. Its central location and romantic rooms with TV and Internet access make this B&B one of the town's best options. Breakfast buffet included. Singles €60-90; doubles €80-130; triples €100-150. ❹

Ostello della Gioventù Villa Francescatti, Salita Fontana del Ferro 15 (☎045 59 03 60; www.villafrancescatti.com). Take bus #73 or night bus #90 to P. Isolo. From the Arena, turn on V. Anfiteatro, cross Ponte Nuovo on V. Carducci, turn left on V. Giusti, then right on V. San Giovanni in Valle. Follow yellow signs uphill. Quiet, out-of-the-way. Breakfast included; dinner €8, with vegetarian options. Laundry €2.50. Check-in by 5pm. Checkout 9am. Curfew midnight, extended for opera-goers. Reservations accepted for family rooms (€19 per person per night). Dorms €17. Cash and traveler's checks only. ❶

Locanda Catullo, V. Vco. Catullo 1, 2nd fl. (☎045 80 02 786; locandacatullo@tiscali. it). Follow V. Mazzini to V. Catullo. Turn left on Vco. Catullo. Family-run. Ideal refuge from the bustle of the nearby P. Erbe. Rooms are simple and spacious. Reception 9am-11pm. Singles €40; doubles €55, with bath €65; triples €81. Cash only. ❸

Casa della Giovane (ACISJF), V. Pigna 7 (☎045 59 68 80; www.casadellagiovane.com). From P. delle Erbe, turn right on C. Sant'Anastasia and take 1st left on V. Rosa; V. Pigna is the 3rd street on the right. Peaceful atmosphere with friendly, English-speaking staff, a communal kitchen, lounge, and courtyard. Bedrooms and shared showers aren't fancy but are comfortable and well kept for the price. No private keys or lockers. Linens provided. Laundry wash only €1.60. Reception open 1pm-9am. Curfew 11:30pm, except for opera-goers (present ticket upon return). Reserve ahead by email. Women only. Dorms €18; singles €28; doubles €46, with bath €25; triples €60/69. Cash only. ❶

Hotel Europa, V. Roma 8 (☎045 59 47 44; www.veronahoteleuropa.com), close to P. Brà. Centrally located, offering comfortable, modern rooms with A/C, TV, minibar, phone, and private bathrooms. Breakfast included. Parking €15. Wheelchair-accessible. Singles €107; doubles €180; triples €198. AmEx/MC/V. ❺

Hotel Torcolo, Vco. Listone 3 (☎045 80 07 512; www.hoteltorcolo.it). Quaint pink building on a quiet side street just around the corner from the Arena. Rooms equipped with A/C, TV, phone, fridge, safe, and private bath make this an unbeatable bargain. Maintains an intimate, homey feel for travelers seeking modest accommodations. Wheelchair-accessible. Singles €60; doubles €90; triples €110. MC/V. ❹

Hotel Scalzi, 5 V. Corso Scalzi (☎045 59 04 22; www.hotelscalzi.it). Convenient location near the train station and newly renovated rooms justify higher rates. Elegant lobby and well-equipped rooms with TV, private baths, and balconies. Single €80; doubles €100; 4- to 5- person apartments €200. AmEx/MC/V. ❺

FOOD

Verona is famous for its wines, among them the dry white *Soave* and the red *Valpolicella*, *Bardolino*, *Recioto*, and *Amarone*. Local specialties include *gnocchi* and *pasta e fagioli* (pasta and bean soup). **PAM,** V. dei Mutilati 3, sells essentials. From P. Brà, pass through the arch to C. Pta. Nuova, and turn right on V. Mutilati. (Open M-Sa 8am-8:30pm. AmEx/MC/V.)

THE VENETO

▓ **Enoteca dal Zovo,** Vco. San Marco in Foro 7 (☎045 80 34 369; www.enotecadalzovo.it), off C. Pta. Borsari. This small winery occupies a converted chapel with original frescoes still adorning the ceiling, though cluttered shelves of bottles make the space seem more like an apothecary. Owner Oreste dal Zovo serves impressive wines, welcoming visitors like old friends. Open daily 8am-8pm. Cash only. ❶

▓ **Antica Osteria al Duomo,** V. Duomo 7/a (☎045 80 04 505), on the way to the *duomo*. Small, laid-back restaurant with dark wood interior has a few cozy tables and a bar, and serves excellent, simple cuisine like *tagliatelle* with shrimp and zucchini. Customers enjoy drinks outside on the quiet street when the interior gets too crowded. Primi €6.50-7. Secondi €7-15. Cover €1.50. Open M-Sa 11am-3pm and 7-11pm. MC/V ❶

San Matteo, Vco. del Guasto 4 (☎045 80 04 538; fax 59 39 38), from P. delle Erbe on C. Pta. Borsari, walk 5min., and turn left. Housed in a beautiful, centrally located former church with simple, elegant interior. Primi €7.50-11. Secondi €9-17. Cover €1.50. Open daily noon-2:30pm and 6pm-12:30am. AmEx/MC/V. ❸

Ristorante/Pizzeria Redentore, V. Regaste Redentore 15 (☎045 80 05 932), right across Ponte Pietra. Patio seating offers splendid views of the Adige River, *duomo,* and Torre dei Lamberti. Generous portions and wide vegetarian selection make this a popular spot. Pizza €3.50-7.50. Primi €6.50-8.50. Secondi €7-9.50. Cover €1.30. Open Tu-Su noon-2pm and 6pm-midnight. MC/V. ❶

Ristorante San Eufemia, V. Emilei 21/B (☎045 80 06 865; www.s.eufemia.it). From V. Rosa, make a left on V. Francesco Emilei and walk until you reach the tiny Vco. San Eufemia. Specializing in seafood dishes (€10-20) and traditional Veronese cuisine (like homemade *bolognese* with grilled vegetables over spaghetti, €20), this restaurant makes for a romantic pre-opera dinner with outdoor, candlelit seating. Primi €6-20. Secondi €8-16. Cover €2. Open June-Aug. daily noon-2:30pm and 7pm-1am; Sept.-May M-Sa noon-2:30pm and 5-11pm. AmEx/MC/V. ❸

Caffè Tubino, C. Pta.Borsari 15/D (☎045 80 31 313), near the intersection of C. Pta. Borsari and V. Fama. Housed in a 17th-century *palazzo*. Serves healthy doses of coffee and kitsch with rich brews and floor-to-ceiling wall of teacups. Seating is scarce, but come for the popular ground coffee (€18-25 per kg). Espresso €0.90. Cappuccino €1.40. Open daily 7:30am-8:30 pm. Cash only. ❶

◉ SIGHTS

▓**SHAKESPEAREAN HUBRIS.** Shakespeare buffs still flock to Verona for its role as the setting of *Romeo and Juliet,* hoping to absorb some love from the Bard's ill-fated couple. At the **Casa di Giulietta,** tourists pose on the stone balcony, but the house is best admired from the outside, where vastly more entertaining lovers' graffiti has built up. The Veronese authorities have protected the building from further poetic injury by slyly installing plastic sheets where people write, replacing them every two months with no young Romeo the wiser. Contrary to popular belief, the Capulet family never lived here, so save your money and skip the inside. *(V. Cappello 23. ☎045 80 34 303. Open M 1:30-7:30pm, Tu-Su 8:30am-7:30pm. Ticket office closes 6:45pm. €4, students and seniors €3. Cash only.)* A canopy shades the walkway into the **Museo Degli Affreschi,** which displays Veronese artwork, including an excellent collection of Italian frescoes from the 10th to 16th centuries. The museum's garden houses the faux **Tomba di Giulietta,** a cave with a single window illuminating the sepulcher. It will take only a moment to mourn at the *tomba*—which like the Capulet house is lined with lovers graffiti—but stay a minute longer in the atrium courtyard, a quiet place to rest your feet after touring the art inside. *(V. del Pontiere 35. ☎045 80 00 361. Open M 1:30-7:30pm, Tu-Su 8:30am-7:30pm. Ticket office closes 6:45pm. €3, students and seniors €2.)* The **Casa di Romeo,** reportedly once home to the Montecchi (Montague) family, sits around the corner from P. dei Signori at V. Arche Scaligeri 2. The villa is privately owned and closed to the public.

▨ PIAZZA ERBE AND PIAZZA DEI SIGNORI. Tourists and school groups swarm to P. Erbe, which features a market selling fruit and tacky souvenirs. Shops and restaurants line the *piazza;* in its center, pigeons hop around tiers of the **Madonna Verona's Fountain.** The nearby **Berlina**—a platform on which medieval convicts were punished by being pelted with produce—is also a crowd pleaser. P. delle Erbe lies near **Via Mazzini,** where pink marble leads local glitterati to Gucci and Louis Vuitton along the city's fashion row. The **Arco della Costa** (Arch of the Rib) connects P. delle Erbe to **Piazza dei Signori.** A whale rib, prophesied to fall on the first passing person who has never told a lie, still dangles from the arch, and a statue of Dante stands in the center of the *piazza.* The 15th-century **Loggia del Consiglio** sits in the *piazza* just behind Dante's back. The della Scala family lived in the **Palazzo degli Scaligeri,** and the medieval **Tombs of the Scaligeri,** on V. Arche Scaligeri, are through the arch in P. dei Signori.

ROMEO, ROMEO, WHEREFORE ART THOU ROMEO? Juliet & Co. provides excellent full- and half-day walking tours of Verona for groups (€105-210, up to 30 people). Individuals may join alternative walking tours (1¼hr), which run daily from Apr. 1 to Nov. 5 and depart from P. Brà at 5:30pm. (☎045 81 03 173; www.julietandco.com. €10; no booking required.)

THE ARENA. Red velvet curtains and an eroding stone archway welcome visitors to this AD first-century Roman amphitheater, home to the annual **Verona Opera Festival.** For the best view and the lowest price, opt for original stone slab seating above. The age and authenticity of the arena is slightly thrown off by the concession stands and souvenir tables that draw hoards of tourists, especially during opera season. (*In P. Brà.* ☎045 80 03 204. Open M 1:30-7:30pm, Tu-Su 8:30am-7:30pm. Closes 4:30pm on opera nights. Ticket sales end 1hr. before closing. Wheelchair-accessible. €4, students and seniors €3, children 8-13 €1.)

BASILICA DI SANT'ANASTASIA. Verona's largest Gothic church hides artistic treasures behind its crumbling brick doors. Colorful stain-glass at the apse complements the beautiful 15th- and 16th-century frescoes lining the walls, including those of the Lavagnoli Chapel to the left of the main altar. Floral patterns and geometric designs on the ceiling lend to the church's majestic feel. To the right, the Cappella Pellegrini depicts the life of Christ with Michele da Firenze's series of 24 terra-cotta reliefs. (*At the end of C. Sant'Anastasia. For info, call the Associazione "Chiese Vive" at* ☎045 59 28 13. Open Mar.-Oct. M-Sa 9am-6pm, Su 1-6pm; Nov.-Feb. Tu-Sa 10am-1pm and 1:30-4pm, Su 1-5pm. €3, students €2.50. Cash only.)

DUOMO AND ENVIRONS. History lives beneath the floorboards of this 12th-century *duomo,* which houses treasures that include ancient Roman thermal baths and two previous basilicas. The excavation of one of the older basilicas, the Church of Saint Elena, is accessible through the *duomo,* just to the left of the apse. Titian's *Assumption of the Virgin,* which is a less potent version of his later Assumption that now hangs in Venice, is in the first chapel on the left. (*At the end of V. Duomo. From the basilica, turn on V. Massalongo, which becomes V. Duomo.* ☎045 59 28 13. Open Mar.-Oct. M-Sa 10am-5:30pm, Su 1-5:30pm; Nov.-Feb. Tu-Sa 10am-1pm and 1:30-4pm, Su 1:30-5pm. €3, students €2.50. Cash only.)

TEATRO ROMANO AND ENVIRONS. A crumbling **Roman theater** comes alive with productions of Shakespeare's works translated into Italian (see **Entertainment,** see next page). Behind the theater's seats, precarious Roman stairs weave up a small hillside, offering a romantic view of Verona's housetops and cypress trees. Built in 1480, the city's **archaeological museum**—formerly a Jesuit monastery—now displays Roman and Greek artifacts from local excavation sites. In the center sits the **Grande Terrazza,** a quiet, leafy garden lined with Roman bas-reliefs. *(V. Regaste Redentore 2. Cross Ponte Pietra from the centro, and turn right. ☎045 80 00 360; fax 80 10 587. Open M 1:30-7:30pm, Tu-Su 8:30am-7:30pm. Ticket office closes 6:45pm. €3, students and groups of 20 or more €2. Cash only.)* Behind a brown facade, the gates of the 16th-century ▓**Giardino Giusti** open onto a spacious hillside dotted with trickling, moss-covered fountains and rows of meticulously trimmed hedges—including **Il Labirinto,** a thigh-high hedge maze, which children and adults alike can explore. The cypress-lined avenue winds upward toward a series of picturesque porticoes and curving balconies with breathtaking views of Verona. *(Down V. Santa Chiara from Teatro Romano at V. Giardino Giusti 2. ☎045 80 34 029. Open daily Apr.-Sept. 9am-8pm; Oct.-Mar. 9am-7pm. €5, students €2.50, under 18 free. Cash only.)*

MY FAIR VERONA. The **Verona Card** (day pass €8, 3 days €12) is an excellent money saver, which includes free ATV bus rides and entry to most of the city's museums, churches, and sights. Purchase it at participating museums, churches, or *tabaccherie.* Churches also offer their own pass (€5, students and seniors €4), permitting entrance to the basilica, *duomo,* S. Fermo, S. Zeno, and S. Lorenzo. For more information, visit www.comune.verona.it.

CASTELVECCHIO AND ENVIRONS. The 14th-century *castello* was built as a defense by the della Scala family, whose coat of arms lines the interior walls. These days, the castle is a **museum** of sculptures and paintings, among them Pisanello's celebration of natural paradise in *Madonna della Quaglia* and works by Mantegna and Bellini. Perhaps most interesting is the castle itself. Its maze-like design leads visitors up stone staircases and over partially covered bridges to a lovely elevated view of the **Fiume Adige.** The interior courtyard houses a peaceful garden. *(From P. Brà, take V. Roma to C. Castelvecchio 2. ☎045 80 62 611; www.comune.verona.it/castelvecchio/cvsito. Open M 1:30-7:30pm, Tu-Su 8:30am-7:30pm. Last entry 45min. before closing. €4, students €3. Audio tour in English, German, and Italian €4. Cash only.)* Scipione Maffei's devotion to preserving stone inscriptions is enshrined in the nearby **Museo Lapidario Maffeiano,** where much of the collection of Greek, Roman, and Etruscan art is over 2000 years old. *(P. Brà, 3 at the corner of V. Roma and C. Pta. Nuova. ☎045 59 00 87. Open Tu-Su 8:30am-2pm. €3, students €2. Cash only.)*

SAN ZENO MAGGIORE. Named for Verona's patron saint, who converted the city to Christianity in the AD fourth century, this massive brick church is one of Verona's finest examples of Romanesque architecture. An urn in the subterranean crypt holds Zeno's remains, and one particularly beautiful balcony among the church's multiple levels features statues of Christ and the 12 apostles. *(From Castelvecchio, walk up Rigaste San Zeno and turn left at the piazza on V. Barbarani, then right on V. San Procolo to the church on the right. For info, call the Associazione "Chiese Vive" at ☎045 59 28 13 or visit www.chiesaverona.it. Open Mar.-Oct. M-Sa 8:30am-6pm, Su 1-6pm; Nov.-Feb. Tu-Sa 10am-1pm and 1:30-4pm, Su 5pm. Ticket sales end 15min. before closing. €2.50. Cash only.)*

♫ ENTERTAINMENT

The Arena di Verona is the venue for the world-famous ▓**Verona Opera Festival,** which attracts opera enthusiasts in droves every year from June to August. Past productions have included Verdi's *Nabucco, Aida,* and *La Traviata;* Puccini's *La Bohème;* and Rossini's *The Barber of Seville.* The 2009 opera season runs from June 19 to Aug. 30. (Tickets and info at V. Dietro Anfiteatro 6/B, along the side of the Arena. ☎045 80 05 151; www.arena.it. Open M-F 9am-noon and 3:15-5:45pm, Sa 9am-noon. Open on performance days and Sundays during opera season 10am-9pm. Admission €19-198; seats range from general admission on stone steps to reserved "gold" membership seating. AmEx/MC/V.) Also in summer, the **Teatro Romano,** V. Regaste Redentore 2, close to the Ponte Pietà, stages dance performances and Shakespearean plays performed in Italian. June brings the **Verona Jazz Festival.** (Info ☎045 80 66 485 or 045 80 66 488; www.estateteatraleveronese.it. Ticket office at Palazzo Barbieri, V. Leoncino 61. Open M-Sa 10:30am-1pm and 4-7pm. Tickets €11-21.)

CAORLE ☎0421

The small fishing town of Caorle (kah-OR-leh, pop. 10,000) has been nicknamed "Little Venice," and with its winding *calli* (narrow pedestrian streets) and brightly colored buildings, it's easy to see why. While it may remind visitors of its colossal cousin, which is just a 2hr. train ride away, Caorle has a charm all its own. Stroll through the quiet stone streets of the Old City, sample the seafood fresh from local docks, and sunbathe on miles of shoreline. What it lacks in cultural attractions, Caorle makes up in casual charm.

TRANSPORTATION. Caorle is 45min. by bus from the nearest train station in Portogruaro. The **bus station,** Vle. Chiggiato, is a 5min. walk from the *centro.* (☎0421 38 36 75. Ticket office open M-F 6am-7:50pm, Sa-Su 7:10am-8:30pm.) **Buses** run from Portogruaro (ticket office open M-F 6:20am-7:10pm, Sa-Su 6:20am-7:30pm) to Caorle (17 per day 5:45am-10:30pm, €3.10). Buses also run directly from Caorle to Venice (1-2hr., 19 per day 5am-8pm, €4.70). From Portogruaro, **trains** run to Trieste (1hr., 23 per day 1:07am-midnight, €6.60) and Venice (1 hr., 20 per day 5:37am-10:38pm, €4). The ticket office is open daily 6:05am-5:25pm and 5:40-7:40pm. Local bus lines connect the central bus station with Porto Falconera on the western end of town, **airport** Marco Polo, and Traghetto on the eastern end. (Tickets €1, available at tourist office and *tabaccherie.*) Rent **bikes** at **Noleggio Cicli,** V. Santa Margherita 17. (☎0421 338 887 4240. €3 per hr., €10 per day, €25 per week. Open daily 9am-10pm, depending on weather. Cash only.) Bikes are also available at **Da Fiammetta,** V. Istria 3. (☎338 86 01 794. €3.50 per hr., €10 per day, €30 per week. Open daily 9am-midnight.)

ORIENTATION AND PRACTICAL INFORMATION. From the bus station, take **Via San Giuseppe,** then turn right on **Via Altinate** and left on **Strada Nuova** to reach **Piazza Papa Giovanni,** which marks the northeastern border of Caorle's Old City. The **tourist office,** Calle Delle Liburniche 16, just off the *piazza,* offers great maps, hotel and B&B listings, a list of Internet access points, and info on local and regional attractions. (☎0421 81 085. Open daily 8am-2pm and 4-10pm.) In an **emergency,** call the **police** (☎0421 81 345). The nearest **hospital** is in Portogruaro (☎041 76 41), but the **clinic** on Vle. Buonarroti has 24hr. first aid and an on-call doctor. **Pharmacy Montanari** is located at Rio Terra 30. (☎0421 81 044. Open daily 8:45am-12:30pm and 4:30-10:30pm.) For **Internet** access, head next door to **Central Photo** at Rio Terra 38. (☎0421 81 039. Open May-Sept. daily 9am-12:30pm and 4:30-11pm; Oct.-Apr. Tu-Su 9am-noon and 3:30-7pm. €2 per 30min., €3 per hr., €5 for 2hr.) The **post office** is at Calle Lunga 1. (☎0421 21 99 11. Open M-F 8:30am-2pm, Sa 8:30am-1pm.) **Postal Code:** 30021.

ACCOMMODATIONS AND CAMPING. Caorle offers scores of hotels on or near the beach. Expect that a beach chair, umbrella, and some pension package will be included in your nightly rate. From the bus station, turn left

STONE COLD CREATIVITY

Along the boardwalk that begins at the historic Santuario della Madonna and stretches along the town's beautiful coastline to the east, Caorle is developing an art tradition to match its beach scene. Every other year in late June, five sculptors from around the world arrive in the small fishing town to work one of the hundreds of shoreline stones into a personal creation. The project, called Viva Scogliera (Long Live the Stones), allows locals and visitors an unobstructed view of the creative process: during selected hours, the five sculptors allow the public to look on as they continue to transform the boardwalk.

Initiated in 1993, Viva Scogliera began as an annual event; in 2003, town officials decided to alternate years, worrying that they might run out of stones! Now, the competition takes place only during even-numbered years.

Jin Hee Lee, a South Korean sculptor, takes credit for the stone that has come to symbolize the project: an exaggerated nose and pair of lips, entitled "Self-Portrait." The dramatic 1994 sculpture "Umanità," by Italian artist Franco Maschio, features a man reaching off a cliff for the outstretched hand of a falling comrade. To browse the sculptures, start at the Madonna and meander down the boardwalk, stopping briefly to take in each of the labeled stones against the blue-green Adriatic Sea.

on C. Chiggiato, then right on V. Falconera to reach family-friendly **Albergo Villa Venezia ❷**, V. Falconera 13, which has simple, comfortable rooms and a bustling dining area. The real draws, however, are the friendly staff and winning location—less than 5min. from both the bus station and the beach. (☎0421 21 23 13; www.villavenezia.caorle.it. Free bike rental. €25-30 per person; varies seasonally. Half- and full-board available. Breakfast €5. MC/V.) To get to **Hotel Meduna ❸**, V. Nicesolo 11, from the bus station, turn left on C. So Chiggiato, then right on V. Nicesolo; the hotel is on the corner. English-speaking owner Roberto offers clean, spacious, and quiet rooms with bath, phone, A/C, balcony, and satellite TV. The hotel also features an elegant lobby and open dining area where meals are served for those on half- and full-pension plans. (☎0421 21 22 96; www.hotelmeduna.com. Breakfast included. Beach equipment included. Min. 3-night stay. €35-45 per person; prices vary seasonally. AmEx/MC/V.) Just a few blocks from the center and Spiaggia di Ponente, **Camping Santa Margherita ❶**, V. Duca degli Abruzzi, is a hike from the bus station and Old City, but only steps away from the shoreline of Spiaggia di Ponente. From the bus station, take local bus #98-99 toward Traghetto (every hr. 7:30am-10:30pm, €1) and ask for Camping S. Margherita, or walk 20-25min. down Lungomare Venezia from the *centro*. A supermarket and restaurant/bar are located on the premises of this quiet, shaded spot. (☎0421 81 276; www.campingcaorle.it. Open Mar.-Oct. 5. Reception open 8:30am-noon and 3-6:30pm. €3.70-7.65 per person; €6.80-18 per tent site. AmEx/MC/V.)

◖ **FOOD.** True to its reputation as a fishing town, Caorle specializes in fresh seafood straight from the Adriatic. Sit at one of the aging wood tables at laid-back **Ristorante Pizzeria de Mauri ❸**, P. San Pio X. The simple menu offers grilled fish and delicious seafood pasta, like *spaghetti pescatore* (€7.50), at slightly lower prices than its nearby competitors. (☎0421 81 279. Primi €6-7.50. Secondi €7-16. Open daily 9:50am-2:10pm and 6:30pm-midnight. MC/V.) Your stay in Caorle wouldn't be complete without a visit to **Caffe Charlotte ❶**, where servers clad in glittery, silver vests prepare warm crepes with sinful fillings (€2.50-4). Try their popular nutella-filled crepe or the adventurous *dulce de leche* with meringue and Irish cream. (☎0421 338 327 9958. Open daily 4pm-midnight.) For ocean views and the daily catch, make the 20min. trip down Lungomare Venezia to **Picnic ❸**, V. Timavo 6, on the western shore. Eat in your bathing suit at the cafe's outdoor tables, or cover up for the classy interior. (☎0421 21 15 75. Primi €6.50-12. Secondi €5.50-13. Cover €1.50. Open daily 7am-midnight. MC/V.) The closest supermarket is **Super M,** V. delle Orate 47, which can be entered around the corner on V. Calamari. (☎0421 81 167. Open M-F 8am-1pm and 3:30-8:30pm, Sa-Su 8am-8:30pm. MC/V.) On Saturday from 8:30am-1pm, there is an **outdoor market** behind the bus station, which sells fresh fruits, vegetables, meats, and local cheeses.

⚓ ⊙ BEACHES AND SIGHTS. Vacationers from Italy, Austria, and Slovenia converge in Caorle during the summer months to share adjacent beach umbrellas and wait in line at one of the town's many *gelaterie.* The town's two main beaches, **Spiaggia di Levante** and **Spiaggia di Ponente,** extend to the left and right, respectively, from the *centro* as you face the water. Access to both beaches is free, but you must either pay for a chair and umbrella, or stay at one of the many hotels that provide them. Spiaggia di Levante has shallower water and fewer crowds, but it's all relative on summer weekends—expect squealing children wherever you spread your towel. For a less chaotic seaside experience, check out the **lagoon** on the western shore. Undisturbed by hordes of beachgoers, the lagoon, which once inspired Ernest Hemingway's novel *Across the River and Into the Trees,* is home to abandoned thatched-roof fishermen's huts. A **walking** and **biking** path runs along the lagoon, then turns back eastward to join the main road heading into town. This route offers particularly striking views, but well-marked bike paths run all over town. Just be aware in the areas immediately surrounding the *centro;* you'll have to swerve around crowds of pedestrians. If you have more than a passing interest in the lagoon, consider **Motonave Arcobaleno's** boat tour, which thoroughly explains the history of Caorle's port and lagoon. (☎0421 21 04 28. Boats run Apr.-Sept. and depart from Caorle's fishing port. 2½hrs., 9am and 2:30pm. €14, ages 2-10 €8. Ask at the tourist office for more details.) Be sure to spend some time between beach sessions exploring the narrow, winding streets of Caorle's *centro storico.* While *gelaterie* and souvenir shops have taken over the main pedestrian thoroughfares, the stunningly bright pastels of the buildings remain. The **Santuario della Madonna dell'Angello,** a striking sight at the tip of the *centro* against the blue-green Adriatic, contains a beloved statue of the Madonna that watches over Caorle and its fishermen. The Santuario's ornate ceiling, decorated with floral motifs and oceanic paintings, is spectacular to behold by candlelight. (Open daily 7am-10pm. Free.) Slightly inland from the sanctuary, **Cathedral St. Stefano** provides an example of Romanesque-Byzantine architecture and holds the skull of the martyr St. Stephen. Adjacent to the cathedral is its **campanile.** Equally as formidable along the skyline as the sanctuary's tower, this site was once a watchtower over the ocean. (Cathedral open daily 7am-10pm. No admittance to *campanile.* Free.)

▨ NIGHTLIFE. Caorle offers its fair share of bars, but those looking for loud music and dancing should head to **Don Pablo,** Lungomare Venezia 1. In the daytime, customers enjoy sandwiches and drinks on the open terrace overlooking the water as techno music blares in the tropical-themed and cartoon-decorated interior. On Tuesdays, the adjoining *discoteca* caters to the late-night crowd with Latin music, while Saturday is disco night. Low lighting, fruity cocktails (€7), and a crowded dance floor make this the most popular spot around. (☎0421 81 054. €8 cover includes first drink. *Discoteca* open Tu and Sa 11pm-4am; restaurant open daily 8am-2pm. AmEx/MC/V.) Those looking for a good drink—or a few—should head to **Drizze Scotte,** P. P. Giovanni 11. Packed at all hours, this lounge has sleek furnishings along the *piazza,* loud music, and cold drinks that flow all night long. (☎0421 320 882 0399. Mixed drinks €6. Beer €2.50-5. Open daily 8am-2pm and 5pm-4am.)

TREVISO ☎ 0422

Treviso (treh-VEE-zoh; pop. 80,000), provincial capital of the Veneto and a low-cost flight hub, has two nicknames: *Città d'Acqua* (City of Water) and *Città Dipinta* (Painted City). The city's most noticeable feature, however, is its wealth. While fashion aficionados peer at the glitzy storefronts in the birthplace of Benetton, anyone can enjoy the local specialty—tiramisu—at outdoor tables and explore the cobblestone lanes that weave through the *centro storico*.

⌐ TRANSPORTATION

Budget Airlines: Treviso airport (TSF; www.trevisoairport.it). The ACTV Line 6 bus runs from the airport to the Treviso train station (10-15min.; every 15-20min. 6:09am-10pm; €1, €2 on board). **RyanAir** flies to **Rome, Barcelona, Dublin, London,** and **Paris.**

Trains: P. Duca d'Aosta, (☎0422 89 20 21), south of the *centro.* **Luggage storage** €3 for 1st 12hr., €2 per each additional 12hr. Open M-F 7am-8pm, Sa-Su 8:30am-6pm. Cash only. Ticket counter open daily 6am-8pm. To: **Trieste** (2hr., 27per day 5:58am-11:45pm, €10), **Udine** (1hr., 32per day 12:27am-11:30pm, €6.40), and **Venice** (30min., 55 per day 5:07am-11:30pm, €2.40). Trains to **Milan** or **Padua** connect in Venice.

Buses: Lungosile A. Mattei 21 (☎0422 57 73 11), off C. del Popolo where it crosses the river. From the train station, turn left on V. Roma. La Marca (☎0422 57 73 11; www.lamarcabus.it; ticket window open daily 6:30am-7:30pm) serves the Veneto region and the Palladian Villas, sending buses to **Padua** (1hr., 35 per day 5:25am-8:15pm, €4) and Vicenza (1-2hr., 11 per day 6:15am-5:10pm, €4.20). ACTV (☎0415 28 78 86; informazioni@actv.it) runs buses to **Venice** (1hr., 40 per day 4:10am-10:45pm, €2.60). All buses run slightly reduced service on the weekend.

◼✈✿ ORIENTATION AND PRACTICAL INFORMATION

Treviso lies 30km inland from Venice. Surrounded by the Sile River, the old city walls encompass Treviso's *centro storico* and most points of interest. From the train station, the ACTV (intra-city) bus hub is across from **Piazza Duca d'Aosta.** Left of the buses, **Via Roma** leads to the river; it then becomes **Corso del Popolo,** crosses the river, and enters **Piazza della Borsa.** From there, a walk up **Via XX Settembre** leads to **Piazza dei Signori,** Treviso's main square. Pedestrian-dominated **Via Calmaggiore** leads to the *duomo.*

Tourist Office: P. Monte di Pietà 8 (☎0422 54 76 32; www.provincia.treviso.it). Palazzo dei Trecento's side from P. dei Signori. Open M 9am-12:30pm, Tu-F 9am-12:30pm and 2-6pm, Sa 9am-12:30pm and 3-6pm, Su 9:30am-12:30pm and 3-6pm.

Beyond Tourism: Centro Giovani, P. Duomo 23 (☎0422 58 00 71; www.progettogiovani.it). Offers info on employment and study opportunities. Open Tu 10am-12:30pm and 3:30-6pm, W 10am-12:30pm, Th 3:30-6pm, F 3:30-6pm and 8:30-10:30pm.

Police: V. Carlo Alberto 37 (☎0422 57 71 11).

Hospital: Ospedale Civile Ca' Foncello is at P. Ospedale 1 (☎0422 32 21 11).

Pharmacy: P. Duomo 29 (☎0422 54 12 46). Posts after hours rotation. Open M-F and Su 8:45am-12:30pm and 3:45-7:15pm, Sa 8:45am-12:30pm.

Internet Access: Atta and Sons, Vle. D'Alviano Bartolomeo 52 (☎0422 54 54 77), on the northern edge of the town. €1.50 per hr. Also has telephones and Western Union. Open M-Th and Sa-Su 7:30am-8:30pm. Cash only.

Post Office: P. Vittoria 1 (☎0422 65 32 11), at the end of V. Cadorna, off C. del Popolo. Open M-Sa 8:30am-6:30pm. **Postal Code:** 31100.

THE VENETO

◤ ACCOMMODATIONS

Wealthy Treviso's accommodations are no friend to the budget traveler.

Albergo Il Focolare, P. Ancilotto 4 (☎/fax: 0422 56 601.), behind Palazzo dei Trecento. Sunny, pleasant rooms with flowers and pastel decor have TV, A/C, phone, and private bath in a prime location. If you're willing to splurge, Il Focolare is worth it. Breakfast included. Reception 7am-midnight, though guests may enter later with key. Reservations recommended. Singles €75; doubles €100; triples €115. AmEx/MC/V. ❺

Hotel Aurora, Ple. Ospedale 23 (☎0422 40 66 22; www.hotelauroratreviso.com). Take bus #1 to the Ospedale stop and walk 5min. to Ple Ospedale. Modern, sunny, and neat rooms with A/C, phone, TV, minibar, and private baths. Rare value is worth the trip from the *centro*. Singles €45; doubles €65; triples €80; quads €100. AmEx/MC/V. ❸

19 Borgo Cavour, 19 Borgo Cavour (☎380 25 89 743 or 41 91 45; www.cre-attivi.it), a 2min. walk heading left on Borgo Cavour from the *duomo*. Hallways lined with paintings lead to 3 spacious rooms decked out in modern, minimalist decor with private baths. Multi-lingual owner and designer Luca welcome guests with his vast knowledge of the area. Breakfast included. Singles €70; doubles €100; triples €140. MC/V. ❺

Hotel Continental, V. Roma 16 (☎0422 41 12 16), 5min. from the train station and *centro*. With friendly service and an old-fashioned feel, this hotel boasts 80 elegantly furnished rooms with private baths, phone, TV, minibars, and A/C. Palatial lobby. Wi-Fi €3 per hr. Singles €79-97; doubles €96-110. AmEx/MC/V. ❺

Locanda Da Renzo, V. Terraglio 108 (☎0422 40 20 68; www.locandadarenzo.it.). From the train station, turn right, climb the stairs to the overpass, and head right down Strada Terraglio for 10-15min.; or, take bus #7, 8, or 11 (€0.80). Ask the driver for Da Renzo or the Borgo Savoia stop. The small but comfortable rooms of this villa share a breakfast nook and quiet courtyard. All rooms have shower, A/C, TV, and phone. Breakfast included. Internet €2 per hr. Reception 7am-midnight. Singles €55; doubles €75; triples €95. AmEx/MC/V. ❹

◖ FOOD

Treviso is famous for its cherries, which ripen in June; radicchio, a bitter and spicy vegetable that peaks in December; and tiramisu. There's a **produce market** in Borgo Mazzini, near the northeastern walls of the *centro*. (Tu and Sa 7:30am-12:30pm.) For basics, head to the **PAM** supermarket, V. Zorzetto 12, off C. del Popolo. (☎0422 58 39 13. Open M-Sa 8am-8pm, Su 9am-1pm. AmEx/MC/V.)

La Vera Terra, V. Girolamo di Treviso 5 (☎0422 41 02 03), near Hotel Carlton. Hearty vegetarian dishes in an smooth, Zen-like atmosphere. Try the spicy quinoa with Kiziki and carrot (€6.50) or the falafel with hummus and sweet curry (€8). Primi €6.50-15. Secondi €8-18. Cover €2. Open M-Sa 12:30-2:30pm and 8-10:30pm. Their market next door sells groceries and vitamins. Open M-Sa 9am-9pm. MC/V. ❹

Enoteca Odeon La Colonna, V. Campana 27 (☎0422 58 35 99). Fish specialties include black ravioli filled with salmon and ricotta in saffron and wild fennel sauce (€11). Outdoor seating overlooks the river. Primi €8-11. Secondi €16-18. Cover €3. Open Tu-Sa 12:30-2:30pm and 7:30pm-12:30am, Su 7:30pm-12:30am. V/MC. ❹

All'Oca Bianca, V. della Torre 7, (☎0422 54 18 50; www.allocabianca.com) off V. Calmaggiore. Excellent fish from a fresh, seasonal menu. Try famous pasta and beans or the vegetarian antipasto plate. Primi €6-7. Secondi €7-16. Cover €2. Open M-Tu and F-Su 12:30-2pm and 7:30-10pm, Th 7:30-10pm. AmEx/MC/V. ❸

Brek, C. del Popolo 25 (☎0422 59 00 12). Self-service chain with a wide selection of fresh cuisine at reasonable prices. Salad bar, pasta station, and grill. Primi €4. Secondi €4-7. Open daily 11:30am-3pm and 6:30-10pm. AmEx/MC/V. ❶

⊙ SIGHTS

The busy, boutique-laden Calmaggiore stretches from beneath the arcades of the P. dei Signori to the unusual pillars marking the entrance to the seven-domed Neoclassical **duomo**. Its Renaissance chapels were restored in 1947 after World War II damage. Check out the **Annunciation Chapel,** which features Titian's masterpiece of the same name, to the right and behind the main altar. (Open M-Sa 7:30am-noon and 3:30-7pm, Su 7:30am-1pm and 3:30-8pm. *Duomo* free. Modest dress required. Capella illumination €0.30.) From V. XX Settembre, skirt the right side of the busy, cafe-lined loggias of P. dei Signori to find the marble staircase of the **Palazzo dei Trecento.** Originally the town's municipal building, it is now a memorial to the 1944 Good Friday air raid that devastated the small town. A marble plaque under the stairs commemorates local citizens killed in concentration camps. (☎0422 65 82 35. Closed to the public. Contact the tourist office for info about group tours.)

⊙ NIGHTLIFE

Al Botegon, Vle. Burchiellati 7 (☎0422 54 83 45). Fresh sandwiches and appetizers by day; young crowd at night. Huge wine selection (€1.50-2.30). Open M 9:30am-2:30pm and 5pm-midnight, Tu and Sa 8am-3pm and 5pm-2am, W-F 8:30am-2:30pm and 5pm-2am, Su 8:30am-midnight. Cash only.

Mamamia, Borgo Mazzini 50 (☎0422 333 258 6753). Hip crowd and chic patio with neon cube lanterns and geometric seating. Mixed drinks (€5), beer (€2.50-4), and spritz (€2; after 11pm €3) served with tasty *cicchetti*. Open Tu-Su 6pm-2am. Cash only.

BELLUNO   ☎0437

On the southeastern border of the Dolomites, Belluno (beh-LOO-no; pop. 37,000) is ideal for outdoorsmen on a budget. You won't find obnoxious tourists or souvenir stands here, just quiet *piazze* and locals who all seem to know each other. Easy train access combined with inexpensive dining and lodging make Belluno a great base for exploring the beautiful snow-covered peaks.

▐ TRANSPORTATION. Belluno runs trains to a number of cities, but plan ahead because some lines run much less frequently than others. The station is in Ple. della Stazione. **Trains** run to Padua (1hr., 11 per day 6:13am-9:37pm, €6.10) via Conegliano (1hr., 8 per day 6:04am-7:45pm, €3), on the Venice-Udine line. Some scheduled trains run directly to Conegliano, but many require a change in Ponte nelle Alpi. (☎0437 89 20 21. Ticket office open daily 5:50am-7:50pm.) Belluno's bus station, across Ple. della Stazione, serves the pre-Alps to the west and the eastern Dolomites. **Buses** (www.dolomitibus.it) run to Calalzo (1hr., 12 per day 6:13am-8:05pm, €3.70), Cortina (2hr., 13 per day 6:10am-8:05pm, €4.40), and Feltre (40min., 14 per day 6:20am-7:10pm, €4.40). Service is greatly reduced on Sunday; check station for schedules. (Ticket office ☎0437 94 11 67. Open M-F 7am-12:15pm and 3-6pm, Sa 7am-12:15pm. When closed, buy ticket from tourist office.) Orange local buses (€1.10) stop in Ple. della Stazione. For a **taxi,** call ☎0437 94 33 12 or ☎334 970 2141 after 9pm.

◪ PRACTICAL INFORMATION. The city center, **Piazza dei Martiri,** is a 5min. walk from the train and bus stations in **Piazzale della Stazione.** From the train terminal, cross the parking lot and follow **Via Dante** through **Piazzale Battisti** and across **Via Caffi** to **Via Loreto.** Turn left on **Via Matteotti** so that P. dei Martiri is in sight. The **tourist office** is in P. del Duomo. Cross the garden in P. dei Martiri and pass through **Porta Dante** onto **Via XXX Aprile.** (☎0437 94 00 83; www.infodolomiti.it. Open M-Sa 9am-12:30pm and 3:30-6:30pm, Su 9am-12:30pm.) Services include: the **Club Alpino Italiano office,** P. San Giovanni Bosco 11 (☎0437 93 16 55; www.caibelluno.it; open F 8-10pm; also Jan.-Mar. Tu 6-8pm); banks and **24hr. ATMs** along P. dei Martiri; the **police** (☎0437 94 55 11); **Farmacia Dott. Perale,** P. Vittorio Emanuele 12 (☎0437 252 71; open in summer M-F and Su 8:45am-12:30pm and 4-7:30pm, Sa 8:45am-12:30pm; in winter M-F 8:45am-12:30pm and 3:30-7pm; AmEx/MC/V); the **hospital,** Vle. Europa 32 (☎216 111); **Internet** access at **Ki-Point,** V. Feltre 192 (☎0437 94 05 33; €1.30 per 15min., €3 per hr; open M-F 8:30am-1pm and 3:30-7:30pm, Sa 8:30am-12:30pm; cash only); the laundromat **Lavafacile,** P. Piloni 18 (Wash €2 per load; open daily 8:30am-10pm); and the **post office,** P. Castello 14/A (☎0437 95 32 11; open M-F 8:30am-6:30pm, Sa 8:30am-1pm; reduced hours in Aug.) **Postal Code:** 32100.

█▐ ACCOMMODATIONS AND FOOD. Central locations and cliff-side balconies come at low nightly rates, with an abundance of B&B options. Inquire at the tourist office about accommodations and *affittacamere.* Built in 1843, **Albergo Cappello e Cadore ❸,** V. Ricci 8, welcomes guests into newly renovated rooms that are snug but cheerful and equipped with minifridge, TV, telephone, private bathroom (some with jacuzzi), and A/C. Turn left on Vle. Volontari Libertà from the station, and then turn right on V. Fantuzzi, which changes to V. Jacopo Tasso; V. Ricci branches off to the left. (☎0437 94 02 46; www.albergocappello.com. Breakfast included. Internet access €1 per hr. Wheelchair-accessible. Singles €45; doubles €80-85. AmEx/MC/V.) Comfortable rooms, a home-cooked breakfast, and free Internet access are just a few of the perks at **La Cerva B&B ❷,** V. Paoletti 7/B. Exit the train station heading to the left and following Vle. Volantari Libertà, then turn left on V. Fantuzzi. After crossing the rotary at V. Col di Lana, look for V. Paoletti on the right. (☎0437 33 88 25 36 08; www.lacerva.it. Singles €20, with breakfast €23; doubles €35. Extra bed €8.50. Cash only.) The rooms at **Casa per Ferie Al Centro ❷,** P. Piloni 11, may not have the frills of B&B options, but the price is right, considering the central location. Turn right on Vle. Fantuzzi and follow it as it becomes V. Jacopo Tasso. Look for Casa al Ferie on the left at P. Piloni. All rooms have bath and phone, and the self-service restaurant in front offers cheap meals in a cafeteria atmosphere. (☎0437 94 44 60; casaferie@diocesi.it. Breakfast €3.60. Singles €29; doubles €42. Prices drop with weeklong stays. AmEx/MC/V.) At the end of a little side street, **B&B Centro Storico ❸,** V. Torricelle 6, offers three small, comfortable rooms and a terrace overlooking the mountains. From P. Emanuele, take V. Rialto south, which becomes V. Mezzaterra, turn left on V. S. Croce, and right on V. Torricelle. (☎0437 94 20 92; giocard13@virgilio.it. Breakfast included. Singles €35; doubles €60. Discount with longer stays. Cash only.)

Dining options in the *centro* are plentiful and inexpensive. **La Trappola Birreria e Spaghetteria ❷,** Ple. Cesare Battisti 6, serves massive portions of excellent pasta in steaming pots brought to your table. Sit outside at picnic tables or indoors amid whimsical pictures of boozing monks. (☎0437 274 17. Primi €6-8. Open M-Th 11am-3:30pm and 5:30pm-2am, F 11am-3:30pm and 5:30pm-3am, Sa 4pm-3am. AmEx/MC/V.) Descend through the red-walled bar into **Ristorante Taverna ❸,** V. Cipro 7, where a variety of pastas and local specialties like vegetable and fish *spiedino* (kebab) are served in the traditional dining room. (☎0437 251 92. Wine from €2-3 per glass; €12-13 per bottle. Primi €7-8. Secondi €8-18. Cover €2. Open M-Sa noon-3:30pm and 7pm-midnight. MC/V.) **Al Mirapiave ❷,** V. Matteotti 29, satisfies big appetites with more than 60 types of pizza, a balcony, and dramatic views of the Dolomites. (☎0437 94 18 13. Pizza €3.50-9. Pasta €5-10. Cover €1. Open M and W-Su 11:30am-3:30pm and 6pm-1am. MC/V.) Although the small shop might not look like much, locals swear by **Il Gelato ❶,** Ple. Cesare Battistie 3/B, for its enormous scoops and flavor variety. (☎0437 94 33 32. Cones €0.90 for one scoop. Open daily 10am-10pm. Cash only.) **Super A & O,** P. dei Martiri 9/10, has a hot deli as well as groceries. (☎0437 94 20 00. Open M-Tu and Th-Su 8am-1pm and 4-7:30pm, W 8am-1pm. V.)

🄶 SIGHTS. Changes in the city's government can be traced through the architecture of the Piazza del Duomo. In the mid-17th century, academics gathered in the nearby **Palazzo dei Giuristi,** whose benefactors' busts line the facade. Since 1876, the building has housed the **Museo Civico,** which exhibits its local artifacts ranging from prehistory to the 20th century. Metal flowers, Caffi's Venetian scenes, and sprawling paintings by Belluno native Sebastino Ricci are the real highlights. (☎0437 94 48 36. Open Tu-Su 10am-1pm and 4-7pm. Last entry 20min. before closing. €3; students, over 60, or groups of 10 or more €1.50; under 6 free.) Since 1838, the town government has been housed in the **Palazzo Rettori,** P. del Duomo 38, next to the tourist info office. The vast **Parco Nazionale Dolomiti Bellunesi** (Bellunese Dolomites National Park) starts at the city's northern edge. (☎0439 33 28; www.dolomitipark.it.) For a more high-flying travel package, the **Botanical Garden of the Eastern Alps** rests at the top of a chairlift on the western slope of nearby **Monte Faverghera.** In July and August, buses from Belluno service the chairlift, which zooms 1500m up the mountain, at Ple. Nevegal. Both bus and chairlift schedules are unpredictable, so consult the tourist office for the latest info. (☎0437 94 48 30. Garden open June-Sept. Tu-F 9am-noon and 1-5pm; Su 9:30am-5:30pm. €1.50, 14 and under €0.80. Chairlifts run from July-Aug. M-Sa 8:30am-noon and 2-5pm, Su 8:30am-5pm. €7.50, ages 10-14 and over 60 €5.50, under 8 free.)

YOU DRIVE ME CRAZY. Due to unpredictable bus and chairlift schedules, both the Parco Nazionale Dolomiti Belunesi and the Botanical Garden of the Eastern Alps are nearly impossible to reach without a car. Consider renting one to take in all the views.

🄷 HIKING. Belluno offers excellent, well-marked hiking trails; one of the best is along the *altavia,* stretching north to south from Belluno to Lago di Braies. Hiking the entire *altavia* (about 125 km) would take about 8 days, but the hike along the first stretch, from Belluno to **Rifugio #7,** can be done in a day. From Belluno's P. dei Martiri, take V. Jacopo Tasso, which changes to Vle. Fantuzzi, and then V. Col di Lana. Follow this for about 1km until a sign points right, toward Bolzano; walk uphill about 9km. The paved road is easily cycled or walked in about 3hr., ending at **Casa Bortot** (707m). Get a bite to eat at the restaurant here—it's the last stop before Rifugio #7. Follow the small gravel path to the left, leading to the Parco Nazionale Dolomiti Bellunesi, or the start of **Altavia #1.** The route is well-marked and sticks close to the river gorge, with views of waterfalls and deep pools etched out of the boulders. For info on the *altevie,* visit www.dolomiti-altevie.it. For more info on hiking, visit the tourist office or the **CAI office (Practical Information, p. 352)** If you want to see Belluno's surroundings in all their majesty but would rather leave the hiking boots behind, just take the leisurely walk down V. Dino Buzzati on the western edge of the *centro storico.* Don't forget your camera: gorgeous views of the Dolomites, Piava River, and the bell tower of the *duomo* await.

NIGHTLIFE. The crowd hits **Cafe Loreto**, V. Loreto 5, early as customers "pre-game" with a wide assortment of *aperitivi* served from 7-8pm (on the house with your purchased drink). Enjoy mixed drinks, wine (€0.70-2), and beers (€2-4) in comfortable, modern seating as jazz plays in the background. (Open Tu-Su 8am-2am. Cash only.) **Enoteca Mazzini,** P. Mazzini 10, recalls evenings of yore with its wooden floors, black-and-white photos of Belluno, and hand-drawn caricatures. Savory appetizers such as ham and cold pasta are brought out in stages as customers sip their drinks (€1.40-5). The cozy upstairs seating is a nice alternative to the outdoor tables, which can be especially crowded at lunch and during the evening. (Open daily 9am-3pm and 5pm-2am. Cash only.) Tiny **Astor Cafe**, P. di Marti 27, consistently draws a young crowd to its small tables overlooking the river. Inside, slot machines and mirror-lined walls give the place a retro feel. (Look for the "In and Out" sign off the main *piazza*. Wine starting at €0.70. Open M-Th 7:30am-11pm, F-Sa 7:30am-1am.)

TIP

CLUB ALPINO ITALIANO (CAI). Those intending to do a serious amount of hiking in Italy should consider purchasing a Club Alpino Italiano membership. CAI runs many mountain *rifugi,* and members pay half-price for lodgings. *Rifugi,* which generally operate from late June to early October, may also rent out *vie ferrate* hiking equipment essentials. Membership is €35, under 18 €11. Purchase one at a CAI office, V. Petrella 19, 202124 Milan. (☎02 205 7231; bring a passport photo. Supplement for new members €5.20, surcharge for shipment of membership card outside the EU €10.)

THE VENETO

TRENTINO-ALTO ADIGE

The Mediterranean feel of Italy's southern and eastern regions fades under Germanic influences in the jagged peaks of the Dolomites in Trentino-Alto Adige (tren-TEE-noh AL-toh ah-DEE-jay). One glance at the conifers and snow-covered peaks of *Le Dolomiti* (leh doh-loh-MEE-tee) explains why backpackers and skiers still swarm the area. At the onset of the 19th century, Napoleon conquered this part of the Holy Roman Empire, but eventually relinquished it to the Austro-Hungarian Empire. Trentino and the Südtirol (South Tyrol) came under Italian control at the end of WWI, a transition that created hybridized linguistic patterns and cultural traditions. Though Germany thwarted Mussolini's brutal efforts to Italianize the region, Benito did manage to give every German name an Italian equivalent, which explains the dual street and town names used today. From *wurst* stands in Bolzano's *piazze* to the German-speaking locals in Bressanone, Trentino-Alto Adige's Germanic aura bears witness to a deep-rooted Austrian culture, which still thrives today.

HIGHLIGHTS OF TRENTINO-ALTO ADIGE

DISCOVER Il Mart, Italy's largest modern art museum, in Rovereto, housing over 12,000 pieces by masters such as Warhol, Lichtenstein, and Rosenquist (p. 361).

CHILL OUT with Bolzano's Ötzi the Iceman from the 4th millennium BC (p. 365).

CHANGE IT UP with Germanic flair in Bressanone, which borders Austria (p. 366).

TRENT (TRENTO, TRIENT) ☎0461

Pedestrian-friendly streets and an idyllic mountain location give Trent (TRENtoh; pop. 111,000) a small-town feel. The city represents a historical intersection between Italian and Nordic cultures. While the delicious strudel in Trent's bakeries attests to the town's proximity to Austria, the colorful buildings and *piazze* are quintessentially Italian. Named "Alpine City of the Year" in 2004 for its local pride and carefully preserved culture, Trent is growing in prominence in contemporary culture and hosts annual festivals and events. Easily explorable, it combines a vibrant student life with excellent nearby hiking options.

⬕ TRANSPORTATION

Trains: V. Dogana (☎0461 89 20 21). Ticket office open daily 5:40am-8:30pm. Info office open M-F 8:30am-12:15pm and 1:15-4:30pm. To: **Bologna** (3hr., 12 per day 1am-9:27pm, €15); **Bolzano** (45min., 33 per day 1:55am-10:59pm, €2.89); **Venice** (3-4hr., 12 per day 7:05am-5pm, €10); **Verona** (1hr., 2 per hr. 4am-9:48pm, €4.65).

Buses: Atesina and **Trentino Transporti** (☎0461 82 10 00; www.ttspa.it) on V. Pozzo next to the train station. Info office open M-Sa 7am-7:30pm. Bulletin board at the back of the station posts line suspension alerts. Buses run to **Riva del Garda** (1hr., every 2hr. 5:57am-7:50pm, €3.20) and **Rovereto** (50min., every hr. 5:57am-7:50pm, €2.70).

Public Transportation: Atesina runs local buses. Tickets (€0.90 for 70min. ticket; €2.30 for 24hr. ticket) available at the bus station, train station, or *tabaccherie.*

Cableways: Funivia Trento-Sardagna (☎0461 23 21 54), on Lung'Adige Monte Grappa. From bus station, turn right on V. Pozzo; take 1st right on Cavalcavia di San Lorenzo. Cross bridge over train tracks, and cross the intersection to the red-and-yellow building to the right of the tracks. To 🚠**Sardagna** on Mt. Bondone (4min.; every 15-30min.; €0.90 for a 70min. ticket; €1.20 for 2 hr. ticket; €2.30 for 24hr. ticket.) May bring up to 3 bikes per person, €0.90 per bike. Open daily 6:35am-10:30pm. Cash only.

Taxi: RadioTaxi (☎0461 93 00 02).

Bicycle Rental: Moser Cicli, V. Calepina 63 (☎0461 23 03 27). Mountain bikes €15 per day. Open Tu-Su 9am-noon and 3-7pm. MC/V.

⚡🛈 ORIENTATION AND PRACTICAL INFORMATION

The **bus** and **train** stations are on the same street, between the gardens next to the Adige River and the circles-of-hell statue of **Piazza Dante**. The *centro* lies east of the Adige. From the stations, walk right to the intersection of **Via Pozzo** with **Via Torre Vanga**. V. Pozzo becomes **Via delle Orfane** and then the curving **Via Cavour** before it reaches **Piazza del Duomo** in the *centro*. **ATMs** are nearby.

Tourist Office: APT, V. Manci 2 (☎0461 21 60 00; www.apt.trento.it). Turn right from the train station and left on V. Roma, which becomes V. Manci as it intersects V. Alfieri. **Tours** leave from the office. No reservation required. Limited to groups of 10 or fewer. Tours July-Aug. Th and Sa 3pm, Sept.-June Sa 3pm; €3. Castle tours July-Aug. Th and Sa 10am; Sept.-June Sa 10am; €3. Open daily 9am-7pm.

Bookstore: Libreria Disertori, V. Diaz 11 (☎0461 98 14 55), near V. Battisti. A slim selection of mostly classic English books, including Shakespeare. Open M 3-7pm, Tu-Su 9am-noon and 3-7pm. AmEx/MC/V.

Police: Vle. Verona, outside the *centro* to the south.

Pharmacy: Farmacia dall'Armi, P. Duomo 10 (☎0461 23 61 39). Serving the city since 1490. After-hours rotation posted in window. Open July-Aug. M-Sa 8:30am-12:30pm and 3-7pm; Sept.-June M-Sa 8:30am-7pm. Cash only.

Hospital: Ospedale Santa Chiara, Largo Medaglie d'Oro 9 (☎0461 90 31 11 or 91 43 09), up V. Orsi. From the bus stand directly in front of train station, take bus #2.

Internet Access: The city of Trent provides free Wi-Fi through **WilmaNet.** Sign up at one of 2 registration offices: **ITAL GM,** 15 V. del Suffragio (☎0461 19 20 141; trento@wilmanet.it) or **URP,** 3 V. Belenzani and 2 Via Manci (☎0461 88 44 53; comurp@comune.trento.it). Anyone with valid ID may register. Most of the city is connected.

Post Office: V. Calepina 16 (☎0461 98 47 15), offers fax services and money exchange just off P. Vittoria. Open M-F 8am-6:30pm, Sa 8am-12:30pm. **Postal Code:** 38100.

🏠 ACCOMMODATIONS

🏨 **Ostello Giovane Europa,** V. Torre Vanga 11 (☎0461 26 34 84; www.gayaproject.org). Exit train station and turn right; hostel is the white building on the corner of V. Pozzo and V.

Torre Vanga. Centrally located clean dorms offer private bath, sunny terraces, desks, and phones. €10 deposit gains access to games and a foosball table. Library study area stocked with a multitude of books and brochures. Breakfast included. 3-course dinner €9. Laundry €4.50; dry €2.50; soap €1. Reception 7:30am-11pm. Check-out 10am. Curfew 11:30pm; ask for door code to return later. Reservations recommended. Dorms €14-16; singles €25; doubles €42; triples €54. AmEx/MC/V. ❶

Hotel America, V. Torre Verde 52 (☎0461 98 30 10; www.hotelamerica.it). Located 5-10min. from both the train station and the town center. Cozy, well-furnished rooms with bath, TV, A/C, and minibar. Balconies with hanging plants offer beautiful views of Trent and Castello del Buonconsiglio to the east. Breakfast included. Attached restaurant with a daily *menù* for €20. Wi-Fi €2 per 30min., €3.50 per hr., €9 for 4hr. Singles €70; doubles €108; triples €120. AmEx/MC/V. ❺

Aquila d'Oro, V. Belezani 76 (☎0461 98 62 82; www.aquiladoro.it). Provides luxurious bedrooms with free Wi-Fi, private bath, parking, and breakfast in its spacious restaurant downstairs. Though the price is high, the central location and palatial feel may be worth the splurge. Singles €77-85; doubles €153-170. ❺

Albermonaco, 25 V. Torre d'Augusto (☎0461 98 30 60; www.albermonaco.it). Just a short walk from the beautiful Castello del Buonconsiglio, this handsome inn provides spacious rooms, pool access, parking, Internet access, and breakfast. The inn's major perk is the view of nearby mountains. Singles €68; doubles €100; triples €110. ❺

🔆 FOOD

Trentino cuisine owes much to the local production of sterling cheeses like *nostrano*, *tosela*, and the highly prized *vezzena*. *Piatti del malgaro* (herdsman's plates) include cheeses, polenta, mushrooms, and sausage. A Germanic undercurrent surfaces in the exceptional local version of *apfelstrudel*. **Supermercati Trentini** lies across P. Pasi from the *duomo* at P. Lodron 28. (☎0461 22 01 96. Open Tu-Su 9am-8pm, M 2:30-8pm. MC/V.)

▨ Osteria Il Cappello, P. Lunelli 5 (☎0461 23 58 50). From the station, turn right, then left on V. Roma. After 4 blocks, turn right on V. San Pietro, then take the tunnel near #27 into P. Lunelli. This classy restaurant overlooking a private courtyard serves traditional Trentino cuisine like cream of asparagus with crisp *sfogliatine* (€8.50). Delicious assortment of breads and a good selection of wines (€3-5.50 per glass). Primi €8.50-9.50. Secondi €14-17. Cover €2. Open Tu-Su noon-2pm and 7:30-10pm. AmEx/MC/V. ❹

▨ Alla Grotta, Vco. San Marco 6 (☎0461 98 71 97). Huge pizzas heaped with toppings make this busy spot perfect for those in search of a filling meal or late-night drink. Pizza and primi €4.10-7.20. Open Tu-Su noon-3pm and 6:30-11:30pm. MC/V. ❷

Ristorante Al Vò, Vco. del Vò 11 (☎0461 98 53 74; www.ristorantealvo.it). From the station, turn right and walk to V. Torre Vanga. Turn left and continue for 200m; Ristorante Al Vò is on the right. Outdoor seating, friendly staff, and a brightly lit interior complete this casual dining experience. Try the *spaghettini* with mushrooms for a taste of traditional Trentino cuisine. *Menù del giorno* €15. Primi €6.50. Secondi €8.50. Cover €1.20. Open M-Sa 11:30am-2:30pm and 7-9:30pm. AmEx/D/MC/V. ❸

La Cantinota, V. San Marco 22/24 (☎0461 23 85 27). From the station, turn right and then left on V. Roma, which becomes V. San Marco. Sip sparkling wine in the elegant upstairs dining room or indulge in traditional gnocchi with pesto, arugula, and green beans in the trattoria downstairs. Primi €7-12. Secondi €12-14. Restaurant open Sept.-July M-W and Su noon-3pm and 7:30-11pm, F 7:30-11pm. MC/V. ❹

La Gelateria, V. Belanzani 50, near P. del Duomo. This colorful *gelateria* serves up intimidatingly large scoops of rich gelato—exotic flavors include violet and 2 different types of pistachio. 3 huge scoops €2.40. Open daily 11:30am-11:30pm. Cash only. ❶

◉ SIGHTS

PIAZZA DEL DUOMO. Trent's P. del Duomo offers everything from religious history to modern shops and services. At the **Fontana del Nettuno** in the center of the *piazza*, a majestic Neptune waves his trident as merpeople spit incessantly at his feet. Nearby stands the **Cattedrale di San Vigilio.** Its majestic interior housed the historical Council of Trent (1545-1563), which standardized Catholic traditions during the Counter-Reformation. Dark, rich art adorns the massive incense-filled building, illuminated by sunlight and clusters of votive candles. *(Open daily 7-11:45am and 2:45-7pm. Free.)* Underneath, the **Basilica Paleocristiana di San Vigilio,** entered from the left of the altar, displays religious artifacts and statues uncovered in excavations near the *duomo*. *(Open M-Sa 10am-noon and 2:30-5:30pm. €1.50, ages 12-18 €1. Free admission with ticket to Museo Diocesano.)*

MUSEO DIOCESANO TRIDENTINO. The **Museo Diocesano** was officially reopened by Pope John Paul II in 1995 after renovations were made to the tapestries, paintings, and illuminated manuscripts from regional churches. The museum offers insight into the importance of the diocese, local history, and politics. The eight elaborate Flemish tapestries on the museum's second floor that depict the Passion of Christ once decorated the hall where sessions of the Council of Trent were held. *(P. del Duomo 18. ☎0461 23 44 19; www.museodiocesanotridentino. it. Open M and W-Su 9:30am-12:30pm and 2-5:30pm. Hours extended during exhibitions. Ticket counter closes 15min. before museum. €4, groups of 20 or more €2.50. Entrance includes access to Basilica Sotteranea di San Vigilio. Free audio tours in English, French, German, and Italian.)*

FREE TRENTO. Consider buying the Trento Card for free access to all museums (including special exhibitions), guided tours of wine cellars, public transportation, bike rental, discounts in fitness and wellness centers, and tours of the city. €10 for 24 hours; €15 for 48 hours. Available at the tourist office. Call ☎0461 21 60 00 for more information.

CASTELLO DEL BUONCONSIGLIO. Made up of buildings from different eras of Trentino history, the Castello del Buonconsiglio looms over the city from its dominant position east of the *centro*. At the end of the *castello's* rooftop garden, the **loggia's** ceiling features Diana depicted as the moon and Apollo as the sun with scenes from Greek, Roman, and Hebrew history and mythology in the lunettes. Stairs lead down from the loggia to the **Fossa dei Martiri,** the *castello's* old moat and the execution site of famed martyrs Cesare Battisti, Damiano Chiesa, and Fabio Filzi in 1916. Tours of the **Torre dell'Aquila,** which depart from the loggia, offer a glimpse into the court life of the Trentino Middle Ages. *(From V. Belenzani, turn right on V. Roma and continue as it becomes V. San Marco; the castello is in front of you as the road ends. ☎0461 23 37 70; www.buonconsiglio.it. Castle open Tu-Su 9:30am-5pm. Tours 10 per day 10:30am-5:15pm. €7, students and under 18 or over 60 €4. Torre d'Aquila additional €1. Ticket price includes admission to museum and Tridentino, an excavation of Roman ruins under P. Battisti. Free audio tours in multiple languages. Guided tours €1.)*

♫ ◉ ENTERTAINMENT AND NIGHTLIFE

While Trent is fairly quiet at night, local bars and lively restaurants provide visitors with some action. At **Osteria Trentina,** V. Roma 48, cozy seating and live jazz keeps a hip young crowd happy. (☎0461 23 88 41. Wine €2-3.50. Open M-Th 10am-10pm, F 10am-2:30pm and 6pm-2am, Sa 6pm-2am. Cash only.) **Supercin-**

ema Vittoria, 72 V. G. Manci, screens the latest hits and offers deals on Monday. (☎0461 23 52 84; www.cineworld.info. Tickets €7.50.)

ROVERETO   ☎0464

An easy daytrip from Trent, the town of Rovereto (ro-veh-REH-toh; pop. 35,858) offers picturesque views at every turn, but without crowds of camera-toting tourists. Cobblestone alleys weave around frescoed buildings, decorative stone fountains dot the *piazze*, and mountain breezes waft delicately through the streets. Rovereto offers the best of both worlds: while the surrounding countryside offers opportunities for biking, hiking, walking, and horseback-riding, the Museo d'Arte Moderna e Contemporanea, or Il Mart, houses the largest collection of modern art in Italy and is the *centro*'s star attraction.

◪◪ TRANSPORTATION AND PRACTICAL INFORMATION. The train station is at P. Orsi 11. (☎0464 89 20 21. Ticket office open M-F 5:50am-7:30pm, Sa 9am-6:30pm. AmEx/MC/V.)**Trains** run to: Bologna (3hr., 11 per day 6:03am-9:44pm, €10); Bolzano (1hr., 29 per day 6:14am-11:36pm, €7); Trent (15min., 34 per day 6:14am-11:36pm, €2.40); Verona (1hr., 31 per day 6:03am-10:20pm, €3.36). The **bus station,** C. Rosmini 45, runs buses frequently to Riva del Garda (1hr., 24 per day 6:55am-10:50pm, €2.40) and Trent (50min., 29 per day 5:07am-6:56pm, €4.15). Check station for schedules. (☎0464 43 37 77. Open M-Sa 6:30am-7:15pm. MC/V.) For a **taxi,** call Radiotaxi (☎0464 48 00 66. Open 24hr.) The **APT tourist office,** C. Rosmini 6/A, has maps and info on lodging and nearby activities. (☎0464 43 55 28; www.aptrovereto.it. Open M-F 9am-12:15pm and 2:30-6:30pm, Sa 9am-12:45pm.) In case of emergency, call the **police,** V. Sighele 1 (☎0464 48 46 11). **Farmacia Thaler** is at V. Dante 3. (☎0464 42 10 30. Open M-F 8:30am-12:30pm and 3-7:30pm.) The **post office,** V. Largo Posta 7, is just up C. Rosmini from the bus station. (☎0464 40 22 10. Open M-F 8am-6:30pm, Sa 8am-12:30pm. MC/V.) **Internet** access at **Paradise SAS,** 9 V. Don Rossaro. (☎0464 48 07 64. €1.50 per hr. Open daily 9:30am-midnight.) **Postal Code:** 38068.

◪◪ ACCOMMODATIONS AND FOOD. Budget hotels are scarce in quiet Rovereto, but ◪**Ostello di Rovereto ❷,** V. delle Scuole 18, is an excellent option. To reach the hostel, follow C. Rosmini until you arrive at V. Stoppani. Turn right and follow until the road becomes V. delle Scuole. Close to the *centro*, the hostel has spacious, modern rooms with terraces, free lockers, and private bathrooms. Other perks include Internet access (9am-noon and 3-9pm), parking, and bike rental. Breakfast included. (☎0464 48 67 57; www.ostellorovereto.it. Reception closes at 10pm. Check-out 10am. Singles €23; doubles €42; triples €63; quads €90; quints €90. MC/V.) On the more upscale end of housing options, the elegant **Hotel Rovereto ❺,** C.Rosmini 82/D, is conveniently located between the train station and town center. The hotel's clean, spacious rooms have showers and TV. Breakfast is served in the elegant restaurant downstairs. (☎0464 43 52 22; www.hotelrovereto.it. Singles €95; doubles €115.)

Up a narrow staircase from P. delle Erbe, **Vecchia Trattoria Birrara Scala della Torre ❷,** serves traditional Trentino cuisine with both an interior courtyard and a private dining room in the front. Festive lighting, potted plants, rustic furniture, and colorful tiling complement authentic cuisine. Specialties include *spätzle* (small Tylorean dumplings) in tomato and cream sauce, with mushrooms and cheese (€8). (☎0464 43 71 00. Most dishes €8-14. Bread and cover €2. Open daily noon-2:30pm and 7:30-10pm. AmEx/MC/V.) Cozy cafe **Silvani ❶,** V. Mazzini 48, offers a wide assortment of delectable pastries. What Silvani lacks in variety of gelato (€1), it more than makes up for with the generous portions.

(☎0464 433 657. Ferrari Perle wine by the glass €4. Open daily 7:30am-10pm.) **Trentini** supermarket, V. Mazzini 65, stocks basics. (☎0464 42 11 87. Open M 8:30am-1:30pm, Tu-Sa 8:30am-12:30pm and 3:15-7:15pm. V.)

🎦🎭 **SIGHTS AND NIGHTLIFE** An unlikely sight in a small town, the enormous 🏛**Museo d'Arte Moderna e Contemporanea** (commonly known as "Il Mart"), C. A. Bettini 43, is the largest modern art museum in Italy. A majestic, circular courtyard covered by a glass skylight welcomes visitors, while inside a winding staircase leads to the permanent collection: 6000 sq. m of sleek rooms housing over 12,000 pieces. Fortunato Depero's *La Rissa* anchors the Futurist wing, 20th-century Italian pieces and American works such as Warhol's *Four Marilyns* and Lichtenstein's *Hot Dog* round out the collection. There is also an impressive collection of installation artwork and sculpture. (☎0464 43 88 87; www.mart.trento.it. Open Tu-Th, Sa-Su 10am-6pm, F 10am-9pm. €10, under 18 and over 65, free. Audio tours in English, German, or Italian €5. AmEx/MC/V.)

The **Castello di Rovereto,** V. Castelbarco 7, has served mostly military purposes since its construction in the fourth century. From P. Podestà, follow V. Della Terra (near the cannon), turn right on V. Castelbarco, and head up the stairs. The **Museo della Guerra** (Museum of War) now fills the *castello* with war materials ranging from medieval spears to bombshells from WWII. The collection also includes a set of Samurai armor. Above the museum, an observation deck affords a stunning view of Rovereto and the Dolomites. (☎0464 43 81 00; www. museodellaguerra.it. Open July-Sept. Tu-F 10am-6pm, Sa-Su 9:30am-6:30pm; Oct.-June Tu-Su 10am-6pm. €5.50, ages 6-18 €2. MC/V.) About an hour walk from the *centro*, the **Campana della Pace** (Bell of Peace), on V. Miravalle, tolls 100 times each night at 9pm in memory of war victims and in a call for global tolerance and peace. The bell was cast in 1924 from 226 tons of bronze recycled from the cannons of the 19 nations involved in WWI, and was later blessed by Pope Paul VI. (☎0464 43 44 12. Open daily Nov.-Feb. 9am-4:30pm; Mar. and Oct. 9am-6pm; Apr.-Sept. 9am-7pm. €2, children 6-14 €0.50. Cash only.) The **Museo Civico,** Borgo Santa Caterina 41, provides tours of the astronomical observatory on Monte Zugna and of the dinosaur tracks in southern Rovereto. From various places along the mountain trail, these ancient prints are still visible in the gray hillside. (☎0464 43 90 55; www.museocivico.rovereto.it. Open Tu-Su 9am-noon, 3-6pm. Planetarium show Sa and Su 4:45. Adults €3.60, under 18 and over 60 €2.50, children €1.55. Call to arrange a tour. Wheelchair-accessible.)

Nightlife in Rovereto is fairly tame, but **Bacchus,** V. G. Garibaldi 29, keeps patrons out late with drinks like "the Shakerati" (€4). Customers at keg-shaped tables enjoy funky music in the warmly lit interior. Once it gets crowded, many head outside. (Open M, Th, Su 10:30am-1:30pm and 4:30-9pm, W 4:30-9pm, F-Sa 11am-1:30pm and 4:30pm-midnight. Cash only.) By day, **Caffè de Min,** V. Dante 6, is just another place to grab pasteries or gelato (€2), but a long, hardwood bar and plush booths bring local patrons in for drinks starting around 7pm. (☎0464 43 77 76. Wine by the glass €3-4. Open Tu-Su 7:30am-midnight.)

BOLZANO (BOZEN) ☎0471

Bolzano (bohl-ZAH-no; pop. 100,000) is most famous for 5000-year-old Ötzi the Iceman, a partially decayed body found frozen in 1991, held in the South Tyrol Museum of Archaeology. The best sights in the city, however, don't charge admission. Winter hikers climb to the snowy peaks, while summer visitors bike along the crystal-green Talvera River, wander up the stone pathway to Castel Roncolo, or gaze at the steep hills, resplendent with rows of grape

TRENTINO-ALTO ADIGE

vines. Whether it is the *duomo*'s mixed architecture or the city's two languages, Italian and German, Bolzano seems to rise above national borders.

▌ TRANSPORTATION

Trains: in P. Stazione (☎0471 48 89 93). Ticket office open daily 6am-8:50pm. Info office open M-Sa 8am-7pm, Su 9am-1pm and 2-5pm. Customer service open daily 7am-9pm. To: **Bologna** (3hr., 16 per day 5:11am-3:36am, €20); **Bressanone** (30min., 33 per day 4:32am-10:40pm, €3.25); **Trent** (45min., 36 per day 1am-10:49pm, €3); **Venice** (3hr., 1 per day, €16); **Verona** (1hr., 31 per day 3:36am-9:31pm, €10); **Munich, DEU** (4hr., 8 per day 2:25am-6:32pm).

Buses: SAD, V. Perathoner 4 (☎0471 45 01 11), between train station and P. Walther. Bus station and tourist office distribute bus schedules for travel to the western Dolomites. **Luggage storage** available. MC/V.Office open M-Sa 7am-7:25pm, Su 7am-1:15pm.

Funiculars: 3 cableways, located at the edges of Bolzano, carry visitors to nearby mountain towns. For info, visit either the tourist office or the alpine info office.

  Funivia del Colle, V. Campiglio 7 (☎0471 97 85 45). The world's oldest cableway leads from V. Campiglio to **Colle** or **Kohlern** (9min., every 30-60min., daily June-Sept. 7am-noon and 1-7:30pm, Oct.-May 7am-noon and 1-7pm. €3, round-trip €4; children under 14 and adults over 65, €1.50; bikes €2.) No baggage or dogs allowed.

  Funivia San Genesio, V. Rafenstein 15 (☎0471 97 84 36), off V. Sarentino, across the Talvera River, near Ponte Sant'Antonio. Connects Bolzano to **Salto's** high plateaus (8min., every 30 minutes, daily from mid-June to mid-Sept. 10am-12:30pm and 2:30-7pm, from mid-Sept. to mid-June 9am-12:30pm and 2:30-6pm. €3.50; €2 per bike.)

Public Transportation: SASA (☎0471 45 01 11). All lines stop in P. Walther or the station at V. Perathoner 4. Buy tickets (€1) at *tabaccherie* or from machines near stops.

Taxi: Radiofunk Taxi, V. Perathoner 4 (☎0471 98 11 11; www.ratabz.it.) 24hr.

Bike Rental: Run by the **Cooperativa Sociale** (☎0471 97 55 92), on Vle. Stazione, right off P. Walther. Main office at V. Carduci 9. 1st 6hr. €1, over 7hr. €2. Whole day €5. Deposit required. Open M-Sa Apr.-Oct. 7:30am-7:50pm. Cash only.

✦ ▌ ORIENTATION AND PRACTICAL INFORMATION

The *centro storico* lies between the **train station** and the **Talvera River** *(Talfer Fluss)*. All major *piazze* are within walking distance. Visitors should consider renting bikes, Bolzano's transportation of choice. Street and *piazze* names appear in Italian and German, and most maps mark both. From the bus stop, follow **Via Alto Adige** *(Südtirolerstrasse)* to **Piazza Walther** *(Waltherplatz)* and the *duomo*. Farther along, **Piazza del Grano** leads directly to **Via Portici** *(Laubenstrasse)*. Here, German and Italian merchants set up shop on opposite sides of the arcade. To reach **Ponte Talvera**, take V. Portici past **Piazza delle Erbe.**

Tourist Office: AST, P. Walther 8 (☎0471 30 70 00; www.bolzano-bozen.it). Offers 2hr. guided tours of the city's museums and churches (M and Sa 10:30am, €5), and horseback-riding trips. Also publishes *Bolzano a Passeggio*, a guide to 14 walks in the surrounding hills. Open M-F 9am-1pm and 2-7pm, Sa 9am-2pm. **Alpine Info: Club Alpino Italiano (CAI),** P. delle Erbe 46, 2nd fl. (☎0471 97 81 72). Ring bell. Info on hiking, climbing, and tours. Open Tu, Th, F 1-5pm, W 11am-1pm, 5-7pm.

Currency Exchange: Banca Nazionale del Lavoro, P. Walther 10, next to tourist office. Good rates. Open M-F 8:20am-1:20pm and 2:30-4pm.

Bookstore: Athesiabuch, 41 V. Portici (☎0471 92 72 85). Well-stocked bookstore also carries CDs, software videogames, and magazines. English section is limited to mostly classics. Open M-F 9am-7pm, Sa 9am-6pm.

TRENTINO-ALTO ADIGE

Laundromat: Lava e Asciuga, V. Rosmini 81, near Ponte Talvera. Wash €3 (€5 for 2 loads), dry €3. Detergent €1. Open daily 7:30am-10:30pm.

Pharmacy: Farmacia all'Aquila Nera, V. Portici 46/B. Open M-F 8:30am-12:30pm and 3-7pm, Sa 8:30am-12:30pm. After-hours rotation posted outside.

Hospital: Ospedale Regionale San Maurizio (☎0471 90 81 11), on V. Lorenz Böhler.

Internet Access: MultiKulti, V. Dott Streiter 9 (☎0471 05 60 56; www.multikulti.info), 1 street past V. Portici. €3 per hr. Also offers international calling, money transfer, and fax. Open M-Sa 10am-10pm, Su noon-10pm. Cash only. **Caffè Brennpunkt,** V. Brennero 7 (☎0471 98 29 53), is a slick bar with 2 even slicker flat-screen computers. €1 per 15min. Open M-W and Su 7:30am-8pm, Th-F 7:30am-1am, Sa 7:30am-2pm.

Post Office: Palazzo della Posta 13 (☎0471 32 22 81), by the *duomo*. Open M-F 8am-6:30pm, Sa 8am-12:30pm. **Postal Code:** 39100.

TIP | **RIDOTTO!** Bolzano offers two Museum Cards, which grant holders the *ridotto* price of entry to the city's museums and sights. With the purchase of any museum ticket, you receive a booklet of one-time use cards for many of the city's important museums. Alternatively, pay €2.50 for a card and receive a 20% discount every time you visit one of the city's surrounding museums and castles. Check the tourist office or participating museums for details.

ACCOMMODATIONS AND CAMPING

The tourist office lists affordable *agriturismi* options, but most require private transportation—rent a bicycle and enjoy the countryside or reserve ahead for the inexpensive accommodations in the *centro*.

 Youth Hostel Bolzano, V. Renon 23 (☎0471 30 08 65; www.ostello.bz). From train station, turn right onto V. Renon. Squeaky clean rooms, friendly staff, and bountiful amenities make this new hostel a great deal. Kitchen access until 10pm. Excellent breakfast buffet included. Showers in the room, lockers, and linens free. Laundry €2 wash, €2 dry. Internet access €2 per hr. Reception 8am-4am. Check-in 1pm. Check-out 9am. Dorms €19.50; singles €22. €2 surcharge for 1-night stay. AmEx/MC/V. ❶

Garni Eisenhut-Cappello di Ferro, V. Bottai 21 (☎0471 97 83 97; www.cappellodiferro. com). 1 block north of P. Walther, follow V. Bottai out of P. Municipio. Accommodating, English spoken. Small, comfortable rooms with bath and TV. Breakfast included; ½- and full pension options available. Singles €50; doubles €80. Extra bed €25. MC/V. ❸

Hotel Regina, V. Renon 1 (☎0471 97 21 95; www.hotelreginabz.it), 5min. from P. Walther. From the train station, take a right; hotel is across the street. Snug rooms mostly overlook a busy street, which makes for a noisy stay, though some have views of the green mountains that loom over Bolzano. All rooms have private bath, TV, and phone. Breakfast and linens included. Internet access €1.50 per 30 min. Parking €1.50 per hr. Singles €55-65; doubles €83-100; triples €108-120. MC/V. ❹

Schwarze Katz, Stazione Magdalena di Sotto 2 (☎0471 97 54 17; schwarze.katz@ virgilio.it), near V. Brennero, 20min. from the city center. From the train station, turn right at V. Renon; keep left as you pass the cable car station, and look for signs; walk uphill into the steep driveway. Simple, spacious rooms in this family-run hostel have TV and free Internet access. Most rooms use shared bathrooms. Breakfast included. Reception open in summer M-Sa 7am-10pm; in winter M-F 7am-midnight, Sa 7am-9pm. Reservations recommended. Singles €25-30; doubles €60. AmEx/MC/V. ❷

Moosbauer, V. San Maurizio 83 (☎0471 91 84 92; www.moosbauer.com). Take SAD bus toward Merano; ask driver to stop at Moosbauer. Beautifully tended, off-the-beaten-path campground has pool, bar, restaurant, Internet cafe (€0.10 per min.), market, and playground. Friendly English-speaking staff has brochures on local activities. Convenient to nearby trails for hikers looking for a relaxing stay. Showers included. Laundry €3, dry €3. Reception open 8am-9pm daily. Reservations require a €50 down payment and 3-night min. stay. Entrance fee €5.50-6 per car. Tent/RV sites €12.50-16, includes water and electricity. €7.50-8.50 per adult, €5-6 per child, €3.50-4 per dog, €5.50-6 per tent. No tent rentals. 10% discount for those staying 10 days with cash payment. MC/V. ❶

Hotel Luna (Mondschein), V. Piave 15 (☎0471 97 56 42 www.hotel-luna.it info@hotel-luna.it). From P. Walther, walk to V. Portici. Turn right until it becomes V. Piave; Hotel Luna is on the left. Elegant garden terrace provides a peaceful refuge from the bustle of the *piazza.* Spacious rooms with TV, minibars, private bath, and Internet. Breakfast €11; half and full board available. Singles €95; doubles €142. ❺

Hotel Feichter, V. Grappoli 15 (☎0471 97 87 68; www.hotelfeichter.it). Sunny, conveniently located hotel with small, yet quaint rooms and peaceful views of the rooftops and mountains of Bolzano. Hallways lined with flowers, decorative tiles, and bookshelves with American books make for a homey feel. Breakfast included. Parking €5 per day. Singles €55; doubles €85; triples €105. ❹

Hotel-Garni Adria, V. Perathoner 17 (☎0471 97 57 35; www.hoteladria-bz.it). Modest hotel with a modern feel 5min. from the train station. Sunny, spacious rooms overlook a busy street. Rooms have TV, private bath, minibar, and safe. Breakfast included. Singles €48; doubles €79; triples €90. ❹

🅵 FOOD

For a full smorgasbord of Bolzano's hybrid cuisine, start with a bowl of *rindgu-lasch* (beef stew); then try *wurst* (spicy sausage), *speck* (smoked bacon that tops pizzas and breads across mainland Italy), and Hearty *knödel* (dumplings). For dessert, chose from three types of flaky strudel: *apfel* (apple), *topfen* (soft cheese), and *mohn* (poppyseed). An all-day **market** in P. delle Erbe and along V. della Roggia has sold fine produce, cheese, baked goods, and meats since 1295. (Open M-F 7am-7pm, Sa 7am-1pm.) A **Despar** supermarket, is on the corner of V. della Rena. (☎0471 97 07 46. Open M-F 8:15am-7:15pm, Sa 8am-6pm.)

▨ Hopfen & Co., P. delle Erbe 17 (☎0471 30 07 88, www.boznerbier.it). Housed in an 800-year-old building. No-frills pub, perfect for beer lovers and carnivores. Hearty Bavarian menu. At night, a young clientele spills out onto the street, gathering in nearby vacated vendor stands. Beer from €1.90-4.50. Specialty plates for 2 (€12-23) leave customers satisfied. Cover €1. Open M-Sa 9:30am-1am. MC/V. ❷

Exil Lounge, P. del Grano 2 (☎0471 97 18 14). To the *wurst*-intolerant traveler's delight, this colorful cafe in the heart of town offers a diverse selection of healthy salads and sandwiches. Perfect lunch treats include baguettes with grilled vegetables, mozzarella, and pesto as well as yogurt bowls with granola and seasonal fruit. Extensive tea, wine, and drink list. Open M-W 10am-midnight, Th-Sa 10am-1am. Cash only. ❷

Lowengrube, P. Dogana 3 (☎0471 97 68 48). The name of this Bolzano favorite, which opened in 1543, translates from German to "the place of the lion." Cheerful Austrian decor surrounds crowds of locals who attest to its popularity as a lunch spot. Primi €6.50-8.50. Secondi €12-19.50. Beer €1.60. Open daily 8am-1am. MC/V. ❸

Hostaria Argentieri, V. Argentieri 14 (☎0471 98 17 18). Flower-lined patio and quiet, candlelit tables provide a romantic evening at this upscale fish restaurant. Customers choose from a limited but tasty, handwritten menu. Primi €3.50-10. Secondi €7.50-30. Cover €1.50. Open M-Sa noon-2:30pm and 7-10:30pm. AmEx/MC/V. ❹

Trattoria Bar Nadamas, P. delle Erbe 44. What little nightlife Bolzano has to offer is centered around P. delle Erbe, mostly due to its cheap drinks. A slightly more mature crowd of locals and tourists fill the spacious, wood-furnished interior before gathering outside, drinks in hand. At lunch, enjoy bruschetta (€4.70), salads (€4-10.50) and a wide selection of *antipasti* (€4-8.20). Glasses of wine and beer from €1. Open M-Sa 9am-1am. Kitchen open noon-2:30pm and 7-10:30pm. ❷

🔄 SIGHTS

DUOMO. The bell tower's spined hollow spire and the ornate masonry around its eaves demonstrate Bolzano's transition from Romanesque to Gothic religious architecture, while paintings, frescoes and statues line the walkways inside. *(P. Walther. Open M-F 10am-noon and 2-5pm. Free.)*

CHIESA DEI FRANCESCANI. Gateways lined with cypress trees and flowers lead into this church's cool, silent interior. At the apse, three vibrant stainglass windows are a sight to behold for patrons seated in the wooden pews. *(V. dei Francesca 1. Open M-F 8:30am-noon and 2:30-6pm, Sa-Su 8:30am-noon. Free.)*

SOUTH TYROL MUSEUM OF ARCHAEOLOGY. Tourists at this museum file by the giant refrigerator that houses **Ötzi**, the 5000-year-old Neanderthal discovered by hikers in the Alps in 1991. Ötzi has his own floor, where English-language displays chart the extensive investigations archeologists have made of his daily life. *(V. Museo 43, near Ponte Talvera. ☎0471 32 01 00; www.iceman.it. Open Tu-Su 10am-5:30pm; July-Aug. and Dec. also open M. Wheelchair-accessible. €8, students and seniors €6, under 6 free. Multilingual audio tours €2.)*

CASTEL RONCOLO. This medieval fortress looks more like a Disney wonderland. Lavish wall frescoes narrate the legend of Tristan and Isolde. The winding stone path to the castle and the connector between the museum's two wings offer spectacular views of the mountains and city below. *(V. Sant'Antonio 15. Take city bus #12 from P. Walther to the Funivia stop, then go up V. Weggerstein to V. San Antonio. Ask at the ticket desk about the free bus for tourists back to P. Walther. ☎0471 32 98 08; www.roncolo.info. Open Tu-Su 10am-6pm. Gates for frescoes close 5:30pm. €8; groups of 10 or more, students, and seniors €5.50. Guided tour supplement €2.70.)*

🥾 HIKING

Bolzano is technically located at the beginning of the Alps, despite local allegiance to the Dolomites. The hiking here pales in comparison with that of the Alps to the west or the Dolomites to the east. The **CAI office** (p. 362) has helpful info on outdoor activities. The best hikes can be accessed by the three *funivie* that surround the town and run straight to vista level. While **Funivia del Renon** and **Funivia del Colle** have limited marked trails, **Funivia**

THE LOCAL STORY

A MAVERICK ICEMAN

In September 1991, Erica and Helmut Simon were hiking through the Tyrolean region of northeastern Italy, enjoying the scenery and getting some exercise. In between their photo ops and trail mix stops, they discovered something a little out of the ordinary: a fully-clothed but completely frozen human being.

As it turned out, the body belonged to a man from the late Neolithic Age (3300-3100 BCE), whom bolzanini have nicknamed Ötzi and taken under their wing in Bolzano's South Tyrol Museum of Archaeology. Though some too-cool locals insist that only tourists are interested in this human artifcat, most take a sense of pride in the fact that Ötzi has made his way to their town.

In his real form, Ötzi isn't much to look at: he's a skeleton in a refrigerator. Plus, he's a little guy—at the time of his death, he stood only 5 feet, 2 inches tall and weighed only 132 pounds. His shoe size was 5½! (It turns out that this was about normal size in those days.)

But the museum has taken special care to portray him in a more flattering light, creating a replica on which a soft spotlight shines. Ötzi's no Prince Charming, but he's armed with a heavy coat, trusty tools, and a look of determination.

To see Ötzi, visit Bolzano's South Tyrol Museum of Archaeology.

San Genesio services extensive marked trails of moderate difficulty. On Funivia del Renon, the ride itself is an attraction, as it gives a bird's-eye view of curving grape arbors. All three *funivie* offer free maps that should suffice for the easier hikes. Drop by the San Genesio **tourist office,** Schrann 7 (☎0471 35 41 96; www.jenesien.net) before starting out. The pleasant walk from the San Genesio Funivia to the Edelweiss rest house, to the Tachaufenhaus, and then back to the *funivie* via the Locher rest house, makes for a pleasant 4hr. hike. Even on the easiest hikes, take precautions against dehydration and sun exposure.

▧ NIGHTLIFE

While most of Bolzano's activities center around hiking, camping, and bicycle trips through the city and surrounding mountains, those seeking a fun evening should head to **Piazza Erbe,** where hordes of young people gather on the street. With beer from **Hopfen & Co.** (p. 364), a lively crowd, and an informal atmosphere, visitors are sure to enjoy themselves on a warm summer evening.

BRESSANONE (BRIXEN)   ☎0472

Bressanone's (breh-sa-NO-neh; pop. 20,000) Alpine valley dazzles visitors with unobstructed views of green mountains, crystalline rivers, and rows of pastel houses. Its layout blends patches of urbanity with vast expanses of green space, where cobblestone roads wind around swirling rivers and cool shade trees. Pedestrians can stroll through the town center's quiet walkways, exploring the towering *duomo* and small shops nearby, but the real appeal for travelers is the area's hiking, biking, and skiing.

> **TIP** **CULTURE SHOCK.** Culturally and linguistically, the northern Dolomites have belonged to Germany and Austria for centuries. This means that most natives' first language is German, then Italian, with English a distant third.

◨ TRANSPORTATION. Bressanone is a daytrip by train or bus from Bolzano or Trent. **Trains** run to: Bolzano (30min., every hr. 12:36am-10:12pm, €3.25); Brennero (45min., every hr. 5am-11:11pm, €4.65); Trent (1hr., 14 per day 12:30am-10pm, €4.65); Verona (2hr., 15 per day 6:30am-9pm, €10); Munich, DEU (4hr., 7 per day 5am-7pm, €50);. Train info is available at ☎0472 89 20 21 or www.trenitalia.com. (Ticket office open M-Su 6:30am-8pm.)

◪ ▰ ORIENTATION AND PRACTICAL INFORMATION. To reach the *centro* in **Piazza del Duomo,** turn left from the bus and train stations onto **Viale Stazione,** walk 500m past the tourist office, and when Vle. Stazione becomes **Via Bastioni Minore,** turn immediately right through the arch to enter the courtyard of the **Palazzo Vescovile.** P. del Duomo is to the left. The **tourist office,** Vle. Stazione 9, distributes town maps and info on suggested hikes, and lists hotel vacancies throughout. (☎0472 83 64 01; www.brixen.info.) Open M-F 8:30am-12:30pm and 2-8pm, Sa 9am-12:30pm.) **ATMs** line V. Bastioni Maggiore at the end of Vle. Stazione. **Luggage storage** is available at the *edicola* in the *biglietteria* for roughly €2, though this may vary with number of bags; negotiate with the man behind the counter. (Open M-Sa 6am-7pm, Su 8am-noon.) Find **Internet** access at the **Biblioteca Civica,** P. Seminario 4, which charges €1 per 30min. to use its computers. (☎0472 26 21 90. Open M-Sa 9am-7pm.) A sign in the window of **Farmacia di Corte Principevescovile,** V. Portici Minori 2/A, posts a list of after-hours rotations. (Open daily 8am-12:30pm and 3-7pm.) The **hospital** (☎0472 81 21 11) is on V.

Dante, toward Brenner. The **police station** is located on V. Vittorio Veneto 13 (☎0472 83 61 31). **Currency exchange** is available at Bressanone's **post office,** behind the tourist office at V. Cassiano 4/B. (☎0472 27 20 01; fax 27 20 40. Open M-F 8am-6:30pm, Sa 8am-12:30pm.) **Postal Code:** 39042.

📷 **ACCOMMODATIONS.** Bressanone's more expensive hotels are near the river. Head from P. del Duomo into P. Vescoville then turn left on V. Bruno to find **🏠Ostello della Gioventù Bressanone ❶**, V. Bruno 2. Friendly staff, remarkably clean rooms, and large bathrooms make it an excellent choice for budget travelers. Take advantage of its great views and proximity to the *duomo*, as well as the multitude of brochures available in the lobby for local activities. (☎0472 27 99 99; www.ostello.bz. Generous breakfast buffet in a sunny dining hall, linens, and lockers included. Towels €1. Laundry €2.50. Reception M-Sa 8am-8pm, Su 8am-6pm. Dorms €19.50 with shared bathroom, €27 with private bath. €2 surcharge for 1-night stay. MC/V.) From the tourist office, take a right onto V. Roma from V. Bastioni, left onto V. Fienili, and right onto V. Tratten for **Pensione Mayrhofer ❹**, V. Tratten 17. This small hotel provides a quiet stay just outside the *centro*. Perks include patio-seating breakfast overlooking a secluded garden, comfortable rooms with TV and Internet access, and free access to a nearby pool. (☎0472 83 63 27; www.mayrhofer.bz. Parking €3 per day. Reservations recommended. ½-pension €53 per person; B&B €41 per person. €5 surcharge for singles; lowered prices for longer stays. MC/V.) Near P. del Duomo, **Cityhotel Tallero ❹**, V. Mercato Vecchio 35, offers a classier alternative to the town's cheaper, no-frills options. Well-lit, modern rooms are equipped with telephones, TV, safe, and Internet access, making for a comfortable stay. (☎0472 83 05 77; www.tallero.it. Breakfast included. Singles €60; doubles €92-108. MC/V.)

🍴 **FOOD.** At the 100-year-old **Fink ❹**, Portici Minor 4, waitresses in traditional garb serve a nice selection of entrees on the outdoor patio, but their real speciality lies inside, where homemade jams, thick slices of cake and strudel (€2.40), and chocolate and candies are sold from behind the counter. Sip Alto Adige wines from €2.90 per glass and regional beer from €2.30. (☎0472 83 48 83. Primi €6.50-9.30. Secondi €9.50-14.50. €1.50 cover includes homemade bread. Open M and Th-Su 11am-10pm. AmEx/MC/V.) Bressanone's oldest restaurant, **Finsterwirt ❹**, Domasse 3, specializes in elegant dining on the tiny Vco. del Duomo off the main *piazza*. The dark

FROM THE ROAD

WHIPPED CREAM AND WHIPS

Strolling among cookie-cutter cafes on Via Portici Maggiore, visions of warm *apfelstrudel* dancing in my head, I was lured into the sweet-smelling *pasticceria*, **Rosa d'Oro** (see next page). Hoping to flatter the owner, I mustered a compliment in broken Italian about the interesting menu. *"Interessante?"* he retorted, a mischievous gleam in his eye.

Before I knew it he had dragged me to a back room and shut the heavy door behind us. I found myself before a wall of swords, rusty chains, and jagged wheels. There was no turning back now, so I decided to conquer the language barrier and extract the story behind these bizarre instruments. Didn't they belong in a prison, or at the very least, a museum?

In a whirlwind of words and gestures, the owner proudly explained that the vicious artifacts were originally torture devices used by the Inquisition. Of course. Up a staircase behind the unassuming *pasticceria*, Adolf Schiner has established a tiny museum where visitors can "admire" the gruesome goodies.

Leaving through the vault-like door, I wandered bleary-eyed back toward the delectable pastries and back into reality. Interesting might have been an understatement.

- *Julia Rooney*

V. Portici Maggiori, 7 (☎0472 83 50 67). Open M-F 9am-10pm, Sa 9am-4pm.

TOP TEN LIST

FOODS YOU'VE PROBABLY NEVER HEARD OF

Trentino-Alto Adige is a culinary crossroads. Bordering Switzerland to the West and Austria to the East, this region's cuisine mixes a strong Austro-German undercurrent with typical Italian fare and even a subtle hint of Slovenia farther off to the east. While Trent's menu is heavenly for the visitor's palate, the names themselves aren't always quite so tasty. Here's a guide to some of Northwestern Italy's most popular foods, so that the unknowing vegetarian doesn't mistakenly order sassaka thinking it's salad.

1. Jota: a stew made with sauerkraut, beans, and sausage.

2. Porcina: boiled pork with mustard and horseradish.

3. Gubana: cake filled with raisins, dried fruits, almonds, grappa, honey, and citron.

4. Frico: slow-cooked cheese, often with potatoes and onions.

5. Palatschinken: apricot and chocolate-filled pancakes.

6. Kipfel: crescent-shaped dumplings made from potato dough.

7. Kaiserfleisch: smoked pork with horseradish and sauerkraut.

8. Muset and Brovade: pork sausage and turnips soaked in wine.

9. Cjarsons: tortellini pasta filled with creamy ricotta.

10. Sassaka: layered pork fat and bacon with onion.

wood interior and intimate dining rooms upstairs provide the perfect complement to chef Hermann Mayr's delicious South Tylorean seafood menu. (☎0472 83 53 43; www.finsterwirt.it. Primi €9-10. Secondi €12-18. Soup €6-7. Open daily 10:30am-3pm and 5:30pm-midnight. AmEx/MC/V.) Sit indoors or under the canopy at **Torre Bianca ❷**, V. Torre Bianca 6, which serves a wide variety of pizzas (€5.20-9) and traditional Tyrolean food on a quiet street in the *centro*. Walk past the left side of the cloister's *campanile*, and pass through the arch. (☎0472 83 29 72. Cover €1.20. Open M and W-Su 9am-11:30pm. MC/V.) Huge slices of cake (€3), cups of ice-cream, fruit, and chocolate sauce are just some of the reasons to drop by *pasticceria* **Rosa d'Oro,** V. Portici Maggiori 7 7/a. Inside, owner Adolf Schiner has established a tiny museum (see **Whipped Cream and Whips,** p. 367) to house his collection of Inquisition-era torture instruments. (☎0472 83 50 67. Open M-F, 9am-10pm, Sa 9am-4pm. Cash only.) There's a **Despar** supermarket, V. Bastioni Minori 4. (☎0472 83 70 32. Open M-Sa 8am-7pm. MC/V.)

◨ ⚲ SIGHTS AND HIKING. To kick off your sightseeing, head to **Piazza del Duomo.** A few meters south of the *piazza*, look for a golden lamb-topped monument in P. Palazzo, where the pale yellow **Palazzo Vescovile,** completed in 1595, houses the **Museo Diocesano.** Its predominantly ecclesiastical collection traces the development of Western Christianity. The majestic interior courtyard features over two dozen terra-cotta sculptures constructed around 1600 that depict various members of the royal Hapsburg family. Ask for the info brochure in English. (☎0472 83 05 05. Open Mar. 15-Oct. 31 Tu-Su 10am-5pm; Dec. 20-Jan. 31 daily 2-5pm. €6, students and groups €5.) The candy-colored **duomo** is as colorful inside as out; huge chandeliers illuminate the golden altar and the Baroque and Neoclassical frescoes. To the right of the *duomo*, the peaceful **cloister** displays traditional Stations of the Cross, which contrast with the stunningly ornamented organ in the back. The garden holds a WWI and WWII monument dedicated to local soldiers. (*Duomo* open 6:30am-6pm; cloister 6:30am-noon and 3-6pm. Guided *duomo* tours Easter-Nov. 1 M-Sa 10:30am; meet just left of the main doors. Free.) For a break from central Bressanone's boutiques and pedestrians, follow Ponte Aquila behind the *duomo* and cross the bridge to the winding footpaths east of the **Altstadt** (old town), where shops and pastel houses huddle along quiet streets. The *Plose Plateau*, towering over Bressanone at heights of over 2000m, is a popular skiing area made accessible by the **Sant'Andrea Cable Car** (10min.; 2 per hr. July 7-Oct. 3 M-F 9am-6pm, Sa-Su 9am-6pm; round-trip €7, bikes €3), which operates from the nearby hillside town of Sant'Andrea. SAD bus #126 makes roundtrips between the Bressanone train station and Sant'Andrea (20min., 7 per day 7:15am-7:20pm) and Bressanone *centro* (7:15am-7:25pm, round-trip €2). Buy tickets at *tabacherrie* or the bus station. From the upper cablecar station in Valcroce, **trail #30** leads along the smooth terrain of the Plose's western slope, and **trail #17** follows the meadows on the Plose's southern slope. For a longer, more strenuous hike, traverse **trail #7** along the summits of Monte Telegrafo and Monte Fana, reaching altitudes of 2600m. Before tackling this hike, check the weather and plan for possible overnights in *rifugi* (hiker huts), such as the **Plose** (☎0472 52 13 41) and **Rossalm** (☎0472 52 13 26; www.rossalm.com), which also offer hot meals. Be prepared to face rough terrain and high altitudes. A multilingual tourist office brochure details three 3-6hr. hikes on the Plose.

For a more leisurely and lower altitude option, the hike to the strikingly beautiful **Abbey Novacella,** V. Abbazia 1, in Varna runs along River Isarco. Cross Ponte Aquila and walk north along the river, then follow **trail #16,** which brings you through the tiny town of **Varna** and to the Abbey (1½-2hr. round-trip). The abbey, founded in 1147, contains examples of Gothic, Romanesque, Baroque, and Rococco art and decor. (☎0472 83 61 89. Museum visits for groups of 10 or more at 10, 11am, 2, 3, 4pm. €2.50.)

🎵 **NIGHTLIFE Discomax Club,** V. Laghetto 30, is a rare find in a town with few loud and late bars. Special dancing nights throughout the week (most from Th-Su) offer hours of Latin, disco, and oldies tunes. (☎0472 80 21 90; www. discomax.com. Drinks start at €3. Happy hour F 9-10pm. Open Th 9pm-2am, F-Sa 11pm-4am.) Though a bit out of the way, **BarSport,** V. Dante 14, offers late nights filled with beer, video games, darts, and *calcio*. (☎0472 83 15 37. Internet access €7 per hr. Open M-Sa 10am-midnight.)

TRENTINO-ALTO ADIGE

FRIULI-VENEZIA GIULIA

Bounded by the Veneto to the west and Slovenia to the east, Friuli-Venezia Giulia (free-OO-lee veh-NETS-ya JOOL-ya) was once several distinct provinces united only by a common clergy in the sixth through 15th centuries. The Hapsburgs claimed the area in the early 1700s as an economic stronghold for Austria and Hungary. Since then, the region has changed hands multiple times, with each new occupant leaving its mark on local cuisine, culture, and architecture. Its natural beauty also draws from varied sources; serene lakes and jagged peaks characterize the north, while dramatic views of the Adriatic Sea shape the coastal regions. James Joyce wrote the bulk of *Ulysses* in the coffeehouses that still dot Trieste, while Ernest Hemingway found inspiration for *A Farewell to Arms* in the region's Carso cliffs. Although smaller towns retain their idyllic charm, Friuli-Venezia Giulia's cultural mixing pot and growing metropolises are what make it one of Italy's most cosmopolitan provinces.

HIGHLIGHTS OF FRIULI-VENEZIA GIULIA

INDULGE in the cuisine of Trieste, Italy's gateway to central Europe (p. 370).

SNAP a photo against the stunning backdrop of the Laghi di Fusine (p. 384).

RUMMAGE through ruins at Aquileia, a former Roman city on the Adriatic (p. 376).

SUNBATHE on the beautiful beaches of Lignano (p. 379).

TRIESTE ☎ 040

After volleying between Italian, Austrian, and Slavic allegiances for hundreds of years, Trieste (tree-YE-steh; pop. 241,000) has finally settled down, celebrating its 50th anniversary as an Italian city in 2004. Yet subtle reminders of Trieste's Central European past remain in its architecture, cuisine, and artwork. Locals strut along bustling waterfront *piazze*, while the natural beauty of the Carso cliffs and the Adriatic Sea complement Trieste's constant excitement.

▶ TRANSPORTATION

Flights: Aeroporto Internazionale di Ronchi dei Legionari (Gorizia) V. Aquileia 46 (☎0481 77 32 24; www.aeroporto.fvg.it. Ticket office: 04 81 77 32 32), 20km from the centro. **Bus-Navetta** runs from the city to the airport (☎340 230 6444) and also has an outer city bus (☎040 42 50 20).

Trains: P. della Libertà 8 (☎040 89 20 21). Ticket counter open daily 6:05am-7:50pm. Info office open daily 7am-9pm. Trains run to **Udine** (1-2hr., 32 per day 5:02am-9:16pm, €6.70) and **Venice** (2hr., 29 per day 4:30am-9:25pm, €8.20).

Buses: P. della Libertà 11 (☎040 42 50 20), next to train station. Ticket office open M-Sa 6:25am-7:40pm, Su 6:30-11:05am. Buses depart for **Udine** as well as destinations in Croatia, Serbia, and Slovenia.

Friuli-Venezia Giulia

Ferries: Depart on a number of lines for **Albania.** Schedules and tickets can be found at Agemar Viaggi, P. Duca degli Abruzzi 1/A (☎040 36 37 37; fax 63 81 72; albania.bk@ agemar.it), on the east side of C. Cavour. Open M-F 8:30am-1pm and 3-6:30pm.

Public Transportation: ACT buses travel to **Carso, Miramare,** and **Opicina.** Trieste Trasporti office located at V. d'Alviano. (www.triestetrasporti.it. Open M-Th 8:30am-3:30pm, F 8:30am-1pm. Purchase tickets at *tabaccherie*. €1 per hr., €3.30 per 24hr.)

Taxis: RadioTaxi (☎040 30 77 30).

⚡🔋 ORIENTATION AND PRACTICAL INFORMATION

The center of Trieste is a grid, bounded on the east by **Via Carducci,** which stretches south from **Piazza Oberdan** toward the historical Capitoline Hill. To the west, **Corso Italia** runs from the spectacular **Piazza dell'Unità d'Italia,** a vast square beside the harbor. The two streets intersect at busy **Piazza Goldoni.** Along C. Italia, just steps from P. dell'Unità d'Italia, lies **Piazza della Borsa,** the place where *triestini* come to see and be seen.

Tourist Office: APT, P. dell'Unità d'Italia 4/B (☎040 34 78 312; fax 34 78 320), has great info and lists of *manifestazioni* (artistic events). Open daily 9am-7pm. Audio tours (€4, 2 for €7; free with the FVG card) of the city available.

Luggage Storage: At the train station (☎040 83 06 68). 1st 12hr. €3, each 12hr. thereafter €2. Max. 2 bags. Open 7am-9pm. Storage also available at the bus station. €2.50 for 24hr. below 0.75 cubic meters, €3 for 24 hr. above 0.75 cubic meters.

Currency Exchange: Deutsche Bank, V. Roma 7 (☎040 63 19 25). Open M-F 8:20am-1:20pm and 2:35-3:35pm.

Pharmacy: Farmacia alla Borsa, P. della Borsa 12/A (☎040 36 83 56). Open M-F 8:30am-1pm and 4-7:30pm, Sa 8:30am-1pm. Posts after-hours rotations.

Internet Access: Bar Unità, Capo di P. Monsignor Antonio Santin 1/B (☎040 36 80 33). €4 per hr. Open M-Th and Su 6am-midnight, F-Sa 6am-3am. **Maranzina Service,** V. Milano 22/C (☎040 34 78 246; lucamaranzina@libero.it), off V. Carducci. €2 per hr. Offers fax, photocopy, and money transfer. Open M-Sa 9am-9pm. Cash only.

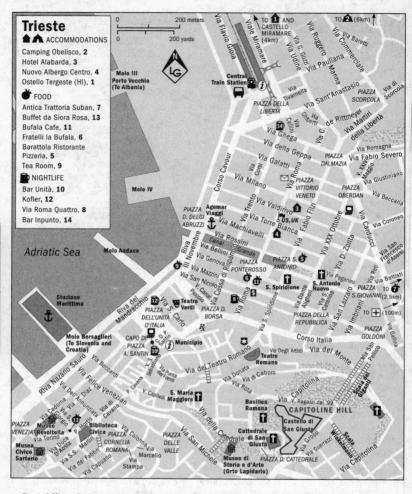

Trieste
🏠🏕 ACCOMMODATIONS

Camping Obelisco, **2**
Hotel Alabarda, **3**
Nuovo Albergo Centro, **4**
Ostello Tergeste (HI), **1**

🍎 FOOD

Antica Trattoria Suban, **7**
Buffet da Siora Rosa, **13**
Bufala Cafe, **11**
Fratelli la Bufala, **6**
Barattola Ristorante
Pizzeria, **5**
Tea Room, **9**

🍸 NIGHTLIFE

Bar Unità, **10**
Kofler, **12**
Via Roma Quattro, **8**
Bar Inpunto, **14**

FRIULI-VENEZIA GIULIA

Post Office: P. Vittorio Veneto 1 (☎040 67 64 282), along V. Roma. From the train station, take 3rd right off V. Ghega. Open M-Sa 8:30am-7pm. **Postal Code:** 34100.

🏠🏕 ACCOMMODATIONS AND CAMPING

Nuovo Albergo Centro, V. Roma 13 (☎040 34 78 790; www.hotelcentrotrieste.it). Centrally located hotel with sunny, spacious rooms with minibar, phone, fan or A/C, and satellite TV. Breakfast included. Internet access €4 per hr. Parking €14. Reception open 7:30am-midnight. Reservations require a deposit and are recommended for summer and weekend stays. Singles €37, with bath €52; doubles €54/72. AmEx/MC/V. ❸

Hotel Alabarda, V. Valdirivo 22, 3rd fl. (☎040 63 02 69; www.hotelalabarda.it). From the station, head down C. Cavour and turn left on V. Valdirivo. Cheerful staff offers simple, clean rooms with satellite TVs. Breakfast included. Internet access free for 1st 30min., €2.50 per hr. thereafter. Singles €35, with bath €55; doubles €55-75. AmEx/MC/V. ❸

Ostello Tergeste (HI), V. Miramare 331 (☎040 22 41 02; ostellotrieste@hotmail.com), 4km from the *centro*. Cross V. Miramare from the station to take bus #36 (every 10 min., last bus at 9pm, €1); ask for the Ostello stop and then walk 7min. to the hostel. Despite small rooms without locks, breathtaking views of the Gulf of Trieste from the patio and balcony make for a pleasant stay. Guests share a common bathroom. Breakfast included; dinner €9.50 on a lovely vine-covered patio that overlooks the water. Lockers €10 deposit. Reception 8-10am and 3:30pm-midnight. Lockout 10am-3:30pm. Midnight curfew. Dorms €16. HI members only. Cash only. ❶

Camping Obelisco, Strada Nuova per Opicina 37 (☎040 21 16 55; fax 21 27 44; campeggioclubtrieste@tin.it), in Opicina. Take Capolinea Tram di Opicina from P. Oberdan to Obelisco stop and follow the signs up the hill. Showers, bar, and parking. Sporting activities organized for guests. No tents provided. Reception Tu-Sa 9am-1pm and 2-6pm. €3.70-4.50 per person; €2.50-3 per tent. MC/V. ❶

🗂 FOOD

Trieste's cuisine has distinct Central European overtones, evident in the region's *sauerkraut*, strudel, and *iota* (sauerkraut, bean, and sausage stew). There's no shortage of quality seafood restaurants along Riva Nazario Sauro and Riva Gulli. The *alimentari* on V. Carducci provide an ideal place to eat on the cheap, while the hundreds of city cafes offer a chance to people-watch. There's a giant **PAM** supermarket, V. Miramare, across from the train station. (☎040 42 61 004. Open M-Sa 8am-8pm, Su 9am-9pm. MC/V.) At Trieste's covered **market**, V. Carducci 36/D, on the corner of Vle. della Majolica, dishware booths and magazine vendors peddle their wares amid vendors hawking fruits and cheeses. (Open M 8am-2pm, Tu-Sa 8am-5pm.)

▨ **Buffet da Siora Rosa,** P. Hortis 3 (☎040 30 14 60). This family-run joint has served *triestini* favorites since it opened over 50 years ago. Try their porcini mushroom and pork sausage doused in *senape, kren,* and *crauti* (mustard, horshradish, and sauerkraut with cumin and juniper; €12.80). Other regional specialties prepared in their open kitchen include *jota* (bean soup with onions and turnips marinated in wine), goulash, and bread gnocchi. *Panini* €2.90-4.50. Cover €1. May-Sept. *piazza* seating service charge 10%. Open M-F 8am-9:30pm. Reservations recommended. MC/V. ❷

▨ **Antica Trattoria Suban,** V. Comici 2 (☎040 54 368). Take bus #35 from P. Oberdan. Austro-Hungarian and Italian dishes are heavenly. Try the house specialty of crepes with basil (€7). Primi €6-8. Secondi €11-16. Cover €2.50. Open M 7-10:30pm, W-Su noon-3pm and 7-10:30pm. Closed Aug. Reservations recommended. AmEx/MC/V. ❸

Bufala Cafe, V. Roma 14 (☎040 06 44 208). If the dark lighting and loud tropical music don't hold allure, then the thick *panini* (€2.50-6), pizza (€2), and fresh focaccia (€1.80-2.50) surely will. The menu is simple with filling picks like *"Pizza ripiena"* (pizza stuffed with tomatoes and veggies; €3.50). Friendly service accompanies cheerful decor, making for a great lunch spot. Open M-Sa 7:30am-11pm. Cash only. ❶

Tea Room, V. Luigi Cadorna 2A. Come for huge *panini* (€1.80-3.50) in this old-fashioned bar where cozy red leather booths welcome customers. Posters on the walls and lamps fashioned from wine bottles add to the funky decor. Late hours make it a great night spot. Beer €2.50-4. Mixed drinks €3-10. Open Tu-Su 7am-2am. Cash only. ❷

Fratelli la Bufala, V. Roma 12 (☎040 34 81 316). Colorful decor and food inspired by (what else?) buffaloes. The *mozzarella di bufala*, imported fresh from Naples, is the main attraction of dishes like *"La Filatina,"* a filet of cheese with tomatoes, basil, olive oil, pepper, and oregano (€9). Perhaps their best deal, however, is their rotating lunch menù, which includes primo, secondo with contorno, and bread all for €10 (served M-F). Pizza €5-11. Open daily noon-3:30pm and 7-11:30pm. AmEx/MC/V. ❷

Barattolo Ristorante Pizzeria, P. Sant'Antonio 2 (☎040 63 14 80; www.albarattolo. it). Overlooks the Canal Grande. Choose from a huge, multilingual menu specializing in pizza, meat, and fish. Try favorites like *schiacciata* (a pizza stuffed with grilled vegetables, *grana* cheese, garlic, and basil; €9.20). Pizza €6.60-10.50. Primi €6.50-12. Secondi €5.50-20. Cover €1. Service 15%. Open daily 8:30am-midnight. AmEx/MC/V. ❸

SIGHTS

THE CENTRO

 MUSEO REVOLTELLA. Also known as the **Galleria d'Arte Moderna,** this museum displays temporary modern art exhibits and an extensive permanent collection that includes the work of Italian artists Francesco Hayez, Domenico Morelli, and Giacomo Favretto. The Revoltella Palace, built in 1858 under the direction of Friedrich Hitzig, is an ornate building with an older collection of Neoclassical works, while the more stark Brunner Palace holds modern works by artists such as still life painter Giorgio Morandi and proto-surrealist Giorgio De Chirico. Don't miss Magni's **Fontana della Ninfa Aurisiana,** a marble fountain of a woman representing Trieste. *(V. Diaz 21. ☎67 54 350; www.museorevoltella.it. Open M and W-Sa 9am-1pm and 4-7pm, Su 10am-7pm. Ticket sales end at 6:15pm. Guided tours Su 11am. Special tours of 20 or more people, €2. €5, students €3.)*

> **TIP**
>
> **TRIESTE FOR VIPS.** A great way to experience Trieste is the **T For You Card.** The card (€10) is valid for 48 hours, and allows free admission to all civic museums, use of special motor ships, "Trieste by Bus" tours, and admission to the race-course, lighthouse, and beach resort at Grignano. Discounts are also offered at hotels, restaurants, shops, and theaters. Purchase one at the Central Travel Office, P. Unita d'Italia 6, or consult the tourist office.

CITTÀ NUOVA. The oldest areas in southern Trieste (the *Castelvecchia,* or "Old City") sport a tangle of roads in no discernible pattern. In the 1700s, Empress Maria Theresa of Austria commissioned a *città nuova* plan, which 19th-century Viennese urban planners implemented between the waterfront and the **Castello di San Giusto.** The resulting grid, lined with Neoclassical palaces, centers around the **Canale Grande,** where colorful rowboats bob past the pedestrian-only paths. Facing the canal from the south is the majestic Serbian Orthodox **Chiesa di San Spiridione,** an AD ninth-century church with blue domes and frescoes of biblical characters. *(Open Tu-Sa 9am-noon and 5-8pm, Su 9am-noon. Modest dress required.)* The vast **Piazza dell'Unità d'Italia,** Italy's largest waterfront square, provides a full view of the Adriatic coastline. On the eastern side of the *piazza,* the Municipio (Town Hall) faces the **Mazzoleni Fountain of the Four Continents,** which represents the world as it was known at the time of the fountain's completion in 1750.

PIAZZA DELLA CATTEDRALE. Climb to this hilltop *piazza* for a spectacular view of downtown Trieste and the Adriatic. At the edge of the *piazza,* a majestic statue covered in flowers and ribbons commemorates Trieste's fall in the War of Liberation. Across the street is the restored **Cattedrale di San Giusto,** created in the 14th century from two parallel churches: the original *Cattedrale* and **Santa Maria Assunta.** Inside, gray walls and humble archways are set off against glittering blue and gold mosaics at the main altar. Climb the *campanile* next door for a nice breeze and views of the city and Gulf. *(The site is reached by bus #24. ☎040 30*

93 62. Open M-Sa 8am-noon and 2:30-6:30pm, Su 8am-8pm; closed to tourists Su mornings for mass. Cathedral free. Campanile €1.50, children under 6 years free. Printed guides €7.)

TEATRO ROMANO. In the AD first century the Emperor Trajan commissioned this amphitheater where both gladiatorial games and dramatic performances were staged. Although weeds have overtaken the structure and the nearby supermarket reduces its majesty, when illuminated after dusk, the theater still manages to impress. *(On V. del Teatro Romano, off C. Italia. From Capitoline Hill, descend toward P. Ponterosso. Free.)*

CITY ENVIRONS

■CASTELLO MIRAMARE. Archduke Maximilian of Austria commissioned this luxurious castle in the mid-19th century, intending its carefully tended flowers and lush greenery as a meditative respite from the bustle of the city. Each of the castle's carefully preserved rooms contains explanatory panels in English. Miramare's towers are easily visible from the Capitoline Hill in Trieste and most points along the **Barcola,** a boardwalk extending 7km between the Castello and Trieste. *(Take bus #36 to Ostello Tergeste and walk along the water for 15min. ☎040 22 41 43. Open M-Sa 9am-7pm, Su 8:30am-7pm. Ticket office open daily 9am-6:30pm. €4, EU citizens ages 18-25 €2, EU citizens under 18 or over 65 free. Guided tours in English €3.50; audio tours in multiple languages, including English €3.50, 2 for €5. Gardens open daily Apr.-Sept. 8am-7pm; Mar.-Oct. 8am-6pm; Nov.-Feb. 8am-5pm. Free.)*

NATURAL MARINE RESERVE OF MIRAMARE. Up the gentle slope from the Castello, in the gardens of **Castelletto Miramare,** this small World Wildlife Federation museum has an aquarium and scuba tours just off the Mediterranean shore. *(☎040 22 41 47; www.riservamarinamiramare.it. Museum open daily 9am-7pm. Scuba diving Sa-Su; snorkeling daily during the summer. Land dive €20, night dive or boat dive €28. Equipment and tank €5 each. Scuba certification and reservation required. Must be in groups of 6-10; ask to be grouped with others if your group is smaller than 6. Call ahead to inquire about guided tours. Museum €2.50; students, youth between 6-18, and seniors €2. With guide €4.50/3.)*

NAPOLEONICA AND GROTTA GIGANTE. The tram to Opicina from P. Oberdan, which started running in 1902, is one of Europe's oldest. It clatters up a steep climb from Trieste, past vineyards and breathtaking views of the Adriatic coastline. Hop off at the Obelisk stop to meet up with the **Napoleonica,** a popular trail that cuts along the sides of the Carso cliffs. At the end of the tram route, local bus

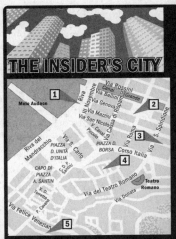

THE INSIDER'S CITY

JAMES JOYCE'S TRIESTE

During his self-imposed exile from Ireland between 1904 and 1920, James Joyce, author of *Ulysses* and *Finnegan's Wake*, lived off and on in Trieste, leaving behind a wake of monuments to his life.

1. At the **Greek Orthodox Church of San Nicolò,** Joyce attended services simply to observe the rituals. (Open daily 9am-12:30pm, 3:30-7:30pm.)
2. In 1905 Joyce lived at P. Ponterosso 3. Continue a few steps and say hello the man himself—a **statue** of him sits on the bridge of the Canal Grande.
3. V. Roma 32 was the site of the **Berlitz School,** where Joyce taught English for two years. On the second floor of V. Roma 30 lies one of Joyce's many flats.
4. Take a meal at the dimly lit **Osteria da Marino,** V. del Ponte 5, where Joyce met friends. (Open M-F 11:30am-3pm and 6:30pm-4am, Sa-Su 6:30pm-4am.)
5. End your odyssey at the **Joyce Museum,** V. Madonna del Mare 6.

#42 takes you close to **Grotta Gigante,** where guided tours in Italian descend into the base of the world's largest touristed cave. Its 500 stairs wind in and around the 107m interior, which could fit St. Peter's Basilica comfortably inside. *(V. Donota 2. Bus #42 arrives in the small parking lot across V. Nazionale from the tram stop. Buy tickets in town for return journey. ☎ 040 32 73 12; www.grottagigante.it. Open Tu-Su Nov.-Feb. 10am-noon and 2-4pm; Mar. and Oct. 10am-4pm; Apr.-Sept. 10am-6pm. 50min. guided tours start every hour Oct.-Mar. and every 30min. Apr.-Sept. €8, groups of 25 or more €6.50.)*

RISIERA DI SAN SABBA. Italy's only WWII concentration camp occupied this abandoned factory outside Trieste, where an estimated 3000-5000 prisoners were put to death. The *risiera* now houses a museum detailing Trieste's role in the Slovenian-born resistance movement fighting Nazi occupation. *(V. Giovanni Palatucci 5. Take bus #8, 10, 19, 20, 21 or 23 from P. Goldoni and ask for the "Risiera" stop. ☎ 040 82 62 02. Open daily 9am-7pm. Free. Brochure in English €1.)*

FARO DELLA VITTORIA. Towering over the Gulf, this lighthouse pays tribute to those lost at sea during WWI. Inaugurated in 1927 in Vittorio Emanuele III's presence, the 70m tower incorporates the anchor of the first ship to enter the harbor after Italy's liberation. *(Strada del Friuli 141. Bus #42, 44, 45, 46. ☎ 040 41 04 61. Open Apr.-Sept. M, Tu, and Th-Su 9-11am and 4-6pm; Oct.-Mar. Sa-Su 10am-3pm. Free.)*

🎵 📷 ENTERTAINMENT AND NIGHTLIFE

On the second Sunday in October, Trieste stages the annual **Barcolana,** a regatta that blankets the harbor with thousands of billowing sails. The acclaimed **Teatro Verdi** hosts opera and ballet for six weeks from July to mid-August. Buy tickets or make reservations at the **box office,** Riva III Novembre 1. Enter on the P. Giuseppe Verdi side of the building. (☎ 040 67 22 298; www.teatroverdi-trieste. com. Open Tu-Su 9am-noon and 4-7pm. Tickets €8-40. AmEx/MC/V.)

The night heats up early at ◼**Via Roma Quattro,** whose name is also its address. Funky orange decor, lively music, and comfy outdoor seating distinguish this central spot, where young trendsetters come for drinks. Thick *panini* (€3.50) stuffed with veggies and sliced meat also make it a great lunch spot. (☎ 040 63 46 33. Beer €2-4.10. Mixed drinks €3.50-6.20. Open M-Sa 7:30am-11pm. AmEx/ MC/V.) Trieste's *glitterati* are out in full force along the bars of **Capo di Piazza Monsignor Antonio Santin,** part of the pedestrian district that connects P. della Borsa and P. dell'Unità d'Italia. On summer evenings, the crowd gravitates toward fresh mixed drinks (€2.50-8), beer (€2-5), and *piazza* seating at **Bar Unità,** Capo di P. M. A. Santin 1/B, on the southwestern corner of P. dell'Unità d'Italia. (☎ 040 36 80 33. Internet access €4 per hour. Open M-Th and Su 6am-midnight, F-Sa 6am-3am. Cash only.) **Bar Inpunto,** V. Ghega 6, sports a dark interior with hanging plants, loud music, and sleek booths. (☎ 36 47 56; www.inpuntomu-sicbar.com. Beer €2.40-5. Mixed drinks €3-5.50. Open M-Sa 6am-2am. Cash only.) At **Kofler,** Riva del Mondracchio 14, Paulaner signs and a lion emblem adorn the walls. Huge interior accommodates a crowd at night and the bar up front serves an extensive menu of beer (€3-8), wine (€2.80-5), and hard liquor (€2.80-6.20). What's more, the view of the Adriatic can't be beat. (☎ 040 37 912. Open M-Th 7pm-2am, F-Sa 7pm-2:30am, Su 6:30pm-1:30am. MC/V.)

GRADO AND AQUILEIA ☎ 0431

Grado (GRA-doh; pop 8700), an island beach resort renowned for its *terme* (thermal) spas, and Aquileia (ah-kwee-LAY-ah; pop. 3300), named a UNESCO world heritage sight for its extensive Roman ruins, lie at opposite ends of the Italian vacation spectrum. However, they're only 15km apart and linked by frequent buses, so visitors can take a dip in the Adriatic on Grado's sloping coast and explore the ruins of Aquileia's ancient port in the same day.

TRANSPORTATION. For both Grado and Aquileia, Cervignano is the nearest city with a train station, on the Trieste-Venice line. From the Cervignano **train station,** frequent **buses** depart for V. Giulia Agusto in Aquileia's *centro* (15min., 32 per day with reduced service on weekends 6:20am-11:15pm, €1.65; tickets available at the *tabaccheria* down the street). From Grado (bus station open daily 6am-10pm), buses run to Aquileia (15min., 35 per day 5:35am-11:15pm, €1.20), Trieste (1hr., 6 per day 6:15am-7:05pm, €4.40) and Udine (1 hr., 21 per day 5:35am-9pm, approximately every hour). In Grado, **city buses** 37A and 37B (every 30min.; €1) stop at major points on the island as well as at many spas and hotels along its south side.

ORIENTATION AND PRACTICAL INFORMATION. From the bus station in Grado, take **Via Roma;** continue on **Via Venezia,** then turn left on **Via Dante Alighieri** to reach the **tourist office,** V. D. Alighieri 72, which provides maps of Grado and listings of spa treatments and prices. (☎0431 87 71 11; www.turismo.fvg.it info. grado@turismo.fvg.it. Open daily 9am-7pm.) The Aquileia **APT Tourist Office**is a short walk from the bus terminal on V. Giulia Augusta in the center of town. (☎0431 91 94 91. Open M-F 9am-7pm.) Find the Grado **police** at V. Goldoni 8 (☎0431 80 161). **Pharmacy Madonna di Barbana** is at V. Orseolo 1. (☎0431 80 058. Open daily 8:30am-12:30pm and 4-8pm.) Find **Internet** access at **Nova Internet Café,** P. Carpaccio 26. (☎0431 87 70 22. €0.08 per minute. Open daily 6am-8pm. Cash only.) The **post office** at V. Caprin 34 has an **ATM.** (☎0431 80 206. Open M-F 8:30am-2pm, Sa 8:30am-1pm.) **Postal Codes:** 34073 (Grado); 33051 (Aquileia).

ACCOMMODATIONS AND CAMPING. A variety of lodgings can be found in Grado; however, the hostel in Aquileia is the best budget option. In sleepy Aquileia, just minutes from the bus station, **Domus Augusta (HI) ❶,** V. Roma 25, has clean dorms, a spacious common area, and bicycles to rent. (☎0431 91 024; www.ostelloaquileia.it. Breakfast and linen included. Laundry available. Reception 2-11:30pm. Check-out 10am. Lockout 10am-2pm. Curfew 11:30pm. Doubles €18.50, €4.50 charge for single use; family rooms, €17. MC/V.) **Villa Romana Meuble ❸,** Vle. Dante 20, is a good bargain right near the action. The hotel features a lounge, bar, and private garden for those who have had enough of the beach. Rooms each come with bath, telephone, fridge, and A/C. (☎0431 82 604 in summer, 0431 39 00 74 in winter; www.grado.it/villaromana. Breakfast included. Singles €35-40; doubles €70-80. MC/V.) Seconds from the ruins of Porto Fluviale, **Camping Aquileia ❶,** V. Gemina 10, provides campers with electricity, warm water, laundry, toilets, pool, and a restaurant. There's also a market across the street. (Apr. 25-Sept. 15 ☎0431 91 042; Sept. 16-Apr. 24 ☎0431 91 95 83; www.campingaquileia.it. Reception 8am-8pm. €5-7 per person. 70 sq. m sites €8-10.50; 140 sq. m sites €16-21. Doubles with bath €19-21 per person; 2-person bungalows €42-48.50; 4-person bungalows €60-72. MC/V.)

FOOD. Locals in Grado know that **⬛Savial ❹,** Campo S. Niceta 14, is the best place for huge variety and generous helpings. More than 50 types of pizza (€4-8.50) and traditional pasta dishes make this the most popular spot in the winding streets of the Old City. (☎0431 85 160. Primi €6-9.50. Secondi €9-16. Cover €1.80. Open daily noon-2pm and 4:30-10:30pm. MC/V.) Enjoy fish specialties like seabass with prosecco and pine nuts (€15) at **Ristorante Taverna Al Canevon ❹,** Calle Corbatto 11. The garden and cozy tables make for a romantic night out. (☎/fax 0431 81 662. Primi €7.50-15. Secondi €13-16. Cover €2.50.

FRIULI-VENEZIA GIULIA

Open M-Tu and Th-Su 12:30-2:30pm and 6:30-10:30pm. AmEx/MC/V.) If hunger strikes while you're checking out ruins in Aquileia, stop by **Pizzeria alla Basilica ❷**, V. della Stazione, behind the tourist office off V. Giulia Augusta. A wood-burning stove churns out crisp pizzas with generous toppings. (☎0431 91 74 49. Pizzas €3.50-7.50. *Menù* with antipasto, pizza, dessert, and drink €20. Open M-Tu and Th-Su noon-3pm and 6:30-10:30pm. AmEx/MC/V.) There's a **Coop** supermarket in Grado, Vle. Europa Unità 35. (☎0431 81 237. Open M-F 8am-1pm and 5-7:30pm, Sa 8am-7:30pm, Su 8am-1pm. AmEx/MC/V.)

◪SIGHTS. Visitors to Aquileia may want to begin their visit with a walking tour of the center and its archaeological sites, offered by the tourist office. The floor of the ◪**basilica,** a remnant of the original building, is a giant mosaic containing over 700 sq. m of geometric patterns and images of animals, cherubs, and field workers; don't miss the charming depiction of Jesus as a rooster battling Satan, a turtle, who retreats into his shell just to the right of the entrance. Beneath the altar, 12th-century frescoes illustrate the trials of Aquileia's early Christians as well as scenes from the life of Christ. Catwalks overlooking the remarkable floor guide visitors to the **Cripta degli Scavi** in the back and the **Cripta degli Affreschi** near the entrance, both home to half-covered mosaics and artifacts. (☎0431 91 067. Basilica open daily 9am-7pm. Guided visits Su 10:30-11:30am. Free; crypt entrance €3, under 10 free.) The nearby **campanile** was constructed in 1031 from the remains of a Roman amphitheater. Visitors sweat their way up 127 steep, sharply turning steps before enjoying unobstructed views of the countryside and shoreline. (Open daily 9am-1pm and 2:30-6pm. €1.50.) Head behind the church to the cemetery where rows of metal crosses and a poignant statue of a fallen soldier occupy the quiet space. **Porto Fluviale,** a cypress-lined alley behind the basilica, is listed as one of UNESCO's most valuable World Heritage Sites. It conveniently leads to Roman ruins at the forum. Frequent placards in Italian, English, and French explain the ruins along the tranquil path. The **Museo Archeologico,** at the corner of V. Augusta and V. Roma, features the preserved remains of a boat used by Roman citizens as well as an ancient bronze chandelier. (☎0431 91 016. Open M 8:30am-2pm, Tu-Su 8:30am-7:30pm. €4, EU citizens ages 18 to 25 €2, EU citizens under 18 or over 65 free. Cashier closes 30min. before closing.) From the Museo Archeologico, walk down V. G. Augusta, take a right on V. Gemina, and follow signs to the **Museo Paleocristiano** in P. Pirano to see mosaics that document the region's transition from paganism to Christianity. (☎0431 91 131. Open Tu-Su 8:30am-1:45pm. Free.)

◪ NIGHTLIFE. Nightlife in Grado centers around the Old City and V. Dante Alghieri, though for a beach town it is surprisingly tame. A few bars stay open late, but the streets and the beach are usually full of families and couples interested in enjoying a social evening out, rather than dancing the night away. **Bar Persona,** Galleria Esplanade (at the corner of V. Dante Alghieri and V. Venezia), is a small, laid-back bar with lively music. Brick archways and a wooden counter give the place a rustic feel. Customers sit on the patio, leisurely watching passersby as they sip drinks and enjoy *panini*. (Beer €3-4.50. Wine €1.50-5. Open daily 10:30am-2:30pm and 5:30-11:30pm. Cash only.)

◪ OUTDOOR ACTIVITIES. Visitors willing to pay top dollar come to Grado for spa treatments at the *terme*, a set of spas along the lagoon on Grado's south side. Those reluctant to splurge on eternal youth can still enjoy the beach along the *terme*. Tickets are available along V. Regina Elena; prices vary by time of day and season, and depend on extra beach services. **Parco delle Rose,** behind the Tourist Office, offers entrance along with shower access and emergency ambulance service (€4). Don't miss the **free beach,** at the western end of the island 15min. beyond the *centro storico.*

LIGNANO   ☎0431

There isn't a *duomo* in sight nor a medieval *centro storico* to wander—just miles and miles of sandy beaches packed with bronzed Italians and pale German visitors. One of Italy's best resort towns, Lignano (leen-YA-no; pop. 6000) is packed with fun-seeking beachgoers. The energetic atmosphere of Lignano can make even the most scholarly visitor forget about the lack of museums and churches and simply relax on the beach.

▐ TRANSPORTATION. Lignano is best accessed by a 40min. bus ride from the nearest **train station** in Latisana. **Buses** run from Latisana to Lignano (every 30min.-1hr., depending on time of day; 32 per day 6:30am-11:30pm; €2.55) and from Lignano to Latisana (every hr. 5:50am-10:30pm). Lignano's **bus station,** Vle. Gorizia 26, is around the corner from the **AIAT Tourist Office** in the center of town where you can pick up maps, brochures, and flyers about local events and frequent beach parties around the island. (☎0431 71 373. Open daily 6:30am-1pm and 3-9:30pm.) For a **taxi,** call **Radiotaxi** ☎0431 70 782.

▐▐ ORIENTATION AND PRACTICAL INFORMATION. The island of Lignano is divided into three areas: **Riviera** in the west, **Pineta** in the middle, and **Sabbiadoro,** where all the action is, in the east. In Sabbiadoro, **Viale Centrale, Via Latisana,** and **Viale Europa** run the length of the island to the town center. **Lungomare Trieste** begins after Camping Sabbiadoro and runs along the coast. In the center of town, Vle. Centrale turns into **Viale Venezia, Via Tolmezzo,** and finally, **Via Udine.**

The **AIAT tourist office,** V. Latisana 42, distributes detailed maps and bus schedules and offers a list of free **Wi-Fi** hot spots for those who register with ID. (☎0431 71 821; www.infolignano.it. Open daily 9am-7pm.) Find the **police** at Vle. Europa 100 (☎0431 40 91 22). Pick up designer sunscreen at **Farmacia De Roia,** V. Tolmesso 3 (☎0431 71 263. Open daily 8:30am-12:30pm and 4-10pm. MC/V.) A medical **clinic** is at Parco S. Giovanni Bosco 20/A, off V. Tolmezzo (☎0431 71 001). The **post office,** Vle. Gorizia 37/39, is near the tourist office. (☎0431 40 93 33. Open M-F 8:30am-7pm, Sa 8:30am-1pm.) **Postal code:** 33054.

▐▐ ACCOMMODATIONS AND CAMPING. When deciding between hundreds of indistinguishable resorts that line the beach, look out for special services—like free daily passes for a chair and umbrella at the beach—that not every hotel offers. Most hotels also offer good pensions (approx. €5-10 per meal), which definitely beat the bills at Lignano's touristy restaurants. **◪Hotel Castiglione ❸,** Lungomare Trieste 126, offers free beach chair and umbrella passes, *pensione* plans (€10-12 extra for full board), and bikes at no extra fee. Only 30m from the beach, Castiglione welcomes guests to comfortable, modern rooms, each with private bath, A/C, TV, phone, and safe. (☎0431 71 551; www.castiglionehotel. it. Breakfast included. €38-61 per person. 10% discount for week stay. MC/V.) **Pensione Zen ❷,** Ple. San Giovanni Bosco 15, is a cheaper, family-run option at the center of the action, offering basic rooms, some with terraces. A beach umbrella pass is included in the daily rate. (☎0431 71 237. Breakfast €5. Open May-Oct. Singles €20-40, with bath €31-42; doubles €35-50/36-60. Cash only.) At family-oriented **Camping Sabbiadoro ❶,** V. Sabbiadoro 8, you'll have access to a pool, supermarket, restaurant, Internet, bike rental, and a beach. Walk 20min. from center of town, or ask the driver for Camping Sabbiadoro on the bus from Latisana. (☎0431 71 455; www.campingsabbiadoro.it. €4.80-9 per person, children age 3-12 €3-5; €7.20-14.50 per tent. AmEx/MC/V.)

🔲 **FOOD.** The ratio of *gelaterie* to vacationer is high in Lignano. Try out Lignano's best *gelateria*, **Tropicana Gelateria ❶**, V. Tolmezzo 37, for frappes (€3), *macedonia* (€3.50-4.50), and gelato (1 scoop €1) topped with fresh fruit. (Open daily 10:30am-late. Cash only.) Those not on a *pensione* plan can try out **O Sole Mio ❹**, V. Udine 62, for great wood-oven pizza and classic pasta dishes. Run by the same family for three generations, the laid-back restaurant caters mostly to families and locals. (☎0431 71 364. Pizza €4.50-9.50. Primi €4.50-15. Fish €4-18. Cover €1.20. Open daily 10:30am-1am, closed Th in winter. AmEx/MC/V.) Famous for its *tramezzini*, **Time Out ❶**, Vle. Gorizia 48, is a great stop before hitting the beach. Tons of sandwiches (€1.50-2) stuffed with veggies and meat served inside or at outdoor tables. (☎0431 72 12 35. Open M-Sa 7:30am-9pm in summer.) A **PAM** Supermarket is located at V. Carnia 17. (Open M-Sa 8:30am-1pm and 4-8pm, Su 8:30-1pm and 4-7:30pm.)

🔲🔲 **BEACHES AND NIGHTLIFE.** The **free beach** on the southern side of Lignano Sabbiadoro stretches the full length of Lungomare Trieste, but be prepared to shell out a little extra for a beach chair or umbrella if it's not included in your hotel's rates. In summer, the young children and the elderly fade with the setting sun as Lignano's night scene gets going along **Via Tolmezzo** and **Via Udine.** Before hitting the dance floor, sip a tall drink at **Tango,** V. Gorizia 5. Neon lights, fruity mixed drinks (€5-7), and buff bartenders keep customers feeling hip and happy. (Open daily 5pm-4am.) **Bar Italia,** V. Udine 99, serves frozen drinks and cocktails beneath palm trees and tropical decor. Customers spill onto the street and into next-door. Some of the best *discoteche* in Lignano require some planning, as they are located a bus-ride away and often require reservations. **Kursaal,** Lungomare Riccardo Riva 1, hosts Mukambo night Sundays (6pm-midnight) from May to August on its private beach and terrace. Saturday night is *"La Noche Escambrosa,"* hosted in a fiery red room with DJ and bar (10pm-5am). Reserve in advance for entrance. Cover is around €10 and often includes a free drink. (☎800 17 87 02.)

CIVIDALE DEL FRIULI ☎0432

On the banks of the Natisone River, tiny Cividale (chee-vee-DAH-leh; pop. 11,000) is perhaps the most enchanting town in Friuli. Founded by Julius Caesar as Forum Iulii, Cividale eventually became the capital of the first Lombard duchy in AD 568 and later flourished as a meeting point for artists and nobility during the Middle Ages. Cividale, a mere 20min. train ride from Udine, draws visitors with its well-preserved medieval monuments and natural beauty.

🔲🔲 **TRANSPORTATION AND PRACTICAL INFORMATION.** Cividale is best reached by **train** from Udine (20min., 25 per day 6:33am-11:33pm, €2.10). Buy tickets in the Udine train station. The train station, Vle. Libertà 43, is near the *centro*. (☎0432 73 37 16.) For a **taxi**, call ☎3396 59 10 14. To reach the *centro* from the station, take **Via Guglielmo Marconi.** Turn left through the stone gate, **Porta Arsenale Veneto,** when Vle. G. Marconi ends. Cross **Piazza Dante** and turn right on **Via San Pellico,** then left on **Largo Boiani;** the *duomo* is straight ahead. To reach the **tourist office,** P. Paolo Diacono 10, take C. Giuseppe Mazzini from P. Duomo to its end. The office offers free **Internet** access and serves as an **Informagiovani** to help young people find work. (☎0432 71 04 60; www.cividale.net. Open daily 9:30am-noon and 3:30-6pm.) In case of emergency, contact the **police,**

P. Armando Diaz 1 (☎0432 70 61 11). Services include: **Farmacia Minisini,** Largo Boiani 11 (open M 3:30-7:30pm, Tu-F and Su 8:30am-12:30pm and 3:30-7:30pm, Sa 8:30am-12:30pm; MC/V); **Ospedale Cividale,** P. dell'Ospedale, south of the Natisone river (☎0432 70 81); and the **post office,** Largo Boiani 37-39 (☎0432 70 57 11; open M-F 8:30am-7pm, Sa 8:30am-1pm). **Postal Code:** 33043.

⌗⌂ ACCOMMODATIONS AND FOOD. Quiet Cividale lacks a wide variety of budget accommodations, but the tourist office lists available *affittacamere* (rooms for rent). **Casa Franca,** V. Alto Adige 15, is a 10 minute walk from the train station. Turn left from the station, then left on V. Bottego and follow it until it becomes V. San Moro; V. Alto Adige is the first street on the left. This large accommodation has two doubles, one single, a shared bathroom, kitchen, and lounge. (☎0432 73 40 55. Breakfast €5. Price upon request; call ahead. Cash only.) Find warm service at the family-run **Locanda Al Pomo d'Oro ❹,** P. San Giovanni 20, a restored medieval inn from the sixth century. Though close to the *centro*, the secluded atmosphere makes for a quiet, cozy stay. Rooms have TV, fridge, safe, and private bath. (☎0432 73 14 89; www.alpomodoro.com. Breakfast included. Wheelchair-accessible. Check-in by 6pm. Singles €60; doubles €80. AmEx/MC/V.) The few rooms at **B&B La Casa Dai Toscans ❸,** C. Mazzini 15, are spacious, sunny, and elegantly furnished with private bath and TV. Traditional or American breakfast served in a cozy breakfast nook. (☎3490 76 52 88; www.lacjasedaitoscans.it. Singles €40; doubles €70. Cash only.)

Regional culinary specialties include *stakanje* (a puree of potatoes and seasonal vegetables) and *gubana* (a large fig- and prune-filled pastry laced with *grappa*). Try the flaky *gubana* (€0.75) at ▧**Cattarossi V. di Blasutig Alberto ❶,** C. Paolino d'Aquileia 10, where owner Alberto has amassed a loyal following over the last few decades with his consistently mouth-watering pastries. (☎0432 73 21 52. Open M-Sa 7:30am-11pm and 3:30-8pm, Su 8:30am-1pm and 2:30-8pm. Cash only.) **Antica Osteria alla Speranza ❸,** P. Foro Giulio Cesare 15, across from the post office, offers delicious plates like *linguine al pesto di Rucola* (€7) under frescoed ceilings or among hanging plants in its back courtyard. (☎0432 73 11 31. Primi €7. Secondi €9-12. Cover €1.20. Open M, W-F, and Su 10am-2:30pm and 5pm-midnight, Sa 9am-2:30pm and 5pm-midnight. MC/V.) For more upscale dining, **Alla Frasca ❸,** V. Stretta de Rubeis 11, serves traditional pasta in elegant booths or at outside tables under a leafy canopy. (☎0432 73 12 70; www.allafrasca.it. Primi €7-8. Secondi €12-19. Cover €2. Open Tu-Su 10:30am-3pm and 6:30pm-midnight. AmEx/MC/V.) **Coopca,** V. Adelaide Ristori 15, sells groceries. (☎0432 73 11 05. Open M and W 8:30am-12:45pm, Tu and Th-Su 8:30am-12:45pm and 4-7:30pm. Cash only.)

◼ SIGHTS. The dark, gray-stone interior of the *centro*'s 15th- and 16th-century **duomo** houses the Renaissance sarcophagus of Patriarch Nicolò Donato, left of the entrance. Five stained-glass windows at the apse illuminate the dim church and the magnificent silver altarpiece of Pellegrino II dating from 1194-1204. Annexed to the *duomo* is the **Museo Cristiano,** displaying the *Battistero di Callisto*, commissioned by the first Aquileian patriarch in Cividale, and the *Altar of Ratchis*, a Lombard sculpture from AD 740. (☎0432 70 12 11. *Duomo* and museum open M-Sa 9:30am-noon and 3-6pm, Su 3-6pm. Free.) Circle around the right side to the back of the *duomo* and follow Riva Pozzo di Callisto to the bottom of the stairs where signs point to **Tempietto Longobardo,** an AD 8th-century sanctuary whose original purpose remains a mystery. Built on the remains of a Benedectine convent, it houses a remarkable collection of frescoes and stucco figures. *The Procession of Virgins and Martyrs*, which stares down from a high perch, is rumored to have been painted by a Muslim who fled westward to avoid persecution for his religious art. Follow the rocky ledge overlooking the emerald green Natisone River to the museum's entrance. (☎0432 70 08 67. Open Apr.-Sept. M-F 9:30am-12:30pm and 3-6:30pm, Sa-Su 9:30am-1pm and 3-7:30pm; Oct.-Mar. M-F 9:30am-12:30pm and 3-5pm, Sa-Su 9:30am-12:30pm and 2:30-6pm. €2.50, students €1.) The elegant Venetian **Superintendent's Palace,** P. Duomo 13, designed by Andrea Palladio, houses the **Museo Archaelogico Nazionale.** Recovered mosaics from Roman and Early Christian times, tombstones of Jewish residents, and Romanesque reliefs occupy the ground floor, while the extensive collection of jewelry found at Longoboard funerary sites occupies the first. English and Italian explanations trace the Longobard rule in Cividale up to the Carolingian period in the AD ninth century. (☎0432 70 07 00. Open M 9am-2pm, Tu-Su 8:30am-7:30pm. Last entry 30min. before closing. Tickets €2, ages 18-25 €1, under 18 and over 65 free.) From the *duomo,* follow C. Paolino d'Aquileia to **Ponte del Diavolo,** a 15th-century stone bridge set between cliffs 22m above the **Natisone River.** The bridge, now a symbol for the city itself, was named for Lucifer, who allegedly allowed the bridge to stand in exchange for the first soul to cross. The tricky townspeople got the better of Lucifer by sending an unsuspecting cat across first. Head behind the Chiesa San Martino for another lookout point on the river from the balcony along the steep banks. From there, turn off C. P. d'Aquileia on Vle. Monastero Maggiore right before the bridge to explore the dim, steep stone tunnels of **Ipogeo Celtico,** Monastero Maggiore 10, an ancient Roman prison with open-jawed skulls engraved in the walls, remnants of its former use as a graveyard. (Open Tu-Su 7am-3pm. Free.) For the key, visit **Bar all'Ipogeo,** Monastero Maggiore 2, or call the **Informagiovani** (☎0432 71 04 60).

■ **NIGHTLIFE.** Cividale doesn't offer much in the way of nightlife, but the town's center is the place to find what little there is. By night, ▨**Caffe San Marco** attracts a youthful yet refined clientele with its swanky red-and-silver lounge, live jazz, and late hours. (☎0432 73 10 01. Beer €2.30-4.30. Wine €1.50-3. Open M-Th 7:30am-1am, F 7:30am-3am, Sa-Su 8:30am-3am. Cash only.) **Bea Caffe,** 16 V. Alessandro Manzoni, is an eclectic hub with hanging lanterns, American rock music, *calcio* paraphernalia, and posters of Mt. Rushmore. Although the eye-catching interior is tough to turn down, small tables are also available outside. (Beer €2. Open daily 7am-2am. Cash only.)

TARVISIO   ☎0428

Pristine wilderness and a mix of Italian, Austrian, and Slovenian cultures set Tarvisio (tar-VEE-see-oh; pop. 5000) apart from other ski resort towns in Italy. In the winter, Tarvisio bustles with nordic enthusiasts from nearby Central European countries. The mountains of Carnia and the majestic Fusine Lakes are the centerpieces of summer tourism as well. Eager backpackers delight in the many hiking and biking opportunities and the picture-perfect views. In the *centro,* a large, daily market brings shoppers from across the border to stalls hawking Italian clothing and accessories.

▣ **TRANSPORTATION.** The city of Tarvisio is 2km from the **train** station, Tarvisio Boscoverde. **Buses** run from the train station to Tarvisio Città (7min., 10 per day, M-F 7:23am-6:08pm; Su 2 per day 10:15am and 4:25pm, €1). Buses run from Tarvisio Città to Udine (1hr., 6 per day 5:30am-6:25pm, €7.40), typically with a transfer in Carnia or Gemona, and Trieste (3hr., 7 per day, 5:01am-7pm, €14). Purchase tickets at the train station or *tabaccherie.* Both train and bus services are greatly reduced on Sunday. For timetables, call the Boscoverde's ticket office (☎0428 64 46 94) or ask at the tourist office. Ticket office open M-Sa 8:30am-noon and 2:30-5:30pm, Su 9am-1pm.The area around Tarvisio has little public transportation—to explore the area thoroughly, rent a car. For **car rental,** call Mauro Collini at **Maggiore** (☎3472 60 26 36). For a **taxi,** call Luciana Zossi (☎3487 14 74 93) or Basile Lino (☎3405 68 36 71).

⬛▮ ORIENTATION AND PRACTICAL INFORMATION. Tarvisio is essentially three long, parallel streets that come together at each end of the *centro*. Approaching Tarvisio from the east, **Via Diaz** splits into **Via Romana, Via Roma,** and **Via Vittorio Veneto.** The large covered market extends down V. V. Veneto after V. Roma ends. The **tourist office,** V. Roma 12, across the street from the bus stop, offers bus and train schedules and a stash of glossy brochures. (☎0428 21 35 or 0428 28 65; www.tarvisiano.org. Open M-Sa 9am-1pm and 3-7pm, Su 9:30am-12:30pm and 4-7pm.) For **emergencies,** call the **police,** V. Giovanni Paolo II, (☎29 80) or an **ambulance** (☎0428 29 31). A **pharmacy,** V. Roma 22, is across the street from Hotel Adriatico. (☎0428 20 46. Open M-Sa 9am-12:30pm and 3-7pm. MC/V.) A **clinic** is located on V. Veneto, and the nearest **hospital** is in Gemona (☎0432 98 91). **Internet** access in town can be found at the computer in the lobby of **Hotel Nevada,** V. Kugy 4, right next to the tourist office. (☎0428 23 32. €3 per 30min., €5 per hr. Open daily 9am-9:30pm.) The **post office,** V. V. Veneto 18, is near Tarvisio's school building. (☎04 28 21 92. Open M-F 8am-1:30pm, Sa 8am-12:30pm.) **Postal code:** 33018.

▮◻ ACCOMMODATIONS AND FOOD. Many accommodations shut down during June, the lowest point of ski season; however, you can use this as an opportunity to take advantage of the summer bargains. A great budget choice is **Hotel Adriatico ❷,** V. Roma 51. Rooms are small but have TV, bath, and a mountain view. (☎0428 26 37; fax 63 246. Breakfast included M-Sa. Singles €25; doubles €50. MC/V.) A more upscale option is the quaint **Hotel Haberl ❹,** V. Kugy 1, which features free Internet access and rooms with bath, TV, and a patio. (☎0428 23 12 or 0428 2233; www.hotelhaberl.com. Wheelchair-accessible. Breakfast €5. Singles €50; doubles €70; triples €90. Extra bed €15. MC/V.)

Plenty of restaurants can be found on V. V. Veneto around the covered market, but better meals are often closer to the *centro*. At **Raibl ❶,** V. IV Novembre 12, sit on the outside patio and choose from over 30 varieties of pizza (€4-8), including their special with fresh tomatoes, *mozzarella di bufala*, olive oil, parmesan, and basil. Walk on V. Roma toward the *duomo*; V. IV Novembre goes up the hill to the left after the tourist office. (☎0428 22 47; www.hotelraibl.com. Open Tu-Su noon-10pm. Primi €4.50-9.50. Cover €0.50. AmEx/MC/V.) Reward yourself after a long day of hiking (or shopping) with one of the seafood specialties, like the filet of *sogliola* (sole) with appetizers (€9), at **Ristorante Adriatico ❷,** V. Roma 51. The dining room's tall windows reveal green hills and snow-capped peaks beyond. (☎0428 26 37. Open M-Sa 7am-10pm. Primi €4-7.50. Secondi €9-12.50. MC/V.) You'll know the town's best *gelateria* by the colored flags and the crowds of locals sitting on the patio outside at **Bar Commercio,** P. Unita 1, just before the tourist office. One-scoop cones (€1) and sundaes (€2.50-4.50) are great buys. *Panini*, snacks, and bus tickets are also available for purchase. (☎0428 21 33. Open daily 7am-midnight. Cash only.)

◙▰ SIGHTS AND OUTDOOR ACTIVITIES. The main sights in the center of Tarvisio are the market and the *duomo*. The **market,** run primarily by Neopolitans who have migrated north, draws crowds from Austria and Slovenia with its reasonably priced leather goods, jewelry, shoes, and discounted clothing.

FRIULI-VENEZIA GIULIA

Local artisans face competition from the more upscale boutiques across the street. (www.mercatotarvisio.it; open M-Sa from 9am-6:30pm, although some stalls may have different hours.) The **Tarvis Card** offers discounts at the market and the boutiques and allows holders to accumulate points toward prizes like a free, week-long vacation in Tarvisio (www.tarviscard.it; free with any purchase). Constructed in 1445, **Chiesa di San Pietro e Paolo**, in P. Unità, is a rare example of a fortified church, protected by a high stone wall meant to defend against Turkish invasions in 1474. The hushed and soothing interior features wall frescoes of King Charles V and the Last Judgement, but the real highlight is the pale yellow **duomo**, a striking sight against the mountains beyond. Fragments of Roman monuments are scattered behind the church. (Open 24hr. Free.)

Tarvisio's main draw is undoubtedly the abundance of **hiking** and **skiing** opportunities in the Julian Alps. The largest ski resort near Tarvisio is actually in Austria: **Pramollo-Nassfeld** has 101km of trails and 30 lifts. When hitting the slopes, carrying a passport is a good idea for non-Italian citizens. (☎+43 0428 58 241; www.nassfeld.at. Lift ticket at 9am €37; prices decrease later in the day.) The tourist office is the best resource for info about ski resorts and discounted outdoor activities. Hiking excursions generally take visitors into the western half of the Julian Alps. For package tours of the area and detailed trail maps, contact **Consorzio di Promizione Turistica**, above the tourist office at V. Roma 12. (☎0428 23 92; www.tarvisiano.org. Open M-F 9am-1pm and 3-7pm.)

▶ **DAYTRIP FROM TARVISIO: LAGHI DI FUSINE.** Worth every effort to explore, the ▧**Fusine Lakes** ("LA-gee dee Foo-SEE-neh") are stunning natural creations. Hedged in the south by the glacier-covered Mangart Mountains (2677m) and surrounded by forest in all other directions, the lakes act like a mirror on clear days, and the effect is deeply serene. A two hour hike circling **Lake Superiore, Lake Inferiore,** and traversing **Massi Marinelli** and **Pirona** offers some of the best vistas. **Buses** depart the school on V. V. Veneto. (5 per day M-Sa 6:40am-5:25pm, last bus back to Tarvisio 5:50pm. Consult tourist office for up-to-date schedules. Round-trip €2.40, buy tickets from **Bar Commercio** or any *tabaccheria*. Cash only.) By **car**, take freeway A-23 or #12. From the parking lot near Lake Superiore, **trail #1** will lead you around both lakes, with **Hotel Edelweiss** and **Chalet Belvedere** along the way. Coming around **Lake Inferiore,** at the section that links the two lakes, you may either follow the original route around a forested region and back to the parking lot or opt for the less traveled path, which leads to a scenic cow pasture. The slightly more difficult **Trail #2** (approximately 3½hr.) starts at Lake Superiore and circles through the **Alpe Vecchia,** running parallel to the Slovenian border. Much of the route traverses forests where local black blueberries and baby strawberries grow. In winter, part of the route becomes a ski trail, while during the summer expect to see grazing horses and cows. Both trails require proper footwear and preparation; consult the tourist office before setting out.

For lodging, **Capana Edelweiss** ❸, V. dei Laghi 6, offers solitude in the forest of the Fusine Lakes. The charming cottage and restaurant sits on the shore of Lake Inferiore, but there is not much else in the area. A car is a good idea if you choose to stay, since bus service is infrequent. (☎0428 61 050. Breakfast included. Row boat rental €4.50 per 30min. Call ahead. Singles €40; doubles €70 with full or half-board available. Cash only.) After trekking all day, break for a snack and enjoy the view from the porch of **Osteria Belvedere** ❷, at Lake Inferiore. (☎3498 12 10 52. Specializes in grilled meat. Primi €4.50-8. Cover €1. Open April 25-October 31 daily 9:30am-8pm. Also rents rowboats, €4.50 per 30min.)

EMILIA-
ROMAGNA

Italy's wealthiest wheat- and dairy-producing region, Emilia-Romagna (eh-MEE-lya ro-MAN-ya) spans the Po River Valley's fertile plains and is home to some of the peninsula's finest culinary traditions. Gorge on Parma's famous *parmigiano-reggiano* and prosciutto, Bologna's fresh *spaghetti alla bolognese* and *mortadella*, and Ferrara's *grana* cheese and *salama*. Complement the local specialties with regional wines like the sparkling red *Lambrusco*. Although the Romans originally settled this region, most of the visible ruins are medieval, and today's travelers find urban scenes that have escaped the oppressive tourism of other major Italian cities. Visitors will enjoy enough peace and quiet to contemplate Emilia-Romagna's art and natural beauty.

HIGHLIGHTS OF EMILIA-ROMAGNA

SAVOR Modena's renowned balsamic vinegar (p. 399).

BIKE along Ferrara's 9km medieval wall (p. 393).

ABSORB the Byzantine influence through Ravenna's world-famous mosaics (p. 410).

PARTY with students and backpackers at the notorious clubs in Rimini (p. 415).

ESCAPE Italy for majestic views off San Marino's Castello della Guaita (p. 425).

BOLOGNA   ☎051

Affectionately referred to as the *grassa* (fat) and *dotta* (learned) city, Bologna (bo-LOHN-ya; pop. 370,000) has a legacy of excellent food, education, and art.

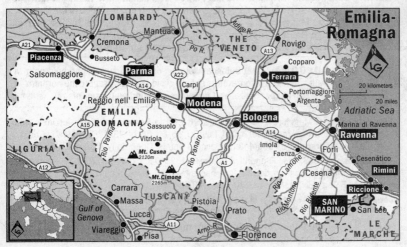

While the Po Valley provides tables with hearty egg pasta and savory local wines, Bologna's museums and churches house priceless artistic treasures. The city is also home to Europe's oldest university—a law school founded in 1088 to settle disputes between the Holy Roman Empire and the Papacy. After taking in free sights, unbelievable food, and the lively student-based nightlife, travelers leave Bologna more than satisfied with their taste of *la dolce vita*.

▮ TRANSPORTATION

Flights: Aeroporto Guglielmo Marconi (☎051 64 79 615; www.bologna-airport.it), at Borgo Panigale, northwest of the *centro*. The Aerobus (☎051 29 02 90) runs to the airport from Track D outside the train station and makes stops at several locations in the *centro* (every 15min. 5:20am-11:40pm, €5).

Trains: Ticket office open 5:30am-11:30pm. Info office (☎051 89 20 21). Open daily 7am-9pm. West platform disability assistance (☎199 30 30 60) is open daily 7am-9pm. To: **Florence** (1hr., 38 per day 5:15am-10:08pm, €5.10); **Milan** (3hr., 40 per day 4:12am-10:16pm, €19); **Rome** (3hr., 46 per day 12:44am-8:46pm, €32); **Venice** (2hr., 30 per day 3:18am-11:20pm, €8.20).

Buses: Terminal Bus (☎051 24 21 50), next to ATC ticket counter, provides Eurolines bus service. Open M-F 9am-6:30pm, Sa 8:30am-6pm, Su 3-6:30pm. Cash only.

Public Transportation: ATC (☎051 29 02 90) runs efficient buses that get crowded in the early afternoon and evening. Intra-city tickets (€1) are good 1hr. after onboard validation; 24hr. tickets €3. Purchase at newsstands, self-service machines, or *tabaccherie*. Buses #11, 20, and 27 run from the train station, up V. Indipendenza and down V. Rizzoli and from there, along V. S. Stefano, V. Barberia and Strada Maggiore, respectively.

Car Rental: Hertz, V. Amendola 16/A (☎051 25 48 30). Turn right from the train station, and left on V. Amendola. 25+. Open M-F 8am-8pm, Sa 8am-1pm. AmEx/MC/V.

Taxis: C.A.T. ☎051 53 41 41. **RadioTaxi** ☎051 37 27 27. 24hr.

✦ ▮ ORIENTATION AND PRACTICAL INFORMATION

From the train station, turn left on **Viale Pietro Pietramellara,** and head to **Piazza XX Settembre.** From there, take **Via dell'Indipendenza,** which leads to **Piazza del Nettuno;** behind it is **Piazza Maggiore,** the *centro*. At P. del Nettuno, V. dell'Indipendenza intersects **Via Ugo Bassi,** which runs west, and **Via Rizzoli,** which runs east to **Piazza Porta Ravegnana. Via Zamboni** and **Strada Maggiore** lead out of this *piazza*.

 NO BOLOGNA. Treat Bologna like a big city—use caution, and hold onto your wallet. At night, solo travelers should avoid the train station, the northern part of V. dell'Indipendenza, and the areas surrounding the university.

Tourist Office: P. Maggiore 1/e (☎051 23 96 60), in Palazzo del Podestà. Offers free accommodation booking through **CST** (☎800 85 60 65 or 23 47 35; www.cst.bo.it), guided city **tours,** and a list of Internet access points. Open daily 9:30am-7:30pm.

Budget Travel: CTS, Vle. Filopanti 4/M (☎051 23 73 07 or 23 75 01). Resources include ISICs (€10), train tickets, tour packages, and discounts on air and sea travel. Open M-F 9am-12:30pm and 2:30-6pm. MC/V.

Luggage Storage: At the train station. Max. bag weight 20kg. €3.80 for 1st 5hr., €0.60 per hr. up to 12hr., €0.20 per hr. thereafter. Open daily 6am-10pm. Cash only.

English-Language Bookstore: Feltrinelli International, V. Zamboni 7/B (☎051 26 80 70). Wide selection. Open M-Sa 9am-7:30pm. AmEx/MC/V.

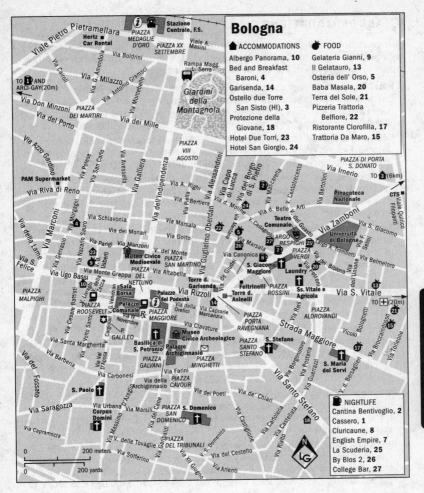

Bologna

🏠 ACCOMMODATIONS
Albergo Panorama, **10**
Bed and Breakfast
  Baroni, **4**
Garisenda, **14**
Ostello due Torre
  San Sisto (HI), **3**
Protezione della
  Giovane, **18**
Hotel Due Torri, **23**
Hotel San Giorgio, **24**

🍴 FOOD
Gelateria Gianni, **9**
Il Gelatauro, **13**
Osteria dell' Orso, **5**
Baba Masala, **20**
Terra del Sole, **21**
Pizzeria Trattoria
  Belfiore, **22**
Ristorante Clorofilla, **17**
Trattoria Da Maro, **15**

■ NIGHTLIFE
Cantina Bentivoglio, **2**
Cassero, **1**
Cluricaune, **8**
English Empire, **7**
La Scuderia, **25**
By Blos 2, **26**
College Bar, **27**

EMILIA-ROMAGNA

GLBT Resources: ARCI-GAY, V. Don Minzoni 18 (☎051 64 94 416; www.cassero.it). Library and counseling center. Open M-F 9am-7pm. **Cassero** nightclub downstairs (p. 393).

Laundromat: Lavarapido, V. Petroni 38/B, off P. Verdi, near V. Zamboni. Wash €3.40 per 8kg. Detergent €0.60. Open M-Sa 9am-9pm, Su 10:30am-9pm. Cash only.

Police: P. Galileo 7 (☎051 16 40 11 11).

24hr. Pharmacy: Farmacia Comunali AFM Bologna, P. Maggiore 6 (☎051 23 85 09).

Internet Access: Sportello Iperbole, P. Maggiore 6 (☎051 20 31 84). Wi-Fi, limit 3 hr. per day. Reserve a few days ahead for free Internet on public computers, limit 2hr. per week. Open M-F 8:30am-7pm, Sa 8:30am-2pm, 3-7pm; last use at 5:30pm.

Post Office: P. Minghetti 4 (☎051 80 31 60), southeast of P. Maggiore, off V. Farini. Exchanges currency. Open M-F 8am-6:30pm, Sa 8am-12:30pm. **Postal Code:** 40100.

ACCOMMODATIONS

Bologna's hotels are pricey and fill up quickly, especially during the September high season; reservations are recommended. The most affordable establishments are located near **Via Ugo Bassi** and **Via Marconi**.

Hotel Due Torri, V. degli Usberti 4 (☎/fax: 051 26 98 26 or 23 99 44). White flowers and glittering lights adorn the lobby of this charming hotel. Slightly cramped but well-furnished and quiet rooms have minibar, TV, phone, A/C, and free Internet access. Breakfast served amid floral decor. Singles €60-79; doubles €80-90. AmEx/MC/V. ❹

Hotel San Giorgio, V. Moline 17 (☎051 24 86 59; www.sangiorgiohotel.it). Conveniently located. Elegant, gold lobby. Spacious rooms with bath. Satellite TV. Breakfast included. Free Internet. Singles €55-60; doubles €85-90; triples €100-110. AmEx/MC/V. ❹

Albergo Panorama, V. Livraghi 1, 4th fl. (☎051 22 18 02; www.hotelpanoramabologna. it). From P. del Nettuno, take V. Ugo Bassi; take the 3rd left. Large rooms have TV. Breakfast included. Reception 7am-10pm. Check-in by 6pm. Singles €50; doubles €60-70, with private bath 80; triples €80-85/120; quads €90-95/140. MC/V. ❹

Ostello due Torre San Sisto (HI), V. Viadagola 5 (☎/fax 051 50 18 10), off V S. Donato, in Località di S. Sisto. Take bus #93 from V. Marconi 69 (15min., M-Sa every 30min. 6:05am-8:20pm). For late night service take 21B from in front of the train station (M-Sa every hr. 8:44pm-12:44am). On Su, take #301 from bus station (6 per day 7:30am-8pm). Exit at S. Sisto. Comfortable, but out-of-the-way hostel with basketball court, satellite TV, and DVDs. Breakfast included. Free lockers in room. Laundry €2.60 per load. Internet access €3.50 per hr. Wheelchair-accessible. Reception 7:30-10am and 3:30-11:30pm. Lockout 10am-2pm. Dorms €16; singles €23, with bath €25; doubles €38; family rooms €18 per person. HI-member discount €3. AmEx/MC/V. ❶

Bed and Breakfast Baroni, V. Morgagni 9 (☎340 29 41 752; www.bedandbreakfast-baroni.it). From V. Marconi, take a left onto V. Riva di Reno then a right onto V. Morgani. Centrally located B&B offers 3 colorful rooms in quiet area near the *centro*. Breakfast €5. Singles €35-45; doubles €55-65. AmEx/MC/V. ❹

Protezione della Giovane, V. S. Stefano 45 (☎051 22 55 73). Past the church, on the right. Buzz and climb the large staircase at the end of the hall. Frescoed ceilings and French windows. Check-in or call between 10am and 5pm. Curfew 10:30pm. Reservations recommended. 2- to 3-bed dorms €15. Women only. MC/V. ❶

Garisenda, Galleria Leone 1, 3rd fl. (☎051 22 43 69; www.albergogarisenda.com). Take V. Rizzoli and turn right into the gallery. A hallway lined with antiques leads to 7 spacious rooms with basic furnishings. Unbeatable location. Breakfast €5. Reserved parking €7 per day. Singles €45-55; doubles €65-85, with bath 85-110. Extra bed €30. MC/V. ❸

FOOD

Bologna is known for its stuffed pastas, such as tortellini in meat sauce or with ricotta and spinach, and for its salamis and hams, which include *mortadella*, a sausage-like creation that bears little resemblance to American bologna. Restaurants cluster on side streets near the *centro;* circle by **Via Augusto Righi, Via Piella,** and **Via Saragozza.** The area around **Via Petroni** has smaller, cheaper joints that cater mostly to students. Indoor **Mercato delle Erbe,** V. Ugo Bassi 27, sells produce, cheese, meat, and bread. (Open in summer M-W 7am-1:15pm and 5-7:30pm, Th and Sa 7am-1:15pm, F 7am-1:15pm and 4:30-7:30pm; in winter M-W and F 4:30-7:30pm. Cash only.) Buy essentials at **PAM** supermarket, V. Marconi 28/A. (Open M-Sa 7:45am-8pm, Su 9am-8pm. AmEx/MC/V.)

Osteria dell'Orsa, V. Mentana 1/F (☎051 23 15 76; www.osteriadellorsa.com). Serves simple, fresh cuisine like homemade pasta (€6), panini (€5), *piadine* (round flatbread; €4-5), and big salads (€7). Try healthy, veggie-filled options like the "Macro" with brie, mushroom, arugula, corn, and artichoke (€5). Communal seating perfect for students before a night on the town. Wine €4 per 0.5L. Open daily noon-1am. MC/V. ❶

Terra del Sole, V. Petroni 3/B (☎051 26 26 08). Small and student-friendly. Delicious Bolognese cuisine with a healthy twist. Daily menu of fresh pasta (€4.50), calzones (€2.20), and salads (€3.80). Try the *sformato pitta,* a savory baked gratin made from potatoes, onions, olives, capers, tomatoes, and ricotta (€3). Limited seating—try the nearby Piazza Verdi. Open M-F 11am-8pm. Cash only. ❶

Pizzeria Trattoria Belfiore, V. Marsala 11/A (☎051 22 66 41). Traditional Bolognese pasta and pizza (€2.60-6) served on a quiet street beneath soft, yellow arches and bamboo curtains. Try savory classics like tortelloni with ricotta, spinach, and tomatoes (€7) or *garganelli* with cream, prosciutto, and peas (€6.50). Primi €6-7.50. Secondi €7-9. Cover €2. Open M, W-Su 12:30-2:30pm and 7:30-12:30am. AmEx/MC/V. ❸

Ristorante Clorofilla, Strada Maggiore 64/C (☎051 23 53 43). "Eat your way to good health" is the motto at this wholesome organic eatery. The signature is couscous with tofu, vegetables, and tomato sauce (€6.50). Hot entrees €6-7.50. Salads from €4.50. Fresh juices €2.30. Cover €1. Organic beer and wine from €2.80. Open Jan.-July and Sept.-Dec. M-Sa noon-3pm and 7:30-11pm. AmEx/MC/V. ❷

Gelateria Gianni, V. Montegrappa 11 (☎051 23 30 08), at the corner of V. degli Usberti. Madly popular chain with 99 unthinkably decadent flavors, which include the "Samurai" (mascarpone, ricotta, and powdered cocoa). 1 scoop €1.80-2.20; 3 scoops €2.80-3.30. Open M-Tu and Th-Su noon-midnight. Cash only. ❶

Il Gelatauro, V. S. Vitale 98/B (☎051 23 00 49). This upscale *gelateria* churns out classics like *stracciatella* (vanilla with a chocolate swirl) as well as a large selection of creamy nut flavors like pistachio, almond, and pine nut (2 flavors €2.10; 3 flavors €2.40). Also has gourmet chocolates, truffles, and pastries. Open Jan.-July and Sept.-Dec. M 8am-7pm, Tu-Th 8am-11:30pm, F-Su 8am-11pm. Cash only. ❶

👁 SIGHTS

PIAZZA MAGGIORE. Aristotle Fioravanti, designer of Moscow's Kremlin, remodeled the Romanesque Palazzo del Podestà, now the boxy, brick home of varied cafes and shops that line its loggia. The 15th-century building is a feat of engineering: the weight of the palace rests entirely on columns. Directly across the *piazza* sits the **Basilica di San Petronio,** designed by Antonio da Vincenzo in 1390. The *bolognesi* originally plotted to make their basilica larger than St. Peter's in Rome, but the Vatican ordered that the funds be used to build the nearby Palazzo Archiginnasio. The cavernous Gothic interior hosted both the Council of Trent and ceremony where Pope Clement VII gave Italy to German Kaiser Karl V in 1530. Golden panels and cherubs fill the **Cappella di San Petronio,** left of the entrance, where opulence contrasts the basilica's predominantly bare walls. From the base of the nave nearby, a marble track dotted with constellation symbols and a single gold line extends across the church's floor to create the **world's largest zodiac sundial.** Don't miss the main altar, which elevates ornate stone statues toward the arches above. The tiny museum contains models of the basilica, beautiful chalices, and illuminated books. (*P. Maggiore 3.* ☎ *051 22 54 42. Open daily 7:45am-12:30pm and 3-6pm. Modest dress required. No bags or backpacks. Museum open M 9:30am-12:30pm and 3:30-6:30pm. Free.*)

EMILIA-ROMAGNA

GIVING BACK

IF YOU CAN'T TAKE THE HEAT, GET OUT OF THE KITCHEN

To take a little of the "fat" city home with you, try a class at any of Bologna's short-term culinary schools. Consult the tourist office for a complete listing.

La Vecchia Scuola Bolognese (☎051 64 93 627; www.lavecchiascuola.com), the mother of local cooking schools, offers a 4hr. course topped off by a fabulous meal. Master the art of fresh pasta with help from a professional, English-speaking staff. When all is said and done, you'll get to eat your own pasta creations; if your attempts don't quite succeed, you'll still be served the school's menu of *bolognese* specialties.

La Cucina di Petronilla, V. San Vitale 53 (☎051 22 40 11), offers group classes or one-on-one lessons upon request. The courses focus on wine pairing with food and cooking regional dishes. The chef believes in healthy organic cuisine, but fear not: it's still hearty *bolognese* fare.

La Cantina Bentivoglio (☎051 26 54 16; www.affari.com/bentivoglio), a classy restaurant offering delicious local cuisine and live jazz as well as demonstrations (though not lessons) of the pasta-making process. The price and length of demonstrations vary, so call ahead to book a custom demo with the restaurant.

PALAZZO ARCHIGINNASIO. This *palazzo*, the first seat of the city's university, features thousands of names and coats-of-arms of past students. The building, constructed to consolidate the schools of the university, now houses the **Biblioteca dell'Archiginnasio,** the university's main reading room and a city library with over 800,000 texts. Above the central courtyard's 30 arches sits the **Teatro Anatomico,** a lecture hall where bronze statues of famous doctors blend into the woodwork. A marble table marks where dissections took place beneath the starry ceiling decorations. (*V. Archiginnasio 1, next to the Museo Archeologico. Follow signs from P. Maggiore.* ☎051 27 68 11. *Palazzo open M-F 9am-6:45pm, Sa 9am-1:45pm. Closed 1st 2 weeks of Aug. Free.*)

PIAZZA DEL NETTUNO. This *piazza* contains Giambologna's 16th-century stone-and-bronze fountain *Neptune and Attendants.* Affectionately called "The Giant," a nude Neptune reigns over a collection of water-babies and sirens spraying water from every bodily orifice. According to local legend, Pope Pious IV, who commissioned the statue, was disturbed by the large original size of Neptune's manhood and ordered Giambologna to change it. Giambologna, who agreed to alter the actual member, had the last laugh: standing near the steps of Sala Borsa, it appears as if Neptune is at his original—ahem—grandeur. Nearby, a wall of portrait tiles commemorates the Bolognese resistance to Nazi occupation, while a Plexiglas plaque lists the names and ages of the more recent victims of the 1974, 1980, and 1984 Bologna train bombings.

PINACOTECA NAZIONALE. The Pinacoteca displays religious artwork dating from the Ancient Roman era to the 18th century, with pieces by Giotto, Titian, and Giovanni Battista. **Gallery 15** contains works by Raphael and his Florentine followers, while **Gallery 24** has *Sampson Victorious* by Bologna's own Guido Reni, and floor-to-ceiling *Pietà detta dei Mendicanti.* **Gallery 26** displays Francesco Albani's beautiful *Madonna e Bambino,* and **Gallery 22** holds several large canvases, including Vasari's *Christ in Casa di Marta.* (*V. delle Belle Arti 56, off V. Zamboni.* ☎051 42 09 411; www.pinacotecabologna.it. *Open Tu-Su 9am-7pm. Last entry 30min. before closing. €4, EU students €2, under 18 and over 65 free. Cash only.*)

PALAZZO COMUNALE. Nicolò dell'Arca's terra-cotta *Madonna* and Alessandro Menganti's bronze statue of Pope Gregory XIV adorn the outside of this *palazzo*. The **Collezioni Comunali d'Arte** houses regional art from the 13th to the 20th century. The Rusconi wing displays furnishings from ornate

Bolognan homes, to the gorgeous **Sala Boschereccia,** where walls painted with serene landscapes and playful winged angels surround Baruzzi's 19th-century statue of Apollo. *(P. Maggiore 6. Office ☎ 051 21 93 526 or 21 93 629. Open Tu-F 9am-3pm, Sa-Su 10am-6:30pm. Free.)* If you're looking for secular art, don't miss the **Museo Morandi,** which displays luminous oil paintings and watercolors. It also features the reconstructed V. Fondazza studio of early 20th-century painter, Giorgio Morandi, along with his landscapes and muted oil still-lifes of jugs, cups, and bottles. *(P. Maggiore 6. ☎ 051 219 33 32 or 219 36 29; www.museomorandi.it. Wheelchair-accessible. Open Tu-F 9am-3pm, Sa-Su 10am-6:30pm. Free.)*

MUSEO CIVICO MEDIOEVALE. This collection contains all things *bolognese*, including images of its patron saints, wax seals of local nobility, an impressive set of sepulcher lids, and weaponry. Watch for a 17th-century dagger that shatters after stabbing its victims and the 17th-century Roman *Sileno con Otre*, a rare example of an obese antique marble statue. In the basement, funerary slabs depicting classroom scenes immortalize celebrated Bolognese professors. *(V. Manzoni 4. Off V. dell'Indipendenza, near P. Maggiore. ☎ 051 219 39 30; www.comune. bologna.it/iperbole/MuseiCivici. Open Tu-F 9am-3pm, Sa-Su 10am-6:30pm. Free. Audio tour €4.)*

THE TWO TOWERS. After seismic shifts left Bologna with an unexpectedly tilted **Torre degli Garisenda,** the city strove for new heights with the 97.2m **Torre degli Asinelli.** Visible from all over the city, the towers have become Bologna's architectural symbols. Climbers mount 498 narrow wooden steps past four landings to a breezy perch where a sea of red rooftops, Gothic church spires, yellow villages, and miles of uninterrupted horizon sit stories below. *(P. Pta. Rave-gana, at the end of V. Rizzoli. Open daily 9am-6pm. Last ticket sale 5:40pm. €3. Cash only.)*

MUSEO CIVICO ARCHEOLOGICO. This museum of local artifacts brims with Roman inscriptions, red-and-black Greek pottery, and two dirt-covered, mummified Etruscans. The enormous Etruscan section is filled with jewelry and other tiny ornaments. The basement's Egyptian collection has items from 2640 BC, including stone reliefs from the tomb of Pharaoh Horemheb. *(V. Archiginnasio 2. Follow signs from P. Maggiore. ☎ 27 57 211; www.comune.bologna.it/Musei/ Archeologico. Open Tu-F 9am-3pm, Sa-Su 10am-6:30pm. Free. Audio tour €4.)*

CHURCHES

▓CHIESA SANTO STEFANO. This cluster of buildings and courtyards was shaped from remains of Egyptian temples honoring the goddess Isis. Four of the seven churches of the original Romanesque basilica, known collectively as "Holy Jerusalem," remain. Built to hold the relics of Saints Vitalis and Agricola, the **Cripta** now contains the tomb of Martin the Abbot. In the small **Chiesa di San Sepolcro,** another of Bologna's patron saints, St. Petronio, is entombed in the towering **Edicola del Santo Sepolcro,** supposedly modeled from Christ's sepulcher in Jerusalem. In the rear courtyard is the **Cortile di Pilato** (Basin of Pilate), where the governor reportedly absolved himself of responsibility for Christ's death. *(In P. S. Stefano. Follow V. S. Stefano from V. Rizzoli. ☎ 051 22 32 56. San Stefano open daily 7am-noon and 3:30-6:45pm. Santo Sepolcro open M-F 9am-noon and 3:30-6pm, Sa-Su 9am-1pm and 3:30-6:30pm. Modest dress required. Both churches free.)*

CHIESA DI SANTA MARI DEI SERVI. Glittering red votives and faded patches of fresco conceal the bottom half of this soaring basilica from street-level view. Inside the well-preserved Gothic structure, octagonal columns support an unusual blend of arches and ribbed vaulting. Cimabue's *Maestà* hangs in a dimly lit chapel behind an exquisite altar that was sculpted by Giovanni Antonio Montorsoli, a pupil of Michelangelo. *(Take Strada Maggiore to P. Aldrovandi. ☎ 051 22 68 07. Open daily 7:30am-12:30pm and 3:30-7:45pm. Free.)*

EMILIA-ROMAGNA

CHIESA DI SAN DOMENICO. Tall marble columns line San Domenico's clean interior, but its signature minimalism stops at the two transept chapels. In the Cappella di San Domenico, St. Dominic's body lies in a marble tomb sculpted by Nicolò Pisano and Michelangelo. Across the nave in the Cappella del Rosario, 15 small paintings by Fontana, Carracci, and others depict the mysteries of the rosary and frame a statue of the Virgin beneath a painted ceiling of playful angels. Because St. Dominic is largely credited with institutionalizing the rosary as a conventional form of prayer, this chapel is especially notable. *(From P. Maggiore, follow V. Archiginnasio to V. Farini. Turn right on V. Garibaldi. ☎051 64 00 411. Open daily 9:30am-12:30pm and 3:30-5:30pm. Free. English tours daily upon request.)*

CHIESA DELLE SANTISSIME VITALE E AGRICOLA. With its polygonal brick spire jutting over the walls of local homes, this small church incorporates shards of capitals and columns into its facade. A lavish gold altar illuminates the otherwise dimly lit interior, and underneath the building, an 11th-century crypt holds paintings by Francia and Sano di Pietro. Look for a sculpture of Christ based on the **Shroud of Turin's** (p. 169) anatomical clues. *(V. S. Vitale 50. ☎051 22 05 70. Open daily 8am-noon and 4-7:30pm. Chapel free. Crypt €1.)*

CHIESA DI SAN GIACOMO MAGGIORE. This church's exterior blends Romanesque and Gothic styles, but it's the artwork inside that makes it worth a visit. Nextdoor, the **Oratorio di Santa Cecilia** contains a fresco cycle depicting St. Cecilia's marriage and martyrdom. *(Follow V. Zamboni to P. Rossini. ☎051 22 59 70. Church open daily 7am-noon and 3:30-6pm. Enter Oratorio from V. Zamboni 15. Oratorio open daily in summer 10am-1pm and 3-7pm; in winter 10am-1pm and 2-6pm. Both free.)*

🎵 🎭 ENTERTAINMENT AND NIGHTLIFE

Every year from June to September, Bologna sponsors an ▣entertainment festival of dance, music, cinema, and art. Many events are free; some cost €5. The tourist office has programs. The **Teatro Comunale,** Largo Respighi 1, hosts world-class operas, symphonies, and ballets. To order tickets ahead, call or sign up outside the ticket office two days before performances. In summer, the theater hosts free concerts at 9pm. Pick up a schedule at the tourist office. (☎051 52 99 99; www.comunalebologna.it. Box office open Tu-F 3-7pm, Sa 10am-noon and 3-7pm. 10% surcharge for pre-order. AmEx/MC/V.)

Bologna's student population accounts for the city's large number of bars, pubs, and nightclubs. A mass of them are on **Via Zamboni,** near the university. Call ahead for hours and cover; info changes frequently. In June and July, clubs close and the party scene moves outdoors. The tourist office has a list of outdoor music venues. Don't expect much activity in August—even the outdoor *discoteche* close as locals head to the beach.

▨ **College Bar,** Largo Resphigi 6/D (☎051 349 003 7366). From the music to the inexpensive drinks to the Carl Jung books placed inconspicuously above the bar, this place screams college. Live music ranging from jazz to techno performed daily by students. From 10am-5pm choose any 2 drinks for €3.50, or at 5pm try their special "4x3" shot deal: 4 shots made from 3 liquors, all for €2.50. Open daily 10am-3am. Cash only.

Cluricaune, V. Zamboni 18/B (☎051 26 34 19). Huge, multi-level Irish pub adorned with old bicycles attracts local students with extensive beer selection. Beer from €2. Mixed drinks €4.50. Happy hour 7:30-8:30pm; W 7:30-10:30pm. Open June-Aug. M-Th noon-2am, F-Sa noon-2:30am; Sept.-May daily 4pm-2am. MC/V.

La Scuderia, P. Verdi 2 (☎051 65 69 619; www.lascuderia.bo.it). A large fresco of the deposition graces the entrance to this huge student hangout. Live music. Free Wi-Fi. Nightly buffet 6-8pm. Beer €2.70. Mixed drinks €6. Spritz €4. Student discount 30%. Open M-Th 8am-8pm, F-Sa 6pm-3am. AmEx/MC/V.

Cassero, V. Don Minzoni 18 (☎051 64 94 416; www.cassero.it). Take V. Marconi to P. dei Martiri and turn left on V. Don Minzoni. This popular club draws chatty crowds of students and locals into cavernous dance hall. Popular with the gay community. Arcigay card required for entrance (€15 per year; tourists can purchase a 1-month card for €8 (see **Practical Information,** p. 386). Beer €3. Mixed drinks €7. W night free and features pop music. F and Sa feature techno. Cover €10; join the guest list online for €5 discount. Open in summer daily 9pm-6am; in winter W-Su 9pm-6am. Cash only.

English Empire, V. Zamboni 24, near the University. Drawing crowds of loyal patrons, this bar mixes old-world pub with bumping club music and flashing lights. Under the motto of "one day of pleasure is worth two of sorrow," enjoy *piadine* and crepes (€4.50) or hamburgers, fries, and pizza with a variety of drinks. Great Tu deal: 2 drinks for €5. Mixed drinks €5, after 6:30pm €6. Beer €3.50/4.50. Open daily noon-3am. Cash only.

By Blos 2, V. Marsala 17/19 (☎051 22 63 86). Pink lights, a bubbling fish tank, cow-print columns, and flatscreen TVs decorate the otherwise modern decor of this spacious restaurant/bar. Enjoy pizza (€3.50-6) by day and stick around for a night of *aperitivi,* mixed drinks, beer, and wine (€3.50-7). Live music daily Sept.-May. Open M-Th 8am-1am, F 8am-3am, Sa 5pm-3am, Su 3pm-1am. AmEx/MC/V.

Cantina Bentivoglio, V. Mascarella 4/B (☎051 26 54 16), near Largo Respighi and the Teatro Comunale. Caters to a classier crowd with pricey food and cheap drinks. Relaxed atmosphere. Umbrella-covered patio. Extensive wine list (glasses from €8). Live jazz nightly Sept.-May; outdoors Th-F. Cover €1.20. Open daily 8pm-2am.

FERRARA ☎0532

Rome has its mopeds and Venice its boats, but Ferrara (feh-RA-ra; pop. 130,000) has its *biciclette.* In a city with more bicycles than people, girls in stilettos, businessmen with cell phones, and elderly ladies cycle through low arches and narrow streets of the area outside the *centro.* On the city's outskirts, biking aficionados can spend an afternoon cycling a 9km bike path that skirts crumbling medieval walls, while rambling medieval streets, art museums, and an ominous *castello* offer eye-candy and adventure to the exercise-phobic crowd.

▐ TRANSPORTATION

Trains: Ticket office open daily 6:15am-8:30pm. (☎0532 89 20 21. AmEx/MC/V.) To: **Bologna** (30min., 43 per day 1:41am-10:10pm, €3.10); **Padua** (1hr., 31 per day 4am-11:50pm, €4.60); **Ravenna** (1hr., 14 per day 6am-11:38pm, €4.50); **Rome** (3-4hr., 23 per day 1:41am-8pm, €34); **Venice** (1hr., 30 per day 4am-11:50pm, €6.20).

Buses: Rampari S. Paolo and Corso Isonzo. Ticket office open daily 6:40am-6:50pm. **ACFT** (☎0532 59 94 11), **GGFP,** and most other buses leave from the train station. To **local beaches** (1hr., 12 per day 7:30am-9:15pm, €4.30), **Bologna** (1hr., 15 per day 5:20am-7:50pm, €3.40), and **Modena** (2hr., 13 per day 5am-7:32pm, €4.65).

Taxis: RadioTaxi (☎0532 90 09 00). Open 24hr.

Bike Rental: Pirani e Bagni, P. Stazione 2 (☎0532 77 21 90). €2 per hr., €7 per day. Open M-F 7am-8pm, Sa 6am-2pm. Cash only.

▣ ▮ ORIENTATION AND PRACTICAL INFORMATION

To get to the **centro storico,** turn left from the train station on **Viale Costituzione,** which becomes **Viale Cavour** and runs to the **Castello Estense.** Alternatively, take bus #2 to the Castello stop or #1 or 9 to the post office (every 15-20min.; line 1 6:48am-8:20pm, line 2 7am-8:50pm, line 9 5:37am-8:30pm, €1). Turn right after the *castello* onto **Corso Martiri della Libertà.**

EMILIA-ROMAGNA

Ferrara

ACCOMMODATIONS
Pensione Artisti, **6**
Estense Campground, **1**
San Girolamo dei Gesuati, **7**
Student's Hostel Estense, **8**

FOOD
Pizzeria da Alice, **9**
Fuocolento, **10**

Osteria al Brindisi, **4**
Ristorante Italia Big Night da
Giovanni, **3**

NIGHTLIFE
Ludovico, **11**
Peperosa, **12**
Enobar Estense, **13**
Tsunami, **14**
La Cantina del Duca, **15**

Tourist Office: Castello Estense, near P. Castello (☎0532 20 93 70; www.ferrarainfo. com). Open M-Sa 9am-1pm and 2-6pm, Su 9:30am-1pm and 2-5pm.)

Banks: at Banca Nazionale del Lavoro, C. Pta. Reno 19 ☎0532 78 16 11. Open M-F 8:20am-1:20pm and 2:35-4:05pm, Su 8:20-11:50am. Currency exchange available.

Police: C. Ercole I d'Este 26 (☎0532 41 86 00), off Largo Castello.

Pharmacy: Fides, C. Giovecca 125 (☎0532 20 25 24). Open 24hr. AmEx/MC/V.

Internet Access: Ferrara Internet Point, V. Aleardi 17 (☎0532 20 70 05), beside the *duomo*. Printing, photocopy, and fax services. €6 per hr., students €3. Open M-Tu and Th 9am-1pm and 3:30-8:30pm, W and F-Sa 9am-1pm and 3:30-10pm. Cash only.)

Post Office: Vle. Cavour 27 (☎0532 29 72 11), 1 block toward the train station from the *castello*. Open M-F 8am-6:30pm, Sa 8am-12:30pm. **Postal Code:** 44100.

EMILIA-ROMAGNA

ACCOMMODATIONS AND CAMPING

Student's Hostel Estense, C. Biagio Rossetti 24 (☎0532 20 11 58; www.ostelloferrara. it). From the train station, turn left on Vle. IV Novembre. Continue onto C. Pta. Po. until it becomes C. Biagio Rossetti; hostel is on the left. Enthusiastic staff, excellent location, and perks like bike rental (€5), free Wi-Fi, and free lockers make this hostel a steal. Private garden. Breakfast included. Laundry €3. Check-out 10:30am. Reservations recommended. Dorms €15; singles and doubles €40; triples €45. Cash only. ❶

Pensione Artisti, V. Vittoria 66 (☎0532 76 10 38). From C. Martiri della Libertà, turn left at the cathedral, right on V. San Romano, left on V. Ragno, then immediately left. Accommodating staff offers spacious rooms with stone floors, large windows, and sinks. Guests share access to an ivy-covered garden, bikes, minibar, and a small kitchen. Curfew 12:30am. Singles €28; doubles €48, with bath €60. Cash only. ❷

San Girolamo dei Gesuati, V. Madama 40 (☎0532 20 74 48; www.sangirolamodeigesuati.com). Former convent feels more like a sanctuary than a hotel. Large garden, spacious dining room, and sunny lounge complement peaceful rooms that come with bath, A/C, phone, TV, and minibar. Breakfast included. Internet €6 per hr. 24hr. reception; payment between 7am-11:30pm. Singles €42, with ½-pension €55; doubles €78/104; triples €95/134; quads €112/164. AmEx/V/MC. ❸

Estense Campground, V. Gramicia 76 (☎/fax 0532 75 23 96), 1km from the *centro* (a 30min. walk or a €7-8 taxi ride). Take bus #1 to P. San Giovanni (€1), then V. Gramicia for 15min. through the traffic circle. From the *castello,* take C. Ercole I d'Este, turn right on C. Pta. Mare and then left on V. Gramicia. A quiet spot northeast of the *centro* near some of Ferrara's best bike paths. Bike rental €5-7 per ½-day. Reception 8am-10pm. Closed mid-Jan. to late Feb. €5 per person, under 8 free; €6.50-8 per car and tent site. Electricity €3.50. Hot showers free. MC/V over €50. ❶

FOOD

Aside from fresh seafood, Ferrara's specialties include *cappellacci di zucca* (pasta stuffed with pumpkin and parmesan), *salama da sugo* (pork, spices, and wine), and *pasticcio alla ferrarese* (sweet bread stuffed with macaroni and meat sauce). Corpus Domini nuns invented Ferrara's *pampepato* (chocolate cake with almonds, candied fruit, and icing). For wine, try the sparkling **Uva d'Oro** (Golden Grape). There's a **Conad** supermarket at V. Garibaldi 53. (☎0532 20 78 68. Open M-Sa 8:30am-8pm, Su 9am-1pm. AmEx/MC/V.) **Ferrara Frutta,** a local produce market, is located at P. Castello 24-26. (☎0532 20 31 36. Open M-W, F, and Su 8am-1pm and 5-7:30pm, Th and Sa 8am-1pm. Cash only.)

Osteria al Brindisi, V. Guglielmo degli Adelardi 11 (☎0532 20 91 42), near the *duomo.* Reputedly the world's oldest *osteria*, al Brindisi has welcomed such luminaries as Titian, Cellini, and Pope John Paul II since 1435. Waiters climb ladders to reach the countless rows of dusty wine bottles. Excellent vegetarian options and hearty salads. At lunch, try the *Lavoro menù* (*ferranese* macaroni pie, salad, and wine; €12). Primi €7-9. Secondi 7-15. Cover €2. Open daily 11am-1am. *Enoteca* open 8:30am-1am. AmEx/MC/V. ❸

Pizzeria da Alice, V. Palestro 89/91 (☎0532 24 85 81). Well-priced pies with especially generous toppings. A sky-light, wood ceilings, and hanging plants make the patio a summery escape. €6 lunch special (M-F) includes pizza and drink. Antipasti €5-10. Pizza €3-7. Cover €0.50. Open daily noon-3pm and 7pm-1am. Cash only. ❶

Fuocolento, V. Saraceno 87 (☎0532 21 08 13). Upscale Mediterranean and *ferrarese* cuisine. Serves savory plates like *straccetti* with spinach, beef in balsamic vinaigrette, and pine nuts (€8). Primi €8-12. Secondi €12-18. Cover €3. Open Tu-F 8-10:30pm, Sa-Su 12:30-2:30pm and 8-10:30pm. MC/V. ❹

Ristorante Italia Big Night da Giovanni, V. Largo Castello 38 (☎0532 24 23 67). Inspired by the Italian brothers in the film *Big Night,* this *ristorante* presents elegant dishes like ricotta, spinach, and radicchio with salmon ragout (€13) on a bamboo-lined patio or in the De Chirico-themed interior. Primi €11-19. Secondi €18-23. Cover €3. Open daily 12:15-2:30pm and 7:15-10:45pm. AmEx/MC/V. ⑤

🅖 SIGHTS

Leonello d'Este, ruler and patron of the arts, molded Ferrara into an important artistic center with its own school of painting, the *Officina Ferrarese.* Works by Pisanello, Piero della Francesca, and Titian grace the city's palaces and monuments. Those yearning for natural beauty can ride or walk down the 9km concourse that runs atop the medieval wall.

> **MUSEUM MANIA.** The **Cumulativo Arte Antica** (€8, reduced €5) offers entrance to Museo della Cattedrale, Museo Laidario, Palazzina Marfisa d'Este, and Palazzo Schifanoia. The **Cumulativo Arte Moderna** (€7.50) offers entrance to Museo Boldini, Museo dell'Ottocento, Museo Filippo de Pisis, and Padiglione d'Arte Contemporanea. Finally, the **Museum Card** (€14, reduced €10), combines the Arte Antica and the Arte Moderna and is valid for the entire year. Purchase cards at participating museums.

◪**CASTELLO ESTENSE.** This castle debuted as a small fortress in the 14th century and has been carefully preserved, complete with drawbridges over a murky green moat. Today, excellent English panels guide visitors through the castle, a reminder of the distinguished *ferrarese* court life. The tour tracks the city's development to regional military and cultural prominence. The red-tiled **Garden and Loggia of the Oranges,** Eleanor of Aragon's terrace, was added later. Descend the narrow staircases to the dank prisons where everyone from doomed lovers to the most high-ranking prisoners of the court were sequestered before their beheadings. Upstairs, large tilted mirrors allow visitors to see the magnificent frescoes that grace the palace's ceilings, without craning their necks. Though a steep climb, the tower provides a spectacular view of the city's red-tiled rooftops. (☎0532 29 92 33. Open Tu-Su 9:30am-5:30pm. €10, under 18 and over 65 €8. Supplement for Estense tower €1. Audio tour in English, French, German, and Italian €5. Garofalo show daily 9:30am-7:30pm, ticket window closes at 6:30pm. Cash only.)

◪**DUOMO SAN ROMANO.** Dedicated to the city's patron saints, the 12th-century cathedral is a stunning masterpiece of loggia, rose windows, and bas-reliefs. Trompe l'oeil paintings decorate the domed ceilings and columns, while gold-inlaid cornices accent the walls. An otherwise dark altarpiece houses an illuminated crucifix, while the fresco on its ceiling, inspired by Michelangelo's *Last Judgment,* is barely visible. Biagio Rosetti designed the arches and terra-cotta apse, and Leon Battista Alberti fashioned the pink *campanile.* A dim interior houses the beautiful **Santuario Beata Vergine delle Grazie,** a gleaming side altar illuminated by red votives and soft white bulbs on candlesticks. Across the street, the **Museo della Cattedrale** displays the church's precious works, including Jacopo Quercia's *Madonna of the Pomegranate.* (Museum across the street from the duomo, through the courtyard on V. S. Romano. Museum ☎0532 24 49 49. Duomo open M-Sa 7:30am-noon and 3-6:30pm, Su 7:30am-12:30pm and 3:30-7:30pm. Free. Museum open Tu-Su 9am-1pm and 3-6pm. Last entry 30min. before closing. €5, students €3. AmEx/MC/V.)

PALAZZO DEI DIAMANTI. Built in 1493 by Rossetti, the *palazzo* is easily recognizable by the many white pyramidal studs that cover its facade. Inside is the **Pinacoteca Nazionale,** an art collection that includes a series of tablets by El Greco, which depicts scenes from Christ's life. Don't miss the Bastianino's *La Resurrezione di Cristo,* whose softly rendered figures seem to blur into each other. The first of Scarsellino's *Last Suppers* extends across three darkly painted canvases, while the version displayed in the following room is stouter and more luminous. The final **Room of Honor,** completed in 1450, is a spectacular finish to the collection with its geometric ceiling and the massive frescoes that line its walls. *(C. Ercole I d'Este 1. Just before the intersection with C. Rossetti. ☎ 0532 20 58 44. Open Tu-W and F-Sa 9am-2pm, Th 9am-7pm, Su 9am-1pm. Last entry 30min. before closing. €4, students ages 18-25 €2; under 18 and over 65 free. Cash only.)*

PALAZZO MASSARI. Once a 16th-century residence, the *palazzo* now houses three separate museums. **Padiglione d'Arte Contemporanea** has temporary modern art exhibitions. **Museo d'Arte Moderna e Contemporanea Filippo de Pisis** has displays paintings and sculptures by *ferrarese* artists. **Museo Ferrarese dell'Ottocento/ Museo Giovanni Boldini** shows a range of 18th- through 20th-century works; Boldini's intimate works are the highlights. *(C. Porta Mare 9. Turn right off C. Ercole I d'Este. ☎ 0532 24 49 49. Museums open Tu-Su 9am-1pm and 3-6pm. Last entry 30min. before closing. Filippo de Pisis €3, students €2. Ottocento and Boldini €5/3. Combined ticket €8/3. Cash only.)*

SINAGOGHE E MUSEO EBRAICO. The city's Jewish museum documents the history of Ferrara's Jewish community, including a display of the keys that once locked the gates that separated the ghetto from the rest of the city. The synagogue is still used for Shabbat and high holiday services. *(V. Mazzini 95. From the duomo, the museum is on the left side of the street. ☎ 0532 21 02 28. Open M-Th and Su 10am-1pm. Guided tours Su-Th 10, 11am, and noon. Admission with guided tour. €4, students €3.)* Inquire at the synagogue for directions to the **Cimitero Ebraico (Jewish Cemetery),** where most of Ferrara's 19th- and 20th-century Jewish community is buried. The tourist office also provides a map of Jewish sights throughout the city. *(From the castello, head down C. Giovecca, turn left on V. Montebello, and continue to end.)*

PALAZZO SCHIFANOIA. The word Schifanoia translates to "shunning boredom," and in its day this palace was entirely dedicated to court entertainment. The 15th-century **Hall of the Months,** a Renaissance fresco series representing each month, its astrological sign, and its corresponding Greek deity, is the *palazzo*'s main attraction. *(V. Scandiana 23. ☎ 0532 64 178. Open Tu-Su 9am-6pm. €5, students and over 65 €3. With Palazzina Marfisa €8/5. Cash only.)*

BIRD'S-EYE VIEW. For a different perspective, survey Ferrara from atop the medieval walls that surround the city—by bike. There's a paved road below this gravel path, but both are flat, making for a stress-free ride around town.

MUSEO ARCHEOLOGICO NAZIONALE. The courtyard of the **Palazzo di Ludovico il Moro** was built in 1495 for a d'Este court official. Glass cases display artifacts from Ferrara's own mysterious Atlantis, called **Spina**—the Greek-Etruscan city that disappeared into the Adriatic Sea 2000 years ago. *(V. XX Settembre 122. From P. Trento Trieste, follow V. Mazzini, which becomes V. Saraceno, to the end; turn left on V. Mayr, then right on V. Borgovado. ☎ 0532 66 299; mnafe@tiscalinet.it. No English explanations. Open Tu-Su 9am-2pm. €4, ages 18-25 €2, under 18 and over 65 free. Cash only.)*

PALAZZINA MARFISA D'ESTE. The furniture in this brick dwelling is positioned as if the *palazzina* were still in use. Note the walnut benches supported by Ionic columns, which have been called one of the most perfect creations of 16th-century Tuscan furniture. *(C. Giovecca 170. Follow C. Giovecca from Largo Castello,* *or take bus #9. ☎0532 20 74 50. Open Tu-Su 9am-1pm and 3-6pm. €3, students €2. Combined ticket with Palazzo Schifanoia and Museo della Cattedrale €8/5. Cash only.)*

CASA ROMEI. After a legal tug-of-war, this Renaissance showpiece, halfway house, and onetime demolition candidate opened as a museum in 1952. Giovanni Romei—an ambitious merchant, administrator to the *ferraresi* lords, and husband of princess Polisenna d'Este—constructed the brick *palazzo* to bolster his reputation in 1440. It now stands as a prototypical 15th-century aristocratic home. Its rooms, which wind around a sunny interior courtyard, are filled with ceiling frescoes, artwork from destroyed churches, and the remains of one of Ferrara's oldest thermal baths. *(V. Savonarola 30. Follow V. Adelardi left of the duomo until it becomes V. Savonarola. ☎0532 24 03 41. Open Tu-Su 8:30am-7:30pm. Last entry 30min. before closing. €3, EU students €1.50, under 18 and over 65 free. Cash only.)*

🎧 NIGHTLIFE

As in Padova and Bologna, its college town neighbors to the north and south, nightlife in Ferrara peaks during the school year when university students fill the city's cobblestone side streets, especially on Wednesday nights when students flood P. della Cattedrale. Still, summer brings outdoor tables with groups that linger late into the evening over drinks.

Peperosa, V. San Romano 99 (☎0532 76 31 70). Draws in a hip crowd with hanging crystals and plastic fish, incense, and dim lighting. A non-traditional menu includes infused teas (€3) and mixed drinks with freshly squeezed juices (€5). Daily *aperitivo* buffet with drinks. Open M-W and F 5pm-2am, Sa-Su 4pm-2am. AmEx/MC/V.

Enobar Estense, P. Cattedrale 7. Small bar in the *centro* that caters to a crowd of students and 30-somethings. Sleek black stools, blue lighting, and Warhol-esque paintings decorate the interior, but the real draw is the open *piazza* where customers mingle as they sip. Beer €2-5. Wine €3.50-5. Mixed drinks €6. Open daily noon-2am. Cash only.

Tsunami, V. Savonarola 2 (☎0532 21 11 03), the corner of V. Terranuova, close to the university. Flatscreen TVs and zebra-striped bar stools draw a young crowd. Small plates and a long list of mixed drinks (€5). Beers €2.50-4. Happy hour Sept.-June Tu 10-11pm. Open M-Tu and Th 7:30am-1am, W and F-Sa 7:30am-2am. Cash only.

Ludovico, Palestro 7. Laid-back with bright red walls, an exposed beam ceiling, and stunning views of Piazza Ariostea. Spritz €2.50. Beer €2.50-3.50. Mixed drinks €5. Wine €3-4.50. Open daily 11am-2am. Cash only.

La Cantina del Duca, V. della Luna 30 (☎0532 24 57 58), on P. Repubblica. Cafe by day, bar by night. Minimalist decor in front leads to an equally sparse and spacious lounge where crowds drink and socialize. Beers €2.50-5. Mixed drinks €5-7.50. Open M 11am-3pm, Tu-Sa 11am-3pm and 6pm-midnight. MC/V.

🎉 FESTIVALS

On the last Sunday of May, Ferrara revives the ancient **Palio di San Giorgio** (☎0532 75 12 63; www.paliodiferrara.it.). Dating from the 13th century, this event begins with a lively procession of delegates from the city's eight *contrade* (districts), followed by a series of four races held in P. Ariostea: the boys' race, the girls' race, the donkey race, and the great horse race. During the last full week of August, street performers display their talents at the **Busker's Festival** (☎0532 24 93 37; www.ferrarabuskers.com). Finally, those seeking oddity will appreciate the countless methods of eel preparation at the annual **Eel Festival,** celebrated at the beginning of October in the province of Comacchio. (Info ☎0532 33 10 161; www.comune.comacchio.fe.it.)

MODENA ☎ 059

From the quiet but colorful sidestreets in the *centro*, you might be fooled into thinking Modena (MO-deh-na; pop. 170,000) a mere charming backwater. But just outside, in the stunning UNESCO-protected Piazza Grande, you'll find picturesque beauty amped up by a rollicking nightlife and great shopping. Modena is a small town that packs a big punch, boasting Luciano Pavarotti, the nearby Ferrari and Maserati factories, and internationally renowned *aceto balsamico di Modena* (balsamic vinegar). With its famous attractions, ornate structures, tantalizing cuisine, and cultural history, Modena is undoubtedly worth a stop.

⌐ TRANSPORTATION

Trains: (☎059 89 20 21), P. Dante Alighieri. Info office open daily 8am-7pm; ticket office open daily 5:30am-11:10pm. Trains run to: **Bologna** (30min., every 30min. 4:47am-12:55am, €5.70); **Milan** (2hr., every hr. 4:37am-10:04pm, €10); **Parma** (30min., 2 per hr. 4:37am-10:53pm, €3.50); **Verona** (4hr., 8 per day 6:10am-8:22pm, €5.10).

Buses: ATCM (☎199 11 11 01 or 800 11 11 01; www.atcm.mo.it) in V. Fabriani, off V. Monte Kosica to the right of the train station. Open M-F 7am-7:30pm, Sa 7am-2pm, Su 8:30am-12:30pm and 2:30-6:30pm. Buses go to Maranello (every 1-2hr.; €2.18, €1 extra on bus) and also run throughout the city.

Taxis: (☎059 37 42 42). 24hr.

▋⑦ ORIENTATION AND PRACTICAL INFORMATION

From the **train station,** take bus #7 (dir.: Policlinico) or 11 (dir.: Zodiaco) to **Piazza Grande** and the *centro*. On foot, take **Via Galvani** from the station and turn right on **Viale Monte Kosica.** A left on **Via Ganaceto** leads to **Via Emilia,** Modena's main thoroughfare. Continue through **Piazza Matteotti** to **Piazza della Torre,** which opens onto P. Grande. V. Emilia changes names from **Via Emilia Ovest** on the west side to **Via Emilia Centro** in the center to **Via Emilia Est** in the east.

Tourist Office: P. Grande 14 (☎059 20 32 660; www.comune.modena.it), located in the Palazzo Comunale building close to V. Emilia Centro. Open M 3-6pm, Tu-Sa 9am-1pm and 3-6pm, Su 9:30am-12:30pm. **Modenatur,** V. Scudari 10 (☎22 00 22; www.modenatur.it), located on the other side of the building from the tourist office. Organizes guided tours inside the province of Modena, offers tourist info, and arranges themed tours of the city's automobile factories, culinary specialties, and castles. Open M 2:30-6:30pm, Tu-F 9am-1pm and 2:30-6:30pm. MC/V.

Beyond Tourism: Informagiovani, P. Grande 17 (☎059 20 65 83). Geared toward younger travelers. Provides travel info, job listings, alternatives to tourism, and Internet (1-time €1.50 registration fee, Wi-Fi free after that; €2 per hr.). Open M-F 9am-1pm and 3-6:30pm, Sa 9:30am-12:30pm. Closed W afternoon.

Currency Exchange: Credito Italiano, V. Emilia Centro 102 (☎059 21 80 86). Open M-F 8:20am-1:20pm and 2:45-4:45pm, Sa 8:20am-12:45pm. **ATMs** at **Unicredit Banca,** P. Grande 40. Open M-F 8:20am-1:20pm and 3-4pm, Sa 8:20am-12:45pm.

Laundry: Washing Point, 31 V. Piave. Open daily 8am-9:30pm.

Ambulance: ☎059 34 31 56.

Pharmacy: Farmacia del Collegio, corner of V. Emilia Est and V. San Carlo, near P. Grande. Open M-F 8:30am-1pm and 3:30-7:30pm, Sa 8:30am-1pm. AmEx/MC/V.

Internet Access: Informagiovani (see **Beyond Tourism,** above). **Internet Point,** P. Grande 34 (☎/fax 21 20 96). €1 per 15min. Open M-Sa 10am-8pm.

EMILIA-ROMAGNA

Post Office: V. Emilia Centro 86 (☎059 20 53 211). Open M-F 8am-6:30pm, Sa 8am-12:30pm. **Postal Code:** 41100.

ACCOMMODATIONS

Ostello San Filippo Neri (HI) ❶, V. Sant'Orsola 48-52, is Modena's best budget option. Walk down V. Galvani from the station, turn right along Vle. Monte Kosica, left on V. Ganaceto, and take another left on V. Sant'Orsola. The friendly staff and low bed-to-room ratio makes for a hotel-like hostel experience. (☎/fax 23 45 98; hostelmodena@hotmail.com. Wheelchair-accessible. Free bike rental with passport and €20 deposit. Check-out 9:45am. Lockout 10am-2pm. Dorms €19; doubles €40. AmEx/MC/V.) To find **Hotel Modena ❹**, V. Ramazzini 59, from the station, turn left on V. Ganaceto, right on V. Cerca, and walk straight. Rooms are spacious, all with TV, sink, phone, and shared bath. (☎059 22 36 34. Reception 7am-1am. Reservations recommended. Singles €42; doubles €62; triples €82. Discounts for longer stays. AmEx/MC/V.) **Locanda Sole ❸**, V. Malatesta 45, has rooms with sink, TV, desk, and closet. From V. Ganaceto, turn right on V. Emilia, then left to reach this quiet, centrally located hotel. (☎059 21 42 45; fax 43 99 016. Closed 3 weeks in Aug. Singles €35; doubles €60. Cash only.)

FOOD

Modena specializes in *prosciutto crudo* and sparkling *Lambrusco* red wine, but its most prominent product is fragrant *aceto balsamico* (balsamic vinegar), a thick condiment worlds away from the stuff back home. Be sure to taste the difference between the traditional and wannabe styles. **✖Mercato Coperto di Via Albinelli**, down V. Albinelli, was built by the city in 1931 to house a food market that's been around since medieval times. Vendors sell fresh produce, flowers, and even squid. (Open June-Sept. M-F 6:30am-2pm and 4:30-7pm, Sa 6:30am-2pm; Oct.-May M-F 6:30am-2pm, Sa 6:30am-2pm and 4:30-7:30pm. Cash only.)

> **THE BITTER TRUTH.** Traditional Italian *aceto balsamico* (balsamic vinegar) is not what you're used to finding on the shelves of your local supermarket. Originating in the hills of Modena nearly 1000 years ago, authentic *aceto balsamico di Modena* is made from a top-secret recipe; the complex process, which can take years, likely contributes to the skyrocketing costs of the true product—a good bottle can run hundreds of euro. At restaurants, you'll find it drizzled over a fresh salad, and other less-expected place, too—adding a zing to your strawberries or flavoring creamy gelato.

Caffeteria Giusti, V. Farini 83 (☎059 21 91 32). This shop is famous as a supplier of *aceto balsamico* and sparkling wine. Free tasting of both traditional and non-traditional balsamic vinegars (bottles €38-85) aids in this difficult decision. Friendly staff also serves up coffee and snacks. Open M-Sa 7:30am-midnight. AmEx/MC/V. ❶

Ristorante Uva' d'Oro, P. Mazzini 38 (☎059 42 20 103). This popular restaurant gets busy at night, and for good reason. Regional specialty *fileto al balsamico* (filet of meat with balsamic; €15) is prepared to perfection. House wine €4 per L. Primi €5-10. Secondi €5-18. Cover €2. Open M-Sa noon-2:30pm and 7:30-10pm. AmEx/MC/V. ❷

Trattoria da Omer, V. Torre 33 (☎059 21 80 50), off V. Emilia, across from P. Torre. Grandma's kitchen goes gourmet. All dishes, including *scaloppe* and *salmone*, are €8. Open M-Sa 1-2pm and 7:30-midnight. Reservations recommended. AmEx/MC/V. ❷

Caffè Concerto, P. Grande 26 (☎059 22 22 32; www.caffeconcertomodena.it). Delicious food or beverages whenever a craving strikes. Transforms into a popular piano bar

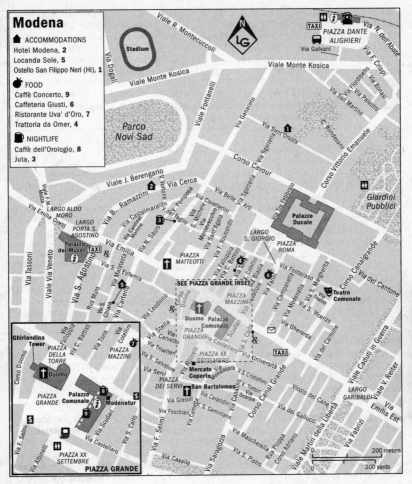

Modena

▲ ACCOMMODATIONS
Hotel Modena, **2**
Locanda Sole, **5**
Ostello San Filippo Neri (HI), **1**

● FOOD
Caffè Concerto, **9**
Caffeteria Giusti, **6**
Ristorante Uva' d'Oro, **7**
Trattoria da Omer, **4**

▮ NIGHTLIFE
Caffè dell'Orologio, **8**
Juta, **3**

at night. All-you-can-eat lunch buffet noon-3pm €15. Primi €10-14. Secondi €10-16. Open daily 8am-3am. AmEx/MC/V. ❸

◉ SIGHTS

DUOMO. Modena's towering Romanesque *duomo* is built over the grave of its patron saint, San Geminiano. Guards used to signal the opening of the city gates from the *duomo*'s 87m tower. The brick arched interior has a lovely simplicity, and the church houses San Geminiano's encased arm, which is paraded around in a religious procession in January. Legend holds that he prevented Attila the Hun from destroying the city by shrouding it in mist. Sculptor Wiligelmo and his students decorated most of the *duomo*'s red Veronese marble with carvings of local Roman, biblical, and Celtic themes. Scenes from the Old Testament and San Geminiano's travels frame the door. Visit the 3D clay nativity scene in a cave on the right wall. *(P. Grande. ☎059 21 60 78; www.duomodimodena.it. Open daily 7am-12:30pm and 3:30-7pm. Free.)* The **Museo del Duomo** allows visitors to see gold chalices, crosses, and embroidered ecclesiastical robes that in centuries past were paraded only on holy feast days. *(V. Lanfranco 6. ☎059 43 96 969. Open Tu-Su Apr.-Sept. 9:30am-12:30pm and 3:30-7pm; Oct.-Mar. 9:30am-12:30pm and 3:30-6:30pm. €3.)*

> **MO' MODENA.** To save on museums, buy a combined ticket. A 2-day ticket costs €6 and allows admission to civic museums, Este Gallery, and the Cathedral museums.

PALAZZO DEI MUSEI. Inside the *palazzo*, the **Biblioteca Estense** holds a collection of exquisitely illuminated 14th- to 16th-century books, including a 1501 Portuguese world map. The library's **Sala Campori,** accessible by appointment only, houses the **Biblia di Borso d'Este,** a 15th-century, 1200-page Bible partially illustrated by Emiliano and painter Taddeo Crivelli. The different parts of the *palazzo* close for weeks at a time on a rotating schedule. *(On Largo Sant'Agostino at the western side of V. Emilia. ☎059 22 22 48; www.cedoc.mo.it/estense. Exhibits open M-Sa 9am-1pm. Call the library in advance to see the Sala Campori and Biblia di Borso d'Este. €2.60, under 19 or over 65 free.)* Above the library, the **Galleria Estense** displays huge canvases like Velázquez's *Portrait of Francesco d'Este* and Bernini's bust of the same subject, a triptych by El Greco, and a crucifix by Guido Reni. *(☎059 43 95 711; www.galleriaestense.it. Open Tu-Su 8:30am-7:30pm. €4.)* In the **Archaeological Ethnological Civic Museum** and the **Civic Art Museum,** large glass cases contain musical instruments, 19th-century scientific instruments, and artifacts from the Americas, Asia, and Africa. *(Both museums ☎059 20 01 00. Open Tu-Sa 9am-noon and 3-6pm, Su 10am-1pm and 3-7pm. Closes at 6pm during winter. €4, students €2.)*

GHIRLANDINA TOWER. This 95m tower, built in the 13th century, incorporates Gothic and Romanesque elements. Though it's currently being restored, visits are still occasionally offered through the tourist office. Climb to the top for a view of Modena's stucco rooftops. A photo collection at the base commemorates those who died fighting the Nazis and Fascists during WWII. *(P. Torre, off P. Grande. Open Apr.-July and Sept.-Oct. Su 9:30am-12:30pm and 3-7pm, or by reservation. €2.)*

FERRARI FACTORY. Modena's flashiest claim to fame is the Ferrari, created in 1940 by Enzo Ferrari, which makes its home southwest of Modena in **Maranello,** a 40min. bus ride from Modena (round-trip €4). Check at the tourist office for schedule of buses to and from Modena. View antique and modern Ferraris, Formula One race cars, trophies, and exhibits on founder Enzo Ferrari at the **Ferrari Galleria.** On small TV screens, watch a live feed of the complex's recreated Grand Prix, where owners race by invitation only. *(Galleria at V. Dino Ferrari 43. From Ferrari factory bus stop, continue along the road in the same direction as the bus for 200m; turn right at Galleria Ferrari sign. ☎0536 94 32 04; galleria@ferrari.it. Open daily June-Sept. 9:30am-7pm; Oct.-May 9:30am-6pm. €12, seniors and students under 18 €10.)* The Maserati Factory is closed to the public, but you can visit the museum if you book at least 10 days ahead. *(V. Corletto 320. ☎059 51 06 60.)* **Modenatur** (p. 399) organizes tours for car enthusiasts to these sites. *(☎059 21 82 64; www.motorsite.it. Tours from €35.)*

FESTIVALS AND NIGHTLIFE

In May, Modena demonstrates its love of all things fast with the **Land of Motors** festival, featuring parades of both vintage and ultra-modern cars and other spectacles in P. Grande. *(Info ☎059 20 66 60.)* The **Millemiglia** vintage car race that finishes in Brescia also passes through Modena in May. In June and July,

Modena stages the **Serate Estensi** (☎059 20 32 707; www.comune.modena.it/ seratestensi), a week-long festival recreating the city's history of Estense rule with jousting, art shows, street theater, dances, fireworks, and a Renaissance costume show. Lastly, the **Fiera Antiquaria**, Emilia-Romagna's largest antique market, with over 300 exhibitions, is held the fourth Saturday of each month and the following Sunday. **Juta,** V. del Taglio 91, welcomes the majority of Modena's 20-somethings after 10pm, with ultra-current music and edgy decor. (☎059 21 94 49. Sangria €4. Sa-Su DJ-spun music from 8pm. Cover €1.50. Open Tu-Th noon-1am, F-Sa noon-2am, Su 5pm-1am. AmEx/MC/V.) **Caffè dell'Orologio,** Piazzetta delle Ova 4, next to the tourist office, has an upscale atmosphere. Relax with an espresso or indulge in an evening drink. (☎338 92 56 608. Mixed drinks from €6-7. Open M and W-Su 8am-midnight. Cash only.)

PARMA   ☎0521

Although a trip to Parma (PAR-ma; pop. 180,000)—where platters overflow with aged parmesan cheese and rosy-pink prosciutto—will certainly never leave the taste buds unsatisfied, Parma's artistic excellence is not confined to the kitchen. In the 16th century, Mannerist painting flourished under native artists Parmigianino and Correggio. The city was also the birthplace of composer Giuseppe Verdi, who resided in Parma while writing some of his greatest works. Pervasive French influences inspired Stendhal to choose the picturesque town as the setting of his 1839 novel *The Charterhouse of Parma*. If your tastes are less literary, have no fear—Parma's nightlife, though confined to a few central streets, rivals that of much larger cities. Summer nights find students and travelers alike enjoying the bars, live music, and theatre.

▌▔ TRANSPORTATION

Flights depart from **Giuseppe Verdi Airport,** V. dell'Aeroporto 44/A (☎98 26 26; fax 99 20 28). Parma lies on the Bologna-Milan line. **Trains** leave the station in Ple. Carlo Alberto della Chiesa (☎0521 89 20 21 or 77 14 26; ticket office open daily 5:55am-12:05am) to: Bologna (1hr., 3 per hr. 4:11am-12:18am, €5); Florence (2hr., 6:46am-9:24pm, €10); Milan (1hr., 3-5 per hr. 5:14am-10:36pm, €7.40); Modena (30min., 4 per hr. 5:46am-11:51pm, €3.50); Rome (4hr., 6:46am-11:51pm); Turin (3hr., 5 per day 5:53am-10:36pm, €11.70). **Buses** to nearby towns including Bardi, Busseto, and Colorno stop at P. Carlo Alberto della Chiesa 7/B, at the InfoBus booth. (☎0521 27 32 51. Ticket office open M-Sa 6am-7:15pm, Su 7am-1pm.) **Intra-city buses** run throughout Parma, and stop in front of the train station. For bus rides between 8pm and 1am, reserve a ride with ProntoBus (☎800 977 900; www.tep.pr.it; around €3). Call a **taxi** (☎0521 25 25 62) for 24hr. service. **Rent a car** at the airport from Avis (☎0521 29 12 38). For **bike rental,** check out Parma PuntoBici, Vle. P. Toschi 2. (☎0521 28 19 79; www.parmapuntobici.it. Bikes €0.70 per hr.; €10 for 1st day, €5 each day thereafter. Electric bikes €1/20/10. Open M-Sa 9am-1pm and 3-7pm, Su 10am-1pm and 3-7pm.)

▟◢ ▞ ORIENTATION AND PRACTICAL INFORMATION

To get to the city, exit the station with the fountain on your right. Turn left on **Viale Bottego** and right on **Strada Garibaldi.** Follow it 1km into town. Turn left on **Strada Mazzini** to reach **Piazza Garibaldi,** the *centro*. **Strada della Repubblica, Strada Cavour,** and **Strada Farini,** Parma's main streets, branch out from this *piazza*.

   Tourist Office: Strada Melloni 11/A (☎0521 21 88 89; www.turismo.comune.parma.it). From train station, walk left on Vle. Bottego, turn right on Strada Garibaldi, then left on Strada Melloni. Open M 9am-1pm and 3-7pm, Tu-Sa 9am-7pm, Su 9am-1pm.

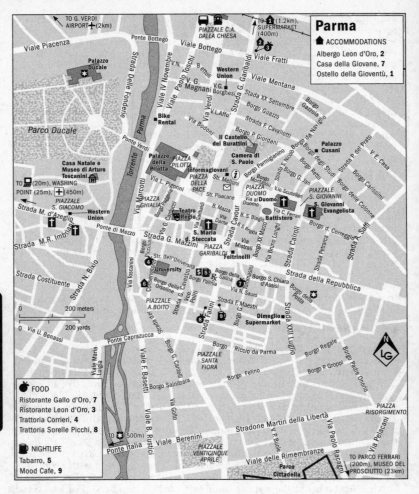

Parma

🏠 ACCOMMODATIONS

Albergo Leon d'Oro, **2**
Casa della Giovane, **7**
Ostello della Gioventù, **1**

🍎 FOOD
Ristorante Gallo d'Oro, **7**
Ristorante Leon d'Oro, **3**
Trattoria Corrieri, **4**
Trattoria Sorelle Picchi, **8**

🍷 NIGHTLIFE
Tabarro, **5**
Mood Cafe, **9**

EMILIA-ROMAGNA

Beyond Tourism: Informagiovani, Strada Melloni 1 (☎0521 21 87 49; http://informagiovani.comune.parma.it), next to the tourist office. Posts jobs, volunteer work, and apartment listings. English spoken. Free **Internet** access and study room. Open M-Tu and F-Sa 9am-1pm and 3-7pm, W 9am-1pm, Th 9am-7pm.

Bank: Banca Antonveneta, Strada dell'Università 2, just off P. Garibaldi. Open M-F 8:20am-1:20pm and 3-4pm, Sa 8:20-11:50am. Also has **24hr. ATM.**

Western Union: Infinitho, Strada M. D'Azeglio 23/A (☎0521 23 45 55; www.hopera.net), just across the river over Ponte di Mezzo from V. Mazzini. Internet access €1.10 per 15min., students €0.90; €4/3 per hr. Skype and webcam access also available. Open M-W and F-Sa 8:30am-9pm, Th 8:30am-2pm. AmEx/MC/V. .

Laundromat: WashingPoint, Strada Massimo D'Azeglio 108a. Wash and dry €2. Detergent €1. Open daily 8-10pm.

Police: Vle. Villetta 12/A (☎0521 21 87 40).

Pharmacy: Farmacia Guareschi, Strada Farini 5/C (☎0521 28 22 40). Open M-F 8:30am-12:30pm and 3:30-7:30pm. After-hours rotation posted outside.

Hospital: Ospedale Maggiore, V. Gramsci 14 (☎0521 70 21 11 or 70 31 11), over the river past the Parco Ducale. For emergencies go to entrance on V. Abbeveratoria.

Internet: Free at **Informagiovani** (see **Beyond Tourism,** above). **Web'n'Wine,** Strada M. D'Azeglio 72/D (☎0521 03 08 93; www.webnwine.it), across the river. €2.50 per 30min. English spoken. Open M-Th 9am-8pm, F 9am-9pm, Sa 10am-8pm.

Post Office: On Strada Melloni across from the tourist office. Open M-F 8:30am-5pm, Sa 8:30am-12:30pm. Currency exchange also available. **Postal Code:** 43100.

ACCOMMODATIONS

Ostello della Gioventù (HI), V. San Leonardo 86 (☎0521 19 17 547; www.ostel-loparma.it). From the train station, turn left onto V. Bottego. Make a right onto Strada G. Garibaldi. The bus stops on the other side of the street, in front of the fountains. Take bus 2, 2N, or 13 (until 8pm; if later, use ProntoBus). Or, to walk, turn left onto Strada G. Garibaldi, which becomes V. S. Leonardo. Hostel on left immediately after highway overpass. Beautiful, new, and easily accessible. Young, English-speaking staff, large common areas, laundry (€6), and Internet (€3.50 per hr.). Dorms €19; doubles €41. ❶

Albergo Leon d'Oro, Vle. Fratti 4a (☎0521 77 31 82; www.leondoroparma.com), 1 block from the train station, just after the intersection with Strada Garibaldi. Required advance payment may seem unorthodox, but guests will find elegant rooms with large windows and big beds. Shared modern bath. Restaurant downstairs. Singles €35-60; doubles €60, with private bath €80; triples €105. AmEx/MC/V. ❸

Casa della Giovane, Strada del Conservatorio 11 (☎0521 28 32 29; www.casadellagio-vane.it). From Strada Mazzini, turn left on V. Oberdan; hotel is on the right. Only accepts female guests aged 14-26. Religious community. 2 beds per room and shared bath. Fridge access. Breakfast and lunch or dinner included. Free laundry. Check-out 10am. Curfew M-Tu, Th-F, and Su 10pm; W and Sa 11pm. €25 per person. Cash only. ❷

FOOD

Parma's cuisine is rich, delicious, affordable, and renowned throughout Italy. Aged parmesan cheese and *prosciutto crudo* fill the windows of the *salume-rie* (delicatessens) along V. Garibaldi. Local *Malvasia* is the wine of choice. When exported, this sparkling white loses its natural fizz, so carbon dioxide is usually added to compensate—sip a glass here to sample the real thing. An **open-air market** displays its goods at P. Ghiaia every Wednesday and Saturday morning, and Wednesday and Friday nights during summer. It offers local varieties of cheese, meats, and vinegar. **Dimeglio** supermarket is located at S. XXII Luglio 27/C. (☎0521 28 13 82. Open daily 8:30am-1:30pm and 4:30-8pm.) **ECU Convenience** market is on V. San Leonardo 17. (Open daily 8:30am-1pm and 4pm-7:30pm. Closed Th afternoon. AmEx/MC/V.)

Trattoria Sorelle Picchi, Strada Farini 27 (☎0521 23 35 28), several blocks from P. Garibaldi. Food served out of a *salumeria* of the same name. This local secret cooks traditional dishes including roasted pheasant, homemade lasagna, and sweet-and-sour onions. Let the waitstaff advise on specialties and starters, like the mixed prosciutto plate (€9). Primi €8-9. Secondi €10-15. Cover €2. *Salumeria* open 8:30am-7pm. *Trattoria* open M-Sa noon-3pm. AmEx/MC/V. ❸

Trattoria Corrieri, Strada del Conservatorio 1 (☎0521 23 44 26; www.trattoriacorrieri. it). Rustic decorations surround a narrow ivy-draped courtyard. Vibrant atmosphere and modest prices keep tables full. Majestic pasta is made fresh daily. Primi €7.50-9. Secondi €7.50-10. Open noon-2:30pm and 7:30-10:30pm. AmEx/MC/V. ❸

Ristorante Gallo d'Oro, Borgo della Salina 3 (☎0521 20 88 46). From P. Garibaldi, take Strada Farini and turn left. Eat in a 16th-century stone building. Wines €3 per ¼-bottle, €4 per ½-bottle, €7-11 per bottle. Primi €6.50-9. Secondi €6.50-9.50. Cover €2. Open M-Sa noon-2:30pm and 7:30-11pm. AmEx/MC/V. ❷

Ristorante Leon d'Oro, V. Fratti 4a (☎0521 77 31 82; www.leondoroparma.com), off Strada Garibaldi. Features platters of colorful antipasto, typical *parmigiano* meals, and desserts. Primi €8. Secondi €18. Cover €2. Open daily May-Sept. 12:30-2pm and 8-10pm. Reservations recommended Sa-Su. AmEx/MC/V. ❸

👁 SIGHTS

PALAZZO DELLA PILOTTA. Built in 1602, the *palazzo*'s grandeur suggests the ambitions of the Farnese dukes; today, the *palazzo* houses several museums, accessible through the courtyard. Though there have been no actual performances in the theater since the curtain last fell in 1732, the elegant, wooden **Teatro Farnese,** completed in 1618, underwent restorations in the 50s to repair damage inflicted by WWII bombs. Beyond the theater, the **Galleria Nazionale** contains numerous medieval polyptychs and portraits, including Leonardo da Vinci's *Testa d'una Fanciulla* (Head of a Young Girl), as well as a gallery devoted to Parmigianino and Correggio. The **Museo Archeologico Nazionale** displays bronzes, and sculptures of ancient origin. *(From Strada Cavour, turn left on Strada Pisacane and cut across P. della Pace to P. Pilotta. ☎0521 23 37 18. Open June-Sept. Su 9:30am-12:30pm and 4-7pm. Closed in afternoon Aug. €2.)*

DUOMO, BATTISTERO, AND MUSEO DIOCESANO. Parma's 11th-century Romanesque *duomo* balances paintings of clouds with austere masterpieces like the Episcopal throne and Benedetto Antelami's bas-relief *Descent from the Cross* (1178). The stunning *duomo* features Correggio's Virgin ascending to heaven. *(In P. Duomo. From P. Garibaldi, follow Strada Cavour, and turn right on Strada al Duomo. ☎23 58 8. Open daily 9am-12:30pm and 3-7pm. Free.)* The pink-and-white *battistero* (baptistry) displays medieval frescoes of enthroned saints and apostles some represented with animal heads that rise from each of the dome's 16 sides. *(☎0521 23 58 86. Open daily 9am-12:30pm and 3-6:30pm. €4, with Museo Diocesano €5.)* Diagonally across the *piazza*, the Museo Diocesano holds examples of 12th- and 13th-century sculpture while preserving Roman ruins in the basement. *(In P. Duomo. ☎20 86 99; www.cattedrale.parma.it. Open daily 9am-12:30pm and 3-6:30pm. €3.)*

IL MONASTERIO DI SAN PAOLO. This aged monastery holds an impressive fresco above the **Camera di San Paolo,** which depicts the coat of arms of the Abbess, under whose direction the monastery prospered. Don't miss the ceiling frescoes of what seem to be heavily muscled babies cavorting with decapitated animals. *(V. Melloni 3. From P. Garibaldi, head up Strada Cavour, turn left on Strada Melloni, and follow the signs. ☎53 32 21. Open Tu-Su 8:30am-1:30pm. Last entry 1pm. €2, ages 18-25 €1, under 18 or over 65 free.)* The complex of St. Paul also houses **Il Castello dei Burattini** (Puppet Castle), densely showcasing a collection of over 1500 puppets in a few small but well-arranged rooms. *(☎0521 031 631; fax 0521 218 876; www.castello-deiburattini.it. Open Tu-Su Apr.-Oct. 9am-7pm; Nov.-Mar. 9am-5pm. €2.50, students €1.50.)* Just around the corner, the **Pinacoteca Stuard** holds 270 paintings from the 14th-19th centuries. Near the entrance you'll see the prized *Madonna in trono con Bambino* by Maestro della Misericordia (c. 1350-75). *(Borgo Parmigianino 2. ☎0521 50 81 84. Open M and W-Sa 9am-6:30pm, Su 9am-6pm. €4, under 25 and over 65 €2.)*

CHIESA DI SAN GIOVANNI EVANGELISTA. This 10th-century church is a long-standing Italian classic. The dome was famously frescoed by Correggio, while frescoes by Parmigianino run along the left nave and over the first, second, and fourth chapels. The belltower was constructed in 1613. *(In P. San Giovanni, behind the duomo. ☎0521 23 53 11. Open daily 8am-noon and 3-7:45pm. Monastery closes 6pm. Reservations recommended for guided tours. Free.)*

CHIESA MAGISTRALE DI SANTA MARIA DELLA STECCATA. Built in 1521 to house a miraculous picture of the Virgin Mary, the church now frames the icon with red marble columns. This Renaissance church also features impressive frescoes by Parmigianino. Call ahead to see the **Crypt of the Farnese Dukes** and pay respect to the famous Alexander, whose helmet and sword still sit above his tomb, and Antonio Farnese, the last Duke of Parma. *(P. Steccata 9, up V. Garibaldi. ☎0521 23 49 37. Open daily 9am-noon and 3-6pm. Free.)*

TEATRO REGIO. Commissioned by Marie Louise in 1821, the Teatro Regio is known worldwide. Its Neoclassical facade is complemented by Borghesi's decorations inside. The four-tiered Baroque balconies feature red velvet seats interrupted only by the large crowned ducal box that faces the stage. *(V. Garibaldi 16, next to P. della Pace. ☎0521 03 93 93; www.teatroregioparma.org. Open M-Sa 10:30am-noon. Guided tours in Italian every 30min. Advance booking recommended. €2, students €1.)*

PARMIGIANO AND PROSCIUTTO FACTORIES. Cheese enthusiasts interested in seeing the origin of 38kg blocks of Parmigiano should contact the **Consorzio del Parmigiano-Reggiano** to arrange a 2hr. tour of factories around Parma. Tours are offered infrequently and only on weekdays, are inaccessible by public transportation, and must be booked in advance. *(Strada dei Mercati 9. ☎0521 29 27 00; sezionepr@parmigiano-reggiano.it.)* Visits to a prosciutto factory are usually available only during the **Proscuitto Festival** in the first week of September. *(For more info, call the Consorzio del Prosciutto di Parma. ☎24 39 87; fax 24 39 83.)* A somewhat more feasible and satisfying option is the **Museo del Prosciutto di Parma.** *(V. Bocchialini 7. 23km outside Parma in Langhirano, accessible by bus #12. ☎0521 85 83 47 and ☎33 56 66 4220. Open Sa-Su 10am-6pm. €3; Parma ham tasting €3; "typical products tasting" €9.)* The **Parmigiano-Reggiano Museum** is in Soragna. *(☎22 81 52. Open Mar.-Oct. M-F only by reservation, Sa-Su 9:30am-12:30pm and 3-6pm; Nov.-Feb. only by reservation. €5, includes tasting.)*

OTHER SIGHTS. Although many French palaces were destroyed during WWII, Marie Louise's gardens remain by the Baroque **Palazzo Ducale** in Parco Ducale. *(West of Palazzo della Pilotta, across Ponte Verdi. Park open daily in summer 6am-midnight; in winter 7am-8pm. Free. Palazzo ☎53 76 78; call in morning. Open M-Sa 9:30am-noon. €3, students and under 25 €2.)* Across the river, the **Palazzo Cusani,** or Casa della Musica, first served as the seat of the University of Parma and later as the Mint of the Duchy of Parma. Today, it houses a museum. *(Ple. San Francesco 1. Follow Borgo del Parmigianino from the tourist office, then turn right on V. Daimazia. ☎0521 03 11 70. Open July to mid-Aug. M-Sa 9am-1pm and 3-7pm; Sept.-June Tu-Sa 9am-6pm, Su 9am-1pm.)*

📷 🎵 NIGHTLIFE AND ENTERTAINMENT

At night, *parmigiani* stroll along Strada Farini, or the intersection of Strada Maestri and V. Nazario Sauro, where the truly vibrant nightlife rivals that of a much larger city. Bars and street performers densely pack along this central strip. A gaggle of merrymakers spill out of **Tabarro,** Strada Farini 5/B, where glasses of wine (€2.50-5) are served along with the vegetable bowls. (☎0521 200 223; www.tabarro.net. Open Tu 6:30pm-1am, W-Th noon-3pm and 6:30pm-1am, F-Sa noon-3pm and 6:30pm-2am, Su 6pm-midnight. Cash only.) For a chilled-out vibe and a mostly white decor, head to **Mood Cafe,** P.le S. Apollonia 3/A. (☎0521 181 3841. Mixed drinks €6. Open M 8:30am-9pm, Tu 8:30am-3pm, W-Th

7am-3pm and 6pm-midnight, F 7am-3pm and 6pm-2am, Sa 6pm-2am. Cash only.) For even more casual revelry, enjoy the balmy nights and cool green grass in front of P. Pilotta.

The **Teatro Regio** is one of Italy's premier opera houses, hosting operatic, cultural, and theatrical extravaganzas throughout the year. (Strada Garibaldi 16/A, next to P. della Pace. ☎0521 03 93 93; www.teatroregioparma.org.) The opera season runs from November to April, while the popular **Verdi Festival,** honoring the native composer with local concerts and operas, takes place each year usually in October at the *teatro.* The **Parma Poesia Festival,** debuted in 2005, organizes a week of poetry readings, lectures, and slams throughout the city in June. In May, the city hosts **Parma Danza,** an international festival of ballet and modern dance. **Grande Estate** brings classical music, opera, jazz, and tango concerts to Ple. della Pilotta in July. (☎0521 21 86 78. Tickets €10-35.) Info for all events may be obtained at the teatro's ticket office. The **Cinema Astra,** V. Rondizzoni 1 (☎0521 96 05 54; www.cinema-astra.it), also hosts the summer movie festival Estive Astra in June and July. (All movies begin at 9:30pm. €5-6, students €4.) Last but not least, the annual **Prosciutto Festival** takes over the city and the surrounding area during the first two weekends in September; contact the Consorzio del Prosciutto di Parma for annual scheduled events. (☎0521 24 39 87; www.festivaldelprosciutto.it or www.finestreaperte.it.)

PIACENZA   ☎ 0523

One of the first Roman colonies in northern Italy and Julius Caesar's long-time headquarters, Piacenza (PEE-ah-CHEN-za; pop. 95,132) has the atmosphere and perfect walkability of a small town with the shopping and museums of a big city. Shoppers seeking the latest fashions wander down Corso Vittorio Emanuele II and Via XX Settembre. Those looking for respite relax in Piazza Duomo or pack Piazza dei Cavalli during concerts. Modern art enthusiasts enjoy the collection of Italian work at the Galleria Ricci Oddi. Though Piacenza is reluctant to encourage a tourist economy, it was recently voted one of Italy's most hospitable cities and is an ideal stop on the way to Parma or Milan.

⌐ TRANSPORTATION. Trains from P. Marconi to: Bologna (2hr., 7 per day 5:31am-11:46pm, €7.70); Milan (1hr., 66 per day 4:15am-11:12pm, €5); Parma (45min., 3 per hr. 5:31am-11:46pm, €3.35); Turin (2hr., 10 per day 4:46am-11:12pm, €9.40). The ticket office (☎0523 89 20 21) is open daily 5:25am-11:40pm. **City buses** (☎0523 39 06 11; www.tempi.piacenza.it; €1) leave from the front of the station on Borgo Sant'Ambrogio; a map of routes is posted inside the station. For a **taxi,** call ☎0523 59 19 19. **Car rental** is available from Europcar, close to the station at V. Alberoni 93. (☎0523 33 22 76. Open M-F 8:30am-1pm and 3-7pm, Sa 8:30am-1pm. AmEx/MC/V.) **Bike rental** is available at APCOA Parking Italia, on V. S. Ambrogio. Through their *park e bici* (for those with cars) and *centro in bici* (for pedestrians) programs, free bikes are available throughout the city for the day. Go to APCOA and a €5 deposit will give you a key to unlock one of the bikes found throughout the *centro.* Upon returning the key, you are repaid your deposit.

▪▪ ⁊ ORIENTATION AND PRACTICAL INFORMATION. From the **train station,** cross the *piazza* to **Viale dei Mille,** and turn right on **Via Giulio Alberoni.** Make a right at **Via Roma** and then turn left on **Via Daveri,** which leads to **Piazza Duomo.** From there, a right on shop-lined **Via XX Settembre** leads straight to **Piazza dei Cavalli.** The **IAT tourist office,** P. dei Cavalli 7, is on the left side of **Palazzo Gotico.** (☎0523 32 93 24; www.comune.piacenza.it. Open Tu-Sa 9am-1pm and 3-6pm, Su 9am-noon.) **Banca Agricola Mantovana** is at V. Cella 70. (Open M-F 8:20am-1:20pm and 2:50-3:50pm, Sa 8:20-11:20am.) For those seeking tourism alternatives, the **Centro Informagiovani,** P. dei Cavalli 2, has info on volunteer work, study abroad, professional associations, and travel. They also have free **Internet** access and Wi-Fi after a brief registration. (☎0523 49 22 24. Open M-F 8:30am-1pm and 3-6pm, Th 8:30am-6pm, Sa 9am-noon.) **Farmacia Dr. Parmigiani,** P. Duomo 41, posts after-hours rotations. (Open daily 8:30am-12:30pm and 3:30-7:30pm. AmEx/MC/V.) In case of emergency, call the **police,** V. Rogerio 3 (☎0523 49 21 00). A **hospital,** Ospedale G. da Saliceto, is on V. Taverna 49 (☎0523 30 11 11). The **post office,** V. Sant'Antonino 38-40, **exchanges currency.** (☎0523 31 64 68. Open M-F 8am-6:30pm, Sa 8am-12:30pm.) **Postal Code:** 29100.

⌐⌐ ACCOMMODATIONS AND FOOD. There are few affordable accommodations in Piacenza, though the tourist office can help with reservations. From C. Vittorio Emanuele, turn right on V. del Tempio to reach **Protezione della Giovane ❸,** V. Tempio 26. This nun-run establishment welcomes women only. (☎0523 32 38 12. Breakfast included. Reception 6:30am-10:30pm. Curfew M-Th and Su 10:30pm, F-Sa midnight. Reservations strictly required. Singles €25. 1-person apartments €425 per month; 2-person €790. Cost per week estimated based on monthly rate. Cash only.) Many of Piacenza's other affordable accommodations can only be reached with a lengthy bus ride to the city outskirts. Be sure to ask the tourist office where to disembark for your hotel, as few bus drivers speak English.

Enjoy dinner either outdoors or in the charming dining room at **Osteria del Trentino ❸,** V. del Castello 71, off P. Borgo, past the police station, which offers seasonal meat and fish dishes. (☎0523 32 42 60. Primi €7-11. Secondi €9-16. Cover €2. Open M-Sa noon-3pm and 7:30-10:30pm. MC/V.) At the foot of the lavish *duomo* is the surprisingly affordable **L'Orologio da Pasquale ❸,** P. Duomo 36. With its simple white patio furniture, this restaurant is a relaxing place for a cheese platter or dessert with a quarter-liter of house wine (€4). For full meals, the large menu of *primi* (€6.50-10) and *secondi* (€8-14) is priced comparably to surrounding restaurants. (☎0523 32 46 69. Open M-W and F-Su 12:30-2:30pm and 7:30-11pm. AmEx/MC/V.) A popular Spanish restaurant, **Taberna Movida ❷,** V. Daveri 8, offers tapas in a modern setting. (☎0523 31 81 31; www.tabernamovida.it. Tapas and entrees €4.50-14.50. Open M-F 12:30-2:30pm and 7:30pm-1am, Sa 7:30pm-2am, Su 5pm-1am.) A very convenient **Sigma** supermarket is located on the second floor of the mall to the left of the train station. (Open M 5am-9pm, Tu-Sa 9am-9pm, Su 9:30am-8pm. MC/V.) In the *centro,* **Punto Supermercato** is on XX Settembre, across from the Basilica di San Francesco. (Open M-Sa 8am-7:45pm. AmEx/MC/V.) An open-air **market** is held every Wednesday and Saturday morning in P. Duomo and P. dei Cavalli.

◎♫ SIGHTS AND ENTERTAINMENT. Piazza dei Cavalli, the central square, is named for the two 17th-century equestrian statues that grace the *piazza* in tribute to Duke Rannucio I and his father, Duke Alessandro Farnese. The true jewel is the Gothic **Palazzo del Comune,** or **Il Gotico.** The impressive *palazzo* was constructed in 1280 when Piacenza led the Lombard League, one of Italy's most powerful trade groups. A monument to war veterans sits under the *palazzo,* directly across from the **Palazzo del Governatore.** Completing the trio of impressive buildings is the **Basilica di San Francesco,** whose *Capella della Concezione di Maria* (1594) and vibrant altarpiece (1663) stand out against the rest of the basilica's modest decoration. (Open daily 6:30am-noon and 2:30-6:30pm. Free.) In P. Duomo, the town's *duomo,* constructed between 1122 and 1233, contains a wealth of frescoes dating to the 12th century. A side chapel holds the embalmed body of San Giovanni Battista Scalabrini. The ▓**crypt,** a spooky maze of narrow columns, holds the bones of Santa Giustina d'Antiocha at its center and two dark tombs at the rear. (Open daily 7:30am-12:30pm and 4-7:30pm. Modest dress required. Free.) A great collection of obscure modern Italian art can be found in **Galleria Ricci Oddi**, V. San Siro 13, which displays art from the early 1800s to the present. Works are divided among 19 rooms by the region of the artist's birth. The collection includes **Bruzzi's** scenes of the countryside and **Michetti's** episodes of villagers in landscapes. (☎0523 32 07 42; www.riccioddi.it. Open Tu-Su 10am-noon and 3-6pm. €4, students €3. Free last Th of every month.) The commanding **Palazzo Farnese**, P. Cittadella 29, houses the **Museo Civico**, the **Pinacoteca**, the **Museo del Risorgimento**, and the **Museo delle Carrozze.** The Museo Civico's Etruscan and Roman collection from the AD second and third centuries is a highlight, while the most notable work in the Pinacoteca is a Botticelli fresco depicting Christ's birth. (☎0523 49 26 58; www.musei.piacenza.it. Visit by guided tour in Italian only: Tu-Th 9:30am; F 9:30am and 3:30pm; Sa-Su 9:30, 11am, 3, 4:30pm; July-Aug. all 9:30am tours begin at 10am. Museo Civico and Pinacoteca €4.80, students €4; Museo delle Carrozze €2.50/2. All museums €6/4.80.)

RAVENNA   ☎0544

Ravenna's (ra-VEH-na; pop. 150,000) mosaics appear everywhere, from under your drink at the bar to behind the glass windows of tourist shops, and, of course, at every major sight. The streets paved with colored stones are almost entirely car-free, and travelers walk past monuments like Dante's tomb (to the chagrin of the Florentines, who maintain an empty sepulcher for their exiled son). For the artistically and academically inclined, Ravenna is filled with churches and historic monuments that date from its Byzantine glory under Justinian and Theodora, all within walking distance from the compact *centro*. Yet Ravenna knows how to kick back and relax—its proximity to the shore also attracts plenty of vacationers who want nothing more than a spot in the sun.

⊏ TRANSPORTATION

Trains: Station in P. Farini. Open daily 3:50am-12:35am. Ticket counter open daily 6:05am-8:35pm. AmEx/MC/V. To: **Bologna** (1hr., 13 per day 5:05am-8:35pm, €5), **Ferrara** (1hr., 11 per day 4:13am-9:33pm, €4.50) with connections to **Florence** and **Venice**, and **Rimini** (1hr., 22 per day 12:31am-9:35pm, €3).

Buses: **ATR** (regional) and **ATM** (municipal) depart from outside the train station. Office (☎0544 68 99 00) open in summer M-Sa 6:30am-8:30pm, Su 7am-8:30pm; during school year M-Sa 6:30am-7:30pm, Su 7:30am-7:30pm. AmEx/MC/V. To: **Lido Adriano** (Line 80, 20min.; every 30min.; 5:40am-8:10pm; for evening service take Line 75: 8:40pm-midnight, every 30 min.; €1) and **Marina di Ravenna.** (Line 60 and 70. 20-30min.; every 30min. 5:40am-7:55pm; €1.) Tickets (1-day pass €3 valid for all buses) are sold at the booth marked "PUNTO" to the right when you exit the station. Return tickets can be bought on board with a surcharge.

Taxis: RadioTaxi (☎0544 33 888), in P. Farini.

▣✦❼ ORIENTATION AND PRACTICAL INFORMATION

The train station is in **Piazza Farini** at the eastern end of town. **Viale Farini** leads from the station to **Via Diaz**, which runs to **Piazza del Popolo**, the *centro*.

Tourist Office: V. Salara 8 (☎0544 35 404; www.turismo.ravenna.it). Walk to the end of P. del Popolo, turn right on V. Matteotti, and follow the signs. Free bike rental; ID required. Office open M-Th 8:30am-7pm, F 8:30am-11pm, Su 10am-6pm.

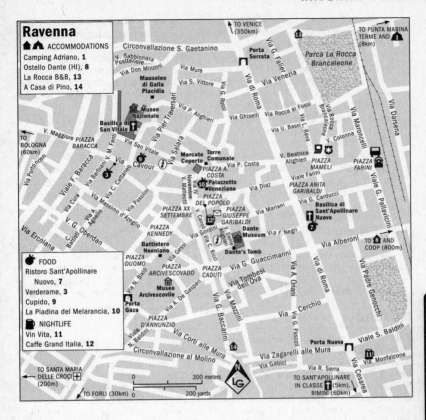

Ravenna

🏠🏔 ACCOMMODATIONS
Camping Adriano, **1**
Ostello Dante (HI), **8**
La Rocca B&B, **13**
A Casa di Pino, **14**

🍎 FOOD
Ristoro Sant'Apollinare
    Nuovo, **7**
Verderame, **3**
Cupido, **9**
La Piadina del Melarancia, **10**

📺 NIGHTLIFE
Vin Vita, **11**
Caffe Grand Italia, **12**

EMILIA-ROMAGNA

Youth Center: Informagiovani, V. Massimo D'Azeglio, 2nd floor (☎0544 48 24 56; www. racine.ra.it/informagiovani/ravenna). Work, volunteer, travel info, and free Internet (max. 30min.) for students. Open Tu and Th 10am-1pm and 2-6pm, W and F-Sa 10am-1pm.

Luggage storage: left of the station. Lockers €2-5. 24hr. max. Open M-Sa 7am-7:30pm.

Laundry: Fast Clean Laundry, V. Candiano 16. Open daily 7am-10pm.

Police: P. Mameli (☎0544 48 29 99).

Hospital: Santa Maria delle Croci, Vle. Randi 5 (☎0544 28 51 11).

Internet: free for students at **Informagiovani** (above). **Internet and Phone Center,** V. Rocca Brancaleone 4/6, (☎0544 33 744). €2 per hr. Open daily 9am-9pm.

Post office: P. Garibaldi 1 (☎0544 24 33 11), off V. Diaz before P. del Popolo. Offers currency exchange. Open M-F 8am-6:30pm, Sa 8am-12:30pm. **Postal Code:** 48100.

🏠🏠 ACCOMMODATIONS AND CAMPING

🏠 **Ostello Dante (HI),** V. Nicolodi 12 (☎0544 42 11 64; hostelravenna@hotmail.com). Take bus #70 (every 20-30min. 5:40am-7:55pm; get off at stop 249), 80 (every

30-40min. 5:40am-8:10pm; get off at stop 121), or the red or yellow line from V. Pallavicini, across from the station. This hostel offers foosball tables, a lounge area, books, board games, and bike and cooler rental. Rooms are named after cantos from Dante's *Inferno*. Kitchen access and safes available. Breakfast included. Laundry wash €2.50, dry €2.50. Internet access 1st 15min. free, €3 per hr. thereafter. Wheelchair-accessible. Reception 7-11am and 2:30-11:30pm. Lockout 11am-2:30pm. Curfew 11:30pm; €1 key card to enter later. Dorms €14; singles €24; doubles €21; family rooms €16 per person. HI-member discount €3. MC/V. ●

La Rocca B&B, V. Rocca Brancaleone 116 (☎0544 45 34 88), across from beautiful Rocca Park. From the station, turn left onto V. Maroncelli, then left again until you reach V. Rocca Brancaleone. Accommodating owner offers 3 quiet rooms with A/C, fan, TV, and balcony. Breakfast included. Singles €30; doubles with bath €50. Cash only. ❷

A Casa di Pino, V. Baccarini 37 (☎0544 38 524; www.acasadipino.it). Take bus #3 to Borgo San Rocco, or any other bus to Piazza Caduti. Cheerful former hotel owner. Sunny apartment stocked with classic American movies. Guests have their own bathroom, access to TV (until 10pm), and fan. Breakfast included. Curfew around 11pm; arrange ahead of time. Singles €34; doubles €54. Cash only. ❸

Camping Adriano, (☎0544 43 72 30; www.campingadriano.com). From the train station, take bus #80 (every 30-40min. 5:40am-8:10pm) to V. dei Campeggi 7, in Punta Marina Terme, 8km from the *centro*. 4-star, family-friendly facilities with bocce courts and a pool and soccer field. Near public beach. Reception daily 8:30am-1pm and 3-9pm. Reservation required for bungalows. Camping open mid-Apr. to late Aug., bungalows open until mid-Sept. €5.10-10.30; per person, €7.50-17.50 per tent. MC/V. ●

🍴 FOOD

The distinctive flavors of *ravennese* salt, extra-virgin olive oil, and chestnuts characterize Ravenna's cuisine. Accompany a filling meal with a full-bodied *Albana* or *Trebbiano* wine. For dessert, try *zuppa inglese*, a combination of biscuits and custard with a splash of cordial. There's a **Coop** across the street at V. Aquileia 110, near the hostel. (Open M-Sa 8am-8pm. AmEx/MC/V.) In the *centro*, there's a **Plenty Market,** V. Roma 150. (Open M-Sa 7:30am-8:30pm, Su 10am-1:30pm. ☎0544 21 71 16. MC/V.) Fruit, meat, and cheese stands fill the covered **market** at P. Andrea Costa 2, up V. IV Novembre from P. del Popolo. (Open M-Th and Sa 7am-2pm, F 7am-2pm and 4:30-7:30pm. Cash only.)

Cupido, V. Cavour 43/A (☎0544 37 529). Hearty plates of freshly made pasta and sandwiches near local sights. Warm *piadine* (€3.20-4.50) filled with both sweet and savory; try the ricotta mousse with balsamic strawberry vinagrette (€4.30). Pizza €2.70-6.30. Primi €5.50. Open Tu-F 11am-8pm, Sa 7am-8pm, Su 7am-3pm. AmEx/MC/V. ●

La Piadina del Melarancio, V. IV Novembre 31 (☎0544 21 20 71). Sells hot *piadine* (€4), fresh milk, and local wine. Classics like *parma* and *squaquerone* cheese (€4.50) hit the spot. Panini €2.50-4. Open M-T and Th-Su 10:45am-8:30pm. AmEx/MC/V. ●

Verderame, V. Cavour 82 (☎/fax 0544 32 248). Dried flowers, hand-painted menus, and mosaic tabletops complement famous hot chocolate. Try invigorating blends like "Chocolate Pick Me Up" (liquor, chocolate, whipped cream, and *nocciolo;* €6). Open in summer M-Sa 8:30am-8pm, Su 2-8pm; in winter M-Th 8:30am-8pm, F-Sa 8:30am-midnight, Su 10am-8pm. Cash only. ●

Ristoro Sant'Apollinare Nuovo, V. di Roma 53 (☎0544 35 679), turn right by the basilica entrance. Grab lunch at the self-service counter for a cheap meal. Daily menu with traditional pastas like gnocchi with 4 cheeses. 4-course lunch *menù* €8. Primi €4-5.50. Secondi €4-6. Open M-F noon-2:30pm. AmEx/MC/V. ❷

👁 SIGHTS

█BASILICA DI SAN VITALE. The glimmering jewel in mosaic-crazy Ravenna, this remarkable basilica overwhelms viewers with its ornate tile work and the dusty warmth that seems to float on the earth-colored frescoes. Peer up at the colorful mosaics that decorate the apse; at the center, Christ Pantocrator is depicted in lush blue and gold, while to the side a scene with Theodora and Justinian is rendered in bright aqua, scarlet, and green. At the center, rosy paintings grace the walls as warm light streams through the quartz windows. *(V. S. Vitale 17. From tourist office, turn right on V. Cavour, then again on V. Argentario. ☎ 0544 21 62 92. Open daily Apr.-Sept. 9am-7pm; Mar. and Oct. 9am-5:30pm; Nov.-Feb. 9:30am-5pm. Individual ticket not available; included in the Ravenna Card pass.)* Mosaics cover the interior of the tiny **█Mausoleo di Galla Placidia,** where a single lamp illuminates 570 gold stars set against a night sky, arranged in concentric circles around a cross. Three stone sarcophagi are said to contain the remains of Costanzo III, Empress Galla Placida, and Valentiniano III. *(Behind S. Vitale. Same hours as basilica.)*

DAY AND NIGHT, NIGHT AND DAY. American jazz musician Cole Porter, after having toured Ravenna by night in 1920, was allegedly so struck by the beautiful light in the Mausoleo di Galla Placida that he composed the song "Night and Day" with the structure's starry ceiling in mind.

█BASILICA DI SANT'APOLLINARE IN CLASSE. A bus ride from the town center, this church at first seems simple, with dark wood beams and unlabeled marble columns. But keep exploring: the real draw is the massive mosaic above the apse, where Sant'Apollinare and flocks of sheep fill the enormous half-dome. *(In Classe, south of the city. Take bus #4 or 44; both stop across from the train station. ☎ 0544 34 424. Open daily 8:30am-7:30pm. Last entry 30min. before closing. €3, EU students 18-25 €2, under 18 and over 65 free. Free entry Su mornings. Cash only.)*

DANTE'S TOMB AND THE DANTE MUSEUM. Ravenna's most popular monument is the unassuming, green-domed tomb of Dante Alighieri, who died in Ravenna in 1321 after being exiled from his native Florence. A suspended lamp that has burned with Florentine oil since 1908 illuminates a relief of Dante leafing through books. The nearby Dante Museum contains Wostry Carlo's illustrations of Dante's works, the poet's bones in a fir chest, 18,000 scholarly volumes on his works, and the trowel and hammer that laid the cornerstone of Rio de Janeiro's *Dante Monument.* However, the peaceful garden outside provides a nice respite from the city streets. *(V. D. Alighieri. From P. del Popolo, cut through P. Garibaldi to V. D. Alighieri. Museum ☎ 0544 33 667. Tomb open daily Apr.-Sept. 9:30am-6:30pm. Free.)*

RAVENOUS FOR ART. Individual tickets to 5 of Ravenna's monuments are not available, but the **Ravenna Card** (€8.50, students €7.50) provides admission to 5 museums and monuments for 7 days: the Basilica di San Vitale, Basilica di Sant'Apollinare Nuovo, Battistero Neoniano, Mausoleo di Galla Placidia, and Museo Arcivescovile. From Mar. 1 to June 15, Mausoleo di Galla Placidia costs an extra €2. A group ticket to Basilica di Sant'Apollinare in Classe, Mausoleo di Teodorico, and the Museo Nazionale costs €8. For info on the churches, contact the **Ufficio Informazioni e Prenotaxioni dell'Opera di Religione della Diocesi di Ravenna,** V. Canneti 3. (☎ 0544 54 16 88; fax 54 16 80. Open M-F 9am-12:30pm and 3:30-6pm.)

MUSEO NAZIONALE. This former Benedictine monastery features Roman, early Christian, Byzantine, and medieval works, like the sixth-century bronze cross from the roof of San Vitale's cupola and the original apse vault of Sant'Apollinare in Classe. Discovered in the 70s during excavations, the original vault featured peacocks, doves, and fruit trees, but the renovators eventually went with the existing design of herds of lambs instead. *(On V. Fiandrin Ticket booth to the right of Basilica di San Vitale's entrance. Museum is through courtyard. ☎0544 34 424. Open Tu-Su 8:30am-7:30pm. Last entry 30min. before closing. €4, EU students ages 18-25 €2, under 18 and over 65 free. Cumulative tickets with Basilica di Sant'Apollinare in Classe and Mausoleo di Teodorico €8, reduced €4. Cash only.)*

BASILICA DI SANT'APOLLINARE NUOVO. This sixth-century basilica makes quite an impression with white tile floors, graceful columns, crushed seashell mortar, and gilded coffers. A dynamic procession of white-robed mosaic figures leads to the apse where a soft gray-green ceiling houses beautiful sculptures. Beside the rustic exterior of chipping brick, a tall, circular *campanile* spirals up six stories over the church's sloping, red-tiled roof. *(On V. di Roma. ☎0544 21 95 18. Open daily Apr.-Sept. 9am-7pm; Mar. and Oct. 9:30am-5:30pm; Nov.-Feb. 10am-5pm.)*

BATTISTERO NEONIANO. Originally a Roman bath, today, this pint-sized baptistry welcomes visitors into a deep blue interior decked out in gold floral designs. The 12 apostles, rendered in blue and yellow, circle the domed ceiling while good luck coins litter the bottom of the baptismal font in the center. Seating along the sides allows visitors to gawk for the five brief minutes they are allowed inside. *(From P. del Popolo, follow V. Cairoli, turn right on V. Gessi, and head toward P. Arcivescovado. Duomo open daily 7am-noon and 2:30-6:30pm. Baptistry open daily Apr.-Sept. 9am-7pm; Mar. and Oct. 9:30am-5:30pm; Nov.-Feb. 10am-5pm.)*

MUSEO ARCIVESCOVILE. This one-room museum offers an up-close look at the city's most celebrated art form, displaying detailed religious mosaics that were rescued from the now-destroyed Ursian Basilica. To the left of the entrance, the eyes of four mosaic faces look in different directions. At the center, an ivory throne given to Justinian by Maximilian impresses all with its exceedingly ornate carvings. *(To the right of the Battistero Neoniano. ☎0544 21 52 01. Open daily Apr.-Sept. 9am-7pm; Mar. and Oct. 9:30am-5:30pm; Nov.-Feb. 10am-5pm.)*

🎵 🌿 ENTERTAINMENT AND FESTIVALS

Many bars and cafes stay open late around P. del Popolo. Watch for the **Organ Music Festival,** held annually in late July in the basilica, and the **Ravenna Festival,** which brings together some of the world's most famous classical performers each June and July. (Info office at V. D. Alighieri 1. ☎0544 24 92 11; www.ravennafestival.org. Open M-W and F-Sa 10am-1pm, Th 4-6pm; during festival. M-Sa 10am-1pm and 4-6pm, Su 10am-1pm. Box Office Ravenna Live at G. Raspni 9. ☎0544 24 92 44. Tickets from €10. Reserve ahead for popular events.) In the second week of September, Dante's legacy comes to life with the exhibits and theatrical performances of the **Dante Festival** (☎0544 30 252).

Vin Vita, V. Monfalcone 10 (☎0544 47 14 18). Funky leopard seats, a shiny bar, and spacious seating. F and Sa *discoteca* nights with live music in the laid-back lounge. Every Su, starting at 6pm, *aperitivi* (€2.50-4) served with live house music. Beer €2. Wine €3-4. Open daily 6pm-2am. AmEx/MC/V.

Caffe Grand Italia, in P. Popolo (☎0544 217 529). Classy, silver bar with soft lighting and great mixed drinks. Live music. Dishes like ricotta ravioli with braised endive and *bruciatini* in cheese fondue (€8.50) by day. Primi €8. Secondi €11-15. Mixed drinks

€6. Wine €4-6. Open in summer M-Th and Su 6:30am-midnight, F-Sa 6:30am-3am; in winter M-Tu, Th and Su 6:30am-midnight, F-Sa 6:30am-3am. AmEx/MC/V.

RIMINI   ☎0541

Given the lack of surprise on doormen's faces when they let in mojito-stained lodgers at 3am, Rimini (REE-mee-nee; pop. 136,000) is clearly a city that's used to playing fast and loose. Inland, the *centro storico* preserves its Roman heritage with *piazze* overshadowed by immense monuments. But the town shows its true colors on buses crammed with rowdy drunk teens and during colorful midnight explosions of impromptu fireworks. Beaches, pastel-colored hotels, and wide boardwalks filled with clothing vendors and fortune-tellers all contribute to an atmosphere in which it's perfectly acceptable—and even admirable—to collapse into bed and wish the rising sun "good night."

⌐ TRANSPORTATION

Flights: Miramare Civil Airport (☎0541 71 57 11; www.riminiairport.com), V. Flaminia 409. Mostly charter flights. Serves many European cities. Bus #9, across from the train station, goes to the airport (every 30min. 6:09-1:01am-10:52pm and 1:02am, €1).

Trains: P. Cesare Battisti and V. Dante Alighieri (☎0541 89 20 21). Info office open daily 7:30am-8:30pm. Ticket office open daily 5:15am-10:15pm. To: **Ancona** (1hr., 44 per day 12:14am-11:02pm, €5); **Bologna** (1hr., 44 per day 2:30am-10pm, €7); **Milan** (3hr., 23 per day 2:56am-10:22pm, €28); **Ravenna** (1hr., 23 per day 3:33am-10:58pm, €4); **Riccione** (10min., 37 per day 12:30am-11:03pm, €1.10). AmEx/MC/V.

Buses: Buy both intercity and municipal tickets at ticket booth across from train station. Open daily 5:50am-12:20am. Municipal bus tickets available (90min. pass €1, purchased onboard €1.50; 24hr. pass €3; 72hr. pass €5.50; 7-day pass €11). 24hr. service to many inland towns (€1.03-3.36). Local bus #11 travels to Riccione. **TRAM intercity bus station** (☎0541 30 05 11 ; www.tram.rimini.it), at V. Roma in P. Clementini, near the station. From the train station, follow V. D. Alighieri, and take 1st left.

Taxis: RadioTaxi (☎0541 50 020). Available 24hr.

Car Rental: Avis, Vle. Trieste 16/D (☎0541 51 256; fax 56 176), off V. Amerigo Vespucci. Bus #11: stop 12. 21+. Prices starting at €66 per day. Open M-F 8:30am-1pm and 3-7:30pm, Sa 8:30am-1pm and 4-7pm. AmEx/MC/V.

Bike/Scooter Rental: P. Kennedy 6 (☎0541 27 016). Bikes €3 per hr., €10 per day; pedal-powered cars €30 per hr.; scooters from €20 per hr.; €60 per day. Open Apr.-Sept. daily 9am-midnight. AmEx/MC/V.

✦🛈 ORIENTATION AND PRACTICAL INFORMATION

To reach the beach from the train station in **Piazzale Cesare Battisti,** turn right from the station, take another right into the tunnel at the yellow arrow indicating "*al mare,*" and follow **Viale Principe Amedeo.** To the right, **Viale Amerigo Vespucci,** the hub of Rimini activity, runs one block inland along the beach. **Bus #11** runs from the train station to the beach and continues along Vle. Vespucci and V. Regina Elena (every 15min. 5:22am-2am). Buy tickets at the kiosk in front of the station or at *tabaccherie.* To reach the **centro storico,** follow **Via Dante Alighieri** from the station to **Piazza Tre Martiri.** The center of Rimini is **Marina Centro** with **Rivabella** to the northwest and **Bellariva** to the southeast. **Rimini Sud** (south) branches out from the main city along the coast and comprises the neighborhoods of Marebello, Rivazzurra, and Miramare. **Rimini Nord** (north) goes toward the less-visited Viserba, Viserbella, and Tre Pedrera.

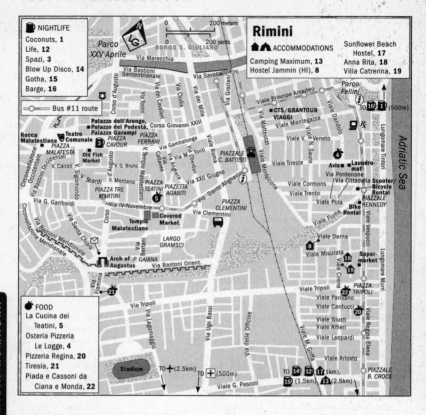

NIGHTLIFE
Coconuts, **1**
Life, **12**
Spazi, **3**
Blow Up Disco, **14**
Gotha, **15**
Barge, **16**

—○— Bus #11 route

Rimini

ACCOMMODATIONS
Camping Maximum, **13**
Hostel Jammin (HI), **8**

Sunflower Beach
Hostel, **17**
Anna Rita, **18**
Villa Catrerina, **19**

FOOD
La Cucina dei
Teatini, **5**
Osteria Pizzeria
Le Logge, **4**
Pizzeria Regina, **20**
Tiresia, **21**
Piada e Cassoni da
Ciana e Monda, **22**

EMILIA-ROMAGNA

Tourist Offices: IAT, P. Fellini 3 (☎0541 56 902; www.riminiturismo.it), at the beginning of V. Vespucci. Bus #11: stop 10. Open in summer M-Sa 8:30am-7:15pm, Su 8:30am-2:15pm; in winter M-F 9am-1pm and 3:30-7pm, Sa 9am-1pm. Branch: Ple. Cesare Battisti 1 (☎0541 53 399), on the left after the train station. Open in summer M-Sa 8:15am-7:15pm; in winter M-Sa 8:30am-6:30pm.

Budget Travel: CTS/Grantour Viaggi, V. Matteucci 2/4 (☎0541 51 001 or 55 525). Open M-W and F 9am-12:30pm and 3:30-7pm, Th 9am-4pm, Sa 9am-12:30pm.

Luggage Storage: Self-service lockers in train station. €3-5 for 1st 6hr., €1 per hr. thereafter. Coins only. Call ☎0541 23 428 for problems.

Laundromat: Lavanderia Trieste Express, Vle. Trieste 16 (☎0541 26 764). 5 kg wash €10, dry €10. No self-service. Open M-Sa 8:30am-12:30pm and 3-7:30pm.

Police: C. d'Augusto 192.

Pharmacy: Farmacia del Kursaal, V. Vespucci 12/E (☎0541 21 711). Open daily 8:30am-1pm and 4-10pm. AmEx/MC/V.

Hospital: Ospedale Infermi, V. Settembrini 2 (☎0541 70 51 11 or 78 74 61).

Internet: Central Park, Vle. Vespucci 21 (☎0541 27 550). €1 per 10min., €2 per 30min., €5 per 80min. Open daily 9am-2am. MC/V.

Post Office: C. d'Augusto 8 (☎0541 78 16 73), off P. Tre Martiri, near the Arch of Augustus. Currency exchange available. Open M-F 8am-6:30pm, Sa 8am-12:30pm. Branch at P. Marvelli 3. Open M-F 8am-1:30pm, Sa 8am-12:30pm. **Postal Code:** 47900.

◪ ◪ ACCOMMODATIONS AND CAMPING

With 1146 hotels and 62,000 beds, Rimini overwhelms visitors with its array of cookie-cutter accommodations. The smaller streets off Vle. Vespucci and Vle. Regina Elena between bus #11 stops 12 and 20 are filled with more hotels than homes. Prices peak in August, and reservations are necessary far in advance. If plans fall through, however, the tourist office provides booking services.

▨ **Sunflower Beach Hostel,** Vle. Siracusa 25 (☎0541 37 34 32; www.sunflowerhostel. com), 20min. from the station and 15min. from Marino Centro. Bus #11, stop 24. Funky hostel in the heart of the party scene. Fully equipped kitchen, laundry, bar, garden, and common room. Weekly pizza and pasta parties. Breakfast included. Free lockers, Wi-Fi, and bike rental. Check-in after 2pm. Check-out 11am. Open Mar.-Oct. Dorms €14-23, with bath €16-24; singles €24-44/26-47; doubles with bath €42-60. AmEx/MC/V. ❶

▨ **Anna Rita,** V. Misurata 24 (☎0541 39 10 44; www.hotelannarita.it). Bus #11, stop 13. A cut above its neighbors, this family-oriented hotel just steps from the beach offers top-notch services including free Wi-Fi, beach umbrellas, bicycle rentals, and parking. Comfortable rooms with bath, phone, TV, safe, and A/C. Buffet breakfast, takeout lunch, and dinner included. €31-53 per person during the summer (€10 surcharge for singles); in winter €20 (only bed and breakfast). Reservations recommended. AmEx/MC/V. ❸

Hostel Jammin (HI), Vle. Derna 22 (☎0541 39 08 00; www.hosteljammin.it). Bus #11, stop 13. Ideal place for beachgoers and party-seekers, just minutes from the action. Boasts excellent amenities. Central lounge features perpetually playing music videos, a well-stocked bar, and an outdoor patio. Breakfast included. Free bike rental for 1st 4hr., €1 per hr. thereafter. €10 key deposit. Lockers €1 per 24hr. Internet access €1 for 1st 15min., €3 per hr. thereafter. Reception 24hr. Closed Jan. Dorms €21; singles €33; doubles €29 per person; triples €28; quads €24, with bath €26. AmEx/MC/V. ❷

Villa Caterina, V. Cirene 21 (☎0541 30 78 50; www.villacaterina.it). Newly renovated hotel on a quiet street near the beach. Snug and simple rooms have TV, phone, safe, A/C, and private bath; some have balconies. Breakfast in an elegant dining room. Private garden. Free bike rental. Open Apr.-Sept. €28-42 per person, full pension €36-60. Stays shorter than 3 days 20% surcharge; single rooms €8 extra. AmEx/MC/V. ❷

Camping Maximum, Vle. Principe di Piemonte 57 (☎0541 37 26 02; www.campingmaximum.com). Bus #11, stop 33. Across from the beach on the way to Riccione, this lively campground is sandwiched between seaside hotels. Showers and electricity free. Wi-Fi €4 per hr. Reception 7am-10pm. Open May 20-Sept. 20. €7-10 per person, €4-5 per child; €8.50-12 per tent; €2.50-4 per car; bungalows €60-130. AmEx/MC/V. ❶

◪ FOOD

Rimini's covered **market** between V. Castelfidardo and the **Tempio** sells fresh produce, fish, meat, bread, and cheese. (Open M-Sa 7:30am-7:30pm.) If you don't see what you're looking for, check out **STANDA** supermarket, Vle. Vespucci 133, between P. Kennedy and P. Tripoli. (Open daily 8am-10:30pm. AmEx/MC/V.) On Saturday nights, reservations are advisable at nicer, popular restaurants. For a quick lunch or late-night snack, grab a *piada*, a typical Emilia-Romagna dish of pita-like bread topped with ingredients like *prosciutto crudo*, arugula, and *squacerone* (a soft, regional cheese); or a *cassoni*, similar but sealed like a quesadilla and stuffed with cheese, meat or vegetables.

Piada e Cassoni da Ciana e Monda, Vle. Don Giovanni Bosco (☎348 563 2992). From P. Tripoli, walk down Vle. Tripoli and turn left on V. D. G. Bosco. The beach is littered with *cassoni* and *piade* joints, but this humble, family-owned spot is the real thing. Try classics like sausage, smoked bacon, and mozzarella or a vegetarian option with tomatoes, mushrooms, artichokes, and mozzarella. *Cassone* €2.50-5. *Piade* €0.70-4.50. Open June-Sept. Tu-Su 11:30am-2pm and 4-11pm. Cash only. ❶

La Cucina dei Teatini, P. Teatini 3 (☎0541 28 008, reservations 340 12 41 107), just off V. IV Novembre, near the temple. This romantic restaurant in the *centro* serves Italian plates with a healthy twist. Enjoy dishes like baked lamb with potato *pâté*, yogurt, and cucumbers (€18) or one of the *"energia"* plates (€9.50). Pasta €9-9.50. Meat €15-22. Open M-Sa 12:30-2:30pm and 7:30-11pm, Sa 7:30-10:30pm. MC/V. ❸

Pizzeria Regina, Vle. Regina Elena 37 (☎0541 38 85 96). Big helpings of dishes like sliced beef with *rucola* and balsamic vinaigrette (€12). Great late-night stop. Pizza €3-8. Primi €6. Secondi €5.50-12. Meat or fish *menù* with primo, secondo, contorno and bread €13-15. Cover €0.50. Open in summer daily 11am-5am. AmEx/MC/V. ❷

Tiresia, V. XX Settembre 41 (☎0541 78 18 96; www.osteriatiresia.it). From the Arch of Augustus, walk 5min. down V. XX Settembre. Dim lighting, cobblestone floors, rustic exposed beam ceilings, and a quiet garden out back set the tone for a laid-back, romantic night in the *centro storico*. Homemade pasta €9.50-11. Secondi €11-20. Contorni €4.50-10. Open Tu-Su 6pm-2am. AmEx/MC/V. ❸

Osteria Pizzeria Le Logge, Vle. Trieste 5 (☎0541 55 978). On a shady street off the crowded beachfront. Tasty pizza (€2-11) and seafood dishes like *strozzapretti* (gnocchi) with prawns, mushrooms, onions, and a brandy cream sauce (€8.70). Grapevines and palm awnings on the deck generate a romantic, slightly upscale feel. Primi €6.70-11. Secondi €7.50-15. Cover €1.50. Open M-Tu and Th-Su 7pm-1am. AmEx/MC/V. ❶

◎ ⌒ SIGHTS AND BEACHES

TEMPIO MALATESTIANO. Rimini's cultural life once relied largely on Sigismondo Malatesta, a 15th-century lord who refurbished the *tempio* with funereal chapels for himself and his fourth wife. The simple white interior with a dark, wood ceiling houses beautiful frescoes. To the right of the apse, Piero della Francesca's *Sigismondo Pandolfo Malatesta in preghiera davanti a San Sigismondo* shows Malatesta kneeling in front of his Rimini castle, the family dog lying dutifully behind. In the first chapel, a statue of the ruler sits atop two elephants—the family emblem. The apse holds a painted crucifix by Giotto, Rimini's only work by the artist. The small brick protrusion on the exterior was added by Leon Battista Alberti to resemble the Arch of Augustus (below) as per Malatesta's orders. *(On V. IV Novembre. Follow V. D. Alighieri from the train station. ☎0541 51 130. Open M-Sa 8:30am-1pm and 3:30-7pm, Su 8:30am-1pm. Modest dress required. Free.)*

ARCH OF AUGUSTUS. Built in 27 BC to celebrate Caesar Octavian Augustus's recent completion of the Via Flaminia, this impressive arch now triumphantly marks the entrance to Rimini's *centro storico*. The top of the arch, probably destroyed in an earthquake, was refinished with medieval brick ramparts, while marble pillars depicting the gods and an inscription honoring Augustus survive today. *(Follow V. IV Novembre to P. Tre Martiri, and turn left on C. d'Augusto.)*

PIAZZE. Shops and bars surround the 18th-century *pescheria* (fish market) under the brick arches in **Piazza Cavour.** The four stone fish in the corners of the arcade once spouted water used to clean the daily catch. Perpendicular to the municipal building lies the modern **Teatro Comunale,** whose auditorium was destroyed in WWII. In the center of the *piazza*, the 1543 **Fontana della Pigna** contains an inscription by Leonardo da Vinci. In the center of the square, a militant Pope Paul V sits on his throne, his fierce gaze doing little to ward off pigeon admirers. Farther south lies **Piazza Tre Martiri.** Once a medieval jousting venue, the *piazza* now houses outdoor cafes, an 18th-century bell tower, and the mint-green domes of the **Chiesa di Sant'Antonio di Padova.**

BEACHES. Though hotels own most of the shore, a minimum charge of about €3.50 will buy a lounge chair and use of whirlpools, volleyball courts, lockers, and other facilities. The fun continues into the night with bars and live music. Vendors by the beach offer watersports equipment. A **free beach,** located at the top of the shore, is less picturesque and has no storage or lounge amenities, but the price is right and the waves are huge.

NIGHTLIFE

Rimini is notorious for the nonstop partying at clubs near the *lungomare* in Rimini Sud. A bustling nightlife scene lights up the *centro storico* by the old fish market. From P. Cavour, follow **Via Pescheria,** where pubs and bars stay open until 3am—but the real action that attracts a younger crowd of vacationers is outside the *centro storico*, near the port, where *discoteche*, pubs, and clubs glitter. Many clubs offer free bus service (check the travel agency in P. Tripoli at stop 14 for schedules; ☎0541 39 11 72; open M-Sa 8:30am-7pm, Su 9am-noon), but there is also a **Blue Line bus** (☎0541 74 35 94; www.bluelinenus. com; from June to early Sept. every 20min. 2:20am-5:40am; 1-night pass €4, 1-week €14) for late-night discogoers. It has color-coded lines depending on the *discoteca* destination and travels up the coast hitting **Miramare, Rivazzurra, Bellaria, Rivabella, Marebello, Cattolic,** and **Riccione.** Buy tickets onboard. The last bus leaves at 5:40am, after which bus #11 resumes service. During the high season, **bus #11** is an institution—by midnight, expect a crowd of strangers singing drinking songs, comparing outfits, and cheering. The route runs from Rimini to the bus station in Riccione, where Blue Line buses allow easy access to seven more nightclubs grouped together in a valley. Clubs change their hours and prices frequently, and many close in winter.

>
> **CLUB HOPPING.** Nightlife in Rimini has a quick turnover rate, so it's tough to stay on top of what's popular. Ask around (especially on bus #11), follow the crowds, and if a venue is not to your liking upon arrival, just hop back on the bus—there is a world of Rimini still to discover.

Life, Vle. Regina Margherita 11 (☎0541 37 34 73), in Bellariva. Bus #11, stop 22; offers a free bus service. One of the busiest night spots, this *discoteca* draws partygoers to its movie-poster strewn bar upstairs and expansive dance floor below. DJs play American and foreign hits popular with the international crowd. Mixed drinks €5-7.50. Shots €3-4. Cover €7-12 and includes 1 drink. Open daily 11pm-4am. Cash only.

Blow up Disco, Vle. Regina Elena 209 (☎0541 38 60 60 or 335 706 3445; www. blowupdisco.it). Bus #11 to stop 21; offers a free shuttle service. Covered walkway and an upstairs lounge lead to a pulsing dance floor with lit floors, marble columns, mirrors, and neon couches. R&B, house, and Top 40 play late into the night. Partygoers tend to be young tourists, ready to experience the best of Rimini nightlife. W night guest DJ. Mixed drinks €7. Cover €10, includes 1 drink. Open daily 9:30pm-4am. Cash only.

Coconuts, Lungomare Tintorin 5 (☎0541 52 325 or 339 658 5135; www.coconuts.it). Bus #11, stop 10. Walk through Parco Fellini and 5-10min. down Lungomare Tintori. Expansive interior surrounded by comfy lounge seating, dancing platforms, and scattered bars. Attracts a young, classy crowd. Leafy plants, hardwood floors, and colorful lighting generate a tropical vibe as chic male dancers and bikini-clad women strut the dance floor. Street bar opens at 8pm, but don't expect things to start up before 9:30pm. Su features pop music. W, F and Sa have live house music. *Aperitivo* buffet at 6pm. Mixed drinks €4-8. Open daily 6pm-4:30am. MC/V.

Barge, Lungomare Tintori 13 (☎0541 70 98 45,; www.thebarge.eu). Laid-back spot near the water with a friendly, young staff. Live music. The outside enclave off the main street attracts a crowd of varied musical tastes: classic rock, jazz, and blues performed on the stage in front W, F, and Sa nights. Beer €4.50. Mixed drinks €6. Shots €4. Open M-F 7pm-4am, Sa-Su noon-3pm and 7pm-4am. AmEx/MC/V.

Gotha, Vle. Regina Margherita 52 (☎0541 47 87 39; www.gotha-rimini.com). Bus #11 to stop 28. Laid-back yet social alternative to busy neighboring *discoteche.* Large lounge surrounded by palm leaves, exotic cloths, and colored lights. R&B, pop, and Latin music. Slightly more mature crowd. From mid-July to late Aug., crowds pack the dance floor Th nights. Mixed drinks €7. Shots €4. Open daily 9pm-4am. AmEx/MC/V.

Spazi, (☎0541 23 439), in P. Cavour. More traditional spot perfect for a relaxed drink before hitting the *discoteche.* Attracts a slightly older clientele with an extensive wine list, trendy bar, and patio. Wine €3-6 per glass. €10 special includes 1 chalice of wine and 1 plate of sushi. Open M-Sa 7am-1am, Su 4pm-1am. AmEx/MC/V.

▶ DAYTRIP FROM RIMINI

SAN LEO

San Leo is accessible from Rimini by buses operated by Ferrovie Emilia-Romagna. Only 1 bus (#165; noon; €2.60) goes directly from Rimini to San Leo; bus 160 stops every 30-60 min. at Pietracuta, where a connection is available to San Leo. Ask at the tourist office for a schedule. Connecting trips €2 for the 1st leg, €1.40 for the 2nd. Buy Ferrovie Emilia-Romagna tickets outside the train station and connection tickets on the van.

Surrounded by craggy cliffs atop the Apennines, San Leo (SAN LAY-oh) began as a Kingdom of Italy under King Berngard II. Later it served as the Papacy's maximum-security prison, **La Fortezza** (The Fortress), which most famously held Count Cogliostro, imprisoned for causing innumerable scandals in the European court. Today, the tiny hamlet offers a tranquil alternative to the swarming streets of nearby Rimini and San Marino. It takes only a few hours to explore the entire area, but plan to linger a little longer to indulge in San Leo's timeless charm. Just before P. Dante Alighieri, signs point up a rocky path that zigzags steeply to La Fortezza. Inside, glass cases contain 14th- to 19th-century military artifacts, but the history of famous prisoners is more interesting. The surrounding countryside views alone are worth the trip. (☎0541 91 63 02. Open daily 9am-6pm. €8, students and over 65 €5, ages 6-14 €3. Cash only.) Across from the tourist office sits **La Pieve,** a tiny church made of sandstone blocks that contains one row of pews and a simple brick apse; in the basement's crypt, a softly illuminated statue honors Santa Maria Assunta, to whom the church is dedicated. (Open daily 9:20am-12:30pm and 2:30-7:30pm. Free.) If you're not tired out by the trip up to La Fortezza, work those legs a little more with a climb up **Torre Campanaria,** past La Pieve to the right. A cool breeze and views of the valley and the fortress reward those who make the climb. (Open Mar.-Sept. daily 9am-noon and 3:30-6:30pm. €3.)

Though ideal as a daytrip from Rimini, San Leo has a few good lodging options. **Albergo Rocca's ❹** welcoming, English-speaking owner Ivo lets six small and charming rooms with bath, but the real draw is the outdoor terrace that looks out over the rooftops of San Leo. (☎0541 91 62 41. Restaurant downstairs serves breakfast. Reception noon-11pm. Call ahead for Aug. stays. Singles €55; doubles €60-65; triples €75-85; quads €90-105. AmEx/MC/V.) **Albergo Castello ❹,** in the main *piazza*, has 14 rooms with TV, phone, and bath. Call ahead to reserve one of the rooms with great valley views. (☎0541 91 62 14; albergo-castello@libero.it. Breakfast included. Reception 7:30am-10pm. Singles €50; doubles €65; triples €80; quads €95. AmEx/MC/V.)

Il Bettolino ❸, V. Montefeltro 4, serves piles of pasta in the quiet interior or at canopied tables along the street. Ask to sit by the window; you won't regret it. (☎0541 91 62 65. Pizza €4-7. Primi €6.50-9. Secondi €7-15. Cover €1.50. Open M-Tu and Th-Su noon-3pm and 7-10:30pm. AmEx/MC/V.) After exiting the tourist office, turn left for **La Corte ❷,** V. Michele Rosa 74, which offers traditional dishes, like the specialty *ravioli al formaggio di fossa* (€8). The attached gelateria has gelato from €1.70 per scoop and crepes for €3. For lighter eaters, the *conini* (tiny gelato cones dipped in chocolate) are just €0.50. (☎0541 91 61 45; osterialacorte@liberto.it. Primi €6.50-8. Secondi €6.50-9.50. Cover €1.50. Gelateria open daily Mar.-Oct. 9am-midnight. Restaurant open daily 12:15-2:30pm, 7:30-11pm. MC/V.) The **tourist office** is at P. D. Aligheri 14. (☎0541 91 63 06 or 92 69 67; fax 92 69 73. Open daily July-Aug. 9am-6pm; Sept.-June 9am-4pm.)

RICCIONE
☎0541

In Riccione (ree-CHYO-neh; pop. 33,000), a tangible rift exists between the shaded residential lanes and the steamy beachfront streets, where wide-eyed vacationers wander boardwalks lined with video arcades, sex shops, and a constant stream of busy disco-bars and hotels. The city itself is humming with electricity and neon until early in the morning, but the true partygoers make the trek to the hillside of world-renowned *discoteche* just a bus ride away.

[icons] TRANSPORTATION AND PRACTICAL INFORMATION. The **train station** is between Ple. della Stazione and Ple. Vittorio Veneto. (☎0541 89 20 21. Station and ticket booth open daily 6am-7:45pm. Binario #1 open 24hr.) Trains run to Bologna (1hr., 24 per day 5:23am-11:36pm, €6.80), Pesaro (20min., 36 per day 12:41am-10:17pm, €2.20), and Rimini (10 min., 38 per day 5:05am-11:36pm, €1.10). **Local bus #11** (€1, onboard €1.50) runs from Riccione to Rimini.

To get to the **beach,** exit the train station toward Ple. V. Veneto, walk down **Viale Martinelli,** and turn left on **Via Gramsci;** head right on V. Ceccarini for 2 blocks to **Piazzale Roma.** The public beach is on the other side of the *piazzale*. An **IAT tourist office,** Ple. Ceccarini 10, offers accommodations booking. (☎0541 69 33 02, bookings ☎69 78 36; iat@comune.riccione.rn.it. Open daily June-Aug. 8am-10pm; Sept. 8am-8pm; Oct.-May 8am-7pm.) In case of emergency, call the **police,** Vle. Sirtori 2 (☎0541 42 61 00). The **hospital,** Ospedale G. Ceccarini, is at V. Cervi 48 (☎0541 60 85 11). **Internet access,** printing, fax, and photocopy services are available at **Phone Center and Internet Point,** V. Amendola 17/D. (☎0541 69 38 11. €1 per 15min. Open M-Tu and Th-Su 11am-10pm. Cash only.) The **post office,** V. Corrodoni 13, offers currency exchange. (☎0541 47 39 11. Open M-F 8am-6:30pm, Sa 8am-12:30pm.) **Postal Code:** 47838.

[icons] ACCOMMODATIONS AND FOOD. Hotel reservations are essential for the high season; for the rest of the year, there are plenty of bargains. To reach **Hotel Nancy ❷,** Vle. Boito 12, take bus #11 to stop 43, continue to Ple. Azzarita and turn right onto V. Boito. Bright and comfortable rooms near the beach and *centro* have TV, A/C, balcony, safe, and private bath. (☎0541 64 82 62; www.hotelnancy.net. Breakfast included. Free bike rental. 3-night min. stay. Reception 24-hr. €25-43 per person; with full board €33-55; 10% surcharge for singles. AmEx/MC/V.) **Hotel Laila ❸,** Vle. Tasso 137 is a centrally located, social hotel, just 100m from the beach. Take bus #11 to stop 42, proceed onto V. Alfiero and then turn onto V. Tasso. Rooms have private bath, phone, TV, and balcony. (☎0541 64 06 26; www.hotellaila.it. A/C €4 euro. Free bike and beach equipment. 3-night min. stay. Reception 24hr. in Aug. Half- or full-pension plan only, with special gluten-free menus and buffet breakfast. Half pension €31-60 per person; full pension €35-64. €6 surcharge for singles. AmEx/MC/V.) **Hotel Garden ❸**, V. Bixio 24, a short walk from the beach, offers guests free bike rental and bright blue-and-white rooms with TV, phone, safe, bath, and balcony. (☎0541 60 15 00; www.hotelgardenonline.com. Breakfast included. A/C €3. Reception 24hr. Half- and full-pension available. €28-45 per person. €5 surcharge for singles. 10% surcharge for extra bed. For week-long stays, €10 deal offers A/C, beach equipment and wine/water with meals. MC/V.)

In a town with so many tourists, conformity reigns in countless cafes and pizzerias. On one of the main pedestrian malls, the self-service **Hot Café ❶**, Vle. Dante 170/A, offers a well-priced pasta *menù* and flatscreen TV near street-side seating. (☎0541 64 63 28. Piade €5-6. Piadine €3.50-6. Thick tramezzini €3. Self-service pasta bar with primi €6-8. Open daily 6:30am-3am. AmEx/MC/V.) For a break from bright lights and fast-paced joints, turn onto Vle. Diaz from P. Unità and then right to find **Com' una Volta ❸**, V. Galliano 6. Enjoy ravioli with butter and sage (€7) or a rich plate of tortellini with prosciutto, peas, and cream (€7) on the vine-covered terrace or in the warmly lit interior. (☎0541 60 58 00. Primi €5-8. Secondi €6-16. Open in summer daily noon-3pm and 7pm-midnight; in winter Tu-Su noon-3pm and 7pm-midnight. MC/V.) Lounge seating, yellow tables, and funky chandeliers lend an upscale, decorative feel to **Cristall,** V. Dante 36, where you'll find hearty seafood plates like *pasatelli* with clams, butter, and lemon juice. (☎0541 60 54 04; www.ristorantecristallo.it. Primi €7-11. Secondi €11-20. Open daily in summer 7:30am-12:30am; in winter 7:30am-3:30pm and 6:30pm-12:30am. AmEx MC/V.) Named for The Beatles' "Strawberry Fields," the lyrics scrawled across the wall, **Campi di Fragole ❶**, V. Dante 180, is a reprieve from Riccione's cookie-cutter *gelaterie*, and the stifling summer humidity. After sampling the freshly made gelato, tag the graffiti-covered mirrors with neon gel pens from the counter. (Cones €1.60-3. Open daily Mar.-Sept. 10am-2am. Cash only.) **Supermarket Angelini** is at Vle. Dante 18. (Open M-Sa 7:45am-1:15pm and 4-11pm, Su 7:45am-1:15pm. AmEx/MC/V.)

🅼 **NIGHTLIFE.** Riccione's real action is in the clubs, conveniently nestled together in a valley accessible by bus. From the bus station near the waterfront, take bus #46 to the *"discoteche"* stop—from there, signs point to a half-dozen hot spots. Even easier to reach, though, is 🆆**Hakuna Matata**, Vle. d'Annunzio 138, a classy restaurant by day and hopping club by night, with the carefree attitude of the Disney tune it is named for. Take bus #11 to stop 37. (☎0541 64 12 03. Primi €8-9. Secondi €9-15. Mixed drinks €5-6. Call for reservations. Discoteca open W, F, and Sa 24hr. AmEx/MC/V.) Not for the faint of heart, **Sasa Green,** Vle. Ceccarini 57, serves some of the priciest mixed drinks in town in its emerald-green hall. Gold couches, mirrored walls, crystal chandeliers, and a bright orange bar complete the classy decor. (☎0541 69 24 62 or 331 85 59 530; www.greenbarriccione.it. Happy hour with DJ F, Sa, and Su 6pm. Mixed drinks around €20. Open 24hr. in summer; in winter daily 9am-1:30am. AmEx/MC/V.) It's pricey and it's far, but 🆆**Baia Imperiale**, in Cattolica on V. Panoramica 41, is a must-see for the incredible—almost surreal—scale of its party. Take the Blue Line's *"linea gialla."* In a gigantic faux-Roman complex, complete with imitation baths and temples, world-famous DJs spin records for hundreds of young and sweaty clubgoers, who keep alive the memory of the bacchanalian ancient Romans. (☎0541 95 03 12; www.baiaimperiale.net. Cover from €10, usually including at least one drink. Women enter free W before 1am.) For those weary of the *discoteca* scene, check out **Zanzibar "La Chianina,"** Vle. Tasso 21, where dim lighting, orange curtains, and modern seating suggest the romantic more than the risqué. The late-night crowd enjoys mixed drinks (€6) and beer (€3-4) to the sounds of everything from jazz to pop. (☎339 246 7674. Open daily noon-3pm and 7pm-5am. AmEx/MC/V.) In Miramare, **L'Altro Mondo Studio's,** V. Flaminia 358, is well off the beaten path. Lights illuminate a huge floor lined with portals, sliding doors, and steel platforms. A young international crowd grooves to house and techno, pausing only for the 2am laser show. Avoid heading to this club alone; the 15-20min. walk to the bus route is mostly unlit. (☎0541 37 31 51; www.altromondo.com. Cover approx. €15. Open daily 11pm-4am. Cash only.)

SAN MARINO ☎0549

San Marino (san ma-REE-no; pop. 30,000) is one of two independent states inside Italy—the other is the Vatican. Officially titled the Serenissima Repubblica di San Marino ("The Most Serene Republic of San Marino"), it was founded in AD 301 by Marinus, a pious stone cutter who fled to Mt. Titano to escape the advances of an overly affectionate girl. The winding cobblestone streets of San Marino may be wrought with jewelry shops and *piadinerie* aimed at roping in the busloads of daily tourists, but this stifling commercialism is more than made up for by stunning views of rolling hills and the patchwork countryside.

 STAYING IN TOUCH WITH SAN MARINO. San Marino's country code is ☎328. It is necessary to dial it only when calling from outside Italy. Within Italy and San Marino, just dial the city code (☎0549).

TRANSPORTATION

Trains: The closest train station is in Rimini (p. 415).

Buses: Fratelli Benedettini (☎0549 90 38 54) and Bonelli (☎0541 66 20 69) companies run from San Marino's *centro* to Rimini's train station (45min., 12 per day 6:30am-7pm, €3.70) and from Rimini to San Marino (11 per day 7:30am-7pm).

Funicular: connects Borgo Maggiore to the *centro storico* (☎0549 88 35 90). Every 15min. July to mid-Sept. 7:50am-1am; from mid-Sep. to Oct. 8am-7pm; Nov.-Dec. 8am-6:30pm; Jan.-Feb. 7:50am-6:30pm; Mar.-Apr. 7am-5:30pm; May-June 8am-8:30pm. €2.80, round-trip €4.54, 12 rides €8.

Taxis: in P. Lo Stradone. ☎0549 99 14 41.

ORIENTATION AND PRACTICAL INFORMATION

San Marino consists mostly of long streets that zig-zag up a steep hill; walk up any stretch to reach one of the many *piazze*, where stunning views of the countryside await. Street signs direct you to hotels, restaurants, and sights. From the bus, exit to the left, climb the staircase, and pass through the **Porta San Francesco** to begin the ascent. **Via Basilicus** leads to **Piazza Titano.** From there, turn right to **Piazza Garibaldi,** then follow **Contrada del Collegio** to **Piazza della Libertà.**

Tourist Office: Contrada del Collegio 40. (☎0549 88 29 14; www.visitsanmarino.com. Open M-F 8:30am-6:30pm, Sa 9am-1pm and 1:30-6:30pm. Cash only.)

Currency Exchange: San Marino mints coins interchangeable with the euro, though they're more collector's items than anything else. Pick them up at the **Coin and Stamp Office,** P. Garibaldi 5. (☎0549 88 23 70. Open July-Aug. daily 8:15am-6pm; Sept.-June M and Th 8:15am-6pm, Tu-W, and F 8:15am-2:15pm. MC/V.)

EMILIA-ROMAGNA

THE LOCAL STORY

SOFT TOUCH

San Marino, a tiny independent nation in Emilia-Romagna, has always done things a little differently. Perhaps that's why their soccer team's nickname, La Serenissima (The Most Serene One), isn't intended to terrify anyone. Its nickname may not inspire much fear in opponents, but—truth be told—the team itself really doesn't either. Since 1990, when San Marino's soccer team busted into the world of international play, the team has recorded only one victory. In San Marino's debut, she fell flat in a 0-4 loss to Switzerland, a country with 250 times as many people.

Still, it's astounding that the country even manages to field a team on the international stage. The country itself is the size of most Italian small towns and has less than 30,000 residents.

Losing history aside, San Marino does hold the bragging rights for one wacky *calcio* record: the fastest goal ever scored in World Cup history. Just 8.3 seconds after the opening whistle, La Serenissima's Davide Gualtieri scored a goal that put his country ahead of England. Undoubtedly reeling from the early setback, the British got their act together and scored a few retribution goals, defeating San Marino 7-1. San Marino's greatest moment came in 2004, when she beat that perennial powerhouse (ahem) Liechtenstein 1-0 in a friendly match.

Police: ☎0549 88 77 77.

Internet Access: Caffè del Titano, Piazzetta del Titano 4 (☎0549 99 24 73). €1 per 15min. Open daily Apr.-July 7am-7pm; Aug. and Nov.-Mar. 7am-6pm. AmEx/MC/V.

Post Office: Vle. Onofri 87 (☎0549 88 29 07). Open M-F 8:15am-4:45pm, Sa 8:15-11:45am. Cash only. **Postal Code:** 47890.

🏠 ACCOMMODATIONS

Hotel Rosa, V. Lapicidi Marini 23 (☎0549 99 19 61; www.hotelrosasanmarino.com). From Salsita alla Rocca, follow signs for the Museo delle Cere. Excellent services in a prime location. Rooms have TV, phone, minibar, A/C, private bath, safe, and radio. Breakfast included. Internet access available in the bar. Reception 9am-11pm. Singles €45-55; doubles €65-110. AmEx/MC/V. ❸

Hotel Joli, Vle. Federico d'Urbino 36/B (☎0549 99 10 09), 5min. from the bus station. From P. Calcigni, climb the stairs, turn right onto Ple. lo Stradone and continue until it becomes Vle. Federico Durbino. Professional service. Elegant, sunny rooms with TV, radio, phone, shower, A/C or fan, and minibar. Restaurant downstairs. Breakfast included. Free Wi-Fi. Singles €42-75; doubles €68-110. AmEx/MC/V. ❸

Bellavista, Contrada del Pianello 42/44 (☎0549 99 12 12). Bellavista offers simple rooms with private bathroom and TV, and—as the name suggests—great views of the mountains nearby. Reception 8am-8pm. Singles €40; doubles €60. AmEx/MC/V. ❸

Hotel La Rocca, Salita alla Rocca 33 (☎0549 99 11 66; fax 99 24 30), down the street from the *castello*. Kind staff offers 10 spacious rooms with TV, private bath, phone, and fantastic views. There's also a restaurant downstairs. Breakfast included. Reception daily 9am-4pm. Singles €50-59; doubles €65-79; triples €85-100. AmEx/MC/V. ❹

🍴 FOOD

Find basics at **Alimentari Chiaruzzi,** Contra del Collegio 13, between P. Titano and P. Garibaldi. (☎0549 99 12 22. Open daily Aug. 7:30am-midnight; Sept.-July 7:30am-7:30pm. AmEx/MC/V.)

Buca San Francesco, Piazzetta Placido Feretrano 3 (☎0549 99 14 62) past Porta San Francesco. Sample regional pasta like the *Tris della Buca* (ravioli, *tagliatelle*, and cheesy lasagna in a light *ragù*) for €8. Primi €5-8. Secondi €6-9. Offerta Buca includes *lasagne, escalope* of veal, and fries €10. Bar open daily 8am-6pm. Restaurant open daily noon-3:30pm; closed Tu in winter. AmEx/MC/V. ❷

La Capanna, V. Salita alla Rocca 47 (☎0549 99 05 44). Reward yourself for the steep climb to the castles with a well-priced meal and spectacular views of the hills. Pizza heaped with toppings and classic pasta. Pizza €4.40-7. Primi €5.50. Cover and service included. Open Apr.-Oct. daily 9am-1am. AmEx/MC/V. ❶

Da Pier, Contrada S. Croce 5 (☎0549 99 03 76). Scrumptious dishes at surprisingly low prices. *Menù* of the day includes ravioli, gnocchi, or lasagna, roast or cutlet, 2 contorni, fruit salad, and wine (€16). For the less hungry, there's pizza (€3.60-7.25) or home-made pasta (€5.20-6.20). Open daily 8:30am-10pm. V. ❷

Il Loco, V. Basilicius 8 (☎0549 99 05 98). Before hopping on the bus, grab a bite at this self-service restaurant, which offers a 3-course meal for €8.30. Individual plates like *cannelloni* with ricotta and vegetables or baked lasagna €4.30-7. Open daily Aug. 9am-10pm; Sept.-July 9am-6pm. Cash only. ❶

👁 🎋 SIGHTS AND FESTIVALS

Guards clad in festive red-and-green uniforms stand outside the late 19th-century **Palazzo Pubblico,** which serves as the seat of San Marino's parliament. The marble interior features the **Sala del Consiglio** (Hall of the Council), from which the city is still run amid a depiction of Justice (holding a broadsword) and Peace (at a slight disadvantage, holding an olive branch). The changing of the guard takes place in front of the *palazzo* from April to September at half past the hour from 8:30am to 6:30pm. (P. della Libertà. ☎0549 88 31 52, museum 88 26 74. Open daily June-Sept. 8am-8pm; Oct.-May. 9am-12:30pm and 2-5:15pm. Last entry 30min. before closing. €3. Cash only.) Two of the three points along San Marino's defensive network are open to the public, but just traveling between them offers many of the same views for free. The first tower is the **Castello della Guaita,** which offers stunning views of the country's hills and cypress trees from atop winding pathways. Climb to the tower, where lovers have scratched their names into the rafters. Be careful as you ascend the steep staircase. (Follow signs from P. della Libertà. ☎0549 99 13 69. Open from Apr. to mid-Sept. daily 8am-8pm; from mid-Sept. to Oct. M-F 9am-5pm, Sa-Su 9am-6pm; Nov.-Mar. daily 9am-5pm. Last entry 30min. before closing. €3, combined with Castello della Cesta and Museum of Ancient Arms €4.50. AmEx/MC/V.) Follow signs along the trail to the highest peak of Mt. Titano, where the **Castello della Cesta** offers the best views of the distant Adriatic and the Castello della Guaita. Inside, the **Museo delle Armi Antiche,** an arms museum, displays a selection of fierce weapons ranging from 15th-century tridents to medieval helmets. (☎0549 99 12 95. Same hours as Castello della Guaita. €3, with Castello della Guaita €4.50. Cash only.) Castle fanatics can follow the trail to the third tower, **Torre del Montale,** a squat, mossy turret closed to the public. Nearby, stone outcroppings offer quiet views of the hills and ocean.

In late summer, a **medieval festival** brings parades, food, musicians, and jugglers to San Marino. September 3 is San Marino's day of independence; the **Palio delle Balestre,** or crossbowman's show, commemorates this event; increased bus service makes daytripping easy. (Early Sept.; for specific dates and info, call☎0549 88 29 98 or the tourist office, p. 423)

TUSCANY
(TOSCANA)

Popular culture has glorified Tuscany (tos-CAH-nah) as a sun-soaked sanctuary of frescoes, cypress trees, and bottles of *vino*. For once, pop has gotten it right. In Tuscany, every town was home to a Renaissance master, every highway provides vistas of ancient hills, and every year, the *Chianti Classico* flows at local celebrations of the region's illustrious history with costumed parades and festivals. The concentration of art, coupled with some of Italy's best cuisine, including famous meaty dishes like *bistecca alla fiorentina* from Florence and *cinta senese* from Siena, rightfully lures millions of visitors each year. Wander through medieval sidestreets of hill towns, marvel at the genius of Brunelleschi's dome in Florence, and get caught up in the fanfare of Siena's *palio* festival. While it's tempting to confine a visit to Tuscan rivals, Florence and Siena, don't overlook the majesty of the smaller towns that cling to their medieval roots, the tranquility of the wine country, and Elba's island paradise.

> ### HIGHLIGHTS OF TUSCANY
>
> **ADMIRE** the towering marble statues in Florence's Piazza della Signoria (p. 443).
>
> **PRETEND** to live in medieval times in the small town of Cortona (p. 475).
>
> **TASTE** local reds and whites in the vineyards of Tuscan wine country (p. 466).
>
> **ABSORB** the sun on pebbly stretches of Elban coastline (p. 496).
>
> **SIGH** as the sun sets gloriously over the Ponte Vecchio in Florence (p. 446).

FLORENCE (FIRENZE)   ☎ 055

Sopping-wet, war-weary, emaciated, and plagued, Florence (Fee-REN-zeh; pop. 400,000) could not escape the floods, wars, famine, and Black Death that haunted Europe during the early Renaissance. However, by the late 14th century, Florence was able to etch itself into the history books. Florentines Boccaccio, Dante, and Giotto created trend-setting masterpieces and, in the 15th century, Florence gained further artistic distinction as the Medici family amassed a peerless collection, supporting masters like Botticelli, Brunelleschi, Donatello, and Michelangelo. This incredible input of creative spirit generated a kind of beauty that, unlike the plague, has survived through the ages. The city that inspired the old masters is timeless, unflagging, and yours to behold.

◼ INTERCITY TRANSPORTATION

Flights: Aeroporto Amerigo Vespucci (FLR; main line ☎055 30 615, 24hr. automated flight info line 30 61 700; www.aeroporto.firenze.it) in the suburb of Peretola. Mostly domestic and charter flights. **SITA,** V. S. Caterina da Siena (☎055 80 03 73 760), runs buses (20min., 5:30am-11pm, €4.50) to and from the Florence airport.

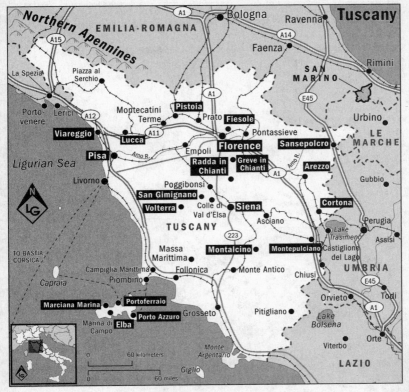

Trains: Stazione Santa Maria Novella, just north of Santa Maria Novella. Info office open daily 7am-9pm (after-hours ☎055 89 20 21). **Luggage storage** and lost property services available. Trains every hr. to: **Bologna** (1hr., 5:48am-1:47am, €4.70-6.80); **Milan** (3hr., 6am-1:47am, €29); **Rome** (3hr., 5:55am-10:55pm, €30); **Siena** (1hr., 5:31am-11:07pm, €5.70); **Venice** (3hr., 5:18am-1:47am, €16).

Buses: 3 major bus companies run out of Florence. Offices near P. della Stazione. Intercity buses depart from P. della Stazione, or in front of the train station.

> **NOT SO DIRETTA.** When busing it with SITA's frequent, convenient buses, be sure to check the schedule to see if the bus is a *"rapida"* or *"diretta."* As counter-intuitive as it is, the *diretta* is not direct and makes many stops. The *rapida* is faster and nearly as panoramic.

SITA, V. S. Caterina da Siena (☎055 80 03 73 760). Office open M-Sa 5:50am-8:30pm, Su 6:15am-7:55pm. MC/V. To: **Arezzo** (2hr., 3 per day, €4.30); **San Gimignano** (1hr., 14 per day, €6); **Siena** (1hr., 2 per day, €6.50); **Volterra** (2hr., 6 per day, €7.50) via **Colle Val D'Elsa.**

LAZZI, P. Stazione 4/6r, (☎055 35 10 61). Departures from P. Adua. Office open M-Sa 6:10am-8:15pm, Su 7am-7:20pm. To: **Lucca** (1hr., every hr. 7am-8:15pm, €5); **Pisa** (1hr., every hr. 6am-8:15pm, €6.10); **Pistoia** (1hr., every hr. 7am-6pm, €3); **Prato** (1hr., every hr. 6am-11pm, €3).

CAP, Largo Alinari 10 (☎055 21 46 37). Office open M-F 9am-12:30pm and 2:30-7pm, Sa 9am-12:30pm. To **Prato** (1hr., 6:40am-8pm, €2.20).

FOOD

all'Antico R. Di' Cambi,	19 A4
Dante,	50 B4
Carabè,	20 D2
Hemingway,	21 A5
La Mangiatoia,	22 B6
Ristorante Il Vegetariano,	23 D1
Trattoria Contadino,	27 B3
Trattoria Zà-Zà,	28 D2
Trattoria Mario,	29 D2
Lorenzo il Magni co,	51 C2
Mamma Toscana,	52 C2

NIGHTLIFE

Central Park,	30 A3
Enoteca Fuori Porta,	31 E6
Meccanò,	32 A3
The Gate Pub,	53 A4
La Dolce Vita,	54 B4
Dublin Pub,	55 C2
Twice,	56 E4
Bebop Music Club,	57 E2

CHURCHES

Badia,	34 D4
Basilica di San Lorenzo,	35 C3
Duomo,	36 D3
Orsanmichele,	37 D4
San Marco,	38 D2
Santa Croce,	39 E5
Santa Maria del Carmine,	40 B5
Santa Maria Novella,	41 C3
Santa Trinità,	42 C4

TUSCANY

FORTEZZA DA BASSO

Via delle Ghiacciaie
Via Cittadella
Via G. Monaco
V.I. Peri
Viale Strozzi
Viale Strozzi
Via della Fortezza
PIAZZA INDIPEND
Via Fratelli Rosselli
Via Valfonda
Via della Scala
Via Jacopo da Diacceto
Via Almanni
Via Guelfa
Via Faenza
Via Fiume
Santa Maria Novella Station
Box Of ce
LAZZI
Mercato Centrale
PIAZZA MER CENT
TAXI
CAP
Via Nazionale
Alinari Card Store
PIAZZA DELLA STAZIONE
PIAZZA DELL' UNITA ITALIANA
Via de' Panzani
Via dei Cerreta
PIAZZA S. MARIA NOVELLA
Via d. Belle Donne
Via de' Pecori
Via dei Sole
Lavarapido
Via de' Orti Oricellari
Via del Prato
Via Palestro
Via S. Lucia
Via Palazzuola
Via dei Finiguerra
Via dell' Albero
SITA
Via S.C. da Siena
Via de' Canacci
Via della Scala
Hertz
Maggiore
Avis
Via Ognissanti
Via Montebello
Via Curtatone
Lungarno Amerigo Vespucci
PIAZZA D'OGNISSANTI
Via de' Fossi
Palazzo Rucellai
Via della Vigna Nuova
Palazzo Strozzi
Via degli Strozzi
Via de' Tornabuoni
Via Porta Rossa
REPUBE
Teatro Comunale
Corso Italia
Via Garibaldi
Via Solferino
BUS
Ponte A. Vespucci
Lungarno S. Rosa
Via d. Ancenella
Via Pisana
Arno R.
Lungarno Soderini
Ponte Alla Carraia
Lungarno Corsini
Lungarno Acciaiuoli
Ponte S. Trinita
Via L. Bartolini
PORTA SAN FREDIANO
Viale L. Ariosto
Via dell'Orto
P. dei Nerfi
Via Cardatori
Via del Tessitori
V. d. Piazo d'Oro
Borgo San Frediano
PIAZZA NAZARIO SAURO
Via di Santo Spirito
Ponte Vecchio
Borgo San Jacopo
Via S. Monaca
PIAZZA DEL CARMINE
Borgo Stella
Via Serragli
OLTRARNO
Via de' Guicciardini
Via S. Agostino
PIAZZA SANTO SPIRITO
Via dell'Ardiglione
PIAZZA DEI PITTI
Palazzo Pitti
Via della Chiesa
Via del Campuccio
Via delle Caldaie
Via Mazzetta
Via Maggio
PIAZZA S. FELICE
Giardino Torrigiani
Via S. Maria
Borgo Tegolaio
PIAZZA T. TASSO
Via Villani
Via dei Serragli
Via Romana
Giardino di Boboli
Forte Belved

0   300 meters
0   300 yards

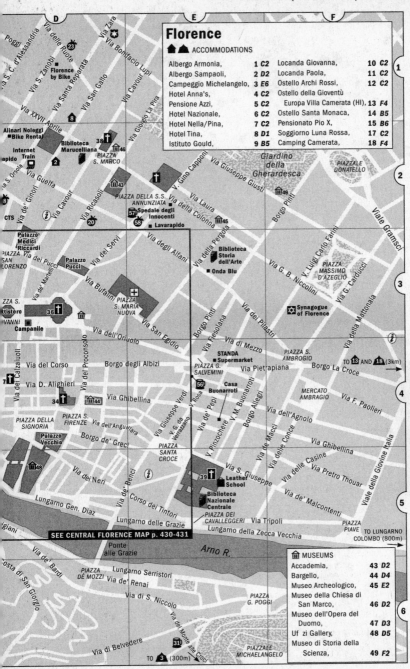

Florence

🏠 ACCOMMODATIONS

Albergo Armonia,	**1 C2**
Albergo Sampaoli,	**2 D2**
Campeggio Michelangelo,	**3 E6**
Hotel Anna's,	**4 C2**
Pensione Azzi,	**5 C2**
Hotel Nazionale,	**6 C2**
Hotel Nella/Pina,	**7 C2**
Hotel Tina,	**8 D1**
Istituto Gould,	**9 B5**
Locanda Giovanna,	**10 C2**
Locanda Paola,	**11 C2**
Ostello Archi Rossi,	**12 C2**
Ostello della Gioventù	
Europa Villa Camerata (HI),	**13 F4**
Ostello Santa Monaca,	**14 B5**
Pensionato Pio X,	**15 B6**
Soggiorno Luna Rossa,	**17 C2**
Camping Camerata,	**18 F4**

SEE CENTRAL FLORENCE MAP p. 430-431

T U S C A N Y

🏛 MUSEUMS	
Accademia,	**43 D2**
Bargello,	**44 D4**
Museo Archeologico,	**45 E2**
Museo della Chiesa di San Marco,	**46 D2**
Museo dell'Opera del Duomo,	**47 D3**
Uf zi Gallery,	**48 D5**
Museo di Storia della Scienza,	**49 F2**

PIAZZA DELLA STAZIONE

A · B · C

TO 32 (500m) Via S. Antonino

Via S. Faenza

6

Via del Canto de'

PIAZZA DELL'UNITÀ ITALIANA

S. Maria Novella

Capelle dei Medici

Basilic San Lor

Via Avelli

Via Amorino

PIAZZA MADONNA ALDOBRANDINI

Via del Melarancio

Via della Scala

Via Benedetta

3

1

Via del Giglio

Via de' Conti

Via F. Zannetti

Via de'Panzani

Via dell'Alloro

PIAZZA S. MARIA NOVELLA

33

Via dei Banchi

2

Via dei Cerretani

4

Via Palazzuolo

Via del Trebbio

Via dei Rodinelli

Via Teatina

Via de' Vecchietti

Via de' Pecori

Via del Porcellana

Via delle Belle Donne

Via Antinori

Via degli Agli

PIAZZA ANTINORI

Via de' Pescioni

Via Brunelleschi

27

Via del Sole

PIAZZA OTTAVIANI

Lavarapido

Via della Spada

Via dei Corsi

Via Campidoglio

Via

0   100 meters
0   100 yards

Via de' Fossi

Via del Moro

Via dei Palchetti

15

Palazzo Rucellai

Via della Vigna Nuova

Via del Purgatorio

Via dell'Inferno

Via de Tornabuoni

Palazzo Strozzi

PIAZZA STROZZI

Via degli Strozzi

PIAZ DELL REPUBL

Borgo Ognissanti

Lungarno Amerigo Vespucci

20

BM Bookstore

PIAZZA CARLO GOLDONI

Via del Parione

Sassetti

Via degli Anselmi

31

Via Pellicceria

Via

Ponte Alla Carraia

24

Lungarno Corsini

Via Parioncino

S. Trinità

Via Monalda

PIAZZA DAVANZATI

Via Porta Rossa

Palazzo Davanzati

22

Via delle Terme

Me N

UK

PIAZZA SANTA TRINITA

8

9

FOOD

Acqua al 2,	10	E4
Il Borgo Antico,	11	A6
Danny Rock,	12	F4
Gelateria dei Neri,	13	E5
Grom,	14	D3
Il Latini,	15	B3

50 Rosso,	33	B1
La Loggia degli Albizi,	16	F3
Osteria de' Benci,	17	E6
Perche No!,	18	D4
Trattoria Anita,	19	E5
Tre Merli,	20	A3
Vivoli,	21	F4
Osteria dell'Olio	34	C2

Borgo S. S. Apostoli

Chiassa Cornino

Lungarno Acciaiuoli

Via Por Santa Maria

Arno R.

23

Ponte Vecchio

Via di San Spirito

Via de Coverelli

PIAZZA FRESCOBALDI

Borgo San Jacopo

PIAZZA ANGOLIERI

Via Mar a

Santo Spirito

St. Mark's Church of England

OLTRARNO

Via del Vellutini

Via Toscanella

Via dello Sprone

Via Ramagliant

Via Barbadori

Via de' Bardi

Via del Presto di San Martino

Via Maggio

Via del Vellutti

Via Squazza

Via Michelozzi

PIAZZA SANTO SPIRITO

11

Via Gucciardini

Costa di San Giorgio

PIAZZA D. FELICITA

5

TO PALAZZO PITTI (200m)

TUSCANY

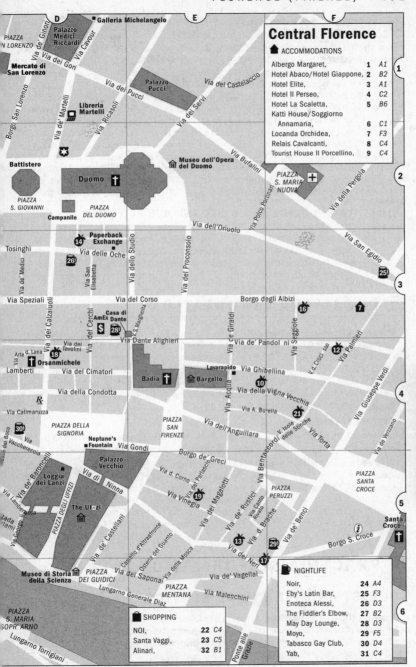

Central Florence

ACCOMMODATIONS

Albergo Margaret,	1	A1
Hotel Abaco/Hotel Giappone,	2	B2
Hotel Elite,	3	A1
Hotel Il Perseo,	4	C2
Hotel La Scaletta,	5	B6
Katti House/Soggiorno Annamaria,	6	C1
Locanda Orchidea,	7	F3
Relais Cavalcanti,	8	C4
Tourist House Il Porcellino,	9	C4

TUSCANY

SHOPPING

NOI,	22	C4
Santa Vaggi,	23	C5
Alinari,	32	B1

NIGHTLIFE

Noir,	24	A4
Eby's Latin Bar,	25	F3
Enoteca Alessi,	26	D3
The Fiddler's Elbow,	27	B2
May Day Lounge,	28	D3
Moyo,	29	F5
Tabasco Gay Club,	30	D4
Yab,	31	C4

▪ ORIENTATION

From the front steps of **Stazione Santa Maria Novella**, a short walk down **Via de'
Panzani** and a left on **Via dei Cerrentari** leads to the **duomo**, in the heart of the city.
Most streets in Florence lead to this instantly recognizable dome, which soars
high above every other city structure and makes getting lost a little easier to
remedy. **Via dei Calzaiuoli**, dominated by throngs of pedestrians, leads south from
the *duomo* to the statue-filled **Piazza della Signoria**, in front of the **Palazzo Vecchio**
and the **Uffizi Gallery**. The other major *piazza* is the **Piazza della Repubblica**, down
Via Roma from the *duomo*. Major streets run north from this *piazza* toward the
duomo and south toward the shop-lined **Ponte Vecchio** (literally, "Old Bridge").
The Ponte Vecchio is one of five bridges that cross from central Florence to the
Oltrarno, the district south of the **Arno River**. When navigating Florence, note that
most streets change names unpredictably, often every few blocks. For guidance, grab a free map from the tourist office across from the train station.

> **TIP** **WHAT'S BLACK AND WHITE AND RED ALL OVER?** Florence's
> streets are numbered in red and black. Red numbers indicate commercial
> establishments, and black (or blue) numbers denote residences (including
> most sights and hotels). Black addresses appear here as a numeral only,
> while red addresses are indicated by a number followed by an "r."

▪ LOCAL TRANSPORTATION

Public Transportation: Orange **ATAF buses** run 6am-1am. Buy tickets at any newsstand,
tabaccheria, or coin-operated ticket dispenser. €1.20 for 1hr., €4.50 for 4 tickets, €5
for 1 day, €12 for 3 days. Validate ticket onboard using the orange machine or risk a
€50 fine. The ATAF info office (☎055 80 04 24 500; www.ataf.net) is to the left of the
train station. Open M-F 7:15am-1:15pm and 1:45-7:45pm, Sa 7:15am-1:15pm. Bus
#7 to Fiesole, #13 to Ple. Michelangelo. Bus #17 goes to area hostels.

Taxis: (☎055 43 90, 47 98, 44 99 or 42 42).

Car Rental: at airport.

Avis (☎055 31 55 88; www.avisautonoleggio.it), at airport. 25+. Open daily 8am-11pm.

Maggiore (☎055 31 12 56; www.maggiore.it), at airport. 23+. Open daily 8:30am-10pm. .

Bike and Scooter Rental: Alinari Noleggi, V. S. Zanobi 38r (☎055 28 05 00; www.alinari-
rental.com). Bikes €14-18 per day; scooters €35 per day. Open M-Sa 9:30am-1:30pm
and 2:45-7:30pm, Su and holidays 10am-1pm and 3-6pm. MC/V. **Florence by Bike,** V.
S. Zanobi 120/122r (☎055 48 89 92; www.florencebybike.it). Bike rental includes helmet, locks, spare tubes, pump, insurance, maps, and suggested itineraries. Bikes €3.70
per hr., €14-35 per day; scooters €65-95 per day. Reserve ahead. Open Apr.-Oct. daily
9am-7:30pm; Nov.-Mar. M-Sa 9am-1pm, 3:30-7:30pm. AmEx/MC/V.

▪ PRACTICAL INFORMATION

TOURIST AND FINANCIAL SERVICES

Tourist Offices: Informazione Turistica, P. della Stazione 4 (☎055 21 22 45; tur-
ismo3@comune.fi.it), directly across the *piazza* from the station's main exit. Open M-Sa
8:30am-7pm, Su and holidays 8:30am-2pm. **Branches:** at airport (☎055 31 58 74); V.

TUSCANY

Cavour 1r (☎055 29 08 32 or 29 08 33); Borgo Santa Croce 29r (☎055 23 40 444); V. Alessandro Manzoni 16 (☎055 23 320).

Budget Travel: CTS, V. de'Ginori 25r (☎055 28 95 70). Transalpino tickets and ISICs available. Open M-F 9:30am-1:30pm and 2:30-6pm, Sa 9:30am-12:30pm. MC/V.

Consulates: UK, Lungarno Corsini 2 (☎055 28 41 33). Open M-F 9am-1pm and 2-5pm. **US,** Lungarno Amerigo Vespucci 38 (☎055 26 69 51). Open M-F 9am-1pm.

American Express, V. Dante Alighieri 22r (☎055 50 98; www.americanexpress.com). Cashes personal checks for cardholders. Free mail and Travelers Cheques for members. Lost Travelers Cheques ☎055 80 08 72 000, lost cards 067 22 80 371. Open M-F 9am-5:30pm.

LOCAL SERVICES

Luggage Storage: At the far end of the train station, toward the bus depot. €4 for 1st 5hr., €0.60 per hr. 6-12hr., €0.20 per hr. thereafter; Max. 5-day. Open daily 6am-midnight. Cash only.

Lost Property: Ufficio Oggetti Rinvenuti (☎055 23 52 190), next to the baggage deposit in train station. **Lost and Found,** V. Circondaria 19 (☎055 32 839 42/43).

English-Language Bookstores: ◪**Paperback Exchange,** V. delle Oche 4r (☎055 24 78 154; www.papex.it). Offers store credit for used books. Special section features novels about Brits and Americans in Italy. Free Wi-Fi for customers. Open M-F 9am-7:30pm, Sa 10am-7:30pm. Closed 2 weeks in mid-Aug. AmEx/MC/V. **BM Bookstore,** Borgo Ognissanti 4r (☎055 29 45 75; bmbookshop@dada.it). Open Mar.-Oct. M-Sa 9:30am-7:30pm, Su afternoons; Nov.-Feb. M-Sa 9:30am-7:30pm. AmEx/MC/V.

Box Office: V. Alamanni 39r (☎055 21 08 04; www.boxol.it). Sells tickets for performances in Florence and Fiesole, including rock concerts. Online and phone reservations only with credit cards (AmEx/MC/V). Open Mar.-Nov. M-F 10am-7:30pm, Sa 10am-1pm; Nov.-Feb. M 3:30-7:30pm, Tu-Sa 10am-7:30pm. Pick up a listing of events in any tourist office or buy the city's entertainment monthly, *Firenze Spettacolo* (€2).

Laundromats: Wash and Dry Lavarapido, V. dei Servi 105r, 2 blocks from the *duomo.* **Branches:** V. della Scala 52-54r, V. del Sole 29r, and V. Ghibellina 143r. Self-service wash and dry €7. Detergent €1. Open daily 8am-8pm. **Onda Blu,** V. degli Alfani 24r. Self-service wash and dry €7. Detergent €1. Use exact change. Open daily 8am-10pm.

EMERGENCY AND COMMUNICATIONS

Police: Central Office (Questura), V. Zara 2 (☎055 49 771 or 49 77 602). **Tourist Police: Ufficio Stranieri,** V. Zara 2 (☎055 49 771). For visa or work-permit problems. Open M-F 9:30am-1pm. To report lost or stolen items, go around the corner to **Ufficio Denunce,** V. Duca d'Aosta 3 (☎055 49 771). Open M-Sa 8am-8pm.

Pharmacies: Farmacia Comunale (☎055 28 94 35), by track #16 at the train station. **Molteni,** V. dei Calzaiuoli 7r (☎055 28 94 90). Both open 24hr. AmEx/MC/V. **Tourist Medical Service,** V. Lorenzo il Magnifico 59 (☎055 47 54 11). English-speaking doctors on call 24hr. Office visits €50; daytime house calls €70, night €85.

Internet Access: Internet Train, V. Guelfa 54/56r. 15 locations in the city. €4.30 per hr., students €3.20 per hr. Most open M-F 9am-midnight, Sa 10am-8pm, Su noon-9pm. AmEx/MC/V.

Post Office: (☎055 27 36 480), on V. Pellicceria, off P. della Repubblica. Open M-Sa 8:15am-7pm. **Postal Code:** 50100.

⌐ ACCOMMODATIONS

Because of the constant stream of tourists, it is best to reserve a room at least 10 days ahead, especially for visits in the summer or during Easter. Most *pensioni* (boarding houses) prefer reservations in writing with at least one night's deposit; others simply ask for a phone confirmation. To avoid unlisted service fees, don't book reservations over the Internet. The best prices are almost always obtained directly from hotel owners, and haggling works at smaller establishments. Florence has so many budget accommodations that it's usually possible to find a room without a reservation, but last-minute options are often of a lower quality. Hotel owners are typically willing to suggest alternatives if their establishments are full, so don't hesitate to ask. Complaints should be lodged with the **Tourist Rights Protection Desk**, V. Cavour 1r (☎055 29 08 32/33; open M-Sa 8:30am-6:30pm, Su 8:30am-1:30pm.) or the **Servizio Turismo**, V. Alessandro Manzoni 16 (☎055 23 320; uff.turismo@provincia.fi.it. Open M-F 9am-1pm). The city strictly regulates hotel prices, so proprietors must charge within the approved range for their category and must also post these rates in a place visible to guests. For **long-term housing** in Florence, check bulletin boards; classified ads in *La Pulce*, published three times weekly (€2), or *Grillo Fiorentino*, a free monthly paper. Reasonable prices range €200-600 per month.

HOSTELS

Ostello Archi Rossi, V. Faenza 94r (☎055 29 08 04; www.hostelarchirossi.com), 2 blocks from the train station. A legacy of a hostel where the walls aren't covered in floor-to-ceiling frescoes but with the signatures and wise words of past visitors. Convenient location. Ceramic tiles and brick archways complement a welcoming courtyard and dining/TV room. Wheelchair-accessible. Breakfast included; dinner €5-6. Laundry €6. Free Internet access. Luggage storage available. Room lockout 11am-2:30pm; no hostel lockout. Curfew 2am. Reserve online a week ahead, especially in summer. 9-bed dorms €22; 6-bed dorms €24; 4-bed dorms €26; singles €35. MC/V. ❷

Istituto Gould, V. dei Serragli 49 (☎055 21 25 76; www.istitutogould.it), in Oltrarno. Take bus #36 or 37 from the station to the 2nd stop across the river. The building is not well marked; look for the signs of the larger Istituto Gould complex, then buzz yourself into the courtyard. Run by a Protestant church with profits supporting local charities. 97 beds, great common spaces, and a large courtyard create a truly comfortable atmosphere. Reception M-F 8:45am-1pm and 3-7:30pm, Sa 9am-1:30pm and 2:30-6pm. 4-bed dorms €16-23; singles €36-43; doubles €52-62. MC/V. ❷

Ostello della Gioventù Europa Villa Camerata (HI), V. Augusto Righi 2-4 (☎055 60 14 51; fax 61 03 00; firenze@ostellionline.it). Take bus #17a/b outside train station (near track #5), or from P. dell'Unità; ask for Salviatino stop. Walk 10min. up driveway. Despite its large size, plenty of opportunities for private relaxation exist in this beautiful but remote villa. Bar. TV with English-language movies M-Su at 9pm. Breakfast included; dinner €10. Laundry €5.20. Max. 3-night stay. Reception 7am-12:30pm and 1pm-midnight. Lockout 10am-2pm. Strict midnight curfew. 4-bed dorms €20-22; 3-bed dorms €23-25; 2-bed dorms €30-32.50. HI-members discount €3.50. MC/V. ❷

Ostello Santa Monaca, V. S. Monaca 6 (☎055 26 83 38; fax 28 01 85). Follow directions to Istituto Gould, but turn right on V. S. Monaca. 114 beds stacked in high-ceilinged rooms. Kitchen facilities. Breakfast €3.50; lunch or dinner €10.50. Hot water for showers 7-9am and 2-11pm. Laundry €7 per 5kg. Internet access €3 per hr. Max. 7-night stay. Reception daily 6am-1pm and 2pm-1am. June-Sept. check-in 9am. Lockout 10am-2pm. Curfew 2am. 16- to 22-bed dorms €17; 10-bed dorms €18; 8-bed dorms €18; 4-bed dorms €19. AmEx/MC/V. ❶

Pensionato Pio X, V. dei Serragli 106 (☎055 22 50 44; www.hostelpiox.it), just beyond Istituto Gould, in the courtyard on the right. Bright rooms in a quiet area, with 3-6 beds per room. Co-ed shared bath. Internet cafe and kitchen facilities available. Check-out 9am. Curfew 1am. Dorms €17. Cash only. ❶

HOTELS

PIAZZA SANTA MARIA NOVELLA AND ENVIRONS

Budget accommodations in these two areas provide convenient access to the *duomo* and *centro storico*—for better or worse.

Hotel Abaco, V. dei Banchi 1 (☎055 23 81 919; www.abaco-hotel.it). Convenient location, helpful staff, and extravagant rooms. Each room is a masterpiece named after a Renaissance great. All rooms have phone and TV. Breakfast and A/C €5 each or free when bill is paid in cash. Laundry €7. Wi-Fi available. Valet parking €24 per day. Doubles €65-75, with bath €75-90; triples €110; quads €135. Let's Go discount 10% Nov.-Mar. except holidays. Accepts traveler's checks. MC/V. ❺

Albergo Margaret, V. della Scala 25 (☎055 21 01 38; www.dormireintoscana.it/margaret). Enthusiastic English-speaking staff runs large rooms with terrace, TV, A/C, and ivory decor. Curfew midnight. June-Aug. singles €60; doubles €70, with full bath €90. Discounts Sept.-May and for longer stays. Cash only. ❹

Soggiorno Luna Rossa, V. Nazionale 7, 3rd fl. (☎055 23 02 185). Wake up to the morning sun streaming through the spectacular stained glass windows of this central Florence establishment. Budget-conscious travelers sleep in small rooms, and share even smaller baths, but comforts like TV, fans, and Internet are available. Breakfast included. Single bed €25; singles €38; doubles €88; triples €100; quads €140. Cash only. ❷

Hotel Elite, V. della Scala 12 (☎055 21 53 95; fax 21 38 32). Exit train station right on V. degli Orti Oricellari, which leads to V. della Scala; turn left. Family owners make reservations for guests at the Uffizi and other sights. Wooden stairs lead to 10 well-maintained rooms, all with TV, phone, and A/C. Quieter rooms in the back have enormous bathrooms. Reception is sporadic, so arrange arrival time beforehand. Singles with shower €50, with bath €70; doubles €75/90; triples €110; quads €130. MC/V. ❹

Hotel Giappone, V. dei Banchi 1, 3rd floor (☎055 21 00 90; www.hotelgiappone.com). Classic hotel with huge rooms equipped with TV and A/C. Small shared baths. Internet available. Singles €55, with bath €75; doubles €60/90; triples €90/110. MC/V. ❹

OLD CITY (NEAR THE DUOMO)

Closest to Florence's major monuments, this area is full of expensive, upscale accommodations. Follow V. de' Panzani from the train station, and turn left on V. dei Cerretani to reach the *duomo*.

▨ **Locanda Orchidea,** Borgo degli Albizi 11 (☎055 24 80 346; www.hotelorchideaflorence.it). Turn left off V. Proconsolo from the *duomo*. Dante's wife was born in this 12th-century *palazzo*. Rooms have marble floors and famous Renaissance prints. English spoken. Clean shared baths. Singles €55; doubles €75; triples with shower €100; quad €120. Prices drop €20-35 in low season. Cash only. ❹

▨ **Hotel Il Perseo,** V. dei Cerretani 1 (☎055 21 25 04; www.hotelperseo.com). Exit the train station and take V. de' Panzani, which becomes V. dei Cerretani. Aussie-Italian couple and English-speaking staff welcome travelers to a recently renovated 3-star hotel with 20 sophisticated rooms and large, gleaming baths. All have fans, satellite TV, and Wi-Fi; some have views of the *duomo*. Intimate bar and TV lounge decorated with proprietor's art. Breakfast included. Valet parking €24 per day. Singles €110; doubles €155; triples €180; quads €210; suite €250. AmEx/MC/V for min. 2-night stay. ❺

Relais Cavalcanti, V. Pellicceria 2 (☎055 21 09 62), steps from P. della Repubblica. Mother-daughter owners welcome guests to gold-trimmed rooms with antique wardrobes and lace curtains. Look for the cookie jar and English-language magazines in the shared kitchen. Rooms have bath, A/C, phone, TV, and fridge. Free luggage storage. Singles €70-100; doubles €90-125; triples €120-155. Let's Go discount 10%. MC/V. ❺

Tourist House Il Porcellino, P. del Mercato Nuovo 4 (☎055 28 26 86; www.hotelporcellino.com). In one of Florence's oldest buildings. Brick arches poke out from white walls in rooms, each with wrought-iron bed, handpainted furniture, full bath, TV, and phone. Rooms can be noisy; request one at the back. Pay for portion of stay in advance. Reservations recommended in summer. Singles €59-90; doubles €79-135. AmEx/MC/V. ❺

VIA NAZIONALE AND ENVIRONS

From P. della Stazione, V. Nazionale leads to budget hotels that are a short walk from both the *duomo* and the train station. The buildings on V. Nazionale, V. Faenza, V. Fiume, and V. Guelfa are filled with inexpensive establishments, but rooms facing the street may be noisy due to throngs of pedestrians. Use caution walking alone in this area at night.

▨ **Katti House/Soggiorno Annamaria,** V. Faenza 21 (☎055 21 34 10; www.kattihouse.com). From the train station, take V. Nazionale for 1 block, and turn right on V. Faenza. Knowledgable owners welcome guests to 5 large rooms furnished with 400-year-old antiques. Well-maintained private and shared baths. Wi-Fi, A/C, fridge, and TV available. The adjacent apartment, **Soggiorno Annamaria,** V. Faenza 24, can be rented by room or in entirety. Singles €40-50; doubles €50-60; triples €60-75. Prices drop significantly Nov.-Mar. Call directly for best rates. Cash only. ❺

Hotel Nazionale, V. Nazionale 22 (☎055 23 82 203; www.nazionalehotel.it). From train station, turn left on V. Nazionale. Sunny, spacious rooms overlook a busy street. Comfortable beds. A/C. Breakfast €6. Singles €45-60, with bath €55-75; doubles €79-99/85-115; triples €109-129/115-139. Extra bed €25. MC/V. ❺

Via Faenza 56. These 4 *pensioni* under the same roof, all with the same amenities, are among the best deals in the area. From V. Nazionale, turn left on V. Faenza.

Pensione Azzi (☎055 21 38 06; www.hotelazzi.com), enter on ground fl. next door to main building. Presents itself as an artists' inn with stylish prints on the walls, but all travelers will appreciate the accommodating management, tasteful furniture, relaxing terrace, and large rooms with bath and Internet. Wheelchair-accessible. Breakfast included. Dorms 25-35. Singles €50-100; doubles €80-130; triples €105-165. Extra bed €25. AmEx/MC/V. ❹

Hotel Anna's (☎055 23 02 714; www.hotelannas.com), 2nd fl. The only 2-star option in the main building features 7 large, generic rooms with private bath, safes, satellite TV, minibar, phone, and A/C. Breakfast €5. Singles €40-60; doubles €80-130. Extra bed €20. AmEx/MC/V. ❹

Locanda Paola (☎055 21 36 82), 3rd fl. 28 beds in 7 bright, minimalist rooms with plush armchairs. Breakfast and Internet access included. Curfew 2am. Dorms €33. MC/V. ❸

Albergo Armonia (☎055 21 11 46), 1st fl. American film posters and antique, black and white photos adorn 7 basic rooms with high ceilings and wooden beds. Shared baths. Internet access available. Min. 2-night stay. Singles €42; doubles €50-60; triples €75; quads €100. Extra bed €25. Prices drop in winter. Cash only. ❹

Via Faenza 69. 2 comfortable, no-frills accommodations under the same roof:

Locanda Giovanna (☎/fax 055 23 81 353; www.albergogiovanna.it), top floor. 7 small, well-kept rooms, some with garden views. Cross your fingers when you ring the bell; there is no designated reception time, but the attentive owner is usually on-site. Singles €35, with bath €40; doubles €60/70; triples €60/85. Prices drop about €5 in winter. Cash only. ❸

Hotel Nella/Pina (☎055 26 54 346), 1st and 2nd fl. Basic, functional rooms with wood paneling and clean shared bath. Nella rooms have A/C, phone, and satellite TV. Singles €47-55, with bath €60; doubles €65-85. Extra bed €20. Let's Go discount 10%. AmEx/MC/V. ❹

NEAR PIAZZA SAN MARCO AND THE UNIVERSITY

This area is quieter than its proximity to the *centro* and university would suggest. All accommodations listed are within a few blocks of the beautiful Chiesa di San Marco. To reach this neighborhood from the train station, turn left on V. Nazionale and right on V. Guelfa, which intersects V. S. Gallo and V. Cavour.

▨ **Albergo Sampaoli,** V. S. Gallo 14 (☎055 28 48 34; www.hotelsampaoli.it). Well-lit rooms with Wi-Fi, DVDs, and fans. Large common room. Fridge available on each floor. 24hr. reception. Singles €25-48, with bath €35-74; doubles €44-55/45-84; triples €75-120; quads €90-140. Extra bed €25. 5% discount with reservation. MC/V. ❷

Hotel Tina, V. S. Gallo 31 (☎055 48 35 19; www.hoteltina.it). Family-run *pensione* with pleasant blue color scheme welcomes guests into large carpeted rooms with comfortable plush furniture, A/C, and phones. Doubles with shower €45-75; with bath €70-80; triples €65-90; quads €80-120. Extra bed €25. MC/V. ❹

IN THE OLTRARNO

Across the Arno and only 10min. from the *duomo*, this area offers a respite from the busy *centro*. Arguably the nicest part of Florence, considering its proximity to historic sites like the Chiesa di San Spirito and natural attractions like the Boboli gardens, all frequented by the trendy student population.

▨ **Hotel La Scaletta,** V. Guicciardini 13 (☎055 28 30 28; www.hotellascaletta.it). Cross the Ponte Vecchio and continue on V. Guicciardini. 2-star hotel. Gorgeous rooms have antique furnishings, A/C, hardwood floors, and bath. Rooftop terrace with spectacular view of Boboli Gardens. Breakfast included. Singles €60-110; doubles €75-150; triples €90-170; quads €110-190. *Let's Go* discount €10 with cash payment. MC/V. ❹

CAMPING

Campeggio Michelangelo, V. Michelangelo 80 (☎055 68 11 977; www.ecvacanze.it), beyond Ple. Michelangelo. Take bus #13 from the station (15min., last bus 11:25pm). Chain campsite is family-geared and very crowded, but offers a distant vista of the city and a shaded olive grove. Market and bar available. Internet access €7.50 per hr. Linen

TUSCANY

€2. Towels €1. Laundry €7. Reception daily 7am-11pm. Apr.-Nov. tent rental €15.50. €9-11 per person, €12 per tent includes one vehicle. MC/V over €100. ❶

Camping Camerata, Vle. Augusto Righi 2/4 (☎055 60 14 51; fax 055 61 03 00). Located next to Villa Camerata. Follow directions above. Surrounded by natural beauty on the Fiesole hill, this is the only campsite open throughout the year in Florence. €6 per person; €12 per tent. Space can be made available for campers or caravans. ❶

◖ FOOD

Florentine cuisine developed from the peasant fare of the surrounding countryside. Characterized by saltless bread and rustic dishes prepared with fresh ingredients and simple recipes, Tuscan food ranks among Italy's best. White beans and olive oil are two staple ingredients. A famous specialty is *bruschetta*, toasted bread doused with olive oil and garlic, usually topped with tomatoes and basil. For *primi*, Florentines favor the Tuscan classics *minestra di fagioli* (a white bean and garlic soup) and *ribollita* (hearty bean, bread, and black cabbage stew). Florence's classic *secondo* is *bistecca alla Fiorentina* (thick sirloin steak); locals order it *al sangue* (very rare; literally "bloody"), though it's also available *al punto* (medium) or *ben cotto* (well-done). The best local cheese is *pecorino*, made from sheep's milk. Other popular ingredients include shrimp and *cinghiale* (wild boar). A liter of house wine usually costs €3.50-6 in a trattoria, but stores sell cheap bottles (€2.50). Avoid ordering soda at restaurants; it often costs over €3 per can, though prices may not be marked on menus. The local dessert is *cantuccini di prato* (hard almond cookies with egg yolk) dipped in *vinsanto* (a rich dessert wine made from raisins).

Buy fresh produce at the **Mercato Centrale,** between V. Nazionale and S. Lorenzo. (Open June-Sept. M-Sa 7:30am-2pm; Oct.-May Sa 7am-2pm and 4-8pm.) For basics, head to the **STANDA,** V. Pietrapiana 1r. Turn right on V. del Proconsolo and the first left on Borgo degli Albizi. Continue through P. G. Salvemini; the supermarket is on the left. (Open M-Sa 8am-9pm, Su 9am-9pm. MC/V.) Beware of overpriced *alimentari* along V. Faenza. **Ruth's Kosher Vegetarian,** V. Luigi Carlo Farini 2/A, serves kosher fare on the second floor of the building to the right of the synagogue. (☎055 24 80 888; kosherruth@katamail. com. Primi €7. Secondi €9-18. Open M-F and Su 12:30-2:30pm and 7:30-10:30pm. AmEx/MC/V.) Several health-food markets cater to vegetarians, two of which draw inspiration from the American book **Sugar Blues.** One is at V. XXVII Aprile 46r/48r, 5min. from the *duomo*. (☎055 48 36 66. Open M-Sa 9am-1:30pm and 5-7:30pm, Su 9am-1:30pm. Closed 1 week in Aug. V.) The other, renamed **Ha-Tha Maya,** is next to the Istituto Gould, in the Oltrarno at V. dei Serragli 57r. (☎055 26 83 78. Open Sept.-July daily 8am-1:30pm and 4-7:30pm; Aug. M-F and Su 8am-1:30pm and 4-7:30pm, Sa 8am-1:30pm. MC/V.)

OLD CITY

Osteria de' Benci, V. de' Benci 13r (☎055 23 44 923), on the corner of V. dei Neri. Owners serve small but savory portions of Tuscan classics like *carpaccio* (thinly sliced raw beef; €15) at this local hot spot. Primi €9. Secondi €10-15. Cover €3.30. Open M-Sa 1-2:45pm and 7:30-11:45pm. Reservations recommended. AmEx/MC/V. ❹

Acqua al 2, V. della Vigna Vecchia 40r (☎055 28 41 70), behind the Bargello. Its location and reputation for unique dishes beckon travelers and locals alike to this closet-sized restaurant. Salads from €7.50. Primi €8-12. Secondi €10-22. Cover €1. Service 10%. Open daily 7pm-1am. Reservations strongly recommended. AmEx/MC/V. ❸

Trattoria Anita, V. del Parlascio 2r (☎055 21 86 98), behind Palazzo Vecchio. American tourists pile into this casual Tuscan restaurant for authentic cuisine at reasonable prices. Primi €5.50-7. Secondi €7-14. Generous lunch *menù* €7. Cover €1. Open M-Sa noon-2:30pm and 7-10pm. AmEx/MC/V. ❷

Danny Rock, V. de' Pandolfini 13r (☎055 23 40 307), 3 blocks northwest of the Bargello. Casual pizzeria with outdoor patio and large dining room favored by local students; turns into a hot night spot after hours. Check the seasonal specials, as they often feature toppings from different Italian regions. Pizza from €5. Cover €2. Open M-Th 12:15-3pm and 7:30pm-1am, F 12:15-3pm and 7:30pm-1:30am, Sa 7:30pm-2am, Su noon-3pm and 7:15pm-1am. Closed July-Aug. Su mornings. MC/V. ❷

Osteria dell'Olio, P. dell'Olio 10r (☎055 21 14 66; www.osteriadellolio.com). 300 years ago P. dell'Olio was home to an open air market for olive oil vendors. Today, this upscale *osteria* bottles house oil and uses only quality local products in its original dishes, like *gnocchi alle barbine rosse* (red gnocchi made with beets and simmered in a gorgonzola cheese and pear sauce; €16). Primi €15-26. Secondi €28-30. 30% student discount. Open daily noon-3:30pm and 7pm-midnight. ❺

SANTA MARIA NOVELLA AND ENVIRONS

▨ **Trattoria Contadino,** V. Palazzuolo 71r (☎055 23 82 673). Casual, homestyle meals. Dining room has black-and-white decor and a relaxed atmosphere. You're sure to leave feeling stuffed, as the only option is a multi-course *menù* that includes primo, secondo, bread, and house wine (€10). Open M-F noon-9:40pm. AmEx/MC/V. ❷

Il Latini, V. dei Palchetti 6r (☎055 21 09 16; www.illatini.com). Mostly popular with an older crowd; young people are greeted with a warning, "no pizza." Classic dimly lit restaurant with attentive staff. Primi €5-10. Secondi €14-22. Open Tu-Su 12:30-2:30pm and 7:30-10:30pm. Reservations recommended. AmEx/MC/V. ❸

Tre Merli, V. del Moro 11r (☎055 28 70 62). Another entrance on V. de' Fossi 12r. Sumptuous meals served in an eclectic dining room close to the river. *Let's Go* readers enjoy a 10% discount. *Menù* includes primo, secondo, wine, and water (€15). Primi €6.50-12. Secondi €12-19. Cover €2. Open daily 11am-10:30pm. AmEx/MC/V. ❸

50 Rosso, V. Panzani 50r (☎055 28 35 85). Gracious owners Massimiliano and Francesco recently opened this *birreria*/snack bar and have already changed the way food *"porta via"* (to go) is made. Choose from a wide selection of pizza (€2) and sandwiches (€2-2.50) or build your own at no extra charge. Open daily 7:30am-midnight. ❶

THE STATION AND UNIVERSITY QUARTER

▨ **Mamma Toscana,** V. S. Antonino 34r (☎055 28 22 496). Preparing some of the best food in Florence, award-winning head chef, Michelangelo, modestly smiles and advises, *"Mangia, mangia!"* Enjoy specialties like *risotto Michelangelo* (€6), buttery rice with tender shrimp surrounded by mussels. Primi €4-8. Secondi €6-10. Cover 10%. Open M and W-Su noon-3:30pm and 6-10:30pm, Tu 6-10:30pm. AmEx/MC/V. ❷

Trattoria Zà-Zà, P. del Mercato Centrale 26r (☎055 21 54 11). Tightly packed outdoor patio is decent enough for a summer dinner at this 30-year-old establishment, but comparable prices with better views can be found near the *duomo*. Specializes in traditional Tuscan grilled meats. Primi €8-11. Secondi €10-22. Cover €2. Open daily 11am-11pm. Reservations recommended. AmEx/MC/V. ❷

Trattoria Mario, V. Rosina 2r, around the corner from P. del Mercato Centrale. Crowded tables and outgoing staff help you to get acquainted with fellow diners. Great pasta and enthusiastic following of Florentines and foreigners. Primi €3.10-6. Secondi €3.10-11. Cover €0.50. Open M-Sa noon-3:30pm. Closed most of Aug. Cash only. ❶

Ristorante Il Vegetariano, V. delle Ruote 30r (☎055 47 50 30), off V. S. Gallo. True to its name, this self-service restaurant is a vegetarian's dream. Enjoy filling dishes in the peaceful bamboo garden. Salads €4-5. Primi from €5. Secondi from €6. Open Sept.-July Tu-F 12:30-3pm and 7:30pm-midnight, Sa-Su 7:30pm-midnight. Cash only. ❷

THE OLTRARNO

all'Antico Ristoro Di' Cambi, V. S. Onofrio 1r (☎055 21 71 34; www.anticoristorodi-cambi.it). Prosciutto hangs from the beautifully restored 5th-century ceilings. Choose among over 100 types of wine (€10-300 per bottle). Knowledgeable waitstaff can advise on the best selection for your meal. Primi €6-8. Secondi €7-18. Cover €1. Open M-Sa noon-10:30pm. Closed 2 weeks in mid-Aug. AmEx/MC/V. ❷

Il Borgo Antico, P. S. Spirito 6r (☎055 21 04 37). Trendy spot frequented by students. Pastas and fantastic salads (€7) with fresh ingredients like shrimp, avocado, and mozzarella. Perfect for a late dinner. Pizza €7. Primi €7. Secondi €13-18. Cover €2. Open daily noon-midnight. Reservations recommended. AmEx/MC/V. ❹

La Mangiatoia, P. S. Felice 8r (☎055 22 40 60). Cross Ponte Vecchio, continue on V. Guicciardini, and pass Palazzo Pitti. Grab a table in the back dining room, or sit at the stone counter to watch the cooks baking pizza in a brick oven. Satisfying pasta and quality local fare. Extensive takeout menu. Pizza €5-8.50. Primi €4-6. Secondi €5-9. Cover €1.50. Open Tu-Su 11am-3pm and 6:30-10pm. AmEx/MC/V. ❷

Dante, P. Nazario Sauro 12r (☎055 21 92 19; fax 055 27 41 471; www.trattoria-dante.com). Artful plate settings and courteous service await in this hidden local favorite. Primi €7-18. Secondi €16-28. Open M-Tu and Th-Su noon-3pm and 7-10:30pm MC/V. ❹

GELATERIE AND PASTICCERIE

Lorenzo il Magnifico, V. Sant'Antonino 37r (☎055 28 78 12). Choose from 60 home-made flavors ranging from fig sorbet to dark chili pepper chocolate. Although the *gelateria* is new, owners have extensive experience in the food industry and are already gaining fame for the authenticity and quality of their gelati, said to be Italy's best. Undoubtedly the best in Florence. Cups €1.50-4. Open daily noon-11pm. ❷

Grom, V. del Campanile (☎055 21 61 58), off P. del Duomo. The kind of gelato you'll be talking about in 50 years. As fresh as it gets; sublimely balanced texture. Large store is standing-room only and flooded with tourists and locals. Cups €2-5. Open daily Apr.-Sept. 10:30am-midnight; Oct.-Mar. 10:30am-11pm. ❶

Hemingway, P. Piatellina 9 (☎055 28 47 87; www.hemingway.fi.it). Delightful selection of chocolate drinks and sweets. Free Wi-Fi weekdays until 9pm. Coffee €3.50-6.50. Mixed drinks €7. Chocolate tasting €8. Teas, crepes, milkshakes, and other sweets available. Open M-Th 4:30pm-1am, F-Sa 4:30pm-2am, Su 3.30pm-1am. MC/V. ❶

Gelateria dei Neri, V. dei Neri 20-22r (☎055 21 00 34). Watch as dozens of delicious flavors are mixed before your eyes. *Crema Giotto* (a blend of coconut, almond, and hazelnut) is incredible. Gelato from €1.50. *Granita* from €1.50. Cash only. ❶

Vivoli, V. Isole delle Stinche 7r (☎055 29 23 34), behind the Bargello. The household name of Florentine *gelaterie*. Pint-sized interior and even smaller portions, but specialties like *crema caffè* (a shot of espresso in a creamy gelato-lined mug; €3.50) are like nothing you've tasted before. Pay first and order with receipt. Cups from €1.80. Open Tu-Sa 7:30am-1am, Su 9:30am-1am. AmEx/MC/V. ❶

Perché No!, V. dei Tavolini 19r (☎055 23 98 969). Light flavors like green tea. Cups from €2. Open M and W-Su in summer 10am-1am; in winter 10am-8pm. Cash only. ❶

Carabè, V. Ricasoli 60r and P. S. Jacopino 9r (☎055 28 94 76; www.gelatocarabe.com). Enjoy pistachio, *nocciola,* and the unusual *susine* (plum). 3rd-generation owners Antonio and Loredana get the lemons for their *gelato di limone* from Sicily every week. The *granita* (from €2.50) is outstanding. Cups from €2. Open daily May-Sept. 9am-midnight; Oct. and Mar.-Apr. noon-midnight. Cash only. ❶

La Loggia degli Albizi, Borgo degli Albizi 39r (☎055 24 79 574). A hidden treasure, this bakery offers an escape from tourist throngs. Pastries from €0.80. Coffee from €0.80, served at table €1.50. Open M-Sa 7am-8pm. ❶

AVOID THE ARTIFICIAL. Gelato is said to have been invented in Florence centuries ago by the Buontalenti family; you'll want to make sure you get the most authentic kind. Before shelling out €1.50 for a *piccolo cono* (small cone), assess the establishment's quality by looking at the banana flavor: if it's bright yellow, it's from a mix—keep walking. If it's slightly gray, real bananas were used. Likewise, steer clear of bright yellow lemon gelato; fresh lemons make white-colored gelato. Metal bins also signify homemade gelato, whereas plastic tubs indicate mass production.

ENOTECHE (WINE BARS)

Enoteca Alessi, V. delle Oche 27/29r (☎055 21 49 66; fax 23 96 987), 1 block from the *duomo*. Among Florence's finest, stocking over 1000 wines in the cavernous interior. Doubles as a chocolate and candy store. Offers nibbles between sips. Cheese and meat platters €11-34. Wine €4.50-10 per glass. Open M-F 11am-7pm. AmEx/MC/V. ❷

Enoteca Fuori Porta, V. del Monte alle Croci 10r (☎055 23 42 483; www.fuoriporta.it), in the shadows of San Miniato. This more casual *enoteca* is free of tourists but crowded with young Italians. Reasonable meals of traditional Tuscan pasta, with an extensive *bruschette* (€1-2.50) and *crostoni* (€4.50-7.50) menu. On the way down from Ple. Michelangelo, it's a great alternative to the expensive hilltop cafes. Cover €1.50. Open Sept.-July daily noon-4pm and 7-10pm; Aug. M-Sa noon-4pm and 7-10pm. MC/V. ❷

◙ SIGHTS

Considering the *duomo* views, the perfection of San Spirito's nave, and the overwhelming array of art in the Uffizi Gallery, it's hard to take a wrong turn in Florence. For comprehensive listings on museum openings, check out www.firenzeturismo.it. To avoid interminable waits for Florence's most renowned attractions, make phone reservations by calling **Firenze Musei.** (☎055 29 48 83; www.firenzemusei.it. Open M-F 8:30am-6:30pm, Sa 8:30am-12:30pm.)

PIAZZA DEL DUOMO AND ENVIRONS

▧**DUOMO (CATTEDRALE DI SANTA MARIA DEL FIORE).** In 1296 the city fathers commissioned Arnolfo di Cambio to erect a cathedral so magnificent that it would be "impossible to make it either better or more beautiful with the industry and power of man." Arnolfo succeeded, designing a massive nave with the confidence that by the time it was completed (1418), technology would have advanced enough to provide a solution to erect a dome. It was Filippo Brunelleschi, after studying Classical methods of sculpture, who devised the ingenious techniques needed to construct a dome large enough for the nave. For the *duomo*'s sublime crown, now known simply as **Brunelleschi's Dome,** the architect designed a revolutionary, double-shelled structure that incorporated self-supporting, interlocking bricks. During construction, Brunelleschi built kitchens, sleeping rooms, and lavatories between the two walls of the cupola so the masons would never have to descend. The **Museo dell'Opera del Duomo** (see opposite page) chronicles Brunelleschi's engineering feats in an in-depth exhibit. A 16th-century Medici rebuilding campaign removed the *duomo*'s incomplete Gothic-Renaissance facade. The walls remained naked until 1871, when Florentine architect Emilio de Fabris won the commission to create a facade in the Neo-Gothic style. Especially when viewed from the southern side, the patterned green-white-and-red marble walls are impressively grand.

Today, the *duomo* claims the world's third-longest nave, after St. Peter's in Rome and St. Paul's in London. It rises 100m into the air, making it as high as the surrounding Tuscan hills and visible from nearly every corner of the city. Though ornately decorated on the outside, the church's interior is rather chilly and stark; unadorned dark stone was believed to encourage humble devotion. One notable exception to this sober style is the extravagant frescoes on the dome's ceiling, where visions of the apocalypse glare down at visitors in a stunning display of color and light. Notice, too, Paolo Uccello's celebrated monument to the mercenary captain Sir John Hawkwood on the cathedral's left wall and his *trompe l'oeil* clock on the back wall. This 24hr. timepiece runs backward, starting its cycle at sunset, when the *Ave Maria* is traditionally sung. *(Duomo open M-W and F 10am-5pm, Th 10am-4pm, Sa 10am-4:45pm, Su 1:30-4:45pm; 1st Sa of the month 10am-3:30pm. Shortest wait at 10am and just before opening. Mass daily 7am, 12:30, and 5-7pm. Free. Ask inside the entrance to the left about free guided tours in English.)* Climb the 463 steps inside the dome to Michelangelo's lantern for an expansive view of the city from the external gallery. Halfway up, visitors can enjoy a view of the dome's frescoed interior from just inches away. *(Entrance on southern side of the duomo. ☎ 055 23 02 885. Open M-F 8:30am-7pm, Sa 8:30am-5:40pm. €6.)*

 YOU GOT SCHOOLED. Sadly, capital letters at most museums in Florence remind visitors that there are NO STUDENT DISCOUNTS. The price of a ticket should not keep anyone from seeing the best Renaissance art collections in the world. Choose carefully and plan to spend a few hours at each landmark. Also since most labels are in Italian, consider investing in cheap English-language audio tours, as their descriptions provide a valuable context for understanding the works. In the summer, ask at the tourist office about **Sere al Museo,** evenings when certain museums are free from 7-10pm.

BATTISTERO. Though built between the fifth and ninth centuries, the octagonal *battistero* was believed in Dante's time to have been a Roman temple. The building's exterior has the same green- and white-marble patterning as the *duomo*, and the interior contains magnificent 13th-century, Byzantine-style mosaics. Dante was christened here, and later gained inspiration for his *Inferno* from the murals of damnation. Florentine artists competed fiercely for the commission to create the famous **bronze doors,** which depict scenes from the Bible in exquisite detail. In 1330 the winner, Andrea Pisano, left Pisa to cast the first set of doors, which now guard the southern entrance (facing the river). In 1401 the cloth guild announced a competition to choose an artist for the remaining two sets. Two young artists, Brunelleschi and Ghiberti, were asked to work in partnership to enter the competition, but the uncompromising Brunelleschi left in an arrogant huff, allowing Ghiberti to complete the project alone. Their separate entries into the competition are displayed side by side in the **Bargello** (p. 446). Ghiberti's project, completed in 1425, was so admired that he immediately received the commission to forge the final set of doors. The **◪Gates of Paradise,** as Michelangelo reportedly called them, are nothing like Pisano's earlier portals. Originally intended for the northern side, they so impressed the

Florentines that they were moved to their current eastern position facing the *duomo*. Best admired in the morning or late evening after the tourist crowds have thinned, the doors are truly a masterpiece, each panel a work of art itself. Even Leonardo da Vinci assumed a role in the structure's execution, finishing the terra-cotta models. *(Opposite the duomo. ☎ 055 23 02 885. Open M-Sa noon-7pm, Su and 1st Sa of the month 8:30am-2pm. Mass M-F 10:30 and 11:30am. €3. Audio tour €2.)*

CAMPANILE. Also called "Giotto's Tower," the 82m bell tower next to the *duomo* has a marble exterior that matches neighboring monuments. Three great Renaissance minds contributed to its construction: Giotto drew the design and laid the foundation in 1334, Andrea Pisano added two stories, and Francesco Talenti completed construction in 1359. The 414 steps to the top offer stunning views of the *duomo*, baptistry, and city. The best time to make the trek is in the early morning, to avoid the smog. *(☎ 055 23 02 885. Open Nov.-May daily 8:30am-6:50pm; June-Oct. M-Th and Su 8:30am-6:50pm, F-Sa 8:30am-10:20pm. €6.)*

ORSANMICHELE. Built in 1337 as a granary, Orsanmichele was converted into a church after a great fire convinced city officials to move grain operations outside the city. The loggia structure and ancient grain chutes are still visible from the outside. Secular and spiritual concerns mingle in the statues tucked into small niches of the facade. Works include Ghiberti's *St. Matthew* (1419-20) and a copy of *St. John the Baptist* (1414-16), Donatello's *St. George* (1416) and *St. Mark* (1411), and Giambologna's *St. Luke* (1405-10). Inside, a Gothic tabernacle designed by Andrea Orcagna encases Bernardo Daddi's miraculous *Madonna* (1347). The top floor occasionally hosts special exhibits. *(V. Arte della Lana, between the duomo and P. della Signoria. ☎ 055 28 49 44. Open Tu-Su 10am-5pm. Free.)*

MUSEO DELL'OPERA DEL DUOMO. Most of the *duomo*'s art resides in this less-crowded, modern museum, including a late *Pietà* by Michelangelo, up the first flight of stairs. He started working on it in his early 70s, and the soft curves and flowing lines of the marble and the limpness of Christ's body are said to reflect the artist's conception of his own mortality. Allegedly, Michelangelo severed the statue's left arm with a hammer in a fit of frustration. An over-eager apprentice touched up the work soon after, leaving lines visible on Mary Magdalene's head. Also in the collection are Donatello's wooden *St. Mary Magdalene* (1455), Donatello and Luca della Robbia's *cantorie* (choir balconies with bas-reliefs of cavorting children), and four frames from the baptistry's original Gates of Paradise. A huge wall displays all of the paintings submitted by architects in the 1870 competition for the *duomo*'s facade. *(P. del Duomo 9, behind the duomo. ☎ 055 23 02 885. Open M-Sa 9am-6:50pm, Su 9am-1:00pm. €6. Audio tour €4.)*

PIAZZA DELLA SIGNORIA AND ENVIRONS

From P. del Duomo, V. dei Calzaiuoli, one of the city's oldest streets, leads to P. della Signoria. Built by the Romans, V. dei Calzaiuoli now bustles with crowds, chic shops, street vendors, and *gelaterie*.

UFFIZI GALLERY. Giorgio Vasari designed this palace for Duke Cosimo in 1554 and called it the "Uffizi" because it housed the Medici's administrative offices (*uffizi*). An impressive walkway between the two branches of the building, full of street performers, human statues, and vendors hawking trinkets and prints, leads from P. della Signoria to the Arno River; the street is surrounded every morning by art-hungry tourists waiting to enter the museum. Beautiful statues overlook the walkway from niches in the columns; play spot-the-Renaissance-man and try to find da Vinci, Machiavelli, Petrarch, and Vespucci.

NO ART FOR YOU. To avoid disappointment inside the museum, keep in mind that a few rooms are usually closed each day and famous pieces often go on temporary loan, so not all works are always on display. A sign outside the ticket office lists the rooms that are closed for the day.

Before visiting the main gallery on the second floor, stop to see the **Cabinet of Drawings and Prints** on the first floor. This exhibit includes rare sketches by Botticelli, Leonardo, Raphael, and Michelangelo. Upstairs, in a U-shaped corridor, is a collection of Hellenistic and Roman marble statues. Arranged chronologically in rooms off the corridor, the collection promises a thorough education on the Florentine Renaissance, as well as a sampling of German and Venetian art. Framing the entrance to **Room 2** are three magnificent Madonnas by Renaissance forefathers Cimabue, Duccio di Buoninsegna, and Giotto. **Room 3** features art from 14th-century Siena, including works by the Lorenzetti brothers and Simone Martini's *Annunciation*. **Room 4** contains several works from Bernardo Daddi, including *Madonna with Child and Saints*. **Rooms 5** and **6** hold examples of International Gothic art, popular in European royal courts. Check out the rounded war-horses in the *The Battle of San Romano*, Paolo Uccello's noble but slightly jumbled effort to conquer the problem of perspective. **Room 7** houses two paintings by Fra Angelico (also called Beato Angelico) and a *Madonna and Child* (1426) by Masaccio. Domenico Veneziano's *Sacra Conversazione* (1445) is one of the first paintings of Mary surrounded by the saints. Piero della Francesca's double portrait of Duke Federico and his wife, Battista Sforza, stands out for its translucent color and honest detail. (A jousting accident gave the Duke's nose its unusual hooked shape.) **Room 8** has Filippo Lippi's *Madonna and Child with Two Angels* (1440). **Room 9** includes works by Botticelli and Pollaiolo.

Rooms 10-14 are a shrine to Botticelli—the resplendent *Primavera* (1478), *Pallas and the Centaur* (1482), *Birth of Venus* (1485), and *Madonna della Melagrana* (1487) glow from recent restorations. **Room 15** moves into the High Renaissance with Leonardo da Vinci's *Annunciation* (1480) and the remarkable, unfinished *Adoration of the Magi* (1481). **Room 18**, the tribune designed by Buontalenti to hold the Medici treasures, has a mother-of-pearl dome and a collection of portraits, most notably Bronzino's *Bia dei Medici* (1542), Vasari's *Lorenzo il Magnifico* (1485), and del Sarto's *Woman with the Petrarchino* (1528). Also note Rosso Fiorentino's oft-duplicated *Musician Angel* (1515). **Room 19** features Piero della Francesca's pupils, Perugino and Signorelli. **Rooms 20** and **22** detour into Northern European art. Note the contrast between Albrecht Dürer's lifelike *Adam and Eve* (1504) and Lucas Cranach's haunting, more surreal treatment of the same subject. Bellini's *Sacred Allegory* (1490) and Mantegna's *Adoration of the Magi* (1495) highlight **Room 23**.

Room 25 showcases Florentine works, including Michelangelo's only oil painting in Florence, *Doni Tondo* (1503). Raphael's *Madonna of the Goldfinch* (1505) and Andrea del Sarto's *Madonna of the Harpies* (1517) rest in **Room 26**. **Room 27** holds the incredible art of Jacopo Pontormo, including the moving *Portrait of a Musician* (1518). **Room 28** displays Titian's sensual *Venus of Urbino* (1538). Parmigianino's Mannerist-style, eerily lovely, and regal *Madonna of the Long Neck* (1534), now in **Room 29**, was discovered unfinished in the artist's studio following his death. Works by Paolo Veronese and Tintoretto dominate **Rooms 31** and **32. Room 33**, in fact a corridor, holds Vasari's *Vulcan's Forge* (1545). **Room 34** is dedicated to Paolo Veronese, and **Room 35** to Tintoretto. The staircase vestibule, **Rooms 36-40**, contains an ancient Roman marble boar, inspiration for the brass Porcellino in Florence's Mercato Nuovo.

Rooms 41 and **43-45** house works by Rembrandt, Goya, Rubens, and Caravaggio, currently on display after lengthy restorations. The Uffizi architect, Vasari, designed a **secret corridor** running between the Palazzo Vecchio and the Medici's Palazzo Pitti. The corridor runs through the Uffizi and over the Ponte Vecchio, housing more art, including a special collection of artists' self-portraits. The corridor is opened sporadically and requires both a separate entrance fee and advance booking. (*Off P. della Signoria. ☎055 23 88 651. Open Tu-Su 8:15am-6:35pm. €10, EU citizens 18-25 €5. Save hours of waiting by reserving tickets in advance for €4 extra. Pick up reserved tickets at Door 1 before entering at Door 3 on the other side of the walkway. Audio tour €4.65. 1½hr. guided tour €29. Online reservations at www.florence-tickets.com.*)

MAKE FRIENDS WITH THE UFFIZI. If you plan on visiting 3 or more museums in Florence, consider obtaining an **Amici degli Uffizi card.** Students under 26 pay €25 for the card (regularly €60) and receive free admission to the Uffizi and all state museums in Florence (including the Accademia and Bargello). It includes one visit to each of the museums and gets you to the front of the line. For more information, call Amici degli Uffizi, V. Lorenzo il Magnifico 1, ☎055 47 94 422, or email amicidegliuffizi@waf.it.

PALAZZO VECCHIO. Arnolfo del Cambio designed this fortress-like *palazzo*, built between 1299 and 1304, as the seat of the *comune*'s government. The massive brown stone facade has a thin, square tower rising from its center and turrets along the top. Its apartments once served as living quarters for members of the *signoria* (city council) during their two-month terms, where they prayed, ate, and lived together in complete isolation from the outside world. The building later became the Medici family home. In 1470, Michelozzo decorated the **courtyard,** now open to the public. He filled it with religious frescoes and placed ornate stone pediments over every door and window. The courtyard also has stone lions and a humbling replica of Verrocchio's 15th-century *Putto* fountain. Once inside the palace, visitors can take advantage of numerous tour opportunities. The worthwhile **Activities Tour Ticket** includes both the "Secret Routes" and "Invitation to Court" tours. "Secret Routes" fulfills Clue® fans' fantasies of hidden passages with visits to stairwells tucked in walls behind beautiful oil paintings, an area between the ornate ceiling and the roof of the Salone del Cinquecento, and the private chambers of Duke Cosimo I dei Medici. "Invitation to Court" includes reenactments of Medici court life, complete with a tour guide playing Cosimo's wife, Eleonora di Toledo, decked out in Renaissance finery. "The Encounter with Giorgio Vasari" tours through the **Monumental Apartments** with a guide playing the part of Vasari, Duke Cosimo's court painter and architect and a biographer of Renaissance artists. The apartments house the *palazzo*'s extensive art collections. The rooms contain 12 interactive terminals with virtual tours of the building's history and detailed computer animations. (*☎055 27 68 224 or 27 68 558. Office open M-W and F-Su 9am-6pm, Th 9am-2pm. Tours daily in English and French. 20-person group max. Reservations required. "Monumental Apartments" tour €6, ages 18-25 €4.50; Activities tour €8/5.50.*)

The city commissioned Michelangelo and Leonardo da Vinci to paint opposite walls of the **Salone del Cinquecento,** the meeting room of the Grand Council of the Republic. Although they never completed the frescoes, their preliminary sketches for the *Battle of Cascina* and the *Battle of Anghiari* were studied by Florentine artists for years. The Salone's ceiling is so elaborately decorated with moldings and frescoes that an intricate network of beams between the ceiling and roof suspend each wall painting. The tiny **Studio di Francesco I,** designed by Vasari, has a plethora of Mannerist art, with paintings by Bronzino and Vasari, and statuettes by Giambologna and Ammannati. The mezzanine holds Bronzino's portrait of the poet Laura Battiferi and Giambologna's *Hercules and the Hydra*. (☎055 27 68 465. *Open M-W and F-Su 9am-6pm, Th 9am-2pm. Palazzo Vecchio €6, ages 18-25 €4.50; courtyard free. Combined ticket with Cappella Brancacci €8/6.*)

PIAZZA DELLA SIGNORIA. With the turreted Palazzo Vecchio to the west and a corner of the Uffizi Gallery to the south, this 13th-century *piazza* is now one of the city's most frequented areas. The statues in the *piazza* are as spectacular as those inside any of the neighboring buildings. Although many are replicas, all these sights can be enjoyed gelato in hand, outside the confines of a traditional museum. With the construction of the Palazzo Vecchio, the square blossomed into Florence's civic and political center. In 1497, religious zealot Girolamo Savonarola convinced Florentines to light the Bonfire of the Vanities in the *piazza*, barbecuing some of Florence's best art, including (according to legend) all of Botticelli's secular works held in public collections. A year later, disillusioned citizens sent Savonarola up in smoke on the same spot, marked today by a comparatively discreet commemorative disc near the ◪**Fountain of Neptune.** Monumental sculptures cluster around the Palazzo Vecchio, including Donatello's *Judith and Holofernes* (1460), a copy of Michelangelo's *David* (1504), Bandinelli's *Hercules* (1534), and Giambologna's equestrian *Cosimo I* (1567). The massive *Neptune* (1560), to the left of the Palazzo Vecchio, so revolted Michelangelo that he decried the artist: "Oh, Ammannato, Ammannato, what lovely marble you have ruined!" But perhaps that was just jealousy. The 14th-century stone **Loggia dei Lanzi,** adjacent to the *palazzo*, originally built as a stage for civic orators, is now one of the best places in Florence to see world-class sculpture for free, including Giambologna's spiraling composition of *The Rape of the Sabines*. Indeed, as a sign near the entrance proclaims, the towering works of marble are "on par with the gallery in the Uffizi."

THE PONTE VECCHIO. Built in 1345, this is Florence's oldest bridge. In the 1500s, butchers and tanners lined the bridge and dumped pig's blood and intestines in the river, creating an odor that, unsurprisingly, offended the powerful bankers as they crossed the Arno on their way to the office. In an effort to improve the area, the Medici clan kicked out the lower-class shopkeepers, and goldsmiths and diamond-cutters moved in. Today, their descendants line the street in medieval-looking boutiques, and the bridge glitters with rows of necklaces, brooches, and charms. While technically open to vehicles, it is chiefly tourists and street musicians who swamp the roadway. The Ponte Vecchio was the only Florentine bridge to escape German bombs during WWII. A German commander who led his retreating army across the river in 1944 couldn't bear to destroy it, choosing instead to make it impassable by toppling nearby buildings. From the neighboring **Ponte alle Grazie,** the heart-melting ◪**sunset view** of the Ponte Vecchio showcases its glowing buildings and Arno River beneath.

THE BARGELLO AND ENVIRONS

◪**THE BARGELLO.** In the heart of medieval Florence, this 13th-century brick fortress was once the residence of Florence's chief magistrate. Later it became a brutal prison with public executions held in its courtyard. In the 19th century, the Bargello's former elegance was restored, and it now gracefully hosts the spectacular, yet largely unfrequented **Museo Nazionale,** a treasury of Florentine sculpture. On the second floor and to the right is the spacious, high-ceilinged **Salone di Donatello,** which contains Donatello's bronze *David* (c. 1430), the first free-standing nude since antiquity. This "nude" David chose to discard his clothes, but still posed in hat and boots. David's playful expression and youthful posture provide quite the contrast to Michelangelo's determined figure of chiseled perfection in the Accademia. Donatello's earlier marble *David*, fully clothed and somewhat generic, stands near the left wall. On the right, two bronze panels of the *Sacrifice of Isaac* submitted by Ghiberti and Brunelleschi to the baptistry door compete for attention. The next floor contains dramatic works by Andrea del Verrochio, Leonardo da Vinci's teacher, as well as a vast collection of small bronzes and coins. Dominating the ground floor are early works by Michelangelo, including a debauched *Bacchus* (1496), an intense bust of *Brutus* (1540), and an unfinished *Apollo* (1530). Baccio Bandinelli's *Adam and Eve* (1504), in the same room, seem to have been captured in a moment of relaxed conversation. The spacious courtyard is filled with plaques of noble Florentine families' coats of arms. (*V. del Proconsolo 4, between the duomo and P. della Signoria.* ☎*055 23 88 606. Open daily 8:15am-6pm. Closed 2nd and 4th M of each month. €7. Audio tour €4.*)

BADIA. The Badia was the site of medieval Florence's richest monastery. Buried in the interior of a quiet residential block, the church's simple facade belies the treasures within. Filippino Lippi's stunning *Apparition of the Virgin to St. Bernard*, one of the most appreciated paintings of the late 15th century, hangs in eerie gloom to the left of the church. Note the beautiful frescoes and Corinthian pilasters, and be sure to glance at the intricately carved dark wood ceiling. Visitors are asked to walk silently among the white-robed monks. (*Entrance on V. Dante Alighieri, off V. Proconsolo.* ☎*055 26 44 02. Officially open to tourists M 3-6pm, but respectful visitors can walk through the church at any time.*)

MUSEO DI STORIA DELLA SCIENZA. This impressive and unique collection is well worth a visit to offset the art overload. It boasts scientific instruments from the Renaissance, including telescopes, astrological models, clock workings, and wax models of anatomy and childbirth. The stellar **Room 4** displays a number of Galileo's tools, including his embalmed middle finger and the objective lens through which he first observed the satellites of Jupiter in 1610. Detailed English guides are available at the ticket office. (*P. dei Giudici 1, behind Palazzo Vecchio and the Uffizi.* ☎*055 26 53 11. Open M and W-F 9:30am-5pm, Tu and Sa 9:30am-1pm; Oct.-May also 2nd Su of each month 10am-1pm. €6.50, under 18 €4.*)

CASA DI DANTE. This residence is reputedly identical to Dante's original home. Those who can read Italian and who have a fascination with Dante will

TOP TEN LIST

WORD UP

You bought the bilingual dictionary, and you've probably got the Italian curse words down, but to *really* get in with locals, you've got to know some Tuscan slang. From picking up *una bella Italiana* in a club to respectfully telling street peddlers to scram, local lingo escapes translation and goes beyond clichéd idioms. Here are the top ten you'll need to fit in under the Tuscan sun.

1. Ganzo/a! (adj.) Cool. She/He is cool! *Lei è ganza!*

2. Bono (adj.) Hot. Zack/Kelly is hot! *Zack/Kelly é bono/a!*

3. M'attizza (v.) I'm hot for X. I'm hot for Lisa! *Lisa m'attizza.*

4. Mannaggia! (int.) Oh no. Oh no! I lost my *Let's Go!* Now I can't find that popular restaurant, The Max! *Mannaggia! Ho perso il mio Let's Go! Ora non posso vedere il ristorante popolare, The Max!*

5. Secchione (n.) Nerd. Screech is a nerd. *Screech è un secchione.*

6. Accipicchia! (int.) Wow. Wow, check out that dragon! *Accipicchia, che dragone!*

7. Incasinato (adj.) Screwed. I'm screwed. *Io sono incasinato(a).*

8. Donnaiolo (n.) Playboy. Slater is a playboy. *Slater è un donnaiolo.*

9. Spettagolare (v.) Gossip. Let's gossip about Skinner! *Spettagoliamo su Skinner!*

10. Cicciobomba (n.) Fatso. Jessie is a Fatso. *Jessie è un cicciobomba.*

enjoy this place, otherwise it's probably not worth the money. Displays trace the poet's life from youth to exile and pay homage to the artistic creation that immortalized him; check out Giotto's early but representative portrait of Dante on the third floor. Nearby is a facsimile of the abandoned and melancholy little church where Beatrice, Dante's unrequited love and spiritual guide in *Paradiso*, attended mass. *(Corner of V. Dante Alighieri and V. S. Margherita, 1 block of the Bargello. Ring bell to enter. ☎ 055 21 94 16. Open Tu-Su 10am-5pm. €4, groups over 15 €2 per person.)*

PIAZZA DELLA REPUBBLICA AND FARTHER WEST

After hours of contemplating great Florentine art, visit the area that financed it all. In the early 1420s, 72 banks operated in Florence, most in the area around the Mercato Nuovo and V. Tornabuoni. With a lower concentration of famous sights, this area is more residential and commercial, though still crowded with visitors. Surrounding cafes and stores are often overpriced.

CHIESA DI SANTA MARIA NOVELLA. Constructed between 1279 and 1360, this Dominican *chiesa* boasts a Romanesque-Gothic facade, considered one of the greatest masterpieces of early Renaissance architecture. Made of Florentine marble, it is geometrically pure and balanced, a precursor to the Classical revival of the high Renaissance. The church was originally home to Dominican friars, or *Domini canes* (Hounds of the Lord), who took a bite out of sin and corruption. Thirteenth-century frescoes covered the interior until the Medici's commissioned Vasari to paint new ones. Vasari spared Masaccio's powerful **Trinity,** the first painting to use geometric perspective. The **Cappella di Filippo Strozzi,** to the right of the high altar, contains frescoes by Filippo Lippi, including a cartoonish Adam, a woolly Abraham, and an excruciating *Torture of St. John the Evangelist*. Brunelleschi's *Crucifix* in the **Gondi Chapel** is a response to Donatello's *Crucifix* in **Santa Croce** (p. 451), which Brunelleschi thought too full of "vigorous naturalism." A Ghirlandaio fresco series covers the **Tournabuoni Chapel** behind the main altar. *(☎ 055 26 45 184. Open M-Th 10am-5pm, F-Sa 1-5pm, Su 9am-5pm. Ticket office closes at 4:30pm. €2.70, ages 13-18 €1.50.)*

PIAZZA DELLA REPUBBLICA. The largest open space in Florence, this *piazza* teems with crowds and street performers at night. An enormous arch filling in the gap over V. Strozzi marks the square's western edge. Overpriced cafes, restaurants, and *gelaterie* line the rest of the *piazza*. In 1890 the *piazza* replaced the **Mercato Vecchio** as the site of the city market, but has since traded market stalls for the more fashionable Guess and Pucci. The inscription *"Antico centro della città, da secolare squalore, a vita nuova restituito"* (the "ancient center of the city, squalid for centuries, restored to new life") makes a derogatory reference to the fact that the *piazza* is the site of the old Jewish ghetto. When the "liberation of the Jews" of Italy in the 1860s allowed Jews to live elsewhere, the ghetto slowly diminished. An ill-advised plan to demolish the *centro's* historical buildings and remodel Florence destroyed the Old Market, but an international campaign successfully thwarted the razing of the entire ghetto, leaving the present-day gathering space as a vibrant center for city life. Today the *piazza* is entirely commercial. A small, lighted carousel sits in the center of the *piazza*, rather than a typical fountain. After sunset, P. Della Repubblica is as busy as P. del Duomo, as young people, families, and vendors chat by moonlight.

CHIESA DI SANTA TRINITÀ. Hoping to spend eternity as they had lived—in elite company—the most fashionable *palazzo* owners commissioned family chapels in this church. The facade, designed by Bernardo Buontalenti in the 16th century, is almost Baroque in its ornamentation, and is an exquisite example of late-Renaissance architecture. Scenes from Ghirlandaio's *Life of St. Francis*

(1486) decorate the **Sassetti chapel.** The famous altarpiece, Ghirlandaio's *Adoration of the Shepherds* (1485), is in the Uffizi. The one here is a convincing copy. *(In P. di Santa Trinità. ☎ 055 21 69 12. Open M-Sa 7am-noon and 4-7pm, Su 7am-noon. Free.)*

MERCATO NUOVO. Under their Corinthian-columned splendor, the loggias of the New Market have housed gold and silk traders since 1547. Today, gold falsely glints among the wares of vendors selling imitation designer purses, belts, and clothes. The Italian government reminds visitors that it is illegal to purchase knock-off goods, so make selections carefully. Pietro Tacca's pleasantly plump statue, *Il Porcellino* (The Little Pig; 1612) appeared some 50 years after the market opened. Rub its snout and put a coin in the pig's mouth; if the coin drops neatly into the grate below your luck is golden, but it still won't turn your "Fendi" purse into real leather. *(Off V. Porta Rossa, between P. della Repubblica and the Ponte Vecchio. Vendors hawk wares from dawn to dusk.)*

PALAZZO DAVANZATI. As Florence's 15th-century economy expanded, its bankers and merchants flaunted their new wealth by erecting grand edifices. The great boom began with construction of this *palazzo*, whose cavernous interior houses the **Museo della Casa Fiorentina Antica.** In 2005, the building's interior was reopened after extensive renovations. The courtyard is adorned with antique furniture, restored frescoes, and wooden doors and ornaments, giving visitors a small glimpse of the 15th-century merchants' luxury. Check out the trap doors on the floor in the Sala dei Pappagalli. The courtyard below was open to the public, and the holes in the floor look down over the very spots of entrance below, so the rich families could monitor visitors and drop heavy stone balls (kept in wall niches nearby) if need be. *(V. Pta. Rossa 13. ☎ 055 23 88 610. Open daily 8:50am-1:50pm. Closed 1st, 3rd, and 5th M and 2nd and 4th Su of each month. Videos about the palazzo screened at 10, 11am, and noon on 4th fl. Free.)*

SAN LORENZO AND FARTHER NORTH

ACCADEMIA. No matter how many pictures of Michelangelo's triumphant sculpture you've seen, seeing ▓**David** in the marble flesh will blow you away. From five feet away, Michelangelo's painstaking attention to detail—like the veins in David's hands and at the backs of his knees—bring the statue to life. The sheer size of the work, and the fact that Michelangelo used a piece of stone abandoned by another artist, gives new appreciation to Michelangelo's genius. In a series of unfortunate events, the statue's base was struck by lightning in 1512, damaged by anti-Medici riots in 1527, and was finally moved here from P. della Signoria in 1873 after a stone hurled during a riot broke David's left wrist in two places. If this real *David* seems a bit different from the copy in front of the Palazzo Vecchio, there's a reason: Michelangelo intended the David to be positioned on a high pedestal and therefore exaggerated his head and torso to correct for distortion from viewing far below; in the Accademia, the statue stands on a relatively high pedestal and appears less top-heavy. If you can manage to pull your eyes away from David, look for Michelangelo's four *Slaves* (1520) and a *Florence (Firenze*, 1499) lining the hall. Even today, it is hotly debated whether the statues were meant to appear unfinished. Chipping away only enough to show the figures emerging from the marble, Michelangelo remained true to his theories about "releasing" his figures from the living stone. Also worth a look are Botticelli's paintings of the Madonna as well as works by Uccello. Two panel paintings, Lippi's *Deposition* (1504) and Perugino's *Assumption* (1504), sit in the room just in front of the rotunda. The Serviti family, who commissioned the two-sided panel, disliked Perugino's depiction so much that they only displayed Lippi's portion in their church. *(V.*

TUSCANY

Ricasoli 60, between the San Marco and San Annunziata. Line for entrance without a reservation begins at V. Ricasoli 58. The line is shortest early in the day. ☎ 055 23 88 609. Open Sept.-May Tu-Su 8:15am-6:50pm; June-Aug. Tu-Th and Sa-Su 8:15am-6:50pm, Sa 8:15am-10pm. Last entry 45min. before close. Most areas wheelchair-accessible. May-Sept. €14; Oct.-Apr. €7.)

◼**MUSEO DELLA CHIESA DI SAN MARCO.** Remarkable works by Fra Angelico adorn the Museo della Chiesa di San Marco, one of the most peaceful and spiritual places in Florence. A large room to the right of the courtyard contains some of the painter's major works. The 2nd floor houses Angelico's most famous *Annunciation*, across from the top of the stairwell, as well as the monks' quarters. Every cell in the convent contains its own Fra Angelico fresco, each painted in flat colors and sparse detail to facilitate the monks' somber meditation. To the right of the stairwell, **Michelozzo's library,** based on Michelangelo's work in San Lorenzo, is a simple space for reflection. In **Cells 17** and **22,** underground artwork peeks through a glass floor, excavated in the medieval period. Look also for Savonarola's cells, at the end of the northwest corridor, which display some of his relics. On the way out, the **Museo di Firenze Antica** of Florence's ancient roots is worth a quick visit. These two rooms showcase numerous archaeological fragments, mostly pieces of stone work from Etruscan and Roman buildings in the area. Be sure to peek into the church itself, next door to the museum, to admire the elaborate altar and vaulted ceiling. *(Enter at P. di San Marco 3. ☎ 055 23 88 608. Open M-F 8:15am-1:50pm, Sa 8:15am-6:50pm, Su 8:15am-7pm. Closed 2nd and 4th M and 1st, 3rd, and 5th Su of each month. English guides available near the entrance. €4, EU citizens 18-25 €2, over 65 or under 18 free.)*

BASILICA DI SAN LORENZO. In 1419 Brunelleschi designed this spacious basilica, another Florentine example of simple, early-Renaissance lines and proportion. Because the Medici lent the funds to build the church, they retained artistic control over its construction. Their coat of arms appears all over the nave, and their tombs occupy the two sacristies and the Cappella dei Principi behind the altar. The family cleverly placed Cosimo dei Medici's grave in front of the high altar, making the entire church into his personal mausoleum. Donatello created two **pulpits,** one for each aisle; his *Martelli Sarcophagus* in the left transept takes the form of a wicker basket woven in marble. Michelangelo designed the exterior, but, disgusted by the murkiness of Florentine politics, he abandoned the project and headed to Rome, which accounts for the basilica's still unadorned brown-stone facade.*(☎ 055 26 45 184. Open Nov.-Feb. M-Sa 10am-5pm; Mar.-Oct. M-Sa 10am-5pm, Su 1:30-5pm. €3.50, includes entrance to Laurentian Library.)*

The **Cappelle dei Medici** (Medici Chapels) consist of dual design contributions by Matteo Nigetti and Michelangelo. Michelangelo created and sculpted the entire **New Sacristy**—architecture, tombs, and statues—in a mature, careful style that reflects his study of Brunelleschi. Designed to house the bodies of four Medici, the room contains two impressive tombs for Medici Dukes Lorenzo and Giuliano. Lounging on the tomb of the military-minded Lorenzo are the smooth female Night and the muscle-bound male Day, both left provocatively "unfinished." Michelangelo rendered the hazier Dawn and Dusk with more androgynous figures for Giuliano's tomb, which is closer to the entrance. Some of the artist's sketches are in the basement. *(Walk around to the back entrance in P. Madonna degli Aldobrandini. ☎ 055 23 88 602. Open daily 8:15am-5pm. Closed 1st, 3rd, and 5th M and 2nd and 4th Su of each month. €6.)* The adjacent **Laurentian Library** houses one of the world's most valuable manuscript collections. Michelangelo's famous entrance **portico** confirms his virtuosity; the *pietra serena* sandstone staircase is one of his most innovative architectural designs. *(☎ 055 21 07 60. Open daily 8:30am-1:30pm. Free with entrance to San Lorenzo.)*

MUSEO ARCHEOLOGICO. Unassuming behind its bland plaster facade, the archaeological museum has a surprisingly diverse collection. Its rooms teem with collections of statues and other monuments of the ancient Greeks, Etruscans, and Egyptians. A long, two-story gallery devoted to Etruscan jewelry runs the length of the plant-filled courtyard. In almost any other city in the world, this museum would be a major cultural highlight, but in Florence, it's possible to enjoy it without large crowds. Don't miss the *Chimera d'Arezzo*, a bronze sculpture from the late 5th century BC in **Room 14**. *(V. della Colonna 38. ☎ 055 23 57 50. Open M 2-7pm, Tu and Th-Su 8:30am-7pm, W 8:30am-2pm. €7.)*

PIAZZA SANTA CROCE AND ENVIRONS

◪**CHIESA DI SANTA CROCE.** The Franciscans built this church as far away as possible from their Dominican rivals at Santa Maria Novella. Started in 1210 as a small oratory, the ascetic Franciscans ironically produced what is arguably the city's most splendid church, with a unique Egyptian cross layout. Breathtaking marble sculptures adorn the grand tombs of Florentine luminaries on both sides of the main aisle, frozen in expressions of grief and mourning. The Renaissance greats buried here include Michelangelo, who rests near the beginning of the right aisle (his tomb is by Vasari, but his body is actually buried under the floor slightly to the left); Galileo, directly opposite in the left aisle; and Machiavelli, farther down and on the right. Donatello's *Crucifix* (1412-13), which left Brunelleschi awestruck, is in the Vernio Chapel of the left transept under heavy scaffolding; the artist's gilded *Annunciation* (1435) is to the right of humanist Leonardo Bruni's tomb. The Florentines who banished Dante in 1302 eventually prepared a tomb for him here. Dante died in Ravenna in 1321, however, and the literary necrophiles there never returned his body. To the right of the altar, the frescoes of the **Cappella Peruzzi** vie with those of the **Cappella Bardi**. Giotto and his school painted both, but unfortunately, the works are badly faded. While wandering the church, note the water mark eight feet up the walls, an enduring reminder of the 1966 flood. *(☎ 055 24 66 105 or 23 02 885. Open Mar. 15-Nov. 15 M-Sa 9:30am-5:30pm, Su and holidays 1-5:30pm. €5, under 18 €3.)*

The **Museo dell'Opera di Santa Croce**, which forms three sides of a peaceful courtyard, is accessible from the right aisle of the church. At the end of the cloister next to the church is Brunelleschi's ◪**Cappella Pazzi**, a humble marvel of perfect proportions. Its decorations include Luca della Robbia's *tondi* (circular paintings) of the apostles and Brunelleschi's moldings of the evangelists. Across the courtyard down a gravel path, a former dining hall contains Taddeo Gaddi's fresco *The Tree of the Cross* and his rendition of the *Last Supper*. Also in the room is Cimabue's *Crucifixion*, left in a tragic state by the 1966 flood, when the water actually carried it out into the *piazza*. *(Enter through the loggia in front of Cappella Pazzi. Hours same as church. Admission included in ticket to church.)*

SYNAGOGUE OF FLORENCE. This synagogue, also known as the **Museo del Tempio Israelitico**, sits behind a hefty iron gate and is resplendent with Sephardic domes and horseshoe arches. David Levi, a wealthy Jewish businessman, donated his fortune in 1870 for the construction of "a monumental temple worthy of Florence," in recognition of the fact that Jews were newly allowed to live and worship outside the old Jewish ghetto. Architects Micheli, Falchi, and Treves created one of Europe's most beautiful synagogues. *(V. Luigi Carlo Farini 4, at V. Pilastri. ☎ 055 24 52 52 or 24 52 53. Open M-Th and Su 10am-6pm, F 10am-2pm. €4, students €3. Includes free, informative hourly tours; book in advance at the ticket booth or the tourist office.)*

CASA BUONARROTI. This small museum houses two of Michelangelo's most important early works, *The Madonna of the Steps* and *The Battle of the Cen-*

taurs, both completed when he was just 16 years old. The panels illustrate his growth from bas-relief to sculpture. Some of his rare sketches are on rotating display. *(V. Ghibellina 70. From P. S. Croce, follow V. dei Pepi and turn right on V. Ghibellina. ☎ 055 25 17 52. Open M and W-Su 9:30am-2pm. €6.50, students €4.)*

THE OLTRARNO

The far side of the Arno River is a lively, unpretentious quarter filled with young people. Though you'll likely cross over the Ponte Vecchio on the way to the Oltrarno, consider coming back over the **Ponte di Santa Trinità,** which affords excellent views of the Ponte Vecchio, or dally a bit in **P. di Santo Spirito,** which thrives with markets in the day and street artists at night.

▨**PALAZZO PITTI.** Luca Pitti, a 15th-century banker, built his *palazzo* east of Santo Spirito against the Boboli hill. The Medici family acquired the *palazzo* and the hill in 1550 and enlarged everything they could. During Italy's brief experiment with monarchy, the structure served as a royal residence. Today, the **Palazzo Pitti** is fronted with a vast, uninhabited *piazza* and houses a gallery and four museums, providing enough diversions for a lengthy and unhurried visit. *(Ticket office is on the right before the palazzo. ☎ 055 29 48 83. 3-day ticket €12.50.)*

The ▨**Galleria Palatina** was one of only a few public galleries when it opened in 1833. Today, it houses Florence's second most important collection (after the Uffizi). Its artistic smorgasbord includes works by Botticelli, Canova, Caravaggio, del Sarto, Perugino, Raphael, Rubens, Tintoretto, Titian, Vasari, Velasquez, and Veronese. The **Appartamenti Reali** (Royal Apartments), at the end of the *galleria*, are lavish reminders of the time when the *palazzo* served as the Royal House of Savoy's living quarters. The apartments hold a few Renaissance and Baroque greats. For a change of pace, check out the early 19th-century proto-Impressionist works of the Macchiaioli group in the **Galleria d'Arte Moderna.** *(☎ 055 23 88 616. Open Tu-Su 8:15am-6:50pm. Combined ticket for Palatine Gallery, Royal Apartments and Modern Art Gallery €8.50, EU students €4.25.)*

Find out if the clothes make the Medici in the **Galleria del Costume,** a decadent display of the family's finery. The **Museo degli Argenti** on the ground floor exhibits Medici family treasures, including cases of precious gems, ivories, silver, and Lorenzo the Magnificent's famous vase collection. The *salone* depicts a floor-to-ceiling fresco of blind Homer and the nine Muses leaving Mount Parnassus, alluding to scholars who fled to Tuscany from Greece after the Turkish invasion of 1453. An elaborately landscaped park, the ▨**Boboli Gardens** is an exquisite example of a stylized Renaissance garden and provides open spaces with beautifully groomed lawns and impressive marble statues. A large oval lawn sits just up the hill behind the palace, marked by an Egyptian obelisk. Labyrinthine avenues of cypress trees lead eager wanderers to bubbling fountains with graceful nudes. Be sure to see the fountain of a portly Bacchus, sitting astride a very strained turtle. While the gardens seem like the perfect picnic spot, visitors are unfortunately prohibited from bringing in outside food. The **Museo della Porcellana,** hidden behind the gardens, exhibits fine porcelain from the Medici collection. *(☎ 055 23 88 709. Gardens open daily June-Aug. 8:15am-7:30pm; Sept.-Oct. and Apr.-May 8:15am-6:30pm; Nov.-Feb. 8:15am-4:30pm; Mar. 8:15am-5:30pm. Museo degli Argenti and Museo della Porcellana open daily 8:15am-7:30pm. Closed 2nd and 4th M and 1st, 3rd, and 5th Su of each month. Combined ticket for all 4 sights €10, EU students €4. Cash only.)*

CHIESA DI SANTA MARIA DEL CARMINE. Inside this church, the ▨**Brancacci Chapel** holds Masaccio's stunning 15th-century frescoes, declared masterpieces in their own time. Fifty years later, a respectful Filippino Lippi completed the cycle. Masolino's *Adam and Eve* and Masaccio's pain-filled *Expulsion from Eden* stand face to face, demonstrating the latter's innovative depiction of human forms. With such monumental works as the *Tribute Money*, this chapel became a school for many later Renaissance artists, including Michelangelo himself. *(P. del Carmine 14. ☎ 055 27 68 224. Church open daily 9am-noon. Chapel open M and W-Sa 10am-5pm, Su 1-5pm. Reservation required for Chapel. Church free. Chapel €4, 18-25 €3, under 18 €1.50. Combined ticket with Palazzo Vecchio €8/6/3.)*

SAN MINIATO AL MONTE AND ENVIRONS

▓**PIAZZALE MICHELANGELO.** Though the *piazzale* itself is a bit of an eyesore, the romantic view alone demands a visit. At sunset, waning light casts a warm glow over the city. Make the challenging uphill trek at around 8:30pm during the summer to arrive in time for sunset. The large *piazza* doubles as a parking lot, home to hordes of tour buses on summer days, and occasionally hosts concerts as well. *(Cross Ponte Vecchio, and turn left. Walk through the piazza, and turn right on V. dei Bardi. Follow it uphill as it becomes V. del Monte alle Croci, where a staircase to the left heads to the piazzale. Or take bus #13 from P. S. Maria Novella or any other point en route.)*

▓**SAN MINIATO AL MONTE.** One of Florence's oldest churches, San Miniato's marble facade and 13th-century mosaics provide a prelude to the incredible interior. The floor inside is patterned with lions, doves, and astrological signs. The **Chapel of the Cardinal of Portugal** holds a collection of superb Luca della Robbia terracottas. *(Take bus #13 from the station or climb stairs from Ple. Michelangelo. ☎ 055 23 42 731. Open daily Mar.-Oct. 8am-7pm; Nov.-Feb. 8am-1pm and 2:30-6pm. Free.)*

◻ SHOPPING

Florentines design their window displays (and their goods) with flair. Watch for store windows to flood with *saldi* (sales) signs in January and July. In July and August, Florentine families rush to the beach for the weekend and nearly all stores close early on Saturday, and some close for all of August.

V. Tornabuoni's swanky **boutiques** and the well-stocked goldsmiths on the Ponte Vecchio serve a sophisticated clientele. Join this crowd at **Santa Vaggi,** Ponte Vecchio 2/6r and 20r. (☎ 055 21 55 02. Charms start at €25. 18k gold earrings start at €40. Open Sept.-Oct. and Dec.-July daily 9am-7:30pm; Nov. and Aug. M-Su 9am-7:30pm. AmEx/MC/V.) Florence makes its contribution to *alta moda* with a number of runway shows, including the biannual **Pitti Uomo** (info ☎ 055 23 580), a menswear exhibit in January and June.

The city's artisan traditions thrive at the open-air **markets. San Lorenzo,** the largest, cheapest, and most touristed, sprawls for several blocks around P. S. Lorenzo. In front of the leather shops, stands stock all kinds of goods—bags, clothes, food, toys, and flags. High prices are rare, but so are quality and honest dealings. (Open daily 9am-dusk.) For everything from pot-holders to parakeets, shop at the market in **Parco delle Cascine** on Tuesday morning, which begins four bridges west of the Ponte Vecchio at P. Vittorio Veneto and stretches along the Arno River. For a flea market that specializes in old furniture and postcards, visit **Piazza Ciompi,** off V. Pietrapiana from Borgo degli Albizi. (Open Tu-Sa.)

Alinari, Largo Alinari 15, stocks the world's largest selection of art prints and high-quality photographs from €25, as well as a selection of journals and *carta fiorentina*, paper covered in intricate floral designs typical of Florence The impressive artwork are enlarged prints of historic negatives found in Italian archives. (☎ 055 23 951; www.alinari.it. Open M 2:30-6:30pm, Tu-F 9am-1pm and 2:30-6:30pm, Sa 9am-1pm and 3-7pm. Closed 2 weeks in Aug. AmEx/MC/V.)

Florentine **leatherwork** is affordable and internationally renowned. Some of the city's best artisans work around P. S. Croce and V. Pta. Santa Maria. The **Santa Croce Leather School,** in Chiesa di Santa Croce, offers first-rate products at reasonable prices as well as the chance to observe craftsmen making bags and jackets. (Enter through the church or V. S. Giuseppe 5r. ☎055 24 45 34 and 24 79 913; www.leatherschool.it. Open Mar. 15-Nov. 15 daily 9:30am-6pm; Nov. 16-Mar. 14 M-Sa 10am-12:30pm and 3-6pm. AmEx/MC/V.) **NOI,** at V. delle Terme 22, produces leather apparel of superb quality for a hotshot clientele, but also carries some affordable goods. (Wallets from €25. Bags €60-200. Jackets from €250. *Let's Go* discount 10%. Open daily 9:30am-7:30pm. AmEx/MC/V.)

BARGAIN BABY! Even when prices are marked, don't hesitate to haggle. As a general rule, start with half the price offered or at least show disinterest to get the price lowered. Only propose a price you are willing to pay. Brush up on your Italian shopping phrases, as vendors are more likely to lower the price for shoppers who "talk the talk." Bargain only if paying with cash.

♫ 🌺 ENTERTAINMENT AND FESTIVALS

Florence disagrees with England over who invented modern soccer, but every June, the various *quartieri* turn out in costume to play their own medieval version of the sport, known as **calcio storico.** Two teams chase a wooden ball in *piazze* around the city; unsurprisingly, matches often blur the boundary between athletic contest and riot. Check newspapers or the tourist office for the exact dates and locations of historical or modern *calcio*, and always book tickets ahead. In 2007, the event was suspended due to rowdiness in previous years; check with the tourist office for the most updated information. The **stadio,** north of the *centro*, hosts modern soccer matches. Tickets (from €10 in the bleachers, from €40 in the smaller, less crowded stands along the sidelines) are sold at the box office and at Marisa, across the street from the stadium. Take bus #25 from the station to the **Giardini del Drago** for a pick-up game of soccer.

The most important of Florence's traditional festivals celebrates the city's patron saint, **San Giovanni Battista,** on June 24. A tremendous fireworks display in Ple. Michelangelo starts around 10pm—grab a spot anywhere along the Arno and watch for the specially coordinated combinations of red, purple, and white fireworks in honor of Florence's Series-A soccer team. The summer is also packed with music festivals, starting in May with the classical **Maggio Musicale.** Take in an evening of opera or ballet with locals in the **Teatro Comunale.** (Box office: C. Italia 16. ☎055 21 35 35. Open Tu-F 10am-4:30pm and Sa 10am-1pm. Tickets €15-150.) To avoid an obstructed view, always ask to see a seating chart before simply springing for the cheapest seats.

In summer, the **Europa dei Sensi** program hosts **Rime Rampanti** (☎055 34 85 80 48 12), a series of nightly cultural shows featuring music, poetry, and food from a chosen European country. Call the info office for reservations. The same company also hosts **Le Pavoniere** (☎055 30 81 60), a pseudo beach party with live music, pool, bar, and pizzeria, in the **Ippodromo delle Cascine** (along the river and past the train station). The **Festa del Grillo** (Festival of the Cricket) is held the first Sunday after Ascension Day, which is 40 days after Easter. Crickets in wooden cages are sold in the Cascine Park to be released into the grass—Florentines believe a cricket's song brings good luck.

🎵 NIGHTLIFE

For reliable info, consult the city's entertainment monthly, *Firenze Spettacolo* (€2), found at newsstands. *Firenze Notte* is also a reliable source (www.

firenzenotte.it). **Piazza Santo Spirito** in Oltrarno has live music in the summer. For clubs or bars far from the *centro* that stay open late, keep in mind that the last bus may leave before the fun train comes to a halt. Taxis are rare around the popular discos, so plan ahead and make sure you have the number of a taxi.

BARS

▧ **Bebop Music Club,** V. de'Servi 76r (☎055 21 87 99; www.bebopclub.com). Live music every night makes Bebop the ultimate party destination. The black and red mod club showcases established cover bands of American groups, a local favorite house band, and Indie Club Sessions at open mike Mondays. When the music gets too loud, head to a private room for a strong cocktail (€7) or challenge internationals to a game of beer pong. Standing-room only on Tu Night Beatles Tribute. Open daily 8:30pm-2am. Shows start at 11pm; soundcheck 9-10pm. No cover.

Moyo, V. de' Benci 23r (☎055 24 79 738; www.moyo.it), near P. S. Croce. Hip spot crowded with young Italians. Fresh salads and tasty burgers. Try the *insalata Moyo* (lettuce, strawberries, nuts, and feta; €7). Lunch from €7. Evening mixed drinks come with free, self-serve snacks. Wi-Fi available. Open daily 8am-3am. AmEx/MC/V.

Noir, Lungarno Corsini 12r (☎055 21 07 51). Buzzing with locals, this bar serves refreshing mojitos (€7). Pay for your drink at the bar and take it outside to enjoy by the Arno. Best for smaller groups looking for a hip but tamer evening. Beer from €3.50. Mixed drinks €6-7. Open daily 11am-1am. Closed 2 weeks in Aug. AmEx/MC/V.

May Day Lounge, V. Dante Alighieri 16r (☎055 23 81 290; www.maydayclub.it). A club with a purpose (a collective of local students) but welcoming to all. Spend nights reading poetry, looking at original artwork, and conversing. Special mixed drinks include apple-kiwi martinis (€5) and a variety of more typical mixed drinks (€7). Beer €3. Happy hour 8-10pm. Open M-Sa 8pm-2am. Closed most of Aug. No cover. Cash only.

The Fiddler's Elbow, P. S. Maria Novella 7r (☎055 21 50 56). Ex-pat bartenders serve beer (€5 per pint) to convivial foreigners. Don't be surprised if impromptu karaoke breaks out in the wee hours. Happy hour noon-9pm. Open daily 11am-1am. MC/V.

Eby's Latin Bar, V. dell'Oriuolo 5r (☎055 33 86 50 89 59). Listen to Latin music on the palm-covered patio while sipping fresh-fruit mixed drinks blended with seasonal ingredients. Fantastic nachos, burritos, and sangria. Beer €1.40-4.50. Mixed drinks €5.50-7. Lunch special: burrito and drink €4.50. Happy hour M-F 6-10pm, drinks €3.50. Open from the 3rd week of Aug. to July M-Sa 11am-3am.

Dublin Pub, V. Faenza 27/r (☎/fax 055 27 41 571; www.dublinpub.it). Described by the Irish manager as the "most authentic Irish pub outside of Ireland." Attracts Americans and locals. Pile in to people watch at the door or check out the televised soccer game. Beer €5. Mixed drinks €6. Wine €3. Free food. No cover. Open daily 5pm-2am.

La Dolce Vita, P. Del Carminelo. A slightly older crowd enjoys this smoky, crowded bar. Comfortable outdoor seating takes on new meaning as couches surround tables beneath lighted umbrellas in the *piazza*. Drinks €7. Open Tu-Su 5pm-2am.

The Gate Pub, Borgo San Frediano 131. For low-cost beer of buzz-guaranteed portions, cross the river to an authentically Italian Irish pub. Locals and well-informed travelers guzzle pints (€4.50) and shots (€1.50) on wooden benches while singing along to Irish rugby songs. Happy hour daily until 9pm. Open daily 5pm-2am.

DISCOS

Twice, V. Verdi 57/r (☎055 24 76 356; www.twiceclub.com). Come here late for a packed crowd of tourists, backpackers, and a healthy portion of Italians. Separate indoor smoking lounge. Beer €6. Mixed drinks €8. Open daily 9pm-4am. MC/V.

Central Park, V. del Fosso Macinante 2 in Parco delle Cascine (☎055 35 35 05). 4 open-air dance floors pulsate with hip-hop, reggae, and Italian "dance rock." Favored by teens and university students. Well-dressed bouncers and management keep things under control. Beer €9. Mixed drinks €11. Cover €20; no cover for foreign students before 1am. Open in summer Tu-Su 8pm-3am. AmEx/MC/V.

Meccanò, V. degli Olmi 1 (☎055 33 13 71), near Parco delle Cascine. Meccanò and Central Park are Florence's most popular discos, with Meccanò catering to a slightly older crowd. Open-air dance floors and sparkling grounds make for sophisticated fun. Special nights include soul, hip-hop, house, and reggae; call for schedule. Cover €16 includes 1 drink; each subsequent drink €7. Open Tu-Sa 11pm-4am. AmEx/MC/V.

Tabasco Gay Club, P. di Santa Cecilia 3r (☎055 21 30 00), in tiny alley across P. della Signoria from Palazzo Vecchio. This dark basement club features smoke machines, strobe lights, and low-vaulted ceilings. Caters to gay men. 18+. Cover €10, after 1am €13; includes 1st drink. Mixed drinks €8. Beer €6. Open Tu-Su 10pm-4am. AmEx/MC/V.

Yab, V. Sassetti 5r (☎055 32 81 96 75 39; www.yab.it). 2 bars, disco lights, neon floors, and an 800-person capacity make it clear this is the place for a good time. Very respectable and clean atmosphere, with no shorts or tanks for guys. A free van drives attendees to their hotels at any point during the night. Students free W. Fashion night Th. Cover with drink €8. Open Sept.-May M and W-Sa 11:30pm-4am; June-Aug M 11:30-4am.

▣ DAYTRIPS FROM FLORENCE

FIESOLE

A 30min. bus ride from Florence. Catch the ATAF city bus #7 (€1) from the train station every 30min.; it stops at P. Mino da Fiesole in the centro. The tourist office, V. Portigiani 3 (☎055 59 87 20; www.comune.fiesole.fi.it), is next to the Teatro Romano, half a block off P. Mino da Fiesole, directly across the piazza from the bus stop. Office provides a free map with museum and sights listings. Open Mar.-Oct. M-Sa 9am-6pm, Su 10am-1pm and 2-6pm; Nov.-Feb. M-Sa 9am-5pm, Su 10am-4pm.

Fiesole (FEE-yeh-SOH-leh; pop. 15,000) is the site of the ancient Etruscan settlement that later extended down the hill to become Florence. Fiesole's clean, cool breezes have long been a welcome escape from the sweltering summer heat of the Arno Valley as well as a source of inspiration for famous figures: Alexander Dumas, Anatole France, Paul Klee, Marcel Proust, Gertrude Stein, and Frank Lloyd Wright all had productive sojourns here. Leonardo da Vinci even used the town as a testing ground for his famed flying machine.

Facing away from the bus stop, walk across P. Mino da Fiesole and down V. Dupre half a block to the entrance of the **Museo Civico,** V. Portigiani 1 (☎055 59 477). One ticket provides admission to three associated museums—the Teatro Romano, Museo Civico Archeologico, and Museo Bandini. The **Teatro Romano** includes the perfectly rectangular foundations of Etruscan thermal baths and the toppled columns and sturdy archways of temple ruins. The well-preserved amphitheater is gussied up with modern sound equipment and spotlights for summer concerts. The amphitheater grounds lead into the **Museo Civico Archeologico,** housing an extensive collection of Etruscan artifacts, well-preserved Grecian urns, a reconstructed tomb with a skeleton, and vases from *Magna Graecia* (southern Italy, once the Greek Empire). Hop across the street to breeze through the **Museo Bandini,** V. Dupre 1, which holds a collection of 15th-century Italian paintings, including works by Cortona's Signorelli, and from the studios of Giotto and the della Robbias. (☎055 59 477. Ruins and museums open Apr.-Oct. daily 9:30am-7pm; Nov.-Mar. M and W-Su 9:30am-7pm. Last entry 30min. before close. €13, students and over 65 €10. MC/V.)

A short, steep walk uphill to the left of the bus stop leads to the **Convento Francesco** and **public gardens.** The panorama of the valley below is perhaps the only context in which Florence's massive *duomo* appears small. The monastery contains a frescoed chapel and a tiny museum, which includes items brought back by Franciscan missionaries, precious Chinese pottery and jade figurines, and an Egyptian mummy. (☎055 59 175. Open June-Sept. Tu-F 10am-noon and 3-6pm, Sa-Su 3-6pm; Oct.-May Tu-F 10am-noon and 3-5pm, Sa-Su 3-5pm. Free.) The **Estate Fiesolana** (☎800 41 42 40; www.estatefiesolana.it), from June through September, fills the Roman theater with concerts, opera, theater, and film.

Accommodations in Fiesole are expensive, so a daytrip is more budget-friendly. The town is also a great lunch spot. Take in fantastic Arno Valley views over coffee (from €0.80) or gelato (from €1.60) at **Blu Bar ❷**, P. Mino 39. The table charge can be expensive, so enjoy your snack at the bar or take it outside to appreciate the full grandeur of your surroundings. (☎055 59 72 35. Pizza €5.50-7. Crepes €7. Mixed drinks €10. Min. charge for table service €3.10. Open Apr.-Oct. daily 8am-1am; Nov.-Mar. Sa-Su 8am-midnight. AmEx/MC/V.)

GREVE IN CHIANTI

SITA buses run to Greve from Florence (1hr., every hr. 7am-8pm, €3.30; reduced service Su and holidays). There are 2 stops in Greve; get off at the first at P. Trento. From P. Trento, either continue to walk in the direction of the bus on Vle. Vittorio Veneto, turning right at the first stop light on V. Battisti, leading to the main piazza, P. Matteotti, or walk in the opposite direction to reach the tourist office (☎055 85 46 287), a hut at Vle. Giovanni da Verazzano 59. Find maps and general info on area wineries. Open Tu-F 9:30am-1pm and 2:30-7pm.

Welcome to Chianti country, where the cheese and olive oil are exquisite and the wine is even better. The tiny town of Greve (GREV-ay; pop. 12,855), is the hub of it all. To find out what that *Chianti Classico* (key-AN-tee CLAS-see-ko) is all about, get your taste buds ready and sip with the best. Just down Vle. Vittorio Veneto and on the right in P. delle Cantine, a wine lover's paradise awaits at ◪**Le Cantine di Greve in Chianti,** P. delle Cantine 2, which is part wine museum, part *enoteca*. Recently opened in 2000, the Cantine use a new technology for wine tasting where the bottles rest in vacuum-valves that enable over 150 bottles to be tasted at once, including a wide range of local *Chianti Classico* and *Supertuscan*. They also stock *Nobile*, *Brunello*, and *Bolgheri*, wines from other Tuscan towns. Grab a tasting card in denominations of €10, 15, 20, or 25, and insert the card above the wine you wish to taste; tastes start around €1, depending on the type of wine. Helpful staff will help you navigate the stands that pack the brick-arched, stone-walled basement. (☎055 85 46 404; fax 85 44 521. Open daily 10am-7pm. Free admission. AmEx/MC/V.) Many other *enoteche* in town offer free wine tastings of 3-5 wines in the hopes that you'll whip out the wallet. The selection at **Enoteca del Chianti Classico,** P. S. Croce 8, is especially impressive. (☎055 85 32 97. Open daily in summer 9:30am-7:30pm, in winter 9:30am-12:30pm and 3:30-7:30pm. AmEx/MC/V.)

For a list of local vineyards and help booking accommodations, head to **Chianti Slow Travel Agency,** P. Matteotti 11 (☎055 85 46 299. Open daily 9am-1pm and 2:30-6:30pm). **Officina Marco Ramuzzi,** V. Italo Stecchi 23 (☎055 85 30 37), offers scooter and mountain bike rentals. Accommodations in the *centro* are scarce and many nearby villas are not easily accessible by public transportation. However, **Albergo del Chianti ❺**, P. Matteotti 86, belies this generalization at a price. Located in the main *piazza*, the hotel offers 16 clean, comfortable rooms with bath, minibar, telephone, A/C, and TV. The rustic lobby and adjoining bar open onto an outdoor oasis: a lovely patio, garden, and swimming pool. (☎055 85 37 63; www.albergodelchianti.it. Breakfast included. Singles €75; doubles €100.) For a truly Tuscan meal, the well-known **Mangiando, Mangiando ❸**, P. Matteotti 80, will do the job with traditional plates such as *cinta senese* (boar) under a wood-beamed ceiling or under outdoor umbrellas. (☎055 85 46 372. Primi €7.50-10. Secondi €15-18. Open Tu-Su in summer 11am-11pm, in winter noon-

3pm and 7-10:30pm. MC/V.) For fresh, local goods, **Macelleria**, P. Matteotti 69-71, is as authentic as it gets. Choose from the wide array of meats and cheeses or pop into the back room to taste several varieties for free. Private tastings that include 8 wines, 3 salamis, 2 cheeses, and 1 olive oil, are offered for €8. Wine tastings start at €10. (Open M-Sa 8am-1pm and 3:30-7:30pm, Su 10am-1pm and 3-7:15pm. AmEx/MC/V.) Dirt cheap picnic eats can be found at **Coop**, Vle. Vittorio Veneto 76. (☎055 85 30 53. Open M-Sa 8am-1pm and 4-8pm. MC/V.) Pick up fresh bread and sweets (from €1.50) at **Forno**, P. Matteotti 89. (Open daily in summer 7am-1pm and 5-8pm; in winter 5-8pm. Cash only.)

SIENA ☎0577

Siena's (see-EH-na; pop. 50,000) vibrant character and local energy make it a distinctly Tuscan city. Locals are fiercely proud of their town's history, which dates back to the 13th century. The city's vehement (and still palpable) rivalry with Florence resulted in grandiose Gothic architecture and soaring towers, though the arrival of the Black Death stunted much potential for innovation. These days, the Sienese celebrate their heritage with festivals like the semi-annual *Palio*, a riotous display of pageantry in which jockeys race bareback horses around the central square. In the heart of the Tuscan wine country, Siena also is an ideal base for exploring the surrounding vineyards and vines.

▐ TRANSPORTATION

Trains: In P. Rosselli. 15min. by bus #3, 4, 7, 9, 10, 17, 77 from the *centro*. Buy tickets from vending machines by station entrance or at ticket office (€1). Ticket office open daily 6:30am-1:10pm and 1:40-8:10pm. Trains to **Florence** (1hr., 16 per day 5:44am-9:22pm, €5.90) and **Rome** (3hr., 20 per day 5:40am-8:21pm, €12.60) via **Grosseto.**

Buses: TRA-IN/SITA (☎0577 20 42 46; www.trainspa.it). Some intercity buses leave from P. Gramsci, but most leave from the train station. Ticket offices are in the underground terminal in P. Gramsci and at the train station. Open daily 6:15am-8:15pm. To reach the train station from P. Gramsci, take bus 4 or 9 to Ferrovia. Tickets can be purchased at the underground ticket office or at the local *tabaccheria* (€0.95). To: **Arezzo** (7 per day, €5.20); **Florence** (every hr., €6.70); **Montalcino** (7 per day, €3.30); **Montepulciano** (4 per day, €4.70) via **Buonconvento** or **Torrenieri; San Gimignano** (31 per day, €5.40) via **Poggibonsi; Volterra** (M-F 4 per day, €2.50; get off at Colle Val d'Elsa). **TRA-IN** also runs buses within Siena. Buy tickets (€0.95, valid 1hr.) at the office in P. Gramsci or a vendor that displays a TRA-IN sign. All buses have reduced service Su.

Taxis: RadioTaxi (☎0577 49 222), in P. Indipendenza and P. Matteotti.

Rentals: Siena Perozzi Rental, V. dei Gazzani 16 (☎0577 28 83 87) and V. del Romitorio 5 (☎0577 28 08 39; www.perozzi.it), off P. la Lizza. Rents mountain bikes (€10 per day, €50 per week), scooters (€26-52/€150-260), and cars (€50-115 per day). Must have a valid license. Rates include insurance. A deposit of €300 or credit card number is required. Open M-Sa 9am-7pm and Su 10am-1pm.

▐ ▐ ORIENTATION AND PRACTICAL INFORMATION

From **Piazza Gramsci,** the main bus stop, follow **Via Malavolti** into **Piazza Matteotti.** Cross the *piazza* and continue straight on **Via Banchi di Sopra,** heading through the heart of town. Continuing downhill, pass through one of the several archways that lead to **Piazza del Campo,** Siena's *centro storico,* also known as **Il Campo.** The **Palazzo Pubblico,** the tourist office, and the best people-watching in the town are located here. To get to the *centro* from the **train station,** cross the street and take one of the buses listed above. These buses stop in **Piazza del Sale** or P. Gramsci. Some buses stop just before P. Gramsci, which makes it difficult to know where to get off; ask the bus driver. From either *piazza*, follow the signs to Il Campo. From the bus station in Piazza San Domenico, follow the signs to P. del Campo. **Piazza del Duomo** lies 100m west of Il Campo.

Tourist Office: APT, P. del Campo 56 (☎0577 28 05 51; www.terresiena.it). Knowledgeable staff offers brochures, some at a nominal fee. Open Mar. 16-Nov. 14 daily 9:30am-1pm and 2:30-6pm; Nov. 15-Mar. 15 M-Sa 8:30am-1pm and 3-7pm, Su 9am-1pm. **Prenotazioni Alberghi e Ristoranti** (☎0577 28 80 84/84 80; fax 28 02 90), in P. S. Domenico, reserves accommodations (€2). Also books reservations for 2hr. walking tours of Siena (M-F 3pm; reserve by 1pm; €20) and San Gimignano. Open M-Sa 9am-7pm, Su 9am-noon. AmEx/MC/V.

Budget Travel: CTS, V. Sallustio Bandini 21 (☎0577 28 50 08). Student travel services. Open M-F and Su 9am-12:30pm and 3:30-7pm. MC/V.

Laundromat: Express Wash, V. Pantaneto 38. Self-service. Wash €3.50, dry €3.50. **Onda Blu,** V. Casato di Sotto 17. Wash €3 per 7kg, dry €3. Both open daily 8am-10pm.

English-Language Bookstore: Libreria Ticci, V. delle Terme 5/7 (☎0577 28 00 10). Extensive selection. Open M-Sa 9am-7:30pm. AmEx/MC/V. **Feltrinelli,** V. Banchi di Sopra 64 (☎0577 44 009). Classics, popular fiction, and English-language magazines. Open M-Sa 9am-7:30pm, Su 11am-1:30pm and 3:30-7:30pm. AmEx/MC/V.

Luggage Storage: At TRA-IN ticket office beneath P. Gramsci. €3 per 12hr., €5 per day. No overnight storage. Open daily 7am-7pm. Cash only.

Police: on V. del Castoro (☎112) near the *duomo*.

Pharmacy: Farmacia del Campo, P. del Campo 26. Open M-F 9am-1pm and 4-8pm. Posts after-hours rotations. MC/V.

Hospital: V. Le Scotte 14 (☎0577 58 51 11). Take bus #3 or 77 from P. Gramsci.

Internet Access: Cafe Internet/International Call Center, V. Cecco Angiolieri 16 (☎0577 41 521). €2 per hr. Open M-Sa 8:30am-11pm, Su 9am-11pm. Cash only. **Internet Train,** V. di Città 121 (☎0577 22 63 66). Wi-Fi available. €5 per hr. Open M-F 10am-8pm, Sa-Su noon-8pm. MC/V. **Branch** at V. Pantaneto 54 (☎0577 24 74 60). €5 per hr. Open M-F 10am-10pm, Su 2-8pm. MC/V.

Post Office: P. Matteotti 36. Open M-Sa 8:15am-7pm. **Postal Code:** 53100.

🕪 🕪 ACCOMMODATIONS AND CAMPING

Finding a room in central Siena can be difficult and expensive in the summer. Book months in advance for the Palio (p. 464). For visits over a week, *affittacamere* (room rental) are a popular option. Tourist offices can provide a list of these private rooms and help with booking.

Casa Laura, V. Roma 3 (☎0577 22 60 61; fax 22 52 40), 10min. from Il Campo, in the university area. Ring 3rd doorbell down, labeled *"Bencini Valentini."* Sacrifice immediate access to downtown Siena for spacious, well-priced rooms. Some with bath. Kitchen access available. Singles €35-40; doubles €65-67; triples €70; quads €75. MC/V. ❸

Piccolo Hotel Etruria, V. Donzelle 3 (☎0577 28 80 88; www.hoteletruria.com). A stone's throw from Il Campo. Small, family-run establishment maintains 20 immaculate rooms with phone, TV, and hair dryer. Breakfast €5. Curfew 1am. Singles €48, with bath €53; doubles €86; triples €114. Extra bed €28. AmEx/MC/V. ❹

Ostello della Gioventù "Guidoriccio" (HI), V. Fiorentina 89 (☎0577 52 212), in Località Lo Stellino, a 20min. bus ride from town. Take bus #10, 17, or 15 from P. Gramsci. Bus #15 stops at front door. For buses #10 and 17, continue from stop in bus's direction and take 1st right. Hostel is on the right, 50m down. Mostly 2- to 4-person rooms in this

100-bed hostel. Breakfast €1.73; dinner €9.83. Key deposit €1. Lockout 9:30am-3pm. Curfew midnight. Reservation recommended. Dorms €14.45. Cash only. ❶

Albergo Tre Donzelle, V. Donzelle 5 (☎0577 28 03 58; fax 22 39 33). Basic rooms have simple wood furnishings and lots of space. Close to Il Campo. Curfew 1am. Singles €38; doubles €49, with bath €70; triples €70/85; quads €84/104. AmEx/MC/V. ❸

Albergo Bernini, V. della Sapienza 15 (☎0577 28 90 47; www.albergobernini.com). 9 antique-laden rooms have picture-perfect views of the *duomo.* Outdoor patio is lined with plants, which makes for the perfect setting for a serenade by the accordion-playing owner. Breakfast €7. Curfew midnight. July-Sept. singles with bath €80; doubles €68, with bath €88. Extra bed €15. Oct.-June prices drop 20%. Cash only. ❺

Locanda Garibaldi, V. Giovanni Dupré 18 (☎0577 28 42 04). Heavy carved wood doors and plenty of free brochures welcome guests to the lobby of this economical hotel. Most rooms with bath. Restaurant/bar in lobby. Curfew midnight. Reservation recommended. Doubles €75. Extra bed €10. Cash only. ❸

Hotel Domus, V. Camporeggio 37 (☎0577 44 177; fax 47 601), next to Santuario di Santa Caterina and Chiesa San Domenico. Though a quieter area during the day, 2 nearby restaurants prevent an uninterrupted night's sleep. Run by nuns. Bare rooms have bath, stone floors, A/C, and floral sheets. Ask ahead of time for a *duomo* view. Curfew 1:30am. Singles €42; doubles €65; triples €80; quads €95. Cash only. ❹

Camping Colleverde, Strada di Scacciapensieri 47 (☎0577 28 00 44). Take bus #3 or 17 from train station or bus #8 (both every 30min.) from P. del Sale; confirm stop with driver. Grocery store, restaurant, and pool (open 10am-6pm). Reception 7:30am-11pm. Open from late Mar. to mid-Nov. €8 per adult, €4.30 per child; €4 per tent. MC/V. ❶

⬛ FOOD

Siena specializes in rich pastries. The most famous is *panforte,* a concoction of honey, almonds, and citron, once baked as a trail mix for the Crusaders. For a lighter snack, try *ricciarelli,* soft almond cookies topped with powdered sugar. Sample either (€2.20 per 100g) at the **Bar/Pasticceria Nannini,** V. Banchi di Sopra 22-24, Siena's oldest *pasticceria,* which has evolved into a chain. (Open M-Th 7:30am-9pm, F-Sa 7:30am-10pm, and Su 8am-9pm.) The local meat specialty, *cinta senese,* is also popular. Siena's **open-air market** fills P. La Lizza each Wednesday (8am-1pm). For groceries, head to **Conad,** in P. Matteoti (open M-Sa 8:30am-8:30pm, Su 9am-1pm and 4-8pm; MC/V), or **Pam,** in the mall next to the train station (open M-Sa 8:30am-9:30pm, Su 9am-9pm. AmEx/MC/V).

⬛ Trattoria Papei, P. del Mercato 6 (☎0577 28 08 94), on the far side of Palazzo Pubblico from Il Campo. Shaded, outdoor tables and a large, stone-arched dining room can get crowded and noisy. Vast range of homemade pasta dishes, including scrumptious *pici alla cardinale* (spaghetti with tomato-pepper sauce and pancetta; €7), and traditional dishes like savory *coniglio all'arrabbiata* (rabbit with hot spices; €9). Cover €2. Open Tu-Su noon-3pm and 7-10:30pm. AmEx/MC/V. ❸

Osteria La Chiacchera, Costa di San Antonio 4 (☎0577 28 06 31), next to Santuario di Santa Caterina. Frequented by young Italians and savvy tourists, the restaurant offers delicious food at low prices in a casual and lively atmosphere. Primi €5-6. Secondi €8-12. Open M and W-Su noon-3:30pm and 7pm-midnight. AmEx/MC/V. ❷

Il Cucchiaio di Legno, V. Calzoleria 12 (☎0577 28 90 10), off V. Banchi di Sotto. This relatively new establishment is already attracting a crowd—drawing in tourists and locals with the aromas of great Italian eats. Although a relatively generic menu, there are plenty of options, including steak (€3.50 per 100g). Primi €5.50-7. Secondi €8.50-13. Open daily noon-2:30pm and 7:30-10:30pm. ❸

Siena

ACCOMMODATIONS
Albergo Bernini, **5**
Albergo Tre Donzelle, **10**
Camping Colleverde, **2**
Casa Laura, **15**
Locanda Garibaldi, **18**
Ostello della Gioventù
  "Guidoriccio" (HI), **1**
Piccolo Hotel Etruria, **14**

FOOD
Il Cucchiaio di Legno, **12**
Gelateria Brivido, **17**
Osteria La Chiacchera, **6**
Osteria Il Grattacielo, **4**
Trattoria Papei, **19**
Nonno Mede, **8**

NIGHTLIFE
Bar Porrione, **21**
Barone Rosso, **13**
Caffè del Corso, **22**
Tea Room, **20**
Maudit Music Pub, **23**
Gallery, **24**

Nonno Mede, V. Camporeggio 21 (☎0577 24 79 66), down the hill to the left of Chiesa San Domenico. Choose from an extensive pizza menu and enjoy the expansive outdoor seating area that has great views of the *duomo* and picturesque Siena rooftops. Serves everything from mixed vegetables to stuffed rabbit. Pizza €5.50-7. Primi €6-7.50. Secondi €10-15. Open daily noon-3:30pm and 7pm-1:30am. MC/V. ❶

Osteria Il Grattacielo, V. dei Pontani 8 (☎0577 33 46 31 14 60), between V. dei Termini and V. Banchi di Sopra. The perfect place to enjoy native culinary delights, including baby artichokes, olives, sun-dried tomatoes in oil, and hunks of salami and *pecorino*. Half the fun here is ordering—add ingredients to your base meal by pointing at jars of food to create your dream lunch. A full meal with wine runs under €10. Open M-F 8am-2:45pm and 5:30-7pm, Sa 8am-2:45pm and 5:30-6pm. Cash only. ❷

Gelateria Brivido, V. dei Pellegrini 1-3 (☎0577 28 00 58). Gelato in flavors like kiwi and watermelon are presented in spiraling towers served standing-room only. Cones come plain or chocolate-dipped (€2-5.50). Open daily 10am-midnight. Cash only. ❶

SIGHTS

IL CAMPO. Siena radiates from the **Piazza del Campo,** a shell-shaped square designed for civic events and affectionately referred to as "Il Campo." The *piazza's* brick paving is divided into nine sections, representing the city's medieval Council of Nine. Dante's *Inferno* referred to the square in the account of the real-life drama of Provenzan Salvani, a heroic Sienese merchant who pan-handled in Il Campo to pay a friend's ransom. Later Sienese mystics used the *piazza* as a public auditorium. Today, Il Campo is framed by restaurants and cafes overlooking the monstrous clock tower, and provides the perfect hang-out for tourists and locals alike. Twice each summer, the **Palio** (p. 464) morphs the mellow Campo into a chaotic arena as horses race around its edge. At the top of the slope is the **Fonte Gaia,** a rectangular marble fountain nestled into the slanted *piazza.* The water here emerges from the same 25km aqueduct that has refreshed Siena since the 14th century. Standing at the bottom of the *piazza* is the imposing **Palazzo Pubblico,** with its looming *campanile,* the **Torre del Mangia.** In front of the *palazzo* is the **Cappella di Piazza,** which was started in 1348, but took 100 years to complete due to the Black Death's untimely arrival.

▨PALAZZO PUBBLICO. This impressive medieval building was home to Siena's Council of Nine in the Middle Ages. It still houses city government offices, but the main draw is its **Museo Civico.** While the Sienese art pieces here range from medieval triptychs to 18th-century landscapes, the greatest treasure is the col-lection of late-medieval to early-Renaissance painting in the distinctive Sienese style. The large and airy **Sala del Mappamondo,** named for a lost series of astro-nomical frescoes, displays Simone Martini's *Maestà,* which combines religious overtones with civic and literary awareness. The Christ Child is depicted hold-ing a parchment inscribed with the city motto of upholding justice, *"Expertus fidelem,"* and the steps of the canopied throne are engraved with two stanzas from Dante's *Divine Comedy.* In the next room, the **Sala dei Nove** holds Ambro-gio Lorenzetti's famous frescoes, the *Allegories of Good and Bad Government and their Effects on Town and Country,* with opposing visions of damnation and utopia on the right and left walls. *(Open daily Mar.-Oct. 10am-6:15pm; Nov.-Feb. 10am-5:30pm. €7, EU students €4.50, under 11 free. Cash only.)* The Palazzo Pubblico's other star attraction is the **Torre del Mangia,** named for the gluttonous bell-ringer, Giovanni di Duccio, also called *"Mangiaguadagni"* (Eat the profits). At 102m, Italy's tallest secular medieval monument is Siena's equivalent of the North Star. Lost tourists need only search for the tower's ornate top to orient them-selves. After 500 dizzying and narrow steps, persistence pays off underneath the tower's highest bell: from the top, Siena's tile rooftops, farmlands, and vine-yard hills form an enchanting mosaic. Arrive early, as it gets crowded in the afternoon. *(Open daily Mar. 16-Oct. 10am-6:15pm; Nov.-Mar. 15 10am-4pm. €6. Cash only.)*

▨DUOMO. Atop one of the city's seven hills, the *duomo* is one of few com-pletely Gothic cathedrals south of the Alps. Construction began in 1229, and the entire structure was completed over a hundred years later. The dome was built in 1263, and the bell tower by 1313. A huge arch, part of a striped wall facing the front of the cathedral, is the sole remnant of Siena's 1339 plan to con-struct a new nave, which would have made this *duomo* the largest church in all Christendom. The effort ended when the Black Plague decimated the work-ing population in 1348. One of the *duomo*'s side aisles has been enclosed and turned into the **Museo dell'Opera Metropolitana.** Statues of philosophers, sibyls, and prophets, all by Giovanni Pisano, hold sway beneath impressive spires.

The bronze sun on the *duomo*'s facade was the creation of San Bernadino of Siena, who wanted the feuding Sienese to relinquish their emblems of nobility to unite under this symbol of the risen Christ. Alas, his efforts were in vain—the Sienese continue to identify with the animal symbols of their *contrade* (dis-tricts). The marble floor, like the rest of the *duomo,* is ornate, depicting such diverse and often violent themes as the *Slaughter of the Innocents.* Michelan-gelo, Donatello, Pinturicchio, and Bernini are just a few of the many renowned

TUSCANY

artists who worked on the floor, called "the Unveiled Floor" because it is only open to the public mid-August through October. Halfway up the left aisle is the **Piccolomini Altar,** designed by Andrea Bregno in 1503. The statue was built to host a very special holy relic—St. John's right arm. The lavish Libreria Piccolomini, commissioned by Pope Pius III in 1492, houses elaborately illustrated books of his uncle, Pius II. On the right, the **Papal Chapel of Madonna del Voto** houses two Bernini statues. *(Open daily 1st 2 weeks in Mar. and Oct. 10:30am-7:30pm; Mar. 16–Sept. 10:30am-8:00pm; Nov.-Feb. 10:30am-6:30pm. Open holidays Mar.-Oct. 1:30-6pm and Nov.-Feb. 1:30-5:30pm. Modest dress required. €4-5.50. Cash only.)*

Outside and downhill lies the 15th-century **baptistry.** Inside, lavish and intricate frescoes depict the lives of Christ and St. Anthony. The central part of the ceiling, known as the *"Vecchietta,"* depicts scenes from the Apostles Creed. The baptistry's centerpiece is the hexagonal Renaissance baptismal font (1417-31) of marble, bronze, and enamel. Panels include Ghiberti's *Baptism of Christ* and *Prediction of John the Baptist,* as well as *Herod's Feast* by Donatello. *(Open daily Mar. 15-Sept. 9:30am-8pm; 1st 2 weeks in Mar. and Oct. 9:30am-7:30pm; Nov.-Feb. 10am-5pm. Modest dress required. €3. Cash only.)*

X MARKS THE SPOT. If you look closely, you'll notice a small cross two-thirds of the way up the stairs that lead from P. S. Giovanni to the entrance of the *duomo.* This mark is neither a trick of the pavement, nor is it graffiti. Legend has it that this step is where St. Catherine of Siena tripped and fell down the stairs in the 14th century, supposedly pushed by the devil. Despite the steepness and severity of the marble steps, she walked away without a scratch: *un miracolo* worthy only of a saint, as any Sienese will tell you.

CRIPTA. Recently rediscovered in 1999, these 700-year-old underground rooms were not tombs but a preparation for pilgrims entering the *duomo.* These 13th-century depictions of the Old and New Testament are attributed to the pre-Duccio Sienese painters, including Diotisalvi di Speme, Guido da Siena, and Guido di Graziano. Due to the absence of light, climatic instability, and human intervention, the colors remain vibrant and detailed. *(In P. del Duomo, entrance halfway down stairs, to the left of the baptistry. Open daily Mar. 15-Sept. 9:30am-8pm; 1st 2 weeks in Mar. and Oct. 9am-6pm; Nov.-Feb. 10am-5pm. €6, students €5. Ticket includes audio guide in French, German, Italian, or English. Cash only.)*

MUSEO DELL'OPERA METROPOLITANA. This museum holds all the art that won't fit in the *duomo.* The first floor contains some of the foremost Gothic statuary in Italy, all by Giovanni Pisano. Upstairs the 700-year-old *Maestà,* by Duccio di Buoninsegna, originally served as a screen for the cathedral's altar. Other notable works are the Byzantine *Madonna dagli Occhi Grossi,* paintings by Lorenzetti, and two altarpieces by Matteo di Giovanni. Follow signs for the **Panorama dal Facciatone,** in Room 4, to a balcony over the nave. A very narrow spiral staircase leads to a tiny tower for a beautiful, unadvertised view of the entire city. *(Museum entrance outside of duomo. Exit portals and turn left. Open daily Mar.-Sept. 9:30am-7:30pm; Oct. 9:30am-7pm; Nov.-Feb. 14 10am-4:30pm. €6. Cash only.)*

OSPEDALE DI SANTA MARIA DELLA SCALA. Built as a hospital in the 13th century, the *ospedale* is now a museum displaying its original frescoes, chapels, and vaults. The **Sala del Pellegrinaio,** or the Pilgrims' Hall, used as a ward until the late 20th century, contains an expressive fresco cycle by Vecchietta, which tells the history of the hospital's construction. The **Sagrestia Vecchia,** or *Cappello del Sacro Chiodo,* houses masterful 15th-century Sienese frescoes. On the way downstairs, duck into the dim underground chapels and vaults, sites of rituals and "acts of piety for the dead" performed by various *contrade*. One level down is the entrance to the **Museo Archeologico,** included in admission to the *ospedale*. Established in 1933 to preserve Etruscan artifacts from the Siena area, the museum is now almost entirely housed in the eerie, medieval, underground water works of the city. Signs point the way through dank, labyrinthine passageways before emerging into rooms with well-lit displays of Etruscan pottery and coins. *(Opposite the duomo. Open daily Mar.-Nov. 10:30am-6:30pm; Dec.-Feb. 10:30am-4:30pm. Last entry 30min. before closing. €6, students €3.50, under 11 free. Cash only.)*

PINACOTECA NAZIONALE. Siena's superb art gallery displays works by every major artist of the highly stylized Sienese school. Masters represented include seven followers of Duccio—Simone Martini, the Lorenzetti brothers, Bartolo di Fredi, Bartolomeo Bulgarini, Sano di Pietro, and Il Sodoma. The museum is refreshingly free of tourist hordes, although the collection is best geared toward art-lovers. *(V. S. Pietro 29, in the Palazzo Buonsignori down V. del Capitano from the duomo. Open M 8:30am-1:30pm, Tu-Sa 8:15am-7:15pm, Su 8:15am-1:15pm. €4, EU citizens and students 18-26 €2, EU citizens under 18 or over 65 free. Cash only.)*

SANTUARIO DI SANTA CATERINA. This sanctuary honors Sienese St. Catherine, who had a miraculous vision of Christ coming to her with a ring and proposing marriage. Known for her outspoken manner, Mary persuaded Pope Gregory XI to return to Rome from Avignon in 1377; in 1939 she was proclaimed one of Italy's patron saints. The brick buildings and airy courtyards, converted into a Renaissance loggia, branch into Baroque chapels. The **Chiesa del Crocefisso,** on the right, is impressive, but don't overlook the beautiful but smaller **Oratorio della Cucina,** on the left. *(Entrance at the intersection of Costa di San Antonio and V. dei Pittori, down from P. S. Domenico on V. della Sapienza. Open daily 9am-12:30pm and 3-6pm. Free.)*

OTHER SIGHTS. Siena's Franciscan and Dominican basilicas rival each other from opposite ends of town. The **Chiesa di San Domenico** contains Andrea Vanni's portrait of Saint Catherine and several other dramatic frescoes that illustrate her miraculous acts. The exquisite chapel inside, dedicated to Santa Caterina, was built in 1460 to store her preserved head and half of one of her fingers, still on display today for the curious and non-squeamish. *(In P. S. Domenico. Open daily Nov.-Apr. 9am-1pm and 3-5:30pm; May-Oct. 7am-1pm and 3-7pm. Modest dress required. Free.)* Those interested in the Palio may enjoy one of Siena's 17 **contrada museums.** Each neighborhood organization maintains its own collection of costumes, banners, and icons. *(Most require an appointment at least 1 week in advance; inquire at the tourist office for information.)* Take a break from sightseeing for a stroll within the brick walls of the **Fortezza Medicea,** filled with fountains and towers. *(Just north of P. Gramsci on Vle. Cesare Maccari. Open from dawn to dusk. Free.)*

🎵 📷 ENTERTAINMENT AND NIGHTLIFE

Siena's ☗**Palio,** hands-down the highlight of the town's entertainment, overtakes the city twice each year, on July 2 and August 16, transforming Siena into an exciting frenzy as people pack Il Campo to watch the bareback horse race. Even when it doesn't involve barbaric races, Siena's nightlife is kept booming by the large population of local and foreign students. A great place to sample regional wines is **Enoteca Italiana,** in the Fortezza Medicea near the entrance off Vle. Cesare Maccari, where fine wines are sold by the bottle or by the glass, from €3.50. (☎0577 22 88 13. Open Apr.-Sept. M noon-8pm, Tu-Sa noon-1am; Oct.-Mar. M-W noon-8pm, Th-Sa noon-1am. AmEx/MC/V.) **Accademia Musicale Chigiana,** V. di Città 89 (☎0577 22 091; www.chigiana.it) organizes classical music concerts throughout the year.

▨ **Caffé del Corso,** V. Bancha di Sopra 25 (☎/fax 0566 22 66 56; www.caffedelcor sosiena.it.) Cheap eats upstairs; bar downstairs that doubles as an outdoor dance floor in summer. Mixed drinks €2.50-5. 3-shot specials €5. Open daily 8am-3am.

▨ **Gallery,** V. Pantaneto 16-22 (☎0577 34 05 73 16 32). A central bar that serves a variety of drink specials from a bottle pyramid illuminated by colored fluorescent lights. Beer €4.50. Mixed drinks €6. Open Tu and Th-Sa 6pm-3am.

Barone Rosso, V. dei Termini 9 (☎0577 28 66 86; www.barone-rosso.com). A study-abroad crowd sprinkled with locals. Lively themed parties. Live music F and Sa; reduced prices for international students W. Open daily 9pm-3am. AmEx/MC/V.

Maudit Music Pub, Vc. della Manna 25 (☎0577 46 818). Follow V. Salicotto, the left center street leading off P. il Campo facing the clock tower, and turn left onto Vc. della Manna. A mostly teenage crowd chills at this pub, known for its great pizza (€4.50), cheap drinks (€2.50-5), and live music. Open 8pm-2am.

Bar Porrione, V. Porrione 44, off P. del Campo. Large bar, with limited indoor and outdoor seating. Plays contemporary American music but sells traditional Italian drinks, including *Negroni* (€3.50). If drinking and mingling with locals gets tiring, there are arcade machines in back. Open daily 10am-3am.

Tea Room, V. di Pta. Giustizia 9 (☎0577 22 27 53), down a small staircase to the left behind P. Mercato. Though alcoholic beverages are available, many customers choose from an extensive menu of desserts and exotic teas. Melt into the cushions of a comfy couch near the fireplace or grab a tiny candlelit table for 2. Tea and other drinks from €4. Open Tu-Su 9pm-3am. Closed for 2 months in summer.

◤ DAYTRIPS FROM SIENA

RADDA IN CHIANTI

Buses connect Siena to Radda in Chianti (1hr., 4 per day, round-trip €5.80). Buses leave from Siena's train station. Take bus 9 to station from Piazza Gramsci. Buses also connect Radda to Florence, though schedules are sporadic; call ☎800 37 37 60 for info. (1hr.; 3 per day; last bus to Florence 6:15pm, last bus to Siena 6:40pm.) In the morning, buses arrive at and depart from V. XX Settembre. In the afternoon, return buses to Florence and Siena leave from a stop across the street about 100m down. Stand in front of the orange sign, and flag down the bus as it approaches.

Siena lies within easy reach of the Chianti region, a harmonious landscape of green hills, ancient castles, tiny villages, and of course, uninterrupted expanses of vineyards. In the Middle Ages, the small countryside towns of Castellina, Radda, and Gaiole formed a military alliance against French and Spanish invaders, adopting the black rooster as their symbol. Today, the rooster adorns bottles of Chianti, which are famous throughout the world. Peaceful **Radda in Chianti** (RAD-da; pop. 1668) just 30km from Siena, makes a great base for exploring the surrounding countryside. Every year on the 2nd of June, the town comes together for **Radda in the Glass.** For this one-day event the *enoteche* provide ample bottles of Chianti on outdoor tables along V. Roma as rosy-cheeked citizens and lucky visitors make frequent stops with glasses in hand. For more info on touring nearby wineries, vacation rentals, and excursions to the countryside, inquire at **A Bit of Tuscany,** V. Roma 39, next to Camere di Giovannino. Private tours begin at €60 for 5hr. Larger, public tours are more economical, if slightly less revealing. (☎73 89 48. Open M-F 10am-1pm and 2:30-6pm.) If you can get out of town, most wineries in the area give free tastings, though a stroll down V. Roma also reveals numerous **enoteche** willing to let you sample for free. Cellar tours often require reservations—tourist offices provide bookings.

Located in the center of town, the outgoing staff at **La Bottega di Giovannino** ❷, V. Roma 37, serves filling plates on a breezy outdoor patio or in a wine-bottle laden dining room. Pair pasta with a glass of *Chianti Classico* (from €3.50). The Bernardoni family lovingly maintains their restaurant and also offers transportation and tours for groups of seven or fewer to local wineries. (☎73 80 56; www.labottegadigiovannino.it. Primi €6. Secondi €6-9. Open M and W-Su 8:30am-10:30pm. MC/V.) After a rigorous day of wine-tasting, relax in the public gardens outside the city walls, near P. IV Novembre. Inside the reputable **Porciatti Alimentari** ❷, P. IV Novembre 1-3, master butchers sell aged, handmade salami, pork sausages, and cheese that are also available for tasting. Across the street and down Camminamento Medievale, a medieval passage-way from the 14th century, is **Casa Porciatti,** run by the same owners. Savor the free samples of wine, *grappa*, and olive oil, or schedule a tasting with a larger group (6-8 people) for €8-12. (☎73 80 55; www.casaporciatti.it. Wine from €6 per bottle. *Alimentari* open May-Oct. M-Sa 8am-1pm and 4-8pm, Su 8am-1pm; Nov.-Apr. M-Sa 8am-1pm and 4:30-7:30pm. *Casa* open M-Sa 10:30am-7pm, Su 10:30am-12:30pm and 3-7pm. MC/V.) The innovative **Pizzeria da Michele** ❸, P. IV Novembre 4, down a flight of stairs from the main bus stop, has valley views and a menu that changes seasonally to incorporate the freshest produce. (☎73 84 91. Pizza served only at dinner. Primi €7-12.50. Secondi €12-16. Cover €2. Open Tu-Su noon-2:30pm and 7pm-midnight. AmEx/MC/V.) The cheapest place to pick up wine is the **Coop** supermarket, V. Roma 26, which stocks bottles from €2.50. (Open M-Tu and Th-Sa 8:30am-1pm and 4-8pm, W 8:30am-1pm. MC/V.)

 HIGH TIMES. Many hotels in the Tuscan wine country consider Sept. and Oct. to be their high season (instead of the typical July and Aug. tourist peak in Italy) because of the grape harvest. Prices can jump to €10-30 per night. Of course, you may not care so much after a couple of glasses of bubbly.

MONTEPULCIANO

A bus is the easiest way to reach Montepulciano; the train station is 10km out of town, with no reliable bus linking it to the city. A TRA-IN bus connects Siena to Montepulciano (1½hr., M-Sa 5 per day, €4.70), some via Buonconvento. The Ufficio delle Strade del Vino, P. Grande 7, provides maps and bus schedules, makes free arrangements for hotels and nearby affittacamere, and sells tickets for wine and olive-oil tours. (☎0578 71 74 84; www.stradavinonobile.it. Open M-Sa 10am-1pm and 3-6pm.) The tourist office in P. Don Minzoni, off V. Sangallo, sells maps (€0.50) and provides free brochures. Internet available for €3.50 per hr. (☎0578 75 73 41. Open daily 9:30am-12:30pm, M-Sa 3-7:30pm.)

Situated atop a limestone ridge, this small, medieval hamlet is Tuscany's high-est hill town. Sixteenth-century *palazzi* and *piazze* grace Montepulciano's (Mohn-teh-pool-CHYA-no; pop. 5,000) narrow streets and walkways. After cen-turies of neglect following the Renaissance, this walled town is now wealthy and heavily touristed, largely as a result of its traditional *Vino Nobile* and its famous red wine industry. Visitors busy themselves browsing the wine stores and tasting free samples. Enjoy a few sips at the shop at **Porta di Bacco,** on the left immediately inside the city gates. (Open daily 9am-8pm.) **Alimentari** selling local Tuscan products line V. Gracciano nel Corso. For a delicious selection of typical Tuscan food, visit **Osteria Acquacheta** ❷, V. del Teatro 22, off V. di Voltaia nel Corso, where you savor a platter of *pecorino fresco al tartufo* (soft pecorino cheese with truffles; €5.20) while chatting up fellow diners. (Primi €5.20-7.50. Secondi €3 per 100g. Open M and W-Su 12:30-3pm and 7:30-10:30pm. MC/V.) Try the *pollo e coniglio all'Etrusca* (Etruscan-style chicken and rabbit; €10.40) at **Il Cantuccio** ❸, V. delle Cantine 1-2, where tuxedo-clad waiters serve elegant dishes under dim lights. (☎0578 75 78 70. Primi €7.50-10. Secondi €9-16. Service 12%. Open Tu-Su 12:30-2:30pm and 7:30-11pm. MC/V.) **Ristorante ai Quattro Venti ❸**, P. Grande 2 (☎0578 71 72 31), in the heart of the central *piazza*, provides outdoor seating overlooking the *duomo*. Try the heavenly *ribollita* (€8), a vegetable soup with fresh bread. (Open Su-W and F-Sa 12:30-2:30pm and 7:30-10:30pm. Primi €7.60-8.20. Secondi €8.30-15. MC/V.) The **open-air market** is every Thursday in P. del Mercato, in parking lot #5 off V. delle Lettere. For cheap groceries head to **Conad**, V. Bernabei 4/A, 50m downhill from Chiesa Sant'Agnese. (☎0578 71 67 31. Open M-Sa 8:30am-8pm. MC/V.)

From P. Grande, follow V. Ricci to V. della Mercezia. Turn left down staircase before Piazzetta di S. Francesco. Follow signs, through the city walls, and along V. di San Biagio. The **Chiesa di San Biagio,** built on a wide, grassy plateau, is a stunning example of high-Renaissance symmetry. The cavernous interior was redone in the 17th century in overwrought Baroque, but the simplicity of the original still shines through. The surrounding area has stunning views of the rolling Tuscan hills and the houses poised in between. *(Open daily 9am-1pm and 3:30-7pm. Free.)* Montepulciano's main square, **Piazza Grande,** is surrounded by the **Palazzo Tarugi** to the north, an unfinished *duomo* to the south, the **Palazzo Contucci** to the east, and the 14th-century **Palazzo Comunale** to the west. The exterior of the *duomo*, Santa Maria Assunta (1594-1680), is somber, with simple, bare walls that contrast with several great oil paintings. Note the Sienese master Taddeo di Bartolo's poignant *Assumption of the Virgin* above the altar. (Open daily 9am-12:30pm and 2:30-6:30pm. Free.) Since most lodgings in Montepulciano are pricey three- or four-star hotels, *affittacamere* (rooms for rent) are the best option if you absolutely must spend the night.

A PLAN A DAY KEEPS THE HIKING AWAY. On its way to Siena, the southbound bus stops twice in Montepulciano. The 1st stop is at V. dell'Oriolo, in a parking lot at the higher end of the city. From the bus stop, climb the stairs along V. delle Mura to arrive at V. dell'Opio nel Corso. The 2nd stop is at the bus station at the bottom of the hill. Before entering Montepulciano, know which stop you want. While the trek offers great views, hiking is never fun with a gargantuan backpack.

SAN GIMIGNANO ☎0577

The hilltop village of San Gimignano (san jee-meen-YA-no; pop. 7000) looks like an illustration from a medieval manuscript. Churches and the town's 14 famous towers, all that remain of the original 72, loom above the city's walls. The impressive towers date back to a period when prosperous families battled each other, using their towers to store grain for sieges. They were also conveniently used for dumping boiling oil on attacking enemies. After WWII, the skyline began to lure tourists, whose tastes and wallets resuscitated production of the golden *Vernaccia* wine. Despite hordes of daytrippers and an infestation of souvenir shops, the fortress-top sunsets, nighttime gelato strolls, and ample spots for lounging on *piazza* steps make an overnight stay worthwhile.

⬛ TRANSPORTATION

Trains: the nearest station is in Poggibonsi. MiniBuses go from the station to town (20min.; M-F every 30min. 6:05am-8:35pm, Sa-Su every hr. 7:35am-8:20pm; €1.80).

Buses: TRA-IN, Ple. Martiri Montemaggio (☎800 57 05 30 or 20 42 46; www.sienamobilita.it), outside Pta. San Giovanni. Schedules and tickets are at Caffè Combattente,

V. S. Giovanni 124, on the left after entering the city gates, at *tabaccherie,* or at the tourist office. Change at Poggibonsi for **Florence** (1hr., every hr., €6). Buses also run to **Siena** (1hr., every 1-2hr., €5.40), departing at Poggibonsi and in Ple. Martiri Montemaggio, across from the bottom of V. S. Giovanni.

Bike and Car Rentals: Bruno Bellini, V. Roma 41 (☎0577 94 02 01; www.bellinibruno. com). Bikes €7-11 per hr., €15-21 per day. Scooters from €32-35 per day. Cars from €60 per day. Open daily 9am-1pm and 3-7:30pm. AmEx/MC/V.

✈ ⁊ ORIENTATION AND PRACTICAL INFORMATION

Buses to San Gimignano stop in **Piazzale Martiri Montemaggio,** just outside the city walls. To reach the *centro,* pass through **Porta San Matte,** climb the hill, and follow **Via San Giovanni** to **Piazza della Cisterna,** which merges with **Piazza del Duomo.** The town's other main street, **Via San Matteo,** extends from the other side of P. del Duomo. Addresses in San Gimignano are marked in both black stencil and etched clay tiles; most establishments go by the black, so these are listed.

Tourist Office: Protur, P. del Duomo 1 (☎0577 94 00 08; www.sangimignano.com), has *affittacamere* listings and bus tickets. Audio tours of the town €5. Free maps and help with hotel bookings. 2hr. tours of wineries Tu and Th 5pm with tastings (€18, with transportation €20); reserve by noon the day before. Open daily 10:30am-1pm and 3-6pm.

Accommodations Services: Associazione Strutture Extralberghiere, P. della Cisterna 6 (☎/fax 0577 94 31 90). Patient staff makes free reservations for private rooms. Call a week ahead to stay in the countryside; the *centro* is easier to book. Open Mar.-Nov. daily 10am-1pm and 3-6pm. MC/V.

Currency Exchange: Tourist office and post office offer best rates. **ATMs** scattered along V. S. Giovanni, V. degli Innocenti, and P. della Cisterna.

Carabinieri: (☎0577 94 03 13), in P. Martiri.

Pharmacy: P. della Cisterna 8, on the far left coming from V.S. Giovanni (☎0577 94 03 69; at night ☎348 00 21 710). Open M-Sa 9am-1pm and 5-7:30pm. AmEx/MC/V.

Internet Access: Edicola La Tuscia, V. Garibaldi 2, outside the gates to the right of Pta. San Matteo. €5 per hr. Open daily 7:30am-1pm and 2:30-7:30pm. Cash only.

Post Office: P. delle Erbe 8, behind the *duomo.* Open M-F 8:15am-4pm, Sa 8:15am-12:30pm. **Postal Code:** 53037.

⌂ ⌂ ACCOMMODATIONS AND CAMPING

San Gimignano caters to wealthy tourists, and most accommodations are well beyond budget range. *Affittacamere* provide an alternative to overpriced hotels, with most doubles with bath from €70. An abundance of signs for "*Camere/Rooms/Zimmer*" hang in souvenir shops, restaurants, and other storefront windows along main streets. The tourist office and the Associazione Strutture Extralberghiere have lists of budget rooms.

▨ **Camere Gianni Cennini,** V. S. Giovanni 21 (☎0577 347 074 8188; www.sangiapartments.com). Enter through Pta. San Giovanni. Reception is at the *pasticceria* at V. S. Giovanni 88. Each room is lovingly decorated by the young English-speaking owner, with large baths and scenic views of the surrounding vineyards. Kitchen use €15. Reservations recommended. Singles €45; doubles €55-60; triples €70; quads €85. MC/V. ❹

Albergo Il Pino, V. Cellolese 4 (☎/fax 0577 94 04 15), just off V. S. Matteo before exiting Pta. S. Matteo. 7 spacious rooms owned by the restaurant downstairs have hand-sewn comforters, antique furnishings, comfy sofa chairs, and TV. Reservations recommended. Singles €45; doubles €55. AmEx/MC/V. ❹

TUSCANY

Hotel La Cisterna, P. della Cisterna 23 (☎0577 94 03 28; www.hotelcisterna.it). Panoramic views of San Gimignano from atop a hill in a central *piazza*. All 49 large rooms have bath, A/C, and satellite TV. Breakfast included. Singles €62-78; doubles €87-100, with view €100-118, with balcony €107-140. Extra bed €25-30. AmEx/MC/V. ❺

Podere Sant'Elena, Loc. Racciano 42/A (☎0577 94 19 62; www.poderesantelena. com). Bed and breakfast in a colonial house offers luxuries sure to spoil, including on-site pool and freshly baked pastries served every morning. Though located in a converted barn, sound-proof rooms are spacious and private, and equipped with A/C, bath, TV, and phone. Singles €80-100; doubles €90-105. Extra bed €35. ❺

Camping Boschetto di Piemma (☎0577 94 03 52; www.boschettodipiemma.it), at Località Santa Lucia 38/C, 2km downhill from Pta. San Giovanni. Buses (€0.50) run from Ple. Martiri Montemaggio; confirm destination with driver before boarding. Small, wooded sites close together, but near community pool. Bar and market on premises. Tennis €4 per hr. Hot showers free. Reception daily 8am-1pm and 3-11pm. €6.50-9.40 per person; €5-9 per tent; €2-3 per car. Apartment for 2 people €70-80. For stays longer than 3 nights, 15% discount begins with 4th night. AmEx/MC/V. ❶

◖ FOOD

San Gimignano specializes in *cinghiale* (boar) and other wild game, though it also caters to less daring palates with mainstream Tuscan dishes at high prices. A weekly **open-air market** is in P. del Duomo and P. della Cisterna. (Open Th 8am-1pm.) Purchase the famous *Vernaccia di San Gimignano*, a light, sweet white wine, from **La Buca**, V. S. Giovanni 16, for around €4.50 per bottle. This cooperative also offers tastes of terrific sausages and meats produced on its own farm. The boar sausage *al pignoli* (with pine nuts; €2.07 per 100g) and the oddly satisfying *salame con mirto* (salami with blueberry) are delicious. (☎0577 94 04 07. Open daily Apr.-Oct. 9am-8pm; Nov.-Mar. 10am-6pm. AmEx/MC/V.)

▨ **Trattoria Chiribiri,** P. della Madonna 1 (☎0577 94 19 48). From the bus stop, take 1st left off V. S. Giovanni and climb a short staircase or follow your nose down the sidestreet. Especially fragrant is the *zuppa di pollo,* an old-fashioned chicken soup served Italian style. Unusually affordable local fare. Primi €5.50-7.50. Secondi €7-15. Open M-Tu and Th-Su Mar.-Oct.11am-11pm; Nov.-Feb. noon-2pm and 7-10pm. Cash only. ❷

Pluripremiata Gelateria, P. della Cisterna 4 (☎0577 94 22 44), to the immediate left after the hill. Visitors and locals pack in and surround 3 counters that hold award-winning gelato flavors. Try the *champelmo,* a mix of champagne and grapefruit, or the *Vernaccia,* a gelato version of the region's famous wine. Cups from €1.50. 3 flavors in a chocolate-lined cone €2.50. Open daily 11:30am-9pm. Cash only. ❶

Ristorante Perucà, V. Capassi 16 (☎0577 94 31 36). Behind V. S. Matteo. Charming benches, lanterns, and cheery staff welcome diners to a quiet spot hidden from the tourist bustle. The menu varies seasonally, but is always heavy with secret family recipes that fuse traditional Tuscan fare with atypical spices and ingredients. Primi €5-9. Secondi €10-18. Cover €2. Open daily noon-2:30pm and 7-10:30pm. MC/V. ❸

La Stella, V. S. Matteo 77 (☎0577 94 04 44). Food made with produce from the restaurant's own farm and served in the long, narrow dining room. Extensive wine list includes *Vernaccia* and other local favorites. Primi €6-9.50. Secondi €8-14. *Menù turistico* €15. Cover €2. Open Apr.-Oct. M-Tu and Th-Su noon-3pm and 7-10pm; Nov.-Mar. M-Tu and Th-Su noon-2pm and 7-9pm. AmEx/MC/V. ❸

◖ SIGHTS

Famous as the *Città delle Belle Torri* (City of the Beautiful Towers), San Gimignano has always appealed to artists. During the Renaissance, they came

TUSCANY

in droves, and the collection of their works complements San Gimignano's cityscape. Indeed, it's hard not to be impressed by the proud towers and the humble, winding streets caught in their shadows.

◪PIAZZA DELLA CISTERNA AND PIAZZA DEL DUOMO. P. della Cisterna (1237), surrounded by towers and palaces, is the center of life in San Gimignano. It neighbors P. del Duomo, site of the impressive tower of the **Palazzo del Podestà.** To the left, tunnels and intricate loggias fill the Palazzo del Popolo. To the right of the *palazzo* rises its Torre Grossa, the town's highest tower and the only one visitors can climb. Also in the *piazza* stand the twin towers of the Ardinghelli, truncated due to a medieval zoning ordinance that regulated tower envy by prohibiting structures higher than the Torre Grossa. A perch on one of the steps in either *piazza* offers opportunities to watch scenery and people.

PALAZZO COMUNALE. A frescoed medieval courtyard leads to the entrance to the **Museo Civico** on the second floor. The first room of the museum is the **Sala di Dante,** where the bard spoke on May 8, 1300, in an attempt to convince San Gimignano to side with the Florentines in their ongoing wars with Siena. On the walls, Lippo Memmi's sparkling *Maestà* overwhelms the accompanying 14th-century scenes of hunting and tournament pageantry. Up the stairs, Taddeo di Bartolo's altarpiece, *The Story of San Gimignano*, tells the tale of the city's namesake saint, originally a bishop of Modena. Within the museum lies the entrance to the 218-step climb up ◪**Torre Grossa.** While the final steps are precarious (watch your head on the low ceiling at the top), they are well worth the climb, as the tower offers views of half a dozen of San Gimignano's towers, the ancient fortress, several *piazze*, and the Tuscan landscape stretching to the horizon in all directions. *(Palazzo del Popolo, Museo Civico, and Tower open daily Mar.-Oct. 9:30am-7pm; Nov.-Feb. 10am-6pm. €5, students €4.)*

BASILICA DI SANTA MARIA ASSUNTA. The bare facade of this 12th-century church seems unfit to shelter such an exceptionally frescoed interior. Off the right aisle, the **Cappella di Santa Fina** is covered in Ghirlandaio's frescoes of the life of Santa Fina, the town's ascetic saint who was stricken with a fatal disease at the age of 10. *(In P. del Duomo. Open Apr.-Oct. M-F 9:30am-7:30pm, Sa 9:30am-5pm, Su 12:30-5pm; Nov.-Jan. and Mar. M-Sa 9:30am-5pm, Su 12:30-5pm. €4, under 18 €2. Cash only.)*

FORTEZZA AND MUSEO DEL VINO. Follow the signs past the Basilica di Collegiata from P. del Duomo to this tiny, crumbling fortress. The courtyard has a small cafe, and outdoor seating on the turret offers a beautiful view of the countryside. Park benches enclosed by trees make for a great picnic or lounge spot when visitors clear out in the evening. There are weekly screenings of movies in the courtyard at night from June to August. Pop into the modest wine museum to brush up on your knowledge of *Chianti Classico* and *Vernaccia*. *(Fortezza open dawn until dusk. Museo del Vino ☎0577 94 03 59. Open daily Mar.-Oct. 11:30am-7:30pm; closed W afternoon. Movie schedule and info at the tourist office. €6, children €4.)*

MUSEO PENA DI MORTO AND MUSEO DELLA TORTURO. The Museum of Torture is filled with ancient instruments of castigation, including a Medieval electric chair. Admire the pain that must have been felt before human rights laws and lethal injection, and have fun with interactive displays; a head in a guillotine is always a great photo op. *(V. S. Giovanni 12b. Open 9:30am-8pm. €4.)*

VOLTERRA ☎0588

Atop a huge bluff known as Le Balze, Volterra (Vol-TER-ra; pop. 12,000) is surrounded by a patchwork of green and yellow farmland, strong Etruscan walls, and the rivers Bra and Cecina. Once an important Etruscan settlement, the town shrunk to its current size during the Middle Ages, when outlying parts fell from the eroding hillside. Volterra's Roman amphitheater and famous alabaster work blend centuries of Tuscan tradition with a friendly and much-visited atmosphere. If you've ever wondered why the Tuscan countryside is so popular with visitors, take a short walk to Volterra's perimeter and admire the sprawling vista—you'll understand what all the fuss is about.

TRANSPORTATION

The **train station** that services Volterra is in the nearby town of Cecina. To get there, take the CPT **bus** to Saline (6 per day, Aug. and Su 2 per day; €1.80) and transfer to another CPT bus to Cecina (5 per day, Aug. and Su 2 per day; €1.60) for trains to Pisa (€4) and the coast. **Buses** (☎0588 86 150) are more convenient and centrally located in P. Martiri della Libertà, with daily departures to Florence and Siena (1hr., 4 per day, €7.30) via Colle Val d'Elsa (50min., 5 per day, €2.30). Buses are not timed to meet each other; make plenty of time for connections. Buses also run to Pisa (2hr., 10 per day, €4.90) via Pontederra. Buy tickets at Associazione Pro Volterra, at *tabaccherie*, or at vending machines near the bus stop. No tickets can be purchased on board. For **taxis,** call ☎0588 87 257.

ALL ABOARD! Buses from Volterra are infrequent, often departing just a few times each day. Check bus departures the night before, or you might find yourself spending an unexpected night inside these historic Etruscan walls.

ORIENTATION AND PRACTICAL INFORMATION

To get from the bus stop in **Piazza Martiri della Libertà** to the town center, turn right from the bus stop crossing the *piazza*, and turn left on **Via dei Marchesi** which becomes **Via Ricciarelli** and leads to **Piazza dei Priori,** the central *piazza*.

Tourist Office: Consorzio Turistico, P. dei Priori 19 (☎0588 87 257; www.volterratur.it). Audio walking tours (€5) with suggested footpath itineraries, free hotel and taxi reservations, and *affitacamere* listings. Open daily 10am-1pm and 2-6pm. **Associazione Pro Volterra,** V. Turazza 2 (☎0588 86 150; www.provolterra.it), just off P. dei Priori, sells CPT bus tickets and provides schedule and fare info on trains to Pisa and buses to Florence, Pisa, Saline, San Gimignano, and Siena. Open M-F 9am-noon and 3-6:30pm.

Currency Exchange: Cassa di Risparmio di Volterra, V. Matteotti 1, has a 24hr. exchange machine and an **ATM** outside. Also in P. Martiri della Libertà. Open M-F 8:20am-1:20pm and 2:35-3:35pm, Sa 8:20-11:20am.

Pharmacy: Farmacia Amidei, V. Ricciarelli 2 (emergencies ☎0588 86 060). Open M-Tu and Th-Sa 9am-1pm and 4:30-8pm, Su for emergencies (extra fees apply).

Hospital: (☎0588 91 911), on Borgo San Lazzaro.

Internet Access: ▨Web and Wine, V. Porte all'Arco 11/13 (☎0588 81 531; www.webandwine.com). Surf the web with a glass of *Chianti* or one of 32 different kinds of hot chocolate. High ceilings, glass tables and floors, and views of Etruscan ruins. €4 per hr. Open daily 8:30am-1am. MC/V.

Post Office: P. dei Priori 14 (☎0588 86 969). Open M-F 8:15am-6pm, Sa 8:15am-12:30pm. **Postal Code:** 56048.

ACCOMMODATIONS AND CAMPING

La Torre, V. Guarnacci 47 (☎0588 80 036 or 348 724 7693). From bus stop, turn right into town, then left and immediately right on V. Matteoti, which becomes V. Guarnacci after it crosses V. Gramsci. Arrange arrival ahead of time (no doorbell or formal reception hours). Great *affittacamere* in the *centro storico.* Rooms sport comfy beds, large bath, and TV. Owner supplies free maps, free coffee, and free advice. Kitchen access. Call ahead or book through tourist office. Singles €35; doubles €45. Cash only. ❸

Affittacamere Renzi, P. Martiri della Libertà 8 (☎0588 86 106 or 86 133). Friendly locals rent 1 double and a large apartment, with private bath and thoughtful furnishings. Quiet locations and views of countryside. Minutes from P. dei Priori. Double €50; apartment with kitchen and terrace €65. Reserve ahead. AmEx/MC/V. ❷

Seminario Vescovile, Vle. Vittorio Veneto, 2 (☎0588 86 028; fax 90 791), in Ple. Sant'Andrea, next to the church. Follow directions to La Torre, but turn right on V. Gramsci. Walk through P. XX Settembre, then turn left. Exit city through Pta. Marcoli, and follow the road. Turn left on Vle. V. Veneto until Ple. Sant'Andrea. High arched ceilings, frescoed doorways, and views of the walled city and Tuscan countryside. 1- to 4-person rooms. No unmarried couples. Breakfast €3. Reception 8am-midnight. Curfew midnight. Reservation required. Rooms €15 per person, with bath €20. AmEx/MC/V. ❶

Albergo Etruria, V. Matteotti 32 (☎0588 87 377). Walk into town, turn left, then make the 1st right on V. Matteotti. Sophisticated decor of ivory walls and modern furniture. Rooms offer TV, phone, and views of the courtyard. Breakfast included. Singles €62-72; doubles €82-92; triples €102-115. AmEx/MC/V. ❹

Hotel La Locanda, V. Guarnacci 24/28 (☎0588 81 547; www.hotel-lalocanda.com). A former palace turned convent turned 4-star hotel next to the Amphitheatre Romano. Rooms adorned with local artwork. All have bath, satellite TV, fridge, Internet access, and safe. Breakfast included. Doubles for single use €71-86; doubles €89-109, wheelchair-accessible €85; suite with massaging shower and sauna €250. AmEx/MC/V. ❺

Le Balze, V. Mandringa 15 (☎0588 87 880). Exit through Pta. San Francesco and bear right on Strada Provincial Pisana. Turn left on V. Mandringa after 20min. Pool and bar. Sells bus tickets (every hr. 7:14am-8:09pm). Showers included. Reception 8am-10pm. July-Aug. €9 per person, €12 per tent; Sept.-Oct. and Apr.-June €7/9. AmEx/MC/V. ❶

◨ FOOD

Sample *salsiccia di cinghiale* (wild boar sausage) and *pecorino* (sheep's milk cheese) at any of the *alimentari* along V. Gaurnacci and V. Gramsci. For a sweet snack, try *ossi di morto* (bones of the dead man), a local candy made of egg whites, sugar, hazelnuts, and a hint of lemon, or *pane di pescatore* (fisherman's bread), a dense and delicious sweet bread similar to fruit cake and filled with nuts and raisins. **Despar,** V. Gramsci 12, sells groceries. (Open M-F 7:30am-1pm and 5-8pm, Sa 7:30am-1pm. MC/V.)

Pizzeria/Birreria Ombra della Sera, V. Guarnacci 16 (☎0588 85 274). Watch chefs toss dough and hope it lands on your plate. Takeout available. Salad €7. Pizza €5-7.50. Pasta €6-8. Cover €1. Service 10%. Open Tu-Su noon-3pm and 7-10pm. MC/V. ❷

L'Ombra della Sera, V. Gramsci 70 (☎0588 86 663), off P. XX Settembre. Local favorite. Candlelit, outdoor patio on busy V. Gramsci makes for great people-watching on a summer evening. Rich Volterran fare. Try *coniglio a forno* (baked rabbit; €12.50). Primi €8-11. Secondi €11-14. Cover €1.50. Service 10%. Open June-Aug. daily noon-3pm and 7-10pm; Sept.-Oct. and Mar.-May Tu-Su noon-3pm and 7-10pm. AmEx/MC/V. ❸

La Pizzicheria da Pina, V. Gramsci 64 (☎0588 87 394). Serves regional wine and savory spreads in an underground Roman cave. Upstairs store sells wine from €6 per bottle, olive oil €6.20, and balsamic vinegar €17. Panini €6-8. Piatti €6-15. Open daily Mar.-Nov. 9:30am-8:30pm; Oct.-Feb. 9am-1pm and 4-8pm. AmEx/MC/V. ❶

Trattoria Il Poggio, V. Porte all'Arco 7 (☎0588 85 257). Pasta with meat sauces and a "medieval" tourist *menù* (€14). Local cheeses, breads, and sweets are highlights.

Medieval wall paraphernalia like huge crossed axes and metal shields. Pizza €5-8. Primi €6-8. Secondi €8-14. Open M and W-Su noon-3pm and 6:30-10pm. AmEx/MC/V. ❷

👁 SIGHTS

PINACOTECA COMUNALE. Dimly lit rooms with few labels display Volterra's best art in this graceful museum. The first floor showcases two dramatic works: Rosso Fiorentino's spectacular *Deposizione della Croce*, in which Christ's greenish body spills from the canvas onto the frame, creating the mesmerizing illusion that his subjects are not confined to the flat surface. Luca Signorelli's even richer *Annunciazione* is filled with finely realized architectural details. *(V. dei Sarti 1, up V. Buonparenti from P. dei Priori. ☎ 0588 87 580. Open daily Mar.-Nov. 9am-7pm; Dec.-Feb. 9am-2pm. €8, students €5, under 6 free. Combined ticket that includes Pinacoteca, Museo Etrusco, and Museo dell' Opera del Duomo di Arte Sacra sold at each. Cash only.)*

PIAZZA DEI PRIORI. This busy *piazza* is surrounded by sober, dignified *palazzi*. The **Palazzo dei Priori**, Tuscany's oldest government palace, presides over the square. Regal coats of arms line the walls of the first floor. Jacopo di Cione Orcagna's damaged *Annunciation with Four Saints* occupies the right wall of the council hall and antechamber, which are open to the public. *(Open Mar.-Nov. daily 10:30am-5:30pm; Nov.-Mar. Sa-Su 10am-5pm. €1.)*

CATTEDRALE DI SANTA MARIA ASSUNTA. Construction began on Volterra's pre-Romanesque cathedral in the 12th century and continued for 300 years. By the time the choir at the end of the nave was completed, architects had already switched to a Gothic design, indicated by the transition from rounded to pointed arches. The chapel off the left transept holds frescoes by Rosselli, including the luminous *Missione per Damasco*. *(In P. S. Giovanni, down V. Turazza from P. dei Priori. Open daily 8am-12:30pm and 3-7pm. Free.)*

MUSEO ETRUSCO GUARNACCI. The Etruscan museum displays over 600 finely carved funeral urns from the fourth to the first centuries BC. The first floor **(Room XV)** holds the museum's most famous piece, the elongated bronze figure dubbed *L'Ombra della Sera* (Shadow of the Evening). The farmer who unearthed it used it for years as a fireplace poker until a visitor recognized it as an Etruscan votive figure. In **Room XIX**, the famous *Urna degli Sposi* depicts a visibly embittered married couple. *(V. Minzoni 15. From P. dei Priori, head down to V. Matteotti, turn right on V. Gramsci, and follow it to V. Minzoni. ☎ 0588 86 347. Open daily mid-Mar. to Oct. 9am-7pm; Nov. to mid-Mar. 9am-1:45pm. €8, students €5. Pieces are not well displayed and lack explanatory signs; audio tour available in English €3. Cash only.)*

ROMAN AMPHITHEATER. These impressive ruins include partly grass-covered stone seating and Corinthian columns salvaged from the stage. The admission fee allows you to walk along the edge of the ruins behind metal rails, but the vantage point from V. Lungo le Mura is free and just as gratifying. *(Just outside the city walls next to Pta. Fiorentina. From P. dei Priori, follow V. delle Prigioni, turn right at the T-junction and left on V. Guarnacci. Proceed out the arch and through the parking lot to the left. Open Mar. 16-Oct. daily 10:30am-5:30pm; Nov.-Mar. 15 Sa-Su 10:30am-4:30pm. €2. Cash only.)*

PALAZZO VITI. This private residence is still home to heirs of the wealthy Viti family, but 12 rooms are open to the public. The furnishings and alabaster collections date from the 15th century to the present, and the beautiful interior was used as a backdrop by Italian director Luchino Visconti for his 1964 film *Vaghe stelle dell'Orsa* (Sandra). A visit to the downstairs *cantine* and a small tasting of wine, cheese, and salami is included. *(V. dei Sarti 41, down the street from the Pinacoteca. Open daily 10am-1pm and 2:30-6:30pm. €5, students €3. Cash only.)*

MONTALCINO ☎0577

Sitting atop a hill, overlooking vineyards and stately clusters of cypress trees, Montalcino (mohn-tal-CHEE-no; pop. 5118) appears to be just another Tuscan wine town with a view. But unlike some of its neighbors, Montalcino has a relatively low tourist influx, allowing visitors to wander into vineyards and stroll along narrow alleys and steep stairways that have changed little since medieval times. A former Sienese stronghold, its heavy walls are evidence of its prior belligerence, but the tiny town has long since traded war-mongering for wine-making, producing heavenly, albeit pricey *Brunello di Montalcino*, a red wine considered Italy's finest. Sample the *Brunello* in the numerous wine shops, or leave Montalcino's city walls to tour a winery.

🖪🚻 **TRANSPORTATION AND PRACTICAL INFORMATION.** To reach Montalcino, take one of the TRA-IN **buses** from Siena's train station (1hr., 7 per day, €3.30). The last bus to Montalcino departs at 10:20pm; the last return to Siena departs at 8:30pm from Montalcino's P. Cavour. From Montepulciano (1hr., €3.30), change buses at Torrenieri. Contact the Pro Loco **tourist office,** Costa del Municipio 8, for info on vineyard tours, free maps, hotel booking, and currency exchange. From P. Cavour, walk up V. Mazzini to P. del Popolo. The office is under the clock tower. (☎0577 84 93 31; www.prolocomontalcino.it. Open Apr.-Oct. daily 10am-1pm and 2-5:50pm; Nov.-Mar. Tu-Su 10am-1pm and 2-5:40pm.)

🚻🄲 **ACCOMMODATIONS AND FOOD.** Hotel rooms are expensive and scarce in Montalcino. *Affittacamere* are generally well-kept and run €42-52 for a double with bath. The tourist office provides a list of all hotels and *affittacamere* in the area. Call ☎0577 22 21 46 for information. **Anna Affittacamera ❹,** V. S. Saloni, provides elegance at a luxurious price. Rooms have ceiling frescoes, comfortable beds, TV, and bath. Check in at Hotel Giglio, V. S. Saloni 5. (☎0577 84 86 66; fax 84 81 67. Reservation recommended. Singles €50; doubles €70; apartment with kitchen and courtyard €75-90. AmEx/MC/V.) Closest to the bus stop is **Albergo Il Giardino ❸,** P. Cavour 4, where a gregarious staff and large well-kept rooms make this an ideal, economical choice. (☎0577 84 82 57; www.albergogiardino.it. Singles €42; doubles €55; triples €75. Cash only.) **Il Barlanzone Affittacamere ❸,** V. Ricasoli 33, rents four color-coordinated rooms and an apartment with TV, large bath, and an unobstructed view of the fortress. Enter through the *enoteca* on the corner. (☎0577 84 61 20. Doubles €55; apartments €75. 10% discount for 1-week stay. MC/V.)

Montalcino's wine menus are generally twice as thick as the food menus. *Enoteche* line V. Mazzini, the town's main street, all offering huge selections of *Brunello* and tasty snacks like *bruschette* or cheese and meat plates (€3-7). Before committing for lunch, first indulge in the free samples offered by most establishments. In the rustic and brightly painted **Taverna Il Grappolo Blu ❸,** Scale di V. Moglio 1, a memorable ravioli with *pecorino* cheese and *ragù* (€8) is just one of many superior options. (☎0577 84 71 50. Primi €6-8. Secondi €8-15. Cover €2. Open daily noon-3pm and 7-10pm. AmEx/MC/V.) At **Maria Pia's Re di Macchia ❹,** V. Soccorso Saloni 21, complement a typical Tuscan dish such as *pinci* (large spaghetti) with wild boar *ragù* (€9) and a bottle of *Il Consiglio di Antonio* (€15), one of Montalcino's four premier wines. (☎0577 84 61 16. Primi €8. Secondi €13-16. Cover €2. Open M-W and F-Su noon-2pm and 7-9pm. AmEx/MC/V.) The best deals on *Brunello* (€18-28) are at the **Coop,** at V. Sant'Agostino and V. della Libertà. (Open M-Sa 8:30am-1pm and 4-8pm. MC/V.)

🄶🎶 **SIGHTS AND ENTERTAINMENT.** The ▨**Abbazia di Sant'Antimo** is in Castelnuovo, a town 10km from Montalcino on the same La Peschiera route as the Fattoria dei Barbi (€1.40; return 8am, 2:30, and 5:30pm). The walk from Castelnuovo to the abbey takes about 8min. and passes the sloping hills and cypress trees characteristic of the Tuscan countryside. Legend has it that Charlemagne founded the abbey in AD 780 after he was miraculously saved from the plague that scourged his army. The 12th-century structure is one of Tuscany's most beautiful Romanesque structures. Inside, monks celebrate mass in **Gregorian chant** seven times per day (during which the church is closed to the public). Chants float through speakers throughout the day. (☎0577 83 56 59; www.antimo.it. Open M-Sa 10:15am-12:30pm and 3-6:30pm, Su 9:15-10:45am and 3-6pm. No photos during prayer. Free.)

Back in town stands Montalcino's 14th-century **fortezza,** which sheltered a band of republicans escaping the Florentine siege of Siena in 1555. The fortress is almost perfectly preserved, with five towers and part of the town walls incorporated into the structure. Two interior courtyards, one shaded by foliage, the other sunny and cheered by geraniums, make nice picnic spots. Many visitors bypass the fortress itself in favor of the sophisticated **Enoteca La Fortezza,** which sells cheese plates (€10) and local wines (€3-12 per glass; *Brunello* €6.50-12). A climb up the stairs, through the turret, and onto the panoramic walls is €3.50, but you can enjoy great views from the ground for free. (Fort and *enoteca* open daily Apr.-Oct. 9am-8pm; Nov.-Mar. 10am-6pm.) To appreciate the vineyards, use the **local shuttle service,** La Peschiera (☎0564 95 31 34), to visit **Fattoria dei Barbi.** Shuttles depart daily from P. Cavour at 1:45 and 2:45pm and return at 2:25 and 5pm. Ask the driver to stop at the *Fattoria.* Tours of the cellars are followed by a tasting of three different kinds of *Brunello.* Tastings (€10-20) are available any time during open hours; ring the bell for service. The winery also includes an expensive restaurant that is open for lunch and dinner. (☎0577 84 11 11; www.fattoriadeibarbi.it. Open July-Aug. M-F 10am-1pm and 2:30-7pm, Sa-Su 2:30-7pm; Sept.-June M-F 10am-1pm and 2:30-6pm, Sa-Su 2:30-6pm. Free 30min. tours given M-F every hr. 11am-noon and 3-5pm.)

Every year since 1957, on the last Sunday in October, Montalcino celebrates the **Sagra del Tordo.** Each of the city's four *quartieri* (districts; Borghetto, Pianello, Ruga and Travaglio) participates in the event. This festival evolved from a medieval tradition where archery contests took place after the men returned to their houses following a day of hawk hunting.

CORTONA ☎ 0575

Though its tranquil streets may suggest otherwise, the ancient town of Cortona (cor-TOH-na; pop. 23,600) once rivaled Perugia, Arezzo, and even Florence in power and military dominance. After appropriation in 1411 by Naples, Cortona was sold to the rival Florentines, and citizens of Cortona enjoyed peace and prosperity. Impressive art collections and architecture from this period of grandeur linger within the small city's walls, including two altarpieces by Fra Angelico and the paintings of Luca Signorelli. Cortona, a small town with few notable sights, was recently as the setting of *Under the Tuscan Sun.*

▐▀ TRANSPORTATION

Trains depart **Camucia-Cortona station** to Florence (every hr., €7) and Rome (2hr., every 2hr., €9.40). **LFI buses** (☎0575 30 07 48) run to Cortona's P. Garibaldi from this station (15min., €1) and from **Terontola train station** (30min., every hr.). Buses also stop in P. Garibaldi from Arezzo (1hr., 12 per day, €2.70). Buy LFI bus tickets from the tourist office or *tabaccherie.* For **taxis,** call ☎335 81 96 313.

✈ ⊇ ORIENTATION AND PRACTICAL INFORMATION

Buses stop at **Piazza Garibaldi** at the base of the city. Enter the city by following **Via Nazionale,** which leads to **Piazza della Repubblica.** Follow the road at the far right side of the *piazza* to reach **Piazza Signorelli,** Cortona's main square. The **tourist office,** V. Nazionale 42, provides maps, bus schedules, and bus, train, and tour tickets. (☎0575 63 03 52; www.apt.arezzo.it. Open in summer M-Sa 9am-1pm and 3-7pm, Su 9am-1pm; in winter M-F 9am-1pm and 3-6pm, Sa 9am-1pm. No tickets sold Sa-Su.) **Currency exchange** and a 24hr. **ATM** are available at **Banca Etruria,** V. S. Margherita 5. (Open M-F 8:20am-1:20pm and 2:35-3:35pm, Sa 8:20-11:50am.) In case of emergency, call the **police** at V. Dardano 9 (☎0575 63 72 25). **Farmacia Centrale** is at V. Nazionale 38. (☎0575 60 32 06. Open M-Sa 9am-1pm and 4:30-8pm. MC/V.) Reach the **hospital** at ☎0575 63 91. **Telenet,** V. Guelfa 25, offers **Internet** access, as well as a **Western Union,** phone center, cell phone rental, and shipping services. (☎0575 60 10 96. €1 for 1st 15min., €3.50 per hr. with subscription bought on-site. Open M-Sa 9am-8:30pm. MC/V.) **Lamentini Internet,** V. Nazionale 33, has fewer services but longer hours. (☎0575 335 687 2330. €5 per hour. Open M-Sa 10am-8pm, Su 10am-6pm. MC/V.) **Nocentrini Libri,** V. Nazionale 32, stocks books in English, including classics, bestsellers, and travel guides. (Open daily 9am-1pm and 3-8pm. MC/V.) The **post office** is uphill from P. della Repubblica at V. Benedetti 2. (☎0575 60 30 21. Open M-F 8:15am-1:30pm, Sa 8:15am-12:30pm.) **Postal Code:** 52044.

⌂ ACCOMMODATIONS

🛏 **Ostello San Marco (HI),** V. Maffei 57 (☎0575 60 13 92; www.cortonahostel.com). From the bus stop, walk 5min. uphill on V. S. Margherita and follow signs curving left to the hostel. A stone, wood-beamed, medieval lobby lends amiable cheer to this clean, well-kept hostel. Breakfast included. Dinner €10. Open to individuals mid-Mar. to Nov., to groups year-round. Dorms €14; singles €18. Cash only. ❶

Casa Betania, V. Gino Severini 50 (☎0575 62 829; fax 60 42 99), downhill from P. Garibaldi. Cross Vle. Cesare Battisti and take an immediate right through the gates. Although rooms are plain, large windows admit copious amounts of Tuscan sunshine. Breakfast €5. Singles €35; doubles €48; triples €60. MC/V. ❸

Hotel San Luca, P. Garibaldi 1 (☎0575 63 05 04; albergosanluca@technet.it). Take in spectacular views of the Chiana Valley from your private terrace. Richly decorated rooms with A/C, bath, minibar, phone, safe, and TV are meticulously maintained. Singles €78; doubles €113; triples €143; quads €173; quints €188. AmEx/MC/V. ❺

Istituto Santa Margherita, V. Cesare Battisti 15 (☎0575 63 03 36; fax 63 05 49). Downhill on V. G. Severini from P. Garibaldi; on the corner of V. C. Battisti. A former college, with antique furniture, wide hallways, and large baths. Breakfast €3. Singles €32; doubles (no unmarried couples) €46; triples €56; quads €66. Cash only. ❸

⎈ FOOD

You won't have to search long for a bustling, home-style Tuscan trattoria in Cortona; tables spill onto the streets surrounding the town's main *piazze.* The best beef in Tuscany is raised in the surrounding valleys, so consider making a modest splurge on *bistecca alla Fiorentina* (Florentine beef steak). Complement dinner with the fine, local white wine, *Bianco Vergine di Valdichiana.* Penny-pinchers can pick up a €2.50 bottle at **Despar,** P. della Repubblica 23, which also stocks basic groceries and picnic supplies, including cheap *panini.* (☎0575 63 06 66. Open Apr.-Oct. M-Sa 7am-1:30pm and 4-8pm, Su 9am-1pm;

TUSCANY

Nov.-Mar. M-Tu and Th-Sa 7am-1:30pm and 4:30-7:30pm, W 7am-1:30pm. AmEx/ MC/V.) On Saturday, P. Signorelli hosts an open-air **market.** (Open 8am-1pm.)

Trattoria La Grotta, P. Baldelli 3 (☎0575 63 02 71). Off P. della Repubblica at the end of V. Nazionale. While the cramped seating in this alleyway retreat doesn't exactly set the mood for fine dining, the extensive menu offers a selection of Tuscan treats. Primi €6-8. Secondi €6-35. Cover €1. Open M and W-Su noon-2:30pm and 7-9:30pm. MC/V. ❷

Trattoria Dardano, V. Dardano 24 (☎0575 60 19 44; www.trattoriadardano.com). Follow the succulent smells to lively conversation that carries down the street. Simple, filling dishes include a variety of affordable steaks (€3 per 100g). Primi €5-7. Secondi €5-8. Cover €1. Open M-Tu and Th-Su noon-2:45pm and 7:15-9:45pm. Cash only. ❷

Ristorante Preludio, V. Guelfa 11 (☎0575 63 01 04; www.ilpreudio.net). Chandeliers and candlelit tables provide an elegant environment in which to enjoy upscale dishes like stuffed *crespelle* with duck and spicy tomato (€9). Primi €8-10. Secondi €13-14. Cover €2. Open Tu-Su 12:30-3pm and 7:30-10:30pm. AmEx/MC/V. ❸

Gelateria Snoopy, P. Signorelli 29. Themed *gelateria* in the heart of Cortona, complete with Charlie Brown and Snoopy pictures on the wall, serves a generous ▨ **4 scoops** for €2.50; 5 for €3. Open daily 10am-midnight. Cash only. ❶

👁 SIGHTS

MUSEO DELL'ACCADEMIA ETRUSCA. Perfectly preserved Egyptian sarcophagi and mummies, Roman coins, and golden altarpieces are displayed to fantastic effect in this extravagant collection. Also check out oil paintings by native sons Luca Signorelli and Pietro Berrettini (known as Pietro da Cortona), as well as those of Futurist Gino Severini. The first floor's main hall houses an unusual 4th-century BC Etruscan chandelier decorated with intricate allegorical carvings. The **Medici Room,** lined with coats of arms, holds two 1714 globes by Silvestro Moroncelli; one depicts the "Isola di California" floating in the Pacific, the other sports vivid illustrations of all the constellations. *(P. Signorelli, inside the courtyard of Palazzo Casali, at the far right of P. della Repubblica. ☎0575 63 72 35. Open Apr.-Oct. daily 10am-7pm; Nov.-Mar. Tu-Su 10am-5pm. Guided tours available by reservation only. €7, groups of more than 15 €4 per person, students €2. Cash only.)*

MUSEO DIOCESANO. This humble museum packs some of the Italian Renaissance's greats. Admire the grace of the golden wings in Fra Angelico's stunning *Annunciation* (c. 1436) in **Room 3** of the upstairs gallery. Luca Signorelli's masterpiece, *The Deposition* (1502), which combines classical Roman and medieval detail, hangs in **Room 1.** Works by the Sienese Pietro Lorenzetti, such as his fresco *The Way to Calvary* in **Room 2** and his meticulously rendered *Crucifix* in **Room 3,** are also impressive. Severini's modern interpretations of traditional biblical scenes line the stairwell. *(From P. della Repubblica, pass through P. Signorelli and follow the signs. ☎0575 62 830. Open daily 10am-7pm. €5, groups of more than 15 people and children under age 15 €3. English audio tour €3. Cash only.)*

FORTEZZA MEDICEA. As the highest point in Cortona, the *fortezza* offers incomparable views of the Val di Chiana and Lake Trasimeno. The courtyard and bastions contain temporary art installations and shrines decorated with mosaics based on Severini's series in the Museo Diocesano line the uphill path. On the way, the unassuming white marble facade of the **Basilica di Santa Margherita** bursts into bold combinations of primary colors—blue ceilings are fancifully dotted with gold stars. The body of Santa Margherita (1247-1297) rests in a glass coffin at the center of the altarpiece. *(Trek to the top of V. S. Margherita from P. Garibaldi. To reach the fortress, take a right out of the church and climb the small uphill road.*

TUSCANY

☎ *0575 60 37 93. Fortress open daily July-Aug. 10am-1:30pm and 2:30-7pm; Apr.-June and Sept. 10am-1:30pm and 2:30-6pm. Modest dress required. €3, under 12 €1.50. Basilica free.)*

PALAZZI AND PIAZZE. In P. della Repubblica, the 13th-century **Palazzo Comunale** serves as a bold backdrop for the surrounding shops and cafes. At night, people gather on the steps to enjoy their gelato, people-watch, and enjoy the show at P. Signorelli's outdoor theater. **Palazzo Casali,** to the right and behind the Palazzo del Comune, dominates P. Signorelli. Only the courtyard walls lined with coats of arms remain from the original structure; the facade and interlocking staircase are 17th-century additions. **Piazza del Duomo** lies to the right and downhill from the Palazzo Casali. The simple, 16th-century **Cattedrale di Santa Maria** houses paintings by Signorelli and del Sarto as well as an impressive Baroque-canopied high altar and a rich, dark-wood pulpit built in 1524. *(Open daily Mar.-Oct. 7:30am-1pm and 3-6:30pm; Nov.-Mar. 8am-12:30pm and 3-5:30pm. Free.)*

❉ FESTIVALS

When August 14 rolls around, Italian cows start to tremble. Yes, it's time for the **Sagra della Bistecca** (Steakfest), the most important town festival, when the populace shares superb steak in the public gardens behind the church of San Domenico. The next culinary extravaganza follows during the third weekend of August with the **Festa dei Porcini,** when mushroom-lovers flock for tastings. Tickets are sold at the garden entrance. In early June, neighborhoods commemorate a local nobleman's 1397 marriage with religious ceremonies, period dress, and the **Giostra Dell'Archidado,** a crossbow challenge in which participants compete for the *verretta d'oro* (golden dart). Musical and theatrical events come in July, when Cortona absorbs the spillover from the Umbria Jazz Festival. Relax in the gardens or enjoy a *passeggiata* in the park, which screens **movies** in their original language (usually English) weekly from mid-June through September. (Visit www.teatrosignorelli.com for lists of films and info. Films start 9:45pm. In bad weather, screenings in Teatro Signorelli. €5.)

AREZZO ☎ 0575

It was Michelangelo himself who said, "Any talent I have is a result of the fine air of your town, Arezzo." Indeed, for its size, Arezzo (ah-RET-so; pop. 92,000) has seen a veritable treasure trove of artists and thinkers. Aside from Michelangelo, the town was also home to Renaissance titans Piero della Francesca, poet Petrarch, humanist Leonardo Bruni, and artist and historian Giorgio Vasari. It's also the hometown of Roberto Benigni, director and star of the Oscar-winning *La Vita è Bella* ("Life is Beautiful"; 1997), who shot much of the film in the surrounding countryside. Escape the busy *centro* with a stroll outside the eastern portion of the medieval city walls; catch striking views of the countryside and glimpses of backyard olive trees, vegetable gardens, and flowerbeds.

▐ TRANSPORTATION

Arezzo lies on the Florence-Rome train line. From P. della Repubblica, **trains** run to Florence (1hr., 2 per hr. 4:30am-9:50pm, €5.40) and Rome (2hr., every 1-2hr. 6:30am-10:11pm, €11.70). The ticket booth is open M-Sa 5:50am-8:50pm and self-service ticket machines are open 24hr. To the left of the train station, TRA-IN, SITA, and LFI **buses** run to Sansepolcro (1hr., every hr., €3.30) and Siena (1hr., 4 per day, €5.20). Call ☎ 0575 38 26 51 for more info. Buy tickets at ATAM ticket office, in front and to the left of train station exit across from the bus depot. (☎ 0575 800 38 17 30. Open daily 5:50am-8:50pm.) For **taxis,** contact 24hr. **RadioTaxi** (☎ 0575 38 26 26). **Car rental** is available at **Autonoleggi Royal,**

V. Marco Perrenio 21. (☎0575 35 35 70. 21+. Open M-F 8:30am-12:30pm and 3:30-7:30pm, Sa 8:30am-12:30pm. Manual and automatic available.)

■ 🔢 ORIENTATION AND PRACTICAL INFORMATION

Via Guido Monaco, which begins directly across from the **train station** at **Piazza della Repubblica**, parallels **Corso Italia**; together they form the backbone of the commercial district. To get to the *centro storico*, follow V. G. Monaco from the station to the traffic circle at **Piazza Guido Monaco**. Turn right on **Via Roma** and then turn left on the pedestrian walkway C. Italia, which leads to the old city. **Piazza Grande** lies to the right, 250m up C. Italia.

Tourist Office: Centro Servizi Turistici, P. Emiciclo Giovanni Paolo II (☎0575 18 22 770; www.arezzoturismo.it) is located on the opposite side of town from the train station, but is the better of the two offices. Facing the entrance to the *duomo*, turn left and enter the adjacent building. Walk through the short hallway to the right, down the escalator, and the office is on the right. Services include hotel, airline and tour bookings, **luggage storage,** and **Internet** access. Open daily 9:30am-7pm. **APT,** P. della Repubblica 28 (☎0575 20 839; www.apt.arezzo.it). Turn right after exiting the train station. Free maps and brochures of the town and nearby valleys. Open Apr.-Oct. M-Sa 9:30am-1pm and 3-7pm, Su 9am-1pm; Nov.-Mar. M-Sa 10:30am-1pm and 3-6pm, Su 9am-1pm.

Budget Travel: CTS, V. V. Veneto 25 (☎0575 90 78 08), sells Eurail passes and plane tickets. Open M-F 9am-1pm and 3-7:30pm, Sa 9am-1pm.

Currency Exchange: Banks line V. G. Monaco between the train station and P. G. Monaco. **Banca Nazionale del Lavoro,** V. G. Monaco 74, has a 24hr. **ATM.** Open M-F 8:20am-1:35pm and 2:50-4:05pm, Sa 8:20-11:50am.

Police: V. Leone Leoni 16 (☎0575 35 931).

Pharmacy: Farmacia Comunale, Campo di Marte 1 (☎0575 90 24 66), next to Conad supermarket on V. V. Veneto. Open 24hr.

Hospital: Ospedale Civico, V. Pietronenni (☎0575 30 51).

Internet: InformaGiovani, P. G. Monaco 2 (☎0575 37 78 68; informagiovani@comune.arezzo.it). Free. 30min. max. Open M-Sa 9:30am-7:30pm, 1st Su of mo. 3:30-7:30pm.

Post Office: V. G. Monaco 34 (☎0575 33 24 11). **Currency exchange** (€0.50 commission). Open M-Sa 8:15am-7pm. **Postal Code:** 52100.

▛ ACCOMMODATIONS

Hotels fill to capacity the first weekend of every month due to the **Fiera Antiquaria** (Antique Fair). Finding a cheap room can pose a challenge given the expensive chain hotels that crowd Arezzo. The best option, **Foresteria San Pier Piccolo ❷,** V. Bicchieraja 32, is located in the old city, a short walk from Arezzo's main sights. Rooms in this 14th-century Benedictine convent have changed a little over the years. Spartan stone walls and wooden furniture have been supplemented with electricity, renovated baths, and TV. (☎0575 32 42 19; fax 37 04 74. Breakfast €3. Reception 7am-11pm. Curfew 11pm. Singles €24, with bath €35; doubles with bath €75; triples with bath €95. Cash only.) To get to **Albergo Cecco ❸,** C. Italia 215, follow V. G. Monaco from the train station, turn right on V. Roma and right again on C. Italia. The no-frills rooms are great for the budget-minded who care about location. (☎0575 20 986; fax 35 67 30. Breakfast €3. Singles €30, with bath €42; doubles €64-70; triples €80; quads €95. AmEx/MC/V.)

◖ FOOD

An open-air **market** takes place in P. Sant'Agostino on weekdays until 1pm. Head to **La Mozzarella,** V. Spinello 25, to the right and across the street from the train station, for a great variety of cheeses. (Open M-F 8am-1pm and 4-8pm, Sa 8am-1pm. Cash only.) **Eurospar**, V. G. Monaco 82, carries basic groceries. (Open daily 8am-8pm, closed W afternoon.)

> **TIP** **PUZZLING PANE.** No, that bread isn't stale, just unsalted. Traditional Tuscan bread is made without salt because, historically, salt was so valuable it was used as currency. Before you dig into that breadbasket, know that Tuscan bread is best enjoyed with other dishes and sauces. If you're in a grocery store buying bread and want the salted kind, ask for *pane salato*.

Antica Osteria L'Agania, V. Mazzini 10 (☎0575 29 53 81; www.agania.com). Sample wine from local vineyards (€4 a bottle) in an *osteria* that feels like a family kitchen. Primi and secondi €5-7. Open Tu-Su noon-3pm and 7-11pm. AmEx/MC/V. ❷

Trattoria Il Saraceno, V. Mazzini 6/a (☎0575 27 644), off C. Italia. *Arezzese* specialties like duck and *pecorino* cheese in honey (€10). Pizza €6-8. Primi €7-8. Secondi €8-12. Cover €2. Open M-Tu and Th-Su 12:05-3:10pm and 7-9:30pm. AmEx/MC/V. ❸

Paradiso di Stelle, V. G. Monaco 58 (☎0575 27 448). Great homemade gelato (from €1.60) and even better crepes (from €2.50). Open May-Sept. M-F 11am-11pm, Sa 11am-midnight; Oct.-Apr. M-F 11am-8:30pm, Sa 11am-11pm. Cash only. ❶

Osteria del Borghicciolo, Corso Italia 35. The staff swears the only secret to its great-tasting eats is authentic Italian extra virgin olive oil. Enjoy a 4-course meal for two (€18). Open daily noon-3:30pm and from 7pm until the crowd leaves. ❸

👁 SIGHTS

BASILICA DI SAN FRANCESCO. This extraordinary 13th-century basilica houses elaborate 15th-century frescoes like Piero della Francesca's ◼**Leggenda della Vera Croce** (*Legend of the True Cross*) in the *Bacci* chapel behind the main altar. It tells the story of the first crucifix and its role in early Christianity. The narrative begins with the death of Adam and proceeds to major events such as Emperor Constantine's conversion in the AD fourth century. St. Francis kneels at the foot of the cross. (*Walk up V. G. Monaco from train station and turn right into P. S. Francesco. Basilica open daily 8:30am-noon and 2-7pm. Free. Chapel containing della Francesca's frescoes open Apr.-Oct. M-F 9am-6:30pm, Sa 9am-5:30pm, Su 1-5:30pm; Nov.-Mar. M-F 9am-5:30pm, Sa 9am-5pm, Su 1-5pm. Groups of 25 admitted every 30min. Last entry 30min. before closing. Reservation required. Call ☎0575 20 630 or 0575 35 27 27, or visit the office to the right of the church. €6, EU students 18-25 €4, art students or EU citizens under 18 €2. Cash only.*)

◼**CASA VASARI.** Colors swirl on the elaborate ceilings of the Casa Vasari, built by the artist and historian himself, is decorated without restraint. Vibrant portrait-frescoes by Michelangelo and del Sarto cover the walls. In one room, Vasari's depictions of the muses the ceiling is crowned with, one of which is a likeness of his fiancée, Niccolosa. He even painted himself taking in the view from one of the *casa*'s windows. (*V. XX Settembre 55. Just off V. S. Domenico. Ring bell to enter. ☎0575 40 90 40. Open M and W-Sa 8:30am-7:30pm, Su 8:30am-1:30pm. Last entry 30min. before closing. €2, EU students €1. Cash only.*)

PIAZZA GRANDE (PIAZZA VASARI). This *piazza*, which surrounds a small fountain decorated by the garden club of Arezzo, contains the **Chiesa di Santa Maria della Pieve,** a spectacular Romanesque church built in the 12th century. Elegant columns and rounded arches frame a 13th-century portico. On the elevated presbytery sits Pietro Lorenzetti's brilliantly restored *Annunciation* and *Madonna and Child.* Below lies the 11th-century church upon which the

Pieve was built. The adjoining pock-marked **tower** is known appropriately as the "Tower of 100 Holes." *(Open M-Sa 8am-noon and 3-7pm, Su 8:30am-noon and 4-7pm. Free.)* Surrounding *palazzi* enclose P. Grande with pleasing proportionality. The 14th-century Romanesque **Palazzo della Fraternità** and 16th-century Baroque **Palazzo delle Logge Vasariane** recall past eras. For a livelier version of history, attend the monthly **antique fair** or the semi-annual **Giostra del Saracino** each summer. To reach **Parco "Il Prato,"** a grassy retreat of flowers, picnic areas, and ancient statues, follow C. Italia to V. dei Pileati. *(Open daily until dusk. Free.)*

DUOMO. The massive 13th-century *duomo* sits high on the hill of Arezzo. Built in the Tuscan Gothic style, the cathedral houses Arezzo native Piero della Francesca's *Maddalena* and Bishop Guido Tarlati's tomb on the left side of the nave near the altar. Carved reliefs relate stories of the iconoclastic bishop's unconventional life. The seven elaborate stained-glass windows were designed by French artist Guillaume de Marcillat. The *Capella della Madonna del Conforto*, off the austere nave, holds a notable terra-cotta *Crucifixion* by Andrea della Robbia. *(Up V. Andrea Cesalpino from P. S. Francesco. ☎0575 23 991. Open daily 7am-12:30pm and 3-6:30pm. Modest dress required. Free.)*

CHIESA DI SAN DOMENICO. The church's true gem is the Cimabue's ▪crucifix (1265-70) which hangs over the main altar. It is the artist's oldest and best preserved work. Other significant pieces in the simple, wood-timbered interior include Spinello Aretino's *Annunciation* and a Marcillat rose window depicting St. Augustine. *(Take V. A. Celaspino from P. S. Francesco, turn left at P. Libertà on V. Ricasorli, then right on V. di Sassoverde, leading to the church. Open daily 8:30am-1pm and 3:30-7pm. Hours may vary. Closed to public during mass. Free.)*

🌼 FESTIVALS

Whether you're up for haggling or merely wish to browse, Arezzo's **antique fairs,** which take place in and around P. Grande on the first weekend of every month, paint a living portrait of the town's history and variety. Furniture and religious paraphernalia would be tough to lug through customs, though sundry bric-a-brac can make unique souvenirs. The **Giostra del Saracino** (☎0575 37 74 62; giostradelsaracino@comune.arezzo.it), a medieval joust, is on the third Saturday of June and the first Sunday of September, though flags begin to plaster uncovered surfaces and celebrations engulf the town for the entire week before the event. In a Crusade-era ritual, knights representing the four quarters of the town charge a wooden effigy of a Turk with lances drawn.

▶ DAYTRIP FROM AREZZO

SANSEPOLCRO

Sansepolcro is most easily accessible by SITA bus from Arezzo (1hr., every hr., €3.30). Some routes require a change in Le Ville; ask the driver. The bus stops just outside the walls of the old city. From the bus stop, enter the old city on V. Nord Aggiunti. Follow the street 5 blocks, until you pass the Museo Civico on the right. Turn right under an arch on V. Matteotti, and take the first left into P. Garibaldi. Sansepolcro's tourist office, V. Matteotti 8, is on the right. (☎/fax 0575 74 05 36. Open Apr.-Sept. daily 9am-1pm and 3:30-7pm.)

Retreat into this sleepy, one stoplight town that embraces its artistic past, even if it lacks the renown or the number of sites possessed by nearby attractions. Nestled in the Tiber River valley at the foot of the Apennines, Sansepolcro's (sahn-seh-POHL-croh; pop. 15,693) claim to fame is its native early Renaissance painter, Piero della Francesca. The **Museo Civico,** V. Nord Aggiunti 65, displays some of della Francesca's finest works. *The Resurrection* (1450-1463) features a triumphant Jesus who towers above sleeping guards, resting one foot on his coffin and staring intently at the viewer. Study the guard in red on the lower right—it's actually della Francesca's self-portrait. *(Open daily June 15-Sept. 15 9:30am-1:30pm and 2:30-7pm; Sept. 16-June 14 9:30am-1pm and 2:30-6pm. Last entry 20min. before closing. €6, ages 19-25 and over 65 €4.50, ages 10-18 €3. Groups €4.50 per person. Audio tour €2. AmEx/MC/V.)* The left chapel of the Romanesque **duomo**, V. Matteotti, just off P. Torre di Berta, shelters the town's other cherished sight, the mysterious **Volto Santo** (Holy Face), a large wooden crucifix depicting a blue-robed Jesus. Believed by some to be much older than its 12th-century attribution, the Holy Face's Assyrian features suggest Middle Eastern origins. Scholars speculate that the same artist produced the much-celebrated *Volto Santo* in Lucca. (Open daily 8:30am-noon and 3:30-6:30pm. Free.)

Trattorie and pizzerias spot V. XX Settembre, around V. Matteotti and parallel streets. A more upscale cafe that has reasonable prices is modern and trendy **K Cafe ❷**, V. XX Settembre 73, where customers sip cappucinos and admire modern art on the walls. (☎0575 74 29 39. Salads €5. Primi and secondi €6-7. Open Su-Tu and Th-Sa 7am-1:30pm and 7:30pm-1am.) Customers pack the more intimate **Enoteca Guidi ❸**, V. Luca Pacioli 44, for gourmet dishes. (☎0575 73 65 87. Primi €8-10. Secondi €9-12. Cover €1. Open M-Tu and Th-Su 12:30-2:30pm and 7:30-10:30pm. AmEx/MC/V.) **Ristorante Ventura ❸**, V. Nord Aggiunti 30, is a great stop for those seeking a bite without the hassle of hunting for one. Indulge in one of many meat offerings. (☎0575 74 25 60. Primi €8. Secondi €8.50-15. Open Tu-Sa 12:30-2:15pm and 7:30-9:30pm, Su 12:30-2:15 pm. AmEx/MC/V.)

PISTOIA ☎0573

Many travelers regard Pistoia (pee-STOY-yah; pop. 84,000) as merely a stop on the train between Florence and Lucca. Truth be told, it's a small, but surprisingly urban Tuscan city that is worth the visit, though there are few real tourist attractions. In 1177 the town joined several other Italian city-states in declaring its independence, but was soon surpassed by its neighbors in military, political, and economic strength. Thereafter, Pistoia became a murderous backwater, whose inhabitants Michelangelo maligned as "enemies of heaven." Lending its name to the pistol and pistole dagger, the town's bloody reputation spawned an enduring mythology. Today's more peaceful residents prefer to haggle over produce prices in the markets of P. della Sala.

▌ TRANSPORTATION

Pistoia is accessible by train or bus. The **train station** is in P. Dante Alighieri. **Trains** run to: Florence (40min., 2-4 per hr. 4:40am-11:12pm, €2.80); Pisa (1hr., every 2hr. 6:52am-11:30pm, €4.50); Rome (4hr., every hr., €30-40) via Florence; Siena (2hr., 16 per day 5:51am-9:12pm, €7.50-13); Viareggio (1hr., every 2hr. 5:55am-10:47pm, €4.50). COPIT **buses** run from the train station to Empoli (1hr., 6:30am-6:50pm, €2.70) and Florence (1hr., 5:22am-9:05pm, €2.70). Buy tickets at COPIT vendors or across from the train station at V. XX Settembre 71. Call RadioTaxi (☎0573 53 44 44) for a **taxi**. Panconi Andrea, V. Cesare Battisti 21, rents mountain **bikes** for €15 per day. (☎0573 22 395. Open M-F 8am-1pm and 3:30-8pm, Sa 8am-1pm. AmEx/MC/V.)

▞ ▌ ORIENTATION AND PRACTICAL INFORMATION

To reach the *centro* from the **train station**, walk up **Via XX Settembre**, and continue straight as it changes names to **Via Vanucci** and then to **Via Cino**. At P. Gavinana turn right on **Via Cavour**, then left on **Via Roma**, which leads to **Piazza del Duomo**, the heart of town. Local **buses #1** and **3** (€1, taken from the station) stop at the corner of V. Curtatone e Montanara and V. degli Orafi. From there, follow V. degli Orafi straight to P. del Duomo. An **APT Tourist Office**, P. del Duomo 4, is in Palazzo dei Vescovi. The staff distributes free maps and brochures and helps book accommodations. (☎0573 21 622; fax 34 327. Open daily 9am-1pm and 3-6pm.) **Currency exchange** is available at **Cassa di Risparmio di Pistoia e Pescia**, V. S. Matteo 3. (☎0573 36 91. Open M-F 8:20am-1:20pm and 2:50-3:50pm.) A **pharmacy** is at V. Cino 33. (☎0573 36 81 80. Open M-Sa 8:30am-1pm and 3:30-8pm. MC/V.) For the **hospital**, call ☎0573 35 21. **Internet** access is available at **Telnet Internet Point**, V. Carducci 25. (☎0573 99 35 71. €3.50 per hr. Open M-F 9:30am-1pm and 3:30pm-midnight, Sa 9:30am-1pm and 3:30-8pm; 2nd and 4th Su of the month 3:30-8pm. Cash only.) The **post office**, V. Roma 5-11 (☎0573 99 52 11), up the road from the bank, provides currency exchange. (Open Sept.-July M-Sa 8am-7pm; Aug. M-F 8:15am-7pm, Sa 8:15am-12:30pm.) **Postal Code:** 51100.

ACCOMMODATIONS AND FOOD

Most accommodations are near the train station and somewhat expensive. *Affittacamere* listings are available from the tourist office, but most of the cheaper rooms are in localities far from town. One good option is ▨**Bed & Breakfast Canto alla Porta Vecchia ❸**, V. Curtatone e Montanara 2. As one happy patron wrote in the guest book, staying at Canto alla Porta Vecchia is living like a real Pistoian. Take V. XX Settembre from the train station; the road changes names several times before becoming V. Curtatone e Montanara. There is no sign, so watch for the address in front. Walk up the steps to buzz in. Friendly owners Anna and Giovanni serve complimentary drinks and guests gather on the terrace to chat. Carved wooden beds, red satin couches, antique furniture, and original sketches furnish the four frescoed rooms. (☎/fax 0573 27 692. Singles €35; doubles €60, with bath €75. Cash only.) Up the street to the left, **Albergo Firenze ❹**, V. Curtatone e Montanara 42, offers basic rooms with A/C, satellite TV, minibars, phones, private baths, high ceilings, and lace curtains. (☎0573 23 141; www.hotel-firenze.it. Breakfast included. Internet access free. Singles €45-62; doubles €60-88. Extra bed €25. AmEx/MC/V.)

Trattoria dell'Abbondanza ❸, V. dell'Abbondanza 10, serves an excellent *insalate di Farro* (€6), a summer salad of oil-soaked lentils, basil, tomatoes, parsley, and garlic in a fresh, white-walled dining room or at outdoor tables in a quiet alley. (☎0573 36 80 37. Primi €6-8. Secondi €10-16. Open M-Tu and F-Su 12:15-2:15pm and 7-10:30pm, Th 7-10:30pm. MC/V.) **Il Duomo ❶**, V. Bracciolini 5, is low key and casual, and offers plates of pasta from €4.50. It's self service; order at the counter and take your tray to one of the long tables in the rear dining room. Catch up on news with locals or with the small TV in the corner. (☎0573 31 948. Open daily 10:30am-3:30pm. MC/V.) Multilingual menus present the ample choices at **Ristorante San Jacopo ❸**, V. Crispi 15, where the emphasis is on meaty Tuscan dishes. (☎0573 27 786. Primi €6-11. Secondi €9-15. Open Tu-Sa 12:15-2:30pm and 7-10pm, Su 12:15-2:30pm. AmEx/MC/V.)

Grocery stores and specialty shops line the side streets. Bargain hunters browse the **open-air market** in and around P. del Duomo for deals on items from shower curtains to silver. (Open W and Sa 8am-1pm. Fewer vendors show at these hours the rest of the week.) P. della Sala has hosted a produce **market** since medieval times. (Open daily 8am-7pm.) A **Dimeglio** supermarket is at V. Veneto 5, across from the train station. (Open M-Sa 8am-8pm. MC/V.)

TUSCANY

👁 SIGHTS

PIAZZA DEL DUOMO. Activity in Pistoia converges on the flat cement slabs of P. del Duomo. The green-and-white marble **Cattedrale di San Zeno** houses early Renaissance art tucked into pocket-sized niches on multiple floors, as well as San Zeno's greatest treasure, the ◪**Dossale di San Jacopo.** Between 1287 and 1456, nearly every significant Tuscan silversmith (including the young Brunelleschi) lent a hand to this altarpiece, a tremendously ornate affair off the right aisle, with relief work detailing biblical scenes and a procession of saints in a plain chapel. (☎0573 25 095. *Open M-Sa 7am-12:30pm and 3:30-7pm, Su 9am-1pm and 3:30-7pm. Altar open M-Sa 10am-12:30pm and 3-5:30pm; Su 8-9:30am, 11-11:30am, and 4-5:30pm. Modest dress required. €2.*) Across from the *duomo* is the octagonal **baptistry,** designed by Andrea Pisano in the 14th century. Nino and Tommaso Pisano's sculpture *Virgin and Child* (1308) graces the facade above the entrance. (*Open Tu-Su 10am-1pm and 3-6:30pm.*) The **campanile,** adjacent to the *duomo,* has sounded the hour since the 12th century, although the clock face and spire weren't added until the 16th century. From its 66m pyramid-shaped spire, vistas reach Florence on clear days. (☎0573 33 49 31 77 10. *Open Sa 11am and 4pm, Su noon and 5pm. €5.*)

PALAZZO COMUNALE. To the left of the *palazzo*'s central balcony, an arm reaches out, brandishing a club above the black marble head below—a tribute to the Pistoian victory over the Moorish King Musetto in 1115. Inside, the **Museo Civico** houses artwork dating to the 13th century. The archways and Gothic windows of the courtyard are also worth a look. (*Next to the duomo facing the piazza.* ☎0573 37 12 96. *Open Tu-Sa 10am-6pm, Su 9:30am-12:30pm. Museum €3.50, students €2. Combined ticket for museo, the Centro Marini, and other museums €6.50/5.20. Cash only.*)

CENTRO MARINO MARINI. Escape a Renaissance overdose with a visit to this modern collection celebrating one of Italy's most renowned 20th-century artists, native Marino Marini. The collection's pieces include his tactile sculptures (many of the sensuous Pomona, ancient Roman fertility goddess), studies, and vibrant paintings. (*C. Silvano Fedi 30, in the Palazzo del Tau.* ☎0573 30 285; www.museomarinomarini.it. *Open M-Sa May-Sept. 10am-6pm; Oct.-Apr. 10am-5pm. €3.50. Cash only.*)

CHIESA DI GIOVANNI FUORCIVITAS. Originally built outside the city, the single-naved interior of this 12th-century church is a vast space with vibrant, stained-glass windows that punctuate stark stone walls. The exterior's dark green-and-white stripes are characteristic of the Pisan school of architecture. The church contains a Romanesque relief of *The Last Supper* on the lintel. Giovanni Pisano's baptismal font and Guglielmo de Pisa's pulpit are among Europe's finest 13th-century carvings. (*At the intersection of V. Cavour and V. Crispi.* ☎0573 24 784. *Open daily 7:30am-6:30pm. Modest dress required. Free.*)

CHIESA DI SANT'ANDREA. This Romanesque church was built in the AD eighth century. In 1298 Giovanni Pisano carved the pulpit, now considered his masterpiece. Supported by seven red-marble columns, the pulpit's white-marble panels have delicately carved figures illustrating the Nativity, Adoration of the Magi, Massacre of the Innocents, Crucifixion, and Last Judgment. (*Exit P. del Duomo by V. del Duca, from the corner opposite the duomo, and continue on it as it changes to V. dei Rossi and then V. Sant'Andrea.* ☎0573 21 912. *Open daily 7:30am-6pm. Free.*)

�֎ 📷 FESTIVALS AND NIGHTLIFE

Europeans seeking to wash away their troubles converge the second weekend in July in P. del Duomo for the **Pistoia Blues** concert series. Past performers have included Ben Harper, Santana, Jethro Tull, Gregg Allman, and Joe Cocker. (☎0573 99 46 59; www.pistoiablues.com.) During the festival, the city allows free camping in designated sites near the stadium. On July 25, Pistoia holds the **Giostra dell'Orso** (Joust of the Bear). In accordance with 13th-century custom, 12 contemporary knights from four competing districts joust a defenseless, bear-shaped target, earning points for the accuracy of their lunges. Pistoians and visitors fill the stands in the P. del Duomo, cheering on their favorite knight and recording wins and losses on the free scorecards given out by the city (☎0573 37 16 90; cultura@comune.pistoia.it). With Staropramen, Hopf Weizen, and Bass on tap, **Vecchia Praga,** P. della Sala 6, at the end of V. del Lastrone, is a beer-lover's haven. Mixed drinks, wine, and light food are also available to the mostly Italian crowd. (☎0573 31 155. Pints €3.50. Open daily noon-1am.)

LUCCA   ☎0583

Lucca (LOO-ka; pop. 9000) dabbles successfully in every area of tourist pleasure. Bikers rattle through the town and on the tree-lined promenade that runs atop its medieval walls, the well-heeled take on the trendy boutiques along the main streets, and art lovers admire the Romanesque churches and elegant architecture of the *centro*. Picturesque *piazze* appear every few blocks, along with notice boards advertising concerts, most of which are operas by Lucca's own Giacomo Puccini. Tranquil and compelling Lucca is a Tuscan gem.

▐ TRANSPORTATION

Trains: (☎0583 89 20 21), in Ple. Ricasoli. Info kiosk open daily 5:30am-8:10pm. To **Florence** (1½hr., 2-3 per hr. 5:07am-10:32pm, €4.90), **Pisa** (30min., 1-3 per hr. 7:08am-12:24am, €2.30), and **Viareggio** (16min., every hr. 6:51am-11:31pm, €2.30). For other major cities, change in Pisa. For Cinque Terre, change in Viareggio.

Buses: Lazzi (☎0583 46 49 63), in Ple. Verdi. To **Florence** (1hr., every hr. 6:25am-7:45pm, €4.90) and **Pisa** (50min., every hr. 5:48am-8:10pm, €2.50).

Taxis: in P. S. Maria (☎0583 49 41 90); in P. Napoleone (☎0583 49 16 46); in Ple. Ricasoli (☎0583 49 49 89); in Ple. Verdi (☎0583 58 13 05).

Bike Rental: Cicli Bizzari, P. S. Maria 32 (☎0583 49 60 31), 2 doors down from the regional tourist office. Basic bikes €2.50 per hr., €12.50 per day; mountain and racing bikes €3.50/17.50; tandem bikes €5.50 per hr. Open daily 9am-7:30pm. Cash only. **Antonio Poli,** P. S. Maria 42 (☎0583 49 37 87; www.biciclettepoli.com), on the other side of the regional tourist office, offers virtually identical prices. Open daily 8:30am-8pm. AmEx/MC/V.

▐ ▐ ORIENTATION AND PRACTICAL INFORMATION

To reach the *centro storico* from the **train station,** cross the road and turn left on Vle. Regina Margherita. Enter the city through the arches to the right of **Porta San Pietro,** then head left on **Corso Garibaldi.** Turn right on **Via Vittorio Veneto,** and follow it one block to **Piazza Napoleone** (also called **Piazza Grande**). Continue walking on V. V. Veneto to reach **Piazza San Michele** in the center of town. If arriving by bus, walk to the right through **Piazza Verdi,** follow **Via San Paolino** toward the center of town, and turn right on V. V. Veneto to reach P. Napoleone.

Tourist Office: Centro di Accoglienza Turistica (☎0583 58 31 50; www.turislucca. com), in Ple. San Donato. Schedules guided tours (M, Th, Sa 3pm; €10). Self-guided audio tours (€9-12) and bike rental (€2.50 per hr.). Open daily 9am-7pm. **Branch:**

(☎0583 49 57 30) in P. Curtatone, right of the train station. Provides luggage storage (€1.50 per bag per hr.). Open daily 10am-6pm. **Agenzia per il Turismo,** P. S. Maria 35 (☎0583 91 99 31), between the bike shops. Open daily 9am-8pm.

Currency Exchange: UniCredit Banca, P. S. Michele 47 (☎0583 47 546). Open M-F 8:20am-1:20pm and 2:35-4:05pm, Sa 8:20am-12:45pm. **24hr. ATM** available on corner of V. S. Paolino and P. S. Michele, 50m away from bank.

Laundry: Lavanderia Niagara, V. Michele Rosi 26 (☎0583 335 629 2055). €6 per 7kg. Open daily 8am-10pm.

Pharmacy: Farmacia Comunale, in P. Curtatone. Open 24hr.

Hospital: Campo di Marte (☎0583 97 01).

Internet: Mondo Chiocciola Internet Point, V. del Gonfalone 12 (☎0583 44 05 10). €5 per hr. Wi-Fi available. Open M-Sa 9am-1pm and 3:30-8:30pm. Cash only.

Post Office: V. Vallisneri (☎0583 43 351). Open M-Sa 8am-7pm. **Postal Code:** 55100.

◤ ACCOMMODATIONS

Bed and Breakfast La Torre, V. del Carmine 11 (☎/fax 0583 95 70 44; www.roomslatorre.com). Family-run. Call when you arrive for free pickup. 3 locations in the heart of the *centro* with large, bright rooms and well-kept bathrooms. Some with canopied beds. Delicious homemade breakfast included. Free Internet access. Singles €35, with bath €50; doubles €50/80. Apartments equipped with kitchen, parlor, and TV also available for rental on a weekly basis. 2 people €700; 4 people €840. MC/V. ❸

Ostello per la Gioventù San Frediano (HI), V. della Cavallerizza 12 (☎0583 46 99 57; www.ostellolucca.it), 15min. from P. Napoleone. Walk 2 blocks on V. Beccheria, then turn right on V. Roma and left on V. Fillungo. After 6 blocks, turn left into P. S. Frediano and right on V. della Cavallerizza. Good-sized rooms and great common spaces with high ceilings and plenty of couches. Breakfast €3; dinner €10. Towels €1.50. Linens included. Laundry available. Reception daily 7:30-10am and 3:30pm-midnight. Checkout 9:45am. Lockout 10am-3:30pm. Dorms €18-20; 2- to 6-person rooms with bath €50-135. HI-member discount €3. Cash only. ❶

Affittacamere San Frediano, V. degli Angeli 19 (☎0583 46 96 30; www.sanfrediano. com). Follow signs to hostel; but turn left on V. degli Angeli. English spoken. Light spills into well-kept rooms with TV and antique furniture; some have A/C. Shared baths. Breakfast included. Singles €38, with bath €65; doubles €48-80. AmEx/MC/V. ❹

Zimmer La Colonna, V. dell'Angelo Custode 16 (☎/fax 0583 44 01 70), off P. Maria Foris Portam. Colonnaded hallways lead to spacious rooms with TV and antique decor. Clean shared baths. Doubles €45, with bath €65. Extra bed €16. AmEx/MC/V. ❹

Piccolo Hotel Puccini, V. di Poggio 9 (☎0583 55 421; www.hotelpuccini.com). Rooms decorated with framed playbills from Puccini's operas. 3-star hotel. Comfortable rooms have bath, TV, phone, and safe. Singles €65; doubles €90. AmEx/MC/V. ❺

Da Elisa Alle Sette Arti, V. Elisa 25. Ornately-tiled *affitacamere* and 3 shared baths. Art-deco furnishings. Kitchen available. Breakfast €7. Singles €47; doubles €100. ❹

Residence Santa Chiara, V. S. Chiara 12. Huge rooms with tiled floors in a 16th-century building. Terrace overlooks the gardens of Elisa Bonaparte's former home. Safes, A/C, common area, and buffet breakfast included. Doubles €70. AmEx/MC/V. ❸

La Gemma di Elena Bed and Breakfast, V. della Zecca 33. 6 plush rooms, some with fireplace, terrace, TV, and private bath. Internet access and common room available. Breakfast included. Singles €35; doubles €55. Extra bed €15. AmEx/MC/V. ❸

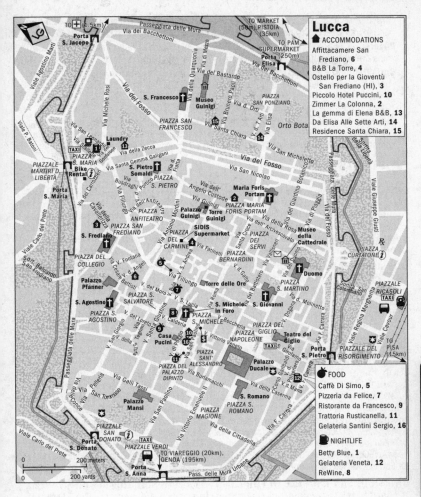

Lucca

🏠 ACCOMMODATIONS

Affittacamere San
   Frediano, 6
B&B La Torre, 4
Ostello per la Gioventù
   San Frediano (HI), 3
Piccolo Hotel Puccini, 10
Zimmer La Colonna, 2
La gemma di Elena B&B, 13
Da Elisa Alle Sette Arti, 14
Residence Santa Chiara, 15

🍴 FOOD

Caffè Di Simo, 5
Pizzeria da Felice, 7
Ristorante da Francesco, 9
Trattoria Rusticanella, 11
Gelateria Santini Sergio, 16

🌙 NIGHTLIFE

Betty Blue, 1
Gelateria Veneta, 12
ReWine, 8

TUSCANY

🍴 FOOD

An **open-air market,** outside and to the left of Pta. Elisa, overtakes V. dello Stadio
(W and Sa 8am-1pm). **SIDIS,** P. del Carmine 2, stocks basic groceries. (Open M-
Tu, Th-Sa 8am-1pm and 4:30-8pm, W and Su 4:30-8pm. MC/V.)

   Ristorante da Francesco, Corte Portici 13 (☎0583 41 80 49), off V. Calderia between P.
   S. Salvatore and P. S. Michele. Ample patio seating. Ideal for a light meal. Try the *zuppa
   di verdure* (vegetable soup; €5). Pizza €7-8. Primi €5-6. Secondi €7-12. Wine €7.20
   per L. Cover €1.50. Open Tu-Su noon-2:30pm and 8-10:30pm. MC/V. ❷

   Trattoria Rusticanella, V. S. Paolino 32 (☎0583 55 383). Tavern with house-bottled
   wines and homemade jams. The *ciancino* platter includes appetizer, wine, foccacia,

bruschetta, and *pecorino* (€8.50). 3-course lunch *menù* €15. Pizza from €5. Primi €5-6. Secondi €7-26. Cover €1. Open M-Sa 11am-3pm and 6-10:30pm. MC/V. ❷

Pizzeria da Felice, V. Buia 12 (☎0583 49 49 86). *Pizza al taglio* (slices; from €1.40) flies over the countertop into the hands of hungry locals. Open daily 10am-8:30pm. ❶

Caffè Di Simo, V. Fillungo 58 (☎0583 49 62 34). Amped-up style amid a row of designer boutiques. Bow-tied waiters serve delicious coffee and bite-size cakes (€1.50), while mellow jazz plays in the background. Coffee €1, at table €2.40. Primi €5-7. Secondi €8. Open Tu-Sa 9am-8pm. Lunch served noon-2:30pm. MC/V. ❶

Gelateria Santini Sergio, P. Cittadella 1 (☎0583 55 295), has been wowing hungry passersby since 1916. Exotic, homemade flavors like mandarin and banana leave a creamy taste in your mouth. Cups and cones €2-5. Open daily noon-10pm. ❶

◼ SIGHTS

▨**BALUARDI.** No tour of Lucca is complete and no journey into the city possible without passing the perfectly intact medieval city walls, or *baluardi* (battlements). The shaded 4km pedestrian path along the walls, which passes grassy parks and cool fountains, is perfect for a breezy, afternoon picnic or a sunset view. Rent a bike and try to master the Luccan art of simultaneously biking and chatting on your cell phone, or simply admire the city's layout as you stroll.

DUOMO DI SAN MARTINO. Though the building was supposedly begun in the sixth century and rebuilt in AD 1070 by Pope Alexander II, the majority of the building that stands today is the result of another reconstruction, which took place between the 12th and 15th centuries. The multi-layered, arched facade of this asymmetrical *duomo* is the oldest feature of the present structure. The 13th-century reliefs that decorate the *duomo's* exterior include Nicola Pisano's *Journey of the Magi and Deposition.* Matteo Civitali, Lucca's famous sculptor, designed the floor and contributed the S. Martino statue to the right of the door. His prized *Colobium,* in the left aisle, houses the 11th-century **Volto Santo** (Holy Face). Reputedly carved by Nicodemus at Calvary, this wooden crucifix is said to depict the true image of Christ. Other highlights include Tintoretto's *Last Supper* (1590), the third painting on the right, and *Holy Conversation* by Ghirlandaio, in the sacristy off the right aisle. The **Museo della Cattedrale,** left of the *duomo,* houses religious objects from the *duomo. (P. S. Martino. From P. Napoleone, take V. del Duomo. Duomo and sacristy open M-F 9:30am-5:45pm; Sa 9:30am-6:45pm; Su between masses 9-9:50am, 11:30-11:50am, and 1-5:45pm. Duomo free. Sacristy €2. Museum open Apr.-Oct. daily 10am-6pm; Nov.-Mar. M-F 10am-2pm, Sa-Su 10am-5pm. €4; combined ticket for Sacristy, Museo della Cattedrale, and Chiesa di S. Giovanni €6. Audio tour €1. Cash only.)*

CHIESA DI SAN MICHELE IN FORO. Given its current setting in a busy *piazza,* it's hard to tell that construction on this church actually began in the AD eighth century on the site of a Roman forum. Once inside, the church's large, stone interior holds beautiful and dramatic oil paintings, such as Lippi's bold *Saints Helen, Roch, Sebastian, and Jerome* toward the end of the right aisle, and Luca della Robbia's *Madonna and Child* near the front. Original religious statues were replaced in the 19th century with likenesses of prominent political figures: Cavour, Garibaldi, and Napoleon III. *(Open M-Sa 9am-noon and 3-6pm, Su 9-10:30am and 3-6pm. Modest dress required. Free.)*

CHIESA DI SAN GIOVANNI. The simple plaster dome of this unassuming church holds a recently excavated AD second-century Roman complex, complete with mosaic pavement, the ruins of a private house and bath (the church's foundations), a Longobard burial site, and a Paleochristian chapel, as well as a 10th- to 11th-century crypt. *(From P. S. Martino, walk past San Giovanni, and around*

the corner to the right. Open Mar.-Nov. daily 10am-6pm; Dec.-Feb. Sa-Su 10am-5pm. Nave free.
Museum €6. Combined church and baptistry €2.50. Cash Only.)

TORRE GUINIGI AND TORRE DELL'ORE. These are two of the 15 remaining towers from medieval Lucca's original 250. Narrow **Torre Guinigi** rises above Lucca
from the stone mass of Palazzo Guinigi, which is closed to the public. Crouch
through a small door to reach a set of 227 stairs, seven little oak trees, called
"lecci," provide a shaded view of the city and the hills beyond. *(V. Sant'Andrea 41.*
From P. S. Michele, follow V. Roma for 1 block, turn left on V. Fillungo and right on V. Sant'Andrea.
☎ *0583 31 68 46. Open daily June-Sept. 9am-11pm; Oct.-Jan. 9am-7pm; Feb.-May 9am-5pm. €5,*
students €3. Cash only.) For some more exercise, climb the 207 steps of the **Torre**
delle Ore (Hour Towers/Clock Towers), where you can see the inner workings
of the city's tallest timepiece. *(V. Fillungo 24. Open daily in summer 10am-7pm; in winter*
10:30am-5pm. €3.50, students €2.50. Combined ticket for both towers €6/4. Cash only.)

PIAZZA NAPOLEONE. Also called "Piazza Grande" by locals, this *piazza* is the
town's administrative center. The 16th-century **Palazzo Ducale** now houses government offices. At night, *lucchese* pack the *piazza* for *passeggiate* (strolls).

PIAZZA ANFITEATRO. Closely packed buildings, 3-star hotels, and upscale restaurants create a nearly seamless, oval wall around this *piazza*, originally
an ancient Roman amphitheater. Though the ruins are now nearly 3m below
the ground, some of the original arches are visible on the outer walls of the
buildings. Locals and tourists mingle over coffee and conversation close to
but free of the hyperactivity of Piazza Napoleone.

BASILICA DI SAN FREDIANO. Multiple additions led to San Frediano's proud,
Romanesque structure. Originally constructed in the AD sixth century with the
facade facing west, it was rebuilt in the first half of the 12th century with an
eastward orientation. The gleaming Byzantine mosaic atop the facade is striking. *(Open daily in summer 9:30am-noon and 3-6pm; in winter 9am-noon and 3-5pm. Free.)*

PALAZZO PFANNER. Palazzo Pfanner's sumptuous garden oasis, complete with
an octagonal fountain and statuary of mythical figures, was designed by Filippo
Juvarra in the 18th century. While the view from the wall is free, sitting in
the garden makes you feel like royalty. The *palazzo* now serves as a museum
that showcases 18th- and 19th-century costumes and old medical instruments
belonging to Dr. Pietro Pfanner, the surgeon who owned the *palazzo* and gave
it his name. *(V. degli Asili 33. From the Basilica di San Frediano, take V. S. Frediano to V. Cesare*
Battisti and turn left. Take a right onto V. degli Angeli to reach V. degli Asili. ☎ *0583 95 40 29. Open*
daily Mar.-Oct. 10am-6pm. Palazzo €2.50, students €2; garden €2.50/2; both €4/3.)

ORTO BOTANICO. For a change of pace, retreat to the calming paths of Lucca's
botanical gardens. Created in 1820 by duchess Maria Luisa of Bourbon, the garden was originally linked to the Royal University of Lucca for scientific study. A
broad main avenue leads to a pond and marshy plants before branching off into
smaller, more isolated trails. *(☎ 0583 44 21 60. Open daily Apr. 10am-1pm and 3-5:30pm;*
May-June 10am-1pm and 5-7pm; July-Aug. 10am-1:30pm and 2:30-7pm; Sept. 10am-1pm and
3-6pm; Oct. 10am-1pm and 3-5pm; Nov.-Mar. by reservation only 9:30am-12:30pm. €3, ages
6-14, over 65 and groups larger than 15 €2. Last entry 30min. before closing.)

🎭 🎆 NIGHTLIFE AND FESTIVALS

At its heart, Lucca is a sleepy Tuscan town. For evidence, look no further than
Gelateria Veneta, V. V. Veneto 74, the epicenter of nighttime activity. The place to
see and be seen on summer nights and on Saturdays year-round, Veneta offers
interesting flavors and swanky seating. The whipped mousse flavors are sensational. (☎ 0583 46 70 37. Cones €1.90-3. Granita €2.60. Open daily 10am-2am.

MC/V.) For liquid refreshment, trendy **ReWine,** V. Calderia 6, has an expansive wine selection. (☎0583 48 427. Antipasti and primi €7.50. Wine approx. €15 per bottle. Open M-Sa 7am-1am, Su 3:30pm-1am. AmEx/MC/V.) Located slightly away from the *centro's* action but still buzzing with life is **Betty Blue,** V. del Gonfalone 16, an Internet cafe by day, bar by night. (www.betty-blue.eu. Wine from €3. Mixed drinks €6. Open daily 10am-1am.)

Lucca's calendar is jam-packed with artistic and musical performances, especially in summer. The **Summer Festival** (☎0584 46 477; www.summer-festival. com) takes place in July and features performances by the likes of Elton John, Norah Jones, Steely Dan, and Lauryn Hill. **Teatro Comunale del Giglio's** opera season is in late September; their ballet season takes place in January. The king of Lucca's festivals is the **Settembre Lucchese** (Sept. 13-22), a lively jumble of artistic, athletic, and folkloric presentations. On July 12 and September 14, Lucca also holds an annual **Palio della Balestra,** a crossbow competition dating from 1443 and revived for tourists in the early 1970s.

PISA   ☎050

Millions of tourists arrive in Pisa (PEE-zah; pop. 85,379) each year to marvel at the famous "Leaning Tower," forming a gelato-slurping, photo-snapping mire. Though a little worn around the edges, the heart of Pisa is as alive as ever. Home to three universities, Pisa thrives as a haven for exuberant, opinionated students. After that inevitable Kodak moment before the leaning tower, take some time to wander the sprawling university neighborhood through P. dei Cavalieri and P. Dante, along alleys lined with elegant buildings and impassioned political graffiti mostly directed at intercity rivals.

▤ TRANSPORTATION

Flights: Galileo Galilei Airport (PSA; ☎050 50 07 07; www.pisa-airport.com). Trains that make the 5min. trip (€1.10) between train station and airport coincide with flight departures and arrivals. Trains for airport depart on track 14; find access at the end of platform 1. Bus **LAM ROSSA (red line)** runs between the airport, train station, and other points in Pisa and its environs (every 20min., €1). To: **Barcelona** (2hr., 2 per day), **London** (1hr., 11 per day), and **Paris** (2hr., 3 per day). Not a major Italian airport. Try Milan or Rome for more options and cheaper flights.

Trains (☎050 89 20 21). In P. della Stazione, at southern end of town. Info office open daily 7am-9pm. Ticket booth open 6am-9:30pm; self-service ticket machines available 24hr. MC/V. To: **Florence** (70min., 2 per hr. 4am-11:16pm, €5.40); **Genoa** (2hr., every hr. 6am-3:09am, €8); **Livorno** (20min., every hr., €1.70); **Rome** (4hr., 1-2 per hr. 5:45am-2:19am, €22-28). Regional trains to **Lucca** (25min., every 30min. 6:20am-9:20pm, €2.30) also stop at Pisa's **San Rossore** (€1.10), close to the *duomo* and the youth hostel. If leaving from S. Rossore, buy tickets at *tabaccherie.*

Buses: Lazzi (☎055 35 10 61; www.lazzi.it) and **CPT** (☎800 01 27 73; www.cpt.pisa. it) in P. Sant'Antonio. Ticket office open M-Sa 7am-8:20pm. To: **Florence** (2hr., every hr., €7.80) via **Lucca** (40min., every hr., €2.30); **La Spezia** (3hr., 4 per day, €7.80); **Livorno** (1hr., 5am-8:30pm, €2.50); **Volterra** (1hr., 7 per day, €5.20) via **Pondedera.**

Taxis: RadioTaxi (☎050 54 16 00).

Car Rental: Avis (☎050 42 028), **Hertz** (☎050 43 220), and **Maggiore** (☎050 42 574) have offices at the airport.

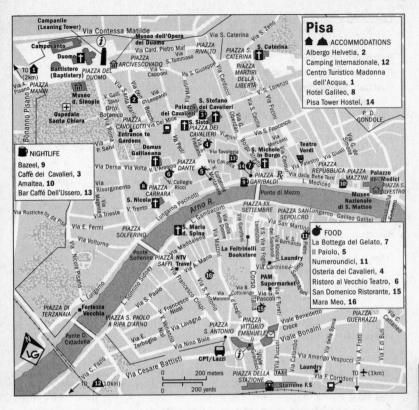

Pisa

🏠 ▲ ACCOMMODATIONS
Albergo Helvetia, **2**
Camping Internazionale, **12**
Centro Turistico Madonna
dell'Acqua, **1**
Hotel Galileo, **8**
Pisa Tower Hostel, **14**

🛏 NIGHTLIFE
Bazeel, **9**
Caffè dei Cavalieri, **3**
Amaltea, **10**
Bar Caffè Dell'Ussero, **13**

🍴 FOOD
La Bottega del Gelato, **7**
Il Paiolo, **5**
Numeroundici, **11**
Osteria dei Cavalieri, **4**
Ristoro al Vecchio Teatro, **6**
San Domenico Ristorante, **15**
Mara Meo, **16**

📷 🔢 ORIENTATION AND PRACTICAL INFORMATION

Pisa lies near the mouth of the **Arno River,** which splits the town. Most sights lie to the north of the Arno; the main **train station** is to the south. To reach the **Campo dei Miracoli (Piazza del Duomo)** from the station, take the bus marked LAM ROSSA (red line; €1). Alternatively, opt for a pleasant 30min. walk by starting straight up **Viale Gramsci,** through **Piazza Vittorio Emanuele II,** and stroll along the busy **Corso Italia.** Cross **Ponte di Mezzo,** and follow the river left for a distance, then turn right on **Via Santa Maria.**

Tourist Office: P. V. Emanuele II 16 (☎050 42 291; www.turismo.toscana.it). English spoken. Open M-F 9am-7pm, Sa 9am-1:30pm. **Branch** (☎050 56 04 64) to the right of the Leaning Tower. Open M-Sa 9am-6:30pm.

Budget Travel: New Taurus Viaggi, V. Francesco Crispi 25/27 (☎050 50 20 90), sells international tickets. English spoken. Open M-F 9am-12:30pm and 3:30-7:30pm, Sa 9am-12:30pm. AmEx/MC/V.

Luggage Storage: At the train station, on the left at the end of Platform #1. Self-service lockers available for small pieces. €3 per bag per day. Open 6am-9pm. Cash only.

English-Language Bookstore: La Feltrinelli, C. Italia 50. Open M-Sa 9am-8pm, Su 10am-1pm and 4-8pm.

Laundromat: Bucato Point, V. Filippo Corridoni (☎050 800 08 04 03), 50m from train station. Wash €3.50, dry €3.50 per 7kg. Detergent €1. Open daily 8am-10pm. Cash only. **Lavanderia,** V. Carmine 20. Wash €3.50, dry €3.50. Open daily 7am-11pm.

Police: ☎050 58 35 11.

Pharmacy: Farmacia, Lugarno Mediceo 51 (☎050 54 40 02). Open 24hr.

Hospital: Santa Chiara (☎050 99 21 11), on V. Bonanno near P. del Duomo.

Internet Access: Internet Point 77, V. Filippo Corridoni 77, near the train station. €3 per hr. Open daily noon-10pm. **Koine,** V. dei Mille 3/5 (☎050 83 07 01). Students €3 per hr. After 9pm €2 per hr. Open M-F 10am-midnight, Sa-Su 1pm-midnight. MC/V.

Post Office: P. V. Emanuele II 8 (☎050 51 94 11), near the station, on the right of the *piazza.* Open M-Sa 8:15am-7pm. **Postal Code:** 56100.

🏠 🏕 ACCOMMODATIONS AND CAMPING

In Pisa, flashing hotel and *albergo* signs cater to tourist hordes. You'll pay for location—rooms closer to sights are sure to be pricier. Hotel and campground listings are available at the tourist office (see **Practical Information,** p. 458).

Albergo Helvetia, V. Don Gaetano Boschi 31 (☎050 55 30 84), off P. Arcivescovado. Close to major sights and the university quarter. Small, generic rooms have TV, ceiling fans, phone, and shared bath. English-speaking staff. Breakfast €5. Reception 8am-midnight. Singles €35, with bath €50; doubles €45/62. Extra bed €15. Cash only. ❸

Hotel Galileo, V. S. Maria 12, 1st fl. (☎050 40 621; hotelgalileo@pisaonline.it). Stellar rooms in the university district, all with frescoed ceiling, minifridge, TV, and antique tiling and furniture. Shared bath is well-kept. Singles €40, with bath €45; doubles €48/60; triples €63/75. Extra bed €15. Cash only. ❸

Centro Turistico Madonna dell'Acqua, V. Pietrasantina 15 (☎050 89 06 22), 2km from the Tower. Board LAM ROSSA (red line; 4 per hr., last at 9:45pm; €0.85) bus outside Hotel Cavalieri in *piazza;* request *ostello* stop. Near an old Catholic sanctuary and a marshy creek. Basic rooms. Kitchen available. Linens €1. Reception daily 6-9pm. Check-out 9am. Dorms €15; doubles €30; triples €54; quads €64. MC/V. ❶

Pisa Tower Hostel, P. Garibaldi 2, 2nd fl., above La Bottega del Gelato. In the heart of Pisa, this newly opened hostel offers small rooms with steel frame beds, long windows, and Tuscan landscape paintings. Free linens and towel. Cash payments on arrival. 4-bed dorms €49; singles €55; doubles with shared bath €80. Dorms for women only. ❹

Camping Internazionale (☎050 35 211), 10km away on V. Litoranea in Marina di Pisa, across from its private beach. Take CPT intercity bus from P. S. Antonio to Marina di Pisa (buy ticket in CPT office entering P. Sant'Antonio from P. V. Emanuele II; €1.50). Small, partially shaded sites with clean shared bath. On-site bar and market. Best for those who are satisfied seeing Pisa's sights as a daytrip. Open May-Sept. €7 per person, €5 per child; €7.50 per tent. July-Aug. prices increase by €1-2. AmEx/MC/V. ❶

🍴 FOOD

Steer clear of the overcrowded cafes with mandatory service charges near the Tower and head for the river or the universities, where the restaurants offer a more authentic ambience and consistently high quality. An **open-air market** spills into the streets near P. Vettovaglie. Bakeries and *salumerie* fill Pisa's residential quarter. There's also a **Pam** supermarket, V. Pascoli 8, just off C. Italia. (Open M-Sa 7:30am-8:30pm, Su 9am-1pm. AmEx/MC/V.)

Il Paiolo, V. Curtatone e Montanara 9 (☎050 42 528), near the university. Always packed with rambunctious students, especially at night. Dim yellow lighting, benches, and great music make for a fun atmosphere. Primi and secondi €5-8. Cover €1. Open M-F 12:30-3pm and 8pm-2am, Sa-Su 8pm-2am. MC/V. ❷

Numeroundici, V. S. Martino 47 (☎050 27 282; www.numeroundici.it). Choose a sandwich (€2.50) from the chalkboard menu at this casual establishment and enjoy it on wood benches in the dining room filled with Tibetan lanterns. Self-service. Primi €4. Secondi €6. Dinner specials €10. Open M-F noon-11pm, Sa 6-10pm. Cash only. ❶

Ristoro al Vecchio Teatro, P. Dante 2 (☎050 20 210). Enjoy fresh Pisan cuisine *al fresco* or in the dining room of one of the city's oldest buildings. Try the *risotto di verdure miste,* a buttery dish with artichoke, garlic, and peppers. Primi and secondi €6-9. Cover €1.50. Open Sept.-July M-Sa noon-3pm and 8-10pm. AmEx/MC/V. ❷

Osteria dei Cavalieri, V. S. Frediano 16 (☎050 58 08 58). Classy setting caters to the sophisticated diner. Relax after a busy day at this Slow Food spot. Sample traditional *spaghetti all'arrabbiata* (spicy pasta with tomato and herbs). Primi €7.50-10. Secondi €12-17. Open M-F 12:30-2pm and 7:45-10pm, Sa 7:45-10pm. MC/V. ❸

La Bottega del Gelato, P. Garibaldi 11, right off Ponte di Mezzo. The usual suspects as well as a few original flavors like Cannoli. Decide before reaching the counter, or you'll be swallowed by the crowd, which is busiest after sundown. 2 generous scoops €1.50; 4 for 2.50. Open daily 11am-1am. Cash only. ❶

San Domenico Ristorante, C. Italia 139 (☎050 12 94 96), through the alcove to the right. Hot chocolate, pastries, and a vibrant evening piano bar. Hearty dishes of pasta and meats (€10-14). Open daily noon-2:30pm and 5-10pm. Open late F and Sa. ❷

Mara Meo, V. S. Croce 58 (☎050 058 331 7233). The best deal around for a quick bite. Brick dining room has colorful ceramic furnishings. Serves pizza, coffee, dessert, and ice cream. Huge slices of *pizza margherita* €1. Open daily 11am-9pm. ❷

◉ SIGHTS

▨LEANING TOWER. The white stone buildings of the **Piazza del Duomo,** aptly renamed Campo dei Miracoli (Field of Miracles) by poet Gabriele D'annunzio, stretch across the well-maintained greens of the *piazza,* which houses the Leaning Tower, *duomo,* baptistry, and *Camposanto* (cemetery). Look closely: all of the buildings lean at different angles, thanks to the mischievous, shifty soil. No matter how many postcards you see of the Tower, nothing quite compares to witnessing the 5.5° tilt in person. Bonanno Pisano began building the tower in 1173, and construction was repeatedly delayed as the soil shifted and the building began to lean. The tilt intensified after WWII, and thanks to tourist traffic, it continues to slip 1-2mm every year. In June 2001, the steel safety cables and iron girdles that imprisoned the Tower during years of stabilization efforts were finally removed. One year later, the Tower reopened, albeit on a tightly regulated schedule: once every 30min., guided groups of 30 visitors are permitted to ascend. *(Make reservations at the ticket offices in the Museo del Duomo, online, or next to the tourist info office. Tours depart daily June-Aug. 8:30am-11pm; Sept.-May 8:30am-7:30pm. Assemble next to info office 10min. before scheduled entry. Free baggage storage. Children under 8 not permitted, under 18 must be accompanied by an adult. €15. Cash only.)*

 LUNAR LEANER. The wait to climb the Leaning Tower can sometimes take hours out of your day. To escape the crowds, save the ascent until after sundown; the tower is open during the summer until 11pm. You'll get a unique view of the city illuminated by moonlight.

▨BATTISTERO. The baptistry, an enormous barrel of a building unfairly overshadowed by the all-too-famous leaning legend, was begun in 1153 by a man known as Diotisalvi ("God save you"), its design inspired by the church of the Holy Sepulchre in Jerusalem. Blending architectural styles, it incorporates Tuscan-Romanesque stripes with a multi-tiered Gothic ensemble of gables, pinnacles, and statues. Guido Bigarelli's **fountain** (1246) dominates the center of the ground floor. Nicola Pisano's **pulpit** (1260) recaptures the dignity of classical antiquity and is one of the harbingers of Renaissance art in Italy. Each of the building's four portals face one of the cardinal directions. The dome's acoustics are astounding: a choir singing in the baptistry can be heard 2km away. A staircase embedded in the wall leads to a balcony just below the dome; farther up, a space between the interior and exterior of the dome yields views of the surrounding *piazza*. *(Open daily Apr.-Sept. 8am-7:30pm; Oct. and Mar. 9am-5:30pm; Nov.-Feb. 9am-4:30pm. €5; combined ticket to multiple sites €10.50.)*

CAMPOSANTO. Built in 1277, this cloistered courtyard cemetery greets visitors with over 600 tombstones, covered with earth that Crusaders brought back from Golgotha and Roman sarcophagi that date from the AD third century. The sarcophagi reliefs inspired Pisano's pulpit in the baptistry. Fragments of enormous frescoes shattered by WWII Allied bombs line the galleries. The **Cappella Ammannati** contains haunting frescoes of Florence succumbing to the plague; its unidentified, 14th-century creator is known as the "Master of the Triumph of Death." *(Next to the duomo. Open daily Apr.-Sept. 8am-7.30pm; Oct. and Mar. 9am-5:30pm; Nov.-Feb. 9am-4:30pm. €5; combined ticket €10.50. MC/V.)*

DUOMO. The *duomo*'s dark green-and-white facade is the archetype of the Pisan-Romanesque style. Begun in 1064 by Buscheto (who is now entombed in the wall), the cathedral is the *campo*'s oldest structure. Enter the five-aisled nave through Bonanno Pisano's richly decorated bronze doors. Although a 1595 fire destroyed most of the interior, the cathedral was masterfully restored; original paintings by Ghirlandaio hang on the right wall, Cimabue's spectacular gilded mosaic **Christ Pantocrator** graces the apse, and bits of intricately patterned marble Cosmati pavement remain. Giovanni Pisano's last and greatest **pulpit** (1311), designed to outdo his father's in the baptistry, sits regally in the center. *(Open daily Apr.-Sept. 10am-8pm; Oct. and Mar. 10am-7pm; Nov.-Feb. 10am-1pm and 3-5pm. €2. Cash only.)*

PIAZZA DEI CAVALIERI. Designed by Vasari and built on the site of the Roman forum, this *piazza*, originally a home and place of that belonged to the Knights of St. Stephen, is now the site of the **Scuola Normale Superiore,** one of Italy's premier universities. The **Palazzo della Carovana** displays a magnificent facade, intricately detailed with Medicean coats of arms and zodiac signs. To the right, the **Church of Santo Stefano del Cavalieri,** dedicated to Order founder Cosimo, is capped with a wood ceiling carved by Bartolomeo Atticciati (1606). The wrought-iron baskets on either end of the **Palazzo dell'Orologio** (Palace of the Clock) were once receptacles for the heads of delinquent Pisans. In the *palazzo*'s **tower,** Ugolino della Gherardesca was starved to death in 1208 along with his sons and grandsons, as punishment for treachery. This murky episode in Tuscan politics is commemorated in Shelley's *Tower of Famine,* as well as in Dante's *Inferno* with gruesome, cannibalistic innuendos.

MUSEO NAZIONALE DI SAN MATTEO. Thirty rooms hold an important collection of medieval art by Masaccio, Fra Angelico, and Simone Martini. Sculptures by the Pisanos and a bust by Donatello also grace this converted Benedictine convent. *(Off P. Mazzini on Lugarno Mediceo next to the Palazzo dei Medici. ☎ 39 050 54 18 65. Open Tu-Sa 8:30am-7pm, Su 8:30am-1:30pm. Last entry 30min. before closing. €5. Cash only.)*

MUSEO DELL'OPERA DEL DUOMO. For more on the monuments of the *Campo dei Miracoli,* try the Museo dell'Opera del Duomo, which gives excellent historical detail on the art and construction of the famous buildings of P. del Duomo. Lots of Pisano family work is displayed, including the 13th-century sculpture *Madonna del Colloquio* (Madonna of the Conversation) by Giovanni, which was named for the expressive gazes exchanged between mother and child. The collection also includes Egyptian, Roman, and Etruscan art. *(Behind the Leaning Tower. ☎ 050 56 05 47. Open daily Apr.-Sept. 8am-7:20pm; Oct. 9am-5:20pm; Nov.-Feb. 9am-5pm; Mar. 9am-5.20pm. €5; included in €10.50 combination ticket. MC/V.)*

CHIESA DI SANTA MARIA DELLA SPINA. This tiny Gothic church on the south side of the Arno offers a glimpse at masterpieces by Andrea and Nino Pisano. Originally built between 1063 and 1230, the Church of Saint Mary of the Thorn later housed a thorn from the Crown of Thorns in 1333. *(From the Campo dei Miracoli, walk down V. S. Maria and over the bridge. Open Mar.-Oct. Tu-F 10am-1:15pm and 2:30-5:45pm, Sa-Su 10am-6:45pm; Open Nov.-Feb. daily 10am-12:45pm and 3-4:30pm. €2.)*

ENTERTAINMENT AND NIGHTLIFE

Occasional concerts take place in the *duomo*. For info, call the **Opera della Primaziale Pisana,** P. del Duomo 17 (☎050 38 72 229; www.opapisa.it). On the last Sunday in June, the **Gioco del Ponte** (☎050 92 91 11) revives the city's medieval pageantry tradition. Pisans divide into multiple teams, pledging their allegiance to their respective neighborhoods. Pairs of teams converge on the Ponte di Mezzo and joust until one side conquers the bridge. The night before the holiday for the city's patron saint (Nicholas) on June 16, the **Luminara di San Ranieri** brings the illumination of Pisa (including the tower) with 70,000 lights.

Three universities flood Pisa with lively students, but as summer approaches the nightlife gradually recedes. During the school year, watch students reclaim the tourist-packed *centro* after the sun goes down. Bars and cafes line the north side of the Arno, and students turn virtually every horizontal surface into seating. Bass lines blare from **Bazeel,** Lungarno Pacinotti 1. (Beer €3.50-4. Mixed drinks €4-6. Open daily 7pm-1am.) Farther down the Arno in P. Cairoli, **Amaltea** offers candlelit outdoor seating and wine for about €5 a glass. (Open daily 7:30pm-1:30am.) Wander deeper into the university neighborhood on P. dei Cavalieri to find **Caffè dei Cavalieri,** V. Corsica 8A. Arrive during *aperitivo* hour (approx. 6-7pm) for drinks from €3, or relax after dinner with beers from €3. (☎050 55 39 25. Open daily 7am-1pm.) Rowdy **Caffè dell'Ussero,** Lungarno Pacinotti 27, has served strong drinks (€5-7) and beer (€4-6) to generations of happy students since it opened in 1794. (☎050 58 11 00. Open daily 2pm-2am.)

DAYTRIP FROM PISA

VIAREGGIO

Trains connect Pisa and Lucca to Viareggio (Lucca 17min., Pisa 20min.; 6am-11pm; €2.30). The train station is at the bottom of V. Mazzini. To reach the beach, cross the street and take V. Mazzini to the end. Turn left on V. Regina Margherita. Lazzi buses (☎0583 46 233) connect Viareggio to Lucca (45min., every hr., €2.50) and Pisa (20min., 20 per day, €2.50). All buses stop in P. Mazzini, the town's main square near the waterfront. There's a tourist office at the train station. Open Tu 9:30am-1pm, W-Sa 9:30am-1pm and 4-6pm. The main tourist office, V. Carducci 10, posts train schedules. ☎050 96 22 33; www.aptversilia.it. Open M-Sa 9am-2pm and 3-7pm, Su 9am-1pm.

The resort town of Viareggio (vee-ah-REJ-yo; pop. 57,514) sits at the foot of the Riviera. Packed trains of young Italians arrive each morning to slather on oil and soak up the sun, but usually return to the inland cities by evening to avoid the costly accommodations. Most of Viareggio's shoreline has been roped off by private beach owners that charge as much as €15 for admission. Walk to the left facing the water across the canal along Vle. Europa, 20min. from P. Mazzini, to locate the **free beach,** at the southern edge of town. Or, take city bus #10 (1-2 per hr.; tickets €0.85, on board €1.50) from the train station and save precious tanning time. Bus #10 also returns from the beach to the station. Farther down the shore is **La Lecciona,** which has a reputation as an unofficial gay beach. Revelers flock annually to Viareggio to celebrate **Carnevale.** The town is famous for its colorful parades, hilarious performances, and riotous parties.

Few budget accommodations exist amid Viareggio's splendor; travelers are better off finding a bed in nearby Pisa or Lucca. Viareggio's pricey restaurants cater to a wealthy clientele and there are few supermarkets. Pasta dishes typically cost €10-16 and meat dishes €12-36. Even *gelaterie* have cover charges of upward of €1.50. Pack a picnic before hitting the beach.

ELBA ☎ 0565

According to legend, the enchanting island of Elba (EL-ba; pop. 28,000) grew from a precious stone that slipped from Venus's neck into the Tyrrhenian Sea. Since then, Elba's extensive 150km coastline has seen its share of visitors. Renowned since Hellenic times for its mineral wealth, the island also derived considerable fame for its association with Napoleon. The "Little Emperor" was sent into his first exile here in 1814, creating both a temporarily war-free Europe and the famous palindrome: "Able was I ere I saw Elba." The island's turquoise waters, dramatic peaks, and rich vegetation can take the breath away of conqueror and commoner alike. Pebble beaches, fashion boutiques, and amateur moped riders dot this Italian retreat, from the justifiably touristed Portoferraio, to the clear waters of Marciana Marina. Make like the Italians and trade city dirt for Elba's sweet, salty air—a bit of Tuscany, untamed.

TRANSPORTATION TO ELBA. Elba's **airport** (☎056597 60 11; fax 97 60 08) in Marina di Campo, sends flights to Florence, Milan, Monaco, Munich, Pisa, Rome, Vienna, and Zurich. The best way to reach Elba is to take a **ferry** from Piombino Marittima (also called Piombino Porto) on the mainland to Portoferraio. Ferries also dock at Porto Azzuro, on the opposite side of the island. Both **Toremar** (ferry 1hr., €8-11; hydrofoil in summer 30min., €8-10) and **Moby Lines** (1hr., 5am-10pm, €10-14) run about 20 trips to Elba per day. The ticket offices of Toremar (☎0565 31 100; www.toremar.it) and Moby Lines (☎0565 22 12 12; www.moby.it) are in the Stazione Marittima at the ferry docks in Piombino; buy tickets for the next departing ferry at these offices or at the Trenitalia booth in the Campiglia Marittima train station. Allow 10min. to descend from the ticket office to the dock.

Some **trains** on the Genoa-Rome line travel to Piombino Marittima, but most stop at Campiglia Marittima. From Campiglia Marittima, a connecting **intercity bus** (25min., €1.80), timed to meet incoming trains, connects to Piombino Marittima. Meet the bus in front of the station.

PORTOFERRAIO ☎ 0565

As the island's main port, Portoferraio (por-TOH-feh-RYE-oh; pop. 11,000) is Elba's liveliest city and contains most of its essential services. Visitors and locals alike spill from the pink, peach, and yellow buildings of the *centro* that seem to carpet the steep hillsides. Lively, restaurant-inundated *piazze* overlook the nearby harbor, filling the air with the smell of local cuisine and the sound of Italian conversation at all hours of the day.

▐ TRANSPORTATION

Ferry service is at Toremar, Calata Italia 32 (☎0565 96 01 31; portoferraio@ toremar.it), and Moby Lines, V. Elba 12 (☎0565 91 41 33; moby.portoferraio@ moby.it). Buy tickets at the travel agency, Calata Italia 22, across from the docks, in order to compare prices and schedules. Portoferraio is accessible by bus from Elba's other towns. ATL, V. Elba 22, across from the Toremar landing, runs **buses** to Marciana Marina (every hr., 7:15am-8pm) and Porto Azzuro (every hr., 5:10am-8pm). For other schedules, ask the office. (☎0565 91 43 92. Open June-Sept. daily 8am-8pm; Oct.-May M-Sa 8am-1:20pm and 4-6:30pm, Su 9am-12:30pm and 2-6:30pm. Tickets €2-2.50. Day pass €7, 6-day pass €19.) For **taxis** call ☎0565 91 51 12. Rent Chiappi, Calata Italia 38, rents **cars** (€45-65 per day). (☎0565 91 66 87; www.rentchiappi.it. Open daily 9am-7:30pm. MC/V.)

▐▐ ORIENTATION AND PRACTICAL INFORMATION

Though it's Elba's largest city, Portoferraio has a tiny *centro*. **Calata Italia** runs parallel to the harbor and **Via Manzoni** runs perpendicular. The first right off V. Manzoni is **Via Vittorio Emanuele**. From Calata Italia, a right turn on **Viale Elba** goes further inland toward services like banks and grocery stores. V. V. Emanuele turns into **Calata Mazzini**, which curves with the borders of the harbor; follow street signs and turn left through a brick arch, **Porta Medicea**, to **Piazza Cavour**. Cut through the *piazza* to reach **Piazza della Repubblica**, the center of town.

Tourist Offices: APT, Calata Italia 43 (☎0565 91 46 71; www.aptelba.it). From the Toremar docks facing away from the water, proceed left on Calata Italia. Open in summer M-Sa 9am-7pm, Su 9am-noon and 3-7pm; in winter daily 8am-1pm and 4-6:30pm.

Boat Excursions: Visione Sottomarina (☎0565 32 87 09 54 70) runs trips along the coast (€18) in glass-bottomed boats for prime views of the seafloor. Arrive 20min. early for decent seats. Tickets sold onboard or through tourist office. Morning tours depart from Portoferraio, afternoon tours from Marciana Marina.

Parks and Nature: Parco Nazionale Arcipelago Toscano, Vle. Elba 8 (☎0565 91 94 94). Has maps and info on hikes. Office open Tu-Th 9am-noon, Sa-Su 9am-2:30pm.

Internet Access: Da Ciro Bar, V. V. Emanuele 14 (☎0565 91 90 00), across from the Toremar dock. €3 per 30min., €5 per hr. Open daily 9am-10pm. AmEx/MC/V.

Post Office: V. Manganaro 7M (☎0565 93 47 31), around the left side of the building. Open M-F 8:15am-7pm, Sa 8:15am-12:30pm. **Postal Code:** 57037.

▐ ACCOMMODATIONS

Uphill from a heavenly beach, ▨**Albergo Le Ghiaie ❹**, Località Le Ghiaie, has comfortable rooms with bath. Great common areas foster a sense of community. Mornings start with coffee on the wooden terrace. From the harbor, take V. Manzoni and bear left on V. Cairoli. (☎0565 91 51 78. Breakfast included. Private parking. Singles €40-45; doubles €80-85; triples €110; quads €125. AmEx/ MC/V.) The small, no-frills rooms at **Hotel Nobel ❷**, V. Manganaro 72, are a decent option for a tight budget in high season. Follow V. Elba from the port for 10min. until it merges with V. Manganaro; the hotel is on the right. (☎0565 91 52 17; fax 91 54 15. Singles €20-34, with bath €42; doubles €44/62; triples with bath €78. AmEx/MC/V.) **Acquaviva ❶**, Località Acquaviva, has good camping on a picturesque site roughly 4km west of the *centro*. Take the bus toward Viticcio (8am, 12:30, 3, 6pm; €1) from Portoferraio and ask the driver to stop at the

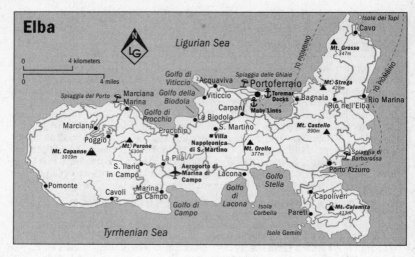

Elba

Ligurian Sea

0   4 kilometers

0   4 miles

Isole dei Topi

Cavo

TO PIOMBINO

Mt. Grosso
347m

Golfo di
Viticcio   Acquaviva   *Spiaggia delle Ghiaie*

Spiaggia del Porto   Marciana
Marina   Golfo della
Biodola   Viticcio   Portoferraio   Mt. Strega
428m

Golfo di
Procchio   La Biodola   Carpani   Toremar
Docks   Bagnaia   TO PIOMBINO   Rio Marina

Marciana   Procchio   Moby Lines   Rio nell'Elba

Poggio   S. Martino   Mt. Castello
390m

Mt. Perone
630m   Villa
Napoleonica
di S. Martino

Mt. Capanne
1019m   La Pila   Mt. Orello
377m   Spiaggia di
Barbarossa

S. Ilario
in Campo   Aeroporto di
Marina di
Campo   Lacona   Porto Azzurro

Pomonte   Marina
di Campo   Golfo
Stella

Cavoli   Golfo
di
Lacona   Capoliveri

Golfo di
Campo   Isola
Corbella   Pareti   Mt. Calamita
413m

Tyrrhenian Sea   *Isole Gemini*

campground *(campeggio)*. Located on the beach, the site has a bar, restaurant, and grocery store. (☎0565 91 91 03; fax 91 55 92; www.campingacquaviva.it. Reserve via fax. €7.30-14 per person, €6-15 per tent, €2-3.50 per car. MC/V.)

🔋 FOOD

Two Elban specialties of note are *schiaccia*, a flat sandwich bread cooked in olive oil and studded with onions or black olives, and *aleatico*, a sweet liqueur. Elba as a whole suffers from an infestation of overpriced, tourist-trap restaurants, but Portoferraio has options for value-conscious diners. Dwarfed by ships, **Ristorante Stella Marina** ❸, V. Vittorio Emanuele 1, in a parking lot across from the Toremar dock, offers courteous service and fabulous seafood dishes at busy tables. Try some *tagliolini ai frutti di mare* (pasta with mussels, clams, shrimp, and octopus; €10), or splurge on Elban lobster (€14). The pasta-dominated vegetarian menu is reasonably priced (€6.50-9). (☎0565 91 59 83. Primi €9-12. Secondi by weight. Cover €2.50. Open May to mid-Nov. Tu-Su noon-2:30pm and 7:20-10:30pm. AmEx/MC/V.) **Il Garibaldino** ❷, Calata Mazzini 1, is a popular find right on the waterfront. (☎0565 91 47 51. Pizza €3.50-5. Primi €5.50-8.50. Secondi €6.50-18. Open daily 12:30-2:30pm and 7-10:30pm. AmEx/ MC/V.) **Trattoria-Pizzeria Napoletana da Zucchetta** ❸, P. della Repubblica 40, is a casual spot in the *centro storico* with outdoor seating and affordable pizza. (☎0565 91 53 31. Pizza €3-8. Primi €7-11. Secondi €9-25. Open M-Tu and Th-Su 11:30am-3pm and 6-11:30pm, W 6-11:30pm. MC/V.) For groceries, head to the centrally located **Conad**, P. Pietri 2/4, off Vle. Elba, next to the Banca di Roma. (Open from M-Sa 7:30am-9pm, Su 8am-1:30pm and 4:30-8:30pm. AmEx/MC/V.)

🔵🔲 SIGHTS AND BEACHES

Inside Emperor Napoleon's one-time residence, the **Villa dei Mulini,** rest his personal library, letters, several silk chairs once graced by his imperial derriere, and the sovereign Elban flag that he designed. (☎0565 91 58 46. Ticket office open July-Aug. M-Sa 9am-7pm, Su 9am-1pm; Sept.-June closed Tu. €5; 3-day combined ticket with Villa Napoleonica €9. Cash only.) Monogrammatic Ns emblazon the **Villa Napoleonica di San Martino,** placed there after Napoleon's death. Note especially the Sala Egizia, with friezes depicting his Egyptian campaign. (Take bus #1 5km out of Portoferraio. ☎0565 91 46 88. Ticket office open July-Aug. M-Sa 9am-7pm, Su 9am-1pm; Sept.-June Tu-Sa 9am-7pm, Su 9am-1pm.) The **Museo Archeologico della Linguella** glorifies Elba's seafaring history, displaying finds from ancient trading boat wrecks dating back to the AD 5th century. (In the Fortezza del Lingrella, up the hill from the Villa dei Mulini in the *centro storico*. ☎0565 91 73 38. Open daily Sept.-June 10am-1pm and 3-7pm; July-Aug. 10am-2:25pm and 6pm-midnight. €3, children and individuals in large groups €2. Cash only.) The **Medici Fortress,** looming over the port, is worth a quick peek. Cosimo dei Medici, Grand Duke of Tuscany, founded the complex in 1548. The structure was so imposing that the dreaded Turkish pirate Dracut declared the building impenetrable and called off his planned attack in 1553. (Open Tu and Th-Su 10am-1pm and 3:30-7:10pm. €3, children €2. Cash only.)

Many large signs from the harbor point to **Spiaggia delle Ghiaie,** so, unsurprisingly, every day its shores are quickly covered with the chairs and towels of the masses grabbing their piece of the precious rocky, white beach. Bring a towel and claim a spot to avoid roped-off areas and their corresponding fees. Come for sun, not serenity: music-blasting restaurants and a kiddie park in the vicinity make this a beach exclusively for jamming tanners. For those who wish to tan in tranquility, farther east and down a long flight of stairs from the Villa dei Mulini is the sandy and more secluded **Spiaggia delle Viste.** Appropriately named for its views, this beach is framed with cliffs and is the perfect spot to take a dip in the crystal-blue water.

MARCIANA MARINA   ☎0565

The pebbly border of Marciana Marina's (mar-CHEE-ya-na ma-REE-na; pop. 1700) waterfront is known as the most beautiful beach destination on the island. Explore the lopsided rocks, stake out a sunny niche, and bring along goggles to observe schools of fish in the still waters. Many stretches of shoreline are accessible only by boat: the nicest ones lie between Sant'Andrea and Fetovaia, along the western border of Elba, an area reputed to contain the island's clearest waters. The town itself, though tiny, accommodates hordes of sunbathing tourists and daytripping families.

⌗⏚ TRANSPORTATION AND PRACTICAL INFORMATION. Reach Marciana Marina from Portoferraio by car, boat, or bus ride (45min., €2). The **tourist office** stands near the shore in P. Vittoria. (Open July-Aug. M-W and F-Su 10am-1pm and 8-11pm.) For information about boat excursions, pop into **Agenzia Brauntour Viaggi,** V. Felice Cavallotti 10. (☎0565 99 68 73; abviaggi@abvaiggi.it. Open high season M-Sa 9am-1pm and 4-8pm, Su 9am-1pm; low season M-F 9am-12:30pm and 3:30-7pm, Sa-Su 9am-12:30pm.) The **post office** is at Vle. Lloyd 37. (Open M-F 8:15am-1:30pm, Sa 8:15am-12:30pm.) **Postal Code:** 57033.

⌗⏚ ACCOMMODATIONS AND FOOD. The tourist office offers info on *affittacamere* during July and August, though these fill quickly and other options are pricey, making Marciana Marina an ideal spot for a daytrip. **Hotel Imperia ❸,** V. Amedeo 12, is steps from the sea. Bright rooms, an upbeat staff, and an extensive breakfast buffet can't be beat. Book ahead for a room with a balcony at no extra cost. (☎0565 99 082; www.hotelimperia.it. Breakfast included. July-Aug. €35-55 per person. Additional €15 for single. Half pension €47-80. Prices drop significantly Sept.-June. AmEx/MC/V.) Follow V. Amedeo away from the harbor on a slight incline for 15min., and turn right on Località Ontanelli to reach **Casa Lupi ❹,** Località Ontanelli 15. The immaculate rooms all have bath,

TUSCANY

and the carefully tended rose garden looks out over the mountains and the sea. (☎/fax 0565 99 143. Breakfast €6. Singles €42; doubles €70. Cash only.)

Placate a growling stomach in P. Vittoria where a slew of good restaurants serve cheap and filling seafood dishes. Diners fall for **First Love ❷**, V. G. Dussol 9/13, at first bite. Enjoy the limited but very tasty selection of fish and pasta or join the boisterous night crowd for a drink. (☎0565 99 355. Primi €7-8. Secondi €7.50-17. Open daily 7pm-2am. MC/V.) For a filling snack, head to **dall'Elba al Tramonto ❶**, V. Aurelio Saffi 9. This perfect alternative to a formal restaurant serves crepes for breakfast, lunch, and dinner. Every confection has a suggested beer and wine to complement its particular flavor. Simple crepes start at €2.50. For takeout, ring the bell at the window on V. Amadeo. (Open daily 7am-midnight. MC/V.) Fifty meters up V. Amedeo from Hotel Imperia, **Conad**, V. Cerboni 4, supplies basics. (Open M-Sa 8am-1pm and 4-7:30pm, Su 8am-1pm. MC/V.)

◪ **SIGHTS.** If sun and sand are what you crave, stake out a spot on Marciana Marina's **Spiaggia del Porto**, a sandy beach that runs the length of the harbor along Vle. Regina Margherita. For a different perspective, head inland to **Monte Capanne**, Elba's highest peak at 1019m, a literally uplifting excursion. The mountaintop offers views of the entire island, with sea and sky blending in a periwinkle haze. On clear days, the view extends all the way to Corsica; otherwise, the far-off island appears to float in a mist of passing clouds. The strenuous 2hr. uphill trek is poorly marked (maps available at the parks office in Portoferraio), but a ride in the small open cage of a **cable car** can shorten the trip—those afraid of heights should opt for the hike. (☎0565 90 10 20. Cable car open for ascent Apr. 14-Oct. 10am-12:15pm and 2:45-5:30pm, for descent 10am-12:45pm and 2:45-6pm. €10, round-trip €15. Cash only.) To reach Monte Capanne, take the bus (15min., €1) from Marciana Marina toward Marciana. Ask the driver to stop at Monte Capanne; look for a parking lot and the "Cabinovia" signs that point to the lifts. Be sure to buy a round-trip bus ticket, as there are no *tabaccherie* near the mountain and you can't buy a ticket onboard.

PORTO AZZURRO ☎0565

The gleaming waters of Porto Azzurro (POR-toh Ad-ZUR-ro; pop. 3200) surround a beautiful, low-key beach town. While the town has its fair share of postcard racks and tourist shops, there are also plenty of great restaurants and dramatic coastal views. Dense and colorful flora, intimidating cliffs, and produce farms can all be found within a kilometer of the harbor. Brave the crowds at the tiny, crowded beach off the main drag, or hop over to **Barbarossa** beach for glistening waters, a younger crowd, and a bit more towel space. To reach the beach, skirt the port and take the narrow steps leading to a dirt trail (25min.) that climbs the hill and overlooks the water. For flat terrain, head through the campgrounds on Vle. Italia and curve around on the highway, V. Provinciale Est (20min.). Get to the beach faster by taking the bus headed to Marina di Campo (ask the driver if it stops at Barbarossa).

If staying overnight, camping is by far the cheapest option; prices vary by month. The first three weeks in August are considered the high season. Campgrounds are in **Località Barbarossa**, near Barbarossa beach. Follow the directions above to Barbarossa or take the less scenic, faster route by following Vle. Italia out of town and turn right at the sign for the campground. Near the beach, family-run **Arrighi ❶** offers amenities like safes, a supermarket, and a common area with A/C. Internet and Wi-Fi are available for an additional fee. (☎0565 95 568; www.campingarrighi.it. Laundry €6. Open Easter-Oct. €6-14 per person, €5.50-19 per tent, €2-2.80 per car. MC/V.) Away from the beach, a 5min. walk down a dirt path inland and to the west of Camping Arrighi brings you to **Il Gabbiano ❶**, with shaded grounds near the road. (☎0565 95 087. €6-10 per person, €7-12 per tent. No cars July-Aug.; low-season €9.50 per car. Cash only.)

Porto Azzurro has an abundance of restaurants; choosing one will be more difficult than finding one. Picnickers will fare best at the **Coop,** Vle. Italia 32. (Open Ma-Sa 8am-1pm and 4-8pm, Su 8am-1pm.) **La Creperia ❶**, V. Marconi 2, off V. 25 Aprile, is just right for a quick crepe (€2.20-3.60). The extensive menu will satisfy cravings for both the sweet and the savory. (Open daily Apr.-Oct. 11am-2am. Cash only.) **Ristorante Bella M'Briana ❸**, V. D'Alarcon 29, serves more elegant meals in a waterfront setting. (Primi €6.50-8. Secondi €9-20. Cover €2. Open daily noon-3pm and 7-11pm. AmEx/MC/V.) Wind down the evening with the mellow, late-night crowd at **Bar Tamata,** V. Cesare Battisti 3. (☎0565 34 83 05 88 63. Open daily 6pm-2am; reduced winter hours. Cash only.) Brazilian **Morumbi,** 2km down the road to Capoliveri, is one of the island's hottest and largest discos, with indoor and outdoor dance floors, a pizzeria, and a pagoda. (☎0565 92 01 91. Weekend cover €8-10. Open June 30-Sept. 15.)

Piazza Giacomo Matteotti, right from the Porto Azzurro bus stop, harbors the town's glitziest restaurants, most casual *gelaterie*, and funkiest shops. Grab a seat on a bench facing the water and enjoy the sun and activity of the *centro*. Elba is renowned for its abundance of natural resources including its extensive mineral deposits. The Etruscan mineral and marine biology museum, **Piccola Miniera,** V. Provinciale Est 34, offers tours that include wine tastings, mineral showcases, and marine life exhibits. Tickets range from €3-9 depending on activities included in the tour. (Open daily 9am-1pm and 2:30-6:30pm. MC/V.)

UMBRIA

Because of its wild woods and fertile plains, craggy gorges and gentle hills, Umbria (OOM-bree-ah) is known as the "green heart of Italy." Cobblestoned villages and lively international universities are scattered throughout the region, bringing a distinct vitality to the land. Three thousand years ago, Etruscans settled this regional crossroads between the Adriatic and Tyrrhenian coasts. One thousand years later, Christianity transformed Umbria's architecture and regional identity. St. Francis shamed the increasingly extravagant Church with his legacy of humility, pacifism, and charity that persists in Assisi to this day. The region also produced medieval masters Perugino and Pinturicchio and holds Giotto's greatest masterpieces. Umbria's artistic spirit gives life today to the internationally acclaimed Umbria Jazz Festival and Spoleto Festival.

HIGHLIGHTS OF UMBRIA

HIKE to Eremo delle Carceri to meditate at the sanctuary of St. Francis (p. 520).

EAT GELATO with locals on the steps of Cattedrale di San Lorenzo (p. 507).

WATCH a performance at the historic Teatro Romane in medieval Gubbio (p. 511).

PERUGIA   ☎ 075

The citizens of Perugia (peh-ROO-ja; pop. 162,000) rose to political prominence after chasing the *Umbri* tribe into surrounding valleys. Wars with neighboring cities dominate Perugia's history, but periods of peace and prosperity led to the stunning artistic achievements for which the city is known today. The city's own Pietro Vannucci, a painter and mentor to Raphael, is known as "Perugino" because of his association with the town. While not as pristine as neighboring cities, well-worn Perugia is loved by visitors and locals for its convenient big-city amenities and easily navigable small-town layout. Whether through the renowned jazz festival, the decadent chocolate, the religious art, or the student-driven university atmosphere, Perugia displays its character with pride.

▐ TRANSPORTATION

Trains: Perugia lies on the Foligno-Terontola line. It is serviced by 2 stations.

    Stazione Fontiveggio, in P. Vittorio Veneto. Info booth open daily 7am-8pm. Ticket window open daily 6:10am-8pm. To: **Arezzo** (1hr., every hr., €4); **Assisi** (25min., every hr., €2.05); **Florence** (2hr., 6 per day, from €8); **Foligno** (40min., every hr., €3); **Orvieto** (1hr., 11 per day, €7) via **Terontola** (40min., €6); **Rome** (2hr., 7 per day 6am-6pm, €11); **Spoleto** (1hr., every hr., €4.50); Terni (1hr., 19 per day 7:31am-12:30am, €4.85).

    Perugia Sant'Anna, in Ple. Bellucci. Commuter rail runs to **Sansepolcro** (1hr., 18 per day 6:18am-7:40pm, €4.50), **Terni** (1hr., 14 per day 6:06am-6:58pm, €4.40), and **Todi** (1hr., 5 per day 6:53am-7:41pm, €3.05).

Buses: APM (☎80 05 12 141; www.apmperugia.it), in P. dei Partigiani. To: **Assisi** (1hr., 7 per day 6:40am-7.05pm, €3); **Chiusi** (1hr., 8 per day 6:20am-6:35pm, €5.40); **Gubbio** (1hr., 16 per day 6:40am-8:08pm, €4.50); **Siena** (1hr., M-F 8:30am and 5:30pm, €11); **Todi** (1hr., 10 per day 6:30am-7:30pm, €5.40). Reduced service Su. Additional

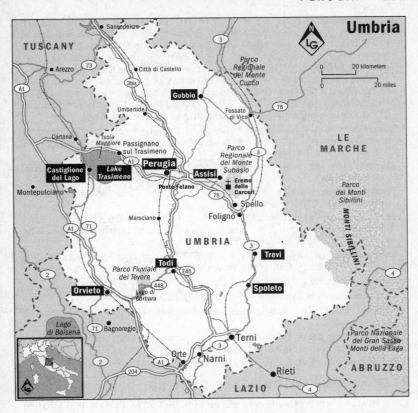

buses leave from the train station. Tickets at Radio Taxi Perugia (☎075 50 04 888), to the right of the train station. **City buses** in P. dei Partigiani, down a series of escalators through Rocca Paolina from P. Italia. Bus #6 (€1) runs to the train station.

Taxis: In P. Italia and P. Vittorio Veneto or call **Radio Taxi** (☎075 50 04 888).

Car Rental: Hertz, P. Vittorio Veneto 2 (☎075 50 02 439; hertzperugia@tiscali.it), in the train station. Open M-F 8:30am-12:30pm and 3-7pm, Sa 8:30am-1pm. AmEx/MC/V.

✴ 🛈 ORIENTATION AND PRACTICAL INFORMATION

From Fontiveggio train station, buses #6, 7, 9, 11, 13, and 15 run to **Piazza Italia** (€1). The **Minimetro** (E1) is a fun alternative and goes to Pincetto, near Piazza Matteotti. Otherwise, it's a 2km trek uphill to the *centro*. To get to P. Italia from the **bus station** in **Piazza dei Partigiani** or from the nearby **Perugia Sant'Anna** train station at **Piazzale Belucci**, follow the signs to the **escalators** (open 6:15am-1:45am; free) that run beneath the old city and through the *Rocca Paolina*. From P. Italia, **Corso Vannucci,** the main shopping thoroughfare, leads to **Piazza IV Novembre** and the *duomo*. Behind the *duomo*, Via Rocchi winds downhill to **Piazza Braccio Fortebraccio** and the university district. Just off C. Vannucci is Via Baglioni, which leads to **Piazza Matteotti,** the municipal center.

Tourist Office: IAT di Perugia, P. Matteotti 18 (☎075 57 36 458; fax 57 20 988). The office offers free maps and pamphlets on accommodations, restaurants, and cultural events. If in stock, a free ✂**Perugia Little Blue** guide in English is especially helpful for long-term stays and exploration. Open daily 8:30am-6:30pm. **Info Umbria,** Largo Cacciatori delle Alpi 3/B (☎075 57 57; www.infoumbria.com), next to the bus station in P. dei Partigiani; provides free maps and free bookings for many hotels, as well as tickets for the **"Perugia City Tour."** On-board tour audioguide provides info on sites in English, French, German, and Italian. Open M-F 9am-1pm and 2:30-6:30pm, Sa 9am-1pm. Tour €13. Check www.umbriabest.com for information on the town and events.

Budget Travel: CTS, V. del Roscetto 21 (☎075 57 20 284; www.cts.it), off V. Pinturicchio toward the bottom of the street. Offers vacation deals to ISIC cardholders. Open M-F 9:30am-1pm and 3-6:30pm. AmEx/MC/V.

Currency Exchange: Banks have the best rates; those in P. Italia and P. dei Partigiani have 24hr. **ATMs.**

Luggage Storage: In Stazione Fontiveggio. €3 for 1st 12hr., €2 for each additional 12hr. Open daily 8am-7:30pm. Cash only.

English-Language Bookstore: L'Altra Libreria, V. Rocchi 3 (☎075 57 36 104). Small selection of classics, travel guides, and, in the summer months, trendy titles. Open M-Sa 9am-1pm and 3:30-8:30pm, Su 10:30am-1pm. AmEx/MC/V.

Laundromat: 67 Laundry, V. Fabretti 7/A. Wash €3.50 per 8kg, dry €2 per 20kg. Open daily 8am-9pm. **Bolle Blu,** C. Garibaldi 43. Wash €3.50 per 8kg, dry €3. Open daily 8am-10pm.

Police: V. Cortonese 157 (☎075 50 621).

Pharmacy: Farmacia San Martino, P. Matteotti 26 (☎075 57 22 335).

Hospital: (☎075 57 81) for specific concerns. **Ospedale Silvestrini** (☎075 57 86 400) for emergencies.

Internet: Coffee Break, V. Danzetta 22, off V. Baglioni near P. Matteotti. Free Wi-Fi. Internet €1 per hr. Open M-Sa 8am-11:30pm, Su 11am-11pm. AmEx/MC/V.

Post Office: P. Matteotti 1. Open M-Sa 8am-6:30pm. **Postal Code:** 06110.

🏠 🏠 ACCOMMODATIONS AND CAMPING

Reserve ahead when crowds descend on Perugia for the Umbria Jazz Festival in July and the Eurochocolate Festival in late October.

Ostello Ponte Felcino, V. Maniconi 97 (☎075 59 13 991; www.ostellopontefelcino.com). Settled in the gardens of Ponte Felcino just outside of Perugia, this well-kept hostel gives its guests a taste of authentic small town Umbrian life. Bus service is frequent into P. dei Partigiani. Clean rooms, complimentary breakfast, and spacious common areas. Internet access available. Dinner €10. Dorms €16; singles €22; doubles €36. ❷

Ostello della Gioventù/Centro Internazionale di Accoglienza per la Gioventù, V. Bontempi 13 (☎075 57 22 880; www.ostello.perugia.it). 300-year-old frescoes and helpful staff adjacent to lively P. IV Novembre in downtown Perugia. Kitchen, library, lockers, spacious showers, lobby phone, and TV room. Linens €2. 2-week max. stay. Check-in 4-11:30pm. Check-out 7:30-9:30am. Lockout 9:30am-4pm. Curfew midnight, in summer 1am. Open Jan. 16-Dec. 14. Dorms €15. AmEx/MC/V. ❶

Hotel Priori, V. Vermiglioli 3 (☎075 57 23 378; www.hotelpriori.it), located directly off V. dei Priori. 55 large rooms centrally located near historic street. Private terrace is ideal for relaxing and lounging. Take advantage of off-season prices. Singles €45-70; doubles €65-95; triples €85-125; quads €100-145. ❹

Albergo Anna, V. dei Priori 48 (☎/fax 075 57 36 304; www.albergoanna.it), off C. Vannucci. Ornate 17th-century rooms, some with ceramic fireplaces and views of city rooftops. Breakfast €2. Singles €40-50; doubles €65-80; triples €70-90. MC/V. ❹

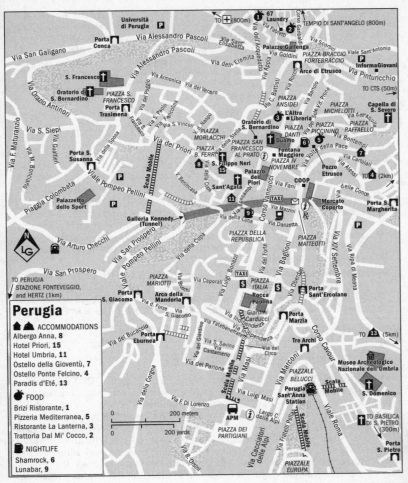

Perugia

🏠🏠 **ACCOMMODATIONS**
Albergo Anna, **8**
Hotel Priori, **15**
Hotel Umbria, **11**
Ostello della Gioventù, **7**
Ostello Ponte Felcino, **4**
Paradis d'Eté, **13**

🍴 **FOOD**
Brizi Ristorante, **1**
Pizzeria Mediterranea, **5**
Ristorante La Lanterna, **3**
Trattoria Dal Mi' Cocco, **2**

🌙 **NIGHTLIFE**
Shamrock, **6**
Lunabar, **9**

Hotel Umbria, V. Boncambi 37 (☎075 57 21 203; www.hotel-umbria.com), off P. della Repubblica. 17 rooms with small beds, high ceilings, and standard hotel furnishings, including TV, phone, and bath. Reservations recommended, especially in summer. Singles €40-50; doubles €75; triples €90; quads €120. AmEx/MC/V. ❸

Paradis d'Eté, Strada Fontana 29H (☎/fax 075 51 73 121), 8km from the city, in Colle della Trinità. Take a city bus from P. Italia (dir.: Colle della Trinità. 30min.. every 2hr.), and ask the driver to stop at the campground. Free hot showers and pool access in summer. €7 per person; €5.50 per tent; €3 per car. AmEx/MC/V. ❶

🍴 **FOOD**

No visit to Perugia is complete without a taste of the world-famous chocolate at **Perugina,** C. Vannucci 101. (Open M 2:30-7:45pm, Tu-Sa 9:30am-7:45pm, Su and holidays 10:30am-1:30pm and 3-8pm.) While you're at it, try the *torta di formaggio* (cheese torte) or *mele al cartoccio* (apple pie) at sweet-smelling **Ceccarani**, P. Matteotti 16. (☎075 57 21 960. Open M-Sa 7am-8pm, Su 9am-1:30pm.) Check out the **covered market** in P. Matteotti. Entrance is below street level, to the right of the post office off Via Baglioni. (Open M-Sa 7am-7:30pm.) The Italian chain, **Coop**, P. Matteotti 15, stocks essentials. (Open M-Sa 9am-8pm. MC/V/ AmEx.) Complement meals with one of the region's native wines: *Sagrantino Secco*, a dry red, or *Grechetto*, a light white.

☒ Trattoria Dal Mi' Cocco, C. Garibaldi 12 (☎075 57 32 511). Secluded local favorite. Leaves diners happily stuffed. Full course meal (€15) includes antipasti, primi, secondi, daily special, bread, dessert, and a glass of liqueur. Open Tu-Su 11am-2pm and 8:15-10pm. Reservations recommended. MC/V. ❷

Pizzeria Mediterranea, P. Piccinino 11/12 (☎075 57 21 322). From P. IV Novembre, walk to the right of the *duomo*, and turn right shortly before Ostello della Gioventù. A college crowd descends by night for typical pizza at reasonable prices (€4-12). Cover €1.10. Open daily 12:30-2:30pm and 7:30-11pm. MC/V. ❶

Brizi Ristorante, V. Fabretti 75 (☎075 57 21 386). From P. IV Novembre, walk right of the *duomo*, veer left through P. Danti, and right down V. Rocchi to P. Braccio Fortebraccio. On far side of *piazza*, turn left on V. Fabretti. Skip the *menù* and order well presented pasta and carnivorous offerings, like the delicious lamb (€6-7.50). Cover €1.50. Open M and W-Su noon-3pm and 7:30-10pm. MC/V. ❷

Ristorante La Lanterna, V. Rocchi 6 (☎075 57 26 397), near the *duomo*. Enjoy pizza (€7) baked *forno a legna* (wood oven), as well as rich pasta (€8-11) and meat dishes (€10-16). A romantic setting with elegant, brick-vaulted rooms managed by accommodating waiters. Cover €2. Open M-W and F-Su noon-3pm and 7-10pm. AmEx/MC/V. ❸

👁 SIGHTS

PIAZZA IV NOVEMBRE AND ENVIRONS

☒PIAZZA IV NOVEMBRE. The social center of Perugian life, P. IV Novembre presents a pageant of young, lively locals, students, tourists, and resident internationals against a backdrop of monuments. Perugia's most popular sights frame the *piazza*; the **Duomo**, the **Galleria Nazionale Dell'Umbria**, and most other monuments lie no more than a 15min. walk away. The **Fontana Maggiore** (1278-80), designed by Fra' Bevignate and decorated by Nicola and Giovanni Pisano, sits in the center of the *piazza*. Bas-reliefs depicting both religious and Roman history cover the double-basin fountain. Beginning at dusk, the *piazza* plays hosts to a diverse assortment of people enjoying the summer night air, savoring gelato, and conversing on the ancient city steps.

PALAZZO DEI PRIORI AND GALLERIA NAZIONALE DELL'UMBRIA. The 13th-century windows and turrets of this *palazzo*, on the left when facing the Fontana Maggiore, are remnants of an embattled era. This building, one of the finest examples of Gothic communal architecture, shelters the grandiose **Galleria Nazionale dell'Umbria**. The collection contains a number of 13th- and 14th-century religious works by Duccio, Fra Angelico, Taddeo di Bartolo, Guido da Siena, and Piero della Francesca. Among these early masterpieces, Duccio's skillful rendering of delicately translucent garments in his *Virgin and Child and Six Angels* in **Room 2** is worth a closer look. Another highlight is della Francesca's detailed *Polyptych of Saint Anthony* in **Room 11**. Native sons Pinturicchio and Perugino share **Room 15**. The two right panels of *Miracles of San Bernardino of Siena* are Pinturicchio's. Note his rich tones that contrast with Perugino's characteristic soft pastels of the two panels on the right. Downstairs, three rooms display Baroque and Neoclassical works as well as a collection of jewelry and textiles. *(In P. IV Novembre at C. Vannucci 19. ☎ 075 57 21 009; www.gallerianazionaleumbria. it. Open Tu-Su 8:30am-7:30pm. Last entry 1hr. before closing. Closed Jan. 1 and Dec. 25. €6.50; reduced €3.25. Cash only.)* To the right of the Galleria sits the **Sala dei Notari,** once the citizens' assembly chamber. Thirteenth-century frescoes adorn the eight Romanesque arches, which support the vault. Note the scene on the fourth arch on the left of the crow and the fox from Aesop's fables. *(Up the steps. Sometimes closed for public performances. Open June-Sept. Tu-Su 9am-1pm and 3-7pm. Free.)*

DUOMO (CATTEDRALE DI SAN LORENZO). The rugged facade of Perugia's imposing Gothic *duomo* was begun in the 14th century, but builders never completed it. Though not as ornate as other cathedrals in Tuscany and Umbria, the groin-vaulted interior and 15th- to 18th-century embellishments, lit by small chandeliers, are quite elegant. The church is also said to hold the Virgin Mary's wedding ring, snagged from Chiusi in the Middle Ages, though the average visitor is unlikely to catch a glimpse of the guarded treasure. *(P. IV Novembre. Open M-Sa 8am-1pm and 4-8pm, Su 4-5:45pm. Modest dress required. Free.)*

COLLEGIO DELLA MERCANZIA AND COLLEGIO DEL CAMBIO. The walls of the audience chambers on either side of Palazzo dei Priori are covered in magnificent wood paneling and elaborate frescoes. The elegantly carved bench in the *Collegio della Mercanzia* (Merchants' Guild) is a tribute to the Republic of Perugia, marking an advancement from the previous feudal system. In the *Collegio del Cambio* (Exchange Guild), the **Sala dell'Udienza** (audience chamber) holds Perugino's frescoes, which portray heroes, prophets, and even the artist himself. The members of Perugia's merchant guild have met in this wood-paneled structure since the 14th century. *(Collegio della Mercanzia: C. Vannucci 15, adjacent to the police station. ☎ 075 57 30 366. Open daily Mar.-Oct. and Dec. 18-Jan. 3 Tu-Sa 9am-1pm and 2:30-5:30pm, Su and holidays 9am-1pm; Nov.-Dec. 17 and Jan. 4-Feb. Tu and Th-F 8am-2pm, W and Sa 8am-4:30pm, Su 9am-1pm. €1. Collegio del Cambio: C. Vannucci 25. ☎ 075 57 28 599. Open M-Sa 9am-12:30pm and 2:30-5:30pm, Su 9am-1pm. €4.50. Cash only.)*

VIA DEI PRIORI. Don't be fooled by the street's present-day calm and stone-like serenity. Via dei Priori, which begins under the arch at Palazzo dei Priori, was once one of medieval Perugia's goriest streets: the spikes on the lower walls of the street were once used to impale the rotting heads of executed criminals. The Neoclassical **Chiesa di San Filippo Neri,** begun in 1627 and built in the form of a Latin cross, resides solemnly in P. Ferri; Santa Maria di Vallicella's heart is kept to the right of the altar. *(Open daily in summer 7am-noon and 4:30-7:30pm; in winter 8am-noon and 4-6pm. Free.)* **Piazza San Francesco al Prato** is a grassy square used for lounging and strolling. At its edge the 15th-century **Oratorio di San Bernardino** serves as a retreat from urban commotion. *(Next to Chiesa di San Francesco, down V. San Francesco. Open daily 8am-12:30pm and 3:30-6pm. Free.)*

THE NORTHEAST

VIA ROCCHI. From behind the *duomo*, medieval V. Rocchi, both the city's oldest street and a former aqueduct, winds through the northern city and straight underneath the impressive **Arco di Etrusco,** a perfectly preserved Roman arch built on Etruscan pedestals. Walk straight through P. Braccio Fortebraccio, the youth hang-out where V. Rocchi turns to C. Guiseppe Garibaldi, and follow it for 10min. toward the humbling **Tempio di Sant'Angelo** (also known as **Chiesa di San Michele Arcangelo**), a fifth-century circular church constructed with stone and wood taken from ancient pagan buildings. The **Porta Sant'Angelo,** an arch and tower that welcomes visitors to the city, stands nearby, its top level offering a view of all of Perugia. *(Past Palazzo Gallenga, to the right near the end of C. Garibaldi.* ☎ *075 57 22 624. Open daily 10am-noon and 4-6pm.)*

CAPPELLA DI SAN SEVERO. San Severo is home to *The Holy Trinity and Saints,* one of many collaborations by Perugia's favorite mentor-student tag team, Perugino and Raphael, who painted the lower and upper sections, respectively. Opposite the chapel, a *piazza* wall holds a plaque with a quote from Dante's *Paradiso* praising the city. *(In P. Rafaello.* ☎ *075 57 33 864. Open Apr.-Oct. M and W-Su 10am-1:30pm and 2:30-6pm; Nov.-Mar. 10:30am-1:30pm and 2:30-5pm. €2.50.)*

POZZO ETRUSCO. With a depth of 36m, the Etruscan Well dates to the third century BC and was once Perugia's main water source. Perugians were forced to use the well again during WWII, when bombs destroyed outside water lines to the city. Descend damp stairs to the footbridge spanning the well just meters above the water. *(P. Danti 18, across from the duomo. Look for the "Pozzo Etrusco" sign above a small alleyway and follow the cobblestone alley down to the left.* ☎ *075 57 33 669. Open Apr.-Oct. Tu-Su 10am-1:30pm and 2:30-6:30pm; Nov.-Mar. Tu-Su 11am-1:30pm and 2:30-5pm. Free.)*

THE EAST SIDE

BASILICA DI SAN PIETRO. This 10th-century church consists of a double arcade of closely spaced columns that lead to a choir. Its art-filled interior contains solemn, majestic paintings and frescoes depicting saints and soldiers, all in brilliant color on a dramatic scale. Look for Perugino's *Pietà* along the northern aisle. At the far end through the arch is a small garden; its lower section offers a must-see view of the surrounding countryside. *(V. Borgo XX Giugno, past P. San Pietro. Entrance to church is on the far left side of the courtyard; garden is through courtyard on right. Open daily 7:30am-12:30pm and 3-6pm. Free.)*

CHIESA DI SAN DOMENICO. This cathedral, though a relatively unremarkable example of Italian architecture, is Umbria's largest. The Gothic rose window brightens the otherwise simple, cream-colored interior, rebuilt in 1632. The intricately carved **Tomb of Pope Benedict XI** (1325) rests in the Capella del Santissimo Sacramento to the right of the high altar. *(From P. Giordano Bruno, follow the main road, C. Cavour. Open daily 7am-noon and 4-7:30pm. Free.)*

GIARDINI CARDUCCI. These romantic public gardens are named after the 19th-century poet Giosuè Carducci. From the garden wall, enjoy a splendid panorama of the Umbrian countryside; a castle or an ancient church crowns every hill. *(Behind P. Italia at the far end of C. Vannucci, off P. IV Novembre. Free.)*

ROCCA PAOLINA. The underground remains of a grandiose fortress, the *Rocca* was built by the architect Antonio Sangallo il Giovane on the order of Pope Paolo III Farnese. Several escalators descend through the brick structure, connecting the upper (P. Italia) and lower (P. dei Partigiani) parts of the city. Nearby, the **Museo della Rocca Paolina** offers information and exhibits illuminating the Rocca's history. *(Entrances beneath P. Italia and across from bus station in P. dei Partigiani. Open daily 6:15am-1:45am. Free. Museum open daily 10am-1:30pm and 2:30-6pm. €1)*

◼ ❀ NIGHTLIFE AND FESTIVALS

Perugia provides more nightlife opportunities than any other city in Umbria, and its large student population keeps clubs packed nearly every night of the week from September to May. Unfortunately, in summer many nightlife establishments shut down, and most are reachable only by car or bus. During the academic year, join the nightly bandwagon at **Piazza Braccio Fortebraccio,** known as **Piazza Grimana** to locals, where free buses depart for several nearby clubs (starting at midnight). In the city, students congregate at all hours on the steps of **Piazza IV Novembre** to people-watch or chat over pizza and wine. Bottles aren't allowed on the steps after 8pm and on-site police enforce this rule, but never fear—neighboring cafes happily dole out drinks in plastic cups.

To find **Lunabar/Ferrari,** V. Scura 1/6, follow the loud music emanating from an entrance under the neon "Hotel Umbria" sign off C. Vannucci. In a city where traditional nightlife is a bit hard to find, Lunabar is a rowdy yet sophisticated relief for anyone looking to drink, dance, and mingle with the college population. (☎075 57 22 966; www.lunabarferrari.it) **Shamrock,** P. Danti 18, is down a small side street on the way to the Pozzo Etrusco. Bite into juicy bacon burgers (€3.50) at this Irish pub. (☎075 57 36 625. Drinks €3.50. Happy hour 6-9pm. Open daily 6pm-2am). Late-night cafes along **Via Mazzini, Corso Vannucci,** and **Piazza Matteotti** are a popular alternative to bar-hopping.

Every July, the 10-day ◪**Umbria Jazz Festival** draws world-class performers like B.B. King, Herbie Hancock, James Brown, and Alicia Keys. Grab a snack and a bottle of wine and head to one of the free outdoor concerts, or dance all night by the stage in P. IV Novembre. (Info ☎800 46 23 11; www.umbriajazz.com. Ticket office, C. Vannucci 39. Open M-F 10am-1pm and 3-7pm, Sa 10am-1pm. During festival, open daily 10am-7pm. Tickets €17-68, some events free.) In September, the **Sagra Musicale Umbra** occurs in many Umbrian cities and fills Perugia's churches with religious and classical music. Check Palazzo Gallenga or www.sagramusicaleumbra.com for event listings. During the 10-day **Eurochocolate Festival** (www.eurochocolate.perugia.it) at the end of October, chocolate becomes the focus of fanciful creations, and throngs of chocolate devotees wait for their free samples. On the first Sunday of the festival, throughout Perugia sculptors hack away at huge blocks of chocolate to make *Pietà*, the face of Berlusconi, or animals of every kind—stand close and grab the shavings.

◪ DAYTRIPS FROM PERUGIA

LAKE TRASIMENO AND CASTIGLIONE DEL LAGO

The easiest way to Castiglione del Lago from Perugia is by bus (1hr., 6 per day, €4.80) from P. dei Partigiani. Buses stop in P. Guglielmo Marconi. From there, walk up the stairs into P. Dante Alighieri, which leads up to the city entrance. The tourist office, P. Mazzini 10, is in the only square in town. (☎075 96 52 484. Open M-Sa 9am-1pm and 3:30-7pm, Su 9am-1pm and 4-7pm.) To exchange currency or for an ATM, head to bank Monte dei Paschi di Siena, V. Vittorio Emanuele 57-61. (Open daily 8:20am-1:40pm and 2:20-3:30pm.)

Thirty kilometers west of Perugia, Lake Trasimeno (trah-see-MEH-no) is a refreshing oasis. After advancing down the Alps in 217 BC during the Second Punic War, Hannibal's elephant-riding army routed the Romans just north of the lake, killing 16,000 soldiers. Sadly, neither elephants nor bloodshed can be found in Castiglione del Lago today. A system of ferries connects the main town with Passignano sul Trasimeno, Tuero, San Feliciano, and Lake Trasimeno's two largest islands—Isola Maggiore and Isola Polvese.

 LOVE THE LAKE? If you plan to spend a long time exploring Lake Trasimeno, consider participating in the **Museo Aperto** museum tour, sponsored by the region's tourist offices. One ticket costs €5 and includes admission to attractions in Castiglione del Lago, Città della Pieve, Pacicino, and Panicale. A €3 supplement includes a tour on Isola Maggiore. Inquire at the tourist office in any of the four towns to buy tickets or book tours.

Castiglione del Lago (ca-steel-YON-ay del LA-go; pop. 14,500) is now a much quieter town than in past centuries, when it was conquered by Arezzo, Cortona, and finally Perugia in 1184. Clinging to a limestone promontory covered in olive groves, its medieval walls enclose two main streets and a single *piazza*. At the end of V. Vittorio Emanuele, next to the hospital, stand the **Palazzo della Corgna** and the medieval **Rocca del Leone.** The 16th-century *palazzo* is notable for its frescoes, particularly those in **Sala delle Gesta d'Ascanio** by Niccolò Circignani, the Italian painter known as Pomarancio. Follow a dark passageway to view the Lake from the *Rocca*. The courtyard of the crumbling *Rocca* is free and open to the public, and its grass lawn sometimes serves as a venue for open-air concerts during the summer. (☎96 58 210. Open daily Mar 21.-Apr. 9:30am-1pm and 3:30-7pm; May-June 10am-1:30pm and 4-7:30pm; July-Aug. 10am-1:30pm and 4:30-7pm; Sept.-Oct. 10am-1:30pm and 3:30-7pm; Nov.-Mar. 20 9:30am-4:30pm. Combined ticket €3.) Visitors can also catch a ferry to nearby **Isola Maggiore,** one of Lake Trasimeno's only inhabited islands. From V. Belvedere, take V. Giovanni Pascoli to Vle. Garibaldi. Tickets can be purchased on board.

Budget lodgings are scarce in Castiglione del Lago's immediate vicinity, but **Il Torrione ❹,** V. delle Mura 2/4, right on V. Battisti just inside the gates, is a worthy option. The large garden overlooking the lake leads to four rooms and two apartments with bath and fridge. (☎ 075 95 32 36; www.trasinet.com/iltorrione. Reserve ahead in summer. Singles €65; doubles €80. Cash only.) **La Torre ❹,** V. Vittorio Emanuele 50, offers nine well furnished rooms with bath, TV, A/C, and fridge in the heart of the old town. (☎075 95 16 66; www.trasinet.com/latorre. Breakfast €5. Singles €50; doubles €65-75; triples €80. AmEx/MC/V.) Gourmet food shops line the busier streets, while cheap pizzerias, where prices average €3-8 per person, crowd V. Vittorio Emanuele. With beautiful views and an attentive waitstaff, **La Cantina ❷,** V. V. Emanuele 93, offers a fancier dining experience full of Umbrian cuisine and seafood specialities from the Lake. (Pizza €4-8. Primi €6-9. Secondi €10-18. *Menù* €12.50. Cover €1.80. Open June-Sept. W-Su 12:30-3pm and 7pm-1am; Oct.-May W-Su 12:30-3pm and 7-10:30pm. AmEx/MC/V.) With prices typical of this ritzy retreat, **Ristorante L'Acquario ❸,** V. V. Emanuele 69, offers a variety of lunch *menù* for €30. Try a Trasimeno original: pasta with black truffles or *tagliatelle* with lake fish eggs and perch fillets. (☎075 96 52 432. Primi €8-12. Secondi €9-16. Open M-Tu and Th-Su noon-2:30pm and 7-10:30pm; Nov.-Feb. closed M. MC/V.)

TODI

APM (☎075 89 42 939 or 800 51 21 41) runs buses to and from Perugia (1hr.; M-Sa 10 per day; last bus from Todi 4:58pm, last bus from Perugia 7:30pm; €5.40). The bus station is in P. della Consolazione, near Tempio di Santa Maria della Consolazione. Todi is also accessible by train from Ponte Rio (45min., 7 per day 6:30am-1pm and 3:30-8pm, €2.70). Last train leaves from Terni at 8:10pm and from Perugia 8:50pm; city bus C runs to the station at P. Jacopone until 7:45pm. (€1, €1.50 on board.) The IAT Tourist Office, P. del Popolo 38, has free maps, schedules, and info on history, restaurants and lodgings. (☎075 89 42 526. Open M-Sa 9:30am-1pm and 3:30-6:30pm, Su 10am-1:30pm.)

At the foot of Todi's (TO-dee) lush hills sits the Renaissance **Tempio di Santa Maria della Consolazione,** whose elegant domes are thought to have been based on architectural genius Bramante's early draft for St. Peter's Basilica in Rome. The orderly geometric shapes of the central dome are pleasing alone, and even more impressive when seen alongside the Baroque altarpiece and the 12 surrounding statues. (Open daily Apr.-Oct. 9am-12:30pm and 2:30-6:30pm; Nov.-Mar. 9:30am-12:30pm and 2:30-5pm. Free.) From P. della Consolazione, follow a sinuous, cypress-lined dirt path (Serpentina della Viale) to V. della Vittoria or the less curvy V. della Consolazione to reach **La Rocca,** a ruined 14th-century castle that fronts a large, but generic public **park** with picnic tables and a basketball court. (Open daily Apr.-Oct. 6:30am-10pm; Nov.-Mar. 7am-7pm.) From the park, enter Piazza IV Novembre and follow V. della Rocca to the towering **Tempio di San Fortunato.** Built by the Franciscans between the 13th and 15th centuries, the church, dedicated to Todi's patron saint, features a high vaulted ceiling with decorative medallions and aged frescoes like *The Madonna and Jesus With Angels* by Masolino da Panciale in the fourth chapel on the right. Peek into the sixth chapel on the right and the fifth chapel on the left to see of vestiges of magnificent frescoes from the 14th century. Part of the original church is currently used as a school, but ask the guardian for permission to view the cloisters for unobstructed **360 degree views of Todi.** (Open Tu-Su 9am-1pm and 3-7pm. Free.) From San Fortunato, follow P. Jacopone to the **Piazza del Popolo,** encircled by three palaces-turned-municipal-centers, two souvenir shops, two *gelaterie,* and a 900-year-old church. The 12th-century **duomo** is at the far end of P. del Popolo atop a flight of broad stone steps. The 16th-century rose window at the rear brightens up the interior. (Open daily 8:30am-12:30pm and 2:30-7pm. Mass daily in summer 11:30am and 6pm; in winter 6pm. Free.)

Staying in Todi is an unnecessary expense, as cheaper accommodations are easily found in nearby Perugia. **☒Crispolti Holiday House ❸**, V. Santa Prassede 36, near P. del Popolo. Walking down V. del Duomo, turn right on V. S. Prassede, and wind to the right until you reach V. Cesia; the Holiday House is ahead on the left. This hostel-style accommodation provides private and dormitory rooms in an old monastery. Crispolti offers a bar, inexpensive restaurant, meeting room, terrace overlooking the Umbrian countryside, TV room, and Internet access. (☎075 89 44 827; www.crispoltiholidayhouse.com. Breakfast included. Dorms €25-40; singles €35-60; doubles €70-90; triples €90-120; quads €120-160. Group discounts available. MC/V.) You'll find **Pizzeria al Vicoletto ❷**, V. Vicoletto 11, on the sidestreet between P. Garibaldi and P. Jacopone. This small pizzeria provides a relief from tourist-infested *gelaterrie* that double as souvenir-shops. Italian radio soothes local patrons as they munch on pizza by the slice (€1.20) in the stone alleyway. (Open M and W-Su 8:35am-2:30pm and 4-9pm.) **Antica Hosteria de la Valle ❷**, V. Ciuffelli 17-21, serves meals in a stately dining room of brick and wood. The menu, as well as the local art displayed on the walls, changes bi-weekly. (☎075 89 44 848. Primi €8-14. Secondi €10-16. *Menù* €20-22. Cover €1. Open Tu-Su 12:30-2:30pm and 7:30-10pm. MC/V.)

GUBBIO
☎075

Roman remains, a thriving ceramics trade, historical festivals and the artistic feats of a local painting school all find themselves packed together in the medieval alleyways of Gubbio (GOO-bee-yo; pop. 32,000). The town's famous 300-100BC Eugubine Tablets, one of the only existing records of the ancient Umbrian language, offer a glimpse into Umbria's history and provide important evidence of an Umbrian and Roman alliance against invading Etruscans. The town's mountain backdrop offer unrivaled views, and serves as a convenient daytrip from Perugia for travelers who wish to avoid the high prices.

🚋 🛈 TRANSPORTATION AND PRACTICAL INFORMATION

The nearest **train station** is in **Fossato di Vico,** 15km away and on the Rome-Ancona line. Trains run to Ancona (1hr., 14 per day, from €4.30), Rome (2hr., 12 per day, €10.12), and Spoleto (1hr., 10 per day, €3.36). **APM buses** (☎075 50 67 81) run to and from Perugia (1hr.; M-F 9 per day, Sa-Su 4 per day; €4.50) and are much more convenient than the train. The bus is the easiest way to reach Gubbio from Fossato (M-Sa 11 per day, Su 5 per day; €2). Tickets are sold at the newsstand in P. Quaranta Martiri, at the Perugia bus stop, and at the newsstand in

Fossato's train station. If stranded in Fossato without bus service, call a **taxi** (☎075 91 92 02 or 033 53 37 48 71; €28 per 20min.). In Gubbio, **taxis** (☎075 92 73 800) are available in P. Quaranta Martiri.

Tiny Gubbio's medieval streets are easily navigable. Buses stop in **Piazza Quaranta Martiri,** where you can find a 24hr. **ATM.** A short walk up **V. della Repubblica,** on the far right of P. Quaranta Martiri from the bus stop, is the **ITA Tourist Office,** V. della Repubblica 15, which offers bus schedules and maps. (☎075 92 20 790; www.gubbio-altochiascio.umbria2000.it. Open Mar.-Oct. M-F 8:30am-1:45pm and 3:30-6:30pm, Sa 9am-1pm and 3:30-6:30pm, Su 9:30am-12:30pm and 3:30-6:30pm; Oct.-Mar. M-F 8:30am-1:45pm and 3-6pm, Sa 9am-1pm and 3-6pm, Su 9:30am-12:30pm and 3-6pm.) V. della Repubblica crosses **Corso Garibaldi,** the second major street on the right. **Farmacia Luconi** is at C. Garibaldi 12. (☎075 92 73 783. Open M-Sa Apr.-Sept. 9am-1pm and 4:30-8pm; Oct.-Mar. 9am-1pm and 4-7:30pm.) Signs point uphill to **Piazza Grande,** the civic headquarters. The **hospital** can be reached at ☎075 92 391. The **post office** is at V. Cairoli 11. (☎075 92 73 925. Open M-F 8am-1:30pm, Sa 8am-12:30pm.) **Postal Code:** 06024.

📷📷 ACCOMMODATIONS AND FOOD

A private garden and enthusiastic staff make ◼**Residenza di Via Piccardi ❸**, V. Piccardi 12, an ideal place to relax. Six comfortable rooms each have bath and TV. (☎075 92 76 108; e.biagiotti@tiscali.it. Breakfast included. Check-in before 8pm. Singles €35; doubles €50; triples €60. Extra bed €10. Cash only.) Directly across the street is another option, **Residenza Le Logge ❹**, V. Piccardi 7/9, where rooms feature religious art and small bath. For a splurge, ask for the huge suite with a whirlpool tub. (☎075 92 77 574; www.paginegialle.it/residenzalelogge. Singles €35-45; doubles €52-80, with bath €65-100. AmEx/MC/V.) Walk up from P. Quaranta Martiri on V. della Repubblica, and turn right on V. Gioia to reach **Hotel Grotta dell'Angelo ❸**, V. Gioia 47. Bright, large, and cheery rooms make this an ideal stay that's worth the extra penny. (☎075 92 71 747; www.grottadellangelo.it. Breakfast €5. Singles €38-42; doubles €55-60. AmEx/MC/V.)

Sample local delicacies at **Prodotti Tipici e Tartufati Eugubini ❶**, V. Piccardi 17, including *salumi di cinghiale o cervo* (boar or deer sausage), cheese, and the region's white-truffle oil. (☎075 92 71 751. Open Apr.-Jan. 7 daily 10am-1:30pm and 3:30-8pm. MC/V/AmEx.) Take advantage of the chance to interact and learn from friendly locals at the **outdoor market** in P. Quaranta Martiri. Purchase homegrown seasonal produce and other *prodotti tipici* of Gubbio. (Open M-Sa 7am-1pm.) Enjoy regional truffles and other specialties amidst 14th-century decor at **La Cantina Ristorante/Pizzeria ❸**, V. Francesco Piccotti 3, off V. della Repubblica. (☎075 92 20 583. Pizza €4.50-7. Primi €6.50-12. Secondi €7-14. 4-course meal €14. Cover €1. Restaurant open Tu-Su noon-2:30pm and 7-10pm. Pizzeria open noon-3pm. MC/V.) The stone dining room of **San Francesco e il Lupo ❹**, V. Cairoli 24, serves homemade pizza and has a wine cellar with over 200 labels. (☎075 92 72 344. Pizza €4-7.50. Primi €8-13. Secondi €8-24. Cover €2. Open M and W-Su noon-2pm and 7-10pm. AmEx/MC/V.) The health conscious **Bar Jolly ❷**, V. della Repubblica 4, comes as close to a night scene as can be found in medieval Gubbio with its midnight closing time. The menu includes a variety of sandwiches, pasta, and creative salads (€5.50-7). Try the *Insalatone Esotica*, which comes with mozzarella, pineapple, olives, nuts, and kiwi. (Open daily noon-midnight.) Dine under elegant stone vaulted ceilings in the dining room of **Ristorante La Lanterna ❸**, V. Gioia 2. The menu selections offer staples of Eugubine fare such as mushrooms and truffles. (☎075 92 76 694. Primi €7-10. Secondi €8-14. Open M-W and F-Su noon-3pm and 7:30-10:30pm. MC/V.)

👁 SIGHTS

PIAZZA QUARANTA MARTIRI. In the middle of the *piazza* stretches the **Giardino dei Quaranta Martiri** (Garden of the 40 Martyrs), a memorial to those slain by the Nazis in reprisal for the assassination of two German officials. Across the *piazza* from the bus stop stands the **Chiesa di San Francesco**, which was completed in 1256 and is one of the places rumored to be the site where St. Francis experienced his conversion. The left-hand apse holds the *Vita della Madonna*, a partially destroyed, 15th-century fresco series by Ottaviano Nelli, Gubbio's most famous painter. The frescoes are skillfully rendered and the 15th-century *campanile* rises gracefully outside. (*Church open daily 7:15am-noon and 3:30-7:30pm. Free.*) Via Matteotti runs from P. Quaranta Martiri, outside the city walls, to the **Teatro Romano,** built at the end of the first century BC. While restorations are a modern addition, a sense of power and stability still seems to emanate from the semi-circular stone tiers. Productions are staged in July and August. (*Vle. del Teatro Romano. Tickets €15.*) The nearby **Antiquarium** displays impressive Roman mosaics found in the city and preserved foundations beneath your feet.

PALAZZO DEI CONSOLI. This white stone palace (1321-1330) was built for Gubbio's high magistrate. Inside, the **Museo Civico** displays a collection of Eugubinian and Roman artifacts. In a room upstairs, the **⬛Tavole Eugubine** (Eugubine Tablets), are comparable to the Rosetta Stone for their linguistic significance. Five of these seven bronze tablets, dating from 300 to 100 BC, are showcased as rare proof of the ancient Umbrian language, as well as an Umbrian and Roman alliance against the Etruscans. The last two tablets are in Latin. An illiterate farmer discovered them in 1444 in an underground chamber of the Roman theater just outside the city walls; he was subsequently tricked into swapping them for a worthless piece of land. The texts spell out the social, religious, and political organization of early Umbria, and they describe how to read religious omens from animal livers. (*P. Grande. ☎ 075 92 74 298. Open daily Apr.-Oct. 10am-1pm and 3-6pm; Nov. to mid-Mar. 10am-1pm and 2-5pm. €5, ages 7-25 €3, under 7 free.*)

DUOMO. The pink Gothic *duomo*, sitting up on a hill from P. Grande, was built in the 13th and 14th centuries on the site of a Romanesque church. The interior is simple, with a single pitched-roof nave. Notable are the 12th-century stained-glass windows, art by Perugino's student Dono Doni, and Antonio Tatoti's *Adoration of the Magi*. (*Open daily Apr.-Sept. 9am-6pm; Oct.-Mar. 10am-5pm. Free.*)

MONTE INGINO. See the sights from a new perspective by hopping into the shaky cages of the **⬛funivia**, a standing chairlift, which, in six short minutes, climbs to an unparalleled view of Gubbio's medieval rooftops and the Umbrian hills. Climb the hill behind the *funivia*'s drop-off point to reach the **Basilica and Monastery of Sant'Ubaldo**, which houses the saint's preserved body in a glass case above the altar. The stained glass at the entrance tells the story of his life; the three *ceri*, large wooden candles carried in the **Corsa dei Ceri** procession each May, are also on display. Each December, lights transform the entire hill into the world's largest Christmas tree (documented in the Guinness Book of World Records). Follow the dirt trail behind the basilica up to the scaffolding where the star is placed atop the "tree," and then continue up to an ancient but well-preserved tower for spectacular 360-degree vistas of the Umbrian mountains and valleys. (*To reach the funivia, exit Pta. Romana to the left. From the uphill entrance to the basilica, bear left and continue upward on a dirt path to the top of the mountain. Chairlift open June M-Sa 9:30am-1:30pm and 2:30-7pm, Su 9am-7:30pm; July-Aug. daily 9am-8pm; Sept. M-Sa 9:30am-1:30pm and 2:30-7pm, Su 9:30am-1:30pm and 2:30-7:30pm; Mar. M-Sa 10am-1:30pm and 2:30-5:30pm, Su 9:30am-1:30pm and 2:30-6pm; Apr.-May M-Sa 10am-1:30pm and*

2:30-6:30pm, Su 9:30am-1:30pm and 2:30-7pm; Oct. daily 10am-1:30pm and 2:30-6pm; Nov.-Feb. M-Tu and Th-Su 10am-1:30pm and 2:30-5pm. €5, round-trip €6. Cash only.)

☀ FESTIVALS

The annual **Corsa dei Ceri,** 900 years old and still going strong, takes place every May 15, the day of patron Saint Ubaldo's death. Three *ceri* (candles) are carved like hourglasses and topped with little statues of saints. Each one corresponds to a distinct section of the populace: the masons (Sant'Ubaldo), the farmers (Sant'Antonio Abate), and the artisans (San Giorgio). After 12hr. of furious preparation and frenetic flag-twirling, squads of *ceraioli* (candle runners) clad in Renaissance-style tights lift the heavy objects onto their shoulders and run a wild relay race up Monte Ingino. This raucous festival turns Gubbio's quiet streets into a chaotic stomping ground bristling with intense ritual fervor. Visitors will be entranced; locals will almost certainly be drunk. During the **Palio della Balestra,** held in P. Grande on the last Sunday in May, archers from Gubbio and nearby Sansepolcro have gathered for a fierce crossbow contest since 1139. The contest provides an excellent excuse for Gubbio to throw a huge party every year and maintain an industry in medieval-weaponry toys.

ASSISI

☎ 075

Assisi's (ah-SEE-zee; pop. 25,000) serene atmosphere and renowned spirituality stem from the legacy of its favorite son and Italy's patron saint, St. Francis. The 12th-century monk founded the Franciscan order and sparked an ascetic revolution within the Catholic Church. Franciscan monks and nuns, dressed in brown *cappucci* robes, still inhabit Assisi. Fervent religiosity, however, is hardly a prerequisite for a visit. Many people come simply for the city's intricate architecture. The Basilica di San Francesco is the most-frequented sight in Umbria, housing the saint's relics and Giotto's renowned fresco series of St. Francis. While local ruins attest to Assisi's Etruscan and Roman roots, grand palaces and majestic castles from a later era tower above tile roofs. Assisi's stone archways reveal patchwork panoramas of the Umbrian countryside, accompanied by the sounds of birds and ringing bells.

⌨ TRANSPORTATION

Trains: Station 15min. walk from Basilica di Santa Maria degli Angeli. Assisi is on the Foligno-Terontola line. No formal ticket office. Purchase tickets at the newsstand. (☎075 80 40 272. AmEx/MC/V.) **Luggage storage** available. Trains to **Florence** (2hr., 7 per day 5:48am-7:19pm, €9), **Perugia** (30min., 1-2 per hr. 5:54am-10:45pm, €2.05), and **Rome** (2hr., 7 per day 6:18am-5:47pm, €9).

Buses: Intracity buses leave from P. Unità d'Italia. SULGA (☎075 50 09 641; www.sulga.it) runs buses to **Florence** (2hr., 7am and 6pm, €11) and **Rome** (3hr., 1:45 and 4:30pm, €17). APM (☎800 51 21 41) runs to **Foligno** (1hr., M-Sa 10 per day 6:55am-7:10pm, €4) via **Spello and Perugia** (1hr., 12 per day 6:30am-6:25pm, €3). Buy tickets at newsstands. SENA (☎075 72 83 203) runs from Basilica di S. Maria degli Angeli to **Siena** (2hr., 2 per day, €9). Buy tickets on board.

Public Transportation: Local buses (2 per hr., €0.90) run along **Linea A** from the train station and next to Santa Maria degli Angeli bus stops at P. Unità d'Italia, Largo Properzio, and P. Matteotti. Buy tickets on board or at *tabaccherie* in the train station or across from Santa Maria degli Angeli. **Minibuses** (€0.90) run around the inner city to select points on the outside along 2 lines, A and B.

Assisi

◆ ACCOMMODATIONS

Camere Martini, 10
Hotel La Rocca, 3
Ostello Fontemaggio, 1
Ostello della Pace (HI), 12
Hotel San Ru no, 7

● FOOD

Pizzeria da Andrea, 5
Pizzeria Otello, 8
Ristorante An teatro Romano, 2
Trattoria da Erminio, 4
Osteria Piazzetta dell'Erba, 6
Ristorante La Laterna, 9

UMBRIA

TO ↑ (800m),
EREMO DELLE
CARCERI (4km)

Porta
Cappuccini

Viale Umberto I

LARGO
PROPERZIO

TO SAN DAMIANO (1.5km)

Porta
Nuova

Parco
Regina
Margherita

Viale Umberto I

Via degli Acquedotti

Viale Vittorio Emanuele II

150 meters
150 yards

Rocca
Minore

An teatro
Romano

teatro Romano

Via dell'Anfiteatro

Via Eremo delle Carceri

PIAZZA
MATTEOTTI

Via Borgo Aretino

TO SAN DAMIANO

Via San Damiano

TO SAN DAMIANO (1km)

Porta
Perlici

Via Villamena

Vicolo Bovi

Via del
Comune Vecchio

Cattedrale
S. RUFINO

Via Dono Doni

Via S. Gabriele dell'Addolorata

Sermei

Via S. Chiara

PIAZZA
S. CHIARA

Basilica di
S. Chiara

Via delle Font di Moiano

Via della Rocca

Via porta Perlici

Via Monte Cavallo

V. del Torrione

PIAZZA
S. RUFINO

Corso Mazzini

Chiesa
Nuova

Via S. Agnese

Via Porta Moiano

Porta
Moiano

Colle del
Paradiso

S. Lorenzo

Via delle Rose

S. Maria
delle Rose

Via S. Rufino

Via S. Rufino

Via S. Antonio

PIAZZA
DEL
COMUNE

Palazzo
dei Priori

S. Maria
Maggiore

S. Apollinare

Porta del
Sementone

Rocca
Maggiore

Via Fortini

Via G. Jacopone

Via G. Jacopone

Foro
Romano

Via
Rocchi

Via S.
Gregorio

Via Bernardo da Quintavalle

Via Antonio Cristofani

Traversa degli Ancajani

Tempio di
Minerva

Via A.
Fortini

Via del Seminario

P. Garibaldi

Via S. Apollinare

Via Aluigi

Via S. Paolo

Via San Francesco

Vicolo degli Esposti

Via degli Ancajani

Via D.
Aromatari

Viale Abornoz

Via del Colle

Via G.P. Nicolini Vescovo

Via degli
Ancajani

Via S. Pietro

Via Borgo

TO ↑ (200m)

Viale Vittorio Emanuele II

Via santa Croce

Via Metastasio

Via Fontebella

Via Giorgetti

Peggia
San Pietro

PIAZZA
S. PIETRO

S. Pietro

Porta
S. Pietro

PIAZZA
S. PIETRO

Oratorio dei
Pellegrini

Pinacoteca

S. Giacomo
de Muro Rupto

Via Borgo

PIAZZA
UNITÀ
D'ITALIA

Via G. Marconi

TO (5km)
AND BASILICA DI SANTA
MARIA DEGLI ANGELI (5km)

Porta S.
Giacomo

Via S. Giacomo

Via S. Andrea

Via Frate Elia

Porta
S. Francesco

Via C. Merry del Val

Basilica di
San Francesco

PIAZZA SUPERIORE
DI S. FRANCESCO

PIAZZA
INFERIORE
DI S. FRANCESCO

Taxis: In P. del Comune (☎075 81 31 93), P. Santa Chiara (☎075 81 26 00), P. Unità d'Italia (☎075 81 23 78), and the train station (☎075 80 40 275).

✈ ❼ ORIENTATION AND PRACTICAL INFORMATION

Towering above the city to the north, the **Rocca Maggiore** can help orient those lost among Assisi's winding streets. The bus from the train station stops first at **Piazza Unità d'Italia**; get off here for direct access to the Basilica di San Francesco. Stay on the bus until **Piazza Matteotti** to access the *centro* from above. To reach **Piazza del Comune**, take Via del Torrione from P. Matteotti to **Piazza San Rufino**; take the downhill left in the *piazza*, and then walk down **Via San Rufino**. From P. del Comune Via Portica becomes V. Fortini, V. del Seminario, and, finally, V. San Francesco and connects P. del Comune to the Basilica di San Francesco. Heading in the opposite direction from P. del Comune, Corso Mazzini leads to the **Basilica di Santa Chiara**.

Tourist Office: P. del Comune 22/23 (☎075 81 25 34; www.umbria2000.it). From V. S. Rufino, office is at far end of *piazza*. Provides brochures, bus info, train schedules, and a decent map. Open M-Sa 8am-2pm and 3-6pm, Su and holidays 10am-1pm.

Currency Exchange: For traveler's checks, try **Banca Toscana**, in P. San Pietro. Open M-F 8:20am-1:30pm and 2:15-3:35pm, Su 8:20-11:50am. **Unicredit Banca**, in P. del Comune. Open M-F 8:20am-1:20pm and 2:35-4:05pm. **ATMs** outside.

Luggage Storage: In train station. €2.70 per 12hr. Open daily 7am-7:30pm. MC/V.

Hospital: Ospedale d'Assisi (☎075 81 391), on the outskirts of town. Take the Linea A bus from P. del Comune and get off at stop 7 (Ospedale).

Pharmacy: Farmacia Antici dei Caldari, P. del Commune 44/45.

Internet Access: Bar, V. Portica 29B (☎075 81 62 46). €2 for 1st 15min, €1 per each additional 15min. Print and copy €.30/page. Open daily 9am-11pm. Cash only. **Caffe Minerva**, P. del Comune 15/16 (☎075 81 24 75). €3 per 30min., €5 per hr. Open daily 7am-midnight. Cash only.

Post Office: Largo Properzio 4, outside Pta. Nuova. Open M-F 8am-1:30pm, Sa 8am-12:30pm. Cash only. **Postal Code:** 06081.

▐ ACCOMMODATIONS AND CAMPING

Reservations are crucial around Easter and Christmas and strongly recommended for the Festa di Calendimaggio. If you don't mind an 11pm curfew, ask the tourist office for a list of **religious institutions** that provide cheap rooms, although most require an extended stay. The tourist office also provides a list of *affittacamere*, rooms for rent in private residences, for longer visits.

Camere Martini, V. Antonio Cristofani 6 (☎/fax 075 81 35 36; cameremartini@libero.it). Well-furnished rooms—many with balconies—provide perfect views of Assisi's sights and the Umbrian countryside. Central location, soft beds, TV, and large bathrooms. Laundry €5. Singles €25; doubles €40; triples €55; quads €65. Cash only. ❷

Hotel San Rufino, V. Porta Perlici 7 (☎075 58 12 803). Take V. S. Rufino through P. S. Rufino, and veer left onto V. Porta Perlici. A centrally-located medieval building renovated in 1992. Richly decorated rooms with baths and great views. TV room and bar downstairs. Singles €45; doubles €55; triples €70; quads €83. AmEx/MC/V. ❸

Ostello della Pace (HI), V. di Valecchie 177 (☎075 81 67 67; www.assisihostel.com). From the train station, take the bus to P. Unità d'Italia. From P. Unità d'Italia, walk downhill on V. Marconi. Turn left at sign and walk for 500m down a curving paved road bordered by olive groves. Bright rooms accommodate up to 8 people. Friendly hostel offers common rooms, board games, library, Internet access, and musical instruments. Breakfast included. Pack Lunch €6.50. Dinner €10. Laundry €3.50. Reception 7-9:30am and 3:30-11:30pm. Lockout 9:30am-3:30pm. Curfew 11pm. Reservations recommended. HI card required; can purchase at hostel. Dorms €16; singles with bath €18. MC/V. ●

Ostello/Hotel/Camping Fontemaggio, V. Eremo delle Carceri 24 (☎075 81 36 36; fax 075 81 37 49). V. Eremo delle Carceri begins in P. Matteotti and leads through Pta. Cappuccini; follow it 1km up the road, and then bear right at the sign. Trekkers who manage the slightly exerting hike are rewarded with well-kept hotel, hostel, campground and bungalows. On-site restaurant. Breakfast €5. Check-out 10am. Curfew 11pm. Reservations recommended. Hostel: dorms €22. Hotel: singles €35; doubles €52; triples €72.50; quads €96. Campground: camping €5.50 per person; €4.50 per tent; €2.50 per car. 4- to 8-person bungalows €50-140. MC/V. Hostel ❷/Hotel ❸/Campground ❶

Hotel La Rocca, V. Pta. Perlici 27 (☎075 81 22 84). From P. Rufino follow V. Pta. Perlici until you reach the old arches. Situated near the *centro*. Generically furnished rooms have bath, TV, and telephone; some recently renovated rooms have view of the Rocca. Restaurant and bar downstairs. Singles €45; doubles €53; triples €73. AmEx/MC/V. ❹

◪ FOOD

Pasticceria Santa Monica, V. Portica 4, right off P. del Comune, sells delectables native to Assisi. Mouth-watering *torrone* (a sweet nougat of almonds and egg whites; €4.00 per 100g) and the divine *brustengoli* (a cake packed with raisins, apples, and pine nuts; €3.50 per 100g) are well-priced treats among the city's often marked-up sweets. (Open daily 10:30am-11pm. Cash only.) For fresh produce on weekdays, head to the **market** on V. San Gabriele dell'Addolorata. The only grocery stores in town are small *alimentari* scattered around the city's center, which cater primarily to misled tourists with their stocks of high-priced Umbrian *prodotti tipici*. The nearest supermarket, **Issimo**, is a steep hill hike away, located in P. Garibaldi, near the Basilica di Santa Maria degli Angeli. (Open daily 7:30am-1pm and 4:30-8pm. MC/V.)

▨ Pizzeria Otello, V. Sant'Antonio 1 (☎075 81 51 25). On the far right of the Palazzo dei Priori from Via Portica. Arrive early for a spot at one of the long wooden tables to taste one of the popular pizzas (€5.50-8). Or try the deliciously creamy *strangozzi al tartufo* (pasta with truffles; €7). Open daily noon-3pm and 7-10:30pm. AmEx/MC/V. ❶

Osteria Piazzetta dell'Erba, V. San Gabriele dell'Addolorata 15A/B. While this Slow Food restaurant asks patrons to savor every morsel, the terrace service is snappy. Artfully prepared plates include refreshing salads (€8) and hearty pastas (€10). Secondi €15-19. Cover €1.50. Open Tu-Su 12:30-2pm and 7:30-10pm. AmEx/MC/V. ❹

Pizzeria da Andrea, P. San Rufino 26 (☎075 81 53 25). From P. del Comune, walk up V. S. Rufino. Look for the *pizza al taglio* sign on the right side of the *piazza*. Pizza €1.50. Panini €3. Also sells meats and cheeses, as well as gourmet food products like homemade pasta, cookies, and wine. Open Tu-Su 8:30am-8:30pm. Cash only. ❶

Ristorante La Lanterna, V. S. Rufino 39 (☎075 81 63 99). Located up a quaint stone alley off busy V. San Rufino, La Lanterna is great for meat eaters looking for authentic Italian *carne*. Outdoor patio and indoor seating available. Antipasti €6. Primi €8. Secondi €9-16. Open noon-3pm and 6-10pm. AmEx/MC/V. ❷

Trattoria da Erminio, V. Monte Cavallo 19 (☎075 81 25 06). A wood fire sends the savory aroma of roasting meat into the street. Antipasti €2.50. Primi €6-11. Secondi €8-13. Cover €1.80. Open M-W and F-Su noon-2:30pm and 7-9pm. AmEx/MC/V. ❷

Ristorante Anfiteatro Romano, V. Anfiteatro Romano 4 (☎075 81 30 25), off P. Matteotti. Hearty portions of Umbrian fare in an elegant outdoor dining area. For shelter, exchange the vine-rimmed patio for the delightfully over-decorated interior. Primi €5-9. Secondi €5.50-10. Cover €1.60. Open Tu-Su noon-2:30pm and 7-9pm. MC/V. ❷

UMBRIA

⊙ SIGHTS

At age 19, St. Francis (1182-1226) abandoned his military and social ambitions, rejected his father's wealth, and embraced asceticism. His love of nature, devoted humility, and rejection of the Church's worldliness earned him a huge European following and posed an unprecedented threat to the decadent papacy and corrupt monastic orders. St. Francis continued to preach chastity and poverty until his death. Since then, the Church and various artists have glorified the modest saint in countless cathedrals, many of which are found in Assisi.

◼BASILICA DI SAN FRANCESCO. A major pilgrimage site, Basilica di San Francesco is one of Italy's greatest spiritual and artistic attractions. When its construction began in the mid-13th century, the Franciscan order protested, complaining that the elaborate church was an impious monument to the conspicuous consumption that St. Francis had scorned. Brother Elia, the vicar of the order, insisted that a double church be erected, the lower level built around the saint's tomb, the upper level used for services. The walls of the upper basilica are covered with Giotto's renowned **Life of St. Francis** fresco cycle. The dimension and volume the painter brings to his figures was not depicted by previous artists of this age. Cimabue's magnificent *Maestà* (displaying the Virgin and child surrounded by four angels and St. Francis) graces the right transept. Pietro Lorenzetti decorated the left transept with his outstanding *Crucifixion, Last Supper, and Madonna and Saints.* **St. Francis's tomb,** the inspiration for the entire edifice, lies below the lower basilica; the coffin itself was hidden in the 15th century from war-mongering *Perugini,* and it wasn't rediscovered until 1818. The stone coffin rests on the altar of the lower basilica, surrounded by the sarcophagi of four of the saint's dearest friends. (☎075 81 90 084; www.sanfrancescoassisi.org. Info window open M-Sa 9am-noon and 2-5:30pm. Lower basilica and tomb open daily 6am-6:45pm. Upper basilica open daily 8:30am-6:45pm. Modest dress required: no shorts or sleeveless shirts. Free. Tours given by monks arranged in advance for groups of 20 or more, €2.50 per person; call or visit info window across from entrance to lower basilica. Audio tour €4.)

BASILICA DI SANTA CHIARA. St. Claire (1194-1253) was one of the first followers of St. Francis. Since the Franciscan Order already took care of the pious men, St. Claire opened the door to women bent on poverty and celibacy by establishing the Order of Poor Ladies. The Basilica di Santa Chiara's pink-and-white stone flying buttresses seen on the left side of the basilica are notable, but it is the surrounding **courtyard** with fountains and views that make it dazzling. Standing on the site where St. Francis attended school, the church shelters the tomb and relics of St. Claire, as well as the crucifix that supposedly spoke to St. Francis, instigating his conversion. Nuns in the convent are sworn to seclusion. (☎075 81 22 82. Open daily 6:30am-noon and 2-6pm. Modest dress required. Free.)

ROCCA MAGGIORE. The craggy Rocca Maggiore is situated uphill from the *duomo.* The hike up is well worth the view of the town and the Basilica di San Francesco from the gravel lot outside the fortress. For a nominal fee, step into the shade of the fortress and the eerie 50m tunnel to Torre Poligonale. The ◼**view** is breathtaking—miles of countryside stretch in all directions. The Colle del Paradiso, V. della Rocca 3, is on the hike towards Rocco Maggiore, and is a wonderful (free) alternative. (From P.S. Rufino, go down V. Porta Perlici and ascend the winding staircase to the left. Rocco open daily 9am-8pm. Colle open May-Oct. 10am-6pm. Last entry 30min. before closing. Closed in bad weather. €3.50, students €2.50; combined ticket for Pinacoteca, Foro Romano, and Rocca €4.50/3.50. Cash only.)

CATTEDRALE DI SAN RUFINO. V. S. Rufino climbs steeply from P. del Comune between closely packed houses, opening onto P. S. Rufino to reveal the cathedral at the far end of P. S. Rufino. If you don't see the bell tower at first, you'll definitely hear it. Inside, peach-colored pilasters frame a bright white central dome. Peer through glass tiles on the floor into the Roman ruins below. (☎ 075 81 22 83; www.assisimuseocattedrale.com. Open daily 7am-12:30pm and 2-6pm. Free.)

TEMPIO DI MINERVA. Above Foro Romano, between the city's *campanile* and a cafe, six crumbling Roman columns frame the interior of the Tempio di Minerva. Check out the gold altarpiece and glorious painted ceiling of this majestic Roman temple turned Christian church. (Open daily 7am-7pm. Free.)

OTHER SIGHTS. From Basilica di San Francesco, V. S. Francesco passes medieval buildings and their 16th-century additions on its path toward the center of town. Not far from the basilica, the pink facade of the **Palazzo Vallemani** houses the **Pinacoteca,** a museum containing works by important Umbrian artists like Dono Doni, as well as a collection of Renaissance frescoes retrieved from city gates and various shrines. (Pinacoteca ☎ 075 81 20 33. Open daily Mar.-May and Sept.-Oct. 10am-1pm and 2:30-6pm; July-Aug. 10am-1pm and 2:30-7pm; Nov.-Feb. 10:30am-1pm and 2-5pm. Admission to each €3.50, students €3. Cash only.) Up the street, the one-room **Oratorio dei Pellegrini** (Pilgrim's Oratory) holds colorful frescoes. Built in 1457, the oratory was used to care for poor pilgrims who came to visit the tomb of St. Francis. At the end of the street, P. del Comune sits on the **Foro Romano.** Enter from the crypt of St. Nicholas on V. Portica, and walk among the columns and statues of the old Roman forum. The area that stretches the length of the *piazza* above was the original ground level of the town, and in Roman times, stairs led from this area to the **Tempio di Minerva** in P. del Comune. (Forum ☎ 075 81 30 53. Open daily Mar.-May and Sept.-Oct. 10am-1pm and 2-6pm; July-Aug. 10am-1pm and 2:30-7pm; Nov.-Feb. 10:30am-1pm and 2-5pm. €3.50 each, students €3. Cash only.)

※ FESTIVALS

Assisi's ecclesiastical enthusiasm is contagious during church holidays, as all of Assisi's religious festivals are steeped in tradition. **Holy Week** commences on Palm Sunday with elaborate services, ushering in a week's worth of prayer and piety in the town. A play reenacts the Deposition from the Cross on Holy Thursday, and traditional torch-lit processions, virtually unchanged since medieval times (except for the camera flashes), trail through town on Good Friday. Vigils are held on Holy Saturday and grand masses of celebration take place in churches throughout town on Easter Sunday. Assisi welcomes spring with the **Festa di Calendimaggio** (1st Th-Sa of May). A queen is chosen and dubbed *Primavera* (Spring), while the upper and lower quarters of the city compete in a musical tournament. Ladies and knights overtake the streets in celebration of the young St. Francis, who wandered the streets of Assisi singing serenades at night. According to legend it was on one such night that he encountered a vision of the *Madonna della Povertà* (Lady of Poverty). October 4 marks the **Festa di San Francesco,** which kicks off in Basilica di Santa Maria degli Angeli, the site of St. Francis's death. Aside from various religious ceremonies, the highlight of this celebration is the offering of oil for the cathedral's votive lamp. Each year a different region of Italy, whose traditional dances and songs are performed during the festival, offers the oil. In addition to these festivals, classical music concerts and organ recitals occur once or twice each week from April to October in various churches.

◆ DAYTRIPS FROM ASSISI

EREMO DELLE CARCERI AND MONTE SUBASIO

From P. Matteotti, exit Assisi through Pta. Cappuccini, and walk straight on V. Eremo delle Car-ceri, following signs for "Campeggio Fontemaggio." Once you reach the road for the campsite, don't turn off; continue to walk uphill along V. Fontemaggio. Follow the dirt trail next to the paved road uphill. Eremo is about 4km away. Open daily in summer 6:30am-7pm; in winter 6:30am-5pm. Taxis make the climb for €12-15 from the centro.

To experience the spiritual tranquility known to St. Francis, embark on the intense, but rewarding 1hr. hike up Monte Subasio, revealing the forested sanctuary of Eremo delle Carceri (EH-re-mo DE-leh CAR-che-ree), where St. Francis often retired in prayer. Though cars crowd the front gates, once inside, visitors can follow quiet paths that lead through the building and among the trees. The central courtyard gives access to the Grotta di San Francesco, a series of tiny cells and chapels where St. Francis slept and prayed. Modest dress is required, so bring a scarf or other appropriate attire in addition to hik-ing clothes. Pray with the friars during prayer sessions, held at 7:30am, 12:15, and 5:30pm. The trails continue past the building and run through St. Francis's preferred retreat, Monte Subasio (MON-tay soo-BA-zee-yo). Navigate with a Kompass map (€7.50), available at any Assisi bookshop or newsstand.

OTHER RELIGIOUS SITES AROUND ASSISI

Several churches associated with St. Francis and St. Claire surround Assisi. A 15min. stroll down the road outside Pta. Nuova leads to the **Convent of San Dami-ano,** where St. Francis supposedly heard his calling and later wrote the *Canticle of the Creatures.* The entrance to the convent is inside, by the church's altar. Duck inside to see the modest sanctuary and its frescoes and take a moment of reflection. (☎075 81 22 73. Open daily 10am-noon and 2-6pm. Free.) The train to Assisi passes **Basilica di Santa Maria degli Angeli.** From Assisi, take the frequent bus line C to the Santa Maria degli Angeli stop. St. Francis built the small stone **Cappella Porziuncola,** which stands in the middle of the giant nave of the basilica, and died in the tiny **Cappella del Transito.** According to legend, St. Francis flung himself on the thorny rosebushes in the garden outside to overcome the temp-tation to break his ascetic ways, permanently staining the leaves red. Through the rose garden is the **Museo di Santa Maria degli Angeli,** which houses relics from the Porziuncola chapel. (☎075 80 51 430. Basilica open daily 6:15am-1pm and 2:30-7:30pm. Museum open daily 9am-12:30pm and 3-6pm. Free.)

SPOLETO ☎0743

The magnificent gorge and medieval walls that surround Spoleto (spo-LEH-toh; pop. 38,000) shelter a town full of Roman ruins and friendly locals. Travelers have always admired Spoleto's dramatic gorge, spanned by the 14th-century Ponte delle Torri, but it wasn't until 1958 that Spoleto's tourist industry took off. In that year, the Italian composer Giancarlo Menotti selected the city as the trial site for a summer arts festival, and his *Festival dei Due Mondi* (Festival of Two Worlds) has attracted summer visitors there ever since.

◆ TRANSPORTATION

Trains: The station (☎0743 48 516) is in P. Polvani. Ticket window open M-F 7:10-11am and 2-5pm. To: **Ancona** (2hr., 12 per day 6:16am-10:09pm, €8.20); **Assisi** (40-60min., 19 per day 5:40am-10:09pm, €3.30); **Orte** (1hr., 15 per day 5:06am-9:23pm,

€3.90); **Perugia** (2hr., 19 per day 5:40am-10:09pm, €4.20); **Rome** (1hr., 18 per day 5:06am-9:23pm, €7.50). Trains to Assisi and Perugia often run via **Foligno.**

Buses: SSIT (☎0743 21 22 09; www.spoletina.com). Departs P. della Vittoria for **Foligno** (40min., M-F 5 per day 7:04am-7:40pm, €3.10), **Monteluco** (6 per day 8:45am-6:20pm mid-June to early-Sept., €1.40), and **Perugia** (1½hr., 3 per day 6:20am-2:05pm €5.80). Schedule and tickets available at *tabaccherie* around the *piazza.*

Taxis: P. della Libertà (☎0743 22 58 09) and at the train station (☎0743 22 04 89).

▚ ⚑ ORIENTATION AND PRACTICAL INFORMATION

Piazza della Libertà is most easily accessible from the train station. Take a white and orange SITA bus (direct to *centro*, €0.90). Buy tickets in the station at the newsstand, marked with a yellow "Lotto" sign. From **Corso Mazzini**, turn left up **Via del Mercato** to **Piazza del Mercato**, a cafe-laden marketplace. **Via del Municipio** runs from P. del Mercato to **Piazza del Municipio** and **Piazza Campello**, and **Via Saffi** leads to **Piazza del Duomo**. Most of the city sights are in these *piazze.*

Tourist Office: P. della Libertà 7 (☎0743 23 89 20 or 22 07 73; www.comune.spoleto. pg.it). Open Apr.-Oct. M-F 8:30am-1:30pm and 4-7pm, Sa-Su 9:30am-12:30pm and 4-7pm; Nov.-Mar. M-Sa 9:30am-1:30pm and 3:30-6:30pm, Su 9:30am-12:30pm; during Spoleto Festival daily 8:30am-1:30pm and 4-8pm.

Luggage storage: in the train station. €3 per 12hr. per bag. Open daily 5:30am-11pm.

Police: V. dei Filosofi 57 (☎0743 23 22 00).

Pharmacy: Farmacia Betti, V. Trento e Trieste 63 (☎0743 22 31 74), on the way to town from the train station. Open M-F 9am-1pm and 4-8pm.

Hospital: V. Madonna di Loreto, outside the southwestern walls of the *centro.*

Internet Access: Spider Service, V. Porta Fuga 11 (☎0743 22 51 65). €0.80 per 10min. With card, €2 per hr.; inquire at desk. Open M-Sa 9am-10pm.

Post Office: Vle. Giacomo Matteotti 2 (☎0743 40 373). Open M-F 8am-6:30pm, Sa 8am-12:30pm. **Postal Code:** 06049.

▛ ACCOMMODATIONS

Well-priced options clutter the *centro*'s periphery, but finding accommodations during the summer music festival may be more trying. Contact **Conspoleto**, P. della Libertà 7, for help finding a room. (☎/fax 0743 22 07 73; www.conspoleto. com. Charges commission. Open M-Sa 8:30am-1:30pm and 4-7pm.)

▨ **Ostello di Villa Redenta,** Villa Redenta 1 (☎0743 22 49 36; www.villaredenta.com). From the train station, walk up Vle. Trento e Trieste and make the 1st left at the parking lot; veer left onto V. San Tommaso, then right onto V. delle Tre Madonne. With its expansive garden, feels like a country residence. Spacious rooms have private bath and TV. Breakfast included. Free laundry and Internet access. Wheelchair-accessible. Reception 8am-1pm and 3:30-8pm. Singles €25-30; doubles €60; triples €68-80; quads €78-90. 6-bed dorms in winter, €22. Cash only. ❷

Istituto Bambin Gesu, V. Montrone/Via S. Angelo 4 (☎0743 40 232). From P. della Liberta, take Vle. G. Matteotti just past the post office. Turn left on V. B. Egio. Veer left onto V. degli Abeti, descend the stairs, and turn right onto V. Monterone. Spacious and peaceful rooms in a 16th-century monastery. Breakfast included. Call ahead to check availability and arrange arrival. Singles €25; doubles €30, with bath €35. Cash only. ❷

Hotel Clarici, P. della Vittoria 32 (☎0743 22 33 11; www.hotelclarifici.com). From the station walk 10min. up Vle. Trento e Trieste and turn into P. Garibaldi; hotel is to the right. Modestly furnished rooms in a central location with balconies, phone, TV, A/C, and private bath. Breakfast included. Free Wi-Fi. Singles €45-65; doubles €70-120. MC/V. ❸

Albergo Due Porte, P. della Vittoria 5 (☎0743 22 36 66), just outside the city walls, 10min. from the train station toward the *centro*. Head down Vle. Trento e Trieste, and bear right into P. della Vittoria. Large rooms with bath, TV, A/C, and phone. Breakfast included. Free parking. Wheelchair-accessible. Singles €35; doubles €60; triples €85; quads €100. Discount with longer stays. AmEx/MC/V. ❸

⬛ FOOD

Rare is the Spoleto restaurant that doesn't boast its own version of the town's signature dish: *strengozzi alla spoletina*, a zesty take on pasta with tomato sauce. Other specialties include the same pasta garnished with a generous portion of flavorful shaved truffles. An **outdoor market** runs along V. Cacciatori delle Alpi, which stretches south from Ponte G. Garibaldi on Friday mornings. For groceries, head to **Vega Sigma Supermarket,** V. Cesare Micheli 1, off P. Garibaldi. (Open M-W and F-Su 8am-1pm and 4:45-7:45pm, Th 8am-1pm. MC/V.)

Ristoritrovo ConTe, V. Porta Fuga 43 (☎0743 22 52 21). If the strains of karaoke or the squawking parrot outside don't draw you in, then surely the magenta walls and 1m tall pink wine bottles will. This wacky restaurant dishes up the famous *strengozzi* with mushrooms, garlic, chili pepper, and tomatoes (€7.50). Pizza €4.30-7. Primi €6-15. Secondi €8-16. Open Tu-Su 11am-2:30pm and 7-11pm. Cash only. ❸

Ristorante Apollinare, V. Sant'Agata 14 (☎0743 22 32 56; www.ristoranteapollinare. it). Former 10th-century convent serves fresh local cuisine. 3- and 5-course *menùs* (€25-35) are some of Umbria's best. Try mouthwatering roasted, stuffed rabbit with olive sauce and grilled raddichio (€13). Primi €8-20. Secondi €10-24. Desserts €5-7. Open daily noon-2:30pm and 7-10:30pm. Closed Tu in winter. AmEx/MC/V. ❸

Ristorante Sabatini, C. Mazzini 52-54 (☎0743 22 18 31). Photos of famous past customers line the otherwise simple walls of this expansive restaurant. Look for shots of Niki Lauda or Scalfaro as you enjoy dishes like pork fillet soaked in red wine, rosemary, and wild juniper berry sauce (€11). Excellent vegetable contorni €4. Primi €8-12. Secondi €8-13. Open Tu-Su 12:30-2:30pm and 7-10pm. AmEx/MC/V. ❸

Osteria del Trivio, V. del Trivio 16 (☎0743 44 349; www.osteriadeltrivio.it). From V. Garibaldi, turn left on V. del Trivio. Festively decorated with paintings and musical instruments. Some of the best food in town. Menu features traditional *strengozzi* with fava beans, bacon, and *pecorino* cheese (€9) and beef fillet in Sagranino wine (€15). Primi €8-13. Secondi €8-15. Open daily 12:30-2:30pm and 7-10pm. AmEx/MC/V. ❸

Taverna dei Duchi, V. Saffi 1 (☎0743 44 088). The restaurant is unmarked, so look for green walls with stone arches. All manner of Umbrian specialities, most often including truffles. Don't fill up on the focaccia before trying the *strengozzi al rancetto* (with onion, bacon, and pecorino cheese; €6), a tomato-less take on the local favorite. 3-course *menù* (€16) is a good deal. Pizza €5.50-11; dinner only. Primi €5.50-11. Secondi €7-11. Open M-Th, Sa-Su noon-3pm and 7-10pm. MC/V. ❸

Osteria dell'Enoteca, V. Saffi 7 (☎0743 22 04 84). At this stylish *osteria*, diners enjoy traditional *strengozzi* (€9) or richer dishes like *tortellini alla montanara* with meat, truffle sauce, gorgonzola, and bacon (€9). Primi €6.50-12. Secondi €6.50-13. Cover €1. Open M and W-Su 11:15am-3pm and 7-11pm. AmEx/MC/V. ❷

◉ SIGHTS

ROCCA ALBORNOZIANA AND PONTE DELLE TORRI. The Rocca, a papal fortress up V. Saffi from P. del Duomo, was a high-security prison until 1982. During WWII, 94 Italian and Slovenian prisoners staged an escape to join partisans in the Umbrian hills. The complex's only drama now is in the restored 15th-century frescoes of the **Camera Pinta.** (☎0743 46 434. Museum open Tu-W and Su

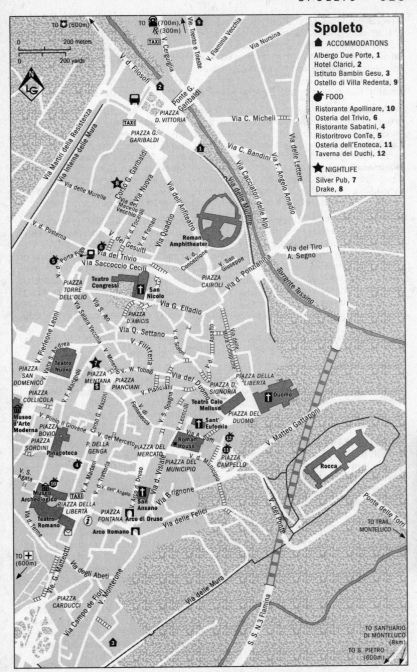

Spoleto

🏠 **ACCOMMODATIONS**

Albergo Due Porte, **1**
Hotel Clarici, **2**
Istituto Bambin Gesu, **3**
Ostello di Villa Redenta, **9**

🍴 **FOOD**

Ristorante Apollinare, **10**
Osteria del Trivio, **6**
Ristorante Sabatini, **4**
Ristoritrovo ConTe, **5**
Osteria dell'Enoteca, **11**
Taverna dei Duchi, **12**

⭐ **NIGHTLIFE**

Silver Pub, **7**
Drake, **8**

UMBRIA

9am-1:30pm, Th-Sa 9am-7:30pm. €6, ages 18-25 €3, under 18 and over 65 free. Rocca open M 10am-6pm, Tu-W and Su 9am-6pm, Th-Sa 9am-3:30pm. €6, ages 15-25 and over 60 €5, ages 7-14 €2.50, under 6 free. Combined ticket €7.50/6.50/3.50/free. Tower €2. Guided tours in Italian offered Sa-Su 11am and 3pm; call to reserve.) On the far side of the Rocca is the massive **Ponte delle Torri,** a stunning 14th-century engineering feat on an ancient Roman aqueduct. Ten 80m arches support the bridge, and the view across the Tessino Gorge is riveting. Several hikes start at the end of the bridge. (Free.)

MONTELUCO. The 800m trail along Spoleto's steep "mountain of the sacred grove" begins across Ponte delle Torri and winds through a canopied forest, passing abandoned mountain shrines and the churches of **San Giuliano** and **San Pietro.** At the peak of Monteluco, you'll find hotel-restaurants, a flat grassy picnic-ready clearing, and the tiny, 13th-century **Santuario di San Francesco di Monteluco,** once the refuge of St. Francis of Assisi and St. Bernadine of Siena. (Open 9am-noon and 3-6pm. Free.) Rain can turn the path into a rocky stream; to avoid slippery terrain, it's best to hike there on a sunny day or take a bus. Wear proper footwear and get a trail map from the tourist office before leaving.

DUOMO. Spoleto's Romanesque cathedral was built in the 12th century and later expanded by a 1491 portico and 17th-century interior redecoration. Inside, brilliantly colored scenes by Fra Filippo Lippi fill the domed apse, such as The Coronation in the half-dome of the main apse and a nativity scene on the lower right side. The 15th-century Cappella dell'Assunta is covered in eroding frescoes, while the more lavish 17th-century Cappella della Santa Icone stands to the right of the main apse. Lorenzo dei Medici commissioned Lippi's tomb, which was decorated by the artist's son, Filippino, and is now in the right transept. The soaring campanile features a mixture of styles and materials: stone blocks, fragments of inscriptions, friezes, and other remnants of the Roman era combine to form this structure. (Down the steps from Casa Romana. Open daily 8:30am-12:30pm and 3:30-7pm. No visits during Mass M-Sa 9am and 6pm; Su 9, 11:30am, 6pm.)

CASA ROMANA. This small AD first-century Roman house, once home to Emperor Vespasian's mother Vespasia Polla, features well-preserved mosaic floors and other artifacts. (V. di Visiale 9. Beneath city hall. From P. del Duomo, take stairs opposite duomo entrance, then take a right and follow the yellow sign. ☎0743 23 42 50. Open daily Mar. 16-Oct. 14 10am-8pm; Oct. 15-Mar. 15 daily 10am-6pm. €2.50, ages 15-25 and over 65 €2, ages 7-14 €1; with Museum of Modern Art and Pinacoteca €6/4/1.50, valid for 3 days.)

CHIESA DI SANT'ANSANO AND CRIPTA DI SAN ISAACO. Built on the ruins of a Roman temple dating to the first century BC, Sant'Ansano has a Renaissance facade and interior. Haunting frescoes detail scenes from the life of St. Isaac, who lives in an AD sixth-century sarcophagus at the center of the room. (Heading away from P. Mercato on V. dell'Arco di Druso, the church is on the left hand corner. ☎0743 40 305. Open daily Apr.-Oct. 9am-noon and 3-7pm; Nov.-Mar. 9am-noon and 3-6pm.)

MUSEUM OF MODERN ART. A refreshing alternative to ancient ruins and holy frescoes, this collection includes early works by Moore, Consagra, Pomodoro, and Leoncillo. The museum's first room is dedicated to American artist Alexander Calder, whose Teodelapio now stands in Spoleto's P. della Stazione. (Follow V. Mercato as it turns into V. Giovane, and go downstairs; the museum lies straight ahead. ☎0743 46 434. Open Mar. 16-Oct. 14 daily 10:30am-1pm and 3:30-7pm; Oct. 15-Mar. 15 M and W-Su 10:30am-1pm and 3-5:30pm. €4, ages 15-25 and over 65 €3, ages 7-14 €1.50.)

OTHER ROMAN RUINS. Spoleto's ruins, a testament to the city's prominence in Roman times, are found mainly near P. della Libertà. Take V. S. Agata from the piazza to reach the entrance of the **Museo Archeologico Statale,** which houses a small collection of Roman artifacts found in the area. Admission includes the opportunity to explore the **Roman Theater,** which hosts concerts and plays dur-ing the summer festival. *(☎0743 22 32 77. Open daily 8:30am-7:30pm. €4, EU citizens ages 18-25 €2, EU citizens under 18 or over 65 free.)* The **Arco Romano,** at the top of V. Monterone, once marked the town's entrance. Off P. Fontana, the **Arco di Druso** commemorates Emperor Druscu's military triumphs. Though closed to the public, the **amphitheater** stands just beyond the Roman walls.

▓ FESTIVALS

▓ **Spoleto Festival (Festival dei Due Mondi)** (☎800 56 56 00; www.spoletofestival.it.), 2 weeks in late June and early July. One of the world's most prestigious international arts events with concerts, operas, ballets, films, modern art shows, and craft fairs. Pur-chase tickets beginning in late April by contacting the box office, P. della Libertà 10 (☎0743 89 21 01; www.ticketone.it Open daily from April 22 to June 26 W and F 10:30am-1:30pm and 4-7pm, Sa 10:30am-12:30pm and 4-7pm. During the festival M-F 10:30am-1:30pm and 4-7pm, Sa-Su 10:30am-12:30pm and 4-7pm. Call center open M-F 9am-8pm, Sa 9am-5:30pm). Ages 25 and under or over 60, 20% discount.

Vini nel Mondo, during the last weekend of June. Citywide wine tastings and musical and theatrical performances.

Spoleto Estate, throughout Aug. and Sept. Cultural events pick up where the Spoleto Festival leaves off. Schedules available at the tourist office.

Stagione del Teatro Lirico Sperimentale A. Belli di Spoleto, P. Bovio 1 (☎0743 22 16 45), from late Aug. to Sept. Renowned experimental opera season.

▓ NIGHTLIFE

Down **Corso Garibaldi,** crowds gather in the early evening in the busy **Piazza Vit-toria** where cafes serve *aperitivo* buffets and dish up creamy gelato. Young people and couples hang out on the *piazza's* central fountain.

Drake, C. Garibaldi 92 (☎0743 49 311). Serves hot pizza and cold drinks, or cold *panini* and hot drinks. The Dark Violet is a hot mix of absinthe, sambuca, blue cura-cao, and orange juice (€6). During winter, *discobar* downstairs opens with a DJ on Su, live music on Sa, and Latin W. Mixed drinks €4-6. Beer €2.50-5. Open Tu-Su 11:30am-3:30pm and 6:30pm-3am. AmEx/MC/V.

Silver Pub, V. Felice Cavalloti (☎0743 22 10 00). From P. della Liberta, follow V. Mazzini to the left. Imposing wood doors open up to an off-beat bar with a huge selection of mixed drinks (€5-6) and beer. Yellow walls, a steep spiral staircase, live music, and an even livelier crowd make this one of Spoleto's most popular spots. Happy hour daily 8-10pm. Karaoke F. Open M-Tu and Th-Su 8pm-3am. Cash only.

▓ DAYTRIP FROM SPOLETO

TREVI

From Spoleto, take a train to Trevi. Dir: Perugia or Ancona, 10min., 17 per day 12:10am-10:09pm, €1.75. From the station, take an orange municipal bus to town. Buses run to P. Mazzini, the main piazza at the top of the hill. M-Sa 6 per day 7:30am-6:15pm, return buses M-Sa 5 per day 6:55am-5:40pm; €0.70.

Removed and unhurried compared to the more trafficked Umbrian towns, Trevi (TREH-vee; pop. 7800) rests among sloping olive groves atop a hill. Most sights are easily reached from **Piazza Mazzini,** the *centro.* The **Pinacoteca Rac-colta d'Arte di San Francesco** houses a collection of Renaissance religious art. The unique **Museo della Civiltà Dell'Ulivo** offers a history of the city's staple olive oil industry as well as samples and recipes. Follow V. San Francesco from P.

Mazzini to reach the museums, both at Lungo Don Bosco 5. (☎0742 38 16 28; www.sistemamuseo.it. Open June-July Tu-Su 10am-12:30pm and 3:30-7pm; Aug. daily 10am-12:30pm and 3-7:30pm; Sept. and Apr.-May Tu-Su 10am-12:30pm and 2:30-6pm; Oct.-Mar. F-Su 10am-12:30pm and 2:30-5pm. €4, students €2.50.) The **Flash Art Museum,** V. Placido Riccardi 4, showcases avant-garde art in a 15th-century *palazzo*. The small museum, which is associated with the contemporary Italian art magazine, *Flash*, hosts rotating exhibits of modern art. (☎0742 38 10 21; www.treviflashartmuseum.org. Open Tu-Su 4-7pm.) The **Illumination Procession,** one of Umbria's oldest religious festivals, takes place on January 28.

Ristorante Maggiolini ❷, V. San Francesco 20, near the museums off P. Mazzini, has an intimate interior and a bar for sampling Trevi's olive oil. (☎0742 38 15 34. Primi €6-8. Secondi €6-12. Open M and W-Su noon-3pm and 7-10:30pm. MC/V.) The Pro Loco **tourist office,** P. Mazzini 5, offers assistance in renting one of the abundant *affitacamere*, a better deal than any of Trevi's expensive hotels. (☎0742 78 11 50; www.protrevi.it. Open daily 9am-1pm and 3:30-7:30pm.) To reach the office from P. Garibaldi, take V. Roma to P. Mazzini.

ORVIETO ☎0763

A city upon a city, Orvieto (or-vee-YEH-toh; pop. 20,705) was built in layers: medieval edifices rest upon ancient subterranean remains. In the 8th century BC, Etruscans burrowed for *tufa* (a volcanic stone out of which most of the medieval quarter is built), leaving behind an entire city beneath the ground surface. Six centuries later, Romans sacked and reoccupied the plateau, calling their "new" city, strangely enough, *urbus ventus* (old city), from which the name Orvieto is derived. Today, the town is a tourist destination made popular by its spectacular underground chambers, distinctly Medieval ambiance, and refreshing *Orvieto Classico* wine. To escape the crowds, skip the shops on C. Cavour and head to the side streets, where local artisans display their wares.

▐ TRANSPORTATION

Situated between Rome and Florence, **trains** from Orvieto run to **Arezzo** (1hr., every hr. 7:30am-11:22pm, €6.10), **Florence** (2hr., every hr. 7:30am-8:33pm, €10.40) via **Cortona** (45min.), and **Rome** (1hr., every hr. 4:30am-11:28pm, €7.10). **Buses** leave from P. Cahen and the train station. **COTRAL** (☎0763 73 48 14) runs buses to **Viterbo** (8 per day 6:20am-5:45pm, €2.80). Purchase tickets at *tabaccherie*. **ATC** buses (☎0763 30 12 24) stop in P. Cahen and go to **Perugia** (1hr., 5:55am, €6.65) and **Todi** (1hr., 1:05pm, €5.40). Purchase tickets at the funicular ticket office, at *tabaccherie* on C. Cavour, or on the bus with a surcharge. The **funicular** ascends Orvieto's hill, connecting the train station with the city's historical center at P. Cahen (every 10min.; one-way ticket including bus ride €0.95, day ticket €3.70, 10% group discount). The tickets for the funicular are valid for 1hr., which allows for multiple journeys between the hilltop and the *centro storico*. For a **taxi**, call ☎0763 30 19 03.

◀ ⚡ ORIENTATION AND PRACTICAL INFORMATION

Across from the **train station**, located in **Piazza G. Matteotti**, the funicular travels up the hill to Piazza Cahen. From there, **Corso Cavour** runs slightly uphill from P. Cahen to **Piazza della Repubblica**. About 10min. from P. Cahen, C. Cavour crosses **Via del Duomo.** At this intersection, turn left down V. del Duomo to reach the *duomo*. If you continue instead two blocks down C. Cavour, a right turn on **Via della Piazza del Popolo** will bring you to **Piazza del Popolo.** Many of the city's most popular restaurants, hotels, and shops can be found between V. Duomo and the P. della Repubblica along C. Cavour. The **tourist office** is at P. del Duomo

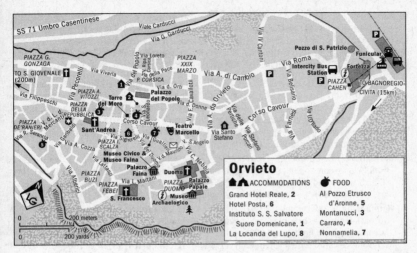

Orvieto

🏠🏠 ACCOMMODATIONS

Grand Hotel Reale, **2**
Hotel Posta, **6**
Instituto S. S. Salvatore
  Suore Domenicane, **1**
La Locanda del Lupo, **8**

🍎 FOOD

Al Pozzo Etrusco
  d'Aronne, **5**
Montanucci, **3**
Carraro, **4**
Nonnamelia, **7**

24. (☎0763 34 17 72. Open M-F 8:15am-1:50pm and 4-7pm, Sa-Su and holidays 10am-1pm and 3-6pm.) The office next door sells the **Orvieto Unica card** (€18, students €15), which includes an underground tour, round-trip ticket for funicular-minibus, 5hr. of parking, and entrance to select sights, as well as discounts at participating businesses. (☎0763 34 06 88, www.cartaunica.it.) **Luggage storage** is available at the train station. In an **emergency**, call the **police** (☎0763 34 00 88), in P. della Repubblica. The **hospital** (☎0763 30 71) is in Località Cicania. A **post office** (☎0763 39 83 49) is on V. Ravelli, off C. Cavour. (Open M-Sa 8:10am-4:45pm; last day of the month 8:10am-noon.) **Postal Code:** 05018.

■ ACCOMMODATIONS

Grand Hotel Reale, P. del Popolo 27 (☎0763 34 12 47; hotelreale@orvietohotels.it). An opulent 13th-century *palazzo* with old-world flair. Once housed King Umberto. Fine artwork and views of the Palazzo del Popolo show off the hotel's class. Rooms have TV and phone; more expensive rooms have magnificent frescoes and luxurious Murano glass light fixtures. Breakfast €8. Singles €66; doubles €90; triples €117; quads €140. V. ❹

La Locanda del Lupo, C. Cavour 231 (☎0763 34 13 88 or 34 41 03; www.lalocandadellupo.it), halfway between the intersection of P. Cahen and V. del Duomo. Breakfast €2.50; discounted meals for guests in the restaurant below. Singles €30; doubles €60; triples €90; quads €120. Ask for student or group discount. AmEx/MC/V. ❸

Hotel Posta, V. Luca Signorelli 18 (☎0763 34 19 09; www.orvietohotels.it). Converted *palazzo* located off C. Cavour and V. del Duomo. Breakfast €6. Reservations recommended. Singles €31, with bath €37; doubles €43/56; triples €60/75. Cash only. ❸

Instituto S. S. Salvatore Suore Domenicane, V. del Popolo 1 (☎0763 34 29 10). Convent situated in a corner of P. del Popolo, removed from the more heavily trafficked areas of town. Features religious art and a lovely 3-level garden. Reservations recommended. Apr.-Sept. singles €35; doubles €55. Oct-Mar. €30; doubles €45. Cash only. ❹

▪ FOOD

Orvieto was once known as *Oinarea*, or the "city where wine flows." The stream is still rocking steady. Pair a light bottle of *Classico* with local treats like baked *lumachelle* (snail-shaped buns with ham and cheese), *tortucce* (fried bread dough), or *mazzafegate* (sweet or salty sausages). Also prevalent are *tartufi* (truffles), served frequently and at reasonable prices in many dishes—sometimes even grated tableside. The sociable **Panini Imbottiti**, V. del Duomo 36, sells bottles of *Classico* from €2. (Open daily 8:30am-9pm. Cash only.)

Carraro, C. Cavour 101 (☎0763 34 28 70; carraro@orvieto.tin.it), before the intersection with V. del Duomo, as you walk toward Torre del Moro. This shop sells homemade truffle spread (small jar €5) as well as a variety of fresh cured meats, cheeses, and baked goods. Indulge in wild boar and truffle sausage (€24 per kg) and award-winning *cenerino* cheese (€22 per kg). Picnic lunch for under €5, bottles of Orvieto Classico for €8.50. Open M-Tu and Th-Su 7:15am-1:30pm and 4:30-8:30pm. MC/V. ❷

Montanucci, C. Cavour 21 (☎0763 34 12 61; barmontanucci@libero.it). Spacious, worldly, and conveniently located cafe has everything you need. The bar sells gelato (€2.50-3.50) and a staggering variety of chocolates (from €1), as well as some lighter fare (*insalate* €6). Wi-Fi available. Open daily 6am-12:30am. ❶

Nonnamelia, V. del Duomo 25 (☎0763 34 24 02). Creative recipes and quaint wooden decorations make for a pleasant dining experience. Try the *maialino da latte agliaromi* (suckling pig and herbs) and choose from a wide variety of pizzas. Pizza €3.50-9. Primi €5.50-8. Secondi €7-14. Open daily 11:30am-3:30pm and 7-11pm. AmEx/MC/V. ❷

Al Pozzo Etrusco d'Aronne, P. dei Ranieri 1/A (☎0763 34 44 56). Basic hearty food served in an intimate space off the beaten path, complete with an Etruscan well and outdoor *piazza* seating. Primi €5.50-8.50. Secondi €7-12. Free Wi-Fi. Open Tu-Su 12:30-3:30pm and 7:30-10:30pm. AmEx/D/MC/V. ❸

🄖 SIGHTS

🄳**DUOMO.** Orvieto's architectural claim to fame, the striped *duomo* is nothing short of dazzling. Designed in the late 13th century by Sienese architect Lorenzo Maitani, the facade is an excellent example of the Italian Gothic style. Its carved marble pillars, sculptures, and mosaics miraculously avoided bombings during both World Wars and today continue to awe admirers with elaborate details and brilliant colors. The bottom level features carved bas-reliefs of the Genesis and Old Testament prophecies as well as the final panel of Maitani's *Last Judgment*. Surrounding a rose window designed by Andrea Orcagna (1325-1364) are bronze and marble sculptures that illustrate the Christian canon. Thirty-three architects, 90 mosaic artisans, 152 sculptors, and 68 painters worked for over 600 years to improve the *duomo*, and the work continues—bronze doors were installed in 1970. (☎0763 34 11 67. *Duomo open in summer M-Sa 7:30am-12:45pm and 2:30-7:15pm, Su and holidays 2:30-6:45pm; closes in winter 1-2hr. earlier. Crypt open M-F 10am-noon. Modest dress required. Free.*) The **Cappella della Madonna di San Brizio,** also called the *Cappella Nuova*, off the right transept, includes Luca Signorelli's floor-to-ceiling frescoes of the Apocalypse. His vigorous craftsmanship, mastery of human anatomy, and dramatic compositions inspired Michelangelo in his work on the Sistine Chapel. Also note da Fabriano's *Madonna and Child* and the marble *Pietà* by di Scalza. Opposite the San Brizio chapel is the **Cappella Corporale,** which features stunning frescoes by Ugolino di Prete Ilario and holds the gold-encrusted *Reliquario del Corporale* (chalice-cloth), said to have been soaked with Christ's blood, from the 1263 miracle of Bolsena. (*Mass 9am daily; Su 8:30, 10:30am, noon, 6pm. €5, under 18 and over 65 €4, under 10 free. The ticket grants admission to the Museo Archeologico Nazionale and the Museo dell'Opera del Duomo. Audio tour €1.*)

PALAZZO PAPALE. Pope Clement VII rejected King Henry VIII's petition to annul his marriage with Catherine of Aragon in this austere, 13th-century "Palace of the Popes." Set back in the *palazzo* is the **Museo Archeologico Nazionale**, where visitors can examine Etruscan art from the area and walk into a restored tomb decorated with faded AD 4th-century frescoes. *(To the right facing the duomo. www.archeopg.arti.beniculturali.it. Open daily 8:30am-7:30pm. €3, with entrance to Etruscan Necropolis €5; students 18-25 €1.50; EU citizens under 18 or over 65 free.)* Above the archaeological museum is the **Museo dell'Opera del Duomo,** which displays art and cultural artifacts from the 13th to 17th centuries. Featured pieces include Simone Martini's *Politico di San Domenico*, Andrea Pisano's *Madonna and Child*, and Francesco Mochi's marble *Annunciation*. *(☎0763 34 35 92; www.opsm. it. Open Apr.-Sept. daily 9:30am-7pm; Nov.-Feb. M and W-Su 9:30am-1pm and 3-5pm; Mar. and Oct. M and W-Su 9:30am-1pm and 3-6pm. €5; €4 reduced.)*

UNDERGROUND CITY. The ancient Etruscan town Velzna occupied the soft *tufa* of the cliff below modern Orvieto. Although Velzna was sacked by the Romans, its cisterns, mills, pottery workshops, quarries, pigeon coops, wine cellars, and burial sites lie preserved underground. **Underground City Excursions** runs the most complete and accessible tours of the city's dark, twisted bowels. *(☎0763 34 48 91; www.orvietounderground.it. 1hr. tours depart the tourist office daily 11am, 12:15, 4, and 5:15pm. English guided tours 11:15am and 4:15pm. €5.50, students €3.50, under 5 free.)*

CHIESA DI SAN GIOVENALE. Built in AD 1000, the city's oldest church was dedicated to its first bishop, who is represented in a fresco near the entry. Directly next to the doors on the left is a 14th-century "Tree of Life"—a family tree of the church's founders. The church's courtyard offers spectacular ◪**views** of the countryside below. Graves of victims of the Black Death of 1348 fill the slope below P. San Giovanni. *(From P. della Repubblica, walk downhill along V. Filippeschi, which turns into V. Malabranca. The church is at the end of the street on the right.)*

MUSEO CIVICO AND MUSEO FAINA. Directly opposite the *duomo*, these museums hold an extensive collection of Etruscan artifacts. Exhibits include collections of over 3000 coins, bronze urns, Roman ornaments, and figure vases attributed to Athenian artists from the 6th century BC. **Palazzo Faina,** in which the collections are housed, also sports beautifully frescoed ceilings. *(P. del Duomo 29. ☎0763 34 15 11 www.museofaina.it. Open Apr.-Sept. daily 9:30am-6pm; Oct.-Mar. Tu-Su 10am-5pm. €4.50; students and over 65, families of 4, or groups of at least 15 €3.)*

❀ FESTIVALS

Though nightclubs are virtually nonexistent in Orvieto, the city has no shortage of festival fun. Look for craft fairs, food- and wine-tasting events, antique car shows, and theater and music festivals. Spring brings the **Palio dell'Oca,** which has tested equestrian skills since medieval times. On Pentecost Orvieto celebrates the **Festa della Palombella.** At noon, Campo della Fiera lights up with fireworks when a white dove descends across a wire to ignite the explosives. The dove, which symbolizes the Holy Spirit, is entrusted to the last woman married in the church. First Communions and confirmations, sacraments in the Catholic Church, are also celebrated on this day. In June the **Procession of Corpus Domini** celebrates the Miracle of Bolsena when a communion wafer was transformed into flesh and blood. A week of medieval banquets and dancing precedes the 700-year-old procession. From December 28 to January 1, **Umbria Jazz Winter** swings in theaters, churches, and palaces, with the grand finale in the *duomo*. For details and pamphlets concerning festivals, contact **Servizio Turistico Territoriale IAT dell'Orvietano,** P. Duomo 24 (☎0763 34 19 11 or 34 36 58), or **Informazioni Turistiche** (☎0763 34 17 72; fax 34 44 33), at the same address.

UMBRIA

LE MARCHE

Green foothills separate the umbrella-laden beaches along the Adriatic from the craggy inland Apennines in Le Marche (LAY MAR-kay), one of Italy's most under appreciated regions. In its rural towns, remains of the Gauls, Picenes, and Romans hint at a fascinating past, but the present is alive and well among friendly locals and picturesque side streets. The legacy of Raphael and Donato Bramante in Urbino, the palm-lined boardwalk of San Benedetto del Tronto, the winding streets of Ascoli Piceno, and the hidden beauty of Ancona are just a few of the highlights of this geographically and historically diverse region. Just as it has charmed the knickers off artists in the past, it'll charm the sleek, white capris off you and your fellow stylin' travelin' band members.

HIGHLIGHTS OF LE MARCHE

BAKE on the untouristed beaches of the sleepy town of Fano (p. 534).

CLIMB up to the grand hilltop Palazzo Ducale in Urbino (p. 537).

STROLL along Pesaro's promenade for some of Italy's best Adriatic views (p. 530).

PESARO
☎ 0721

Pesaro (PEZ-ah-ro; pop. 92,000) strikes a balance between its neighbors—hip Rimini and laid-back Fano—offering a blend of culture, couture, and seaside serenity. While the bright blue Adriatic delights beachgoers, the *centro* charms visitors with street concerts and back-alley shops. Come here to buy a smokin' bikini, then stake your claim on the sandy shores to justify your purchase.

▐ TRANSPORTATION

Trains: at the end of V. Risorgimento and Vle. della Liberazione. Ticket counter open daily 6:10am-8:30pm. AmEx/MC/V. To: **Ancona** (1hr., 31 per day 12:59am-11:46pm, €3.25); **Bologna** (2hr., 34 per day 4:43am-11:18pm, €7.90); **Fano** (10min., 22 per day 6:27am-11:13pm, €1.35); **Rimini** (30min., 41 per day 4:43am-11:18pm, €2.70).

Buses: 50 ft. from the train station (☎0721 32 401). Open M-Sa 7:30am-1pm. Buses #10, 11, 14, 20, 30, 40, 50, 60, 70, 130, and C/S stop at Ple. Giacomo Matteotti and run to **Fano** (25min., every 15-30min. 6:35am-9:05pm, €1.40) and **Gradara** (55min., M-F 6:05am-7:05pm every hr., Su every 2hr.; €1.60). ADRIABUS (☎0721 54 96 20) runs to **Urbino** from the train station (55min.; M-Sa 20 per day 6:15am-8:15pm, Su 9 per day 8:15am-8:15pm; €2.75). **Bucci** runs to **Rome's** Tiburtina station from Ple. G. Matteotti (4hr., 6am and 2pm, €22). Buy tickets on board. Cash only.

Taxis: Available 24hr. at the train station (☎0721 31 111 or 45 44 25), P. del Popolo (☎0721 31 430), and Ple. G. Matteotti (☎0721 34 053).

Bike Rental: in Ple. d'Annunzio, at the intersection of Vle. Trieste and Vle. G. Verdi (☎347 75 29 634). €3 per hr., €9 per day. Open May to Sept. 8:30am-midnight. Cash only.

✳ ▐ ORIENTATION AND PRACTICAL INFORMATION

From the train station, take **Via Risorgimento** and walk straight through P. Garibaldi and up V. Branca to reach **Piazza del Popolo**, the relaxed *centro storico*. **Corso XI Settembre** runs west toward Chiesa di Sant'Agostino, while **Via San Francesco** runs east toward **Piazzale Giacomo Matteotti** and the bus station. **Via Rossini** runs straight toward **Largo Aldo Moro,** which leads to **Viale della Repubblica, Piazzale Libertà,** and the sea. **Viale Trieste** runs along the beach.

Tourist Offices: IAT, V. Rossini 41 (☎0721 69 341; iat.pesaro@regione.marche.it). Open M-Sa 9am-1pm and 3-6pm, Su 9am-1pm. **Provincial tourist office** (☎800 56 38 00; www.comune.pesaro.it), off Largo Aldo Moro. Open M-Sa 9am-1pm and 4-7pm, Su 9am-1pm.

Luggage storage: near the "Taxis" sign outside the station. 1st 12hr. €3, each additional 12hr. €2. Open daily 6am-11pm.

Police: ☎0721 42 551.

Hospital: Ospedale San Salvatore, Ple. Cinelli 4 (☎0721 36 11).

Pharmacy: V. Rossini 42 (☎0721 67 121), right off Largo Aldo Moro. Open daily 8:30am-12:30pm and 4pm-8pm. MC/V.

Internet: Max3D, V. Passeri 54/56. (☎0721 35 122). €3 per hr. Open M 3:30-8pm, Tu-Sa 9:30am-1pm and 3:30-8pm. Cash only.

Laundry: New Blue City, Vle. Fiume 10 (☎0721 87 47 408). Wash €2, dry €3. Open daily 7:30am-midnight.

Post Office: P. del Popolo 28 (☎0721 43 22 85). Open M-F 8am-6:30pm, Sa 8am-12:30pm. **Postal Code:** 61100.

ACCOMMODATIONS AND CAMPING

Pesaro is a low-season steal, but bargains are harder to find come summer.

Hotel Holiday, Vle. Trento 159/161 (☎0721 34 851), on a quiet street minutes from the beach. Rooms have floral ceilings, sunny balconies, phone, private bath, minibar, safe, TV, and fan. Breakfast, lunch, and dinner included. 3-night min. stay. Reception 7am-10pm. €38-58 per person; €6 surcharge for singles. AmEx/MC/V. ❸

Hotel Continental, Vle. Trieste 70 (☎0721 31 808; www.hotelcontinental.it). Colorful flags greet guests at this cheery hotel, practically on the sand. Sunny rooms with private bath, phone, TV, and balcony. Great services include buffet breakfast, communal TV rooms, free beach umbrellas, and daily *aperitivo* buffet. €41-62 per person; €6 surcharge for singles. MC/V. ❸

San Marco, Vle. XI Febbraio 32 (☎0721 31 396; www.hotelsanmarcopu.it). From the station follow V. Risorgimento, bear right into Ple. Garibaldi, and turn right onto Vle. XI Febbraio. Eager staff offers sparse but spacious rooms with Internet access, phone, and TV. A/C €6 about extra. Breakfast included. Wheelchair-accessible. Singles €42-55; doubles €68-83; triples €84-103; quads €100-115. AmEx/MC/V. ❸

Camping Panorama, (☎0721 20 81 45; www.campingpanorama.it), is near a national park and a beach, 7km north of Pesaro on Strada Panoramica S. Bartolo toward Gabicce Mare. Take bus #14 (M-Sa 5 per day, Su 2 per day) from the train station or Ple. Matteotti and ask for Camping Panorama. On-site pool, market, and laundry. Hot showers free. Open May-Sept. €6-9 per person; €16 per tent. Electricity €2.50. Cash only. ❶

◗ FOOD

There's a **Standa** supermarket at V. Canale 41. (Open M-Sa 7:30am-8:30pm, Su 8am-1:30pm. AmEx/MC/V.) **Mercato delle Erbe**, at the San Domenico Convent off V. Branca, sells flowers, bread, meat, fruit, and *piadine*. (Flower and bread stands open M-Sa 7am-8:30pm; *piadine* and food open M and W-Su 5-8:30pm.)

Trattoria da Sante, V. Bovio 27 (☎0721 33 676.www.trattoriadasante.com). Follow C. XI Settembre north from P. del Popolo, and turn left on V. Bovio. Heaping portions of delicious seafood pasta on a quiet side street off the *centro*. Try the filling *menù* of grilled fish, antipasto, primo, contorno, coffee, wine, and dessert (€30). Primi €6-8. Secondi €8-11. Cover €1. Service 15%. Open Tu-Su noon-2:30pm and 7-10:30pm. Reservations recommended Sa-Su. Cash only. ❸

Gelateria del Porto, Vle. Fiume 12 (☎0721 35 350). Retreat into the acqua blue interior after a hot day on the sand. Sorbets like *azzurro* (to match the bright walls) or richer flavors like "scrok!" (vanilla, *pinoli,* and caramel) are served in homemade chocolate-dipped cones (€1.50-4). Open M-Sa 7am-midnight, Su 7am-5pm. AmEx/MC/V. ❶

Sando Kan, V. Tebaldi 14 (☎339 830 4045), just off V. Branca coming from P. del Popolo. Warm red lights and intimate tables provide a cozy setting for classic Indian plates like *kukar daal* (lentils with chicken and basmati rice; €9), or *malaee kofta* (ground pork with cream and lemon; €13). Open Tu-Su 12:30-2:30pm and 7-11pm. Cash only. ❷

Harnold's, Ple. Lazzarini 34 (☎0721 65 155), 3 doors down from Teatro Rossini. From P. del Popolo, follow V. Branca away from the sea. Affordable fare ranges from extra thick *panini* and salads to the "Big Ben" (double-decker cheeseburger; €4.80). The food, prices, and feel-good atmosphere are worth the wait at the busy outdoor tables on summer nights. Panini €2-4.80. Open daily 8am-3am. Closed Su Oct.-Mar. MC/V. ❶

◉ SIGHTS

PIAZZA DEL POPOLO. Pesaro's main square holds the massive **Palazzo Ducale,** commissioned in the 15th century by Alessandro Sforza. *(Open to visitors during exhibitions only. Ask the tourist office about scheduled events.)*

MUSEI CIVICI. Rich clay deposits from the nearby Folgia River have made the crafting of ceramics a long-standing tradition in Pesaro. Within the Musei Civici, the **Museo delle Ceramiche** showcases centuries of local ceramics, which range from prehistoric artifacts to colorful contemporary works. In the same building, Pesaro's **Pinacoteca** holds the fiery *Fall of the Giants* by Guido Reni and four still-lifes by Benedetto Sartori. Don't miss Bellini's remarkable *Incoronazione della Vergine*, surrounded by 15 panels depicting scenes ranging from Christ's Nativity to St. George's somewhat unimpressive slaying of an iguana-sized ◪dragon. *(V. Toschi Mosca 29. From P. del Popolo, head down C. XI Settembre with Palazzo Ducale on your left, and turn right on V. Toschi Mosca. ☎0721 38 75 41; www.museicivicipesaro. it. Open July-Aug. Tu and Th 9:30am-12:30pm and 4-10:30pm, W and F-Su 9:30am-12:30pm and 4-7pm; Sept.-June Tu-W 9:30am-12:30pm, Th-Su 9:30am-12:30pm and 4-7pm. €4, ages 15-25 and over 65 €2, under 15 free. Combined ticket with Casa Rossini €7/€3. Cash only.)*

CASA ROSSINI. Gioachino Rossini's birthplace is now a museum with his old photographs, theatrical and opera memorabilia, and piano. *(V. Rossini 34. ☎0721 38 73 57. Same hours as Musei Civici. €4, under 26 or over 65 €2, under 15 free. Cash only.)*

♫ ◙ ENTERTAINMENT AND NIGHTLIFE

Pesaro hosts the **Mostra Internazionale del Nuovo Cinema** (The International Festival of New Films) from late June to July (☎0721 44 56 643; www.pesarofilmfest.

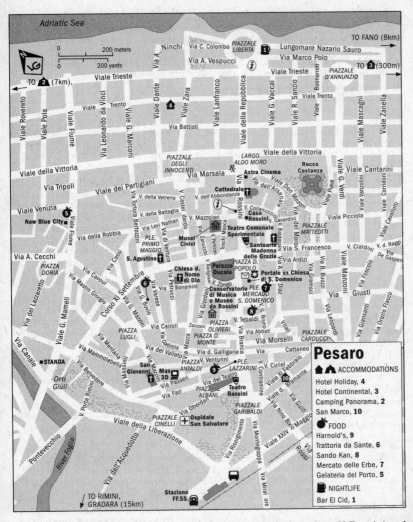

Pesaro

♦ **ACCOMMODATIONS**
Hotel Holiday, **4**
Hotel Continental, **3**
Camping Panorama, **2**
San Marco, **10**

🍎 **FOOD**
Harnold's, **9**
Trattoria da Sante, **6**
Sando Kan, **8**
Mercato delle Erbe, **7**
Gelateria del Porto, **5**

🌙 **NIGHTLIFE**
Bar El Cid, **1**

it). Live theater and movie screenings are held in buildings along V. Rossini and at the **Teatro Comunale Sperimentale** (☎0721 38 75 48), an experimental theater on V. Rossini. Native composer Rossini founded the Conservatorio di Musica G. Rossini, P. Olivieri 5, which sponsors artistic events year-round. Contact **Teatro Rossini,** Ple. Lazzarini 29 (☎0721 38 76 21), off V. Branca, for show times and prices. The annual **Rossini Opera Festival** runs from early August through September. Reserve tickets at Teatro Rossini's box office starting April 18. (☎0721 38 001; www.rossinioperafestival.it. Info line open M-F 10am-1pm and 3-6pm. Theater open M, W, and F 8:30am-1:30pm and 3:30-5:30pm. Ticket office open 9:30am-12:30pm and 4:30-7:30pm and 1hr. before performances.)

The perfect spot for a light lunch during a day of beaching, **Bar El Cid,** Ple. della Libertà, offers a great summer salad buffet from noon-3pm and breezy beachside seating. Try the packed Nizzarda salad with tuna, tomato, mozzarella, olives, mushrooms, eggs, and radicchio (€6). Return at night to sample the extensive drink list. (☎0721 31 891. Salad buffet and bread €5. Mixed drinks €5.50. Beer €3-4. Open daily Mar.-Oct. 7am-2am. Cash only.)

DAYTRIPS FROM PESARO

FANO

Fano is accessible from Pesaro by train (10min., 22 per day 6:27amm-11:13pm, €1.35) and by bus (every 15min.-hr., €1.40). To get to the beach, exit the train station right on V. Cavallotti and turn right on V. Cesare Battisti. To reach P. XX Settembre, the centro, turn left on V. Garibaldi from V. Cavallotti then right on C. Giacomo Matteotti.

Fano (FA-no; pop. 62,000) is a sleepy town stretching 20km along the coast from Pesaro to some of Italy's quietest seaside retreats. Even in summer, vacationers are scarce on the northern beaches; farther inland, a quiet *centro* offers relatively untouristed churches and restaurants serving seafood specialties. Marking the western entrance to these streets is the **Arco d'Augusto,** named for the city's founder, Augustus. Nearby stands a larger-than-life bronze statue of the man himself and the crumbling brick walls he built to protect his small city. Hotels reserve most of the private shoreline for their guests, but there is a rocky **public beach;** the first entrance sits across from Vle. Adriatico 150. Though this beach is convenient, you'll need some padding to sunbathe comfortably. (Open daily 5am-11pm. Free.) If you schedule your trip well, you might find yourself at the **July Jazz by the Sea,** which in the past has hosted artists like Wynton Marsalis. At **Al Pesce Azzuro ❷,** Vle. Adriatico 48/A, a brightly painted ship's hull welcomes visitors to this funky, self-service restaurant on the beach's northern end. (☎0721 80 31 65. *Menù* €10. Open Apr.-Oct. Tu-Su noon-2pm and 7:30-10pm.) Inland, **La Vecchia Fano ❸,** V. Vecchia 8, serves authentic *fanese* plates like *tagliolini al farro* (wheat pasta; €6.50). From V. Garibaldi, turn left through P. Costanzi on V. Cavour, then right on V. Vecchia. (☎/fax 0721 80 34 93. Primi €6.50-11. Secondi €6.50-20. Cover €2. Open Tu-Su noon-2:30pm and 7:30-10:30pm. AmEx/MC/V.) A **PuntoSMA** supermarket is at V. Garibaldi 53. (Open M-Sa 8am-8pm. MC/V.) The **tourist office** is at Vle. Battisti 10. (☎0721 80 35 34; www.turismofano.com. Open M, W, and F-Sa 9am-1pm, Tu and Th 3-6pm.)

GRADARA

Gradara is accessible from Pesaro by bus (55min., every hr. 6:05am-7:05pm, €1.60). To reach the walled city, walk uphill from the bus stop on V. Mancini. At the city gates, the main road becomes V. Umberto Primo and reaches P. V Novembre. For a complete investigation of the city walls, follow V. Circonvallazione around the castello.

The picturesque walled city of Gradara (gra-DA-ra; pop. 3400), 13km inland from Pesaro, sits atop a hill that surveys the surrounding landscape for miles—a beautiful patchwork of olive trees, vineyards, and sunflowers. Gradara's history is less sunny—it is ripe with stories of war and conquest. The impeccably restored *castello* at the heart of the city was built by Pietro and Ridolfo de Grido in the beginning of the 12th century, but construction was finished by the Malatestas after their conquest of the city in the first half of the 13th century. In 1289 lovers Paolo and Francesca were murdered here; their tragic story was famously immortalized in the fifth canto of Dante's *Inferno* and less famously in the name of a restaurant on the way to the castle. In 1494, Lucrezia Borgia came to Gradara to marry Giovanni Sforza, after the Sforzas conquered Gradara in the 16th century. In 1920, the castle was restored to appear as it had under the Sforzas 400 years ago, complete with dark-wood furniture and heavy drapes around four-post beds. At night, ▓views from the castle are spectacular; they take in the entire seaside, from the crystal coastline of Rimini to the sparkling San Marino lights. In summer, these vistas are often paired with music and dance performances in the *castello*'s courtyard, next to the moat and drawbridge. (☎0541 96 46 73. Open daily in summer 10am-1pm and 2-11pm; in winter 9am-1pm and 2:30-6:30pm. Ticket office closes 45min. before *castello*. Night visits by guided tour only July-Aug. W-Sa 9-11:30pm. *Castello* tickets €4, EU citizens ages 18-25 €2; night visits €8/5.) Next to the tourist office, the **Museo Storico** displays a decent collection of medieval arms and an exhibit about the daily life of a farmer in the Middle Ages. (☎0541 96 95 86. Open daily 9:30am-12:30pm, 2-7pm, and 8:30-11:30pm. €2.) **Osteria della Luna ❸**, V. Umberto Primo 6, on the way up to the castle, offers traditional dishes like *crostini al tartufo e porcini*. Be sure to sample some of the famous regional San Giovese wines. (☎0541 96 98 38. Primi €6.50-9.50. Secondi €12-18. Open daily 11:30am-3pm and 5pm-midnight; closed M Nov.-Mar. MC/V.) For in-depth tours or info on upcoming performances, visit the **tourist office,** Pro Loco Gradara, in P. V Novembre. (☎0541 96 41 15; www.gradara.org. Open M-Sa 9am-1pm.)

URBINO   ☎0722

With picturesque stone dwellings scattered along steep city streets and a turreted palace ornamenting its skyline, Urbino (oor-BEE-no; pop. 15,500) encompasses all that is classically Italian. The cobblestone streets and *piazze* lead to many artistic treasures and Renaissance monuments, including Piero della Francesca's *Ideal City* and Raphael's childhood home. This cultural beauty within the city walls is rivaled only by the magnificence of surrounding mountains and valleys. A huge university population and stream of international visitors continually bolster Urbino's vitality: when classes are in session, the town's population swells from 9,000 to nearly 30,000.

⌐ TRANSPORTATION

Buses stop in Borgo Mercatale and serve train stations in Pesaro and Fano. ADRIABUS (☎0722 37 67 11) runs to P. Matteotti and the depot outside the train station in Pesaro (45min.-1hr.; M-Sa 20 per day 6:20am-8:35pm, Su 9 per day 7:35am-8:35pm; €2.75) and Fano Pincio (1½hr.; 18 per day 5:40am-8:10pm, service reduced on Su). Buy tickets onboard. Bucci (☎0722 32 401; www.autolineebucci.it) runs buses to Rome (4hr., 6:15am and 3pm, €25). **Taxis** are in P. della Repubblica (☎0722 25 50) and at the bus stop (☎0722 32 79 49).

✚ ▓ ORIENTATION AND PRACTICAL INFORMATION

A short walk up **Via Mazzini** from **Borgo Mercatale** leads to **Piazza della Repubblica**, the city's hub, from which **Via Raffaello, Via Cesare Battisti, Via Vittorio Veneto,** and **Corso Garibaldi** radiate. Another walk uphill on V. V. Veneto leads to **Piazza Rinascimento** and the **Palazzo Ducale.**

Tourist Office: V. Puccinotti 35 (☎0722 26 13; www.marcheturismo.it), across from Palazzo Ducale. Free guided **tours** Mar.-Sept. Sa-Su 10:30am; Aug. Sa-Su 10:30am and 3:30pm. Open M and Sa 9am-1pm, Tu-F 9am-1pm and 3-6pm. Info booth (☎0722 26 31) in Borgo Mercatale. Open M-Sa 9am-6pm, Su 9am-1pm.

Laundromat: Powders, V. Battisti 35 (☎0722 21 96). Wash €3.75 per kg. Dry €2. Open M-Sa 9am-8pm. Cash only.

Police: V. S. Provinciale Feltresca 9. ☎0722 37 89 00.

Hospital: V. Bonconte da Montefeltro, off V. Comandino (☎0722 30 11).

Internet Access: Due Mila Net, V. Mazzini 17 (☎/fax 0722 37 81 95). €4 per hr., students €2.50 per hr.; min. 3hr. Open M-Sa 9am-10pm. Cash only.

Post Office: V. Bramante 28 (☎0722 37 791), off V. Raffaello. Currency exchange and **ATM** available. Open M-F 8am-6:30pm, Sa 8am-12:30pm. **Postal Code:** 61029.

ACCOMMODATIONS AND CAMPING

Pensionato Maria Immacolata, V. Mazzini 30 (☎0722 28 53), steps from the bus station and P. della Repubblica. High ceilings, a peaceful inner courtyard, and beautiful stone floors. Shared baths. Reception 7am-10pm. Curfew 10pm. Singles €18; doubles €32. Women only. Cash only. ❶

Pensione Fosca, V. Raffaello 67 (☎0722 32 96 22 or 339 54 05 640), on the top floor. From P. della Repubblica, turn left onto V. Raffaello and climb hill. Central location, kind proprietress, and unbeatable value. Shared bath. Call ahead to arrange check-in time. Singles €21; doubles €35; triples €45. Cash only. ❷

Albergo Italia, C. Garibaldi 32 (☎0722 27 01; www.albergo-italia-urbino.it), just off P. della Repubblica. A charming staff welcomes you to spotless modern rooms with wood floors and furniture, beautiful countryside views, and excellent services. Rooms have private bath, minibar, TV, and A/C. Breakfast included. Free Wi-Fi; computer with Internet access €1 per 15min. Wheelchair-accessible. Singles €47-70; doubles €70-120; triples €120-145; quads €160. Discounts with longer stays. AmEx/MC/V. ❹

Hotel Raffaello, Vicolino S. Margherita 40 (☎0722 47 84 or 48 96; www.albergorafello. com). From P. della Repubblica, turn left on V. Raffaello, left on V. S. Margherita, and right on the 1st side street. Tall blue ceilings, checkered marble floors, and bright decor give this hotel an eclectic feel. Historic location near the House of Raphael. Snug rooms have minibar, A/C, TV, phone, private bath, radio, and views of the hills. Breakfast included. Internet. Reception 7:30am-midnight. Singles €50-70; doubles €90-115. MC/V. ❹

Piero della Francesca, V. Comandino 53 (☎0722 32 84 28; fax 32 84 27), in front of the hospital. Bus #1 from Borgo Mercatale or a 15min. walk from P. della Repubblica. Modern rooms have bath, TV, phone, and balconies with views of the misty hills. Reception 24hr. Singles €31; doubles €52; triples €68. AmEx/MC/V. ❸

Camping Pineta, Località San Donato (☎0722 47 10; www.camping-pineta-urbino.it), 2km from Urbino. Take bus #4 or 7 from Borgo Mercatale; request to stop at camping. Private sites with city views. Open from 1 week before Easter to Sept. Reception 9am-10pm. €8-9 per person; €14-16 per tent. Electricity €2. Showers free. Cash only. ❶

FOOD

Urbino's *caciotta* is a delicate cheese that pairs well with a glass of *Bianchello del Metauro*. **Supermarket Margherita,** V. Raffaello 37, has meats and cheeses. (☎0722 32 97 71. Open M-Sa 7:30am-1:55pm and 4:30-8pm. MC/V.)

▨ **Il Portico,** V. Mazzini 7 (☎0722 43 29; www.porticourbino.it). A maze of exposed brick leads to the warm interior of this family-run restaurant, which serves Mediterranean food and wine. Try the especially popular *fiori di zucchine ripieni* (stuffed zucchini; €4.50), or a hearty portion of spaghetti with mussels and pecorino cheese (€8). Live music Tu and Sa-Su. Open Tu-Su noon-3pm and 7-11pm. Cover €2. AmEx/MC/V. ❷

▨ **Pizzeria Le Tre Piante,** V. Voltaccia della Vecchia 1 (☎0722 48 63). From P. della Repubblica, take V. Veneto, turn left on V. Nazario Sauro, right on V. Budassi, and left down the stairs onto V. Foro Posterula. Join locals on the terrace for fine fish and pasta. Try the *tagliatelle* with beans, rucola, and *pendoini* (€6.80), while watching the sun set over the

Apennines. Pizza €3.50-6.50. Primi €6.80-7.50. Secondi €8-15. Cover €1.50. Open Tu-Su noon-3pm and 7-11:30pm. Cash only. ❸

La Trattoria del Leone, V. Battisti 5 (☎0722 32 98 94). Brick archways and simple yellow walls provide a cozy space to enjoy regional dishes liked salted beef with orange, walnuts, and parmesan (€7.50). Vegetarian dishes include spaghetti with eggs, breadcrumbs, and parmesan in vegetable broth (€7.50). Primi €7. Secondi €6.50-12. Cover €2. Open M-F 6:30-11:30pm, Sa-Su 12:30-2:30pm. AmEx/MC/V. ❷

Ristorante Ragno d'Oro, Vle. Don Minzoni 2/4 (☎0722 32 77 05). Follow Vle. Raffaello to the statue at the top of the hill and turn right on Vle. Don Minzoni. Students and locals hike to the top of the hill, where the town's best pizza and *piadine* awaits. Try the signature Ragno d'Oro, with mozzarella, spinach, ricotta, and speck ham (€7); wash it down with the German beer on tap. Pizza €3.50-7.50. Primi €6-8. Secondi €7-17. Cover €1.50. Open Apr.-Oct. daily 9am-2:30pm and 7:30-midnight. AmEx/MC/V. ❸

Un Punto Macrobiotico, V. Pozzo Nuovo 4 (☎0722 32 97 90). From P. della Repubblica, take C. Battisti and then 1st right. Small, community-minded socially conscious market. Serves delicious organic food. Prices vary with the daily menu. Rice dishes €3-8. Open M-Sa 12:30-2:30pm and 7:30-9pm. Students eat ½-price. Cash only. ❶

Caffè del Sole, V. Mazzini 34 (☎0722 26 19). Popular student hangout serves *panini,* drinks, and hearty helpings of local personality. Walls decorated with sun motifs, a mural of clinking wine glasses, and a giant mouth on the back wall. Sept.-May W nights jazz concerts. Open M-Sa 7am-2am. AmEx/MC/V. ❶

👁 SIGHTS

PALAZZO DUCALE. The turreted silhouette of the Renaissance *palazzo* in P. Rinascimento dominates Urbino's skyline. A stairway inside leads to the **Galleria Nazionale delle Marche,** in the former residence of Duke Frederico da Montefeltro. The gallery contains an extensive Italian art collection, including works like Piero della Francesca's *The Ideal City.* In the last rooms, Berruguete's *Portrait of Duke Federico with a Young Guidubaldo,* Raphael's *Portrait of a Lady,* and Paolo Uccello's narrative panel *The Profanation of the Host* are on display. The building also contains the **Museo Archeologico's** collection of Roman art and artifacts. (☎0722 32 26 25. Open M 8:30am-2pm, Tu-Su 8:30am-7:15pm. Last entry 1hr. before closing. €8, EU students 18-25 €4, under 18 and over 65 free.)

CASA NATALE DI RAFFAELLO. Raphael's birthplace is now filled with period furnishings and paintings. The only piece in the museum attributed to Raphael himself is a fresco of the Virgin and Child in the room where the artist was born. Within these walls, Raphael began learning the trade from his father, Giovanni Santi. A celebrated painter in his own right, Santi's *Annunciation* hangs in the next room. (V. Raffaello 57. ☎0722 32 01 05. Open M-Sa 9am-1pm and 3-7pm, Su 10am-1pm. Last entry 20min. before closing. €3. Cash only.)

DUOMO. Beside Palazzo Ducale sits the stark facade of the *duomo.* White and mint-green walls, as well as paintings like Veronese's fantastic *Translazione della Santa Casa e Sant'Andrea,* decorate the interior. Next door, the **Sale del Castellare** has free art exhibits. (Open daily 9:30am-1pm and 2:30-6:30pm. Free.)

ORATORIO DI SAN GIOVANNI BATTISTA. From P. della Repubblica, take V. Mazzini and turn right up the small path on the right, following the sign. The 1416 Gothic frescoes that decorate the oratory on V. Barocci, include a gorgeous floor-to-ceiling Crucifixion and panels depicting events from the life of St. John. Its painters, the Salimbeni brothers Giacomo and Lorenzo, are said to have drawn their sketches with lamb's blood. (☎347 67 11 181. *Open M-Sa 10am-12:30pm and 3-5:30pm, Su 10am-12:30pm. €2. Cash only.*)

NIGHTLIFE

The main *piazze* stay lit well into the night, when people head to cafes for one last shot of espresso (or tequila, as the case may be). Students keep the party scene going strong until well after 3am during the school year, but come summer, Urbino slows down as its median age rises drastically. Bars are stocked with German beers, hard liquor, and even the occasional bottle of absinthe.

Daunbailo, V. Posta Vecchia 7. An artsy spot with checkered ceiling, red and turquoise walls, and snapshots from Audrey Hepburn's days in *Roman Holiday*. Live music Tu nights. Monthly photo exhibits. Beer €3.50. Wine €2.50. Mixed drinks €4.50. Open Tu-Sa 6pm-2am, Su 6pm-1am. Cash only.

The Bosom Pub, V. Budassi 24 (☎0722 47 83). Dark wood paneling and beer paraphernalia. Beer from €2.50. Wine €5 per bottle. Mixed drinks €2-6. Happy hour Tu and F-Sa from 10pm-midnight, with beer as cheap as €1 and 2 sangrias for €3. Open daily June-July 8pm-2am; Aug.-May 6pm-2am. Cash only.

Caffè del Corso, C. Garibaldi 3 (☎0722 24 77). Fuschia walls and brick archways lead to comfy modern seating. Creative drinks like hot China martinis (€2.50) and Jamaican coffee (espresso, rum, sugar, and cream; €3.50). Meals during the day €3.50-6.50. Mixed drinks €4.50. Beer €3-4.50. Open daily 6am-2am. Cash only.

Tanto Piacere, V. V. Veneto 29 (☎347 75 64 292). Draws a genial crowd to a simple, jazz-filled, white-brick interior. Appetizer buffet 6:30pm. Beer €2.50-3.50. Wine €2-4. *Bruschette* €3-6. *Crescia* €2-6. Open Tu-Su 10am-2am. Cash only.

FESTIVALS

In July the town resounds with Renaissance music during the **Antique Music Festival.** Saturdays are amateur nights—bring your ancient lute and rock out. The third Sunday of August brings the **Ceremony of the Revocation of the Duke's Court.** Jousting matches erupt on the eve of the festival. The **Festa dell'Aquilone,** held on the first Sunday in September, is a fierce kite-flying competition between different cities. (The rain date is the 2nd Su of Sept.)

ANCONA   ☎071

Midway down the boot, Ancona (an-CO-na; pop. 102,000) is still kickin' as Northern Italy's major transportation hub for boats to Croatia, Greece, and Slovenia. Though most travelers only pass through on their way to more exotic locales, those who choose to linger will enjoy the centuries-old *duomo*, a lively *centro storico*, and the sparkling water along Ancona's concrete beach.

TRANSPORTATION

Trains: P. Rosselli. To: **Bologna** (2hr., 36 per day 1:26am-8:40pm, €11); **Milan** (3-5hr., 18 per day 1:59am-7:13pm, €34); Pesaro (45min., 38 per day 4:27am-10:35pm, €3.25); **Rimini** (1hr., 44 per day 1:32am-10:35pm, €4.80); **Rome** (3-4hr., 11 per day 3:36am-7:05pm, €13.80); **Venice** (5hr., 22 per day 2:34am-8:40pm, €27.50). Ticket office open daily 5:55am-8pm. AmEx/MC/V.

Ferries: Stazione Marittima (☎071 20 78 91). Call the day before departure to confirm; cancellations can occur. Reserve ahead in July and Aug., when prices jump by up to 30%. The following companies all accept AmEx, MC, and Visa:

Adria (☎50 21 16 21; www.adriaferries.com). To: **Durazzo, Albania** (18 hr., €70).

ANEK (☎071 20 72 346; www.anekitalia.com). To: **Igoumenitsa, GRC** (16hr.) and **Patras, GRC** (22hr., €60). 20% youth discount, 10% for families and those over 60; 30% for round-trips.

Jadrolinija (☎071 20 43 05; www.traghetti.amatori.com) To: **Split, HRV** (10hr.; €48).

SEM Maritime Co (SMC) (☎071 20 40 41; www.marittimamauro.it). To: **Split, HRV** (9hr.; €38-44).

SNAV (☎071 20 76 116; www.snav.it) To: **Spalato, HRV** (4hr.; €63).

THE FERRY FAIRY. To find all of the most up-to-date info on ferries from Ancona, check out www.doricaportservices.it.

✚🛈 ORIENTATION AND PRACTICAL INFORMATION

The train station is a 25min. walk from **Stazione Marittima**. Buses #1, 1/3, and 1/4 head along the port toward Stazione Marittima and up **Corso Stamira** to **Piazza Cavour**, the *centro*. Buy tickets (€1) at *tabaccherie*. For Stazione Marittima, disembark at **Piazza della Repubblica**, walk back toward the water, and turn right on the waterfront. Ancona has no central tourist office, but city info, maps, accommodation listings, and brochures can be found at V. Gramsci 2/A. (☎320 01 96 321. Open May-Oct. daily 10am-1pm and 4-8pm.)

Youth Center: InformaGiovani, C. Garibaldi 111 (☎071 54 958, ext. 8; www.anconagiovane.it). Offers 1hr. free Internet access. No Internet within 30min. of closing. Open M, W, and Sa 10am-12:30pm, Tu and Th-F 10am-12:30pm and 4:30-6:30pm.

Luggage storage: Stazione Marittima. Open daily 8am-8:30pm. €1 per bag per day for 1st 2 days; €2 per bag each day thereafter. Cash only.

Pharmacy: Farmacia Central, C. Mazzini 1 (☎071 20 27 46). Open daily 7:45am-12:30pm and 4:30-11pm. AmEx/MC/V.

Police: ☎071 22 881.

Hospital: Ospedale Regionale Umberto I, V. Conca-Torrette (☎071 59 61).

Internet: Informagiovani (see above). Internet cafes crowd the *centro*, charging around €1.50 per 2hr.

Post office: P. XXIV Maggio 2, off P. Cavour (☎071 50 12 260). Open M-F 8am-6:30pm and Sa 8am-12:30pm. **Postal Code:** 60100.

🛏 ACCOMMODATIONS

Ostello della Gioventù (HI), V. Lamaticci 7 (☎/fax 071 42 257), from the train station, cross the *piazza* and turn left. Quiet with convenient access to the train station. Clean, spacious rooms with wooden bunk beds. Kind, welcoming staff. Reception 6:30-11am and 4:30pm-midnight. Check-out 9:30am. Lockout 11am-4:30pm, but owner is occasionally flexible. Curfew midnight. Dorms €17. AmEx/MC/V. ❶

Albergo Gino, V. Flaminia 4 (☎/fax 071 42 179, 42 562, or 41 157), on the right side of the *piazza*. Simple, sunny rooms with private bath and TV. Breakfast included. Singles €35; doubles €47; triples €60; quads €80. AmEx/MC/V. ❸

Pensione Euro, C. Mazzini 142 (☎/fax 071 20 34 22). Central location. A cheery hallway leads to modestly furnished but spacious rooms with TV and large windows; most have private bath. Reception 5:30am-midnight. Singles €25; doubles €40-50; triples €60-69. Discount for longer stays. Cash only. ❷

Hotel Roma & Pace, V. G. Leopardi 1 (☎071 20 20 07 or 20 73 743). From P. Roma, turn left onto C. Garibaldi and take the 1st left onto V. Leopardi. With elegant, old-fashioned decor and modern comforts, this 19th-century building contains grandly furnished rooms, all with private bath, TV, A/C, and phone. Breakfast included. Internet access €6 per hr. Singles €59; doubles €95; triples €112; quads €124. AmEx/MC/V. ❹

🔳 FOOD

For groceries, hit up **DìperDì**, V. Matteotti 115 (open M-W and F 8:15am-1:30pm and 5-7:35pm, Th 8:15am-1:30pm, Sa 8:15am-1pm and 5-7:40pm. Cash only) or **STANDA**, C. C. Alberto 2, near the station (open daily 8am-9pm).

🔳 **La Cantineta**, V. Gramsci 1 (☎071 20 11 07). Locals crowd tightly packed tables. Don't be deceived by the average-looking exterior—a genial, welcoming staff offers large portions of regional cuisine like *stoccafisso* (cod; €14) or *tacchino* (turkey) *alla milanese* (€5) at reasonable prices. At least among locals, this secret is out—come early or be prepared to wait. Open M and W-Su noon-2:40pm and 7:30pm-midnight, Tu and Th noon-2:40pm. Primi €4-13. Secondi €5-15. Cover €1.50. AmEx/MC/V. ❷

🔳 **Pizzeria Papa**, C. Mazzini 60 (☎339 75 72 238). Smells of baking bread waft from this tiny pizzeria near the water. Pizza (€0.50-1.20; pies €4-5) comes loaded with toppings. A fresh, warm, and cheap favorite among locals. Calzones €1.50. Open daily in summer 9am-2pm and 5-9pm; in winter 10am-2pm and 4-8pm. Cash only. ❶

Roma & Pace, V. G. Leopardi 1 (☎071 52 278). Relaxed but social self-service restaurant. More extensive dinner menu has dishes liked grilled *sardoncini* on a bed of arugula (€9). Pizza €4-7.50. Primi €7. Secondi €9-13. AmEx/MC/V. ❸

Enopolis, C. Mazzini 7 (☎071 20 71 505; www.enopolis.it). Genial staff. Extensive regional and foreign wine selection. Downstairs, a labyrinth of stone hallways houses live music and rotating art exhibits. Organic *menù* features *spaghetti al farro con Adriatic Sarde*, *brodetto di pesce*, apple tart, and wine (€35). Primi €11. Secondi €16. Cover €2. Wine €5 per glass. Open Tu-Su 9:30am-midnight. AmEx/MC/V. ❹

👁 🔳 SIGHTS AND BEACHES

Above the city in Piazzale del Duomo stands the 🔳**Cattedrale di San Ciriaco**, a Romanesque church built above the remains of an early Christian basilica and an even earlier Roman temple to Venus. From P. Cavour, follow C. Mazzini to the port and turn right on V. Gramsci at P. Repubblica. Continue to P. del Senato and climb 247 steps to the cathedral. Look in the basement on the left for the tomb of S. Ciriaco and a rather gruesome view of the body; don't miss the fantastic views of Ancona and the Adriatic. (☎071 52 688. Open daily in summer 8am-noon and 3-7pm; in winter 8am-noon and 3-6pm. Free.) The 16th-century **Palazzo Ferretti** houses Le Marche's foremost archaeological museum, the **Museo Archeologico Nazionale delle Marche**, V. Ferretti 6, an impressive collection including the Ionian Dinos of Amandola, Greek pottery, and jewelry unearthed in the 1900s. From Palazzo Bosdari, continue toward the *duomo*. (☎071 20 26 02. Open Tu-Su 8:30am-7:30pm. €4, ages 18-25 €2, under 18 and over 65 free. Cash only.) From P. Roma, head down C. Garibaldi toward the port. Turn right at P. Repubblica onto V. Gramsci and go straight until you reach Ancona's art gallery, the **Pinacoteca Comunale Francesco Podesti**, in the Palazzo Bosdari, V. Pizzecolli 17. The gallery features works by the Camerte school including Crivelli's *Madonna con Bambino* and Titian's *Apparition of the Virgin*. The top floor features contemporary and 18th- and 19th-century paintings. (☎071 22 25 041. Open in winter Tu-F 9am-7pm, Sa 8:30am-6:30pm, Su 10am-1pm and 4-7pm; from mid-June to mid-Sept. M 9:30am-noon, Tu-Sa 9am-7pm, Su 10am-1pm and 4-7pm.€4.60, ages 16-25 €3.50, under 16 free. Cash only.)

Far from the port's industrial clutter, cool off at the unorthodox **Passetto Beach.** Sunbathers relax on the concrete sidewalk near ladders that drop directly into the sapphire waters. Above the beach, hundreds of stairs lead to the WWII memorial, **Monumento ai Caduti.** (P. IV Novembre. Take bus #1/4 from the station or from P. Cavour along Vle. della Vittoria to the shore. Free.)

NIGHTLIFE

Being the traveler's city that it is, Ancona doesn't offer quite as extensive evening activities as its coastal neighbors do. Crowds head to **Piazza Roma** for drinks and many bars and cafes have *aperitivo* buffets in the early evening.

Osteria Teatro Strabacco's, V. Oberdan 2/2A (☎071 56 748; www.strabacco.it). Since 1978, its motto has been *"fino all'ora del cappucino"*—finish at the cappucino hour—in other words, at breakfast. Eclectic restaurant lined with murals and twinkling lights. With 873 vintages, the snug *osteria* houses an alleged 10,000 bottles. Primi €7-10. Wine €5 per glass. Open Tu-Su noon-3pm and 7:15pm-3am. AmEx/MC/V.

Note di Vino, C. Mazzini 106 (☎393 05 99 972). Extensive wine list. Upbeat music plays at outdoor white tables that overlook a marble fountain. Wine €4-10 per glass. *Aperitivo* buffet starts at 6pm. Open Tu-Su 6pm-midnight. Cash only.

Classi Cafe, C. Mazzini 19 (☎071 20 30 00). Funky music and a hip crowd. Buffet at 6pm. Mixed drinks €6. Beer €3.50-4.50. Open daily 8am-late. Cash only.

FIND PASSETTO PASSÉ? If Passetto Beach doesn't satisfy your cravings for sand, the towns north and south of Ancona have excellent beaches. Ask at the tourist office. Keep in mind that the beaches to the north of Ancona are sandy but have murky water (still clean; just the effect of sand mixing with the water), while beaches to the south are rocky with clear water.

ASCOLI PICENO   ☎0736

According to legend, Ascoli Piceno (AS-co-lee pee-CHAY-no; pop. 55,000), "the city of a hundred towers," was founded by Sabines who were guided westward out of central Italy by a *picchio* (woodpecker), now the city's feathered mascot. By other accounts, Ascoli was the metropolis of the *Piceno*, a Latin tribe that controlled much of the coastal marshes and had the woodpecker as its totem. However it came to be, Ascoli offers charming stone streets and *piazze* that overflow with ancient towers and stately *palazzi*. As you savor the city's signature anise-flavored liqueur, *anisetta meletti*, you will undoubtedly also drink in some of the city's proud pre-Roman culture.

TRANSPORTATION

The **train station** is in Ple. della Stazione, at the end of V. Marconi. (Ticket counter open M-F 8am-noon and 3-6pm.) **Trains** run to San Benedetto (30min., M-Sa 16 per day 5:31am-8pm, €2.50) but require a transfer at the Porto d'Ascoli station from July to early September. **Buses** leave from Vle. Gasperi, behind the *duomo*. Start (☎0736 34 24 67 or 800 44 30 40; www.startspa.it) sells bus tickets at **Agenzia Cameli,** adjacent to the station. (☎0736 26 11 54. Ticket office open M-Sa 9am-12:45pm and 4-7pm, Su 9-9:30am and 4-4:30pm.) Buses run to Acquasanta Terme (1hr., 12 per day 5:10am-7:15pm, €2), Rome (3hr.; M-Sa 4 per day 3:20am-4:30pm, Su 4 per day 3:20am-5:30pm; €15), and San Benedetto (1hr.; M-Sa 34 per day 5:10am-11:35pm, Su 15 per day 7am-11:30pm; €2.50).

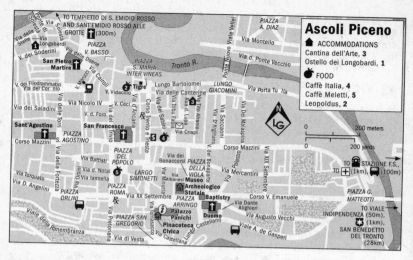

Ascoli Piceno

ACCOMMODATIONS
Cantina dell'Arte, 3
Ostello dei Longobardi, 1

FOOD
Caffè Italia, 4
Caffè Meletti, 5
Leopoldus, 2

⚔🛈 ORIENTATION AND PRACTICAL INFORMATION

From the **train station,** walk one block to Viale Indipendenza, turn right, and continue straight to Piazza Giacomo Matteotti. Turn right on **Corso Giuseppe Mazzini;** follow it into **Piazza del Popolo.** To reach the main bus stop from P. Matteotti, turn left onto Vle. de Gasperi; the stop is behind the *duomo.* Next to the *duomo* lies **Piazza Arringo,** which leads into **Via XX Settembre** and **Piazza Roma.** From there, **Via del Trivio** leads back to C. Giuseppe Mazzini and P. del Popolo. The **tourist office,** or **Centro Visitatori,** P. Arringo 7, offers maps, comprehensive guides (€5; in English, French, German, and Spanish), and info about festivals and transportation (☎0736 29 82 04; www.comune.ascolipiceno.it. Open daily 9:30am-6:30pm). Head to **Banca Nazionale del Lavoro,** C. G. Mazzini 160, on the corner with C. Trento e Trieste, for currency exchange. (☎0736 29 61. Open M-F 8:20am-1:20pm and 2:30-4pm, Sa 8:20am-11:50pm.) The **police** are at V. della Repubblica 8 (☎0736 35 691). **Farmacia Dott. Sebastiani,** at P. Roma 1, posts a 24hr. rotation. (☎0736 25 91 83. Open daily.) The **hospital** is on V. Monticelli (☎0736 35 81). **Interage,** V. Pietro Marucci 10, offers **Internet.** (☎0736 24 04 79. €3 per hr. Open M-Sa 9am-12:30pm and 3:30-7:45pm. Closed in summer Sa afternoon.) Ascoli's **post office,** V. Crispi 2, provides currency exchange. (☎0736 24 22 83. Open M-F 8am-6:30pm, Sa 8am-12:30pm.) **Postal Code:** 63100.

🏠🍴 ACCOMMODATIONS AND FOOD

The best deal in town is the pleasant ⭐**Ostello dei Longobardi (HI) ❶,** V. Soderini 26. In an 11th-century building, this quiet hostel offers 16 beds in two single-sex dorms. Ask friendly staffer Luigi for a tour of the haunted tower—one of the city's 192 towers. Feel free to borrow a bike, and be sure to sign the latest of a stack of guestbooks, with signatures dating back to 1949. From P. del Popolo, take C. Mazzini to P. Sant'Agostino, and turn right on V. delle Torri, then left on V. Soderini. (☎0736 26 18 62. Dorms €15. Cash only.) In the heart of town, **Cantina dell'Arte ❸,** V. della Lupa 8, is a picturesque hotel decorated with family photos. Follow C. Trento e Trieste to P. Santa Maria Inter Vineas; turn right on V. delle Canterine, then right on V. della Lupa. Rooms have marble floors, bath,

TV, and phone. (☎0736 25 56 20; www.cantinadellarte.it. Breakfast and either lunch or dinner included at restaurant. Reservations recommended. Singles €30; doubles €50; quads €70-75; quint with kitchen €100. AmEx/MC/V.)

Ascoli's cuisine relies on local produce—wild mushrooms, onions, capers, garlic, fennel, and anise—but still maintains low prices. *Olive all'ascolana* (olives stuffed with meat) is a true delight, not to be missed as an antipasto. Savory, anise-flavored cakes topped with powdered sugar are a holiday favorite, and the region's wines include *Rosso Piceno* and *Falerio dei Colli Ascolani*. **Leopoldus ❷**, V. Vidacilio 18, a gorgeous establishment, both looks and smells authentic. Their *olive all'ascolana* (€5) and lamb chops (€6) are equally delicious. (Pizza €4-7. Open Tu-Sa 12:20-3pm and 7:30pm-midnight. Weekend reservations are a must. AmEx/MC/V.) There's no better place to try local *anisetta meletti* (€3.50 per glass, €12.40 per bottle) than **Caffè Meletti ❶**, P. del Popolo 20, the 100-year-old cafe where Silvio Meletti introduced his now-famous liqueur. A variety of other anise-flavored sweets are also available, including bags of biscuits from €3. (☎0736 25 96 26; caffemeletti@virgilio.it. Open daily in summer 7:30am-midnight. AmEx/MC/V.) The fare at **Caffè Italia ❶**, V. C. Mazzini 184, is unparalleled, from vegetarian *panini* (with coffee and a glass of regional wine, €3.60), to delicious fruit salads (€2) which are always fresh. (☎393 957 7298. Open M-F 7am-8:30pm, Sa 7am-1pm and 6pm-midnight, Su 7pm-midnight.) An **open-air market** is in P. San Francesco, behind P. del Popolo. (Open M-Sa 8am-1pm.) **Tigre** supermarket is at P. Santa Maria Inter Vineas 1, at the end of C. Trento e Trieste. (Open M-W and F-Sa 8:30am-1:30pm and 5-8pm, Th 8:30am-1:30pm, Su 8:30am-1:30pm and 4:30-8pm. MC/V.)

🄶 SIGHTS

PINACOTECA CIVICA. Medieval and Renaissance works by Crivelli, Titian, Van Dyck, and Reni line the walls and frescoes cover the ceilings in the **Palazzo Arringo.** Check out lifelike *Il Pastorello*, a statue of a small boy from 19th-century Italy used to critique child labor. As you peruse Pietro Brenda's *I Rifuti dei Mari*: notice how the dead man's feet appear to shift subtly to point toward the viewer no matter his or her angle and how the waves seem to change size. *(To the left after exiting the tourist office in P. Arringo. Enter the garden courtyard, turn right immediately, then go left up the staircase. ☎ 29 82 13. Open daily 9am-1pm and 3-7pm. €5. Cash only.)*

DUOMO. Flanking one end of **Oration Square** in P. Arringo, Ascoli's travertine *duomo* combines Classical, Romanesque, and Baroque styles and holds work from the fifth to 18th centuries. A Roman basilica serves as the transept, topped by an eighth-century octagonal dome. Inside, freshly restored frescoes decorate the ceiling, while stairs on the left descend into the dim **Cripta di Sant'Emidio,** where shimmering mosaics and gorgeous sculptures adorn the tomb of Ascoli's first bishop and patron saint. According to legend, the head of the decapitated martyr is housed in Chiesa di Sant'Emidio alle Grotte (see next page), and the tomb holds only his body. *(Open daily 7am-2pm and 3:30-7:45pm. Free.)*

MUSEO ARCHEOLOGICO STATALE. Inside the 15th-century **Palazzo Panichi** is a three-floor museum with a collection of Greek and Roman artifacts, some excavated from the nearby city of San Benedetto del Tronto. The most impressive piece is a mosaic floor that depicts the face of a boy on one side and the face of an old man on the other. The museum also shows written examples of *Piceno*, the language of the area adapted from ancient Greek that predates Latin. *(P. Arringo 28. ☎ 25 35 62. Open Tu-Su 8:30am-7:30pm. €2, students €1.)*

PIAZZA DEL POPOLO. In what was once a Roman forum, the cafes, boutiques, and city offices at this vast *piazza* still buzz with activity. The pavement is made of travertine, an off-white mineral that has also been used to construct the city's major buildings and squares for over two millennia. The eastern end of the Romanesque-Gothic **Tempio di San Francesco** contains a wood crucifix, the only art saved from a 1535 fire. The church's "singing columns," low columns that flank the outer door on the V. del Trivio side, make a dull popping sound if you draw your hand across them. *(Open daily 8am-noon and 3:30-7:30pm. Free.)*

OTHER SIGHTS. From P. del Popolo, turn left onto C. Mazzini and right on V. del Trivio. Bear left on V. Cairoli, which becomes V. delle Donne, then pass the church on the left and follow the tiny pedestrian way, V. Solestà, as it curves right. V. Solestà leads to the single-arched **Ponte di Solestà**, one of Europe's tallest Roman bridges. Cross the bridge and take V. Rigante to the right. Take a right on Vle. M. Federici, left on V. Carso, and follow it under the roadway to **Chiesa di Sant'Emidio alle Grotte** (a 15min. walk from the bridge), whose Baroque facade is crafted from rock. Though closed to the public, the **catacombs** hold the remains of the first Ascoli Christians and, allegedly, Sant'Emidio's head.

❄ FESTIVALS

Insanity reigns during Ascoli's **Carnevale** on the days preceding Ash Wednesday. On the first Sunday in August, the **Tournament of Quintana** honors the city's patron Saint Emidio; 1500 local enthusiasts don medieval garb and onlookers watch man-on-dummy jousting and a torch-lit procession. The tournament culminates in a fierce competition in which the town's six neighborhoods battle for the coveted winner's banner, the *palio*. Ascoli is also renowned for its fireworks displays, especially those on August 4 and 5, the eve and celebration of Saint Emidio. On the 3rd Sunday of each month except July, an **Antique Market** unfolds in the *centro* from 8am-10pm. Stop by any tourist office or *tabaccheria* to pick up the free magazine, *What's Ap*, for an extensive list of summer events.

SAN BENEDETTO DEL TRONTO ☎0735

With over 7000 palm trees and nearly as many children playing under their waving fronds, San Benedetto (san beh-neh-DEHT-toh; pop. 50,000) draws summering Italian families and over 200,000 tourists. Don't come expecting cultural enrichment—the only *castelli* you'll find are made of sand.

⌐ TRANSPORTATION

The **train station** is at Vle. Gramsci 20/A. Ticket counter open daily 6:40am-8:35pm. (AmEx/MC/V.) **Trains** run to Ancona (1hr., 27 per day 12:25am-9:26pm, €4.50), Ascoli Piceno (30min., 14 per day 7:18am-9:50pm, €2.50), Bologna (3hr., 11 per day 12:39am-5:11pm, €17), and Milan (5-6hr., 6 per day 12:38am-4:42pm, €39). Start (☎0735 34 24 67 or 800 44 30 40; www.startspa.it) runs **buses** from the train station and Porto d'Ascoli to Ascoli Piceno (1hr.; 33 per day M-Sa 6am-12:40am, 15 per day Su 7am-12:40am; €2.50). Buy tickets at the train station. **Local buses** stop in front of the train station. Bus #2 departs across from the station (every 15-20min. 5:57am-12:45am, €0.80). Buy tickets from the newsstand in the train station. **Taxis** (☎0735 58 41 27) run from the train station.

✦ ⁊ ORIENTATION AND PRACTICAL INFORMATION

Buses #4 and #5 follow Vle. dello Sport, which traverses the heart of the city. **Viale Trieste**, the *lungomare* (promenade), undergoes various name changes. **Via Trento,** which becomes **Via Volta,** runs parallel to the *lungomare*.

Tourist Office: V. del Mare 203 (☎0735 75 17 98; www.rivieradellepalme.it). Take bus #2 to the rotunda and turn right. The office is in a brown building, facing the shore. Open June-Sept. M-Sa 9:30am-1:30pm and 4:30pm-midnight, Su 4:30pm-midnight.

Laundromat: Iris Lavanderie, V. dei Laureati 52. Self-service laundry and free detergent. Wash and dry €5. Open M-F 8:30am-1pm and 3:30-7:30pm, Sa 8:30am-1pm.

Police: P. Battisti 22 (☎0735 89 22 11).

24hr. Pharmacy: Farmacia Mercuri, Vle. de Gasperi 61/63, posts a 24hr. rotation outside. (☎0735 78 01 51. Open M-Sa 9am-1pm and 5-8pm.)

Hospital: Ospedale Civile (☎0735 79 31), on V. Manara.

Internet Access: Easy Connect, V. Roma 120 across from the train station. €1.50 per hr.; open daily 10am-10pm. Also at **ConoCafe,** V. dei Laureati 9 (☎0735 75 78 55). €1.50 per hr.; Open M-Th and Su 6am-10pm, F-Sa 6am-midnight.

Post Office: V. Roma 125 (☎0735 59 58 41). Outside train station. Currency exchange and an **ATM.** Open M-F 8am-1:30pm, Sa 8am-12:30pm. **Postal Code:** 63039.

▮▮ ACCOMMODATIONS AND CAMPING

Hotel Le Soleil, V. A. Volta, 119 (☎0735 81 768; www.lesoleil.it). Proximity to the beach and San Benedetto's *porto turistico*. Slightly narrow rooms come with a fridge, TV, bathroom, parking, bicycles, and a breakfast complete with fresh pastries and prosciutto. Singles €35-50; doubles €50-70; triples €65-85. MC/V. ❸

Hotel Ferrara, V. Cola di Rienzo 25 (☎/fax 0735 65 97 77). At the end of V. dei Laureati, turn right on V. Francesco Ferrucci. Walk 1 block and turn left onto V. Cola di Rienzo. Friendly owners and neat rooms with baths, TV, fridge, and a balcony. Breakfast, Internet, parking, and bicycle rental included. Open May-Oct. Singles €30-50; doubles €44-68; triples €56-85. Reception hours 7am-midnight. AmEx/MC/V. ❸

Ostello IPSIA, Vle. dello Sport 60 (☎0735 78 12 63). From the train station, take bus #4 or 5. 10min. from the beach. A dormitory during the year, only open July-Aug. Each room has three beds and a bath. Breakfast included. Min. 3-night stay. Dorms €25. ❷

Camping Seaside, V. dei Mille 125 (☎0735 65 95 05; www.seaside.it). Take bus #2, or walk from Vle. Rinascimento, turning right onto V. A. Negri and bear left on V. dei Mille. Has a pool, market, and restaurant. Open June-September. €7-10 per adult, €3-5 per child ages 3-7, €12-18 per site, €2.50-5 per car. Hot showers free. MC/V. ❶

▮▮ FOOD AND NIGHTLIFE

When hunger strikes, head to one of the beachside food spots that turn into *discoteche* by night. There's an **open-air market** on V. Montebello (Tu and F mornings). **Tigre** supermarkets are everywhere; find one at V. dei Laureati 41a. (Open in summer M-Sa 8am-1:30pm and 4:30-8:30pm, Su 8:30am-1pm. AmEx/MC/V.)

Alex, on the *lungomare* at *concessione* #87 (☎0735 75 80 21; www.chaletalex.it). Offers comfortable, beachside seating and a seafood *menù*, including antipasto, primo, secondo, salad, wine, water, and coffee for €20. *Discoteca* open nightly until 1am. Mixed drinks €5-8. Open Easter-Nov. noon-1am. Kitchen closes 10pm. AmEx/MC/V. ❸

Americo Village, on the *lungomare* at *concessione* #88, (☎0735 65 55 25 www.americovillage.com). This Porto d'Ascoli chalet offers offers a restaurant, *gelateria*, cabins, and a private beach with a volleyball court. Transforms nightly into a bar with themed patio lounges. Beer €2.50. Mixed drinks €5-6. Wine €4-5. ❸

Bagni Andrea, on the *lungomare* at *concessione* #8, (☎0736 83 834; www.bagniandrea.com.). Offers a romantic dining experience and specializes in seafood. Antipasti from €15. Primi €10. Secondi €10-18. Th-Su piano bar 10pm. Open daily 1-3pm and 8:30-11pm. Late-night Latin and swing disco closes at 4am. Reservations recommended Sa-Su night. AmEx/MC/V. ❹

Birlandia, V. dei Laureti 60/c (☎0735 65 53 34; www.birlandia.tk). Don't miss out on the house beer (€3) and pizza (€5.50). Boasts a 30,000 bottle cap collection on the ceiling and close to 200 beers from all over the world. Owner Cosimo challenges any patron to drink his secret mixed drink *"Il Cosimino"* for a photo on the pub's wall. Beer bottles €4.50; tap €3. Pizza €4.50-6.20. Open Tu-Su 8pm-3am. €1 off pints and bottles on Thursdays, plus €3 cocktails. MC/V. ❶

Medusa, V. Trieste 13, gives this restaurant and bar well-deserved prominence early along the *lungomare*. On weekend nights Medusa blasts the loudest music for those who like to live it up on the 2-story beach lounge. Open daily mid-June to Sept. 9am-midnight. Mixed drinks €3-7. Wine €1. ❸

🏖 BEACHES

San Benedetto's palm-lined beaches and *lungomare* cover a lot of distance, starting with **Beach #1** near the train station and continuing through **Beach #114,** which is actually in Porto d'Ascoli. Each number corresponds to a *concessione,* the business in front of each beach. The free beaches, or *spiaggie libere,* in San Benedetto are superb, so don't waste money paying for private ones. Free **Beach #13,** located next to chalet Claudia, is one of the widest, and has both a large playground and an information booth in front of it. The most popular choice by far is the free beach at the **Giardino delle Palme,** with an inviting park and shady palm trees. The spot with generally the fewest people is all the way at the end of the promenade. Numerous cabanas rent storage cabins (from €5.20) and umbrellas (from €6). From San Benedetto's train station, cross the street and take bus #2 to the seaside, or turn left on V. Gramsci and left again on V. Monfalcone toward the beach. Vle. Trieste, the *lungomare,* intersects V. Monfalcone and runs along the shore, changing from Vle. Marconi to Vle. Europa/Scipioni, and then to Vle. Rinascimento. From start to finish the *lungomare* is about an hour's walk, or a leisurely 20min. bicycle ride.

ABRUZZO AND MOLISE

The foothills of the Apennine mountains are home to medieval fortresses, Roman rubble, and sprawling wilderness. The people of this region have been shepherds since the Bronze Age, and only in the last half-century has their way of life begun to transform. Millennia-old shepherds' paths weave through the countryside, and the villages sustain a sleepy lifestyle largely similar to that of their ancestors. About two hours from the Eternal City and still predominantly untouched by tourism, these highlands offer natural beauty and a unique retreat from bustling urban life. A single region until they split in 1963, Abruzzo (ah-BROOTS-oh) and Molise (mo-LEEZ-eh) lie at the juncture of Northern and Southern Italy. Abruzzo offers crystal lakes, lush pines, and unique wildlife, especially in its national park. The smaller Molise, inhabited long ago by Samnite highlanders, is home to wondrous ruins, medieval festivals, and especially flavorful food. These regions may not fit in with the stereotypical image of Italy, but if you seek an unexpected twist on *la dolce vita*, look no farther.

HIGHLIGHTS OF ABRUZZO AND MOLISE

GLIMPSE herds of wild horses on the Gran Sasso d'Italia (p. 550).

EXPLORE Ovid's homeland of Sulmona (p. 551).

SET UP CAMP in Abruzzo National Park after an arduous day of hiking (p. 554).

ESCAPE to Puglia to bathe in the azure waves of the Tremiti Islands (p. 561).

L'AQUILA
☎0862

As the story goes, in 1254, 99 lords from 99 castles banded together to erect L'Aquila ("The Eagle"; LA-kwee-la; pop. 65,000), Abruzzo's capital. Some historians claim the city plan mimics that of Jerusalem, perhaps a result of Frederick II's desire to create a new seat for Catholic Christianity following the decline of Rome. Dubbed the "Salzburg of the South," this city has rediscovered its charm, echoing its glory days now that over 40,000 students crowd its streets and hikers ascend its nearby mountains.

⌐ TRANSPORTATION

The **train station** (☎0862 41 92 90) is on the outskirts of town. (Ticket office ☎0862 41 28 08. Open M-Sa 6:15am-8:15pm, Su 7am-2pm.) **Trains** go to Sulmona (1hr., 11 per day 6:23am-8:47pm, €4.50) and Terni (2hr., 11 per day 6:15am-8:04pm, €6). L'Aquila has two **bus** systems: blue ARPA regional buses and orange municipal buses. ARPA buses (☎0862 199 166 952) stop at the station near P. Duomo and go to: Avezzano (50min., M-Sa 38 per day 5:50am-8:30pm, €4.90); Pescara (1hr., M-Sa 20 per day 6am-9:10pm, €7.50); Rome (1hr., M-Sa 33 per day 4:40am-8pm, €9.10); Sulmona (40min., M-Sa 6 per day 6:20am-7:15pm, €4.50). The yellow **municipal buses** stop at AMA markers and serve surrounding towns and sights. (☎0862 31 98 57; www.ama.laquila.it. One-way €0.90, 1hr. €1.10, 1-day pass €2.10.) Tickets are available at *tabaccherie*, newsstands, bars, and the bus

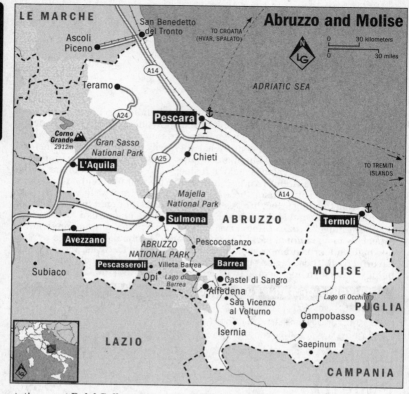

Abruzzo and Molise

station, past P. del Collemaggio on V. Giacomo Caldora. A subway runs from the station to P. del Duomo. Find **taxis** (☎0862 22 115) at the bus station.

⁂ 🗽 ORIENTATION AND PRACTICAL INFORMATION

Take bus #M11, 5, or 8 from the train station to **Via XX Settembre** to reach the *centro*. On foot, follow signs to *"Fontana delle 99 Cannelle"* to the right and hike 2km uphill. C. Federico II becomes **Corso Vittorio Emanuele II**, the main street which stretches between **Piazza del Duomo**, the heart of L'Aquila's *centro storico*, in the south, and the **Castello Cinquecentesco** and the **Fontana Luminosa** in the north. Beyond P. del Duomo, the street continues as Corso Federico II until reaching the gardens of the **Villa Comunale** and **Via XX Settembre**. Pick up a map at the tourist office; L'Aquila's often unlabeled streets are difficult to navigate.

Tourist Office: APT, V. XX Settembre 8 (☎0862 22 306). Stocks free maps. Open M-Sa 9am-1pm and 3-6pm, Su 9am-1pm. There is also an office in the front of P. del Duomo, (☎0862 23 021; www.centrostorico.laquila.it). Open daily 10am-9pm.

Police: at V. del Beato Cesidio.

Pharmacy: right next to the *duomo*. Open 9am-1pm and 4:30-8pm.

Internet Access: Duomo.net, V. Cimino 25. Opposite the *duomo* on the *piazza*. Open M-Sa 9am-10pm, Su 4pm-10pm. Internet €3 per hr., students and over 65 €2.50.

Post Office: in P. del Duomo (☎0862 63 71). Exchanges currency. Open M-F 8am-6:30pm, Sa 8am-12:30pm. **Postal Code:** 67100.

ACCOMMODATIONS

Centro Spiritualita Sant'Agostino, V. Tre Spighe 9 (☎347 490 5672). From P. Duomo, take C. V. Emanuele to the Fontana Luminosa, and turn left on V. Tre Spighe. The monastery was built in 1375, but guests stay in a modern building with a garden, TV and reading room, and communal kitchen. Breakfast included. €25 per person. Cash only. ❷

Casa Ospitalita' San Giuseppe, P. Pasquale Paoli 12 (☎0862 42 05 66 or 41 07 55). Offers similar accommodations to the Centro Spiritualita Sant'Agostino. €25-30 per person. Reservations required. Cash only. ❷

Porto Rivera Hostel, Ple. della Stazione 27 (☎0862 29 56 85; www.portariverahostel. it). Clean, well-lit rooms have full bath, phone, TV, and minibar. Wheelchair-accessible. Breakfast included. Singles €40; doubles €55; triples €74; quads €87. MC/V. ❸

Bed and Breakfast "da Charlie," V. Monte Brancastello 22 (☎347 85 97 938). A 10min. ride on bus #79 or 81 from La Fontana Luminosa to "Cianfrano". Named after the owner's dog. Offers clean rooms and cheap food with a great city view. Breakfast included. Reservations required. Singles €25; doubles €40-45. ❷

FOOD

Torrone, a honey and almond nougat, is L'Aquila's specialty. Find everything from fresh fruit and cured meats to clothes at the busy **market** in P. del Duomo. (Open M-Sa 8am-noon.) A **STANDA supermarket**, C. Federico II 1, is two blocks from V. XX Settembre. Enter at the corner of V. Monteguelfi and V. Sant'Agostino. (☎0862 26 482. Open M-Sa 8am-9pm. AmEx/MC/V.)

La Stella Alpina, V. Crispomonti 19 (☎0862 41 31 90). 2nd to none. Lunch special (€7) buys pizza and a drink. Primi €5-7. Open Tu-Su noon-3pm and 7:30-midnight. ❶

Darkover, V. dell'Arcivescovado 17 (☎0862 40 60 20). The cool, maze-like interior is decorated with mythical Chinese characters, but Darkover maintains its Italian flavor. Try the specialty, *arrosticini* (lamb kebab; €5). Pizza €4-8. Open daily 7:30-midnight. ❷

L'Insalata Ricca, C.V. Emanuele 81 (☎0862 26 642; www.linsalataricca.it). Nearly 50 fresh, unique salads (€4-7.50). A nightly grand buffet (€7) is serves typical *abruzzese* produce. Antipasti €3-7. Primi €5.50-7. Secondi €8-16. MC/V. ❷

Caffè Europa, C. V. Emanuele II 38 (☎333 41 47 377). Chocolate-drizzled *caffè macchiato* (€8-10) are worth a try. Open 6:30am-9:30pm. Cash only. ❶

SIGHTS

BASILICA DI SANTA MARIA DI COLLEMAGGIO. At the request of Pietro da Marrone (later Pope and Saint Celestine V), L'Aquila began constructing this church in 1287. The pink-and-white checkered facade is the symbol of the Knights Templar, a group with origins in medieval times that is now linked to the Freemasons. Notice the number eight and the serpent made by circles on the floor design, both Templar symbols. Despite its controversial cross, the basilica's claim to fame is its **Holy Door**—the first of only seven in the world. The door is opened only once a year on August 28th; those who walk through it are said to have their sins absolved. *(From P. del Duomo, take C. Federico I past V. XX Settembre or the tram to the bus station and turn left onto V. di Collemaggio after Villa Comunale. Open in summer daily 8am-12:30pm and 3-8pm; in winter hours vary. Modest dress required. Free.)*

CHIESA DI SAN BERNARDINO. Built in 1454 and restored after an earthquake in 1703, San Bernardino peers over the mountains south of L'Aquila. The interior boasts four beautiful ceiling paintings and the tomb of San Bernardino, complete with a Templar cross. Years ago, schoolchildren from the saint's hometown of Siena would make a pilgrimage to L'Aquila on May 20 to bring oil to light the lamp in front of the church's mausoleum for the rest of the year. *(To reach both the stairway and the church, walk down V. S. Bernardino from C. V. Emanuele II. Open daily 7:30am-noon and 3:30-8pm. Modest dress required. Free.)*

CASTELLO CINQUECENTESCO. In the 16th century, Spanish viceroy Don Pedro da Toledo built the castle at the end of C. V. Emanuele II, to defend himself against the rebelling *aquilesi*. Never attacked, the *castello* is more active today in its role as the **Museo Nazionale di Abruzzo,** showcasing Roman sarcophagi, Renaissance tapestries, and a million-year-old mammoth skeleton, discovered locally in 1954. *(Located at V. Colecchi 1.* ☎ *0862 63 31; www.psaelaquila.it. Open Tu-Su 8:30am-7:30pm. €4; ages 18-25 €2; EU university students, under 18, and over 65 free.)*

FONTANA DELLE 99 CANNELLE. Commissioned in 1272, water streams from the mouth of 99 unique heads at L'Aquila's oldest monument. *(Take C. Federico II and bear right on V. XX Settembre. Follow the small V. Borgo Rivera down the hill.)*

▶ DAYTRIPS FROM L'AQUILA

GRAN SASSO D'ITALIA. The snow-capped Gran Sasso d'Italia ("The Rock of Italy"), the highest mountain ridge within Italy's borders, looms 12km north of L'Aquila. Take a funicular midway up the Sasso (and above the tree line) to a flat plain, **Campo Imperatore,** home to herds of wild horses, shepherds, never-ending landscapes, and a hotel built to imprison Mussolini. On a clear day, you can see both of Italy's coasts from the **Corno Grande,** the highest peak in the range at 2912m. The trail map (€8), available at the Club Alpino Italiano, newsstands in town, and at the base of the mountain, is useful for planning hikes. *Sentieri* (paths) are marked by difficulty, and only the more taxing routes reach the top. The peaks are snowy from September to June, when only experienced mountaineers should venture all the way up. In winter, Gran Sasso teems with **skiers.** The trails around the funicular are among the most difficult, offering one 4000m and several 1000m drops. Ten trails descend from the funicular and the two lifts. Purchase a weekly pass at the *biglietteria* at the base of the funicular. **Campo Felice,** at nearby Monte Rotondo, has 16 lifts, numerous trails of varying difficulty, and a ski school. *(In summer a funicular ascends the 1008m to Campo Imperatore, making Sasso an easy afternoon excursion from L'Aquila, although driving offers a far more picturesque ride than the 10min. funicular. The funicular is closed during parts of June and Oct.* ☎ *0862 60 61 43. Every hr. 8:30am-5pm, €7. Trails start at the upper funicular station. Contact Club Alpino Italiano at* ☎ *0862 24 342 or www.cai.it for current conditions. For info on mountain guides, inquire at the tourist office or Club Alpino Italiano. To reach Campo Felice from L'Aquila, take yellow bus #76 or blue shuttle M6 from the bus station. 30min., 12 per day, €1. Buy tickets at tabaccherie or the station. For ski info, contact Campo Felice at* ☎ *0862 60 61 43. Lift tickets €14-25. Ski rentals around €10.)*

OTHER DAYTRIPS. If skiing is not on your itinerary, **ARPA buses** run to centuries-old towns within 50km of L'Aquila. Ask at the bus station for the most up-to-date schedules. Buses to Castel del Monte (40km, €3.50) stop in medieval towns like Santo Steffano di Sessanio (25km), where the Medici family built an economic stronghold for wool trade in the 15th century. Their legacy is manifested in the grand **Torre Medicea** that still stands today in Santo Steffano. The same bus also stops in Calascio (30km), where the millenary Norman castle **La Rocca Calascio** stands at an altitude of 1500m. Take AMA buses to the town of Stiffe and gaze at the stalactite-filled **Grotte di Stiffe.** *(*☎ *0862 86 142; www.grottestiffe.*

it. Open 10am-1pm and 3-6pm. Complex has two museums, picnic grounds, and a bathing area on Lago di Sinizzo.) Buses to San Vittorino (7km west) take you near the **Sitio Amiternum**, an archaeological site with a first-century Roman theatre. AMA Bus #16 goes to Fossa, where you can walk through a necropolis. Near Campo Felice is Rocca di Mezzo, the town with the greatest number of hotels and restaurants in the **Sirente Velino Regional Park.** A park information office is found here at the Piazza dell'Oratorio. *(☎0862 91 61 25; www.parcosirentevelino.it.)*

SULMONA
☎0864

Hidden deep in Abruzzo's Peligna Valley, medieval Sulmona (sool-MO-nah; pop. 26,000) is encircled by the hulking Apennines. The charming inhabitants of this small town churn out *confetti* (Sulmona's signature candy) and profess pride in their famous native son, the poet Ovid (43 BC-AD 17). The letters "SMPE," adorned on Sulmona's streets and inscribed on its buildings, are shorthand for the poet's famous proclamation, *"Sulmo mihi patria est"* ("Sulmona is my homeland"). A stroll around the public gardens, a hike in the surrounding mountains, or an amble through nearby hamlets are excellent afternoon diversions when the town shuts down for *siesta.*

▐ TRANSPORTATION

Trains: Station (☎0864 34 293), 2km outside the city, 30min. by foot from the *centro.* Serves Rome-Pescara and Carpione-L'Aquila-Terni lines. To: **Avezzano** (1hr., 3 per day 6:30am-2:03pm, €3.50); **L'Aquila** (1hr., 7 per day 6:54am-8:45pm, €3.40); **Naples** (4hr., 4 per day 6:32am-3:44pm, €14-16); **Pescara** (1hr., 15 per day 6:23am-9:30pm, €3.40); **Rome** (1-2hr., 7 per day 5:55am-8:10pm, €7-12). Bus A (5:30am-9:30pm, €0.70) runs from the *centro.* Return bus departs from the public gardens.

Buses: ARPA (☎0864 20 91 33) runs from its main stop at the hospital past Porta Napoli to Castel di Sangro in Abruzzo National Park (1hr.; 10 per day 6:40am-6:10pm, reduced service Su; €4, buy ticket on bus).

Taxis: ☎0864 31 747 from the *centro* or ☎0864 31 446 from the train station.

▐▐ ORIENTATION AND PRACTICAL INFORMATION

Viale Stazione runs from the train station to Sulmona proper (2km). In town, it becomes **Viale Roosevelt** and continues past the public gardens where it becomes **Corso Ovidio,** the main thoroughfare. C. Ovidio runs past **Piazza XX Settembre** (with the statue of Ovid), and **Piazza Garibaldi** (with the medieval aqueduct), and then exits the *centro storico* through **Porta Napoli.** From P. XX Settembre, the northbound **Via de Nino** becomes **Via Giovanni Pansa** as it reaches the **Ponte Capograssi.**

Tourist Office: APT tourist office, C. Ovidio 208 (☎/fax 0864 53 276). Multilingual staff. Free city maps and hotel, B&B, and restaurant listings. Club Italiano Alpino maps (€5-7) and guided **tours** of the countryside. Open M-Sa 9am-1pm and 4-7pm, Su 9am-1pm. **UST tourist office,** across the street in Palazzo dell'Annunziata (☎0864 21 02 16; www.comune.sulmona.aq.it). Helpful English-speaking staff. Detailed hiking info, train and bus schedules, Club Alpino Italiano maps, free city maps, and references for local mountain guides. Open daily 9am-1:30pm and 4-8pm.

Police: ☎0864 35 661.

Internet: .COM, C. Ovidio 90 (☎0864 56 491). €3 per hr. Open daily 9am-1pm and 4-8pm.

Bike Rental: V. G. Pansa 15 (☎0864 32 324). €9 per day; must return by 8pm. Open M-Sa 10am-1pm and 4:30-7pm.

NO WORK, ALL PLAY

‍E INDULGENT KNIGHT

‍While the Giostra Cavalleresca ‍(see opposite page) is easily Sul-‍mona's claim to fame, the weeks ‍leading up to the joust have their ‍"fare" share of traditional treats ‍as well. The weekend before, the ‍town celebrates La Panarda, a ‍24-course feast featuring typical ‍abbruzese cuisine and an endless ‍flow of local wine.

When the sun sets over a dec-‍orated piazza, guests are invited ‍to unbuckle their belts and enjoy ‍their portate (dishes), surrounded ‍by Renaissance entertainment. ‍Flag shows, dances, and live ‍music accompany the seemingly ‍interminable banquet. As the ‍night progresses, waiters in cos-‍tume serve a bounty of seasonal ‍fruits, cold cuts, Pecorino cheese, ‍hearty soups, handmade pastas, ‍and succulent roasted lamb.

In antiquity, such joyous feasts ‍were held in honor of good har-‍vests and weddings. Recently, ‍Panarde-goers have indulged in ‍as many as 77 portate. The eat-‍ing pace is always slow and each ‍dish is more delectable than the ‍previous. Skip lunch and bring ‍the whole family—this feast typi-‍cally lasts from 8pm-2am and is ‍enough to feed an entire cavalry.

Contact Associazione Cultural ‍Sestiere Porta Manaresca (☎ ‍348 92 36 896) or the Sulmona ‍UST tourist office (☎/fax 0864 53 ‍276). Reservations recommended ‍month ahead. Banquet €45.

Post Office: in P. Brigata Maiella (☎0864 62 47 292). **ATM** available. Open M-F 8am-6:30pm, Sa 8am-12:30pm. **Postal Code:** 67039.

▶ ACCOMMODATIONS

Make reservations for July and August stays, since this region is popular with mountain bikers and hikers. The tourist office provides a list of B&Bs.

▣ **Hotel Italia,** P. Salvatore Tommasi 3 (☎0864 52 308). Family-run, vine-covered former *palazzo*. Medieval-inspired ambiance. 27 antique-filled rooms, some with balconies and mountain views. Singles €25, with bath €33; doubles €43/54. Cash only. ❷

Bed and Breakfast "La Dimora", C. Ovidio 238 (☎0864 95 02 98; www.bandbladimora.com). Well located 15th-century *palazzo*. 4 rooms on 3rd floor come with A/C, free Wi-Fi, and breakfast. Owner Oscar is eager to help trekkers arrange tours or plan excursions in Abruzzo. One of Sulmona's best. Singles €30-40; doubles €60-90; triples €80-110. Cash only. ❸

Albergo Stella, V. Panfilo Mazara 18 (☎0864 52 653; www.hasr.it), off C. Ovidio. Service-oriented staff and spacious, pleasantly decorated rooms with bath, phone, and TV. *Enoteca* connected to the restaurant. Breakfast included. Free Internet access. Singles €40-50; doubles €70-80. AmEx/MC/V. ❹

▶ FOOD

Before the *confetti* after party, you'll need something substantive; don't worry, Sulmona doesn't disappoint in this area either. A morning **market** takes place in P. Garibaldi (W and Sa). Buy basics at the **CONAD supermarket** on V. Papa Giovanni XXIII, 22. (Turn right after crossing Ponte Capograssi. Open 8am-8:30pm. MC/V.)

▣ **Ristorante Al Quadrivio,** V. Odorisio 4 (☎0864 55 533), off V. Panfilo Mazara. The best-kept secret for traditional *Abruzzese* cuisine. Try the *budino ubriaco* (bread pudding soaked in *ratafia* liqueur; €2.50). Handmade pasta €6. Primi €6. Secondi from €7. Open M-Sa 7:30-11pm, Su noon-3pm and 7:30-11pm. MC/V. ❷

Hostaria dell'Arco, V. D'Eramo, 58 (☎0864 21 05 53). For a relaxed, intimate experience, head to the cheapest restaurant in town that still offers quality, traditional dishes. The lamb (€7) is delicious. Vegetable antipasti buffet €8. Dessert €2-3. Open M-Sa 1-2:30pm and 8-11:30pm, Su 1-2:30pm. AmEx/MC/V. ❷

Ristorante Gino, P. Plebiscito 12, (☎0864 52 289). Beloved by locals. Simple dishes made with farm-fresh ingredients. Try *risotto* (€7), made with delectable *pecorino* cheese. Primi €7. Secondi €9-12. Open M-Sa 12:30-2:45pm. MC/V. ❸

👁 SIGHTS

CATTEDRALE DI SAN PANFILO. The center of this Romanesque-Gothic church was built 1000 years ago on the ruins of a temple dedicated to Apollo and Vesta. Its crypt contains 14th-century frescoes. *(At the end of the Villa Communale.)*

CHIESA DELLA SANTISSIMA ANNUNZIATA. Adjacent to the cherub-decorated church, a 15th-century Gothic *palazzo* houses the UST tourist office (p. 551) and a very small **museum** presenting rare local Renaissance goldwork. There is also a collection of wood statues from local churches. *(From the public gardens, follow C. Ovidio to the church.* ☎*0864 21 27 11. Open July-Aug. Tu-F 9am-1pm, Sa-Su 6-8:30pm and 9:30-11pm; Sept.-June Tu-Sa 9am-1pm. €1.)* In the same building, the **Museo Civico** features the intact ruins and artifacts of an ancient Roman house. *(Open Tu-Su 9am-1pm and 3-7pm. Free.)*

PIAZZA GARIBALDI. The colossal *piazza* surrounds Renaissance-era **Fontana del Vecchio,** which flows with mountain water channeled from a nearby **medieval aqueduct** that is still intact. With the towering Apennines as its backdrop, P. Garibaldi is a favorite hangout, particularly in the evening.

PELINO FACTORY. When you feel the *confetti*-induced sugar-high start to wear off, replenish your supply of these colored, sugar-coated almonds right from the source. The Pelino family has been making *confetti* since 1783 with traditional machinery; some of it is displayed in the free museum. The candy's universal appeal is evident in pictures of St. Pio and prior popes eating *confetti* shaped like religious icons. *(V. Stazione Introdaqua 55. Turn right after Porta Napoli onto V. Trieste, continue 1km down the hill as it becomes V. Stazione Introdaqua, and enter the Pelino building on the left.* ☎*0864 21 00 47; www.pelino.it. Open M-Sa 8am-12:15pm and 3-6:30pm.)*

🎐 FESTIVALS

The city itself dons medieval garb during the last week of July for the **Giostra Cavalleresca di Sulmona,** when beacon-bearing knights ride figure-eights around P. Garibaldi. Each knight's crest represents one of the seven *borghi* (neighborhoods) of medieval Sulmona. Purchase a seated ticket (€5-12) from the ticket office (☎0864 340 51 846 26; open daily 10am-12:30pm and 5-8pm) in the Rotunda San Francesco, off P. Garibaldi, or stand on tip-toe in the crowd to watch for free. In preparation for the big event, the *borghi* host public festivals on June weekends. The first weekend of August brings the **Giostra Cavalleresca di Europa,** which features international knights (tickets €3-8).

🥾 HIKING

The mountains of **Majella National Park** (also spelled "Maiella") tower over Sulmona. The park's headquarters (☎0871 40 851) are in **Guardiagrele.** From the *centro,* several trails are easily accessible by ARPA bus or on foot. The Sulmona tourist offices have info on the capricious bus schedules; keep mid-afternoon service gaps in mind. High on the cliffs, visit the cave retreat of the saintly hermit who became Pope Celestine V, the only pope to renounce his post. It's a fairly easy hike (round-trip 1hr.) from the town of Badia, which is accessible by bus from Sulmona's public gardens (20min.; 11 per day 7:35am-7:40pm, reduced service Sa-Su; €1, purchase tickets at *tabaccherie*). Several longer routes can be reached from Campo di Giove, accessible by bus from Sulmona (25min.; 4 per day 6:30am-6pm, reduced service Sa-Su; €2.20). For hiking info,

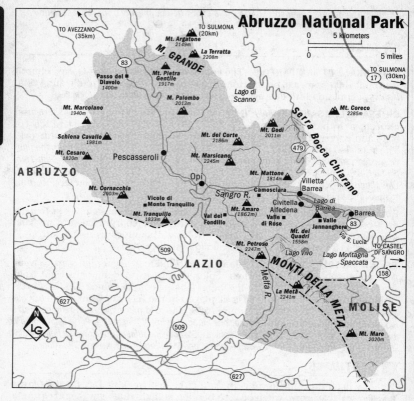

Abruzzo National Park

consult the UST tourist office (p. 551) and the **Club Alpino Italiano** (☎0842 10 635) for maps (€5-7). The difficulty levels in the Club Alpino Italiano guide refer to mountaineering experience, not hiking experience—so hikes of "moderate difficulty" may be challenging for those not used to mountain climbing. Take advantage of buses since trailheads are tough to find on foot; ask the driver to let you off directly at the trailhead.

ABRUZZO NATIONAL PARK

Parco Nazionale d'Abruzzo, Lazio, e Molise contains the highest peaks in the Apennines, which provide spectacular views of lush woodlands and crystal-clear lakes as frigid as they are pristine. The park's 44,000 hectares bristle with wildlife. Grazing horses, white *abruzzese* sheep-dog packs, herds of *chamois* (hoofed, goat-like animals with horns), and aloof *marsicano* brown bears are the current proprietors of abandoned castles and pre-Roman ruins. This immaculate refuge is interrupted by only five towns: Barrea, Civitella Alfedena, Opi, Pescasseroli, and Villetta Barrea. Enter the park from Castel di Sangro in the south, or from Avezzano in the northeast. Pescasseroli, the park's administrative center and largest town, provides the best base for exploration. The other four towns are tiny and a bit uneventful—especially Barrea and Civitella

ABRUZZO
AND MOLISE

Alfedena—but this does not detract from their beauty. Though the wild creatures and landscapes are diverse, the park's human inhabitants are unified in their unfailing warmth and generosity.

TRANSPORTATION AND PRACTICAL INFORMATION

Trains run from Avezzano to Pescara (2-3hr., 7 per day 6:13am-8:10pm, €6.90), Rome (2hr., 13 per day 4am-8:50pm, €6), and Sulmona (1hr., 10 per day 6:13am-8:10pm, €3.90). An ARPA **bus** (☎0863 26 561 or 0863 22 921) runs from Avezzano through the park to Castel di Sangro on the other side (2hr., M-Sa 5 per day 6:40am- 7pm, €5.20), making five stops en route: Pescasseroli (1hr., €3.90); Opi (1hr., €4.20); Villetta Barrea (2hr., €4.20); Civitella Alfedena (2hr., €4.20); Barrea (2hr., €4.40). Buses also run to Pescasseroli from Rome (3hr., 7:45am, one-way €14). All services are reduced or nonexistent on Sunday.

AVEZZANO
Conveniently located on the edge of the park, Avezzano is well-positioned near train stations serving other regions and bus stations serving the park. The **post office** is next to the train station. (Open M-F 8am-1:30pm, Sa 8:30am-12:30pm.)

PESCASSEROLI
Tourist Office: Centro Accoglienza Turistici, Vico Consultore 1 (☎0863 91 13 242; www.parcoabruzzo.it). Sells essential park map (€6). Open daily 10am-1pm and 3-7pm. Buses stop in front of the **IAT Info Office,** Viale Principe di Napoli (☎0863 91 04 61; www.pescasseroli.net). Provides info on buses, trekking excursions, lodgings, and restaurants. Open daily 9am-1pm and 3-6pm.

Police: ☎0863 91 07 16.

State Forest Division: Call ☎1515 in case of an environmental emergency.

Bank: next to IAT (☎0863 91 951). Open M-F 8:25am-1:25pm and 2:40-4:10pm.

Public Toilets: V. Sorgenti, near the IAT. Free.

Pharmacy: Farmacia del Parco, P. V. Emanuele 12 (☎0863 91 07 53). Posts a 24hr. rotation. Open M-W and F-Su 9am-1pm and 4:30-8pm.

Guardia Medica: call ☎0863 91 06 75.

Internet Access: Punto Internet is at I Traversa di Fiume Sangro 6 (☎0863 91 10 64). €2.50 per 30min., €4 per hr. Open daily 9:30am-1pm and 4-8pm.

Post Office: V. Piave 1/A (☎0863 91 07 31), in front of the IAT office. Open M-F 8am-1:30pm, Sa 8am-noon. **Postal Code:** 67032.

> **BUS-TED!** Not all ARPA buses passing through Abruzzo National Park stop at all 5 towns in the park. All buses stop at Pescasseroli, but if you are trying to reach Opi or Civitella Alfedena, get a schedule from the tourist office in Pescasseroli, and confirm the destination with your driver before boarding the bus. A better option is renting a car. Be sure to pick up the free *Guide to Abruzzo's Hidden Wonders* at the park's tourist office.

ACCOMMODATIONS AND CAMPING

PESCASSEROLI
Abruzzo National Park's largest and most popular town, tranquil Pescasseroli (PES-ca-SE-ro-lee; pop. 2212) is a convenient base for exploring the rest of the park. Solo travelers may have a hard time finding a single, as establishments

generally only offer double rooms, especially in August; bring friends or come ready to camp. Inquire at the IAT office about *affittacamere* (rooms for rent).

▨ **Di Clemente Elena,** V. Isonzo 2 (☎0863 91 05 06). Welcoming Elena offers blonde wood rooms with bath, TV, and hand-stitched quilts. Singles €20-30; doubles €36-60; triples €50-80; quads €55-90. Cash only. ❷

Il Piccolo Principe, Vle. Principe di Napoli 43/a (☎0863 91 753), visible from the IAT office. Family-run. 10 clean, simple rooms with TV. Terrace is perfect for sunbathing. Singles €35; doubles €45-70; triples €60-90. No singles in Aug. Cash only. ❸

Hotel Valle del Lupo, (☎0863 91 05 34; www.wel.it/hvalledellupo). From the rotunda in Vle. Cabinovia, follow signs for 1.5km to V. Collacchi. Hospitable cabin far from town has 11 rooms with TV. Breakfast, access to public pool in the *centro storico,* and a private park guide included. English spoken. Owners arrange discounted horseback rides at the nearby Vallecopa ranch. Singles €45; doubles €60-70; triples €90-105. Cash only. ❸

Campeggio dell'Orso, (☎0863 91 95 or 339 76 43 656), 1km from Pescasseroli on the road to Opi. Friendly, English-speaking Geraldo maintains quiet, family-oriented grounds. A good base for hikes. Some houses with hostel beads and kitchen available. Bring linens. €8.50 per person, €4 per child ages 5-10. Hostel bed €12. Cash only. ❶

Camping San Andrea, (☎0863 912 725 or 335 595 6029) about 100m from Campeggio dell'Orso. Bigger, more crowded site. €6 per person. 3-person bungalows €55; 4-person €70. Gates open 8am-1pm and 4-8pm. ❶

BARREA

Entering from the south makes Barrea (bah-REH-ah; pop. 769) the first breathtaking highlight of Abruzzo National Park. Known as "the pearl" of the Park for its picturesque location on **Lago di Barrea,** its historic streets meander down the steep mountainside before slowly giving way to forest in the valleys below. SS 83 becomes V. Roma as it enters Barrea, and later becomes V. Sarentina as it winds down and out of town. Straight past V. Roma is V. Duca delgi Abruzzo, a small street that leads to the *centro storico.*

Ostello dagli Elfi, V. Leonardo di Loreto 54 (☎0864 88 408; www.albergodaglielfi.it). Breakfast area overlooks Lago di Barrea at the cheapest option in town. Staff organizes excursions in the park. Internet access available. Open year-round. Dorms €15, with breakfast €18; singles €25/27; doubles €40/45; triples €55/65; quads €70/80. ❶

Camping "La Genziana", (☎0864 88 101; www.pasetta.it), less than 1km from Ostello dagli Elfi, on the way to Castel di Sangro. Within sight of the K trailhead. Owned and operated by famous K2-Pakistan climber T.D. Pasetta. €7.20 per person, €3 per child; €8 per tent; €3 per car. Hot showers €1. Open year-round. ❶

◩ FOOD

PESCASSEROLI

Though small, the town of Pescasseroli packs a culinary punch. Be sure to sample assorted sweets in the town's many excellent pastry shops. Rural Pescasseroli's restaurants close early, so plan dinner accordingly. For hiking sustenance, head to the many *alimentari* and produce shops in the *centro,* most of which make fresh *panini* (€3.50). A **supermarket** is at the start of Vle. San Lucia, to the left when walking into the city. (Open daily noon-2pm and 4-8pm.)

▨ **La Dolceria dell'Orso,** V. Valle Cicala 5c (☎340 14 34 303). Sample a boundless supply of free almond-, chocolate-, and honey-laden samples from the tiny shop's friendly owner. Open M, W, and F-Su 9am-1pm and 3-8pm; Tu and Th 3-8pm. Cash only. ❶

da Giuseppe, IX Traversa Sangro 3 (☎0863 91 22 05). Always packed. Primi €5-7. Open M-W and F-Su 12:30-2:30pm and 7:30-9:30pm. ❷

Picchio, V. Lungo Sangro. Walk from P. Vittorio Emanuele through V. Traversa Sangro. to this spacious pizzeria. Meat is cooked on a traditional log grill. Pizza €3-6. Primi €6-8. Secondi €5-14. Open M, Tu and Th-Su 12:15-3pm and 7-10pm. MC/V. ❷

Ristorante Peppe di Sora, V. Benedetto Croce 1. *Abruzzese* dishes and specialty desserts. *Ferratelle farcita* (thin stuffed waffles; €2.50) are a delight. Primi €7-9. Secondi €6-12. Desserts €2.50. Open Tu-Su 12:30-10pm, and daily in August. AmEx/MC/V. ❷

BARREA

Al Borgo Antico, V. Stratta (☎338 947 0784). Follow your nose to the fully-loaded pizzas (€3-6) and attentive servers at this small local establishment. Primi €6. Secondi €3.50-7. Open Tu-Su 12:30-3pm and 7:30pm-midnight. Cash only. ❶

Ristorante Tana dell'Orso, V. Duca degli Abruzzo 66 (☎0864 88 125). A town staple since 1962. Serves fair portions of house-made *gnocchetti* (€6) in a quiet setting. Primi €6. Secondi €5-9. Open daily 12:30-2:30pm and 8-10:30pm. AmEx/MC/V. ❷

Bar Centrale, V. Duca degli Abruzzo 23 (☎0864 88 405). Local crowds and late-night fun. Beer €2. Mixed drinks €3-4. Open daily 7am-midnight. Cash only. ❶

NOT TO BE CONFUSED WITH. Remember that Barrea and Villetta Barrea are 2 different locations separated by 10km; Civitella Alfedena and Alfedena are also different. Before setting out from Pescasseroli, verify with the bus driver the correct stop for your intended destination. From Avezzano, Civitella comes before Alfedena, just 10min. after Villetta Barrea.

HIKING, SIGHTS, AND OUTDOOR ACTIVITIES

The ascent from Avezzano to Pescasseroli is breathtaking; this trail, which marks the beginning of the park, passes by fields of poppies, fertile valleys, and rocky outcrops. The indispensable trail map (€6) from the **Centro Accoglienza Turistici** in Pescasseroli (see **Practical Information,** p. 555) indicates prime stakeout points for catching a glimpse of bears, deer, wolves, and eagles. The park teems with trails, but bear in mind that due to the sheer number of paths, even a map can't always keep you from getting lost. This overview of hikes should not be counted as a map substitute. Be sure to consult professionals who know the area before setting off. Clever coordination of hikes with the ARPA bus schedule can enable hikers to embark from any of the park's major towns.

From Pescasseroli, the short trail **BN1** passes castle ruins at **Monte Ceraso** (50min.; moderate difficulty), or the 5hr. round-trip **C3** takes you on a hike of medium-difficulty to the beautiful **Valico di Monte Tranquillo** (1673m). From Opi, the **FN1** trail (50min.) takes you through the highly-praised **Val del Fondillo.** True adventurers starting from Opi can take on one of the park's highest peaks, **Monte Marsicano** (2245m), with the steep and arduous **E6** trail (7-8hr. round-trip). From Civitella Alfedena, explore the **G** trails (about 1hr.; varying difficulties), which pass by **Camosciara,** or take the **I1** (3hr.; difficult) to **K6** (3hr.; difficult) through the beautiful **Valle di Rose** to see the park's largest herd of chamois. K6 is one of the more difficult trails deep into the Valle di Rose, yet it makes for a leisurely hike from Barrea to the Valle Iannanghera (1hr.; easy), where it meets trails **J2** to return by the lakeshore to Barrea (1hr.; easy) and **I4** (1hr.; easy) to hike to Civitella Alfedena. From June to early September, this area can only be explored with a guide (€8-10 per person). Go to an *ufficio di zona* the day before a planned excursion for more info about the trails or to obtain a permit and reserve a guide. From Barrea, the **K5** trail (4hr. round-trip) runs through a forested valley to the **Lago Vivo,** which dries up from June to October.

If the park's creatures prove elusive, check out Pescasseroli's family-friendly **Centro di Visita,** Vle. Colle dell'Orso 2, off V. S. Lucia, heading toward Opi, which has a museum and a small zoo. (☎0863 91 131. Open daily 10am-1pm and 3-7pm. €6, children €4.) **Ecotur,** V. Piave 7, second floor., in Pescasseroli, offers organized excursions throughout the park, many of which include wildlife viewing. (☎0863 91 27 60; www.ecotur.org. Hikes €10. Wolf-watching €20. Bear-watching €50. Open daily 9am-1pm and 4-7:30pm; closed Su in winter.) **La Camosciara,** V. G.B. Antonucci in Civitella Alfedena, organizes hikes of the G trails, mountain bike trips, and horseback rides. (☎0864 89 01 35;www.camosciara. com). Fishing in Lago di Barrea is restricted. Obtain a license (€10 per day) or inquire about seasonal subscriptions at the **Centro Operativo Servizio Educazione** in Villetta Barrea (☎0864 89 102. Open M-Sa.) In winter, this area offers excellent downhill skiing and snowboarding, with challenging slopes and heavy snowfall. Package deals called *Settimane Bianche* (White Weeks) provide accommodations, lift tickets, and half pension. For ticket info, call **Gestione Impianti Sportivi Pescasseroli** (☎0863 91 11 18). For the snow bulletin, call ☎0862 66 510. Pescasseroli's website (www.pescasseroli.net) also has winter sports info.

PESCARA   ☎085

The central transportation hub for Abruzzo and Molise, Pescara (pes-CAH-rah; pop. 122,000) holds little in the way of aesthetic appeal in the city. The beach, however, is a different world, with relaxed sunbathing, clean waters, and fun nightlife. Italian vacationers swarm to this 20km shoreline in July and August but leave its lackluster buildings deserted during the rest of the year. Even so, travelers waiting for a domestic train or a boat to Croatia can manage to find something worthwhile besides the beach. Museums, restaurants, and a celebrated jazz festival in mid-July offer a high-brow alternative to sunbathing.

▐▅ TRANSPORTATION. Domestic and international **flights** leave from **Aeroporto d'Abruzzo** (☎085 899 130 310) on V. Tiburtina. Bus #38 (€1) runs between the train station and the airport. **Trains** run from Stazione Centrale on C. V. Emanuele to: Bari (3-4hr., 6 per day 2:41am-8pm, €22.50-32); Lecce (6hr., 11 per day 3:01am-5:30pm, €20.20-44); Milan (6hr., 13 per day midnight-5:48pm, €26.50-50); Naples (5-7hr., 11 per day 3:32am-8:08pm, €16-36); Rome (4hr., 5 per day 6:21am-7:04pm, €11.70); Sulmona (1hr., 14 per day 4:50am-8:38pm, €3.90); Termoli (1hr., 11 per day 6:32am-8:43pm, €4.70-8). ARPA **buses** (☎085 42 15 099) run from the train station to L'Aquila, Avezzano, Rome, and Naples via Sulmona. Consult the info booth in front of the train station for schedules. **Ferries** depart from just beyond the harbor in the old city. Buy all tickets at the Stazione Marittima inside the port. In summer, SNAV (☎085 45 49 089; www. snavoli.it) runs ferries to the Croatian islands of Hvar and Spalato (€36-95). Jetline (☎085 45 16 241) runs ferries to the Tremiti Islands (2½hr., 7am, €21.).

▐▐ ORIENTATION AND PRACTICAL INFORMATION. Buses and trains stop at **Stazione Centrale** on **Corso Vittorio Emanuele,** the main street of the new city *centro.* To the right, C. V. Emanuele extends toward the **River Pescara.** Across the bridge to the right is the tiny old city, and a short walk to the left leads to the harbor. Straight across the bridge is an extensive public park. **Viale della Riviera,** the main stretch of beach parallel to C. V. Emanuele, is especially lively at night, with restaurants, bars, and live music. From the train station, take C.

Umberto I, which extends from the train station to the main square, **Piazza della Rinascita.** Services include: the **APT tourist office**, C. V. Emanuele 301 (☎085 42 90 01; www.abruzzoturismo.it; open M-Sa 8:30am-1:30pm and 4-8pm, Su 8:30am-1:30pm); **police,** V. Pesaro 7 (☎085 20 571); the **hospital**, V. Fonte Romana 8 (☎085 42 51); the **pharmacy**, V. Firenze 187; **Internet access** at *gelateria* **Sloppy Joe** (V. Marco Polo 2/4; €3 per hr; open daily 7am-2am); and the **post office**, C. V. Emanuele 106, between the station and the river. (☎085 27 541. Open M-F 8am-6:30pm, Sa 8am-12:30pm.) **Postal Code:** 65100.

▌▐ ACCOMMODATIONS AND FOOD. Most hotels in Pescara have similar prices and amenities. Staying near the beach gives easy access to restaurants and nightlife. A good option is **Hotel Lido ❸**, Lungomare Matteoti 83, a clean hotel with a helpful owner. (☎085 27 084. Singles €40-45; doubles €70-75; triples €90-95.) **Villa della Pavone ❹**, V. Pizzoferrato 30, is run by a couple of empty-nesters who have turned their house into a charming and fully-equipped B&B. The leafy garden hides a peacock and a bird sanctuary. To get there, walk away from the river on V. Enzo Ferrari, the street behind the train station, and turn left on V. Pizzoferrato. Towels, breakfast, and Internet are included. (☎085 42 11 770; www.villadelpavone.it. Bikes €2 per day. Singles €40-50; doubles €70-80; triples €80-100. Reserve through tourist office for a discount.)

Pescara's food is generally either from the sea or from a traditional *abruzzese* recipe. Local wines, including the white *Trebbiano* and red *Montepulciano*, satisfy broad tastes. On summer weekends, reservations for beach-side restaurants are essential. Excellent seafood is typically featured on the daily selections at **▩Wine and Wine ❷**, V. Chieti 14, off C. V. Emanuele just before the river. This very welcoming family-run *enoteca* invites guests to dine surrounded by racks of wine bottles. There is never a menu, only what is freshest from the market. (☎085 42 23 180. Open M-Sa 10am-10pm. Dinner reservations strongly recommended. AmEx/MC/V.) The award-winning traditional cuisine at the medieval-themed **Hostaria I Templari ❸**, V. Caserme 38, specializes in fresh Abruzzese vegetable platters, pastas, and cheese. Try their succulent *stinco di maiale alla templare*, (pork on the bone cooked in beer and wine, €12). (Dinner reservations suggested.☎085 64 172; www.itemplari.it. Primi €8. Secondi €10-13. Open Tu-Su 6pm-2am. MC/V.) From the train station, follow C. Umberto and turn right at

ON THE MENU

POOR MAN'S GOURMET

Dishes that were once reserved for the rural poor have remained close to the hearts and stomachs of southern Italy. Passed down through generations, the treasured recipes have made their way onto restaurant menus that tout them as "typical" cuisine.

Polenta, a cakey starch, made by stirring cornmeal into a boiling pot of water, originated in the hills of Teramo, Abruzzo. It was served with "poor sauce"—seasonings lacking meat—and spread over a large dish for the whole family to share. Leftovers were easily reheated in garlic and oil, but if no oil remained, polenta could be toasted and eaten like bread.

The poor fishermen of the Amalfi Coast would prepare seafood dishes using equal or greater portions of **potatoes.** The cheap, filling vegetable would make up for the small quantity of fish.

To conserve oil, the families of the Salento Peninsula would boil half of the pasta in water and fry the rest. With chick peas and a mix of vegetables, **ciceri e tria** provided maximum flavor in the absence of meat and cheese.

Also in Puglia, *baresi* farmers filled their empty stomachs with **pane di grano duro,** a coarse bread made from leftovers grains. To soften it and add flavor, they would dip it in water sprinkled with salt and top it with *pomodorini* (small tomatoes).

the *piazza* to find **Tigre** supermarket, V. Nicola Fabrizi 59. (☎085 42 16 896. Open M-Sa 8:15am-8:30pm, Su 9am-1pm. MC/V.)

⑤ ♫ SIGHTS AND ENTERTAINMENT. All the typical attractions of a seaside resort crowd Pescara's vibrant **beach:** basketball, soccer, volleyball, music, windsurfing, and sunbathing. Bikers and joggers make use of miles of board-walk next to the beach. Laziness, meanwhile, comes at a cost: about €5-7 to sunbathe, depending on the location. There's a paltry public stretch where C. Umberto meets the sea, marked by a large fountain. Take the first right across the bridge to reach **Museo delle Genti d'Abruzzo,** V. delle Caserme 24, which celebrates 4000 years of *abruzzese* history. Chronological galleries show the development of local crafts from the Paleolithic era to the present. (☎085 45 10 026; Open July-Aug. M-F 9am-1pm, Tu-Su 7-11pm. Sept.-June M-Sa 9am-2pm. €5, EU students and citizens under 18 or over 65 €2.) The **Museo Civico "Cascella,"** Vle. Marconi 5345, showcases artwork by members of the influential Cascella family. (☎085 42 83 515. Tu and Th 9am-1pm and 4-6pm, W and F-Su 9am-1pm. €2.50, EU citizens ages 18-24 €1.50, EU citizens under 18 or over 65 free.)

To get the latest scoop on the always-pumping nightlife scene, pick up the monthly *Giorno e Notte* at restaurants and stores around the city. To party beachside, join the hordes packed into **Hai Bin,** Vle. della Riviera 44, for cheap beer (from €2.50) served by 21 taps. (☎085 421 3042. Open daily 7pm-late. AmEx/MC/V.) For an amazing night with good-looking people and a live DJ, try **Nettuno,** Vle. della Riviera 30. (☎085 42 21 542; www.nettunobeach.com. Primi €7-8. Secondi €7-15. Dance music Th and Sa nights. Open daily 7am-4am.)

TERMOLI   ☎0875

Despite its pristine coastline and attractive *centro storico* jutting out over turquoise waters, Termoli (TER-mo-lee; pop. 30,000) is less visited than other coastal towns. While the town is home to many beachside resorts, most travel-ers—likely deterred by the high cost of a night's stay—visit only briefly before an early ferry to the Tremiti Islands. If you stay, leave the beach long enough to see the **duomo** and the **Castello Svevo** in the lively Borgo Vecchio historic area.

The **train station** lies at the western end of town. **Trains** run to: Bari (5 per day 7:44am-9:03pm, €13-21); Milan (8 per day 2:20am-11:20pm, €40); Naples (11:24am, €12.34); Pescara (10 per day 4:55am-8:15pm, €4.40-10). Across the street, **Via Mario Milano** extends to **Lungomare Colombo,** a hotel-lined waterfront strip. Turning right on this street leads to the **Borgo Vecchio** and the **port;** ferry docks and ticket offices are on the breakwater past the fishing boats. Larivera Lines (☎0875 82 248) sends **ferries** from the port to the Croatian islands. For a **taxi,** call (☎0875 77 03 296). The **AAST tourist office,** at the back of P. Bega, offers maps, directories, and brochures for Termoli's lesser-known attractions. From the station, turn right on C. Umberto I. At the galleria, walk through the underpass and to the right to the back of the building. Buzz the office, then take stairway A to the second floor. Ring again to enter. (☎0875 70 39 13; aast-termoli@virgilio.it. Open M-F 8am-2pm and 3-6pm, Sa 9am-1pm.) In case of emergency, dial ☎0875 71 591, the **carabinieri** (☎0875 70 63 40), or **police** (☎0875 57 15 51). A **pharmacy** is attached to the train station (open M-F, Su 8:30am-1pm and 5-8:30pm). For **Internet** access, try **Adriatica 2000,** V. Mario Pagano. (€3 per hr. Open M-F 9am-1pm and 3:30-9pm, Su 5-9pm.) The **post office** at V. M. Milano 7/b has an **ATM.** (Open M-F 8am-6:30pm, Sa 8am-1:30pm.) **Postal Code:** 86039.

Though a 15min. walk from the *centro*, **▧Hotel Giorgione ❷,** V. Rio Vivo 84/90, provides guests with clean, colorful rooms and the complete beach experience. Make use of the hotel's private beach, solarium, volleyball court, beach bar, latin dance classes, and nightly entertainment. Take C. Umberto and turn right on C. Vittorio, which becomes V. di Rio Vivo. Giorgione is after the rotunda, facing Rio Vivo beach. (☎0875 70 64 26; giorgionete@virgilio.it. Breakfast included. Singles €25-60; doubles €50-85; triples €65-105; quads €80-120; quints €95-135. MC/V.) **Modena ❸**, V. Vespucci, is a simple, modern hotel near the beach. Enjoy great sunsets away from the city bustle. (☎0875 70 64 24. Singles €30-40; doubles €50-70.) **Villa Ida ❸**, V. Mario Milano 27, offers spacious, well-lit, comfortable rooms with A/C, phone, TV, and bath. (☎0875 70 66 66. Breakfast included. Singles €35-44; doubles €52-65; triples €74-87.)

Dining options in Termoli are varied and spread out. From the train station, follow C. Umberto I, turn left on C. Nazionale, right on V. Alfano, then left on V. Ruffini to find **Anema e Cuore ❶**, V. Ruffini 56/60. The restaurant offers a wide selection of pizza (€3.50-7) and canopied outdoor seating. (☎0875 71 47 72. Cover €1. Primi €5-7. Secondi from €7. Open daily noon-3:30pm and 6:30pm-1am. AmEx/MC/V.) For authentic Greek food and a great view of the sunset, grab a table at **Ristorante Il Batello Ebbro ❶**, off P. Duomo on Vico VI Duomo. (☎0875 70 32 61. Dishes from €5.50.) Cool cafe **Down Town ❶**, C. Nazionale 24, hosts DJs, karaoke nights, and festivals on select Thursday, Saturday, and Sunday nights throughout the summer. (☎0875 345 219 4140. Beer €2. Mixed drinks €3.50. Open daily 7:30am-1:30pm and 6pm-2am) The younger revelers pack into **Plaza Cafe ❶**, V. Margherita 3, for cheap beer (€1.20) and pastries (€0.70). From May to Sept., the owner sets up an outpost down the street on P. San Antonio, where the beer flows amid outdoor foosball tables and a great beach view. From C. Nazionale, turn left on V. Roma to the *piazza*, and the cafe is on the end farther from the beach. Beer is only €1 F-Su at the cafe. For groceries, go to **Sisa Supermercato Limongi**, V. Adriatica 5, just off V. M. Milano. (☎0875 70 72 53. Open M-Sa 7:30am-1:45pm and 5-9pm, Su 8:30am-1:30pm. MC/V.)

▶ DAYTRIP FROM TERMOLI

THE TREMITI ISLANDS

Ferry service from Termoli, operating late Apr. to Sept., is slower but cheaper than hydrofoils. Navigazione Libera (☎0875 70 48 59; www.navlib.it) runs ferries (1hr.; departs 9:15am, returns 5pm; €11) and hydrofoils (50min.; first departure 8:40am, last return 6:45pm; €17.15-18.50). Tirrenia Adriatica (☎0875 70 53 43; www.tirrenia.it.) runs ferries (1hr.; first departure 9am, last return 6pm; €15.80-17.70). Expect delays. Ferries dock on San Nicola, which means passengers must take small motorboats across the water to the dock at San Domino (2min., €2.50). Only the hydrofoils dock directly at San Domino.

Covered with lush vegetation, rich in natural resources, and surrounded by crystalline azure waters, the four Isole Tremiti (EE-so-leh TRE-mee-tee; pop. 370) are a relatively well-kept secret. Just 35km from the Gargano Peninsula, Puglia's Isole Tremiti make for a relaxing daytrip. **San Domino**, the largest island in the archipelago, is dubbed the "Green Pearl of the Adriatic" because of its rich flora. Its neighbor, **San Nicola**, the only island populated year-round, was most famously home to Emperor Augustus's daughter, Julia, who was exiled there in the AD first century for her adulterous behavior. Though its monastery makes it the most historical island, San Nicola has little else to offer. The last two islands, **Caprara** and **Cretaccio**, are small and desolateo. Scuba divers around Caprara will encounter a massive underwater statue of St. Pio.

San Domino has a small but excellent ☑**free beach** to the left of the port. Entrance is free, so don't feel forced to give in to **Il Pirata**, a beachside restaurant and bar, which offers umbrellas (€5) and beach chairs (€5). **Hiking** paths snake through the thick pine forest; the main trail (#1) circles the entire island in approximately 45min. Many lead down to the small, rocky coves along the coast, where vacationers sometimes swim in sapphire waters sans suits. If you join them, be mindful of sea urchins, slippery rocks, and jellyfish. The **Marlin Tremiti Diving Center,** up the hill and to the left in San Domino Villagio, in the back of the Hotel Eden complex, offers **scuba diving** instruction for all experience levels. (☎0882 46 37 65; www.marlintremiti.it. 1 dive with equipment and guide €55; without equipment €35. 1 week of lessons €350. Open daily March-Nov. 8am-9pm.) **M.G.M.** (☎0882 368 700 0341), in a kiosk in San Domino's port, offers glass-bottom boat tours of the archipelago's natural caves, one including all the islands for €15, and another covering only San Nicola and San Domino for €5.

Food on the island is expensive, so consider getting an excellent pizza slice (€1.50) at **Rossana ❶**, right by the port. (☎0882 46 32 98. Open daily 8am-3pm.) Otherwise, try **Ristorante Al Faro ❸**, V. Aldo Moro 22, in San Domino, which serves a short but excellent menu of local seafood dishes. (☎0882 339 221 1771. Primi €6-8. Secondi €10-14. Open daily 8-10:30pm. MC/V.) **Ristorante da Pio ❸**, V. Moro 12, serves fresh fish caught by the owner's family boat. *Spaghetti al sugo di arragosta* (pasta and lobster; €14) is especially good. (☎0882 46 32 69. Primi €8-14. Secondi €10-15. Open daily May-Oct. 12:30-2pm and 8:30-10:30pm. AmEx/MC/V.) If not, try the always-busy **Ristorante Bel Mare ❷**, San Domino Marina 1, on San Domino's beach to the left of the port, where customers choose their favorite seafood and pasta dishes from a large self-service counter. (☎0882 339 687 4457. Primi €7. Secondi €7-8. Open daily June-Sept. 12:30-3pm. Cash only.) The cheapest food option is the **Mini-Market Shop 88** by San Domino's *centro*. Choose some picnic food and sit down by any of the wooded areas around the island. (☎0882 46 32 36. Open daily 8:30am-11pm.) Those who spend a night on the island can find their groove at relaxing **Diomede**, P. San Pertini 1. (☎0882 46 34 03; www.discotecadiomeda.it. Happy hour daily 6:30-8pm. Beer €4. Wine €4. Mixed drinks €6-7. Open daily Apr.-Oct. 8am-3am.)

For tourist info, visit the Termoli **AAST office** (p. 560). Pick up a copy of the *Tutto in Tosca* guide, found in every store on the island, for a map as well as hotel, restaurant, and activity offerings. A **first aid station,** V. Federico II, can be found at the San Domino port—it's the 2nd building on the left when heading uphill on the main road. (☎0882 46 32 34. Open daily in summer 8am-8pm.) A **pharmacy,** V. Garibaldi 23, is in San Domino. (☎0882 46 33 27. Open daily June-Sept. 9am-1pm and 5-8pm; Oct.-May 9:30am-12:30pm and 5-7:30pm.) A **post office** is at the Municipio building on the main road, in front of the Marlin Tremiti diving center (M-F 10:30am-1:30pm). **Postal code:** 71040.

CAMPANIA

Campania (cam-PAH-nee-ah) is a land of contrasts, where a chaotic, modern city, a wealth of remarkably preserved Roman ruins, and a coastline of peaceful villages all coexist. The beautiful *centro storico* in Naples draws visitors to the area, and the nearby islands' emerald waters embrace them when the city's frenetic disorder overwhelms. Nearby, the preserved ancient cities of Pompeii and Herculaneum attest to the destructive power of Mt. Vesuvius, which remains a constant—and yes, very active—threat. One of Italy's poorest regions, Campania has withstood natural disasters and foreign invasions, but its people have managed to cultivate and sustain a unique, carefree attitude—the region's true treasure.

HIGHLIGHTS OF CAMPANIA

DESCEND underneath the city of Naples to tour catacombs and aqueducts (p. 575).

PEER into the crater of Mt. Vesuvius, mainland Europe's only active volcano (p. 586).

RECOVER from all your ailments at Ischia's therapeutic hot springs (p. 594).

SIP *granita* or *limoncello* in the shade of Amalfi's lemon groves (p. 609).

NAPLES (NAPOLI) ☎081

From zipping Vespas to bustling crowds, Naples (in Italian, "NAH-po-lee"; pop. 1,000,000) rarely rests. Neapolitans spend every waking moment out on the town, eating, drinking, carousing, and laughing. Surrounded by the ancient ruins of Pompeii and the gorgeous Amalfi Coast, Naples—Italy's third-largest city—is the anchor of Campania. The city has a reputation for crime and grime, but on the bright side, UNESCO recently declared its historical center the most architecturally varied in the world. As the birthplace of pizza and home of tantalizing seafood and pasta, Naples is world-renowned for culinary delights. Whereas Milan flaunts sophistication and Venice emanates mystique, Naples wallows in cheerful chaos. This is a city with personality that doesn't tolerate ambivalence—either you can't stand it or you can't get enough.

✈ INTERCITY TRANSPORTATION

Flights: Aeroporto Capodichino (NAP), V. Umberto Maddalena (☎081 848 88 87 77, info line 081 78 96 259; www.gesac.it), northeast of the city. A white **Alibus** travels between the port near P. Municipio, Stazione Centrale, and the airport (15-20min., 6:30am-11:30pm, €3.10). City bus **3S** runs from P. Garibaldi to the airport (€1). Buy tickets at any newsstand or *tabaccheria*. Cheaper than the Alibus and with many more stops, the city bus is a target for pickpockets. **Taxis** run to and from the airport for €19 (p. 566). **Alitalia** (☎081 848 865 643), **British Airways** (☎081 199 71 22 66), **Lufthansa** (☎081 199 40 00 44), and **Easy Jet** (☎081 848 88 77 66) fly to Naples.

Trains: Naples is served by 3 train companies from **Stazione Centrale,** P. Garibaldi (www.napolipiazzagaribaldi.it). **Luggage storage** is available but insecure.

Circumvesuviana (☎081 800 05 39 39; www.vesuviana.it). To **Herculaneum** (€1.80), **Pompeii** (€2.40), and **Sorrento** (€3.30). Trains depart every 30min. 5:09am-10:42pm.

CAMPANIA

Ferrovia Cumana and **Ferrovia Circumflegrea** (☎081 800 00 16 16). Trains from Montesanto to **Cumae** and **Puzzuoli** (every 20min.). Info booth in Stazione open daily 7am-9pm.

Trenitalia (☎081 56 72 430; www.trenitalia.it). Ticket office open daily 6am-9:40pm. To: **Milan** (8hr., 15 per day 6am-9:50pm, €39-50); **Rome** (2hr., every hr. 4am-9:22pm, €11-38); **Salerno** (45min., every hr. 6am-10:57pm, €3.30); **Syracuse** (10hr., 3 per day 9:42am-11:30pm, €31).

Ferries: The daily newspaper *Il Mattino* (€0.90) has up-to-date ferry schedules. Port taxes may apply. Hydrofoils depart from **Mergellina, Molo Beverello,** and **Pozzuoli,** and ferries from **Stazione Marittima** (on **Molo Angioino**) and **Molo Beverello.** Molo Angioino is for longer trips to **Sicily** and **Sardinia.** Molo Beverello is at the base of P. Municipio. Take the R2, 152, 3S, or Alibus from P. Garibaldi to P. Municipio.

Alilauro (☎081 49 72 252 or 081 49 72 249; www.alilauro.it). Ticket offices at Molo Beverello and Mergellina. Open daily 6am-7pm. Ferries to **Ischia** (15 per day 6:25am-6:50pm, €10-20).

Caremar (☎081 55 13 882; www.caremar.it). Ticket office on Molo Beverello. Open daily 6am-10pm. Ferries and hydrofoils to **Capri** (ferry 1hr., 3 per day 7:35am-6:40pm, €4.80-10; hydrofoil 1hr., 4 per day 5:40am-9:10pm, €9.60-15), **Ischia** (ferry 1hr., 8 per day 6:25am-9:55pm, €4.80-12; hydrofoil 1hr., 6 per day 7:50am-8:20pm, €9.60-15), and **Procida** (ferry 1hr., 7 per day 6:25am-9:55pm, €4.80-12; hydrofoil 40min., 5 per day 7:40am-8:20pm, €7.90-14).

Metro del Mare (☎081 199 600 700; www.metrodelmare.com). Ticket office at Molo Beverello and Mergellina. 3 Lines run between Bacoli and Salerno (€17), Bacoli and Sorrento (€6), and Monte di Procida and Salerno (€18). Stops at Pozzouli, Napoli Mergellina, Napoli Beverello, Ercolano, Torre del Greco, Torre A. Pompeii, Sorrento, Capri, Positano, and Amalfi, among others.

SNAV (☎081 42 85 111; www.snav.it). Ticket office at Molo Beverello and Mergellina. Open daily 9am-7pm. Hydrofoils Apr.-Oct. go to **Capri** (1hr., 10 per day 7:10am-6:10pm, €17), **Ischia-Casamicciola Terme** (1hr., 4 per day 8:20am-6:45pm, €16), and **Procida** (40min., 4 per day 8:20am-6:40pm, €14). Ferries go to **Palermo** (10hr., 8pm, €27) from Stazione Marittima.

Siremar (☎081 58 00 340). Ticket office at Molo Angioino. Open daily 9am-7pm. Depart from Stazione Marittima. 2 ferries per week in summer, 3 in winter. To **Lipari** (12hr.), **Stromboli** (8hr.), and **Vulcano** (13hr.). Prices vary.

Tirrenia (☎081 199 123 199). Ticket office at Molo Angioino. Open daily 8:30am-1:15pm and 2:30-5:30pm. Ferries to **Cagliari** (16hr.; depart weekly, 2 per week in summer) and **Palermo** (11hr., depart daily). Required supplemental port tax. Schedules and prices vary.

> **STREET SMARTS.** When crossing busy streets in Naples, keep in mind that if you make eye contact with the driver of an oncoming vehicle, it is assumed that you will stop and wait for the car to pass.

ORIENTATION

In Naples, hectic modern grime rubs shoulders with historic architectural gems. To the east, the area around **Stazione Centrale** is dangerous; beware of pickpockets and exercise extra caution at night. From **Piazza Garibaldi** (right outside the station), take a left on C. Garibaldi and walk until it ends at the water in P. Guglielmo Pepe. With the water on your left, V. Nuova Marina turns into V. Cristoforo Colombo and later V. Ferdinando Acton, which leads to **Piazza del Plebiscito,** the historic and social center of Naples. From here, turn away from the water onto **Via Toledo,** the town's shop- and restaurant-lined main drag. This street passes through the disordered **Spanish Quarter** on its way to **Piazza Dante** and **Piazza Salvo D'Aquisto** (also known as **Piazza Carità**), which lie on the western extreme of the **centro storico (Spaccanapoli).** A right off V. Toledo on V. Maddaloni (which later becomes V. Capitelli, V. Benedetto Croce, and V. S. Biagio dei Librai) leads through the central *piazze* of the historical district, **Piazza Gesù Nuovo** and **Piazza San Domenico Maggiore.** Lots of hip, unique restaurants and hangouts are found around the university in **Piazza Ruggero Bonghi.** A short funicular ride

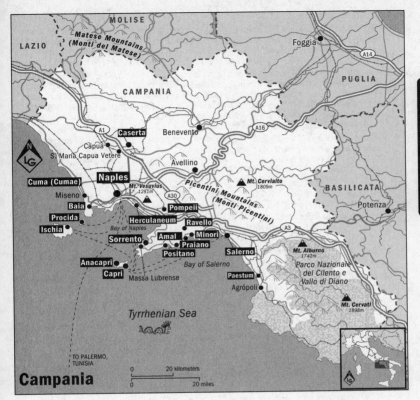

CAMPANIA

Campania

from V. Toledo will take you to the **Vomero** district, away from the chaos of central Naples. Returning back down V. Toledo to P. del Plebiscito, turn right at the water to reach upscale boutique restaurants and shops tucked away on the side streets off **Riviera di Chiaia** in the **Chiaia** district. The nearby **Piazza dei Martiri** offers good nightlife. **Mergellina,** the beautiful and relaxed waterfront district, is accessible by foot along V. Caracciolo or by Metro line #2. **Posillipo,** is also pleasant and even farther along the wild, wild west.

⅀ LOCAL TRANSPORTATION

One **UnicoNapoli ticket** (☎081 55 13 109; www.napolipass.it) is valid for all modes of transportation in Naples: **bus, metro, train,** and **funicular.** Tickets are available at *tabaccherie* in three varieties: 1½hr. (€1.10), full day (€3.10), and weekend (€2.60). The buses and metro stop running around midnight, and the *notturno* (nighttime) buses are unsafe and unreliable. Transportation in Naples's environs includes the **Metro del Mare** (see **Intercity Transportation,** p. 563), the **Circumvesuviana** train to the areas around Mt. Vesuvius and the **metro** to Pozzuoli. All buses and trains in Campania are on the **UnicoCampania** system (www.unicocampania.it). Ticket costs depend on the *fascia* (zone) of your destination (€1-5). The daily newspaper, *Il Mattino,* has schedules, which change constantly.

Public Transportation:

Buses: Public buses are orange. Stops have signs indicating routes and destinations. **R1** travels from P. Bovio to Vomero (P. Medaglie d'Oro), and **R2** runs from P. Garibaldi to P. Municipio. **3S** connects the 3 stations: the airport, Stazione Centrale in P. Garibaldi, and Molo Beverello, where boats leave for islands in the Bay of Naples and other more distant destinations.

Metro (Info ☎800 56 89 866; www.metro.na.it.) To cover long distances (e.g., from the train station to P. Cavour, Montesanto, or Mergellina), use the efficient Metro that runs west to Pozzuoli from P. Garibaldi. Go to platform #4, 1 fl. underground at Stazione Centrale. Line #1 stops at **Piazza Cavour** (Museo Nazionale), **Montesanto** (Cumana, Circumflegrea, funicular to Vomero), **Piazza Amedeo** (funicular to Vomero), **Mergellina,** and **Pozzuoli.** Transfer at P. Cavour for line #2. For **Procida** or **Ischia,** take the Metro to Pozzuoli.

Funiculars (Info: ☎800 56 89 866; www.metro.na.it). 3 connect the lower city to Vomero: **Centrale,** most frequently used, runs from V. Toledo to P. Fuga; **Montesanto** from P. Montesanto to V. Morghen; **Chiaia** from V. del Parco Margherita to C. Cimarosa. Centrale and Chiaia make intermittent stops at C. V. Emanuele. A 4th, **Mergellina,** connects Posillipo to Mergellina. 6 per hr., M-Tu 6:30am-10pm, W-Su 6:30am-1:30am.

Taxis: Consortaxi: ☎081 20 20 20. **Cotana:** ☎081 570 70 70. **Napoli:** ☎081 44 44 44. **Partenope:** ☎08155 60 202. Only take official taxis with meters, and inquire about prices up front; even well-known companies have been known to charge suspiciously high rates. For all taxis, the meter starts at €3 M-Sa, €5.50 Su and at night (10pm-7am); each additional 65m costs €0.05. There is also a €0.50-1 surcharge for luggage. Service to and from the airport is set at €19. Other fixed tariffs must be agreed upon before meter starts. Tariffs double for trips beyond the city limits.

Car Rental: Avis (☎081 75 16 052; www.avisautonoleggio.it), in the airport. Open M-F 8am-7:30pm, Sa 8:30am-1pm and 4-6pm, Su 9am-1pm. Extra 12% tax on cars rented at airport. AmEx/MC/V. **Hertz,** V. Ricciardi 5 (☎081 20 62 28 or 199 91 12 211). Branch at airport, V. Scarfoglio 1 (☎081 78 02 971). Open M-F 8am-1pm and 2-7pm, Sa 8am-noon. AmEx/MC/V. **Maggiore** (☎081 84 88 67 067; www.maggiore.it), in Stazione Centrale. Open M-F 8am-1pm and 3-7pm, Sa 8:30am-1:30pm. AmEx/MC/V.

NAPLES'S NOTORIETY. Although violent crime is rare in Naples, theft is not. For the love of San Gennaro, be smart: don't carry money in wallets or purses, don't wear flashy jewelry or flaunt a camera, and hold onto your bags, especially on buses. Be wary of "scooter robberies," where Vespas speed up behind you and grab your goods before you even realize what hit you. When choosing accommodations, always ask to see a room before paying; never stay anywhere that feels unsafe. At night, avoid the areas around Stazione Centrale and the Spanish Quarter. Women should not make eye contact with strangers and should avoid traveling alone.

🔁 PRACTICAL INFORMATION

TOURIST AND FINANCIAL SERVICES

Tourist Office: EPT, P. dei Martiri 58 (☎081 41 07 211; www.eptnapoli.info). Offers booking services, free maps, and the indispensable 📖**Qui Napoli,** a twice-monthly publication tourist publication with event schedules. Make sure to ask for *Zero 81,* which also lists all cultural, musical, and artistic events happening every night in the city. English spoken. Open M-F 9am-2pm. **Branches:** Stazione Centrale (☎081 26 87 79). This office is very busy; go elsewhere for more attentive service. Open M-Sa 9am-7pm, Su 9am-1pm. Stazione Mergellina (☎081 76 12 102). Open M-Sa 9am-7pm. **AASCT** (☎081 25 25 714; www.inaples.it) at Galleria Umberto in P. del Plebiscito, offers friendly info on accommodations and sights. English spoken. Open M-Sa 9:30am-1:30pm and 2:30-6:30pm, Su 9:30am-1:30pm. **Branch:** P. Gesù Nuovo (☎081 55 12 701). Open M-Sa 9:30am-1:30pm and 2:30-6:30pm, Su 9am-1:30pm.

Budget Travel: CTS, V. Mezzocannone 25 (☎081 55 27 960; www.cts.it), off C. Umberto on the R2 line. Student travel info, ISIC and FIYTO cards, and booking services. Open M-F 9:30am-1:30pm and 2:30-6pm, Sa 9:30am-12:30pm. Branch at V. Cinthia 36 (☎081 76 77 877.) Open May-Sept. M-F 9:30am-1pm and 4-7pm, Sa 9:30am-1pm, Oct.-April M-F 9:30am-12:30pm.

Consulates: Canada, V. Carducci 29 (☎081 40 13 38). Open M-F 9am-1pm. **UK,** V. dei Mille 40 (☎081 42 38 911). Open in summer M-F 9am-12:30pm and 2-4pm. **US,** P. della Repubblica 2 (☎081 58 38 111, 24hr. emergency 033 79 45 083), at the western end of Villa Comunale. Open M-F 8am-1pm and 2-5pm.

Currency Exchange: Stazione Centrale has expensive 24hr. currency exchange. Smaller offices along C. Umberto I charge more reasonable fees, as do the banks along V. Toledo and in P. Municipio and P. Garibaldi. Decent rates at **Thomas Cook** in the airport. Open M-F 9:30am-1pm and 3-7pm. **Branch:** P. Municipio 70 (☎081 55 18 399).

 LUG YOUR LUGGAGE. The luggage storage in Stazione Centrale is extremely unsafe; bring your bags to your hostel locker or hold onto them!

LOCAL SERVICES

English-Language Bookstores: Feltrinelli, V. S. Tommaso d'Aquino 70/76 (☎081 55 21 436; www.lafeltrinelli.it), just north of the Municipio. Open M-F 9am-8pm, Sa 9am-2pm and 4-8:30pm. AmEx/MC/V. **Libreria Universal Books,** C. Umberto I 22 (☎081 25 20 069; unibooks@tin.it), off C. Umberto I. Open daily 8:30am-1pm and 4-7pm. MC/V.

Laundromats: Onda Blu City, V. M. Zannotti 11/B, off C. Umberto I. Wash and dry from €7. **Internet** €1 per 30min. Open daily 8am-8pm. Cash only.

EMERGENCY AND COMMUNICATIONS

Police: ☎081 113. **Ambulance:** ☎081 118.

Tourist Police: Ufficio Stranieri, V. G. Ferrairis 131 (☎081 60 64 111), near Stazione Centrale. Helps tourist who have been victims of crime. Assists with passport problems.

Pharmacy: ☎081 26 88 81, at Stazione Centrale by Trenitalia ticket windows. Open 24hr., except some Sa and holidays. **Farmacia Helvethia,** C. Umberto I 290/c (☎081 55 48 894; fax 554 19 20), across from station. Open 5pm-1pm daily.

Hospital: Incurabili (☎081 25 49 422), near the Museo Archeologico Nazionale. ⓂCavour (Museo). From the Metro, the emergency ward is directly up V. Maria Longo.

Internet: Internet points cluster around V. Mezzocannone.

Mouseclub, V. Pignatelli 45 (☎081 55 10 763; www.mouseclub.it). Take V. Toledo from P. Municipio. Turn right at V. Capitelli. V. Pignatelli is the 2nd right after P. Gesù Nuovo. Bar, lounge, and Internet cafe. €1.50 per hr. Open M-Sa 10am-6pm.

Internet Point, V. de Sanctis 27, 20m from the Cappella San Severo. €2 per hr., 1hr. free after 10hr. Open daily 9am-9pm.

Lemme Lemme By Internet Bar, P. Bellini 74 (See **Nightlife,** p. 580). Offers Internet access at €2 per hr. and free Wi-Fi to clients. €3 per hr. without purchase.

Post Office: ☎081 55 24 233. In P. Matteotti, at V. Diaz. Take the R2 line, a view into true Neapolitan life like nothing else. Notoriously unreliable *fermoposta.* **Branches** in Galleria Umberto I (☎08155 23 467) and outside Stazione Centrale. Open M-F 8:15am-6pm, Sa 8:15am-noon. **Postal Code:** 80100.

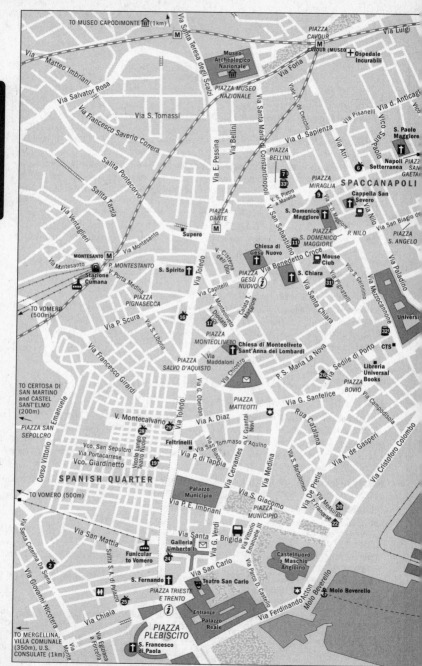

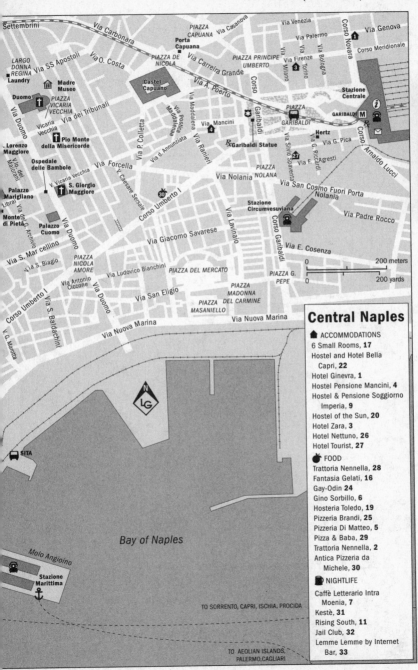

CAMPANIA

Central Naples

🏠 **ACCOMMODATIONS**
6 Small Rooms, **17**
Hostel and Hotel Bella
   Capri, **22**
Hotel Ginevra, **1**
Hostel Pensione Mancini, **4**
Hostel & Pensione Soggiorno
   Imperia, **9**
Hostel of the Sun, **20**
Hotel Zara, **3**
Hotel Nettuno, **26**
Hotel Tourist, **27**

🍎 **FOOD**
Trattoria Nennella, **28**
Fantasia Gelati, **16**
Gay-Odin **24**
Gino Sorbillo, **6**
Hosteria Toledo, **19**
Pizzeria Brandi, **25**
Pizzeria Di Matteo, **5**
Pizza & Baba, **29**
Trattoria Nennella, **2**
Antica Pizzeria da
   Michele, **30**

🍺 **NIGHTLIFE**
Caffè Letterario Intra
   Moenia, **7**
Kestè, **31**
Rising South, **11**
Jail Club, **32**
Lemme Lemme by Internet
   Bar, **33**

CAMPANIA

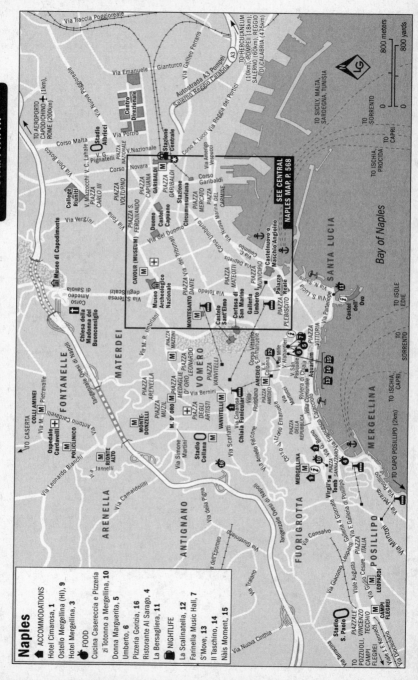

Naples

ACCOMMODATIONS
Hotel Cimarosa, **1**
Ostello Mergellina (HI), **9**
Hotel Mergellina, **3**

FOOD
Cucina Casereccia e Pizzeria
  zi Totonno a Mergellina, **10**
Donna Marguerita, **5**
Umberto, **6**
Pizzeria Gorizia, **16**
Ristorante Al Sarago, **4**
La Bersagliera, **11**

NIGHTLIFE
La Scalinatella, **12**
Farinella Music Hall, **7**
S'Move, **13**
Il Taschino, **14**
Naìs Moment, **15**

SEE CENTRAL
NAPLES MAP P. 568

Bay of Naples

ACCOMMODATIONS

Hotels litter the seedy, hectic area around **Stazione Centrale.** Don't trust anyone who approaches you in the station—people working on commission are happy to lead naïve foreigners to unlicensed, overpriced hotels. Stazione Centrale has several comfortable and inexpensive options that are quiet despite their bustling surroundings, but be especially careful when returning at night. The **centro storico** and **Piazza del Plebiscito** areas are more expensive but also more relaxed. **Vomero,** albeit farther from the sights, provides tranquility and views. **Mergellina,** even farther from the hub, is even calmer. Be cautious when selecting a place to stay, and if possible, make reservations in advance. Don't surrender documents or passports before seeing a room, always agree on the price in writing before unpacking, and look for an intercom system or night attendants. Keep in mind that rooms with views of the city are rarely insulated from the noisy streets below. The tourist office has a pamphlet of accommodations. For camping, check out nearby **Pozzuoli** (p. 587) and other towns on the Bay of Naples.

STAZIONE CENTRALE

Hostel Pensione Mancini, V. P. S. Mancini 33, 2nd fl. (☎081 55 36 731; www.hostelpensionemancini.com), off far end of P. Garibaldi, 5min. walk to station. Attentive owners share their extensive knowledge of Naples. Clean and spacious rooms. New common room and kitchen. English spoken. Breakfast included. Free luggage storage, lockers, and Wi-Fi. Reception 24hr. Check-in and check-out noon. Reservations suggested 1 week in advance. Excellent for late-night arrivals. With *Let's Go* discount, co-ed and female dorms €13-16; singles €25-35, with bath €40-50; doubles €40-50/50-60; triples €60-70/70-80; quads €70-80/75-90. AmEx/MC/V. ❶

Hotel Zara, V. Firenze 81 (☎081 28 71 25; www.hotelzara.it). Spacious, renovated rooms, all with TV, A/C, and bath; some with Internet access and radio. Breakfast €4. Internet €4 per hr. Reservations recommended. Singles €35; doubles €45, with bath €50-65; triples €75-80; quads €100. 5% *Let's Go* discount. AmEx/MC/V. ❸

Hotel Ginevra, V. Genova 116, 2nd fl. (☎/fax 081 28 32 10; www.hotelginevra.it). Exit P. Garibaldi on C. Novara, turn right on V. Genova. Close to the train station. Clean, comfortable, and family-run. Owners can reserve private tours of Naples for guests. English spoken. Breakfast €5. Reservations recommended. Singles €30-35, with bath €45; doubles €55/65; superior doubles, with minibar, safe, bath, TV, and A/C €75; triples €65, with bath €75, superior €85. 10% *Let's Go* discount. AmEx/MC/V. ❸

Hotel Tourist, V. Silvio Spaventa 11 (☎081 28 60 09; www.touristhotelnapoli.it), by P. Garibaldi. Despite the name, this hotel is anything but a trap. Rooms are a bright contrast to those at most hotels immediately near the station and have TV, phone, A/C, and bath. Guests may leave their bags in the safety of reception on checkout day. Breakfast included. Singles €40-60; doubles €60-80; triples €80-100. MC/V. ❹

CENTRO STORICO (SPACCANAPOLI)

6 Small Rooms, V. Diodato Lioy 18, 3rd fl. (☎081 79 01 378; www.6smallrooms.com). From P. Dante, turn left on V. Toledo, left on V. Senise, and right on V. Lioy. Larger rooms than the name would suggest. Kitchen and English video collection available. Breakfast included. Free lockers, Internet, and Wi-Fi. Key deposit €5 to return after midnight curfew. Dorms €18-20; single with bath €30-40; doubles €40-45, with bath €55-60; triples €65-75; quad 85-95. 10% *Let's Go* discount. MC/V. ❷

Hostel and Pensione Soggiorno Imperia, P. Miraglia 386, 6th fl. (☎081 45 93 47; www.soggiornoimperia.it). Take R2, exit at the University, take V. Mezzocannone through P. S. D. Maggiore. Buzz 1st green doors to left on P. Miraglia. Climb 6 flights to reach this peaceful

16th-century *palazzo* and its 9 big, bright rooms. Breakfast and towels included. Laundry €3. Reception open 24hr. Reserve ahead and confirm a few days before arrival. Dorms €15-18; singles €25-30; doubles €45-50, with bath €65; triples €55-60 with shared bath. MC/V. ❸

Hotel Nettuno, V. Sedile di Porto 9, 4th fl. (☎081 55 10 193; www.albergonettuno.com). Take R2, exit at P. Bovio, walk onto V. Sanfelice, and turn right at V. Sedile di Porto. Conveniently located near C. Umberto I, yet removed enough to offer tranquility. Modern rooms have TV, phone, A/C, and bath. Breakfast included. Internet available. Reception 24hr. Singles €45-55; doubles €55-75; triples €75-80; quads €90-100. MC/V. ❸

PIAZZA DEL PLEBISCITO AND ENVIRONS

▨ **Hostel and Hotel Bella Capri,** V. Melisurgo 4 (☎081 55 29 494; www.bellacapri.it). Take R2 bus from station, exit at V. De Pretis. Top-notch hostel offers clean, safe, and fun accommodations for all. Laid-back atmosphere and helpful owner who likes to organize pizza outings. All rooms have A/C and TV; some have bay views. Flatscreen satellite TV and DVDs in the common room; common kitchen. English spoken. Breakfast included. Free lockers, luggage storage, and high-speed Internet access. Laundry €5. Reception 24hr. With *Let's Go* discount, co-ed and female dorms €15-19; singles €35-45, with bath €50-60; doubles €45-55/50-70; triples €60-70/70-90; quads €90-100; family rooms €100-140. AmEx/MC/V. ❶

▨ **Hostel of the Sun,** V. Melisurgo 15 (☎081 42 06 393; www.hostelnapoli.com). Take R2 bus from station, exit at V. De Pretis. Buzz #51. Exuberant staff provide free maps and advice. Pub crawls and free pasta nights twice a week provide surefire entertainment. Common room has satellite TV, DVDs, Skype phone, and library. All private rooms have TV, DVD, and A/C. Kitchen and fridge available. Breakfast included. Free lockers, Internet, and Wi-Fi. Laundry €3. Dorms €18-20; doubles €50-55, with bath €60-70; triples €75-80/70-90; quads €80-90. 10% *Let's Go* discount. MC/V. ❷

MERGELLINA

Ostello Mergellina (HI), V. Salita della Grotta 23 (☎081 76 12 346; fax 76 12 391; info@ostellonapoli.com). ⓂMergellina. Make 2 sharp rights after Metro stop. After overpass, turn right onto driveway, which is unlit at night. Located in a quiet, beautiful part of the city. Laundry €6. Lockout 10am-2pm. Curfew 12:30am. Reserve ahead July-Aug. Dorms €16; singles €25; doubles €40; family rooms €17 per person. MC/V. ❶

Hotel Mergellina, V. Giordano Bruno 115 (☎081 24 82 142; www.hotelmergellina. com). ⓂMergellina or bus #152. Rooms offer TV, phone, bath, and stunning bay views. Breakfast included. Singles €80; doubles €110; triples €130. MC/V. ❹

VOMERO

Hotel Cimarosa, V. Cimarosa 29, 5th fl. (☎081 55 67 044; www.hotelcimarosa.it). Take the funicular from P. Plebiscito, exit at the station. Go around the corner to the right. Buzz to enter (in the same building as the Centrale funicular station). Spacious, ultra-modern rooms have flatscreen TV, phone, safe, minibar, and A/C in a secluded, off-the-beaten path location. Great views of harbor and the city. English spoken. Breakfast included. Free Wi-Fi. Check-out 11am. Curfew 1am. Singles €80-89; doubles €105. MC/V. ❹

◪ FOOD

PIZZERIAS

If you ever doubted the legendary Neapolitan pizza, the city's pizzerias will take that doubt, beat it into a ball, throw it in the air, spin it on their collective finger, punch it down, cover it with sauce and mozzarella, and serve it *alla margherita*. The *centro storico* is full of excellent choices.

CENTRO STORICO

🔣 **Gino Sorbillo,** V. dei Tribunali 35 (☎081 44 66 43; www.sorbillo.it), in the *centro storico* near Vco. San Paolo. The original owner created both the *ripieno al forno* (calzone) and 21 pizza-making children. Reservation may reduce your wait time. Both floors are always abuzz with customers. Basic *marinara* (€3) and *margherita* (€3.50) never tasted so good, yet this is the one place to feast on an everything calzone *fritto al forno* (literally "fried in the oven"). Pizza €2.50-5. Service 10%. Open M-Sa noon-4pm and 7pm-1am. Closes 3 weeks in Aug. AmEx/MC/V. ❶

🔣 **Pizzeria Di Matteo,** V. dei Tribunali 94 (☎081 45 52 62), near V. Duomo. A brick oven churns out some of the best *marinara* around (€2.50). Pizzas burst with flavor and the building bursts with Neapolitans—get on the waiting list and try some of the fried zucchini while you wait. Pizza €2.50-6. Open M-Sa 9am-midnight. Cash only. ❶

PIAZZA DEL PLEBISCITO AND ENVIRONS

Pizzeria Brandi, Salita Sant'Anna di Palazzo 1 (☎081 41 69 28; www.brandi.it), off V. Chiaia. In 1889, Raffaele Esposito invented the *margherita* for Queen Margherita in Brandi's oven to symbolize Italy's flag with green basil, red tomato sauce, and white mozzarella. Famous patrons include Luciano Pavarotti, and Gérard Depardieu. *Margherita* €6.90, with *mozzarella di bufala* €9.40. Cover €1.80. Service 12%. Open M and W-Su 12:30-3pm and 7:30pm-12:30am. Reservations recommended. AmEx/MC/V. ❶

Pizzeria Gorizia, V. Glan Lorenzo Bernini 31 (☎081 57 82 248; www.gorizia1916.com), off P. Vanvitelli in Vomero. A *pizzaiolo* with 60 years of experience still dazzles the young crowd that packs into Gorizia for cheap *margherita* on-the-go (€3) or seated at air conditioned tables (€5). Cover €1. Open Tu-Su 12:30pm-1am. AmEx/MC/V. ❶

RESTAURANTS AND TRATTORIE

Local seafood enjoys an exalted place in Neapolitan dishes. Devour plentiful *cozze* (mussels) with lemon or in soup. Savor *vongole* (clams) in all their glory, and don't miss their more expensive cousin, the *ostrica* (oyster). Try not to gawk as true Neapolitans suck the juices from the heads of *aragosta* (lobster) or devour *polipo* (octopus). For fresh fruits and seafood, the lively **market** on V. Soprammuro, off P. Garibaldi, is the place to go (open M-Sa 8am-1:30pm). Fruit stands, grocery stores, and pastry shops line V. Tribunali in *centro storico*. The waterfront offers a combination of traditional Neapolitan fare and a change of culinary pace; take the Metro or C25 bus to P. Amedeo, on the Mergellina waterfront, for informal, hearty seafood. A large supermarket, **Supero**, Vco. S. Domenico Soriano 20. (Open M-Sa 8:30am-8pm, Su 8:30-1:30pm. MC/V.)

CENTRO STORICO (SPACCANAPOLI)

🔣 **Hosteria Toledo,** Vco. Giardinetto 78/A (☎081 42 12 57), in the Spanish Quarter. Serves Neapolitan comfort food. Tons of antipasti, pasta, and seafood options. If you can't decide, try the chef's surprise—it rarely disappoints. Primi and secondi €5-12. Cover €2. Service 10%. Open M and Th-Su noon-4pm and 7pm-midnight. MC/V. ❷

Trattoria Nennella, Vco. Lungo Teatro Nuovo 105 (☎081 41 43 38), in the Spanish Quarter. Family-run trattoria with fantastic daily *menù* (primo, secondo, contorno, fruit, and wine; €10). Local cuisine at an unbeatable value attracts hordes of Neapolitans nightly. Open Jan.-July and Sept.-Dec. M-Sa noon-3pm and 7-10:30pm. Cash only. ❷

Pizza e Baba, V. Montecalvario 3 (☎081 41 52 44; www.pizzaebaba.com), off V. Toledo. Fresh fish and Neapolitan fare at fair prices. The cool staff and even cooler temperature are a welcome relief from the summer grind. More secluded seating available in renovated basement rooms used as shelters during WWII. *Margherita* €3.50. Primi €6-13. Secondi €6.50-12. Cover €1.50. Open daily noon-midnight. AmEx/MC/V. ❷

Antica Pizzeria da Michele, V. Caesare Sersale 1/3 (☎081 55 39 204; www.damichele.net), at the corner of V. Colletta. From P. Garibaldi, take C. Umberto I and turn right. Huge line outside is an even better indication of quality than the legion of reviews. Serves only *marinara* and *margherita* pizzas. Chefs toss pies with superhuman grace and dexterity. Pizza €4-5. Open M-Sa 10am-11pm. Cash only. ❶

PIAZZA DEL PLEBISCITO AND CHIAIA

⬛ **Donna Margherita,** Vco. Il Alabardieri 4-6 (☎081 40 01 29; www.regina-margherita.it). Quality food with a romantic flair close to great nightlife. Simple and elegant Neapolitan decor. Pizza €3.50-€7. Primi €6-15. Open daily noon-4pm and 7pm-1am. MC/V. ❷

Umberto, V. Alabardieri 30/31 (☎081 41 85 55; www.umberto.it). Ⓜ Amedeo. V. Alabardieri leads out of P. dei Martiri. Swanky but affordable. Serves Neapolitan fare. House special is *tubettoni d'otreddeta* (tube pasta stuffed with seafood; €11). Gluten-free menu available. Primi €6-10. Secondi €8.50-15. Open Tu-Su 12:30-3pm and 7:30pm-midnight. Closed for 3 weeks in Aug. Reservations recommended. AmEx/MC/V. ❷

Ristorante Pizzeria 'a Taverna 'e zi Carmela, V. Niccolò Tommaseo 11-12 (☎081 76 43 35 81), on the corner of V. Partenope. On a breezy side street next to the waterfront. Big with locals for excellent seafood, especially *polipo* (octopus). Ask waiters for *frutti di mare* suggestions to get the best dishes of the day. Primi €3.50-12. Secondi €5-12. Open in summer daily 11:15am-1:30pm and 7:30pm-1am. Cash only. ❷

La Bersagliera, Borgo Marinari 10 (☎081 76 46 016; www.labersagliera.it), seaside by Castel dell'Ovo. Now in it's 4th generation, this family-owned gem of the *lungomare* serves typical Neapolitan dishes in an elegant setting. Prepare your taste buds for the *tagliatelle alla Bersagliera* (€12), pasta with seafood as fresh and salty as the bay it overlooks. Pasta €7-12. Fish secondi €9-15. Cover €2. Reservations suggested for seafront tables. Open M, W-Su noon-3:30pm and 7:30pm-midnight. AmEx/MC/V. ❸

MERGELLINA

Ristorante Al Sarago, P. Sannazzaro 201/b (☎081 76 12 587). Ⓜ Mergellina. Seafaring Neapolitans feel right at home dining in the midst of an aquarium, a brick pizza oven, wine racks, and paintings of the port. The unbeatable marine ambiance is best enjoyed with *spagetthi alla Sarago* (€10), a pasta dish made with every edible treasure the sea has to offer. *Margherita* pizza €5. Primi €4-10. Secondi €7-12. Cover €1.55. Service 13%. Open M-Sa noon-4pm and 7pm-1am, Su noon-4pm. AmEx/MC/V. ❸

Cucina Casereccia e Pizzeria Zi Totonno a Mergellina, P. Sannazzaro 69 (☎081 66 65 64). Ⓜ Mergellina. All imaginable sea creatures are fried, sautéed, and stewed to perfection. *Zuppa di cozze* (mussel soup; €7) comes heaped with succulent mussels and octopus. Tempting antipasti selections (€3.50). Open Tu-Su noon-1am. AmEx/MC/V. ❷

GELATERIE AND PASTICCERIE

Naples's most beloved pastry is *sfogliatelle*, filled with sweetened ricotta, orange rind, and candied fruit. It comes in two forms: the popular *riccia*, a flaky-crust variety, and a softer, crumblier *frolla*. Look for creamy textures and muted colors for the most authentic tastes.

⬛ **Fantasia Gelati,** V. Toledo 381 (☎081 55 11 212), in the *centro storico*. Also at P. Vanvitelli 22. Comes close to gelato perfection. The shop's fruit flavors, including heavenly *arancia* (orange) and tangy papaya, are made with real juices, yielding tart, refreshing results. Over 50 flavors and very generous scoops. Cones €1.50-5; gluten-free €2. Open in summer daily 7am-1am; in winter Tu-Su 7am-11pm. Cash only. ❶

Gay-Odin, V. Toledo 427 (☎081 55 13 491; www.gay-odin.it), in the *centro storico*. Also at V. Vittoria Colonna 15/B (☎081 41 82 82) off P. Amedeo in Chiaia, and V. Benedicto Croce 61 (☎081 55 10 794) near P. Plebiscito. Chocolate treats at this shop include *foresta,* a sweet and crumbly chocolate stalk (from €1 for a small twig to €9 for a trunk best shared with friends). Also offers 12 flavors of gourmet chocolate gelato. Open M-Sa 9:30am-1:30pm and 4:30-8pm, Su 10am-2pm. AmEx/MC/V. ❶

Storico Gran Caffè Gambrinus, V. Chiaia 1 (☎081 41 75 82; www.caffegambrinus. com), off P. del Plebiscito. No visit to the impressive *piazza* is complete without a stop at this equally grand coffee spot. Established in 1860 and renovated in the Liberty style in 1890, the *caffè* still prepares hazelnut cream coffee (€1.80), historically sipped by Ernest Hemingway, Oscar Wilde, Italian presidents, and Neapolitans alike. Frozen desserts from its spectacular *gelateria* start at €4.50. Open 7am-10pm. MC/V. ❶

Storico Gran Caffè Gambrinus, V. Chiaia 1 (☎081 41 75 82; www.caffegambrinus. com), off P. del Plebiscito. No visit to the impressive *piazza* is complete without a stop at this equally grand coffee spot. Established in 1860, the *caffè* still prepares the hazelnut cream coffee (€1.80) once sipped by Ernest Hemingway and Oscar Wilde. Frozen desserts from its spectacular *gelati* start at €4.50. Open 7am-10pm. MC/V. ❶

Scaturchio, P. San D. Maggiore 19 (☎081 55 16 944; www.scaturchio.it), in the *centro storico*. Tucked quietly into a *piazza*, this is the perfect place to enjoy divine desserts and watch Neapolitans pass. A contender for the city's best *sfogliatelle* (€1.40). The wintertime specialty is *ministeriale,* a chocolate and rum pastry (€1.50). Excellent gelato (cones from €2). Open daily 7:20am-8:40pm. AmEx/MC/V. ❶

◉ SIGHTS

The city's exquisite architecture narrates the story of Greek, Roman, and Spanish conquest. The Museo Archeologico Nazionale and the Museo di Capodimonte have excavations in site. The Palazzo Reale's apartments and the city's castles give a taste of 18th-century royal Neapolitan life.

CENTRO STORICO (SPACCANAPOLI)

Naples's most renowned neighborhood is replete with brilliant architecture. Major sights get lost among ornate banks, *pensioni,* and *pasticcerie,* so watch for shoebox-sized signs on buildings. To get to the *centro storico* from P. Dante, walk through Pta. Alba and past P. Bellini before turning down V. dei Tribunali, the former Roman road that now contains some of Naples's best pizzerias.

NAPOLI SOTTERRANEA (CATACOMBS AND UNDERGROUND OF NAPLES). The underground of Naples, started by the Greeks in the seventh century BC, was used until the 1960s; the catacombs of San Gennaro, San Gaudioso, and San Severo provide a glimpse of ancient Neapolis. Fascinating guided tours (1hr.) of the city's subterranean alleys set visitors crawling through narrow underground passageways, grottoes, and catacombs. On your walk beneath the historic center, you'll explore Roman aqueducts, witness Mussolini-era graffiti from the area's days as a bomb shelter, and enter Neapolitan homes to see how ancient Roman theaters have been incorporated into architecture over the ages. (*P. S. Gaetano 68. Take V. Tribunali and turn left right before San Paolo Maggiore. ☎081 29 69 44; www.napolisotterranea.org. Tours in English, French, and German every 2hr. Open M-F noon-4pm, Sa-Su and holidays 10am-6pm. €9.30, students €8. 10% Campania Artecard discount.*)

MUSEO ARCHEOLOGICO NAZIONALE. This former seat of the University of Naples in a 17th-century *palazzo* is one of Europe's oldest museums. A guidebook, audio tour, or guided tour is worth the price. The museum's Farnese Collection displays sculptures from Pompeii and Herculaneum as well as imperial portraits and colossal statues from Rome's Baths of Caracalla. The massive Farnese Hercules depicts the hero after his last labor—another mythical account adds an extra labor to the traditional 12, the 13th including sleeping with 100 women in one night. Check out the ◪**Farnese Bull,** one of the largest surviving statues from antiquity. Sculpted from a single slab of marble, the figure was reworked by none other than Michelangelo. The mezzanine contains a room of exquisite mosaics from Pompeii, most noticeably some delicious-looking fruits and the ◪**Alexander Mosaic,** which depicts a young, fearless Alexander the Great routing the Persian army. Though most have heard of the lovely Aphrodite, the **Gabinetto Segreto** (Secret Cabinet), introduces her lesser-known counterpart, Hermaphrodite, who was blessed with a curvy feminine form and handy masculine member. The collection specializes in erotic art from Pompeii, which includes everything from images of godly love to phallic good luck charms. (Ⓜ*P. Cavour Maseo. Turn right from station, walk 2 blocks. ☎081 44 22 149; www.archeona.arti. benicultura.it. Open M and W-Su 9am-7:30pm. €6.50, EU students €3.25, under 18 or over 65 free. Included on Campania Artecard. Audio tour €4, €2.50 with Campania Artecard.)*

BARGAINAPOLI. The **Campania Artecard** is a worthwhile investment for those taking a few days to tour regional sights. It grants free admission to any 2 of 48 participating museums and sites in and around the city (including Pompeii), and half-price admission to the rest. Free public transportation, special weekend transportation, and discounts on audio tours are also included. Artecards are available at the airport, train stations, travel agencies, and all the museums and sites included on the card throughout the region. (☎800 60 06 01; www.campaniartecard.it. Sights and transportation in Naples and Campi Flegrei €13 for 3 days, ages 18-25 €8; in all of Campania €25 for 3 days, €18 reduced; €28/21 for 1 week.)

DUOMO. Naples's *duomo* lies on V. Duomo, its modest 19th-century facade conceals an ornate interior. Inaugurated in 1315 by Robert of Anjou, the *duomo* has been subject to many additions and renovations. Inside to the right, the main attraction is the **Cappella del Tesoro di San Gennaro,** decorated with Baroque paintings. A beautiful 17th-century bronze grill protects the high altar. The reliquary contains the saint's head and two vials of coagulated blood. According to legend, disaster will strike the city if the blood does not liquefy on the day of the Festa di San Gennaro (**Entertainment and Festivals,** p. 580). Behind the main altar of the church lies the saint's crypt, decorated with Renaissance carvings in white marble. The underground excavation site, also open to visitors, contains an intimate tangle of Greek and Roman roads constructed over several centuries. (*Walk 3 blocks up V. Duomo from C. Umberto I, or take the bus #42 from P. Garibaldi. ☎081 44 90 97. Open M-Sa 8:30am-noon and 4:30-6:30pm. Chapel free; excavation site €3.*)

CAPPELLA SAN SEVERO. The chapel, founded in 1590, is now a private museum. Several remarkable 18th-century statues inhabit its lovely corridors, including the ◪**Veiled Christ** by Giuseppe Sanmartino. Because the chapel's founder, Prince Raimondo of the San Severi, reached Grand Master status in the Free Masons, allusions to Masonry are laced throughout the Christian artwork. These include the swastika labyrinth design, which represents the exploration of universal mysteries. Three major symbols of Masonry can be found at the Veiled Christ's feet: a hammer, a compass, and pliers. Legend claims that the chapel's builder—an alchemist as well as a Grand Master—murdered his wife and her lover by injecting them with a poison that preserved their veins, arteries, and vital organs. (*V. De Sanctis 19, near P. San D. Maggiore.* ☎*081 55 18 470; www.museosansevero.it. Open M and W-Sa 10am-5:40pm, holidays 10am-1:30pm. Admission €5, students under 25 €4, high school students €2, under 9 free. Campania Artecard discount 20%.*)

CHIESA DI SANTA CHIARA. The bright and spacious Santa Chiara was built in the 1300s by the rulers of the house of Anjou. Since then, it has been renovated several times, most recently after a WWII bombing, which destroyed the floor on the left side. The church is littered with sarcophagi and tombs from the Middle Ages, including the 14th-century tomb of Robert of Anjou. The first chapel to the left is dedicated to Neapolitan-born Salvo D'Acquisto, who sacrificed his life during WWII. German troops, enraged at losing one of their own, rounded up 26 women and children to pay dearly for it—Salvo offered his life in the place of theirs, and the Germans conceded. Check out the garden, archaeological site, and monastery, adorned with Gothic frescoes and *majolica* (brightly painted clay) tiles. (*From P. Dante, take V. Toledo and turn left on V. B. Croce. Church in P. Gesù Nuovo.* ☎*081 55 21 597; www.santachiara.info. M-F 9:30am-5:30pm, Su 9:30am-2pm.*)

CHIESA DI GESÙ NUOVO. After its 15th-century construction for the Prince of Salerno, the church passed into the hands of the Jesuits. Its simple facade belies the opulent Baroque interior with inlaid marble floors and colorful ceiling frescoes. The magnificent main altar, featuring a triumvirate of marble statues and a towering gold sun, is overwhelming. Outside the church, a soaring spire glorifies the lives of Jesuit saints. (*Across from Chiesa di Santa Chiara.* ☎*081 55 18 613. Open daily 7am-12:30pm and 4-7:30pm. Modest dress required. Free.*)

PIO MONTE DELLA MISERICORDIA. This chapel was built by a group of nobles to help the sick and needy, house pilgrims, and help ransom Christian slaves held by infidels. The main archway holds Caravaggio's *Seven Works of Mercy*. Outside in the *piazza* stands a spire dedicated to San Gennaro, who saved the city from plague in 1656. (*V. Tribunali 253, 1 block after V. Duomo.* ☎*081 44 69 44; www.piomontedellamisericordia.it. Open M-Tu and Th-Su 9am-2pm. €5; EU students, over 65, and under 14 €3; with Campania Artecard €4. Call to book a tour Tu, Th, Sa 9:30am-1:30pm.*)

IN RECENT NEWS

TRASH TALK

After nearly a decade of trash problems, Naples may finally be cleaning up its act—and its streets. In 2008, the amount of uncollected garbage exceeded 7,000 tons in the metropolitan region around Naples, enough for the EU to finally put its foot down on the boot. Prime Minister Silvio Berlusconi has made it a priority to rescue Naples's nearly defunct municipal waste disposal system from the hands of the Camorra (the Neapolitan Mafia) and to reverse the dumping trend that health experts warned would breed infectious diseases and rat infestations, and thus an increase in cancer and genetic defects.

As attempts to export the city's trash have yielded no sustainable solution, both citizens and politicians are pushing for the latest but not last resort: a *termovalorizzatore*, or incinerator. The chosen model would be located in a former US military space in Agnano (northwest of Naples). Engineers affirm that the state-of-the-art technology, which can burn up to 250,000 tons per year, would pose low risks for the area—and even produce electricity from the combustion process.

Meanwhile, Naples's tourist industry is less than healthy as a result. World-renowned museums, cathedrals, and pizza pies are often skipped over by tourists who fear contact with the *immondizia* (Italian for the trash problem), and assume trash and pickpockets are all that the city has to offer.

CHIESA DI SAN DOMENICO MAGGIORE. Many renovations to this 13th-century church have resulted in the 19th-century spiked Gothic interior visible today. To the right of the altar in the Chapel of the Crucifix hangs the 13th-century painting that allegedly spoke to St. Thomas Aquinas when he lived in the adjoining monastery. Fine Renaissance sculptures decorate the side chapels, but many have been moved to the Capodimonte museum. *(P. S. Domenico Maggiore. ☎ 081 45 91 88. Open daily 8:30am-noon and 4:30-7pm. Free.)*

PIAZZA DEL PLEBISCITO AND CHIAIA

◪PALAZZO REALE. Statues of Neapolitan rulers decorate this 17th-century *palazzo*, now home to the **Museo di Palazzo Reale.** The museum holds opulent royal apartments with Bourbon furnishings, but its artwork pales in comparison to its views of the Bay of Naples and Vomero, which towers majestically in the distance. *(P. Plebiscito 1. ☎ 081 40 05 47; www.pierreci.it. Open M-Tu and Th-Su 9am-7pm. €4, EU students €2, under 18 and over 65 free. Included on Campania Artecard.)* The *palazzo* is also an intellectual mecca, housing the 1,500,000-volume **Biblioteca Nazionale,** which contains carbonized scrolls from the Villa dei Papiri (p. 585) in Herculaneum. *(☎ 081 78 19 231. Visits with reservation M-F 10am-1pm.)* Also in the *palazzo* is the famous **Teatro San Carlo,** built in 1737 and reputed to have better acoustics than La Scala in Milan. For info on performances, see **Entertainment and Festivals,** p. 580. *(Theater entrance on P. Trieste e Trento. ☎ 081 79 72 331; www.itineranapoli.com.)*

CASTELNUOVO O MASCHIO ANGIONO. It's impossible to miss this five-turreted landmark that dominates the Neapolitan skyline. Built in 1284 by Charles II of Anjou as his Naples residence, the fortress's most stunning feature is the soaring triumphal entrance marked by reliefs that commemorate the arrival of Alphonse I of Aragon in 1443. Don't miss WWII bullet holes left on the northern wall. Though actual exhibitions are limited—with the exception of a huge bronze helmet standing about 3m tall—the castle offers wonderful views of Naples. The splendid Cappella Palatina, also called the Chapel of St. Barbara, is a cool retreat from the castle's windy open churchyard. *(P. Municipio. Take the R2 bus from P. Garibaldi, or walk from centro storico. ☎ 081 42 01 241. Open M-Sa 9am-7pm. €5.)*

CASTEL DELL'OVO (EGG CASTLE). This massive, yellow brick Norman castle was built on a large chunk of tufa rock. Virgil—who was believed in medieval times to possess magical powers—is said to have put an enchanted egg in the foundation. According to legend, if the egg breaks, the city will crumble. Originally a monastery, the structure was converted to a fortress to defend against invaders at the end of the AD fifth century. It offers beautiful views, especially during sunset. *(Borgo Marinari. Take bus #1 from P. Garibaldi or P. Municipio to San Lucia and walk across the jetty. ☎ 081 24 00 055. Open M-Sa 8:30am-6pm, Su 8am-2pm.)*

GALLERIA UMBERTO I. Though now a shopping mall busy with vendors selling designer knockoffs, this 19th-century building is one of Naples's most beautiful. Designed by Emanuele Rocco and inspired by a similar gallery in Milan, this space became a meeting place for Allied soldiers toward the end of WWII and is now honored in John Horne Burns's *The Gallery* and Norman Lewis' *Naples '44*. *(P. Trieste e Trento. Most stores open daily 10am-1pm and 4-8pm.)*

CAPODIMONTE

◪MUSEO DI CAPODIMONTE. This museum is housed in a 16th-century royal *palazzo* inside a beautiful pastoral park where youngsters play soccer and lovers, well, play. As if its plush royal apartments were not reason enough to visit, the palace holds the **Italian National Picture Gallery.** The ◪**Farnese Collection**

on the first floor is full of masterpieces, many of them removed from Neapolitan churches for safekeeping. Among these incomparable works are Bellini's *Trasfigurazione* (Transfiguration), Masaccio's *Crocifissione* (Crucifixion), and Titian's *Danae*. The second floor traces the development of the Neapolitan realist style, from Caravaggio's visit to Naples (his funky *Flagellation* is on display) to Ribera and Luca Giordano's adaptations. *(Take bus #178, C63, R4, M4, or M5 from Archaeological Museum and exit at the gate to the park, on the right. Park has 2 entrances, Pta. Piccola and Pta. Grande.* ☎ *081 74 99 109. Open M-Tu and Th-Su 8:30am-7:30pm. Museum €7.50, after 2pm €6.50. Free mandatory bag check.)*

BASILICA DELL'INCORONATA MADRE DEL BUON CONSIGLIO. Although it opened for worship in 1960, this basilica is modeled after St. Peter's in Rome. Built above the catacombs of San Gennaro, it sustained unusual damage during the 1980 earthquake. Most famously, the head of the Madonna statue fell from the tall facade but did not shatter. *(V. Capodimonte 13. All buses to Museo di Capodimonte stop at the basilica and catacombs upon request.* ☎ *081 19 97 91 46; www.basilicaincoronata.it. Open daily 8am-12:30pm and 4:30-7:30pm. Free.)*

CATACOMBE DI SAN GENNARO. The catacombs were once the resting place of San Gennaro's beheaded body. Though most of the lower level is unexcavated, archaeologists know that the grotto was first used by early Pagans as a ceremonial, burial, and orgy site. In the AD third century, it became a Christian cemetery, stratified by social class: rich families had caves adorned with frescoes, while the poor rested on the floors and walls. The small holes along the walls held torches, a necessity before the AD fifth century Basilica Minore's window was carved. Few bodies remain in the upper level; the last time the catacombs suffered from overcrowding was during WWII when they were used as a shelter. *(V. Capodimonte 16. Gated entrance is left of the basilica.* ☎ *081 74 43 714. 30min. tours in English every hour; minimum 2 people per tour. Jan.-July and Sept.-Dec. Tu-Sa 9am-noon and 2-3pm, Su 9am-noon; Aug. Tu-Sa 9am-noon. No afternoon tours in Aug. €5, children 6-15 €3.)*

VOMERO

MUSEO NAZIONALE DI SAN MARTINO. Once the monastery of St. Martin, the cloisters are now home to an excellent museum of Neapolitan history and culture. Highlights include Riberia's *Deposition of Christ*, considered one of his finest works, and the *Nativity* by Guido Reni. The monastery also sports a lavish chapel festooned with Baroque marbles and statuary. Numerous balconies and a multi-level garden have views of the city. *(*☎ *081 22 94 589; www.pierreci.it. Open M-Tu and Th-Su 8:30am-7:30pm. €6, EU students €3. Included on Campania Artecard.)* The massive **Castel Sant'Elmo** next door was built to deter rebellion and hold political prisoners. The Castel is included on a ticket to San Martino but isn't otherwise worth a visit. *(From V. Toledo, take the funicular to Vomero and turn right on V. Cimarosa. Continue straight up 2 flights of stairs, along V. Scarlatti, and then veer left, walking for about 10min., keeping right on V. Tito Angelini; Castel Sant'Elmo and Ple. San Martino are on the right.* ☎ *848 80 02 88; www.civita.it. Open M-Tu and Th-Su 8:30am-6:30pm. €3, EU students €1.50, EU citizens under 18 or over 65 free. Special exhibits around €6. Included on Campania Artecard.)*

MUSEO DUCA DI MARTINA. Ceramics fans should visit this crafts gallery inside the lush gardens of the **Villa Floridiana** for 18th-century Italian and Asian porcelain. Though on the smaller side, this collection is thoughtfully presented and full of treasures. *(V. Cimarosa 77. Take funicular from V. Toledo to Vomero, turn right from the station, then left on V. Cimarosa. Enter the gardens and keep walking downhill.* ☎ *081 22 94 589; www.pierreci.it. Open M and W-Su 8:30am-1:30pm. €2.50, EU students €1.25, EU citizens under 18 or over 65 free. Campania Artecard discount 10%.)*

🛍 SHOPPING

A thriving black market and low prices make Naples an enticing place for shopping—as long as you keep in mind that the street vendor's livelihood depends on his craftiness, so given the chance to outwit you, he will. If a transaction seems too good to be true, it is. **Never buy electronic products from street vendors.** Even brand-name boxes have been known to be filled with newspaper or rocks and CDs and DVDs are often blank. Two words about bargaining: do it. In the dog-eat-dog world of unregulated transactions, bargaining is the law.

Via Santa Maria di Constantinopoli, south of the Archaeological Museum, has old books and antique shops. **Spaccanapoli** and its side streets near the Conservatorio house small music shops with inexpensive manuscripts. **Via Toledo, Corso Umberto I,** and **Via Duomo** provide high-class shopping for a lower budget, and the streets south of **San Lorenzo Maggiore** house Neapolitan craftsmen. **Piazza Martiri** offers major Italian designers, and **Galleria Umberto** has plenty of high-end stores. The most expensive shopping district is in the hills of **Vomero** along the perpendicular **Via Scarlatti** and **Via Luca Giordano.** Many artisans' workshops inhabit the streets nearby, hawking everything from wrought iron to delicate cameos. Most markets are open Monday through Saturday (from 9am to 2pm). Two weekends of every month (1 per month June-July), the **Fiera Antiquaria Neapolitana,** along V. Francesco Caracciolo on the waterfront, hosts flea markets filled with ancient artifacts. Though such items come with hefty price tags, hundreds of shoppers wander through the stands browsing stamps, books, coins, and art. (☎081 62 19 51. Open daily 8am-2pm.) From early December to early January, Neapolitan artisans gather along the Spaccanapoli and surrounding streets to create fine handmade porcelain nativity scenes. Renowned throughout Europe, this spectacle draws a huge international crowd.

🎵 🎎 ENTERTAINMENT AND FESTIVALS

Once famous occasions for revelry, Naples's religious festivals are now excuses for sales and shopping sprees. On September 19 and the first Saturday in May, the city celebrates the **Festa di San Gennaro.** Join the crowd to watch the procession by the *duomo* in May and see the patron saint's blood miraculously liquefy in a vial. In July, P. S. Domenico Maggiore holds concerts and the **Neapolis Festival** hosts pop concerts at Arena Flegrea in Campi Flegrei. **Teatro San Carlo** (☎081 79 72 331 or 79 72 412) at Palazzo Reale hosts symphony (Oct.-May) and opera (Dec.-June) performances. Gallery tickets should be purchased in advance (from €12). Consult the ticket office and *Il Mattino* for schedules. Catch a soccer match at **Stadio San Paolo** in Fuorigrotta for a truly accurate portrait of Neapolitan life. **Napoli,** in Serie A (the first division) attracts spectators for matches from September to June. (☎081 23 95 623. Ⓜ Campi Flegrei, or buses 152, M1, or SEPSA. Tickets from €15.)

🎭 NIGHTLIFE

Travelers hoping to dance the night away may be surprised by the lack of discos, but Naples is not without nightlife. Come summer, young Neapolitans pack the *piazze* by the hundreds, especially on Sundays. The 🅂**evening aperitivo,** a pre-dinner drink accompanied by light fare, is an institution among older crowds. To maximize your enjoyment of the city's bustling nocturnal scene, follow this crash course in *piazza* personalities. At night, **Piazza Gesù Nuovo** and **Piazza Duomo** are crammed with university students who firmly believe in the "healing powers" of certain botanicals. **Via Santa Maria La Nova** are also always packed with crowds looking for a late night hot dog or low priced liquor (beer usually €1). The area around **Piazza dei Martiri** in Chiaia has the most bars, while the *aperitivo* culture thrives on **V. Giuseppe Ferrigni.** Bars in the quieter **Piazza Bellini** host a relaxed mix of locals and tourists. The *piazza* is also a gathering point for the gay community. The young and chic gather at **Piazza Vanvitelli,** just a short metro or funicular ride alongside **V. Toledo.** Beware: buses and funiculars may not run past 11pm. *Il Mattino* and *Zero 81* guides print decent club listings. From September through June, **Angels of Love** attracts world-renowned DJs to host parties for upward of 5,000 people in the outskirts of Naples. Grand scale bashes of this kind are typically accessible only by car or taxi (☎330 86 83 23 or 339 68 23 066; www.angelsoflove.it).

CENTRO STORICO

Rising South, V. S. Sebastiano 19 (☎081 333 653 4273; www.risingsouth.it), near P. Gesù Nuovo. *Enoteca*, bar, cultural association, cinema—this club does it all. Plush, Oriental carpets, vintage chandeliers, and a soundproof main hall carved from tufa set the scene at this student favorite for term-time fun. Mixed drinks €3-6. Open as a bar Sept.-May Tu-Su 10pm-3am (depending on weather) and for special events in summer.

Kestè, V. S. Giovanni Maggiore Pignatelli 27 (☎08 15 51 39 84), near the university. Alternative feel that attracts all strata of Neapolitan society. Enjoy eating outside by the garden or dancing inside to a live DJ Tu-Su. Local bands play every Su from 11pm. Beer €3. Open Sept.-July daily 9:30pm-late. Cash only.

Jail Club, V. Sedile di Porto 65 (☎081 347 170 3585; www.jailclub.it), near the university. The club and the feel are both underground, as live DJs spin progressive, punk, hardcore metal, gothic, and Indie rock. Well-known for its beer fests (free beer 11pm-1am). Cover charge varies. Open Th-Su 11pm-late. Cash only.

Caffè Letterario Intra Moenia, P. Bellini 70 (☎081 29 07 20; www.intramoenia.it). Appeals to an intellectual crowd, with books laid out for skimming. Gay friendly. Beer €3.50-6. Mixed drinks €6-7. Caprisian delight €7. Open daily 10am-2am. Cash only.

Lemme Lemme By Internet Bar, P. Bellini 74 (☎081 29 52 37). Located in one of Naples's more peaceful *piazze*, this bar has art expos, Internet access, and outdoor seating. The vibe is right. Live music F Oct.-Apr. Internet and Wi-Fi discounts for clients. Beer €3-5, mixed drinks €6. *Aperitivo* hour 7pm. Open M-Sa 9:30am-3am, Su 5pm-3am. Cash only.

PIAZZA PLEBISCITO AND CHIAIA

S'Move, Vco. dei Sospiri 10 (☎081 76 45 813; www.smove-lab.net), off V. G. Ferrigni. Puts a new spin on disco music with a different techno DJ every night. 2 levels are always crowded enough to spill out into the street. Beer from €3. Mixed drinks from €5. Open daily 6pm-4am. Closed 2 weeks in Aug. MC/V.

La Scalinatella, V. S. Pasquale 51 (☎081 25 12 478). Well-dressed Neapolitans and tourists mingle up the flight of stairs that give La Scalinatella its name. Stays glamorous until the sun also rises. Mixed drinks €6. Open F-Su 11pm-late. Cash only.

Il Taschino, V. Ferrigni 31 (☎081 338 110 4513). The narrow street becomes almost impassable at the height of this *baretto*. You might as well stay. Bartender DJs serve creative stiff drinks (€4-5). *Aperitivo* hour 7pm. Open Tu-Su 6pm-4am. Closed in Aug. Cash only.

Nàis Moment, V. G. Ferrigni 29 (☎081 65 80 466). A bookstore with a bar in the center of the most popular street in Chiaia. €5 drinks are served by the Nàis People, down-to-earth staff who will invite you to peruse the merchandise or access the Internet for free while you drink. It should make for a *Nàis* night. Open daily 5pm-midnight. Closed in Aug. MC/V.

Farinella Music Hall, V. Alabardieri 10 (☎081 42 38 455). Enormous upscale bar and *discoteca*, packed in winter for live jazz concerts. In summer, the hall is a relaxing prelude to a night on the *piazze*. A hip, young crowd watches sports on the big-screen TVs. Mixed drinks from €5, after 7:30pm from €7. AmEx/MC/V.

🏃 OUTDOOR ACTIVITIES

The **waterfront** streets of Naples afford city-dwellers a great opportunity for relaxation. A 4km rocky shoreline stretches from V. Nazaro Sauro in the P. del Plebiscito area through V. Caracciolo in Mergellina. Ignoring the nearby ports, Neapolitans claim these rocks as their escape from the city, bathing in the sun and casually dipping into the bay or swimming around the Castel dell'Ovo. Kiosks at **P. Nazaro Sauro** sell refreshing drinks and even lemon-sprayed, salted tripe late into the night. Downstairs in the *piazza*, easygoing locals let **rowboats.** (☎081 331 986 9809. Open daily 7am-9pm. €20 for 2hr., but counteroffers are highly recommended.) Currents are generally mild, and **swimming** in the open water is both refreshing and cleaner than near the shore. Find shade and enjoy a picnic at the **Villa Communale,** a large public park which stretches along V. Caracciolo opposite to the waterfront. (Open daily 7am-midnight. Free.) Waterfront bars abound along V. Partenope. If you're famished after a swim, **Bar dell'Ovo,** V. Partenope 6, outdoes its surrounding competitors with an *aperitivo* hour (7pm), a *discoteca* (Nov.-May Th-Su midnight-5am), an electrifying bar crew, and outdoor seating characteristic of the *lungomare*. (☎081 24 74 653. Beer €3. Wine €4. Mixed drinks €4.50. Open 8am-3am. Cash only.)

🔀 DAYTRIPS FROM NAPLES

POMPEII (POMPEI)

On the morning of August 24, AD 79, a deadly cloud of volcanic ash from the eruption of nearby Mt. Vesuvius overtook Pompeii (pom-PAY), engulfing the city in black clouds. Many fled, but others—including the famous historian Pliny the Elder—unaware of the severity of the eruption or scared their property would be stolen, decided to stay. Mere hours after the eruption, stately buildings, works of art, and human bodies were sealed in casts of ash—natural tombs that went undisturbed for centuries. Today, visitors to the site bear witness to an intimate record of the town's demise. Since excavation efforts began in 1748, archaeologists have continually turned up discoveries in their ongoing mission to understand life in the Roman era. Most of the interesting artifacts from Pompeii are in Naples's Museo Archeologico Nazionale (p. 576), meaning that the site itself consists mostly of buildings and streets. To get more out of your trip to Pompeii, preface it with a visit to the museum's extensive Pompeii collection and listen to the audio tour.

🚍 🔀 TRANSPORTATION AND PRACTICAL INFORMATION

The quickest route to Pompeii (25km south of Naples) is the Circumvesuviana **train** (☎081 77 22 444). Board at Naples's Stazione Centrale (dir.: Sorrento; 40min., 2 per hr. 5:40am-10:40pm, €2.30) or from Sorrento's station. Get off at "Pompei Scavi." The **Porta Marina** entrance to the city is downhill to the left. Trenitalia trains also leave from the Naples station, stopping at modern Pompeii en route to Salerno (30min., every hr., €2.20). The Trenitalia station is a

10min. walk from the excavations' eastern entrance; to reach it, walk to the end of V. Statale until it becomes V. Sacra and turn left on V. Roma.

The excavations stretch along an east-west axis, with the modern town (and its hotels and restaurants) at the eastern end. Stop by the **tourist office**, V. Sacra 1 (☎081 85 07 255; www.pompeiisites.org), or the info booth at the site for a free map. From the Pompei Scavi stop, take a right; follow the road down the hill to the **branch office**, P. Porta Marina Inferiore 12. (☎081 800 013 350. Both offices open M-F 8am-3:30pm, Sa 8am-2pm.) Free **luggage storage** and an **ATM** are available at ruins entrance. There is a **police station** and a **post office** (☎081 85 06 164; open M-F 8:30am-1:30pm and Sa 8:30am-noon) at the entrance, P. Esedra 1. Another police station at P. Bartolo Longo, where V. Roma ends.

👁 SIGHTS

A comprehensive exploration of Pompeii takes all day. A popular tourist attraction year-round, Pompeii's **ruins** are most crowded in the spring when they are visited by throngs of school groups. A trip in early summer or fall is best for avoiding the crowds. (Ruins open daily Apr.-Oct. 8:30am-7:30pm; Nov.-Mar. 8:30am-5pm. Last entry 1hr. before close. Tickets €11, EU students €5.50, EU citizens under 18 or over 65 free. No re-entry. Wheelchair access through the eastern entrance at P. Anfiteatro.) Those planning to visit several sites should consider buying a three-day archeological pass to Pompeii, Herculaneum, Opionti, Stabia, and Boscoreale. (€20, EU citizens €10. Sold at site ticket office.) The budget-conscious in search of an engaging tour should consider the excellent audio tours, available at the site's entrance, to supplement the free map. (€6.50, 2 tours for €10, children's tour €4.50.) Independent guides gather solo travelers by the ticket office to form tour groups. Informative guided tours are crowded and expensive (2hr., €90 for 3 people).

NEAR THE FORUM. The **basilica** walls are to the right upon entering the ruins. Before the eruption, lawyers and prominent citizens fought battles on this floor. Walk farther down V. Marina to reach the **forum,** ringed by a marble colonnade. Once dotted with statues of emperors and gods, this site was the city's commercial, civic, and religious center. Glass display cases house gruesome body casts of Vesuvius's victims, contorted in shock and agony. The **Tempio di Giove**—largely destroyed by an earthquake 17 years before the eruption—stands at the upper end of the forum and offers a view of Mt. Vesuvius. To the left, the **Tempio di Apollo** contains copies of the statues of Apollo and Diana (originals displayed in the **Museo Archeologico Nazionale,** p. 576) and a column topped by a sundial. With the Tempio di Giove behind you, the **Tempio di Vespasiano** across the forum retains a delicate frieze depicting preparations for a sacrifice. To the right, the **Building of Eumachia** has a door frame carved with animals and insects.

NEAR THE HOUSE OF THE FAUN. At the **Forum Baths,** notice rooms allotted for servants who accompanied their patrons to watch their belongings. The **House of the Faun** has yielded stunning treasures, among them a dancing bronze faun and the spectacular Alexander Mosaic (originals in the **Museo Archeologico Nazionale,** p. 576). The building's opulence leads archaeologists to believe that it was the dwelling of one of the richest men in town. The **House of the Vettii** was the home of two brothers whose rivalry is apparent on every wall. A famous painting of the fertility god Priapus, flaunting his very ample endowment, is in the vestibule. Phalli were considered lucky and believed to scare off evil spirits in ancient times. Notice the ruts worn in the stone roads by chariot wheels passing through. *(Exit the forum through the upper end by the cafeteria; Forum Baths are on the left. A right on V. della Fortuna leads to the House of the Faun. Continuing on V. della Fortuna, turn left on Vco. dei Vettii to reach the House of the Vettii on the left.)*

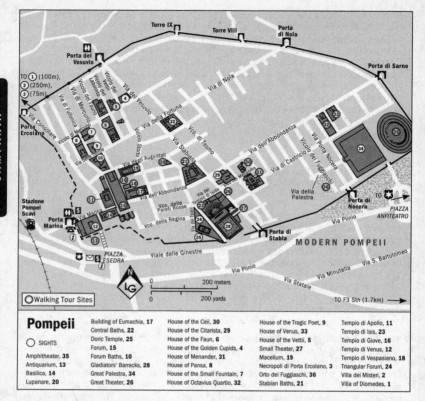

Pompeii

○ SIGHTS

Amphitheater, **35**
Antiquarium, **13**
Basilica, **14**
Lupanare, **20**

Building of Eumachia, **17**
Central Baths, **22**
Doric Temple, **25**
Forum, **15**
Forum Baths, **10**
Gladiators' Barracks, **28**
Great Palestra, **34**
Great Theater, **26**

House of the Ceii, **30**
House of the Citarista, **29**
House of the Faun, **6**
House of the Golden Cupids, **4**
House of Menander, **31**
House of Pansa, **8**
House of the Small Fountain, **7**
House of Octavius Quartio, **32**

House of the Tragic Poet, **9**
House of Venus, **33**
House of the Vettii, **5**
Small Theater, **27**
Macellum, **19**
Necropoli di Porta Ercolano, **3**
Orto dei Fuggiaschi, **36**
Stabian Baths, **21**

Tempio di Apollo, **11**
Tempio di Isis, **23**
Tempio di Giove, **16**
Tempio di Venus, **12**
Tempio di Vespasiano, **18**
Triangular Forum, **24**
Villa dei Misteri, **2**
Villa of Diomedes, **1**

NEAR THE BROTHEL. The racier side of Pompeii can be found at the small brothel, or **Lupanare** (literally, dwelling of she-wolves). Beware if you've got young travelers in tow: the brothel is unsurprisingly covered in pornographic imagery. The **Stabian Baths** were privately owned and therefore fancier than the Forum Baths; the women's side has an impressive marine-creature mosaic. More body casts—some of the site's most gruesome and impressive—rest in dusty glass cases. *(From Vco. dei Vettii, cross V. della Fortuna over to Vco. Storto, and turn left on V. degli Augustali to reach Lupanare. Baths are on the main avenue, V. dell'Abbondanza.)*

 SOME DON'T LIKE IT HOT. The sites at Pompeii provide few water fountains and little shade. Bring lots of water to avoid heat stroke. If you need medical attention, flag down a guide or call ☎113. Remember, you are walking a whole city! Don't think that because it's ancient, it's small.

NEAR THE GREAT THEATER. The **Great Theater,** built during the second century BC, was already somewhat destroyed by the time the volcano erupted. Many stone-walled cells, thought to have been **Gladiators' Barracks,** line the edges of the field in front. The nearby **Small Theater** was used for music and poetry. North of the theaters stands the **Tempio di Isis,** Pompeii's monument to the Egyptian goddess. At the end of the street, take a left to re-connect to the main road. The altar was built to ward off evil spirits, which Romans believed gathered at crossroads. *(Across V. dell'Abbondanza from the baths, V. dei Teatri leads to the theaters.)*

NEAR THE AMPHITHEATER. Red graffiti covers the walls along V. dell'Abbondanza with everything from political slogans to insults to declarations of love. At the end of the street await the **House of Octavius Quartio** and **House of Venus,** where gardens have been replanted according to modern knowledge of ancient horticulture. Nearby is the impeccably preserved **amphitheater** (70 BC), which once held crowds of 20,000. The spectators determined whether a gladiator would live or die during battle with a casual thumbs-down or thumbs-up. In the **Orto dei Fuggiaschi,** some of the body casts of fleeing victims display expressions and individual facial features. Also nearby, the **Great Palestra's** columns still surround a courtyard that once housed exercise sessions for local boys and now offers a great place to rest under the shadows of surrounding trees.

VILLA DEI MISTERI. Outside the city walls, the **Villa dei Misteri** is the best-preserved Pompeiian villa; gape at the extravagant atrium and the varied architecture—all "Four Styles" of Pompeii are displayed. The *Dionysiac Frieze* depicts a bride's initiation into the cult of Dionysus. Nearby, the famed **Cave Canem mosaic** still guards the entry to its master's villa, known as the **House of the Tragic Poet.** Head through the *porta* for a great view of the entire city. *(For the Villa go to western end of V. della Fortuna, turn right on V. Consolare, and walk up Villa delle Tombe.)*

HERCULANEUM (ERCOLANO)

To reach Herculaneum, take a Circumvesuviana train from Naples's Stazione Centrale to "Ercolano Scavi" (dir.: Sorrento; 20min.). Walk 500m downhill to the ticket office. The Municipal Tourist Office, V. IV Novembre 82, is on the way (☎081 78 81 243; open M-Sa 9am-2pm). Archaeological site: ☎081 85 75 347; www.pompeiisites.org. Open Apr.-Oct. daily 8:30am-7:30pm; Nov.-Mar. 8:30am-5pm. Last entry 1hr. before close. €11, EU students €5.50, EU citizens under 18 or over 65 free. Audio tours (in English, French, German, Italian, or Spanish) are especially enlightening. 1-2hr.; €6.50, 2 for €10; under 18 €4/7. Grab an illustrated guidebook (€4-6) at the shops that flank the entrance, or pick up the free Brief Guide to Herculaneum and map at the entrance. Free mandatory bag check.

Neatly excavated and intact, the remains of this prosperous Roman town hardly deserve the term "ruins." Buried in superheated volcanic tuff instead of the ash that covered Pompeii, Herculaneum (in Italian, "ehr-co-LA-no") is much more intact—many buildings still have second stories—and better preserved than its larger and more famous neighbor. Exploring the houses—complete with frescoes, furniture, mosaics, and small sculptures can make a tourist feel more like a house guest; artifacts displayed in their original contexts lend to a very rewarding and informative experience.

Though archaeologists long held the opinion that most of Herculaneum's residents escaped the eruption that destroyed Pompeii, a 1982 discovery of skeletons huddled in a boathouse suggests that a large part of the population was buried while attempting to get away. Much of the city remains un-excavated, and only about a quarter of the city is open to the public. One of the more opulent buildings is the **House of Deer,** named for the grisly statues of deer being mauled by packs of dogs. Here, archaeologists also found the statues *Satyr with a Wineskin* and *Drunken Hercules,* a majestic marble representation of the hero struggling to relieve himself. The **palestra,** a gym and exercise complex, complete with a large vaulted swimming pool, still holds shelves once laden with massage oils and the *strigili* (back scrapers) used to clean skin after a rubdown. The **House of Neptune and Amphitrite** is famous for a stellar mosaic. The house is connected to a remarkably well-preserved **wine shop.**

Dating to the second century BC, the **Samnite House** is one of the oldest buildings in Herculaneum. Down the street, the three-floored **House of the Wooden Partition** still has a door in its elegant courtyard and a clothes press around the corner. Outside the site lies the **theater,** perfectly preserved though buried underground. A well dug in 1709 unearthed the theater and catalyzed excavation of the rest of Herculaneum; unfortunately, the theater was soon stripped of its valuable decorations. (☎081 73 24 311. Occasionally open for visits; call to check.) The extravagant 250m-long **Villa dei Papiri,** 500m west of Herculaneum, earned its name in 1752 when papyrus scrolls were found inside; the highly damaged works are still being studied and restored—thus far, no classics have been found. (Rarely open to the public; Campania Artecard holders can view the site by special arrangement. Contact municipal tourist office at ☎081 78 81 243 for details. Scrolls on display at Biblioteca Nazionale, p. 578.)

MOUNT VESUVIUS (MONTE VESUVIO)

Take Circumvesuviana train from Naples's Stazione Centrale to "Ercolano Scavi" (dir.: Sorrento; 20min.). Vesuvio Express buses (☎081 73 93 666) run from Herculaneum up to the crater of Vesuvius (every 30min. or as soon as van is filled; round-trip €10). Buy tickets next to the Ercolano Vesuviana station; buses leave from outside station. The "Vesuvius" stop is part way up the crater; it's a 20-30min. walk to the top. Open in summer 9am-5pm; in winter 9am-3pm. Wear proper footwear and bring water. €6.50.

A semi-challenging hike to the top of the only active volcano on mainland Europe is completely worth it. From the top, enjoy great views of the Bay of Naples and impressive flora growing on the lava. In the good old days, visitors could clamber about in the crater to their hearts' content; the rules changed a little when a Belgian tourist accidentally took a fatal plunge in 1998. Now you'll have to settle for peering inward from Vesuvius's steep lip. Each fiery belch (over 50 since the famous AD 79 eruption that buried Pompeii) has helped widen and deepen the aperture. Vesuvius hasn't blown its top since March 31, 1944—the longest it has lain dormant in several centuries. A geological station closely monitors tectonic rumblings, and local governments are always ready with a comprehensive evacuation plan. In the summer of 2003, a geological station near the site detected significant subterranean activity, prompting much speculation and concern. The next eruption is expected to be the most violent since 1631, when 3000 people died.

REGGIA DI CASERTA (PALACE OF CASERTA)   ☎0823

Caserta is accessible by trains to and from Naples (40min., 8 per day 5:40am-11:05pm). Buy the Fascia 4 Unico Campania pass (€2.90). The Caserta train station is also a major local stop. The Reggia is directly opposite the train station. EPT tourist offices operate inside the Reggia and at C. Trieste 43, at the corner of P. Dante. (☎0823 55 00 11. Both offices open M-F 9am-4pm.) For Capua, take the train to "Santa Maria Capua Vetere," walk straight 1 block, and make the 1st left. Take the next left on V. Achille, walk 150m, and turn right on V. Eugenia Ricciardi, which becomes V. Amfiteatro. Or take the blue bus from the Caserta train station to P. Adriano near the ruins. Naples-bound buses leave from an intersection 1 block north of Capua train station.

Few palaces, no matter how opulent, hold a candle to Caserta's glorious royal palace, ◪**La Reggia** (lah REH-jya), which was built over a period of 100 years and rivals Versailles. A world apart from Pompeii's brutality and Naples's quiet churches, the palace and its grounds resonate with a love of art and a passion for beauty that have earned it recognition as a UNESCO World Heritage site. Lovely grounds lead already impressed visitors up to the breathtaking palace. Completed in 1775, the expansive lawns, fountains, sculptures, and carefully pruned trees culminate in a 75m man-made waterfall—the setting of the final scene of *Star Wars* (1977). On the 3km walk through the park, visitors can peer into the azure, fish-filled pools, from which royals and servants alike once caught their dinner. The impressive waterworks were made possible by an aqueduct from neighboring mountains made at the time of construction. Nearby, the lush **English Gardens,** complete with fake ruins inspired by Pompeii, are an excellent picnic spot. Instead of walking 30min. to the waterfall, consider taking a horse-and-buggy ride from the garden entrance (€10 per person) or a less-romantic trip on one of the park's mini-buses (€1). The **palazzo** itself boasts 1200 rooms, 1742 windows, and 34 staircases, yet somehow avoids superfluity. Frescoes and intricate marble floors adorn the royal apartments, some boasting beds guarded by sculptures of scary mythical beasts. (☎0823 32 14 00. Open M and W-Su 9am-7:30pm; park open 9am-6:30pm. Gardens €2, *palazzo* and gardens €6. Included on Campania Artecard.)

CAMPI FLEGREI

SEPSA buses run from P. Municipio in Naples to the towns of Campi Flegrei (www.info-campiflegrei.it). Use the blue SEPSA bus (dir.: Monte di Procida/Torregaveta), or the yellow SEPSA bus #152. To Baia, take the blue or yellow SEPSA bus from ⓂPozzuoli (30min.). Don't be confused by signs on the Ferrovia Cumana; this rail line no longer goes through Baia. In Baia, buy an Unico Napoli Fascia 1 ticket (€1.80) for access to any transportation all day. To Cumae, take a SEPSA bus (dir.: Miseno-Cuma) from the train station at Baia to the last stop in Cumae (15min., €0.60) and walk to the end of V. Cumae. The "Cuma" stop on the Ferrovia Circumflegrea is in the modern town, far from the archaeological sites. Get to Pozzuoli using the Ferrovia Cumana, Ferrovia Circumflegria, or Naples Metro.

The Campi Flegrei (CAM-pee fle-GREY), a group of tiny coastal towns west of Naples nestled among lakes and inactive volcanoes, were immortalized in Virgil's *Aeneid* as Aeneas's landing point in Italy (in Cumae). Their hot springs, intricate bath houses, and supposed gate to hell (according to the ancient Greeks) now form the backdrop for a residential center and beautiful bay away from the craziness of Naples. Perched on a hill overlooking the bustling port center of **Baia,** where SEPSA buses drop passengers off, is the town's main attraction: luxurious **Roman Baths,** remarkable for their well-preserved mosaics and ceilings. At the base of the hill sits the gem of the bath houses, known as the **Tempio di Mercurio,** or the Temple of Echoes. (☎081 86 87 592. Open Tu-Su 9am-7pm. 2-day archaeological pass grants admission to the baths, the Archaeological Museum in Baia, the *scavi* (caves) in Cumae, and the amphitheater in Pozzuoli. €4. Sold at participating sites. Included on Campania Artecard.) A short bus ride from the center of Baia takes you to the **Museo Archeologico dei Campi Flegrei,** which contains a small collection of ancient artifacts, including many from the underwater city. The museum is located inside the Castello di Baia, built in 1495 to control the Bay of Pozzuoli, and offers a panoramic view from the top. (☎081 52 33 797. Open Tu-Sa 9am-1hr. before sunset, Su 9am-7pm. €4. Entrance with archaeological pass or Campania Artecard.) For a cooler view of ruins, try the glass-bottomed boat *Cymba* out of Baia's port to see the ▣**Submerged Roman City.** (☎320 83 50 145. Departs Mar.-Nov. Sa noon, 3pm; Su 10am, noon, 3pm. Does not run on days with murky water. Call ahead to confirm departure. €10, ages 5-12 €7, under 5 free. 10% *Let's Go* discount.)

The highlight of the excavations at **Cumae (Cuma)** is the **Antro della Sibilla,** a cave used as a pizza oven until 1932, when archaeologists realized what it really was. Stroll through the cave and see where the mythical Sibyl, the most famous oracle this side of Delphi, gave her prophecies. Then gape at the **Augustan Tunnel,** a route used for transportation inland from the coast and rumored to have been connected to Rome. (☎081 85 43 060. Open daily 9am-1hr. before sunset. €4, ages 5-10 €2.) According to legend, the **Tempio di Apollo** was constructed by

Daedalus, who came to Cumae after escaping captivity in Crete with his hand-made wings. Little remains of the original temples; the hike is worthwhile only for those who want to see the view that captivated Daedalus.

Beneath Solfatara, a short walk from the waterfront, is the first-century ⚑**Flavian Amphitheater,** the third largest in Italy. The remarkably well-preserved structures below have given engineers an idea of how the Romans raised a caged beast up to the floor of the stadium. (☎081 52 66 007. Open M and W-Su in summer 9am-8pm; in winter 9am-3pm. €4, EU students €2. Entrance with archaeological pass or Campania Artecard.) Near the busy port of **Pozzuoli** is the famous volcanic crater **Solfatara,** accessed either by hiking from the center of Pozzuoli (following frequent signs) or by riding bus #152. Solfatara was once believed to be a portal to Hades, but nowadays there is not much to admire. (☎081 52 62 341; www.solfatara.it. Open daily 8:30am-1hr. before sunset. €5.50, children 5-10 €4.) **International Camping ❶,** offers a night's stopover in purgatory before you enter the underworld. (☎081 52 62 341. Reception 6am-11pm. Ring bell after hours. Camping €7.60 per person, €6.50 per student, €3.80 per child; high season €9.40/8/4.70. 2-person bungalows €46, 3-person €55, 4-person €66; high season €51/62/74. Campania Artecard discount 20%.)

BAY OF NAPLES

Home to the pleasant islands of Capri, Ischia, and Procida, and the coastal town of Sorrento, the Bay of Naples could hardly seem further away from the city that shares its coast. On Capri, expensive shops and pristine waters are the playground of the rich, while Ischia's hot springs and therapeutic waters beckon those seeking health of mind and body. Procida, the quietest island, has winding streets and empty shores that retain an unadulterated mystique. Merge with crowds at the famous villas and grottoes, but come back later for a private dip. Back on solid ground, Sorrento is both a good base for island-hopping and a coastal destination in its own right. Above all, in the Bay, just take it easy.

SORRENTO   ☎081

Built on cliffs above the glittering Bay of Naples, Sorrento (so-REN-toh; pop. 18,000) is a maze of tiny alleys and quiet side streets. Its *piazze* and roads are overrun with tourists strolling and window shopping in the *centro storico* and Marina Grande. Majestic sunsets and street music are the perfect end to a perfect day. A convenient base for daytrips, Sorrento boasts plentiful accommodations, swift transportation connections, and proximity to the Amalfi Coast.

⌐ TRANSPORTATION

The Sorrento tourist office has ferry, bus, and train schedules.

Trains: Circumvesuviana railway (☎081 77 22 484), just off P. Lauro. 40 trains per day (5:01am-11:26pm) to **Herculaneum** (45min., €1.90), **Naples** (1hr., €3.30), and **Pompeii** (30min., €1.90).

Ferries and **hydrofoils:** Port is accessible from P. Tasso by bus (€1.10). Ticket offices open just before boats depart.

Linee Marittime Partenopee: (☎081 80 71 812; www.consorziolmp.it). Hydrofoils to **Capri** (20min., 17 per day 7:20am-6:20pm, €15) and **Naples** (35min., 6 per day 7:20am-4:25pm, €12). Ferries to **Positano** (20min., 11am, €8.50).

Caremar: (☎081 80 73 077; www.caremar.it). Ferries to **Capri** (1hr., 4 per day 7am-7pm, €10).

Metro del Mare: (☎081 199 600 700). Ferries to **Amalfi** (30min., 4 per day 7am-3:10pm, €11).

Buses: SITA buses from Circumvesuviana station are the best way to travel south. 29 buses to **Amalfi** (1½hr., €2) and **Positano** (40min., €2). Buses run 6:30am-midnight. Buy tickets (€1.10) at a bar, *tabaccherie,* or the hotel in P. Lauro.

Public Transportation: runs orange local buses every 20min. Buy tickets (€1.10) at a bar, *tabaccherie,* or the hotel in P. Lauro.

Car and Scooter Rental: Rent A Car, V. S. Cesareo 105 (☎081 87 82 801). Scooters start at €33 per day. Insurance included. Driver's license and credit card required. 18+. Open daily 8:30am-9:30pm; last hire 7:30pm. AmEx/MC/V.

✴🛈 ORIENTATION AND PRACTICAL INFORMATION

Most of Sorrento rests atop a flat shelf that descends steeply into the Bay of Naples. Festooned with flags from the home countries of its visitors, **Piazza Tasso** is at the town's *centro.* Steep stairways and roads connect it to **Marina Piccola. Corso Italia** runs through P. Tasso; facing the sea, the train and bus stations are in **Piazza Lauro** to the right, and the old city is to the left. **Via San Cesareo** runs parallel to C. Italia on the old-city side of P. Tasso.

Tourist Office: V. Luigi De Maio 35 (☎081 80 74 033; www.sorrentotourism.com). From P. Tasso, take Luigi De Maio to the far end of P. S. Antonino and continue toward the port. Office is to the right in the Circolo dei Forestieri compound. Free maps. Open M-Sa Apr.-Sept. 8:30am-6:30pm; Oct.-Mar. 8:30am-4:10pm.

Currency Exchange: Western Union kiosk, V. S. Cesareo 26 (☎081 87 73 552). Open in summer daily 10am-2pm and 4-10pm.

English-Language Bookstore: Libreria Tasso, V. S. Cesareo 96 (☎081 80 71 639; www. libreriatasso.com). Stocks classic texts, including the incomparable 📖**Let's Go.** Open M-Sa 9:30am-1pm and 5-9:30pm, Su 11am-1pm and 5:30-9:30pm. MC/V.

Laundromat: Wash and Dry, V. Fuoro 3. Wash and dry €8.50. Open daily 8am-8pm.

Police: Vco. Terzo Rota (☎081 80 74 433).

Hospital: Ospedale Civile di Sorrento, C. Italia 129 (☎081 53 31 111).

Internet: Insolito, C. Italia 38/e (☎081 87 72 429). €5 per hr. Open daily 8am-4am.

Post Office: C. Italia 210 (☎081 87 81 495), near P. Lauro. Also has an **ATM.** Open M-F 8am-6:30pm, Sa 8am-12:30pm. **Postal Code:** 80067.

🏠🏚 ACCOMMODATIONS AND CAMPING

Reasonably priced accommodations make Sorrento a convenient gateway to the Amalfi Coast and destinations farther south. Reserve ahead in summer. To avoid being overcharged, ask hotel managers for an official price list.

🏨 **Ulisse Deluxe Hostel,** 22 V. del Mare (☎0818774753; www.ulissedeluxe.com). From the station, take a left on Corso Italia, follow it nearly to the end, and turn right on the staircase after the hospital. Classy hostel with professional staff, gorgeous lobby, well-stocked bar, and spa, pool, and fitness center. A/C €5. Pool and fitness center €8. Breakfast €5. 2-person dorms low-season €18; high-season €25. Doubles €23/35. ❶

Ostello Le Sirene, V. degli Aranci 160 (☎081 80 72 925). Centrally located yet protected from tourists. Offers small dorms with private bath. Next to a bar and railroad track. Common room with large TV. Internet access €5.20 per hr. Breakfast included. Kitchen. Dorms €16-25; doubles €40-70; triples €60-90. Extra bed €20. Cash only. ❶

Seven Hostel, V. Iommella Grande 99 (☎081 878 67 58; www.sevenh.eu), in Sant'Agnello. From the train station in Sant'Agnello, turn left on V. Balsamo then right on V. Paola Zanzani. V. Iommella Grande is 5min. away on the right. Top-notch dorms with

CAMPANIA

A/C; some with bath. Also offers library, pool, restaurant, and rooftop bar and lounge. Scenic terrace popular for its nightly happy hour. Free lockers, Internet access, and Wi-Fi. Breakfast included. Wash €4; dry €4. Co-ed and all-female dorms available. 6-, 8-, 10-, and 12-bed dorms €19-26. AmEx/MC/V. ❷

Hotel Linda, V. degli Aranci 125 (☎081 87 82 916; www.hotellinda.com). Simple, comfortable rooms near the train station. In-room breakfast €5. Singles €25-30; doubles €45-50, with bath €60-75; quad €80-90. MC/V. ❸

Hotel Cavour, V. Capo 37 (☎081 80 71 513; www.hotelcavoursorrento.com). Take bus A from P. Tasso towards Punta del Capo. Grand amenities include a pool, solarium, and bar. Each room has TV, phone, balcony, and bath. Breakfast included. Open Mar.-Oct. €40-50 per person; ½-pension €50-65. MC/V. ❸

Villaggio Campeggio Santa Fortunata, V. del Capo 39 (☎081 80 73 579; www.santafortunata.com). Bus A from P. Tasso. Spacious, wooded seaside campground with private beach, pool, hot showers, market, and restaurant. Nightly family entertainment and *discoteca* in July-Aug. Internet access €5 per hr. Free Wi-Fi by the pool and restaurant. Laundry €4.50. €6-10 per person; children under 11 free; tents €5-7; dorms €13-19; 2- to 6-person bungalows €20-45 per person. Cash only. ❶

Nube D'Argento, V. Capo 21 (☎081 87 81 344; www.nubedargento.com). Comfortable, clean campground. Market, pool, playground, and restaurant. €8-11 per person, €5-10 per tent. 2-person bungalow €50-85; triples €60-95; quads €65-115. AmEx/MC/V. ❶

Hotel Elios, V. Capo 33 (☎081 87 81 812), halfway to the Punta del Capo. Take bus A from in front of the flags of P. Tasso. The 14 rooms are ordinary, but 2 large terraces and a hilltop location make for great views. A 30min. walk from Sorrento's bus and train stations. Kitchen available. Open Mar.-Nov. Singles €45-50; doubles €65-75; triples €85-95; quads €105-115. Cash only. ❸

⚫ FOOD

Seek out Sorrento's restaurants for substantial portions of affordable Italian fare. Local favorites include *gnocchi alla Sorrentina* (potato dumplings in tomato sauce, mozzarella, and basil) and *cannelloni* (pasta stuffed with meat or cheese). **Fabbrica Liquori,** V. S. Cesareo 51, has free samples of *nocillo*, a dark walnut liqueur, and *limoncello*, its lemony cousin. (Open daily 9am-10pm.) Follow V. S. Cesareo from P. Tasso for a **market** where sweet, ripe fruit awaits. There's a giant **STANDA** supermarket on C. Italia 225. (Open M-Sa 8:30am-1:20pm and 5-9pm, Su 9:30am-1pm and 5-8:30pm. AmEx/MC/V.) The organic food market **Mondo Bio,** V. degli Aranci 146/148, has a small restaurant with daily organic offerings. (☎081 80 75 694. Open M-Sa 8:30am-8:30pm. MC/V.)

▨ Sedil Dominova, V. S. Cesareo 70 (☎081 87 81 351). In front of a charming dome. True to its slogan: "good service with a smile." Delicious *gnocchi alla sorrentina* (€6.50) and pizza (€5-8). Arrive early to avoid lines. Open daily 7-11:30pm. AmEx/MC/V. ❶

▨ Ristorante e Pizzeria Giardiniello, V. dell'Accademia 7 (☎081 87 84 616; ristoranteilgiardiniello@libero.it), 2nd left from V. Giuliani, off C. Italia. Try Mamma Luisa's delightful *linguini al cartoccio* (with seafood; €7). Secluded tables among bamboo plants. Pizza (€4-7) with house-made olive oil. Primi €4-7. Secondi €6-12. Cover €1. Open Apr.-Nov. daily 11am-midnight; Dec.-Mar. M-W and F-Su 11am-midnight. AmEx/MC/V. ❷

Il Leone Rosso, V. Marziale 25 (☎081 80 73 089; www.theredlion.it). From P. Tazzo follow the signs and make a right onto V. Marziale. A roaring atmosphere of fun backpackers and Italian vacationers. Packed every night; in summer, reserve a day ahead or expect lines. Primo, secondo, side, dessert, and *limoncello* €18. Primi €6-11. Secondi €7-15. Open daily noon-12:30am. AmEx/MC/V. ❷

Da Cataldo, Marina Grande (☎081 87 82 170; www.dacataldo.it). Moderately-priced cuisine in a romantic seaside setting. Chefs let you pick out your fish and choose any sauce upon request. Antipasto, primo, and secondo *menù* €15. Primi €5-14. Secondi €8-15. Open Apr.-Sept. daily noon-3:30pm and 7-11:30pm; Mar. and Oct. Tu-Su noon-3:30pm and 7-11:30pm. AmEx/MC/V. ❷

Chantecler's, V. S. Maria della Pietà 38 (☎081 80 75 868; www.chanteclers.com), off P. Tasso. Bar-grill with a variety of drinks, cheap food, and fun clientele. Primi €6. Secondi €7-12. Beer €3.50. Mixed drinks €4. Open nightly 7:30pm-late. AmEx/MC/V. ❷

Pizzeria da Franco, C. Italia 265 (☎081 87 72 066). As one of the town's informal gathering spots, this pizzeria is always full. Try the Sorrento-renowned antipasti (€5-8) or one of the *panini* (€3-6). Open daily 11am-2am. Cash only. ❶

Ristorante Verdemare, V. Capo 70 (☎081 87 82 589; www.ristoranteverdemare.com). A popular spot for family dining, removed from the busy *centro*. Pasta €5-10. Fish and meats €5.50-13. Open daily 12:30-2:45pm and 7:15-11:45pm. AmEx/MC/V. ❷

👁 🎭 SIGHTS AND NIGHTLIFE

Sorrento's popularity among tourists is not unjustified, although neighboring towns offer more serenity. If you're willing to conquer the stairs (about 5min.), the **Marina Grande,** far from the crowds swarming around P. Tasso, provides a pleasant setting for relaxation after a long day of walking or daytripping. A walk to **Punta del Capo** leads to the ruins of **Villa di Pollio Felice** clustered around a beautiful cove. Take bus A from P. Tasso to the end of the route, then take the footpath to the right of the stop. Bring a suit and a towel for a memorable swim in the turquoise pools, but don't expect much sand. Farther down the road on bus A in Massa Lubrense is **Puolo Beach,** a 300m stretch of sandy shore spread with umbrellas and chairs. At night, don't miss the sunset from P. della Vittoria. After dark, the **old city** heats up as English-speaking crowds consistently pack all restaurants around **Piazza Tasso.**

The English Inn, C. Italia 57 (☎081 80 74 357; www.englishinn.org.) Perfect for those nostalgic for Anglo-Saxon culture. A fun-loving crowd gathers after 10:30pm on summer nights to dance to blasting music and return the next morning for a breakfast (€7) of eggs, sausages, and bacon. Drinks €3-8. Open daily May-Sept. 8am-4am.

Danielle's Club, near the flags of the *piazza* (☎081 87 73 992; www.bagattelle.net). One of Sorrento's oldest clubs. A disco groove and karaoke still attract tourists to its decent bar. Beer €5. Mixed drinks €7. Open daily Mar.-Oct. 9pm-5am.

Photo Bar, V. Correale 19 (☎081 87 73 686; www.photosorrento.com). Hands-down the most stylish bar in Sorrento. Garden and creative interior with giant color photos. Sip creative mixed drinks (from €8) and munch on complimentary fresh antipasti while photography flashes on giant screens overhead. Open daily 6:30pm-3am.

Insolito, C. Italia 38/e (☎081 87 72 429; www.insolitosorrento.it). Caters to chic locals who wish to lounge and dance surrounded by large screens and beautiful bartenders. Beer €4. Mixed drinks €5-8. Open daily 8am-4am.

Casino de la Vallee, C. Italia 263 (☎081 87 85 568; www.casinosorrento.it). Underground casino club. Cover-free *discoteca* from 9pm. 18+. Open daily 11am-5am.

PROCIDA ☎081

Calmly rippling waters and bobbing fishing boats complete the perfect island serenity of Procida (PRO-chee-da; pop. 11,000), a setting so ideal that it was chosen for numerous films, including Italian favorite 🎬**Il Postino.** The flattest and smallest of the major islands in the Bay of Naples at just 10 sq. km, Procida is also the least touristed. From fresh seafood to tangy lemons, Procida will awaken your senses to life's simple pleasures. Surrounded by kind and generous islanders, it's almost possible to forget the mainland throngs of tourists.

▐ TRANSPORTATION

Ferries and hydrofoils: All boats dock at Marina Grande, near the ticket offices. Confirm times and seasonal prices at port ticket offices.

Caremar (☎081 89 67 280; www.caremar.it). To **Ischia** (ferries: 25min., 10 per day 7:30am-11pm, €6.30; hydrofoils: 15min., 3 per day 10:35am-3:45pm, €7.10), **Naples** (ferries: 1hr., 5 per day 7:15am-8pm, €8.50; hydrofoils: 40min., 6 per day 6:50am-4:30pm, €9-11), and **Pozzuoli** (ferries: 35min., 3 per day 8:55am-6:05pm, €6.60; hydrofoils: 15min., 8:25am, €7.10). MC/V.

Procida Lines (☎081 89 60 328). Hydrofoil to **Pozzuoli** (30min., 7 per day M-Sa 4am-5:30pm, €7.50). Cash only.

SNAV (☎081 89 69 975; www.snav.it). Hydrofoils to **Naples** (40min., 4 per day 7:35am-5:40pm, €14) and **Ischia** (40min., 8 per day 7:50am-9:10pm, €4). Cash only.

Buses: SEPSA buses (€0.80 at *tabaccherie* or bars located near stops, €1.10 onboard) depart from the port and serve the entire island. Frequency and times vary by season; see schedules posted at many *tabaccherie*. All buses stop at the different beaches.

L1 covers the middle of Procida: passing hotels, campgrounds, and **Chiaiolella** port, the site of the liveliest restaurants and beaches. (Every 20min. 6:10am-11pm. June-Sept. until 3am.)

C1 follows nearly the same route but also covers the less-populated northwestern part of the island. (Every 40min. 6:50am-8:25pm.)

C2 serves Procida's northeastern part. (Every 40min. 6:55am-8:25pm. June-Sept. until 1:10am.)

L2 serves Procida's southeastern part. (Every hr. 6:25am-8:25pm. June-Sept. until 2:50am.) Bus drivers rarely call out stops; ask your driver to remind you when your stop approaches.

Taxis: ☎081 89 68 785. Taxi stand near the docks. Walking around Procida can be an adventure, as cars and scooters don't like to share the narrow streets with pedestrians. Flatten up against the nearest wall when they come speeding along.

▐ PRACTICAL INFORMATION

Services include: **Graziella Travel,** V. Roma 117, which rents bikes (€8 per day) and scooters (€25 per day), and has **Western Union** services (☎081 89 69 594; www. isoladiprocida.it; English spoken; open June-Sept. M-F 9am-1pm and 4-8pm, Sa 9am-8pm; Oct.-May M-F 9am-1pm and 4-8pm); the **carabinieri,** V. Libertà 70 (☎081 89 67 160); the **emergency clinic,** V. V. Emanuele 191 (☎081 89 69 058); the **pharmacy, Madonna delle Grazie** (☎081 896 88 83); **Internet access** at **Bar Capriccio,** V. Roma 99, to the left of the ferry ticket office when facing away from the water (☎081 89 69 506; €3.50 per hr.; free Wi-Fi for customers; open daily 6am-3am); and the **post office,** at the corner of V. V. Emanuele and V. Liberta.(☎081 89 60 740. **ATM** outside. Open M-F 8am-1:30pm, Sa 8am-12:30pm.) **Postal Code:** 80070.

▐ ▐ ACCOMMODATIONS AND CAMPING

Spending an inexpensive night on Procida is difficult, so non-camping budget travelers may want to make the island a daytrip from Naples.

▩ **La Rosa dei Venti,** V. Vincenzo Rinaldi 32 (☎081 89 68 385; www.vacanzeprocida.it). Take the C2 bus to V. Regina Elena. 20 cottages with kitchenette and dining area, surrounded by flowers. Makes busy Naples seem worlds away. Family donkeys and private beach. Barbecue available. Breakfast included. Free Internet. Pets allowed. Refundable security deposit €100. 2- to 6-person cottage €25-45 per person. AmEx/MC/V. ❸

Hotel Residence Tirreno, V. Faro, 34 (☎081 89 68 341; www.tirrenoresidence.it). Take bus C1. With 2 locations, one by V. Faro and another one right by the sea on V. Salette, this hotel offers relaxation. Huge lemon grove, sundeck, pool, free domestic and international calls, and free Internet access. Rooms €25-50 per person. AmEx/MC/V. ❸

Hotel Le Grand Bleu, V. Flavio Gioia 37 (☎081 89 69 594; www.isolaprocida.it/legrandbleu). Take bus L1 or L2, or book at Graziella Travel for free shuttle. Guesthouses are conveniently located and include bike rental, Wi-Fi, satellite TV, A/C, and private balconies. Open June-Sept. 7-night min. stay in August. Rooms €20-40 per person. MC/V. ❸

Hotel Savoia, V. Lavadera 32 (☎081 89 67 616; hotelsavoiaprocida@virgilio.it). Take bus L2. Beautiful tiles, rooms with TV, A/C, private terraces, pool access, and great views make for an idyllic stay. Breakfast €4. Singles €60-75. AmEx/MC/V. ❺

Campeggio La Caravella (☎081 81 01 838) and **Campeggio Vivara** (☎081 89 69 242), adjacent to each other on V. IV Novembre. Take bus L1 or C1. Clean, pleasant grounds with snack bar and flowers. 15min. from beach at Ciraccio. Open May 1-Sept. 15. Reserve in June for Aug. €6 per person; €6 per tent. Shower €0.50. Cash only. ❶

☐ FOOD

Like accommodations, Procida's dining options are not designed for the budget-minded, but seek and you shall find. For snacks, try the small **CRAI** market, V. Roma 3, near the port. (Open M-Sa 8am-2pm and 5-9pm, Su 8am-1pm. MC/V.) Restaurants can be found in the **Porto** and **Chiaiolella** parts of town. After dinner, ask for chilled *limoncello* made from Procidan lemons.

Il Galeone, V. Marina Chiaiolella 35 (☎081 89 69 622). Open-air seating, delicious cuisine, and attentive service distinguish this family-run restaurant from the more touristy ones along the port. Seafood antipasti €6-9. Primi €8-10. Secondi €6.50-13. Daily *menù* €16. Cover €1.50. Open M-Tu and Th-Su 10:30am-midnight. MC/V. ❸

La Locanda del Postino, V. Marina Corricella, 43 (☎081 810 18 87). This was the restaurant used in 1994 for *Il Postino,* and its relaxed beauty explains why. Primi and secondi €6-15. Daily *menù* €12-15 includes fresh fish. Open M and W-Su 9am-1am. ❷

Graziella, V. Marina Corricella 14 (☎081 89 67 479). Escape the spotlight of La Locanda del Postino and head here for delicious seafood, like *spaghetti sapore di mare* (€10). Primi €5-10. Open Apr.-Nov. daily 9am-2am. ❷

Ristorante Lo Sfizicò, V. Roma 81 (☎081 89 69 931; www.ristorantesfizico.it). Enjoy a steaming plate of *gnocchi all Sorrentina* (€6) while you watch the boats dock. Primi €7-10. Secondi €6-10. *Menù* €15. Cover €1.50. Open July-Sept. daily noon-3:30pm and 7:30-1am; Oct.-June Tu-Su noon-3:30pm and 7:30-1am. AmEx/MC/V. ❷

Vefio, V. Libertà 57 (☎081 89 68 256; www.vefio.it). Meaning "balcony" in the local dialect, Vefio boasts prominent upstairs views, crisp brick-oven pizza (€3.50-7), and lemon-based desserts. Free Wi-Fi available. Cover €1. Open Tu-Su 4pm-1am. MC/V. ❶

Fishbone, V. Marina Chiaiolella 22 (☎081 89 67 422). Come to Fishbone for Procidan fare just above the water. Try the succulent rabbit (€8), a highlight of island cuisine. Pizza €2.50-8. Primi €9-15. Secondi €8-12. Cover €2. AmEx/MC/V. ❷

Ristorante Mimante, V. V. Emanuele 227 (☎081 89 69 385). Relax in the restaurant's secluded garden while you listen to live music at night. Primi €6-15. Secondi €8-15. Cover €1.50. Open Tu-Su 10am-1pm and 5pm-2am. AmEx/MC/V. ❷

La Pergola, V. Rinaldi 37 (☎081 89 69 534). This family-run restaurant invites you to dine inside a shady citrus garden, or join its nightly piano bar in Aug. Daily *menù* includes fresh fish, home-grown vegetables, and rabbit. Primi €7-15. Secondi €10-18. Cover €2. Service 10%. Open Tu-Su 8-10:30pm. Reserve ahead. MC/V. ❸

🌀 🌺 SIGHTS AND FESTIVALS

Procida has several **beaches,** most of which remain pleasantly uncrowded. The dark sand and calm waters of **Ciraccio** stretch across the western shore and are sprinkled with drink and snack stands. Ciraccio's western end, near Chiaiolella, is at the end of line L1. Another popular beach is **Chiaia,** on the southeastern cove, accessible by L1, L2, and C1. Perhaps the prettiest of them all, **Pozzo Vecchio** (also known as *Il Postino* Beach, nicknamed after the movie that was filmed here) rests amid striking layered cliffs. **The Procida Diving Center,** V. Giovanni da Procida, at Marina di Chiaiolella, runs scuba diving tours and lessons. (☎081 339 435 8493; www.procidadiving.it. 1 dive and full equipment rental €28. Lessons €50. All levels welcome. Open M-Sa 9am-1pm and 3:30-7pm.) To reach the **Abbazia San Michele Arcangelo** (Abbey of St. Michael the Archangel), take bus #C2, or face a steep uphill trek. From the left of the port facing away from the water, take V. V. Emanuele and turn left on V. Principe Umberto. The abbey is believed to have been founded exactly in the year 1000. Its plain yellow facade guards splendid 15th-century gold frescoes, while scroll work and stately archways prove a jarring contrast to the quiet, unassuming island outside the gates. Take a moment to admire the deeds of St. Michael emblazoned on the domes. (☎081 89 67 612; www.abbaziasanmichele.it. Open Tu-Sa 10am-12:45pm and 3-6pm. Free.) En route to the abbey, the medieval walls of **Terra Murata** are downhill from the monastery, on V. S. Michele. Though Procida's oldest settlement, the area's winding streets now teem with scooters. The lookout point outside the walls opens onto the idyllic marina of **Corricella;** pack a picnic and enjoy the breeze. The view is especially beautiful at night. Lemons are everywhere you turn in Procida and are honored for their place in Procidan culture at the **Festa del Limone** (late May). Besides delicious lemony treats, the festival features a fashion show and—of course—a lemon debate.

📷 NIGHTLIFE

Nightlife on the island emanates from the string of restaurants and bars along the Marina Grande on V. Roma. Young procidans hang around **Bar Capriccio,** V. Roma 99, for the pop music, cheap pizza (€1.50), beer (€2), and frosty milkshakes for €3. (Open daily 6am-3am; reduced hours in winter. Internet and Wi-Fi available.) You're sure to have a good time at the only *discoteca* in Procida, **Number Two.** Short dresses, €4 beer, and a packed dance floor are typical elements of a weekend night at this hopping club. Located at V. Libertà 64, its larger parties are advertised throughout the island and cost €5-20. (www.numbertwo.biz. Open July-Aug. F-Su 9pm-late.)

ISCHIA ☎081

Ischia's (EES-kya; pop. 60,000) combination of sea, sand, and sky presents a rich, earthy beauty so perfect you'll never want to leave. The island, once an active volcano, now houses hot springs, ruins, and lemon groves that give it a refreshing tranquility. Ischia first captivated Phoenicians 7000 years ago and later gained mention in both *The Iliad* and *The Aeneid;* the island's green waters were more recently featured in the film *The Talented Mr. Ripley.* When tourists, particularly Germans, crowd the island in August, Italians turn to the therapeutic hot springs and thermal spas to cure their ailments. Whether or not you frequent its springs, Ischia is sure to leave you refreshed.

▐ TRANSPORTATION

Ferries: From Ischia, ferries and hydrofoils run to **Pozzuoli, Naples, Procida, Capri,** and **Sorrento.** Most ferries arrive and leave from **Ischia Porto,** generally known as "Ischia," where the main ticket offices are located. Ferries also arrive and depart from **Casamicciola,** on the northern side of the island, and from **Forio,** Ischia's largest town. Take the #1, 2, or CS bus from Ischia Porto to reach both departure points. Schedules and prices are subject to change. Call individual ferry lines for details or check online.

Caremar (☎081 98 48 18; www.caremar.it). Runs to **Naples** (ferries: 1hr., 8 per day 6:45am-8:10pm, €11; hydrofoils: 1hr., 6 per day 6:50am-7:10pm, €16), **Pozzuoli** (ferries: 1hr., 3 per day 8:30am-5:35pm, €3.60), and **Procida** (ferries: 35min., 8 per day 6:45am-7:30pm, €6.30; hydrofoils: 20min., 4 per day noon-7:10pm, €7.10). Most Caremar ferries leave from Ischia Porto. Ticket offices open 30min. before departure of 1st boat.

Medmar (☎081 55 13 352; www.medmar.it). Runs ferries to **Naples** (1hr., 4 per day 6:40am-10pm, €9-10) and **Pozzuoli** (1hr., 11 per day 2:30am-8:30pm, €9-10). Ticket offices open 30min. before departure of 1st boat.

Alilauro (☎081 99 18 88; www.alilauro.it). Runs hydrofoils to: **Capri** (40min., 10:40am, €16); Mergellina station in **Naples** (45min.; 6 per day 8am-6:50pm, €12); Molo Beverello station in **Naples** (45min.; from Ischia Porto 10 per day 6:35am-6:50pm, €16; from Forio 8 per day 7am-6:30pm, €13); **Sorrento** (daily 5:20pm, €19).

Buses: Orange **SEPSA buses** (www.sepsa.it) depart from the intersection on V. Iasolino and V. Baldassarree Cossa. Take a right from Molo 1 or a left from Molo 2 and walk along the port, following the road as it curves away from the port. The main lines are CS, CD, and #1. **CS** circles the island counterclockwise, hitting Ischia Porto, Casamicciola Terme, Lacco Ameno, Forio, Panza Cava Grado (Sant'Angelo), Serrara, Fontana, Buonopane, and Barano. **CD** follows the same route in a clockwise direction. (Both CS and CD every 15-30min., 4:20am-1am.) **Bus #1** follows the CS route as far as Cava Grado (Sant'Angelo) and then comes back (every 15-20min; in summer 5:05am-2:30am, in winter 5:05am-1am). Other routes are shorter, run less frequently, and stop earlier; use them for reaching specific sites or more remote locations. Don't expect breathing space; island buses are packed with passengers until the end of the night.

Taxis: The pricey **Microtaxi** fleet (☎081 99 25 50) and **taxis** (☎081 33 31 093) wait at a taxi stand in front of the ticket offices on V. Iasolino.

DAYTRIPPER. The **Unicolschia Pass** for all public transportation is a great deal for daytrippers. (1hr. €1, 1½hr. €1.20, 1 day €4, 2 days €7.)

◼ ⁊ ORIENTATION AND PRACTICAL INFORMATION

Most of Ischia's points of interest lie on the coast, connected by the S.S. 270 (the main road); the inner island is mainly mountainous wilderness. In **Ischia Porto,** the main harbor town, **Corso Vittorio Colonna** runs parallel to **Via de Luca** from the port. Nearby **Ischia Ponte** is a small island connected by a footbridge. Counterclockwise, **Casamicciola, Lacco Ameno,** and **Forio** continue along the coast. In the south, **Fontana,** reached by the CS and CD bus lines, is a good departure point for **Monte Epomeo.** An **AACST tourist office** is on V. Iasolino in Ischia Porto. Turn left from the port; the office is in the Terme Comunali. (☎081 50 74 231 or 50 74 211; www.ischiaonline.it. **Luggage storage** €3 per 2hr. Open M-Sa 9am-2pm and 3-8pm.) Other services include: the **police,** V. delle Terme 78 (☎081 507 47 11; open M, W, and F 9am-noon, Tu and Th 9am-11am), two blocks from V. de Luca in Ischia Porto; **Ospedale Anna Rizzoli,** V. Fundera in Lacco Ameno (☎081 50 79 111 or 507 92 24; accessible by bus #1, CS, or CD); **Internet** access at the **Pointel Store,** P. Trieste e Trento 9 (€3.60 per 30min., €6 per hr.; open M 4:30-8:30pm,

Tu-Sa 9:30am-1pm and 4:30-8:30pm); and the **post office,** V. Mazzella 446, which has a branch at V. Alfredo De Luca 42. **Postal Code:** 80077.

ACCOMMODATIONS AND CAMPING

Despite its immense popularity, Ischia has several budget options in Forio, making it the most affordable base for an island visit. Hotels in Ischia Porto, Casamicciola Terme, and Lacco Ameno tend to be very expensive, since many hotels have pools fed (allegedly) by hot springs, and views fit for a queen. Ischia's thriving tourist crowd ensures the presence of hotels everywhere, and among these, some truly fit the wallet of a budget-minded traveler.

FORIO

Ring Hostel, V. Gaetano Morgera 72 (☎081 99 71 36; www.ringhostel.com). Whether it's organizing midnight excursions to hot springs or planning group dinners, the kind staff makes sure this hostel is a 2nd home. Housed in a 19th-century convent; some rooms have domed ceilings and tiled floors. Common room with guitar, Xbox, flat-screen satellite TV, and DVD collection. Don't miss sunset from the roof. Bar open 8pm-late. English spoken. Breakfast included. Free Internet access. Laundry €4. Bikes available. Dorms €17-21; singles €30; doubles from €56. 10% *Let's Go* discount. ❶

Residence La Rotonda Sul Mare, V. Aiemita 29 (☎081 98 75 46; www.larotondasul-mare.com). With a private patio suspended over the waters of San Francesco Bay, La Rotonda pampers its sea-loving guests in 10 unique residences. The snack bar and lounge has direct access to a private shore and sundeck. English spoken. Breakfast included. Prices €25-50 per person. 10% *Let's Go* discount. AmEx/MC/V. ❸

Hotel Poggio del Sole, V. Baiola 193 (☎081 98 77 56; www.hotelpoggiodelsole.it), at the foot of Mt. Epomeo. Features a vineyard and a restaurant, "La Casereccia." Rooms have TV, safe, fridge, A/C, and either balcony or terrace overlooking the Mediterranean. Pool, jacuzzi, parking, shuttle service, and solarium. Breakfast included. €25-50 per person. 10% *Let's Go* discount. AmEx/MC/V. ❸

Hotel Villa Verde, V. Matteo Verde 34 (☎/fax 081 98 72 81; www.villaverdehotel.it). Follow directions to Pensione di Lustro, continuing on V. Filippo di Lustro and then turning left on V. Matteo Verde. Located in the center of Forio, yet still provides peaceful atmosphere with a rooftop patio, garden, and sweeping views of the port and Monte Epomeo. Clean, spacious rooms with A/C, safe, phone, and TV; 12 have balconies. Breakfast included. July rooms €40 per person; Aug. €45; June-Sept. €35; Oct.-May €30. ❹

ISCHIA PORTO

Eurocamping dei Pini, V. delle Ginestre 34 (☎081 98 20 69). Take bus #13 from Ischia Porto. Ideal for budget travelers; a clean family-friendly campground with a restaurant. No dogs. €7-10 per person; €6-10 per tent. Bungalows €12.50-25 per person. ❶

Valery Hotel, V. Cossa 48 (☎081 99 10 94; www.hotelvaleryischia.com). From Ischia Porto bus station, ascend the main street and turn right; go upstairs to reception. Offers lovely terraces with the best view of the island. 15 basic rooms have bath, TV, fridge, and safe. A/C and Internet available. Restaurant *menù* €10. With *Let's Go* discount, singles €30; doubles €50; triples €75; quads €100. MC/V. ❸

Albergo Fagianella, V. Mirabella 34 (☎081 98 19 91 256), in a residential area near the beach. Spacious rooms with TV sand private baths. €30-40 per person. MC/V. ❸

Albergo Macri, V. Iasolino 78/a (☎081 99 26 03 or 081 33 34 386; www.albergo-macri.it), along the docks, near where buses board. A quiet and conveniently located hotel, barely evading the hordes of tourists on V. Porto. 22 basic rooms have comfortable beds and spotless baths. Breakfast included. Guests are given 10% discount at thermal parks. Singles €35-45; doubles €65-75; triples €85-105. MC/V. ❸

Apartments in Ischia, V. Castello 4 (☎081 98 25 94 or 347 05 64 203; EDP1@interfree.it). Call English-speaking staff for directions. 6 apartments have terrace and beach access. 2-night. min. stay. From €25 per person with *Let's Go* discount. Cash only. ❷

Hotel Villa Ciccio, V. Quercia 26 (☎081 99 32 30; www.villaciccio.it). From Porto Ischia bus station, a short walk uphill to the right along V. Quercia. Facilities make Villa Hermosa a bargain. Quiet, romantic garden surrounds thermal swimming pool and patio. All rooms with terrace or balcony, minibar, safe, and phone. Breakfast included. Singles €65-80; doubles €50-90. ½-pension €75 per person. Cash only. ❹

FOOD

Ischia's seafood and fruit are excellent, but the true local delicacy is *coniglio* (rabbit), served *all'ischitana* (with parsley). In addition to the lip-smacking *limoncello*, try *il rucolino* (an herbal liquor). There's a **DìperDì** at V. Matteo Verde 33. (Open daily 8am-1:30pm and 5-9pm. Closed F morning. AmEx/MC/V.)

▨ **La Casereccia,** V. Baiola 193 (☎081 98 77 56), in Forio. Optimal food, a relaxing ambience, and friendly service. Pasta, seafood, and *limoncello* will not disappoint. Mama Tina's *raviolini* are popular. *Spaghetti con cozze* (with mussels) €7. Primi and secondi €5-10. Open daily noon-3pm and 8pm-midnight. ❷

▨ **Castillo de Aragona,** (☎081 98 31 53), in Ischia Ponte. Right next to the entrance of the Castello Aragonese. This hidden spot offers amazing views, with tables so close to the beach that they're practically in the water. Fun atmosphere thanks to young clientele. Primi €7-10. Open daily 10am-3am. ❷

Pirozzi, V. Seminario 51/53 (☎081 98 32 17), in Ischia Ponte. Gorgeous view of the marina from terrace seats. Tasty seafood and excellent pizza. *Margherita* €3.50. Cover €1.50. Open daily noon-3pm and 7pm-midnight. AmEx/MC/V. ❷

Ristorante Cocò Gelo, Ple. Aragonese 1 (☎081 98 18 23), on the opposite end of the Castello Aragonese footbridge. For a classier meal in Ischia Ponte, dine at this swanky seaside Ischia staple. Excellent roast beef (€7) and local *coniglio* (€9). Fish €7-12. Open daily 12:30-3pm and 7:30-11pm. AmEx/MC/V. ❸

La Tinaia, V. Matteo Verde 39 (☎081 99 84 48), in Forio. Cheap food among a sea of expensive options. Brick-oven pizza €4.90-9. Crepes €2-5.70. Primi €5-11. Secondi €8.50-11. Open daily 11:30am-midnight. AmEx/MC/V. ❶

SIGHTS

▨**MORTELLA GARDENS.** Lady Suzanna Walton, wife of British composer Sir William Walton (1902-1983), cultivated these exotic gardens with over 800 rare and exotic plants. Named "Best Garden in Italy" in 2004, the park houses stately buildings, including a monolithic, modern sun temple and an incongruous Thai shrine nestled among vines, vivid blooms, and lily-covered pools. Allow at least an hour to fully absorb the beauty; the map given at the entrance will guide you. **Victoria House** has tropical plants and a gigantic Amazonian waterlily, one of the world's rarest flowers. A panorama of Ischia's coast crowns the landscape just above the garden tea house. (*Take the CD or CS bus to the stop before San Franceso; ask driver for V. Calise. Walk downhill, following signs for "spiaggia." Garden entrance is on the right. V. Calise 39. ☎081 98 62 20; www.ischia.it/mortella. Concerts in summer; call for schedule and info. Open Tu, Th, and Sa-Su 9am-7pm. €10, ages 8-12 €8, ages 5-7 €6.*)

CASTELLO ARAGONESE. Perched atop its own tiny island, Ischia Ponte, the Castello sits in lofty isolation. Connected to the rest of the island by a 15th-

GIVING BACK

CAFFÈ FOR TWO

Most tourists are notoriously oblivious to the subleties of other cultures. You can try and try to perfect your *"Grazie Mille"* and *"Prego,"* but there are always a couple things you'll miss. One of the toughies of the Italian tradition is probably its coffee culture—the center of social life, there are as many ins and outs as a *Survivor: Sorority Style.* However, there is one practice thats not only easy to understand, but also a crucial part of Neopolitan spirit.

All you need to do is relax, have a Caffè Napolitano (espresso)—and then order another. No, this isn't dating advice; it's simply *caffè sospeso.*

One of the warmest aspects of Neapolitan culture, *caffè sospeso* is the cultural practice of ordering and paying for two cups of coffee, leaving the second "in suspense" for anyone who is homeless or down on their luck to request it at the bar. This small, anonymous act of charity has kept the cherished afternoon caffè an all-inclusive institution in Neapolitan life.

If you are looking for a simple way to help someone out, in true Neapolitan style, then look no further than the *caffè sospeso* tradition. Just 50 cents will make your own afternoon coffee taste that much sweeter.

century footbridge, this former stronghold hosts both the holy and the gruesome. The castle's **duomo**, largely destroyed by WWII bombing, revels in a heady mix of Roman and Baroque styles. Below, the **crypt** houses colorful 14th-century frescoes by craftsmen from the school of Giotto. The **nuns' cemetery** has a ghastly history: whenever a nun died, the order would prop her decomposing body up on a stone chair as a fragrant reminder to the other nuns of their own mortality. There is nothing of interest inside today—only a couple of empty torture chambers and abandoned rooms—yet its external beauty has appeared in many films, including *The Talented Mr. Ripley.* (Bus #7 runs to Ischia Ponte from Ischia Porto. ☎081 99 28 34. Open daily 9am-7:30pm. €10, ages 9-14 €6.)

BEACHES AND HOT SPRINGS. Nestled on an inlet and surrounded on three sides by tall rock, the stunning **Citara** beach boasts coarse, white sands and azure waters. Leave your frisbee at home; there won't be room for it on the crowded shore. Nearby, the **Negombo gardens** and hot springs offer a pleasant atmosphere. (Baia di S. Montano. ☎081 98 61 52; www.negombo.it. Take bus CD or #2 from Ischia Porto.) **Maronti,** on the island's south side, has calm water, younger crowds, and a great view. (Take bus #5 from Ischia Porto.) For a family-oriented beach, try **Spiaggia Cava dell'Isola,** north of Citara beach. Young crowds will enjoy **Lido di San Montano** and **Spiaggia degli Inglesi** (between Ischia Porto and Ischia Ponte). For a steamier experience, the hot springs at **Sorgeto** in Forio on the far side of the island range from tepid to boiling. Locals claim that the lather formed by rubbing the light-green, porous rocks together is fantastic for the skin, and it doesn't hurt to take their word. Lacco Ameno and Casamicciola Terme are packed with thermal baths. The springs are often closed due to falling rocks; ask the tourist office before setting out. (Reach the beach from Panza by a 20min. hike.)

HIKING

A hike in the mountains of Ischia passes more than just greenery and exquisite flora. Scattered throughout the mountainside woods, centuries-old stone sculptures and over 30 ancient stone homes can be explored. Built as protection from frequent pirate attacks that led many Ischians to slavery, these rock houses were an exercise in creative design—improvising on the mountainous terrain, the locals built their homes directly into the hillside. To keep watch over those reckless pirates, the Ischian men guarded the *torrione* (towers), which are still visible along the waterfront in downtown Forio. Those not interested in the history will be rewarded for the fairly difficult climb with breathtaking views. For a more intense hike, head up the 788m to the top of **Monte Epomeo.** On clear days, the summit overlooks Capri and Terracina. *(Take bus CS or #1 from Forio to "Fontana." Follow trail into woods; after 2hr. of hiking, ruins begin to appear. For horseback excursions, contact companies around Fiaiano, near Ischia Porto.)*

◻ NIGHTLIFE

Ischia's liveliest nocturnal scene is in Ischia Porto, along V. Porto and C. Vittorio Colonna. At *discoteca* **New Valentino,** C. V. Colonna 97, young Italians try to seduce foreigners—or at least try to dance with them. (☎081 99 26 53. Open F-Su 11pm-6am.) For something low-key, head to any of the various piano bars in Forio and Ischia Porto, or go for a leisurely *passegiata* along the ocean front streets of Forio. The **'O Spasso Night Club,** downstairs below Calise Caffè on P. Degli Eroi, holds live entertainment. (☎081 99 12 70. Open daily 10pm-4am.)

C A M P A N I A

CAPRI AND ANACAPRI   ☎081

Nicknamed "the pearl of the Mediterranean," Capri (CA-pree; pop. 7000) has been a destination of the rich and famous for thousands of years. Augustus fell in love with Capri in 29 BC before trading its rocky cliffs for the fertile, volcanic Ischia. His successor Tiberius passed his last decade here, leaving scattered villas and a legacy of idyllic retirement homes. Today's royalty flits between ritzy boutiques and top-notch restaurants. Perched on the hills above Capri, Anacapri (AH-na-CA-pree; pop. 5000) is a relative oasis of budget hotels, lovely villas, and deserted mountain paths. Take time to revel in the relaxed island life while enjoying a languid stroll along Capri's cobblestone paths, a breezy vista from Monte Solaro, or a dip in the Grotta Azzurra.

 FROGGER IT! Keep to the footpaths in Capri if you're planning on walking. The very narrow streets have no sidewalks and vehicles move at high speeds without watching for pedestrians. Walking on the major thoroughfares is strongly discouraged, so take the bus to faraway destinations.

◼ TRANSPORTATION

Ferries and Hydrofoils: Capri's main port is **Marina Grande.** Naples and Sorrento are the main gateways to Capri.

    Caremar (☎081 83 70 700) runs to **Naples** (ferries: 1hr., 3 per day 5:45am-2:50pm, €9.60; hydrofoils: 1hr., 4 per day 10:25am-10:20pm, €15) and **Sorrento** (hydrofoils: 25min., 4 per day 7am-6:15pm, €7.10).

    SNAV (☎081 83 77 577) runs hydrofoils to **Naples** (45min., 7 per day 8:10am-6:10pm, €17).

    Linea Jet (☎081 83 70 819) runs hydrofoils to **Naples** (40-50min., 11 per day 9:35am-7:10pm, €17) and **Sorrento** (25min., 12 per day 9:20am-7pm, €15).

Public Transportation: SIPPIC buses (☎081 83 70 420) depart from V. Roma in Capri for **Anacapri** (every 15min. 6am-2am), Marina Piccola, and points in between. In Anacapri, buses depart from P. Barile, off V. G. Orlandi, for the Grotta Azzurra (Blue Grotto), the *faro* (lighthouse), and more. From Marina Grande to P. Vittoria in **Anacapri** (every hr. 5:45am-10:10pm; €1.40, day pass €6.90). Note that all-day pass is rarely worth it. **Funicular** from Marina Grande to **Capri** (every 10min. 6:30am-1:30am, €1.40).

Taxis: At main bus stop in Marina Grande (☎081 83 70 543), at bus stop in Capri (☎081 83 70 543), or in P. Vittoria, in Anacapri (☎081 83 71 175).

KEEP THE CHANGE. On Capri, tickets (€1.40) are generally bought onboard the bus. Have exact change on hand to avoid holding up the bus; it won't leave until you pay.

ORIENTATION AND PRACTICAL INFORMATION

There are two towns on the isle of Capri: **Capri** proper, near the ports, and **Anacapri**, higher up. Ferries dock at **Marina Grande**, below the town of Capri. To get to Anacapri, either wait in long lines for the funicular, take the bus, or trek for 1hr. up the steep and winding stairway. Expensive boutiques and bakeries line the streets that radiate from **Piazza Umberto. Via Roma**, to the right exiting the funicular, leads to Anacapri. The bus to Anacapri passes through **Piazza Vittoria**, the main square; Villa San Michele and the Monte Solaro chairlift are nearby.

Tourist Office: AAST (☎081 83 70 634; www.capritourism.com). At Marina Grande. Open daily 9am-1pm and 3:30-6:45pm. Branches: Capri, in P. Umberto (☎081 83 70 686), under the clock. Open M-Sa 8:30am-8:30pm, Su 8:30am-2:30pm. Anacapri, V. G. Orlandi 59 (☎081 83 71 524), right from bus stop. Open M-Sa 9am-3pm. All provide free detailed maps, ferry and bus info, and *Capri è...*, a magazine with detailed info on the island's hotels and restaurants. Multilingual staff. Reduced hours Oct.-May.

Currency Exchange: V. Roma 31 (☎081 83 74 768), across from the main bus stop, and in P. Umberto. Also in Anacapri at P. Vittoria 2 (☎081 83 73 146). Open in summer daily 8am-6pm; winter hours vary.

Luggage Storage: Outside Capri's funicular. €4 per bag per day. Open daily in summer 8:30am-8pm; in winter 8:15am-7pm.

English-Language Bookstore: Librerie Studio La Conchiglia, V. Le Botteghe 12 (☎081 83 76 577; www.laconchigliacapri.com), in Capri, off P. Umberto. Open daily in summer 9am-1:30pm and 3-10:30pm; in winter 9am-1:30pm and 3-9pm.

Emergency: ☎081 83 81 205.

Police: V. Roma 70 (☎081 83 74 211), in Anacapri.

Medical Services: Ospedale Capilupi, V. Provinciale Anacapri 5 (☎081 83 81 111), a few blocks down V. Roma from P. Umberto. **Tourist Medical Clinic,** V. Caprile 30 (☎081 83 81 240), in Anacapri. **Ambulance:** ☎081 83 81 205.

Internet Access: Bar Due Pini, P. Vittoria (☎081 83 78 160), in Anacapri. €7 per hr. Open daily 8:30am-6:30pm.

Post Office: Anacapri, Vle. Tommaso. de Tommaso 8 (☎081 83 71 015). Open M-F 8:30am-1:30pm, Sa 8:30am-noon. **Capri,** V. Roma 50 (☎081 97 85 211). Open M-F 8:30am-7pm, Sa 8:30am-1pm. **Postal Codes:** 80071 (Anacapri), 80073 (Capri).

ACCOMMODATIONS

Lodgings in Capri proper are pricey year-round and become even more expensive in the summer; daytrip from Naples or Sorrento to save money. Though cheaper and more serene than Capri, Anacapri will dent anyone's budget. Camping is a great option as long as you make sure you find a legitimate campground; makeshift camping is illegal and heavily fined.

ANACAPRI

Hotel Bussola, V. Traversa La Vigna 14 (☎081 83 82 010; www.bussolahermes.com). Call from P. Vittoria in Anacapri for pickup rather than navigate Anacapri's streets. A new building; imitates the neoclassical style of Pompeii, with statues and mosaics. Mediterranean rooms with flat-screen TV, phone, safe, and bath; some with terrace. A/C €10 per day. Free Wi-Fi. Breakfast included. Singles €70-130; doubles €70-130; triples €85-150; quads €90-180. *Let's Go* discount 8%; reserve via phone or email. MC/V. ❹

Villa Mimosa Bed and Breakfast, V. Nuova del Faro 48/A (☎081 83 71 752; www.mimosacapri.com). 100m on the right past the last stop of the Marina Grande-Anacapri bus. Elegant rooms surround a terrace; all come with satellite TV, A/C, safe, and bath. Breakfast included. Doubles €70-110. 10% *Let's Go* discount Oct.-Mar. MC/V. ❹

Hotel Loreley, V. G. Orlandi, 16 (☎081 83 71 440; www.loreley.it). Convenient location by the funicular/bus stop in Anacapri. Tranquility and relaxation are the order of the day. Large clean rooms with great vistas. Open Mar. 15-Nov. Singles €60-85; doubles €80-120. Extra bed €30. 10% *Let's Go* discount weekdays Sept.-July. AmEx/MC/V. ❺

CAPRI

Villa Palomba, V. Mulo 3 (☎081 83 77 322; www.capri.it/villapalomba), off V. M. Piccola. Friendly owners and great vistas make this relaxed, private spot a nice place even for young travelers. Best deal in Capri. Rooms with TV, minibar, safe, bath, and A/C (€10 per day). Breakfast included. Singles €45-75; doubles €75-125. MC/V. ❹

Hotel La Tosca, V. Dalmazio Birago 5 (☎081 83 70 989; www.latoscahotel.com). Take V. Cimino from P. Umberto, then turn left on V. D. Birago. Soothing terrace facing the Faraglioni rocks. Simple rooms with phone, A/C, and bath. Breakfast included. Open Apr.-Oct. Doubles €70-140. Cash only. ❹

Vuotto Antonino, V. Campo di Teste 2 (☎/fax 081 83 70 230). Take V. V. Emanuele from P. Umberto, turn left on V. Camerelle, right on V. Cerio, and left. In "Villa Margherita." Antique-filled rooms with terraces. Open Mar.-Nov. Doubles €70-105. Cash only. ❸

Albergo 4 Stagioni, V. M. Piccola 1 (☎081 83 70 041; www.hotel4stagionicapri.com). From P. Umberto, walk 5min. down V. Roma. Turn left at the 3-pronged fork in the road; look for green gate on the left. 12 plain and pristine rooms. Pricier doubles enjoy garden access and sea views. Breakfast included. Open Mar.-Nov. Singles €40-70; doubles €70-130. Extra bed €20-25. Ask about *Let's Go* discount. MC/V. ❹

🞖 FOOD

Savor creamy local mozzarella served with sweet red tomatoes, glistening olive oil, and zesty basil in an *insalata caprese*—the island's trademark, which many consider the *sine qua non* (a must-have) of summer dining. Conclude with the indulgent *torta di mandorle* (chocolate almond cake), also known as *torta caprese*. Be discerning around P. Umberto, where restaurants serve overpriced stale pastries. Fruit stands around the island sell delectable goods at low prices. (Open daily 8am-1pm and 4-8pm.) In Anacapri, find fixings at the well-stocked **supermarket,** V. G. Orlandi 299. (☎081 83 71 119. Open M-Sa 8:30am-1:30pm and 5-8:30pm, Su 8:30am-noon.) Interestingly enough, it is often cheaper to buy *panini* at restaurants than at *salumerie*. **Via Giuseppe Orlandi,** running from P. Vittoria, leads past restaurants on the way.

ANACAPRI

🞖 **Al Nido D'Oro,** Vle. T. de Tommaso 32 (☎081 83 72 148), on the way to the bus stop for the Grotta Azzurra. Probably the cheapest restaurant on the island. Extremely popular with islanders for its high-quality *Caprese* cuisine. Pizza and drink €7. Primi €5-8. Lunch *menù* €12. Open M-Tu and Th-Su 11am-3:30pm and 7pm-midnight. ❶

🞖 **Da Giovanni a Gradola,** Località Gradola 8 (☎081 83 73 673). Though not as elegant as its upscale neighbors, this multi-level trattoria offers the same panoramic view of the

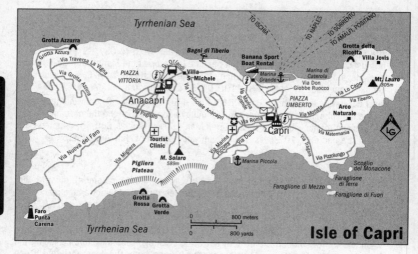

Isle of Capri

Tyrrhenian Sea. Descend its stairs to a free uncrowded beach. *Panini* €5. Primi €8-10. Secondi €10-13. Open from mid-June to Sept. 9:30am-7:30pm. Cash only. ❷

Ristorante Il Cucciolo, V. La Fabbrica 52 (☎081 83 71 917). Try the fresh *ravioli Caprese* (€9). Seaside terrace. With *Let's Go* discount: primi and secondi €6-9. Service 12%. Open daily Mar.-Oct. noon-2:30pm and 7:30-11pm. AmEx/MC/V. ❷

Ristorante Materita, V. G. Orlandi 140 (☎081 83 73 375). Devour delicious pizza (from €6) on a candlelit terrace overlooking Anacapri's most fashionable *piazza*, then linger over house-made *limoncello*. Primi and secondi from €8.50. Cover €2.50. Open Apr.-Oct. daily 11:45am-3:30pm and 6:45-midnight; Nov.-Mar. M and W-Su 11:45am-3:30pm and 6:45pm-midnight. MC/V. ❷

Caffé Orlandi, V. G. Orlandi 83 (☎081 83 82 138). The ideal lunch-spot before a visit to Monte Solaro or a walk around Anacapri's *centro storico*. €10 lunch *menù;* includes salad, primi, and coffee. Open daily Feb.-Dec. 9am-10pm. MC/V. ❷

Vini e Bibite, P. Diaz (☎081 83 73 320). An oasis from the touristy tumult. Primi and secondi €6-13. Service 12%. Open daily noon-3pm and 7pm-midnight. ❸

La Rondinella, V. G. Orlandi 295 (☎081 83 71 223), near P. Vittoria. Enjoy a romantic, candlelit feast under a canopy. Fresh antipasti and seafood offerings, like succulent *gamberoni* (prawns; €21). Dinner reservations suggested. Primi €9-13. Secondi €9-15. Cover €3. Service 10%. Open daily noon-3pm and 7pm-midnight. AmEx/MC/V. ❸

CAPRI

Longano da Tarantino, V. Longano 9 (☎081 83 70 187), just off P. Umberto. Perhaps the best deal in town. Sea view and €18 *menù*. Packed, but service is friendly and efficient. Pizza €4-9. Excellent grilled seafood €10-13. Cover €0.80. Open Mar.-Nov. M-Tu and Th-Su 11:30am-3pm and 7pm-midnight. Reservations recommended. AmEx/MC/V. ❷

Villa Verde, Vico Sella Orta 6/A (☎081 83 77 024; www.villaverde-capri.com). Off V. V. Emanuele, near P. Umberto. Prices reflect the earning power of celeb guests whose pictures adorn the walls. Large portions of fresh fish and lobster. Specialties are *fusilli Villa Verde* (€15) and rich desserts (€5-7). Pizza €5.50-15. Primi €10-25. Secondi €12-25. Service 15%. Open daily noon-4pm and 7pm-1am. AmEx/MC/V. ❹

Aurora Pizzeria, V. Fuorlovado 20-22 (☎081 83 70 181; www.auroracapri.com). Celebs like Michael Douglas and Giorgio Armani come for the *Pizza al Acqua* (€10). Cover €3. Service 15%. Open daily Mar.-Dec. noon-3pm and 7pm-midnight. AmEx/MC/V. ❷

Gelateria Lo Sfizietto, V. Longano 6. Treat yourself to gelato (from €2) made from real fruit for a refreshing break from the Capri sun. Try *Cassatina,* a combo of chocolate chips and dry fruit. Cones from €2. Open daily Mar.-Dec. 10am-11:30pm. Cash only. ❶

👁 ⛰ SIGHTS AND OUTDOOR ACTIVITIES

CLIFFS. An exploration of the island's natural beauty can be a much-needed break from crowded *piazze* and commercial streets. For those who prefer land to sea, various trails starting in Capri lead to stunning panoramas. At the island's eastern edge, a 1hr. round-trip walk connects the **Arco Naturale,** a majestic stone arch, and the **Faraglioni,** the three massive rocks featured on countless postcards. Part of the path is unpaved; wear proper footwear. *(V. Tragara goes from Capri Centro to the Faraglioni, while the path to the Arco Naturale connects to the route to Villa Jovis through V. Matermania.)* Hike a steep uphill path 45min. to the ruins of Emperor Tiberius's magnificent **Villa Jovis.** Tiberius lived here, the largest of his 12 Capri villas, during his more eccentric final years. Always the gracious host, he was prone to tossing displeasing guests over the precipice. Sweeping views from the villa's **Cappella di Santa Maria del Soccorso** are unrivaled. *(Take V. Longano from P. Umberto. Don't miss the left on V. Tiberio, and follow the signs. Open daily 9am-6pm. €2.)*

COAST. Daily **boat tours** explore the gorgeous coast, including the Grotta Azzurra. *(Tickets and info at Grotta Azzurra Travel Office, V. Roma 53, across from the bus stop. ☎081 83 70 466; g.azzurra@capri.it. Ticket office open M-Sa 9am-1pm and 3:30-7pm, Su 9am-12:30pm. See below for info on Grotta Azzurra. Departures from Marina Grande at 9:30, 10:30, 11:30am. €13.)* Cavort in the clear water amid immense lava rocks, or rent a **motor boat** from **Banana Sport,** in Marina Grande. *(☎081 83 75 188 or 330 22 70 64. Open daily 9:30am-6:30pm. 2hr.; May-June and Sept.-Oct. €80; July-Aug. €95. AmEx/MC/V.)* Pebbly **beaches** surround the island. Take a Bagni Tiberio boat (€9 round-trip) from the port or walk between vineyards to **Bagni di Tiberio,** a bathing area within ruins of an imperial villa. A walk along **Marina Piccola** is also nice. *(Take V. Roma from P. Umberto to 3-pronged fork in road; take the left-most fork and head down the path to the left.)*

VILLA SAN MICHELE. Henry James once declared this Anacapri enclave a mix of "the most fantastic beauty, poetry, and inutility." The 20th-century estate displays Roman sculptures from a former Tiberian villa and glorious gardens, which host contemporary art shows and Friday night concerts from June to August. *(Upstairs from P. Vittoria and to the left, past Capri Beauty Farm spa. ☎081 83 71 401. Open daily 9am-6pm. Concert info available at ticket desk and tourist offices. Villa €6.)*

LA GROTTA AZZURRA (THE BLUE GROTTO). The walls of this water-filled cave shimmer vivid blue when sunlight radiates from beneath the water's surface (for this reason, the grotto is more impressive on sunnier days). Watch your head when entering. Some who visit find the water amazing; others don't think it's impressive enough to justify spending €9 on a guided tour (even if there *is* singing involved). Despite the narrow cave opening and the sign warning that swimming is "strictly forbidden," some visitors take dips in the grotto for free after boats stop at 5pm. Check with the tourist office to make sure that the grotto isn't closed due to choppy water. If you rent a boat, consider visiting the **Grotta Verde,** on the other side of the island. *(Take the bus marked "Grotta Azzurra" from the intersection of Vle. T. De Tommaso and V. Catena in Anacapri. The grotto is accessible with the island boat tour as well, but the entrance charge still applies.)*

OTHER SIGHTS. Capri's location makes it ideal for surveying southern Italy's topography. Viewed from the peak of ◪**Monte Solaro,** the Apennines loom ahead to the east and the mountains of Calabria are to the south on the right. The vistas are so stunning that sky and sea actually seem to become one. A 12min. chairlift from P. Vittoria to the summit dangles from precipitous heights. (☎081 83 71 428. *Chairlift open daily July-Sept. 9am-6pm; Mar.-Apr. and Oct. 9:30am-4:45pm. Round-trip €7.)* Alternatively, take the difficult 45min. hike up V. Monte Solaro, which starts from the base near Villa San Michele. A bus from P. Vittoria leads to the **Faro Punta Carena,** Italy's second-tallest lighthouse, and a fairly desolate swimming area. The pedestrian stretch of V. G. Orlandi, off P. Vittoria in Anacapri, leads to the least expensive—yet still pricey—**shopping.**

☒ NIGHTLIFE

Nocturnal action carries a hefty price tag, though Anacapri's prices are slightly lower. In typical Italian fashion, no one bothers heading out until around midnight. **Underground,** V. G. Orlandi 259, is one of the town's most popular night spots, thanks to no cover and €5 mixed drinks. In Capri try **BaraOnda,** V. Roma 8, which enjoys theme nights on most weekends. (☎081 83 77 147. *Drinks €7.)* Both Capri clubs are open all night. Those sufficiently self-assured to hang with dressed-to-kill Italians should remember that buses stop running at 1:40am. For a more sophisticated night, attend a Friday night concert at Villa San Michele.

AMALFI COAST

It happens almost imperceptibly: after the exhausting tumult of Naples and the compact grit of Sorrento, the highway narrows to a two-lane road that zigzags down the coastline. Though the effortless simplicity and sophistication of Positano, Amalfi, and Praiano seduced Emperor Augustus, Ernest Hemingway, and Jacqueline Kennedy Onassis, the region's ultimate appeal rests in the tenuous balance it strikes between man and nature. Whitewashed homes cling defiantly to rock and crazy bus drivers tame even crazier roads. The coast's unassuming grandeur is a reminder to simply relax and enjoy life.

POSITANO ☎089

As birthplace of the modern bikini, Positano (po-zee-TA-no; pop. 4000) has quite a reputation to live up to. In the mid-1900s, the town was a posh haven for artists and literati, attracting visitors such as John Steinbeck, Jack Kerouac, and Tennessee Williams. Positano's classy reputation soon drew millionaires in addition to the writers, painters, actors, and filmmakers who made it famous, and today, its beachfront teems with a diverse crowd of vacationers. Though tourism may have changed Positano since Steinbeck sought solitude along its coast, the town remains a playground for the rich, as well as for the not-so-famous—ordinary travelers seeking its tranquility and beauty.

▤ TRANSPORTATION

Over land, Positano is best reached by **bus.** Blue or green-and-white SITA buses run to Amalfi and Sorrento (June-Sept. 25 per day 7am-9pm, €2). There are two stops in Positano along V. G. Marconi, the main coastal road. Walk downhill from either stop to reach the *centro.* Tickets are sold at Bar Internazionale, by the Chiesa Nuova stop on V. G. Marconi, or at *tabaccherie.* Alternatively, catch a **ferry** or **hydrofoil** from Spiaggia Grande. Linee Marittime Partenopee (☎089 81

19 86) runs daily to Amalfi (ferry 25min., 9 per day 10am-6:30pm, €6; hydrofoil 15min., 3 per day 4-7:15pm, €7.50), Capri (ferry 40min., 8:50 and 10am, €14.50; hydrofoil 25min. 4 per day, 9am-6pm, €16.50), Salerno (ferry 1¼hr., 5:45 and 7:15pm, €10; hydrofoil 40min., 3 per day 4-7:15pm, €12), and Ischia (ferry 2hr., 8:50am, €19). Metro del Mare (☎089 199 600 700) runs hydrofoils daily to Amalfi (20min., 6 per day 8:50am-3:55pm, €9), Napoli Molo Beverello (1½hr., 5 per day 10:40am-7pm, €14), and Sorrento (40min., 4 per day 10:40am-7pm, €9).

✴ ⁊ ORIENTATION AND PRACTICAL INFORMATION

Positano clings to two huge cliffs that overlook the Tyrrhenian Sea. Coming from Sorrento, **Chiesa Nuova** is the first SITA stop in town on **Via Guglielmo Marconi**, in front of Bar Internazionale. From here, if you don't mind the steep downhill walk, take **Viale Pasitea**, or wait for one of Positano's frequent **local buses** marked "Positano Interno" (every 15-30min. 7:15am-midnight, €1.50); the bus route ends in **Piazza dei Mulini**. The second SITA stop is at the intersection of V. G. Marconi and **Via Cristoforo Colombo**; internal buses don't run here, so walk 10min. downhill on V. C. Colombo to reach P. dei Mulini, where V. C. Colombo becomes Vle. Pasitea. Also from P. dei Mulini, **Via dei Mulini** winds through town, past the Santa Maria, and to **Spiaggia Grande**, the main beach. Take the footpath from Spiaggia Grande to get to the cozier **Fornillo** beach on the right.

Tourist Office: V. del Saraceno 4 (☎089 87 50 67; www.aziendaturismopositano.it), near the church. Provides a free map, hotel listings, and ferry and bus schedules. English spoken. Open in summer M-Sa 9am-2pm and 3-8pm; in winter M-Sa 9am-3pm.

Currency Exchange: P. dei Mulini 6 (☎089 87 58 64), on the V. Mulini side of the *piazza*. Decent rates; €1 commission per traveler's check. Open daily in summer 9:30am-1:30pm and 4-9:30pm; in winter 9:30am-1pm and 3:30-7:50pm.

English Language Bookstore: La Libreria, V. C. Colombo 165 (☎089 81 10 77). Open daily Apr.-Oct. 10am-1:30pm and 5-8:30pm. AmEx/MC/V.

Carabinieri: (☎089 87 50 11), near top of the cliffs down the steps by Chiesa Nuova.

Hospital: (☎089 081 533 1111), in Sorrento; a tourist medical clinic is in Amalfi.

Pharmacy: Vle. Pasitea 22 (☎089 87 58 63). Open in summer daily 9am-1pm and 5-9pm; in winter M-W and F-Sa 9am-1pm and 4-8pm.

Internet Access: Conwinum, V. Rampa Teglia 12 (☎089 81 16 87; www.positano.conwinum.it), below Buca di Bacco. €6 per hr. Open daily 9am-11pm.

Luggage Storage: Blu Porter, in front of the pharmacy at Vle. Pasitea 22 (☎089 81 14 96). Prices from €5 per day. Night service available.

Post Office: V. Guglielmo Marconi 320. Open M-F 8am-1:30pm, Sa 8am-12:30pm. **Postal code:** 84017.

◤ ACCOMMODATIONS

Budget travelers might want to make Positano a daytrip from Sorrento or Salerno; there are few cheap accommodations. The tourist office helps arrange *affittacamere* for longer stays.

▨ **Ostello Brikette,** V. G. Marconi 358 (☎089 87 58 57; www.brikette.com). Take an orange Interno bus or SITA bus to "Chiesa Nuova" stop and walk 100m to the left of Bar Internazionale. Rooms with A/C and great terrace views. English-speaking staff provides advice on sights and restaurants. Organic breakfast €1.50-6. Laundry €10. Free Wi-Fi. With *Let's Go* guide, free 30min. Internet access. Lockout 11am-2:30pm. Lights-out M-Th and Su midnight. No curfew for private rooms. Reservation recommended July-Aug. Open from late Mar. to Nov. Dorms €22-25; doubles €65-100. MC/V. ❷

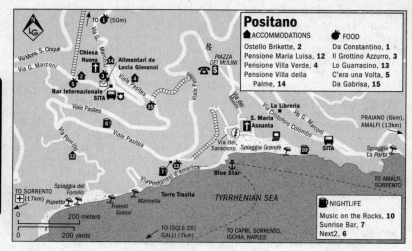

Positita

Positano

🏠 ACCOMMODATIONS
Ostello Brikette, **2**
Pensione Maria Luisa, **12**
Pensione Villa Verde, **4**
Pensione Villa della
Palme, **14**

🍴 FOOD
Da Constantino, **1**
Il Grottino Azzurro, **3**
Lo Guarracino, **13**
C'era una Volta, **5**
Da Gabrisa, **15**

🌙 NIGHTLIFE
Music on the Rocks, **10**
Sunrise Bar, **7**
Next2, **6**

Pensione Villa Verde, Vle. Pasitea 338 (☎089 87 55 06; www.pensionevillaverde.it). Take Interno bus to "Casale." 12 simple rooms overlooking Positano; all with terrace and bath. TV and A/C available upon request. Breakfast included. Open Mar.-Dec. €30-50 per person. Ask for *Let's Go* cash discount. AmEx/MC/V. ❸

Pensione Maria Luisa, V. Fornillo 42 (☎089 87 50 23; www.pensionemarialuisa.com). Take the Interno bus to V. Fornillo. English-speaking owner. Bright, comfortable rooms with bath, fridge, and seaside terrace. Free beach towel rental. Free Internet access with *Let's Go*. Singles €50; doubles €70-80; triples €90-100. Cash only. ❹

Pensione Villa delle Palme, Vle. Pasitea 252 (☎089 87 51 62; www.positanovilladellepalme.com). In the same building as Saraceno d'Oro restaurant, with an easily accessible beach. Rooms full of quirky antiques; all with bath, TV, and balcony or terrace. Breakfast €5. Doubles €75-85; triples €100-110. Cash only. ❹

Casa Guadagno, V. Fornillo 36 (☎089 87 50 42; fax 81 14 07). Take the Interno bus to V. Fornillo. All rooms have bath, minifridge, and terrace with seaside views. Internet access €2 per hr. Free Wi-Fi. Free breakfast on terrace. With *Let's Go* discount, doubles €85-90; triples €110; quads €120. Reservation recommended. Cash only. ❹

🍴 FOOD

In Positano, high prices generally reflect high quality: homemade pasta, fresh produce, and excellent seafood are the norm. The **Alimentari de Lucia Giovanni,** V. G. Marconi 512, sells fresh sandwiches, cheese, and produce. (☎089 87 50 99. Open daily M-Sa 7am-2pm and 4-9pm, Su 7am-2pm. Cash only.)

▨ **Da Constantino,** V. Corvo 95 (☎089 87 57 38). From Ostello Brikette, walk upstairs, and turn right when you hit the real road, or take the bus to Nocelle. Amazing views, sea breezes, and occasional live music. Try the specialty *crespolini al formaggio* (cheese crepes; €9). A vegetarian buffet is available (€9.50). Pizza from €4. Primi €5-10. Secondi €8-13. Open in summer daily noon-3:30pm and 7pm-midnight; in winter M-Tu and Th-Su noon-3:30pm and 7pm-midnight; closed Nov.-Jan. AmEx/MC/V. ❷

▨ **C'era una volta,** V. G. Marconi 127 (☎089 81 19 30), near Ostello Brikette. Local and backpacker favorite. *Pizza margherita* €4. Live outdoor music F-Su. Primi €6-9. Secondi €5-11. Open daily May-Jan. noon-2:30pm and 7pm-midnight. AmEx/MC/V. ❶

Il Grottino Azzurro, V. G. Marconi 304 (☎089 87 54 66), across from the "Chiesa Nuova" bus stop. Excellent fish and seafood priced right. Linger for hours in simple but inviting interior. House-made white wine €2. Fresh seafood from €9; spaghetti with squid €11. Homemade pasta dishes €8-10. Killer tiramisu €3. Cover €2. Open M-Tu and Th-Su 12:30-2:30pm and 7:30-10:30pm. Closed from Dec. to mid-Feb. MC/V. ❷

Lo Guarracino, V. Positanesi d'America 12 (☎089 975 794). To avoid over-priced restaurants by Spiaggia Grande, take the stairs on the way to Fornillo Beach; the restaurant is to the right. Pizza €10; takeout €5. Primi and secondi €9-16. Reservations suggested for seaside tables. Open daily noon-3pm and 7pm-midnight. AmEx/MC/V. ❷

Da Gabrisa, Vle. Pasitea 219 (☎089 81 14 98). Bright, breezy dining room and great service. Savor the grilled vegetable antipasto with tender pumpkin and plump mozzarella (€8). *Pasta alla norma* (pasta in tomato sauce with eggplant; €8) is a savory treat. Primi €7-16. Secondi €7-15. Open daily 12:30-2:30pm and 6-11pm. AmEx/MC/V. ❸

🔵🏖 SIGHTS AND BEACHES

Tourists in Positano often peruse crowded boutiques and sidewalk kiosks, or take boat excursions along the coast and to neighboring islands, as well as the **Emerald** and **Blue Grottoes** (p. 603). For most, Positano's beaches are its main attraction. Your best bet for serene and secluded relaxation, and a waterside post-beach meal, is **Fornillo Beach,** hidden from the docks and downtown chaos by a shady, rocky walkway. Take **Via Positanese d'America,** a footpath that starts from the right side of the port facing the water and winds past **Torre Trasita.** There's a free beach left of La Marinella. Though crowded, the only free area of the expansive **Spiagga Grande** is next to the docks. Outside the entrance, **Blue Star** (☎089 81 18 88; www.bluestarpositano.it) rents motorboats and rowboats, and provides boat tours of the Blue and Emerald Grottoes. For a short, free boat ride, jump on any of the small, white boats off Spiaggia Grande, which pass restaurants that can only be reached by sea.

Positano offers tremendous **hikes** for those with quads of steel. **Montepertuso,** a high mountain pierced by a large *pertusione* (hole), is one of three perforated mountains in the world (the other two are in India). Hike the 45min. trail or take the bus, which leaves from P. dei Mulini near the port. From Montepertuso, take the **Path of the Gods** (4hr.), which explores the surrounding area. Ask the tourist office for a map. The three **Isole dei Galli,** peeking out of the waters off Positano's coast, were allegedly home to Homer's mythical Sirens, who lured unsuspecting victims with their spellbinding songs. While swimming around these beautiful islands is permitted, setting foot on them is not.

🎭🎵 ENTERTAINMENT AND NIGHTLIFE

Positano's Art Festival includes fashion shows, art exhibitions, dance, and music concerts at different spots in the city (Apr.-Oct.; contact tourist office for more info). The swanky piano bar and disco, **Music on the Rocks,** on the far left side of the beach facing the water, packs well-dressed locals and visitors into a large cave with one side open to the water. Celebrities like Denzel Washington and Lenny Kravitz have been known to drop in. (☎089 87 58 74. Mixed drinks from €12. Cover varies: M-Th and Su often free, Sa €25.) Catch the sun falling behind the mountains from **Next2,** Vle. Pasitea 242, and then stick around for a drink (€4-8) and lounge music. (☎089 81 23 516. Open daily Apr.-Nov. 8pm-2am.) Watch Positano light up for an enchanting night from **Sunrise Bar,** V. Pasitea 119, with light music and modern lounging over a breathtaking terrace. (☎089 87 50 10. Beer €4. Wine €3. Mixed drinks €8. Open daily 5pm-1am.)

CAMPANIA

PRAIANO

☎ 089

The quiet town of Praiano (pry-AH-no; pop. 2000), a sparsely-populated expanse scattered over 10km of stunning coastline, is a welcome change from the heavily-touristed Amalfi Coast. From crumbling towers to beautiful sunsets, unjustly-overlooked Praiano has a refreshingly authentic feel; come here for a vacation from your vacation.

✦ 🔁 ORIENTATION AND PRACTICAL INFORMATION

Praiano is less a town than a loose conglomeration of hotels and restaurants. You can reach it by bus from Positano (15min.), or by a 1hr. walk. The town is skirted to the south by **Via Gennaro Capriglione** which turns into **Via Roma; Via Giuglielmo Marconi** and **Via Umberto I** run parallel. The **tourist office,** V. G. Capriglione 116, has an **ATM** (☎089 87 45 57). Other services include: a **hospital** in Sorrento (☎089 081 533 1111); a **pharmacy** at V. G. Capriglione 142 (☎089 87 48 46); and **Internet** access a **Dimensione Futuro,** V. G. Capriglione 27. (€4 per hr.; open M-F 9am-1pm and 5-9pm, Sa 9am-1pm). The **post office** is at V. Capriglione 80 (Open M-F 8am-1:30pm, Sa 8am-12:30pm). **Postal code:** 84010.

🏠 📷 ACCOMMODATIONS AND CAMPING

There's no cheap hostel in Praiano, but the town does offer affordable housing options that are intimate, especially if you're traveling with a friend.

Pensione Continental, V. Roma 21 (☎089 87 40 84). In the secluded, cliffside Villagio "La Tranquilità." 10 antique Mediterranean rooms and 15 modern, Caribbean-themed cottages with phone, safe, bath, and terrace; most have fridge. Private beach and restaurant. Scenic campsite (€20 per night; bring your own tent; free hot showers). Breakfast €7. A/C €10 per day. Internet access €5 per hr. Open Apr.-Nov. Singles €45-65; doubles €55-90. Extra bed €15. AmEx/MC/V. ❹

Il Gelsomino, V. Roma 1 (☎089 87 44 68; www.ilgelsominopraiano.com). Spacious, nicely decorated rooms and kind staff. Min. 1-week stay in Aug. Breakfast included. Doubles €50-75. Extra bed €15. 10% *Let's Go* discount Sept.-July. Cash only. ❷

Casa Benvenuto Residence, V. Roma 60 (☎089 87 45 75). A kind owner runs 6 huge rooms, each with TV, bath, and views of the Mar Tirreno. Breakfast included. Doubles, triples, and quads €75-80. AmEx/MC/V. ❸

La Conchiglia, V. Marina di Praia 17 (☎089 87 43 13; www.laconchigliapraiano.it). Located on the beach, near restaurants and nightlife. Family-run hotel. Beautiful rooms. Breakfast included. Doubles €60-100. Extra bed €25. Cash only. ❸

🍴 FOOD

Your palate may not know the difference between the food of Praiano and that of its pricier cousins, but your wallet will. There are four *alimentari* along V. Capriglione. (All open M-Sa 7:30am-1pm and 6-10pm.)

Il Pirata, V. Terramare (☎089 87 43 77). To the right of Marina di Praia. Enjoy delicious food right on the edge of a cliff overlooking fun-loving swimmers. Primi €9-11. Internet access €6 per hr. Open daily noon-3:30pm and 7:30-11:30pm. ❷

Petit Restaurant Bar Mare, V. Marina di Praia 9 (☎089 87 47 06). Always delicious, this happening spot is especially popular with young people heading out to dance the night way. Spaghetti with squid €11. *Menù* €18. Primi €8-12. Cover €2. Open daily Mar. 15-Dec. 7:30am-1am. AmEx/MC/V. ❷

👁 👂 SIGHTS AND NIGHTLIFE

Praiano's openness and natural beauty make it the coast's best spot for a scenic **scooter** ride, though the abundance of winding roads often makes rental companies hesitant to loan scooters to first-time drivers. Inexperienced drivers should exercise particular caution while navigating the winding roads. The hotel **Casa di San Gennaro,** V. Capriglione 100, rents scooters from €25 per day. (☎089 81 30 71; milanorental@libero.it. Insurance and helmet included. AmEx/MC/V.) Don't miss **Torre a Mare,** a well-preserved tower that once protected against pirates, but now displays works by sculptor and painter Paolo Sandulli. (Open daily 9am-1pm and 3-7pm.) From Torre a Mare, descend the ramp that leads down V. Terramare to the **free beach** in **Marina di Praia.** Nearby, check out **La Boa Diving Center,** which offers trial dives starting at €60; full immersion with equipment and guide from €80. (☎089 81 30 34; www.laboa.com. Ask about *Let's Go* discount.) Marina di Praia, a 400-year-old fishing village, tucked in a tiny ravine, also hides restaurants, bars, and one of the Amalfi Coast's most popular clubs since the early 60s, **Africana.** Fish swim through the grotto under the glass dance floor, while music echoes off the cave roof above, and boats dock at the stairwell right outside. (☎089 87 40 42. Beer €5. Africana mixed drink €8. Tu women free. No cover M and W-Th with purchase of 1 drink. Cover Tu, F, Su €15-20; includes 1 free drink. Open from mid-June to Sept. daily 10:30pm-3am.)

AMALFI ☎089

Picture-perfect Amalfi (ah-MAL-fee; pop. 5500) lies nestled between the jagged rocks of the Sorrentine peninsula and the azure waters of the Tyrrhenian Sea. Monuments like the fanciful Arab-Norman *duomo* and medieval paper mills are the legacy of a long history of international prominence. Amalfi was the seat of Italy's first sea republic and the preeminent maritime powerhouse of the southern Mediterranean, thanks in part to the compass, invented here by Flavio Gioia. Sadly, Amalfi's universal appeal is also responsible for the throngs of tourists, gaudy souvenir shops that characterize the town today. Consider daytripping from neighboring Atrani (ah-TRAH-nee; pop. 1000) to avoid the exorbitant prices. Southern Italy's smallest town, Atrani is a backpacker haven, offering many budget options.

🚐 TRANSPORTATION

The bus terminal is in P. Flavio Gioia, on the waterfront. SITA **buses** (☎089 26 66 04; www.sitabus.it.) go to Positano (40min., 25 per day 6:30am-11pm, €1.30), Salerno (1hr., 20 per day 6am-10pm, €1.80), and Sorrento (1hr., 29 per day 5:15am-11pm, €2). Salerno- and Ravello-bound buses pass the Atrani bus stop 5min. after leaving Amalfi. Buy tickets from *tabaccherie* (45min., €2; 1½hr., €3; 24hr., €6; 3-day, €15). **Ferries** and **hydrofoils** are at the dock off P. Flavio Gioia. Travelmar (☎089 87 31 90; www.coopsantandrea.it) runs hydrofoils to Minori (5min., 11 per day 7:30am-7:15pm, €2.50), Positano (25min., 7 per day 9:20am-6pm, €6), and Salerno (35min., 6 per day 10:40am-7:10pm, €6). Metro del Mare (☎089 19 96 00 700; www.metrodelmare.com) runs ferries to Sorrento (1hr., 5 per day 10:10am-6:30pm, €11) and Napoli Molo Beverello (2hr., 5 per day 10:10am-6:30pm, €15). For **taxis,** call ☎089 87 22 39.

🔧 ❓ ORIENTATION AND PRACTICAL INFORMATION

Amalfi is in the shape of an upside-down "T;" the top runs along the shore. **Via Lorenzo d'Amalfi,** heads uphill from the shore past the white arch of **Piazza Flavio**

Gioia and the town's main square, **Piazza Duomo**. This main street becomes V. Pietro Capuano, V. Marino del Giudice, and V. delle Cartiere as it passes through the *centro*. **Piazza Municipio** is a 100m walk up **Corso Repubbliche Marinare** (on the left when facing the sea). Ferries and buses stop in P. F. Gioia, the intersection of the two roads. Go through the tunnel on C. Repubbliche Marinare to reach Atrani, 250m down the coast, or follow the public path through the restaurant just next to the tunnel, on the side facing the sea. The pleasant, easy walk takes 10min. A stairway connects Atrani's bus stop to P. Umberto I, the main *piazza*. V. dei Dogi, the city's only street, ends at beautiful **Valle del Dragone**.

The **AAST tourist office**, C. delle Repubbliche Marinare, 27, is through a gate on the left on the road toward Atrani. Grab a free map along with hotel and restaurant listings. Ferry and bus timetables are also available. (☎089 87 11 07; www.amalfituristoffice.it. Open M-F Apr.-Sept. 9am-1pm and 4-7pm; Oct.-May 10am-6pm.) Other services include: the **carabinieri**, V. Casamare 19 (☎089 87 10 22); the **police**, inside the Municipio building on V. dei Dogi; a **pharmacy**, Farmacia Del Cervo, P. Duomo 41 (Open daily 9am-1pm and 5-9pm); and **Internet** access at **L'Altra Costiera**, V. L. d'Amalfi 34, which has three computers and also rents scooters. (☎089 87 36 082; www.altracostiera.com. Internet €5 per hr. Scooters from €45 per day; insurance included. 18+. Open daily Mar.-Nov. 9am-9:30pm.) The **post office**, C. Repubbliche Marinare 35, next to the tourist office, offers an **ATM** and currency exchange. (☎089 83 04 811. Commission €2.58. Open M-F 8am-6:30pm, Su 8am-12:30pm.) **Postal code:** 84011.

ACCOMMODATIONS

Lodgings fill up quickly in August, so reserve far ahead. Those on a budget should consider staying in Atrani, Salerno, or Naples for the lower prices.

NO-TELL MOTEL. Don't accept tips from English-speaking solicitors at the Amalfi bus station waiting for gullible travelers. They hand out info on unregistered hostels. Such hostels—though inexpensive—are illegal, unregulated, often unsanitary, and very unsafe.

ATRANI

A'Scalinatella, P. Umberto 6 (☎089 87 14 92; www.hostelscalinatella.com), 15min. from Amalfi bus station. Simple, affordable rooms year-round. Breakfast included. Dorms €21; doubles €50-60, with bath €73-83; quads with bath €120. ❷

Vettica House, V. Maestra dei Villaggi 96 (☎089 87 18 14 or 338 47 39 200; www.hostelscalinatella.com), 2km away in Vettica. A haven of tranquility amid natural beauty. Bright rooms with bath. Quick access to hiking trails. Kitchen available. Must call ahead; check-in at A'Scalinatella only. With *Let's Go* discount, singles with bath €35-50; doubles €50-60, with bath €60-83; quads €100. Cash only. ❸

L'Argine Fiorito, V. dei Dogi 45 (☎089 87 36 309; www.larginefiorito.it). Built inside a 17th-century pasta factory. Cozy rooms with bath and great balcony views. Pets allowed. Breakfast included. Doubles €80-95. Extra bed €30-35. Call ahead. AmEx/MC/V. ❺

AMALFI

Hotel Lidomare, V. Piccolomini 9 (☎089 87 13 32; www.lidomare.it), through alley across from *duomo*. Cozy rooms have terrace, satellite TV, phone, fridge, A/C, safe, and fantastic hydromassage bath. Small library and sitting room. Breakfast included. In summer singles €65; doubles €130. In winter €55/90. Extra bed €20. AmEx/MC/V. ❹

Villa Lara, V. delle Cartiere 1 (☎089 87 36 358; www.villalara.it). Climb 200 steps through a lemon grove, or take the elevator. English-speaking owner. Modern rooms with TV, mini-bar, A/C, phone, safe, and hydromassage bath; some with terrace. Free Internet. Free breakfast on many scenic terraces. Singles €75-145; doubles €90-195. MC/V. ❺

Hotel Fontana, P. Duomo 7 (☎089 87 15 30; www.hotel-fontana.it). Comfortable, modern rooms overlooking the *piazza* and harbor. All have bath, satellite TV, A/C, and minifridge. Free Wi-Fi. Breakfast included. May-Sept. singles €75; doubles €130; extra bed €40. Oct.-Apr. €50/100/30. Suites available. AmEx/MC/V. ❺

Apartments in Amalfi, V. Sant'Andrea (☎089 87 28 04; www.amalfiapartments.com), next to the *duomo* at Suportico Sant'Andrea. Rents 2 small apartments with views of the sea and the *piazza*. The double fits 4 and the studio is perfect for a couple; they share a terrace. Reserve 1 mo. ahead. 2-person €65; 4-person €90-110. Cash only. ❺

Amalfi

🏠 ACOMMODATIONS
A'Scalinatella, **11**
Vettica House, **8**
Hotel Lidomare, **10**
Villa Lara, **1**
Hotel Fontana, **16**

🍴 FOOD
Al Teatro, **3**
Bar Birecto, **5**
Donna Stella Pizzeria, **2**
Il Chiostro, **6**
Ristorante La Perla, **4**
Il Mulino, **7**
Trattoria e Pizzeria da Meme', **9**
Pasticceria Pansa, **12**
Porto Salvo, **13**
Da Maria, **14**
La Risacca, **15**

CAMPANIA

🔲 FOOD

Indulge in delicious seafood or *scialatelli* (a coarsely cut local pasta). The town's many *paninoteche* are perfect for a tight budget, but so are some of its restaurants. After dining, head to **La Valle dei Mulini,** V. L. d'Amalfi 11, for local *limoncello, meloncello,* and *lemonciok.* (☎089 87 32 88. Bottles €3-9. 10% *Let's Go* discount. Open daily Mar.-Dec. 10am-8:30pm.) Reserve 4 days in advance to visit their museum, garden, and factory.

🔳 **Bar Birecto,** P. Umberto I (☎089 87 10 17; www.ilbirecto.com), in Atrani. Fun-loving bar crew and cheap grub. A popular backpacker hangout. Free snacks and after-meal *limoncello.* Free Internet access and Wi-Fi for clients. €8 *menù.* €6 pizza and drink *menù.* Open Apr.-Oct. daily 7am-3am; Nov.-Mar. M-W and F-Su 7am-9pm. Cash only. ❷

🔳 **Donna Stella Pizzeria,** Salita Rascica 2 (☎089 338 358 8483; www.donnastella.com). From V. Capuano, turn right on Suportico Rua and follow the tunnel on the left to Salita Rascica. The cool hang out for *amalfitani,* with a gorgeous citrus terrace filled with the fruits and herbs. Pizza to rival that of Naples (€5-9). Make reservations or arrive early. Cover €1.50. Open Tu-Su 7-11:30pm. ❶

🔳 **Il Chiostro,** V. dei Prefetturi 2 (☎089 87 33 80). Left of the *duomo,* this is the perfect place for a light lunch or sumptuous dinner. Comfortable and private, the service, food, and ambience are the best Amalfi has to offer. Primi €6-10. Secondi €8-12. Open daily noon-2:30pm and 7-11pm. AmEx/MC/V. ❸

🔳 **Il Mulino,** V. delle Cartiere 36 (☎089 87 22 23; www.ristoranteilmulino.biz). Past the commotion of Amalfi's *centro,* locals know this family-owned restaurant for its spicy, smoked octopus with tomato and *peperoncino* (€7). Worth the wait, all dishes are made from scratch upon ordering. Margherita €5, takeout €3. Primi €5-12. Secondi €7-12. Cover €1.50. Open July-Aug. daily noon-4pm and 7pm-midnight; Sept.-June Tu-Su noon-4pm and 7pm-midnight. AmEx/MC/V. ❸

Trattoria e Pizzeria da Meme', Salita Marino Sebaste 8 (☎089 83 04 549). Inside the 18th-century Chiesa di Santa Nicola. A family-friendly locale; specializes in hand-made pasta. Pizza from €4. Primi €5.50-10. Secondi €6-13. Cover €1.50. Open daily Mar.-Oct. noon-3pm and 6:30pm-midnight. AmEx/MC/V. ❷

Al Teatro, V. E. Marini 19 (☎089 87 24 73). From V. L. d'Amalfi, turn left up Salita degli Orafi. Try the *scialatelli al Teatro* (local pasta with tomato and eggplant; €8). Primi and secondi from €6. *Menù* €15. Cover €2. Open from mid-Feb. to early Jan. M-Tu and Th-Su 11:30am-3pm and 7-11pm. AmEx/MC/V. ❷

Ristorante La Perla, Salita Truglio 5 (☎089 87 14 40), around corner from Hotel Amalfi. Excellent local cuisine in a quiet *piazza*. Homemade pasta with seafood is served in a giant seashell. *Menù* with delightful desserts €20. Primi €6-12. Secondi €8-15. Cover €2. Open Apr.-Oct. daily noon-3pm and 7pm-midnight. MC/V. ❸

Pasticceria Pansa, P. Duomo 40 (☎089 87 10 65; www.pasticceriapansa.it). Enjoy citrus-based pastries like *delizia al limone* (€2) or the Santa Rosa, a cream and ricotta puffs with caramelized orange peel (€1.50). Open daily June-Sept. 8:30am-1am; Oct.-Dec. and Feb.-Apr. 8:30am-10pm. Cash only. ❶

La Risacca, P. Umberto 16 (☎089 87 08 66; www.risacca.com), in Atrani. Caters to older crowds. Free snacks and after-meal coffee. Pizza €4-6. *Panini* €3.50. Free Internet access and Wi-Fi for customers. Open May-Oct. daily 8am-2pm and 4pm-midnight; Nov.-Apr. Tu-Su 8am-2pm and 4pm-midnight. AmEx/MC/V. ❶

Porto Salvo, P. Duomo 8 (☎089 338 188 1800). This is the place for hanging out and eating great pizza and sandwiches (both €3). Thick focaccia with toppings from €4. Order at the counter and enjoy its delicacies out on the beach. Mixed salads and vegetarian *panini* available. Open daily 8:30am-8:30pm. Cash only. ❶

Da Maria, P. Duomo 14 (☎089 87 18 80; www.amalfi-trattoriadamaria.com). Daily seafood specials, with traditional favorites like *scialatelli* and delectable seafood risotto (€13). Live piano music, cooking and *limoncello* production demonstrations in summer weekends. Pizza from €4.50. Primi €9-13. Secondi €10-20. *Menù* from €20. Wheelchair-accessible. Free Wi-Fi for clients. Open June-Sept. daily noon-3pm and 6-11pm; Oct.-May Tu-Su noon-3pm and 6-11pm. Reservations recommended. AmEx/MC/V. ❸

👁 SIGHTS

DUOMO DI SANT'ANDREA. This AD ninth-century Cathedral of Amalfi is the small town's dominant feature. Its facade's intricate geometric designs of vividly contrasting colors, typical of the Arab-Norman style, will transport you to southern Spain. The **bronze doors,** crafted in Constantinople in 1066, are so handsomely wrought that they started a bronze door craze throughout Italy. *(Open for prayer daily 7:30-10am and 7pm, for visiting 10am-6pm. Modest dress required. Free.)*

CHIOSTRO DEL PARADISO (CLOISTER OF PARADISE). This 13th-century cemetery, made for Amalfitan nobles, has 120 striking marble columns and an intricate fresco of the Crucifixion. The elegant, interlaced arches of both the cloister and the church reflect a Moorish influence. The modest church **museum** houses mosaics, sculptures, and the church's treasury. Underneath, the newly restored **crypt** contains the body of the church's namesake, St. Andrew the Apostle, whose remains were brought to Amalfi during the Crusades. *(Left of the Duomo di Sant'Andrea. ☎089 87 13 24. Open daily in summer 9am-9pm; in winter 10am-5pm. Free multilingual guides available. Cloister, museum, and crypt €2.50.)*

FONTANA DI SANT'ANDREA. This fountain does its best to counteract the church's stately influence, featuring a marble female nude with water trickling from her nipples. Those who can put their Freudian complexes aside might venture a drink from the fountain, which was rebuilt in the 19th century according to an original medieval plan. The 9th-century waterfront contains relics of Amalfi's former maritime glory, including examples of Amalfitan currency (the *tari*), and early compasses by Flavio Gioia. *(In P. Umberto I.)*

MUSEO DELLA CARTA (PAPER MUSEUM) This museum was a major paper-producing powerhouse during the Middle Ages. In a 13th-century paper mill, it showcases the history of paper production, including free paper samples made from pressed flowers and the water-powered machines. The ticket covers a 20min. tour with a multilingual guide. *(V. delle Cartiere 24. ☎089 83 04 561; www.museodellacarta.it. Open Mar.-Oct. daily 10am-2pm and 3-6:30pm. €3.50, students €2.60.)*

🏔 HIKING

Amalfi is an excellent departure point for several **hikes** of moderate difficulty that traverse a combination of trails and ancient staircases along the seaside mountains. Hikers often tackle paths from Amalfi and Atrani to the imposing **Monti Lattari,** winding through lemon groves and mountain streams. From Amalfi, the **Antiche Scale** lead past stalactite-heavy caves to the charming village of **Pogerola.** Trek through the **Valley of the Dragons,** named for the torrent of water and mist which plumes like smoke from a dragon and explodes out to sea each winter. However, if you only have time for one excursion, the popular **Path of the Gods** is a 3hr. descent from Bomerano (reachable by bus) to **Positano** (p. 604). The hike consists mostly of down-steps and marvellous views. The beautiful hike from Atrani to **Ravello** (next page) runs through gently bending lemon groves, up secluded stairways, and down into green cliff valleys (1-2hr.). From Ravello, it's only around 1hr. downhill to **Minori's** (next page) beautiful beaches, past quaint village churches and bountiful grapevines. SITA also runs frequent bus service from both Minori and Ravello to Amalfi, so you can ride back after a long walk. Hike past the old paper mills in **Valle delle Ferriere,** which begins at a staircase across the street from the paper museum. Naturally, the hikes can get steep, and a good map is essential (available at Amalfi's tourist office).

THE LOCAL STORY

ROW, ROW, ROW YOUR BOAT

Every year, the four medieval powerhouses of the Italian waters reunite for a traditional crew regatta. Amalfi, Pisa, Genoa, and Venice are the sole members of the Regatta of the Ancient Maritime Republics. Held in one of the four cities, the competition calls for each to send their eight mightiest rowers to go for the glory.

The race started in Pisa's Arno River in 1956 to promote cultural preservation and attract visitors to the area. Since then, the location has rotated yearly to include Genoa's Ligurian Sea and the Venetian Lagoon. Wooden boats have been replaced by fiberglass shells, but the flags remain: blue with a winged horse for Amalfi, scarlet with an eagle for Pisa, white with a griffon for Genoa, and green with a lion for Venice.

In Amalfi this past year, perhaps more important than the actual race was the large procession that preceded it. Three-hundred-and-twenty participants—fully dressed as musicians, captains, bishops, and members of the royal court—paraded down the street portraying important scenes from the Amalfi coast's height of medieval power—a true sight to be seen.

By far the strongest team, Venice's all-time record now amounts to 30 out of a total 53 events.

Held in June or late July. Visit http://www.comune.amalfi.sa.it/regata for more info.

SERIOUSLY, DUDE. Take hikes on the Amalfi coast seriously: bring maps, water, and sturdy hiking boots. Be prepared to climb tons of stairs!

BEACHES AND NIGHTLIFE

Amalfi has two small **beaches;** one sandy, the other rocky. The sandy beach, though not stunning, is a social stretch near the marina. Find better, free options 10min. away in nearby **Atrani** (see **Practical Information,** p. 609). With about 1000 inhabitants today, Atrani is a quiet refuge from Amalfi's crowds during the day. At night, Atrani's P. Umberto offers lively bars and a casual atmosphere just a stumbling distance away from A'Scalinatella. At **La Risacca's (p. 611),** the "Crazy Hour" features beers (€5) and long drinks (1L, €6-8), and occasional live music on weekends in summer. Located beside an old paper mill at the end of Amalfi's V. delle Cartiere, *discoteca* **Roccoco** offers DJ and live music, plus free pasta at midnight. (☎089 87 30 80. Beer, wine, and mixed drinks €5. Open F-Su 10pm-3am.)

DAYTRIP FROM AMALFI

MINORI

SITA buses from Amalfi stop on V. Roma, which becomes V. G. Amendola as it heads 1km northwest to Amalfi. C. Vittorio Emanuele ascends from the sea through the town center.

Decidedly low-key and filled with pleasant seaside cafes, Minori (mee-NO-ree; pop. 3300) is serene and inviting. Its large stretches of beautiful free beaches make it a perfect family spot to relax. Take the time to see the **Villa Marittima Romana,** a first-century BC vacation residence, at the entrance of town. The highlight is a remarkably well-preserved mosaic depicting a bull in the triclinium (dining room). (Open daily until sunset. Free.)

Enjoy traditional fare at the secluded **Ristorante La Botte,** next to the Villa on V. S. Maria Vetrano 15. Try the *dundari,* gnocchi's larger cousin, in a mushroom, tomato, and provolone cheese sauce (€7.50) and the flaky *torta diplomatica.* (☎089 87 78 93. Primi €6-9. Secondi €6.50. Cover €2. Open July-Sept. daily noon-3:30pm and 7pm-midnight; Oct.-June M and W-Su noon-3:30pm and 7pm-midnight. AmEx/MC/V.) For a lunchtime *panino* (€3-6) on the beach, try **Suzy Beach ❶,** P. California (☎328 07 77 285; open daily 8am-11pm; cash only), or grab basics at the **CONDAD** market on V. Traversa S. Giovanni a Mare 8. (☎089 85 35 38. Open M-Sa 7:30am-2pm and 4:30-9pm, Su 7:30am-1pm.) Nightlife on the *lungomare* centers around **Tony's,** V. Roma 76, where a large projector screen, plenty of cheap grub, and a beer fest on the second Thursday of each summer month attract teenage crowds. (Beer and wine €4. Open Apr.-Sept. daily 11am-4pm and 6pm-4am; Oct.-Mar. M-W and F-Su 11am-4pm and 6pm-4am.) For a jazzier time, head to **Modus,** C. V. Emanuele 45, a club and music hall that attracts international talent for live jazz shows. (Beer €4. Wine and mixed drinks €6. Open daily 8:30pm-2am. No show, no cover.) The tourist office, **Pro Loco Minori,** V. Roma 30, has free brochures, maps, and an ATM. (☎089 87 70 87; www.proloco.minori.sa.it. Open daily 8:30am-1:30pm and 4:30-9:30pm.)

RAVELLO   ☎089

Towering above the beach on a terraced cliff, Ravello (ra-VEH-lo; pop. 2500) caters mostly to music aficionados and wealthy vacationers. Founded by Romans in AD 500 and later invaded by the Barbarians and Saracens, the town presides over a patchwork of villages and ravines that tumble into the sea. The gardens of Villa Rufolo inspired both Boccaccio and Wagner. Today, Ravello's year-round performances have earned it the nickname *La Città della Musica*.

☐ ☒ TRANSPORTATION AND PRACTICAL INFORMATION. Take the blue SITA **bus** marked "Ravello-Scala" from Amalfi (20min., 30 per day 6:30am-1am, €2). For a **taxi**, call ☎089 85 80 00. Or, hike along hills and lemon groves from Minori (1hr.), Atrani (1hr., via Scala), or Amalfi (2hr., via Pontone). The **AAST tourist office**, V. Roma 18 bis, off P. Duomo, has brochures, event and hotel listings, hiking info, and a free map. (☎089 85 70 96; www.ravellotime.it. Open daily 9am-8pm.) Other services include: **ATMs** across from Cafe Calce and on P. Duomo 5; **public restrooms** in P. Duomo; the **carabinieri** at V. Roma 1 (☎089 85 71 50), near P. Duomo; a **pharmacy** at P. Duomo 14 (☎089 85 71 89; open daily in summer 9am-1pm and 5-8:30pm, in winter 9am-1pm and 4:30-8pm; closed Dec.); and **Internet** access and Wi-Fi at Bar Calce Due, V. Boccaccio 11. (€1.50 per 15min., €5 per hr.) The **post office**, V. Boccaccio 21, also has an ATM. (☎089 85 86 611. Open M-F 8am-1:30pm, Sa 8am-12:30pm.) **Postal Code:** 84010.

☐ ☐ ACCOMMODATIONS AND FOOD. Given that its main clientele is an older, wealthier crowd, Ravello has mainly opulent options. Among the more affordable options is **Palazzo della Marra ❹**, V. della Marra 3, a beautiful hotel offering four immaculate rooms with terraces. (☎089 85 83 02; www.palazzodellamarra. com. Breakfast included. Doubles €60-80. MC/V.) To get to **Hotel Villa Amore ❹**, V. dei Fusco 4, follow V. S. Francesco out of P. Duomo toward Villa Cimbrone, and take a left on V. dei Fusco. Twelve comfortable rooms, all with terrace and bath share a quiet cliffside garden overlooking the sea. The welcome sign says, "A stay at Villa Amore gives peace to the soul and joy to the heart." (☎089 85 71 35. In-room breakfast included. Reserve 1 month in advance. Singles €50-60; doubles €75-95. MC/V.) For a convenient spot by the bus station, head to the huge rooms of **A Due Passi 4**, V. Boccaccio 1, all of which have TV, private bath and A/C. (☎089 320 840 7605; www.aduepassi.it. Doubles €70-95. Extra bed €20.)

For a snack, head to inexpensive *alimentari* on V. Roma or Vle. della Rimembranza. (Open daily 8am-1pm and 4-8pm.) Ravello has few restaurants; one of the best is ☒**Cumpà Cosimo ❸**, V. Roma 44, which serves delicious food in a cozy dining room. The restaurant's atmosphere is laid-back and perfect for casual meals. The colorful *misto della casa* (€13) mixes six delectable homemade pastas. (☎089 85 71 56. Cover €2. Open daily noon-4pm and 7pm-midnight. AmEx/MC/V.) **La Vecchia Cantina ❸**, V. della Marra 15, affords its young clientele one of the best valley views amid soft music and surprise dishes (€10). (☎089 85 86 203. Margherita €5. Primi €8-11. Secondi €8-18. Cover €2. Open daily Mar.-Sept. noon-3:15pm and 7-11pm. MC/V.)

☐ ☐ SIGHTS AND ENTERTAINMENT. The beautiful churches, ivy-covered walls, and meandering paths of the 13th-century **Villa Rufolo** inspired Wagner's magic garden in the second act of his opera *Parsifal*. The villa puts on a summer concert series with performances in some of its most picturesque spaces, and the main hall frequently exhibits works by big-name artists. Enter through the arch off P. Duomo near the tunnel. (☎089 85 76 57. Open daily in summer 9am-8pm; in winter 9am-6pm. €5, under 12 and over 65 €3.)

The Amalfi Coast's third set of famous **bronze doors**, cast by Barisano of Trani in 1179, is in the portal of Ravello's **duomo**. The doors have 54 panels depicting detailed scenes from the Passion. Two pulpits with elaborate mosaics provide a contrast to the otherwise simple interior. In the **Cappella di San Pantaleone**, an image of the town's patron saint stands to the left of the altar, and San

Pantaleone's blood has been preserved in a cracked vessel since his beheading in AD 290, at Nicomedia. The town commemorates his death annually in a **religious festival** (July 27th), during which the saint's congealed blood mysteriously liquefies. The small **museum** inside the church depicts the *duomo*'s history through pagan and Christian eras with ancient mosaics and sculptures. (Open daily 9am-7pm. €2.) Follow V. S. Francesco out of P. Duomo to **Villa Cimbrone**, V. S. Chiara 26. Renovated by Lord Greenthorpe in the 19th century, the villa is now an expensive hotel (€330-950 per night), made famous by guests such as D. H. Lawrence, T. S. Eliot, Virginia Woolf, Winston Churchill, Jackie Kennedy, and Hillary Clinton. Less famous travelers can still enjoy the majestic gardens, which offer magnificent coastal views. (☎089 85 74 59; www. villacimbrone.com. Gardens open daily 9am-sunset. €6; children €4.)

Throughout the year, internationally renowned musicians perform at classical music festivals. In warm weather, concerts take place in the gardens of Villa Rufolo; in winter they move inside the villa or *duomo*. Each season's festival features a Wagnerian motif and includes film screenings and panel discussions. Tickets are sold at the Ravello Festival Box Office. (V. Richard Wagner 5. ☎089 85 84 22; www.ravellofestival.com. Tickets €20-100. Open daily 10am-8pm.)

SALERNO   ☎089

As capital of the Norman Empire from 1077 to 1127 and home to Europe's first medical school, Salerno (sa-LEHR-no; pop. 144,000) once played host to a proud, powerful culture. During WWII, however, the city was blasted by Allied bombs and much of its medieval past was turned to rubble. Unlike the dreamy villages of the Amalfi Coast, Salerno is an urban reality with an industrial core and a famous university. A cheap base for visiting the Amalfi Coast and Paestum's ruins, Salerno is not wholly without charm of its own; side streets in the old city and the sea front promenade offer pleasant walks and views.

⌐ TRANSPORTATION

Trains: (☎089 25 50 05), in P. V. Veneto. To: **Naples** (45min., 37 per day 3:41am-10:21pm, €5-10); **Paestum** (40min., 17 per day 5:52am-9:55pm, €2.70); **Reggia di Calabria** (3-5hr., 16 per day 2:19am-8:19pm, €21-35); **Rome** (2-3hr., 16 per day 3:25am-8:42pm, €23-33).

Buses: SITA buses leave from the train station for **Amalfi** (1hr., 24 per day 6am-10:30pm, €2) and **Naples** (1hr., 38 per day 5:05am-10:10pm, €3). Buy tickets from *tabaccherie*, and ask where your bus leaves from (either P. Veneto or P. della Concordia). CSTP runs buses from P. della Concordia to **Paestum** (1hr., 12 per day 6:30am-7:30pm, €2.70) and from P. Veneto to **Pompeii** (1hr., 14 per day 6:10am-9pm, €3.20).

Ferries and Hydrofoils: Ferries leave from Molo Masuccio, P. della Concordia, 2 blocks from the train station. Travelmar (☎089 87 29 50) runs to **Positano** (1¼hr., 7 per day 8:40am-5:15pm, €10) via **Amalfi** (35min., €6).

Public Transportation: Orange CSTP buses connect the train station to the rest of the city. For schedules, check the ticket booth in P. Veneto. 1hr. tickets €1, day pass €5.

Taxis: ☎089 75 75 75.

Car Rental: Travel Car, P. Veneto 33 (☎089 22 77 22). Cars from €35 per day. 18+. Open daily 8am-1:15pm and 3-8pm. AmEx/MC/V.

✹ 🛈 ORIENTATION AND PRACTICAL INFORMATION

Salerno's **train station** is in **Piazza Vittorio Veneto**. The pedestrian **Corso Vittorio Emanuele** veers right out of the *piazza*, becoming **Via dei Mercanti** upon reaching the old quarter, the liveliest and most historically interesting part of Salerno. **Via Roma**, home to many of the city's best restaurants, runs parallel to C. V. Emanuele, one block toward the waterfront. Along the waterfront in front of the train station is **Piazza della Concordia,** from which many intercity buses depart, and **Lungomare Trieste,** which runs to Salerno's port, **Molo Manfredi.**

Tourist Office: EPT (☎089 23 14 32), in P. V. Veneto 1, to the right when leaving the station. Friendly staff provides free maps, brochures on hotels and restaurants, and bus and train info. Open M-F 9am-2pm and 3-8pm, Sa 9am-1pm and 3:30-7:30pm.

English-Language Bookstore: La Feltrinelli, C. V. Emanuele 230. Decent selection of classics and new fiction. Open M-F 9:30am-2pm and 4-8:30pm, Sa 10am-2pm and 4-10pm, Su 10am-1:30pm and 5-9:30pm. MC/V.

Public restrooms: 2nd fl. of train station in P. Veneto.

Carabinieri: V. Duomo 17 (☎089 22 56 80).

Hospital: G. da Procida, V. S. Calenda (☎089 69 11 11).

Internet Access: PAK, V. Romualdo Guarna 12b, near the *duomo*. €2.50 per hr. Open M-F and Su 9am-1pm and 4-8pm.

Post Office: C. Garibaldi 203 (☎089 25 72 111). Open M-Sa 8:15am-6:15pm. **Branch,** V. Roma 130, has an **ATM.** Open M-F 8am-1:30pm, Sa 8am-12:30pm. Currency exchange at main office only. **Postal Code:** 84100.

ACCOMMODATIONS

Ostello Ave Gratia Plena, V. Canali (☎089 23 47 76; www.ostellodisalerno.it). Take C. Vittorio Emanuele into the old district, where it becomes V. dei Mercanti; then turn right on V. Canali. Amazing location in a former convent, close to restaurants and nightlife. Clean rooms, large showers, and a great courtyard bar with music and cheap food. Book exchange and tourist information point. Private rooms have bath. Breakfast included. Towels €2. Laundry €3. Internet access €3.50 per hr. Curfew 2am. Single-sex 4- and 8-bed dorms €15; singles €32; doubles €45; triples €67.50. AmEx/MC/V. ❶

Albergo Koinè, V. Angelo. Napolitano 10 (☎089 27 51 051; www.hostelkoine.it). 10min. walk from train station and port. Modern and cool, this hostel was recently renovated and even has an infirmary. Dogs welcome. Laundry €5. Internet access €2. Wheelchair-accessible bath available. Reception 24hr. 4-, 6-, and 10-bed dorms €12. MC/V. ❶

Albergo Santa Lucia, V. Roma 182 (☎089 22 58 28). Simple rooms with TV, phone, bath, and balcony offer unbeatable proximity to the public beach. For a tranquil stay, ask for air-conditioned rooms not facing the street. Operates the Santa Lucia restaurant below. Singles €35; doubles €55; triples €70. ❸

FOOD

Hosteria Il Brigante, V. Linguiti 4 (☎089 22 65 92). From P. Duomo, head up the ramp, look for sign on the left. Laid-back. Handwritten menu boasts "rigorously homemade" dishes like the *pasta alla sangiovannara* (€3), a hodgepodge of pasta, tomato, cheese, and sausage. Open Tu-Su 1:30-2:30pm and 9-11:30pm. Cash only. ❶

Trattoria "da Peppe a Seccia," V. Antica Corte 5 (☎089 22 05 18). Large, yet quaint and intimate restaurant in the heart of the historical center serves cheap, delicious seafood. The fresh squid antipasto (€5) is a must. Pizza €4-6. Primi €5-9. Cover €1.50. Open Tu-Su noon-2:30pm and 8pm-midnight. MC/V. ❷

Santa Lucia, V. Roma 182/184 (☎089 22 56 96). Located in the main street of Salerno's historical center, this restaurant offers the same cool breeze, glamor, and laid-back ambience as its neighbors, but at cheaper prices. Try the *spaghetti alle vongole* (with clams; €7), or choose from a large array of cheap entrees €5-8. Cover €1.50. Open Tu-Su noon-2:30pm and 7-11:30pm. AmEx/MC/V. ❷

👁 🎵 SIGHTS AND ENTERTAINMENT

To take in the evening air, stroll down C. V. Emanuele or sit in the lush gardens of the **Villa Comunale** (open daily 7:30am-midnight). For a bit of history, explore the medieval section, starting at C. V. Emanuele; turn right off V. Mercanti or V. Roma on to V. Duomo, which runs uphill to **Duomo San Matteo.** First constructed in AD 845, the *duomo* was destroyed and rebuilt 200 years later by the Norman leader Robert Guiscard. If its beauty isn't enough of a draw, come to see a tooth from Evangelist Matthew, a hair from the Virgin Mary, and a splinter from the True Cross. (☎089 23 13 87. Open M-Sa 10am-6pm, Su 1-6pm. Modest dress required. Free.) To soak up some rays, take the bus along Lungomare Trieste and head to the beach near the sailboat harbor. Though Salerno is right by the water, its beaches are not the nicest. Instead, you might want to hop on a bus and head to nearby **Vietri sul Mare,** home to hundreds of artisans and a pleasant beach. (Buses #4 and 9; 10min., €0.80.)

The impressive **Teatro Municipale Giuseppe Verdi,** P. Matteo Luciani, hosts concerts as well as theater and ballet performances from October to March. (☎089 66 21 41; www.teatroverdisalerno.it. Concert tickets €10-60; opera and events €17.50-70. Box office open daily 10am-1pm and 5-8pm. MC/V.) Through July, the **Salerno Summer Festival,** at the Arena del Mare near the Molo Manfredi, hosts jazz and blues concerts for all to enjoy. (☎089 66 51 76; www.comune.salerno.it. Concerts usually start 10pm. Prices vary.) At night, younger crowds gather on the seaside promenade near **Bar/Gelateria Nettuno,** Lungomare Trieste 136-138. Purchase a cone (€1.50-2.70) and push up to the counter for some of the most popular flavors in town. (☎089 22 83 75. Beer €1.70. Open July-Sept. daily 7am-2am; Oct.-June M-Tu and Th-Su 7am-2am.) **Galleon,** one of the many pubs along V. Roma, is where yuppie pirates-at-heart come to find their next booty, or at least a cold, €4 beer. (V. Roma 256. Open daily 7pm-3am.) The small bar **Tekabega,** V. Giovanni da Procida 7, packs a nighttime punch with bartender DJs and occasional fanciful feasts at a beach location outside Salerno. Gay-, lesbian-, and transgender-friendly. (www.tekabega.it. Beer €2-4. Mixed drinks €4.50. Wine €3. Open Tu-Su 9pm-4am.)

🔁 DAYTRIP FROM SALERNO

PAESTUM

The simplest way to get to Paestum is by train from Salerno (30min., 17 per day, round-trip €5.80). Exiting the Paestum station, walk under the arch for 7min. until you see the museum and entrance to temples. CSTP buses also travel to Paestum from Salerno's P. della Concordia (1hr., 12 per day 6:30am-7:30pm, round-trip €5.40), stopping at V. Magna Graecia, the main modern road in Paestum. The Paestum train station is abandoned, so buy tickets from tabaccherie. The tourist office in Salerno provides a list of return buses and trains from Paestum.

Not far from the Roman ruins of Pompeii and Herculaneum, Paestum's three **Doric temples** rank among the best-preserved and most complete in the world, rivaling those of Sicily and Athens. These masterfully constructed temples were built without any mortar or cement, yet remained standing after the great earthquake of AD 62 that reduced Pompeii's Temple of Jupiter to rubble. The town began as a Greek colony dedicated to sea god Poseidon, but was taken back by native Lucans and later conquered and expanded by the Romans. The city declined in the Middle Ages when a malaria epidemic ravaged its population. Today, many of the buildings have been reduced to crumbs, but some still feature intricate mosaics on their floors. The **Roman forum,** larger though more dilapidated than the one at Pompeii, lies on V. Sacra. More Roman ruins can be seen in the nearby **amphitheater** and **gymnasium.**

When excavators first uncovered the three temples in the 18th century, they attributed them to the wrong gods. Although recent scholarship has provided new info about the temples' true dedications, the 18th-century names have stuck. There are three entrances: the northernmost (closest to the bus stop) leads to the **Tempio di Cere** (actually built to honor Athena) built around 500 BC and later used as a church in the early Middle Ages. South of the forum lies the fifth-century BC **Tempio di Poseidon-Nettuno** (actually dedicated to Apollo). More sophisticated and complete than the Temple of Ceres, this temple incorporates many of the refinements found in Athens's Parthenon. Small lions' heads (now on display in the museum, see below) served as gargoyles on the temple roof. The southernmost temple, dubbed the **basilica** because it was believed to be a civil Roman building, is also the oldest, dating from the sixth century BC. Its unusual plan, with a main interior section split by a row of columns down the middle, has inspired the theory that the temple was dedicated to two gods, Zeus and Hera, rather than one, although most scholars contend that it was built solely to worship Hera. A **museum** on the other side of V. Magna Graecia, will tell you everything you want to know about Paestum. It houses extraordinary pottery, paintings, and artifacts taken primarily from Paestum's tombs, as well as samples of 2500-year-old honey and paintings from the famous **Tomb of the Diver,** dating from 475 BC. (Temples open daily in summer 9am-7:30pm; in winter 9am-4pm. Restoration work occasionally leaves temples fenced off or hidden. Museum open daily 9am-6pm. Last entry 1hr. before closing. Museum and temples closed 1st and 3rd M of each month for restoration. Museum €4, EU students €2, EU citizens under 18 or over 60 free. Ruins and museum €6.50/€3.30/free. Included on Campania Artecard, p. 576) The often overlooked, modern-day **Paleo-Christian basilica,** right next to the tourist office, is a prime example of Christian incorporation of pagan architectural elements. The **AAST tourist office** in Paestum, V. Magna Graecia 887, is next to the museum. (☎0828 81 10 16. Open daily 9am-1pm and 1:30-5:30pm.)

CAMPANIA

PUGLIA AND CALABRIA

HIGHLIGHTS OF PUGLIA AND CALABRIA

EXPLORE the cerulean waters of Praia a Mare's grottoes of Isola di Dino (p. 651).

CRAWL into the caves of Castellana Grotte, once thought to be the gateway to the underworld (p. 626).

SCRUTINIZE ancient treasure at Reggio di Calabria's Museo Nazionale (p. 643).

RESEARCH wild wolves, and other similarly exciting ecological subjects, in the Parco Nazionale di Calabria, with the Greenwood Cooperative Society (p. 649).

PUGLIA

The often-overlooked Puglia (POOL-ya) region gives Italy its sun-baked southern kick—after all, what's a boot without a heel? Its ports are as animated and international today as they were hundreds of years ago when the Greeks and Romans used them as trade routes to the East, though now they tend to ferry tourists to Greece instead. Besides serving as a useful launching spot, the region harbors cultural treasures all its own: remote medieval villages, cone-roofed *trulli* houses, and ports with a distinct Middle Eastern flavor. Tourism has only recently begun to materialize in rustic, sunny Puglia, which remains a refreshing pause from Italy's more frequented destinations. Travelers to Puglia will welcome its passionate cultural heritage and distinctly southern zest for life.

TRANI   ☎0883

Trani (TRAH-nee; pop. 53,500), with its beautiful architecture, fresh seafood, and breezy seaside strolls, is upper Puglia's unsung hero. The contagious tranquility and local hospitality of this port town bring people back again and again, despite the local government's efforts to resist growth in size and attention. Although its history may be full of traders, Crusaders, and saints, Trani manages to live in the here and now, inviting its visitors to experience life in Italy.

▐▀ **TRANSPORTATION. Trains** run from Bari to Trani (45min., every hr. M-Sa, €2.60) and from Trani to Foggia (45min., €5.10). **Buses** from Trani's P. XX Settembre run to Bari and Foggia (€3) and along the coast to towns like Barletta and Margherita di Savoia. Beware that schedules change frequently.

▐▐ **ORIENTATION AND PRACTICAL INFORMATION.** From the train station, walk down **Via Cavour,** the first street perpendicular to the train station, through **Piazza della Repubblica** all the way to **Piazza Plebiscito,** which is right in front of the relaxing Villa Comunale, and turn left to get a view of the port. Walk down the street that borders the port to **Piazza Trieste,** where you'll find the I.A.T **tourist office,** P. Trieste 10, 2nd fl. (☎0883 58 88 30). The office provides helpful

Puglia, and Calabria

guides, free detailed maps, a list of accommodations, and honest restaurant recommendations. (Open M-F 8am-1:30pm and 3:30-6pm. For winter hours, call ☎0883 50 60 20). In an emergency, contact **Polizia Stradale,** Vle. Padre Pio (☎0883 48 21 11); **Polizia Municipale,** C. Imbriani 119 (☎0883 58 80 00); or the **carabinieri,** C. Imbriani 147 (☎0883 58 04 00). **Pharmacies** are available throughout the city, including one right outside the train station by V. Cavour and another on P. della Repubblica. A **hospital** can be found on Vle. Padre Pio (☎0883 48 21 11). **Internet access,** a phone center, and free maps are available at **Internet Phone Center,** V. Giovanni Bovio 37. (€3 per hr. Open M-W and F-Sa 9:30am-1:30pm and 4:30-10pm, Su 9:30am-10pm). The **post office** is at V. Giovanni Bovio 115 (☎0883 49 01 11; open M-F 8am-6:30pm, Sa 8am-12:30pm). **Postal Code:** 70059.

ACCOMMODATIONS AND FOOD. Accommodations in Trani are varied and quite affordable. The best bet is **Tre Re ❶,** V. Casale 58. This small hostel's cleanliness, location, and hospitable owner make it a great find. (☎0883 40 33 28; www.trere.it. Breakfast included. Free Internet. Singles €16-19, doubles €39-43. Cash only.) Another excellent option is the charmingly personal **Centro Storico ❸,** V. Leopardi 29. This time capsule is a playground for historians and architects, as well as tourists enjoying cathedral views and the unique interior garden. Film directors have tried to use it as a setting various times,

but the owner prefers to maintain its low-key publicity. (☎0883 50 61 76; www.
bbtrani.it. Free Internet cable use. Breakfast included. Reserve in June for Aug.
Singles €35-40; doubles €50-60. Cash only.)

For a view of the port and the cathedral without high prices, head to **Osteria-
Pizzeria Mèditerranèe,** V. S. Marittimi 60. It's one of the few places open for lunch
on weekdays, and its Neapolitan-style pizza is made with prized *mozzarella di
buffala.* (☎0883 48 04 31. Pizza from €3.50. Primi €4-8. Secondi €5-13. *Menù*
€15. Cover €1.50. Open M-Tu and Th-Su 11:30am-5pm and 7pm-2am. MC/V.)

◖S◗ SIGHTS. Trani's main attraction is the **cathedral,** located on V. Archivo near
P. Trieste. The bones of Trani's patron saint, St. Nicholas the Pilgrim, are in
a crypt under the church. (Open M-Sa 8:15am-12:15pm and 3:15-6:30pm, Su
9am-12:45pm and 4-7pm.). The other main monument is the nearby **Castello
Svevo.** Make sure to enjoy the view along the way from the cathedral. Built
by Frederick II, Holy Roman emperor from 1215-1250, the castle was most
recently used as a prison; consequently, it is more impressive outside than
in. Don't rely on the clock at its entrance, as it has been broken for years.
(Open daily 8:30am-7pm. €2, ages 18-25 €1, under 18 and over 65 free.) The
Villa Comunale, past P. Plebiscito, is often an unfairly overlooked sight. It has a
small park, gardens, a mini-aquarium, and most importantly, stunning views
of the whole city. (Open daily 7am-midnight.)

◖ ◗ ENTERTAINMENT AND NIGHTLIFE. Trani is a beautiful city for a stroll,
and evening sunsets by the port only add to its allure. Be sure to watch the sunset between the cathedral and the castle. Though deserted during the day, **Piazza
Teatro** lives up to its name with nightly performances and free street shows in
summer. Young crowds stick around for the large number of *gelaterie,* pizzerie, and cool bars. The closest thing to a *discoteca* in Trani is **◖El Matador,** V.
Cesare Lambertini 15, off V. Cavour. This high-tech bar transforms its floor into
a mini-*discoteca* on weekend nights with freestyle flair and DJ music. (☎348
92 26 919; www.elmatador.it. Beer €2.50. Mixed drinks €4.50. Shots from €2.
Open M-Tu and Th-Su 8am-2pm and 7pm-late.) The Amsterdam-inspired **Before
XXX,** V. Zanardelli 9, drowns out the noise that comes from its entrance on P.
Teatro with Saturday night DJs and Sunday happy hour. (☎349 06 25 933; www.
myspace.com/beforexxx. Open Tu-Su 8pm-3am.) Oyster bar **Il Vecchio e Il Mare**
keeps the lighthouses company at the far right end of V. S. Marittimi, offering a
unique seaside setting than the bars inside the port. Walk in the direction of the
Villa Comunale or look for the free ferry service from V. Zanardelli in summer.
(☎0883 40 37 94; www.dymmy.it/ilvecchioeilmare. F live music. Beer €3. Mixed
drinks €5. Open Tu-Su 6pm-early morning.) The last weekend of July brings the
Trani Film Festival, when movies are shown in different historical buildings of the
city, like the castle and the Monastero di Colonna.

BARI   ☎ 080

Exquisite Puglian cuisine and nightlife, fueled by the city's university population, add to the complexity of Bari (BA-ree; pop. 329,000), the main Italian
transportation hub for travel to Greece. On every street, clothing shops and
gelaterie tempt pedestrians, and the sea is never more than a few blocks away.
Amid the commotion, reckless drivers zoom about the modern city's wide avenues and pickpockets dart down alleys in the small medieval section. Although
Bari does not figure prominently on most itineraries, its cosmopolitan vibes
and urban grit make it a worthwhile divergence from southern Italy's more
touristy cities, if only for a brief visit. Just ask the locals, who say Paris could
be a *piccolo* Bari (little Bari) if it only had the sea.

⊟ TRANSPORTATION

Flights: Palese Airport (☎080 58 00 200; www.seap-puglia.it), 8km west of the city. **Alitalia, Air France, British Airways,** and **Lufthansa** fly to major European cities from Bari. Shuttle bus #16 leaves from P. Aldo Moro (21 per day, 5:10am-8:10pm, €0.80).

Trains: Bari is connected to 4 railways running from **Bari Centrale** (☎080 52 40 148) in P. Aldo Moro. Regional (non-Trenitalia) trains have reduced or no service on Su. Double-check schedules, which change about every six months.

> **Trenitalia** (☎89 20 21; www.trenitalia.com), serves large cities. Trains to: **Foggia** (1-2hr., 26 per day 4am-11:14pm, €7.40); **Lecce** (2hr., 26 per day 5:05am-11:10pm, €8.60) via **Brindisi; Milan** (9-10hr., 11 per day 6:53am-11:57pm, €48); **Rome** (5-7hr., 6 per day 5:15am-6:42pm, €27-36); **Taranto** (1½hr., 16 per day. 3:50am-11:20pm, €6.80).

> **Ferrovie del Sud Est** (☎800 079 090; www.fseonline.it) runs trains from track 11 to **Alberobello** (1½hr., M-Sa 13 per day 6:28am-7:20pm, €4) and **Castellana Grotte** (50min., M-Sa 10 per day 6:28am-8:30pm, €2.30).

> **Ferrotramviaria Nord** (☎080 57 89 542; www.ferrovienordbarese.it). Left of Centrale, exit and re-enter the station. To **Ruvo** (45min., 24 per day 6:22am-10:15pm, €2.30). On Su the Ruvo route is served by bus from P. Aldo Moro.

> **Ferrovie Appulo Lucane** (☎080 57 25 229; www.fal-srl.it), next door to Ferrotramviaria Nord station in P. Aldo Moro. Trains depart for **Matera** (1hr., 8 per day 6:48am-9:57pm, €4) via **Altamura.**

Buses: SITA (☎080 52 16 004; www.sitabus.it), behind station, on Viale Unità d'Italia.

Ferries: Obtain info and tickets at **Stazione Marittima** (☎080 52 19 140), individual company offices, or **Porto di Bari** (☎080 52 82 828; www.porto.bari.it). Take bus #20 to and from railway station. Some companies are listed below, but call ahead; schedules and prices vary, especially on weekends. Check-in at least 2hr. before departure. Visit www.greekferries.gr for more info on ferries to Greece. High season from late July-Aug.

> **Marlines** (☎080 52 31 824 or 080 52 75 409, reservations 080 52 10 266; www.marlines.com). To **Durres, Albania** (schedules vary weekly July-Sept., high season €62-130).

> **Superfast Ferries** (☎080 52 41 527; www.superfast.com), offices in front of port terminal. Sails to **Greece.** To **Corfu** (8hr.; odd days July and early Sept., even days in Aug. 8pm), **Igoumenitsa** (8hr., M-Sa 8pm), and **Patras** (14hr., daily 8pm). The line to **Corfu** is operated by partner company **Blue Star Ferries.** High season €95-430, depending on seating. Discount for Eurail pass holders.

> **Ventouris Ferries,** V. Piccinni 133, c/o P. Lorusso & Co. (☎080 52 17 609 to Greece, ☎080 52 75 499 to Albania; www.ventouris.gr). Windows #18-20 in Stazione Marittima. To **Corfu-Igoumenitsa, Greece** (10hr.; 2 per week Feb.-Apr., at least 5 per week May-Dec., daily in high season; shared cabin of four with bath €83-112) and **Durres, Albania** (7hr., €70-87).

Public Transportation: Local AMTAB **buses** leave from P. Aldo Moro, in front of the train station. Tickets sold at *tabaccherie* (€0.80) or on the bus (€1.50). Bus #20/ makes hourly trips between Stazione Marittima and train stations.

Taxis: RadioTaxi ☎080 53 46 666, leave voice message with departure location and destination. Taxi station ☎080 52 10 600.

⊞ ☷ ORIENTATION AND PRACTICAL INFORMATION

Via Sparano runs from the train station to **Piazza Umberto I,** Bari's main square. The end of V. Sparano intersects **Corso Vittorio Emanuele II** and the edge of the old city. To walk to the port, skirt the old city's winding streets by turning left on C. Vittorio Emanuele II and right at **Piazza della Libertà** onto **Piazza Giuseppe Massari.** Circle the castle, head right, and follow the coast. Otherwise, take the hourly bus #20/ from the station. For a calmer route to the sea (not the port), turn right off V. Sparano on C. Vittorio Emanuele II, continuing past **Corso Cavour** to **Piazza Eroi del Mare.** Then turn right and enjoy a nice stroll down **Lungomare Araldo**

di **Crollalanza.** Above all, make sure to see the beautiful **Piazza del Ferrarese** and **Piazza Mercantile in Il Borgo Antico** (The Old Town) by walking down C. Cavour.

Outside the train station, find the **APT Tourist Office,** P. Aldo Moro 33/A. Inquire about and reserve the free 🏖**Flash Tours** of the province here. (☎080 99 09 34; www.pugliaturismoinfopointbari.com. Open M-Sa 9am-7pm, Su 9am-1pm.) Do laundry at **Clean It,** V. Dante Alighieri 260. (☎080 52 37 096. Internet access €3 per hr. Wash €3.50 per 7.5kg; dry €3.50. Open M-F 11am-3:30pm and 6:30-9:30pm, Sa 11am-4pm.) For a **pharmacy,** try **San Nicola,** C. Cavour 53a. (Open M-F 8:30am-1pm and 4:30-8pm.) Get **Internet** access and tourist info at **Netcafe,** V. Andrea da Bari 11. (☎080 52 41 756; www.netcafebari.it. €4 per hr. Open M-Sa 9am-11:30pm, Su 10am-1pm and 5-9:30pm. Cash only.) In case of emergency, dial the **carabinieri** (☎080 52 45 960). **Policlinino,** the local **hospital,** is at Ple. Giulio Cesare 11 (☎080 54 21 854). The **post office** is at P. Umberto I 31, to the right of P. Battisti, facing away from the train station. It has an ATM outside. (☎080 57 57 187. Open M-F 8am-6:30pm, Sa 8am-12:30pm.) **Postal Code:** 70100.

❗ BARESI, BEWARE. Ancient citizens built the old city as a labyrinth in which to hide from surprise attacks. Today, the old city remains a maze for travelers and is safest when enjoyed in the light of day; turn to one of the many shop owners in P. Perrarese if you get lost. There is no need to venture into the old city at night, but if you do, exercise caution.

 ACCOMMODATIONS AND FOOD

The top-notch hostel 🏖**La Nuova Arca ❷,** C. Alcide de Gasperi 320, is inside the Parco di Cagno Abbrescia, 6km away. Take bus #4 from C. Benedetto Croce behind the station; ask the driver to stop at the park. Facilities for the single-sex rooms include multiple common rooms with A/C, bath, TV, game console, terrace, pianos, pool tables, bicycle rentals, and a chapel. (☎080 56 48 789; www.lanuovarca.com. Internet €3 per hr. Breakfast, towels, and linen included. Reserve in June for July-Aug. Dorms €24; doubles €79; triples €89. Cash only.) A popular choice, **Hotel de Rossi ❸,** V. de Rossi 186, offers clean, bright rooms with TV, phone, A/C, and bath. (☎080 52 45 355. Reserve 1 month ahead. Breakfast included. Singles €35; doubles €60; triples €85. MC/V.)

Eating in the old city's restaurants can feel like a time warp; often restaurants offer neither menus nor itemized checks. The food, however, is inevitably excellent, and the raucous atmosphere, enjoyable. Follow *baresi* students and families to 🏖**Pizzeria Il Rustico ❷,** V. Quintino Sella 95, a hidden gem for hungry travelers. The €9 *menù* includes an amazing antipasto buffet that piles up on your table, a large pizza, drink, and liqueur to top it off. (Open M-Sa 7:30pm-midnight. Cash only.) For a true Italian experience, head to cozy **Vini e Cucina ❷,** V. Vallisa 23, in a prime spot next to P. del Ferrarese. Squeeze into a free seat, let the waiters tell you which of their daily specials you'll be receiving, then sit back and enjoy the authentic ambience and beauty of this *baresi* favorite. (☎330 43 30 18. Antipasti €3. Primi €4.50. Secondi €6.50. Drinks €1. Open M-Sa noon-3pm and 7pm-midnight. MC/V.) Find groceries at **CONAD market,** V. Crisanzio 20/22. (Open M-Tu and Th-Su 7am-3pm and 5-8pm, W 8am-2pm. MC/V.)

◎ SIGHTS

Looks like Mom and Dad were wrong—there really is a Santa Claus, and the 🏖**Basilica di San Nicola** proves it. Sixty *baresi* sailors tomb raided St. Nicholas's remains from Turkey in 1087; the sailors initially refused to cede the body to local clergy, they ultimately gave it up when the Church built this

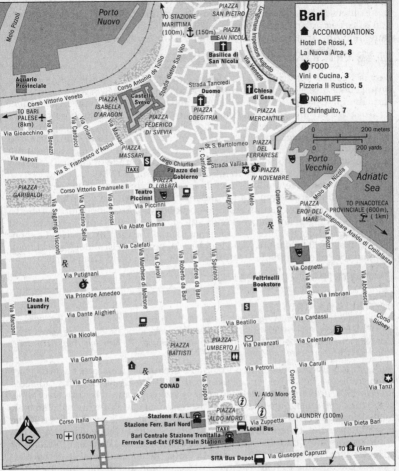

Bari

🏠 ACCOMMODATIONS
Hotel De Rossi, **1**
La Nuova Arca, **8**

🍴 FOOD
Vini e Cucina, **3**
Pizzeria Il Rustico, **5**

🌙 NIGHTLIFE
El Chiringuito, **7**

PUGLIA AND
CALABRIA

spartan basilica as Santa's final resting place. On the back wall, several paintings commemorate the jolly saint's good deeds, including his resurrection of three children who were sliced to bits and plunged into a brine barrel by a nasty butcher. (Open M-Sa 8:30am-noon and 4:30-6:30pm, Su 9:30am-7pm, except during mass. Free.) Just outside the old city, off C. Vittorio Veneto near the water, stands the colossal **Castello Svevo,** P. Federico di Svevia 4, built in the 13th century by Frederick II on Norman and Byzantine foundations. Visitors can't climb the jagged ramparts, but the medieval cellar displays art from the region's cathedrals and castles, and other areas display locally produced modern art. (☎080 52 86 111. Open M-Tu and Th-Su 9am-7pm. €2, ages 18-25 €1, under 18 and over 65 free.) Down Lungomare Nazario Sauro past P. Armando Diaz at V. Spalato 19, on the fourth floor, is the **Pinacoteca Provinciale.** Housed in a beautiful building with a tall clock tower, the gallery displays landscapes and works by Veronese, Tintoretto, Bellini, De Nittis, and Francesco Netti, an acclaimed hometown artist. As well as a vast collection of Greek art from the 1800s. (☎080 54 12 422. Open Tu-Sa 9am-7pm, Su 9am-1pm; Aug. open only in the morning. €2.60, students €0.60.)

ENTERTAINMENT AND NIGHTLIFE

Bari is Puglia's cultural nucleus. **Teatro Piccinni,** C. V. Emanuele 86, offers a spring concert season and year-round opera. (☎080 52 10 878; www.fondazion-eliricabari.it. Open M-F 10:30am-12:30pm and 5-8pm.) Consult the ticket office, *La Gazzetta del Mezzogiorno* (the local newspaper), or the free newspapers *Leggo* and *City* for the latest info. From September through June, sports fans can catch **soccer matches** every Sunday. Tickets start at €15 and are available at the stadium or in bars. On May 7-9, *baresi* celebrate their stolen saint in the **Festa di San Nicola,** featuring traditional foods and a parade of children. There's also a huge **Summer Jazz Festival** in mid-July (☎080 45 55 696).

Bari does not have much of a club scene, but its bars are hopping. Most are open nightly from 8pm until 1 or 2am (3am on Sa) and generally close in August, when the town's university is on holiday. V. Sparano and P. Umberto are packed at night, and on weekends students cram into P. del Ferrarese and other *piazze* along the breezy waterfront east of the old city. To avoid expensive drinks, try **El Chiringuito,** Molo San Nicola, next to P. Eroi del Mare, a main hangout for college students. (☎080 52 40 206. Open daily 11pm-4am.)

◪ DAYTRIPS FROM BARI

CASTELLANA GROTTE

Take the FSE trains from Bari to "Grotte di Castellana Grotte" (1hr., every 50min. 7:07am-5:05pm, €3). ☎080 49 98 211; www.grottedicastellana.it. Caves are across the parking lot and to the left. 50min. English tours in summer 9:30am and 1pm; €10, children €8. 2hr. tour 11am and 4pm; €15/12.

Superstitious locals once feared that these breathtaking natural caverns were an entrance to hell. The Castellana Grotte (CA-ste-LA-na GRO-tay), discovered in 1938, are famed for their impressive size and natural beauty. Over time, stalactites and stalagmites have developed into all sorts of whimsical shapes, including a miniature Virgin Mary, a camel, a wolf, and an owl. Even if the resemblances don't seem obvious, the formations invite the imagination to run wild. Visitors must take one of two **guided tours:** a short 1km jaunt (50min.) or a longer 3km trek (2hr.). Both start at **La Grave,** the enormous pit that was considered the opening to hell. The longer tour culminates in the stunning **Grotta Bianca** (White Cave), a giant cavern filled with white stalactites. No shoes, no go: be sure to wear proper footgear and perhaps bring a light jacket, since the grotto is usually chilly and damp all year.

> **WHAT'S IN A NAME?** Not all trains heading for Castellana Grotte actually stop at the grottoes. The stop "Castellana Grotte" is for the city, 2km away. The next, unmarked stop is for the grottoes. Confirm with the conductor when boarding that the train actually stops at the grottoes.

ALBEROBELLO

Take the FSE train from Bari (1hr., 13 per day M-Sa 6:28am-7:20pm, €4). To reach the trulli from the train station, bear left and take V. Mazzini, which becomes V. Garibaldi, to

P. del Popolo. The tourist office at V. Brigata Regina 11, in the trulli districton the way to the oil museum provides tourist info. (☎080 43 24 419. Open M-Sa 9:30am-1pm and 3:30-7pm.) Visit wwwt.alberobellonline.it for more info on the city.

The mere sight of *trulli*-covered hills—a sea of white limestone structures, strung together, each topped by its own neat conical roof—is well worth the trek out to Alberobello (AL-be-ro-BE-lo; pop. 11,000). The *trulli* are associated with magic and mystery in Italian lore—one glance at the fantastical landscape, populated by gnarled olive trees, rust-colored earth, and the homes themselves, and it's easy to understand why. Unfortunately, the origin of *trulli* in Alberobello proper is far less glamorous. A 17th-century count ordered the construction of these easy-to-dissemble dwellings; he planned to evade taxes by dismantling the houses when imperial inspectors came. Inhabitants inscribed symbols onto the stone roofs, reputedly to ward off evil spirits; many have unexpected meanings. For example, while the trident may seem like an obvious reference to Poseidon, it actually symbolized the Holy Trinity for the *trulli* inhabitants. Likewise, a heart struck by an arrow is not a victim of Cupid, but Mary's pierced heart. While some *trulli* remain occupied, more than 1000 *trulli* qualify as UNESCO World Heritage sights and currently house craftshops and restaurants, which are mostly open to the public.

To get a better idea of the lifestyle of the *trulli* residents before they were replaced by artisans hawking souvenirs, ask at **Casa d'Amore** (the local tourist office). From P. del Popolo, turn left at Eritrea store to P. XXVII Maggio to get to the **Museo del Territorio.** It exhibits artifacts from the town in a complex of 15 adjoining *trulli*. (Open from mid-Sept. to mid-July Tu-Su 10am-1pm and 3:30-7pm. Free. Tour €2.50.) **Sylva Tour** operates out of the museum, offering excursions into the countryside and guided walks around town. (☎080 43 21 838; www.sylvanet.it. Tours in English, French, and German.) To reach the **Trullo Sovrano,** P. Sacramento 10, take C. Vittorio Emanuele from P. del Popolo and continue past the church. The residence for the powerful family of a local priest in the 18th century, this structure is still decorated with its original furniture and details of a *trullo* household. It was declared a national monument in 1923. (☎080 43 26 030. Open daily 10am-7:30pm. €1.50, children under 12 €1.)

I LOVE YOU TRULLI. Most people visit Alberobello for its hills of *trulli*; however, the town's rural location also makes it an excellent starting point for a trip into the *bosco*, a small wooded park with winding paths running through the countryside past dilapidated *trulli*. Be sure to get a map from the tourist office no matter how far you intend to walk. To reach the park, head to the top of the hill of *trulli*, turn right, and follow signs for the *bosco*.

SALENTO PENINSULA

Tourists often overlook Italy's sun-baked heel, home to hidden grottoes, medieval fortresses, and the beautiful beaches of two seas. With roots stretching back to ancient Greece, the Salento modestly bears the laurels of centuries of history. Its art and architecture are some of the best preserved in Italy, its vistas pristine, and its scuba diving superb. Transportation within the peninsula can sometimes be complicated, but a sojourn along the varied coastline or inland among olive groves and vineyards is well worth the careful planning.

PUGLIA AND CALABRIA

BRINDISI

☎ 0831

As Italy's seaside gateway to the East, Brindisi (BREEN-dee-see; pop. 90,000) has always been more of a departure point than a destination. Pompey made his escape from Julius Caesar's army here in the first century BC, and crusaders used the port to sail for the Holy Land. As a port of industry and travel, the city is crowded with travelers who stay only long enough to pick up their ferry tickets. Whether you visit en route to Greece or as a base for a daytrip to beautiful Ostuni, you will find a mix of historic sights and modern Italian flavor.

■ TRANSPORTATION

Airport: Aeroporto del Salento, V. Ruggero De Simone, in Casale. (☎0831 41 17 208); ticket office open daily 6am-11pm (☎0831 41 17 408); Services **Bologna, Rome,** and **Milan** all year. During summer, services and frequency increase.

Trains: Stazione Brindisi Centrale at P. Crispi. Ticket office open daily 8am-8pm at Stazione Marittima. Trains go to: **Bari** (1hr., 17 per day 4:06am-8:33pm, €6.80-13); **Lecce** (20-35min., 35 per day 12:29am-10:22pm, €2.30); **Milan** (9-12hr., 5 per day 7:25am-10:31pm, €44-85); **Rome** (6-9hr., 5 per day 6:25am-10:46pm, €36-45); **Taranto** (1hr., 29 per day 5:07am-10:25pm, €4).

Buses: FSE, at the train station, handles buses throughout Puglia. Marozzi buses travel to **Rome** (7-8hr., 4 per day 11am-10pm, €36). Miccolis runs to **Naples** (5hr., 3 per day 6:35am-7:25 pm, €25.60). Marino runs to **Milan** (12hr., 8:25am or 6:20pm, €56). Buses leave from the centro. Marozzi buses stop by the cemetery 400m outside Porta Lecce. Miccolis and Marino buses stop in front of the Tribunale di Brindisi (courthouse), Viale P. Togliatti 2. Take STP bus line 1 from the train station (every 15-30min., 6am-9:30pm) or follow Corso Roma 2km outside the *centro* as it becomes Cavalcavia de Gasperi, Viale Aldo Moro, and Vle. P. Togliatti. Buy tickets for all companies at the helpful, efficient **Grecian Travel,** Vco. de Lubelli 8 (☎0831 56 83 33; www.greciantravel.it), which is also a CTS budget travel info point. From the Stazione Marittima, take the 2nd right off C. Garibaldi. Open M-F and Su 9am-1pm and 4:30-8pm, Sa 9am-1pm.

Ferries: Ferries leave from **Costa Morena** to various destinations in Greece, including **Corfu** (8hr.); **Igoumenitsa** (10hr.); **Kephalonia** (16hr.); **Patras** (17hr.); **Paxi** (13hr.). Catamarans operated by SNAV, C. Garibaldi 88 (☎0831 52 13 50; www.snav.it), sail to Corfu (4½hr.) and Paxi (6hr.), and are only slightly pricier than ferries. Catamarans leave from Stazione Marittima. Prices for each ferry line are fixed by the transport authority so all agencies charge the same amount for tickets, but some agencies will book passages for a full or nonexistent ferry. To avoid getting scammed, use a reputable agency like Grecian Travel (see above). Well-established ferry lines include **Agoudimos Lines,** C. Garibaldi 81 (☎0831 52 90 91; www.agoudimos-lines.com) and **Endeavor Lines,** C. Garibaldi 49 (☎0831 32 76 67; www.ferries.gr/hml), which offers discounts for Eurail pass holders. Port tax (€10) is not included in ticket price. **Stazione Marittima** provides a free shuttle (every 15min.) to Costa Morena. Check-in 2hr. before departure. Bring your own food to avoid the overpriced fodder found in snack bars on board.

GREECE LIGHTNING. Brindisi is a central port for boats to Greece. To get to Athens, take the ferry from Brindisi to Patras and then a train or bus from Patras to Athens (2hr.; tickets at Brindisi's Stazione Marittima). Ferries also run to Çesme, Turkey (30hr.), and Durres, Albania (9hr.).

Public Transportation: STP buses (☎800 23 20 42; www.stpbrindisi.it) run between the station and port and to destinations around the city. Line A runs between the station and the airport (every 15-20min, 5:30am-11:30pm). **Local ferries** depart from the tourist office on V. Margherita every 10min., crossing Seno di Ponente and landing near Chiesa di Santa Maria del Casale. Purchase bus and ferry tickets at bars and *tabaccherie* (€0.80), or on board (€1.50). A daily urban bus pass is also available (€3).

Taxis: (☎0831 59 79 01). Make sure to take a licensed taxi (white with a bit of blue), as unofficial taxis tend to overcharge. Agree on a price before taking off; remember that drivers generally charge a supplementary fee after 9pm. Taxis from the train station to Costa Morena cost €15, and from there to Stazione Marittima cost €10.

✈️ ℹ️ ORIENTATION AND PRACTICAL INFORMATION

Corso Umberto runs from the train station to **Piazza Cairoli** and through **Piazza del Popolo** and **Piazza della Vittoria**. At P. della Vittoria, it becomes **Corso Garibaldi**, which ends when it meets **Via Regina Margherita** at the port. A right onto V. R. Margherita leads to the **Stazione Marittima**. Keeping straight, the street becomes **Via Flacco** and then **Via Thaon de Revel**.

The **APT Information Office**, V. Regina Margherita 44, provides a free map and advice about local services and sights. (☎0831 52 30 72; www.viaggareinpuglia.it.com. Open July-Aug. daily 8:30am-1pm and 3-11pm; Sept.-June M-F 8:30am-1pm and 3-8pm, Sa 8:30am-1pm.) Reach the **carabinieri** at ☎083115 29 11. A **hospital**, Ospedale di Summa, S. Mesagne (☎083153 75 10) offers emergency care. **Internet access** is available at Webmaniacs, Vico Sacramento 8, off C. Garibaldi. (☎083152 15 32; www.webmaniacs.it. €3 per hr. Open M-Sa 9am-2pm and 4:30-8:30pm.) For an English-language **library**, try Piazzo, C.Garibaldi 38/A (☎0831 56 20 47). The **post office** is at P. Vittoria 10. (☎0831 22 52 11. Open M-F 8am-6:30pm, Sa 8am-12:30pm.) **Postal Code:** 72100.

🏠 🍴 ACCOMMODATIONS AND FOOD

With Brindisi's popularity as a point of entry and departure, budget accommodations tend to fill up quickly in summer. Reserving one month ahead is advisable. The best option is **⬛Hostel Carpe Diem ❶**, V. Nicola Brandi 2, outside the *centro* in Casale. Call for free pick-up and drop-off, or take bus 3D or 4 from the train station. The multilingual, fun-loving owner Maurizio invites you to seize the day and night in Brindisi, with shuttle rides to the beach and advice on the hottest nightlife. (☎338 32 35545; www.hostelcarpediem.it. Pool table, mini gym, and bicycle rental available. Breakfast included. Free lockers and Wi-Fi; Internet €4. Laundry €6. Curfew 3am. Reception 24hr. With *Let's Go* discount, dorms €15; singles €25; doubles €40, with bath €50; triples €54; quads €68. AmEx/MC/V.) Cheaper rooms can be found at **Hotel Venezia ❶**, V. Pisanelli 4, which is equidistant from the train station and Stazione Marittima. From the train station, pass the fountain and take a left off C. Umberto onto V. San Lorenzo da Brindisi, following the signs pointing right on V. Pisanelli. Twelve basic rooms have quirky decor and shared baths. (☎0831 52 75 11. Singles €16; doubles €26, with bath €36; triples €45; quads €52. Cash only.)

Avoid the restaurants and cafes on C. Garibaldi near the port, where the ubiquitous *menù turistico* yields small, bland portions and steep drink prices. Better options lie on nearby side streets. The fishermen's shack **Iaccato ❷**, Viale. Flacco 32, right on the water, has an unbeatable location. Look for the building with the green awning. Bold pizzas (€6-10) are topped with combinations of fresh seafood. (☎083152 40 84. Primi €7-8. Secondi €7-12. Cover €1.20. Open daily noon-3pm and 7-11pm. MC/V.) **Ristorante Pizzeria Skipper ❷**, V. Dogana 2, enjoys popularity thanks to its proximity to the Stazione Marittima, reasonable prices, and outdoor seating on a waterfront *piazza*. Try the *orecchiette al forno* (€8), pasta baked in the pizza oven. (☎0831 52 32 36. Pizza €4-8. Primi €7-12. Secondi €7-15. Cover €2. Open daily noon-1am. MC/V.) An **open-air market,** off

P. della Vittoria on V. Fornari, sells fresh fruit, vegetables, and dairy products. (Open M-Sa 7am-1pm.) Pick up supplies for your ferry ride at **DiperDì** supermarket, C. Garibaldi 106, one block from the port. (☎0831 56 25 66. Open M-Sa 8am-1:30pm and 5-9pm, Su 9am-1pm. MC/V.)

👁 🎵 SIGHTS AND ENTERTAINMENT

Turning left at the seaside end of C. Garibaldi, V. R. Margherita passes the **Scalinata Virgiliana,** a set of marble steps, great for restful gelato-eating or people-watching. The huge column at the top, recently restored, once marked the end of the Appian Way. Figures of Jove, Neptune, Mars, and tritons grace the top of the **column,** a replica of the original marble capital. The column's twin, which once stood on the adjacent base, now resides in Lecce. V. Colonne runs behind the column to P. Duomo. Inside the 11th-century **duomo** (heavily restored in the 18th century), find relics and a mosaic floor. (Open daily 7am-noon and 4:30-7:30pm. Free.) Nearby, the **Museo Archeologico** traces Brindisi's history through various artifacts, although the display is currently limited to just a few rooms as the museum undergoes restoration. (☎0831 56 55 01. Open Tu and Th 9am-1pm and 3:30-7:30pm, W and F 9am-1pm, Sa 3:30-7:30pm, Su 9am-12:30pm. Free.) Follow signs from the train station to the outskirts of town to see the **Chiesa di Santa Maria del Casale** and its 13th-century frescoes, including one of Mary blessing the Crusaders. (Open daily 7am-noon and 4-7pm. Free.)

In the rush to board a ferry, most tourists miss out on Brindisi's nearby **▩beaches.** The crystalline waters of **Punta Penne** and **Apani** are perfect for swimming and scuba diving and are accessible by STP lines 4 (1 per hr., 6:20am-10:10pm) and 4\(1 per hr., 8:10am-8:10pm). At night, all tables along V. R. Margherita fill up and the lit-up port becomes its own attraction. **Vertigo Cafe,** V. R. Margherita 39, is the place to see and be seen. Purchase a gelato cone (€1.80-2.50) and join the madness at the counter in exchanging a receipt for a delicious treat. (Open daily 6am-3am.) Farther down the port in the direction of the Castello Svevo is the medieval themed **L'Aragonese,** V. Thaon de Revel 15. The pub's breezy location on the water also gives it the freedom to blast the loudest music, attracting younger crowds year-round. (☎340 29 39 497. Beer €2.50-4. Mixed drinks €4. Wine €3. Open May-Sept, daily 8pm-5am, Oct.-Apr. M-Tu and Th-Su 8pm-5am.) The equally-popular bar **Gruit,** V. Carmine 120, boasts three varieties of house brew. Large windows let you peer into the bar's brewery, which houses seven 2200L tanks. (☎346 57 36 327; www.gruit.it. Oct.-May live music Th. Beer €3-5. Mixed drinks €6. Open M and W-Su 8pm-2am.)

▶ DAYTRIP FROM BRINDISI

OSTUNI

Ostuni is on the train line between Bari (1hr., 26 per day 5:05am-11:10pm, €4.10) and Brindisi (40min., 17 per day 4:06am-8:33pm, €2.30). From the train station (☎0831 30 12 68), take the orange city bus 2.5km to P. della Libertà at the centro (15min.; M-Sa every 30min., Su every hr. 7am-9:30pm). Buy tickets at the train station bar (€0.80) or onboard (€1.50). Buses are not numbered, so tell the driver your intended destination before boarding. The APT Tourist Office, Corso Mazzini 8 (☎0831 30 12 68), just off P. della Libertà, provides maps of the centro storico and a booklet of the town's historical info. Open June-Aug. M-F 8:30am-2:30pm and 3:30-8:30pm, Sa 8:30am-1:30pm and 6:30-8:30pm; Sept.-May M-F 8am-2pm and 3:30-6:30pm, Sa 9:30am-12:30pm.

Rising from a landscape of sea, dark-red earth, and olive trees, the *città bianca* (white city) of Ostuni (oh-STOO-nee; pop. 33,000) appears unworldly. The *centro storico's* thick, whitewashed walls protect the city from the ocean wind and lend a fairy-tale touch to serpentine streets. The terrace at the top of C.

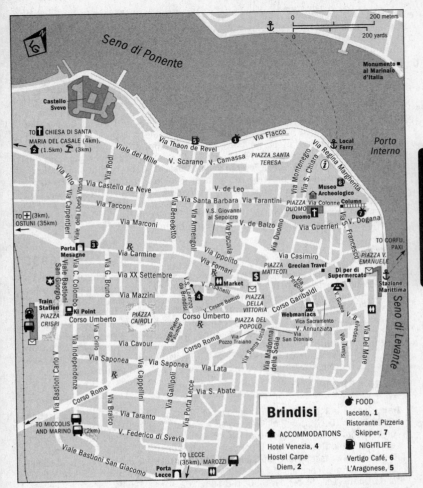

Brindisi

🍴 FOOD
Iaccato, **1**
Ristorante Pizzeria
Skipper, **7**

🏠 ACCOMMODATIONS
Hotel Venezia, **4**
Hostel Carpe
Diem, **2**

🍸 NIGHTLIFE
Vertigo Café, **6**
L'Aragonese, **5**

V. Emanuele provides a view of the old city. Just off P. della Libertà, **Comune di Ostuni**—apart from being the city's administrative center—also displays the works of Onofrio Bramante, whose 🖼️**paintings** provide a pictorial history of Puglia starting around 10,000 BC. (2nd floor. Open M-Sa 8am-2pm and 4-7pm. Free.) From P. della Libertà, V. Cattedrale runs through the *centro storico*, leading to the **Convento delle Monacelle** (Convent of Little Nuns), V. Cattedrale 15. Behind its Baroque facade and under its white-tiled dome, the convent houses an **archaeological museum** with a 24,500-year-old human skeleton. Crowning Ostuni's hill on V. Cattedrale, the **duomo** was among the last Byzantine buildings erected in southern Italy. The Spanish-Gothic facade, with its intricate *rosette*, contrasts sharply with Norman styles more common in Puglia. (Open daily 7am-noon and 4-7pm, except during mass. Modest dress required. Free.) Though several kilometers from the *centro*, Ostuni's praiseworthy **beaches,** accessible from P. della Libertà by STP bus, have free sections. (☎800 23 20 42; www.stpbrindisi.it. July-Aug. take a bus toward "Torre Canne." 6 per day 5:50am-2:25pm, €1. *Tabaccherie* in the square post schedules. Ask bus driver to tell you when you have reached your destination.) The closest beach is **Villanova,** but the most popular is **Costa Merlata.** On August 25-27, Ostuni celebrates the **Festa di Sant'Oronzo**—in honor of the saint who saved the city from a plague— with the **Cavalcata,** a parade of red-and-white costumed horses and riders.

Fresh seafood abounds in Ostuni, but *antipasti* and grilled meats are true local delights. For lunch or dinner, try one of the many small taverns or *osterie* in the old city. Medieval meat-lovers will find bounty and joy at **Osteria Pantagruel ❷,** V. Zaccaria 9, where a €16 *menù* includes a typical *pugliese* antipasto, salad, unlimited meat, pastries, and *caffè*; minimum 2 people. (☎347 10 68 224. Primi €6-7. Secondi €3-12. Cover €1. Open daily 12:30-3:30pm and dinner 7:30-10:30pm. Cash only). **Taverna della Gelosia ❸,** deep within V. Tanzarella Vitale at V. Andriola 26, has one of the best *antipasti* culinary tours in town. Try the *pasta nera* (pasta cooked in black olive oil, served in a bread bowl; €10) or delight your senses with any combination of *pugliese antipasti.* (☎0831 33 47 36; www.tavernadellagelosia.it. Primi €10-13. Secondi €11-15. Cover €2.50. Open daily June-Sept. 12:30-2:30pm and 8pm-midnight. MC/V.)

LECCE ☎0832

One of Italy's hidden pearls, Lecce (LEH-chay; pop. 90,000) is where Italians go when foreign tourists take over their country. Historical invaders have included Cretans, Romans, Saracens, and Swabians; Spanish Hapsburg influence during the 16th and 17th centuries inspired beautiful Baroque buildings that now line Lecce's streets. Most of the city's churches and palaces are sculpted from *tufigna*—soft, locally quarried "Lecce stone" that hardens when exposed to air. At night, the illuminated buildings make for a memorable *passeggiata* (promenade). The "Florence of the South" and home to some of the country's best beaches, is a great starting point for a tour of the Salento Peninsula.

🚍 TRANSPORTATION

Trains: Lecce is the southeastern terminus of the state railway. The **Trenitalia Station** (☎0832 30 10 16) is in P. Massari. Buses #24 and 28 (€0.80) leave from the station on V. Oronzo Quarta. Trains to **Bari** via **Brindisi** (1-2hr., 13 per day 5:30am-8:03pm, €8.60-13) and **Rome** (6-9hr., 5 per day 6am-10:20pm, €30-54). FSE trains (☎0832 66 81 11; www.fseonline.it) cross the Salento Peninsula. The *biglietteria* is on the right end of Binario 1. Trains run M-Sa to **Gallipoli** (1hr., 11 per day 6:56am-8:50pm, €3.40) and **Otranto** (1hr., 11 per day 6:56am-8:50pm, €2.90) via **Maglie.** Schedules are subject to frequent change; consult www.salentointrenoebus.it for detailed schedules.

Buses: The **FSE Station** (☎0832 34 76 34; www.fseonline.it), on V. Boito, is easily accessible by bus #4 (€0.80) from the train station. FSE buses depart daily from the FSE Garage, across from the train station on the left, and stop at the FSE station on their way out of town. Tickets are available in the train station bar. To **Gallipoli** (1hr., 5 per day, €2.90) and **Taranto** (2hr., 5 per day 7am-4pm, €4.58). STP (☎0832 22 84 41), on V. San Nicola, heads to smaller towns of the Salento Peninsula. Pick up a schedule at the tourist office. In July-Aug., Salento in Bus (☎0832 35 03 76; www.salentointrenoebus.it) is the most convenient way to traverse the peninsula, with green-line buses running to **Gallipoli** (1hr., 7 per day 7:05am-9:53pm, €3.50) and red-line buses to **Otranto** (1hr., 9 per day 7:13am-12:23am, €3.50), and other peninsular towns such as Santa Maria di Leuca and Porto Cesareo. Buses stop on V. Pitagora, by the train station. Local buses (€0.80 in *tabaccherie*, €1.50 onboard) service the *centro* and metropoli-

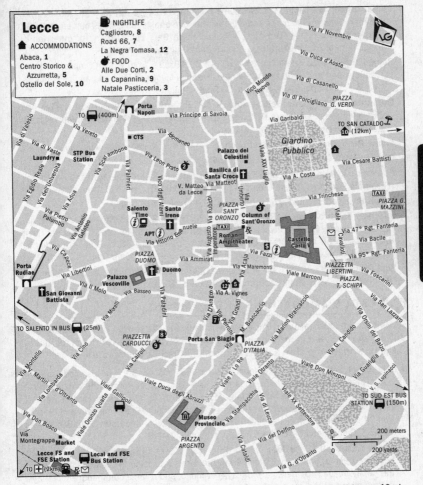

Lecce

ACCOMMODATIONS

Abaca, **1**
Centro Storico &
Azzuretta, **5**
Ostello del Sole, **10**

NIGHTLIFE

Cagliostro, **8**
Road 66, **7**
La Negra Tomasa, **12**

FOOD

Alle Due Corti, **2**
La Capannina, **9**
Natale Pasticceria, **3**

PUGLIA AND CALABRIA

tan area. Line #32 to the coastal town San Cataldo starts at Porta Napoli (every 40min., 6:50am-8:40pm) and makes a stop in front of the Palazzo Uffici Financieri on Viale Gallipoli, the 2nd right off Viale Oronzo Quarta from the train station.

Taxis: (☎0832 24 79 78) at the train station; (☎0832 30 60 45), in P. Sant'Oronzo.

✈ 🔋 ORIENTATION AND PRACTICAL INFORMATION

Lecce lies 35km southeast of Brindisi. From the **train station,** take **Viale Oronzo Quarta** until it becomes V. Cairoli. Turn left on V. Paladini, and wind around the **duomo.** To the left, **Via Libertini** passes **Piazza Duomo** and Chiesa di San Giovanni Battista, eventually exiting the old city walls through Porta Rudiae. To the right lies **Via Vittorio Emanuele II,** which passes **Piazza Sant'Oronzo,** Lecce's main square, with the Roman amphitheater and *castello* beyond.

Tourist Office: APT Lecce, V. V. Emanuele 24 (☎0832 24 80 92; www.viaggareinpuglia. it), near P. Duomo. Free maps and a comprehensive booklet on Lecce's numerous B&Bs. Open in summer daily 9am-1pm; in winter M-Sa 9am-1pm. Dozens of other tourist offices, both public and private, around P. Sant'Oronzo.

Budget Travel: CTS, V. Palmieri 89 (☎0832 30 18 62). From P. Sant'Oronzo, take V. V. Emanuele, and turn right onto V. Palmieri. Provides flight and train info and sells tickets. Open M-F 9am-1pm and 4-8:30pm, Sa 9am-noon.

Laundromat: Lavanderia Self-Service, V. dell'Università 47, between Pta. Rudiae and Pta. Napoli. Wash €3-8, dry €1.50 per 12min. Detergent €1. **Western Union** services. Open M-Sa 8am-8:30pm, Su 8am-1pm.

Public Restrooms: In P. Sant'Oronzo, on the corner with V. Imperatore Augusto.

Carabinieri: V. Calabria (☎0832 27 98 64).

Pharmacy: In train station (☎0832 28 85 52). Open M-Sa 8:30am-1pm and 5-8:30pm. **Farmacia Ferocino,** P. Sant'Oronzo 57 (☎0832 30 91 81), posts a 24hr. rotation.

Hospital: Ospedale Vito Fazzi (☎0832 66 11 11), on V. San Cesario.

Internet: Salento Time, V. Regina Isabella 22 (☎0832 30 36 86; www.salentotime. it. €2.50 per hr. Student discount. Also has **bicycle** rentals (€2 per hr., €10 per day); includes info on bike tours of varying difficulty. Open daily 10am-9pm. Info Point at Castello Carlo V is open June-Sept. M-F 9am-9pm, Sa-Su 9:30am-9pm.

Post Office: ☎0832 27 41 11. In Piazzetta Libertini, across from the castello. Open M-F 8am-6:30pm, Sa 8:30am-1:30pm. **Postal Code:** 73100.

🏠 📷 ACCOMMODATIONS AND CAMPING

B&Bs offer an alternative to impersonal hotels and the tourist office lists afford-able *affittacamere* (rooms for rent). Consider staying in the youth hostel in San Cataldo, whose only drawback is limited night public transporation.

🛏 Ostello del Sole, V. Amerigo Vespucci 45 (☎0832 65 08 90; www.ostellodelsole.it), 12km away in San Cataldo. Take bus #32. In a pinewood in front of the public beach, this newly-renovated hostel offers large dorms with A/C, free lockers, and communal baths. The campsites include hot showers and free parking. Bring your own tent. Reception 24hr. Reserve 2 weeks ahead. 4-bed dorms €15-25, 2-bed dorms €20-30; singles €25-30. Campsites €8-18 plus €5-6 per person. MC/V. ❶

Abaca, V. Cavalloti 19 (☎0832 24 05 48 or 338 72 00 435). Buses #24, 27, and 28 from the train station stop 1 block away. The owner's passion for ballet is reflected in the dainty decor. Nice views, a terrace, A/C, fridge, and a large communal kitchen and bathroom add to the appeal. €20-40 per person. Discounts for extended stays. ❷

Centro Storico, V. Andrea Vignes 2/B (☎338 58 81 265; www.bedandbreakfast.lecce. it). From P. S. Oronzo, take V. Augusto Imperatore until it becomes V. Federico D'Aragona; V. A. Vignes is on the left. Centrally located, this charming B&B boasts a sunroof with city views. 5 big rooms all have A/C, TV, and refrigerator. Breakfast included. Free Wi-Fi. Reservations recommended. Singles €35-40, with bath 50-80; doubles €52-57, with bath €70-109. Extra bed €20. AmEx/MC/V. ❸

Azzurretta, V. A. Vignes 2/B (☎338 25 85 958; www.bblecce.it). Shares management and 16th-century building with Centro Storico. 3 spacious rooms and 1 apartment with kitchen have big, sunny windows, A/C, TV, balcony, and shared sunroof. Breakfast included. Free Wi-Fi. Reservations recommended. Singles €33-38; doubles €61-70; apartment €39-70. Extra bed €17-19. Cash only. ❸

🍴 FOOD

Leccese food is a delight. Regional specialties range from hearty *cicerietria* (chickpeas and pasta) and *pucce* (sandwiches made with olive-bread rolls) to *confettoni* (traditional chocolate candies).

▓ **Alle Due Corti,** Corte dei Giugni 1 (☎0832 24 22 23; www.alleduecorti.com), at the corner with V. Prato. Dedicated to the preservation of *leccese* culture through cuisine—it's so authentic, even Italians can't read some of the dialect on the ever-changing menu. The vegetable *antipasti* are excellent (€6-9). Primi €5-8. Secondi €6-10. Cover €1.50. Reservations recommended. Open M-Sa noon-2pm and 8pm-12:30am. MC/V. ❷

La Capannina, V. Cairoli 13 (☎0832 30 41 59), between the train station and P. Duomo. If you've ever dreamed of eating in the Parthenon, this is likely as close as you'll get. Attentive service in a nearly private *piazza* surrounded by columns, which are illuminated at night. Try the pasta specialty *orecchiette alla casereccia* (with meat, tomato, and cheese sauce; €5.20). Pizza €3.50-6.20; dinner only. Primi €5.20-7.50. Secondi €5.85-12. Cover €1.30. Open Tu-Su noon-3pm and 7pm-midnight. MC/V. ❷

Natale Pasticceria, V. Trinchese 7 (☎0832 25 60 60), off P. Sant'Oronzo. This copper-frosted pastry shop is full of so many pastries, candies, flavors of gelato, and eager customers that your head will spin. Take a number and try the pistachio if the crowds haven't already devoured it. Cones and *granita* €1.80-3. Local, cream-filled delights from €0.80. Open daily 8:30am-midnight. MC/V. ❶

📷 SIGHTS

Lecce's close-knit *centro storico* is visually enchanting. Get an education in Baroque architecture by touring its churches and *palazzi*, which are a 10min. walk apart, but can take hours to enjoy.

BASILICA DI SANTA CROCE. Constructed between 1549 and 1695, this church is a masterpiece of *leccese* Baroque. Most of the area's architects contributed their skills to its ▓**facade** at some point. Inside, the lighting, artwork, and ambience are captivating; look closely to see the profile of Gabriele Riccardi, the basilica's original designer, hidden between the upper window and the column to its left. *(From P. Sant'Oronzo, head down V. Umberto I. Open daily 9am-noon and 5-8pm, except during mass. Modest dress required. Free.)*

DUOMO. Though construction began in 1114, the *duomo* was renovated between 1661 and 1662 by Giuseppe Zimbalo, nicknamed "Lo Zingarello" (The Gypsy) for his tendency to wander aimlessly from one project to another. Except for two *leccese* altars, the stained-glass-bedecked interior dates from the 18th century. At night, when crowds flood the *piazza*, misty streams of light pour out of the *campanile* that rises from the left side of the cathedral. Opposite, the Palazzo Vescovile (Bishop's Palace) has been remodeled several times since its 1632 construction. On the right, with a Baroque well in its center, stands the seminary, designed by Cino in 1709. *(From P. S. Oronzo, take V. V. Emanuele. Duomo open daily 7am-noon and 5-7:30pm. Free.)*

ANCIENT ATTRACTIONS. The **Column of Sant'Oronzo** is one of two that marked the termination of the Appian Way in Brindisi (p. 628). Today, it is topped by a saint, and towers melodramatically over P. Sant'Oronzo. Nearby, the ruins of a second-century **amphitheater** recede into the ground. In its prime, the structure held 20,000 spectators; these days, people gather there on summer nights to flirt or just eat gelato. The **Castello Carlo V,** built on 13th-century foundations, was fortified by King Carlo V in the 16th century. In the midst of heavy archeological excavation and restoration, it only houses small art exhibits for the foreseeable future. (Open M-F 9am-1pm and 4-8:30pm, Sa-Su 9:30am-1pm and 4-8:30pm. Free.) Near the station, the **Museo Provinciale** contains a large collection of Apulian ceramics and figurines from the fifth century BC, as well as rotating art exhibits. (*V. Gallipoli 28.* ☎ *0832 68 35 03. Wheelchair-accessible. Open M-Sa 9am-1:30pm and 2:30-7:30pm, Su 9am-1:30pm. Free.*)

BEACHES. A relaxing daytrip of sand and sun at one of many beaches is just a short trip from Lecce. The nearest access points to the coast are San Cataldo's free beaches, accessible by bus #32. Try the small but beautiful **Torre dell'Orso**, a vacationer's hot spot with many free stretches. (*Blue line #101. 1 hr., 8 per day.*) Popular with locals, **Santa Cesarea Terme** has a wide expanse of clear, pale blue ocean lapping against many caves and coves. (*Blue line, change in Maglie.*) At the tip of the peninsula, the rocky enclaves of **Santa Maria di Leuca** offer small, untouristed beaches and an important lighthouse marking the divide between the Adriatic and the Ionean seas. (*Blue line.*) North of Gallipoli, Porto Cesareo's coast is dotted with towers crumbling into the sea. Bordered by tiny islands, the area is perfect for exploring with kayaks or boats. (*Pink line dir.: Gallipoli.*)

OTHER SIGHTS. The wildly intricate **Chiesa di San Giovanni Battista del Rosario** was Lo Zingarello's last work. The artist, who used dramatic Baroque norms as a basis for innovation, decorated the columns with unfettered glee. Inside the church, 15 altars surround a Roman cross design, testifying to Lo Zingarello's disdain for moderation. (*From P. Duomo, take V. Libertini. Open Tu-Su 9am-12:30pm and 4-7:30pm. Free.*) The ornate **Porta Napoli** once stood on the road to Naples. The arch was erected in 1548 in honor of Holy Roman Emperor Charles V, whose coat of arms adorns the front. (*From P. Duomo, take V. Palmieri.*)

NIGHTLIFE AND FESTIVALS

Don't be fooled by the quiet that takes over Lecce every afternoon; by night, the city wakes from a long *siesta* as people stroll its sidewalks and mingle in its many *piazze*. To join the fun, head to **Via d'Aragona** or **V. Trinchese**, which are crammed with young barhoppers on weekends. Major *piazze*, such as **Piazza Duomo** and **Piazza Sant'Oronzo**, often have live music on weekends. Most nightclubs, especially ones which open only for summer, are on the coast and are thus only accessible by car. For up-to-date info on the hottest nightlife options, consult the publication *Salento in Tasca*, available at local bars. **La Negra Tomasa**, V. d'Aragona 2, is at the core of the street's pub scene, with a definite student following for its Monday-night pizza happy hour and Friday-night live music in winter. (☎0832 33 27 68. Beer €3-4.50. Mixed drinks €6. Open M-Tu and Th-Su 6:30pm-2:30am.) Despite its private, exclusive feel, **Cagliostro**, V. Cairoli 25, has a chill interior and relaxed outdoor seating, making it a favorite for all crowds. (☎083230 18 81. Nov.-May live jazz music Tu and Th 9pm-midnight. Draft beer and mixed drinks from €2.50. Open daily 7pm-3am.) Though lacking authentic Italian charm, **Road 66**, V. dei Perroni 8, near Pta. San Biagio, emulates American bars with its gas-station decor. Try the Road 66 (€3.50), a special fire shot. (☎0832 24 65 68. Beer €2.50-4. Mixed drinks €5. Open daily 6pm-2am.)

The inner courtyard of **Palazzo dei Celestini**, next to Basilica di Santa Croce, hosts rock and classical music concerts in summer. Keep an eye out for posters or ask at the APT office for more info. On the second and third weeks of August, Lecce hosts **La Notte della Taranta**, a festival dedicated to the *pizzica*— Lecce's own *tarantella* dance—which culminates in a grand final concert (☎0832 82 18 27; www.lanottedellataranta.it/eng. Free.)

GALLIPOLI   ☎0833

Ideal as a brisk daytrip from Lecce or a prolonged seaside vacation, Gallipoli (ga-LEE-po-lee; pop. 20,000) boasts a wealth of assets: gorgeous beaches, excellent seafood, and a charming maze of historical homes and churches. Gallipoli's old city is perched on a small island that juts into the sparkling Ionian Sea. Throughout its history, outsiders have coveted the island's strategic location; foreign remnants include a Greek fountain and an Aragonese Castle. Today, Gallipoli's residents maintain a carefree island mentality, and the old city has retained an air of authenticity. Despite its growing popularity as a vacation spot, its whitewashed alleys and clear waters remain largely undiscovered.

TRANSPORTATION AND PRACTICAL INFORMATION. Gallipoli is southwest of Lecce, and is best reached by **train** from Lecce. FSE trains run M-Sa (1hr., 11 per day 6:56am-8:50pm, €3.40). In July and August, Salento in Bus (☎0832 35 03 76; www.salentointrenoebus.it) runs to the town hall in the *città nuova* (1hr., €2.30 at info points, €3.30 onboard) on the green line; catch it in Lecce on V. Gallipoli, in front of Bar Rossa Nera. The train station is in the *città nuova;* to reach the *città vecchia*'s main *piazza,* **Piazza Imbriani,** from the train station, turn right on C. Roma, cross the bridge, and turn right. From there, the main road, **Via Antonietta de Pace,** runs past the *duomo,* on the left, to the other side of the island. The **IAT Tourist Office,** P. Imbriani 10, offers advice on travel around the Salento Peninsula, and has free maps. (☎0833 26 25 29. Open daily 8:30am-1pm and 4-8:30pm.) In case of emergency, contact the **carabinieri,** P. Malta 2 (☎0833 26 74 00), or the **police** (☎0833 26 77 11). **Farmacia Provenzano** is at V. A. de Pace 59. (☎0833 26 64 12. Open M-Sa 8:30am-12:30pm and 4-8pm.) The **Ospedale Sacro Cuore di Gesù** (☎0833 27 01 11) is at V. Alezio 12. **Internet Café,** V. Bartolo Ravenna 2/A, is 200m to the immediate right of the train station. (☎0833 26 25 47. €4 per hr. Open M-F and Su 8:30am-1:30pm and 4:30-8:30pm, Sa 8:30am-1:30pm.) The **post office,** V. Quartini 1, is on the first right after crossing the bridge from the *città vecchia* to the *città nuova.* (☎0833 26 75 11. Open M-F 8am-6:30pm, Sa 8am-12:30pm.) **Postal Code:** 73014.

ACCOMMODATIONS AND FOOD. Gallipoli's hotels are expensive, particularly in July and August. The seaside ◪**La Riviera Bed and Breakfast ❸,** Riviera Sauro 7, decorated with intricate frescoes, has rooms with A/C, phone, bath, and flat-screen TV, some boasting a terrace with views of the Ionian sea. (☎0833 26 10 96; www.bedandbreakfastlariviera.com. Breakfast included. Free Wi-Fi. Singles €50, only available Sept.-May; doubles €60-80, in Aug. €120; triples €80-110/150; quads €100-130/160. Cash only.) Take the green line minibus (20min., 10 per day 8:31am-10:16, €1) from V. Kennedy in the *città nuova* to ◪**Camping Baia di Gallipoli ❶,** Litoranea per Santa Maria di Leuca. With a 2400-person capacity, this large village has a campground, bar, restaurant, pool, private beach, and bungalows. (☎0833 27 32 10; www.baiadigallipoli.com. Free Wi-Fi. Reception 8am-1pm and 4-8pm. €6-18 per person. Bungalows €45-115.)

Escape the crowds and inflated prices of the city center by heading to the family-run **Osteria La Pentola degli Gnomi ❷,** V. Consalvo di Cordoba 8. Enjoy Salentine specialties like *purè di fave e cicorie* (bean and chicory; €7) in a breezy inner courtyard. From the train station, turn left on C. Roma. V. C. di Cordoba is the fourth street on the right. (☎0833 26 41 60. Primi €7-10. Secondi €6-12. Open July-Sept. daily 10:30am-3pm and 7pm-midnight; Oct.-June M-Tu and Th-Su 10:30am-3pm and 7pm-midnight AmEx/MC/V.) **Trattoria L'Angolo Blu ❸,**

V. Carlo Muzio 45, offers local seafood specialties. Enjoy perfect *al dente* pasta in the cool, stone-walled interior. (☎0833 26 15 00. Primi €6-8.50. Secondi from €7. Cover €1.50. Open daily noon-3pm and 7pm-1am. MC/V.)

🄲 **BEACHES.** By day, Gallipoli's cobbled streets are a colorful jungle of markets and produce vendors, its walls draped in fishing traps and fresh laundry. By night, the city is set aglow with lights. Residents make their evening *passeggiata* along the promenade encircling the *città vecchia;* the promenade passes by the port as well as the island's small, uncrowded, and completely free beach: **Seno della Purità.** The turquoise waters make for excellent swimming. Three miles down the coast, beaches encircle the emerald **Baia Verde,** with free sandy strips interspersed along private beaches. Three miles from Gallipoli's *città vecchia,* Baia Verde is accessible by bus #5 (€0.70) or by walking along the coastal seawall, bearing right after crossing the bridge. The walk passes many tiny beaches carved into the *tufa,* and offers excellent views of the coastline.

🄶 🄻 **SIGHTS AND ENTERTAINMENT.** Aside from its beaches, the city contains many layers of historical relics. All the churches in the *città vecchia* are open daily in July and August 10am-noon and 5-9pm, except during mass. Lookout for IAT tour guides inside the main churches who give ▧**free tours** daily (info ☎0833 26 42 42). On V. Duomo, find the ornate exterior of the city's 17th-century **Baroque Cattedrale di Sant'Agata.** Its arched walls and ceilings are covered with intricate murals, and the inside boasts 700 square meters of impressive paintings on canvas. (Open daily 8am-noon and 4-9pm. Free.) Just before the *duomo* lies the **Museo Diocesano,** V. A. de Pace 51, containing religious art from the *duomo* and other churches in Gallipoli. Its large terrace offers great views of the *città vecchia* and harbor. (☎0833 51 26 90. Open June-Sept. Tu-Su 5:30-11pm; Oct.-May Tu-F 9am-12:30pm, Sa-Su 9am-12:30pm and 3:30-6:30pm. €2.50, children and seniors €1.50, under 12 free.) Farther up the street on V. della A. de Pace 108, the **Museo Civico** contains a variety of relics and artwork from the town's past. (Open M-F 10am-1pm and 4-8pm, Sa-Su 10am-1pm and 5-9pm. €1.) Before crossing the 17th-century bridge to the *città vecchia,* find the recently restored Greek fountain, also known as the **Fontana Ellenica,** to the left.

The free publication *Night & Day* lists Gallipoli's restaurants, bars, and distant *discoteche.* In the evening, don't miss the ▧**sunset** from Riviera Sauro, when the brilliant Salentino sun slips beneath the horizon in a thrilling finale of pink and orange. Continue to the other side of the old city to reach bar **Ritrò,** Riviera Armando Diaz 1/3. Candle-lit and canopied, the daily *aperitivo* hour (6:30-8pm) is the perfect place to try a live *riccio di mare* (sea-urchin) with your drink. (☎0833 26 39 01; www.ritroristobar.com. Beer €3-4. Mixed drinks €5. Wine €3. Open daily in summer 10am-3am; in winter M-Tu and Th-Su 10:30am-3pm and 7pm-midnight.) From July 23-25, the city honors its patron saint with the **Festa di Santa Cristina.** Aside from a sea procession with the saint's statue, locals gather at this time for the traditional challenge of *"la cuccagna"*, which involves grabbing a flag at the end of a greased pole suspended over the port waters. The *Museo Diocesano*, along with museums from Otranto and Lecce, also hosts **Arte Mare,** a series of concerts, art displays, and discussions from the beginning of July to the end of August.

OTRANTO   ☎0836

Although throngs of Italian tourists descend upon Otranto (OH-tran-toh; pop. 5300) and drive already high prices even higher in summer, its winding streets, gorgeous coastline, and medieval sights merit a visit in any season. This town is a testament to the power of faith; impressed by the piety of the 800 *Martiri d'Otranto* (Martyrs of Otranto) who chose to die rather than renounce their religion, Turkish pirates who had conquered the city in 1480 gave up Islam in favor of Christianity. Today, the martyrs' bones—and the mosaic-adorned cathedral that houses them—attract some visitors, but most make their pilgrimage to bathe in Otranto's warm, clear waters.

TRANSPORTATION AND PRACTICAL INFORMATION. Otranto is 40km southeast of Lecce. Rustic FSE **trains** run M-Sa from Lecce (1hr., 11 per day 6:56am-8:50pm, €2.90) to Maglie via Otranto. In July and August, the red line of **Salento in Bus** (☎0832 35 03 76; www.salentointrenoebus.it) runs straight from Lecce's V. Gallipoli (in front of Bar Rossa Nera) to Otranto's *castello* (2hr., €3.50). For a **taxi** to areas around Otranto, call ☎0836 80 46 88.

From the station, walk straight and bear right to reach the main beach, along **Lungomare Terra d'Otranto**; after the **public gardens**, V. Vittorio Emanuele leads to **Piazza de Donno** and the entrance to the *centro storico*. Enter through the city gate, and turn right on **Via Basilica** to reach the **duomo**. The **AIT Tourist Office**, across from the Castello Aragonese, offers advice on lodgings and transportation to towns on the peninsula. (☎0836 80 14 36. Open Apr.-Sept. M-Sa 8:30am-1pm and 4-8:30pm; Oct.-Mar. Tu and Th 8am-2pm and 4-6pm.) For the **carabinieri**, V. 800 Martiri 10, call ☎083680 10 10. **Farmacia Ricciardi** is at Lungomare T. d'Otranto 73. (☎0836 80 10 36. Open M-Sa 8:30am-1pm and 4:30-10pm, Su 9am-noon and 6-8pm.) For medical **emergencies**, call ☎0836 80 16 76. Stop for **Internet** access at **Giardini Caffè**, V. V. Emanuele 911. (☎338 64 88 100. €3.50 per hr. Open daily 10am-1pm and 5pm-midnight.) The **post office** is by the stoplight on V. Pantaleone. (☎0836 80 02 11. Open M-Sa 8:15am-6pm.) **Postal Code:** 73028.

ACCOMMODATIONS AND FOOD. Lodgings in Otranto are very expensive, especially from mid-July to August when most hotels require that guests eat at their restaurants and all require reservations. The tourist office can help find *affittacamere*, and camping is a fun, cheap alternative. **Hotel Meublé Il Gabbiano ❸**, V. Porto Craulo 13, though far from the *centro storico*, offers tranquility and proximity to the beach. Simple rooms have phone, ceiling fan, and sometimes a balcony. (☎0836 80 15 57; www.hotelmeublegabbiano.it. Open Apr.-Oct. Singles €35-45, not available in Aug.; doubles €50-80, Aug. €100; triples €65-95/115. Cash only.) **Camping Idrusa ❶**, V. del Porto 1, is in a forest before the port and offers a market and bar. (☎0836 80 12 55; www.campingidrusa.it. Reception 8am-noon and 3-5pm; gate shut 11pm-7am. Pets allowed. €6-8 per person; €6-10 per tent. Free hot showers. Electricity €2. Cash only.)

A gate in the Castello Aragonese walls on V. Immacolata leads to the refuge of Otranto's picturesque sailboat harbor, where **Ai Bastioni ❷** offers seaside seating. The location and the food—only the freshest from the port—make the cool maritime decorations almost superfluous. (☎0836 80 15 57. Primi €5-10. Secondi €9-15. Cover €2.50. Open July-Mar. daily noon-3pm and 5-11pm; Apr.-June M-Tu and Th-Su noon-3pm and 5-11pm. MC/V.) A Sicilian family runs **Ristorante Il Vicolo ❷**, Lungomare T. d'Otranto 87, nearly ensuring authentic island cuisine and quality seafood. (☎0836 80 26 44. Primi €4-9. Secondi €6-12. Cover €1.50. Open in summer daily noon-3pm and 7pm-midnight; only open W-M in winter. MC/V.) The public gardens sport numerous snack stands; try the delicious *noccioline zuccherate* (candy-coated nuts; €1). For essentials, visit the **market** by P. del Donno which sells fruit, meat, and fish (open daily 8am-1pm), or the **supermarket** on the way from the train station to the beach.

□ SIGHTS. The *centro storico*, which hosted Dante while he wrote parts of the *Divine Comedy*, guards many of Otranto's proudest historical sites. The first stop on a tour of the old city should be the **■duomo** (also called the cathedral), which is lined by a phenomenal 11th-century floor mosaic of the Tree of Life. The mosaic depicts religious and historical figures from Adam to Alexander the Great and King Arthur. Another section depicts the 12 zodiac signs and seasonal agricultural work. Equally impressive is the colorful gilded porcelain ceiling, which is well worth straining your neck to see. In the **Cappella dei Martiri,** a small chapel above the *duomo*'s crypt, to the right of the altar, three glass cabinets display the skulls and bones of all 800 *otrantini* who died for their faith at the hands of Turkish pirates. (*Duomo* open daily 8am-noon and 3-6:30pm, except during mass. Modest dress required. Free.) Take C. Garibaldi to P. del Popolo, and follow the signs up the stairs on the left to find aging frescoes of the Garden of Eden adorning the small, musty interior of the beautiful Byzantine **Chiesa di San Pietro,** V. Martiri d'Otranto. (Open daily 10am-noon and 3-6pm.) The huge **Aragonese castle,** with its imposing walls and now-dry moat, may not be exciting inside, but it could still withstand a siege. (☎339 74 325 60. Open daily 9:30am-1pm and 4-10pm. €2, children and seniors €1.) Every Wednesday a **market** surrounding the castle sells local arts and foods. (Open 9am-1pm.) For a relaxing stroll, grab a friend and head to the **Santuario Santa Maria dei Martiri.** Walk straight out of the old city onto V. 800 Martiri, off P. Castello to the left (5min.). Peer into the church's Baroque interior and intricate white altar. With stone steps, a freshly restored exterior, and a beautiful view of the surrounding seaside and landscape, the church provides a respite from the beach buzz. The peaceful sanctuary also memorializes one of the darkest moments in Otranto's history—the decapitation of the *martiri d'Otranto*.

◪ 🖵 BEACHES AND ENTERTAINMENT. In August, Otranto's **beaches** show less shore than skin as Italian vacationers stake claims to every patch of sand. For those seeking fewer crowds, the fine sand and azure waters are just as enjoyable in early summer. The **free** public strips interspersed along the *lungomare*, farther along V. degli Haethey, and all the way to the right on Lungomare Kennedy are the most accessible, but also the most crowded. Also consider the beaches north of Otranto, accessible by the red bus line. The beach closest to V. Pantaleone Presbitero provides bathrooms and changing facilities (€5), as well as umbrellas and chairs (€10). While not actually a beach, one of the best places to swim is in the concrete stretch in front of Lungomare degli Eroi. If exploring the depths of the briny blue sounds more appealing than sunbathing, scuba diving is available by appointment at V. San Francesco di Paola 41/43. (☎/fax 0836 80 27 40; www.scubadiving.it. 1 dive €32. 10% *Let's Go* discount on merchandise and dives. Open daily 9:30am-1pm and 4:30-8pm.)

After dark, Otranto's *lungomare* fills with people walking along the waterfront and hitting up the pubs near P. del Popolo in the *centro*. Enjoy the sunset while strolling above the water on V. Bastioni, then settle for a drink at **Giro di Boa,** V. Scupoli. (☎0836 80 12 92. Beer €2.50-4. Mixed drinks €5.50. Open daily Apr.-Sept. 7pm-2am.) **L'Alternativa,** V. Scupoli, is the perfect people-watching option off P. del Popolo. (☎338 37 79 684. Beer €2-3.50. Mixed drinks €5.50. Open daily 7pm-2am.) Every year on August 13-14, Otranto enjoys fireworks, free concerts, and a lot of food for the **Festa dei Martiri d'Otranto,** a festival held in honor of the town's martyrs. On the first Sunday in September, the town celebrates the **Festa della Madonna dell'Altomare** (Festival of the Virgin of the High Seas) with a lengthy seafaring procession and fireworks.

CALABRIA

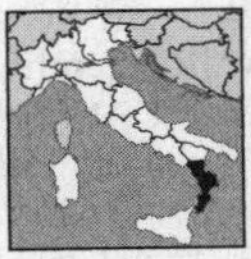

Sometimes called the last great oasis of the Mediterranean, Calabria (ca-LAH-bree-ah) is an undiscovered land of inspiring history and unspoiled natural beauty. Long stretches of beaches lie on the coast, and untamed mountain wilderness reigns in the interior. As one of Italy's less developed regions, it is one of the few places that has not become completely overrun with camera-toting tourists. Two and a half millennia ago, when the northern cities that now belittle Calabria were but small backwaters, the region was of international importance, home to leading philosophers, artists, and athletes. Fortunately for local pride, traces of this illustrious past remain in abundance, from the castles that dot the coast to the stunningly intact Greek bronze statues still on display in Reggio di Calabria's Museo Nazionale della Magna Graecia. What Calabria lacks in urban bustle, it makes up for in quiet natural beauty and a relaxed attitude that the North simply cannot match—or understand for that matter.

REGGIO DI CALABRIA ☎0965

Though often regarded as a mere departure point for Sicily, Reggio and its environs actually comprise some of the finest landscapes and friendliest people in Italy. The provincial capital of Reggio di Calabria (REH-jo dee Ca-LA-bree-ya; pop. 185,000) was one of the earliest and proudest Greek settlements on the Italian mainland, but it slid into neglect and disarray following centuries of raids and natural disasters. After a devastating 1908 earthquake, a new city arose from the rubble, crowded with designer stores and turn-of-the-century *palazzi*. A vibrant and manageable city, Reggio offers magnificent sunsets, the amazing Riace Bronzes, and a serene evening stroll along the *lungomare*. The nearby towns of Scilla and Locri offer one of Italy's most attractive beaches and finest collections of archaeological treasures.

TRANSPORTATION

Flights: Aeroporto dello Stretto (☎0965 64 05 17) is 5km south of town. **Orange buses** #113, 114, 115, 125, or 131 run from P. Garibaldi outside Stazione Centrale to the airport (€1). Flights service Bologna, Florence, Milan, Rome, Venice, and Turin.

Trains: Stazione Centrale (☎0965 27 120), on P. Garibaldi at the south end of town. Info office open daily 7am-9pm. Trains run to: **Cosenza** (2hr., 14 per day 5:05am-7:35pm, €13.60); **Naples** (4hr., 12 per day 5:45am-11:40pm, €22); **Rome** (8hr., 14 per day 5:45am-11:40pm, €30); **Scilla** (30min., 20 per day 5:05am-8:35pm, €5.50); **Tropea** (2hr., 10 per day 5:10am-8:35pm, €11).

Buses: Most buses run from P. Garibaldi.

Lirosi: (☎0965 57 552) runs buses to **Florence** (12hr.; M, W-F, and Su 6:45pm; €47) and **Rome** (8hr.; 7am, 11:45am, and 10pm; €35). Buy tickets at Agenzia Viaggi Simonetta, C. Garibaldi 551. (☎0965 81 40 24. Open M-F 9am-8pm, Sa 9am-1pm. AmEx/MC/V.)

Costaviola: (☎0965 75 15 86; www.costaviolabus.it) runs buses to Scilla (45min., 12 per day 7:20am-8:10pm, €3). Buy tickets onboard.

Ferries and hydrofoils: depart from the port at the northern end of the city and serve Messina and the Aeolian Islands.

Trenitalia: (☎0965 81 76 75), to the left of the port. Office open daily 6:30am-8:15pm.

Ustica: (☎090 66 25 06 or 090 36 40 44), to the right of Trenitalia. Office hours vary.

NGI (General Italian Navigation Line): (☎335 84 27 784), across from Onda Marina to the right of the port entrance. Open M-F 12:30-10pm, Sa 12:30-8pm.

⊞ 🛈 ORIENTATION AND PRACTICAL INFORMATION

Reggio's main thoroughfare is **Corso Garibaldi,** which runs parallel to the sea and to all the major sights. Facing away from **Stazione Centrale,** walk straight through **Piazza Garibaldi** to C. Garibaldi; a left turn leads to the *centro.* At the end of C. Garibaldi and down Vle. Genoese Zerbi is Reggio's **port,** from which hydrofoils and boats depart. One block to the left of the station, the twin roads **Corso Vittorio Emanuele III** and **Viale Matteotti** trace the *lungomare.* City buses run continuously up and down C. Garibaldi and northward along the two roads. At its center, C. Garibaldi becomes a pedestrian route, perfect for an evening *passeggiata* past the many bars and designer outlets that line the street.

Tourist office: APT, V. Roma 3, 1st fl. (☎0965 21 171). Provides info and free maps. Open M-W 7:30am-1:30pm and 2-4pm, Th-F 7:30am-1:30pm. Branches: at Stazione Centrale (☎0965 27 120) and airport (☎0965 64 32 91).

Currency exchange: Banca Nazionale del Lavoro, C. Garibaldi 431 (☎0965 85 11). Open M-F 8:20am-1:20pm and 2:35-4pm.

Police: (☎0965 53 991), near Stazione Centrale.

Hospital: Ospedale Riuniti (☎0965 39 111), on V. Melacrino.

Internet Access: Online Internet Point Multiservices, V. De Nava 142 (☎0965 23 902). €4 per hr., students €3 with student ID. Open daily 9am-1pm and 4-8:30pm.

Post office: V. Miraglia 14 (☎0965 31 52 68). Open M-F 8:30am-6:30pm, Sa 8am-12:30pm. **Postal Code:** 89121.

🛏 ACCOMMODATIONS

Cheap, quality accommodations are difficult to find in Reggio, but they exist.

🏠 **B&B La Pineta,** Vle. G. Zerbi 13/B (☎0965 59 37 13; www.bblapineta.info). A diamond in the rough; simple rooms on the *lungomare.* All have bath and TV; doubles have A/C. Reserve ahead July-Aug. Singles €35; doubles €50; triples €60. Cash only. ❸

B&B Le Stanze di Anna e Catarina, V. Chiesa Pepe, 11/13 (☎333 19 879 25; www. lestanzediannaecaterina.it). Hidden within a maze of curving streets and parked cars. The epitome of budget luxury. Elegant wardrobe, stunning collection of impressionist paintings, and colorful themed rooms. Terrace, TV lounge, reading room and A/C. Free Wi-Fi. Reservations recommended. Singles €35-40; extra bed €10. Cash only. ❸

Hotel Mundial, V. Gaeta 9 (☎0965 33 22 55; hotelmundial@virgilio.it). Offers relatively cheap rooms near the train station. All rooms with bath, TV, A/C, and phone. Singles €40; doubles €55; triples €60; quads €80. Cash only. ❹

B&B Villa Maria, V. Marina Arenile 3 (☎0965 37 26 33), in Gallico Marina. Take bus #110 from P. Garibaldi, walk to the waterfront (10min.), and turn right, or call to be picked up. The B&B is on V. Marina Arenile behind the "Ottica" shop. Offers rooms near the coast with shared terrace. Singles €30-€40, extra bed €25. Cash only. ❸

🍴 FOOD

Chefs in Reggio serve *spaghetti alla calabrese* (pasta with pepper sauce), *capocollo* (ham spiced with local hot peppers), *frittole* (pork cooked in a boiler), and *pesce spada* (swordfish). Bars along C. Garibaldi often offer baked goods, so sweeten the day with a few of the region's beloved *biscotti.* Stock up on groceries at **Dì per Dì** supermarket, past the museum where V. de Nava crosses V. Roma. (☎0965 81 12 79. Open M-Sa 8am-1:30pm and 5-8:30pm. MC/V.)

■ **Cordon Bleu,** C. Garibaldi 205 (☎0965 33 24 47). Despite chandelier lighting and a haughty French name, this versatile joint serves cheap tavola calda goodies (from €1.50), as well as more sophisticated meat and vegetable entrees. Primi €5-6. Secondi €6-8. Open daily 6:30am-11pm. Kitchen open 11am-9pm. AmEx/MC/V. ❷

Lord Byron, V. del Plebiscito 20 (☎0218 33 908 02). Everything from the *rosticceria* is €1, including *calzoni, arancini, pizza a taglio, schicciate,* and *sfoglie.* Open 24hr. ❶

La Taverna dei Templari, V. del Torrione 35 (☎349 16 614 25). A medieval menu and feudal decorations make this pizzeria stand out from all the rest. €16 dinner *menù* would make any knight burst his armor. Enormous pizzas €3.50-6. Open 8pm-4am. ❸

◉ SIGHTS

The preeminence Reggio di Calabria enjoyed in antiquity as a great Greek polis may have passed, but the ■**Museo Nazionale** preserves the city's historical claim to fame with one of the world's finest collections of art and artifacts from Magna Graecia (Greater Greece). In the first floor galleries, a wealth of *amphorae* and *pinakes* (wine jars and votive tablets) depict scenes from mythology and daily life. The floor above the gallery has a large coin collection and a 2300-year-old novelty sarcophagus shaped like a huge, sandaled foot. Downstairs, treasures formerly submerged in the Ionian Sea, such as pottery and broken statues, comprise the **Sezione Subacquea** (Underwater Section). If the Subacquea is the centerpiece, ■**I Bronzi di Riace** are the crown jewels. Rescued from the sea in 1972, the Riace Bronzes are among the best (and arguably the most valuable) ancient Greek sculptures in the world. Dating from the fifth century BC, they depict nude male warriors in stunning detail. Muscular and assured, the bronzes share gallery space with the realistic **Head of the Philosopher,** which some cite as the Greek tradition's first life-like portrait. A display documents the bronzes' restoration process. (P. de Nava, on C. Garibaldi toward the Stazione Lido. ☎0965 89 69 72 or 0965 31 62 42. Open Tu-Su 9am-8pm. Last entry 30min. before closing. €6, ages 18-25 €3, under 18 or over 65 free.) **Castello Aragonese** is said to date from 536 BC and has provided the city with protection ever since. It was greatly enlarged under the rule of Ferdinand of Aragon and Charles V, who sought to defend the city from Turkish invasions. Today the castle provides magnificent views of the city and Calabria's neighboring Sicily. (P. Castello; take V. degli Ottimati up from C. Garibaldi. ☎0965 36 21 11. Open daily, hours vary.) For more stunning views, enjoy a stroll through the **Parco della Rotonda,** across from Chiesa San Paolo. (Take either V. del Salvatore or V. E. Cuzzocrea away from the sea, turn right at V. Udine, and then walk until you see the park. Open 10am-12:30pm and 5-8pm. Free.)

◤ ♫ BEACHES AND ENTERTAINMENT

As the day cools, *reggiani* mingle on the ■**lungomare,** a long narrow, botanical garden stretching along the seaside that Italian author Gabriele d'Annunzio immortalized as the "most beautiful kilometer in all of Italy." When they desire a dip, travelers and locals head to the beach near **Lido Comunale.** Playgrounds, an elevated boardwalk, and monuments to the city's more famous citizens dot the *lungomare,* while the quiet beauty of a sunset behind the misty blue mountains of nearby Sicily provides the final natural touch to a pleasant afternoon swim. Private beaches come alive at night and play host to Reggio's youth. Calabrians finish the summer with the humongous **Festival of the Madonna della Consolazione.** This four-day festival, beginning the second Saturday of September, starts with an enormous parade led by men carrying an effigy of the Holy Virgin, and concludes with an elaborate fireworks display over the ocean.

◆ DAYTRIPS FROM REGGIO DI CALABRIA

▨SCILLA

Scilla is accessible from Reggio by train (30min., 20per day, €5.50) or by bus (45min., 12 per day, €3). Scilla's train station does not sell tickets, so purchase a round-trip ticket from Reggio or ask at nearby bars for regional train tickets.

Walk along the beach and listen for mermaids singing; local legend has it that merfolk still dwell off the Scillan coast. Homer immortalized Scilla's (SHEEL-la; pop. 5134) great cliffs in *The Odyssey* as the home of the menacing Scylla, a terrible monster with six heads, 12 feet, and a fierce temper. Even fiercer was the monster's snare—as ships fled nearby Charybdis, a hazardous whirlpool in the straits where Sicily and Italy meet, Scylla would wait patiently and then devour the vessels as they sailed past. Travelers today are greeted instead by a resort town filled with beach umbrellas and untroubled tourists. Only 23km from Reggio, Scilla's languorous pace and distinctive geography (it is built directly into cliffs which enclose a sandy beach) can make the real world seem far away—especially when the meteorological oddity *Fata Morgana* creates a natural magnifying glass out of the light over the sea, making the Sicilian city of Messina appear to be floating just above the water. Former hippies seeking the good old days should look no further than this oceanic retreat; **Dalì City Scilla ❷**, V. Porto 6, offers *panini* (€3.50-4), salads (€5), and a variety of drinks (€2-7) in a seaside shack. Electric guitars hang from the ceiling, posters of Jimi Hendrix, Janis Joplin, and the Beatles cover both the inside and outside, and classic rock erupts from the stereo system. (☎0965 79 01 96. Hours vary, so listen for the music.) **Zanzibar Gelateria ❶**, V. Spirito Santo 1, specializes in *granita* (Italian flavored ice) and old-fashioned gelato. (☎339 33 272 35; open afternoons, hours vary). Those craving seafood should try **La Pescatora ❷**, V. Cristoforo Colombo 32. (☎0965 17 54 147. Primi €4-7.50. Secondi €7-11.50. Open M-Tu and Th-Su noon-3:30pm, 8-11:30pm. AmEx/MC/V.)

THE IONIAN COAST AND ASPROMONTE NATIONAL PARK

Trains and buses along the Ionian Coast and to Aspromonte often have erratic schedules and multiple connections; allow ample travel time when planning an itinerary. Consult the tourist office in Reggio for more info. Those looking to hike in Aspromonte should call the National Park ☎ 74 30 60 for park conditions and to arrange excursions.

From Reggio to Riace, the Ionian Coast (CO-sta Ee-YO-nee-ya) offers miles of beaches. White sands, rocks, and dunes cater to every taste and provide a contrast to the mountains visible in the distance. Even the more established sites at the villages of **Bianco, Bovalino Marina,** and **Soverato** are relatively unknown. Although it holds the title of the kidnapping capital of the world, **Aspromonte** provides miles of trails to get lost in natural wonder and not the trunk of someone's car. **Montalto,** the primary peak, is a 2½hr. drive from Reggio and then a 30min. hike. One can also visit the **Garibaldi Mausoleum,** which commemorates where Garibaldi was wounded by the Piedmontese, enshrining the hero's body near the tree he leaned upon when he was injured.

COSENZA   ☎0984

One of the most important cultural and industrial centers of Calabria, Cosenza (co-SEN-za; pop. 71,680) is full of intrigue. From the plundered riches that King Alaric I supposedly buried in the city's Busento River in AD 410 to the Norman-style castle built by the Saracens, Cosenza's treasures mirror its unusual history. Though often ignored by tourists due to its inland location, Cosenza's labyrinthine *centro storico*, massive student population, and thriving nightlife make it worth a stopover. The best time to visit is in spring, when university is in session, Teatro Rendano echoes with plays, and weather is moderate.

SUNDAY SERVICES. Transportation options from Cosenza are severely reduced Su. City buses run less frequently, and Ferrovie della Calabria trains and buses do not run at all. Act like a local and lay low.

TRANSPORTATION. Trains depart from **Stazione Cosenza** (☎0984 39 47 46), on V. Popilia, 4km north of the city center. The ticket office is open daily 6:10am-12:42pm and 1:50-8:22pm. Trains go to Naples (4hr., 13 per day 4:35am-6:25pm, €17.30) and Reggio di Calabria (2hr., 15 per day 4:35am-9:25pm, €13.60). Ferrovie della Calabria sends trains to Camigliatello (1hr., M-Sa 9:18am, €3). It also sends blue **regional buses** to Camigliatello (45min., M-Sa 8 per day 6:50am-7:05pm, €2) and San Giovanni (2hr., M-Sa 10 per day, €3) from the station on V. Autostazione and the Stazione Cosenza. The ticket office is opposite the train ticket window and is open daily 6am-2:20pm and 4-7:30pm. All orange **city buses** stop at P. Matteotti. Tickets (€0.77) are sold at kiosks (main kiosk at V. Trieste with C. Mazzini, near P. dei Bruzi) and at most *tabaccherie*. Buses #4T, 22, and 23 serve the *centro storico*, departing from P. Bruzi and stopping in P. Prefeturra (every 30min. 5:30am-11pm). Buses #17 and 27 run between P. Matteotti and the train station (every 7min. 5am-midnight). Routes are posted on yellow street signs in P. Matteotti and at all bus stops. (Info ☎800 24 24 00.)

ORIENTATION AND PRACTICAL INFORMATION. The **Busento River** divides the city into two parts: the traffic-heavy new city, north of the Busento, and the relaxed *centro storico*, south of the river. **Corso Mazzini**, the main pedestrian thoroughfare and shopping center, begins near the river at **Piazza dei Bruzi**, continues through **Piazza Kennedy**, and ends in **Piazza Bilotti**. To get to C. Mazzini, hop on any bus to **Piazza Matteotti** and, facing away from the bus stop, walk one block up **Corso Umberto** to P. dei Bruzi. The bus station is on **Via Autostazione**, to the right off P. Bilotti at the end of C. Mazzini, where the *corso* splits seven ways. Cosenza's *centro storico* lies across the **Ponte Mario Martiri**. A maze of medieval stone buildings, the old city has winding streets and cobblestone staircases. The only discernible street, the narrow **Corso Telesio**, begins in **Piazza Valdesi**, near the Busento, and climbs to the statue of Telesio in the **Piazza XV Marzo** (also called **Piazza Prefettura**).

For tourist info, head either to the **Agenzia Informagiovani,** V. Francesco Acri 1/C-1/E, next to Morrone Park (☎0984 74 044), or the town hall, P. dei Bruzi 1 (☎0984 81 31). Be aware that opening hours are sporadic. In case of emergency, call the **police** in P. dei Bruzi, behind the town hall (☎0984 25 422). **Farmacia Berardelli,** C. Mazzini 40, posts after-hours rotations. (☎0984 26 452. Open M-F 8:30am-1pm and 4:30-8pm.) The **Ospedale Civile dell'Annunziata** (☎0984 68 11) is on V. Felice Migliori. **Libreria Mondadori,** C. Mazzini 156, has a small selection of English-language bestsellers. (☎0983 79 58 14. Open M-F 9am-1pm and 4:30-8:30pm, Sa 9am-1pm. AmEx/MC/V.) For **Internet** access, head to **Web Point,** P. Campanella 32. (€2 per hr. Open daily 9am-1pm and 4:30-9pm.) The **post office,** V. Veneto 41, is at the end of V. Piave, off C. Mazzini. (☎0984 22 162. Open M-F 8am-6:30pm, Sa 8am-12:30pm). **Postal Code:** 87100.

ACCOMMODATIONS AND FOOD. Ostello Re Alarico ❶, Vico II Giuseppe Marini Serra 10, is the perfect base for exploring the old city and its surroundings. To get there, cross the Crati River from the old city and follow V. G. M.

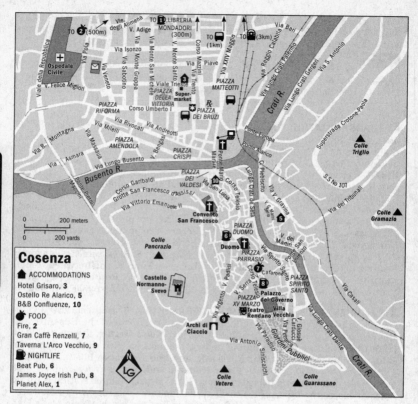

Cosenza

🏠 ACCOMMODATIONS
Hotel Grisaro, 3
Ostello Re Alarico, 5
B&B Confluenze, 10

🍴 FOOD
Fire, 2
Gran Caffè Renzelli, 7
Taverna L'Arco Vecchio, 9

🌙 NIGHTLIFE
Beat Pub, 6
James Joyce Irish Pub, 8
Planet Alex, 1

Serra until the brown sign for V. II Giuseppe. The hostel offers ornately furnished eight-bed rooms, a bar, lounge, kitchen, and courtyard. (☎0984 79 25 70; www.ostellorealarico.com. Internet €3 per hr. Light breakfast included. Dorms €17. AmEx/MC/V.) Also located in the historic center, **B&B Confluenze** ❷, Vico IV Santa Lucia 48, boasts four modern rooms with heating and historic feel. (☎320 372 6087. Internet, telephone, and laundry access. Reservations required. Singles €25-35; doubles €50-70. Cash only.) To reach **Hotel Grisaro** ❸, V. Monte Santo 6, walk one block up C. Mazzini from P. dei Bruzi, then turn left on V. Trieste and look for V. Monte Santo. Rooms are spacious and comfortable, with TV, and balcony. (☎0984 27 952; fax 27 838. Wheelchair-accessible. Reservations recommended. Singles with exterior private bath €29, with interior bath €36; doubles €52; triples €67; quads €78. MC/V.)

Cosenza's cuisine is a crossroads of flavor, drawing on fresh prosciutto and rich mushrooms of the Sila forests, plentiful fish from the Tyrrhenian Sea, and the fruit of the region's orchards. For a proper meal, hike up the stone steps next to Teatro Rendano to reach **Taverna L'Arco Vecchio** ❷, P. Archi di Ciaccio 21. Outfitted in elegant wood, this versatile restaurant offers guests a range of salads (€6-8), pizzas (€3-10), and entrees in a garden dining area. Enjoy the large wine selection and the marvelous location by the city's old arch. (☎0984 72 564. Primi €4-8. Secondi €3-6.50. Cover €1.50. Open M-Sa 1-3pm and 8-11pm.

Reservations recommended. AmEx/MC/V.) For a cheaper, more filling feast, check out **Fire ❶**, V. degli Alimena 125 (off C. Mazzini), a hybrid pizzeria, *rosticceria*, and *tavola calda* serving up enormous portions at low prices. Order the *"pranzo completo,"* a two-course lunch with sliced bread and a cold drink (€7). Hurried patrons order the *pizza margherita* (€0.70) and a wildberry *granatina* (€0.70) to go. (☎348 08 18 210. Open daily noon-8pm, though hours sometimes vary. Cash only.) Owned and operated by the same family since 1803, **Gran Caffè Renzelli ❶**, C. Telesio 46, specializes in homemade sweets; their *varchiglia alla mocale* is a chocolate-covered almond treat still made by nuns with a recipe from the 1300s. The *gran caffè* is as pretty as it is powerful, with steamed milk, cocoa, and *vov*, an egg liqueur. (☎0984 26 814; www.grancafferenzelli.it. Mini pizza *rustica* €1. Gelato €2.60. Cover €0.50. Open daily 7am-midnight. Closed Tu in winter. Cash only.) For fresh, juicy produce, stop at **Cooper Frutta**, Vle. Trieste 33, a block from C. Mazzini; and for everything else at **Cooperatore Alimentare,** next door at Vle. Trieste 35. (Both open M-F 7am-8pm, Sa 7am-2:30pm.)

🏛️🎭 **SIGHTS AND NIGHTLIFE. Via Corso Mazzini,** filled with expensive shops and restaurants, is the place to see and be seen. Be sure to stroll through during the late afternoon, when the whole city comes alive. For an older, less crowded sight, cross Ponte Mario Martiri into the old city and head left up C. Telesio to reach the **duomo.** Alternatively, take bus #22 or 23 to P. Prefettura; facing away from P. del Governo, turn right down C. Telesio. Originally erected in 1140 with a Romanesque design, the church had to be entirely rebuilt in 1184 after an earthquake. When the *duomo* was reconsecrated in 1222 after yet another earthquake, Frederick II gave the city a gilt **Byzantine crucifix** containing a splinter allegedly from the True Cross. Now the cross is in the Galleria Nazionale at the Palazzo Arnone; call ahead to see it. Inside the *duomo* is Cosenza's most prized work of art after the famed cross—*La Madonna del Pilerio*, a 12th-century painting in the Byzantine style. It is in a Baroque chapel, the first to the left side of the church entrance. (☎0984 79 56 39. Open daily mornings and late afternoons.) Back in P. Prefettura, the **Teatro Rendano,** Calabria's most prestigious performance venue, was constructed in 1895 and destroyed by WWII bombing. It has since been restored to its former glory, and its plush interior has even showcased the likes of José Carreras. Reservations for non-*calabresi* or unconnected foreigners are extremely difficult to get during opera season (Oct.-Dec.); seats for theater season (Jan.-May) may be somewhat easier to come by. The Rendano also hosts regional performance groups during summer, with readily available tickets. (☎0984 81 32 20. For plays, tickets are sporadically available from 10am-1pm and 5-8pm on performance day. Tickets from €18, student discounts available.) While you're up there, peek inside the **Biblioteca Civica di Cosenza,** directly to the right of Teatro Rendano. This library houses extensive collections on the history of Cosenza and Calabria, as well as striking paintings and an Internet point. (Open M-F 9am-1:45pm, Tu and Th 9am-1:45pm and 3:30-6:15pm. Free.) To reach the fairy-tale manor on a hill, **Castello Normanno-Svevo (Norman Castle),** walk up the stairs to the left of the *teatro* about 200m, turn left at P. Archi di Ciaccio, and continue up the stairs opposite Taverna L'Arco Vecchio. Or, take bus 4T to the village and follow signs a steep 10-15min. climb uphill. The castle predates most of the *centro storico* and, in its ruined state, testifies to the city's tumultuous past. Originally built by the Saracens but refurbished by Frederick II after the *cosentini* tried to overthrow him, the castle offers postcard views of the city. The *castello* has since functioned as a barracks, a prison, and a seminary and is now open to all visitors. (Open daily 8am-8pm. Currently undergoing long-term renovations. Free.)

Revelers from surrounding towns flock to Cosenza, as it is the region's night-life hub. ▧**Beat Pub**, P. Duomo 4/6, right next to the *duomo*, is huge, with more than 50 Belgian beers. (☎0984 29 548. Beers from €2. Open daily 7:30pm-3am. AmEx/MC/V). **Planet Alex**, P. XI Settembre 12, off C. Mazzini, is a disco-pub in the new city that blasts dance music. (☎0984 79 53 37. Live music Th-F in winter. Open M-Sa 7am-2am, Su 5pm-2am. AmEx/MC/V.) Get a taste of the Emerald Isle at the **James Joyce Irish Pub**, V. Cafarone 19, a lively bar that's packed on weekends. (☎0984 22 799. Open daily from 8pm. AmEx/MC/V.)

CAMIGLIATELLO AND SILA MASSIF ☎0984

"Its nature will amaze you," states a billboard near the Sila Massif train station. Indeed, the 1850 sq. km plateau is an untainted landscape of fertile green mountains, prismatic lakes, and woods that burst with wildflowers in the spring. Covering the widest part of the Calabrian peninsula, Sila was once a single forest, exploited from its earliest days to provide fuel and material for the buildings of Rome. Today, the area offers some of Italy's most spectacular natural settings and a wealth of activities to satisfy intrepid explorers. Camigliatello (cah-MEE-lyah-TEH-loh; pop. 700), a resort town, offers bus connections and access to hikes and ski slopes, making it the best base for exploring Sila.

▤▨ TRANSPORTATION AND PRACTICAL INFORMATION. Trains to Sila-Camigliatello run from Cosenza (1hr., 9:18am, €2) but are often erratic; **buses** from Cosenza are usually more reliable (40min., 9 per day 6:30am-7pm, €2). Find bus schedules at the tourist office and buy tickets at **Bar Pedace,** the bar closest to the bus stop. Info on Sila and surrounding attractions, events, and trails can be found at the **Pro Loco** tourist office, V. Roma 5, uphill from the train station and bus stop. (☎0984 57 81 59. Open Tu-Su 9:30am-1pm and 3:30-7:30pm.) **Banca Carime** is at V. del Turismo 73. (☎57 80 27. Open M-F 8:30am-1:15pm and 2:30-3:30pm.) In case of **emergency**, call the **guardia medica** (☎0984 57 83 28), near the bus stop. The **post office,** on V. Tasso, is at the intersection of V. del Turismo and V. Roma, next to Hotel Tasso. (☎0984 57 80 76. Open M-F 8am-1:30pm, Sa 8am-12:30pm.) **Postal Code:** 87052.

▥▢ ACCOMMODATIONS AND FOOD. Hotel Meranda ❸, V. del Turismo 29, offers clean modern rooms in a secluded area just off the main road. Facilities include an elegant restaurant and *discoteca*, plus TV, telephone, heating, and A/C in every room. Prices rise during ski season. (☎0984 57 80 22; fax 57 92 93. Breakfast included. Singles €30-60; doubles with half pension €48-65, full pension €53-70. Extra bed €35-52. AmEx/MC/V.) Buses run from Camigliatello to campground **La Fattoria ❶**, 54.5 km from Camigliatello, which boasts a pizzeria, bowling alley, and minigolf course. (☎0984 57 83 64. Tent provided. €5.60 per person. Cash only.) The classy **Hotel Cristallo ❸**, V. Roma 91, has 43 rooms with private bath and seven two-room apartments for families, as well as a large conference room, restaurant, stylish *discoteca*, and games rooms. (☎0984 57 80 13; www.hotelcristallosila.it. Singles €35-55; doubles €55-85. AmEx/MC/V.)

▧**Le Tre Lanterne ❸**, V. Roma 142, is a popular spot specializing in Sila's famous porcini mushrooms. (☎0984 57 82 03. Pizza from €3.50. Primi €6-8. Secondi €8-12. Cover €1.50. Open Tu-Su noon-3pm and 7-11pm. AmEx/MC/V.) Dine by lantern light at Ristorante Hotel Lo Sciatore ❸, V. Roma 128, where patrons savor creamy mushroom risotto in a dining room with a wooden ski-lodge feel. Starving patrons should ask about the ever-varying but always enormous *pranzo turistico* (€15), and oenophiles should examine the extensive wine list, provided they have some extra money. (☎0984 57 81 05. Wood-oven pizza €3-6.50, Sa and Su only. Primi €6. Secondi €7.50. Cover €1.60. Open daily 12:30-3pm and 7:30-10pm. AmEx/MC/V.) La Casa del Fungo ❷, on P. Misasil, just next door to Campanaro, sells locally-grown mushrooms. (Open daily 9am-8:30pm. Closed Tu in winter. Cash only.) Picnic grounds lie 10min. from the *centro*, up V. Tasso. There are a number of *salumerie* overflowing with cheeses, meats, and mushrooms, like Antica Salumeria Campanaro, P. Misasi 5, across from the post office (☎0984 57 80 15. Open daily 9am-9pm. MC/V.)

⊠ NIGHTLIFE. Bar Le Bistro ❶, V. C. Alvaro 68, off V. Roma and across from the bus stop, has it all. With six virtual slot machines, two driving arcades, billiards, and a foosball table, not to mention a variety of assorted liquors from Italy and abroad (from €2), this bar is your best bet for a good time. *Caffè freddo* (€0.70) is a favorite, as are the sweet and salty snack offerings. (☎0984 06 807 68. Open daily 3pm-midnight. Cash only. A local hot spot known for its subdued atmosphere and mouth-watering *cioccolata bianca* (€0.80), Bar Pantusa ❶, V. Roma 202, also has a large selection of low-priced alcohol, ice cream, and snacks. (☎0984 57 84 59. Open 1-9pm. Cash only.).

> **MENACING MUSHROOMS.** When exploring the Parco Nazionale di Calabria, think twice before taking home any of the region's famous wild mushrooms. While the *funghi porcini* are both edible and delicious, other species range from mildly poisonous to lethally toxic. The safest way to enjoy Silan mushrooms is to purchase them in local shops or restaurants.

▟⚞ OUTDOOR ACTIVITIES AND SKIING. Come winter, there's plenty of snow at the **Tasso Monte Curcio Ski Trail**, 2km from town up V. Roma and left at Hotel Tasso. Go right at the fork in the road. In winter, minibuses leave for the trailhead from Camigliatello's bus stop. Buy tickets on board. Though Tasso offers 35km of cross-country skiing, it has only 2km of downhill trails. (☎0984 57 81 36 or 57 80 37. When snow is on the ground, lifts are open daily 9am-4:30pm. Round-trip lift ticket €4, weekends €5; day pass €15/20.) The Sci Club Camigliatello, V. Roma next door to Pro Loco, offers lessons at low prices (www.sciclubcamigliatello.it.) Master skier Fiorino Spizzirri offers both individual and group lessons through his **Scuola Italiana Sci Camigliatello**, V. del Turismo 11 (☎328 95 709 93; www.incamigliatello.it.) Getting to the ⊠Parco Nazionale di Calabria (☎0984 57 97 57), 10km northwest, is tricky, but well worth it. Just two Autolinee Scura (☎0984 31 324) buses head into the park daily, so plan your day accordingly and be prepared to wait. **Altipiani,** V. Roma 146 (☎0984 57 81 54 or 0984 339 26 42 365; www.inaltipiani.it), is a tremendous tourist resource that offers outdoor activities for every season. Hike through the park with a knowledgeable guide, mountain bike the trails with a group of riders of similar ability, hunt for edible mushrooms with experts, or study the lifestyle of wolves and other animals in the Sila forest with professional researchers. English-language group tours of the park are available year-round. Arrange times and prices through reservation. Altipani also rents bikes. (Bikes €12 per half-day, €18 per day. Snowshoes €13 per day. Cross-country skis €18 per day. *Let's Go* discount €3 on all full-day rentals. Cash only.) The ⊠**Greenwood Cooperative Society** (Società Cooperativa Greenwood), V. Pozzillo 21, conducts research in the park and urges *"turismo naturalistico,"* or tourism that helps sustain the environment rather than spoil it. Tourist services include guided treks on foot, mountain bike, and horseback, as well as night excursions and birdwatching. In addition, Greenwood uses volunteers to help with ecological studies and research, such as a full week of studying and tracking wolves with

GPS devices and topographic maps (€350 to cover food, camping, and research supplies). These studies change every season, so explore the Greenwood website to see what's coming up on the ever-expanding environmentally friendly horizon. (☎0984 44 55 26; www.scgreenwood.it. Reservations required.)

PRAIA A MARE ☎0985

Although Praia a Mare (PRY-ah A MAR-eh) has only 6280 year-round residents, come summer, vacationing Italians swarm this beach town and cause the population to swell dramatically. Largely undiscovered by foreigners, this peaceful hamlet boasts glistening sands, cliff diving, and a popular philosophy of repose not found in any major northern city. Home to both the natural beauty of Isola Dino and the non-stop parties of the *Festa di Santa Maria della Grotta*, Praia offers something for everyone. Those who make the trip to lovely Praia often end up staying longer than expected—only to return as soon as possible.

 TRANSPORTATION AND PRACTICAL INFORMATION. The best way to reach Praia is by train. **Trains** depart from the Praia station for: Cosenza (2hr., 16 per day, €7); Naples (3hr., 14 per day, €9); Reggio di Calabria (3hr., 20 per day, €14); Rome (3-5hr., 12 per day, €30). For **taxis**, call ☎338 76 49 71. The best way to get around town is by **bike**: rentals are available at **Bike Motor Points**, P. Italia. (☎0985 72 126. €10 per day.) Praia basically consists of three main streets that run parallel to the ocean. **Via Roma** is the first street outside the train station; next is **Via C. P. Longo**, which becomes **Via L. Giuguie** and the main avenue through town. After that is the **lungomare**, which follows the ocean all the way to the beautiful beaches of Fiuzzi. For maps and info on events in town head to the **IAT tourist office**, V. Amerigo Vespucci 12. (☎0985 72 322. Open daily 8am-8pm.) For currency exchange and an **ATM** right off the main street, go to **Banca di Napoli**, V. della Libertà 14. (☎0985 72 071. Open daily 7am-2pm.) In an emergency, call the **carabinieri** (☎0985 72 020). A pharmacy, **Farmacia Nappi**, can be found at V. C. P. Longo 51. (☎0985 72 009. Open daily 8am-8pm.) **Internet** with free Wi-Fi can be found at the **Museo Communale** on V. Verdi. (☎0985 77 020. Open M-F 8am-noon and 4-10pm, Sa 7pm-midnight.) The **post office** is located in P. Municipio near the town center. (Open M-Sa 7am-1pm.) **Postal Code:** 87028.

> **TIP**
> **WHAT'S IN A NAME?** Praia a Mare also goes by the name Praja; both names show up on maps and train schedules. Trenitalia clumps the Praia a Mare stop with two other towns: look for Praja-Ajeta-Tortora.

ACCOMMODATIONS AND FOOD. Although prices in Praia skyrocket in August, a few budget bargains remain. With a fun community atmosphere, ▓**The Onda Road Beach Hostel ❶**, V. Boccioni 13, is the best bet for backpackers. Martina, Papa, and their dog Sylia welcome foreigners with open arms. The hostel has simple dorms and two doubles. The real deals are their incredible discounts on attractions such as rafting, paragliding, bikes, and the beach clubs. (☎34 70 73 61 69; www.calabriahostel.com. Free pickup from train station. Papa runs Isola di Dino boat tours for about €10 per person. Kitchen available. Breakfast and lunch included. Laundry €3 per load, free for stays longer than 3 nights. Reservations recommended. Dorms €19; doubles €50. Cash only.) For slightly classier digs right in the center of town, head to **Le Arcate ❹**, V. Filippo Turati 25. This modern hotel has large marble-floored rooms, many with balconies overlooking the main street. All rooms have bath, TV, AC, and phone. (☎0985 72 297. Breakfast included. Reservations recommended in Aug. Singles €45-76; doubles €60-150;

triples €75-225. Full pension required in Aug.) For a more intimate experience, the Calabrese hospitality at **B&B Al Vecchio Pioppo** ❸, V. Turati 77, is sure to charm. Four lavishly-furnished rooms offer private baths, AC, refrigerators, and TV. (☎0985 77 73 52; www.alvecchiopioppo.com. Singles €30-45; doubles €60-90. AmEx/MC/V.) Camping can be found a short walk from town near Fiuzzi at **La Mantinera** ❶, V. Giovanni Battista Falcone. With a pool, private beach, amphitheater, and restaurant, the campground truly deserves its self-proclaimed title of tourist village. (☎0985 77 90 23; www.lamantinera.it. Reservations recommended Aug. €4.50-14 per person, €14-97 per tent. Bungalows €330-1350 per week. Prices rise during *Ferragosto*. AmEx/MC/V).

While the eateries in Praia are generally overpriced, the restaurant at **Le Arcate** ❷, V. Filippo Turati 21, provides affordable upscale dining. Try their drink and pizza special for €5. (☎0985 72 297. Pizza from €3.50; dinner only. Primi €4.55-8. Secondi €6.27-14. Cover €1.50. Open 24hr. in summer. AmEx/MC/V). Also be sure to visit **Ciacco Caffè-Gelateria** ❷, V. C. P. Longo 1, the favorite spot in town to beat the heat with a rich gelato. Choose from over 20 flavors, including Nutella, (medium cone €1.50), which was voted best in its class for five straight years. (☎275 72 30 780. Open daily 7am-midnight, or whenever people stop coming. Cash only.) If you're being chased by a coyote, or just in a general hurry, grab a hot slice and a cold drink at **Road Runner** ❶, V. della Libertà. (Pizza from €1. Open daily 5-11pm. Cash only.) There are five supermarkets within the city center, as well as numerous vegetable stands and fish markets. The most convenient is the **Sisa** supermarket located at V. L. Giugni 37 right in the middle of town. (Open daily 9am-1:30pm and 4:30-8:30pm.)

◎◖ SIGHTS AND BEACHES. Just a few meters from the beaches at Fiuzzi lies the massive, craggy **Isola di Dino**, owned by the famous Ferrari family. Though a climb to the tiptop of the isle costs €7, the grottoes underneath are easily accessible by kayak, paddle boat, or motorboat. The truly brave can venture to a natural arch 10min. away by boat that accommodates 22m dives. Novices should not attempt this as serious injury can result! Those less inclined for savage leaps should snorkel in the water around the island. (Boat tours and all other rentals can be arranged at most of the beach clubs. Prices vary by season.) Home of the city's patron, the Blessed Madonna, the **Santuario Madonna della Grotta** is found in a large cave in the cliffs overlooking the city. Follow V. della Grotta up from V. L.

GIVING BACK

DIG IN

Italy may have more than its fair share of ancient artifacts, but most of them are kept behind glass. Travelers who want hands-on experience with ancient pottery should consider volunteering with the Mamertion Foundation, a non-profit archaeological group. The group is currently excavating Monte Palazzi in southeastern Calabria, where a Greek fort stood from the fifth to third centuries BC. While excavations have only just begun, Dr. Paolo Visona and his crew expect to find pottery, terra-cotta figures, and other treasure.

During minimum two-week sessions, volunteers learn how to excavate a site and sift dirt just like the pros. They work closely with Dr. Visona and his crew of students, gaining new information on the life of those who once called the fort home. The work is expected to be somewhat strenuous, but nothing that a budding archaeologist would find too hard.

While the job may be demanding, volunteers will enjoy the comfort of a three-star hotel with pool, and all their meals will be included. Though the work is technically unpaid, there is a US$1500 tax-deductible fee for each two-week session. Regardless of the price, the chance to become an actual archaeologist and work with artifacts—if only for two weeks—pays for itself.

The Mamertion Foundation, *9332 E. McGill Ct., Parker, Ontario (www. mamertiondig.org).*

Giugni. The cave itself houses an ongoing archaeological dig, a modern church, and, of course, the statue of the Madonna, which sits safely in a plexiglass case. You can only get up close and personal with the Virgin Mary by embarking on a guided tour. Legend claims that a 12th-century Christian sea captain chose this cave as the refuge for the statue after his Muslim shipmates, stuck off the coast of Praia, deemed it a curse. The Madonna was later discovered by sheepherders, who later founded Praia a Mare. The cave has been inhabited for the last 14,000 years and has provided archaeologists with a wealth of information regarding the lives and culture of the ancient settlements of Calabria. (For tours call ☎0985 72 061. Open daily 8am-8pm.)

Beaches run the length of Praia all along the *lungomare*, though the nicest ones are located at **Fuizzi** nearest to Isola Dino. Chairs (from €5) and umbrellas (from €5) can be rented from any of the beach clubs. Don't feel intimidated; the beaches are free regardless of the club presence. If sunbathing sounds too tame, **FlyTirreno** offers paragliding excursions. After driving 600m up into the nearby mountains, the pilot takes off for a 20min. flight over Praia and land on the beach directly next to Fuizzi. (☎347 55 70 595. Flights €70, Onda Road Hostel guests €40. Reservations required. Cash only.)

🎵🍸 NIGHTLIFE AND ENTERTAINMENT. Check out **Bar Perfetti,** next door to Bike Motor Points and directly across from Ciacco. The disco bar is the local hangout year-round, but it really fires up during high season, when the owners place a DJ outside, and revelers dance in the street until the sun comes up. When the music stops, cool off with a refreshing *cedrata* for only €2. (Open 7am-midnight Tu-Su, and until 4am in August. Cash only.) If a quieter drink sounds more appealing, visit **Bar Branca,** V. L. Giugni 48, which offers reasonably cheap prices and an assortment of alcoholic and non-alcoholic drinks. (Open daily 7am-1pm and 4pm-whenever people stop coming. Cash only.) Although Praia fills up during summer, it reaches critical mass on August 15 for the **Festa di Santa Maria.** Locals bring the Madonna down from the church and parade it by boat through the harbor. When the Madonna passes revelers on the beach, they light bonfires and ignite a week of festivities that brings thousands more visitors to the already overflowing town.

▶ DAYTRIP FROM PRAIA A MARE

🛶 LAO RIVER RAFTING. The Lao River was once used by the ancient Greeks to send messages quickly from Greece to Sicily. Today, rafters can rush through the very same rapids, pausing only to gape at natural wonders. Located deep within the mountainous interior of Calabria, the Lao River Valley remains largely untouched by man and shimmers with the natural beauty of waterfalls, wildlife, and ancient caverns. Although the river is cold, rafters will be adequately outfitted with wetsuits and rubber shoes and can jump in and float along for the initial phase of the trip. Rafters will brave a few rapids, but nothing overly strenuous; just make sure to hang on to your paddle! **Rafting Yahoooooo,** V. Marconi 11, in Scalea, runs 5hr. tours of the river and will drive guests to the valley from anywhere in Scalea or Praia. Feel free to bring along a camera, as tour guides offer waterproof cases. (☎333 72 58 276; www.raftingcalabria.it. Wetsuits provided. Reservations required. €65 per person, €40 for Onda Road Hostel guests. Group rates available.) While the rafting itself is over an hour by van inland, most of the rafting companies are based in nearby Scalea which can easily be reached by train from Praia. (10min., 15 per day, €1.80.)

SICILY (SICILIA)

An island of contradictions, Sicily's (see-CHEE-lee-ya) complex culture emerges from millennia of diverse influences. Every great Mediterranean empire since the arrival of the Phoenicians in 900 BC has left its mark here. A string of Greek colonies followed Phoenician rule, and even today, the island sports more Greek temples than Greece itself. Roman theaters, Arab mosques, and Norman cathedrals round out the physical remnants of Sicily's past. While Italian culture dominates modern Sicily, the separation with the mainland is far greater than the narrow Strait of Messina suggests. The ancient Greeks lauded the "golden isle" as the second home of the gods, but today it is known to many tourists as the home of The Godfather. The Mafia remains an unspoken presence in Sicilian society, but has lately been largely reduced to mostly petty crime. Regardless of her connotations, Sicily overflows with the rich cultural, culinary, and natural wonders that its position at the center of the Mediterranean truly merits.

HIGHLIGHTS OF SICILY

BASK in the glow of Byzantine gold at Monreale Cathedral near Palermo (p. 660).

INTERACT with archaeologists restoring the world's largest intact mosaic at Villa Romana del Casale in Piazza Armerina (p. 696).

SCALE Mt. Etna (p. 694) in the morning and party all night in Syracuse (p. 699).

COMMUNE with the sultry splendors of Pantelleria's azure-lapped shores (p. 721).

PALERMO ☎091

Both turbulent and exquisite, Italy's fifth largest city is an alluring mix of beauty and decay. A smoggy, gritty metropolis with over 1,000,000 inhabitants, Palermo's (pa-LEHR-mo) pace of life dispels any myth of sleepy Sicily; its racing stream of cars, buses, and scooters set the city's breakneck pace. Those who opt to slow down will be rewarded by Palermo's impressive sights and relics. While poverty, bombings, and centuries of neglect have taken their toll on Palermo, the city is slowly experiencing a revival. The 1993 election of an anti-Mafia mayor brought a temporary end to the Mob's knee-bashing control, and with political reform underway, Palermo is now left at peace, to work on restoring its many architectural treasures.

✈ INTERCITY TRANSPORTATION

Flights: Falcone Borsellino Airport (☎091 70 20 111), at Punta Raisi, 30min. from central Palermo. Prestia & Comande (☎091 58 04 57) runs buses every 30min. from P. Castelnuovo (45min.) and Stazione Centrale (1hr., €4.90). Taxis (☎091 59 16 62) charge at least €40-50 to get to town and are parked outside the airport. For trains, look for the "shuttle to trains" sign. Free shuttles run every 30min. to and from the nearby train station at Punto Raisi. At the station, head left and down the escalator. Trains to Stazione Centrale run every hr. 5:40am-10:40pm (€5).

Trains: Stazione Centrale (☎091 60 31 111; www.palermocentrale.it), in P. Giulio Cesare. Ticket office open daily 5:30am-9pm. Luggage storage available (**Practical**

Sicily

Scilla
Villa Sem.
Reggio di Calabria
Villa San Giovanni
TO AEOLIAN ISLANDS
TO AEOLIAN ISLANDS
Messina
A18
Taormina
Giardini-Naxos
Acireale
Gulf of Catania
Augusta
Ionian Sea
Gulf of Noto
Avola
Capo Passero
TO MALTA
Milazzo
A20
Oliveri
Tindari (Tyndaris)
Patti
Linguaglossa
▲ *Mt. Etna* 3340m
Paternò
Catania
Vizzini
Palazzolo Acreide
Syracuse
Noto
Capo d'Orlando
Randazzo
Bronte
Adrano
A198
Lago di Ogliastro
Cattagirone
Ragusa
Comiso
Modica
Tyrrhenian Sea
Sto Stefano di Camastra
Lago di Pozzillo
Piazza Armerina
Niscemi
Gela
Gulf of Gela
Cefalù
Enna
Pergusa
Villa Romana del Casale
Caltanissetta
Licata
25 miles
25 kilometers
0
0
Termini Imerese
A19
Canicattì
N
A20
Soluntu
Valle dei Templi
Agrigento
TO USTICA
NAPOLI, CAGLIARI
Palermo
▲ *Mt. Pellegrino*
Corleone
Ribera
Sciacca
Mediterranean Sea
Pantelleria
TO TRAPANI
Pantelleria
TO LINOSA, LAMPEDUSA
TO CAGLIARI
Monreale
A29
Lago Poma
Alcamo
Segesta
Salemi
Castelvetrano
Selinunte
Stromboli
Panarea
TO MILAZZO
Gulf of Castellammare
Riserva dello Zingaro
Scopello
A29d
Mazara del Vallo
Salina
Lipari
Vulcano
San Vito lo Capo
Erice
Segesta
Trapani
Marsala
TO PANTELLERIA
Filicudi
Levanzo
Favignana
Egadi Islands
Maretimo
TO TUNIS
Alicudi

Aeolian Islands
(see map p. 668)

(see map p. 668)

Information, p. 657). To: **Agrigento** (2hr., 13 per day 7:35am-8:15pm, €7.60); **Catania** (3hr., 2 per day 8:15am, €12); **Messina** (3hr., 11 per day 4:05am-8:30pm, €11); **Milazzo** (3hr., 17 per day 4:05am-8:30pm, €9.50); **Falcone Borsellino Airport** (40min., every hr. 5am-10:10pm, €5); **Rome** (12hr., 3 per day 7:30am-6:40pm, €42); **Trapani** (2hr., 8 per day 6:38am-6:29pm, €7.40)

SPARE SOME CHANGE. When purchasing train tickets at the Stazione Centrale, avoid using large bill; the machine only gives back change up to €4.50. If your change exceeds €4.50, you will receive a ticket credited to that amount that can be used in the machine at a later date.

Buses: All lines run along V. Paolo Balsamo, by the train station. Facing away from the tracks, turn right and exit with McDonald's on the left and the newsstands on the right; V. P. Balsamo is straight ahead, hidden by an army of buses. When purchasing tickets, ask exactly where the bus will be arriving and find out its logo.

Cuffaro, V. P. Balsamo 13 (☎091 61 61 510; www.cuffaro.it). To **Agrigento** (2hr.; M-Sa 9 per day 5:45am-8pm, Su 8am, noon, and 3:30pm; €7.20. Purchase ticket onboard).

SAIS, V. P. Balsamo 16 (☎09161 66 028; www.saisautolinee.it). To: **Catania** (3hr.) and **Catania Airport** (2hr.; M-Th 12 per day, F 14 per day, Sa 11 per day 5am-8:30pm, Su 7 per day 8:30am-8:30pm; €12.80); **Messina** (3hr.; M-F 7 per day 5am-7:30pm, Sa-Su 4 per day 9am-8pm; €13.70); **Piazza Armerina** (2hr., 4-5 per day 6:15am-9pm, €7.30).

Segesta, V. P. Balsamo 14 (☎09161 69 039; www.segesta.it). Buses marked "Sicilbus," "EtnaTransport," or "Interbus" to: **Alcamo** (1hr.; M-F 7-10 per day 6:30am-8pm, Sa 6 per day 6:30am-8pm, Su 11:30am and 8pm; €5.50, round-trip €8.80); **Rome** (12hr.; Th and Su from Politeama 7pm); from **Stazione Centrale** 7:15pm; €39, round-trip €70); **Terrasini** (1hr.; M-Sa 6 per day 6:30am-8pm, Su 11:30am and 8pm; €2.70, round-trip €4.40); **Trapani** (2hr.; M-F 25 per day 6am-9pm, Sa 16 per day 6am-8pm, Su 10 per day 7am-8pm; €8.20, round-trip €13).

Ferries and Hydrofoils:

Grimaldi Group, Calata Marinai d'Italia (seaport) on the waterfront (☎091 58 74 04; www.grimaldi-ferries.com), on V. del Mare, off V. Francesco Crispi. Ticket office open M-F 9am-1pm. Sporadic ferries to **Salerno** (€35) and **Tunisi** (€80). Call or check schedule online.

Siremar, V. Francesco Crispi 118 (☎091 58 24 03; www.siremar.it), on the last street before the waterfront, between V. Principe di Belmonte and V. Mariano Stabile. Ticket office open M-F 7:30am-12:45pm, 3-3:30pm, and 4-7pm; Sa 7:30am-12pm, 3-3:30pm, and 6:30-7pm; Su 7-8:15am, 3-3:30pm, and 6:30-7pm. Hydrofoils to **Ustica** (1¼hr.; daily 8:15am, 3:30pm, 7pm; €24). Ferries to **Ustica** (2¾hr.; M-Sa 9am, Su 8am; €18.35). Leave from Stazione Marittima.

Tirrenia, V. Molo Vittorio Veneto (☎09160 21 111; www.tirrenia.it), 100m from Grimaldi. Open M-F 8:30am-12:30pm and 3:30-8:45pm, Sa 3:30-8:45pm, Su 5-8:45pm. Ferries to **Naples** (10hr.; Oct.-June 8:15pm, July-Aug. 10am and 8:45pm; €35-80) and **Cagliari** (14hr., F 7pm, €30-60).

Ustica, V. Cap. di Bartolo (☎091 84 49 002; www.usticalines.it), runs hydrofoils twice a day to the Aeolian Islands. Ticket office at end of Stazione Marittima. Open daily 9am-1pm and 5-7pm. All Hydrofoils to: **Alicudi** (2hr., €20); **Filicudi** (3hr., €26); **Lipari** (4hr., €32); **Panarea** (3 hr., €37); **Salina** (3hr., €33); **Stromboli** (4hr., €31.30); **Vulcano** (4hr., €32).

ORIENTATION

Palermo's newer half follows a grid, but older sections near the **train station** form a tangled knot. The station dominates **Piazza Giulio Cesare,** from which two streets define Palermo's central axis. **Via Roma** runs the length of the old city, ending at V. Emerico Amari, to the right of the **Politeama.** On the left side of P. Giulio Cesare, running parallel to V. Roma, **Via Maqueda** meets **Via Vittorio Emanuele** at the **Quattro Canti;** and this intersection forms the *centro storico.* Continue up V. Maqueda to **Piazza Verdi** and **Teatro Massimo.** Turn right at P. Verdi on **Via Cavour** and go past V. Roma to reach the port. At P. Verdi, V. Maqueda becomes **Via Ruggero**

SICILY

Palermo

🏠 ACCOMMODATIONS
Hotel Ariston, 5
Hotel Regina, 13
Hotel Columbia
   Classic, 1
Hotel Concordia, 3
Bed and Breakfast
   Agata, 7

🍎 FOOD
Antica Focaccería
   San Francesco, 12
Il Mirto e la Rosa, 4
Margò Ristorante/
   Pizzeria, 9
Polli alla Brace, 17
Al Manar, 8
Al Carretto, 18

🍷 NIGHTLIFE
I Candelai, 10
Via di Mezzo
Librotéca, 6
Volo, 2
Whisky and Drink, 11

Settimo, which leads to **Piazza Castelnuovo** and the Politeama. From there V. Ruggero Settimo becomes **Via della Libertà** and leads to the **Giardino Inglese.**

🚌 LOCAL TRANSPORTATION

Public Transportation: AMAT city buses. Main terminal in front of Stazione Centrale, under a green awning. Tickets €1.10 per 90 min., €3.50 per day. Buy tickets from *tabaccherie*, or ticket booths. Pick up a **free transit map** from the tourist office or AMAT info booth. Most bus stops are labeled and have route maps posted. Palermo also has the Metropolitana **subway** system, but it's usually faster to take a bus or walk.

Taxis: Station office ☎091 61 62 001. **Autoradio** ☎091 51 27 27. **RadioTaxi** ☎091 22 54 55, in front of Stazione Centrale next to the bus stop.

🔢 PRACTICAL INFORMATION

TOURIST AND FINANCIAL SERVICES

Tourist Office: P. Castelnuovo 34, at the west end of the *piazza* (☎091 60 58 351; www.palermotourism.com). Maps, informative brochures, and *Agenda*, a seasonal info packet. Open M-F 8:30am-2pm and 2:30-6pm. **Branches** at train station (☎091 61 65 914) and airport (☎091 59 16 98). Both open M-F 8:30am-2pm and 2:30-6pm).

Consular Services: UK, V. Cavour 117 (☎091 32 64 12). Open daily 9am-1pm and 4-7pm. **US,** V. Giovan Battista Vaccarini 1 (☎09130 58 57). Open M-F 9am-1pm.

Currency Exchange: At the central post office. **Banca Nazionale del Lavoro,** V. Roma 201. Open M-F 8:20am-1:20pm. **ATMs** on V. Roma and V. Maqueda; the Bancomat 3-plus ATMs are newer and more reliable.

American Express: G. Ruggieri and Figli Travel, V. Emerico Amari 38 (☎091 58 71 44). From P. Castelnuovo, follow V. E. Amari toward the water. Cashes **Travelers Cheques** for cardholders only. Open M-F 9am-1pm and 4-7pm, Sa 9am-1pm.

LOCAL SERVICES

Luggage Storage: In the train station, track #8. €3.90 per bag for 1st 5hr., €0.60 per each additional hr. up to 12hr., €0.20 per each additional hr. thereafter. Open daily 7am-11pm.

Laundromat: L'Oblio, V. Volturno 62 (☎091 333 80 32 82). 1 block west of Teatro Massimo. Wash and dry €8. Detergent included. Open M-F 9am-7pm, Sa 9am-3pm.

EMERGENCY AND COMMUNICATIONS

Police: V. Dogali 29 (☎091 69 54 111).

Pharmacy: Lo Cascio, V. Roma 1 (☎091 61 62 117). Look for green cross near the train station. Open daily midnight-1pm and 4:30pm-midnight. **Di Naro,** V. Roma 207 (☎091 58 58 69), on the right after V. V. Emanuele. Open M-F 8:30am-1pm and 4:30-8pm.

Hospital: Policlinico Universitario, V. del Vespro 147 (☎091 65 51 111).

Internet: Among a multitude of Internet points scattered around the city, the best is **Centro Internet Point,** V. Maqueda 304 (☎091 61 13 576), with 7 fast computers. €0.50 per 15min., €2 per hr.; 15min. minimum.

Post Office: V. Roma 322 (☎091 75 39 392). Massive white-columned building 5 blocks up V. Roma, past V. V. Emanuele. Open M-F 8am-1:30pm, Sa 8am-12:30pm. Branch at Stazione Centrale (☎09180 31 60), next to track 1. Open M-F 8am-6:30pm, Sa 8am-12:30pm. **Postal Code:** 90100.

🏠 ACCOMMODATIONS

When it comes to finding a place to stay, Palermo is pricey. For the sake of comfort and, more importantly, safety, plan on spending a little more in Palermo.

🏨 **Hotel Regina,** V. V. Emanuele 316 (☎091 61 14 216; www.hotelreginapalermo.it), at the intersection of V. Maqueda and V. V. Emanuele, across from Hotel Centrale. 18 no-frills rooms at the best price in town. All have fan; some have balconies. Beach passes available. Curfew midnight. Credit card required for reservation. Singles €28; doubles €54, with bath €64. AmEx/MC/V. ❷

🏨 **Hotel Ariston,** V. Mariano Stabile 139, 6th fl. (☎091 33 24 34; www.aristonpalermo.it). Walk on V. Roma 4 blocks past V. Cavour, or take bus #122 from the station, and get off before V. E. Amari. Between Teatro Massimo and the Politeama. Bright rooms with modern art. All have bath, A/C, TV, safe, and free Wi-Fi. Book in advance. 1st night paid with reservation. Singles €40-49; doubles €50-69; triples €70-85. AmEx/MC/V. ❸

Bed and Breakfast Agata, V. Roma 188 (091 61 16 581 or 347 91 19 815; www.bbagata.it). Hidden B&B offers 20 rooms with high ceilings and original paintings, as well as A/C, TV, phone, and dresser. Breakfast included. Singles €35; doubles €45-50; triples €75-90; quint €100. Student discount 20% for stays longer than 2 nights. MC/V. ❸

Hotel Columbia Classic, V. del Celso 31 (☎/fax 091 61 13 777; www.hotelcolumbiapalermo.com). Although it doesn't look like much from the outside, the inside is a different story—white tiles, sparkling chandeliers, marble stairs, and glass countertops make for a fancy abode. Large rooms come with A/C, private bath, TV, free Wi-Fi, phone, minifridge, and safe. Breakfast area, minibar, and panoramic terrace overlooking Palermo's historical center. Singles €35-45; doubles €65-85. MC/V. ❸

Hotel Concordia, V. Roma 72, 4th fl. (☎091 62 30 635; www.concordiahotel.info). Midway between the Quattrocanti and the train station on a main shopping thoroughfare, Hotel Concordia offers 13 individually decorated rooms with private bath, A/C, satellite TV, fridge, phone, and desk. Breakfast included. Singles €40-50; doubles €70-90; triples €90-100; quad suite €100-110. AmEx/MC/V. ❸

SICILIAN STREET SMARTS. Be careful in Palermo. The city can feel deserted at any time of the day, and some of the streets, particularly in the helter-skelter old city, south of Teatro Massimo, can be hard to navigate. When possible, stay on main streets: Via Roma, Via Maqueda, Via Ruggero Settimo, Via della Libertà, and Via Vittorio Emanuele. These straight thoroughfares will keep you on track, and the steady stream of traffic is reassuring.

◖ FOOD

The best restaurants in town are between Teatro Massimo and the Politeama. Palermo's three bustling food markets provide fresher and more interesting selections than most supermarkets. **Ballarò** dots V. Maqueda and V. V. Emanuele, while **Capo** covers the streets behind Teatro Massimo. **Vucciria,** in the area between V. V. Emanuele and P. San Domenico, completes the trio. All are open Monday through Saturday during daylight hours. Try the *Palermitano* specialty *cassata*, a sweet ricotta pastry. If you don't feel like haggling, head to **Supermercato GS,** Salita Partanna 1. From P. Marina, with Villa Garibaldi on your left, walk straight toward Chiesa di. S. Maria dei Miracoli and turn right when you get there. (Open M-Sa 8:30am-8:30pm. MC/V.)

🍽 **Margò Ristorante/Pizzeria,** P. Sant'Onofrio 3 (☎091 61 18 230). Follow Discesa dei Giovenchi, away from the intersection of V. Maqueda and V. Bari. Taste the best pizza in town (€4-8) or the specialty *ravioli di cernia, spada, e crema di asparagi* (with grouper, swordfish, and cream of asparagus; €8.50). Primi €5.50-9. Secondi €7.50-15. Cover €2. Open Tu-Su 8pm-midnight. AmEx/MC/V. ❸

Al Carretto, Salita Artele 5 (☎091 58 57 85), behind Palermo's Cathedral. Family-style Sicilian fare reminiscent of the Middle Ages. Diners enjoy plates like spaghetti *Vesuvio* (with swordfish, shrimp, and tomatoes; €9) and specialty *risotto ai frutti di mare* (€10) amidst depictions of battling knights and dragons, or under white umbrellas next to the church. 28 styles of pizza €5-7. Antipasti €2-6. Primi €8-10. Secondi €10-15. Salads €4-6. Cover €2. Open daily 10am-3pm and 7pm-midnight. AmEx/MC/V. ❸

Polli alla Brace, C. Tukory 54 (☎091 65 17 023). Follow C. Tukory for 5 minutes from the train station and look to the left. Polli is the best bet in the area for a filling meal at a cheap price. For €5 they offer half of a rotisserie chicken and a heaping selection of Italian sides—more than enough for 2 people. Open daily 5:30-10:30pm. Cash only. ❶

Antica Focacceria San Francesco, V. Alessandro Paternostro 58 (☎09132 02 64). From V. Roma, take V. V. Emanuele toward the port and turn right. This expansive *focacceria* has served delighted patrons in a secluded *piazza* since 1834. Behind the counter sits an infamous vat of *milza* (spleen). While the brave can try it in a *panino* or with *maritata* cheese (€2), the rest can choose from 2 separate menus: 1 features standard Italian fare, the other international cuisine. Complete vegetarian dinner (*panelle, taboulè, involtini di melanzane, cannolo,* drink; €12). 19 salads from €4. Primi €6-12. Secondi €6-18. Cover €1-4. Open daily 12-3:30pm and 6pm-midnight. AmEx/MC/V. ❷

Al Manar, V. S. Isidoro 23 (☎091 32 76 03). Tunisia and Italy unite here, where seafood takes center stage. Try the *couscus con pesce, carne, e verdura* (€8), or go for the swordfish *spiedino manar* (€10). Pizza options include the vegetarian (€5) and the Chef's Specialty (€7), with calamari. Antipasti €3-6. Primi €7-9. Secondi €7-14. Contorni €3-5. Open Tu-Su 11:30am-3pm and 7-11pm. M 11:30am-3pm. AmEx/MC/V. ❷

Il Mirto e la Rosa, V. Principe di Granatelli 30 (☎091 32 43 53; info@ilmirtoelarosa.com). Helpful owner serves traditional fare, including house specialty, *polpette di melanzane* (fried eggplant balls; €5). Primi €7-10. Secondi €6-15. *Menù* €13-21. Open M-Sa 12:30-3pm and 7:30-11pm. AmEx/MC/V. ❷

◐ SIGHTS

Ancient glory, centuries of neglect, and heavy bombing during WWII have made Palermo a city of deteriorated splendor, where ancient and modern ruins stand side-by-side. For much of the 20th century, corrupt politicians and Mafia activity diverted funds and attention from dilapidated landmarks, but recent political changes have made promising strides toward cleaning and rebuilding.

PALERMO FOR POCKET CHANGE. Sightseeing in Palermo can leave you with a bill that makes the Byzantine mosaics look cheap. If you're planning to visit several sights, consider an all-in-one pass from the ticket office of any major museum. Good for 2 days, the passes open the doors to multiple sights at reduced prices. For details on rates and specific deals, go to the tourist office and ask for the free guide, *Palermo e Provincia.*

▨ **TEATRO MASSIMO.** Constructed between 1875 and 1897, the Neoclassical Teatro Massimo is the second-largest indoor stage in Europe, so big that real horses and elephants were used in a production of *Aida.* After 30 years of renovation, the theater reopened for its 100th birthday in 1997. Rumor has it that the restoration was prolonged by Mafia feuding, not by artistic debates. (Incidentally, it was here that Francis Ford Coppola shot the climactic scene in *The Godfather: Part III.*) Guided tours allow visitors to repose in the VIP guest box and view the beautiful Murano flower light fixtures. Operas, plays, and ballets are performed here all year (student discounts available), while the **Festival della Verdura** brings famous performers in July. For this month only, shows move from the Massimo to nearby Villa Castelnuovo. *(On P. Verdi. From Quattro Canti walk up V. Maqueda. ☎ General info 800 65 58 58, tour info 091 60 90 831, box office 091 60 53 580; www.teatromassimo.it. Open Tu-Su 10am-3pm. No entry during rehearsals. 25 min. tours every 30min. in English, French, and German. €5, under 18 or over 65 €3, under 6 free.)*

MONREALE. Palermo's greatest golden treasure isn't in Palermo, but in little Monreale, 8km from the city. The extraordinary Cattedrale di Monreale is an example of Sicilian Norman architecture, a mixture of Arabic and local styles on the northern template. The interior is a masterpiece of Byzantine design; the mystical flavor of the locale is emphasized by the minimal light from the cathedral's windows. Its walls glisten with 6340 sq. m of gold mosaics, the largest display of Byzantine religious art outside the Hagia Sofia. The series of panels over the main altar depicts the massive Christ Pantocrator. Every few minutes someone pays €1 to activate electric lighting in a portion of the church, and the sudden illumination is startling. The Old Testament narrative begins with Genesis at the upper left of the central aisle and continues clockwise with images of Adam and Eve. The quiet **cloister** offers a contrast to the cathedral's solemn shadows. The interior columns are ringed with 228 paired Sicilian columns, alternating with ones decorated by Arabic tiles. Each capital is constructed in Greco-Roman, Islamic, Norman, Romanesque, and Gothic styles. A balcony along the cathedral's apse looks over the cloisters to all of Palermo. Two doors down from the cloister is the entrance to tranquil **gardens.** *(Bus #389 leaves from Palermo's P. Indipendenza for Monreale's P. Vittorio Emanuele. 30min., 3 per hr., €1.10. To get to P. Indipendenza, take bus #109 or 318 from Palermo's Stazione Centrale. Tourist info (☎09164 04 413) to the left of the church. Cathedral open daily 8am-1pm and 2:30-6:30pm. Reduced hours Nov.-Apr. Modest dress required. Free. Balcony open M-Sa 9-12:30pm and 2:30-5:15pm, Su 2:30-5:15pm. €1.50. Tesoro open M-Sa 9am-12:45pm and 2:30-6:15pm, Su 2:30-6:15pm. €1.50. Cloister open daily 9am-6:30pm. €6. Under 10 and over 65 free.)*

SAVE MONEY. The courtyard adjoining the Cattedrale di Monreale charges a steep €6 entry fee. Unless you're an architecture aficionado or especially interested in Doric, Corinthian, and Ionic columns, consider viewing the garden from the terrace of the cathedral (€1.50).

PALERMO'S CATHEDRAL. As a part of their ongoing rivalry, the leaders of Palermo and Monreale competed to construct the most beautiful church. Although many consider Monreale's mosaics to be superior, Palermo's cathedral is still awe-inspiring. Renovated from the 13th to 18th centuries, this structure's exterior shows various styles butting heads. Arabic columns, Norman turrets, and an 18th-century dome crowd the facade and walls. Note the Qur'an inscription on the first left column before the entrance; in 1185 the *palermitano* archbishop chose to plunk his cathedral down on top of a mosque, and this column was part of its stonework. The interior is dominated by saint-lined arches and carved rock walls. The neighboring **archbishop's palace** now serves as the Diocesan Museum of Palermo, and can be visited on the same ticket. *(On V. V. Emanuele. ☎09133 43 73. Cathedral open M-Sa 7am-7pm, Su 8am-1pm and 4-7pm. Treasury and crypt open M-Sa 9:30am-1:30pm and 2:30-5:30pm. Archbishop's museum open Tu-F 9:30am-1:30pm, Sa 10am-6pm, Su 9:30am-1:30pm. Admission €5, €2.50 treasury and crypt only.)*

CAPPELLA PALATINA. This chapel, in the monstrous **Palazzo dei Normanni,** houses a smaller version of the Monreale mosaics. One corner to the far left of the altar was designed by local artisans; Norman kings imported artists from Constantinople to cover the remaining interior in gold and azure. Locally crafted Arabic mosaics complete the effect. Those who prefer this Christ Pantocrator over that of Monreale claim it is softer and more compassionate. *(Take V. V. Emanuele past the cathedral on the right and through the Porta Nuova; take a left just before P. Indipendenza. ☎091 70 56 001. Chapel open M-Sa 8:30am-12pm and 2-5pm, Su 8:30am-12:30pm. Closed*

Easter M. Tu-Th entire palace €6, chapel €4; Under 18 or over 65 €3; M and F-Su special chapel-only rate not available. Guided tours of upstairs Sala di Ruggero every 20min. in Italian.)

CATACOMBE DEI CAPPUCCINI. Over the course of 350 years, the Cappuchin friars preserved remains of over 8000 men, women, and children. Hanging from niches by wires and nails, and lying in glass-sided caskets, many are dressed in their finest and are in various stages of decay. Several notables are buried here—including several bishops and the painter Velázquez—but the most arresting remains are those of Rosalia, a three-year-old girl who lies in her own tiny glass box. *(P. Cappuccini 1. Take bus #109 or #318 from Stazione Centrale to P. Indipendenza. From there, hop on #327. Or, from V. V. Emanuele, pass P. Indipendenza, and turn right on V. Cappuccini, then right again on V. Ippolito Pindemonte. ☎ 091 21 21 17. From P. Indipendenza, about a 20min. walk. Open daily 9am-noon and 1-5pm. €2.)*

THE LEG BONE'S CONNECTED TO THE KNEE BONE. Travelers to Sicily will undoubtedly come across the Trinacria. The island's ancient symbol, an unusual combination of mythological references, consists of 3 legs bent at the knee, that radiate from Medusa's snakey mane. Famous for turning men into stone with her fearsome gaze, Medusa was in charge of protecting the ends of the earth, which in the days of ancient Greece meant Sicily. The sheaves of wheat represent the cultivation of Sicily's fertile soil, and the 3 legs stand for the 3 corners of the triangular island: Capo Pallor at Messina, Capo Passer at Syracuse, and Capo Lille west of Marsala. The leg bent at the knee was a Spartan symbol of power. The Trinacria is most often represented in burnished gold, the color of the sun.

MUSEO ARCHEOLOGICO ANTONINO SALINAS. Hidden in a quiet *palazzo* in the town center, this museum features an impressive collection of Sicilian archaeological treasures. Most impressive are several fine Greek and Roman works, including a large section of the **Punic Temple of Himera,** and the 3rd-century BC Greek **Ram of Syracuse.** Also not to be missed is the recently restored **Mosaico delle Quattro Stagioni,** which depicts the four seasons in a haunting mosaic. Other temple remnants include fantastic renditions of Perseus beheading Medusa and Zeus courting Hera. *(P. Olivella 24. From Teatro Massimo, cross V. Maqueda and head down V. Bara all'Olivella. ☎ 091 61 16 805. Open M, W, Sa 8:30am-1:45pm, Tu and F 8:30am-1:45pm and 3-6:45pm. €4.50, students 18-25 €2, EU residents under 18 or over 65 free.)*

QUATTRO CANTI AND LA FONTANA PRETORIA. The intersection of V. Maqueda and V. V. Emanuele forms the center of the old city at the Quattro Canti (Four Screens). Dividing the old city into four districts, each sculpted corner of this 17th-century *piazza* has three levels. The lowest level has statues of the four seasons; on the middle level are the Spanish viceroys who commanded Sicily and Southern Italy, and on the top level are the city's patron saints. P. Pretoria, down V. Maqueda, houses the Fontana della Vergogna (Fountain of Shame; also called Fontana Pretoria) adjacent to Teatro Bellini. The fountain got its name from irate churchgoers who didn't like staring at monsters and nude figures as they left Chiesa di San Giuseppe dei Teatini across the street. An even more shameful story explains its shameless size. In the early 16th century, a rich Florentine commissioned the fountain for his villa and sent his son to the marble quarries to ensure its safe delivery. In need of cash, the son sold the fountain to the senate of Palermo and shipped it to Sicily, bringing Albert Mobilio's words to mind: "Sicily is a world where deception is only frowned upon to the degree it lacks artfulness." *(630m down V. Maqueda from the train station.)*

SICILY

CHIESA DEL GESÙ (CASA PROFESSA). Nicknamed "Il Gesù," this green-domed church has a dazzling interior and Surrealist ceiling paintings of the Last Judgment, depicting figures with swords beating the unworthy into Hell and a black-clad man waving a pastel flag with "Jesus" written across it. WWII bombing damaged its courtyard and the Quartiere dell'Albergheria, leaving behind bomb-blackened facades. *(In P. Casa Professa, on V. Ponticello, across V. Maqueda. Open daily Sept.-July 7-11:30am and 5-6:30pm, Aug. 7-11:30am. No visits during mass. Free.)*

GALLERIA D'ARTE MODERNA. Recently moved from the foyer of the Politeama to the newly refurbished Piazza Sant'Anna in the historical center, this gallery showcases much newer art than that found in Palermo's churches and museums. The ground floor is dedicated to the great Exhibitions, with works by Francesco Lojacono portraying a new image of Sicily. Move up a floor to see realism in literary themes, and finish with 20th-century Sicilian works of symbolism and modernism. *(V. Sant'Anna 21. ☎ 091 84 31 605. Open Tu-Su 9:30am-6:30pm, last ticket sold one hour before closing. €7, students 19-25 €5, over 60 and under 18 free.)*

PUPPETS. There are no small parts, only small wooden actors. For 300 years, Sicilian-made puppets have taken the stage at the **Museo Internazionale delle Marionette,** which showcases over 3000 examples of Sicilian stage culture. Galleries also display puppets from across the globe; it's a small world, after all. *(P. Niscemi 5. Follow signs from P. Marina. ☎ 091 32 80 60; fax 091 32 82 76. Open M-F 9am-1pm and 4-7pm. Closed 1 week in Aug. 15. €5, under 18 and over 65 €3. Demonstrations on request.)* Catch a puppet show at Vincenzo Argento's **Opera dei Pupi.** Tall, armored puppets reenact the chivalric *Orlando e Ronaldo per la Bella Angelica* and other works. *(V. Pietro Novelli 1. ☎ 091 61 13 680. Shows Sa-Su 5:30pm. €10, children €3.)*

GARDENS. The city's fresh gardens and parks provide relief from Palermo's smog-filled urban jungle. The large **Giardino Inglese,** off V. della Libertà, is not a stiffly organized British garden as its name might suggest, but a paradise harboring picnickers. In summer, the park hosts concerts and carnival rides for children. Down V. V. Emanuele toward the port, the **Giardino Garibaldi** in P. Marina features enormous banyan trees. The large Parisian-style **Villa Giulia,** at the end of V. A. Lincoln, has flower beds and fountains. *(Open daily 8am-8pm.)*

MONTE PELLEGRINO. Monte Pellegrino, an isolated mass of limestone rising from the sea, is Palermo's principal natural landmark, separating the city from the beach at Mondello. Near its peak, the **Santuario di Santa Rosalia** marks the site where young Rosalia sought refuge from her marriage and wandered into ascetic seclusion. After dying there, she appeared as an apparition to a woodsman and told him to carry her bones in a procession believed to have ended the plague that had been destroying Palermo. The bones of Rosalia, who is now the patron saint of the city, can be found in Palermo's cathedral or on parade display every year on July 15. *(Take bus #812 from P. Castelnuovo. Buses every 1hr. 7am-8pm. Last bus back 7:30pm. ☎ 091 54 03 26. Open daily 7am-7:30pm.)*

ACQUAPARK MONREALE. Slip and slide at Sicily's biggest water park, enjoying water chutes, fountains, pools, and restaurants. Fun for the whole family, but it's not as cheap as the beach. *(Contrada Fiumelato, V. Pezzingoli 172. ☎ 091 64 60 246; www. acquaparkmonreale.it. Open daily 9:30am-6pm. €10-18, children 7-13 €7-12; under 7 €2-5.)*

🖺 NIGHTLIFE

Palermo's nightlife is as varied as the city's history. For info on cultural events, pick up *Un Mese a Palermo*, available at any APT office and in News-News. Piazza

Olivella, Via dei Candelai, and Via Spinuzza, are popular nightlife hubs where mobs of young *palermitani* flood the outdoor bars and dance floors every night.

I Candelai, V. dei Candelai 65 (☎333 70 02 942; www.candelai.it). Picks up around midnight. Sip Carlsberg *alla spina* and listen to local cover bands do their best Chuck Berry impression. DJs spin Top 40 hits Th-Sa nights. Open daily noon-3:30pm and 7pm-3am. Closed M in winter. Cash only.

Whisky and Drink, V. di Carducci 38 (☎320 14 11 405), 2 blocks west from P. Castelnuovo. Loud rock music and cheap drinks draw a huge crowd nightly to this popular local bar. Beer €1.50-3. Mixed drinks €3.50-4.50. Open M and W-Su 7pm-3am. Cash only.

Via di Mezzo Librotéca, V. Sant'Oliva 20/22 (☎091 60 90 090; viadmezzo@virgilio. it), from P. Sant'Oliva, walk toward Villa Fillipina, and Librotéca will be around the corner. The name stands for book+tea+coffee, and describes the vibe at this cafeteria-pub. Coffee and tea €1-2.50. Beer €3.50-4. Mixed drinks €3.50-5. Wine €3-4. Open daily 12-3pm and 7pm-1:30am. AmEx/MC/V.

Volo, V. della Libertà 12 (☎091 61 21 284). 2 blocks up from P. Castelnuovo, after V. Giosuè Carducci on the left. Dress to impress at Volo, where the Euro-sleek interior and elegant garden exterior are equally perfect settings for young singles to flit about. Mixed drinks €5. Happy hour with free hors d'oeuvres 6-9pm. Open daily June-Oct. 12:30-3pm and 6:30pm-1:30am. Closed M Nov.-May. AmEx/MC/V.

◪ BEACHES

Mondello Lido is a beach for tourists by day and a playground of clubs and bars by night. All registered hotels provide tickets that must be shown at the entrance. Otherwise, beachgoers pay €8 to set up camp in the area near the Charleston—or sit for free directly on the shoreline. Take bus #101 or 102 from the station to reach the Politeama and V. della Libertà, then bus #806 in the same direction to reach Mondello; the beach is beyond a tree-filled area known as *la Favorita*. Watch for the frequent vendors who wander the sand with all types of goodies. *Ciambelle* (donuts caked in sugar; €1) are an essential beach treat. Mondello starts summer a little early each May with the **World Festival** on the Beach, a full week jam-packed with sports, music, and shows right on the water. Call the tourist office for info.

▶ DAYTRIP FROM PALERMO

USTICA

Accessible by ferry or hydrofoil from Palermo. L'Agenzia Miletello, V. Capitano Vincenzo di Bartolo 15, next to Chiesa S. Fernando Re, is open daily 6:10-6:45am, 9am-1pm and 3:30-6pm (☎091 84 49 002; fax 091 84 49 457). Hydrofoils (1¼hr.; daily 6:45am, 1pm, and 5:15pm; €21.55) and ferries (2¾hr., M-Sa 5pm, €16.35) to Palermo. Orange public minibuses run the perimeter of the island, from P.Vito Longo (every 30min., €1). Many rental shops off P. Umberto I, the centro of Ustica, rent scooters (with helmet and gas) for around €20 per day. Try Servizi Generali di Isidoro, V. Spezeria 3 (☎338 28 45 718; www.servizigeneraliustica.it). Open daily 9am-1pm and 4-8pm. To get to town from the hydrofoil port, turn right, and head up the road until you reach the staircase with an arrow marked "Centro" and follow that to P. Umberto I; with your back to the stairs, P. Capitano Vito Longo will be up and to the right. To reach the town from Cala Cimitero, the ferry port, take the road uphill and turn left at the fork.

The self-proclaimed "diving capital of the world," Ustica (OOS-tee-ca; pop. 1300) has become a bustling tourist port with abundant outdoor and underwater activities. Hiking trails wind around the island's 9km scenic coastline and guided tours explore a prehistoric village and necropolis. The island's most spectacular attractions are arguably the ancient artifacts buried just below the water's surface, catalogued and labeled for divers to explore.

Boat tours are a great way to navigate grottoes along the coastline, including the waters of **Grotta delle Barche** and **Grotta Azzurra,** a nautical graveyard filled with ancient vessels. Small boat owners advertise cheap rides that circle the island; find them at P. Umberto I or at the port. Set a price before embarking; women traveling alone should join a larger group. The island's most popular activity, **scuba diving** off rocky coasts, is quite affordable. **Alta Marea,** on V. Cristoforo Colombo, runs dives from May to October. (☎347 17 57 255; www.alta-mareaustica.it. Boats leave the port daily 9:15am and 3:15pm. Single immersion €35, with full equipment €55; 6 dives €200; 10 dives €300. Diving class €330.) Once submerged, see the **underwater archaeological remains** of Roman anchors and *amphorae* (vases), part of Ustica's underwater archaeology experiment.

If you miss the last hydrofoil back to Palermo, your best bet for a night's accommodation is **Ustica Hotel ❸,** V. Cristoforo Colombo 1. Rooms all come with A/C and private bath; some come with a panoramic view. Breakfast included at the in-house bar. (☎091 84 49 796; www.usticahotelresidence.it. Doubles without view €55-95; with view €65-110. Extra bed €15-25. MC/V.) Satisfy your post-dive hunger at **Ristorante Da Umberto ❸,** P. della Vittoria 7, which serves local dishes like *polpette di finocchio* in *agrodolce* (€9) and "*spaghetti alla Giulietta*" (€8) in an outdoor dining area. (☎ 091 84 49 542; www.isoladi-ustica.com. Antipasti €7-10. Primi €6-8. Secondi €12-18. Contorni €4-6. Dessert €3. Cover €1.50. Open daily noon-3pm and 8pm-midnight. AmEx/MC/V.)

RENAISSANCE MAN. To experience the best Ustica has to offer, you need to know only one man: Gigi Tranchina. A lifelong resident of Ustica, Gigi is a one-man tourist office who knows everything about the island and will gladly coordinate hikes, scooter rentals, and diving trips. Head to **Trattoria da Umberto** to find Gigi himself, or check him out online at his websites: www.usticatour.it and www.isoladiustica.it.

CEFALÙ
☎0921

The Sicilian proverb "good wine comes in small bottles" captures the timeless nature of Cefalù (che-fa-LOO; pop. 14,000), whose sleepy, seaside qualities were featured in the Academy Award-winning film *Cinema Paradiso*. Dominated by *La Rocca*, the imposing fortification rising 278m above the old town, Cefalù is a labyrinth of cobblestone streets. The city's aging terra-cotta and stone buildings cling to the water's edge, just as tourist crowds congregate along the expansive *lungomare* (seafront). Be aware, however, that Cefalù's charms do not come cheaply: the city's reputation as a beach resort, as well as its proximity to Palermo, allow *pensioni* to charge whatever they please.

▐ TRANSPORTATION

Cefalù is best accessed by train; call the tourist office for a complete schedule. The **train station,** located in P. Stazione, offers service to: Messina (3hr., 12 per day 5:15am-9:40pm, €8.10), Milazzo (2 hr., 18 per day, €6.55), and Palermo (1hr., 33per day 5:15am-10pm, €4.70). Sommatinese, V. Cavour 2 (☎0921 42 43 01), runs **buses** throughout the city (from €1.70). Schedules are posted at the train station bar's window and are also available in the tourist office. **Taxis** are available in P. Stazione or by calling ☎0921 42 25 54.

⊞ 🛈 ORIENTATION AND PRACTICAL INFORMATION

From the **train station,** head right on **Via Aldo Moro,** which curves up to the city's biggest intersection. To the left, **Via Roma** cuts through the center of the new city. Straight and to the left, **Via Matteotti** leads into the old city, changing at the central **Piazza Garibaldi** into the boutique-lined **Corso Ruggero. Via Cavour,** across the intersection from V. A. Moro, leads directly to the *lungomare.*

Tourist Office: C. Ruggero 77 (☎0921 42 10 50; fax 42 23 86), in the old city. Brochures, maps, hotel listings, and transportation schedules. Open M-Sa 8am-8pm.

Currency Exchange: Credito Siciliano (☎0921 42 39 22), near train station, at the corner of V. Giglio and V. Roma. Open M-F 8:30am-1:30pm and 2:30-4pm. **ATM** at the **Banca di Sicilia** (☎0921 42 11 03 or 0921 42 28 90), in P. Garibaldi.

Police: ☎0921 92 60 11. Guardia Medica: Vle. Mazzini 8 (☎0921 42 36 23).

Pharmacies: Dr. V. Battaglia, V. Roma 13 (☎0921 42 17 89), in the new city. Open M-F 9am-1pm and 4-8pm. AmEx/MC/V. **Dr. Vacanti,** V. Vazzana 6 (☎0921 42 25 66), across the street from the post office. Open M-F 9am-1pm and 4-8pm. AmEx/MC/V.

Hospital: (☎0921 92 01 11), on Contrada Pietra Pollastra, outside city limits.

Internet: Capriccio Siciliano, V. Umberto I 1 (☎0921 42 05 50; capriccioso@libero.it). €3 for 30min. Open daily 9am-1pm and 3-9pm. **Kefaonline,** P. San Francesco 1 (☎92 30 91). €5 per hr. Open M-F 9am-1pm and 3:30-7:30pm, Sa 9am-1pm.

Post Office: V. Vazzana 2 (☎0921 92 55 40). On the right off the *lungomare,* 2 blocks off V. Roma. Open M-F 8am-6:30pm, Sa 8am-12:30pm. **Postal Code:** 90015.

🏠 🏕 ACCOMMODATIONS AND CAMPING

If you're planning on staying in one place for a week or more, consider renting an apartment from a local. Sealing the deal might take some haggling (and will often requires a basic knowledge of Italian), but it usually pays off in the long run—especially when hotel rates peak during July and August. Look for *"affittasi"* signs in the desired area of residence.

La Fenice Affittacamere, V. Bagno Cicerone 21, 2nd fl. (☎347 23 76 011), near the water. Recently opened. Bright rooms overlooking the ocean are Cefalù's best-kept secret. All come with private bath, A/C, and view. Communal kitchen and living room with satellite TV. English spoken. Breakfast included. Towel and linens provided. €25-35 per person. Cash only. ❸

Locanda Cangelosi, V. Umberto I 26 (☎092142 15 91), off P. Garibaldi. The private apartments are large, clean, and simply adorned. All come with fan and towel; some come with a balcony. Laundry €5 per load. Reservations recommended. Singles €25-30; doubles €35-40; triples €50-60. Cash only. ❸

Camping Costa Ponente (☎0921 42 00 85; fax 0921 42 44 92), west of Cefalù, on Contrada Ogliastrillo. A 45min. walk or short ride on the Cefalù-Lascari bus (round-trip €2.30) from P. Colombo. Swimming pool and hot showers included. July-Aug. €6.20 per person; €6 per tent; €5 per car. Sept.-June €5.50/5/4. ❶

🍴 FOOD

Seafood is undoubtedly Cefalù's specialty, but delicious, formerly land-dwelling cuisine is also easily found. Just off the *lungomare,* next to the post office on V. Vazzana, an **IperSidis** supermarket sells basics, including bathing suits. (☎0921 42 45 00. Open M-Sa 8:30am-8:30pm, Su 9am-1pm.)

🍨 Gelateria di Noto, V. Bagno Cicerone 3 (☎0921 42 26 54; www.gelateriadinoto.it), where the *lungomare* meets the old town. More than 40 flavors of some of Sicily's best gelato. Flavors include black cherry, mint cream, wildberry, *cassata siciliana*, and hazelnut, plus every traditional flavor found in lesser *gelaterie*. Some English spoken. Cones from €1.80. Open daily Apr.-Oct. 7am-1am. Cash only. ❶

Ristorante Trappitu, V. di Bordonaro 96 (☎0921 92 19 72). Offers filling food, including Sicilian sea bass (€14). Seaside seating. Enormous olive press in the middle of the restaurant. Some English spoken. Primi €6-17. Secondi €7-17. Open daily noon-3pm and 7pm-midnight. Cover €1.50. AmEx/MC/V. ❸

CAFFÈ, SICILIAN STYLE. In an attempt to combat the sweltering summer heat, Sicilians have devised a cool alternative to traditional Italian coffee. Called *"caffè freddo"* and available in most cafes, this popular concoction is a mixture of espresso, raw sugar, and ice.

La Brace, V. XXV Novembre 10 (☎0921 42 35 70). Cheap food served in a low-lit setting with jazz. Meat-lovers should go for the *chili con carne* (€8.50), while vegetarians can opt for *rigatoni al rustico* (€6.50). Antipasti €4.50-8.50. Primi €6-9.50. Secondi €6-13. Contorni €2.50-5. Dessert €3-5. Open Tu-Su 1-3:30pm and 7-11pm. MC/V. ❷

Al Vicoletto, P. Duomo (☎0921 42 01 81). Found in an alley next to Il Caffè Duomo, Vicoletto offers respite from the crowds in P. Duomo. Family-style dining, animated staff, and large portions. Sample the *casarecce "Al Vicoletto"* (pasta with tomato, shrimp, and zucchini; €10). 30 styles of pizza €5-10. Antipasti €4-10. Primi €6-10. Secondi €7-15. Service 10%. Open daily 10am-1:30pm and 6pm-11pm. AmEx/MC/V. ❷

👁 SIGHTS

La Rocca stands above Cefalù at the center of the city's history and offers breathtaking views. Take Salità Saraceni to Tempio di Diana, a 20min. uphill hike. From Diana, continue up for another, steeper, 20min. hike to Il Castello. From P. Garibaldi, follow the signs for *Pedonale Rocca* up V. G. Fiore to Vco. Macell between the fountain and Banco di Sicilia. Use caution, as the path is slippery when wet. Medieval fortifications lace the edges, while crumbling cisterns line forgotten avenues. The **Tempio di Diana** first acted as a place of sea worship and later as a defensive outpost. At the top of La Rocca is **Il Castello**, a military fort dating back to the Byzantines. Most remains date from the 12th and 13th centuries AD. (Gates closed 1hr. before sunset.) During the winter months, **Club Alpino Italiano,** Vicolo alle Falde 4 (www.caicefalu.it), coordinates hiking excursions in the area and yoga sessions up on La Rocca.

Tucked away in Cefalù's narrow streets is the city's *duomo*. It was constructed in 1131 after King Ruggero II promised to build a monument to the Savior if he lived through a terrible shipwreck. The dramatic structure combines Arabic, Norman, and Byzantine styles, reflecting the cultures of the craftsmen hired for its construction. Once a potential fortress with towers and firing outposts, it now protects the king's remains and stunning Byzantine mosaics. An enormous Christ Pantocrator mosaic surveys with glistening calm all who enter. The carved pillars of the newly opened cloister depict Biblical stories from Genesis to Revelations. *(Sanctuary open daily in summer 8am-7pm; in winter 8am-5:30pm. Free. Cloister open daily 10am-1pm and 2:30-6pm. €3, €2 per person for groups of 10 or more. Modest dress required.)* Stuffed alligator cases and ancient urns get equal footing in the **Museo Mandralisca,** V. Mandralisca 13. Local 19th-century art connoisseur Baron Mandralisca bequeathed his collection to the city; this included an array of medieval and early Renaissance Sicilian paintings by anonymous artists, including the centerpiece, the *Ritratto di Ignoto*, by 15th-century Sicilian master Antonello da Messina. The image is inescapable in Cefalù—it smirks at tourists from every postcard rack—and the actual painting is surprisingly lively. Upstairs, hundreds of strange shells and old coins shimmer behind glass cases, as well as a half dozen lamps of questionable taste. The lifelike stuffed birds, iguana, and porcupine in the final room will startle any visitor numb from staring at terra-cotta vases and Roman sculptures in the preceding hall. *(Opposite the duomo. ☎0921 42 15 47. Open daily 9am-7pm. €5, €3 per person in groups of 10 or more.)* For some maritime adventure, **Hippokampus Pesca Turismo** offers boat excursions off Cefalù's coast. Participants can admire caves, encounter dolphins, and immerse themselves in the job of a fisherman for a half-day. (3 sessions per day €45-50; includes lunch or dinner of fish, fruit, and wine.)

📷 🍸 BEACHES AND NIGHTLIFE

Mazzaforno and **Settefrati**, Cefalù's most attractive beaches, lie west of town. Take the Cefalù-Lascari bus (round-trip €3) from the train station or the Cefalù-Mazzaforno bus (round-trip €2.40) from P. Colombo. Settefrati boasts white sand, turquoise shallows, and free showers; it is crowded for good reason. The seven stones jutting out from the waves are said to have been placed in memory of seven brothers who died here while trying to rescue their sister from pirates. All the beaches are free, though renting an umbrella and lounge chair costs around €5. Easily-accessible beaches along Cefalù's lungomare near the city center include **Lido di Apollo, Lido Angeli del Mare,** and **Lido Pura Vida.** They all have soft sand, shallow water, and daytime crowds. To splash without sand, take a trip to **AcquaVerde,** a waterpark in nearby Capo San Nicola, which houses slides, pools, fountains, and a health spa. (☎0921 93 11 33; www.hotel-costaverde.it. Open daily 9am-6:30pm. Full day pass €15; half day €10.)

While nightlife is limited, there are a few good hangouts. Head to the open-air garden at **Be Bop Pub,** V. Nicola Botta 4, and sip on something (€2-5) beneath the oleander trees. From P. Duomo, head down C. Ruggiero, toward P. Garibaldi. V. Botta is two streets down on the right. (☎0921 92 39 72. Karaoke Th and Su. Open daily 7:30pm-3am.) With a great seaside location, **Murphy's Pub,** Lungomare G. Giardina 5, offers draft beers (€2-4) and a big-screen TV. Occasional live music during summer or karaoke depending on the crowd. (☎0921 42 25 88. Mixed drinks €4. *Panini* €3-4. Pizza €3.50-9. Open Tu-Su 7:30pm-3am.)

AEOLIAN ISLANDS (ISOLE EOLIE)

Homer believed this unspoiled archipelago to be home to the gods; residents deem them Le Perle del Mare (Pearls of the Sea). In summer, boatloads of visitors arrive from Milazzo to experience the magic of the rugged shores and pristine landscapes of the Isole Eolie (EE-so-leh Ey-OH-lee-yeh). Lipari, the central and largest island, has ancient ruins as well as serves as a perfect base for exploring the other islands. If staying longer, visit nearby Stromboli for its restless volcano, Panarea for its inlets and elitism, Salina for its sheer cliffs over cerulean waters, and Vulcano for its radioactive mud baths and the Great Crater, the long-extinguished home of Vulcan, god of fire. Far more affordable in the low season, the islands see a steep price hike in July and August. Summer reservations should be made well in advance, especially for more elite resorts.

⛴ TRANSPORTATION

The islands lie off Sicily, north of Milazzo, the principal and least expensive departure point. **Trains** run to Milazzo from Messina (30min., 21 per day, €3.10) and Palermo (3hr., 12 per day, €11.60). **Giuntabus** (☎090 67 37 82/57 49) arrives

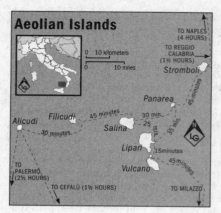

Aeolian Islands

0 10 kilometers
0 10 miles

TO NAPLES (4 HOURS)
TO REGGIO CALABRIA (1½ HOURS)
Stromboli
Panarea
Filicudi 45 minutes 30 min. 25
Alicudi 30 minutes Salina
Lipari 15minutes
Vulcano 45 minutes
TO PALERMO (2½ HOURS)
TO CEFALÙ (1½ HOURS)
TO MILAZZO

in Milazzo's port from Messina (45min.; M-Sa 16 per day, Su 1 per day; €3.60) and from the Catania airport (Apr.-Sept. daily 4pm, €10.50). From Milazzo's train station, the orange **AST bus** runs to the seaport (10min., every 30min., €1). **Hydrofoils** and **ferries** run regularly from mid-June through September to Lipari from Cefalù (3hr., 8pm, €27); Messina (2½hr., 5 per day 7:10am-6:20pm, €18.50); Naples (5hr., 1:05pm, €85); Palermo (4hr., 1-2 per day, €35); Reggio di Calabria (2hr., 4 per day, €24). Hydrofoils run twice as fast as ferries and far more frequently, but for twice the price. Three major hydrofoil and ferry companies serve the islands, all with ticket offices in Milazzo on V. dei Mille, directly across from the docks in the port. **Siremar,** V. dei Mille 18 in Milazzo, sends ferries and hydrofoils to the islands. (☎090 92 83 242; fax 090 92 83 243. Open daily 5:45am-6:30pm.) It also has offices in Lipari (☎090 98 12 193) and Naples (☎081 25 14 740). **Ustica,** V. dei Mille 23 (☎090 92 87 821; www.usticalines.it), in Milazzo, sends hydrofoils to the islands, and it also has an office in Lipari (☎090 98 12 448). Ustica recently bought SNAV Lines, but note that some booths still say "SNAV." **Navigazione Generale Italiana (NGI),** V. dei Mille 26, is a third option (☎090 92 84 091 fax 090 92 83 415) in Milazzo; V. Mariano Amendola 14 (☎090 98 11 955), at Porto Sottomonastero in Lipari. The following table lists ferry and hydrofoil info for both Ustica and Siremar. There is a €1.50 fee to reserve in advance that is not included in the fees listed here. Boats **frequently deviate from schedules,** so be sure to call ahead. Both offices have convenient portable timetable booklets—just ask for an *orario*.

TO	FERRY FROM MILAZZO		HYDROFOIL FROM MILAZZO	
	TIME	HIGH SEASON	TIME	HIGH SEASON
Vulcano	1hr.	7,9am, 6:30pm; €6.30	45min.	6 per day 7:50am-7:10pm, €12.50
Lipari	2hr.	7,9am, 6:30pm; €6.60	1hr.	17 per day 7:50am-7:10pm, €15.80
Salina	3hr.	7, 9am; €4	1hr.	3 per day 7:50am-7:10pm, €14.80
Panarea	4hr.	M and W-Su 2:30pm, Tu and Sa 7am; €4.50	2hr.	2 per day 7:50am and 2:25pm, €15.30

MILAZZO   ☎090

Visitors to Milazzo (mee-LAT-so; pop. 40,000) are all thinking the same thing: "What time does my boat leave?" Once upon a time, only a few boats left Milazzo's port daily. Now, ferries and hydrofoils zip to the Aeolian Islands and Italian mainland every hour. Welcome to Milazzo: get in, get your boat, and get out.

Milazzo gears itself toward travelers on the go, but food doesn't have to be rushed. Bars line the *lungomare,* and fruit vendors line V. Regis in P. Natasi and at the intersection with V. del Sole. Take a travel break at **Lo Spizzico ❶**, V. dei Mille 32, which offers *panini* and *calzoni* at low prices. (☎0272 04 60 837. Open 24 hours. Cash only.) **Blue Pub ❶**, V. Alessandro Manzoni 4, serves pizza in air-conditioned, decorative, Tex-Mex splendor. (☎090 92 83 839. Pizza from €3.50. Cover €1. Open M-W and F-Su 7:30pm-midnight. MC/V.) For a relaxed meal, **Ristorante Al Gambero ❸**, V. Cavour 5/7, has a large, covered patio overlooking the port. (☎090 92 23 337. Pizza from €5.50. Primi €6.50-9. Secondi €10-16.50. Cover €3. Open daily noon-3pm and 7pm-midnight; closed F in winter. AmEx/MC/V.) A large **Despar** supermarket, V. del Sole 20, provides necessities. (Open M-Sa 8:30am-1pm and 5-8:30pm, Su 9am-1pm. AmEx/MC/V.)

City buses and Giuntabuses arrive in **Piazza della Repubblica** across from the Agip gas station close to the port; the train station is a 10min. bus ride away. **Lungomare Garibaldi** runs the length of the port. Turn left down V. Francesco Crispi, right into P. Caio Duilio, and follow the signs to the **tourist office**, P. C. Duilio 20. (☎090 92 22 865; www.aastmilazzo.it. Open M-Sa 9:30am-1:30pm.) A **medical clinic** (☎090 92 81 158) is on V. F. Crispi, next to the **carabinieri** station. A **pharmacy**, Farmacia Vece, P. C. Duilio 4, posts after-hours rotations. (☎090 92 81 181. Open M-F 9am-1pm and 4:30-8:30pm.)

 SITTIN' ON THE DOCK OF THE BAY. Give yourself extra time when planning travel in the Aeolian islands as ferry schedules change daily and are only on time about 30% of the time.

LIPARI ☎090

Centuries ago, pirates ravaged Lipari's (LEE-pa-ree; pop. 10,000) shores. Today, boats and hydrofoils let loose packs of equally ravenous tourists, who pillage the island of overpriced T-shirts and other wares geared toward the foreign masses. They descend in swarms upon its beaches and wallow in its waves like listless merpeople; those who prefer the colors of the sea and mountains to umbrellas and skimpy beachwear hike to nearby private beaches. Inexpensive hotels, divine sunbathing, and excellent archaeological museums make this island an ideal launching pad for further raids in this archipelago.

▐ TRANSPORTATION

Autobus Urso Guglielmo, V. Cappuccini 9 (☎090 98 11 262 or 98 11 026), operates **buses** on most of the island. Ticket office open daily 9am-7:30pm (tickets also available onboard). Lipari island tours (€4) depart daily at 2pm (reservations required). De. Sco., V. Stradale Pianoconte 5, at the end of C. Vittorio Emanuele, rents shiny **scooters**. (☎090 98 13 288 or 368 75 35 590. €18-24 per day; Aug. €30-36. Gas extra. Open daily 9am-8pm. Cash only.) Steps away from De. Sco., Ditta Carbonaro Paola, C. V. Emanuele 21, also rents scooters. Prices are usually negotiable, especially if renting for more than one day. (☎090 98 11 994. €15 per day; Aug. €30. Open daily 9am-1pm and 2:30-8:30pm. Cash only.) For **taxis**, call ☎090 98 86 077 or 090 98 12 216.

▣ ▐ ORIENTATION AND PRACTICAL INFORMATION

The **hydrofoil** and **ferry** port are on the end of the promontory supporting the *castello* and museum. Restaurants and hotels cluster around **Corso Vittorio Emanuele**, the main thoroughfare, and **Via Garibaldi**, which runs mostly parallel to C. V. Emanuele around the base of the *castello*, and are accessible by large stone stairs; C. V. Emanuele ends at the docks. Purchase maps at *tabaccherie*.

Tourist Office: AAST, C. V. Emanuele 202 (☎090 98 80 095; fax 98 11 190; www.aasteolie. info). Info hub for all 7 islands. Ask for *Ospitalità in blu*, which contains helpful visitor info. Open M-F 8:30am-1:30pm and 4:30-7:30pm; July-Aug. also open Sa 8am-2pm and 4-9pm.

Currency Exchange: C. V. Emanuele is lined with banks and **ATMs. Currency exchange** available at **Banco Antonveneta** (☎090 98 12 117; open M-F 8:20am-1:20pm and 2:35-3:35pm) or at the **post office** (cash only). Some of the smaller Aeolian Islands have few or no ATMs; get cash before you leave Lipari.

Luggage Storage: At Ustica hydrofoil office on the port (☎090 347 997 3545). €3 per 12hr. €5 overnight surcharge. Open 8am-8pm.

English-Language Bookstore: Libreria Mimo Belletti, C. V. Emanuele 172 (☎090 98 11 282; mimmobelletti@tiscali.it). Small rack of varied English books, newspapers, and magazines. Open daily 9am-2pm and 4:30-11pm. AmEx/MC/V.

Laundry: Vico Storione 5 (☎090 98 13 177), off C. V. Emanuele. Wash and dry €4 per kg; 4kg min. Open M-Sa 9am-1pm and 4:30-8pm. Cash only.

Ambulance: ☎090 98 95 267. **Carabinieri:** ☎090 98 11 333.

Pharmacies: Farmacia Cincotta, V. Garibaldi 60 (☎090 98 11 472). Open M-F in summer 9am-1pm and 5-9pm; in winter 9am-1pm and 4-8pm. Posts after-hours rotation.

Hospital: (☎090 98 851), on V. Santana. At southern end of C. V. Emanuele, take side street between scooter rental places and turn right on V. Roma. V. Santana is the 2nd left. Open daily 8am-8pm. **Medical Clinic:** ☎090 98 85 226. Office 50m up V. Garibaldi from the waterfront. Open M, W, and F 8:30am-1pm, Tu and Th 3:30-5:30pm.

Internet Access: Internet Point, C. V. Emanuele 185. 7 fast computers. €2 per 15min., €3 per 30min., €5 per hr. Open in summer M-Sa 9:30am-1pm and 5pm-midnight, Su 6pm-midnight; in winter M-Sa 9:30am-1:30pm and 4:30-9pm. **Net C@fe,** V. Garibaldi 61 (☎090 98 13 527). 3 computers. €3 per 30min., €5 per hr. Open daily 9am-1pm and 4:30pm-midnight; in winter M-Th and Sa-Su 9am-1pm and 4:30 pm-midnight.

Post Office: Main branch for Aeolian Islands (☎090 98 10 051), on C. V. Emanuele. Open M-F 8am-6:30pm, Sa 8am-12:30pm. **Postal Codes:** 98052 (Canneto-Lipari); 98055 (Lipari); 98050 (all other islands).

ACCOMMODATIONS AND CAMPING

As soon as you step off the hydrofoil exit ramp, you'll be bombarded with offers for *affittacamere* (room rentals). These are often the most affordable way to enjoy the islands, and some of the best deals are listed below. Ask to see the room before accepting and always obtain a price quote in writing. Prices are often fairly negotiable outside of August, so try bargaining for a better rate.

Villa Rosa, V. Francesco Crispi 134 (☎090 98 80 280; www.liparivillarosa.it). From the port turn right away from the *centro* and walk until you reach a somewhat random gas station. Relax on your private terrace away from the bustle of C. V. Emanuele. 8 rooms with bath, A/C, fridge, and kitchen. Doubles €30-60. ❷

Casa Vittorio di Cassara, Vico Sparviero 15 (☎090 81 15 23 or 338 392 3867; www. casavittorio.com), off V. Garibaldi, near Da Gilberto e Vera. Look for sign leading to the end of the alley and ring the bell. Rooms vary from doubles with shared bath to 5-person apartments in an ideal location. Some have kitchen and sea-view terrace. Rooms €18-45 per person depending on season and length of stay. Cash only. ❷

Affittacamere Marturano, V. Mavrolico 35 (☎090 368 322 4997; www.enzamarturano. it), off C. V. Emanuele. 4 spacious rooms with bath, A/C, fridge, TV, kitchenette, and terrace. Reservations recommended. Doubles €50-85. Cash only. ❹

Affittacamare La Narda, Vico Ulisse 32 (☎090 98 80 431), off C. V. Emanuele. Several simply furnished rooms with shared bath and kitchen, conveniently located near the port and off the main thoroughfare. Singles €30; doubles €40-50. Cash only. ❷

Affittacamere Del Vicolo, Vico Ulisse 17 (☎090 98 11 066; www.affittacameredelvi-colo.it), off C. V. Emanuele. Only a few doors down from La Narda, this *affittacamere* also doubles as a restaurant, Trattoria del Vicolo. Bath, A/C, and shared kitchen; right near the port. Spacious doubles from €35-100, depending on season. Cash only. ❸

Baia Unci, V. Marina Garibaldi 2 (☎090 98 11 909; www.campeggitalia.it/sicilia/baiaunci). Campground near Canneto, 2km from Lipari. 10min. from beach. Self-service restaurant on-site. Open Mar. 15-Oct. 15. €8-15 per person with tent. Cash only. ❶

◪ FOOD

The island's renowned aphrodisiacs, *capperi* (capers), adorn many dishes, while local *Malvasia* dessert wine provides an equally sweet finish. Lipari's lip-smacking cuisine can get expensive, so head to **UPIM** supermarket, C. V. Emanuele 212, for a budget meal. (☎090 98 11 587. Open M-Sa 8am-9:30pm and Su 8am-1:30pm. AmEx/MC/V.) *Alimentari* on C. V. Emanuele sell fruit daily.

Da Gilberto e Vera, V. Garibaldi 22-24 (☎090 98 12 756; www.gilbertoevera.it). Famous for some of Italy's best *panini* with ingredients like prosciutto, capers, tomatoes, olives, mint, etc. Also carries tons of picnic supplies. Panini €4.50. Open daily Mar.-July and Sept.-Oct. 7am-4am; Aug. 7am-6am; Nov.-Feb. 7pm-2am. AmEx/MC/V. ❶

Rosticceria Take Away, C. V. Emanuele 150 (☎090 98 13 126). This local hotspot is perfect for a quick meal on the way to the port or upon arrival in Lipari. 30 types of pizza €1-4. Open Tu-Su 2-10pm. Cash only. ❶

La Cambusa, V. Garibaldi 72 (☎090 349 476 6061). Husband-and-wife team makes this trattoria feel like home. Cluster around outdoor tables with *liparesi* or retreat indoors to enjoy authentic Sicilian flavors. Pasta from €5. Cover €1. Open daily Apr.-Oct. 10am-4pm and 6pm-midnight. Reservations recommended. Cash only. ❸

La Piazzetta, P. Luigi Salvatore d'Austria 13 (☎090 98 12 522; fax 98 13 761), off C. V. Emanuele, next to Pasticceria Subba. Walls and menus boast famous signatures of satisfied celebrity clientele, among them, Audrey Hepburn. Elegant patio extends into a small *piazza*. Pizza €7.50. Primi from €5. Secondi from €8.50. Cover €1. Service 10%. Open daily noon-2pm and 7:45-11pm; closed Tu. Nov.-May. AmEx/MC/V. ❷

Ristorante Sottomonastero, C. V. Emanuele 232 (☎090 98 80 720; www.ritrovosotto-monastero.it). Centrally located. Specializes in Aeolian sweets. Pizza from €4. Primi €5-8. Secondi €5.60-15.50. *Menù turistico* €13. Cover €1.80. Open daily 7am-midnight; late July-Aug. 24hr. Kitchen open noon-2:30pm and 7-11pm. AmEx/MC/V. ❷

◉ SIGHTS

Lipari's best sights—aside from its beaches—are all in the *castello* on the hill, where a fortress with ancient Greek foundations dwarfs the surrounding town. In the vicinity is the **Museo Archeological Eoliano,** whose collection, explained in English and Italian, includes Liparite urns, galleries full of Greek and Sicilian pottery from the fourth and fifth centuries BC, and treasures from underwater exploration. The geological and volcanic section is devoted to the island's natural history. Walk up the stone steps to the right off V. Garibaldi; turn left at the Church of San Bartolomeo. (☎090 98 80 174. Museum open M-Sa 9am-1pm and 3-7pm. Last entry 1hr. before closing. €6, EU residents ages 18-25 €3, EU residents under 18 or over 65 free.) Next door, the tiny **Museo della Marineria e delle Tradizioni Eoliane** houses old fishing instruments and detailed descriptions of early Eolian culture. Knowledgeable guides are overjoyed to give tours and history lessons in Italian or English. (Open M-Sa 9am-12:30pm and 4-6pm. Free.) The **Chiesa di San Bartolomeo** is on the same hill. Built in the 12th century, it was sacked by Barbarossa the Turk in 1544. A new Baroque version, dedicated to St. Bartholomew, is done up in blue hues and topped by a master mural on the ceiling. Stratified Greek, Roman, and Stone Age ruins encircle the building. The park's centerpiece is a contemporary ancient Greek-style theater; ask at the tourist office for programs and ticket prices. Continue walking past the church to find a walkway that leads to Lipari's **harbor vistas.** (Both sites are across from the museum. Open daily 9am-1pm and 3-7pm. Free.) Many agencies near the port offer sightseeing tourist excursions to the other islands from Lipari. Check around for the best prices, which vary considerably by season.

🏖 🎵 BEACHES AND ENTERTAINMENT

From July to September, island **bus tours** (€4) run at 2pm from Autobus Guglielmo Urso (☎090 98 11 262/026) on V. Cappuccini. Reservations are required. A better way to see the coastline is from the water, aboard a rented boat from the hydrofoil port. For still better views, take the Lipari-Cavedi bus to the beaches of nearby **Canneto.** The pebbles are prickly and the sun scorching, so bring sunscreen and flip-flops. Rent a raft, kayak, or canoe from any of the boat rental shacks along the beach at V. Marina Garibaldi (€3-5 per hr., €13-24 per day) to explore the coves flanking **Spiaggia Bianca.** A few kilometers north at **Pomiciazzo,** pumice mines line the road. Farther north at **Porticello,** people bathe at the foot of mines where flecks of stone float on the water's surface. A beach closer to the port is **Porto della Gente.** From the docks at the end of V. Garibaldi, turn left on the *lungomare,* and walk up the hill. Turn right up the stairs and take the first left away from the hotel. Turn right on the next road, and follow it to the shore. These beaches provide views of Salina, Panarea, and Stromboli. For the best vista, take the Lipari-Quattropani bus (7:45, 9:30, 11:45am, 3:30, 5:30pm) to **Pianoconte** and head to **Monte Sant'Angelo.** The mountain path is narrow and overgrown, so ask for directions to avoid getting lost. For a relaxed evening, head to 🍸**Bar Luna Quinta,** V. Francesco Crispi 44, a safe haven for visiting mariners and local artists alike. With your back to the dock, V. F. Crispi runs along the water to your right. (Open daily 7:30pm-late. Cash only.) Summer fever reaches its boiling point (and surpasses the island's capacity) on August 24 with the **Festa di San Bartolomeo,** when parties and pyrotechnics rule.

VULCANO   ☎090

Visitors can usually smell Vulcano (vool-CA-no; pop. 4000) before they see it. The pungent island was believed to be the home of the Greek blacksmiths' god, Vulcan, and the keeper of the winds, Aeolus. Thought to have been the gate to Hell, Vulcano is now known for its volcanic craters and savage landscapes. The largest volcano is the active and heavily touristed Fossa di Vulcano. Geologists forecast an eruption within 20 years. Black beaches, bubbling seas, and natural sulfuric mud spas may make Vulcano seem abrasive, but these untamed natural phenomena usually end up winning over visitors.

🚍 TRANSPORTATION

Hydrofoils and ferries: Ustica ticket office (☎090 98 52 230; www.usticalines.it), directly off the port, next to Cantine Stevenson. **Siremar** (☎090 98 52 149 or 199 123 199; www.siremar.it) at the Porto Levante intersection. Hydrofoils to: **Lipari** (10min., 17 per day 6:35am-8:05pm, €5.80); **Milazzo** (40min., 14 per day 7:10am-7:50pm, €18); **Naples** (6hr., 2:55pm, €80); **Palermo** (4 hr., 7:15am and 4:05pm, €34); Panarea (1hr.,

7 per day 7:30am-6:20pm, €11); **Reggio di Calabria** (2hr., 4 per day 6:35am-6:30pm, €19.50); **Salina** (40min., 14 per day 7:30am-8:20pm, €10.50); **Stromboli** (2hr., 8 per day 7:30am-6:20pm, €18.30). NGI Biglietteria, on V. Provinciale, off P. Levante, sells tickets. (☎090 98 52 401. Open daily 8am-2pm, 3-5:30pm, and 11:30pm-midnight.)

Internal Transportation: Tindaro Scaffidi off the port on V. Provinciale, next to Ritrovo Remigio, runs **buses** (☎090 98 53 073). Infrequent buses run to **Capo Grillo, Gelso Beach, Vulcanello,** and **Vulcano Piano** from the port. Buy a ticket (€2) onboard.

Taxis: from the port call ☎090 339 579 1576 or 338 254 2181.

Bike and scooter rental: Noleggio da Paolo (☎090 98 52 112) and Sprint da Luigi (☎347 76 00 275), a block apart on V. Provinciale, have almost identical prices. Multilingual owners provide maps and other tourist info. Bikes €3-5 for 1st day, €3 per day thereafter. Tandem bike €6 per hr., €10 per day. Minicar €15 per hr., €35 per day, €30 each additional day. Scooters €15-25 per day. Prices jump in August. 18+ for anything with a motor. Paolo accepts AmEx/MC/V, Luigi is cash only.

Boat rental: Blob Oasi, Baia di Ponente (☎090 338 896 9690), on the Sabbie Nere. Lets everything from 2-person for €100 to 17-person for €350. Open daily June-Oct. 9am-7:30pm. Cash only. **Centro Nautico Baia di Levante** (☎090 98 22 197 or 339 337 2795), on the beach behind Ritrovo Remigio, near the hydrofoil dock. 8-person motorboat €100-200 per day. Gas extra. Open daily 8am-11pm. Cash only.

ORIENTATION AND PRACTICAL INFORMATION

Vulcano's casual atmosphere comes across in its lack of posted street names and address numbers. Frequent directional signs and arrows, however, make this pedestrian island easily navigable. Ferries and hydrofoils dock at **Porto di Levante,** on the eastern side of **Vulcanello,** the youngest of the island's three volcanoes. Facing away from the hydrofoil dock at the far left of the port, **Via Provinciale** heads toward the Fossa di Vulcane and its ■**Gran Cratere** (Great Crater). Straight ahead and up a small hill is **Via Porto Levante,** a semicircular road that loops through town and reconnects to the ferry docks. At the small statue of Aeolus, **V. Porto Levante** bends and splits in three directions. The pharmacy is straight ahead, while the **acquacalda** and **Laghetto di Fanghi** are on the right. Continue along to the left of the pharmacy to the black shoreline of **Sabbie Nere.**

Tourist Office: V. Provinciale 41 (☎090 98 52 105). Info on *affittacamere.* Open in Aug. daily 8am-1:30pm and 3-5pm. All other info at **AAST** in Lipari. Head to **Soggiorni Information** (to the left of the NGI biglietteria) or Sprint da Luigi (see above) when the tourist office is closed for maps and info.

Bank: Banco Sicilia, down V. Provinciale from the port (☎090 98 52 335). **ATM** available. Open M-F 8:30am-1:30pm and 3:45-4:45pm.

Police: In an emergency, call the **carabinieri** ☎090 98 52 110.

Pharmacy: Farmacia Bonarrigo, V. Cesare Battisti 180 (☎090 71 75 89; emergency 338 565 6260), at the far end of the *piazza* where V. Provinciale splits off. Open Jan.-Sept. daily 9am-1pm and 4-8pm; Oct.-May M-F 9am-1pm and 4-8pm, Sa 4-8pm.

Internet Access: DeSpar market on V. Lentia, 100m from Cafe Piazzetta. €4 per hr. Open daily 8am-1:30pm and 4-9pm.

Post Office: at Vulcano Piano, down V. Provinciale. Open M-F 8am-1:20pm, Sa 8am-12:20pm. **Postal Code:** 98050.

ACCOMMODATIONS AND CAMPING

Hotel Torre, V. Favaloro 1 (☎090 98 52 563 or 333 92 07 465; www.hoteltorrevulcano.it), down V. Porto Levante from the hydrofoil docks. Close to the acquacalda.

Rooms have bath, A/C, TV, and kitchen, and many offer great views. Doubles €40-80; triples €90-120; quads €120-160. Cash only. ❷

Residence Lanterna Bleu di Francesco Corrieri, V. Lentia 58 (☎/fax 98 52 178), off V. Provinciale. Tranquil apartments with bath, A/C, kitchenette, and terrace. Just 400m from *acquacalda* and mudbaths. Doubles €50-90; extra bed €18-25. Cash only. ❷

Campeggio Togo Togo, V. Porto Ponente (☎/fax 090 98 52 303), on the opposite side of Vulcano's isthmus neck, 1.5km from hydrofoil dock. On-site pizzeria in summer. Reservations recommended for Aug. Open Apr.-Sept. €11 per person, includes tent and light; 4-person bungalow with TV and kitchenette €85. Hot showers €1. AmEx/MC/V. ❶

🍴 FOOD

Granita and gelato are in abundance at the port, but venture off the main roads for a good meal. The aromatic *Malvasia* wine is a delight.

Geco Bar, V. Porto Levante 1 (☎090 347 60 74 091). Hot and cold sandwiches (€3), delicious gelato (€2.50), and desserts. Open daily 7am-midnight. Cash only. ❶

Il Castello, (☎090 98 52 117) on the corner of V. Porto Levante, across from the Laghetto di Fanghi. Self-service options, filling wood-oven pizzas (€4-7), and the ever-changing *menù turistico* (primo, secondo, contorno, drink; €9). Call ahead for the ivy-covered outdoor patio. Open daily noon-3pm and 7-10:30pm. Cover €1. Cash only. ❷

Cafe Piazzetta, Piazzetta Faraglione (☎090 98 53 267), down V. Provinciale from docks. Gelato from €3.80. Mixed drinks from €2.60. Pizza €5-7. Panini from €3. Service 10%. Live music June-Sept. 10pm-1:30am. Open Apr.-Sept. daily 8am-2am. MC/V. ❷

Cantine Stevenson, on V. Porto Levante (☎090 98 53 247). Popular with locals. 60-page wine list. Occasional live music in the summer. Mixed drinks €5.50. Pizza from €6.50. Primi €6.50-12. Secondi €8-14. Dessert €6. Open daily 7pm-3am. AmEx/MC/V. ❸

👁 SIGHTS

GRAN CRATERE. Anyone visiting Vulcano for more than a day should tackle the 1hr. hike to the summit of Fossa di Vulcano. The crater rewards trekkers with views of the island, sea, and volcanic landscape. The hike winds through yellow *fumaroli*, emissions of noxious smoke, and orange rock formations powdered with dust. Between 11am and 3pm, the sun transforms the volcano face into a furnace. Begin the climb during early morning or late afternoon, and bring a hat, sunscreen, sturdy climbing shoes, and plenty of water. Segments of the trail are quite strenuous and should be approached with caution. Obey the signs, and don't sit or lie down, as poisonous gases tend to accumulate close to the ground. If you make it to Vulcanello, follow the lava flow down to reach the extraordinary **Valle dei Mostri (Monster's Valley).** Here, the remnants of Vulcanello's last eruption play tricks on the eyes; many visitors claim to see frightening creatures among the jagged lava rocks. (*To reach the volcano, face away from the port, turn left on V. Provinciale, and follow it until the path with "Cratere" signs appears. Signs point to a turn-off 300m on the left. Hike €3.*)

LAGHETTO DI FANGHI. The murky gray-brown of the water of this natural spa blends with surrounding volcanic rock formations. The putrid smell makes the small lake impossible to miss. Undeterred droves of visitors spread sludge over their bodies for its allegedly curative effects, especially for arthritis. For €2.50 you get a radioactive bath and the added satisfaction of exploring the **Faraglione,** a steaming rock formation overlooking the mudpit. (*Up V. Porto Levante and to the right from the port. Entrance fee €2, organized group discount €1.50, showers €1.*)

SICILY

ACQUACALDA. Vulcano's shoreline bubbles like a hot tub, courtesy of subterranean volcanic *fumaroli*. The sulfuric water has quite an effect on human blood circulation, creating a heavenly sensation upon emerging. Because the mercilessly corrosive acid tends to destroy bathing suits, this is not the place to display the latest in swimwear fashion. Disposable suits are available nearby for €5. *(Directly behind the mud pits.)*

IF EVERYONE JUMPED INTO A RADIOACTIVE MUDPIT, WOULD YOU? Therapeutic or not, the mud is radioactive and high in corrosive sulfuric acid, which can cause severe burning or blistering. Remove all silver and leather accessories, and keep the mud away from your eyes.

SABBIE NERE. If sulfur burns and radioactive mud don't sound appealing, join carefree sunbathers on Vulcano's best beach, where colorful umbrellas dot the curiously black sand. *(Follow V. Provinciale, then take the road that veers left of the pharmacy. Continue along the pastures, past the Hotel Eolie.)*

PANAREA
☎090

The constant stream of white linen and Louis Vuitton luggage on the hydrofoil docks proves petite Panarea (pa-na-RE-ah; pop. 200) is the island for chic repose. With simple buildings and a beguiling elegance, Panarea attracts an older, upscale crowd seeking relaxation. In August, however, rambunctious youth overtake this 3.4 sq. km oasis, forcing the island's once-dignified, beach bars to pump up the volume and party until morning.

TRANSPORTATION AND PRACTICAL INFORMATION. Panarea is accessible by **ferry** and **hydrofoil**. The Ustica (☎090 98 33 44) and Siremar (☎090 98 30 07) offices are at the port. Hydrofoils to: Lipari (1hr., 10 per day 7:10am-8:30pm, €10.40); Milazzo (2hr., 6 per day 7:50am-8:20pm, €16); Naples (5hr., 1 per day 2:30pm, €70); Reggio di Calabria (3hr., 4 per day 9:25am-7:35pm, €22); Salina (30min., 6 per day 8am-6:40pm, €9.40); Stromboli (45min., 6 per day 9:05am-6:40pm, €11); Vulcano (1hr., 8 per day 7:30am-8:20pm, €10). Panarea is a purely pedestrian island. All directional signs list distances by feet rather than kilometers, and street signs and numbers are very rare. The main road, **Via San Pietro,** runs past Chiesa San Pietro along a stone path to **Punta Milazzese. Banca Antonveneta** has an **ATM** on V. S. Pietro, on the left from the port, and **Banca di Sicilia** has one on Hotel Cincotta's patio. In case of emergency, call the **carabinieri** (July-Aug. ☎090 98 31 81; Sept.-June ☎090 98 11 333 in Lipari) or the **medical clinic** (☎090 98 30 40). A 24hr. **golf cart taxi** service called "Pantaxi" (☎090 333 31 38 610), is on V. S. Pietro; a ride to the beach costs €8. A **pharmacy** is at V. Iditella 8. (☎090 98 31 48. Open in summer M-Sa 9am-1pm and 5-9pm; in winter M-Tu and Th-Su 9am-12:30pm.) The **post office** on V. S. Pietro exchanges currency. (☎090 98 30 28. Open M-F 8am-1:30pm, Sa 8am-12:30pm.) **Postal Code:** 98050.

ACCOMMODATIONS AND FOOD. Hotels are small and costly, and prices peak in July and August. Be sure to make reservations well in advance if you're willing to dole out the euro. Turn right from the docks and climb stairs to the white-and-blue houses of **Da Francesco/Pasqualina ❺,** on V. del Porto. All rooms have bath, fan, and sea view. (☎090 98 30 23. Breakfast included. Trattoria on deck. Rooms €70-110 per person. MC/V.) **B&B Da Luca ❹,** V. Iditella, has bath, minibar, TV with DVD, A/C, safe, and terrace. (☎090 333 675 3547; www.bbdaluca.com. Sept.-July €30 per person; Aug. €100 per person. MC/V.)

For the cheapest meal on the island, hike up to **Da Claudia ❷**, V. S. Pietro 3, a *rosticceria* also specializing in sweet treats like *cannoli Siciliani* (€2.50). Their pizza *a taglio* (€2.50) and *calzoni* (€3) are local staples. (☎090 98 34 405. Open daily 7:45am-8:30pm. Cash only.) Down by the water, patrons flock to **Il Geco ❸**, directly in front of the port to the left V. S. Pietro, for *panini* (€6-8), drinks (from €2.50), and 33 types of pizza (€6-12). On the expansive upstairs patio with a view of the water. (☎090 98 32 56. Open daily 7am-midnight. AmEx/MC/V.) **Da Bruno** minimart is by the post office. (☎090 98 30 02. Open daily July-Aug. 7:45am-9pm; Sept.-June 8am-2pm and 5-9pm.) Locals line up at the **panificio** next door for pizza and focaccia. (☎090 98 32 84. Open daily Sept.-July 6:30am-1:30pm and 5-8pm; Aug. 6:30am-9pm.)

◪ 🛏️ BEACHES AND ENTERTAINMENT. Panarea's beaches are largely empty and quiet. Tiny and free of umbrellas, these are some of the archipelago's more intimate coves. From Punta Milazzese, three small beaches extend along the coastline; gradually changing from rocks to sand. Two rights from the *centro* lead to **Calcara** (also known as Spiaggia Fumarole), near the thermal springs at **Acquacalda.** Reach the second beach by walking 30min., following V. S. Pietro's signs for Spiagietta Zimmari. Arrive early to find an empty patch of sand, and stop by the supermarket before heading out, as Spiagietta Zimmari's only food option is pricey. For views of coves and cliffs, embark on a boat tour with **Eolie Mare,** on V. Umberto I. The company also rents boats for private exploration. (☎090 98 33 28. 2-person tour €50. Open 24hr.) **Blue Adventure Guided Charters** offers excursions to Salina, Filicudi, Stromboli, Lipari, and Vulcano, though generally for a steep price. For prices and booking, call ☎39 339 714 0436 or visit www.panareablueadventure.com. For scuba diving and snorkeling, **Amphibia** has an office on the *lungomare*, up the stairs next to the hotel Da Francesco. (☎090 335 61 38 529. Single immersion €36; 3 dives €100; 6 dives €190. Wetsuit rental €15. Office open daily May-Sept. 9am-1pm and 3-7pm. Cash only.) A large map of the island in front of Panea, to the left of the port, marks out three different **hikes** for the adventurous, plus one mountain bike route. There's an easy 1hr. walk through the **Villaggio Preistorico,** a medium 1½hr. hike along the Spiaggia di Calcara, and a difficult 3hr. trek to the Punta del Corvo.

SALINA
☎090

Though close to Lipari and about the same size, Salina (sa-LEE-na; pop. 2300) is far removed from its more developed neighbor. Untouched landscapes and the archipelago's most dramatic beaches make the island a tranquil paradise. Its most astounding rock formations are at Semaforo di Pollara, chosen as a backdrop for Massimo Troisi's film *Il Postino.* Some of Sicily's best restaurants hide on Salina's slopes and in dockside Santa Marina. Ultimately, Salina's serene simplicity is a welcome respite from the crowds on the other islands.

📧 TRANSPORTATION

Porto Santa Marina is Salina's main port, accessible from Lipari by **hydrofoil** (30min., 8 per day, €8.80) and **ferry** (50min., 3 per day, €6.50). The smaller port of **Rinella,** on the opposite side of the island, docks hydrofoils (45min., €6) and ferries (1hr., €4). Hydrofoils run from Salina P. Santa Marina to: Messina (2hr., 1 per day, €24); Milazzo (1hr., 6 per day, €18); Panarea (25min., 5 per day, €9.60); Reggio di Calabria (2 hr., 1 per day, €24); Stromboli (1hr., 6 per day, €16.30); Vulcano (45min., 10 per day, €10.40). Ustica (☎090 98 43 003) and Siremar (☎090 98 43 004) have offices on either side of Chiesa di Santa Marina, in front of the port in P. Santa Marina. Blue CITIS **buses,** V. Nazionale 10 (☎090 98

44 150), in Malfa, stop at the *chiesa*. Monthly schedules are posted outside the Siremar office. Buses run to Pollara (45min., 10 per day 7:30am-6:30pm, €1.80) via Malfa, and Gramignazzi, Leni, Lingua, Malfa, Rinella, and Valdichiesa (13-24 per day 7am-8:30pm). Rent **scooters** from Motonoleggio Bongiorno Antonio, V. Risorgimento 240, in Santa Marina. Facing away from the docks, turn left up the road that curves uphill. Turn right up the first side street to reach the office. Salina's roads are extremely narrow and curvy, and locals drive recklessly, so leave driving to the experts. If you do not rent a scooter, absolutely wear a helmet. (☎090 98 43 409. Mountain bikes €2.50-3.50 per hr., €8-10.50 per day. Scooters €8-8.50 per hr., €26-31 per day. Gas extra. Open daily in summer 8:30am-7:30pm; in winter 8:30am-1:30pm. AmEx/MC/V.)

◩ ⊞ ORIENTATION AND PRACTICAL INFORMATION

The main road, **Via Risorgimento,** runs parallel to the *lungomare*. **Banco di Sicilia,** V. Risorgimento 158-160, cashes traveler's checks, offers currency exchange, and has an **ATM.** (☎090 98 43 365. Open M-F 8:30am-1:30pm.) In case of emergency, call **first aid** (☎090 98 40 005), the **carabinieri** (☎090 98 43 019), or the **police** (☎090 98 43 021). The **pharmacy,** V. Risorgimento 211, is at the end of the street, behind the Ustica office. (☎090 98 43 098. Open M 5-8pm, Tu-F 9am-1pm and 5-8pm, Sa 9am-1pm.) Access **Internet** at **Salina Computer,** V. Risorgimento 110. (☎090 98 43 444. €6 per hr.) The **post office** is at V. Risorgimento 130. (☎090 98 43 028. Open M-F 8am-1:30pm, Sa 8am-12:30pm.) **Postal Code:** 98050.

⌂⌂ ACCOMMODATIONS AND FOOD.
Unfortunately, staying overnight in Salina will cost you. Several hotels line the *lungomare* to the right of the port. Get your money's worth at **Hotel Mamma Santina ❹,** V. Sanità 40, by the port. The hotel offers rooms with satellite TV, A/C, and Internet that overlook a private swimming pool. Chef and owner Mario has been known to give cooking lessons to inquisitive guests. (☎090 98 43 054; www.mammasantina.it. Breakfast included. Doubles €100-210. Half-pension €30 extra per person. 15% surcharge for use of double as single. AmEx/MC/V). Salina's only true budget accommodation, **Campeggio Tre Pini ❶,** V. Rotabile 1, maintains a campground with a market, bar, and restaurant. Take the bus to Rinella, then the hydrofoil to Salina Rinella. (☎090 98 09 155, in winter 92 22 293. Reservations recommended July-Aug. €6-8 per person, €8-11 per tent. AmEx/MC/V.)

Restaurants crowd Santa Marina, the dockside town, and some dishes can be pricey. But given Salina's cuisine, it is inexcusable not to indulge at least for one meal. The finest is at ▧**Ristorante Mamma Santina ❸,** attached to the hotel, where chef Mario welcomes you to the terrace for homemade specialties. *Spaghetti alla Mamma Santina* (€10), a secret family recipe made with 14 fresh herbs and spices, is unbelievable. (Primi €6-10. Secondi €8-12. Open daily noon-3pm and 8pm-midnight. AmEx/MC/V.) **Mare Luna ❷,** V. Torrente Barone 8 (at the end of V. Risorgimento, a 5min. walk to the right of the port), serves delicious *pizza napoletana* in 12 different styles (€5-9), making it a true local favorite. (☎090 98 43 070. Open daily 8pm-midnight. Cash only.) The cheapest way to eat is to assemble a picnic at any *alimentari* on V. Risorgimento.

⋀ OUTDOOR ACTIVITIES.
Viewing Salina's finest sight involves a bus ride (1hr.) from Santa Marina to the striking ▧**Pollara,** a beach in the middle of a half-submerged volcanic crater, 100m below the town's cliffs. While there isn't much of a beach, black sand, crumbling boulders, sandstone walls, and blue water create a beautifully surreal scene. To the far right, a natural rock archway juts out from the water. On the other side of the island, **Valdichiesa** rests at the base of **Monte Fossa delle Felci,** the highest point of the Aeolians.

SICILY

Trails lead from the town 962m up the mountain. For less aerobic activity, relax at **Malfa's beach,** which offers equally tantalizing views—of the huge sulfur bubbles known as *sconcassi*. **Amphibia** offers scuba diving at relatively cheap rates. Turn left from the port, climb the hill for two minutes, and look for the white sign with "Diving" in red lettering. (☎090 335 124 5332 or 335 613 8529; www.amphibia.it. Single immersion €36; night immersion €45; 3-dive package €100. Full-day group adventures, 5 person min., €97.) **Nautica Levante Noleggio,** V. Risorgimento is a 3min. walk to the right of the port and rents small boats, canoes, pedal boats, and beach umbrellas. (☎090 368 675 795 or 338 690 0403; www.nauticalevante.it AmEx/MC/V.)

NIGHTLIFE AND FESTIVALS. For music and dancing during the summer, head right from the port and walk six minutes to reach resort **RapaNui,** which has a *discoteca*, tennis court, and mini hardtop soccer field. Cover and drink prices rise and fall depending on season, but be prepared to drop some cash if you feel the need to dance in this island club. (☎090 98 43 546; www.rapanuiresort. it.) On the first Sunday in June, the population of Salina heads to Pollara for the **Sacra del Cappero.** Each restaurant and volunteering family brings its own special dish in which the *cappero* (caper) is prominently featured. Visitors are invited to contribute their own treats, an easy way to bond with the locals.

STROMBOLI   ☎090

In Italian geology, "strombolic activity" refers to the most violent of volcanic eruptions. In keeping with its title, the island of Stromboli (STROM-bo-lee; pop. 600) harbors the Aeolians' only active volcano—a fact that frightens residents and delights visitors. Though the great Stromboli is always rumbling, the island itself keeps quiet until summer. Sporadic volcanic activity scares away all but the most determined visitors, clearing out hotel rooms and turning the town into a deserted haven, albeit a distinctly ominous one. The adventurous are drawn to nightly guided hikes up the mountain, but if the volcano seems more intimidating than intriguing, renting a boat is another great way to visit.

TRANSPORTATION

Ferries and Hydrofoils: NGI (☎090 98 30 03), along the *lungomare*. Siremar (☎090 98 60 16; open daily 9am-1pm, 3-8pm, and 8:30-10pm for service to Naples), and Ustica (☎090 98 60 03; open daily 8:30am-12:30pm and 4:15-8pm) Hydrofoils run to: **Lipari** (1½hr., 9 per day 7:25am-5:40pm, €17.80); **Milazzo** (2hr., 5 per day 6:15am-6:40pm, €20); **Naples** (4hr., 9:05am and 8pm, €62-70); **Panarea** (45min., 8 per day 7:25am-7:45pm, €11); **Salina** (1hr., 6 per day 8:40am-6:40pm, €15); **Vulcano** (1hr., 8 per day 7:50am-6:40pm, €18).

Boat rentals: available from a number of companies at the port, including **Società Navigazione Pippo.** (☎090 98 61 35. €70 per day. Gas extra. 3hr. boat tours daily 10:30am and 3:10pm; €20. Open daily 8am-10:30pm. Cash only.)

ORIENTATION AND PRACTICAL INFORMATION

On the calmer slopes of smoking Stromboli, the three villages of **Scari, Ficogrande,** and **Piscita** have melded into one stretch called Stromboli. From the ferry docks, the wide *lungomare* is on the right, continuing to the beach and two large hotels. The narrow **Via Roma** heads from the ticket offices, left of Hotel Ossidiana, to the *centro*. Twisting uphill to the left, V. Roma passes the island's only **ATM** next to the Alimentari da Maria, and finally the **pharmacy** (☎090 98 67 13; open M-Sa June-Aug. 8:30am-1pm and 4-8:30pm; Sept.-May

8:30am-1pm and 4-7:30pm), just before reaching **Piazza San Vincenzo.** Pick up an excellent map (€3) at **Totem Trekking,** across from the *duomo.* V. Roma then dips downhill, becoming **Via Vittorio Emanuele,** which then leads to the trail up the mountain. In case of emergency, call the **medical clinic** (☎090 98 60 97) or the **carabinieri** (☎090 98 60 21). The **post office** is open M-F 8am-1:30pm and 8am-12:30pm on the weekend (☎090 98 60 27). **Postal Code:** 98050.

ACCOMMODATIONS

Unlike the more populated islands, the tourist deluge hits Stromboli in August; *affittacamere* may be the best bet for lodging. Ask to see the room before paying, and don't be afraid to check for hot water and comfortable beds.

Casa del Sole, V. Cincotta (☎/fax 090 98 60 17; casa-del-sole@tiscali.it). Follow the side street across from St. Bartholomew's church at the end of V. V. Emanuele. Big dorms face a terrace and shared kitchen. Doubles upstairs. 4 bathrooms downstairs. Dorms €27; doubles €60-70. Prices drop considerably in low season. Cash only. ❷

La Lampara B&B, V. V. Emanuele 27 (☎090 98 64 09; fax 98 67 21). 5 island-themed rooms with TV, A/C, and bath. Breakfast included. €35-50 per person. AmEx/MC/V. ❸

Casa la Pergola di Scibilia, V. Roma (☎090 98 61 27 or 349 38 35 085; www.casa-lapergola.com). Look for signs as you begin to climb the hill. Rents comfortable, clean rooms year round, and is located close to the port. Singles €25-40; doubles €50-75; triples €75-115. Children 4-18 half-priced, under 4 free. Cash only. ❷

FOOD

Grab a pre-hike snack at **Alimentari da Maria,** V. Roma 191, just before the church. (☎090 98 61 49. Open M-Sa 8:30am-1pm and 4:30-8:30pm, Su 9am-1pm. MC/V.) When waiting for your boat ride off the island, enjoy a drink or a gelato (€2.50) from the lively **Beach Bar ❷,** V. Lungomare, which offers a variety of cheap beers and coffee drinks.(☎090 348 730 837. Open 24hr. Cash only.)

L'Osservatorio, V. V. Emanuele (☎090 98 60 13), Punta Labronzo. The food is slightly overpriced, but the spectacular view of nighttime eruptions pays for itself. The restaurant is a serious trek away; bring a flashlight at night and wear sneakers. Taxis also depart for the restaurant from S. Bartolo every hr. 5-11pm. Pizza from €6. Primi from €7. Secondi from €12. Cover €1.50. Open daily 9:30am-midnight. Cash only. ❸

La Lampara, V. V. Emanuele 27, on the left just after P. San Vincenzo. Sample the catch of the day, caught by the owner, by ordering the *frittura di pesce misto* (mixed fried fish; €11). Pizza (reputedly the island's best) from €5. Primi €6-10. Secondi €10-14. Freshly squeezed lemon *granita* (€2). Open Mar.-Nov. daily 6pm-midnight. AmEx/MC/V. ❸

La Trottola ❷, V. Roma 32 (☎090 98 60 46). Dive into the *pizza Stromboli,* a cone-shaped creation that explodes with mozzarella, tomatoes, and olives. Wide variety of classic pizzas (from €4), including 13 vegetarian options. Try the namesake *Trottola pizza* (€7.50). Open daily noon-2:15pm and 6-10:30pm. AmEx/MC/V.

SIGHTS AND OUTDOOR ACTIVITIES

Strombolicchio, a gigantic rock with a small lighthouse, rises an inaccessible 2km in the distance from the beach at **Ficogrande.** The ravages of the sea have eroded the rock from 56m to a mere 42m in the past century. Beachgoers should check out the cove at the end of V. Giuseppe Cincotta, off V. V. Emanuele near Casa del Sole, where volcanic rocks encircle the stretch of black sand. For exciting underwater excursions, look into a scuba course with **Diving Club La Sirenetta,** to the right of the port. Awarded a prestigious five stars by

SICILY

the Scubapro Educational Association, La Sirenetta instructors Daniele and Roberto teach daily diving courses (in English or Italian), from introductory to advanced levels. (☎090 347 596 1499; www.lasirenettadiving.com. Single immersion €25-40; full intro course €80. Office open 9-10am and 6-7pm daily. AmEx/MC/V.) At the ◼**volcano,** rivers of orange lava and molten rock spill over the slope, lighting the **Sciara del Fuoco** (Trail of Fire) at roughly 10min. intervals. While it generally spews continuously, be forewarned that the volcano sometimes needs a rest; call **Magmatrek** (see below) ahead to check up on Stromboli's activity. An ordinance passed in 1990 made hiking the volcano without a guide illegal, and for good reason: a photographer was burned to death after getting too close to the volcanic opening, and in 1998, a Czech diplomat, lost in the fog, walked off the cliff's edge. If such an end is not in your stars, look into an escorted trip with **Stromboli Adventures** (☎090 98 62 64; www.stromboli-adventures.it), or **Magmatrek** (☎/fax 090 98 65 768), both on V. V. Emanuele past the church. (Open daily 10am-1pm and 4:30-6:30pm. Helmets required and provided. Tours offered in English. Departures daily Mar.-June and Sept.-Oct. 3:30pm; July-Aug. 5:30pm. €13.50 to 400m lookout point, €25 to the crater. Reserve at least 2-3 days in advance.) **Totem Trekking,** P. San Vincenzo 4, rents equipment and supplies, and offers Internet access for €2.50 per hr. (☎090 98 65 752. Open daily in summer 10am-1pm and 4:30pm-midnight; Dec. 15-Jan. 8 10am-1pm and 4-7pm. Call year-round to arrange rentals. AmEx/MC/V.) The **Società Navigazione Pippo** (see **Transportation,** p. 678), runs a boat trip (1hr., 8:30 and 10pm, €15) for those who wish to view the volcano from the sea.

> **!** **STOP! IN THE NAME OF LAVA!** Let's Go doesn't recommend, advocate, or take responsibility for anyone hiking Stromboli's volcano, with or without a guide. Posted red triangles with black bars signify "danger."

🎵 ENTERTAINMENT

The plateau of **Piazza San Vincenzo** is Stromboli's geographic center and its most exciting 46 sq. m (besides the crater itself). Each night around 10pm, islanders flock to **Ritrovo Ingrid** for gelato (€1.80-4.70) and reasonably priced mixed drinks. (☎090 98 63 85. Open daily July-Aug. 8am-3am; Sept.-June 8am-1am. Cash only.) Its neighbor, **Ristorante-Pizzeria Il Conte Ugolino,** has a spacious seating area. The moon rising directly over the *piazza* with the volcano in the background is a spectacular sight. (☎090 98 65 765. Cover €3. Service 15%.)

EASTERN SICILY

MESSINA   ☎090

Messina (meh-SEE-na; pop. 240,00) is more than a busy transportation hub. Despite centuries of invasions, plagues, and earthquakes, Messina maintains its immense dignity in points of historical interest and beauty. Those planning to "just pass through" on the way to Sicily should think twice before skipping the sacred *duomo*, the allegorical clock tower, and the Santuario di Montalto.

⌐ TRANSPORTATION

Trains: Stazione Centrale, in P. della Repubblica (☎090 67 97 95 or 147 88 80 88). To: **Milazzo** (30min., 21 per day, €3.10); **Palermo** (3hr., 14 per day, €11); **Rome** (9hr., 7 per day, €45); **Syracuse** (3hr., 14 per day, €9); **Taormina** (40min., 23 per day, €3.30).

Buses: Messina has 4 bus carriers, many of which serve the same routes.

   AST, V. I Settembre 156 (☎090 66 22 44, ask for *"informazioni"*). Buy tickets at the orange minibus in P. del Duomo across from the cathedral or onboard. Serves remote areas in southern Italy.

   Giuntabus, V. Terranova 8 (☎090 67 37 82 or 67 57 49), 3 blocks up V. I Settembre, left on V. Bruno, right on V. Terranova. To **Milazzo** (45min.; M-Sa 16 per day 6am-8pm, Su 1 per day 7:15am; €3.40, €5.20 round-trip). Purchase tickets on bus.

   Interbus, P. della Repubblica 6 (☎090 66 17 54; www.interbus.it), has blue offices next to SAIS. To: **Giardini-Naxos** (1hr., 8 per day, €2.50); **Naples** (1 per week, Su, €22). **Rome** (2 per day, €30); **Taormina** (1hr., 12 per day, €2.50).

   SAIS, P. della Repubblica 8 (☎090 77 19 14). Ticket office to the left when exiting the train station. To: **Catania airport** (1-2hr., 17 per day, €7.30); **Catania** (1hr., 23 per day, €6.50); **Florence** (12hr., 1 per week, €50); **Naples** (22hr., 3 per week., €25); **Palermo** (1hr., 6 per day, €13.30).

Speedboats and Hydrofoils: From **BluVia** (☎090 67 86 51 7), the waterfront wing of Stazione Centrale, Trenitalia sends hydrofoils to **Reggio di Calabria** (25min., M-F 13 per day 6:10am-7:40pm, Sa-Su 7 per day 7:30am-7:40pm, €3) and **Villa San Giovanni** (40min., 2 per hr., €1). From the station facing the *piazza*, turn right and walk toward the waterfront, then look for BluVia signs. Ticket office on the docks. MC/V. **Ustica** (☎090 36 40 44; www.usticalines.it), has offices in a blue building on the waterfront side of V. V. Emanuele, 2km north of the train station off C. Garibaldi. Hydrofoils to: **Lipari** (2.5hr., 5 per day 7:10am-6:20pm, €18.50), **Panarea** (2hr., 3 per day 7:10am-3:25pm, €22), and **Salina** (2hr., 6 per day 7:10am-6:20pm, €22). AmEx/MC/V.

Public Transportation: Orange **Azienda Trasporti Milanesi buses** leave either from P. della Repubblica or from the bus station, 2 blocks up V. I Settembre from the station, on the right. **Bus #79** stops at the *duomo*, museum, and aquarium, and only runs from P. della Repubblica. **Trams** run from the station to the museum (10min., every 10min. 5am-10pm). The same ticket (€1, valid for 3hr.), available at any *tabaccheria* or newsstand, is good for both the ATM buses and the tram.

Taxis: Radiotaxi Jolly (☎090 51 513 or 65 01 11), to the right of the *duomo*.

Car rentals: AVIS Autonoleggi, V. Garibaldi 109 (☎090 67 91 50)

✴ ⚹ ORIENTATION AND PRACTICAL INFORMATION

Messina's transportation center is **Piazza della Repubblica,** in front of the **train station,** home to two tourist offices and several bus lines. The tram leaves from the *piazza,* and ferry and speedboats run from the port right next to the station. **Via Guiseppe la Farina** runs in front of the train station. Beyond the high rises to the left, **Via Tommaso Cannizzaro** leads to the *centro,* meeting palm-lined **Viale San Martino** at **Piazza Cairoli.** At the far right end begins **Via I Settembre,** which intersects **Corso Garibaldi,** which runs along the harbor to both the hydrofoil dock and **Corso Cavour.**

 MIDNIGHT MESSINA. Women should not walk alone in Messina at night, and no one should roam the streets near the train station or the port after 10pm. Stay near the more populated streets around the *duomo* and the university. Be wary of pick-pockets and keep money in a secure place.

Tourist Office: Provincia Regionale, V. Calabria 301 (☎090 67 42 71; aptmeinfoturismo@virgilio.it), immediately to the right when exiting the train station. Well staffed and very helpful, with maps and info on Messina and the Aeolian Islands. Open M-Th 9am-1:30pm and 3-5pm, F 9am-1:30pm.

Currency Exchange: Frattelli Grosso, V. Garibaldi 58 (☎090 77 40 83). Open M-F 8:30am-1pm and 4:30-8pm.

ATMs: Outside the train station and to the right. Also at V. Tommaso Cannizzaro 24, and **Banco di Napoli** on V. V. Emanuele facing the port.

Pharmacy: Farmacia Abate, Vle. San Martino 39 (☎090 63 733, for info on all pharmacies in town 71 75 89). From the train station take V. del Vespro 4 blocks and turn left. All pharmacies open M-F 8:30am-1pm and 4:30-8pm. Posts after-hours rotation.

Hospital: Ospedale Piemonte, Vle. Europa (☎090 22 24 238 or 22 24 347). **Medical Clinic:** V. Garibaldi 242 (☎090 34 54 22). Open M-F 8am-8pm, Sa 10am-Su 8am.

Internet Access: Last Planet Internet and Games, V. Nicola Fabrizi 20, offers 18 computers with fast connections. €2 for 30min. Open M-Th 9am-1:30pm and 3:30pm-midnight, F-Sa 9am-1:30pm and 3:30pm-2:30am, Su 1:30-8:30pm. **Punto Internet,** V. Ghibellina 87, on the small street across V. T. Cannizzaro from Libreria Nunnari e Sfameri. 4 fast computers. €0.05 per min. Open daily 9:30am-1pm and 4-8pm.

Post Office: ☎090 66 86 415. In P. Antonello, off C. Cavour and across from Galleria. Open M-Sa 8:30am-6:30pm. **Postal Code:** 98100.

ACCOMMODATIONS

Although most of Messina's hotels cater to deep-pocketed businessmen, budget accommodations can be found in the neighborhood by the station.

Hotel Mirage, V. Nicola Scotto 3 (☎090 29 38 842). From the train station walk left past the buses and under the overpass and look for the hotel's sign. Simple rooms at an affordable price, perfect for those passing through. Rooms have TV, fan, sink, phone, and shared bath. Singles €21; doubles €37, with private bath €51; triples €41. ❷

Hotel Touring, V. Nicola Scotto 17 (☎090 29 38 851; www.hoteltouring-me.it). Similar to Hotel Mirage, a few doors down. Offers 19 rooms with the added luxuries of AC, heating, and phones. Some of the more expensive rooms come with private bath and TV. Singles €20-40; doubles €40-70; triples €60-90. Prices vary by season. Cash only. ❷

Hotel Cairoli , Vle. San Martino 63 (☎090 67 37 55), off P. Cairoli. Rooms at this older hotel have bath, A/C, TV, and phone. Ask front desk for free breakfast coupon. Singles €45; doubles €80. MC/V. ❸

FOOD

Restaurants and trattorie line V. Risorgimento. To reach this neighborhood, follow V. Tomaso Cannizzaro two blocks past P. Cairoli. Messina is hooked on *pesce spada* (swordfish): baked, fried, or stewed. Another specialty is *caponata*, a dish of fried eggplant, onion, capers, and olives in a red sauce. For dessert, sugary *pignolata* is a decadent treat.

Osteria Etnea, Vle. San Martino 38 (☎090 67 260), three blocks east of the intersection between C. Cavour and V. T. Cannizaro. Signature pasta and fish dishes (from €5). Try the *spaghetti etnea* (€5), a house specialty that packs a delicious shrimp-and-calamari one-two punch. Cover €1. Open M-Sa 11am-3:30pm and 8-11:30pm. MC/V. ❶

Happy Island, C. Cavour 122 (☎090 028 7155 0832). Hip local favorite offers over 15 varieties of pizza *a taglio* ("by the slice"; €1-1.50), as well as volcano-shaped *arancini al ragu* (fried rice balls in meat sauce; €1.50), all to a fun soundtrack of Italian rap and rock music. Open M-F 10am-9pm, Sa 10:30am-3pm and 5:30pm-midnight. MC/V. ❶

SICILY

◉ SIGHTS

Though Messina has lost many of its monuments to both natural and manmade calamities, the town still contains a number of great sights. Churches on the outskirts of the town offer sweeping vistas of the city and port.

PIAZZA DEL DUOMO. Trees provide a shaded, relaxing respite from the city that surrounds this central *piazza*. The great ◪**duomo,** built in Norman times and dedicated to the Virgin Mary in 1197, dominates the square with an enormous marble facade. The long nave stretches past 14 niche sculptures of saints above sweeping tile floors and arrives at a massive altar dedicated to Madonna della Lettera, the city's patron saint. A statue of Archbishop Angelo Paino to the left of the altar commemorates the tireless efforts of the man who twice rebuilt the *duomo,* first after the earthquake of 1908 and again after WWII bombing. **Il Tesoro** (The Treasury) houses the church's most valuable possessions, including gold reliquaries and candlesticks. The *piazza's* highlight is the ornate **Manta d'Oro** (Golden Mantle), a special cover decorated with precious stones and jewels used to drape the picture of the Madonna and Child in the church's altar. After being locked away for three centuries, it is on display once more and is brought out each year for an annual festival (see **Festivals,** p. 684). Plans for the *campanile* began in the early 16th century, and at 90m, it was intended to be Sicily's highest. After being struck by lightning in 1588, restorations continued until 1933, when the tower acquired its clock. At noon, a mechanized lion lets out a few roars and a creaky recording of the Ave Maria booms. Below the clock tower, ancient myth and local lore meet in stone at the ◪**Fontana di Orione,** designed in 1547 by Angelo Montorsoli, a pupil of Michelangelo. The fountain glorifies Orion, the mythical founder of Messina. (*Duomo open daily 7am-7pm. Treasury open Apr.-Oct. M-Sa 9am-1pm and 3:30-6:30pm; Nov.-Mar. M-Sa 9am-1pm. Duomo free. Treasury €3, under 18 €2. Campanile €3.50/2. Combined ticket for treasury and campanile €5/3.50. Guided tours of treasury in English, French, German, and Spanish.*)

MUSEO REGIONALE. A converted spinning mill houses all that was salvaged from the monastery of St. Gregory and the churches throughout the city after the devastating earthquakes of 1894 and 1908. Galleries around a quiet courtyard display the development of Messina's rich artistic tradition. Among more notable pieces are 15th-century *The Polyptych of the Rosary* by local master Antonello da Messina, Andrea della Robbia's terra-cotta *Virgin and Child,* and Caravaggio's life-sized *Adoration of the Shepherds* and *Resurrection of Lazarus.* Just past the entrance, door panels tell the story of the *Madonna della Lettera. (Take the tram from the station or catch bus #78 or 79 from P. Duomo; look for the museum and walk around to the left to find entrance. ☎ 090 36 12 92. Open June-Sept. M and F 9am-1:30pm, Tu, Th, and Sa 9am-1:30pm and 4-6:30pm, Su 9am-12:30pm; Oct.-May M and F 9am-1:30pm, Tu, Th, and Sa 9am-1:30pm and 3-5pm, Su 9am-12:30pm. Last entry 30min. before closing. €4.50, EU residents 18-25 €1.50, EU residents under 18 or over 65 and students free.*)

PORT. The port is more than a place to catch a hydrofoil; Messina's history and former naval prowess still inform the city's character. The enormous **La Madonnina,** a 6m golden statue, surveys the city from a 60m column across the water in the port's center. On the city side, the gleaming **Fontana di Nettuno** graces the intersection of V. Garibaldi and V. della Libertà. The muscular marble god stands triumphant over the chained, muscle-bound she-beasts, Scylla and Charybdis. Directly behind the fountain lies the impressive **Palazzo del Governo,** and to the left across the street sits the **Chiesa San Giovanni,** which boasts a museum brimming with religious treasures, including the ornate Cappella Palatina. (*Open Tu-Sa 9am-1pm and 4-7pm; closed M and Su. Call ☎ 090 42 877 to reserve a guided tour. €1.50.*)

For kids and kids at heart, the **Acquario di Messina** (directly across the street from Chiesa S. Giovanni) holds entire school districts of fish species in colorful tanks, with informative posters along the walls and guides ready to answer any questions. *(Open Tu-Sa 9am-1pm and 3-7pm. €3, students and children €2. Remember that the port can be dangerous after dark, so make this adventure a daytime excursion.)*

FESTIVALS

The **Festa di Madonna della Lettera** on June 3 celebrates Messina's guardian. Parades throughout the city end at the *duomo*, where the sacred *Manta d'Oro* is restored to the altar for one day. Candy and toy vendors flood Piazza Duomo and nearby streets, taking advantage of the business presented by the hordes of tourists who come to photograph the Capello di Maria. If you plan to be in the area on June 3, make hotel reservations well in advance. Later in summer, Messina overflows with approximately 150,000 white-robed pilgrims during the nationally celebrated **Ferragosto Messinese** festival on August 13-15. During the first two days of Ferragosto, two huge human effigies called Mata and Grifone zoom through the city on horseback in the *Processione dei Gianti*.

TAORMINA ☎0942

Legend has it that the sea-god Neptune wrecked a Greek boat off the eastern coast of Sicily in the eighth century BC and that the sole survivor, inspired by the area's beauty, founded Taormina (tah-or-MEE-na; pop. 10,000). Historians tell a different tale: the Carthaginians founded Tauromenium in the fourth century BC, only to have it wrested away by the Greek tyrant Dionysius. Disputed origins aside, Taormina's brilliance is uncontested, with pines and mansions crowning a cliff above the sea. Disoriented, fanny-packed foreigners, hearty backpackers, and elite VIPs all come for a glimpse of what millions of photographic flashes and hyperbolic statements can't seem to dull—a vista that sweeps from boiling Etna to the straits of Messina.

TRANSPORTATION

Taormina is accessible by bus from Messina or Catania. Though trains are more frequent than buses, the train station lies 5km below Taormina, next to neighboring Giardini-Naxos. Buses run from the train station to Taormina and Giardini-Naxos (every 30min., 7:30am-11pm, more frequently in summer).

Trains: ☎0942 89 20 21. To: **Catania** (50min., 25 per day 6:30am-8:25pm, €3.60), **Messina** (1hr., 20 per day 9:50am-8:07pm, €3.60), and **Syracuse** (2hr., 10 per day 7:12am-8:25pm, €10.50).

Buses: Interbus, at the end of V. L. Pirandello (☎0942 62 53 01), off C. Umberto I. (Open daily 6:20am-11:45pm.) To: **Catania** (M-Sa 16 per day 6:30am-7:45pm, Su 12 per day 8:45am-6pm; €4.40, round-trip €6.70); **Isola Bella, Mazzaro,** and **Spisone** (M-Sa 12 per day 6:30am-7:40pm, Su 4 per day 8:40am-5:40pm; €1.70, round-trip €2.20); **Gole Alcantara** (M-Sa 4 per day 9:15am-4:45pm, Su 9:15am; €2.80, round-trip €4.80); **Messina** (M-Sa 5 per day 6:20am-5:40pm, Su 3 per day 8:50am-6pm; €3, round-trip €5.30). Same bus runs to **Giardini-Naxos** and **train station** (dir.: Recanti or Catania; M-F every 30min. 7:30am-11pm; €1.40, round-trip €2.50). The schedule changes monthly, so be sure to grab a copy at the Taormina bus terminal.

Taxis: ☎0942 23 000 or 23 800. From the train station to downtown Taormina €15. Don't pay more than €7 within the city. €3 surcharge 10pm-6am.

Scooter Rental: Cundari Rent, Vle. Apollo Arcageta 12 (☎0942 24 700), around corner from post office at the end of C. Umberto I. Scooters €15-40 per day. 21+.

█◆ ▮ ORIENTATION AND PRACTICAL INFORMATION

To reach the city from the **train station,** hop on the blue Interbus that makes the trip uphill (10min., every 30min. 6:50am-11:35pm, €1.40). Cars are not allowed on Taormina's steep, narrow streets; automobiles can park in a small lot at the base of **Via Luigi Pirandello.** From the bus depot, a short walk on V. L. Pirandello leads to the town's main street, **Corso Umberto I.** The boutique-lined road runs left from a stone arch through four principal *piazze:* **Piazza Vittorio Emanuele II, Piazza IX Aprile, Piazza del Duomo,** and **Piazza S. Antonio.** Small stairways and side streets wind downhill to a more affordable part of the city. Accurate and detailed maps are posted on brown signs throughout the city.

Tourist Office: AAST (☎0942 23 243; www.gate2taormina.com), in the courtyard of Palazzo Corvaja, off C. Umberto I across from P. Vittorio Emanuele II. Offers turquoise brochure *SAT Sicilian Airbus Travel.* Open M-F 8am-2:30pm and 4-7pm.

Tours: CST, C. Umberto I 99-101, 1st fl. (☎0942 62 60 88; csttao@tiscalinet.it). Offers Etna Tramonto, a sunset trip up the volcano (June-Oct. F 4pm; €70) and runs treks to 3000m (M and W June-Sept. 3pm, Oct. 2:15pm; €60); and to 2000m (year-round Tu and Th 8am; €30). AmEx/MC/V. **SAT,** C. Umberto I 73 (☎0942 24 653; www.sat-group. it), operates day-long bus excursions to Mt. Etna from €21.

Currency Exchange: Banks and **ATMs** line C. Umberto I and V. L. Pirandello, as do many currency exchange offices, including **Rocco Frisono,** C. Umberto I 224 (☎0942 24 806), between P. Sant'Antonio and P. Duomo. Open M-Sa 9am-1pm and 4-8pm.

American Express: La Duca Viaggi, V. Don Bosco 39, 2nd fl. (☎0942 62 52 55), in P. IX Aprile. Open M-F Apr.-Oct. 9am-1pm and 4-7:30pm; Nov.-Mar. 9am-1pm and 2-6pm.

Police: ☎0942 23 232. **Emergency:** ☎0942 61 11 11.

Pharmacy: Farmacia Ragusa, P. Duomo 9 (☎0942 23 23). Open M-Tu and Th-Su 8:30am-1pm and 5-8:30pm. Posts after-hours rotations. AmEx/MC/V. **First aid:** ☎0942 62 54 19 or 0942 57 92 97.

Hospital: Ospedale San Vincenzo (☎0942 57 91), in P. San Vincenzo.

Internet Access: Net Point, V. Jallia Bassia 34 (☎0942 62 60 80), down V. del Ginnasio from the public gardens. Wi-Fi, Skype, and photocopies. Internet €2 for 1-20min., €0.10 per min. thereafter. Unlimited Wi-Fi €2. Open daily 9am-9pm.

Post Office: ☎0942 73 230. In P. Sant'Antonio at the very top of C. Umberto I. Cashes traveler's checks. Open M-Sa 8am-6:30pm. **Postal Code:** 98039.

▛ ACCOMMODATIONS

Taormina's popularity as a resort town makes cheap accommodations difficult to find. Those on a tight budget should consider staying in the hostel, or perhaps in nearby Mazzarò, Spisone, or Giardini-Naxos. Hike down steep trails to Mazzarò and Spisone or take the bus or cable cars; service stops around 1am.

▨ **Taormina's Odyssey Youth Hostel,** Traversa A di V. Galiano Martino 2 (☎0942 24 533). A 15min. walk from the intersection of C. Umberto I and V. L. Pirandello. Take V. C. Patrizio to V. Cappuccini. When it forks, turn right onto V. Fontana Vecchia. Follow Greek ship signs. Renowned among backpackers. English-speaking employees. Clean rooms and lockers. Kitchen open 10am-9pm. Towel rental €2. Breakfast included. Luggage storage €1. Reservations recommended. Dorms €18; 1 double €60. Cash only. ❶

Pensione Grazia, V. Iallia Bassia 20 (☎0942 24 776), off V. Giovanni di Giovanni, between the Greek theater and the lush public gardens. 4 cozy doubles (€50-60) with A/C, heating, shared bath, and terraces. Reservations recommended. Cash only. ❷

Inn Piero, V. L. Pirandello 20 (☎0942 23 139; www.hotelinnpiero.com), near base of C. Umberto I. Piero. Rooms have full bath. Breakfast included. Reservations recommended. Singles €50; doubles €70. Sept.-July. student discount 10%. AmEx/MC/V. ❹

Hotel Villa Nettuno, V. L. Pirandello 33 (☎0942 23 797; www.hotelvillanettuno.it). Charming inn with stone steps and garden. All rooms with bath. Breakfast €4. Reservations recommended. Singles €40; doubles €70-80. Extra bed €15. Cash only. ❸

Hotel Villa Astoria, V. L. Pirandello 38 (☎0942 23 943; villaastoria@libero.it), across from the bus stop. All rooms come with balcony and private bath. Singles €45; doubles €65-80; triples €85-100. Cash only. ❹

☐ FOOD

Taormina's restaurants are of consistently high quality; prices vary, though, so shop around. The **SMA supermarket,** V. Apollo Arcageta 21, is at the end of C. Umberto I. (Open M-Sa 8am-9pm, Su 8:30am-12:30pm. Cash and debit only.)

La Cisterna del Moro, V. Bonifacio 1 (☎0942 23 001), off C. Umberto I near P. IX Aprile. Serves incredible food on a secluded terrace with great views. Try the *stuzzichini caserecci* (€12), an antipasto plate of vegetables, meats, and cheese. Cover €1.50. Open daily noon-3pm and 7pm-midnight, closes later in summer. AmEx/MC/V. ❷

Ristorante Il Ciclope, C. Umberto I (☎0942 23 263), 50m past L'Arco dell'Orologio. Locals and tourists alike come to the self-proclaimed "number 1 since 1950" for the "best fish in Taormina." Primi €6.50-9.50. Fish platters €8-15. Cover €2. Open M-Tu and Th-Su 10am-3pm and 7-11pm. AmEx/MC/V. ❸

Granduca, C. Umberto I 172 (☎0942 24 983). According to locals, the views of Etna and the sea from the terrace are the most spectacular in town. Pizza €6-9.50. Primi €9-15. Secondi €16-24. Cover €2. Open 7pm-midnight. AmEx/MC/V. ❸

Pigghia e Potta, V. Giovanni di Giovanni 23 (☎0942 62 62 86), off P. V. Emanuele II. Brightly decorated and friendly hole-in-the-wall serves tasty and cheap takeout. Pizza €2. Pasta €5. Open daily 11am-midnight. Cash only. ❶

Bella Blu, V. L. Pirandello 28 (☎0942 24 239). One of the city's most unique views: cable cars glide down the mountain between clusters of cypress trees that overlook blue water and sandy beaches. Pizza and drink €8.50. Primi €5.50-9. Secondi €4.50-15. Cover €1.50. Open daily 11am-5pm and 6-11pm. AmEx/MC/V. ❷

EAT SHELLFISH WITHOUT SHELLING OUT. For fresh yet cheap seafood, consider taking a short excursion outside the city. In nearby **Forza D'Agro,** a small hillside town 15km from Taormina, locals enjoy excellent fare for a fraction of the price. Though buses stop running early in the evening, a rental scooter or car will get you up the hill and back in under 45min. Ask for directions in the tourist office or at any hotel.

◎ SIGHTS

From P. V. Emanuele II, walk up V. Teatro Greco to Taormina's best treasure: the well-preserved **Greek theater.** Though originally constructed by the Greeks in the third century BC, it was rebuilt and enlarged by Romans in the AD second century. On clear days, it offers an unsurpassed view of Etna, whose sultry smoke and occasional eruptions rival even the greatest Sophoclean tragedies. The cliff-side arena packs 5000 spectators into its seats for annual summer festivals. (☎0942 62 06 66. Open daily May-Aug. 9am-7pm; Apr. and Sept. 9am-6:30pm; Oct. and Mar. 9am-5pm; Nov.-Feb. 9am-4pm. €6, EU residents

18-25 €3, EU residents under 18 or over 65 free.) From P. V. Emanuele II, take C. Umberto I to reach the **duomo**. This 13th-century structure, rebuilt during the Renaissance, now takes center stage. The Gothic interior shelters paintings by Messinese artists and a statue of the Virgin Mary. A two-legged female centaur, Taormina's mascot, crowns the fountain out front. (Hours vary; inquire at the **Museo Sacra** next door.) Behind the tourist office, the grandiose **Chiesa di Santa Caterina** protects a small theater, the Roman **Odeon**. The short walk down V. Giovanni di Giovanni leads to Taormina's tranquil public gardens, the **Villa Comunale**. Filled with vibrant flowers and people relaxing under palms during summer's greatest heat, the gardens look out over Giardini-Naxos below and Etna in the distance. V. Circonvallazione leads away from the crowds to a small stairway that snakes up the mountainside to the **Piccolo Castello**. The **Galleria Gagliardi**, C. Umberto I 187a, debuts contemporary art. Exhibits change every 15 days. (☎0942 62 89 02. Open daily 10am-1pm and 5:30-10pm.)

🕭 NIGHTLIFE

Deja Vu, P. Garibaldi 2 (☎0942 62 86 94), behind the post office. This exotic bar's mixed drinks (from €8) and Turkish coffee (€5-6) seduce partygoers both indoors and out. Open Tu-Su 5pm-3am. MC/V.

O Seven Irish Pub, Largo La Farina 6 (☎0942 24 980), at P. IX Aprile. Massive selection of local and international beer and liquor (from €2), and a nice patio for people-watching on the main thoroughfare. Open Tu-Su 11am-2am. AmEx/MC/V.

Re di Bastoni, C. Umberto I 120 (☎0942 23 037; www.redibastoni.it.). Classy, laid-back vibe goes well with live jazz on F and Su nights. Drinks from €4. Open July-Aug. daily 11am-2am; closed Sept.-June M. AmEx/MC/V.

Morgana Bar and Cocktail Garden, Scesa Morgana 4, off C. Umberto I. Generous staff, purple and white couches inside, and a floral patio out back. Huge assortment of mixed drinks (from €7) and beer (from €2). Open 5pm-1am. MC/V.

La Giara, Vico La Floresta 1 (☎0942 23 360). Turns into Taormina's only dance club every Sa night with Top 40 and techno from 1-5am. Restaurant open M-Tu and Th-Su 7:30pm-midnight, bar open later. Alcohol from €3.50. MC/V.

🕭 🎵 BEACHES AND ENTERTAINMENT

Cable cars take a breezy ride along the funivia from V. L. Pirandello to the beach. (☎0942 23 605. Every 15min. M 8am-1:30pm, Tu-Su 8am-1:30am; €2, round-trip €3.) At the popular **Lido Mazzarò**, lounge-chair rentals (€7.50) from Lido La Pigna include shower, parasol, and changing area—or just enjoy the view with your coffee on the terrace upstairs. Five minutes to the right, there is a beautiful beach where sparkling waters surround the ◨**Isola Bella**, a nature preserve 100m offshore. **SAISTours**, Corso Umberto 222 (☎0942 62 06 71), offers daily bus excursions to Etna and the Alcantara Gorges (from €21), Syracuse (€33), Palermo, and Cefalù (€42). Ask for the *Excursions from Taormina* brochure at the tourist office. **Acquaterra**, V. A. Longo 74 (☎0942 50 30 20; www.acquaterra.com), hosts Alcantara canyoning and river trekking adventures geared toward families and groups (½-day €30-50, full-day €50-80).

Every summer brings ◨**Taormina Arte**, a theater, ballet, music, and film extravaganza with performances from June to August. Shows, held in the Greek Theater, have featured Bob Dylan and Ray Charles. (Box office in P. V. Emanuele II. ☎0942 62 87 30; www.taormina-arte.com.)

⟩⟩ DAYTRIP FROM TAORMINA: GIARDINI-NAXOS

Now the eastern coast's ultimate beach town and a touristy watering hole, Giardini-Naxos (JAR-dee-nee NAX-ohs; pop. 9150) was the first Greek colony in Sicily in 734 BC. Excavations in the 60s unearthed traces of a Greek city built of lava blocks, founded in the shadow of the volcano. Visit the fortress ruins, now overgrown with wildflowers, for a break from the city. The nearby **Museo Archeologico** records the ancient city's earliest days and includes an inscribed ceramic cup, the colony's earliest surviving writing. (☎0942 51 001. *Open daily 9am-7pm. €2, ages 18-25 €1, EU citizens under 18 or over 65 free.*) While there are some public beaches, private beaches rent umbrellas, lounge chairs, and cabanas, and are much less crowded. **Lido di Naxos,** toward the end of the line of private beach clubs, also rents pedal boats and canoes (*€8 and €6 per hour, respectively*). Restaurants crowd the *lungomare* and offer sunbathers pricey options. **Taverna Naxos da Angelo ❷,** V. Naxos 42, is an exception. The staff, fluent in French, English, and German, serves delicious meals and desserts. Try the special *spaghetti alle vongole* (spaghetti with clams) for €6. (☎0942 52 251. *Primi €4.70-6.30. Secondi €5.50-13.50. Cover €1.40. Open M-Tu and Th-Su 11am-4:30pm and 6:30pm-midnight. MC/V.*) Consider heading off the beach for more budget options. Buy necessities at **Sigma supermarket,** V. Casarsa 15. Look for sign on V. Dalmazia, just off V. Naxos. (*Open M-Sa 8:30am-1:30pm and 4:30-9pm, Su 8:30am-1pm.*) Giardini-Naxos shares a train station with its neighbor, Taormina, which is just 5km away. **Interbus** runs from Giardini to the train station and Taormina's bus station. (*☎0942 62 53 01. 35 per day 7:35am-11:35pm; €1.40, €2.30 round trip.*)

CATANIA ☎095

Modern Catania (ca-TA-nee-ya; pop. 500,000) hasn't forgotten its ancient roots. From the stately grace of its *piazze* to its ancient ruins, the city merges tradition with youthful revelry, as university students funnel into its plentiful bars and cafes. Leveled repeatedly, sometimes by invaders but mostly by nearby Mt. Etna, Catania has been rebuilt often since its founding in 729 BC. After the monstrous 1693 earthquake, Giovanni Battista Vaccarini recreated the city with his Baroque *duomo* and *piazze*, which fill daily with eager vendors.

▐ TRANSPORTATION

Flights: Fontanarossa (CTA), C. Sicilia 71 (☎095 34 05 05 or 800 60 56 56). Take Alibus #457 from the train station; purchase bus tickets in kiosk outside station or in *tabaccherie.* The 15min. cab ride to the airport costs about €20.

Trains: ☎095 53 27 19. In P. Papa Giovanni XXIII. To: **Agrigento** (3hr., 4 per day 5:45am-7pm, €10.50); **Enna** (1hr., 7 per day 5:45am-7pm, €5.30); **Messina** (2hr., 24 per day 5:15am-8:20pm, €5.50); **Palermo** (3hr., 3 per day 10:45am-7:15pm, €12); **Rome** (10hr., 5 per day 9:10am-10:20pm, €50); **Syracuse** (1hr., 12 per day 5:15am-9pm, €5.50); **Taormina/Giardini-Naxos** (1hr., 30 per day 4am-8:15pm, €4).

Buses: All companies are on V. D'Amico, across the *piazza* in front of the train station. Because service is significantly reduced Su, weekend travelers may want to opt for the train. Info office inside the train station to the left.

SAIS Trasporti (☎095 53 62 01). To: **Agrigento** (3hr., 20 per day 6:30am-9pm, €11) and **Rome** (14hr.; 8, 9:15pm; €45) via **Naples.**

SAIS Autolinee (☎095 53 61 68) to **Enna** (1hr.; M-Sa 8 per day 6:30am-8pm, Su 3 per day 9am-8pm; €7), **Messina** (1hr.; M-Sa 22 per day 5:15am-8:15pm, Su 5 per day 7am-8:30pm; €7.20), and **Palermo** (3hr., 14 per day 5am-8pm, €13).

Catania

▲ ACCOMMODATIONS
Agorà Youth Hostel, 14
Hotel Bellini, 1
Hotel Biscari, 2
Hotel Gresi, 5
San Demetrio Hotel, 4

◆ FOOD
L' Artigiano del Kebab, 6
Gelateria Zio Pietro, 7
Quattrocanti, 8
Trattoria Casalinga, 9
Agorà Bar and
    Restaurant, 15

◼ NIGHTLIFE
Al Cortile Alessi, 10
Banacher, 3
Trattoria la Paglia, 13
Caffè del Duomo, 12

Ionian Sea

TO PIAZZA EUROPA (300m)
TO PIAZZA EUROPA (20m)

PIAZZALE
ASIA Le Ciminiere
**Museo dello
Sbarco Alleato**

Viale Africa

PIAZZA PAPA
GIOVANNI XXIII
**Stazione
Centrale**
TAXI

Via VI Aprile

Viale d. Libertà
Viale Conte di Torino
Via Conte di Torino
Via d'Amico
Via Archimede
Via Marchese Casalotto
Corso Martiri della Libertà

Via Crispi
Via Colajanni
Via Celeste
PIAZZA
BOVIO
Via M. Ventimiglia
Via Verdi
Via Oberdan
Via G. Bruno
Via Teocrito

Corso Sicilia
PIAZZA DELLA
REPUBBLICA
CTS
SMA
Via Rizzo
Via G. Puccini

PIAZZA
CARLO
ALBERTO
Pescheria
Via Pacini
Via S. Filomena
Via Corridoni
PIAZZA
STESICORO
**Rome
Amphitheater**
PIAZZA DELLA
BORSA

Via S. Euplio

Giardino
Bellini
Villa
Bellini
Largo
Paisello

Via Tomaselli
Via Androne
Via Lago di Nicito
Via Rocca Romana
Via d. Consoli

TO SCOOTER
RENTAL (400m)

Via Umberto I
Via Pacini

Via Etnea
Via Manzoni
PIAZZA
SPIRITO
SANTO
V. Montesano
V. Penninello

Via Antonino di Sangiuliano
Via Crociferi
Via S. Maddalena
Via G. Clementi
Via Gesuiti
Via del Plebiscito
Via San Benedetto

PIAZZA
SAN
FRANCESCO
D'ASSISI
**Museo Belliniano
and Museo
Emilio Greco**
Università
UNIVERSITÀ

**Roman
Theater**
Odeon

PIAZZA
DANTE
Via del Bambino
Via Teatro Greco

S. Nicolò

Via V. Emanuele II
PIAZZA
MACHIAVELLI
Via Garibaldi
Via del Plebiscito

PIAZZA
FALCONE
PIAZZA
LUPO
Corso Martiri della Libertà
Via Antonino di Sangiuliano

PIAZZA
DEI
MARTIRI
Via V. Emanuele II
Via Calì
Via Porta di Ferro
Via San Gattano
Via Anzalone
Via Landolina

Via Teatro Massimo
**Teatro
Massimo**
BELLINI
Via Rapisardi
Via L. Sturzo
Via di Prima
Via S. Orsola
Via V. Coppola
Via S. Gaetano

**Museo Diocesano
and Seminario
dei Chierici**
PIAZZA S.
PLACIDO
Palazzo del Municipio
PIAZZA
DEL
DUOMO
Duomo
**Fontana
dell'Elefante**
Market
PIAZZA
MAZZINI

PIAZZA
UNIVERSITÀ
Mondadori
Bookstore
Via Collegiata
Via Alessi

Via Gisira
Via Auteri
Via S. Calogero
Via Pardo
Via C. Colombo

TO LA PLAYA (5km)
Via del Plebiscito

Via Biondi
PIAZZA
FEDERICO
DI SVEVIA
**Castello
Ursino**

Via S. S. Trinita
Via del Plebiscito

TO (3km)

Ionian Sea
Via Cardinale Dusmet

Porto
Nuovo

Porto
Vecchio

TO (200m)

200 meters
200 yards

Villa
Pacini

SICILY

Interbus and Etna (☎095 53 27 16). Both run to: **Brindisi** (8hr.; 10:15am, 10pm; €40); **Noto** (2hr.; 2, 5:30, 7:15pm; €6.50); **Ragusa** (2hr., 9 per day 6am-8pm, €6.50); **Taormina/Giardini-Naxos** (1hr., 16 per day 7:15am-9:15pm, €4.40).

Ferries: La Duca Viaggi, P. Europa 1 (☎095 72 22 295), up Vle. Africa from train station. To **Malta** (€89). Open M-F 9am-1pm and 4:30-7pm, Sa 9am-noon. **Traghetti Caronte** (☎095 53 77 97) runs to **Salerno** (daily 11:45pm). **Traghetti TTTLines** (☎095 28 13 88) runs to **Naples** (M-F 9:15pm, Sa-Su 7:30pm).

Public Transportation: AMT buses leave from train station in P. Papa Giovanni XXIII. Take Alibus #27 to reach the beach. Tickets (€1; valid 1hr.) are sold at *tabaccherie.*

Scooter Rental: Hollywood Rent by Motoservice, P. Cavour 12 (☎095 44 27 20). Scooters €16-42. Motorcycles €52-93. Cars €62-130 per day. 21+. AmEx/MC/V.

ORIENTATION AND PRACTICAL INFORMATION

Via Etnea, connecting the *duomo* to the **Giardini Bellini,** is Catania's main street. Several main thoroughfares run perpendicular to V. Etnea. From north to south: **Via Umberto I** runs from Piazza Galatea on the water to Villa Bellini; **Corso Martiri della Libertà** runs from the bus and train stations at Piazza Papa Giovanni XXIII and becomes **Corso Sicilia** at Piazza della Repubblica, bisecting V. Etnea at Piazza Stesicoro; **Via Antonino di Sangiuliano** runs past Piazza Bellini and the Teatro Massimo; and **Via Vittorio Emanuele II** leads from the water to Piazza Duomo. **V. VI Aprile** curves south from the train station and turns into **V. Cardinale Dusmet** at P. dei Martiri, leading to Villa Pacini and P. del Duomo.

> **! STREET SMARTS.** As with any city, visitors to Catania should be careful of petty theft. Know where your things are at all times, don't walk around with a map glued to your face, and be wary of manufactured distractions. At night, stick to the populated, well-lit areas along V. Etnea and other main avenues.

Tourist Offices: Municipal Tourist Office, V. V. Emanuele II 172 (☎095 74 25 573 or 800 84 10 42). English-speaking staff provides self-guided tours and theater schedules. Open M-F 8:30am-7pm. **AAPIT,** V. Cimarosa 10 (☎095 73 06 279 or 73 06 222), near the Giardini Bellini. From V. Etnea, turn on V. Pacini before the post office, and follow signs. Open M-F 8am-8pm, Sa-Su 8am-2pm. Annexes at train station (☎095 73 06 255), V. Etnea 63 (☎095 31 17 78 or 73 06 233), and the airport (☎095 73 06 266 or 73 06 277) have the same hours as the main office.

Tours: Acquaterra, P. della Republica 1 (☎095 50 30 20; www.acquaterra.com). Company picks up clients from hotels and runs daily Jeep excursions up Mt. Etna. Half-day trip €50, full-day €59 (lunch and an excursion to the Alcantara River Gorges included).

Budget Travel: CTS, V. Monsignore Ventimiglia 153 (☎095 53 02 23; fax 53 62 46), off P. della Repubblica. Open M-F 9:30am-1pm and 4:30-7:30pm, Sa 9:30am-12:30pm.

American Express: La Duca Viaggi, P. Europa 1 (☎095 72 22 295), up Vle. Africa from train station. Open M-F 9am-1pm and 4-7:30pm, Sa 9am-12:30pm.

Luggage Storage: In train station. €3.50 per 12hr. Open daily 8am-8pm.

English-Language Bookstore: Libreria Mondadori, V. Antonino di Sangiuliano 223/225 (☎095 31 51 60), just down from Teatro Bellini. Brand-new branch of national chain. In-store cafe. Open M and Sa 5pm-2am, Tu-F and Su 9am-2am.

Police: ☎095 53 13 33.

Pharmacy: Crocerossa, V. Etnea 274 (☎095 31 70 53). **Croceverde,** V. Gabriele D'Annunzio 43 (☎095 44 16 62), at the intersection of C. Italia and C. della Provincia. Both open daily 8:30am-1pm and 4:30-8pm. AmEx/MC/V.

SICILY

Hospital: Ospedale Garibaldi (☎095 75 91 111), in P. Santa Maria del Gesù. **Medical Clinic,** C. Italia 234 (☎095 37 71 22). **Ambulance:** ☎095 37 71 22.

Internet Access: Internetteria, V. Penninello 44 (☎095 31 01 39). Wi-Fi and Internet access €1 per 30min. Food €2-7. Open M-Sa 10am-midnight, Su hours vary.

Post Office: V. Etnea 215 (☎095 71 55 111), in the big building next to Giardini Bellini. Open M-F 8am-6:30pm, Sa 8am-12:30pm. **Postal Code:** 95125.

⌐ ACCOMMODATIONS

The plethora of posh stores that lines the streets suggests high hotel prices, but many *pensione* near V. Etnea are affordable. Reserve early for summer travel.

▨ **Agorà Youth Hostel,** P. Currò 6 (☎095 72 33 010; www.agorahostel.com). From the train station follow V. Dusmet until you pass the park (Villa Pacini), then walk uphill on V. Pardo until you reach P. Currò. English spoken. On-site grotto restaurant and wine bar serve food. *Piatto unico* (all-in-one course) and drink €6. Happy hour 5-10pm; 2-for-1 beer and mixed drinks €4. Bike rental €8 per day. Towels €2. Laundry €4. Internet access €2 per hr. Breakfast included. Sept.-July dorms €19; Aug. €20. AmEx/MC/V. ❶

Hotel Bellini, V. Landolina 41 (☎095 71 50 969; www.bellinihotel.com). Convenient to Teatro Bellini. Marble stairs lead to 7 rooms with A/C, TV, and phone. Reservations requested. Doubles €50-55. MC/V. ❷

Hotel Gresi, V. Pacini 28 (☎095 32 27 09; www.gresihotel.com), off V. Etnea before Villa Bellini. Inviting salon, breakfast room, and spacious social bar. Spotless rooms have bath, A/C, TV, and phone. Breakfast €5. Singles €55; doubles €80. AmEx/MC/V. ❹

San Demetrio Hotel, V. Etnea 55 (☎095 25 00 237; www.hotelsandemetrio.com), at the intersection of V. Sangiuliano. 6 enormous rooms have private bath, A/C, phone, and TV. Continental breakfast and laundry service available. Singles €30-60; doubles €41-82. Reservations requested. AmEx/MC/V. ❸

Hotel Biscari, V. Anzalone 7 (☎095 25 00 209), off V.V. Emanuele II. Gold statues and smooth stone floors welcome guests. Large rooms with A/C, TV, and phone. Breakfast included. Small bar in common area. Doubles €60-70; triples €85-95. MC/V. ❸

◲ FOOD

When *catanesi* gather at the table, chances are they'll be dining on eggplant- and ricotta-topped *spaghetti alla norma*, named for Bellini's famous opera. Another hit is the fresh *masculini* (anchovies), alleged aphrodisiacs. The expansive **market** off P. del Duomo and V. Garibaldi features fish, fruit, and sweets vendors. (Open M-Sa morning and early afternoon.) An **SMA supermarket** is at C. Sicilia 50. (☎095 32 60 699. Open M-Sa 8:30am-8:30pm, Su 8:30am-1pm.) **Bar Savia,** V. Etnea 304, across from Bellini Gardens, serves the best *granite di gelsi* (mulberry iced drinks; €1.80) in town. (Open M-Sa 8am-9:30pm.) Perhaps the best deal, however, is the catanese *arancino*—a filling fried rice ball stuffed with meat, available for around €1.50 at any bar with a *"tavola calda"* sign.

▨ **Trattoria la Paglia,** V. Pardo 23 (☎095 34 68 38), near P. Duomo. Share a table with locals and trade tired red sauce for *spaghetti al nero di seppia* (with squid ink; €5). Primi €4-10. Secondi €7-12. Cover €1. Open M-Sa 10am-midnight. AmEx/MC/V. ❷

▨ **Trattoria Casalinga,** V. Biondi 19 (☎095 31 13 19). Popular with local theater-goers, and *casalinghe* (housewives), serves up traditional cuisine *al fresco*. Primi €6-8. Secondi €8-12. Cover €1.50. Open M-Sa noon-4pm and 8pm-midnight. MC/V. ❸

Quattrocanti, V. Etnea 84 (☎095 71 50 885). Popular, modern restaurant right on the main thoroughfare. F night karaoke. Fried calamari €6.50. Primi €3.50-6. Secondi €4-12. Contorni €1.50-2. Beer €1.50-3.50. Open daily 8pm-12:30am. MC/V. ❷

SICILY

L'Artigiano del Kebab, V. V. Emanuele II 94 (☎340 35 83 831). Indian flavors meet classic Sicilian cuisine. *Pranzo completo* (primo, secondo, kebab, and drink) €6. Pizza *a taglio* €2. Indian plates from €4. Primi €4-7. Open daily 9am-midnight. Cash only. ❸

Gelateria Zio Pietro, V. Porto di Ferro 47, off V. Cardinale Dusmet. Local favorite since 1964. 35 flavors include Kit Kat and pistachio. The latter, made from locally grown nuts, is reputedly the world's finest. 2 scoops €1. Open Tu-Su 11am-11pm. Cash only. ❸

👁 SIGHTS

PIAZZA DUOMO. Giovanni Battista Vaccarini's little lava 🏛**Fontana dell'Elefante** (1736) commands the city's attention. Vaccarini carved his elephant (the symbol of the city) without visible testicles. When the statue was unveiled, horrified *catanesi* men, who construed this omission as an attack on their virility, demanded corrective measures. Vaccarini's acquiescence was, well, monumental. Residents claim that visitors may attain citizenship by smooching the elephant's nether regions, but the height of the pachyderm's backside precludes fulfillment of such aspirations. Other buildings on the *piazza*, including the 18th-century Palazzo del Municipio on the left and the former Seminario dei Chierici on the right, are striped black-and-white to mirror the *duomo*'s side. Pose for a picture at the **Amenano fountain** in the southwest corner of the *piazza*, and then visit the **Museo Diocesano,** V. Etnea 8, to see centuries-old priestly vestments. The 1950 restoration of the *duomo* revealed an interior that predates the Baroque makeover. Restorers discovered stumps of the columns and pointed arches of the original apses. The walls of the Norman **Cappella della Madonna** on the *duomo*'s right side surround a 15th-century statue of the Virgin Mary. The body of Catania's beloved priest, the Beato Cardinal Dusmet, lies nearby. To the right of the main door is Bellini's tomb, guarded by a marble angel. The words and music from his *Sonnambula* are inscribed above the tomb and translate as, "Ah, I didn't think I'd see you wilt so soon, flower." (☎095 28 16 35. Open M-Sa 9am-noon and 4-6pm, Su by appointment. Long pants and sleeves are required for men and no short skirts or bare shoulders for women. Free.)

GIARDINI BELLINI AND ENVIRONS. The centerpiece of Catania's restoration sits on V. Etnea and is marked by a fountain and crooked cypresses. These gardens sprawl across small hills and around tiny ponds. Half the city strolls here, gelato in hand, on Sunday afternoons. Below a Victorian bandstand, a plot displays the day's date in perfect grass figures, replanted daily. A few blocks away in P. Stesicoro, modern streets cradle a sunken pit holding ruins of an AD second-century **Roman amphitheater,** with visible tunnels that gladiators once used to enter the arena. Uphill from P. Duomo, at V. V. Emanuele 260, lies the entrance to the **Roman Theater,** built in the AD second century on the grounds of an earlier Greek theater. Passageways lined with the remains of marble columns spill out into the similar but smaller **Odeon,** with another entrance around the back. Mt. Etna's 1669 eruption coated both theaters in lava. (☎095 71 50 508. Open daily 9am-1pm and 3-7pm. €3, EU residents 18-25 €2, under 18 and over 65 free.)

OTHER SIGHTS. Near the train station on Vle. Africa, **Le Ciminiere,** a rescued factory complex, has been restored as a cultural center with free art exhibits, concerts, and home improvement expositions. In addition, the 🏛**Museo Storico dello Sbarco Alleato in Sicilia-Estate 1943** (Historical Museum of the Allied Landing in Sicily—Summer 1943), Ple. Asia, skillfully showcases an oft-ignored event in WWII history. Exhibits highlight the Allied bombing and subsequent invasion of Sicily by American, British, Canadian, and Australian troops, which immediately preceded Mussolini's defeat. The museum depicts a typical Sicilian city square before and after bombing, as well as Axis and Allied propaganda.

Also included are wartime Italian postcards of various saints blessing the fascist troops marching under the fascist banner. (☎095 53 35 40. Open Tu-Su 9:30am-12:30pm, Tu and Th also 3-5pm. Guided tours in Italian, English, or French upon request. €4, under 18 and over 60 €1).
The Museo del Cinema, next door, provides a broad education in cinematic techniques, as well as a closer look at the past films of the once-renowned Catania Industry of Cinema. (☎095 40 11 928. Open W, F, Sa, and Su 9am-1:30pm, Tu and Th 9am-5:30pm. Guided tours every hr. €4, under 18 and over 60 €1.)

BEACHES. The crowded **La Playa** offers a charming view of a nearby power plant. (Take Alibus #27.) Farther from the port is the rugged **La Scogliera,** with jutting cliffs and a not-so-jutting bathing area. (Take bus #534 or #535 from P. Borsellino.)

🎵 📷 ENTERTAINMENT AND NIGHTLIFE

During opera season (Jan.-June), the **Teatro Massimo (Bellini),** V. Perrotta 12, off V. Antonino di Sanguiliano, mesmerizes audiences with its sumptuous setting during opera season. (☎095 71 50 921. Student discounts available on all tickets; contact tourist office. Tours in Italian available upon request. Box office open M-F 9:30am-12:30pm.) In cooler months, *catanesi* love their nightly *passeggiate* (stroll), circulating both P. Duomo and P. Bellini. Cafes pulsate with life on weekends, drawing a sometimes raucous crowd. Local university students and urban 30-somethings frequent local watering holes. In the late evening, students pack the streets around P. Duomo. **Piazza Spirito Santo** offers a little sliver of Ireland every night with three neighboring pubs: **Murphy's Irish Stout, Joyce Irish Pub,** and **Waxy O'Connor's.** Catania's biggest feast day honors the city's patron, **Sant'Agata.** Fireworks and non-stop partying in the first five days of February salvage the city from winter gloom. In the summer, most *catanesi* leave town. Summer crowds typically scooter 15min. away to **Banacher** or **Aci Castello** and nearby **Aci Trezza,** nearly identical nightlife hubs with expensive bars and pretty seaside views. AAPIT's free monthly bulletin *Lapis,* available at the tourist office and in bars, details Catania's nightlife, concerts, and festivals.

Banacher, V. XXI Aprile-S.S. 114 (☎095 27 12 57), a 15min. taxi ride from Catania's *centro.* Crowds dance into the wee hours at what is reputedly Europe's largest outdoor disco. Cover €10. Open Tu-Su 10pm-3am.

Agorà Bar and Restaurant, Piazza Currò 6, next to the hostel. Youth swarm this outdoor favorite by the hun-

THE HIDDEN DEAL

SPOILER ALERT!

While it threatens to be just another overpriced tour, the guided visit at the **Museo Storico dello Sbarco** in Sicily is really much more. In a startling way, it recounts "Operation Husky," the Allied landing in Sicily in 1943 that paved the way for Italy's liberation.

The tour begins with a 12min. video in Italian detailing the historical background; forget the language barrier—the often-horrifying images speak for themselves.

In the first room, curators have reconstructed an entire Catania *piazza,* complete with newspapers from the time, Fascist propaganda, and a typical *catanese* kitchen.

As you enter the second room, air-raid sirens begin to blare, and the guide rushes everyone into an anti-aircraft shelter, where special effects bring history to life. Visitors then reenter the *piazza,* now destroyed by bombings, and guests are left to explore alone. After your heart stops pounding, peruse wax depictions of key events, from the meeting between Roosevelt and Churchill to the signing of the 1943 armistice.

The final room is dedicated to the British war cemetery near Catania, which holds soldiers killed in Sicily. Names of the dead flash onto a screen as a poignant final reminder of war's infinite costs.

Sicilia-Estate 1943, V. le Africa (☎095 53 35 40). Open Tu and Th 9:30am-12:30pm and 3-5pm, W, F, and Sa-Su 9:30am-12:30pm. €4, under 18 and over 60 €1.

dreds. Cheap drinks, loud music, and plenty of company combine for a fun experience sure to last into the morning. Open 9pm-late. MC/V.

Al Cortile Alessi, V. Alessi 30, offers courtyard dining under swaying *nespola* trees and a welcome respite from the buzzing nightlife nearby. Open Tu-Su 8pm-late. AmEx/MC/V.

Caffè del Duomo, (☎095 71 50 556), across from the elephant fountain. Offers gelato and coffee for a low-key night in Catania's main *piazza*, where monuments sparkle under the full moon and blazing street lamps. Open daily 6am-3am. Cash only.

▶ DAYTRIP FROM CATANIA

▨MOUNT ETNA

An AST bus leaves from Catania's central train station at 8am for a 2hr. ride to Rifugio Sapienza. The bus leaves Etna around 4:30pm (schedules vary; round-trip €5). Tours to Mt. Etna by various organizations depart daily from Catania (p. 688) and Taormina (p. 684). From Catania, **Geo Etna Explorer** *(☎349 61 09 957; www.geoetna.it) offers free pick-up from your hotel and a Jeep tour of the volcano (€55, under 18 €35).* **EtnASicilyTouring** *(☎329 09 50 051; www.etnasicilytouring.com) has a half-day excursion to Etna and the Silvestri Mountain craters (€39), a full-day trek up the mountain and through the Alcantara Gorge (€59), and the spectacular Etna by Night (€39). Tours daily, free pick-up from hotel.* **Etna Experience** *(☎349 30 53 021; www.etnaexperience.com) offers a 9hr. Classic Tour that stops at the Bove Valley, the lava caves, the craters and lava flow, and finally the Alcantara Canyons (adults €59, children and students under 26 years old €45). Pick-up from hotel, picnic lunch, and Etna wine included. Reservations required for all tours.*

Mount Etna's lava-seared wilderness is one of Italy's most compelling natural settings. Etna's history of volcanic activity is the longest documented of any volcano—the first recorded eruption was in 1500 BC, though it was probably active long before that. Also Europe's tallest active volcano (3350m), it has long held sway over eastern Sicily's residents: the Greek poet Hesiod envisioned Etna as the home of Typhon, the last monster conceived by Earth to fight the gods before the dawn of the human race. The ancients also claimed its fires were the home of Vulcan, the blacksmith god. Apparently Typhon's aggressions aren't over yet: a 1985 eruption destroyed much of the summit tourist station, and eruptions in 2001 and 2002 sent lava rolling down slopes at 160km per hour. The most recent major eruptions occurred in the fall and winter of 2002-2003 and formed two new craters near the volcano's peak.

DON'T BE A HERO. The trek up Mt. Etna is not for the faint of heart (or the faint of breath). Since you have 6hr. until the bus returns to Catania, you can take your time scaling the volcano. If you decide to bypass the hike for the comforts of the cable car, it's worth it to pay the extra €24 for the shuttle to the *Torre del Filosofo*. The hike to the towers is both steep and dusty.

From the parking lot at Rifugio Sapienza (1900m) where the AST bus stops, you can either hike to the aptly named **Torre del Filosofo** (Philosopher's Tower; 3hr.; 2920m) or take the cable car and an off-road shuttle. (Cable car, off-road shuttle, and guided tour of craters €50; cable car and guided tour only €30). Ask at the information center about times and prices for these excursions, as they vary immensely based on crowds and season. Anyone with sturdy shoes can take a 30min. jaunt to explore the crater in front of the parking area. From the Philosopher's Tower, a 2hr. hike leads to the **craters** themselves. **Valle del Bove,** Etna's first volcanic crater, is on the way down. While the view of the hardened lava, huge boulders, and unearthly craters is incredible, the trail is so difficult and the volcanic activity so unpredictable that sightseers are allowed access only by guided tour. On a certified **tour**, hikers can sometimes hold molten rocks heated by subterranean activity or watch guides burn newspapers on exposed rifts in the rock. Those who brave the trip should take precautions: carry water and bring warm clothing, as winds are ferocious and pockets of snow can linger into mid-July. Windbreakers and hiking boots can be rented at the top of the cable car route for €2 each.

CENTRAL SICILY

PIAZZA ARMERINA ☎0935

Perched in the Erei Mountains, the medieval city of Piazza Armerina (pee-YAT-sa ar-meh-REE-na; pop. 21,000) shows few signs of time's passing. Traditional Sicilian music still echoes from the green *duomo*, and the rhymes of the singing fruit-truck drivers resonate through town at mid-day. Locals are friendly and eager to welcome tourists into their peaceful town—over 30 new B&Bs have opened in the last three years alone. Many streets are little more than winding stone staircases, but the foothills below contain the city's real attraction: the famed Villa Romana del Casale and its remarkably intact ancient mosaics, which are among the largest and most beautiful in the world.

TRANSPORTATION AND PRACTICAL INFORMATION. Buses run to Piazza Armerina from Caltanissetta (1hr., 5 per day 6am-4:25pm, €4.90), Catania (1½hr., 6 per day 8am-3:30pm, €7.90), and Enna (45min., 9 per day 5:45am-4:50pm, €2.90), arriving at the city's northern end in **Piazza Senatore Marescalchi.** Facing away from the Interbus office, walk two short blocks and turn left on **Via D'Annunzio**, which becomes **Via Chiaranda**, then **Via Mazzini**, and finally arrives at **Piazza Garibaldi**, the *centro storico*. There are plenty of helpful signs, so don't worry too much about individual street names. Other services include: the **tourist office**, P. Rosalia 1 (☎0935 68 30 49; open M-F 9am-1pm), in a *palazzo* courtyard, just off P. Garibaldi; **Farmacia Quattrino**, P. Garibaldi (☎0935 68 00 44; open M-F 9am-1pm and 4:30-8pm); the **carabinieri** (☎0935 68 20 14); **Internet** access at **Wilma Wine Bar,** V. Garibaldi 89/91 (☎0935 68 46 09; free for customers; open M-Sa 3:30pm-midnight); an **ATM** on the corner of V. Generale Ciancio and V. Piave, near the station; and the **post office**, V. Salvatore La Malfa 1 (☎0935 98 00 11; open M-F 8:15am-6:30pm, Sa 8am-12:30pm). **Postal Code:** 94015.

ACCOMMODATIONS AND FOOD. Follow the yellow signs to **Ostello del Borgo ❶**, Largo S. Giovanni 6, a renovated 14th-century monastery on V. Umberto I. This hostel offers 20 rooms with dignified furniture and a friendly staff. Private rooms include bath and toiletries. Dorms have cramped but clean showers and toilets down the hall. (☎0935 68 70 19; www.ostellodelborgo.it. Full breakfast included. Wheelchair-accessible. Internet access €3 per hr. Bike rentals €9 per day. Dorms €17 for HI members; singles €45; doubles €60; triples €80; quads €100. AmEx/MC/V.) Located 1km from town, **Bed and Breakfast Pepito ❸**, Contrada da Centova, offers amenities that few can match. Reasonably priced rooms have A/C, TV, and private bath, while the B&B offers a billiard table, a pool, bikes, and horseback riding to all guests. (☎0935 68 57 37; www.pepitoweb.it. Breakfast included. Horseback riding €15 per day. Singles €30-40; doubles €65-70. AmEx/MC/V.) **B&B Paladino ❸**, P. G. Paladino 8, has three simply furnished modern rooms, all with A/C and private bath ideally located near the *centro*. (☎0935

68 85 12; www.bedandbreakfastpaladino.it. Breakfast included. Doubles €50-60; single occupancy doubles or triple €30-35. MC/V.)

A handful of restaurants dot the streets of Piazza Armerina's historic district, though more options are available close to the bus station. Local hotspot **Ristorante Da Giana ❶**, P. Umberto I 9, offers homemade Sicilan specialties at low prices. Try the southern spaghetti *alla Turiddu* (€6), or one of the many dinner pizzas from €3-5. (☎347 30 64 581. Open daily 9am-midnight. Cash only.) **Ristorante Pizzeria Pepito ❷**, V. Roma 140, serves Italian comfort food with a distinct Spanish flair. Enjoy *agnello al forno* (baked lamb; €10) in the upstairs dining room with impressive views of the gardens across the street. (☎0931 68 57 37; www.pepitoweb.it. Primi €5-7. Secondi €7-12. Cover €1. Open daily noon-3pm and 7pm-midnight. AmEx/MC/V.) **Café des Amis ❶**, V. Marconi 22, has outdoor seating and the best *arancini* (fried rice ball stuffed with meat or vegetables) in town. (☎0931 68 06 61; www.cafedesamis.net. Open daily 6:30am-11pm.)

🄶 **SIGHTS.** A fertile valley 5km southwest of town shelters the **Villa Romana del Casale.** This remarkable site, known locally as "I Mosaici," is thought to have been constructed at the turn of the AD fourth century, but a 12th-century landslide kept it mostly hidden for another 800 years. In 1916, famed archaeologists Paolo Orsi and Giuseppe Culterra unearthed 40 rooms of **stone mosaics,** but there are rooms that have yet to be excavated. Glass walls and ceilings protect the mosaics but still allow for a sense of what the villa would have looked like at the height of its glory. Guidebooks from nearby vendors explain the finer points of its construction and history. Enter first through the **baths,** then pass into a large hall on the left to find a mosaic depicting a chariot race; the flying legs are all that remain of the driver, believed to have been Maximenius Herculeus. His great wealth, fondness for the hunt, and side business as an importer of animals are part of the tiles' tale. One of the largest rooms shows the capture of bulls, tigers, and lions, while the floor of the **Triclinium** depicts the Battle of the Giants and the Feats of Hercules. The **Salle delle Dieci Ragazze** (Room of Ten Girls) showcases 10 scantily clad beauties in the most famous of the villa's mosaics. While the **Cubicolo Scena Erotica** is not quite as scandalous as its title suggests, the bare tush and intimate kiss depicted still make it the villa's raciest mosaic. A room off the great hall illustrates the battle between Odysseus and Polyphemus, though the artist fudged the finer narrative details, generously allowing the Cyclops three eyes instead of one. Restoration and excavations are ongoing and a prime opportunity for visitors to interact with the archaeologists as they work. (Buses leave from P. Marescalchi. The 5km walk is well marked with signs pointing to I Mosaici. City buses (€1) run every hr. 9am-noon and 3-6pm. Return buses generally run every hr. from 9:30am-12:30pm and 3:30-6:30pm, though it is not uncommon for the final bus not to make the last trip. Villa ☎0935 68 00 36. Tour office ☎0935 68 76 67, www.guardalasicilia.it. Ticket office open Tu-Su 10am-5pm. €6, ages 18-25 €3, under 18 or over 65 free. Guided tours available for groups. Audio tours €5.)

🄿🌂 **NIGHTLIFE AND FESTIVALS.** For an elegant but relaxed night on the town, head to **Pan e Vinu** wine bar in P. Garibaldi, where the friendly staff and laid-back atmosphere provide a nice complement to the dignified burgundy and dark wood interior. (☎347 74 38 344. Wine from €3 per glass and €12 per bottle. Free appetizers with wine. More elaborate fare €4-12. Open daily 11:30am-3pm and 7pm-1am.) Those seeking loud music and hard drinks head down V. Carducci, where a number of popular bars line the pathway to Piazza Armerina's finest *discoteca*, **Frutto Proibito,** V. Carducci 27. Partygoers rush to pay the steep cover in exchange for several hours of rhythmic madness that are otherwise nonexistent in this quiet town. (Cover €15. Mixed drinks from €5. Open F and Sa midnight-4am.) The nearby **Autodromo di Pergusa** (☎0935 256 60) hosts Grand Prix auto races from March through October. The most important race is the Formula 3 in May. Otherwise, the Autodromo acts as an all-purpose arena, hosting everything from motorcycle races to dog shows.

ENNA   ☎0935

Dubbed *l'ombelico della Sicilia* (the belly button of Sicily), Enna (EN-nah; pop. 30,000) is a mountaintop city of ancient castles, worn stone streets, and some of Sicily's most superb, impressive panoramas. A self-proclaimed "island in the sun," Enna provides a welcome respite from the sun-soaked Sicilian interior.

 TRANSPORTATION AND PRACTICAL INFORMATION. Trains run to Enna from Agrigento (2hr., 4 per day 7am-3pm, €6.50), Catania (1hr., 8 per day 6:30am-5:30pm, €5.40), and Palermo (2hr., 3 per day 11:30am-8pm, €8.60). **Buses** run from the station to the *centro storico* (M-Sa 8 per day 6:25am-8pm, Su 8:45am, 1:10pm; €1.40 on board); buses arrive on V. Diaz, just outside of Enna, from a variety of destinations like Catania (4 per day 6am-5pm, €6.30), Ragusa (8 per day 6am-8pm, €9), Syracuse (10 per day 6am-10pm, €8), Piazza Armerina (9 per day 6am-5pm, €2.90), and Taormina (7 per day 5am-3:30pm, €9). **Via Vittorio Emanuele** runs from the bus station to **Piazza Matteotti,** where **Via Roma** branches in two directions. V. Roma passes **Piazza Vittorio Emanuele** and the *duomo*, going toward Castello di Lombardia. The right fork of V. Roma cuts through residential areas to the **Torre di Federico II.** For info on the city, transportation, and lodgings, head to **AAST,** P. Cloajanni 6. (☎0935 50 08 75. Open M-Tu and Th-F 8am-2pm, W 8am-2pm and 3-6pm.) **Banks** line V. Roma between P. V. Emanuele and P. Umberto I. In case of emergency, call the **carabinieri** (☎0935 50 12 67). **Farmacia del Centro,** V. Roma 315, posts after-hours rotations. (☎0935 50 06 50. Open daily 9am-1pm and 4-8pm.) Speedy **Internet** access is available at **Ciemme,** V. Lombardia 31, next to the Castello di Lombardia. (☎0935 50 47 12. €3 per hr. Open M-Sa 9:30am-8pm.) The **post office,** V. Volta 1, **exchanges currency.** (☎0935 56 23 12. Open M-F 8am-6:30pm, Sa 8am-12:30pm.) **Postal Code:** 94100.

> **ROLL OUT!** Make sure to catch the last evening bus out of Enna. If you don't, you'll have to stay in town and pay an extravagant hotel rate or take a €20 taxi ride to Calascibetta or Pergusa.

ACCOMMODATIONS AND FOOD

Because accommodations are sparse in Enna, the budget-conscious may want to stay in nearby Piazza Armerina or B&Bs in the surrounding area that offer better deals. If you don't mind a trek past the *castello* and away from the city center, the rooms at **Affittacamere da Pietro ❸,** Contrada Longobardo da Pietro, have bath, TV, A/C, and simple, comfortable furnishings. (☎0935 33 647. Singles €35; doubles €50; triples €70. Cash only.) All 76 luxuriously decorated rooms at **Hotel Sicilia ❺,** P. Colajanni 7, come with bath, TV, A/C, minibar, hair dryer, antiques, and Botticelli reproductions. (☎0935 50 08 50; www.hotelsiciliaenna. it. Breakfast included. Singles €62-72; doubles €91; triples €110. AmEx/MC/V.)

Enna's relaxed character extends to its dining, making eating out an enjoyable and lengthy affair. Restaurants cluster along Vle. Marconi, behind V. Roma and P. Crispi. The dining terrace at **⬛Ristorante La Fontana ❷,** V. Vulturo 6, right off P. V. Emanuele, overlooks the gorgeous valley below. Master paintings, most of which are for sale, cover the walls inside. The house specialty, *spaghetti alla donna concetta* (€7), mixes pasta and regional vegetables. Top off a meal with a few handmade *dolci sfingi* before your complimentary glass of *zibbibo*, a local grape liqueur. (☎0935 25 465. Antipasti €7-8.70. Primi €6-7.20. Secondi €8-13. Contorni €2.60. Cover and bread €1.04. Service 15%. Open daily noon-4pm and 7-11pm. AmEx/MC/V.) For a more youthful and modern atmosphere in the town center, **Stuzzicando ❷,** V. Roma 391, offers a variety of dishes served up to the tune of a Top 40s soundtrack. Go for one of 26 pizzas (from €3.50), or sample the house specialty *spaghetti del capitano* (€7), with white wine and *frutti di mare.* (☎0935 50 35 88. Primi €5-7. Secondi €6.50-12. Salads €3.60-6. Dessert from €2. Open daily 6pm-1am. MC/V.) A meal at **Tiffany ❷,** V. Roma 467, feels like home, if your family includes a master chef. Although they offer 30 styles of pizza (€3.50-8), including the namesake Tiffany (€5.50), most come for the mouth-watering seafood dinner plates like *riso ai frutti di mare* and grilled swordfish, both for €9. (☎0935 50 13 68. Antipasti €5-9. Primi €5-9. Secondi €7-10. Open M-W and F-Su noon-4pm and 6:30pm-2am. MC/V.) At **San Gennaro da Gino ❷,** Vle. Marconi 6, nibble from the extensive antipasto buffet (€7-9), move on to the *gnocchetti deliziosi* (€9), and finish with delicious *panna cotta* (€3). (☎0935 24 067. Pizza from €€3-10. Antipasti €8-12. Primi €6-10. Secondi €7-16. Cover €1.50. Open M-Tu and Th-Su 12:30-3pm and 8pm-12:30am. AmEx/MC/V.) Pick up picnic supplies at the **Sisa supermarket,** V. Lombardia 21. (Open M-Tu and Th-Sa 9am-2pm and 5-9pm, W 9am-2pm.)

🔲 🎵 **SIGHTS AND ENTERTAINMENT.** Though over a dozen religious orders have their own churches in Enna, all participated in creating the remarkable **duomo,** which combines as many architectural styles as there are brotherhoods. Note the detailed ceiling carvings and lifelike statues above the altar, as well as the colorful exterior murals. (Open daily 9am-1pm and 4-7pm. Free.) From the *duomo*, take the left fork up V. Roma as it becomes V. Lombardia to the Norman **Castello di Lombardia.** Although grass and vines have overrun its courtyards, the walls and towers of this castle attest to a time when residents of Enna were more engaged in defending their environment than enjoying it. The tallest of the castle's towers, **La Pisana,** offers enviable views of the entire province after a steep climb. On clear days, the imposing silhouette of Mt. Etna shimmers in the distance. The weeping Demeter supposedly mourned the loss of her daughter Persephone to Hades at the **Rocca di Cerere,** on the path leading to the left of the *castello*. Turn left on V. IV Novembre for the **public gardens.** (☎0935 50 09 62. *Castello* open daily Apr.-Oct. 8am-8pm; Nov.-Mar. 8am-5pm. Gates are often open later. Gardens open daily 9am-8pm. Free.) Take the right fork of V. Roma from the *duomo* to take cover at **Torre di Federico II,** on the other end of town from the castle. Once used as a hideout for Sicilian defenders during WWII, the tower is connected to the *castello* by an underground tunnel, the entrance of which is still visible from within the tower. (Open daily 8am-6pm. Free.) Ancient churches hide on almost every corner of the city, as do many interesting museums, most free of charge. If you have some extra time and energy after the castle-area exploration, take a look inside the **Museo della Chiesa di S. Cataldo,** in P. S. Cataldo, at the far end of V. Roma opposite the *duomo* (open daily 9am-1pm and 4-7pm), or the Museo della Sicilia 3M, V. Roma 533 (☎0935 33 85 02 33 61; open M and W-Su 10am-1pm and 3:30-7:30pm.)

Built onto the side of a hill between the castle and the Rocca di Cerere, **New Life Discopub** serves up drinks, music, and superb views of the valley below. Around midnight things loosen up with a popular house DJ and dancing. **Stuzzicando,** V. Roma 391, throws wild Happy Hours once a month, with cheap drinks, live music, and a house DJ for dancing. Call ahead to find out when the next one will occur. (☎0935 50 35 88. Open F 11pm-late.) On July 2, Enna floods the streets and celebrates the **Festa della Madonna** with the procession of three enormous votive statues through the streets of the city, followed by fireworks, music, and traditional *mastazzoli* (apple cookies). The party continues through the summer with the feasts of **Sant'Anna** and **Madonna di Valverde** on the last Sundays of July and August, respectively. Every Easter, the brothers of each religious fraternity parade through the streets in an enormous, sacred procession attended by the whole city.

SOUTHERN SICILY

SYRACUSE (SIRACUSA) ☎0931

Syracuse (SEE-ra-COO-sa; pop. 125,000) blends ancient archaeological treasure with extravagant Baroque beauty. In its golden age, Syracuse was home to some of the greatest contributors to Western culture: Theocritus, Archimedes, and the Greek lyric poet Pindar. After many conquests, the city's fortune waned and Syracuse receded from the spotlight. Today, nighttime crowds meander around the lighted ruins of the Temple of Apollo and the ancient *duomo*, and party from dusk to dawn at the nearby Fontane Bianche.

▶ TRANSPORTATION

Trains: V. Francesco Crispi (☎0931 46 44 67). To: **Catania** (1hr., 18 per day 5am-8:25pm, €5.80); **Messina** (3hr., 9 per day 5am-9:30pm, €9.50); **Milan** (18hr., 5:15 and 5:40pm, €50); **Noto** (45min., 10 per day 5:15am-8:05pm, €3.10); **Ragusa** (2-3hr., 4 per day 5:15am-2:50pm, €8.90); **Rome** (10-13hr.; Tu, Th, Sa-Su 8am and 6pm; €44); **Taormina** (2hr., 10 per day 5am-9:30pm, €8.30).

Buses: AST (☎0931 46 27 11 or 44 92 15), on C. Umberto I near the train station. To **Gela** (4hr., 6:50am and 12:30pm, €9) and **Ragusa** (3hr.; M-Sa 8 per day 7:25am-7:15pm, Su 2:10pm and 8:30pm, €8.50). Interbus, V. Trieste 40 (☎0931 66 710), 1 block from P. delle Poste toward center of Ortigia, 2nd street on left after stone bridge. To **Catania** (14 per day M-F 6:15am-8:30pm, Sa and Su 4 per day 6:18am-7:33pm; €4.70) and **Noto** (1hr.; M-Sa 5 per day 7:50am-5:10pm, Su 4:05pm; €2.85).

Public Transportation: Orange AST buses depart from P. delle Poste. Buses #21 and 22 run past Fontane Bianche every 2-3hr.; buses #23 and 24 do so much less frequently. Tickets (€1) sold in *tabaccherie* and bars displaying an AST sticker in the window.

Taxis: ☎0931 69 722 or 60 980. From the train station to Ortigia costs about €8.

◀▶ ORIENTATION AND PRACTICAL INFORMATION

Ponte Umbertino connects the island of Ortigia to mainland Syracuse. **Ponte Nuovo** (Ponte Santa Lucia), just to the left of Ponte Umbertino facing the mainland, is open even when Umbertino is closed to car traffic. On the mainland, **Corso Umberto I** links the bridge to the train station and passes through **Piazza Marconi**, from which **Corso Gelone** passes through town to the **Archaeological Park**. C. Umberto I continues past **Foro Siracusano** to the train station.

Tourist Office: AAT Office Ortigia, V. Maestranza 33 (☎0931 46 42 55). After crossing Ponte Umbertino, turn right through P. Pancali to uphill C. Matteoti. Turn left on V. Maestranza at the fountain in P. Archimede; office is in the *palazzo's* courtyard across from the pharmacy. English spoken. Open M-Th 8:30am-1:45pm and 3-5:30pm, F

8:30am-1:45pm. **URP,** V. Malta 106 (☎0931 46 88 69; www.provincia.siracusa.it), has a tourist section, with brochures in many languages, detailed maps of Syracuse and surrounding cities, and guides to the nearby historical sights. Open M-F 9am-1pm.

Luggage Storage: In train station. €4 per hr. Open daily 7:30am-1pm and 3-7pm.

English-Language Bookstore and Internet Access: Libreria Gabo, C. Matteotti 38 (☎0931 66 255). Internet access €1.50 per 15min. Open M-F and Su 9am-1pm and 4-8:30pm, Sa 5-8:30pm. AmEx/MC/V.

Tours: Ortigia Passengers, V. dei Mille (☎368 31 70 711; www.ortigiatour.com). Captain Emanuele and his fearless crew sail to the sea caves and along Ortigia's coast, providing passengers plenty of photo ops and a truly memorable experience. Every hr. from 9am-8pm. €10 per person, €40 minimum. Cash only.

Laundry: Lavenderia ad Acqua, C. Umberto I 13, near the bridge to Ortigia. Wash €3.50, dry €1 per 6min. Detergent €1. Open M-Sa 8:30am-8pm.

Police: ☎0931 49 51 11. **Carabinieri:** ☎0931 44 13 44.

Pharmacy: Mangiafico Farmacia, C. Matteotti 53 (☎0931 65 643). Open M-Sa 8:30am-1pm and 4:30-8pm. After-hours rotations posted outside. AmEx/MC/V.

Hospital: Ospedale Generale Provinciale, V. Testaferrata (☎0931 68 555), off C. Gelone. **Guardia Medica,** V. della Giudecca (☎0931 48 46 39). Open daily 8am-8pm.

Post Office: P. delle Poste 15, on Ortigia. Turn left crossing the bridge. Currency exchange available. Open M-F 8:15am-6:30pm, Sa 8am-12:30pm. **Postal Code:** 96100.

> **TIP**
>
> **OLD TIME TOURS.** Ask at the APT tourist office about the Val di Noto train tour (€25), an all-day tour of southeastern Sicily with guided stops in either Noto and Modica or Ragusa and Scicli to admire the history, regional cuisine, and Baroque architecture from a historical steam locomotive.

ACCOMMODATIONS

Many budget accommodations have staked out the area between the station and the bridge to Ortigia. While the price is often right, quality is very uneven. Don't be fooled by big signs and a lot of flyers. This area is somewhat run down, and at night, visitors should stick to the well-lit thoroughfares. Ortigia's options are more expensive, but generally of higher quality.

lolhostel, V. Francesco Crispi 94 (☎0931 46 50 88; www.lolhostel.com). Opened in June 2007, this conveniently located hostel is becoming a true Syracusan legend. ROFL LOLZ! Rooms have A/C. Communal kitchen—I can haz cheezeburger? English spoken. Internet. Free Wi-Fi. Dorms €18-20; singles €35-40; doubles €60-64. Cash only. ❶

Piccolo Hotel B&B "Casa Mia", C. Umberto I 112 (☎0931 46 33 49; www.bbcasamia. it). Former palace in the middle of Syracuse's *centro storico*. Rooms have A/C, bath, TV, and phone. Breakfast included. Free Internet access and bike rentals for guests. Singles €40-50; doubles €60-80; triples €75-90; quads €80-100. AmEx/MC/V. ❸

Sorella Luna, V. Francesco Crispi 23 (☎0931 21 178; www.sorellalunasrl.it). Former convent with exposed-beam ceilings. 12 rooms have phone, A/C, bath, wet bar with minifridge, and TV. Breakfast included. Free Wi-Fi. Singles €45-55; doubles €70-90; triples €85-110; quads €100-125. Extra bed €20. AmEx/MC/V. ❹

Hotel Archimede, V. Francesco Crispi 67 (☎0931 46 20 40; www.archimedehotels. com). Theatrical theme. 14 spacious rooms with A/C, TV, bath, and locker. Continental breakfast included. Wheelchair-accessible. Singles €35-55; doubles €50-85; triples €75-100; quads €100-130. AmEx/MC/V. ❸

SICILY

Hotel Centrale, C. Umberto I 141 (☎0931 60 528; www.hotelcentralesr.com), near the train station. Recently renovated, modern rooms; some with sea views (€5 extra). Rooms have bath, TV, and A/C. Breakfast included. Wi-Fi in the lobby. Singles €45-60; doubles €70-80; triples €90-110. AmEx/MC/V. ❹

🍴 FOOD

Though hotel prices run fairly high, restaurants in Syracuse are affordable. On the mainland, the area around the station and the Archaeological Park offers some of the best deals. Ortigia has an **open-air market** on V. Trento, off P. Pancali, as well as several budget options on V. Savoia and V. Cavour. There is a **Eurospar supermarket** at C. Umberto I 174 (☎0931 44 20 874), just beyond the bus station. (Open M-Sa 8:30am-8:30pm, Su 8:30am-1pm. AmEx/MC/V.)

🔲 **Ristorante Porta Marina,** V. dei Candelai 35 (☎0931 22 553), off V. Cavour. Elegant and affordable. Great selection of seafood in a sleek modern space. The brave start with the *carpaccio polipo* (octopus salad; €8), and then move to the chef's special *risotto alla marinara* (squid, shrimp, shellfish, and tomatoes; €9). Antipasti €6.50-10. Primi €7-16. Secondi €8-18. Open Tu-Su 12:30-3pm and 8-11:30pm. AmEx/MC/V. ❸

🔲 **Trattoria Del Forestiero,** C. Timoleonte 2 (☎335 84 30 736), on the mainland, 10min. from Ortigia. A lively favorite. Try swordfish in marinara sauce (€6). 22 styles of pizza from €2.50-4.50 (dinner only). Primi €3.50-6. Secondi €4.50-7. Cover €1.10. Takeout available. Open M and W-Su 12:30-4:20pm and 7-11pm. Cash only. ❷

Medea Cafe, C. Gelone 136/138 (☎0931 74 30 892). The perfect spot to grab a quick, filling meal before exploring nearby sights. Breakfast pastries €1. Primi €3.50. Secondi €3.50-4.50. Open M-Sa 6:30am-11pm. Cash only. ❶

Trattoria La Finanziera, V. Epicarmo 41 (☎0931 46 31 17). Self-proclaimed "Seafood Specialists". Experience authentic local cuisine with the *fettucine alla siracusana* (€9). Primi €7-15. Secondi €8-15. Extensive wine list €8-15. Generous tourist discount with passport. Open M-Sa 9:30am-4pm and 6pm-midnight. MC/V. ❸

Aziz, V. Trento 10 (☎349 59 78 909), off of C. Umberto I right before the Temple of Apollo. A great late-night local hangout with outdoor seating and an upstairs dining room complete with pillows and hookah (€5). Kebabs €3.50. Couscous €7-13. Open Tu-Su noon-3pm and 8:30pm-midnight. Cash only. ❷

👁 SIGHTS

MAINLAND SYRACUSE

🔲**ARCHAEOLOGICAL PARK.** Three centuries as a strategic city on the Mediterranean left Syracuse with a collection of colossal Greek and Roman monuments. Two theaters, an ancient quarry, and the remains of the world's largest altar share a fenced compound, viewable with a single ticket. The view from the **Greek Theater,** carved into the hillside in 475 BC, competed with the actors for the audience's attention. If the 16,000 spectators watching Aeschylus's original production of *The Persians* got bored, they could look out over the impressive landscape. Greek inscriptions line the walls along the mid-level aisles, and the track for the *deus ex machina*, a large crane that made the gods "fly," is still in place. The **Paradise Quarry** next to the theater derives its name from the gardens that line the base of the chalky cliffs. These quarries provided most of the gray stone that built old Syracuse. Two large caves, the **Orecchio di Dionisio** (Ear of Dionysius) and the **Grotta dei Cordari** (Ropemakers' Cave), were cut in the walls. The latter is closed to the public for safety, but visitors can still hear the famous echoes that ricochet off the Orecchio di Dionisio's walls. Legend claims tyran-

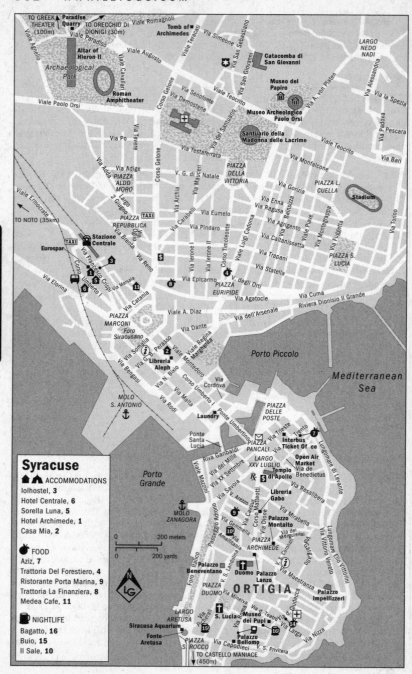

TO GREEK THEATER (100m)
Paradise Quarry
Viale Romagnoli
TO ORECCHIO DI DIONIGI (30m)
Viale Teracati
Via Simeone
Via San Sebastiano
Viale Augusto
Viale Paradiso
Viale Aretusa
Viale Cavallari
Tomb of Archimedes
Via San Giovanni
LARGO NEDO NADI
Altar of Hieron II
Catacomba di San Giovanni
Archaeological Park
Roman Amphitheater
Viale Paolo Orsi
Viale Teocrito
Museo del Papiro
Via A. von Platen
Via Alessandria
Via la Spezia
Via Padova
Via Pescara
Museo Archeologico Paolo Orsi
Via Po
Via Tevere
Via Adda
Via del Santuario
Santuario della Madonna delle Lacrime
Via Bari
Corso Gelone
Via Senofonte
Via Demostene
Via Testaferrata
Viale Teocrito
Viale Monfalcone
Via Torino
PIAZZA ALDO MORO
Via Adige
Via Archia
V. G. di Natale
PIAZZA DELLA VITTORIA
Via Gorizia
PIAZZA L. CUELLA
Viale Ermocrate
TO NOTO (35km)
Largo 2 Giugno
PIAZZA REPUBBLICA
TAXI
Via Carabelli
Via Eumelo
Via Pindaro
Via Enna
Via Ragusa
Via Battisti
Stadium
Stazione Centrale
TAXI
Via Brenta
Via Reno
Via Ierone I
Via Ierone II
Corso Timoleonte
Via Plave
Via Montegrappa
Via Fulgenti
Eurospar
Via Francesco Crispi
Via Marsala
Via Agrigento
Via Caltanissetta
PIAZZA S. LUCIA
Via Elorina
Corso Umberto I
Via Catania
Via Epicarmo
Via Trapani
Via Statella
Hotel Centrale, 6
Via Jolo
Via degli Orti
PIAZZA EURIPIDE
Via Agatocle
Via Cuma
Riviera Dionisio II Grande
PIAZZA MARCONI
Foro Siracusano
Viale A. Diaz
Via Dante
Via dell'Arsenale
Mediterranean Sea
Via Somalia
Viale Regina Margherita
Porto Piccolo
MOLO S. ANTONIO
Via Bengasi
Via G.B. Pegaso
Via Montedoro
Corso Umberto II
Via N. Brio
Libreria Aleph
Via Cordova
Via Malta
Via Rodi
PIAZZA DELLE POSTE
Laundry
Ponte Umbertino
Via Trento
PIAZZA PANCALI
Interbus Ticket Office
Ponte Santa Lucia
Via Trieste
Open Air Market
Via de Benedictus
Riva Garibaldi
LARGO XXV LUGLIO
Tempio di Apollo
Via dei Mille
Via XX Settmbre
Libreria Gabo
Porto Grande
Viale Mazzini
Via Savoia
Via Resalibera
Via Mirabella
Lungomare di Levante
Passeggio Adorno
Via V. Arezzo
PIAZZA ARCHIMEDE
Palazzo Montalto
MOLO ZANAGORA
Via Gemmella
Corso Matteotti
Via del Merguiensi
Lungomare Elio Vittorini
Via Vittoria Veneto
Via Cavour
Via Dione
0 200 meters
0 200 yards
Via Amalfitania
Via Landolina
PIAZZA ARCHIMEDE
Via Resalbera
Palazzo Beneventano
Duomo
Palazzo Lanzo
ORTIGIA
Palazzo Impellizzeri
PIAZZA DUOMO
Via Minerva
Via Roma
PIAZZA MINERVA
S. Lucia
Museo dei Pupi
Via Teatro Greco
Via Larga
Via Giudecca
LARGO ARETUSA
Siracusa Aquarium
Fonte Aretusa
PIAZZA S. ROCCO
Via Picherali
S. Lucia
Via Capodieci
Palazzo Bellomo
V. S. Privitera
TO CASTELLO MANIACE (450m)

Syracuse

🏠🏠 ACCOMMODATIONS
Iolhostel, 3
Hotel Centrale, 6
Sorella Luna, 5
Hotel Archimede, 1
Casa Mia, 2

🍎 FOOD
Aziz, 7
Trattoria Del Forestiero, 4
Ristorante Porta Marina, 9
Trattoria La Finanziera, 8
Medea Cafe, 11

🍺 NIGHTLIFE
Bagatto, 16
Buio, 15
Il Sale, 10

nical Dionysius held political prisoners here so he could eavesdrop on their conversations. *(Open daily from 9am-6pm. Included in park entrance.)* Outside this area lies the **Ara di Ierone II** (the altar of Hieron II, 241-215 BC). Once used for public sacrifices to Zeus Eleuterio, the altar was torn down in the 16th century by the Spanish, who used the stone to build the walls of Ortigia. The enormous steps of the altar's base are still intact. Up the hill is an AD third-century Roman **amphitheater.** *(Take C. Gelone to Vle. Teocrito. Park entrance down V. Augusto to the left; follow signs. Walk through the gauntlet of souvenir stands to reach the ticket office. Info ☎ 0931 65 068. Park and ticket office open daily in summer from 9am-6pm; in winter 9am-2pm. Theater open from July to early May. €8, EU residents 18-25 €3, EU residents under 18 or over 65 free.)*

▨CATACOMBA DI SAN GIOVANNI. Dating from AD 315-360, this subterranean maze has over 20,000 tombs carved into the walls of what used to be a Greek aqueduct. No corpses linger—only ghostly frescoes, an occasional sarcophagus, and a few wall carvings. The adjoining crypt of San Marciano includes the basilica in which Paul the Apostle remained for three days as he preached the gospel throughout Syracuse. *(Across from the tourist office on V. San Giovanni, off Vle. Teocrito from C. Gelone. ☎ 0931 64 694; www.kairos-web.com. Open daily 9:30am-12:30pm and 2:30-5:30pm. Mandatory guided tours every 30min. €5, under 15 and over 65 €3. AmEx/MC/V.)*

DUOMO. The 18th-century exterior of the cathedral looks like the standard Baroque compilation of architectural styles, but the interior holds a secret. A fifth-century BC Temple of Athena first stood on the site, and rather than demolishing the pagan structure, architects incorporated it into their construction. Fluted columns line the interior, recalling the structure's Classical origins. Large, shiny letters proclaim this the **first Christian church** in the West. Legend has it that the temple became a church with the arrival of St. Paul. The first chapel on the right is dedicated to Santa Lucia, the light-bearer and Syracuse's patron saint. Catch a glimpse of her left arm in the elaborate glass reliquary. Hidden from view above the reliquary is a masterpiece of Sicilian silver work, a life-sized statue of Lucia that parades through the streets on her feast day (see **Entertainment,** p. 704). Lest people forget how she died, silversmiths thoughtfully included a dagger protruding from her throat, the punishment dealt the saint by the pagan government of AD 304. *(From P. Archimede, take V. Roma and turn right on V. Minerva. Open daily 8am-7pm. Modest dress required. Free.)*

SANTUARIO DELLA MADONNA DELLE LACRIME. For three days in 1953, a mass-produced statuette of the Madonna reputedly began to weep in the home of the Iannuso family. Since then the number of pilgrims to the site has grown so large that the commanding spire of the **Basilica Madonna delle Lacrime** was built in 1994 according to the plans of Frenchmen Michel Arnault and Pierre Parat. Whether you're a pilgrim or not, the impressive architecture is worth a visit. The **Museum of Lacrymation** and the **Museum of Liturgy** complement the basilica; timetables placed outside the sanctuary tell the statue's tale, from the first teardrop to Pope John Paul's inauguration and papal blessing of the Sanctuary in November 1994. *(On Vle. Teocrito, off V. del Santuario. ☎ 0931 21 446; www.madonnadellelacrime.it. Both museums open daily 9am-12:30pm and 4-6pm. Sanctuary open 8am-noon and 4-7pm; Museum of Lacrymation €1.60, Museum of Liturgy €1, both museums €2. Sanctuary free.)*

MUSEO ARCHEOLOGICO PAOLO ORSI. Named for Sicily's most famous archaeologist, this collection has over 18,000 objects from prehistory through ancient Greece and early Christianity (roughly from 40,000 BC to AD 600). From the introductory room at the museum's core, hallways branch into chronologically arranged galleries. Exquisite kouroi torsos, grimacing Gorgons, elegant vases, and pygmy-elephant skeletons rest in 9000 square meters of dimly lit galleries.

(Vle. Teocrito 66. ☎0931 46 40 22. Open Tu-Sa 9am-7pm, Su 9am-2pm. Last entry 1hr. before close. €6, EU residents 18-25 €3, EU residents under 18 and over 65 free.)

MUSEO ARETUSEO DEI PUPI. The first museum in Italy devoted entirely to puppets focuses on the long, noble tradition of Sicilian puppetry. Visitors make their way through life-like marionettes in traditional Sicilian costume, armed wood soldiers in shining battle gear, and fantastic creatures. Knowledgeable guides offer tours through the museum, around the puppet construction laboratory, and behind the theater facade. An extensive library with books, videos, and audio related to puppetry is available for guests' perusal upon request. When motionless puppets get boring, the **Piccolo Teatro dei Pupi** puts on elaborate puppet shows of traditional Sicilian tales. *(Museum located at P. S. Giuseppe 33. ☎0931 46 55 40; www.pupari.com. Open Mar.-Sept. M-Sa 10:30am-1pm and 4-7pm, Oct.-Dec. M-Sa 11am-1pm and 4-8pm. €2. Theater located at V. della Giudecca 17/19. Performances Jan. and Mar.-Dec. daily at 6:30, 7:30pm. Adults €7, under 18 €5.)*

AQUARIUM. Tucked between Fontana Aretusa and a shady park with a view of the sea, the Siracusa Aquarium is home to an international variety of marine life. Tanks are divided into two sections, the first with freshwater tropical fish and plants, such as those native to African lakes and the Amazon River. The second section houses a mix of the aqarium's strangest, most vibrantly-colored sea-invertebrates and fish. *(Located in Largo Aretusa, directly in front of the fountain. ☎333 16 74 461; www.aquariumsr.it. Open daily 10am-8pm. Adults €4, children €3.)*

TEMPIO DI APOLLO. Standing proudly at the entrance to Ortigia since its construction by the Greeks in the sixth century BC, two intact columns and part of the southern wall of Apollo's Temple are still a sight to behold. Though it is Sicily's oldest Doric temple, it's main role today is to attract tourists to the outdoor markets in the surrounding streets. *(Follow Ponte Umbertino to Ortigia's entrance, walk through P. Pancali, and the temple is visible behind an iron fence from everywhere in Largo XXV Luglio. Oudoor markets begin to the left of the temple and extend nearly to the sea.)*

FONTANE BIANCHE. Like all Italians, *siracusani* fall prey in summer to ancestral instincts that lure them from the cities to beaches like the Fontane Bianche, which offers music on the weekends. *(Take bus #21 or 22. 30min., every 2-3hr., €1.)*

🎵 🎭 ENTERTAINMENT AND NIGHTLIFE

In May and June, the city stages **classical Greek drama** in its ancient amphitheaters. The APT office (see **Practical Information,** p. 699) has details. Tickets for **Istituto Nazionale del Dramma Antico** are available at the theater box office, in the Archaeological Park. (☎0931 48 72 48; www.indafondazione.org. Open M-F 10am-7pm.) During the **Festa di Santa Lucia,** December 13, men clad in green shoulder the silver statue of the city's patron saint in a 6hr. procession from the *duomo* to Santa Lucia al Sepolcro on the mainland. The festival begins with the traditional lighting of a multitude of eye-shaped candles, as St. Lucia is the protector of eyesight. On December 20, the same strong men return the martyr to the *duomo*, concluding the sacred week.

   Piazzetta San Rocco is a nightlife hot spot. The best bar here is the eclectic 🔲**Buio,** V. delle Vergini 16, where the elderly owner blares Tupac and other hip-hop favorites well into the night (☎348 58 54 695). **Il Sale,** hidden away in the courtyard of an old building off V. Amalfitania, hosts live bands and revelers well past 3am (☎339 15 77 381). **Bagatto,** in the small P. S. Giuseppe, often features free, live music and is popular amongst locals for its prime location (☎0931 22 040; show schedule available at www.bagattoilpub.it). **Palalive** (☎0931 79 03 45) hosts sporadic summer concerts at nearby Lido Sayonara.

⚫ DAYTRIP FROM SYRACUSE: NOTO

Noto (NOH-toh) is a Baroque visual pleasure. After a 1693 earthquake shook the Sicilian shore, the noble Landolina and Niccolaci families made Noto their favorite renovation project, restoring its elegance with monumental staircases, putti moldings, and pot-bellied balconies. Noto has a slower pace than other coastal towns, making it a calm retreat from frenzied tourist destinations. In the third week in May, artists work tirelessly from Friday through Sunday for the **Infiorata,** decorating V. Niccolaci with big, bright flower petal murals. Toward the *centro* from C. Vittorio Emanuele and up four flights of giant steps stands the immense **Chiesa di San Francesco all'Immacolata,** which was built in 1704 and houses one of the bloodiest crucifixes in Sicily. *(Explanation in English, French, Italian, and Spanish. Open daily 8am-noon and 2-8pm.)* Visitors to the town will be blown away by the immaculate beige exterior and sparkling white interior of the newly renovated **Cattedrale di Noto,** also on the main thoroughfare. After the cupola and the roof suddenly collapsed on March 13, 1996, the city began rebuilding the church, slowly but surely. Renovations were finally completed on June 18, 2007, and now the cathedral is the undeniable shining gem of Noto, its image on the forefront of every postcard in every souvenir shop. On C. V. Emanuele, stop at the **Teatro Comunale Vittorio Emanuele** to gaze up at its painted balconies and bright, red drapes. *(☎0931 89 66 55. Play season Nov.-May. Open Tu-Su 9am-1pm and 4-8pm. €1.50, show tickets €10-€25.)* From C. V. Emanuele, turn right on V. Niccolaci for a view of the balconies of the **Palazzo Niccolaci,** supported by cherubs, griffins, and seductive sirens. The panoramic view of the city from the top of **Chiesa di San Carlo's** *campanile* is unbeatable. *(Open daily 9:30am-1pm and 3-7:30pm. €1.50, under 18 and students €1.)* **The Hall of Mirrors** at Palazzo Ducezio in P. Municipio on C. V. Emanuele is worth a look if you're into ornate Baroque decorations. The 18th-century frescoes of local history are interspersed with mirrors from which the hall takes its name. *(Open Tu-Su 9am-1pm and 4-8pm. Free.)*

Decent **beaches** are 7km away at **Noto Marina.** Buses depart from the Giardini Pubblici (July-Aug. M-Sa 8:30, 10am, 12:30, 4pm; €1.80). For hungry sightseers, **Ristorante Al Terrazzo ❷,** V. Baccarini 4, right off C. V. Emanuele, offers upscale outdoor dining at affordable prices. *(☎0931 83 97 10. Pizza €4-10. Primi €5-12. Secondi €6-12. Contorni €2-4. Dessert €3. Cover €1. AmEx/MC/V.)* If that stomach begins to grumble on the opposite side of town, indulge in a gelato (€1.50), or *granita* (€2) from **Caffè Arcobaleno ❶,** C. V. Emanuele 54. *(☎0931 30 90 899. Open 24hr. Cash only.)* Noto is accessible by train from Syracuse (45min., 10 per day 5:15am-8:05pm, €3.10). The station is a 15min. walk from Ortigia and can also be reached by **Interbus** (1hr.; 8 per day 7am-5:40pm, return 7 per day 7:40am-4:20pm; €2.85). To reach the *centro* from the train station, follow the road leading uphill and to the right until it ends, then walk one block through the park. A left turn here and a 5min. walk will put you at the far end of the town's main street, C. V. Emanuele.

AGRIGENTO   ☎0922

Agrigento (AH-gree-JEN-toh; pop. 52,000) is a peculiar mix of old and new, from stunningly intact Greek temples to Armani Emporiums, from winding medieval paths to the shiny Mercedes-Benz sedans that traverse them, and from family-run trattorie to the glittering McDonald's across the street. Home to the father of modern medicine, Empedocle, and Nobel Prize-winning author Luigi Pirandello, the city celebrates its roots year-round with traditional parades and festivals. Visitors come explicitly for the Valle dei Templi, and end up staying longer to enjoy the beaches, warmth, and an evening gelato on Via Atenea.

TRANSPORTATION

Trains: The **train station** is in P. Marconi, below P. Aldo Moro. Ticket office open daily 6:30am-8pm. Trains go to **Catania** (3hr.; 12:20pm, 6:50pm; €9.80), via **Enna** (2hr., 4 per day 9am-5pm; €6.50), **Caltanissetta** (1hr. 20min.; 8:15am, 1:50pm; €5.10), and **Palermo** (2hr., 112 per day 4:40am-8:05pm, €6.90).

Buses: Just beyond P. V. Emanuele, buses depart from P. Roselli, where the ticket booth is located. Cuffaro, V. Balsamo 13 (☎0922 091 61 61 510; www.cuffaro.info), runs buses to **Palermo** (M-Sa 8 per day 5:15am-6:30pm, Su 8:15am, 4:30, 6:30pm; €7.50); info available at the bar in P. Roselli. SAIS Trasporti, V. Ragazzi del 99 (☎0922 59 59 33), runs buses to **Caltanissetta** (1hr., M-Sa 11 per day 4:45am-6:15pm, €4.60) and **Catania** (2hr., 12 per day, €11.20). Lumia (www.autolineelumia.it), runs buses to **Trapani** (M-Sa 6:30, 8:30am, 1:40pm; €10.50). Reduced service Su.

Public Transportation: Orange TUA buses depart from the train station. Find tickets (€0.90) valid 1hr. in the station. Buses #2 and 2/ run to the beach at **San Leone**; #1, 1/, 2, 2/, 3, and 3/ run to the **Valle dei Templi**; #1 runs to **Pirandello's house.**

Taxis: At train station, in P. Marconi (☎0922 26 670). A trip to the temples (p. 708) should run about €15 on the meter—just make sure it's running.

ORIENTATION AND PRACTICAL INFORMATION

Agrigento's **train station** is in **Piazza Marconi,** the main stop for all city buses. Walk up the stairs to find the town's lively park-like central square, **Piazza Aldo Moro.** From P. Aldo Moro, the posh **Via Atenea** leads to the *centro storico.* At the far side of P. Aldo Moro is **Piazza Vittorio Emanuele,** just beyond which is the **bus station.** The temples are a bus ride or a long walk away.

Tourist Office: AAPIT kiosk in the train station and **AAST** (☎0922 20 454), adjacent to P. Aldo Moro. English-speaking staff, maps, and brochures. AAST open M-Sa 8:30am-1pm and 3:30-7pm. AAPIT kiosk open daily in summer 9am-1pm and 3:30-7pm; in winter 9am-1pm. Another summer office is in **Valle dei Templi,** adjacent to parking lot. English spoken. Open daily 8:30am-1pm and 3pm-sunset.

English-Language Bookstore: Capalunga, V. Atenea 123 (☎0922 22 338; www.capalunga.com). Art shows, hip decor and a modest selection of English books. Curl up in an egg-shaped window seat overlooking the sea. Customers enjoy free Internet access. Open daily 9:30am-1pm and 6-10pm; July-Aug. closed M.

Carabinieri: P. Aldo Moro 2 (☎0922 59 63 22). **First Aid:** ☎0922 40 13 44.

Pharmacy: Farmacia Averna Antonio, V. Atenea 325 (☎0922 26 093) and **Farmacia Dr Patti,** V. Atenea 129 (☎0922 20 591). Both open M-F 9am-1:30pm and 5-8:30pm. Both also post late-night and weekend rotations.

Hospital: Ospedale Civile (☎0922 44 21 11), 6km from town center toward Palermo on Contrada Consolida, off V. San Michele. Take bus #4 from P. Rosselli.

Internet Access: A.M. Servizi Internet Train, Cortile Contarini 7 (☎0922 40 27 83; www.internettrain.it). 1 block before Chiesa del Purgatorio, make a right onto V. Atenea from P. Aldo Moro. 15 high-speed computers. Wi-Fi and Internet access €3.20 per hr. Open M-Sa 9:15am-1:15pm and 3:30-9pm.

Post Office: P.V. Emanuele (☎0922 59 51 50; fax 0922 22 926). Open M-Sa 8am-6:30pm. **Postal Code:** 92100.

ACCOMMODATIONS

Bed and Breakfast Valle dei Templi, V. Callicratide 164, 5th fl. (☎0922 27 912 or 0922 340 54 59 400). 5 brightly decorated rooms come with desks, dressers, TV, and comfortable beds. Shared kitchen with all the necessities, plus 3 large bathrooms in the hallway. 2 rooms come with A/C, and the others with fans. Free Internet access on the 4th fl. Homemade breakfast included. €20-25 per person. Cash only. ❶

Hotel Concordia, P. S. Francesco 11 (☎0922 59 62 66; www.albergo-concordia.it). Ideal location off V. Atenea and near P. Aldo Moro. 30 cozy, clean rooms with comfortable beds and large windows. All with large private bath, phone, TV, and A/C. Breakfast included. Singles €30; doubles €60; triples €75. MC/V. ❷

Bed and Breakfast Al Centro Storico, V. Saponara 19 (☎0922 59 60 57), off P. Lena in the historic center. 3 elegantly furnished rooms come with A/C, satellite TV, large private bath, and free Wi-Fi. Enormous breakfast included. Doubles €60-70; triples €80-90. Reservations recommended. Cash only. ❷

Hotel Bella Napoli, P. Lena 6 (☎/fax 0922 20 435; hotelbellanapoli@tin.it), off V. Bac Bac. Take V. Atenea 500m uphill, and turn right at the sign for Trattoria de Paris. Cheerful, yellow hallways lead to bright rooms with bath, A/C, phone and TV; some with balcony. Breakfast €3. Singles €35; doubles €65; triples €85. AmEx/MC/V. ❸

Bed and Breakfast Lerux, V. Callicratide 164 (☎0922 27 203 or 0922 333 20 59 606). A 5min. walk from the train station down V. Acrone. Cheap apartment rooms in the residential district. Shared bath and communal TV room. Laundry €3. Reservations recommended. Singles €20-25; doubles €40-48; triples €60-75. Cash only. ❷

Hotel Amici, V. Acrone 5 (☎0922 40 28 31; www.hotelamici.com). Down the stairs and next to the bingo parlor in P. Marconi. Offers 20 quiet rooms with bath, TV, and A/C; some with balcony and sea views. Parking and breakfast included. Singles €40-50; doubles €65-80; triples €75-90; quads €90-120. MC/V. ❹

Camping Nettuno, (☎0922 41 62 68), on the beach at V. l'Acquameno, by the bus stop. Take bus #2 or 2/ from the train station. Market, restaurant, bar, and pizzeria on premises. Free showers. €6 per person; €6 per tent; €3 per car. Cash only. ❶

FOOD

Alimentari cluster near P. Aldo Moro, while the small stairways tucked off V. Atenea lead to authentic, inexpensive trattorie. Indulge your sweet tooth at the candy stalls along V. della Vittoria. The *Sette Soli*, a smooth local wine, provides a nice complement to most meals.

▓ **Trattoria Atenea,** V. Ficani 12 (☎0922 20 247), off V. Atenea. This famed family favorite serves up typical Sicilian specialties like *pasta con sarde* (€3.50) and *risotto alla marinara* (€3.50). Hungry patrons can fill up with the *pranzo della casa* (homemade lunch; €14.50), an enormous meal of the house *cavatelli* and grilled seafood, with salad and a choice of white or red wine. Primi €3.50. Secondi €5.50-7.50. Dessert €3. Open M-Sa noon-3pm and 6pm-midnight. Cash only. ❷

▓ **Trattoria de Paris,** P. Lena 7 (☎0922 25 413), beside Hotel Bella Napoli. Supplies locals with fresh pasta at a deliciously low price. Try the *cavatelli al cartoccio* (homemade pasta with eggplant, basil, ricotta cheese, and tomato sauce; €5), or the *scaloppine al vino bianco* (€6). Primi €5.50. Secondi €6-8. Service 15%. Open M-Sa noon-3pm and 7:30-10:30pm. AmEx/MC/V. ❷

▓ **Manhattan Trattoria/Pizzeria,** Salita degli Angeli 9 (☎0922 20 911), off V. Atenea. Sit inside or outside on terraced steps and enjoy regional specialties like *gnocchi al*

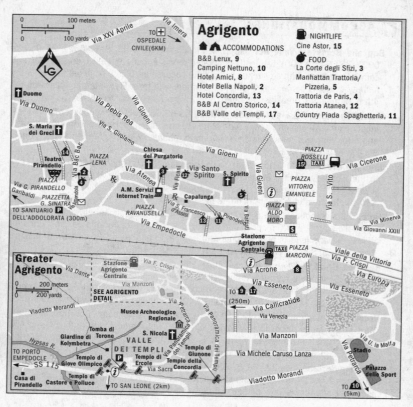

gorgonzola e pistacchio (€6). The chef's specialty ravioli and tortellini options are excellent (€7-8). Antipasto buffet €6. Dinner pizza from €4-7. Primi €5-8. Secondi €6-15. Dessert €1-4. Cover €1.50. Open M-Sa noon-3pm and 7-11pm. AmEx/MC/V. ❷

Country Piada Spaghetteria, V. Pirandello 21 (☎0922 40 28 59). A little piece of the Wild West right in the heart of Agrigento, Country Piada cooks are quick to draw *panini* (€2.60-3) with fun names like Billy the Kid (€2.60) and Smoking Pistol (€3). Full *panino* or *piadina* plates with drinks and *contorno* (€5.50-6). Antipasti €4.50-5. Primi €4-7. Secondi €6. Open Tu-Su 1-3pm and 8pm-midnight. Cash only. ❷

La Corte degli Sfizi, Cortile Contarini 4 (☎0922 349 57 92 922), off V. Atenea. Classic Sicilian dishes served in a lush bamboo-enclosed garden. Go for the house specialty *spaghetti finocchio e sarde* (€7.50), with some local *panelle* (€3) on the side. Pizza €4-8. Antipasti €3-8. Primi €5-8. Secondi €6-13. Dinner *menù* €18-20. Cover €2, pizzeria service 20%. Open M and W-Su 11am-3pm and 6:30pm-midnight. Cash only. ❷

🅖 SIGHTS

🅜**VALLE DEI TEMPLI.** Planted on a ridge below Agrigento's hilltop perch, the five temples revere the invincibility of Greek architecture. Having survived the ravages of time, earthquakes, vicious Punic Wars, and the rise of Christianity, the temples are official UNESCO World Heritage Sites. As sunlight transitions to moonlight, the temples cast eerie silhouettes across the countryside; after dark, they're illuminated by concealed lighting. From the ticket booth right off the road leading to Agrigento, an avenue heads uphill along the ridge, passing the **Tempio di Ercole.** You can climb among one row of solid, squat columns, which is all that remains of the earliest of the temples. Farther along, the perfectly intact pediment and columns of the **Tempio della Concordia** are the Valle's star attraction. Erected in the mid-fifth century BC from limestone, it owes its survival to its use by the Archbishop of Agrigento who, after kicking out the demons Eber and Ray, rededicated the temple to Saints Peter and Paul and transformed it into a Christian church. The road through the valley ends at the fifth-century BC **Tempio di Giunone.** During the ascent, hollows in the rock face to the left mark an early Christian burial site. Down the street lies the entrance to the eternally unfinished **Tempio di Giove Olimpico.** Had Carthaginian troops not interrupted its construction in 406 BC, it would have been one of the largest Greek temples ever built. The toppled partitioned columns and walls have challenged archaeologists for years, but the temple's most interesting sights are the gigantic telamones, 8m sculpted male figures meant to encircle the temple. One of these massive men has been reconstructed at the site. At the end of the path stand four columns of the long since destroyed **Tempio di Castore e Polluce,** also known as the Tempio dei Dioscuri, where sailors and athletes would offer sacrifice for good fortune in their endeavors.

The **Museo Archeologico Regionale,** uphill from the parking lot, has an enormous collection of red- and black-figure vases, terra-cotta votive figures, and funerary vessels from the area's necropolis, as well as a large collection of Paolo Orsi's Agrigento discoveries. Check out a upright telamon and a model projections of how a completed Tempio di Giove Olimpico might have looked. Signs in Italian and English explain each item's significance, and audio tours are offered in many languages (€5). The **Chiesa di San Nicola** near the museum displays the sarcophagus of Phaedra, one of the most impressive AD third-century works. (*30min. walk from the train station. Starting on V. F. Crispi, follow signs downhill and left at the lower intersection. Buses #1/, 2, 2/, 3, or 3/ run from the train station and stop in a dirt parking lot with a snack bar. Make sure to bring lots of water, sunscreen, light clothes, and good walking shoes. Visiting when the park opens or right before it closes is a good way to avoid heat and crowds. Agrigento KREA Touristic Service, ☎ 0922 26 191 or 0922 55 49 18; puntoKREA@libero.it, located at the ticket office, offers guided tours and helpful information in many languages. Temple ☎ 0922 390 92 22 64 36, Museum ☎ 0922 290 22 59 54 48. Lower temples open daily in summer 8:30am-7pm; in winter 8:30am-5pm. Upper temples open daily in summer 8:30am-7pm and 9pm-midnight; in winter 8:30am-7pm. Temples €8; museum €8; combined ticket €10; students 18-24 temples €5, museum 4; under 18 or over 65 free. Parking €2 for 3hr., motorcycle €1.50.*)

GIARDINO DELLA KOLYMBETRA. Originally used as a garden and irrigation basin by the Greeks in 500 BC, the Gardens at Kolymbetra, translated roughly as "the place of giving waters," was used continually as an orchard until the 20th century. Given over to the FAI (Italian Environmental Agency) in the 1990s, the garden is now restored to its formal quiet splendor. Take a break from temple-gazing and enjoy a quiet walk through the shade. (*In a valley next to the Tempio di Castore e Polluce; follow signs to the garden. ☎ 0922 335 12 29 042; www.fondoambiente.it. Open daily July-Sept. 10am-7pm; Apr.-June 10am-6pm; Oct.-Mar. 10am-5pm. €2.*)

CHIESA DI SANTA MARIA DEI GRECI. First constructed by the Normans in the 1100s and remodeled by the Byzantines in the 1300s, Santa Maria dei Greci's real attraction is not what's inside, but what's beneath. Below the pews and through its glass floors, visitors can see a fifth-century BC ancient Greek temple dedicated to Athena and recently excavated ruins of Agrigento's first

Christian church from the AD fifth century. The original Athenian sacrificial altar stands behind the Christian altar in the present church. Down below, pay special attention to the large hole in front of the temple's altar, where the entrance to a tunnel once led all the way to the Valle dei Templi. *(Follow the signs up the hill from V. Bac Bac, off V. Atenea.* ☎ *0922 333 87 02 111. Open M-Sa 9am-1pm and 3-6pm, Su upon request. Modest dress requested. Donations requested.)*

CHIESA DEL PURGATORIO (SAN LORENZO). The legendary craftsman Serpotta employed all of his wizardry to make this church's stucco sculptures look like marble. The statues of the Virtues were intended to help parishioners avoid purgatory by reminding them of its unpleasantries. Church elders did a thorough job—it's pretty hard to ignore the reminders of eternal damnation: an abundance of skulls and crossbones adorn each confessional and countless eery depictions of roasted sinners pepper the walls. You may not want to come here unless you're certain you won't end up in a place like this. *(P. Purgatorio, off V. Atenea, in the centro storico. Open M-Sa 9:30am-7:30pm. €1.50.)*

TEATRO PIRANDELLO. Dedicated to Queen Margherita in 1880, the theater was renamed in honor of Agrigento's favorite son, playwright Luigi Pirandello, on the 10th anniversary of his death in 1946. After brief stints as a movie theater, the building now hosts a variety of plays in the winter months, including many works by Pirandello. There are no plays in the summer, but the 19th-century building designed by local architect Dioniso Sciascia is worth a peek. Look for the four names on the dome ceiling of ancient *agrigentini* famous for the arts. *(☎ 0922 59 02 22. Open M-F 8am-1pm, Tu and Th 3-6pm. Plays Nov.-May. Check the schedule posted at the theater or ask at the tourist office. €2.50, includes tour in English.)*

CASA NATALE DI LUIGI PIRANDELLO. Pirandello aficionados will enjoy a visit to his birthplace, just a few kilometers outside of the city. Treasures include a series of photographs, playbills, script drafts, and various letters from the master to a bevy of friends and loved ones. A huge stone marks his gravesite. Those that don't have a particularly strong interest in Pirandello and the inner-workings of his everyday life may not be thrilled by this sight. *(Take the TUA bus #1 to P. Kaos.* ☎ *0922 51 11 02. Open daily 9am-1pm and 4-7pm. €2, under 18 or over 65 free.)*

🔥📷 FESTIVALS AND BEACHES

The hills surrounding the Valle dei Templi come alive with the sound of music every year on the first Sunday in February, when Agrigento hosts the **Almond Blossom Festival,** an international folk-dancing fest that draws eager visitors from around Italy and the globe. Dancing, music, and huge parades take over the city for a week as thousands journey from all over the world to join in the old-time fun. The **Settimana Pirandelliana,** a week-long outdoor festival of plays, operas, and ballets in P. Kaos, pays homage to the town's beloved son in late July and early August. Overlapping with the celebration of the city's patron saint, San Calogero. (Info ☎ 0922 23 561.) During summer months, some *agrigentini* abandon the town in search of the beach and nightlife at San Leone, 4km from Agrigento by bus #2. Just be careful not to tumble down the **Scala dei Turchi,** the beautiful natural steps that descend to Lido Rossello, another popular beach, after a night of carousing. After a long day at the beach, stroll through the lively Via Atenea in the evening, or catch an Italian or dubbed American flick at **Cine Astor,** P. V. Emanuele. (☎0922 25 866. Nightly shows at 6:30, 8:30, and 10:30pm.) Free classical music concerts often waft lithely through in the sanctuary of the **Monastero di Santo Spirito,** off V. Atenea, throughout the year, making it even more of a restful spot than the name would imply. Call ☎0922 59 85 79 for the concert schedule.

WESTERN SICILY

TRAPANI ☎0923

From the ancient rooftops and buildings adorned with exquisite tilework to the colorful fishing boats and massive ferries just below the horizon, Trapani (TRA-pa-nee; pop. 75,000) is every bit the crossroads between Europe and North Africa it has been for centuries. Reliable transportation and extensive lodgings make Trapani a good base for adventures to Marsala's monuments, Segesta's temple, the Egadi Islands' peaceful nature, Erice's medieval streets, San Vito Lo Capo's beaches, and the natural splendor of Riserva dello Zingaro.

⌐ TRANSPORTATION

Flights: Vincenzo Florio Airport (☎0923 84 25 02), in Birgi en route to Marsala, 16km outside of Trapani. Buses run from P. Malta. Serves **Rome** and **Pantelleria** daily.

Trains: (☎0923 89 20 21), in P. Umberto I. Ticket office open daily 6am-7:45pm. To: **Castelvetrano** (1hr., 10 per day 6:42am-6:40pm, €4.60); **Marsala** (30min., 16 per day 6:42am-9:25pm, €3); **Palermo** (2hr., 11 per day 6am-8pm, €6.90).

Buses: AST, P. Malta (☎0923 23 222) runs to: **Erice** (45min.; M-Sa 8 per day 6:40am-8pm, Su 4 per day 9am-5:30pm; €2.10), **Marsala** (M-Sa 6:50am, 12:50, and 2:10pm; €2.75), and **San Vito Lo Capo** (1hr.; M-Sa 8 per day 6:45am-8pm, Su 4 per day 7:50am-6:45pm; €3.50). **Segesta** (☎0923 21 754) runs to **Rome** (15hr.; Th and Su 5pm, Sa 6am; €49).

DESTINATION	COMPANY	DURATION	FREQUENCY	PRICE
Favignana (Egadi Islands)	Siremar (ferry)	1hr.	3 per day	€3.90
Favignana (E.I.)	Ustica (hydrofoil)	30min.	9 per day	€9.80
Favignana (E.I.)	Siremar (hydrofoil)	30min.	10 per day	€9.80
Levanzo (E.I.)	Siremar (ferry)	1hr.	3 per day	€3.90
Levanzo (E.I.)	Siremar (hydrofoil)	30min.	10 per day	€9.80
Levanzo (E.I.)	Ustica (hydrofoil)	30min.	9 per day	€9.80
Marettimo (E.I.)	Siremar (ferry)	3hr.	1 per day	€8.40
Marettimo (E.I.)	Siremar (hydrofoil)	50min.	3 per day	€18
Marettimo (E.I.)	Ustica (hydrofoil)	50min.	2 per day	€18
Pantelleria	Siremar (ferry)	5hr.	M-F and Su 1 per day	€30
Cagliari (Sardinia)	Tirrenia (ferry)	11hr.	Tu 1 per day	€45
Tunis, Tunisia	Tirrenia (ferry)	8hr.	M, W, F 1 per day	€50
Tunis, Tunisia	Ustica (ferry)	8hr.	M, W, F 1 per day	€44

Ferries: Ferries and hydrofoils to the **Egadi Islands** (Levanzo, Favignana, and Marettimo), **Pantelleria, Sardinia,** and **Tunisia.** Ferries depart Stazione Marittima across from P. Garibaldi; hydrofoils depart farther along V. Ammiraglio Staiti, 150m toward the train station. Buy tickets from travel agents along V. A. Staiti, from ticket booths on the docks, and at Stazione Marittima. The chart above shows high-season (June-Aug.) times and rates; ferries and hydrofoils are less frequent and less expensive in low season.

Ustica: (☎0923 22 200; www.usticalines.it), in a yellow booth at the hydrofoil dock. AmEx/MC/V.

Siremar: (☎0923 54 54 55; www.siremar.it). Ticket offices at a blue-and-white striped waterfront booth, at the hydrofoil dock, and in Stazione Marittima. Open M-F 6:15am-noon, 3-6pm, and 9pm-midnight; Sa 6:15am-noon, 4:15-5:15pm, and 9:30pm-midnight; Su 6-10am, 5-5:45pm, and 9:30pm-midnight. AmEx/MC/V.

Tirrenia: (☎092354 54 33; www.tirrenia.it), in Stazione Marittima. Open M and W-F 9am-1pm and 3-6pm, Tu 9am-1pm and 6-9pm, Sa 9am-noon. AmEx/MC/V.

Public Transportation: Orange **SAU buses** (☎0923 55 95 75). Main terminal at P. Emanuele, 4 blocks from the train station. Tickets (€1) sold at most *tabaccherie*.

Taxis: in P. Umberto I (☎0923 22 808), outside the train station. Near the port in V. Ammiraglio Staiti (☎0923 23 233).

✴ 🔼 ORIENTATION AND PRACTICAL INFORMATION

Trapani is on a peninsula 2hr. west of Palermo. The *centro storico* begins at the outer tip of the hook, grows backward from the peninsula, and spills new streets and high-rises onto the mainland. The train station is in **Piazza Umberto I;** the bus station is behind and to the left in **Piazza Malta. Via Scontrino** runs past the train station; a right from the station leads to an intersection with **Via Garibaldi** at **Piazza Emanuele.** V. Garibaldi becomes **Via Libertà** on its way into the *centro storico.* **Via Torrearsa** is off V. Libertà. **Via Roma,** also off V. Libertà, leads to the port. V. Libertà merges with **Corso Vittorio Emanuele,** which runs to **Torre di Ligny.**

Tourist Offices:

AAPIT (☎0923 29 000; www.apt.trapani.it), off V. Torrearsa. Eager staff. Pick up *Trapani Hotels* for regional accommodations listings. Open M-Sa 8:30am-8pm, Su 9am-noon.

Provincial Tourism Office, V. San Francesco d'Assisi 27 (☎092354 55 11; www.apt.trapani.it), off V. Verdi. Marked "APT" on maps. Open M-Tu and Th-Sa 8am-1pm, W 8am-1pm and 3-6pm.

Currency Exchange: Banks line many of the city's streets. They generally have better rates than the train station. **ATMs** are at Stazione Marittima in the old city and along V. Scontrino in front of the train station.

Emergency: Police, P. Vittorio Veneto (☎0923 59 02 98). **Carabinieri,** V. Orlandini 19 (☎0923 27 122). **Ambulance:** (☎0923 18 09 450.

Pharmacy: Vle. Margherita 9, next to P.V. Veneto. All pharmacies open M-F 9am-1:30pm and 4:30-8pm. Posts after-hours rotation.

Hospital: Ospedale Sant'Antonio Abate, V. Cosenza 81 (☎0923 80 91 11).

Internet Access: Phone and Internet, V. Regina Elena 26/28 (☎0923 28 866; www. trapaniservice.it), next to P. Garibaldi along the *lungomare.* €5 per hr. International phone services and fax. Open M-Sa 10am-1pm and 4-8:30pm.

Post Office: P.V. Veneto 3 (☎0923 43 41 11), in P.V. Veneto on V. Garibaldi. Currency exchange available. Open M-Sa 8am-6pm. **Postal Code:** 91100.

> **✦TIP✦** **KA-CHING!** Before exchanging money, always ask about the commission, which can be as high as €10. No Italian law requires financial institutions to inform clients of exchange fees before finalizing transactions.

🏠 ACCOMMODATIONS

Hotel Moderno, V. Genovese 20 (☎0923 21 247; hotelmodernotrapani@virgilio.it). From P. Sant'Agostino on C. Vittorio Emanuele, turn right on V. Roma and left on V. Genovese. Accommodating staff and modern, well-kept rooms, all with TV and bath. Reception 24hr. Singles €25; doubles €50; triples €67. AmEx/MC/V. ❷

Albergo Messina, C. V. Emanuele 71, 4th fl. (☎/fax 0923 21 198). Tiny family-run hotel in the *centro storico.* All rooms have balcony and fridge. Shared bath. Breakfast €4. Free Internet access. Singles €20; doubles €40. AmEx/MC/V. ❷

Albergo Maccotta, V. degli Argentieri 4 (☎0923 28 418; fax 0923 43 76 93; www.albergomaccotta.it), near P. S. Agostino. Centrally located. Rooms have private bath, phone, TV, desk, and A/C. Free Wi-Fi. Singles €35-40; doubles €60-75. AmEx/MC/V. ❸

Hotel Vittoria, V. Francesco Crispi 4 (☎0923 87 30 44; www.hotelvittoriatrapani.it), off P. V. Emanuele, near train station. Large, luxurious rooms offer modern comforts, including A/C, free Wi-Fi, and, for some, coastal views. Inviting communal area in the lobby. Breakfast included. Singles €65; doubles €100; triples €130. AmEx/MC/V. ❹

Nuovo Albergo Russo, V. Tintori 4 (☎0923 22 166; fax 0923 26 623), off C. V. Emanuele. Comfortable rooms have eclectic decor, bath, A/C, and TV. Breakfast included. Singles €45-52; doubles €76-90; triples €95-115; quads €120-145. AmEx/MC/V. ❹

▐ FOOD

Trapani's cuisine is an exotic blend of North African and Italian flavors. Try the specialty couscous with fish or *biscotti con fichi* (moist, fig-filled cookies). The *centro storico* has *alimentari* and a daily **market** at the intersection of V. Maggio and V. Garibaldi. **Supermercato DìperDì,** V. San Pietro 30, is two blocks up from the port between Chiesa Santa Maria del Gesù and Chisa San Pietro. (☎0923 24 620. Open M-Sa 7:30am-1:30pm and 4:30-8:30pm, Su 8:30am-1pm.)

▨ Trattoria da Salvatore, V. Nunzio Nasi 19 (☎0923 54 65 30), 1 block toward the port from C. V. Emanuele. Serves regional pasta (€6.50) and spicy couscous (€8.50) family-style. Primi €4-8.50. Secondi €7-8.50. Cover €1.50. Open daily noon-3:30pm and 6-11pm; closed Su in winter. AmEx/MC/V. ❷

Ristorante Medina, Vle. Regina Margherita 19 (☎0923 29 028), across from the main gate to Villa Margherita. Popular teen hangout. Middle Eastern cuisine and pizza. Pizza from €1.50. Kebabs €3.50. *Panini* €3.50. Open daily noon-3pm and 7pm-midnight. ❶

Cantina Siciliana, V. Giudecca 32 (☎0923 28 673; www.cantinasiciliana.it), 1st left off V. XXX Gennaio from the port. *Trapanese* cuisine. Antipasti €5-10. Primi €6-10. Secondi €9-13. Contorni €3. Dessert €3. Open daily 12:30-4pm and 7:30-11pm. MC/V. ❸

Trattoria Al Solito Posto, V. Orlandini 30 (☎0923 24 545), 3 blocks east from Hotel Vittoria. Renowned for its authentic Trapanese fare, like the *tonno alla Trapanese* (Trapanese tuna; €12). Lavish seaside dining room. Antipasti €3-10. Primi €5-6.50. Secondi €9-14. Contorni €1.50-4.50. Open daily 1-4pm and 8-10pm. AmEx/MC/V. ❸

Ristorante Antichi Sapori, C. V. Emanuele 191 (☎0923 22 866; www.gliantichisapori. it). Follow C. V. Emanuele until you reach P. Jolanda. Hearty mariner's fare. Market fresh fish. Antipasti €6.50-8.50. Primi €6.50-17. Secondi €7-13.50. Contorni €2-3. Open M and W-Su 12:30-2:30pm and 7:30-10:30pm. AmEx/MC/V. ❷

▣ SIGHTS

CHIESA DEL PURGATORIO. Delicate stone statues blend into the gray exterior of this Baroque church. Inside, 20 nearly life-sized wooden sculptures, known as *i misteri* ("the mysteries"), depict the Passion and the Crucifixion. On Good Friday, the sculptures, each requiring the strength of 14-30 men to move, are dressed up and paraded. The sculptures' 18th-century artists constructed the Roman soldiers to resemble Spanish conquistadors, reflecting Spanish dominance in Sicily at the time. Several statues were damaged in WWII but have since been restored. *(1 block from P. Garibaldi. Open daily 9am-noon and 3:30-6pm. Free.)*

SANTUARIO DELL'ANNUNZIATA. The modern city's main attraction is this enormous, lavishly decorated church, which houses a 14th-century statue of the Madonna of Trapani. Legend has it that a boat carrying the statue was caught in a storm; the captain promised God that if he survived, he would leave it as a gift to the first port at which he arrived. The **Museo Regionale Pepoli,** which features a collection of local sculpture and painting, coral carvings, and folk-art figurines, is in the same complex. *(2 blocks to the right of the train station or a #24, 25, or*

LOCAL LEGEND

LIKE A VIRGIN

Some 700 years ago in Trapani, a Knight Templar named Guerreggio loaded a statue of the Madonna onto a ship bound for Pisa in an effort to protect it from invading Turks. When he tried to set sail, a storm arose, keeping his boat in the harbor. The next day, as sailors tried again to abscond with the statue, yet another storm blew in. So it happened, day after day. Eventually, Guerreggio decided to make the journey alone, entrusting the statue to Carmelite fathers in Trapani. For 50 years, the Madonna stayed in the town's sanctuary, until one day, a few rowdy Tuscans tried to bring the stubborn statue home with them.

As the men drove their oxen toward the port, statue in tow, the animals suddenly charged back into town, running over anything in their path. In the course of the chaos, a blind man about to be crushed regained his sight, a cripple ran out of the way, and a mute screamed in terror. Miraculously, none of those hit by the cart suffered the slightest injury. Madonna herself remains in her sanctuary to this day, ever-ready to fend off marauders.

2 blocks to the right of the train station. Sanctuario ☎0923 53 91 84; museum ☎0923 55 32 69. Santuario open M-Sa 8am-noon and 4-7pm, Su 8am-1pm and 4-7pm; museum open Tu-Sa 9am-1:30pm, Su 9am-12:30pm. €4, ages 18-25 €2, EU residents under 18 or over 65 free.

30 SAU bus ride from P.V. Emanuele. Sanctuario ☎0923 53 91 84; museum ☎0923 55 32 69 or 0923 53 12 42. Santuario open M-Sa 8am-noon and 4-7pm, Su 8am-1pm and 4-7pm; museum open Tu-Sa 9am-1:30pm, Su 9am-12:30pm. €4, ages 18-25 €2, EU residents under 18 or over 65 free.)

TORRE DI LIGNY. At the end of a wide jetty off a promontory, this tower is visible from both of Trapani's ports. By day, the rock walls seem like outcroppings of the rocky surf, as the identically colored brick fortress rises over boulders. By night, the bright lights of the northern coastline reflect off the water. Locals young and old convene on the beaches to either side of the tower to swim and sunbathe from dawn to dusk. The tower houses the **Museo di Preistoria/Museo del Mare,** with shells, artifacts, and underwater excavation pieces. *(☎0923 28 844 or 347 29 60 043. Open M-Sa 9:30am-noon, Su 10:30am-12:30pm. €1.70.)*

VILLA MARGHERITA. At the cusp of the old and new cities, these gardens offer a change of pace from cobblestone and cement. Banyan trees, palms, statues, and fountains surround avenues. Playgrounds and an aviary complete the serene environment. *(Park open July-Aug. 8am-10pm; Apr.-June and Sept.-Oct. 8am-8pm; Jan.-Mar. and Nov.-Dec. 8am-5pm. Free.)* In July, the gardens host the **Luglio Musicale Trapanese,** a festival of opera and dance that draws stars to the temporary stage amid shady trees. *(☎0923 21 454. Shows 9pm. Info booth inside park gates.)*

⚑ DAYTRIPS FROM TRAPANI

SAN VITO LO CAPO

AST buses leave Trapani's P. Malta for San Vito Lo Capo (9 per day 6:45am-8pm, return 8 per day 6:45am-7:40pm; €3.50, round-trip €5.55). AST info ☎0923 23 222.

A popular vacation spot for Italians, Germans, and Spaniards, San Vito Lo Capo (sahn vee-TOH lo CAH-poh; pop. 3900) has remained under the radar of the English-speaking world. While sun worshippers flock to San Vito's 3km of flawless beaches in July and August, the annual **Couscous Fest,** held during the third week of September, is the Olympics of multi-ethnic Mediterranean cuisine. For shade and seclusion, escape to the ▪**Riserva dello Zingaro,** Italy's first nature reserve, to find rare Bonelli's eagles, mountain trails, and prehistoric caves. An unfinished four-lane highway came perilously close to marring the pristine reserve's isolation, but a 1981 environmental rally halted construction. Once in the reserve, follow the road to secluded, pebble beaches that stretch along the coast. The middle two beaches offer the most privacy. Although camping and cars are prohibited on the shore, the hiking is superb. **Bluvacanze,** V. Savoia 166, runs excursions (M-F 9am, return 4pm; €10) and rents **scooters, bikes,** and **cars.** (☎0923 62 10 85; www.bluvacanze.net. Bikes €5 per day. Scooters €30-35 per day. Cars €42-54 per day. Office open daily 9:30am-1pm and 4-7:30pm. Cash only.) **Nautisub Diving Center,** V. Faro 24, offers guided diving and snorkling near the Riserva dello Zingaro for groups and individuals. (☎348 29 40 610 or 328 81 80 748; www.nautisub.it.) For a **taxi,** call ☎328 56 26 098.

Five minutes from the beach, **Eden Camere ❷,** V. Mulino 58, provides clean, simply furnished rooms, all with private bath and A/C. Doubles often come with a full and a twin bed, or a full bed and two bunked twins. (☎0923 97 24 60. Open Apr.-Oct. Singles €25-35; doubles €45-80. Cash only.) **Hotel Sikania ❸,** V. G. Arimondi 128, has colorful rooms near the water with A/C, TV, phone, and minibar. (☎0923 85 13 95; www.hotelsikania.com. €30-60 per person; €20-35 surcharge for singles.)

For a taste of authentic Sicilian and Tunisian cuisine, head to the elegant Arabic-tiled dining area of **Tha'am ❸,** V. Duca degli Abbruzzi 32, off V. Farina near the waterfront. (Antipasti €7-9. Primi €9-15. Secondi €10-17. Contorni €4-5. Cover €2.50. Open daily 12:30-3pm and 7pm-3am. MC/V.) **U Sfizziusu ❷,** V. Lungomare 19, offers dishes like *cuscus con pesce* (couscous with fish; €7.50) on an outdoor patio with great views. (☎348 04 23 967. Primi €7-10. Secondi €6-12. Contorni €3.50-5. Open 24hr. Cash only.)

MARSALA

Trains run from Trapani (30min.; 12 per day; €2.85, round-trip €6.20). AST buses (☎0923 23 222) also run from Trapani (40min.; M-Sa 2:10, 2:50pm, return M-Sa 8:20am, 1:20, 2:20pm; €2.75, round-trip €4.40). From the train station, a right as you face V. A. Fazio and a slight left on V. Roma leads to the centro storico. V. Roma turns into V. XI Maggio then Vle. Vittorio Veneto. The Pro Loco Tourist Office is at V. XI Maggio 100, before Palazzo Comunale and the duomo. (☎0923 71 40 97; www.prolocomarsala.org. Open M-Sa 8:30am-1:30pm and 3-8pm.)

An area of both ancient history and modern convenience, Marsala's (mahr-SA-lah; pop. 77,000) streets are worth a short visit from nearby Trapani. Garibaldi and his red-shirted revolutionaries landed at Marsala in 1860 to launch the Risorgimento; the city honors this event with its **Porta Garibaldi,** an 18th-century gate erected where Garibaldi first entered. Additionally, in the San Pietro complex on V. XI Maggio, the **Museo Civico** features a variety of Garibaldi-related artifacts, including thousands of red shirts. (Open daily 9am-1pm and 4-8pm. €2, under 18 €1, EU residents over 65 free.) The **Museo Archeologico Regionale Baglio Anselmi** guards the famed **Carthiginian warship.** This now skeletal vessel sank in the final battle of the First Punic War (241 BC), in which Rome defeated Carthage and established its naval supremacy. Other galleries display objects from Lilybaeum and the Isle of Mozia, including pottery, funerary decorations, and two life-size sculptures. (☎0923 95 25 35. Open daily 9am-6pm. €3, under 18 €2, EU residents over 65 free.) Enter the **duomo** from the back to visit the **Museo degli Arazzi** (Tapestry Museum), which houses eight tapestries that spin the tale of Vespasian and his Roman legions from 69 AD to the destruction of the holy temple in Jerusalem during the Judean War. Detailed explanations in English and Italian accompany each tapestry. (Open Tu-Sa 9:30am-1pm and 4:30-6pm, Su 9:30am-12:30pm. €2.50.) Exiting the Museo degli Arazzi to the left brings you to the **Quartiere Militare** (Military Quarters). Built in 1576 by Marsala's Civic Council to evade the backlash provoked by the appropriation of Spanish troops, they housed soldiers until 1860. Now the *quartiere* are home to the municipal administration and a daily market. (Officially open daily 8:30am-3pm, though guards often allow visitors after closing time. Free.)

Besides battles and revolutionaries, Marsala is famous for its sweet wine. Samples are available at various *enoteche* scattered throughout the old city.

GIVING BACK

TURISMO DELIZIOSO

Ever wonder how that fish made it onto your plate all the way from the ocean? With *ittiturismo*, a brand new take on sustainable tourism, you can be part of the process. At participating restaurants like **La Tramontana** in Trapani, clientele have the opportunity to go on organized boating excursions and to learn about and experience local fishing custom and culture.

Proceeds from the trips go toward reconstructing and refurbishing old ports, ships, and historical maritime buildings, as well as revamping fishing villages into culinary centers and constructing maritime museums. All efforts are intended to spread socially-conscious fishing practices, a trend currently sweeping through Sicily.

Housed in an ancient palace dating back to 900, La Tramontana is simultaneously bathed in history and on the edge of innovation. You too can help lead the way toward friendlier fishing practices—all you have to do is say the word: *ittiturismo!*

La Tramontana Ittiturismo, V. Carolina 4. ☎0923 54 08 76; www. ittiturismolatramontana.it. Ittiturismo meals are available only on Saturday and Sunday nights, while instruction is given in the morning. Call or check the website for upcoming events and excursions. Prices vary by season.

For something substantial to soak up all that wine, head to **Trattoria Garibaldi ❷**, P. Addolorata 5, fittingly across from Porta Garibaldi. This upscale trattoria, established in 1963, serves vegetarian omelettes (€4) and a wide variety of Italian cuisine in a relaxed yet classy atmosphere. (Antipasti €7-12. Primi €6-10. Secondi €7-16. Contorni €3-4. Cover €2. Open M-F noon-3pm and 7:30-10:30pm, Sa 7-10pm, Su noon-3pm. AmEx/MC/V.) Bars and cafes line V. Roma and V. XI Maggio, most with relaxed outdoor seating and moderate drink and gelato prices. If you decide to spend the night, **Bed and Breakfast Il Mulino ❷**, V. Struppa 55, offers four doubles and a small single with fans and simple furnishings. (☎0923 73 71 92. Breakfast included. Single €25-30; doubles 45-60. Cash only.)

THE TEMPLE OF SEGESTA

Tarantola buses (☎0923 31 020) leave P. Malta in Trapani for Segesta (depart M-Sa 8am, noon and 2pm, Su 10am; 1-2 per day; €3.10, round-trip €5.30). Temple open 9am-7pm; ticket office 9am-6pm. €6, EU residents ages 18-25 €3, EU residents under 18 or over 65 free.

Isolated and untouched, the Doric temple dominates the dramatic valleys and lush vineyards of Segesta (se-JEH-sta), a former Trojan colony. Roam among fifth-century BC ruins or contemplate their majesty from a Lilliputian pedestal. A castle, mosque, and ◼Greek theater cluster near Monte Barbaro. It's worth the bus trip (every 30min., €1.50) to avoid the steep uphill trek in the midday sun, but the 25min. walk is pleasant on cooler days. The Greek theater carved into the hilltop holds dramatic performances from mid-July to August.

ERICE ☎0923

Visitors to tiny Erice (EH-ree-chay; pop. 300) will be charmed by its quiet streets and awed by panoramas that stretch from Pantelleria to Mt. Etna. A center of worship since the fertility cults of Phoenician goddess Tanit-Asarte, today, Erice is home to a beautiful *duomo*—La Chiesa Madrice (the Mother Church). From atop a Castello Normanno tower, it's easy to see why the people of Erice call their home "Il Monte del Dio" *(The Mountain of God)*.

◪◩ **TRANSPORTATION AND PRACTICAL INFORMATION.** The **bus** from Trapani departs P. Malta (45min.; M-Sa 8 per day 6:40am-8pm, last return 9pm; Su 4 per day 9am-5:30pm, last return to Trapani 6:30pm; round-trip €3.20). Buses stop on **Via Conte Pepoli**, at the base of town and near the Castello Normanno. From **Porta Trapani**, a left turn leads to the *duomo*. **Via Vittorio Emanuele** and Erice's *centro*, **Piazza Umberto I**, are straight through Pta. Trapani. From the bus stop, V. Conte Pepoli leads to **Giardino del Balio** (Balio Gardens) and **Castello Normanno**, also known as the Castello di Venere (Castle of Venus). The **AAST Tourist Office** is at V. Guarrasi 1. (☎0923 86 93 88. Open M-F 9am-2pm.)

▐▌ ACCOMMODATIONS AND FOOD. One of the few budget-friendly options is ▐**Ulisse Camere ❸**, V. Santa Lucia 2, five blocks from the bus stop on V. Conte Pepoli. Request a room with a view of the Egadi islands. (☎0923 86 01 55; www.sitodiulisse.it. Reservations recommended. Singles €38; doubles €60; triples €80; quads €95. Cash only.) **Villa San Giovanni ❸**, V. Nunzio Nasi 12, provides simple rooms with full bath, phone, balcony, and views worth every euro. (☎0923 86 91 71; villas.giovanni@libero.it. Breakfast included. Singles €38-45; doubles €75; half-pension €45; full pension €55.) **Ristorante Venus ❸**, V. Conte Pepoli, on the way to the castle, offers great service, savory Sicilian cuisine, and a spectacular view well worth the splurge. (☎0923 86 94 77. Pizza €5-10. Antipasti €3.50-16. Primi €10-13. Secondi €9-22. Contorni €3-7. Dessert €1.50-5. Cover €2.50. Open daily noon-3pm and 7pm-midnight. AmEx/MC/V.) At **La Vetta ❷**, V. Giuseppe Fontana 5, off P. Umberto I, savor Chef Mario's take on regional favorite couscous (€12) and *busiati* (€8), hand-rolled Sicilian pasta. (☎0923 86 94 04. Pizza €6-10. Antipasti €4-12. Primi €8-10. Secondi €8-20. Cover €1.50-2. Open daily Dec.-Sept. noon-3:30pm and 7:30pm-midnight. AmEx/MC/V.)

◗ SIGHTS. Erice fits an impressive number of sights inside its eighth-century BC **Elymian walls**. The **Castello Normanno** (also known as Castello di Venere) was built on the site of ancient temples to fertility goddesses. It served as a prison until 1940; the hollow tub against the wall farthest from the entrance—likely used for human sacrifice—indicates an earlier, more ominous legacy. Inquire at the tourist office about guided tours and winter hours. (Open daily in summer 9am-7pm. Donations requested.) Next to the castle the Spanish-influenced ▐**Torre Medievale** sits precariously on a rocky outcropping. At the castle's base, the **Giardini del Balio** spread green boughs over stone benches. The views from the gardens and castle are incomparable; most of the countryside—the Egadi Islands, Pantelleria, and occasionally Etna and Tunisia—is visible over the horizon. Throughout Erice, 61 churches await exploration; all are accessible by a joint €5 MEMS ticket available at the tourist office and the *duomo*. The 14th-century Gothic **duomo** features an Arab-influenced Neo-Gothic interior. The **campanile** offers wide views, but visit the castle before paying to scale its heights, because any prior thirst for panoramas may be quenched for free on the other side of town. (Open daily Sept.-July 10am-6pm; Aug. 10am-9pm. *Campanile* €2, with *duomo* €3.) In the library in P. Umberto I, the **Museo Comunale di Erice**, houses a small but varied collection related to the city's fertility goddesses. (Open M and Th 9am-1pm and 3-5pm, Tu-W and F 9am-1pm. Free.)

EGADI ISLANDS (ISOLE EGADI) ☎0923

Lying just off Trapani, the archipelago of Favignana, Levanzo, and Marettimo, known collectively as The Egadi Islands (EE-zo-leh EH-ga-dee), is easily accessible by ferry or hydrofoil. Favignana is the largest and most modern of the trio, with plenty of packed beaches. In Levanzo and Marettimo, mules and sheep share plains with cacti, and rugged cliffs climb the coast.

SICILY

⊏ TRANSPORTATION

Siremar (☎0923 92 13 68; www.siremar.it) and **Ustica** (☎0923 92 12 77; www.
usticalines.it) run **hydrofoils** to and from Trapani (Favignana and Levanzo
25-45min., Marettimo 45-60min.; 10 per day 6:15am-8:20pm; Favignana €9.80,
Marettimo €17.30, Levanzo €9.80). Ustica runs hydrofoils between the islands
(Favignana-Levanzo 4 per day 8am-8:50pm, €5.80; Favignana-Marettimo 10am,
2:35, and 4:50pm, €10.30). Siremar runs **ferries** from Trapani to Favignana (1hr.;
M-Sa 7, 10am, and 5:15pm, Su 10am and 5:45pm; €3.90).

FAVIGNANA

Dubbed "The Great Butterfly of the Sea" for its unique shape and bright colors,
Favignana's (fa-veen-YA-na; pop. 3800) appealing beaches make it a summer
playground for Italians. Summer homes line the shore, while short-term vacationers arrive eager for modern conveniences that the sister towns lack.

⊏ **TRANSPORTATION. Buses** are necessary to reach the more remote beaches.
Tarantola buses (☎0923 31020) run from Porto Florio: **Line 1** (June-Sept., 15
per day 8am-7:45pm) to Calamone (5min.), Lido Burrone (8min.), Cala Azzurra
(15min.); **Line 2** (June-Sept., 15 per day 7:45am-10pm) to Calamone and Cala
Rotonda (13min.); **Line 3** (June-Sept., 10 per day 8:30am-7:15pm) to Cala Rossa
(7min.), Lido Burrone, and Calamone. Buy tickets (€0.70) on the bus. Francesca e Rocco, Traversa Calamoni 7, runs **minibus** excursions around the island.
(☎348 58 60 676. Available 24hr. €15 per person, 4-person min.) Noleggio
Isidoro, V. Mazzini 40, rents bikes and scooters. (☎347 32 33 058. **Bikes** €3-5 per
day, **scooters** €15 per day. Driver's license required. Open daily 8am-7pm.)

▰▨ **ORIENTATION AND PRACTICAL INFORMATION.** Hydrofoils and ferries
run from **Porto Florio**. A right out of the port leads to **Piazza Europa** and **Via Vittorio
Emanuele**, which connects P. Europa to the main plaza, **Piazza Madrice. Via Mazzini**
runs parallel to V. V. Emanuele, between the two *piazze*. At P. Madrice, V. V.
Emanuele becomes **Via Roma. Via Nicotera** also runs through P. Madrice. Off V. V.
Emanuele, **Via Garibaldi** heads away from the *piazze;* eventually it becomes **Via
Libertà**. The most beautiful beaches are about 1km away from the port.
  Services include: the **Pro Loco tourist office**, P. Madrice 68 (☎0923 92 16 47;
www.egadiweb.it/proloco; open daily 9:30am-7:30pm); **Compagnia delle Egadi**,
(☎0923 92 21 87; www.compagniadelleegadi.it), which offers boat excursions;
Banco di Sicilia, P. Madrice 12/14 (☎0923 92 13 47; open M-F 8:20am-1:20pm
and 2:50-3:50pm); the **carabinieri** on V. Simone Corleo (☎0923 92 12 02); **first
aid** on Contrada delle Fosse (☎0923 92 12 83); **Farmacia Barone** at P. Madrice 64
(☎0923 92 12 65; open daily 8:30am-1pm and 5-8:30pm),which posts after-hours
rotations; and the **post office**, Guglielmo Marconi 1 (☎0923 92 12 09; open M-F
8am-1:30pm, Sa 8am-12:30pm), off P. Madrice. **Postal Code:** 91023.

▰▱ **ACCOMMODATIONS AND FOOD. Case Vacanze Mio Sogno ❷**, V. Calamoni
2, is a steal. Take V. Libertà and turn left on V. Dante. Somewhat out of the way,
the hotel is castle-like with a small garden. Rooms come with bath, kitchenette,
A/C, TV, and patio. The owner rents scooters (€15-25 per day) and bikes (€3-5
per day) to guests. (☎0923 92 16 76; www.miosogno.com. Reservations recommended in summer. €25-40 per person. Cash only.) **Camping Egàd ❶**, Contrada
Arena, 500m from Lido Burrone, is a comfortable choice. Tents, bungalows
with kitchenettes and bathrooms, and caravans with shared baths are available. A bike rental shop, diving center, restaurant, market, disco, and athletic

facilities are all on-site. (☎0923 92 15 55 or 0923 92 15 67; www.campingegad.it. Look for the port shuttle, or call for pick-up. Showers €0.30. €5.30-7 per person; €4.80-6.80 per tent. 2-person bungalows €36-80; caravans €24-42. Cash only.)

For lunch, try **Alternative Pub** ❶, P. Europa 4, which serves salads and *panini* (both from €2-5) amid nautical decor. The thirsty can brave the Lanterna (€15), a large, colorful, and very potent drink made from a secret recipe. (Non-alcoholic drinks €1-6.50. Open daily 8:30am-late.) For finger-licking pizza (from €4.50), stop by **Pizzeria La Sirenetta** ❶, P. Europa 27. (Open daily Aug. noon-3pm and 7:30pm-midnight; Sept.-July daily 7:30pm-midnight. Cash only.) Funky cafe by day and lively bar by night, **Camarillo Brillo,** V. V. Emanuele 18, offers live music. (Happy hour 6-10pm; drink and hors d'oeuvres €5. Wine €3.50. Breakfast buffet daily 8-10:30am. Open daily Easter-Sept. 8am-3am. Cash only.)

🏖️ 👁️ **BEACHES AND SIGHTS.** The island's most popular beaches are the Lido Burrone, and the rockier Calamone, Cala Rossa, and Cala Azzurra. **Lido Burrone** is the best equipped, with a playground, two restaurants, and a diving center. (Showers €1.50; chair and umbrella rentals €4.) **Cala Azzurra** and **Cala Rossa,** in coves on the eastern-most south and north of the island, respectively, are touted as the most beautiful. Both are free. There are a number of good diving areas along the eastern beach between Punta S. Nicola and Cala Rossa; use caution and common sense. The beach at Punta S. Nicola is perfect for children, with shallow water and soft sand. All beaches are accessible by Tarantola bus (€0.70). The tip of the island around Cala Rotonda and Galera makes a gorgeous boat trip, but it is difficult to access from land. For boats, inquire at the tourist office. Formerly a prison, an Arab lookout tower, and a Norman fortress, the **Castello di Santa Caterina** is a formidable sight above the city.

LEVANZO

Levanzo (LE-van-zo; pop. 220) is the smallest and least-developed of the three Egadi Islands. Little more than a row of white-washed, blue-shuttered buildings, the *centro* is host to two bars above the docks which serve as the island's quiet social center. Head left down the *lungomare* to visit the island's primary attraction, the **Grotta del Genovese,** a cave that contains 14,000-year-old Paleolithic stone cuttings and slightly younger ochre-grease paintings of tuna fish rituals and dancing men. (www.grottadelgenovese.it. €6, ages 5-10 €4.) **Natale Castiglione,** in the ceramics shop of Grotta del Genovese, offers info on the site. (☎0923 92 40 32; nacasti@tin.it. Access to the cave is only permitted with a guide. Reservation at least 1 day ahead required. Boat or jeep excursions around the island €16. Shop open daily 10:30am-4pm.) Down the coastal road, grottoes and beaches await. **Cala Tranate** and **Capo Grosso** (the end of the island where there is a lighthouse) are both about a 1hr. walk. Be careful—the clear water between the rounded rock beach and the neighboring island has a ripping current when the wind picks up. Sandy **Cala Fredda** and **Cala Minnola,** on the south-eastern side of the island, are about a 15 and 20 minute walk, respectively, along the *lungomare* to the right when facing away from the port.

Pensione dei Fenici ❸, up on the hill above the port, offers a comfortable common area and spacious yellow rooms with private baths and A/C. The hotel's **Ristorante Fenici,** serves pizza and local cuisine. (☎/fax 0923 92 40 83. Singles €30-40; doubles €60-80. MC/V.) **Bar Arcobaleno,** V. Galvario 8, serves homemade almond and pistacchio gelato (€2) on a large terrace. (☎0923 92 40 12. Gelato €1.50-3.50. Drinks €0.90-4.50. Open 7:30am-1am. Cash only.) The Ustica and Siremar **hydrofoil** offices are on the dock; Siremar is off the *lungomare*.

MARETTIMO

The most geographically remote of the Egadi Islands, subdued Marettimo (ma-RE-tee-mo; pop. 700) attracts fewer tourists but just as many nature-lovers as the other islands. Because there are few roads, a boat is the best way to see Marettimo's coastal caves. They are available for rent, with a captain, from a number of agencies along the port, such as **Blue Star "I Freschi"** (☎333 71 53 803; www.blustarmarettimo.it) and **Rosa dei Venti** (☎0923 92 32 49; www.isoladimarettimo.it). A guided excursion to the caves should cost between €10-15 with a lunchtime snack included, so be sure to barter if the initial asking price seems high. Beyond the village, only an outstanding set of hiking trails intrude upon the island's rugged environment. The 1½hr. hike to **Pizzo Falcone** (686m), the highest point on the Egadi Islands, starts at the sea road, past the Siremar office. It begins with a paved stone road, after which wooden signs and a clear trail lead the way. Those adventurous enough to make the climb are rewarded with a 365-degree postcard panorama of Marettimo's coast and both of the other islands. The second half of the hike is especially hot and rocky, so bring water and wear sturdy shoes. The Ancient Roman **Case Romane,** stand 25min. up the mountain, between cliffs and greenery at the end of the paved path that leads to Pizzo Falcone. To the right of the little village and past a beach at Punta Troia, a Spanish **castle** rests precariously on a cliff. According to legend, when a prince married one of two sisters, the rejected one threw her sister off the cliff. The heartbroken prince tossed the offending sister down the same route and then followed himself. Locals say that at sunset, the ghosts of the two lovers find each other again at the castle. The curvy hike to the castle takes about 2½hr., but the visit can easily be made by boat.

Though not many budget accommodations exist this far out to sea, if you reserve in advance, you might find a reasonably priced room in one of the following spots. **La Rosa dei Venti ❷**, V. Punta S. Simone 4, to the right from the port when facing the island, rents doubles and apartments with TV, bath, fan, and rooftop terrace. Some come with a dazzling sea view. (☎0923 92 32 52. Doubles €20-30 per person; apartments €40-50 per person. Cash only.) To the right of the dock and up the hill lies **B&B La Terrazza ❸**, V. Pepe 29, which offers a gorgeous rooftop terrace and four moderately sized rooms with private baths and great views. (☎368 76 81 571. Breakfast included. Open Mar.-Oct. €25-40 per person. Cash only.) Find culinary treasures at the pirate-themed **Ristorante Il Pirata ❷**, V. Scalo Vecchio 27, which boasts the island's freshest fish. (☎0923 92 30 27. Antipasti €5-15. Primi €7-10. Secondi €10-25. Contorni €2-3. Cover €2. Open daily noon-4pm and 6pm-midnight. MC/V.) **Al Carrubo ❷**, Contrada Palosa, serves grilled fish and pizza on a large patio that overlooks town. From the Old Port, walk up V. Pepe and continue until Contrada Palosa. Try pizza (€4.50-6.50) made with locally grown herbs and top it off with homemade *cannoli siciliani* (€2.50). (☎0923 92 31 32. Primi €6-15. Secondi €7.50-15.50. Contorni €1-9. Open daily June-Sept. 7:30pm-3am. AmEx/MC/V.) Buy basics at **Alimentare Anastasi Clemente,** V. Mazzini 13. (Open M-Sa 8:30am-1:30pm and 4:30-8pm. AmEx/MC/V.)

A few *piazze* connect the town's maze-like streets. A left turn from the ferry port will lead you up to one of these town centers. From this *piazza*, V. Municipio becomes V. Umberto I, which leads all the way to the Old Port. The **Siremar** office will be on the right and the **Ustica** office is 20m farther down on the left, inside a souvenir shop. There is a **24hr. ATM** on V. Umberto I. A **cultural center** on V. Scalo Vecchio, along the fishing boat docks, has info on all three islands, as well as a local museum. (Open M-Sa 8am-noon and 3-8pm.)

PANTELLERIA ☎ 0923

Known as *"La perla nera dell'Europa"* ("the black pearl of Europe"), Pantelleria (PAN-te-le-REE-ya; pop. 7800) is as African and Middle Eastern as it is European. Visitors who come for the thermal baths are quickly seduced by the breathtaking beauty of black lava rock against verdant vineyards.

▣ TRANSPORTATION

Flights: Contrada Margana (☎0923 91 11 72), 2km from town. Flights from cities like **Rome, Venice, Milan, Palermo,** and **Catania** (14 per day 8am-7:30pm). To: **Pantelleria** (8:45am, 2:25, 5:30pm) and **Trapani** (9:55am, 3:35, 6:40pm; €95 round-trip).

Ferries: Siremar, V. Borgo Italia 65 (☎0923 91 11 04). Runs to **Trapani** (5hr., noon, €30). Open M-F 6:30am-1pm and 5-6:30pm, Sa-Su 6:30am-1pm. AmEx/MC/V.

Island Buses: Infrequent, unreliable buses run M-Sa from P. Cavour to the airport and to **Khamma-Tracino, Scauri-Rekale, Bukkuram, Sibà,** and **Bugeber** (€1 in advance from a *tabaccheria* or bar, €1.20 on-board).

Scooter and Car Rental: Autonoleggio Policardo, V. Messina 31 (☎0923 91 28 44 or 339 42 87 767; noleggiopolicar@tiscalinet.it), off the port, up the street to the right

Isola di Pantelleria

🏠 ACCOMMODATIONS
Hotel Cossyra Mursìa, **6**
La Vela, **7**

🍴 FOOD
Ristorante-Pizzeria Castiglione, **3**
Donne Fugate, **4**

🎵 NIGHTLIFE
Il Goloso, **5**
Tikirriki, **2**

Mediterranean Sea

after the scooter lot. Scooters €20-28 per day; Aug. €43 per day. Cars 21+. €35 per day, €200 per week; Aug. €55 per day. Open daily 8am-1pm and 4-8pm.

ORIENTATION AND PRACTICAL INFORMATION

Ferries arrive at the northwest tip of the teardrop-shaped island at Punta San Leonardo. The town of Pantelleria borders the curved **port**. The main street, **Via Borgo Italia,** changes to **Lungomare Paolo Borsellino** and stretches from the docks to the private sailboat moorings. At the end of Lungomare P. Borsellino beneath the Castello, **Piazza Almanza** becomes **Piazza Cavour.** Most services are here. Roads at either end of the *lungomare* lead along the coast to other small towns. Facing away from the water, to the left are **Bue Marino, Lo Specchio di Venere, Cala Gadir,** and **Arco dell'Elefante.**

Tourist Office: Pro Loco, P. Cavour 10 (☎0923 91 18 38). Look for country flags. Open Apr.-Oct. daily 9am-1pm and 5-8pm.

Budget Travel: La Cossira, V. Borgo Italia 77 (☎0923 91 10 78), where V. Catania meets the *lungomare*. Cheap flights organized from Pantelleria to Trapani and Palermo. Open daily 9am-1pm and 6-7:30pm. AmEx/MC/V.

Currency Exchange: Banca Nuova (☎0923 91 27 32), up V. Catania from the *lungomare*. **24hr. ATM.** Open M-Sa 8:30am-1:30pm and 2:45-3:45pm, Su 8:30-11:45am.

Carabinieri: V. Trieste 13 (☎0923 91 11 09).

First Aid: ☎0923 91 02 55. Open M-F and Su 8am-8pm, Sa 10am-8pm.

Pharmacy: Farmacia Greco, P. Cavour 28 (☎0923 91 13 10). Open M-Sa 8:30am-1pm and 4:30 or 5-8pm, Su 10am-12:30pm and 5-7:30pm.

Hospital: P. Nicolo Almansa (☎092391 01 11), off the *lungomare*.

Internet: Internet Point Da Pietro, V. Dante 7 (☎0923 91 13 67). €0.50 per 5min., €6 per hr., €10 per 2hr. Fax and copy available. Open daily 9am-2pm and 4:30-9:30pm.

Post Office: V. Verdi 2 (☎0923 69 52 32), off P. Cavour. Currency exchange available. Open M-F 8am-1:30pm, Sa 8am-12:30pm. **Postal Code:** 91017.

> **TIP**
> **LEFT IN THE DUST.** Pantelleria's bus system is notorious, frequently leaving travelers waiting for hours on end. A rented car or scooter is the best way to access Pantelleria's treasures, as buses do not serve many parts of the island even when they are on schedule.

ACCOMMODATIONS

Most visitors stay in one of the 3000 *dammusi*, square domed dwellings unique to Pantelleria. White roofs and thick lava-stone walls keep the interiors cool, while cisterns catch rainwater. For both *dammusi* and *affittacamere*, inquire at the bars that line the beach or the tourist office. Some *dammusi* require a minimum stay and most cost from €20-35. Be prepared to haggle. Follow the sea road 10km south from Pantelleria town to Scauri's port on Scauri Scalo, where **La Vela ❸** lets *dammusi* with kitchen, bath, patio, and A/C. A beach, private Turkish bath, and upscale restaurant with sea view should seal the deal. (☎0923 91 18 00 or 349 35 37 154. Reserve 4 months ahead for July-Aug. €30-40 per person. Cash only.) For a comfortable stay near the port, head to **Yacht Marina Hotel ❸,** V. Borgo Italia, which offers rooms with A/C, fridge, minibar, TV, and bath. (☎348 65 79 037; www.pantelleriamarinahotel.com. Doubles €35-70, with ocean view €50-80; suites €80-110/€100-160. AmEx/MC/V.)

🍴 FOOD

Arab domination in the AD eighth century turned Pantelleria away from fishing to the cultivation of its rich volcanic soil. The local specialty is *pesto pantesco*, a sauce of tomato, capers, basil, garlic, and almonds, that tops pasta or bruschetta. The local *passito* and *moscato* grapes yield dessert wines. For the freshest seafood in town, head to **Donne Fugate ❸**, C. Umberto 10, in front of the port. The menu changes daily with chef's special *couscous con pesce e verdure* (fish and vegetable couscous €12) on Fridays. (☎0923 91 26 88. Antipasti €10-15. Primi €12-15. Secondi €15. Contorni €4. Open M-Tu and Th-Su 12:30-3pm and 8pm-midnight. AmEx/MC/V.) **Ristorante-Pizzeria Castiglione ❸**, V. Borgo Italia 81, along the *lungomare*, serves pizza (€4-6.50) in a classic Italian dining room. (☎0923 91 14 48. Primi €7-15. Secondi €8-13. Cover €1. Open in summer daily 11am-3pm and 7:30pm-midnight; in winter M-Tu and Th-Su 11am-3pm and 7:30pm-midnight. AmEx/MC/V.) A **SISA supermarket** sits above the *lungomare* at V. Napoli 18. Hike up the stairs at the bend in the *lungomare*, passing the Banco Nuova sign on the right. (Open M-Tu and Th-Su 8:30am-1pm and 5:30-8:30pm, W 8:30am-1pm. MC/V.)

Pantelleria

🏠 ACCOMMODATIONS
Yacht Marina Hotel, **5**

🍴 FOOD
Ristorante-Pizzeria
Castiglione, **3**

🎵 NIGHTLIFE
Il Goloso, **2**
Tikirriki, **4**

0 — 200 yards
0 — 200 meters

🔆 SIGHTS

🛁BAGNO ASCIUTTO (LA GROTTA DI BENIKULÀ) AND MONTAGNA GRANDE. Near the town of Sibà is a **rock sauna** and the summit of Pantelleria's highest mountain. Signs guide through and beyond Sibà to the sauna; the last 10min. or so must be traveled on foot. Visitors courageous enough to brave the well-behaved swarms of bees that guard the entrance lie face down in a deep, low cave. Bring water and a towel, and be prepared to leave and re-enter several times due to the sauna's stifling heat. Farther along the sauna path, at the foot of Monte Gibele, the **Favara Grande**, a *fumarole* (crater), emits clouds of hot smoke. Most of the trails that leave from the asphalt road are short, and a shady picnic area in a pine grove near the summit is the perfect place to relax after a dry bath or sauna. If the midday heat is already enough, head to Montagna Grande for the view. The road past Sibà leads almost to the top, with views stretching for miles; watch for the lush Ghirlanda Plain. *(Take the Sibà bus from P. Cavour. Both the Bagno and the mountain are clearly marked. By car or scooter, follow signs from Pantelleria for Sibà. Note that on some maps and signs, the Bagno Asciutto is labeled "Grotta di Benikulà.")*

LO SPECCHIO DI VENERE (THE MIRROR OF VENUS). Legend has it that Venus used this lake as a mirror before her dates with Bacchus. Mere mortals may also be lured by a glimpse into the startlingly aquamarine waters, fringed with firm, white mud and sunken into a bowl of green hillside. Sulfur springs warm the water and enrich the mud. Locals know to let the sun dry the therapeutic mud to a white cake on the skin and then to take a long swim through the warm waters to rinse it off. *(From P. Cavour take the bus to Bugeber; ask driver where to exit, and ask about return times. Buses depart Pantelleria M-Sa 7:40am, noon, 2, and 4:10pm. By car or scooter, head to Bugeber, and follow signs for the turn-off. Free.)*

SICILY

LA GROTTA DI SATARIA. At the Grotta di Sataria, stairs lead to a cave once thought to be the home of the nymph Calypso, with whom Ulysses resided for seven years of his odyssey. The 40°C (104°F) water in the thermal pools, only a jump away from the much cooler sea, is believed to cure aching joints. Be careful of the surf in the open water. *(Portions of this site may be blocked off due to falling rocks. Buses depart from Pantelleria toward Rekale M-Sa 9 times per day 6:40am-8:50pm. Be sure to inquire about return times. By car or scooter, follow the road from Pantelleria to Scauri. Free.)*

THE NORTHEASTERN COAST AND L'ARCO DELL'ELEFANTE. In the shadow of the black rock structures lining the coast, visitors crowd the best swimming holes off Pantelleria, located in three small inlets along the northeastern coast. The first, **Cala Gadir,** is one of the more popular *acqua calda* (hot water) spots on the island. Cement encloses the natural pool next to the sea. Even better swimming is down the coast at **Cala Tramontana** and **Cala Levante.** Also perfect for sunbathing, these twin coves are actually one, split by a rocky outcropping. Cala Levante offers a view of the **Arco dell'Elefante,** off to the right; the unofficial symbol of the island, the unusual rock formation looks like a large elephant guzzling up the surf. *(All 3 inlets are on the Khamma-Tracino bus line. Buses leave P. Cavour M-F 9 per day 6:50am-7:40pm. Check return times, as they are subject to change. By car or scooter, follow signs for Khamma and Tracino, then signs for coastal roads.)*

LA PIANA DI GHIRLANDA (THE GARLAND PLAIN). Surrounded by a crumbled lip, this fertile crater makes a beautiful 2hr. hike from Tracino. On the way, scope out the terraces where peasants, working out of small, utilitarian *dammusi,* tend fruit orchards and caper fields. Follow signs to the **Byzantine tombs** at Gabbiana; surrounded by a vineyard, these resting places mark the resting place of a family of four from the early Middle Ages. *(Take the Tracino bus to the Byzantine tombs, then follow signs to trails. By car, take the road leading out of Tracino's P. Perugio.)*

LA GROTTA DEL BUE MARINO. This remarkable swimming area is 2km east of Pantelleria, along the *lungomare.* While snorkelers hug its coast, sunbathers drape towels over volcanic rock. Use extreme caution: the water is shallow in places, and the bottom is lined with jagged rocks. *(By car, follow road from Pantelleria toward Tracino. Or take the Pantelleria-Tracino bus.)*

I SESI. Pantelleria's Bronze Age dwellers left behind the *sesi,* dome-shaped funerary monuments built around 1800 BC. Tunnels in the *sesi* gave access to chambers that stored kneeling corpses. Many have been torn down for building material, but the largest remaining group contains 70 tombs. *(On the road from Pantelleria to Scauri. Rekale-bound buses depart M-Sa 9 per day 6:40am-8:50pm. Inquire about return times. Look for a "zona archeologica" sign to the left, past the Hotel Cossyra Mursìa.)*

🎵 🎭 ENTERTAINMENT AND NIGHTLIFE

Scauri Cineteatro, V. Padre Giovanni Piccirilli 30, plays Italian and dubbed American films nightly. The town's most vibrant nightlife is along the port. **Tikirriki,** V. Borgo Italia 7/9, and **Il Goloso,** V. Borgo Italia 35, both serve waterside tables until about 3am. The lively **U Friscu Café,** C. da Scauri 54, 12km away in Scauri, is the perfect pre-disco party stop. Try the local white wine. (☎092391 83 40. Wine €3 per glass, €15 per bottle. Open daily 6am-4am. Cash only.)

SARDINIA
(SARDEGNA)

An old legend says that when God finished making the world, He had a handful of dirt left over, which He threw into the Mediterranean, stepped on, and—behold—created the island of Sardinia (in Italian, "Sar-DEN-ya"). Another myth claims that Sardinia is truly the land of Atlantis, covered by a tidal wave in the second millennium BC. However Sardinia came to be, control of the island has bounced back and forth between empires for centuries, rendering many of its current inhabitants wary of any type of foreign investment or exploitation. Shuffled between the Phoenicians and the Carthusians, Sardinia got a slight break when the Romans made it an agricultural colony. But by the 13th century, it was again a theater for conflict among the Pisans, the Aragonese, the newly united Spanish, and the Piemontese. Until just decades ago, *padroni* (landlords) controlled the land, and farmers toiled under a system akin to serfdom. Though agriculture is still a significant economic staple, today the island proudly plays host to tourists that come in droves to bask in the perfection of its beaches and the glory of its mountain vistas and to indulge in its unique and delicious cuisine. The architecture, language, and food of Sardinia render it a cultural anomaly—hybrid of African, Italian, and Spanish influences. Though officially a part of Italy, Sardinia is classified as an autonomous region—an administrative manifestation of the island's strong sense of independence.

HIGHLIGHTS OF SARDINIA

RIDE bus #8 from Nuoro to the top of Monte Ortobene where a statue of Christ the Redeemer seems to leap from the summit (p. 748).

SOAK UP the sun on the luxurious beaches of L'Arcipelago della Maddalena (p. 757).

SAIL from Alghero's busy waterfront to the luminescent Grotte di Nettuno (p. 740).

MARVEL at the colorful streets of Orgosolo, where artists have been addressing social issues through enormous murals since 1975 (p. 749).

TRANSPORTATION

FLIGHTS. **Alitalia** flights link Alghero, Cagliari, and Olbia to major Italian cities. Though flights are significantly faster than water travel, exorbitant fares discourage most would-be air passengers. Recently, Ryanair and EasyJet have begun to serve Sardinia's airports. **easyJet** (www.easyjet.com) flies from Olbia to Berlin, Bristol, Geneva, London, and Milan, and from Cagliari to Geneva, London, and Milan. **Ryanair** (www.ryanair.com) flies from Cagliari to Barcelona, Madrid, Milan, and Pisa; from Olbia to Birmingham; and from Alghero to Barcelona, Bremen, Dublin, Dusseldorf, East Midlands Frankfurt, Liverpool, London, Madrid, Milan, Pisa, Rome, and Stockholm.

FERRIES. The cheapest way to reach Sardinia is by ferry from **Civitavecchia, Genoa,** or **Livorno** to Olbia. Civitavecchia, the official port of Rome, is easily reached by train from Rome's Termini station (80min., €4.50). The **ticket offices**

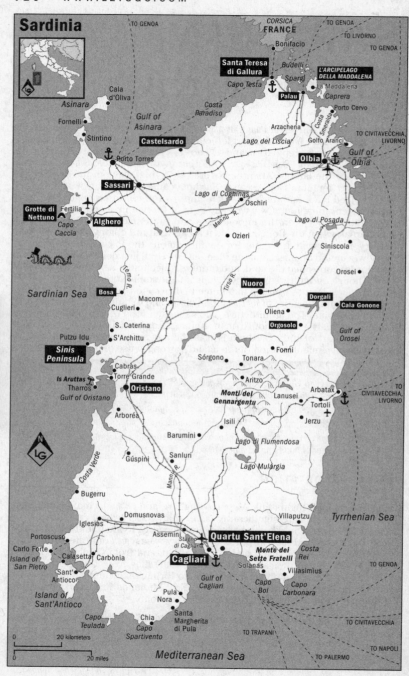

and ferry info centers are at the dock. Exit the train station and make a right, following the signs leading to the *centro* and the ferry terminal. Expect to pay €23-75 each way, depending on the company, season, boat speed, and departure time (night trips, fast ferries, and summer ferries cost more). The cheapest fares are for daytime *posta ponte* (deck class) slots on slow-moving boats, but most ferry companies require that *poltrone* (reserved armchairs) be sold to capacity before they open *posta ponte*. Expect to pay €10-20 more for a *cabina* with a bed, plus €5-15 depending on the season, trip duration, and taxes. Travelers with vehicles, animals, or children should arrive 1hr. before departure; everyone else should arrive 45min. ahead. Transporting vehicles can cost €50-120, depending on the voyage length and the season. The ferry schedule below is for summer service. Winter ferries sell at lower prices and run overnight. Prices and times are extremely variable depending on time of day and the boat speed; call the companies for more info.

ROUTE	COMPANY	DURATION	FREQUENCY	PRICE
Civitavecchia-Olbia	Tirrenia	5-7hr.	M-F 8:30am and 11pm, Sa-Su 3pm	€22-33
Civitavecchia-Cagliari	Tirrenia	12hr.	M-Th and Sa 8:30am	€29-43
		14hr.	F and Su 6:30pm	
Genoa-Olbia	Tirrenia	13hr	M and W-Su 11pm	€23-50
Genoa-Porto Torres	Tirrenia	10hr.	Daily 8:30pm	€30-68
Naples-Cagliari	Tirrenia	15hr.	Th 7:15pm	€29-44
Fiumicino-Golfo Aranci	Tirrenia	4hr.	M and W 8:30am, Tu and Th-Sa 9am	€32-63
Fiumicino-Arbatax	Tirrenia	3hr.	In Aug. M and W 7pm	€38-63
Civitavecchia-Golfo Aranci	Sardinia Ferries	7hr. (C. Shuttle)	8:15am	€17-38
		4hr. (C. Express)	2:15pm	€40-55
Livorno-Golfo Aranci	Sardinia Ferries	8hr.	11pm	€24-48
		6hr.	8:15am	€29-55
Livorno-Olbia	Moby Lines	7-11hr.	Daily 8am, 9:30, and 11:30pm	€20-40
Civitavecchia-Olbia	Moby Lines	4-10hr.	Daily 3 and 10pm	€20-54
Genoa-Olbia	Moby Lines	9hr.	Daily 10pm	€20-59
Genoa-Porto Torres	Moby Lines	10hr	Daily 10pm	€20-59
Bonifacio-S.Teresa	Saremar	1hr.	Daily 8, 11am, 5pm	€8-10
Genoa-Palau	Enermar	11hr.	W and F 7pm	€58-72
			Su 9am	€47
Genoa-Olbia	Grandi Navi	9-10hr.	Daily, times vary	€31-38
Genoa-Porto Torres	Veloci	11hr.	Daily, 2-3 per day	€31-38
Genoa-Palau	Dimaio Lines	12-13hr.	M, W, F-Sa 7pm	€16-70
Salerno-Olbia		15hr.	M, W, F 6:30pm	€20-45
Piombino-Olbia	Linea dei Golfi	6hr.	Aug. 2 per day; Sept.-July days and times vary	€18-23
Civitavecchia-Olbia	SNAV	7-8hr.	Daily 11am and 10pm	€30-40

Tirrenia: (☎89 21 23; www.tirrenia.it). Offices: **Arbatax** (☎07 82 66 78 41); **Cagliari** (☎07 06 66 065); **Civitavecchia** (☎07 66 58 19 25); **Fiumicino** (☎06 65 21 670); **Genoa** (☎01 02 69 81); **Olbia** (☎07 89 20 71 02); **Livorno** (☎05 86 42 47 30), on Calata Addis Abeba-Varco Galvani; **Naples**, Rione Sirignano 2 (☎08 15 51 90 96); **Palermo** (☎09 16 02 11 11); **Porto Torres**, V. Mare 38 (☎07 95 18 10 11).

Sardinia Ferries: (☎19 94 00 500; www.sardiniaferries.com). Offices in: **Livorno** (☎05 86 88 13 80), at the Stazione Marittima; **Civitavecchia** (☎07 66 50 07 14), at Terminal Autostrade del Mare; **Golfo Aranci** (☎07 89 46 780), at the Stazione Marittima.

Moby Lines: (www.moby.it). Offices in: **Olbia** (☎07 89 27 927), Stazione Marittima; **Livorno,** V. Veneto 24 (☎058 68 99 950); **Genoa** (☎01 02 54 15 13), Terminal Traghetti. General help desk (☎19 93 03 040), in English (☎61 11 40 20).

Grandi Navi Veloci: (☎0102 09 45 91). Offices: **Civitavecchia** (☎0766 59 631); **Olbia** (☎0789 20 01 26); **Genoa** (☎0102 54 65); **Porto Torres** (☎0795 16 034).

SNAV: (www.snav.it). Offices in: **Civitavecchia**(☎07 66 36 63 66); **Olbia** (☎07 89 20 00 84); **Naples** (☎08 14 28 55 55).

 TICKET FOR TOMORROW. If you buy your ferry ticket from Palau to Maddalena the day before, you can save 20% on **EneRmaR** tickets. So, if you arrive late in Palau and are planning on visiting La Maddalena the following day, be sure to buy your round-trip tickets for the day before.

CAGLIARI   ☎070

Since the Phoenicians founded the ancient port town of Korales over two millennia ago, several great civilizations have competed for possession of what is now known as Cagliari (CAL-ya-ree; pop. 158,000), Sardinia's largest city and capital. In the 11th century, after defeating the Genoese, the Pisans built the fortified town of Castrum Kolaris, which became one of the most important artistic and cultural centers on the Mediterranean and was later renamed Cagliari. While the city maintains its rich history through its still-functioning Roman amphitheater, Cagliari also incorporates features of modern urban design like the Bastione di San Remy, which offers panoramic views of the port and surrounding territories. If you tire of the throbbing pulse of city life, a 20min. bus ride will transport you to the green water and beachside nightclubs of Il Poetto, one of the most frequented stretches of beach in Sardinia.

▐▀ TRANSPORTATION

Flights: In the village of Elmas. ARST buses run the 8km from the airport to the city terminal at P. Matteotti (30min., 32 per day 5:20am-10:30pm, €1).

Trains: (☎070 89 20 21), in P. Matteotti. Ticket office open daily 6:10am-8:45pm. 24hr. ticket machines. To: **Olbia** (4hr., 6:30pm, €14.60) via **Oristano** (1hr., 17 per day 5:33am-10:02pm, €5.15) or **Macomer; Porto Torres** (4hr., 2 per day, €14.60); **Sassari** (4hr., 4 per day 6:39am-4:38pm, €13.65). Other destinations include **San Gavino, Iglesias, Decimomannu,** and **Carbonia.**

 EXTRA, EXTRA! Sardinia's daily newspaper, L'Unione Sarda, publishes a page titled "Agenda" which lists departure times and contact info for all bus, airplane, train, and ferry routes serving Cagliari, Alghero, Oristano, Olbia, Arbatax, Porto Torres, Palau, Nuoro, Lanusei, and Sassari. Available at any newsstand on the island.

Buses: 2 major bus companies serve Cagliari.

ARST, P. Matteotti 6 (☎070 40 98 324). Office open M-Sa 8-8:30am, 9am-2:15pm, and 5:30-7pm; Su 1:30-2:15pm and 5:30-7pm. Info in the front entrance area, ticket booth in the ARST station next to the McDonald's. When office is closed, buy tickets onboard. To **Bosa** (3hr., M-F 2 per day, €11:50), **Nuoro** (2hr., 3:30pm, €14.50), and **Oristano** (1hr., M-F 2 per day, €6.50). Also serves local towns, including the beaches of **Chia** (1hr.; 9 per day 6:30am-7:35pm, last return 8pm; round-trip €7), **Villasimius** (5 per day 5am-8:10pm, €3).

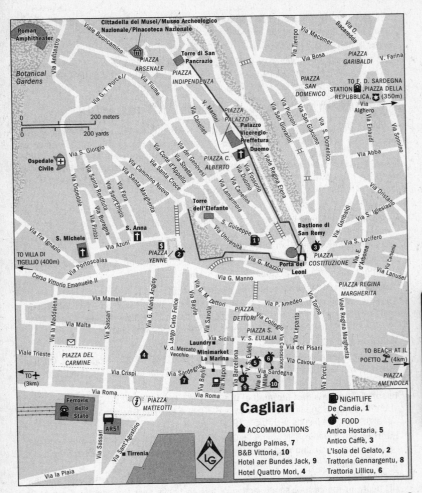

Cagliari

🛏 ACCOMMODATIONS

Albergo Palmas, **7**
B&B Vittoria, **10**
Hotel aer Bundes Jack, **9**
Hotel Quattro Mori, **4**

🎵 NIGHTLIFE
De Candia, **1**

🍴 FOOD
Antica Hostaria, **5**
Antico Caffè, **3**
L'Isola del Gelato, **2**
Trattoria Gennargentu, **8**
Trattoria Lillicu, **6**

FMS (☎070 80 00 44 553; www.ferroviemeridionalisarde.it). Buses leave from ARST station or P. Matteotti. Buses run to smaller towns. To: **Calasetta, Sant'Antioco-San,** and **Giovanni Suergiu** (6 per day 1:43-7:50pm); **Giba** and **Nuxis Santadi** (4:14, 6:19, 6:38pm); and **Iglesias** (14 per day 5:50am-8:47pm). Buy tickets at newsstand across from Farmacia Spanno on V. Roma or at the ticket booth by McDonald's in the ARST station.

Ferries: Tirrenia (☎070 66 60 65). Buy tickets from red building 1 block behind the ARST station. Ticket office open M-F 8:30am-12:30pm and 3:30-6:50pm, Sa 8:30am-12:20pm and 3:30-6pm, Su 4-6pm. **Linea dei Golfi** (☎070 65 84 13), V. Sonnino. Open daily 8am-7pm. Ferries leave from Stazione Marrittima.

Local Buses: (☎070 20 911 or 20 91 200). Orange **CTM** buses run from P. Matteotti. Tickets sold in various *tabaccherie* and newsstands around P. Matteotti and V. Roma, and at the ticket office by the McDonalds in the ARST station. €1 per 1hr., €1.50 per 2hr., €2.30 per day. **Buses P, PQ,** and **PF** go to Il Poetto 5:20am-10:50pm, last return

11:25pm; in the summer, lines **3/P, 9/P, Yellow,** and **Arancio** run to Il Poetto. Pick up a map of the bus routes at the tourist office.

Taxis: Radiotaxi Quattro Mori (☎070 40 01 01), in front of the train station.

Car Rental: Auto Assistance, V. la Plaia 15 (☎070 68 48 874; www.autoassistance.it), in the garage beneath Iper Pan. 21+. Insurance included. Mountain bikes €10 per day; cars from €60 per day. Open M-F 9am-1pm and 4-7pm. AmEx/MC/V.

◼◪ ORIENTATION AND PRACTICAL INFORMATION

Via Roma greets new arrivals to Cagliari, with the **harbor** and **Stazione Marittima** on one side and outdoor cafes on the other. **Piazza Matteotti,** between V. Roma, **V. Sassari,** and **Largo Carlo Felice,** contains the **train station,** the **ARST station,** and the **tourist office.** Across from P. Matteotti, **Largo Carlo Felice** climbs the steep hill leading to **Piazza Yenne,** then ascends even farther to the *centro storico*, also known as the **Castello district.**

Tourist Office: (☎070 66 92 55), in P. Matteotti, across from the train stations. Info on local sights and lodgings. Open M-F 8:30am-1:30pm and 2-8pm, Sa-Su 8am-8pm; in winter hours vary. **EPT,** P. Deffenu 9 (☎070 60 42 41; enturismoco@tiscalinet.it). Open in summer M-Sa 9am-1pm and 5-8pm; in winter hours vary.

Currency Exchange: Banca di Roma, P. Yenne 5, at the corner of C. Vittorio Emanuele II. **ATM** outside. Open M-F 8:20am-4pm, Sa 8:30am-noon.

Luggage Storage: At ARST station. €1 per hr.

Laundry: Ghibli Lavanderia Self-Service, V. Sicilia 20 (☎070 56 55 21 or 349 43 31 129), off V. Baylle, near most budget accommodations. Wash €4 per 6kg, €7 per 16kg; dry €4 per 20min. Detergent €1. Open daily 8am-10pm; last wash 9pm.

Police: ☎070 40 40 40.

Pharmacy: Farmacia Dott. Spano, V. Roma 99 (☎070 65 56 83). Multilingual. Open in summer M-F 9am-1pm and 4:50-8:10pm, Sa 9am-1pm; in winter M-F 9am-1pm and 4:30-7:50pm, Sa 9am-1pm. AmEx/MC/V.

Hospital: Ospedale San Giovanni di Dio, V. Ospedale 54 (☎070 66 32 37), 5min. walk from Chiesa di San Michele. Open daily 8:30am-12:30pm. **Guardia medica:** V. Talente 6. Nights and weekends ☎070 50 29 31.

Internet: Hay Service, V. Napoli 8 (☎070 32 01 81 97 27), off V. Roma. 5 fast computers; fax, photocopy, and Western Union money transfer also available. €2 per 30min., €3 per hr. Open M-F and Su 9am-1pm and 4-8pm.

English Language Bookstore: Ubik, V. Roma, 63-65 (☎070 65 02 56, www.ubiklibri.it). Right in the *centro,* small section of foreign books near the counter. Open M-Sa 9am-8:30pm, Su 10am-1:30pm, 4:30pm-8:30pm.

Post Office: V. Carmine 27 (☎070 60 311). Take V. Sassari from P. Matteotti. *Fermoposta* available. Open M-F 8am-6:50pm, Sa 8am-1:15pm. **Postal Code:** 09100.

◤ ACCOMMODATIONS

Budget hotels and B&Bs dot the area just off V. Roma, between Lago Carlo Felice and Vle. Regina Margherita.

Hotel aer Bundes Jack, V. Roma 75 (☎/fax 070 66 79 70; hotel.aerbundesjack@libero.it). Run by the same couple as B&B Vittoria, this hotel's historic past has been documented in hand-written registers since 1938. 14 rooms with Venetian chandeliers, Victorian molding, phone, radio, and A/C. Private or shared bath available. Check-in on

2nd fl. Breakfast €7. Reservations recommended. Singles €48-58; doubles €70-88, with sea view €88; triples €114. *Let's Go* discount 10%. Cash only. ❹

B&B Vittoria, V. Roma 75, 2nd fl. (☎070 64 04 026 or 349 44 73 556). Airy, spacious rooms with antique decor, Murano glass chandeliers, clean bathrooms, A/C, and radio. Some rooms have TV. Be sure to sample the *Vernaccia*, a special, strong white wine produced by owner Luigi's family near Oristano, at the small bar in the breakfast room. Singles €48; doubles €78. *Let's Go* discount 10%. Cash only. ❹

Hotel Quattro Mori, V. G. M. Angioj 27 (☎070 66 85 35; www.hotel4mori.it). Rooms with wood furnishings, bath, A/C, TV, and fridge. Breakfast included. Reservations recommended. Singles €65-75; doubles €85; triples €120; quads €140. AmEx/MC/V. ❺

Albergo Palmas, V. Sardegna 14 (☎070 65 16 79). 14 large no-frills rooms with sinks. Shared baths. Single €30; double €38, with shower €45; triples €60. MC/V. ❸

FOOD

Many small shops sell fruit, cheese, and bread along V. Sardegna. Try **Mini Market La Marina,** V. Sardegna 43, which has a great bakery. (Open M-Sa 7am-1:30pm and 4:30-8:30pm. MC/V.) Find groceries at the **Iper Pan La Plaia** at V. la Plaia 15. (Open M-Sa 9am-9pm, Su 9am-2pm.) On Sunday mornings, there's a **market** on the far side of the stadium in Borgo Sant'Elia for fresh fruit and seafood.

L'Isola del Gelato, P. Yenne 35 (☎070 65 98 24). Friendly owner Giuseppe presides over this lively island-themed *gelateria* right in P. Yenne. A steady stream of customers flows over the artificial river running beneath the transparent floor. 50+ flavors, including low-fat options for those watching their beach figures. Cups from €1. *Granita* €2. Open Mar.-Nov. daily 9am-2am. Cash only. ❶

Trattoria Gennargentu, V. Sardegna 60/c (☎070 65 82 47). After exploring the sights along V. Roma, join locals here for the seasonal spaghetti with sea urchin and dried mullet fish (€8) or zesty *salsiccia arrosta* (roasted sausage; €5). Primi €4.50-8. Secondi €5-15. Cover €1.60. Open M-Sa 12:30-3pm and 8-11pm. AmEx/MC/V. ❷

Antico Caffè, P. Costituzione 10/11 (☎070 65 82 06). Walls covered in photo collage of patrons who have come for over 150 years in search of appetizers and delicious desserts. Avoid service charge by ordering your drink inside and drinking at the counter. Crepes €3.40-5.60. Sundaes €3.10-7.20. Service 20%. Open daily 7am-2am. Call to reserve a table outside. AmEx/MC/V. ❶

Trattoria Lillicu, V. Sardegna 78 (☎070 65 29 70). Family-run for 80 years. Small but impeccable selection of Sardinian dishes like *anguille* (grilled eels; €9) and snails with tomato sauce (€7). Dining room, with family-style seating, is loud and packed until late; if you're lucky, the guitar-playing owner just might serenade you. A quintessentially *Sardo* experience. Primi €5-8. Secondi €7-12. Cover €1.55. Open M-Sa 1-3pm and 8:30pm-midnight. Reservations strongly recommended. AmEx/MC/V. ❷

Antica Hostaria, V. Cavour 60 (☎070 66 58 70). This beautiful restaurant sports Art Nouveau decor and tuxedo-clad waiters. Start your meal off with a sparkling aperitif (€3). Try house favorite *fregola con arselle* (tiny semolina pasta in clam broth; €8) or veal in *Vernaccia* sauce (€9). Primi €7-12. Secondi €9-13. Cover €2. Open M-Sa 1-3pm and 8-11:30pm. AmEx/MC/V. ❸

SIGHTS

BASTIONE DI SAN REMY. Approaching **Piazza Costituzione,** an enormous arch encases a staircase that seems carved into the hillside. Climb up the graceful double stairway to the expansive terraces of the 19th-century *bastione* for a spectacular view of Cagliari. Take note of the pink flamingoes, the **Golfo degli**

Angeli, and the **Sella del Diavolo** (Devil's Saddle), a massive rock formation. The *bastione* divides the modern city and the medieval Castello district. For a stroll through medieval Cagliari, start at the top of the *bastione* and follow the narrow streets past *aragonese* churches and *piemontese* palaces. *(Take the stairway from P. Costituzione or enter through the elevator on Vle. Regina Elena. Open 24hr. Free.)*

PALAZZO VICEREGIO. Constructed by the Aragonese in 1216 and later used as a seat for Spanish and Savoyard viceroys, this beautiful *palazzo* serves as Cagliari's provincial capital. Portraits inside are by Sardinian masters like Giovanni Marghinotti, and the *palazzo* maintains its original Pisan marble floor and 18th-century furnishings. *(Next to the duomo in P. Palazzo. Open daily 9am-2pm and 3-7pm. Entrance only with tour in English or Italian. Free.)*

DUOMO (CATTEDRALE DI SANTA MARIA). The Pisans constructed this massive Gothic cathedral during the second half of the 13th century, dedicating it to the Virgin Mary and St. Cecilia, whose likenesses can be seen in mosaics above the doors. The *duomo* is modeled after the one in Pisa (p. 490) and filled with art by Pisan masters. Maestro Guglielmo carved the pulpits on either side of the main door in 1162, and Pisano sculpted the four lions at the base of the altarpiece in 1302. The ornate wood balcony to the left, in front of the altar, was constructed for the Piedmontese king, who refused to sit among the people for fear of regicide. Colorful marble inlays conceal 179 niches housing the remains of about 200 martyred saints from Cagliari. *(P. Palazzo 4. ☎070 16 63 837. Open M-F 8am-12:30pm and 4:30-8pm, Su 8am-1pm and 4-8pm. Altar and some chapels currently under restoration. Modest dress required. Free.)*

MUSEUMS. The **Cittadella dei Musei** houses a modern complex of research museums, including the **Museo Archeologico Nazionale.** The extensive collection of Sardinian artifacts from the Nuraghic to Byzantine eras includes Mycenean pottery from 1600 BC; Barumini, jewelry and coins from the times of Punic control, Roman glass works and mosaics, and a 1000-year-old army of tiny bronze figurines. Comprehensive explanations, with wall-text displays in English and Italian, narrate the history of Sardinian occupation. The entire second floor of the museum is devoted to the archaeological history of Cagliari from the Nuraghic to Roman ages. *(P. Arsenale. Take V. Buoncammino to P. Arsenale, go under the arch and turn left. ☎070 68 40 00. Open Tu-Su 9am-8pm. Wheelchair-accessible. €4, students 18-25 €2, under 18 or over 65 free. MC/V.)* The **Pinacoteca Nazionale,** in the same complex as the archaeological museum, displays medieval and Baroque religious paintings and altarpieces, including works by Pietro Cavaro, who is considered as the greatest Sardinian painter of all time. This labyrinthine museum is built around the remains of a 16th-century fortification, discovered during the reconstruction of the Citadel in 1966. The remains are visible on the ground floor. Be sure to visit the anonymously painted **Madonna con Bambino** on the lower floor, which depicts Baby Jesus with flowing golden locks. For a chronological experience, try to visit this museum after visiting the archaeological museum. *(☎070 68 40 00. Open Tu-Su 9am-8pm. Wheelchair-accessible. €2, students 18-25 €1, under 18 or over 65 free. Both museums €5, students €2.50. Get tickets at the Museo Archeologico Nazionale biglietteria. Ticket office open Tu-Su 8:30am-7:15pm.)*

ROMAN AMPHITHEATER. Constructed after the Carthaginians succumbed to the Roman juggernaut in 238 BC, this amphitheater lost its downhill side to the Pisans, who used the wall as a quarry to build their 13th-century monuments. Underground cages once held ferocious animals during the age of gladiators. Today, much of the original seating along the sides remains, and the venue hosts summer performances that are a bit more civilized than the ancient carnage. (V. Fra Ignazio. ☎070 65 29 56; www.anfiteatroromano.it. 30min. guided tours Apr.-Sept. Tu-Sa 9:30am-1pm, Su 10am-1pm. €3.30, students €2.20, over 65 free.)

TORRE DI SAN PANCRAZIO. As Cagliari's highest point, the tower was once used to observe ships and enemies during war, then converted into a medieval prison. Today, visitors can climb the steep stairs, blanketed in pigeon droppings, to the top to view the city below. Despite a great view, it isn't worth the euro. (€4, students €2.50. Guided visit €0.50. Open Tu-Su 9am-1pm and 3:30-7:30pm.)

🎵 🎭 ENTERTAINMENT AND NIGHTLIFE

The **Roman amphitheater** continues to dazzle spectators with theater, dance performances, opera, and concerts in July and August on its large modern stage. Most shows start at 9:30pm and cost €18-50. Buy tickets at the amphitheater starting at 7pm on performance nights or at the box office, at Vle. Regina Margherita 43. (☎070 65 74 28. Open M-F 10am-1pm and 5-8pm, Sa 10am-1pm, Su when there's a show.) **Outdoor movies,** mostly dubbed American films, are screened in July and August around 9pm at the Marina Piccola off Spiaggia del Poetto. Buy tickets (€4) at the Marina. On Sunday mornings, merchants converge for **flea markets** in P. del Carmine and Bastione di San Remy, where visitors hone their haggling skills and find bargain antiques.

Most bars and clubs in the city are open from 9pm to 5am, but they shut down in the summer when students hit the beaches and the dancing moves outdoors. To dance the night away, either find a ride or rent one—most *discoteche* are on the beaches, 15-20km outside of Cagliari. The best night to go out is Friday. For a downtown hot spot that's still parties hard into the summer, check out **De Candia,** V. De Candia 1, and enjoy the DJ or live music and colorful mixed drinks, including *assenzio* (absinthe). The bar is one of several positioned on a terrace on top of the Bastione di San Remy that feature lounging leather couches and hammocks. (☎070 65 58 84. Mixed drinks €6-7. Open daily 7am-4am.) The area around P. Costituzione is usually hopping with street performers and window shoppers. On the first of May, Sardinians flock to Cagliari for the **Festival of Sant'Efisio,** honoring a deserter from Diocletian's army who saved the island from the plague but couldn't save himself from decapitation. A costumed procession escorts his effigy from the capital down the coast to the small church that bears his name.

🏖 BEACHES

Il Poetto, Cagliari's most popular stretch of beach, spans 10km from the Devil's Saddle to the Margine Rosso (Red Bluff). The beach was famous for its pure white sands until the government dumped several tons of coarse brown sand on top to prevent erosion. Locals claim it's ugly, but only because the white sands found in the gorgeous nearby beach towns of **Villasimus** and **Chia** allow them to have high standards. The average traveler will be so focused on the crystal-clear waters that he'll hardly notice the slight imperfection. Behind Il Poetto, the salt-water **Stagno di Molentargius** (Pond of Molentargius) provides a habitat for flamingos. (City buses P, PQ, and PF, as well as the yellow and orange buses Arancio run frequently to the beaches. 20min., €1.) Resist jumping off the bus at the first sight of sand; by remaining on the bus for a few extra stops, you'll avoid crowded areas. For a more remote sunning and swimming area, head to **Cala Mosca,** which is smaller and surrounded by dirt paths. Because some parts of the water contain submerged seaweed-covered rocks, water shoes might be a good idea for squeamish swimmers looking to avoid squishy surfaces. Take bus #5 to Stadio Amsicora, then bus #11 to the beach.

SASSARI ☎079

Sassari (SA-sa-ree; pop. 129,072), the second largest and first independent city in Sardinia, maintained its medieval wall perimeter until the late 1800s, despite constant encroachment by Pisans, Genoese, Aragonese, and Austrians. Sassari is home to the island's first university, the University of Sassari, popularly called "Culleziu." The university's presence has bolstered Sassari's cultural life, crowding its streets with bookstores, museums, tiny restaurants and shops, and plenty of students. Despite its lack of visitor activities, Sassari is quite close to more touristed destinations, such as Castelsardo and Alghero, and is a great place to stay for urban conveniences with easy access to the countryside.

☐ TRANSPORTATION

Trains: In P. Stazione (☎079 89 20 21), 1 block from P. Sant'Antonio. Take bus #8 from P. d'Italia. Buy tickets (€0.80) at *bars*. To: **Alghero** (35min., 11 per day 6am-8:55pm, €2.20); **Cagliari** (3hr., 8 per day 6:36am-6:52pm, €13.65); **Olbia** (2hr., 4 per day 6am-5:08pm, €6.35); **Porto Torres** (20min., 7 per day 7am-6:44pm, €1.40).

Buses:

ARST (☎07 92 63 92 06/03; www.arst.sardegna.it). Buses depart from V. Italia in the public gardens, and the bus station on V. XXV Aprile, in front of the train station. To: **Alghero-Fertilia Airport** (40min.; 9 per day 5am-6:50pm, 5 and 5:30am depart from the bus station at V. Turati; €4); **Castelsardo** (1hr.; 13 per day 7:20am-7:45pm, reduced service Sa-Su; €2.50); **Nuoro** (1hr., M-F 2 per day, €8); **Olbia** (1hr., M-F 2:10pm); **Porto Torres** (20min., 1-2 per day. 5:15am-9:15pm, €1.25); **Santa Teresa di Gallura** (3hr.; 5 per day 7:20am-7:45pm, reduced service Sa-Su; €7.80). Tickets sold at Tonni's Bar, C. Savoia 11, and at the bus station. Cash only.

FDS (☎079 24 13 01; www.ferroviesardegna.it). Buses leave from V. XXV Aprile. Tickets sold at bus stop on C. Vico. To: **Alghero** (50min.; 14 per day 5:50am-8:15pm, reduced service Sa-Su; €3); **Bosa** (2hr., 2 per day); **Castelsardo** (1hr., M-F 11:35am, €1.10); **Fertilia** (1hr.; 10 per day 6:30am-8:15pm, reduced service Sa-Su).

Taxis: RadioTaxi (☎079 26 00 60). 24hr.

Car Rental: Eurorent, V. Roma 56 (☎079 23 23 35; www.rent.it). Ages 18-20 pay a surcharge. Credit card required. Open M-F 8:30am-7pm, Sa 8:30am-noon. MC/V.

✴ 7 ORIENTATION AND PRACTICAL INFORMATION

Many buses stop in the **giardini pubblici** (public gardens) before heading to the **bus station.** Since these gardens are close to Sassari's attractions, get off at **Via Italia** in the park. **Emiciclo Garibaldi,** a small, semi-circular *piazza*, lies ahead past **Via Margherita di Savoia.** To reach the *centro*, head straight through Emiciclo Garibaldi to **Via Carlo Alberto,** which spills into **Piazza d'Italia.** To the right, **Via Roma** runs to the tourist office and the Museo Sanna. To the left lies **Piazza Castello,** packed with people and restaurants. Two hundred meters away, **Corso Vittorio Emanuele,** a major thoroughfare, slices through the *centro storico*.

Tourist Office: V. Roma 62 (☎079 23 17 77; aastss@tiscali.it). Facing the provincial administration building, walk a few blocks to the right of P. d'Italia. Go through the gate and the doorway on the right. English-speaking staff provides maps and transportation schedules. Open M-Th 9am-1:30pm and 4-6pm, F 9am-1:30pm.

Currency Exchange: Banca Commerciale D'Italia, P. Italia 22-23, has an **ATM** outside. Open M-F 8:30am-1:30pm and 2:45-4:15pm, Sa 8:30am-noon.

Luggage Storage: In the bus station. €1.50 per bag per day. Open M-Sa 6am-9:15pm, Su 7am-2:15pm and 5:15-9:15pm. Cash only.

English-Language Bookstore: Giunta al Punto, V. Cavour 16 (☎079 20 13 118). Small selection on 1st fl. of mostly British classics. Open daily 9am-8pm. MC/V.

Pharmacy: Simon, P. Castello 5 (☎079 23 11 44). Open daily 9:10am-8:30pm. Posts after-hours rotations. MC/V.

Hospital: Ospedale Civile, V. Montegrappa 82/83 (☎079 20 61 000).

Internet Access: Net Gate, P. Università, 4 (☎079 23 78 94). 6 computers. €0.08 cents per min. Open M-F 9am-1pm and 3:30-8pm, Sa 9am-1pm.

Post Office: V. Brigata Sassari 11/13 (☎079 28 21 267), off P. Castello. **Currency exchange,** phone cards, and *fermoposta*. Open M-F 8am-6:50pm, Sa 8am-1:15pm. Branch located across the street from V. XXV Aprile's bus station. **Postal Code:** 07100.

■🎴 ACCOMMODATIONS AND FOOD

🏠Casa Chiara ❸, Vco. Matteo Bertolinis 7, a recently renovated B&B located in the *centro storico*, has three large, tastefully decorated rooms (a single, a double, and a triple) all have a TV as well as two clean, shared bathrooms and a kitchen. (☎079 20 05 052 or 333 69 57 118; www.casachiara.net. Breakfast included. Free Wi-Fi. Reservations recommended. €30 per person. Cash only.) Located close to the train and bus stations and the *centro*, **B&B Quattro Gatti ❸,** V. Sant'Eligio 5, so named for the cats that actually live on the premises, has a kitchen, whimsically decorated modern rooms, and a young, sociable owner. Call to arrange free pickup from station. (☎079 23 78 19 or 349 40 60 481. Breakfast, locker, and use of washing machine included. Free Wi-Fi. Singles €27-35; doubles €55-70; triples €80-100. Discounts for longer stays.) **Hotel Leonardo da Vinci ❺,** V. Roma 79, is worth the splurge for a modern hotel with modern amenities. An unremarkable exterior conceals a lavish interior decorated with oriental rugs, granite floors, and hallways lit by chandeliers. Enormous rooms have bath, A/C, phone, minibar, TV, and hair dryer. (☎079 28 07 44; www.leonardodavincihotel.it. Breakfast included. Wi-Fi. Parking €8 per day. Singles €55-80; doubles €75-100; triples €96-130. AmEx/MC/V.)

At **Trattoria La Vela Latina ❸,** Largo Sisini 3, in a *piazza* off V. Arborea, owner Francesco loves his patrons as much as they love his food. Flavorful *cavallo* (horse meat; €9.30) or *asino* (donkey meat; €10) win over even the most timid diners. For something less adventurous, try the fantastic lobster salad or the *riso alla pescatora* for €8. (☎079 23 37 37. Primi €5-7.75. Secondi €7-13. Cover €2. Open M-Sa 1-2:30pm and 8-10:30pm. AmEx/MC/V.) **Il Senato ❹,** V. Alghero 36, is reputedly one of Sardinia's best restaurants and uses only first-rate seasonal ingredients. Don't miss the *dolce della suocera* (the mother-in-law cake; €6) with ricotta, almond, and a caramelized sugar crust. (☎079 27 77 88. Primi €10-15. Fish €8-15 per 100g. Meat €12-17 per 100g. Open M-Sa 1-2:30pm and 8-11pm. AmEx/MC/V.) To reach **Ristorante Trattoria L'Assassino ❸,** V. Ospizio Cappucini 1, from C. V. Emanuele, go down V. Rosello and take a right. This comfortable local favorite serves an extensive menu of interesting Sardinian specialties, like *trippa* (tripe), *cavallo* (horsemeat), and roast suckling pig. (☎079 23 50 41. Primi €3.50-8. Secondi €5-13. 3-course *menù* €20. Cover €2. Open M-Sa 12:30-3:30pm and 7:30pm-midnight. MC/V.) Fresh **produce stands** line V. Rosello from C. V. Emanuele. There is a **Multimarket,** V. Cavour 64, on the corner with V. Manno. (☎079 23 72 78. Open M-Sa 8am-9pm.)

👁️🎵 SIGHTS AND ENTERTAINMENT

The **Museo Giovanni Antonio Sanna,** V. Roma 64, is an informative and fascinating archaeological museum. Extensive collections of artifacts dating from the Neolithic Period to the Middle Ages, including arrowheads, tools, ceramics, bronze statuettes, and Roman sculptures, chronologically detail Sardinia's history. The museum also hosts one of the largest collection of ancient Roman

SARDINIA

lead anchors. (☎079 27 22 03. Open Tu-Su 9am-8pm. €2, ages 18-25 €1, EU citizens under 18 or over 65 free.) From the *centro*, walk down C. V. Emanuele from P. Castello, and turn left on V. al Duomo to P. Duomo to reach Sassari's *duomo*, **Cattedrale di San Nicolò**. Reconstructed in Gothic style in 1480, only the *campanile* remains from the original 13th-century structure. The impressive facade, covered with statues and engravings, conceals a somewhat spartan interior, but you may want to take a peek at some recently uncovered early frescoes that fill the side chapels. (Open daily 8:30am-noon and 4-7:30pm. Mass M-Sa 6pm; Su 9 and 11:30am, 6pm. Modest dress required. Free.)

If it weren't for the **University Pub**, V. Amendola 49/A (☎079 20 04 43), Sassari would be devoid of any kind of youth scene. The subdued, three-tiered pub offers cheap drinks (beer from €2) and overflows with students when school is in session. Try the "Barman" (€5) or the potent, double-malted *biere di demon* for €4.30. (Th karaoke night. Open Sept.-July M and W-Su 8:30pm-1am.) In the third week of May, the lavish **Sardinian Cavalcade** is the island's largest folk festival. The party includes a parade of costumed emissaries from local villages, a horse exhibition, singing, and dancing. On August 14th, **I Candelieri** brings worker's guilds carrying enormous candles through the streets. Each guild has its own costume, and the candles are decked with flowers and streamers.

ALGHERO   ☎079

With a vibrant *centro storico* hanging over the sea, Alghero (al-GEH-ro; pop. 45,000) stretches along Sardinia's northwestern coast. Over the centuries, Alghero has swapped hands between native Sardinians, Spanish Aragonese, and the Ligurian Genoese. As a result, a distinctly Spanish vibe can still be felt—along with Italian, a dialect of Catalán chimes in the streets. Visitors to Alghero can explore rich history, beachside nightlife, and natural wonders like the 70 million-year-old Grotte di Nettuno, only a short bus ride away.

▐ TRANSPORTATION

Flights: Fertilia Civil Airport (☎079 93 52 82), 6km north of the city. Buses run from the *centro* every hr. **Ryanair** (www.ryanair.com) runs domestic flights year-round to **Barcelona, Bremen, Dublin, Dusseldorf, East Midlands, Frankfurt, Liverpool, London, Madrid, Milan, Pisa, Rome,** and **Stockholm.**

Trains: FDS (☎079 95 07 85) on V. Don Minzoni. Take **AP** or **AF bus** from in front of Casa del Caffè in the park (3 per hr.) or walk 1km along port to the station. Taxis €7 from *centro.* Buy tickets at **Trenitalia** stand in the park, and ride the bus to the station for free, or buy from *biglietteria* in station. **Luggage storage** available (€1 per bag per day). To **Sassari** (35min.; 11 per day 6:01am-8:47pm; €2.20, round-trip €3.80).

Buses:

ARST (☎079 800 86 50 42) and **FDS** (☎079 24 13 01). Tickets at stand in the public gardens (☎079 95 01 79). Blue buses depart V. Catalogna, next to park. To: **Bosa** via **Villanova Monteleone**, mountain route (1hr., Sept.-June 2 per day 6:35am and 3:40pm, €4.50); **Bosa** via **Litoranea**, coastal route (1hr. to *centro* and Bosa Marina, 1hr. to Bosa Stazione FDS; June-Sept. 9:55am and 7:30pm, Oct.-May 9am and 1:50pm; €3); **Porto Torres** (1hr.; up to 8 per day 4:45am-8:45pm, reduced service Sa-Su; €2.50); **Sassari** (1hr., 1-2 per hr. 5:35am-7:50pm, €3).

FDS also runs orange **city buses** (☎079 95 04 58). Buy tickets (€0.70) at *tabaccherie.* Buses run from P. della Mercede (in front of the church), stop at V. Cagliari (in front of Casa del Caffè), and go to the airport (20min., 13 per day 5am-10pm; schedule changes monthly). **Line AF** runs between Fertilia and V. Cagliari, stopping at the port (40min.; from Alghero 7am, then every hr. from 8:40am-11:40pm, additional buses M-F between 8:10am and 1:10am; from Fertilia 7:50am then every hr. 9am-midnight, additional weekday buses between 8:30am and 1:30pm). **AP** buses run from Vle. della Resistenza to **train station** (every 30-60min. 6:20am-9pm). **AO** goes from V. Cagliari to the beach and the **hospital** (2 per hr. 7:15am-11:50pm). **AC** runs from V. Liguria to Carmine (2 per hr. 7:20am-7:50pm). Tourist office provides a complete schedule.

Taxis: V. Vittorio Emanuele (☎079 97 53 96), across from the BNL bank. Private cab (☎079 98 92 028). From *centro* to airport about €20. Night prices vary..

Car Rental: Avis, P. Sulis 9 (☎079 97 95 77; www.avisautonoleggio.it), or at the airport (☎079 93 50 64). 25+. Credit card required. Open M-F 8:30am-1pm and 4-7pm, Sa 8:30am-1pm. AmEx/MC/V. **Europcar** (☎079 93 50 32; www.europcar.it), at the airport. Open daily 8am-11pm. AmEx/MC/V.

Bike and Scooter Rental: Cycloexpress di Tomaso Tilocca (☎079 98 69 50; www. cicloexpress.com), near the port at the intersection of V. Garibaldi and V. Spano. Bikes €7-13 per day; tandems €15 per day; electric scooters €15 per day; motor scooters €25-55 per day. Open M-Sa 9am-1pm and 4-8:30pm, Su 9am-1pm. AmEx/MC/V.

◾🛈 ORIENTATION AND PRACTICAL INFORMATION

ARST and FDS buses stop next to the public gardens at the corner of **Via Catalogna** and **Via Cagliari,** on the waterfront one block from the **port.** The tourist office, in **Piazza Porta Terra,** lies diagonally across the small park, on the right beyond the towers of the *centro storico.* The **train station** is a hike from the *centro* (about 1km) but accessible by local orange buses (lines AF and AP).

▨ Tourist Office: P. Porta Terra 9 (☎079 97 90 54; infoturismo@comune.alghero.ss.it), on the right from the bus stop, toward the *centro storico.* Multilingual staff offers an indexed street map, bus and train schedules, tours of the city, and daytrips to local villages. Open Apr.-Oct. M-Sa 8am-8pm, Su 10am-1pm; Nov.-Mar.

Currency Exchange: Banca Nazionale del Lavoro (BNL), V. V. Emanuele 5 (☎079 98 01 22), across from the tourist office, has a **24hr. ATM.** Open M-F 8:20am-1:20pm and 2:30-4pm, Sa 8:20-11:50am. **Currency exchange** also available at the post office.

English-Language Bookstore: Ex Libris Liberia, V. Carlo Alberto 2a (☎079 98 33 22), has a selection of English-language paperbacks. Open daily 9am-midnight. MC/V.

Police: P. della Mercede 7 (☎079 97 20 01). **First Aid:** ☎079 99 62 33.

Pharmacy: Farmacia Puliga di Mugoni, V. Sassari 8 (☎079 97 90 26). Posts afterhours rotations. Open May-Oct. M-Sa 9am-1pm and 5-9pm. AmEx/MC/V.

Hospital: Ospedale Civile (☎079 99 62 33), on V. Don Minzoni in Regione La Pietraia.

Internet Access: Bar Miramar, V. Gramisci 2. 3 computers. €1.60 per 15min., €5 per hr. Open daily 8am-noon and 3pm-3am. Cash only.

Post Office: V. Carducci 33/35 (☎079 97 20 231), has *fermoposta* and currency exchange. Open M-F 8am-6:50pm, Sa 8am-1:15pm. **Postal Code:** 07041.

◣▨ ACCOMMODATIONS AND CAMPING

▨ Hotel San Francesco, V. Ambrogio Machin 2/4 (☎079 98 03 30; www.sanfrancesco-hotel.com). This converted 14th-century church cloister and architectural gem in the heart of the *centro storico* offers 20 rooms with stone walls, bath, A/C, and phone. Enjoy a drink in the small bar, which used to be a monk prison. Ask the informative staff about the classical music festival hosted by the cloister. Breakfast included. Reservation required June-Aug. Singles €49-60; doubles €78-96; triples €99-125. MC/V. ❹

Hotel La Margherita, V. Sassari 70 (☎079 97 90 06; hotel.margherita@tiscali.it), near P. Mercede. 53 spacious rooms with A/C, minifridge, safe, phone, and TV. Internet available. Social terrace with waterfront views, 2 treadmills, and 2 stationary bikes. Free beach umbrellas and lounge chairs at private beach 2km away. Breakfast included. Singles €50-85; doubles €80-125. Extra bed €20. AmEx/D/MC/V. ❹

Bed and Breakfast MamaJuana, Vco. Adami 12 (☎079 33 91 36 97 91; www.mamajuana.it), a cozy B&B in the heart of the *centro storic.* Rooms with wooden ceilings, retro decor, private bath, and TV. Breakfast at nearby bar included. Check-out 10am. Reception 9am-9pm; call ahead. Single €40-60; doubles €60-90. Cash only. ❹

Hostal del'Alguer (HI), V. Parenzo 79 (☎/fax 079 93 20 39 or 93 04 78; alghero@ ostellionline.org), in Fertilia. From the port, take bus AF to Fertilia (every hr., last bus 11:30pm). Turn right, and walk down the street; hostel is on right side of outdoor building complex. Offers sparse but clean furnishings. Bike rental, bar, maps, and info on attractions. Large common room with TV and beach around the corner. Breakfast included; large lunch or dinner €9.50. Laundry €2.50 per 5kg. Internet access €5 per hr. Dorms €18; 4- to 6-bed dorms €18-20; doubles €21-25. HI-member discount €3. ❶

La Mariposa, V. Lido 22 (☎079 95 03 60; www.lamariposa.it), right off the beach, 1.5km from Alghero toward Fertilia. Follow the signs from the *centro.* Offers large grilling pit, restaurant, bar, market, bike rental, diving, and beach access. Laundry €5 per load. Reservations recommended. Open Mar.-Oct. €8-11 per person, €4-8.50 per child; €4-13 per tent; €2-4 per car, €3.50-14 for campers. 2-person bunk-bed cabins €25-38. *Villini* (4 person max) €43-68 for 2 people, €56-88 for 3, €68-135 for 4. Hot showers €0.50. Linen €2.50. Final cleaning €10-15. Apr.-June tents and cars free. AmEx/MC/V. ❶

🄵 FOOD

On Wednesday, there is an **open-air market** on V. Europa and V. Corsica. (Open 8:30am-1pm.) Walk 15min. from the *centro* to check out the wine-lover's paradise that is **Antiche Cantine del Vino Sfuso,** C. V. Emanuele 80. You can sample and purchase local wholesale table wines for a mere €1.50 per L; just bring your own tasting cup. (Open M-Sa 8:30am-1pm and 4:30-8pm. MC/V.) To cool off after a day at the beach, stroll over to 🄲**Gelateria Arcobaleno,** P. Civica 33 (☎079 98 71 52), which serves divine homemade gelato that's perfection in a cup. (Cup €1.50-3. Cash only.) A **Sisa** supermarket is at V. Sassari 49. (☎079 97 31 067. Open M-Sa 8am-8:30pm, Su 8am-1:30pm.) Fresh produce market stalls also line the archways beneath V. Sassari 19-23. (Open M-Sa 7am-1:30pm and 4-8pm.)

Osteria Taverna Paradiso, V. Principe Umberto 29 (☎079 97 80 01). Vaulted stone ceilings and fine cuts of meat like the Argentina Angus filet (€6.50 per 100g) make for charming, casual but classy dining in the *centro.* Try the *Maestro Formaggiaio* (Cheese Master), owner Pasquale's renowned cheese platter (€16). Primi €8.30-12. Secondi €13-20. Cover €1.50. Open daily noon-2pm and 8pm-midnight. AmEx/D/MC/V. ❹

Al Tuguri, V. Maiorca 113 (☎/fax 079 97 67 72; www.altuguri.it). Delicious variations on traditional cuisine give Al Tuguri its stellar reputation. Well-loved for its distinct personality, innovative approach, and personalized service. Emphasis on local and pure ingredients. Try the *triglie* (red mullet fish; €15.80) or the exceptional 5-course *menù* (€40), with a vegetarian option (€34). Primi €12-15. Mandatory secondi €19-23. Open Mar.-Dec. 20 M-Sa 12:30-2pm and 8-10pm. Reservations recommended. MC/V. ❺

Ristorante la Cueva, V. Gioberti 4 (☎079 97 91 83). From P. Porta Terra, take V. Simon, and turn right on V. Gioberti. Housed in an 8th-century building with arched stone ceilings. Savory fare with a distinctly local Catalán twist includes *porcetto sardo* (roast suckling pig; €15), *paella,* and homemade *sebadas* (Sardinian dessert ravioli deep fried and drizzled with honey; €4). Primi €7-20. Secondi €9-20. Open M and W-Su 1-2:30pm and 7:30pm-midnight. AmEx/MC/V. ❸

Cafe Latina, Bast. Magellano 10 (☎079 97 65 41). On the edge of the *centro storico* facing the port. Great place to relax outdoors with a glass of wine and enjoy a view of the beaches and marina. Extensive drink menu and light fare throughout the day, including hours when most restaurants are closed. Open daily 8am-midnight. ❸

Schiaccineria La Buccia, V. Carlo Alberto 10 (☎079 34 93 18 15 75). The aroma corrals customers into this tiny pizzeria. Choose from the pizzas on display or tell them exactly what you want and they'll bake your pizza for you as you wait. Try the delicious proscuitto and asparagus or opt for the sweeter *marmellata* pizza (€4.50). Slices €1.20-2.20. Open daily 11:30am-2:30pm and 5:30-11pm. ❶

◉ SIGHTS

A leisurely walk through the *centro storico* reveals tiny alleys, half-hidden churches, and ancient town walls. The old city is hard to navigate without a map, so stop by the tourist office first. The **Torre di Porta Terra** near the public gardens dominates the entrance to the *centro*. Financed by the Jewish community in the 15th-century and consequently known as the **Torre degli Ebrei** (Tower of the Jews), it now offers visitors a great place to capture views of the town. (Open M-Sa 9:30am-1pm and 5-9pm. €1.50.) Heading down V. Roma, Alghero's *duomo*, **La Cattedrale di Santa Maria**, is at the intersection with V. Principe Umberto. Begun in 1552, it took 178 years to construct, resulting in a unique and stunning Gothic-Catalán-Renaissance facade. Rebuilt in the 19th century, the cathedral has Gothic choirs, a mosaic of John the Baptist, and the original *porta petita* (small door) from the Catalán structure. One block from the *duomo*, down V. P. Umberto, are the 19th-century **Teatro Civico** and **Palazzo Machin**, classic examples of Gothic-Catalán architecture. Backtrack up V. Roma and take a right on V. Carlo Alberto to find **Chiesa di San Francesco**. The simple Neoclassical facade conceals a graceful Gothic interior with beautiful marble altar. (Open M-F 9:30am-noon and 5-6:15pm, Su 5-6:30pm. Modest dress required. Free.) Heading away from the harbor, take V. Carlo Alberto to reach the beautiful **Chiesa di San Michele** at P. Ginnasio, built between 1661 and 1675 and dedicated to the patron saint of Alghero. V. Carlo Alberto ends at P. Sulis and the **Torre dello Sperone**, where French soldiers were imprisoned in 1412 after failing to capture the Catalán fortress. In the 19th century, Sardinian patriot Vincenzo Sulis was a prisoner here, thus giving the *piazza* its name.

⚟ OUTDOOR ACTIVITIES

The countryside around Alghero is filled with spectacular nature reserves, inland mountains, and cliffs plunging into the sea, making it a popular destination for **trekking** and **bicycling**. Inquire at the tourist office for a comprehensive list of itineraries. One of the most popular parks, **Le Prigionette Nature Reserve**, lies at **Porto Conte**, off the Fertilia-Porto Conte highway on the road to Capo Caccia. Buses heading toward the Grotte di Nettuno (see next page) pass by the reserve three times daily. Bike and hiking paths wind through mountains, past sloping valleys dotted with wild horses. The forestry house at the park entrance supplies good maps and advice. (☎079 94 90 60. Open daily 9am-5pm.) FDS buses also lead directly to Porto Conte (30min.; 11 per day 7am-11:30pm; returns 11 per day 7:30am-midnight; €1), where a dirt road leads to **Punta Giglio Reserve**. The road is a difficult but popular route for bikers, ending after 3km at a ▨limestone peak on Punta Giglio. This point has the region's most impressive views, as well as several semi-abandoned WWII barracks for war buffs or curious minds. For those not biking, get off at the Porto Conte stop and walk 300m down the road back toward town, and the entrance is on the right (45-60min.). The low-traffic seaside highway that heads away from Alghero to the Porto Conte area is also popular for biking. For the bike ride, follow the beachside road; V. Garibaldi turns into V. Lido, and then Vle. Maggio. Vle. Maggio leads to the dock at the end of Alghero's coast (8km); cross the bridge onto the highway to Fertilia. Continue along the bike path with the forest on one side and the highway on the other (3km). When the bike path ends, continue along highway for another 3km until Porto Conte. The **Nuraghi di Palmavera** is 3km past Fertilia, along the highway from Alghero to Porto Conte/Capo Caccia. Follow the bike path next to the forest to its end and then go another 200m on the highway. A central tower surrounded by 50 huts forms a limestone complex dating from 1500 BC. (☎079 95 32 00; fax 98 87 65. Open daily Apr.-Oct. 9am-7pm; Nov.-Mar. 9:30am-4pm. €3, over 65 and children €2.) The **S.I.L.T. cooperative**, V. Mattei 14, offers tours of Nuraghi in English by request. (☎079 98 00 40; www.coopsilt.it. Tours run every hr. 9:15am-11:15am and 4-6pm. €2, audio tour €3.)

🎵 🖼 ENTERTAINMENT AND NIGHTLIFE

Alghero comes alive at night. Crowds stream through the *centro storico*'s cramped streets and pour onto the promenade until the early morning hours. In summer, locals in search of warm evening breezes and live music head to the beachside bars along **Lungomare Dante** and along the **waterfront** all the way to Fertilia. Both locals and tourists also enjoy **Poco Loco,** V. Gramsci 8, a gnarly pizza place just past P. Sulis, inland from Lungomare Dante. Famed for its pizza-by-the-meter (€17-27 per m; 0.5m also available), Poco has six bowling lanes (€3.50-6 per game) and Internet for €3 per hr. (☎079 97 31 034; www.pocolo-coalghero.it). Live music in summer W 10:30pm; in winter F-Sa 11pm. Beer from €2. Mixed drinks €5. Open in summer daily 7:30pm-3am or later. MC/V.)

🔲 DAYTRIP FROM ALGHERO

KILLING TIME. The FDS buses leaving at 9:15am, 3:10, and 5:10pm will arrive at Capo Caccia a few minutes past the hour, meaning you'll have to wait around 45min. until the next hourly tour of the Neptune's Grottoes. Also, if relying on the bus for transpotation, take the 9:15am or 3:10pm buses from Alghero since the 5:10 bus will leave you stranded in Capo Caccia.

GROTTE DI NETTUNO. Booming waves echo amidst ancient stalactites and stalagmites in the wondrous **■Grotte di Nettuno** (Neptune's Grottoes). These caves, first discovered by fishermen, have been around for 60 to 70 million years and are one of Sardinia's most frequented tourist destinations. Thanks to modern lighting, the caves come alive when blue, green, and yellow light dances over the rocks. Well-run 45min. tours, conducted in English and Italian, point out whimsical rock formations like Christmas trees, chandeliers, and pipe organs in the bowels of the caves. The caves are in Capo Caccia, a steep promontory that juts out from Porto Conte into a nationally protected marine area. Built in 1954, the steep Escala del Cabirol provides access to the grotto for those adventurous enough to descend the 654 steps that lead to the sea between massive white cliffs. (☎079 94 65 40. Open daily Apr.-Sept. 9am-7pm; Oct. 9am-5pm; Nov.-Mar. 9am-4pm. Groups admitted every hr. for 45 min. tour. €10, children €5. FDS buses run to Capo Caccia. ☎079 95 01 79. 50min.; 3 per day 9:15am-5:10pm, last return 6:05pm; €2. Or take the pleasant Navisarda Grotte di Nettuno ferry tour. ☎079 97 62 02 or 95 06 03; www.navisarda.it. Guide in English and Italian. Boats leave Alghero's Bastione della Maddalena. 2hr. round-trip, with tour of caves; June-Sept. 9 per day 9am-5pm; Apr.-May and Oct. 9, 10am, and 3pm. Round-trip €13, under 13 €7.)

BOSA

☎**079**

Glowing with cheery pastels, Bosa (BO-sa; pop. 7,935) is half medieval city, half Riviera vacation hot spot. Situated on the banks of the Temo River, the only navigable river in Sardinia, Bosa boasts a trademark castle, situated high up on a hill overlooking palm tree-lined streets and spacious *piazze* on the Temo River Valley. Though the *centro storico* is generally a sleepy place, the newer Bosa Marina, 1km from the old city, boasts beautiful beaches, an assortment of seaside bars, and a hostel. If arriving by bus or car from Oristano, you will be treated to some incredible views from the small hill-towns along the way.

TRANSPORTATION. ARST **buses** run from Bosa to Oristano (2hr., M-Sa 5 per day 5:25am-4:05pm, €5.50). Buy tickets at the bar or *tabaccheria* in P. Zanetti. FDS **buses** run to Alghero via Litoranea, the coastal route (1hr., 3 per day, €3), or via Villanove Monteleone, the mountain route (2 hr., 2 per day, €4.50); Nuoro (1hr.; 6 per day 6:06am-7:41pm, reduced service Sa-Su; €5.10); and Sassari (2hr., 3 per day 8:20am-5:20pm, €5.50). Buy tickets at the FDS office in P. Zanetti. (Open daily 6:30pm-midnight.) Buses also run from Bosa to Piazza Palmiro Togliatti in Bosa Marina (5min., 22 per day, €1). For a **taxi,** call ☎079 33 68 11 800. To rent **cars, scooters,** or **bikes,** stop by Euroservice, V. Azuni 23. (☎079 37 34 79. 25+ for car or scooter. Bikes €10 per day; scooters €25-50; cars from €65. Open M-F 9am-1pm and 5-8pm.)

ORIENTATION AND PRACTICAL INFORMATION. Bosa, the city proper, lies across the **Temo River** from **Bosa Marina.** Buses stop in Bosa's **Piazza Angelico Zanetti,** from which **Via Azuni** leads to **Piazza Gioberti** at the base of the *centro storico.* The **Pro Loco tourist office,** V. Azuni 5, at the intersection with V. Francesco Romagna, provides maps and info on the town and surrounding area. Ask for the brochure, which contains a free map. (☎079 37 61 07; www.info-bosa.it. Open M-Sa 10am-1pm.) The **tourist office** for Bosa Marina, Vle. Colombo, is on the *lungomare* about 5min. after the right turn off the main bridge. (☎079 37 71 18; www.agenziailponte.it or www.bosa.it. Open M-F 8:30am-12:30pm and 3:30-7:30pm.) For currency exchange and an **ATM,** head to **Unicredit Banca,** at the corner of V. Lamarmora and V. Giovanni XXIII. (☎079 37 31 18. Open M-F 8:20am-1:20pm and 2:35-4:05pm, Sa 8:20am-12:45pm.) In case of emergency, call the **carabinieri** (☎079 37 31 16), **Red Cross** (☎079 37 38 18), **hospital** (☎079 37 31 07), or **guardia medica** (☎079 37 46 15). **Internet Web Copy,** V. Gioberti 12, has six computers with fast connections (€0.07 per min.) and fax services. (☎079 37 20 49; web.copy@tiscali.it. Open M-Sa 9am-1pm and 5-9pm.) The **post office,** V. Pischedda 1, also has currency exchange. (☎079 07 85 37 31 39. Open M-F 8:15am-6:50pm, Sa 8:15am-1:15pm.) **Postal Code:** 08013.

ACCOMMODATIONS AND FOOD. Located between Bosa *centro* and Bosa Marina, the **Royal Hotel ❸,** Vle. Alghero 27, offers 22 rooms decorated with fresh, Victorian elegance and plenty of flowers. Rooms are equipped with bath, TV, A/C, phone, and balconies. Some even come with hydromassage showers. Breakfast included. (☎079 37 70 37; info@royalhotelbosa.it. €34-44 per person low season, €47-59 high season.) Bosa Marina is home to one of Sardinia's two youth hostels, called simply **Youth Hostel (Ostelle della Gioventú) (HI) ❶,** V. Sardegna 1. After crossing the bridge from the *centro,* take a right on the *lungomare.* V. Sardegna is about 5min. down on the left. Close to the beach, the hostel has clean rooms with large communal bathrooms, and a bar open until midnight. (☎/fax 079 37 50 09, 34 62 36 38 44, or 33 97 75 11 21; valeva-canzesardegna@hotmail.com. Breakfast included. A/C €3 per day. Reception

9am-1pm and 4pm-midnight. Curfew midnight. 5-bed dorms €16; doubles €40. Cash only.) **Albergo Perry Clan ❷**, V. Alghero 3, in Bosa, offers simple rooms with TV, bath, and A/C. From the bus stop, follow V. Daniele Manin, and take first right on V. Giovanni XXIII; the hotel is on the left after P. Dante Alighieri. While farther from the beach, Perry Clan is a good option for travelers who prefer a private bath. (☎079 37 30 74. July-Aug. rooms €60 per person, including mandatory half pension. Sept.-June singles €20-25; doubles €45-50. AmEx/MC/V.)

In a medieval building in the *centro storico*, **Ristorante Borgo Sant'Ignazio ❷**, V. S. Ignazio 33, serves marine delicacies like *nido dello chef* (egg pasta with tomato sauce and local lobster; €12 per 100g) and *azadda iscritta* (€10), a relative of shark. Don't miss the house special *zuppo di pesce* ("fish soup"), a savory seaside specialty throughout Italy chock-full of *frutti di mare* and a mind-boggling variety of fish. (☎079 37 41 29. Primi €8-15. Secondi €10-15. Cover €2. Open in summer Tu-Su 1-3pm and 7:30-11pm. AmEx/MC/V.) Across the bridge from P. Duomo, **Sa Pischedda ❷**, V. Roma 8, offers elegant outdoor dining on a garden patio and candlelit tables which are graced by delicious dishes like *razza alla bosana* (garlicky, sautéed flat fish; €7), *alisanzas al ragu di sorfano e basilico* (pasta with local fish, tomato, and basil; €8), and a selection of brick-oven pizzas. (☎079 37 30 65. Pizza €4.50-11, dinner only. Primi €7-11. Secondi €5 per 100g of fish. Open daily 1-2:30pm and 8-10:30pm. MC/V.) If near the beach and searching for a swashbuckling time, walk the plank down to the **S'Hardrock Cafe ❸**, which features S'Hardinian plates on the deck of a pirate ship. Good, cheesy fun and a great place to unwind and hang out. (Pizza €4-10. Primi €9-12. Secondi €10-17. Open Tu-Su 12:30-3pm and 7pm-1am.) Head to **Sisa** supermarket, P. Gioberti 13, for groceries. (☎079 37 34 23. Open M-Sa 8am-1pm and 5:30-8:30pm, Su 9am-12:30pm.)

◪ ◪ SIGHTS AND BEACHES. Bosa's principal museum, **Casa Deriu**, C. Vittorio Emanuele II 59, exhibits furnishings, tapestries, and family portraits from the wealthy Deriu family's 19th-century home. Examples of filet weaving, unique to Bosa, and traditional Sardinian dress and gold jewelry can be seen on the first floor. The third floor holds a collection of ceramics, prints, and paintings by Melkiorre Melis, a leader in the applied and plastic arts. Art lovers will enjoy the landscapes of Bosa, and surrealist works by Antonio Atza are housed in a permanent collection across the street. (Open Tu-Su 10:30-1pm and 8:30-11pm. €4.50, children €2.) The town's signature **Castello Malaspina** is a short hike uphill through the *centro storico;* take the flower-lined staircase or V. del Castello to see the imposing castle that dates from 1112 and is also home to the early 14th-century **Chiesa Nostra Signora Regnos Altos**. The walk uphill and the entrance fee are well worth the experience that waits at the top, with mountain and ocean views available from the castle. On the second weekend of September, residents celebrate the Virgin Mary by adorning their houses with flowers and small altars, dancing, and parading through the streets. The festival culminates with a mass in the courtyard of the castle. (☎079 33 35 44 56 75. Castle and church open daily 9:30am-1:30pm and 5:30-8:30pm. €2, under 12 €1.)

Local families fill a long stretch of sandy beach in Bosa Marina, where bars line the *lungomare* around the **Aragonese Tower**. The **Bosa Diving Center**, V. Colombo 2 (☎079 37 56 49; www.bosadiving.it), offers snorkeling, scuba diving, and boat tours to nearby grottoes and beaches. Call for more info.

ORISTANO
☎0783

In the AD seventh century, the inhabitants of nearby Tharros repelled invasion after invasion until a band of merciless Moorish pirates forced them to abandon their homes. With the pirates cleared out, the coast is clear for tramping through the ruins of ancient city and gazing at the sea, dotted with seagulls and commercial boats instead of pirate ships. After their abrupt displacement, the residents of Tharros set up camp around modern-day Oristano (oh-rees-TA-no; pop. 35,000), which soon became an independent commercial port protected by Eleanora of Arborea, one of Sardinia's most important saints. The cheery, pastel-colored *centro storico* is a great place to stay while exploring the nearby Sinis Peninsula's Phoenician and Roman ruins at Tharros and the beaches of Is Aruttas and San Giovanni di Sinis. Visiting the town in February is a real treat, as tourists will be able to experience the delightful and unique *"Sartiglia,"* Oristano's special commemoration of *carnevale* featuring traditional costumes, masks, and impressive horseback acrobatics.

▐ TRANSPORTATION

Trains: In P. Ungheria (☎0783 89 20 21), 1km from the *centro*. Ticket counter open 6:20am-8:15pm. **Luggage storage** available. To **Cagliari** (1-2hr., 27 per day 4:49am-9:26pm, €5.15), **Macomer** (1hr., 9 per day 6:38am-9:27pm, €3.30), and **Olbia** (2hr., 1:20 and 7:46pm, €10) via **Ozieri, Chilivani,** or Macomer. To get to **Sassari,** connect via Macomer or Chivilani.

Buses: ARST, V. Cagliari 177 (☎0783 71 185). Ticket office open daily 6am-8pm. To: **Bosa** via **Cuglieri** (2hr., 5 per day 8:05am-7:10pm, €5.50); **Cagliari** (2hr., 7:10am and 2:10pm, €6.50); **San Giovanni di Sinis** (dir.: Is Aruttas; 40min.; July-Oct. 5 per day, 8:25am-6:30pm, last return 7:45pm; round-trip €3); **Scano Montiferro** via **Santa Caterina** (40min., 7 per day 8:05am-7:10pm, round-trip €2.50).

Taxis: At P. Roma (☎0783 70 280) and at the train station (☎0783 74 328). Available 7am-1pm and 3-8:30pm. For 24hr. service, call ☎33 68 13 585.

Car Rental: Avis, V. Liguria 17 (☎0783 31 06 38). 25+. Open M-F 9am-1pm and 4-7pm, Sa 9am-noon. AmEx/MC/V.

Scooter Rental: Marco Moto, V. Cagliari 99/101 (☎0783 31 00 36). €30-50 per day. Open M-F 8:30am-1pm and 4-8pm, Sa 8:30am-1pm. AmEx/MC/V.

◤ ▐ ORIENTATION AND PRACTICAL INFORMATION

To get to the *centro* from the **train station,** follow **Via Vittorio Veneto,** the street farthest to the right, to **Piazza Mariano.** Then take **Via Mazzini** to **Piazza Roma,** the heart of the city. Walk down **Corso Umberto,** bear left at P. Eleanora d'Arborea, and take a right on **Via Ciutadela de Minorca** to reach the tourist office. From the **ARST bus station,** take the exit nearest the ticket office and turn left. You will see brown signs for the Pro Loco tourist office to the right, or you could continue past the *duomo* and up **Via De Castro** to P. Roma.

Tourist Office: Pro Loco, V. Ciutadella de Minorca 8 (☎0783 70 621). Maps and info on local festivals. Open M-F 9am-1pm and 4-8pm, Sa 9am-1pm. **EPT,** P. Eleonora 19 (☎0783 36 831). Info on Oristano and province. Open M-Th 8:30am-1pm and 4:15-6:45pm, F 8:30am-1pm.

Luggage Storage: In ARST station. €1.50 per day. Open daily 6am-7:30pm.

English Language Bookstore: Libreria Canu, V. de Castro 20 (☎0783 78 723). Small collection of contemporary novels. Open M-Sa 9am-1pm and 5-10pm. MC/V.

First Aid: ☎0783 74 333.

Pharmacy: C. Umberto 49/51 (☎0783 70 338). Open M-F 9am-1pm and 5-10pm.

Hospital: V. Fondazione Rockefeller (☎0783 31 71).

Internet Point: V. Verdi 4A and Vco. Tirso 13 (☎0783 71 676). With the tower at your back facing P. Roma, look across the street for the arch in the buildings. Walk through the arch, turn right, and it's on the left. Fax and photocopy here. Must present an ID document to use. Internet €0.10 per min. Open M-Sa 8am-1pm and 4-8:30pm.

Post Office: V. Mariano 4 (☎0783 36 80 15). Currency exchange and fax available. Open M-F 8am-6:50pm, Sa 8am-1:15pm. **Postal Code:** 09170.

ACCOMMODATIONS

Oristano caters primarily to beach-bound travelers, but low competition makes for high prices. Because B&Bs have lower prices, they are a good alternative to hotels but have very limited numbers of rooms and fill up quickly. Reserve well in advance for summer. For info on *agriturismi*, ask at the tourist office or call the **Posidonia Society,** V. Umberto 64, in Riola, 10km from Oristano. (☎0783 41 16 60; www.sardegnaturismo.net. Open daily 9am-1pm and 4-8pm.)

▨ **Eleonora B&B,** P. Eleonora 12 (☎0783 70 435 or 347 48 17 976; www.eleonora-bed-and-breakfast.com). Conveniently located in the *centro storico,* within 2 blocks of bus station and major sights. You can't miss the canary yellow exterior. Friendly owners Paola and Andrea maintain this beautifully decorated Renaissance *palazzo,* which retains its original, 12th-century walls. Spacious rooms, some of which have a loft, private bath, A/C, and TV. Singles €35-70; doubles €60-70. Cash only. ❸

▨ **B&B In Centro,** Vico Tirso 26 (☎0783 78 750). Steps away from P. Roma, this cozy B&B is all about warmth. Owner Maria goes above and beyond to make sure your stay is comfortable and fun. Cute and clean rooms with shared bath. Ample info provided about sights, activities, and attractions in Oristano. Rooms have TV and AC. Breakfast included and served in rooftop garden. Singles €30-35; doubles €25-30. Cash only. ❸

Mariano IV Palace Hotel, P. Mariano 50 (☎/fax 0783 36 01 01). From ARST station, take exit next to the ticket office, turn left, then right on V. Ciutadela de Minorca. Go straight through P. Martini and follow V. Lamarmora to the end. Turn right, then immediately left, and follow signs. Luxurious hotel with oriental rugs, chandeliers, and a frescoed elevator shaft. All rooms have bath, A/C, TV, phone, and minibar; some with balcony. Breakfast included. Singles €65-95; doubles €100-160; triples €115-204. AmEx/MC/V. ❹

Palazzo Corrias, P. Eleonora 4 (☎0783 78 194 or 349 56 81 703; www.palazzocorrias.com). Centrally located in P. Eleonora and housed in an old *palazzo.* 3 enormous rooms with A/C, minibar, and *piazza* views. Common room with TV. Clean shared bath. Breakfast included. Singles €35; doubles €60. Cash only. ❸

FOOD

The **Euro-Drink** market, P. Roma 22, sells inexpensive basics and local products like *mirto* (myrtle liqueur) and *sebadas,* a special type of Sardinian dessert. (Open M-Sa 8am-2pm and 5-9pm. MC/V.) A **Sisa** supermarket is at V. Amiscora 26. (Open M-Sa 8am-8pm. MC/V.)

▨ **Ristorante Craf da Banana,** V. de Castro 34 (☎0783 70 669). Dim lighting and low-arched brick ceilings give this restaurant a cave-like, but romantic atmosphere, and fine cuisine distinguishes it from its peers. Try specialties like the delicious *ravioli della casa* with a meaty wild boar-and-mushroom sauce (€8). Primi €8. Secondi €8-13. Cover €2. Open M-Sa 1-3pm and 8-11pm. Reserve ahead. AmEx/MC/V. ❸

Coco & Dessi, V. Tirso 31 (☎0783 30 07 20). This spacious and thoroughly modern restaurant covers 2 floors, with several dining rooms perfect for group gatherings, and a peaceful patio enclosed by glass doors. Dishes are creative and artistically presented for quite a gourmet experience. Primi €6-9. Secondi €11-15. ❸

Trattoria Da Gino, V. Tirso 13 (☎0783 71 428). Local favorite. Cozy dining room. Menu features spaghetti, ravioli, fettuccini, gnocchi, and risotto in a variety of sauces; as well as meat and fresh fish. Primi €5.50-9. Secondi €7.50-12. Reservations recommended for dinner. Open M-Sa noon-3pm and 8-11pm. MC/V. ❸

Pizzeria La Grotta, V. Diego Contini 3 (☎0783 30 02 06), off P. Roma. Lighthearted atmosphere. Pumps out brick-oven pizzas (€3-8.50). A favorite is the *pizza alla carciofi freschi e bottarga* (with artichoke hearts and fish eggs; €7.50). Takeout available. Cover €1.50. Open daily 7:30pm-12:30am. AmEx/MC/V. ❶

👁 SIGHTS

The whimsical **Chiesa di San Francesco,** in P. Eleonora d'Arborea at the end of V. de Castro, complete with two small, brightly tiled domes, is the largest *duomo* in Sardinia. First built in 1250, it was heavily restructured in the 19th century, leaving little of the original interior intact. One notable remnant is a particularly emotional wooden sculpture depicting Jesus' crucifixion. Created by a 16th-century Catalán teacher, the cross was once attributed to Nicodemus, a friend of Jesus; it was said that such a vivid depiction could only have been captured by an eyewitness. The sacristy houses a 16th-century polyptych, *St. Francis Receiving the Stigmata* and Nino Pisano's 14th-century marble statue of San Basilio. (Open M-Sa 7am-noon. Mass Su 9am. Free.) Adjacent to the cathedral on V. Vittorio Emanuele is the **Archiepiscopal Palace,** the seat of the Curia. Pope John Paul II was once a guest here. A distinctive, almost Oriental, tower, with a beautifully decorated dome, stands next to entrance. A short stroll up C. Umberto reveals the 13th-century **Tower of San Mariano II** in P. Roma. On summer evenings, young *oristanesi* gather in this *piazza* and the adjoining C. Umberto to flirt and sip Ichnusa (a Sardinian beer), while the elderly commandeer benches and enjoy the vivacity around them. Archaeology buffs will love the collection of Nuraghic, Punic, Phoenician, and Roman artifacts at **Antiquarium Arborense,** in P. Corrias, near P. E. d'Aborea, all of which were unearthed at Tharros. The collection includes urns, cups, and earthenware of all shapes and sizes, some dating as far back as 5000 BC. A useful photo guide in English is provided to take you from showcase to showcase. Tabletop models of the ancient port of Tharros and 11th-century Oristano are always on display. (☎0783 79 12 62. Open daily 9am-2pm and 3-8pm. Wheelchair-accessible. €3, under 14 €1.50, students and seniors €1.)

▓ DAYTRIP FROM ORISTANO

THE SINIS PENINSULA

The Sinis peninsula is best reached by bus from Oristano (5 per day from the ARST station; only runs during the summer months). Ask for ticket to San Giovanni di Sinis for the beach (8:25am-6:30pm, last return 7:45pm; round-trip €3). Get off 1 stop earlier at Cabras for town center and archaeological museum. The Penisola del Sinis Isola di Mal di Ventre Info Center is located right in the piazza where the bus stops. Blue and white signs next to the Info Center lead out of the piazza onto the beach. A sign with an arrow points you in the direction of the ruins of Tharros, up the hill around 700m. Because Sinis Peninsula itself is a stretch of protected marine zones, all main commercial buildings are found in the town of Cabras.

Venture outside Oristano to see the impressive sights of the Sinis Peninsula, a Marine Protected Area. Decreed a natural preserve in 1997, only part of the coast is accessible to tourists, the rest being used only for research. The Sinis Peninsula is most famous for its quartz sands, which have been eroded by the winds and granite of the uninhabited Mal di Ventre island, and which look like grains of rice. Ruins from the Roman and early-Christian period of Tharros can be found 700m uphill from where the bus drops you off in San Giovanni di Sinis, at the **Tharros Archaelogical Site.** A large Aragonese tower, a remnant of the period when medieval inhabitants of Sardinia needed to be on constant watch for attacks from the sea, marks the top of the hill. Call a day ahead to reserve a tour of the Tharros ruins in English. (☎0783 37 00 19. Open in summer daily 9am-8pm. €5, includes 1hr. guided tour in Italian.) A ticket to the site also includes admission to the **Archaeological Museum,** V. Tharros, in Cabras, which contains the artifacts from the excavations at Tharros. (☎0783 29 06 36. Open daily in summer 9am-1pm and 4-8pm; in winter 9am-1pm and 3-7pm.)

Located at the tip of the peninsula where the bus unloads, the beach **Spiaggia San Giovanni di Sinis** contains fine sands with bits of dark, volcanic rock. **Spiaggia Funtana Meiga's** sand is shielded by large dunes. The **Park of Seu,** a naturally preserved area of greenery, lies just up the coast. Farther up, **Spiaggia Arutas** is most famous for its pebbly shores. **Mare Morto,** on the other side of the peninsula from San Giovanni di Sinis, is well-known for its wide, sandy, seaweed-littered beaches. Along the curvy part of the coastline, in the Gulf of Oristano, is the **Laguna di Mistras,** where pink flamingos often strut about; bike from San Giovanni toward Cabras along the San Giovanni-Oristano road. Pink flamingos also inhabit the waters beneath the bridge crossing from the peninsula into Cabras. For **diving,** contact Aceti (☎0783 53 747), Aquateam Diving (☎0783 30 34 55), or 9511 Diving Team (☎0783 33 56 05 94 12). For **scuba diving,** contact Ippocampos Scuba Team (☎0783 34 88 05 80 01).

 CURRENT EVENTS. Exercise caution when swimming at the lifeguard-less Spaggia San Giovanni di Sinis and other western beaches, where the undertow is stronger than at the more placid and sheltered eastern shores.

NUORO
☎**0784**

The architecture of this provincial capital, high up in the mountains of central Sardinia, is a mix of the Spanish-influenced buildings and modern block-style apartment complexes. Nuoro (noo-OH-ro; pop. 36,000) is known as a Sardinian center of high culture, home to the island's contemporary art museum, the Museo Arte Nuoro (MAN), and the only government-commissioned ethnographic museum. Locals also proudly tout Nuoro's status as the birthplace and final resting place of Nobel prize-winning author Grazia Deledda. Once you've had your fill of museums, a stomach-churning bus ride or an arduous hike up Monte Ortobene will reveal an imposing statue of Christ the Redeemer and similarly spectacular views of the sea.

 S.O.S. At 8:30pm, buses stop running, and taxis are a rarity. If you plan to be out past this time and are staying outside the *centro,* arrange for transportation home in advance to avoid getting stranded. If you need a taxi in the early hours of the morning (before 9am), arrange for pick-up beforehand.

⌐ TRANSPORTATION

Trains: FDS station (☎0784 30 115), on V. Lamarmora, in P. Stazione. Ticket office open M-Sa 7:30am-5:15pm. To **Cagliari** (3hr., 5 per day 6:24am-6:51pm, €13.50) via **Macomer.** Important: When switching trains in Macomer, note that the FDS station is across the street from the Trenitalia station, and you'll need to switch from the FDS Nuoro-Macomer train to the Trenitalia Macomer-Cagliari train.

Buses:

ARST (☎0784 29 41 73). Buses stop at the ARST station on V. Toscana between Vle. Sardegna and V. Santa Barbara. Tickets available next door at Il Gusto Macelleria, Vle. Sardegna 21 (☎0784 32 408). To: **Cagliari** (2hr., 2:05pm, €14.50); **Olbia** (stops in port, airport, and city, although not all buses make all 3 stops; 1hr., 7 per day 5:30am-5:40pm, €7.50); **Cala Ganone** (1hr., 7 per day 6:53am-7pm, €3) via **Dorgali** (45min.; 8 per day 6:53am-7pm; reduced service Sa-Su; €2.50); **Orgosolo** (30min.; 9 per day 5:50am-6:30pm, last return 7:05pm, reduced service Sa-Su; round-trip €2.50); **Sassari** (4:20 and 7:10pm, €7.50). **Luggage storage** available.

F. **Deplano** buses run from Vle. Sardegna, 1 block to the right of the ARST station, to the **Olbia airport** (☎0784 29 50 30; 1hr., 6 per day 4:15am-5:15pm, €10) and the **Alghero airport** (☎0784 30 325; 2hr.; 11:25am, 3:20, 5pm; €18). Buses coincide with plane arrivals and departures.

Public Transportation: Buy tickets (€1.10) for the local buses at newsstands, *tabaccherie*, or in the train station. **Bus #2** runs from P. Vittorio Emanuele through the *centro* to the train station and the hospital. **Bus #8** runs to the top of M. Ortobene. **Buses #3** and **#9** run between P. V. Emanuele and the ARST station.

Taxis: (☎0784 33 53 99 174 or 368 90 94 71). At night it can be a very long wait, so call ahead. Reserve the night before for taxis before 9am.

Car Rental: Autonoleggio Maggiore, Vle. Monastir 116 (☎0784 27 36 92; fax 20 80 536). 23+. Open M-F 8am-1pm and 4-7pm, Sa 8am-1pm and 4-6pm. AmEx/MC/V.

◢ ▶ ORIENTATION AND PRACTICAL INFORMATION

From the ARST **bus station,** turn right on Viale Sardegna. When you reach **Piazza Sardegna,** take a right on **Via Lamarmora** and follow it to **Piazza delle Grazie** and the *centro.* To get to the tourist office from P. delle Grazie, turn left and follow Via IV Novembre uphill through **Piazza Dante** to **Piazza Italia.** Brown signs will direct you the rest of the way. **Via Roma** leads from P. Italia to **Piazza San Giovanni** and the town's social hub, **Piazza Vittorio Emanuele. Corso Garibaldi** is a major street with shops and cafes that runs out of P. V. Emanuele.

Tourist office: P. Italia 19, (☎0784 23 88 78. Open in summer daily 9am-7pm.) The enthusiastic, English-speaking staff at **EPT** has brochures, maps, and hiking info. Open in summer daily 9am-7pm. There is another tourist office closer to the *centro* at C. Garibaldi 155 (☎0784 38 777, www.puntoinforma.it), with an equally enthusiastic and helpful staff. This office also offers a wealth of information on locations of interest in the island's interior. Ask them to help you set up excursions.

Pharmacy: C. Garibaldi 65, (☎0784 30 143).

Hospital: Ospedale San Francesco, V. Mannironi (☎0784 24 02 49), is on the highway to Bitti. The 24hr. **guardia medica** is on V. Deffenu (☎0784 24 08 48).

Internet: Smile Caffè, V. Piemonte 3, off V. Veneto. €3 per hr. Open Jun.-Aug. M-Sa 7am-10pm.

Post Office: P. Crispi 8 (☎0784 24 52 10) off V. Dante. Open M-F 8am-6:50pm, Sa 8am-1:15pm. Another **branch,** V. Santa Barbara 24 (☎0784 23 28 07), is near the ARST station. Open M-F 8am-6:50pm, Sa 8am-1:15pm. **Postal Code:** 08100.

◤ ◖ ACCOMMODATIONS AND FOOD

Inexpensive hotels are rare in Nuoro, and campgrounds are in distant towns. If you plan to stay in the area, consider B&Bs close to Nuoro or Monte Ortobene, or head to the smaller hamlets in the hills. ◢**Casa Solotti** ❸, in Località Monte Ortobene, a peaceful location in the countryside, has five large rooms that share two bathrooms and a terrace with a mountain view that extends to the sea on clear days. Take bus #8 (every 50min. 8:15am-8pm) from P. V. Emanuele, which stops in front of the Casa at the "Solotti" stop. Welcoming multilingual owner, ◪**Mario,** serves homemade jam, yogurt, and pastries for breakfast. Mario also sometimes takes travelers on an excursion to his family's farm, where you can see an inhabited natural cave, pet domestic animals, and purchase organic cheese. (☎0784 32 86 02 89 75; www.casasolotti.it. Call for free pickup from town. €26-30 per person, depending on time of year. Cash only.)

For a local favorite, visit ◪**Ristorante Tascusi** ❷, V. Aspromonte 15, just off V. Garibaldi, where high quality cuisine comes at surprisingly low prices. The *menù* includes a primo, secondo, side dish, and 0.25L of wine or 0.5L of water for only €10. Come early to beat the crowds. (☎0784 37 287. Open M-Sa noon-3pm and 8-10:30pm. MC/V.) For classy and relaxing dining while enjoying mountain views from the patio, try **Ristorante Ciusa** ❸, V. Francesco Ciusa 55. Menu offers many seafood dishes, tons of pizza, and a magnificently decadent *seadas* with pistacchio gelato for dessert. (☎0784 25 70 52. Primi €8-10. Secondi €12-22. Dessert €5. AmEx/MC/V.) At **Canne Al Vento** ❷, V. Biasi 123, a half hour outside of town, high class and low prices dominate. Guests dine on classic *culurgiones* (ravioli stuffed with potatoes, cheese, and mint; €7) and sip rich espresso. (☎0784 20 17 62. Primi €5-8.50. Secondi €6.70-12.50. Open M-Sa 12:30-3pm and 8-10:30pm. AmEx/MC/V.) A quality bakery, **Antico Panifico Sardo** ❷, V. Ferraciu 73 (☎0784 36 275), off P. delle Grazie, offers some of the best traditional baked goods in town, including hot rolls, *pane carasau* (€5 per kg), and scrumptious *panzerotti* (from €2) filled with cheese, tomato, and a choice of eggplant, mushroom, or ham. (Open M-F 8am-1:30pm and 4:30-8pm, Sa 8am-1:30pm.) **Pellicano** supermarket in P. Mameli has groceries. (☎0784 23 26 66. Open M-Sa 8:30am-2pm and 5-8pm, Su 5-8pm. AmEx/MC/V.)

🅖 SIGHTS

◪**MUSEO DELLA VITA E DELLE TRADIZIONI POPULARI.** Sardinia's largest and highly informative ethnographic museum contains a collection of traditional costumes, hand-woven rugs, musical instruments, and jewelry from around the island. The pieces are arranged in a series of stucco houses circling a flowered courtyard—a reconstruction of a typical Sardinian village. One house contains carnival masks shaped like devils, donkeys, pigs, cows, and goats; don't miss the creepy *Mamuthone* (traditional Sardinian costume masks) or your very own cutout mask in the museum's handout. *(V. Antonio Mereu 56. ☎0784 25 70 35. Open daily July-Sept. 9am-8pm; Oct.-June 9am-1pm and 3-7pm. €3, under 18 and over 60 €1.)*

◪**MONTE ORTOBENE.** The bronze ◪**Christ the Redeemer,** a 1905 statue of the town's symbol, beckons hikers to the peak of this hill, where a shady park and spellbinding views await. After the hike to the statue, walk 20m down the road from the bus stop on Monte Ortobene to see Monte Corrasi, which dwarfs the neighboring town of Oliena. *(Take the sensational bus #8 from P.V. Emanuele 7km to the summit. 14 per day 8:15am-8pm, last return 8:15pm; €1.10. To hike there take the 4.5km trail La Solitudine; start behind Chiesa della Solitudine at the beginning of V. Ortobene, and follow the red-and-white marked "Trail 101." Look for yellow sign saying "Redentore" to reach the statue.)*

MUSEO ARTE NUORO. Affectionately termed the "MAN," this striking white building contains a collection of 20th-century Sardinian art that incorporates both traditional and contemporary themes. The middle two floors hold a permanent collection of works by 20th-century Sardinian painters such as Francesco Ciusa and Antonio Ballero, while the first and fourth floors display rotating exhibits by contemporary artists. *(V. Satta 27. ☎0784 25 21 10; www.museoman.it. Open Tu-Su 10am-1pm and 4:30-8:30pm. €3, students 18-25 €2, under 18 or over 60 free.)*

HOME OF GRAZIA DELEDDA. Locals are fiercely proud of Grazia Deledda, the first female Italian novelist to win a Nobel Prize (for literature; 1926). Nuoro is home to both the house where she was born and the church, Chiesa della Solitudine, where she is buried. Today, the house has transformed into Museo Casa Deledda, which will probably interest only those familiar with her work. *(V. Deledda. Church at base of hill of Monte Ortobene on Vle. La Solitudine. ☎0784 24 29 00. Displays only in Italian. Open daily July-Sept. 8am-9pm; Oct.-June 9am-1pm and 3-7pm. Free.)*

DAYTRIP FROM NUORO

ORGOSOLO. The bus ride alone merits a trip to picturesque **Orgosolo** (or-GO-zo-lo; pop. 4,505) but the town itself is known for its impressive 🖼murals, which range in style from Picasso replicas to controversial political themes. The murals, which cover the buildings along C. Repubblica, are the products of both Sardinian and international influence. The *milanese* anarchist group, Gruppo Dioniso, created the first mural in 1969, and Francesco del Casino, a teacher from Siena, reinvented the mural-painting as an ongoing project in 1975. His works focus on social and political issues, including imperialism, fascism, and commercialism. Artists make new murals focused on modern themes like Sardinian independence; and one chilling mural commemorates the terrorist attacks on the World Trade Center on September 11th, 2001. To eat a traditional meal in the mountains, contact **Cultura e Ambiente,** a local organization that operates excursions into the hills and organizes lunches in a field behind its restaurant, **Supramonte ❸,** in Località Sarthu Thithu, 3km uphill from town. Busloads of tourists come to devour smoked meats, cheese, fresh produce, and pastries off wooden platters. *(☎0784 40 10 15 or 349 17 75 877; www.supramonte.it. Tastings conducted for groups, but individuals may call ahead to join. Transportation provided on request. Lunch €18.)* Though there is no tourist office, souvenir shop owners are quite helpful when navigating through town. Strolling leisurely along C. Repubblica and investigating side-streets will allow you to experience a jamboree of works in this paradise of modern art. For those seeking more details about the paintings, shops sell an English-language picture guide (€12) to the murals. *(To arrive, take an ARST bus from the station in Nuoro, which runs buses approximately every 30 min.)*

> 🟊**TIP** **THE RIGHT SIDE.** When taking the ARST bus from Nuoro to Orgosolo, sit on the right side of the bus. As the bus approaches Orgosolo, a few murals are visible, included one by Francesco Del Casino on 2 large boulders. The painting depicts the half-orange, half-white face of a wide-eyed native, reminding shepherds to always keep a watchful eye over their flocks.

DORGALI   ☎0784

Pint-sized Dorgali (dor-GA-lee; pop. 8035), high up in the mountains and ringed by farms and pastures, offers visitors relaxation and quiet among friendly locals, and access to a vibrant crafts trade that manifests the spirit of traditional Sardinia. Since the tourist boom in the 60s, travelers have trekked to Dorgali to admire craftsmen at work or to indulge in Dorgali's renowned red wine. Though roads connect it to nearby Cala Gonone and archaeological sights, Dorgali's farmers and artisans maintain the town's isolated charm.

🖅🏠 TRANSPORTATION AND PRACTICAL INFORMATION. ARST **buses** stop at V. Lamarmora 59, at the intersection with C. Umberto. Buy tickets at the *tabaccheria* at the intersection of V. Lamarmora and V. Montessori. The schedule is

SARDINIA

posted at the tourist office and *tabaccherie*. Buses run to Cala Gonone (25min., 10 per day 6:20am-7:45pm, €1), Nuoro (45min., 9 per day 6:05am-7:25pm, €2.50), and Olbia port (3hr., 2 per day 6:35am and 5:25pm, €7.50).

Via Lamarmora, which runs uphill from the bus stop, and **Corso Umberto** (perpendicular to V. Lamarmora) are the town's major streets. **Via Roma** descends to **Viale Kennedy,** which runs along the bottom of town. The **Pro Loco tourist office,** V. Lamarmora 108, provides maps and detailed info about Cala Gonone, Dorgali, and nearby attractions. (☎0784 96 243. Open M-Sa May-Sept. 9am-1pm and 4-8pm; Oct.-Apr. 9am-12:30pm and 3:30-7:30pm.) Currency exchange and **ATMs** are at **Banca Intesa,** at the intersection of V. Lamarmora and V. Fleming, and at the post office. (Open M-F 8:30am-1:30pm and 2:45-4:15pm, Sa 8:30am-noon.) In case of emergency, call the **carabinieri** (☎0784 96 114) or the **medical clinic.** (☎0784 93 150. Open M-F 10pm-8am, Sa-Su 24hr.) **Farmacia Mondula,** V. Lamarmora 55, at the intersection with V. Sardegna, posts an after-hours rotation. The closest hospital, **Ospedale Civile San Francesco** (☎0784 24 02 49 37), is in Nuoro, on the highway toward Bitti. Go to **InformaticaMente,** V. Lamarmora 82, for **Internet** access. (☎0784 96 520. €6 per hr. Open M-Sa 9:30am-1pm and 4-8pm.) The **post office** is at the corner of V. Lamarmora and V. Ciusa, across the street from the bus stop. (☎0784 94 712. Open M-F 8am-noon.) **Postal Code:** 08022.

🖼🖳 ACCOMMODATIONS AND FOOD. Accommodations in Dorgali are generally less expensive than those in neighboring beach resorts and in Nuoro. Although none of Dorgali's B&Bs are especially beautiful or outstanding, the clean, simple rooms in these family homes are a cheap place to rest your head after adventure-filled days in the countryside. **B&B di Bardilio Fancello ❷,** V. Azuni 5, keeps four rooms, all with bath, in the town center. A TV room, kitchen, delicious breakfast, and terrace shaded by grape vines make this B&B even more comfortable. (☎/fax 0784 96 335; simfanc@inwind.it. Breakfast included. €25 per person. Cash only.) Surrounded by gardens and fruit trees, the friendly, family-owned **Il Querceto ❹,** V. Lamarmora 4, 10min. downhill from the *centro,* is reminiscent of a countryside retreat. The front entrance and restaurant feature rotating exhibitions by local artists. Forty enormous rooms all have tiled bath, satellite TV, phone, and mountain view (☎0784 96 509; www.ilquerceto. com. Breakfast and dinner included in the restaurant downstairs. Singles €53-69; doubles €88-168; triples €114-162; quads €132-18. AmEx/MC/V.) Follow the signs off V. Lamarmora, 10min. uphill from *centro,* to **Hotel S'Adde ❸,** V. Concordia 38, another family-owned hotel with spacious rooms that have bath, A/C, TV, phone, and private balcony. (☎/fax 0784 94 412; www.hotelsadde.it. Breakfast included; restaurant downstairs. Wheelchair-accessible. Singles €40-70; doubles €70-110; triples €80-120; quads €100-130. AmEx/MC/V.)

For a small town, Dorgali has no shortage of snack bars, but the brick-oven pizzas at 🖼**Il Giardino ❶,** V. Enrico Fermi 59, on the road to Cala Gonone, are a superb and budget-friendly alternative to the all-too-prevalent pre-packaged *panini.* Try the delicious *giardino,* laden with grilled veggies (€8), a bountiful salad (€7.50), or an international selection of beers, including a refreshing white beer (from €2). The house tiramisu (€3.50) is to die for. (☎0784 94 257. Pizza €4.50-8.50. Primi €6.50-10. Secondi €8-16. Wheelchair-accessible. Open M and W-Su 8am-midnight. AmEx/MC/V.) Head to the moderately-priced and friendly **Ristorante Colibri ❸,** V. Gramsci 14, for *penne alla dorgalese* (pasta with pork sauce; €7), the local specialty. From V. Lamarmora, take V. Cerere, which becomes V. Gramsci, to the intersection with V. Flores. (☎0784 96 054. Primi €7. Secondi €10.50-11.50. Cover €2. Open in summer daily 12:30-2:30pm and 7:30-10pm. MC/V.) **Deiana Dolci Sardi ❶,** V. Africa 3, serves handmade sugary Sardinian sweets. Take V. Lamarmora to V. Cavalotti to P. Fancello. (☎0784 95 096.

Pastries €8-20 per kg, most around €10. Bag of 4 pastries approx. €1.50. Open M-Sa 8am-1pm and 4-8pm. Cash only.) Dorgali is also known for its heavy and flavorful red wine. Visit **Cantina Sociale**, V. Piemonte 11, to sample a selection of wines and grappa. (☎0784 96 143. Bottles from €4.) **Supermarket Sia** is on V. Lamarmora 18. (Open M-Sa 8am-1pm and 4-9pm, Su 8am-1pm. AmEx/MC/V.)

⬛❗ SIGHTS AND OUTDOOR ACTIVITIES. With the Supramonte mountains on one side and the Orosei Gulf on the other, Dorgali is an excellent center for embarking on **treks** through the Gorropu Canyon, hikes to the ancient Nuraghic villages of Tiscali and Serra Orrios, or swims along Cala Gonone's **beaches**. It is necessary to have a car to reach most of these sites. Consider renting one at **Prima Sardegna**, V. Lungomare Palmasera 32, in Cala Gonone, which offers rates from 4hr. to 7 days. (☎0784 93 367 or 333 57 62 185; www.primasardegna. com. MC/V.) **Atlantika**, V. Lamarmora 195 (☎0784 32 89 72 97 19; www.atlantika. it), arranges scuba diving, snorkeling, and guided excursions of the Tiscali's Nuraghic village and the Gorropu Canyon. Archaeological tours of the Supramonte of Dorgali, the murals of Orgosolo, and the coast of the Golfo di Orosei are also offered. (Arranges transportation and guide €30-60, depending on length and difficulty of excursions. Usually departs between 8:30 and 9am; returns between 4 and 5pm.) **Cooperative Ghivine**, V. La Marmora 69, arranges guided excursions, hikes, free-climbs, and canyon-climbs of Tiscali, Gorropu, and the Supramonte mountains. (☎0784 34 94 42 55 52 or 338 83 41 618; www. ghivine.com. Tours depart daily 9am-4pm; some available in English. Most tours €35, including transportation. Lunch usually €7.) With 400m tall walls and canyons, the ◼**Goropu Canyon Gorge** is one of Europe's tallest and widest and one of the wonders of inner Sardinia. Large boulders, pink oleander trees, and an underground river that occasionally surfaces form breathtaking views and a spectacular hiking experience. You'll need a car to reach the S'Abba Arva bridge where parking is available. From there, hike up the gorge (2hr.). There are no labeled signs, a guided tour is the best way to explore S'Abba Arva.

A car is also required to reach the base of the ◼**Tiscali**, one of Italy's tallest mountains. From the bottom of the path, it is a 2hr. hike to the top. A Nuraghic village is hidden in a cave on the top of the mountain. The vault has since caved in, leaving the top of the cave open. (Hidden village open daily May-Sept. 9am-7pm; Oct.-Apr. 9am-5pm. €5, children and over 65 €2.) **Serra Orrios Village**, the largest Nuraghic settlement in Sardinia, is 10km away from Dorgali and only accessible by car. Once the island's most important religious center, Serra Orrios contains two small megaron temples and 70 huts. (Guided visits on the hr. 9am-noon and 4-6pm. Call Cooperativa Ghivine for info, reservations, and guided excursions that include transportation and lunch. €5, children and over 65 €3.) The **Ispingoli Cave** holds the longest stalagmite-stalactite column (38m high) in Europe and the second longest in the world. The cave is accessible by car along State Road #125 in the direction of Dorgali/Orosei. Two hundred and eighty steps installed in the 70s descend to the base of the column. Used by prehistoric humans as shelter, the caves now showcase colorful stalagmites and stalactites. (For info and reservations, call Consorzio Atlantika at ☎0784 32 89 72 97 19. Guided visits every hour 9am-noon and 3-5pm; additional tours June-Aug. 1, 6, and 7pm. €7, children and over 65 €3.50.)

⬛ SHOPPING. Dorgali's craft stores are at the heart of its appeal. Tourists wander the tiny streets, observing local artisans weave, mold, and bake their wares. Stores along and around V. Lamarmora display handmade *filigree* jewelry, *tappeti* (wool and cotton weavings), and carvings. Serafina and her mother weave beautiful *tappeti* at **Il Tapetto di Serafina Senette**, P. Asproni 22. (☎0784 95

202. Pieces from €50. Open daily 8:30am-1pm and 4-8pm. MC/V.) At **Ceramica di Tornino Loi**, V. Lamarmora 120, Giovanna sells both traditional plates featuring domesticated animals and other colorful works with cartoon characters and goblins. (☎0784 34 01 26 82 38. Open M-Sa 9:30am-12:30pm and 6-10pm). For belts (from €13), pocketbooks, and a variety of other fine local leatherworks, head to the pleasantly pungent **Pelleterie di Giovanni Ladu**, on V. Cavallotti, off V. Lamarmora (☎0784 95 290. Open daily 8:30am-1pm and 3-11pm).

CALA GONONE   ☎0784

Hugging the coastline at the base of the mountains, Cala Gonone (CA-la go-NO-ne; pop. 1279) was once only accessible by boat. A tunnel carved through the mountains now connects this town to Dorgali, though the contrast between the two is remarkable. As you emerge from the tunnel, the ocean appears as a vast expanse of hazy blue-gray. As word gets out of Cala Gonone's profound beauty and hidden charm, it is quickly becoming one of Sardinia's most popular tourist destinations. Its high mountains, archaeological wonders, postcard-perfect harbor, and secluded beaches—including the famed Cala Luna, where both versions of the film *Swept Away*, the 1975 original and 2001 Madonna remake, were filmed—make it a worthwhile stop on any trip to Sardinia.

◧⏃ TRANSPORTATION AND PRACTICAL INFORMATION. ARST **buses** run to Dorgali (20-25min., 10 per day 6:40am-8:10pm, €1), a bus hub. Buy tickets at Bar La Pinetta on Vle. C. Colombo. Deplano buses (☎0784 29 50 30) leave Cala Gonone for the Olbia airport via Dorgali (4 per day 6:30am-1:15pm; €15, buy tickets onboard). Buses stop in front of the post office on **Via Cala Luna** and at the tourist office on **Viale del Bue Marino. Viale Cristoforo Colombo** leads downhill to the harbor; **Lungomare Palmesare** runs along the seafront. The ◪**tourist office** is on Vle. del Bue Marino. (☎0784 93 696. Open daily Apr.-Sept. 9am-1pm and 3:30-7:30pm; Oct.-Mar. 9am-1pm and 3:30-6:30pm.) An **ATM** is inside the yellow building in the center of the port. In case of emergency, call the **carabinieri** (☎0784 96 114) or the **medical clinic** (☎0784 92 00 32). **New Age Internet Point** is located in P. Verrazzano, off V. Magellano. (€5 per hr., €10 per 4hr. Open M-Sa 9am-12:30pm and 4:30-10pm.) The **post office**, at the corner of Vle. C. Colombo and V. Cala Luna, next to the SISA Supermarket, has currency exchange. (☎0784 93 278. Open M-Sa 8:15am-1:15pm.) **Postal Code:** 08020.

◪⏃ ACCOMMODATIONS AND FOOD. ◪**SOS Ozzastros B&B ❷**, V. Vasco de Gama 7, has large, clean, sunny rooms, each with large double bed, private bath, A/C, and balcony. Common room has large TV and cozy wicker furniture. Cheap alternative to beachside hotels. (☎0784 93 145 or 339 13 78 510. Breakfast included. Open Mar.-Nov. €20 per person; 4-person apartments with kitchen available for longer stays. AmEx/MC/V.) Just steps from the beach, **Hotel Bue Marino ❹**, V. Vespucci 8, offers many spacious rooms with balconies and unobstructed views of the port and the beach. For a truly magnificent view, relax at the hotel's seaside bar across the street from reception. A/C, satellite TV, phone, minifridge, and deposit box in rooms; some even have massage tub. (☎0784 92 00 78 or 347 77 13 099; www.hotelbuemarino.it. Breakfast included. Singles €60-95; doubles €75-150; junior suite €120-190. AmEx/MC/V.) A stay at ◪**Camping Villaggio Calagonone ❶**, V. Callodi 1, just off Vle. C. Colombo, will deceive you into thinking you're no longer near the sea. The peaceful and welcoming campground is set back from the harbor in a mountain-ringed pine grove and features a well stocked market, bar, swimming pool, and tennis court. (☎0784 93 165; www.campingcalagonone.it. Reception 8am-8pm. Tent, parking, and hot showers free. €13-19 per person, €7-10 per child. 2-person campers €35-63, with toilet €39-68; Bungalows with 2-4 beds €48-206. 4-person €57-93/60-130. 4-person bungalows €63-120. MC/V.)

Across from the post office, **Ristorante Self-Service L'Anphora ❷**, V. Cala Luna, is a cafeteria-style restaurant with over 20 pasta dishes, including Sardinian *gulluriones*. (☎0784 93 067. Panini €3. Primi €4-7. Secondi €3-12. *Menù turistiche* €18-23. Takeout available. Open in summer daily 8:30am-midnight. AmEx/MC/V.) **Il Pescatore ❸**, V. Acqua Dolce 7, serves flavorful favorites like *spaghetti alla bottarga* (€9) and several pizzas. (☎0784 83 174. Primi €7-14. Secondi €10-18. Open daily 7-11pm. MC/V.) At the musically themed, **Pub Road House Blues ❷**, V. Palmasera, next to the Prima Sardegna info office, enjoy rocking pizzas (€4.50-8.50), salads (€5.50-6), or beer. (☎0784 93 187. Secondi €9.50-15. Open daily 8am-2am. AmEx/MC/V.) There is a **Sisa** supermarket on the corner of V. Cala Luna and V. C. Colombo by the post office (open M-Sa 7:30am-1:30pm and 4:30-8:30pm, Su 8am-1pm), and a **Sigma** supermarket on Vle. C. Colombo 18 (open M-Sa 7:30am-1pm and 4:30-8pm, Su 7:30am-1pm).

◪◪ BEACHES AND OUTDOOR ACTIVITIES. Cala Gonone is positioned to allow access to several beaches and adventure-sport venues. V. Bue Marino leads 3km along the waterfront, passing long stretches of beach before arriving at the resplendent **Cala Fuili** (cove). Treasured by Italians for its crystal-clear waters and tropical backdrop, and now infamous as the site of Madonna's *Swept Away* remake, **◪Cala Luna** is accessible by boat or foot. Sheltered by limestone cliffs and fuschia oleanders, the cove has maintained its beauty despite the boatloads of tourists that visit daily. To reach Cala Luna, hike a strenuous 2hr. on the 4km trail that departs from Cala Fuili or take the Consorzio Trasporti Marittimi ferry to Cala Luna. (☎0784 93 305; port ticket booth ☎0784 92 00 51. 8 per day 9am-5pm, last return 6:30pm; round-trip €15.)

Consorzio also runs ferries to the elusive **Bue Marino,** accessible only by sea. (Ferry fees include guided tour. Bue Marino: round-trip €17, ages 6-12 €10. Bue Marino and Cala Luna: €24, ages 6-12 €16.) These well-conducted tours are a great value for an opportunity to see beautiful sights that are truly one-of-a-kind. Tour guides lead visitors through cave chambers that conceal natural curiosities, including the dripping stalactites of the **"Candle Room,"** and the **"Mirrors Room,"** in which a large pool of water reflects off the cave walls in a rainbow of colors, owing to variances in mineral composition. (30min. tours offered in English and Italian. July-Sept. 7 per day; May-June 2 per day. Photographs prohibited. €8.) **Atlantika,** V. Amerigo Vespucci or V. Lamarmora 195 in Dorgali (☎0784 93 307 or 328 97 29 719; www.atlantika.it), organizes excursions and tours of the Bue Marino caves and beaches. Atlantika also arranges **scuba diving** and **snorkeling** with certified guides for €25-52.

Prima Sardegna, V. Lungomare Palmasera 32, rents cars (€78-89 per day), scooters (€40 per day), mountain bikes (€5-7 per hr., €16-24 per day, €73-90 per week), and kayaks (single €11 per hr., €24 per day, €109 per week; double €18/42/150). Guides also lead excursions by boat, bike, or foot to natural and archaeological sites. (☎0784 93 367 or 333 57 62 185; www.primasardegna.com. €30-160 per person. Open daily 9am-1pm and 4-8pm. AmEx/MC/V.) Alternatively, to enjoy the grottoes and secluded inlets of white, sandy beaches farther down the coast at your own leisure, rent a **dinghy** for the day from **Centro Informazioni Noleggio di Graziano Mereu.** (Cala Gonone Port, Box # 9. ☎0784 93 048 or 380 32 15 448. Boats from €100 per day. MC/V.) From Cala Luna to Capo Monte Santu, there are several other beach inlets along the coast of the Golf di Orosei. The beach inlets are protected UNESCO World Heritage sites. You can also go **horseback riding** along the hills above the beaches. (Call Sebastiano ☎0784 34

02 49 18 37 or Franco ☎0784 34 96 11 28 50, or visit their booth in the port. €20 per hr., €70-80 per day.) **Dimensione Mare,** Vle. C. Colombo 2 (☎0784 33 88 25 10 40; www.dimensionemare.com), offers scuba diving.

CASTELSARDO   ☎079

When the Arabs invaded Sardinia in the 12th century, the conquerors founded Castelsardo (cah-stel-SAR-doh; pop. 5,679) and left their mark on Sardinia's history forever in the form of the Sardinian flag—four Arab men in white bandanas. Fluttering proudly over the castle's towers, the flag standing sentinel over the expansive sea below. Chill in the *centro storico* at the base of the castle after the endurance-testing hike to the top, or soak up the sun on the rock-strewn beaches a few kilometers down the road in Lu Bagnu.

TRANSPORTATION AND PRACTICAL INFORMATION. ARST **buses** run to Sassari (1hr., 11 per day 5:40am-8:50pm, €2.50) and Santa Teresa Gallura (1hr., 4 per day 8:23am-8:48pm, €5.50) via the *centro* (not the *centro storico*). Tickets can be purchased at La Nuova newsstand in P. Pianedda or at the several *tabaccherie* in the *centro*. From the *centro* bus stop, follow signs for the *centro storico* up **Via Nazionale** to **Via Bastione,** climbing up the steep hillside to reach the **castello.** The **tourist office** is in P. del Popolo, right before the *castello.* (☎079 47 15 06; proloco.castelsardo@tiscali.it. Open M-Sa 10am-12:15pm and 5-7pm.) For a **taxi,** call ☎079 47 01 25. The **post office** is on V. Nazionale. (☎079 47 00 05. Open M-Sa 8am-1:15pm.) **Postal Code:** 07031.

ACCOMMODATIONS AND FOOD. A stay at one of Castelsardo's several cozy B&Bs will guarantee a true Sardinian experience. **Casa Doria** ❸, V. Garibaldi 10, is a beautiful B&B that offers three spacious rooms. (☎079 34 93 55 78 82; www.casadoria.it. Breakfast included. 2 rooms with shared bath €60; double with private bath €70. Extra bed €20. Cash only.) Down the block, the homey **B&B Smorfiosa e Calarina** ❸, V. Garibaldi 42, is spacious and clean, with large beds, private baths, and a terrace with a sea view. (☎079 34 78 61 20 95; www.bb-smorfiosaecalarina.it. Breakfast included. €25-40 per person. Cash only.) **B&B La Pianedda** ❸, V. Mameli 9, is close to both the *centro* and the beach, and provides three clean, colorful rooms with shared bath, A/C, and TV above a ground-floor garden. (☎079 47 01 31 or 320 40 59 729. Breakfast included. Wi-Fi available. €25-35 per person. Cash only.) **Hotel Riviera** ❹, V. Lungomare Anglona 1, is worth the extra cost for its proximity to the sea and the touted Ristorante Fofò. Its modern rooms have A/C, private bath, minifridge, safe, and TV, and the helpful staff helps arrange excursions to local sights. (☎079 47 01 43; www.hotelriviera.net. Complimentary umbrella and deck chair. Breakfast and parking included. Rooms €39-119. AmEx/MC/V.)

This traditional Sardinian town offers a wide variety of restaurants serving up traditional Sardinian cuisine. Locals congregate to watch TV and shoot the breeze at **Trattoria da Maria Giuseppa** ❷, V. Nazionale 20, which serves dishes like Sardinian *gnocchetti* (€7.50) and grilled calamari (€8). The trattoria sits off the main road, which winds up the hill to the *castello* from bus stop. (☎079 47 06 61. Fish €8-15 per 100g. Primi €6-9. Secondi €7-14. Cover €1.50. Open daily noon-2:30pm and 7:30-11:30pm. Cash only.) For nourishment, shade, and a great deal after the trying trek up to the *castello,* dine at **Lu Scubili** ❸, V. Garibaldi 21, a pizzeria with pleasant, shaded tables dotting a cobblestone street. From P. del Popolo, walk all the way down the steps across from the tourist office, and turn left at the bottom. Try typical Sardinian fare, such as fish soup (€11), *cavallo* (horsemeat; €14), and large pizzas (dinner only) with a variety of toppings, including seafood, for €3.50. (☎079 47 05 11. Open M-Sa 12:30-2pm and 7:30pm-midnight. Cover €2. Service 20%. Cash only.) **Supermarkets** and fresh **produce stands** line the streets at the bottom of the hill. Try the smaller, family-owned markets for good prices and great conversation.

◨ ◩ **SIGHTS AND BEACHES.** The **castello**—for which Castelsardo is named—housed the town's *carabinieri* until the 90s. Today, the restored *castello* is home to a museum showcasing the town's long tradition of millinery and fishing through exhibits of historical and local artifacts as well as wicker crafts from Castelsardo. The view from the castle's terrace is worth the entrance fee in itself. To reach the crumbling *castello*, walk to the top of the hill from the *centro*'s bus stop; from there, it's hard to miss. On the way back down, follow V. Bastione to the downhill path along the city walls that leads to grassy knolls, large rock formations, and squawking seagulls. (☎079 47 13 80. *Castello* open daily 9:30am-1pm and 3-8:30pm. €2, children €1.) For your own sample of Castelsardo wicker baskets, check out the artisanal shop, **Vecchio Mercato.** Visit the **beach** by winding down the curving roads from the *centro* and walking along V. Lungomare Anglona, following the signs for *la mare.* Or get off at the ARST bus stop on V. Lungomare Anglona. A 5min. bus ride away, the picturesque and locally flavored ◧**Lu Bagnu** also offers sandy, white beaches and rolling waves perfect for bodysurfing. The private company **Spina Salvatore & Figli** runs orange shuttle buses between Castelsardo and Lu Bagnu. Buses leave from the ARST bus stop on V. Roma, near P. Pianedda (every hr. 6:37am-6:17pm, last return 7pm; €0.70). Castelsardo also has a well-known, wind-swept rock, **la Roccia dell'Elefante,** so named because its profile resembles an elephant with his trunk curled up. The rock is on Strada Statale #134, the road between Castelsardo and Sedini. Check with tourist office for bus schedules.

PALAU ☎0789

Situated on the luminous waters of Sardinia's northern coast, Palau (pa-LA-oo; pop. 4,241) is both an entertaining destination and a portal to the breathtaking Arcipelago della Maddalena. Palau's most famous sight is the Roccia dell'Orso, an enormous granite rock that mistral winds have carved into a bear-shape. It was immortalized in Homer's *Odyssey* with a warning about the ferocious *Lestrigoni* people that lived around it. Palau is now lined with pastel-colored modern buildings; take advantage of its spectacular camping facilities as you explore the incomparable northern Sardinian coastline.

◧◪ **TRANSPORTATION AND PRACTICAL INFORMATION.** The port end of **Via Nazionale,** Palau's single major thoroughfare, contains a white building that houses a bar and ferry ticket offices, with clearly marked bus stops outside. ARST **buses** run to Arzachena (13 per day 12:15am-9:30pm, €2); Olbia (13 per day, €2.50); Porto Cervo (5 per day M-F 5:15am-5:05pm); Santa Teresa di Gallura (7 per day 7:50am-9:25pm, €2); and Sassari (4 per day M-F 5:15am-7pm, Sa-Su only 7pm). Tickets sold onboard. The **ferry** companies EneRmaR (☎0789 70 84 84; www.enermar.it; 15min.; every 30min. 6:15am-11:45pm; round-trip €10, cars €11.50-12.50, bikes €1) and Saremar Ferries (☎0789 70 92 70 or 73 52 98; 15min.; every 30min. 7:30am-7:30pm; round-trip €10, ages 4-12 €8, cars €15.80-24) run between Palau and La Maddalena. Nicos Buses runs **shuttles** to Porto Cervo. (☎079 67 06 13 or 079 63 41 42; www.nicosgroup.it. 45min., departs 9:58am and returns 6pm.) For an expensive **taxi,** call ☎0789 70 92 18.

Palau's ◧**tourist office,** P. Fresi, sits to the right of V. Nazionale when approaching from Stazione Maritime. English-speaking staff offers info on beaches, outdoor activities, and tours of neighboring islands, as well as a wealth of publications about Sardinia and the Palau region. (☎0789 70 70 25; www.palau.it. Open daily 9am-1pm and 4:30-7:30pm.) **Banca di Sassari,** V. Roma 9, has currency exchange and **ATMs** in front. (Open M-F 8:20am-1:20pm and 2:30-3:30pm, Sa 8:20am-12:30pm.) In case of emergency, contact the **medical clinic** (☎0789 70 93 96). **Farmacia Nicolai** is at V. delle Ginestre 19. (☎0789 70 95 16, for urgent needs 0789 70 83 53. Open M-Sa 9am-1pm and 5-8pm. AmEx/MC/V.) The **Guardia Medica Turistica,** V. degli Achei, on the way toward Baia Saraceno from the port (follow signs for Baia Saraceno Camping), provides quick checkups and prescriptions. (☎0789 70 93 96. Open 24hr.) Wi-Fi and **Internet** are available at **Grillo's,** V. Fonte Vecchia 56. (€2 per 15min., €3 per 30min.) Follow the signs to the **post office,** at the intersection of V. Regina Margherita and V. La Maddalena. (☎0789 70 85 27. Open M-Sa 8am-1:15pm, Su 8:15am-12:45pm.) **Postal code:** 07020.

📍 **ACCOMMODATIONS.** Accommodations in Palau can be prohibitively expensive, with the singular exception of the gorgeous campgrounds along the coast near town. If you are desperate for A/C and a break from the beach, you'll have to pay high prices at hotels. **Hotel La Roccia ❺,** V. dei Mille 15, has an airy lobby built around an enormous boulder and themed rooms, like*"Il Faro"* (the lighthouse). Sharing a lovely, small outdoor garden and large breakfast buffet room, all 22 rooms have balcony, A/C, phone, TV, and bath. (☎0789 70 95 28; www.hotellaroccia.com. Breakfast and parking included. Reserve ahead. Singles €48-84; doubles €78-130. Extra bed additional 35%. AmEx/MC/V.) The same company operates two friendly, multilingual-staffed ▨**campsites** in town. Of the two camping options, **Baia Saraceno ❶,** Località Puna Nera 1, is much larger, more self-contained, and farther away from the touristy *centro.* Facing the water, turn right and follow the *lungomare* away from the port (10-15min. walk). Across the docks from the port and behind a man-made forest, Baia Saraceno offers three picturesque beaches 500m outside Palau. This establishment has three clean, large shared bathroom areas, a restaurant, pizzeria, bar, minimarket, and laundry service. The facility has its own diving center and arranges water sports and trips to nearby islands. (☎0789 70 94 03; www.baiasaraceno.com. €8-17.50 per person, ages 4-12 €5.50-13. Electricity €3. 2-person bungalows €26-48, with bath €32-64; 4-person bungalows with kitchen €248-500. 4-person caravan €89. Final cleaning fee €6-25; price varies with accommodation. Check online for detailed price listings and info on RV accommodations. AmEx/MC/V.) On the other side of town and 10min. from the port, Mexican-themed **Acapulco ❶,** Località Punta Palau, has a private beach, a bar with nightly piano music, a pizzeria, and a restaurant. From the port, with the water to the right, follow the *lungomare* up the large hill and follow signs for camping. Friendly and helpful English-speaking staff arranges underwater spear-fishing and excursions to La Maddalena Archipelago. (☎0789 70 94 97; www.campingacapulco.com. Towels €2. Open Mar.-Oct. 15. Reservations recommended in summer. €8-17.50 per person, ages 4-12 €5.50-13. Electricity €3. Hot showers free. Single bungalows with mandatory half pension €44-61; 2-person bungalows with kitchen €45-85; 4-person bungalow with kitchen €65-135. 4-person caravans €45-90. Final cleaning fee €10-30. AmEx/MC/V over €50.)

🍴 **FOOD.** Numerous bakeries and stores line V. Nazionale, and a **market** every Friday (8am-1pm) crowds the harbor with fresh cheeses, meats, clothing, and crafts. ▨**Sicily Creperie ❶,** V. Nazionale 45, is a Nutella haven, with Nutella crepes, Nutella-and-fruit crepes, Nutella-and-gelato brioches, and Nutella frappes for €2.50-4. The friendly staff also serves up fruity gelato, granita, and other Sicilian treats. (☎33 16 44 67 72. Open 9:30am-1pm and 4-10:30pm. Cash only.)

L'Uva Fragola ❶, P. Fresi 4, serve a variety of refreshing salads (€5.50-10.50), spaghetti (€4.50-7), and 39 creative types of pizza (€3.50-8) with toppings like octopus and egg. (☎0789 70 87 65. Cover €1.50. Open daily noon-3pm and 7-11pm. MC/V.) **Ristorante da Robertino ❹**, V. Nazionale 20, a pricey but popular seafood restaurant, serves fresh fish and flavorful pasta, such as spaghetti with shellfish for €11. (☎0789 70 96 10. Primi €6-14. Secondi €15-25. Cover €1.50. Open Tu-Su 1-2:30pm and 8-10pm. Reserve 2-3 days in advance. MC/V.) **Ristorante Il Covo ❸**, V. Sportiva 10/12, serves seafood and traditional, meat-heavy Sardinian cuisine at reasonable prices. The *linguine del pescatore* (assorted seafood spaghetti; €10) is a good call for indecisive patrons. (☎0789 70 96 08. Pizza €3.70-7. Primi €6.80-10. Secondi €5-14.50. 4-course dinner *menù* €30. Cover €2. Open M-Tu and Th-Su noon-2:30pm and 7-11:30pm. AmEx/MC/V.) If your sweet tooth is still aching, try the delectable purple *mora*, an authentic black raspberry gelato, at **La Gelateria dell' Angelo ❶**, tucked in the corner of the pink building at V. Capo d'Orso 2, where V. Nazionale and Capo d'Orso meet. (Open daily 4pm-midnight.) **Supermercati SISA** is at V. Nazionale 104. (☎0789 70 95 04. Open July-Aug. daily 8am-9pm.) Fresh produce is sold on V. Sportiva, across the street from **Grillo's**, V. F. Vecchia 56.

 TIP

BYOTP. If you're staying in a *tukul* (bungalows without private bath), camper, or tent without a private bath at Baia Saraceno or Acapulco, be aware that toilet paper is not provided in the restrooms. Grab a roll before leaving Palau to avoid a messy, or sloppy, situation.

🔲🔲 **SIGHTS AND BEACHES.** The small **Spiaggia Palau Vecchia** is the beach to the left of the port as you face the water. Shady most of the day, it's not the best for those set on tanning. Caramelli buses run to **Porto Pollo** (30min.; 5 per day 8:15am-6:45pm, last return 7:30pm; round-trip €2.50), a beach where Mediterranean seaweed sways under the water. Check out the **Roccia dell'Orso**, a rock that looks like a bear to some, from which you can enjoy stunning views of the countryside and port. (Buses to "Capo d'Orso"; 20min.; 4 per day 9:45am-6pm, last return 6:20pm; round-trip €1.50.) Bring proper footwear for the stair climb (10min.) and perhaps a picnic lunch and a good book, because the return bus doesn't come for roughly 3hr. If you want to see the Roccia without the exercise, look back toward Palau from the ferry to La Maddalena—it can sometimes be seen on the right side of the hill to the left of Palau.

L'ARCIPELAGO DELLA MADDALENA ☎0789

Back in the day, Corsica and Sardinia were one island joined together by a massive land bridge. L'Arcipelago della Maddalena (lar-chee-PEH-la-go DEL-la ma-da-LEH-nah; pop. 11,902), Caprera, and the over 50 smaller islands that surround them are all that remains of this bridge. Though visitors swarm the streets and relax on placid, white-sand beaches, tourism has not spoiled the islands. The entire archipelago was declared Sardinia's first national park in 1996, and ever since, commercial development has been strictly regulated. In addition, Italian patriots mob La Maddalena for their own reasons: their national hero and unifier, Giuseppe Garibaldi (1807-1882), made the nearby island of Caprera his home while in exile. Until January of 2008, La Maddalena was home to a US Navy support base, located on V. Principe Amadeo. The closure of this base after 35 years of operation was an emotional event for the approximately 20,000 Americans who reside in the islands.

SARDINIA

TRANSPORTATION AND PRACTICAL INFORMATION. EneRmaR (☎0789 73 54 68 or 70 84 84; www.enermar.it) and Saremar (☎0789 70 92 70) run **ferries** between Palau and La Maddalena. For a **taxi**, call ☎0789 73 65 00 or 0789 72 20 80. Rent **bikes** and **motor scooters** at Nicola, V. Amendola 18. (☎0789 73 52 66. Bikes €10 per day. Scooters €20-50 per day. Open daily 9am-7:30pm.)

There is no tourist office, but Palau's tourist office usually has brochures featuring La Maddalena's major attractions. For directions, check out the map on a billboard in front of the bus stop at Maddelena's port. **Banco di Sardegna**, on V. Amendola off P. XXIV Febbraio, has currency exchange and a **24hr. ATM**. (Open M-F 8:20am-1:20pm and 2:35-4:05pm.) A **laundromat**, Azzura Lavanderia, is at V. Dei Mille 3, off V. Principe Amadeo, one block past the public gardens. (☎38 99 72 40 27. Wash €4 per 6kg. Open M-Sa 9am-1pm and 4:30-8pm. Cash only.) In case of emergency, call the **carabinieri** (☎0789 73 70 04 or 73 69 43) or the **hospital** (☎0789 79 12 00). There is a **pharmacy** at the corner of P. Santa Maria Maddalena and V. Marsala. (Open M-F and Su 9am-1pm and 5-8:30pm.) **Patsi Net Internet Point,** V. Montanara 4, has three computers with fast connections; turn into the *piazza* to the left, off V. Principe Amadeo, across from the public gardens. Walk uphill and take a left. (☎0789 72 31 04. €6 per hr. Open daily 9am-1pm and 5-9pm. AmEx/MC/V.) The **post office** is in P. Umberto 1, across the street from the main part of the *piazza*. (☎0789 79 09 00. Open M-F 8am-6:50pm, Sa 8:15am-1:15pm.) **Postal Code:** 07024.

ACCOMMODATIONS AND FOOD. Though a 20min. walk from the *centro* and hidden away on a hill, **Hotel Arcipelago ❹**, V. Indipendenza 2, is a good deal. From P. Umberto, follow V. Mirabello along the water until the intersection with the stoplight. Turn left here, then take the first right on V. Indipendenza. Continue uphill, taking the first left onto a branch of the main road. The hotel is around the corner from the grocery store. The flower-lined entrance leads to a tiny, nautically themed lobby and 12 tastefully furnished rooms with TV, phone, and fan. (☎0789 72 73 28. Breakfast included. Reservation required July-Aug. Singles €45-55; doubles €60-85. V.) Up V. Indipendenza, **Hotel La Conchiglia ❹**, V. Indipendenza 3, has seven bright and spacious rooms that offer superb amenities, including A/C, bath, TV, phone, microwave, and minifridge. (☎0789 72 80 90; www.hotellaconchiglialmd.com. Breakfast included. Singles €55-75; doubles €75-125; quads €120-200. AmEx/MC/V.) Tourists and young locals flock to **Garden Bar ❸**, V. Garibaldi 65, thanks to its tasty, varied cuisine and friendly owner Spike. Pass under the painting of the topless mermaid and the fountain with live turtles, and try the *bruschetta* (€1.50-4) for a small snack or something from the vast selection of land and sea fare. (☎0789 73 88 25. Pizza €3.50-8. Primi €6-15. Secondi €6-20. Cover €1.50. Open daily 11:30am-3pm and 5-11pm. MC/V.) For a bite to eat before catching the ferry back to Palau, stop in at **Pizzeria Pappa & Ciccia ❶**, V. Garibaldi, 47, for cheap, topping-heavy pizzas like the "Bad Girl" (€4.50), smothered in almost any topping imaginable. (☎0789 73 68 82. Pizza €3.50-5.50; extra toppings €0.50 each. Open daily 6pm-midnight.) Pick up lunch at the **Despar** supermarket, V. Amendola 6, at the intersection with V. Italia. (☎0789 73 90 05. Open daily 8am-1:30pm and 5:30-8:30pm. MC/V.)

BEACHES AND ISLANDS. The islands surrounding La Maddalena are paradises of natural beauty, well protected from overdevelopment by their national park status. Some claim that these waters, which radiate brilliant shades of green and blue, are the clearest in the world. The nearby island **Razzoli** has magnificent swimming holes, and sightseers can set out by boat to islands like **Santa Maria**, with its long, white-sand cove. Santa Maria's *faro* (lighthouse), a 20min. stroll from the beach down a marked trail, looks out over

SARDINIA

the surrounding islands, including nearby **Spargi**. The waters in Spargi's **Cala Verde** bay shimmer in stunning shades of green. On Spargi's western side, lovers canoodle on **Cala dell'Amore's** unspoiled shores. Around **Cala Corsara**, blustery rock formations reward the adventurous with spectacular vistas. Without a private yacht or powerboat, the only way to explore the archipelago is on a full-day "spaghetti" **boat tour,** so nicknamed because of their pasta lunches. Companies like ☒**Marinella IV** (☎33 92 30 28 42 or 33 37 41 95 28; www.marinellagite. it) send ticket sellers to the docks of Palau mornings and evenings. Packing 50-80 people, the cruises are fun and informative. Guides point out the whimsical rock formations along the way. Tours cost (€35) typically include a pasta lunch, two or three 2hr. stops at beaches along the way (often at Spargi's Cala Corsara and **Cala Santa Maria**), and a quick stop at **Spiaggia Rossa**. Most boats leave between 10 and 11am and return between 5 and 6pm. Purchase tickets one day ahead. Tours are usually less crowded on weekends.

Buses run from La Maddalena to Caprera's Punta Rossa (15 per day 7:10am-7pm, last return 7:30pm; round-trip €2, purchase on bus), giving travelers access to beaches along the eastern peninsula. Catch buses at the port (in P. Colonna Garibaldi; a large monumental column marks the *piazza*) for Caprera or the northern coast of La Maddalena island, toward Ornano. Sunbathers fill the shores of ☒**Spiaggia del Relitto,** where a wide strip of white sand, calm waters, and an expansive swimming cove have made it one of Caprera's largest and most popular beaches. To reach it, follow the main road through Caprera to Punta Rossa or take the bus to the end of the Caprera line. Continue past *Spiaggia Due Mare* on the dirt road for about 1.5km and take a left when you see a sign for *Spiaggia del Relitto*. If Caprera still doesn't satisfy your quest for the perfect panorama, bike or motor along La Maddalena's **Panoramica dei Colmi,** about 25km of paved road circling the island. The road passes by marvelous sea views and attractive beach destinations, including **Cala Lunga** and the watersport-friendly **Cala Spalmatore.**

Buses also run to ☒**Spiaggia Bassa Trinita** from P. Colonna Garibaldi (9 per day 9am-7pm, last return 7:25pm; round-trip €2). The bus ride (10-15min.) alone is worth the trip, as it winds around the coast of La Maddelena with the rocky cliffs to one side and the unspoiled aquamarine beaches of Cala Spalmatore, Porto Massimo, and M. d. Rena to the other. Resist the urge to get off at the first beach; they get less and less touristy as you continue up the island. Bassa Trinita is the most beautiful, with a fine sandy beach, calm waves, and more of the characteristic windswept rock formations jutting out from the waters. From the bus stop, walk down the road immediately to the right (there will be a sign pointing to Baia Trinita) for around 10min.; you will see Baia Trinita carved into a rock when you finally reach it. There are no lifeguards at the beaches, but the water remains shallow for over 50m out. Pick up a book from **La Liberia dell'Isola**, P. Umberto 3, before heading to the beach. La Liberia offers a small selection of classics and mindless beach reads. (☎07 89 73 52 92. Open daily 9am-midnight. AmEx/MC/V.)

SANTA TERESA DI GALLURA ☎0789

It's not immediately clear to new arrivals that Santa Teresa di Gallura (SAN-ta Te-RAY-sa dee ga-LOO-ra; pop. 5000), poised on a hilltop, is in fact near water. But as soon as you crest the hill in the middle of town, the sparkling blue sea will assure you that your bus ticket was well worth the cash. With its narrow streets, social *piazze*, and unbeatable ocean vistas, Santa Teresa is an ideal base for exploring the natural wonders of Capo Testa, a peninsula of wind-sculpted granite with magnificent beaches. Santa Teresa boasts its own sandy beach, Rena Bianca, awarded the prestigious "Blue Flag" for its superior water quality and environmental consciousness. Watch the sunset over the sea from the hill's crest, where the shores of Corsica are visible in the distance.

SARDINIA

TRANSPORTATION

ARST **buses** (☎0789 55 30 00) depart from V. Eleonora d'Arborea, in the parking lot across from the post office, and run to Olbia's *centro* (1hr., 8 per day 6:10am-8:50pm, €4.50), Palau (40min., 8 per day 6:10am-8:50pm, €2), and Sassari (3hr., 5 per day 5:15am-7:15pm, €6.50). TURMO Travel Buses (☎0789 21 487) run to: Cagliari (6hr., 2:30pm, €22.50); Nuoro (3hr., 2:30pm, €7.50); Olbia airport (1hr., 6 per day 6am-6:40pm, €7); Oristano (4hr., 2:30pm, €15); Palau (40min., 6 per day 6am-6:40pm, €2). Buy tickets onboard or at **Baby Bar**, on V. Nazionale, 200m from the bus stop. (Open daily 8am-1pm and 4-6:30pm.) Saremar (☎0789 75 41 56; 1hr., 3 per day 8am-5pm, €12-14 including port tax for Corsica) and Moby (☎0789 75 14 49; 1hr., 4 per day 7am-7pm, €15) run **ferries** to Bonifacio, Corsica. Tickets are available at the office on V. del Porto. For a **taxi**, call ☎0789 75 42 37, 75 44 07, or 74 10 24. **Car rentals** are available from Hertz, V. Nazionale 58. (☎0789 75 56 89; www.gulpimmobiliare.it. Open M-Sa 9am-1pm and 4-7:30pm. Cash only.) **Scooters** and **bikes** can be rented from Global Noleggio, P. San Vittorio. (☎0789 75 50 80; www.globalinformation.it. Mountain bikes €10 per day; scooters €25-50 per day. Open daily 9am-1pm, 3-8pm, and 9:30-11:30pm. AmEx/MC/V.) If motors aren't for you, go **horseback riding** with Li Nibbari, Località da Testa. (☎33 78 17 189. Guided excursions €18 per hr.)

> **TIP**
> **MAKIN' A FUSS OVER THE BUS.** When traveling from Palau to Sassari, remember that every bus has to travel through either Santa Teresa di Gallura or Olbia. Consequently, it makes more sense to spend the night in either place when visiting Sassari instead of traveling back to Palau.

ORIENTATION AND PRACTICAL INFORMATION

The ARST bus stop is at the far end of the parking lot across the street from the post office. Hug the post office corner, walk straight to the intersection, and turn right on **Via Nazionale**. Head for the church in **Piazza San Vittorio**, at the end of the street and turn right again to reach **Piazza Vittorio Emanuele**. The tourist office is on the opposite side of the *piazza*.

Tourist Office: P. Vittorio Emanuele 24, 2nd fl. (☎0789 75 41 27). Provides a pocket-sized map of town and assists with accommodations. Ask about boat, horse, and moped rentals, as well as info about nearby excursions and archaeological attractions. Open M-Sa 9am-1pm and 4-6pm, Su 9am-1pm.

Boat Tours: Consorzio delle Bocche, P. V. Emanuele 16 (☎0789 75 51 12; www.consorziobocche.com), offers tours of the archipelago. Full-day tour daily 9:15am-5pm. Lunch included. €35-40, ages 4-12 €19. Office open daily 9am-1pm and 5pm-12:30am.

Medical Clinic: (☎0789 75 45 92), on V. Carlo Felice, across from bus station. Open 9am-2pm and 4-10pm.

Internet Access: Bar Sport, V. Magnon 6, between P. V. Emanuele and P. San Vittorio. €5 per hr. Open daily 10am-11pm.

Post Office: V. E. d'Arborea (☎0789 73 53 24), near the bus stop. Open M-Sa 8am-1:15pm. **Postal Code:** 07028.

ACCOMMODATIONS

Hotel Moderno, V. Umberto 39 (☎0789 75 42 33; www.modernoweb.it), centrally located off V. Nazionale. 16 comfortable rooms with large clean baths, A/C, and the occasional balcony. Extremely friendly staff. Decor is uber-Sardinian, with light fixtures, bedspreads, and serving dishes designed by local artist Franco Cassellati. Breakfast included. Open Apr.-Sept. Singles €45-65; doubles €62-130. AmEx/MC/V. ❹

Hotel L'Ancora, V. Calabria snc (☎0789 75 45 64; www.hotelancora.it), several blocks from the *centro*. Quaint, pastel-colored rooms with maritime theme, conveniently located near several restaurants. Rooms equipped with TV, phone, A/C, balcony, and bath. Breakfast included. Internet in the lounge. Rooms €37-91. AmEx/MC/V. ❸

Hotel Bellavista, V. Sonnino 8 (☎/fax 0789 75 41 62; www.hotelbellavista.stg@libero. it). Heading toward the ocean, take the 2nd left off P. Liberta onto V. Sonnino. Airy rooms all have large, clean tiled bath, TV, phone, and A/C; many have balconies with sea view. Breakfast €5. Singles €31-35; doubles €50-60. AmEx/MC/V. ❸

Pensione Scano, V. Lazio 4 (☎0789 75 44 47; www.albergoscano.it). Small rooms with TV and private bath. 1st fl. balconies. Breakfast €5. Doubles July €50-55; Aug. €72-78. Extra bed €10-15. AmEx/MC/V. ❸

🔋 FOOD

Shops line V. Aniscara, off P. V. Emanuele. A fruit and clothing **market** by the bus station opens Thursday morning and runs until the early evening. The **Sisa** supermarket, on V. Nazionale, next to Banco di Sardegna, packs the expected goods. (Open M-Sa 8am-1pm and 4:30-8pm, Su 9am-noon. MC/V.)

▨ Ristorante Da Thomas, V. Valle d'Aosta 22 (☎0789 75 51 33). Enjoy fresh local seafood on a relaxed outdoor patio, away from the touristy *centro*. Pair your meal from the sea with a selection from the extensive white wine list. Primi €5-15. Secondi €10-15. Cover €2. Open daily 12:30-3pm and 7-11pm. AmEx/MC/V. ❸

Papè Satan, V. Lamarmora 20/22 (☎0789 75 50 48). Look for signs off V. Nazionale. Neapolitan family cooks diabolically delicious pizza in a traditional brick oven in the courtyard. Try the rich *pizza alla Papè Satan* with cream, butter, mozzarella, and prosciutto (€7.50) or the *spaghetti alle cozze* (spaghetti with mussels; €8). English menu available. Cover €2. Open May-Oct. daily noon-2:30pm and 7-10pm. MC/V. ❷

Marlin, V. Garibaldi 4 (☎0789 75 46 97; www.marlinristorante.it), off V. Imbriani toward the sea, upstairs and to the left. This elegant *enoteca* serves typical seafood pastas and creatively presented dishes to huge dinner crowds lounging on the covered outdoor patio. Pizza only available at dinner. Primi €9-15. Secondi €13-20. Cover €1.65. Open daily noon-2:30pm and 7-11pm. AmEx/MC/V. ❹

Ristorante Azzurra, V. del Porto 19 (☎0789 75 47 89). Friendly staff serves delicious fish and homemade pasta like *tagliatelle* with clams, tuna, eggs, and tomatoes (€9). Over 40 kinds of pizza €5-8.50. Primi €7-13. Secondi €10-18. Cover €2. Open Tu-Su noon-2pm and 7-11pm. AmEx/MC/V. ❹

Gastronomia Pizzeria, Vle. Tibula 13 (☎33 97 47 06 024). Walk down V. Valle d'Aosta, and turn right; walk uphill. Farther away from the *centro*, this pizza shack sells cheap slices by the kilo (about €1.50-2.80 per slice). Also offers seafood and pasta priced by the kilo. Great for a quick bite. Open M-Sa 11am-3:30pm and 7-11pm. Cash only. ❶

👁🔋 SIGHTS AND BEACHES

Long before tourists discovered it, Santa Teresa was home to **Lu Brandali,** one of the region's largest and least disturbed prehistoric villages. Follow V. Nazionale past the end of town, then turn right on the dirt road when you see the brown sign for **Tomba dei Giganti.** From here, a narrow path leads to the massive tomb, communal village graves used between the 14th and 10th centuries BC. Due to their enormous dimensions and stone construction, the tombs were believed to be the final resting place of giants. Overgrown trails wind uphill past the old village dwellings and a pair of towers before culminating at the ruins of a *nuraghe* (prehistoric stone tower). The village is not labeled, so stop by the tourist office for historical information on the site. The whole walk takes 35min.

V. XX Settembre, off P. V. Emanuele, leads to the sea. As the road forks, bear left and continue past Hotel Miramar to reach P. Libertà. The Argonese **Tower of Longonsardo** (built 1358-1577), on the ruins of an ancient *nuraghe*, is framed by a jaw-dropping panorama. Ragged cliffs tumble into the translucent water, and the coastline of Corsica dominates the horizon. For a private, undisturbed dip in the sea, climb down the steep stone steps to reach the sheltered coves on either side of the hill—there's no sand, but the rocks are large enough to lie on, and you're likely to spot several fisherman reeling in their catches. If you do desire a sandy spot, head to the small but popular **Spiaggia Rena Bianca.** Facing the tower, take a left, wind down the street, and walk down the stairs. (Chair €6, with umbrella €12. Paddle boats €10 per hr.; canoes €8 per hr.; kayaks €5-8 per hr. Open daily 8am-7pm. Cash only.)

Some of the town's most notable attractions lie 3km away on the rugged peninsula **Capo Testa.** Take the Sardabus from the post office (10min., 3 per day, round-trip €1.24), but plan accordingly, as the last bus returns immediately after it gets to Capo Testa, and a cab back to town will cost you about €10. You can also bike or walk (45-60min.) along **Via Capo Testa,** off V. Tibula from V. Nazionale. If you're walking, take the opportunity to get off the busy highway and see some astounding vistas by going through the wooden gates on the right of the street; this is Sardinia's **Ente Forest,** which has trails for people and horses that wind through brush and boulders and crest onto views of the coastline that are truly breathtaking. The bus stops at an isthmus called **Spiaggia Rena di Ponente,** where two seas meet to form long parallel beaches ideal for water sports. (Two chairs and umbrella €15. Solo canoes €5 per hr.; doubles €8 per hr.; paddle boats €10 per hr.) Keep walking up the street that runs between the two beaches for 10min. Just before the road bends right at the crest of the hill, squeeze through a one-foot opening in the rocks on the left. Follow the dirt paths up and then down into the valley to reach the remote and stunning ⊠**Valley della Luna.** Once an international hippie commune, it is now home to some 20 dreadlocked hangers-on who live in rock dwellings in the sides of the valley and hang out on the beach. The valley holds abandoned fire rings, rock paintings, and carved posts. For more info about these locations and outdoor activities, stop by the tourist office.

OLBIA   ☎0789

Olbia (OL-bee-ya; pop. 51,045), the Sardinian port closest to the mainland, is a major transportation hub that greets thousands of tourists each day as they arrive on the island by air or by sea. A short distance from Golfo Aranci and a gateway to the fabled Costa Smeralda, Olbia is not just a point of entry but also a stellar base for visiting some of Sardinia's most interesting sites. Take a quick stroll past the shops and restaurants, then head on to experience the sparkling waters, rocky coves and hidden beaches of the Costa Smeralda.

▉ TRANSPORTATION

Flights: Buses #2 and 10 go from **Olbia Costa Smeralda Airport** to the *centro* (€0.80).

Trains: Trenitalia (☎0789 20 21) on V. Pala, just off C. Umberto. Open 6:05am-12:30pm and 1:50-8:15pm. Service to **Golfo Aranci** (25min., 7 per day, €2) and **Sassari** (2hr., 3 per day, €6.35) with connections to: **Alghero, Cagliari, Oristano,** and **Porto Torres** (2hr., 2:08pm, €7.60). Buy tickets from the lobby's machine or in the station.

Buses:

ARST (☎0789 55 30 00 www.arst.sardegna.it), bus stop located at V. Vittorio Veneto across the street from Bar della Caccia's yellow sign, where tickets are sold. To **Palau** (1hr., 12 per day 4:20am-11:15pm, €2.50), **Santa Teresa di Gallura** (2hr., 6 per day 6:15am-8:10pm, €4.50), and **Sassari** (3hr., 6:15am and 8:10pm, €6.50). Buses also run to **Arzachena** (40min., 11 per day 6:25am-11:15pm, €2), where you can catch a bus to **Porto Cervo, Costa Smeralda** (30min., 5 per day 9:10am-5:15pm). Buy tickets at the ticket office in the station (cash only).

Sun Lines, V. Pozzo 23 (☎0789 50 885), the airport (☎348 26 09 881), and Stazione Marittima (☎0789 20 80 82). Shuttle service to **Porto Cervo** and **Palau** from the airport, Stazione Marittima, and P. Crispi (4 per day, €13).

Local buses: Line 1 goes through the *centro* to V. Veneto and V. Aldo Moro, **Line 2** from the airport to the city center and suburban outskirts; **Line 10** is a faster loop from the airport to the *centro*. **Line 4** goes from *centro* to the beaches of the Gulf of Olbia. **Line 5** goes through the *centro* on V. Mameli to the beach in either direction (Porto Rotondo or Porto Istana). **Line 9** goes from the Stazione Marittima to the *centro* and train station. Tickets €0.80 at *tabaccherie*, €1.30 onboard. Bus stops are very visible and have signs that state which buses stop at each location. Local buses are orange, not to be confused with the blue ARST buses.

Ferries: Tirrenia (☎0789 24 691), in Stazione Marittima. **Moby Lines** (☎0789 27 927), in Stazione Marittima.

Taxi: At the airport (☎0789 69 150) and in the *centro* (☎0789 22 718). Expensive, as everyone drives and taxis are considered a luxury service (10min. ride about €25).

Car Rental: Hertz, V. Regina Elena 34 (☎0789 21 274). Open M-F 8:30am-1pm and 3:30-7:30pm, Sa-Su 8:30am-1pm. AmEx/MC/V. Also at the airport (☎0789 66 024). Open daily 8am-midnight. AmEx/MC/V.

🔳🔲 ORIENTATION AND PRACTICAL INFORMATION

Ferries arrive at **Stazione Marittima**, 1km east of the city center on **Viale Isola Bianca**. Be sure to pick up a **map** of Olbia in the information office at the port. ARST buses run from Stazione Marittima to the ARST station on **Via Vittorio Veneto**, as well as **Piazza Margherita**. **Viale Regina Elena** shoots off P. Margherita and leads to **Piazza Crispi**. On the other side of P. Margherita is **Via Porto Romano**, which is lined with shops and snack bars. The street winds across the train tracks and leads to the more industrial **Viale Aldo Moro**, which goes to northern destinations like Golfo Aranci and Porto Rodolfo. The tourist information kiosk gives out free maps in P. Matteotti.

Currency Exchange: Banca Intesa, C. Umberto 191A. Has an **ATM.** Open M-F 8:30am-1:30pm and 2:45-4:15pm, Sa 8:30am-noon.

Pharmacy: C. Umberto 134 (☎0789 21 310). Open M-Sa 10am-5pm.

Hospital: V. Aldo Moro 22 (☎0789 55 22 00).

Emergency: Carabinieri ☎0789 21 221. **Ambulance** ☎0789 55 22 01.

Internet Access: InterSmeraldo, V. Porto Romano 8/B (☎0789 25 366; www.intersmeraldo.com). 9 fast computers in a room with A/C, with bean-bag chairs in the back and 3 DSL ports for laptops. Friendly, English-speaking staff. Fax and copy service available. €2.50 per 30min. Open M-Sa 10am-10pm, Su 5-10pm. Cash only.

Post Office: V. Bari 7 (☎0789 20 74 00). Take V. Acquedotto from C. Umberto to the intersection of V. Acquedotto and V. Bari. Open M-Sa 8am-1pm. **Postal Code:** 07026.

🔳🔲 ACCOMMODATIONS AND FOOD

Olbia is lacking in budget accommodations; your best bet is to head to your ultimate destination right away. For those who need to spend a night and can afford it, Olbia does have some very comfortable establishments. **Hotel Terranova ❹**, V. Garibaldi 3, offers renovated, wheelchair-accessible rooms with A/C, bath, and TV. Try the homey seafood restaurant on the first floor. (☎0789 22 395; www.hotelterranova.it. Breakfast included. Parking €7. Doubles €43-115, depending on season. AmEx/MC/V.) For an affordable and comfortable stay away from the *centro*, choose **Hotel Royal ❹**, V. Aldo Moro 333. Large, neat, sparsely furnished rooms with private bath, TV, phone, and A/C are complemented by an outdoor swimming pool. The *centro* is easily accessible on foot (approx. 15min. walk) or by bus. (☎0789 50 253. Breakfast and parking included. Singles €54-85; doubles €82-126. AmEx/MC/V.) Decorated with roosters and stenciled sunflowers, **Hotel Gallura ❹**, C. Umberto 145, rents rooms with A/C, TV, telephone, and bright baths. Some claim that the pricey restaurant downstairs is Olbia's best. (☎0789 24 629 or 0789 24 648. Breakfast included. Reservations recommended. Singles €50; doubles €85. AmEx/MC/V.)

Many restaurants around C. Umberto advertise an overpriced *menù turistico* and cater to a mostly foreign crowd. Head down the little side streets for a less expensive, more authentic meal. For stained-glass windows and massive portions of hearty Sardinian specialties, head to 🗹**Antica Trattoria ❷**, V. G. Pala 6. Don't miss the spectacular *antipasti* bar (from €4) or the veal in lemon sauce (€6.80). Pizza (from €5) is served at dinner. (☎0789 24 053; www.anticatrattoria.net. Primi €7-9. Desserts €2-4. Cover €2. Open M 7:30-11pm, Tu-Sa 12:30-2:30pm and 7:30-11pm. AmEx/MC/V.) **Gelateria Smeralda ❶**, C. Umberto 124, has the best gelato in town. Try the local specialty *mirto* (myrtle) or the *pere alla grappa*. (☎07 89 26 443. Cones €1-3. Open daily M-Sa 4pm-midnight. Cash only.) **Super Pan Supermarket**, P. Crispi 2, is perfect for stocking up on supplies. Go to the end of V. Regina Elena, turn left, and walk through P. Crispi. (☎0789 26 978. Open M-Sa 8:30am-9pm, Su 8:30am-1:30pm.)

SARDINIA

APPENDIX

CLIMATE

Geographically, Italy lies in a temperate zone and has a predominantly Mediterranean climate. Yet, due to the peninsula's length, temperatures and weather often vary drastically in different parts of the country, based on proximity to the coast or the mountains. Summers in the south near the coast are dry and hot, as the sea and beaches are baked by the warm *sicorro* wind blowing in from North Africa. Moving north and inland, summer temperatures remain hot, but in the absence of a sea breeze, excessive humidity gets added to the mix. Things cool down countrywide in the winter, but to varying degrees, ranging from mild temperatures in the south to freezing fog, frost, and snow in the northern valleys. As a general rule, average temperatures are lower at higher altitudes year-round, especially in the Italian Alps, and wet weather hits most areas of the country from April to June.

AVG. TEMP. (LOW/HIGH), PRECIP.	JANUARY			APRIL			JULY			OCTOBER		
	°C	°F	mm	°C	°F	mm	°C	°F	mm	°C	°F	mm
Brindisi	6/12	43/54	77	11/18	52/64	47	21/29	70/84	14	15/22	59/72	79
Cagliari	7/14	45/57	50	11/19	52/66	31	21/30	70/86	1	15/23	59/73	54
Florence	1/10	34/50	73	8/19	46/66	78	17/31	63/88	40	10/21	50/70	88
Milan	0/5	32/41	44	10/18	50/64	94	20/29	68/84	64	11/17	52/63	125
Naples	4/12	39/54	116	9/18	48/64	62	18/29	64/84	19	12/22	54/72	107
Palermo	8/16	46/61	71	11/20	52/68	49	21/30	70/86	2	16/25	61/77	77
Rome	5/11	41/52	71	10/19	50/66	51	20/30	68/86	15	13/22	55/72	99
Venice	1/6	34/43	37	10/17	50/63	78	19/27	66/81	52	11/19	52/66	77

To convert from degrees Fahrenheit to degrees Celsius, subtract 32 and multiply by 5/9. To convert from Celsius to Fahrenheit, multiply by 9/5 and add 32.

°CELSIUS	-5	0	5	10	15	20	25	30	35	40
°FAHRENHEIT	23	32	41	50	59	68	77	86	95	104

MEASUREMENTS

Like the rest of the rational world, Italy uses the metric system. The basic unit of length is the meter (m), which is divided into 100 centimeters (cm) or 1000 millimeters (mm). One thousand meters make up one kilometer (km). Fluids are measured in liters (L), each divided into 1000 milliliters (mL). A liter of pure water weighs one kilogram (kg), the unit of mass that is divided into 1000 grams (g). One metric ton is 1000kg.

MEASUREMENT CONVERSIONS	
1 inch (in.) = 25.4mm	1 millimeter (mm) = 0.039 in.
1 foot (ft.) = 0.305m	1 meter (m) = 3.28 ft.
1 yard (yd.) = 0.914m	1 meter (m) = 1.094 yd.
1 mile (mi.) = 1.609km	1 kilometer (km) = 0.621 mi.

MEASUREMENT CONVERSIONS	
1 ounce (oz.) = 28.35g	1 gram (g) = 0.035 oz.
1 pound (lb.) = 0.454kg	1 kilogram (kg) = 2.205 lb.
1 fluid ounce (fl. oz.) = 29.57mL	1 milliliter (mL) = 0.034 fl. oz.
1 gallon (gal.) = 3.785L	1 liter (L) = 0.264 gal.

LANGUAGE

Italian is the official language of Italy, and if you plan to get anywhere in the country—physically or otherwise—you should brush up on the language before your trip. While the tourism-driven economy of urban areas has instilled locals with some English familiarity—ranging from knowledge of a few words to complete fluency—the likelihood of meeting an English-speaking Italian drops drastically the farther you travel from heavily touristed areas. In the south, on the islands, and in small towns to the north, tourists with no knowledge of Italian may have to rely entirely on hand gestures, a tactic that is naturally vulnerable to awkward misunderstandings. Be aware that spoken dialects vary greatly between different regions. To get in good with the locals wherever you may be, memorize a few Italian phrases to break the ice, and make sure to end any conversation with a polite, "Grazie" (GRAHT-see-yeh).

PRONUNCIATION

VOWELS

There are seven vowel sounds in standard Italian. **A, i,** and **u** each have one pro-nunciation. **E** and **o** each have two slightly different pronunciations, one open and one closed, depending on the vowel's placement in the word, the stress, and the regional accent. Below are approximate pronunciations.

VOWEL	PRONUNCIATION
a	"a" as in "father" (casa)
e (closed)	"ay" as in "gray" (sera)
e (open)	"eh" as in "wet" (sette)
i	"ee" as in "cheese" (vino)
o (closed)	"o" as in "bone" (sono)
o (open)	"aw" as in "ought" (bocca)
u	"oo" as in "moon" (gusto)

CONSONANTS

C and G: Before a, o, or u, **c** and **g** are hard, as in *candy* and *goose* or as in the Italian *colore* (koh-LOHR-eh; color) and *gatto* (GAHT-toh; cat). Italians soften c and g into **ch** and **j** sounds, respectively, when followed by i or e, as in *cheese* and *jeep* or the Italian *cibo* (CHEE-boh; food) and *gelato* (jeh-LAH-toh; ice cream).

Ch and Gh: H returns **c** and **g** to their "hard" sounds in front of i or e (see above): *chianti* (ky-AHN-tee), the Tuscan wine, and *spaghetti* (spah-GEHT-tee), the pasta.

Gn and Gli: Pronounce **gn** like the **ni** in *onion,* or as in the Italian *bagno* (BAHN-yoh; bath). **Gli** is pronounced like the **lli** in *million,* or as in the Italian *sbagliato* (zbal-YAH-toh; wrong).

Sc and Sch: When followed by **a, o,** or **u,** sc is pronounced as **sk.** *Scusi* (excuse me) yields "SKOO-zee." When followed by an **e** or **i,** sc is pronounced **sh** as in *sciopero*

(SHOH-pair-oh; strike). The addition of the letter **h** returns **c** to its hard sound (sk) before **i** or **e**, as in *pesche* (PEHS-keh; peaches).

Double consonants: When you see a double consonant, stress the preceding vowel; failure to do so can lead to confusion. For example, *penne all'arrabbiata* is "short pasta in a spicy, red sauce," whereas *pene all'arrabbiata* means "penis in a spicy, red sauce."

STRESS

In Italian, the stress generally falls on the penultimate, or next-to-last, syllable. An accent usually indicates when it falls on a different syllable, such as with the word *città* (cheet-TAH; city).

GRAMMAR

GENDER AND PLURALS

Italian nouns fall into two genders, masculine and feminine. The singular masculine ending is usually **o**, as in *duomo*, and the feminine is usually **a**, as in *donna*. Words ending in an **o** in the singular usually end with an **i** in the plural; *conto* (KOHN-toh; bill) becomes *conti* (KOHN-tee). Words ending in an **a** in the singular end with an **e** in the plural; *mela* (MEH-lah; apple) becomes *mele* (MEH-leh). All words ending with **e** take an **i** in the plural; *cane* (KAH-neh; dog) becomes *cani* (KAH-nee). Words with a final accent, like *città*, and words that end in consonants, like *bar*, do not change in the plural. Adjectives, which come after the word they modify, agree with their noun in gender and number.

ARTICLES

In Italian, the gender and number of a noun determine the article that precedes it. **Definite articles** are **il, lo, l', la, i, gli,** and **le.** *Il* is used for most masculine singular nouns (*il gatto;* the cat), while those beginning with a vowel, z, or *s impura* (s plus any consonant) are preceded by the article *lo* (*lo zio;* the uncle; *lo stivale;* the boot). The article *la* is used with feminine singular nouns beginning with a consonant: *la capra* (the goat). For all singular nouns beginning with a vowel, *l'* is the appropriate article: *l'arte* (the art).

In the plural, the article *i* is used for most masculine plural nouns (*i libri;* the books), while *gli* is used with masculine nouns beginning with a vowel, z, or *s impura* (*gli stivali,* the boots; *gli aerei,* the airplanes). *Le* precedes all feminine nouns (*le scarpe;* the shoes).

Indefinite articles are **un, uno, una,** and **un'.** *Un* and *uno* behave like *il* and *lo,* respectively, except that *un* can precede a masculine noun beginning with a vowel: *un gatto* (a cat), *un uomo* (a man), *uno stivale* (a boot). For feminine nouns, *un'* is used before vowels and *una* is used everywhere else: *un'edicola* (a newsstand), *una ragazza* (a girl).

PHRASEBOOK

NUMBERS			
1	uno	8	otto
2	due	9	nove
3	tré	10	dieci
4	quattro	11	undici
5	cinque	12	dodici
6	sei	13	tredici
7	sette	14	quattordici

NUMBERS			
15	quindici	40	quaranta
16	sedici	50	cinquanta
17	diciassette	60	sessanta
18	diciotto	70	settanta
19	dicianove	80	ottanta
20	venti	90	novanta
30	trenta	100	cento

MONTHS*			
January	gennaio	July	luglio
February	febbraio	August	agosto
March	marzo	September	settembre
April	aprile	October	ottobre
May	maggio	November	novembre
June	giugno	December	dicembre

NUMBERS*	
Monday	lunedí
Tuesday	martedí
Wednesday	mercoledí
Thursday	giovedí
Friday	venerdí
Saturday	sabato
Sunday	domenica

*Note: In Italian, days of the week and months are not capitalized unless they come at the beginning of a sentence. *Domenica* (Sunday) is the only day of the week that is of the feminine gender.

GENERAL		
ENGLISH	**ITALIAN**	**PRONUNCIATION**
Hi/Bye (informal)	Ciao	chow
Good day/Hello	Buongiorno	bwohn-JOHR-noh
Good evening	Buonasera	bwoh-nah-SEH-rah
Good night	Buonanotte	bwoh-nah-NOHT-teh
Goodbye	Arrivederci/Arrivederla (formal)	ah-ree-veh-DEHR-chee/ah-ree-veh-DEHR-lah
Please	Per favore/Per piacere	pehr fah-VOH-reh/pehr pyah-CHEH-reh
Thank you	Grazie (formal/polite)	GRAHT-see-yeh
How are you?	Come stai/Come sta (formal)?	COH-meh STA-ee/stah
I am well	Sto bene	stoh BEH-neh
You're welcome. May I help you?/ Please	Prego	PREH-goh
Excuse me	Scusa (formal)/Scusi (informal)	SKOO-zee/-zah
I'm sorry	Mi dispiace	mee dees-PYAH-cheh
My name is	Mi chiamo	mee kee-YAH-moh
I'm on vacation	Sono qui in vacanza	SOH-noh qwee een vah-CAHN-zah
I'm American/British/Irish/Australian/New Zealander	Sono americano(a)/britannico(a)/irlandese/australiano(a)/neozelandese	SOH-noh ah-meh-ree-CAH-noh(nah)/bree-TAH-nee-coh(cah)/eer-lahn-DEH-seh/ah-oo-strah-LYAH-noh(nah)/neh-oh-zeh-lahn-DEH-seh
I live in	Abito a	AH-bee-toh ah
What's your name?	Come ti chiami? Come si chiama Lei (formal)?	COH-meh tee kee-YAH-mee/COH-meh see kee-YAH-mah lay
Yes/No/Maybe	Sì/No/Forse	see/no/FOHR-seh
I don't know	Non lo so	nohn loh soh
Could you repeat that?	Potrebbe ripetere?	poh-TREHB-beh ree-PEH-teh-reh
What does this mean?	Cosa vuol dire questo?	COH-za vwohl DEE-reh KWEH-stoh

GENERAL		
I understand	Ho capito	oh kah-PEE-toh
I don't understand	Non capisco	nohn kah-PEES-koh
Do you speak English?	Parla inglese?	PAR-lah een-GLEH-zeh
Could you help me?	Potrebbe aiutarmi?	poh-TREHB-beh ah-yoo-TAHR-mee
How do you say?	Come si dice?	KOH-meh see DEE-cheh
What do you call this in Italian?	Come si chiama questo in italiano?	KOH-meh see kee-YAH-mah KWEH-stoh een ee-tahl-YAH-no
this/that	questo/quello	KWEH-sto/KWEHL-loh
more/less	più/meno	pyoo/MEH-noh
At what time?	A che ora?	ah keh OHR-ah
What time is it?	Che ore sono?	keh OHR-eh SOH-noh
What time does it open/close?	A che ora apre/chiude?	ah keh OHR-eh AH-preh/kee-OOH-deh
It's noon/midnight	È mezzogiorno/mezzanotte	eh MEHD-zoh-DJOHR-noh/MEHD-zah-NOT-eh
now	adesso/ora	ah-DEHS-so/OH-rah
let's go now	andiamo adesso	ahn-dee-AH-moh ah-DEHS-so
tomorrow	domani	doh-MAH-nee
today	oggi	OHJ-jee
yesterday	ieri	ee-YEH-ree
right away	subito	SU-bee-toh
soon	fra poco/presto	frah POH-koh/PREHS-toh
after	dopo	DOH-poh
before	prima	PREE-mah
late/later	tardi/più tardi	TAHR-dee/pyoo TAHR-dee
early	presto	PREHS-toh
late (after scheduled arrival time)	in ritardo	een ree-TAHR-doh
daily	quotidiano	kwoh-tee-DYAH-no
weekly	settimanale	seht-tee-mah-NAH-leh
monthly	mensile	mehn-SEE-leh
vacation	le ferie	leh FEH-ree-eh

DIRECTIONS AND TRANSPORTATION		
ENGLISH	ITALIAN	PRONUNCIATION
there	lì/là	lee/lah
the street address	l'indirizzo	leen-dee-REET-soh
the telephone	il telefono	eel teh-LEH-foh-noh
street	strada, via, viale, vico, vicolo, corso	STRAH-dah, VEE-ah, vee-AH-le, VEE-koh, VEE-koh-loh, KOHR-soh
speed limit	limite di velocità	LEEH-mee-teh dee veh-loh-chee-TAH
slow down	rallentare	rah-lehn-TAH-reh
one-way street	senso unico	SEHN-soh OOH-nee-coh
large, open square	piazzale	pee-yah-TZAH-leh
stairway	scalinata	scah-lee-NAH-tah
beach	spiaggia	spee-YAH-geeah
river	fiume	fee-YOO-meh
toilet, WC	gabinetto	gah-bee-NEHT-toh
What time does the ... leave?	A che ora parte ... ?	ah keh OHR-ah PAHR-teh
From where does the ... leave?	Da dove parte ... ?	dah DOH-veh PAHR-teh
the (city) bus	l'autobus	LAOW-toh-boos
the (intercity) bus	il pullman	eel POOL-mahn
the ferry	il traghetto	eel tra-GHEHT-toh
the hydrofoil	l'aliscafo	LA-lee-scah-foh
the plane	l'aereo	lah-EHR-reh-oh
the train	il treno	eel TREH-noh
the ticket office	la biglietteria	lah beel-yeht-teh-REE-ah
How much does it cost?	Quanto costa?	KWAN-toh CO-stah

DIRECTIONS AND TRANSPORTATION		
I would like to buy ...	Vorrei comprare ...	voh-RAY com-PRAH-reh
... a ticket	... un biglietto	... oon beel-YEHT-toh
... a pass (bus, etc.)	... una tessera	... OO-nah TEHS-seh-rah
one-way	solo andata	SO-lo ahn-DAH-tah
round-trip	andata e ritorno	ahn-DAH-tah eh ree-TOHR-noh
reduced price	ridotto	ree-DOHT-toh
student discount	lo sconto studentesco	loh SKOHN-toh stoo-dehn-TEHS-koh
the track/train platform	il binario	eel bee-NAH-ree-oh
the flight	il volo	eel VOH-loh
the reservation	la prenotazione	la preh-no-taht-see-YOH-neh
the entrance/exit	l'ingresso/l'uscita	leen-GREH-so/loo-SHEE-tah
I need to get off here	Devo scendere qui	DEH-vo SHEN-dehr-eh kwee

EMERGENCY		
I lost my passport/wallet	Ho perso il passaporto/portafoglio	oh PEHR-soh eel pahs-sah-POHR-toh/por-ta-FOH-lee-oh
I've been robbed	Sono stato derubato/a	SOH-noh STAH-toh deh-roo-BAH-toh/tah
Wait!	Aspetta!	ahs-PEHT-tah
Stop!	Ferma!	FEHR-mah
Help!	Aiuto!	ah-YOO-toh
Leave me alone!	Lasciami stare!/Mollami!	LAH-shah-mee STAH-reh/MOH-lah-MEE
Don't touch me!	Non mi toccare!	NOHN mee tohk-KAH-reh
I'm calling the police!	Telefono alla polizia!	tehl-LEH-foh-noh ah-lah poh-leet-SEE-ah
military police	carabinieri	CAH-rah-been-YEH-ree
Go away, moron!	Vattene, cretino!	VAH-teh-neh creh-TEE-noh

MEDICAL		
I have ... allergies	Ho ...delle allergie	OH ... DEHL-leh ahl-lair-JEE-eh
... a cold	... un raffreddore	oon rahf-freh-DOH-reh
... a cough	... una tosse	OO-nah TOHS-seh
... the flu	... l'influenza	linn-floo-ENT-sah
... a fever	... una febbre	OO-nah FEHB-breh
... a headache	... mal di testa	mahl dee TEHS-tah
My foot/arm hurts	Mi fa male il piede/braccio	mee fah MAH-le eel PYEH-deh/BRAH-cho
I'm on the Pill	Prendo la pillola	PREHN-doh lah PEE-loh-lah

RESTAURANTS		
food	il cibo	eel CHEE-boh
wine bar	l'enoteca	len-oh-TEK-ah
breakfast	la colazione	lah coh-laht-see-YO-neh
lunch	il pranzo	eel PRAHN-zoh
dinner	la cena	lah CHEH-nah
coffee	il caffè	eel kah-FEH
appetizer	l'antipasto	lahn-tee-PAH-stoh
first course	il primo	eel PREE-moh
second course	il secondo	eel seh-COHN-doh
side dish	il contorno	eel cohn-TOHR-noh
dessert	il dolce	eel DOHL-cheh
bottle	la bottiglia	lah boh-TEEL-yah
waiter/waitress	il/la cameriere/a	eel/lah kah-meh-ree-EH-reh/rah
the bill	il conto	eel COHN-toh
cover charge	il coperto	eel koh-PEHR-toh
tip	la mancia	lah MAHN-chyah

APPENDIX

HOTEL AND HOSTEL RESERVATIONS		
hotel/hostel	albergo/ostello	al-BEHR-goh/os-TEHL-loh
I have a reservation	Ho una prenotazione	oh oo-nah preh-no-taht-see-YOH-neh
Could I reserve a single room/ double room (for the 2nd of August)?	Potrei prenotare una camera singola/doppia (per il due agosto)?	poh-TREY preh-noh-TAH-reh oo-nah CAH-meh-rah SEEN-goh-lah/ DOH-pyah (pehr eel DOO-eh ah-GOH-stoh
Is there a bed available tonight?	C'è un posto libero stasera?	cheh oon POHS-toh LEE-ber-oh sta-SAIR-ah
with bath/shower	con bagno/doccia	kohn BAHN-yo/DOH-cha
Is there a cheaper room without a bath/shower?	C'è una stanza più economica senza bagno/doccia?	cheh oo-nah STAN-zah pyoo eko-NOM-ika sen-zah BAHN-yo/ DOH-cha
open/closed	aperto/chiuso	ah-PEHR-toh/KYOO-zoh
sheets/linens	i lenzuoli	ee lehn-SUO-lee
the blanket	la coperta	lah koh-PEHR-tah
the bed	il letto	eel LEHT-toh
Is there heating?	C'è riscaldamento?	cheh ree-skahl-dah-MEHN-toh
Is there air conditioning?	C'è aria condizionata?	che AH-ree-ah con-deet-syon-AH-tah
How much is the room?	Quanto costa la camera?	KWAHN-toh KOHS-ta lah KAM-eh-rah
Is breakfast included?	È compresa la prima colazione?	eh com-PREH-sah la PREEH-mah coh-laht-see-YO-neh
I will arrive (at 2:30pm)	Arriverò (alle due e mezzo)	ah-ree-veh-ROH (ah-leh DOO-eh MED-zoh)
You'll have to send a deposit/ check	Bisogna mandare un anticipo/un assegno	bee-ZOHN-yah mahn-DAH-reh oon ahn-TEE-chee-poh/oon ahs-SEHN-yoh
What is that funny smell?	Che cos'è quest'odore strano?	keh kohz-EH kwest-oh-DOHR-eh STRAH-noh

AMORE		
I have a boyfriend/girlfriend	Ho un ragazzo/una ragazza	Oh oon rah-GAHT-soh/oo-nah rah-GAHT-sah
Let's get a room	Prendiamo una camera	prehn-DYAH-moh oo-nah CAH-meh-rah
Voluptuous!	Volutuoso/a!	VOL-oot-oo-OH-zhoh/zhah
To be in love with	Essere innamorato/a di	Eh-seh-reh een-am-mo-RAH-to/ ta dee
Just a kiss	Solo un bacio	SOH-loh oon BAH-chyoh
Are you single?	Sei nubile?	NOO-bee-leh
You're cute	Sei carino/a (bello/a)	SEY cah-REEN-oh/ah (BEHL-loh/ lah)
I love you, I swear	Ti amo, te lo giuro	tee AH-moh, teh loh DJOO-roh
I'm married	Sono sposato/a	SOH-noh spo-ZA-to/ta
I only have safe sex	Pratico solo sesso sicuro	PRAH-tee-coh sohl-oh SEHS-so see-COO-roh
Leave her alone, she's mine	Lasciala stare, è mia	LAH-shyah-lah STAH-reh, eh mee-ah
Leave right now!	Vai via subito!	vah-ee VEE-ah SOO-beet-oh
I'll never forget you	Non ti dimenticherò mai	nohn tee dee-men-tee-ker-OH mah-ee
The profound mystery of what you just said sets my soul on fire	Il profondo mistero di ciò che stai dicendo mi infuoca il cuore	eel pro-FOHN-doh mee-STEH-roh dee CHOE keh sty dee-CEN-doh mee een-FWOH-cah eel ku-WOR-eh
Not if you're the last man on earth	Neanche se lei fossi l'unico uomo sulla terra	neh-AHN-keh seh lay FOH-see LOO-nee-koh WOH-moh soo-LAH TEH-rah

AT THE BAR		
May I buy you a drink?	Posso offrirle qualcosa da bere?	POHS-soh ohf-FREER-leh kwahl-COHzah dah BEH-reh
a beer	una birra	oo-nah BEER-rah
glass of wine	bicchiere di vino	bee-KYEH-reh dee VEE-noh
liter of wine	litro di vino	LEE-troh dee VEE-noh
I'm drunk	Sono ubriaco/a	SOH-noh oo-BRYAH-coh/cah
Let's go!	Andiamo!	ahn-dee-AH-moh
I don't drink	Non bevo	nohn BEH-voh
Cheers!	Cin cin!	cheen cheen
Do you have a light?	Mi fai accendere?	mee fah-ee ah-CHEN-deh-reh
No thank you, I don't smoke	No grazie, non fumo	noh GRAH-zyeh, nohn FOO-moh
I was here first!	C'ero io prima!	CHEH-roh EE-oh PREE-mah

MENU READER

PRIMI (FIRST COURSE)	
pasta aglio e olio	in garlic and olive oil
pasta all'amatriciana	in a tangy tomato sauce with onions and bacon
pasta all'arabbiata	in a spicy tomato sauce
pasta alla bolognese	in a meat sauce
pasta alla boscaiola	egg pasta, served in a mushroom sauce with peas and cream
pasta alla carbonara	in a creamy sauce with egg, cured bacon, and cheese
pasta alla pizzaiola	tomato-based sauce with olive oil and red peppers
pasta alla puttanesca	in a tomato sauce with olives, capers, and anchovies
gnocchi	potato dumplings
ravioli	square-shaped and often stuffed with cheese or sometimes meat
tagliatelle	thin and flat, these are the northern version of fettuccini
pappardelle	wider and flatter than tagliatelle
polenta	deep-fried cornmeal
risotto	creamy rice dish, comes in nearly as many flavors as pasta sauce

PIZZA	
alla capriciosa	with ham, egg, artichoke, and more
con rucola	with arugula (rocket for Brits)
marinara	with red sauce and no cheese
margherita	plain ol' tomato, mozzarella, and basil
pancetta/speck	bacon
pepperoni	bell pepper; careful not to confuse the Italian bell pepper with the American pepperoni meat, which doesn't exist in Italy!
polpette	meatballs
quattro formaggi	four cheeses
quattro stagioni	four seasons; a different topping for each quarter of the pizza, usually mushrooms, *prosciutto crudo*, artichoke, and tomato
salsiccia	sausage

SECONDI (SECOND COURSES)	
agnello	lamb
animelle alla griglia	grilled sweetbreads
asino	donkey (served in Sicily and Sardinia)
bistecca	steak
cavallo (sfilacci)	horse (served in Sicily and Sardinia)
cinghiale	wild boar
coniglio	rabbit
cotoletta	breaded veal cutlet with cheese
cozze	mussels
fégato	liver
gamberetti/gamberi	shrimps/prawns

SECONDI (SECOND COURSES)

granchi	crab
maiale	pork
manzo	beef
merluzzo/baccalà	cod/dried salted cod
osso buco	braised veal shank
ostriche	oysters
pesce spada	swordfish
pollo	chicken
polpo	octopus
prosciutto	smoked ham, available cured or cooked
salsiccia	sausage
saltimbocca alla romana	slices of veal and ham cooked together and topped with cheese
sarde	sardines
scaloppina	cutlet
seppia	cuttlefish, usually served grilled in its own ink
sogliola	sole
speck	smoked raw ham, lean but surrounded by a layer of fat
tonno	tuna
trippa	tripe (chopped, sautéed cow intestines, usually in a tomato sauce)
trota	trout
vitello	veal
vongole	clams

CONTORNI (SIDE DISHES)

carciofe/carciofini	artichoke/artichoke hearts
carotte	carrots
cavolfiori	cauliflower
cavolo	cabbage
cetriolo	cucumber
cipolla	onion
fagioli	beans (usually white)
fagiolini	green beans
finocchio	fennel
funghi	mushrooms
insalata caprese	tomatoes with mozzarella cheese and basil, drizzled with olive oil
insalata mista	mixed salad with lettuce, cucumbers, and tomatoes
lattuga	lettuce
lenticchie	lentils
melanzana	eggplant
patate	potatoes
piselli	peas
pomodori	tomatoes
spinaci	spinach
tartufi	truffles

ANTIPASTI (APPETIZERS)

bresaola	thinly sliced dried beef, served with olive oil, lemon, and *parmigiano*
bruschetta	crisp slices of garlic-rubbed baked bread, often with raw tomatoes
caponata	mixed eggplant, olives, tomatoes, and anchovies
carpaccio	extremely thin slices of lean, raw beef
crostini	small pieces of toasted bread usually served with chicken liver or mozzarella and anchovies, though other toppings are used
fiori di zucca	zucchini flowers filled with cheese, battered, and lightly fried
insalata di mare/riso	seafood/rice salad
insalata russa	salad of diced vegetables in mayonnaise
melanzane alla parmigiana	eggplant with tomato and parmesan cheese

FRUTTA (FRUIT)	
arancia	orange
ciliegia	cherry
fragola	strawberry
lampone	raspberry
mela	apple
pesca	peach
prugna	plum
uva	grape

DOLCI (DESSERTS)	
gelato	Italian-style ice cream
granita	ice-based fruit or coffee slushee
macedonia	fruit salad
panna cotta	flan
pasta	pastry
sfogliatelle	sugar-coated layers of flaky pastry filled with ricotta
tiramisù	cake-like dessert drenched in *espresso*, layered with *mascarpone*

BIBITE (DRINKS)	
acqua con gas/frizzante	soda water
acqua minerale	mineral water
aranciata	orangeade
bicchiere	glass
birra	beer
caffè	coffee
caraffa	carafe
cioccolata calda	hot chocolate
ghiaccio	ice
latte	milk
limonata	lemonade
spremuta	fresh fruit juice
spumante	sparkling wine
succo	concentrated fruit juice with sugar
tè	tea
tònica	tonic water
vino rosso/bianco/rosato/secco/dolce	red/wine/rosé/dry/sweet wine

PREPARATION	
al dente	firm to the bite (pasta)
al forno	baked
al sangue	rare
al punto	medium
al vino	in wine sauce
fritto/a	fried
ben cotto/a	well done
crudo/a	raw
fresco/a	fresh
fritto/a	fried
piccante	spicy
ripieno	stuffed

INDEX

INDEX